CONSTITUTIONAL COURTS AS POSITIVE LEGISLATORS

A Comparative Law Study

In all democratic states, constitutional courts, which are traditionally empowered to invalidate or to annul unconstitutional statutes, have the role of interpreting and applying the Constitution to preserve its supremacy and to ensure the prevalence of fundamental rights. In this sense, they were traditionally considered "negative legislators," unable to substitute for the legislators or to enact legislative provisions that could not be deduced from the Constitution. During the past decade, the role of constitutional courts has dramatically changed, as their role is no longer limited to declaring the unconstitutionality of statutes or annulling them. Today, constitutional courts condition their decisions on the presumption of constitutionality of statutes, opting to interpret them according to or in harmony with the Constitution to preserve them, instead of deciding their annulment or declaring them unconstitutional. More frequently, constitutional courts, instead of dealing with existing legislation, assume the role of assistants or auxiliaries to the legislator, creating provisions they deduce from the Constitution when controlling the absence of legislation or legislative omissions. In some cases, they act as "positive legislators," issuing temporary or provisional rules to be applied pending the enactment of legislation. This book analyzes this new role of the constitutional courts, conditioned by the principles of progressiveness and of prevalence of human rights, particularly regarding the important rediscovery of the right to equality and nondiscrimination.

Since 1963, Allan R. Brewer-Carías has been Professor at the Central University of Venezuela. He was Simón Bolívar Professor at the University of Cambridge, where he was a Fellow of Trinity College (1985–6); he was Adjunct Professor at the University of Paris II (1990) and at Columbia University in New York (2006–7). He is Titular Member of the International Academy of Comparative Law, where he served as Vice President (1982–2010), and he is a member of the Venezuelan National Academy of Political and Social Sciences, where he served as President (1997–9). He has extensively worked and written on matters of public law and comparative law, particularly on matters of judicial review.

CONSTITUTIONAL COURTS AS POSITIVE LEGISLATORS

A Comparative Law Study

Allan R. Brewer-Carías

Professor of Law, Central University of Venezuela
Academy of Political and Social Sciences, Venezuela
International Academy of Comparative Law

CAMBRIDGE
UNIVERSITY PRESS

CAMBRIDGE UNIVERSITY PRESS
Cambridge, New York, Melbourne, Madrid, Cape Town,
Singapore, São Paulo, Delhi, Tokyo, Mexico City

Cambridge University Press
32 Avenue of the Americas, New York, NY 10013-2473, USA

www.cambridge.org
Information on this title: www.cambridge.org/9781107011656

First published 2011

Printed in the United States of America

A catalog record for this publication is available from the British Library.

Library of Congress Cataloging in Publication data

Brewer Carías, Allan-Randolph.
Constitutional courts as positive legislators : a comparative law study / Allan Brewer-Carias.
p. cm.
Includes bibliographical references and index.
ISBN 978-1-107-01165-6 (hardback)
1. Constitutional courts. 2. Legislative power. 3. Judicial review. 4. Comparative law.
I. Title.
K3370.B735 2011
347′.035–dc22 2011002968

ISBN 978-1-107-01165-6 Hardback

CONTENTS

AUTHOR'S NOTE

This book is the result of the legal research programs conceived by the International Academy of Comparative Law on the occasion of preparing for its quadrennial International Congress of Comparative Law.

For the congresses, every four years, the board of the academy selects nearly fifty important and current law topics or subjects to be studied comparatively. The board requests that the academic community of each country write national reports on each subject, and it assigns the task of producing a comparative law study to a general reporter, who stresses the most important current global trends of the particular subject.

In this case, and for the purpose of the eighteenth International Congress of Comparative Law held in Washington, D.C., in July 2010, organized by the International Academy of Comparative Law with the support of the American Association of Comparative Law, the academy chose within the topic of constitutional law the subject of *Constitutional Courts as Positive Legislators* as one of the current subjects in constitutional law. The academy assigned me the task of preparing the general report on this subject for the congress, and this book is the result of the two years of research and work that I devoted to it. Following the general guidelines that I sent out, the national reporters wrote their national reports, which were the main source of information I had for writing the general report, which of course was complemented by my own research. I received thirty-six national reports from thirty-one countries: nineteen from Europe, including six from Eastern Europe; ten from the American continent (three from North America, five from South America, and two from Central America); one from Asia, and one from Australia. I thank all the national reporters for their cooperation in providing me with precious and current information on the subject.

The general report and the national reports were discussed at the congress. This book integrates those reports in the following parts: Part 1 includes my general report; Part 2 includes the national reports I received on the subject, in English and French, which are the official languages of the academy; and Part 3 includes the synthesis report I prepared for my oral presentation at the eighteenth congress, at the George Washington Law School, in Washington, D.C., on July 27, 2010.

This was not the first time I have had the privilege of being a general reporter for the International Academy's congresses. I was first appointed general reporter by the academy forty-five years ago, on the subject of *Le régime des activités industrielles et commerciales des pouvoirs publiques*, for the seventh International Congress of Comparative Law, held in Uppsala, Sweden, in August 1966. On that occasion, Professor Robert Goldschmidt proposed my name for that task. He was a very well-recognized commercial law professor, who at the time was head of the Private Law Institute of the Central University of Venezuela and head of the Comparative Law Center of the Ministry of Justice. On that occasion he had been appointed general reporter on the subject by the academy, but because it was a public law subject (not a commercial law one), he asked me to allow him to propose my name to the academy, instead of his own, to write the general report. It was thanks to Robert Goldschmidt that I got in touch with the academy, at a time when I was a very young professor, with some books and articles already published but not at all known in the comparative law world. In any case, the appointment from the academy allowed me not only to write an extensive general report on public enterprise in comparative law[1] but also to begin close relations with the academy and all the very distinguished comparatist lawyers with whom I developed close friendships and long-standing academic relations. This was the time of professors Gabriel Marty, C.J. Hamson, John Hazard, Anthony Jolowicz, and Roland Drago, among others, who privileged me with their friendship. The Uppsala general report was published as the book *Les enterprises publiques en droit comparé* by the Faculté international pour l'ensignement du droit comparé, Paris 1968, with a foreword by Professor Roland Drago, who was later secretary-general of the academy.

In subsequent congresses, I was also appointed general reporter for different subjects: *Les limites a la liberté d'information (presse, radio, cinema et télévisión)*, at the eighth International Congress of Comparative Law, in Pescara, Italy, August–September 1970;[2] *Regionalization in*

1 See Allan R. Brewer-Carías, "Le régime des activités industrielles et commerciales des pouvoirs publics en droit comparé," in *Rapports Généraux au VIIe Congrès International de Droit Comparé, Acta Instituti Upsaliensis Jurisprudentiae Comparativae*, Stockholm 1966, pp. 484–565.

2 See Allan R. Brewer-Carías, "Las limitaciones a la libertad de información en el derecho comparado (prensa, radio, cine y televisión)," *Revista Orbita*, nos. 5–6, Caracas 1973, pp. 55–88.

Economic Matters, at the ninth International Congress of Comparative Law, in Tehran, August–September 1974;[3] *La décentralization territoriale, autonomie territoriale et régionalization politique*, at the eleventh International Congress of Comparative Law, in Caracas, August–September 1982;[4] *Les limitations constitutionnelles et légales contre les impositions confiscatoires*, at the thirteenth International Congress of Comparative Law, in Montreal, August 1990;[5] and *Constitutional Implications of Regional Economic Integration*, at the fifteenth International Congress of Comparative Law, in Bristol, United Kingdom, July–August 1998.[6] All these general reports were published in my book *Études de droit public comparé* (published in 2000 by Bruylant in Brussels).

This book, with the general report for the eighteenth International Congress, as mentioned, also includes the national reports as a thematic book, which the academy has encouraged.

I was formally elected an associate member of the academy many years ago, and in 1982, on the occasion of the eleventh International Congress of Comparative Law held in Caracas, which I helped organize, I was elected titular member and vice president, a position that I held for almost thirty years. On the occasion of the 2010 congress in Washington, I decided to step down, giving way to other comparatists from Latin America to join the board.

This work, once more, as general reporter is a good occasion to thank again all the members of the board of the academy for all their support of my academic activities during the almost the half century that has passed since I first delivered a general report at the University of Uppsala. In particular, I express my thanks to Professor Roland Drago, for many decades the secretary-general of the academy, who through his persistent

3 See Allan R. Brewer-Carías, "Regionalization in Economic Matters in Comparative Law," in *Rapports Generaux au IX Congrés International de Droit Comparé, Teherán 1974*, Brussels 1977, pp. 669–696.

4 See Allan R. Brewer-Carías, "La descentralización territorial: Autonomía territorial y regionalización política," en *Revista de Estudios de la Vida Local*, nº 218, Instituto de Estudios de Administración Local, Madrid, April–June 1983, pp. 209–232.

5 See Allan R. Brewer-Carías, "Les protections constitutionnelles et légales contre les impositions confiscatories," *Rapports Généraux XIIIe Congres International*, Académie Internationale de Droit Comparé, Montreal 1990, pp. 795–824.

6 See Allan R. Brewer-Carías, *Las implicaciones constitucionales de la integración económica regional*, Cuadernos de la Cátedra Allan R. Brewer-Carías de Derecho Público, Universidad Católica del Táchira, Editorial Jurídica Venezolana, Caracas 1998.

work positioned the academy among the most recognized institutions in current comparative law.

Beatriz, my wife, went with me to the Uppsala congress in 1966, and she has accompanied me during the past decades in all my academic ventures and relations with the academy. She has been the permanent witness to the hours, days, weeks, and years that the academic life requires; and in the particular case of the work published in this book, she has been even a closer witness in these years of exile in New York – a result of the authoritarian government in Venezuela that since 1999 has seized all branches of government, demolishing with absolute impunity democratic institutions and the rule of law.[7]

It was thanks to her fortitude, support, love, and understanding, that during the difficult months of 2011, I was able to finish this work on time. That is why I dedicate this book to her, with all my love.

New York, July 2011

[7] See Allan R. Brewer-Carías, *Dismantling Democrary. The Chávez Authoritarian Experiment*, Cambridge University Press, New York, 2010.

PART ONE

CONSTITUTIONAL COURTS AS POSITIVE LEGISLATORS IN COMPARATIVE LAW

INTRODUCTION

HANS KELSEN, JUDICIAL REVIEW, AND THE NEGATIVE LEGISLATOR

At the beginning of the twentiest century, Hans Kelsen, in his very well-known article "La garantie juridictionnelle de la constitution (La justice constitutionnelle)," published in 1928, in the *Revue du droit public et de la science politique en France et a l'étranger*, began to write for non-German-speaking readers about constitutional courts as "negative legislators."[1] As Kelsen was one of the most important constructors of modern public law of the twentieth century, it is indeed impossible to write about the opposite assertion – on constitutional courts as positive legislators – without referring to his thoughts on the matter.[2]

1 See Hans Kelsen, "La garantie juridictionnelle de la constitution (La justice constitutionnelle)," *Revue du droit public et de la science politique en France et a l'ètranger*, Librairie Général de Droit et de Jurisprudence, Paris 1928, pp. 197–257. See also the Spanish text in Hans Kelsen, *La garantía jurisdiccional de la Constitución (La justicia constitucional)*, Universidad Nacional Autónoma de México, Mexico City 2001.

2 As all the national reporters, in one way or another, have done in their national reports for subject IV.B.2 of the eighteenth International Congress of Comparative Law, Washington, D.C., July 2010. See the text of all national reports in Part 2 of this book.

In his article, while sharing his experience on the establishment and functioning of the Constitutional Court of Austria in 1920, conceived of as an important part of the concentrated system of judicial review that he had introduced for the first time in Europe,[3] Kelsen began to explain the role of such constitutional organs established outside of the judicial branch of government, but with jurisdictional powers to annul statutes they deemed unconstitutional.

The Austrian system, which was established the same year as that in Czechoslovakia,[4] according to Kelsen's own ideas,[5] sharply contrasted with, at that time, the already well-established and well-developed diffuse system of judicial review adopted in the United States, where for more than a century, courts and the Supreme Court had already developed a very active role as constitutional judges.[6]

It is true that the classic distinction of the judicial review systems in the contemporary world, between the concentrated systems of judicial review and the diffuse systems of judicial review,[7] has developed and has changed, and is difficult to apply in many cases clearly and sharply.[8] Consequently, in almost all democratic countries, a convergence of principles and solutions on

3 See generally Charles Eisenmann, *La justice constitutionelle et la Haute Cour Constitutionelle d'Autriche* (reprint of the 1928 edition, with H. Kelsen's preface), Economica, Paris 1986; Konrad Lachmayer, *Austrian National Report*, p. 1.

4 See Zdenek Kühn, *Czech National Report*, p. 1.

5 Kelsen called constitutional justice his "most personal work." See Theo Öhlinger, "Hans Kelsen y el derecho constitucional federal austriaco: Una retrospectiva crítica," *Revista Iberoamericana de Derecho Procesal Constitucional*, nº 5, Instituto Iberoamericano de Derecho Procesal Constitucional, Editorial Porrúa, Mexico City 2006, p. 219.

6 For the purpose of this general report, the expression "constitutional courts" refers generally to constitutional tribunals or courts – specifically established in many countries as constitutional jurisdictions, with powers to annul with *erga omnes* effects unconstitutional statutes, as well as to supreme courts or tribunals also acting as constitutional jurisdictions, or any court or tribunal when acting as constitutional judges.

7 See generally Mauro Cappelletti, *Judicial Review in Contemporary World*, Bobbs-Merrill, Indianapolis 1971, p. 45; Mauro Cappelletti and J. C. Adams, "Judicial Review of Legislation: European Antecedents and Adaptations," *Harvard Law Review* 79, nº 6, April 1966, p. 1207; Mauro Cappelletti, "El control judicial de la constitucionalidad de las leyes en el derecho comparado," *Revista de la Facultad de Derecho de México* 61, 1966, p. 28; Allan R. Brewer-Carías, *Judicial Review in Comparative Law*, Cambridge University Press, Cambridge 1989; Allan R. Brewer-Carías, *Étutes de droit pubic comparé*, Bruylant, Brussels 2000, pp. 653 ff.

8 See, e.g., Lucio Pegoraro, "Clasificaciones y modelos de justicia constitucional en la dinámica de los ordenamientos," *Revista Iberoamericana de Derecho Procesal Constitucional*, nº 2, Instituto Iberoamericano de Derecho Procesal Constitucional, Editorial Porrúa, Mexico City 2004, pp. 131 ff.; Alfonse Celotto, "La justicia constitucional en el mundo: Formas y modalidades," *Revista Iberoamericana de Derecho Procesal Constitucional*, nº 1, Instituto Iberoamericano de Derecho Procesal Constitucional, Editorial Porrúa, Mexico City 2004, pp. 3 ff.

matters of judicial review has progressively occurred,[9] to the point that nowadays it is possible to say that there are no means or solutions that apply exclusively in one or another system.[10] Nonetheless, this fact, in my opinion, does not deprive the distinction of its basic sense.

In effect, and in spite of criticisms of the concentrated-diffuse distinction,[11] the distinction remains very useful, particularly for comparative law analysis, and it is not possible to consider it obsolete.[12] The basis of the distinction, which can always be considered valid, is established between, on the one hand, constitutional systems in which all courts are constitutional judges and have the power to review the constitutionality of legislation in decisions on particular cases and controversies, without such power necessarily being expressly established in the Constitution, and on the other hand, constitutional systems in which a constitutional jurisdiction is established assigning its exercise to a constitutional court, tribunal or council or to the supreme or high court or tribunal of the country, as the only court with

9 See, e.g., Francisco Fernández Segado, *La justicia constitucional ante el siglo XXI. La progresiva convergencia de los sistemas americano y europeo-kelseniano*, Librería Bonomo Editrice, Bologna 2003, pp. 40 ff.

10 On the effort to establish a new basis for new distinctions, see Louis Favoreu, *Les cours constitutionnelles*, Presses Universitaires de France, 1986; Michel Fromont, *La justice constitutionnelle dans le monde*, Dalloz, Paris 1996; D. Rousseau, *La justice constitutionnelle en Europe*, Montchrestien, Paris 1998.

11 See Francisco Fernández Segado, "La obsolecencia de la bipolaridad 'modelo Americano-modelo europeo-kelseniano' como criterio analítico del control de constitucionalidad y la búsqueda de una nueva tipología explicativa," in *La justicia constitucional: Una visión de derecho comparado*, Ed. Dykinson, Madrid 2009, vol. 1, pp. 129–220; Guillaume Tusseau, *Contre les "modèles" de justice constitutionnelle: Essai de critique métodologique*, Bononia University Press, Universitá di Bologna, Bologna 2009 (bilingual French-Italian edition); Guillaume Tusseau, "Regard critique sur les outils méthodologique du comparatisme. L'example des modèles de justice constitutionnelle," *IUSTEL: Revista General de Derecho Público Comparado*, n° 4, Madrid, January 2009, pp. 1–34.

12 In fact, what can be considered obsolete is the distinction that derives from an erroneous denomination that has been given to the two systems, particularly by many in Europe, contrasting the so-called American and European systems. This ignores that the "European system," which cannot be reduced to the existence of a specialized Constitutional Court, was present in Latin America a few decades before its introduction in the Czechoslovak Constitution and that the "American system" is not at all endemic to countries with common law systems, having been spread since the nineteenth century into countries with Roman law traditions. See Allan R. Brewer-Carías, *Judicial Review in Comparative Law*, Cambridge University Press, Cambridge 1989; Vicki C. Jackson and Mark Tushent, *Comparative Constitutional Law*, 2nd ed., Foundation Press/Thomson West, New York 2006, pp. 465 ff., 485 ff. Also, as has been pointed out by Francisco Rubio Llorente, it is impossible to talk about a European system, when within Europe there are more differences between the existing systems of judicial review than between any of them and the American system. See Francisco Rubio Llorente, "Tendencias actuales de la jurisdicción constitucional en Europa," in *Manuel Fraga: Homenaje académico*, Fundación Canovas del Castillo, Madrid 1997, vol. 2, p. 1416.

jurisdictional power to annul statutes contrary to the Constitution – such courts or the assignment of power to them must be expressly provided for in the Constitution. This is the basic ground for the distinction that still exists in comparative law, even in countries where both systems function in parallel, as it happens in many Latin American countries.[13] It is in this sense that this book refers to the concentrated system and the diffuse system of judicial review.[14]

In this sense, the concentrated system of judicial review, after being adopted since the nineteenth century in many Latin American countries, was adopted in Europe following Kelsen's ideas set forth in the 1920 constitutions of Czechoslovakia and Austria based on the principle of constitutional supremacy and its main guarantee, that is, the nullity and the annulability of statutes and other State acts with similar rank, when they are contrary to the Constitution. Given the general fear regarding the Judiciary and the prevailing principle of the sovereignty of parliaments, the system materialized through the creation of a special constitutional court established outside of the judicial branch of government with the power not only to declare the unconstitutionality of statutes that violate the Constitution but also to annul them with *erga omnes* effects, that is, to expel them from the legal order.

Kelsen's initial arguments were developed to confront the problems that such powers of judicial review in the hand of a new constitutional organ different from the Legislator could arise in Europe regarding the principle of separation of powers and, in particular, its incidence in legislative functions. But the fact was that the system, by that time and without the need to create a separate constitutional court, was already in existence, with similar substantive trends in some Latin American countries such as Colombia and

13 As is, for instance, the case of Brazil, Colombia, Dominican Republic, Ecuador, Guatemala, Mexico, Nicaragua, Peru, and Venezuela, as well as Portugal, and in a certain way Greece, and Canada. See Allan R. Brewer-Carías, "La jurisdicción constitucional en América Latina," in Domingo García Belaúnde and Francisco Fernández Segado (coords.), *La jurisdicción constitucional en Iberoamérica*, Dykinson S.L. (Madrid), Editorial Jurídica Venezolana (Caracas), Ediciones Jurídicas (Lima), Editorial Jurídica E. Esteva (Uruguay), Madrid 1997, pp. 117–161.

14 See Allan R. Brewer-Carías, *Constitutional Protection of Human Rights in Latin America : A Comparative Study of Amparo Proceeding*, Cambridge University Press, New York 2009, pp. 81 ff.

Venezuela, where the annulment powers regarding unconstitutional statutes had been granted since 1858 to supreme courts of justice.[15]

On the other hand, at the time when the concentrated system of judicial review was formulated in Europe, it contrasted sharply with the diffuse or decentralized system of judicial review that had developed in the United States since the 1808 Supreme Court case *Marbury v. Madison*, 1 Cranch 137 (1803), which beginning in the nineteenth century also spread to many Latin American countries, including Argentina, Brazil, Colombia, and Venezuela,[16] and was adopted in some European countries, including Norway,[17] Denmark, Sweden, and Greece.[18]

Summarizing, when Kelsen formulated his arguments in support of the concentrated system of judicial review in Europe, the same system had already existed for more than six decades in Latin America, and the diffuse system had existed for almost a century in North America and later also in Latin America and in some European countries.

But the fact is that it was through Kelsen's proposals and writings that judicial review developed in Europe, eventually contributing to end the principle of parliamentary sovereignty. Kelsen himself not only drafted the proposal to incorporate the new Constitutional Court in the 1920 Austrian Constitution but also was a distinguished member of that tribunal for many years, where he acted as its judge rapporteur. He was then key in implementing the concentrated system of judicial review that over the following decades, and particularly after World War II, developed throughout Europe. Even in France, with its traditional and initial a priori concentrated system of judicial review, the result of the jurisprudence of the Constitutional Council has been considered the "symbolic end of the sovereignty of the law," given the current consideration of the law as "the expression of the general will *within the respect of the Constitution*."[19]

15 On the origins of the Colombian and Venezuelan systems, see Allan R. Brewer-Carías, *El sistema mixto o integral de control de la constitucionalidad en Colombia y Venezuela*, Universidad Externado de Colombia, Pontificia Universidad Javeriana, Bogotá 1995. See Sandra Morelli, *Colombian National Report II*, p. 2.

16 See Allan R. Brewer-Carías, "La jurisdicción constitucional en América Latina," in Domingo García Belaúnde-Francisco Fernández Segado (coords.), *La jurisdicción constitucional en Iberoamérica*, Dykinson S.L. (Madrid), Editorial Jurídica Venezolana (Caracas), Ediciones Jurídicas (Lima), Editorial Jurídica E. Esteva (Uruguay), Madrid 1997, pp. 117–161.

17 See Eivind Amith, *Norway National Report*, p. 1.

18 See Julia Iliopoulos-Strangas and Stylianos-Ioannis G. Koutnatzis, *Greek National Report*, pp. 2–3.

19 See Bertrand Mathieu, *French National Report*, p. 5.

The basic thoughts of Kelsen on the matter, as already mentioned, directed at non-German-speaking readers, were expressed in his 1928 article "The Jurisdictional Guarantee of the Constitution (Constitutional Justice),"[20] in which he considered the general problem of the legitimacy of the concentrated system of judicial review. In particular, he analyzed the compatibility of the system with the principle of separation of powers, based on the fact that an organ of the State other than the Legislator could annul statutes without the decision to do so being considered an invasion of the Legislator's domain.

In this regard, after arguing that "to annul a statute[] is to establish a general norm, because the annulment of a statute has the same general character of its adoption," and after considering that to annul a statute is "the same as to adopt it but with a negative sign, and consequently in itself, a legislative function," Kelsen considered that the court that has the power to annul statutes is, consequently, "an organ of the Legislative branch."[21] Nonetheless, Kelsen finished by affirming that, although the "activity of the constitutional jurisdiction" is an "activity of the Negative Legislator," this does not mean that the constitutional court exercises a "legislative function," because that would be characterized by the "free creation" of norms. The free creation of norms, however, does not exist in the case of the annulment of statutes, which is a "jurisdictional function" that can only be "essentially accomplished in application of the norms of the Constitution," that is, "absolutely determined in the Constitution."[22] His conclusion was that the constitutional jurisdiction accomplishes a "purely juridical mission, that of interpreting the Constitution," with the power to annul unconstitutional statutes the principal guarantee of the supremacy of the Constitution.[23]

20 See Hans Kelsen, "La garantie juridictionnelle de la constitution (La justice constitutionnelle)," *Revue du droit public et de la science politique en France et a l'ètranger*, Librairie Général de Droit et de Jurisprudence, Paris 1928, pp. 197–257. See also Hans Kelsen, "Judicial Review of Legislation : A Comparative Study of the Austrian and the American Constitutions," *Journal of Politics* 4, nº 2, Southern Political Science Association, May 1942, pp 183-200; "El control de la constitucionalidad de las leyes: Estudio comparado de las Constituciones Austríacas y Norteamericana," *Revista Iberoamericana de Derecho Procesal Constitucional*, No 12, Editorial Porrúa, Mexico 2009, pp. 3-17; "Le contrôle de constitutionnalité des lois. Une étude comparative des Constitutions autrichienne et américaine," *Revue française de droit constitutionnel*, nº 1, Presses Universitaires de France, Paris 1999, pp. 17–30.

21 See Hans Kelsen, *La garantía jurisdiccional de la Constitución (La justicia constitucional)*, Universidad Nacional Autónoma de México, Mexico City 2001, p. 54.

22 *Id.*, pp. 56–57. See Allan R. Brewer-Carías, *Études de droit public comparé*, Bruylant, Brussels 2003, p. 682.

23 See Hans Kelsen, *La garantía jurisdiccional de la Constitución (La justicia constitucional)*, Universidad Nacional Autónoma de México, Mexico City 2001, p. 57.

As I argued a few years ago, in reality, constitutional courts do not "repeal" a statute in annulling it, and the annulment they can pronounce is not based on discretionary powers but on constitutional and legal criteria, on the application of a superior rule, embodied in the Constitution. Thus, in no way do they exercise a legislative function. The function of a constitutional court, as argued by Kelsen, is thus jurisdictional; the same that is assigned to an ordinary court but characterized as a guarantee of the Constitution. And, if it is true that constitutional judges in many cases decide political issues when considering the constitutionality of legislative acts, they do so by legal methods and criteria, in a process initiated by a party with the required standing.[24] Only exceptional constitutional courts are authorized to initiate *ex officio* constitutional proceedings.

Eventually, Kelsen, in the same article, summarized the "result" of judicial review in the concentrated system, highlighting that, to guarantee the Constitution, it is indispensable for the unconstitutional statute to be annulled by a constitutional court ruling, that has as a matter of principle and in the interest of legal security, *ex nunc*, *pro futuro* effects (i.e., nonretroactive effects), a rule that nonetheless could be mitigated. Kelsen also considered that the annulment of a statute did not produce the rebirth of old statutes abrogated by the annulled one, a decision that nonetheless he considered could be assigned to the constitutional court, evidencing in such case the "legislative character" of its function.[25]

My purpose in this study is to analyze in comparative law all those situations in which constitutional courts interfere not only with the Legislator and its legislative functions but also with the "constitutional legislator," that is, with the Constituent Power,[26] by assuming, in one way or another, the role of positive legislators. For such purpose, I divide this general report into five chapters. The first analyzes the general aspects of judicial review of the constitutionality of legislation exercised by constitutional courts, as well as

[24] See Allan R. Brewer-Carías, *Études de droit public comparé*, Bruylant, Brussels 2003, p. 685. See also A. Pérez Gordro, *El Tribunal Constitucional y sus funciones*, Barcelona 1982, p. 41. See the comment of Laurence Claus and Richard S. Kay, *U.S. National Report*, pp. 4, 6.

[25] See Hans Kelsen, *La garantía jurisdiccional de la Constitución (La justicia constitucional)*, Universidad Nacional Autónoma de México, Mexico City 2001, pp. 82–86.

[26] I will use the expression "Constituent Power" in order to refer to the will of the people (original constituent power) when approving a Constitution (for instance through a referendum), or to a Constituent Assembly when sanctioning a Constitution, or to any organs of the state with constitutional power to review or change the Constitution. See generally, Pedro de Vega, *La Reforma Constitucional y la Problemática del Poder Constituyente*, Ed. Tecnos, Madrid 2000; Allan R. Brewer-Carías, *Poder Constituyente Originario y Asamblea Nacional Constituyente*, Editorial Jurídica Venezolana, Caracas 1998.

the courts' relation with the Legislator. The second chapter examines cases in which the constitutional courts interfere with the Constituent Power, by enacting constitutional rules and even mutating[27] the Constitution. The third chapter explores the role of constitutional courts that interfere with the Legislator regarding existing legislation, assist the Legislator, complement statutes and add provisions to them through constitutional interpretation, and determine the temporal effects of legislation. The fourth chapter analyzes the role of constitutional courts that interfere with the Legislator regarding absolute and relative legislative omissions and, in some cases, act as provisional legislators. The fifth chapter discusses the role of constitutional courts as legislators on matters of judicial review.

[27] The expresión "constitutional mutation" is used in order to refer to the changes made to the content of a constitutional provision when without formally "reforming" its text, by means of a judicial interpretation it result with a different meaning. See Salvador O. Nava Gomar, "Interpretación, mutación y reforma de la Constitución. Tres extractos," in Eduardo Ferrer Mac-Gregor (coord.), *Interpretación Constitucional*, vol. II, Editorial Porrúa, Universidad Nacional Autónoma de México, México 2005, pp. 804 ss. See also generally on the subject, Konrad Hesse, "Límites a la mutación constitucional," in *Escritos de derecho constitucional*, Centro de Estudios Constitucionales, Madrid 1992, pp. 79–104; and Rogelia Calzada Conde, "Poder Constituyente y mutación constitucional: especial referencia a la interpretación judicial," in *Jornadas de Estudio sobre el Título Preliminar de la Constitución*, Ministerio de Justicia/Secretaría General Técnica/Centro de Publicaciones, Madrid 1988, vol. 11., pp. 1.097–1.111.

Chapter 1

JUDICIAL REVIEW OF LEGISLATION AND THE LEGISLATOR

I. THE SYSTEMS OF JUDICIAL REVIEW AND THE ROLE OF CONSTITUTIONAL COURTS

The result of Kelsen's proposals and their applications in Europe was the development of the concentrated system of judicial review, which attributed specially created constitutional bodies (constitutional courts, tribunals or councils) generally conceived of outside the Judiciary with the power to annul, with *erga omnes* effects, unconstitutional statutes –this was the initial pattern followed after World War II in Germany, Italy, France, Spain, and Portugal. The system developed as the result of a compromise between the need for a judicial review system derived from the notion of constitutional supremacy and the traditional European idea of the separation of powers, which had denied the courts any power to invalidate statutes.

But in spite of the importance of Kelsen's contributions, it is improper to identify the concentrated system of judicial review as a whole with a so-called "European model," because there are also concentrated systems of judicial review in which the exclusive and original jurisdiction to annul statutes, without the creation of a special court or tribunal, has fallen to the existing supreme courts of justice, located at the apex of the Judicial Power, as has been the case, since the nineteenth century, in many Latin American countries.[1] In addition, in many Latin American countries, the judicial

1 The "European model" is referred to the concentrated system of judicial review when the constitutional jurisdiction is assigned to a special constitutional court. Other countries without special constitutional courts also follow the concentrated system of judicial review by assigning the constitutional jurisdiction to existing supreme courts. In this sense, the concentrated system of judicial review has been adopted in Brazil, Bolivia, Colombia, Costa Rica, Chile, Dominican Republic, Ecuador, El Salvador, Guatemala, Honduras, Mexico, Nicaragua, Panama, Paraguay, Peru, Uruguay, and Venezuela. But only in Bolivia, Colombia, Chile, Guatemala, Peru, and Ecuador is the constitutional jurisdiction assigned to special constitutional courts or tribunals. In

review system has developed as a mixed system, combining the diffuse and the concentrated methods that function in parallel,[2] as is also the case in Portugal,[3] Greece,[4] and Canada.[5]

In addition, we must remind that before Kelsen's ideas took root in Europe, also since the nineteenth century, the other main system of judicial review, the diffuse or decentralized one, was developed in the United States as a consequence of the same principle of the supremacy of the Constitution. According to this diffuse system, all judges and courts are empowered to act as constitutional judges, in the sense that when applying the law, they are allowed to decide the law's constitutionality; therefore, they are empowered to decide not to apply a statute that they consider unconstitutional when deciding a particular judicial case or controversy, giving priority to the Constitution. In this system, the courts are empowered not to formally annul statutes with *erga omnes* effects but to only declare their unconstitutionality with *inter partes* effects.

Although the system was first implemented in the United States, and was followed in many common law countries, it cannot be considered a system peculiar to the common law system, and thus incompatible with the civil or Roman law tradition.[6] As mentioned already, it had existed and developed since the nineteenth century in parallel with the concentrated system in many Latin American countries,[7] all of them being part of the Roman law family of legal systems, as well as in some European countries.

the other countries, it is exercised by the existing supreme courts. Only in Bolivia, Costa Rica, Chile, Ecuador, El Salvador, Honduras, Panama, Paraguay, and Uruguay does the system remain exclusively concentrated. In the other countries it has been mixed with the diffuse system, functioning in parallel. See Allan R. Brewer-Carías, *Judicial Review in Comparative Law*, Cambridge University Press, Cambridge 1989; and Allan R. Brewer-Carías, *Constitutional Protection of Human Rights in Latin America: A Comparative Study of Amparo Proceeding*, Cambridge University Press, New York 2009.

2 As in Brazil, Colombia, Dominican Republic, Guatemala, Mexico, Nicaragua, Peru, and Venezuela. See *Id.*

3 See Allan R. Brewer-Carías, *Judicial Review in Comparative Law*, Cambridge University Press, Cambridge 1989; Joaquim de Sousa Ribeiro and Esperança Mealha, *Portuguese National Report*, p. 1.

4 See Julia Iliopoulos-Strangas and Stylianos-Ioannis G. Koutnatzis, *Greek National Report*, pp. 6–7.

5 See Kent Roach, *Canadian National Report*, p. 1.

6 See Allan R. Brewer-Carías, *Judicial Review in Comparative Law*, Cambridge University Press, Cambridge 1989; Vicki C. Jackson and Mark Tushent, *Comparative Constitutional Law*, 2nd ed., Foundation Press and Thomson West 2006, pp. 465 ff., 485 ff.

7 The diffuse system of judicial review has been adopted in Argentina, Brazil, Colombia, Dominican Republic, Guatemala, Mexico, Nicaragua, Peru, and Venezuela. Only in Argentina

In any case, an important aspect to bear in mind is that in diffuse systems of judicial review, when the final decision in a case reaches the supreme court or tribunal, according to the principle of *stare decisis*, the practical effects of the non–application of a statute declared unconstitutional are similar to the practical effects of its annulment, in the sense that even if the statute continues to appear in the books, in practice it is considered null and void.

In addition, even in countries with the diffuse system of judicial review that have not developed the *stare decisis* doctrine, the effects of the supreme court decisions on matters of judicial review are similar, because of the authority that the legal and judicial communities give to supreme court decisions. This is the case in the Netherlands,[8] and also the case in Argentina, where the Supreme Court, since its early decisions, has progressively imposed the doctrine of *stare decisis*.[9] It has been considered as a *de facto stare decisis* doctrine[10] regarding the interpretation of the Constitution and of federal laws, which aims to provide litigants with some degree of certainty as to how the law must be interpreted, a requirement the court finds embedded in the due process clause of the Constitution. In the Argentine *García Aguilera* case decided in 1870, barely eight years after the court's establishment, the Supreme Court held, in a since then oft-repeated statement, that "lower courts are required to adjust their proceedings and decisions to those of the Supreme Court in similar cases,"[11] from which they can depart only if they give "valid motives."[12]

In all the systems of judicial review – whether concentrated or diffuse, hybrid or mixed – what is clear is that the main role of constitutional courts is to interpret and apply the Constitution to test the constitutionality of

does it remain exclusively diffuse. In the other countries, the diffuse system is combined with the concentrated one. See Allan R. Brewer-Carías, *Judicial Review in Comparative Law*, Cambridge University Press, Cambridge 1989; and *Constitutional Protection of Human Rights in Latin America: A Comparative Study of Amparo Proceeding*, Cambridge University Press, New York 2009.

8 See J. Uzman, T. Barkhuysen, and M. L. van Emmerik, *Dutch National Report*, p. 18.

9 Néstor P. Sagües has called this "Argentinean *stare decisis*." See Néstor P. Sagües, "Los efectos de las sentencias constitucionales en el derecho argentino," in *Anuario Iberoamericano de Justicia Constitucional*, Centro de Estudios Políticos y Constitucionales, nº 12, 2008, Madrid 2008, pp. 345–347; *Argentinean National Report II*, p. 3.

10 See Alejandra Rodríguez Galán and Alfredo Mauricio Vítolo, *Argentinean National Report I*, p. 3.

11 Fallos 9:53 (1870), in Alejandra Rodríguez Galán and Alfredo Mauricio Vítolo, *Argentinean National Report I*, p. 4 (footnote 11).

12 See Néstor P. Sagües, *Argentinean National Report II*, p. 3.

statutes and thus preserve the Constitution's supremacy. Thus, constitutional courts are always subordinate to a constitution, not having in principle any power to modify or mutate it or to usurp powers assigned to other State organs. Their essential function is to guarantee the supremacy and integrity of the Constitution by declaring unconstitutional or annulling State acts that violate it, all while being obliged to obey the Constitution by exercising the powers expressly attributed to them in it. Constitutional courts, therefore, are not allowed to assume constituent powers (e.g., issuing decisions that illegitimately modify or mutate the Constitution) or to usurp powers attributed to other constituted powers or organs of the State, like the Executive or the Legislative branches. The contrary is to be considered as a case of the pathology of judicial review.

Regarding other key principles, in general terms, in the exercise of their functions, constitutional courts do so in the course of judicial processes normally initiated by an interested party with due standing in cases or controversies. In the diffuse system it must be a party to the particular case or process, and in the the concentrated system it must be a petitioner with a specific interest to file direct actions on the unconstitutionality of statutes before constitutional courts.[13] As mentioned by Zdenek Kühn, in reference to the Constitutional Court of the Czech Republic, "unlike its short-lived federal predecessor (the Constitutional Court of Czechoslovakia) the Czech Constitutional Court does not have the power to provide generally binding interpretation of the Constitution which would have no connection to either abstract constitutional review or constitutional complaint."[14]

So even in cases of constitutional courts with express constitutional powers to interpret in an abstract way the Constitution, that is, without any reference to a particular action, omission, or decision of a State body, a factual dispute must always exist, for example between two constitutional bodies regarding the interpretation of the Constitution. This is, for instance, the case of Slovakia, where article 128 of the Constitution expressly states that "the Constitutional Court shall give an interpretation of the Constitution or constitutional law if the matter is disputable." The same Constitutional Court of Slovakia has stated that the "Constitutional Court does not decide if the state bodies did break the Constitution by the wrong interpretation" or

[13] See generally Richard S. Kay (ed.), *Standing to Raise Constitutional Issues: Comparative Perspectives, XVIth Congress of the International Academy of Comparative Law, Académie Internationale de Droit Comparé, Brisbane 2002*, Bruylant, Brussels 2005.

[14] See Zdenek Kühn, *Czech National Report*, p. 2.

decide on the constitutionality "of the action, omission or decision of state body, which led to origination of the dispute. The court only provides the interpretation of the disputed part of a constitutional statute."[15]

In Slovakia, petitions for the abstract interpretation of the Constitution can be filed only by some public officials or State bodies[16] and, as mentioned, when a dispute occurs between two State bodies standing against each other with different opinions on the interpretation of a constitutional provision.[17] As a result of the exercise of this competency, the decisions of the Constitutional Court of Slovakia directly complement the normative text of the Constitution, its wording having identical legal power and binding effect as the text of the Constitution itself.[18] This power of judicial review has been used especially since 1993, after the establishment of the Slovak Republic, having an important influence on the shaping of constitutional order of the new State, for instance in matters related to the position and authority of the President of the Slovak Republic.

In Canada, the Constitution can also be interpreted by constitutional courts in an abstract way, without the need for any live cases and controversies. An important feature of the Canadian system of judicial review, is the statutory powers of the federal government to refer abstract legal and constitutional questions to the Supreme Court on a "reference procedure" including those involving the constitutionality of legislation. It has been through this reference procedure that the courts have developed the most important roles as positive legislators, in some cases mutating the Constitution.[19]

A deformation of this possibility of a constitutional court to interpret with binding effects a constitution in an abstract way, that is, without any particular case or dispute involved, at the request of the government or at the

15 The Court has also said: "It follows that the decisions on interpretation of the Constitutional Court of the Slovak Republic does not have and can not have any legal effects in connection with actions, omissions or decisions of state bodies that led to origination of the dispute alike in the cases of proceeding according to art. 125a and art. 152 of the Constitution." See Decision n° II. ÚS 69/99. See Ján Svák and Lucia Berdisová, *Slovakian National Report*, p. 3 (footnote 2).

16 By at least one-fifth of the Members of the National Council of the Slovak Republic, the President of the Slovak Republic, the Government of the Slovak Republic, a court, the Attorney General, or the Public Defender of Rights.

17 "Constitutionally relevant dispute on interpretation of the constitution is a dispute on rights or duties between bodies of the state which have such rights and duties prescribed in the constitution." See Decision n° I. ÚS 30/97. See Ján Svák and Lucía Berdisová, *Slovakian National Report*, p. 3 (footnote 3)

18 See Ján Svák and Lucia Berdisová, *Slovakian National Report*, p. 3.

19 See Kent Roach, *Canadian National Report*, pp. 1, 9.

request of any individual, has been developed by the Constitutional Chamber of the Supreme Tribunal of Venezuela, without any constitutional or legal support. The Chamber, in effect, has "created" a "recourse for the abstract interpretation of the Constitution," whose indiscriminate use has had catastrophic consequences for democracy, given way to an institutional path contrary to democracy and the rule of law.[20] The result has been the reinforcement of an authoritarian government that has developed over the past decade despite its initial electoral origin (1998).[21] This deformation of judicial review powers is also a case of the pathology of judicial review.

In other cases, as an exception to the rule of standing, in some cases constitutional courts can issue rulings also for the abstract interpretation of the Constitution by acting *motu proprio*, that is, without the request of any specific party, whether an individual or a State entity. This is the case, for instance, of the Constitutional Courts in Croatia and in Serbia. In Croatia, the Constitutional Court has cautiously avoided using this power, showing a considerable measure of deference, except in cases where an obviously unconstitutional act has unconstitutionally regulated the Constitutional Court itself.[22] In the case of Serbia, in contrast, the Constitutional Court has often initiated proceedings *ex officio* to assess the constitutionality of statutes, which in practice blurs the difference between requests for judicial review filed by authorities (initiatives) having the needed standing. In addition, when the Court declines to start a procedure on an initiative, it usually states its opinion on the constitutionality of the challenged act. Only when it rejects an initiative for formal reasons does the court not assess the constitutionality of the act in the reasoning of the decision. However, the court can, in any case, put the proceeding in motion independently, even when the initiative has been filed having formal inaccuracies.[23]

[20] See generally Allan R. Brewer-Carías, "Le recours d'interprétation abstrait de la Constitution au Vénézuéla," in *Renouveau du droit constitutionnel. Mélanges en l'honneur de Louis Favoreu*, Paris 2007, pp. 61–70; Brewer-Carías, *Crónica de la "in"justicia constitucional: La Sala Constitucional y el autoritarismo en Venezuela*, Editorial Jurídica Venezolana, Caracas 2007.

[21] See generally Allan R. Brewer-Carías, *Dismantling Democracy. The Chávez Authoritarian Experiment*, Cambridge University Press, New York 2010; Brewer-Carías, "El juez constitucional al servicio del autoritarismo y la ilegítima mutación de la Constitución: el caso de la Sala Constitucional del Tribunal Supremo de Justicia de Venezuela (1999–2009)," in *Revista de Administración Pública*, nº 180, Centro de Estudios Constitucionales, Madrid 2009, pp. 383–418.

[22] See Decision nº U-I-39/2002, Official Gazette *Narodne novine*, nº 10/2002; Sanja Barić and Petar Bačić, *Croatian National Report*, p. 7.

[23] See Boško Tripković, *Serbian National Report*, p. 6.

In other cases, as in Venezuela, the Constitutional Chamber of the Supreme Tribunal has also assumed *ex officio* judicial review powers but in this case without any constitutional or legal authorization, in what can also be considered a case of the pathology of judicial review.[24]

The general principle in any case is that, in general terms, in exercising judicial review, constitutional courts do not act as advisory institutions, without the request of a particular party based on a particular interest, even if the action of unconstitutionality is conceived as an *actio popularis*, that is, a popular action that can be filed by any citizen. In Australia, for example, the High Court held in 1921:

> The Parliament could not confer on a court jurisdiction to give advisory opinions even when such opinions were confined to the validity of enacted legislation and when the determination of the court was "final and conclusive." Under such an arrangement there was no "matter" within the meaning of the Constitution, because there was no "immediate right, duty or liability to be established by the determination of the Court," which would be obliged to make a "declaration of the law, divorced from any attempt to administer that law.[25]

Also in Hungary, in the early phase of court operations, the Constitutional Court declared that it did not undertake answering hypothetical constitutional questions, and in several decisions, it entered to consider how abstract the question raised was. On the one hand, the Court, interpreting its competence narrowly, requires necessary closeness between the statement of facts and the related provision of the Constitution, and it provides interpretation of the Constitution only to resolve a "particular constitutional problem."[26] On the other hand, the Court demands certain distance; it requires that the issue not be closely related to the case and that the decision

[24] See Allan R. Brewer-Carías, "Régimen y alcance de la actuación judicial de oficio en materia de justicia constitucional en Venezuela," *Estudios Constitucionales: Revista Semestral del Centro de Estudios Constitucionales* 4, nº 2, Universidad de Talca, Santiago, Chile 2006, pp. 221–250.

[25] See *In re Judiciary and Navigation Acts (Advisory Opinions* case) (1921) 29 CLR 257; Cheryl Saunders, *Australian National Report*, p. 4.

[26] The Court refused to make a statement about the possibility of raising interest rates on housing loans, because it would have meant interpreting the "constitutional provision in some abstract way unrelated to any individual problem, or . . . a possibility for unbound interpretation." See Decision nº 31/1990, in Lóránt Csink, Józef Petrétei, and Péter Tilk, *Hungarian National Report*, p. 7 (footnote 24).

not become factual,[27] because the Court is not a counsel but the judge of Parliament.[28]

II. CONTROL OF CONSTITUTIONALITY AND CONTROL OF CONVENTIONALITY

In democratic regimes, all judicial review methods have as their main purpose the guarantee of the supremacy of the Constitution. Consequently, when constitutional courts exercise judicial review, they have the task of comparing statutes or primary legislation with the provisions of the Constitution. That is why judicial review is, fundamentally, a constitutional control of legislation or the exercise of judicial control over the constitutionality of legislation.

Nonetheless, the constitutions of many countries, by giving constitutional or supralegal rank to international treaties, also allow the courts, within their constitutional functions of judicial review, the possibility of exercising what can be called "control of conventionality" of statutes, in the sense of guaranteeing the subjection of primary legislation to international conventions, particularly on matters of human rights.[29] This is the case, for instance, in Argentina and Venezuela, where international treaties on human rights have been given constitutional hierarchy, that is, the same rank as constitutional provisions.[30]

27 Upon this, the Court did not interpret whether the petition for the dismissal of the director of public radio can be considered to violate freedom of the press; it could have given, therefore, a statement-of-fact answer for the dispute of the Prime Minister and the President of the Republic. See Decision nº 36/1992, in Lóránt Csink, József Petrétei and Péter Tilk, *Hungarian National Report*, p. 7 (footnote 26).

28 See Decision nº 16/1991, in Lóránt Csink, József Petrétei, and Péter Tilk, *Hungarian National Report*, p. 7.

29 See, e.g., Ernesto Rey Cantor, *El control de convencionalidad de las leyes y derechos humanos*, Editorial Porrúa, Mexico City 2008; Juan Carlos Hitters, "Control de constitucionalidad y control de convencionalidad. Comparación (Criterios fijados por la Corte Interamericana de Derechos Humanos), in *Estudios Constitucionales* 7, nº 2, Santiago de Chile 2009, pp. 109–128; Fernando Silva García, "El control judicial de las leyes con base en tratados internacionales sobre derechos humanos," in *Revista Iberoamericana de Derecho Procesal Constitucional*, nº 5, Instituto Iberoamericano de Derecho Procesal Constitucional, Editorial Porrúa, Mexico City 2006, pp. 231 ff; Víctor Bazán, "Corte Interamericana de derechos humanos y Cortes Supremas o Tribunales Constitucionales latinoamericanos: el control de convencionalidad y la necesidad de un diálogo interjurisdiccional crítico," in *Revista Europea de Derechos Fundamentales*, nº. 16/2, 2010, pp. 15–44.

30 See Allan R. Brewer-Carías, "La aplicación de los tratados internacionales sobre derechos humanos en el orden interno," *Revista Instituto Interamericano de Derechos Humanos*, nº 46, San José, Costa Rica, 2007, pp. 219–271.

In Argentina, even before the 1994 constitutional reform that formally gave "constitutional hierarchy" to a series of enumerated international documents, particularly on matters of human rights (article 75.22), the Supreme Court in *Ekmekdjián v. Sofovich* (1992),[31] on the right to correction (rectification) and response regarding published informations, recognized that international treaties have precedence over internal legislation. Decisions in this vein multiplied after the 1994 constitutional reform in which the Court held that constitutional review includes, as well, comparing internal laws and regulations with international conventions, with the power to declare such laws "unconventional,"[32] that is, contrary to an international convention. In this regard, for instance, the Court compared the provision of the American Convention on Human Rights that guarantees the right to appeal before a superior court as one of the due process rules (article 8.2.h), with provisions of the Argentine criminal legal system that, in some cases, establish a single-instance trial by limiting review of the judgment before the Penal Cassation Court. Consequently, the Supreme Court in the *Casal* case (2005) held that the only way to square the requirement established in the American Convention with the Argentine criminal legal system was to interpret article 456 of the Criminal Procedural Code as allowing an ample review of the prior ruling.[33]

In Venezuela, all international treaties on human rights have the same constitutional hierarchy as the Constitution (article 23) and even prevail in application over the same Constitution if those treaties establish more favorable provisions for the exercise of particular rights. Thus, the Constitutional Chamber of the Supreme Tribunal, during the first years of enforcement of the 1999 Constitution, on many occasions annulled statutes because they were contrary to the American Convention on Human Rights, for instance on matters of the right to political participation and the right to appeal before a superior court in all judicial processes.[34] Unfortunately, this

[31] See Fallos 315:1492 (1992). See Alejandra Rodríguez Galán and Alfredo Mauricio Vítolo, *Argentinean National Report I*, p. 14 (footnote 55). See Néstor Pedro Sagües, *Argentinean National Report II*, p. 19.

[32] See *Mazzeo*, Fallos 330 (2007). See Alejandra Rodríguez Galán and Alfredo Mauricio Vítolo, *Argentinean National Report I*, p. 14 (footnote 57).

[33] Fallos, 328:3399 (2005). See Alejandra Rodríguez Galán and Alfredo Mauricio Vítolo, *Argentinean National Report I*, p. 14 (footnote 59).

[34] See Decision nº 87 of March 13, 2000. "*C. A. Electricidad del Centro (Elecentro) v. Superintendencia para la Promoción y Protección de la Libre Competencia (Procompetencia)*," *Revista de Derecho Público*, nº 81, Editorial Jurídica Venezolana, Caracas 2000, pp. 157 ff. See Carlos Ayala Corao, "Las consecuencias de la jerarquía constitucional de los tratados relativos a derechos humanos," in *Rumbos del Derecho Internacional de los*

constitutional provision of article 23 of the Constitution, in more recent years, has been illegitimately mutated by the same Constitutional Chamber, adopting at the request of the Attorney General, denying the general power of all court to give preference to international treaties on human rights over internal law, and even deciding in 2008 that the rulings of the Inter-American Court on Human Rigths are non-executable in the country.[35]

In effect, in Decision No. 1.939 of December 18, 2008, the Constitutional Chamber of the Supreme Tribunal, in deciding a recourse of interpretation of a decision adopted by the Inter-American Court on Human Rights filed by the Attorney General, rejected the general prevalence of international treaties on human rights regarding internal law, except only when the matter is decided by the Chamber itself.[36] On the other hand, the constitutional rank of international treaties on human rights was proposed to be eliminated in a draft constitutional reform proposal made by a Presidential Council desgned by the President in 2007.[37] Eventually, the proposal was not included in the constitutional reform submitted to popular vote, which that year was rejected by the people. However, what the authoritarian regime was not able to attain thorugh a constitutional reform, in a certain way was carried out by the Constitutional Chamber of the Supreme Court.[38]

As mentioned before, in the same decision, and contrary to the express provision of the same article 23 of the Constitution that established the "direct and immediate application by the courts and other bodies of the State" of human rights treaties, the Constitutional Chamber decided to reserve to itself the power to determine which provisions of treaties would

Derechos Humanos, Estudios en Homenaje al Profesor Antonio Augusto Cancado Trindade, vol. 5, Sergio Antonio Fabris Editor, Porto Alegre, Brazil, 2005.

35 See Decision nº 1.939 of December 18, 2008, Attorney General Office case, http://www.tsj.gov.ve/decisiones/scon/Diciembre/1939-181208-2008-08-1572.html. See comments in Allan R. Brewer-Carías, "La interrelación entre los Tribunales Constitucionales de América Latina y la Corte Interamericana de Derechos Humanos, y la cuestión de la inejecutabilidad de sus decisiones en Venezuela," in Armin von Bogdandy, Flavia Piovesan, and Mariela Morales Antonorzi (coords.), *Direitos humanos, democracia e integração jurídica na América do Sul*, Juris Editora, Rio de Janeiro 2010, pp. 661–701.

36 See the case *Gustavo Alvarez Arias*, http://www.tsj.gov.ve/decisiones/scon/ Diciembre/1939-181208-2008-08-1572.html.

37 See *Consejo Presidencial para la Reforma de la Constitución de la República Bolivariana de Venezuela, "Modificaciones propuestas."* The complete text was published as *Proyecto de Reforma Constitucional. Versión atribuida al Consejo Presidencial para la reforma de la Constitución de la república Bolivariana de Venezuela*, Editorial Atenea, Caracas, July 1, 2007.

38 See Allan R. Brewer-Carías, *Reforma constitucional y fraude a la Constitución. Venezuela 1999–2009*, Academia de Ciencias Políticas y Sociales, Caracas 2009, pp 249–261.

prevail in the internal legal order.[39] With this unconstitutional decision, the Constitutional Chamber illegitimately mutated the Constitution: according to article 23, the authority to apply international treaties on human rights corresponds not only to the Constitutional Chamber but also to all the courts of the Republic when acting as constitutional judges, for instance, when exercising the diffused control of the constitutionality of statutes or when deciding cases of amparo. The intention of the Constitutional Chamber to resereve for itself this aspect of judicial review is not in accordance to the Constitution and to the judicial review system it establishes.

In any case, and referring to the same sort of control of "conventionality" of statutes in democratic countries, this control has developed in all European countries where European Union law, and particularly the European Convention of Human Rights, have prevalence over national law.[40] In particular, the case of the Netherlands must be highlighted. There, as no judicial review of the constitutionality of statutes is allowed in the Constitution, judicial review has developed only as a control of the "conventionality" of such statutes to ensure their subjection to international conventions, specifically on matters of human rights.

In effect, according to article 120 of the Dutch Constitution, "The constitutionality of Acts of Parliament and treaties shall not be reviewed by the courts," which means that judicial review of primary legislation is prohibited, the courts being banned not only from determining the unconstitutionality of statutes but also from declaring them incompatible with the Kingdom Charter.[41] Nonetheless, article 94 of the same Constitution establishes that "Statutory regulations in force within the Kingdom shall not be applicable if such application is in conflict with provisions of treaties that are binding on all persons or of resolutions by international institutions," thus

[39] See *Revista de Derecho Público*, nº 93–96, Editorial Jurídica Venezolana, Caracas 2003, pp. 135 ff.

[40] In the case of Poland, as mentioned by Marek Safjan, "The national court, denying application of a national norm which is contradictory to the European law or interpreting creatively a national norm in the spirit of a European norm *de facto* applies in the legal system a new, earlier non-existent, norm, thus becoming in a way a positive legislator on the level of a specific case." See Marek Safjan, *Polish National Report*, p. 16. Also in Slovakia, according to article 154c of the Constitution, having international treaties, particularly the European Convention of Human Rights, precedence over laws, the courts (including the Constitutional Court) exercise control of conventionality, by giving preference to convention. See Ján Svák and Lucia Berdisová, *Slovak National Report*, pp. 11, 12.

[41] See J. Uzman, T. Barkhuysen, and M. L. van Emmerik, *Dutch National Report*, pp. 2, 5.

leading to the very important development of the system of judicial review of "conventionality" of statutes, particularly on matters of human rights.

Thus, the Dutch system is referred to as a system of "constitutional fundamental rights review by the judiciary" or as "fundamental rights review of parliamentary legislation," that is, regarding the powers of the courts and particularly of the Hoge Raad (High Court) to review acts of Parliament for their compliance with convention rights if the treaty is ratified and insofar as the individual provisions are self-executing.[42] This means that, in the Netherlands, statutes can be reviewed by the courts for their consistency with the written provisions of international law, particularly the UN International Covenant on Civil and Political Rights and the European Convention for the Protection of Human Rights and Fundamental Freedoms (European Convention on Human Rights), which has become the most important civil rights charter for the Netherlands.[43]

Such judicial review has also developed regarding European Union law, which also contains provisions on fundamental rights, in the sense that, because international treaties have precedence over national law, the courts must examine whether national law is compatible with the law of the European Union and, if necessary, either construe national law consistently with European Union law or set it aside if such an interpretation proves impossible under national constitutional law.[44]

In Greece, although the Constitution has no explicit provision for the control of the conventionality of statutes, the courts have held that international treaties have supralegislative status (article 28.1 of the Constitution), which is sufficient basis to exercise control of conventionality if the treaty in question is self-executing, such as the European Convention on Human Rights. In the same sense of the control of constitutionality, if Greek courts find that a statutory provision is inconsistent with international law, that provision cannot be applied in the pending case. However, unconventional legislation remains in effect and thus can be applied in a future occasion.[45]

The situation in the United Kingdom must also be mentioned. The British Constitution is not a single and overarching written document like the

[42] *Id.*, pp. 1, 2, 9, 12, 22.

[43] *Id.*, p. 7.

[44] *Id.*, pp. 2, 31, 32.

[45] See Julia Iliopoulos-Strangas and Stylianos-Ioannis G. Koutnatzis, *Greek National Report*, p. 10.

constitutions of other contemporary democratic states. In addition, it is not possible in principle to formally distinguish a constitutional statute from an ordinary statute. Nonetheless, the British Constitution undoubtedly exists, and it is possible to attach the label "constitutional" to some legal[46] and nonlegal rules,[47] called "conventions of the Constitution," which are considered binding rules of political morality and called the "common law constitution," as a set of legal principles and rules that have been laid down over time, typically by judges.[48] It is possible, therefore, to identify a judicial process of controlling the subjection of statutes to these conventions, which can be called "constitutional review."[49] As it has been summarized by John Bell:

> Britain has neither "specific constitutional or statutory provisions that empower constitutional judges, by means of interpreting the Constitution, to adopt obligatory decisions on constitutional matters" nor specific decisions on constitutional matters. But this would be too simplistic an approach. The nature of a common law constitution is that the basic "rules of recognition" (H. L. A. Hart) are not contained in statute, but are in the common law. The principles are rather like the "fundamental principles recognized by the laws of the Republic" in French law, which are not laid down by statute, but which are judicially identified, even if formally not created by judges. There do arise a number of issues on which ordinary judges have to take decisions which are binding and which could be characterized as constitutional.[50]

In this respect, regarding the conventions to the British Constitution, it is also possible to call this process of constitutional review – of course, in its own historical context – a judicial control of conventionality.

But in other constitutional matters, given the recent evolution of the British Constitution by the creation of a Supreme Court in 2009, it is also possible to distinguish constitutional review powers exercised by the courts. This is the case on matters of devolution, regarding the control of the validity of the legislation of the three devolved assemblies (Wales, Scotland, and Northern

46 An example is the agreement reached by the Prime Ministers of the British Empire in 1931 for the U.K. Parliament to not legislate for Dominions without consent of their parliaments. See John Bell, *British National Report*, p. 1.

47 One example is the Nolan principles (1995), which govern standards in public life and introduce a set of values governing the holders of a range of public offices. See John Bell, *British National Report*, p. 2.

48 See John Bell, *British National Report*, p. 1.

49 *Id.*, p. 2.

50 *Id.*, p .3.

Ireland) that can be referred to the Supreme Court by the British Secretary of State, the British Attorney General, or the national Attorneys General (or equivalent), or by the national courts before which the issue is raised.[51]

But the most important recent developments in the United Kingdom on matters of constitutional review have been regarding the compatibility of British statutes with European Union law, that is, on matters of control of conventionality. An example is the matter decided on the compatibility of a British statute concerning the limits for fishing with European Union law, which was raised and decided by the lowest tier of criminal law courts, the Magistrates' Court.[52] But most important in this process of developing constitutional review in the United Kingdom is the example of the protection and interpretation of human rights, particularly after the Human Rights Act was passed in 1998 to implement the European Convention on Human Rights. The Act is considered by John Bell as a major "constitutional statute on fundamental rights" and can lead "to either the narrowing of the scope of legislation by means of an interpretation, which makes the statute compatible with the Convention, or a declaration of incompatibility, which empowers a minister to amend or repeal an incompatible statutory provision."[53] In addition, the question concerning the compatibility of British law with EU law can be raised before the British courts, and if the matter does not give rise to a serious difficulty in interpretation, the courts can apply European law directly and refuse to apply a British statute.[54] Compatibility with EU law is the only area in which British judges have the power to strike down legislation of Parliament, an approach that was definitively adopted after the European Court of Justice specifically stated that the British courts ought not to apply a British act of Parliament that was incompatible with European legislation.[55]

In any case, the court's decision in these cases does not annul an act of Parliament. As expressed by John Bell:

51 *Id.*, p. 2.

52 *Id.*, p. 3.

53 See N. Bamforth, "Parliamentary Sovereignty and the Human Rights Act 1998," [1998] Public Law 572. See John Bell, *British National Report*, p. 3.

54 Case 283/81, *Srl CILFIT v. Minister of Health*, [1982] ECR 3415. See John Bell, *British National Report*, p. 3 (footnote 14).

55 See *R v. Secretary of State for Transport, ex parte Factortame Ltd.*, [1990] 2 AC 85; *R v. Secretary of State for Transport, ex parte Factortame Ltd (*nº *2)*, [1991] 1 AC 603; *R v. Secretary of State for Employment, ex parte Equal Opportunities Commission*, [1995] 1 AC 1. See John Bell, *British National Report*, p. 3 (footnotes 15–16).

> The Government has to decide whether to propose an amendment of the law to bring it into line with the Convention or to take other action to maintain the incompatibility, e.g. by registering a formal derogation from the Convention. This is the nearest that English judges come to a constitutional review.[56]

As Lord Bingham highlighted in the case *A (FC) v. Secretary of State for the Home Department*:

> The effect is not, of course, to override the sovereign legislative authority of the Queen in Parliament, since if primary legislation is declared to be incompatible the validity of the legislation is unaffected (section 4(6)) and the remedy lies with the appropriate minister (section 10), who is answerable to Parliament.[57]

This case of the House of Lords was issued to decide the challenge filed by a number of individuals regarding their detention without trial on the basis of them being a danger to national security, according to the Anti-Terrorism, Crime, and Security Act of 2001. The House of Lords declared the corresponding provision incompatible with articles 5 and 14 of the European Convention.

This control of "conventionality" of statutes, therefore, as is the case in the Netherlands, is the most common constitutional review procedure in the United Kingdom; it has been applied in numerous cases and is considered the most significant constitutional function that the new Supreme Court will have in the future.[58]

In Sweden, there is a very weak diffuse method of judicial review that has developed after the constitutional reform of 1979, which established the power of judicial review only when Parliament has issued an unconstitutional statute due to a "manifest error."[59] It has only been after the beginning of the Europeanization of Swedish law in the late 1990s that some sort of judicial review has been developed, mainly as a result of the progressive subordination of Swedish law to European law and particularly to the European Convention on Human Rights. Consequently, the most important cases of judicial review have been cases of control of

56 See John Bell, *British National Report*, p. 3.

57 See [2004] HL 56. See John Bell, *British National Report*, p. 5 (footnote 25).

58 See John Bell, *British National Report*, p. 6.

59 Chapter 11, article 14 of the Instrument of Government. See Joakim Nergelius, *Swedish National Report*, pp. 17–18.

conventionality decided by the courts, which have compared national legislation with the provisions of the European Convention on Human Rights.[60]

Finally, also regarding the control of conventionality of statutes, the situation of France must be highlighted. In France, the Cour de Cassation and the Conseil d'État have developed control of conventionality of statutes besides and in parallel to the traditional *a priori* judicial review power of legislation exercised by the Constitutional Council. As it has been summarized by Bertrand Mathieu, it has been due to the requirements imposed by international law, particularly by European Union law and the law of the European Convention on Human Rights that, first, the Cour de Cassation and, later, the Conseil d'État, have proceeded to reject the application of laws deemed *inconventionnelles*, that is, contrary to the conventions. The jurisprudence in such cases have been constructed not only on the basis of article 55 of the Constitution, which assigns the treaties or international agreements regularly ratified or approved superior authority regarding the laws, but also because of the refusal of the Conseil Constitutionnel to examine the *conventionalité de la loi* in accordance with its attributions on matters of control of the constitutionality of statutes.

The consequence of this situation on matters of judicial review has been a clear division of tasks: the control of the constitutionality of laws in an abstract and *a priori* way is exercised by the Conseil Constitutionnel when requested by political authorities,and the control of conventionality of laws is exercised by the ordinary judicial or administrative judges, in specific cases and controversies, particularly regarding fundamental rights and freedoms, which the Conseil Constitutionnel has refused to examine. On this situation, Bertrand Mathieu has referred to the paradox that exists in France between the traditional theory and platonic assertion of constitutional preeminence, and the jurisdictional impotence regarding constitutional provisions.[61]

60 See *Lassagard* case, Administrative Court of Appeal of Jönköping, 1996, which declared that the absence of judicial review in the particular case (agricultural subsidy) was contrary to article 6 of the ECHR; see also *Lundgren* case, Supreme Court, 2005, in which the extension of a criminal judicial procedure was also considered contrary to article 6 of the ECHR. See Joakim Nergelius, *Swedish National Report*, pp. 21–29.

61 See Bertrand Mathieu, *French National Report*, p. 3.

III. THE INTERPRETATION OF THE CONSTITUTION AND THE INFLUENCE OF THE CONSTITUTIONAL COURTS ON CONSTITUTIONAL AND LEGAL REFORMS

The main tool of constitutional courts is the power to interpret the Constitution to ensure its application, enforceability, and supremacy by adapting the Constitution when changes and time require such task but without assuming the role of a constituent power or of the Legislator – they cannot on a discretionary political basis create legal norms or provisions that cannot be deducted from the Constitution itself.[62]

That is why, as a matter of principle, constitutional courts are considered "negative legislators" particularly when deciding to annul statutes,[63] and they cannot act as "positive legislators" in the sense of creating *ex novo* pieces of legislation or introducing "reforms" to statutes. In the words of Laurence Claus and Richard S. Kay, "We will treat judges as engaged in positive lawmaking when they originate a scheme of law as opposed to merely considering, revising or rejecting schemes conceived by other legislative actors" or "for a constitutional court to be positive lawmaker under this terminology would involve the court in considering, propounding, and creating a scheme of regulation of its own conception."[64]

That is, constitutional courts cannot innovate in the legal order in a discretionary way, as they do not have the authority to create new law.[65] As the Federal Supreme Tribunal of Brazil has explained with respect to its decisions that annul statutes:

> The Federal Supreme Tribunal, when exercising the abstract judicial review of objective law positivized in the Constitution of the Republic, act as a virtual Negative Legislator, so its declaration of unconstitutionality comprise an exclusion judgment of control that, based on the attributions assigned to the Tribunal, consists in removing from the positive legal order,

62 See Jorge Carpizo, *El Tribunal Constitucional y sus límites*, Grijley, Lima 2009, pp. 56, 68.

63 In this sense, in some countries, as in Chile, it has been said that the Constitutional Tribunal can act only as negative legislator. See Francisco Zúñiga Urbina, "Control de constitucionalidad y sentencia," *Cuadernos del Tribunal Constitucional*, nº 34, Santiago de Chile 2006, pp. 107, 109.

64 See Laurence Claus and Richard S. Kay, *U.S. National Report*, pp. 3, 5.

65 See Luis Roberto Barroso et al., "Notas sobre a questão do legislador positivo," *Brazilian National Report III*, pp. 19–20; Néstor Pedro Sagües has mentioned that constitutional jurisdiction transforms itself into positive legislation, when it generates infraconstitutional provisions compatible with the Constitution, with the excuse of controlling the constitutionality of the legal order, in *Argentina National Report II*, p. 3.

> the State invalid expression non conformed with the model included in the Constitution of the Republic.[66]

In another case, the same Brazilian Federal Supreme Tribunal, in reviewing Law N° 9.504/97 on the free use of television and radio programs by political parties challenged because considered contrary to the principle of equality, argued:

> The declaration of unconstitutionality in the way it was requested, would modify the system of the law, altering it sense, which is a legal impossibility, because the Judicial Power, when controlling the constitutionality of normative acts, only acts as negative legislator and not as positive legislator.[67]

The consequence of this classical approach is that, constitutional courts being negative legislators, the direct effect of the constitutional courts' decisions excluding from the legal order pieces of legislation, is that the Legislator, in response, very frequently decides to reform the legislation or to enact a new piece of legislation, to comply with the constitutional court criteria.[68] Also, constitutional reforms have occurred after decisions adopted by constitutional courts to follow the doctrine they established.

For instance, in Argentina, Law No. 26,025 was passed to modify the rules applicable to the Supreme Court's appellate jurisdiction (article 117 of Constitution), after the Supreme Court ruled on the unconstitutionality of previous legislation that provided that all cases ordering the government to pay social security benefits were to be appealed before the Supreme Court. Because the rule actually delayed the payment of pensions to elderly people, in *Itzcovich* case (Fallos 2005), the Court declared that the appeal procedure had become unconstitutional in that it affected petitioner's right to a speedy trial.[69]

[66] STF, *DJ*, June 18, 1993, Rcl 385 QO/MA, Rel. Min. Celso de Mello, in Luis Roberto Barroso et al., "Notas sobre a questão do legislador positivo," *Brazilian National Report III*, p. 9.

[67] See STF, *DJ*, December 10, 1999, ADI 1.822/DF, Rel. Min. Moreira Alves, in Luis Roberto Barroso et al., "Notas sobre a questão do legislador positivo," *Brazilian National Report III*, p. 15.

[68] For instance, in the Netherlands, legislation was issued after the *Dutch Citizenship* case (Supreme Court judgment of October 12, 1984, NJ 1985/230). See J. Uzman, T. Barkhuysen, and M. L. van Emmerik, *Dutch National Report*, p. 21.

[69] See Fallos: 328:566 (2005). See Alejandra Rodríguez Galán and Alfredo Mauricio Vítolo, *Argentinean National Report I*, pp. 13–14 (footnote 54).

Something similar happened on matters of marriage law. Although the Argentinean Constitution recognizes the right to marriage, the Civil Code established that divorce did not entail the right to a new marriage, a clause whose constitutionality the courts upheld several times. However, in 1986, the Supreme Court applied what was called a "dynamic," or living constitution, approach considering in *Sejean* case[70] that changes to society's perception of a topic require giving new scope to the right to human dignity, and thus it declared unconstitutional the statute that had been in force for almost a century. This decision was the prelude to reforming the law of civil marriage, which, following the Supreme Court decision, allowed for the possibility of a subsequent marriage.[71]

With respect to Portugal, as mentioned by Joaquim de Sousa Ribeiro, it is a fact that, "even though the Constitutional Court does not play a part in the law making process, many amendments made to existing legislation are the result of its ruling, either to incorporate or to set aside the Court's ruling on the subject."[72]

IV. THE QUESTION OF CONSTITUTIONAL COURTS AS POSITIVE LEGISLATORS

In any case, in the contemporary world, the truth is that judicial review has progressively evolved, surpassing the former rigid character of courts only being negative legislators,[73] as a result of the development of new principles that, at the time of Kelsen's proposals, were not on the agenda of constitutional courts and judges.[74]

70 See Fallos 308:2268 (1986). See Alejandra Rodríguez Galán and Alfredo Mauricio Vítolo, *Argentinean National Report I*, p. 15 (footnote 61).

71 See Alejandra Rodríguez Galán and Alfredo Mauricio Vítolo, *Argentinean National Report I*, p. 5.

72 See Joaquim de Sousa Ribeiro and Esperança Mealha, *Portuguese National Report*, p. 9.

73 See Francisco Fernández Segado, "Algunas reflexiones generales en torno a los efectos de las sentencias de inconstitucionalidad y a la relatividad de ciertas fórmulas estereotipadas vinculadas a ellas," *Anuario Iberoamericano de Justicia Constitucional*, Centro de Estudios Políticos y Constitucionales, nº 12, 2008, Madrid 2008, p. 195.

74 That is why Francisco Javier Díaz Revorio, referring to the European system of judicial review has said, "We are debtors of Kelsen, but not 'slaves' of his ideas," in *Las sentencias interpretativas del Tribunal Constitucional*, Lex Nova, Valladolid 2001, p. 305.

That is why, for instance, in Brazil, the Federal Supreme Tribunal in some cases has considered the same notion of negative legislator that it defended in many previous decisions an "ancient dogma" and a "myth."[75]

Consequently, new principles have developed; for example, the principle of preservation of statutes, derived from the presumption of constitutionality they have, has empowered constitutional courts to interpret statutes according to or in harmony with the constitution,[76] in order to avoid any legislative vacuum, bypassing the need to declare statutes unconstitutional. This is today one of the main tools of constitutional courts when interpreting the constitution, which they have used in some cases, to fill permanently or temporarily the vacuums that annulling the statute could originate.

Another important role that has progressively developed during the past decades, far from the role of declaring null unconstitutional statutes, is the power of constitutional courts on matters of judicial review, not regarding existing legislation, but regarding the absence of statutes or the omissions or abstention incurred by the Legislator when sanctioning statutes.[77]

That is, constitutional courts also control the omissions of the Legislators to produce the legislation that they have the constitutional obligation to sanction. These omissions can be absolute or relative, and judicial review, in both cases, has contributed to the development of new trends in the control of constitutionality of statutes, which converts constitutional courts into a sort of legislative assistant. Nonetheless, in some cases, where judicial review of legislative omissions is not effectively developed, control of those omissions is only possible in an indirect way, by claiming State liability for the absence of a legislative act.[78]

In contrast, the same change of the scope of judicial review has occurred in diffuse or decentralized systems of judicial review, where, in practice, as was stated by Christopher Wolfe, supreme courts, "once a distinctively judicial power, essentially different from legislative power, [have] become merely

[75] See Luis Roberto Barroso et al., "Notas sobre a questão do legislador positivo," *Brazilian National Report III*, p. 22.

[76] See Francisco Javier Díaz Revorio, *Las sentencias interpretativas del Tribunal Constitucional*, Lex Nova, Valladolid 2001, p. 288; See Joaquim de Sousa Ribeiro and Esperança Mealha, *Portuguese National Report*, p. 7.

[77] These judicial review powers do not correspond with Kelsen's pattern of judicial review as negative legislation. See Francisco Javier Díaz Revorio, *Las sentencias interpretativas del Tribunal Constitucional*, Lex Nova, Valladolid 2001, p. 278.

[78] This is what has been envisaged in Greece. See Julia Iliopoulos-Strangas and Stylianos-Ioannis G. Koutnatzis, *Greek National Report*, p. 5.

another variant of legislative power"; considering that, although the Court had never proclaimed it, for the legal profession, "judicial review is an essentially legislative activity"; as such, the controversy is "generally restricted to how this power should be employed, actively or with restraint."[79]

That is why it is sometimes difficult to understand, particularly for non-American lawyers, the exact extent of the expression that any nominee to the U.S. Supreme Court must repeat again and again before the Senate in confirmation hearings: "the task of a judge is not to make law; it is to apply the law."[80] This approach has been considered a "myth" that, as it has been said by Geoffrey R. Stone, must be exposed before there can be a serious discussion about the proper role of U.S. judges:

> Faithfully applying our Constitution's 18th- and 19th-century text to 21st-century problems requires not only careful attention to the text, fidelity to the framers' goals and respect for precedents, but also awareness of the practical realities of the present. Only with such awareness can judges, in a constantly changing society, hope to keep faith with our highest law.
>
> This does not mean judges are free to make up the law as they go along. But it does mean that constitutional law is not a mechanical exercise of just "applying the law."[81]

In any case, it is a fact in the contemporary world that constitutional courts have progressively assumed a more important role assisting the Legislator in its functions and even creating norms that they can deduct from the constitution.[82] In some cases, they are more than auxiliaries to the Legislator; they substitute for it, assuming the role of positive legislators by issuing temporary or provisional rules to be applied on specific matters.

This has occurred, for instance, in many cases by means of the application of the principle of progressiveness and the prevalence of fundamental rights, like the right to equality and nondiscrimination, in the interest of the

[79] See Christopher Wolfe, *The Rise of Modern Judicial Review: From Constitutional Interpretation to Judge-Made Law*, Basic Books, New York 1986, p. 3; Wolfe, *La transformación de la interpretación constitucional*, Civitas, Madrid 1991, p. 15.

[80] This was what Judge Sonia Sotomayor said in the confirmation hearing before the Senate on July 13, 2009. See Peter Baker and Neil A. Lewis, "Sotomayor Vows 'Fidelity to the Law' as Hearings Start," *New York Times*, July 14, 2009, p. A15.

[81] See Geoffrey R. Stone, "Our Fill-in-the-Blank Constitution," Op-Ed, *New York Times*, April 14, 2010, p. A27.

[82] See Iván Escobar Fornos, "Las sentencias constitucionales" in *Estudios Jurídicos*, vol. 1, Ed. Hispamer, Managua 2007, p. 489.

protection of citizens' rights and guarantees, in which cases the interference of the courts in the legislative function has been considered legitimate and according to the constitutional principles and values.

Nonetheless, the legislative agenda of constitutional courts has also included other areas of activism, sometimes with political purposes. For example, in many cases, as has been the case in the former Socialist countries of Eastern Europe, constitutional courts have had an important role implementing, developing, and strengthening the Constitution, and particularly the newly established democratic regime and the rule of law principles.[83]

But in other countries, quite far from the protection of fundamental rights and the consolidation of democratic principles, the danger of constitutional courts encroaching on the legislative power to contribute to the dismantling of the principle of separation of powers is not just a "phantom," as Hamilton pointed out in another context two centuries ago.[84] On the contrary, it has been a tragic reality, particularly in countries ruled by authoritarian governments. In some countries, constitutional courts have assumed with absolute impunity the task of supporting and legitimizing unconstitutional statutes and government acts, in many cases usurping the constituent and legislative powers, of course without any sort of argument to support the partisan judicial decisions taken supposedly in the best interest of the country or for the good of the nation.[85]

Worse, in those cases, it is not a matter of considering "the Judge as Legislator for Social Welfare,"[86] as was the case in the United States at the beginning of the twentieth century, which Benjamin Cardozo considered a necessity,[87] but a matter of the court being an instrument to support an

[83] For instance, in the process of transformation of the former Socialist States into contemporary democratic States subjected to the rule of law. See, for instance, Marek Safjan, *Polish National Report*, pp. 7, 10; Sanja Barić and Petar Bačić, *Croatian National Report*, pp. 18, 21, 28; Boško Tripković, *Serbian National Report*, pp. 1, 14.

[84] He said in Paper nº 81 of *The Federalist*, "The Judiciary Continued, and the Distribution of the Judiciary Authority," that "It may in the last place be observed that the supposed danger of judiciary encroachments on the legislative authority, which has been upon many occasions reiterated, is in reality a phantom." See Clinton Rossiter (ed.), *The Federalist Papers*, Penguin Books, New York 2003, pp. 483–484.

[85] See Christopher Wolfe, *The Rise of Modern Judicial Review: From Constitutional Interpretation to Judge-Made Law*, Basic Books, New York 1986, p. 101; *La transformación de la interpretación constitucional*, Civitas, Madrid 1991, p. 144.

[86] *Id.* pp. 223 ff. and 305 ff.

[87] Benjamin Cardozo recognized "without hesitation that judges must and do legislate," though "only between gaps" of the law. See Benjamin Cardozo, *The Nature of the Judicial Process*,

authoritarian government,[88] and even to restrict constitutional freedoms, which cannot be accepted. This happened, for instance, regarding freedom of expression in Venezuela, in 2001, when the constitutional court *ex officio* restricted the citizens' right to response and to rectification regarding the President of the Republic's media statements;[89] and in 2008, when the same constitutional court decided to confiscate the assets of a private TV station.[90]

In any case, in all the countries that have developed systems to control the constitutionality of statutes, discussions have developed regarding the limits of judicial review, the extent of the effects of the constitutional courts, decisions, and the degree of interference allowed in constitutional states by constitutional courts regarding legislative functions. These discussions have always existed and will continue to exist. They began in all countries with the adoption of judicial review of legislation, and they will continue to exist with constitutional courts, which are the supreme interpreters of the Constitution and have the power to guarantee its supremacy, to interpret statutes according to the Constitution's provisions, to guarantee the enforcement of fundamental constitutional rights, and to resolve conflicts between the different constitutional organs of the State.

The fact is, at the beginning of the twenty-first century, that there is no doubt that constitutional courts are no longer confined to be negative legislators in the traditional way, because their role is no longer reduced

Yale University Press, 1921, pp. 10, 113, 165. See the references in Christopher Wolfe, *The Rise of Modern Judicial Review: From Constitutional Interpretation to Judge-Made Law*, Basic Books, New York 1986, pp. 230, 231, 315, 316.

88 As it has been the case in Venezuela during the past years. See the comments on the most relevant Constitutional Chamber of the Supreme Tribunal decision in Allan R. Brewer-Carías, *Crónica de la "in"justicia constitucional: La Sala Constitucional y el autoritarismo en Venezuela*, Edigtorial Jurídica Venezulana, Caracas 2007; Brewer-Carías, *Reforma constitucional y fraude a la Constitución (1999-2009)*, Academia de Ciencias Políticas y Sociales, Caracas 2009.

89 See Decision nº 1013 of June 12, 2001, *Elías Santana* case. See http://www.tsj.gov.ve/decisiones/scon/Junio/1013-120601-00-2760%20.htm. See the comments in Allan R. Brewer-Carías et al., *La libertad de expresión amenazada (Sentencia 1013)*, Instituto Interamericano de Derechos Humanos, Editorial Jurídica Venezolana, Caracas and San José 2001; "El juez constitucional vs. la libertad de expresión: La libertad de expresión del pensamiento y el derecho a la información y su violación por la Sala Constitucional," in Allan R. Brewer-Carías, *Crónica de la "in"justicia constitucional. La Sala Constitucional y el autoritarismo en Venezuela*, Caracas 2007, pp. 419–468. See also Daniela Urosa Maggi, *Venezuelan National Report*, pp. 16–17.

90 See decision of the Constitutional Chamber nº 956 of May 25, 2007 in Allan R. Brewer-Carías, "El juez constitucional en Venezuela como instrumento para aniquilar la libertad de expresión plural y para confiscar la propiedad privada: El caso RCTV," *Revista de Derecho Público*," nº 110, Editorial Jurídica Venezolana, Caracas 2007, pp. 7–32.

when controlling the constitutionality of statutes, to declare their unconstitutionality, or to annul them when contrary to the Constitution. Constitutional courts have progressively assumed a more active role when reviewing legislative acts vis-à-vis the Constitution.

Nonetheless, what is essential to bear in mind even in cases of new roles and powers is that constitutional courts are, above all, subjected to the Constitution, and as such, they are constituted organs of the State.[91] Thus, they are also subjected to the principle of separation of powers and consequently they are not legislators, as the legislative function is assigned in the Constitution to the legislative body. They can assist the legislators in accomplishing their functions, but they cannot substitute for the legislators and enact legislation.[92] The legislative organs of the States that are contemporary democracies, integrated by representatives elected by universal suffrage, are called to enact legislation through a constitutionally prescribed procedure and are subject to political accountability before the electors. This legislative framework of State action cannot be substituted for by constitutional courts' attempts to legislate in place of the legislators.[93] On the contrary, they risk being considered "illegitimate oligarchies."[94]

That is why, for instance, one can find declarations from constitutional courts themselves explaining their limits, as the Federal Supreme Tribunal of Brazil did in deciding a direct action of unconstitutionality involving article 45.1 of the Constitution, which established the integration of the House of Representatives. The Court said that the only organ that could establish the number of Federal Representatives for each of the Member States was the National Congress, through the corresponding legislation:

91 As stated by the Constitutional Tribunal of Peru: "the fact of the Constitutional Tribunal being the supreme interpreter of the Constitution, does not change its character of constituted power, and as all of them, subjected to the limits established in the Constitution." Decision of February 2, 2006, STC 0030-2005. See Fernán Altuve Febres, *Peruvian National Report II*, pp. 27–28. See also Rubén Hernández Valle, *Costa Rican National Report*, p. 43.

92 See Humberto Nogueira Alcalá, "La sentencia constitucional en Chile: Aspectos fundamentales sobre su fuerza vinculante," *Anuario Iberoamericano de Justicia Constitucional*, Centro de Estudios Políticos y Constitucionales, nº 12, 2008, Madrid 2008, p. 315.

93 As mentioned by Rubén Hernández Valle, "the activity of the courts is not to create law, but to interpret law. Consequently, Constitutional Courts cannot substitute the Legislator will, because constitutional interpretation, in spite of being conditioned by evident political components, is always juridical interpretation." See Rubén Hernández Valle, *Costa Rican National Report*, p. 42.

94 See P. Martens, "Les cours constitutionelles: des oligarchies illegitimes?" in *La Republic des judges*, Actes du Colloque Organize par le Jeune Barreau de Liège le 7 Février 1997, pp. 53–72, quoted by Christian Behrendt, "L'activité du judge constitutionnel comme législateur-cadre positif," summary of the thesis published in *Revue Européenne de Droit Public*, 2010, p. 16.

> The absence of a complementary law (*vacum juris*) that constitutes the necessary normative instrument cannot be filled by any other State act, specially one with jurisdictional character like this Court. The admission of such possibility would imply to transform the Federal Supreme Tribunal, when exercising the concentrated control of constitutionality, into a positive legislator, a role that the Court refuses itself to assume.[95]

But in spite of this self-restraint approach, it is possible to find examples of such illegitimate oligarchies in other countries, like Venezuela, where the Constitutional Chamber of the Supreme Tribunal has attributed to itself a general power called normative jurisdiction, according to which:

> in specific cases where a constitutional infraction arises, the Chamber has exercised jurisdiction in a normative way, giving immediate enforcement to constitutional provisions, establishing its scope or ways of exercise, even in the absence of statutes directly developing them.[96]

It is true that this normative jurisdiction has been mainly used regarding programmatic constitutional provisions referring to fundamental rights, to allow their immediate enforcement, but unfortunately, it has also been used for other purposes by the authoritarian government that has existed in the country since 1999.[97] In any case, the Venezuelan Constitutional Chamber has based its normative jurisdiction on article 335 of the Constitution, which confers to it the role of guaranteeing the supremacy and effectiveness of constitutional provisions and principles and of issuing binding interpretations of the same, arguing that this provision of the Constitution:

> allows the normative jurisdiction particularly regarding programmatic provisions that exists in the Constitution, which would by timely suspended up to when the Legislator could be so kind to develop them, remaining in the meantime without effects.[98]

95 See STF, *DJ*, May 19, 1995, ADI 267 MC/DF, Rel. Min. Celso de Mello. See Luis Roberto Barroso et al., "Notas sobre a questão do legislador positivo," *Brazilian National Report III*, pp. 14. In another case, the Federal Supreme Tribunal reviewed the electoral law (Lei nº 9.504/97).

96 See Decision nº 1571 of August 22, 2001, case *Asodeviprilara*; http://www.tsj.gov.ve/decisiones/scon/Agosto/1571-220801-01-1274%20.htm; Daniela Urosa Maggi, *Venezuelan National Report*, p. 3.

97 See generally Allan R. Brewer-Carías, *Dismantling Democracy: The Chávez Authoritarian Experiment*, Cambridge University Press, New York 2010.

98 See Decision nº 1571 of August 22, 2001, case *Asodeviprilara*; http://www.tsj.gov.ve/decisiones/scon/Agosto/1571-220801-01-1274%20.htm; Daniela Urosa Maggi, *Venezuelan National Report*, pp. 3–4.

For such purpose of exercising its normative jurisdiction, which in its broader sense is an example of a case of the pathology of judicial review, the constitutional court in Venezuela has even rejected the general procedural law principle that requires the courts to act only at the request of a party with standing, assuming it *ex officio*, without any specific party request or judicial controversy developed on the deciding matter.[99]

That is why, as with any power attributed to a State organ with no possibility of itself being controlled, judicial review can also be distorted and abused without any possibility for the citizens or other constitutional organs of the State to control their actions.

The main question that remains to be anwered on this matter of abuse of constitutional jurisdiction remains, *Quis custodies ipso custodiem*?[100] There is no answer, because there are no State organs that can control constitutional jurisdictions, nor can citizens by means of electoral processes.

Constitutional jurisdiction, therefore, is the only State organ not subjected to checks and balance or control, so the abuse of its functions are out of the reach of the enforcement of constitutional provisions. That is why George Jellinek said that the only guarantee regarding the guardian of the Constitution eventually lies in its "moral conscience";[101] and Alexis de Tocqueville was accurate in his observations of the U.S. Federal Constitution:

> The peace, the prosperity, and the very existence of the Union are vested in the hands of the seven Federal judges. Without them the Constitution would be a dead letter. . . .

99 See Allan R. Brewer-Carías, "Régimen y alcance de la actuación judicial de oficio en materia de justicia constitucional en Venezuela," *Estudios Constitucionales: Revista Semestral del Centro de Estudios Constitucionales* 4, nº 2, Universidad de Talca, Santiago, Chile 2006, pp. 221–250; Daniela Urosa Maggi, *Venezuelan National Report*, pp. 4, 5, 22.

100 See Jorge Carpizo, *El Tribunal Constitucional y sus límites*, Grijley, Lima 2009, pp. 44, 47, 51; Allan R. Brewer-Carías, "*Quis Custodiet Ipsos Custodes*: De la interpretación constitucional a la inconstitucionalidad de la interpretación," *Revista de Derecho Público*, nº 105, Editorial Jurídica Venezolana, Caracas 2006, pp. 7–27; *VIII Congreso Nacional de Derecho Constitucional, Perú*, Fondo Editorial 2005, Colegio de Abogados de Arequipa, Arequipa, September 2005, pp. 463–489.

101 See George Jellinek, *Ein Verfassungsgerichtshof fur Österreich*, Alfred Holder, Vienna 1885, quoted by Francisco Fernández Segado, "Algunas reflexiones generales en torno a los efectos de las sentencias de inconstitucionalidad y a la relatividad de ciertas fórmulas estereotipadas vinculadas a ellas," *Anuario Iberoamericano de Justicia Constitucional*, Centro de Estudios Políticos y Constitucionales, nº 12, 2008, Madrid 2008, p. 196.

> Not only must the Federal judges be good citizens, and men of that information and integrity which are indispensable to all magistrates, but they must be statesmen, wise to discern the signs of the times, not afraid to brave the obstacles that can be subdued, nor slow to turn away from the current when it threatens to sweep them off, and the supremacy of the Union and the obedience due to the laws along with them.
>
> The President, who exercises a limited power, may err without causing great mischief in the state. Congress may decide amiss without destroying the Union, because the electoral body in which the Congress originates may cause it to retract its decision by changing its members. But if the Supreme Court is ever composed of imprudent or bad men, the Union may be plunged into anarchy or civil war.[102]

In the same sense, Alexander Hamilton, warned about the "authority of the proposed Supreme Court of the United States," and particularly the following:

> [Its] power of construing the laws according to the *spirit* of the Constitution, will enable that court to mould them into whatever shape it may think proper; especially as its decisions will not be in any manner subject to the revision or correction of the legislative body.

He concluded:

> [T]he legislatures of the several States, can at any time rectify, by law, the exceptionable decisions of their respective courts. But the errors and usurpations of the Supreme Court of the United States will be uncontrollable and remediless.[103]

This is important to bear in mind, particularly in democratic regimes, where the conversion of constitutional courts into legislators violates the principle of separation of powers and transforms them into State organs not subject to political liability. In other words, the blurring of the limits between

[102] See Alexis de Tocqueville, *Democracy in America*, ch. 8, "The Federal Constitution," trans. Henry Reeve, revised and corrected, 1899, http://xroads.virginia.edu/~HYPER/DETOC/1_ch08.htm See also Jorge Carpizo, *El Tribunal Constitucional y sus límites*, Grijley, Lima 2009, pp. 46–48.

[103] See Alexander Hamilton, nº 81 of *The Federalist*, "The Judiciary Continued, and the Distribution of the Judiciary Authority"; Clinton Rossiter (Ed.), *The Federalist Papers*, Penguin Books, New York 2003, pp. 480. See also Laurence Claus and Richard S. Kay, *U.S. National Report*, p. 10.

interpretation and normative jurisdiction "could transform the guardian of the Constitution into sovereign."[104]

The truth is that, in many countries, given the political regime or the condition of the members of constitutional courts, the important instruments designed to guarantee the supremacy of the Constitution, the enforcement of fundamental rights, and the functioning of the democratic regime have been the most diabolical instruments of authoritarianism, legitimizing the actions contrary to the Constitution taken by the other branches of government,[105] and sometimes on their own initiative by the obsequious servants of those in power. These cases, of course, make a mockery of judicial review, because as Mauro Cappelletti affirmed a few decades ago, judicial review is incompatible with authoritarianism and not tolerated by authoritarian regimes that are enemies of freedom.[106] This illness of judicial review, that is also a case of the pathology of judicial review, occurs when constitutional courts, as docile instruments of governments, openly assume the role of the legislator, usurping its powers and functions or, even worse, assuming the role of the constituent power by mutating the Constitution in an illegitimate way.[107] Unfortunately, this has been the case of constitutional courts acting at the service of authoritarian governments, and the Constitutional Chamber of the Supreme Tribunal of Justice in Venezuela is an example. In many aspects, that example shows how serious the illness is that is affecting constitutional jurisdiction and turning constitutional justice into unconstitutional justice.[108]

104 See Francisco Fernández Segado, "Algunas reflexiones generales en torno a los efectos de las sentencias de inconstitucionalidad y a la relatividad de ciertas fórmulas estereotipadas vinculadas a ellas," *Anuario Iberoamericano de Justicia Constitucional*, Centro de Estudios Políticos y Constitucionales, nº 12, 2008, Madrid 2008, p. 161.

105 See Néstor Pedro Sagües, *La interpretación judicial de la Constitución*, LexisNexis, Buenos Aires 2006, p. 31.

106 See Mauro Capelletti, "¿Renegar de Montesquieu? La expansión y legitimidad de la justicia constitucional," *Revista Española de Derecho Constitucional* 6, nº 17, Madrid 1986, p. 17; Francisco Eguiguren and Liliana Salomé, *Peruvian National Report I*, p. 7.

107 See regarding the case of the Constitutional Chamber in Venezuela, Allan R. Brewer-Carías "El juez constitucional al servicio del autoritarismo y la ilegítima mutación de la Constitución: el caso de la Sala Constitucional del Tribunal Supremo de Justicia de Venezuela (1999–2009)," in *Revista de Administración Pública*, nº 180, Madrid 2009, pp. 383–418; "La ilegítima mutación de la Constitución por el juez constitucional y la demolición del Estado de derecho en Venezuela," in *Revista de Derecho Político*, nº 75–76, Homenaje a Manuel García Pelayo, Universidad Nacional de Educación a Distancia, Madrid, 2009, pp. 289–325.

108 See generally Allan R. Brewer-Carías, *Crónica de la "in"justicia constitucional. La Sala Constitucional y el autoritarismo en Venezuela*, Editorial Jurídica Venezolana, Caracas 2007.

Chapter 2

CONSTITUTIONAL COURTS' INTERFERENCE WITH THE CONSTITUENT POWER

Constitutional courts, being constitutional organs leading with constitutional questions, in many cases interfere not with the ordinary Legislator, but with the constitutional legislator, that is with the constituent power, by enacting constitutional rules when resolving constitutional disputes between state organs or even by legitimately making changes to a constitution by means of adapting its provisions and giving them concrete meaning.

I. CONSTITUTIONAL COURTS' RESOLUTION OF DISPUTES OF CONSTITUTIONAL RANK AND ENACTMENT OF CONSTITUTIONAL RULES

The principle of the supremacy of the Constitution, particularly regarding rigid Constitutions, implies that the Constitution and all constitutional rules can be enacted only by the constituent powers established and regulated in the same constitution. This constituent power can be the people, directly expressing their will (e.g., by means of a referendum) or an organ of the State acting as a derived constituent power. The consequence is that no constituted power of the State by itself can enact constitutional rules, except when expressly authorized by a constitution to participate in a constitution-making process.

Nonetheless, in contemporary constitutional law, there are cases in which constitutions authorize, exceptionally and indirectly, organs of the State to enact constitutional rules. For instance, this is the case of parliaments when the constitution has authorized them to enact laws with constitutional rank (i.e., constitutional laws). In other cases, constitutions expressly authorize constitutional courts to enact constitutional rules when deciding conflicts regarding attributions of State organs, for instance on matters of political decentralization. This is particularly true in federal States, which are always constructed on a constitutional system of territorial distribution of powers between the federal (national) and state level, and even in some cases, a municipal level.

When resolving conflicts of competencies between constitutional organs, constitutional courts without a doubt enact constitutional rules. It is in this sense that Konrad Lachmayer, with respect to Austria, says that, since 1925, article 138.2 of the Constitution has enabled the Constitutional Court to act as a positive legislator, giving positive powers to the court in the sensitive area of the division of competences between the Federation and the states (*Länder*). The provision reads as follows: "The Constitutional Court furthermore determines at the request of the Federal Government or a state Government whether a legislative or executive act is part of the competence of the Federation or the States." This means that the Constitutional Court has the final say on the question of whether ultimate authority belongs to the Federation or to the states (*Länder*).

Because in the Austrian concept of a federal state, concurring competences between the federal level of government and the states do not exist, but only exclusive competencies according to a strict separation of powers, the decisions of the Constitutional Court, established in article 138.2 of the Constitution, is understood to be an authentic interpretation of the Constitution, meaning that the Constitutional Court, when deciding conflicts between constitutional entities, "enacts constitutional law."[1]

In other federal states with the same concentrated system of judicial review as Austria, constitutional courts are also empowered to decide on constitutional conflicts between the Federation and the states, and consequently to determine the territorial level of government to which correspond the competence in conflict. This is the case, for instance, of Venezuela, where the Constitutional Chamber of the Supreme Tribunal is empowered to arbitrate constitutional controversies raised between national, state, and municipal bodies (article 336.9 of the Constitution)[2] in a system in which, in addition to exclusive competencies of the three levels of government, there are also concurrent competencies. The decision of the Constitutional Chamber, when determining the level of government that possesses the competency, undoubtedly has constitutional value.

1 See Konrad Lachmayer, *Austrian National Report*, pp. 1–2.

2 See, e.g., Decision nº 2401 of October 8, 2004, "*Gobernador del Estado Carabobo v. Poder Ejecutivo Nacional*," *Revista de Derecho Público*, nº 99–100, Editorial Jurídica Venezolana, Caracas 2004, p. 317.

Nonetheless, this judicial review power can become an instrument for illegitimately mutating the Constitution in a way contrary to its provisions. This happened precisely in Venezuela, in particular, regarding the distribution of competencies between the various territorial levels of government (municipalities, states, and national government), which can be changed only by means of a constitutional reform.[3] Specifically, it happened regarding the competency referred to the conservation, administration and use of roads and national highways, and administration and use of national ports and airports of commercial use, which the Constitution assigns in an "exclusive" way to the states (article 164.10). In 2007, by proposing a constitutional reform, the National Executive intended to centralize this competence of the states,[4] but it was rejected by the people in referendum. Nonetheless, what could not be achieved through popular vote was achieved by the Constitutional Chamber of the Supreme Tribunal in Decision No. 565 of April 15, 2008,[5] issued deciding an autonomous recourse for constitutional interpretation filed by the attorney general. In such ruling, the "exclusive attribution" of the states was converted into a "concurrent" competency that the National Government can revert it in its favor. With this interpretation, the Constitutional Chamber illegitimately mutated the Constitution; usurped popular sovereignty; and changed the federal form of government by mutating the territorial distribution system of powers between the National Power and the states.

[3] See Allan R. Brewer-Carías, "Consideraciones sobre el régimen de distribución de competencias del poder público en la Constitución de 1999," in Fernando Parra Aranguren and Armando Rodríguez García (eds.), *Estudios de Derecho Administrativo: Libro Homenaje a la Universidad Central de Venezuela, Facultad de Ciencias Jurídicas y Políticas, con ocasión del Vigésimo Aniversario del Curso de Especialización en Derecho Administrativo*, vol. I, Tribunal Supremo de Justicia, Caracas 2001, pp. 107–136.

[4] See Allan R. Brewer-Carías, *Hacia la consolidación de un estado socialista, centralizado, policial y militarista: Comentarios sobre el sentido y alcance de las propuestas de reforma constitucional 2007*, Editorial Jurídica Venezolana, Caracas 2007, pp. 41 ff.; Brewer Carías, *La reforma constitucional de 2007 (Comentarios al proyecto inconstitucionalmente sancionado por la Asamblea Nacional el 2 de Noviembre de 2007)*, Editorial Jurídica Venezolana, Caracas 2007, pp. 72 ff.

[5] See Constitutional Chamber, Decision nº 565 of April 15, 2008, case: *Attorney General of the Republic, interpretation recourse of article 164,10 of the 1999 Constitution of 1999*, http://www.tsj.gov.ve/decisio-nes/scon/Abril/565-150408-07-1108.htm. See also Daniela Urosa Maggi, *Venezuelan National Report*, pp. 15–16. See the comments in Allan R. Brewer-Carías, "La ilegítima mutación de la Constitución y la legitimidad de la jurisdicción constitucional: la 'reforma' de la forma federal del Estado en Venezuela mediante interpretación constitucional," in *Memoria del X Congreso Iberoamericano de Derecho Constitucional*, Instituto Iberoamericano de Derecho Constitucional, Asociación Peruana de Derecho Constitucional, Instituto de Investigaciones Jurídicas–UNAM y Maestría en Derecho Constitucional–PUCP, IDEMSA, Lima 2009, vol. 1, pp. 29–51.

The U.S. Supreme Court can also be mentioned regarding the delimitation of the powers of the federal government in relation to the states. In this regard, since 1937, the Supreme Court has developed an expansive constitutional interpretation of congressional authority, according Congress broad authority to regulate under constitutional provisions like the commerce clause of the U.S. Constitution. Article 1, section 8, of the Constitution states, "The Congress shall have the power . . . to regulate Commerce with foreign Nations, and among the several States, and with the Indian Tribes," This provision was initially interpreted in *Gibbon v. Ogden*, 22 U.S. (9 Wheat) I (1824), in which Chief Justice John Marshall, writing for the Court, defined *commerce* to include "all phases of business" and "among the several States" to refer to interstate effects, even if commerce occurs within a state. This clause, "the focus of most of the Supreme Court decisions that have considered the scope of congressional power and federalism,"[6] led to the adoption of very important Supreme Court decisions that were issued after the invalidation of various important pieces of New Deal legislation, like *National Labor Relations Board v. Jones & Laughlin Steel Corp.*, 301 U.S. 1 (1937), *United States v. Darby* 312 U.S. 199 (1941), and *Wickard v. Filburn*, 317 U.S. 111 (1942).

In these decisions, the Supreme Court ceased to distinguish between commerce and other kind of business, such as mining, manufacturing, and production, allowing Congress to exercise control over all business; ceased to distinguish between direct and indirect effects of interstate commerce, allowing Congress to regulate any activity that cumulatively had an effect on interstate commerce; and ceased to consider the Tenth Amendment as a limit on congressional power. Under the test developed, during the following decades, according to Erwin Chemerinsky, it has been difficult to imagine anything that Congress cannot regulate under the commerce clause, so long as it does not violate another constitutional provision.[7] By means of the case law on matters related to the federal State, the Supreme Court's decisions, without doubt, eventually have enacted constitutional rules.

However, in enacting rules about constitutional disputes regarding constitutional distribution of powers in federal States, constitutional courts are not authorized to enact constitutional rules or to give constitutional rank to provisions adopted by constitutional organs of the State not authorized to

6 See Erwin Chemerinsky, *Constitutional Law: Principles and Policies*, Aspen Publishers, New York, 2006, pp. 243 ff.

7 *Id.*, pp. 259–260.

enact constitutional rules. The contrary would be a violation of a constitution, as occurred also in Venezuela, where the Constitutional Court gave constitutional rank and even supraconstitutional rank to provisions that the people had not approved. In effect, after the popular approval of the 1999 Constitution, the National Constituent Assembly adopted a set of "constitutional transition" provisions, not approved by the people, by means of a decree of the "Regime of Transition of the Public Power."[8] In the decree, the Constituent Assembly dismissed all heads of the branches of government, including members of the Supreme Tribunal, and appointed new ones, changing the content of the transition provisions contained in the text of the Constitution. The decree was challenged before the Constitutional Chamber of the Supreme Tribunal of Justice, which issued Decision No. 6, of January 27, 2000,[9] ruling that the National Constituent Assembly had "supraconstitutional" power to create constitutional provisions without popular approval, admitting the existence in the country of two parallel transitional constitutional regimes: the one contained in the transition provisions of the Constitution approved by the people and those approved by the National Constituent Assembly without popular approval. In this way, the Chamber illegitimately changed the Constitution, thus violating popular sovereignty and giving birth to a long period of constitutional instability that still has not ended. This constitutional mutation was ratified by the same Constitutional Chamber in Decision Nº 180 of March 18, 2000.[10]

II. CONSTITUTIONAL COURTS AND JUDICIAL REVIEW OF PROVISIONS OF THE CONSTITUTION AND OF CONSTITUTIONAL REFORMS AND AMENDMENTS

Constitutional courts can also enact constitutional rules when they are empowered to review the Constitution itself, as is the case in Austria, where the Constitutional Court is empowered to confront the Constitution with its

8 *Gaceta Oficial* nº 36.859, December 29, 1999.

9 See *Milagros Gómez et al.* case, in *Revista de Derecho Público*, nº 81, Editorial Jurídica Venezolana, Caracas, 2000, pp. 81 ff., http://www.tsj.gov.ve/decisiones/scon/Enero/06-270100-000011.htm. See also Daniela Urosa Maggi, *Venezuelan National Report*, p. 14.

10 See *Allan Brewer-Carías et al.* case, in http://www.tsj.gov.ve/decisiones/scon/Marzo/180-280300-00-0737%20.htm. See the comments in Allan R. Brewer-Carías, *Golpe de estado y proceso constituyente en Venezuela*, Universidad Nacional Autónoma de México, Mexico City 2002, pp. 367 ff.; Brewer-Carías, "El juez constitucional al servicio del autoritarismo y la ilegítima mutación de la Constitución: El caso de la Sala Constitucional del Tribunal Supremo de Justicia de Venezuela (1999-2009)," *Revista de Administración Pública*, nº 180, Madrid 2009, pp. 383–418. See also Daniela Urosa Maggi, *Venezuelan National Report*, p. 14.

own basic principles, like the principle of democracy, the federal state, the rule of law, separation of powers, and the general system of human rights. Exercising this power, the Austrian Constitutional Court declared in 2001 a constitutional provision itself as unconstitutional, annulling it.[11] The reason for this decision was the ongoing policy of the Austrian legislator to (indirectly) legitimize unconstitutional provisions, which the Constitutional Court had annulled, by creating new constitutional provisions mirroring the former unconstitutional ones. In this case, the Constitutional Court declared void a constitutional provision excluding parts of the Public Procurement Act from its compliance with the Constitution. The scope of review by the Court was limited to the basic principles of the Constitution, holding that the democracy principle and the *Rechtsstaat* principle were violated by exempting constitutional compliance with a significant aspect of legislation (public procurement) in a general manner.[12]

In the same sense, constitutional courts can enact constitutional rules when exercising judicial review over constitutional amendments. For instance, in Colombia, according to article 379 of the Constitution, all constitutional review procedures, including the convening of popular referendum or constituent assemblies are subject to judicial review by the Constitutional Court, which can declare them unconstitutional if they violate rules of procedure.[13] In Ecuador, article 433 of the Constitution assigns the Constitutional Court the power to determine which constitutional review procedure (reform or amendment) must be applied. The Constitution of Bolivia allows the Constitutional Tribunal to decide on actions of unconstitutionality filed against the procedures of partial reform of the Constitution.[14]

Greek courts also have affirmed their power to engage in judicial review of constitutional amendments, although without specifying the exact

11 See, e.g., Constitutional Court, Decision VfSlg 16.327/2001; Konrad Lachmayer, *Austrian National Report*, p. 6 (footnote 20).

12 *Id.*, p. 9.

13 See Mario Alberto Cajas Sarria, "Acerca del control judicial de la reforma constitucional en Colombia," *Revista Iberoamericana de Derecho Procesal Constitucional*, nº 7, Instituto Iberoamericano de Derecho Procesal Constitucional, Editorial Porrúa, Mexico 2007, pp. 19 ff.

14 See Allan R. Brewer-Carías, *Reforma constitucional y fraude a la Constitución. Venezuela 1999-2009*, Academia de Ciencias Políticas y Sociales, Caracas 2009, pp. 78 ff.; Brewer-Carías, "La reforma constitucional en América Latina y el control de constitucionalidad," in *Reforma de la Constitución y control de constitucionalidad. Congreso Internacional, Pontificia Universidad Javeriana, Bogotá Colombia, junio 14 al 17 de 2005*, Pontificia Universidad Javeriana, Bogotá, 2005, pp. 108–159.

constitutional basis or engaging in any meaningful scrutiny of constitutional amendments.[15]

The situation is completely different in cases where constitutional courts exercise judicial review powers regarding reforms or amendments of the Constitution on their merits, not only on matters of procedure. This happens for instance, when the constituent powers try to change constitutional clauses that, according to the express terms of the Constitution, are declared as principles or provisions that cannot be modified or changed. For instance, the Constitution of Brazil establishes: "No proposal of amendment shall be considered which is aimed at abolishing: I. The federative form of State; II. The direct, secret, universal and periodic vote; III. The separation of the Government Powers; IV. Individual rights and guarantees" (article 64, para. 4).

Nonetheless, the powers of a constitutional court to exercise judicial review of the merits of constitutional reforms or amendments, even in cases of clauses that the Constitution stipulates as not modifiable, must be expressly established as one of its competency, as has been established in many countries regarding review on procedural matters concerning constitutional reforms or amendments. On the contrary, the exercise by the constitutional court of judicial review powers not authorized in the Constitution as to the merits of constitutional reforms or amendments would eventually lead the Court to substitute itself for the constituent power. This is what happened, for instance, in Colombia in a decision No. C-141 issued by the Constitutional Court on February 26, 2010, in which the Court annulled Law No. 1,354 of 2009, which convened a referendum to approve reforms to article 197 of the Constitution to allow the reelection for a third period of the President of the Republic.[16] In this case, the Court, in addition to considering various procedural vices affecting the popular initiative of the legislation, and the legislative process followed in the approval of the challenged law, also considered the existence of "vices or excesses in the exercise of the power of constitutional reform." Referring to jurisprudence established since

[15] See Supreme Special Court Judgment nº 11/2003, *DtA* 2009, 553 (555–556); Julia Iliopoulos-Strangas and Stylianos-Ioannis G. Koutnatzis, *Greek National Report*, p. 11 (footnote 85).

[16] Initially the Court published Communiqué nº 9, on February 26, 2010, containing the basic ruling. See http://www.corteconstitucional.gov.co/comunicados/No.%2009%20Comunicado%2026%20de%20febrero%20de%202010.php. See also Sandra Morelli, *Colombian National Report*, pp. 13–16; Germán Alfonso López Daza, *Colombian National Report I*, p. 6. The full text of the decision was later published in 2011. See in http://www.corteconstitucional.gov.co/relatoria/2010/c-141-10.htm.

2003 "under the name of the theory of substitution, the Court confirmed that "it is not feasible any constitutional reform ignoring structural principles or defining elements of the Constitution of 1991," and it affirmed its power to exercise judicial review even regarding the law convening a constitutional reform referendum. As to Law 1,354 of 2009, the Court "found that it ignores some structural axes of the Political Constitution like the principle of separation of powers and the system of checks and balances, the rule of alternation and presidential terms, the right to equality and the general and abstract nature of the laws."[17] The general conclusion of the Constitutional Court's Decision of 2010 to declare the unconstitutionality and to annul Law No. 1,354 was that it was not just "a matter of mere procedural irregularities but of substantial violations of the democratic principle, one of whose essential components is the respect of the forms provided so that the people can express itself."[18]

Regarding this decision of the Constitutional Court, Sandra Morelli has considered it "nothing less than surprising that to find the national body responsible for guarantying the supremacy of the Constitution and its preservation, in sharp contrast with the content of Article 247 of the Constitution that limit[s] its competence to consider vices of procedure when exercising control of constitutionality on the laws convening a constitutional referendum, and that it does it raising the issue that the proposed constitutional reform would constitute a substitution of the constitutional system, in a way that only the primary constituent would be legitimized for such purpose." According to Morelli, "the Colombian constitutional court, on the one hand, is curtailing the powers to reform of the constituted bodies, and on the other, referring to powers, the mutations of the constitution."[19]

In India, the Supreme Court has changed the Constitution on matters of constitutional amendments by establishing substantive limitations on the power of the parliament to amend the Constitution, not provided for in article 368 of the Constitution. In this respect, the Indian Supreme Court, in *Kesvananda Bharti v. State of Kerala*, interpreted an "implied" limitation on the power of Parliament to amend the Constitution, in the sense that it cannot amend the basic features or basic structure of the Constitution.[20] Consequently, judicial review is interpreted as a basic feature of the

[17] *Id.*, p. 19.

[18] *Id.*, p. 20.

[19] *Id.*, p. 22.

[20] See Surya Deva, *Indian National Report*, pp. 5–6.

Constitution,[21] which means that even a constitutional amendment cannot remove the power of judicial review, thus converting the Supreme Court, according to Surya Deva, to "probably the most powerful court in any democracy."[22]

Finally, a case in Venezuela must be mentioned in which the Constitutional Chamber of the Supreme Tribunal of Justice refused to control the constitutionality of a constitutional review procedure that was challenged on grounds of its unconstitutionality. The 1999 Venezuelan Constitution establishes three different and precise procedures for constitutional reforms: the "Constitutional Amendment," the "Constitutional Reform," and the "National Constituent Assembly," depending on the degree and importance of the proposed reforms, the latter being needed for major reforms aiming to transform the State. In 2007, at the initiative of the President of the Republic, the National Assembly sanctioned a "Constitutional Reform" directed to transform the Democratic Decentralized Social State established in the 1999 Consitution into a Socialist, Centralized and Militaristic State.[23] The reform procedure that was followed was challenged before the Constitutional Chamber, but it refused to hear the popular actions filled against it on the grounds that they were "not allowed to be proposed" (*improponibles*) pending the definitive approval of the reform, renouncing to be the guardian of the Constitution'supremacy.[24] Nonetheless,

21 See *Waman Rao v. Union of India*, AIR 1981 SC 271; *S P Sampath Kumar v. Union of India*, AIR 1987 SC 386; *L Chandra Kumar v. Union of India*, AIR 1997 SC 1125. See Surya Deva, *Indian National Report*, p. 6 (footnote 41).

22 See Surya Deva, *Indian National Report*, p. 6.

23 See on the reform proposal Allan R. Brewer-Carías, *Hacia la consolidación de un Estado Socialista, Centralizado, Policial y Militarista. Comentarios sobre el sentido y alcance de las propuestas de reforma constitucional 2007,* Colección Textos Legislativos, nº 42, Editorial Jurídica Venezolana, Caracas 2007; Brewer-Carías, *La reforma constitucional de 2007 (Comentarios al Proyecto inconstitucionalmente sancionado por la Asamblea Nacional el 2 de noviembre de 2007)*, Colección Textos Legislativos, No.43, Editorial Jurídica Venezolana, Caracas 2007; Brewer-Carías, *Reforma constitucional y fraude a la Constitución (1999–2009)*, Academia de Ciencias Políticas y Sociales, Caracas 2009.

24 See Allan R. Brewer-Carías, "El juez constitucional vs. la supremacía constitucional o de cómo la jurisdicción constitucional en Venezuela renunció a controlar la constitucionalidad del procedimiento seguido para la 'reforma constitucional' sancionada por la Asamblea Nacional el 2 de noviembre de 2007, antes de que fuera rechazada por el pueblo en el referendo del 2 de diciembre de 2007," in Eduardo Ferrer Mac-Gregor y César de Jesús Molina Suárez (Coordinarores), *El juez constitucional en el Siglo XXI,* Universidad nacional Autónoma de México, Suprema Corte de Justicia de la Nación, México 2009, Tomo I, pp. 385–435.

it was the people in the December 7, 2007 referendum who rejected the unconstitutional reform.[25]

III. CONSTITUTIONAL COURTS' ADAPATION OF THE CONSTITUTION AND THE QUESTION OF LEGITIMATE CHANGES TO THE CONSTITUTION

The situation is different when constitutional courts adapt constitutional provisions through interpretation. Undoubtedly, one of the main roles of constitutional courts during judicial review of statutes is to interpret the Constitution and to adapt its provisions according to constitutional principles and values, particularly on matters of protecting fundamental rights. In such cases, according to Laurence Claus and Richard S. Kay, constitutional courts "engage in positive constitutional lawmaking," particularly when the rule they "formulate, creates 'affirmative' public duties."[26] Consequently, it is possible to accept judge-made constitutional "mutations," this expression understood to mean "change[s] in the interpretation of a constitutional provision, the meaning of which is altered in spite of the maintenance of the same wording of the Constitution."[27] But in this there are some risks. As I wrote a few years ago, if it is true that "constitutional courts, certainly, can be considered as a phenomenal instrument for the adaptation of the Constitution, and the reinforcement of the rule of law," then it is also true that "they can also be a diabolic instrument of constitutional dictatorship, not subjected to control, when they validate constitutional violations made by authoritarian regimes or when separation of powers is not assured."[28]

These constitutional mutations, when reinforcing the rule of law, generally take place as a consequence of enforcing the fundamental values and

[25] See the comments in Allan R. Brewer-Carías, "La reforma constitucional en Venezuela de 2007 y su rechazo por el poder constituyente originario," in José Ma. Serna de la Garza (coord.), *Procesos Constituyentes contemporáneos en América latina. Tendencias y perspectivas*, Universidad Nacional Autónoma de México, México 2009, pp. 407–449.

[26] See Laurence Claus and Richard S. Kay, *U.S. National Report*, p. 6.

[27] See Salvador O. Nava Gomar, "Interpretación, mutación y reforma de la Constitución: Tres extractos," in Eduardo Ferrer Mac-Gregor (coord.), *Interpretación constitucional*, vol. 2, Editorial Porrúa, Universidad Nacional Autónoma de México, Mexico City 2005, pp. 804 ff. See also Thomas Bustamante and Evanlida de Godoi Bustamante, *Brazilian National Report*, p. 28. See generally Konrad Hesse, "Límites a la mutación constitucional," in *Escritos de derecho constitucional*, Centro de Estudios Constitucionales, Madrid 1992, pp. 79–104.

[28] See Allan R. Brewer-Carías, "La reforma constitucional en América Latina y el control de constitucionalidad," in *Reforma de la Constitución y control de constitucionalidad. Congreso Internacional junio 14 al 17 de 2005*), Pontificia Universidad Javeriana, Bogotá, 2005, pp. 108–159.

principles of the Constitution, particularly the protection of fundamental rights and the strengthening of democratic rule. Nonetheless, they have also occurred in other constitutional matters related to the general organization of the State.

1. *Adapting the Constitution on Matters of Fundamental Rights Guarantees*

Regarding the protection of fundamental rights, the mutation of the Constitution in many countries has resulted from constitutional courts "discovering" fundamental rights that were not expressly listed in a constitution, and consequently enlarging the scope of the constitutional provisions. In this regard, constitutional courts always have had an additional duty over that of the ordinary judge, in that they must defend the Constitution and its foundational values at a given time.[29]

This is why it is considered legitimate for constitutional courts, in their interpretative process, to adapt a constitution to the current values of society and the political system, precisely "to keep the constitution alive."[30] To that end, because a constitution is not a static document, constitutional courts must be creative in effectively applying constitutions that may have been written, for instance, in the nineteenth century, particularly when controlling the constitutionality of legislation according to the evolving social needs and institutions of the country.

This also occurs in the case of more recent constitutions, where fundamental rights sometimes are expressed in a vague, and elusive way, with provisions expressed in ambiguous, but worthy, terms, such as *liberty*, *democracy*, *justice*, *dignity*, *equality*, *social function*, and *public interests*.[31] This leads to the need for judges to have an active role when interpreting

29 This has been particularly true, for instance, in the process of the transformation in the former socialist States of Eastern Europe to contemporary democratic States subject to the rule of law. See, e.g., Marek Safjan, *Polish National Report*, pp. 7, 10; Sanja Barić and Petar Bačić, *Croatian National Report*, pp. 18, 21, 28; Boško Tripković, *Serbian National Report*, pp. 1, 14.

30 See Mauro Cappelletti, "El formidable problema del control judicial y la contribución del análisis comparado," *Revista de Estudios Políticos* 13, Madrid 1980, p. 78; "The Mighty Problem of Judicial Review and the Contribution of Comparative Analysis," *Southern California Law Review*, 53, 1980, p. 409 ff.

31 See Mauro Cappelletti, "Nécessité et légitimité de la justice constitutionnelle," in Louis Favoreu (ed.), *Cours constitutionnelles européenes et droit fundamentaux*, Economica, Presses Universitaires d'Aix-Marseille, 1982, p. 474.

what have been called a constitution's "precious ambiguities"[32] and "majestic generalities."[33]

It is precisely in these matters, as mentioned by Laurence Claus and Richard S. Kay, that the U.S. Supreme Court's elaboration of constitutional principles and values "provides perhaps the most salient example of positive lawmaking in the course of American constitutional adjudication." For instance, the Court interpreted the equal protection clause of the Fourteenth Amendment to expound the nature of equality; it argued about the constitutional guarantee of due process (Amendments V and XIV), and the open clause of Amendment IX, to construct a sense of liberty.[34] As Geoffrey R. Stone has pointed out regarding the text of the U.S Constitution:

> It defines our most fundamental rights and protections in an open-ended terms: "freedom of speech," for example, and "equal protection of laws," "due process of law," "unreasonable searches and seizures," "free exercise" of religion and "cruel and unusual punishment." These terms are not self-defining; they did not have clear meaning even to the people who drafted them. The framers fully understood that they were leaving it to future generations to use their intelligence, judgment and experience to give concrete meaning to the expressed aspirations.[35]

In particular, for instance, it was in *Brown v. Board of Education of Topeka*, 347 U.S. 483 (1954), that this process of mutating the U.S. Constitution began for matters of fundamental rights. It is important to bear in mind that the 1789 U.S. Constitution and the 1791 amendments did not establish the principle of equality and that the Fourteenth Amendment (1868) included only the equal protection clause, which until the 1950s had been interpreted differently.

[32] "If it is true that precision has a place of honor in the writing of a governmental decision, it is mortal when it refers to a constitution which wants to be a lively body." S. M. Hufstedles, "In the Name of Justice," *Stanford Lawyers* 14, nº 1 (1979), pp. 3–4, quoted by Mauro Cappelletti, "Nécessité et légitimité de la justice constitutionnelle," in Louis Favoreu (ed.), *Cours constitutionnelles européennes et droit fondamentaux*, Economica, Presses Universitaires d'Aix-Marseille, 1982, p. 474; L. Favoreu, *Le contrôle juridictionnel des lois et sa légitimité. Développements récents en Europe Occidentale*, Association Internationale des Sciences Juridiques, Colloque d'Uppsala 1984, (mimeo), p. 32.

[33] See *W. Va. State Bd. of Educ. v. Barnette*, 319 U.S. 624, 639 (1943). See Laurence Claus and Richard S. Kay, *U.S. National Report*, p. 12 (footnote 33).

[34] See Laurence Claus and Richard S. Kay, *U.S. National Report*, pp. 12–13.

[35] See Geoffrey R. Stone, "Our Fill-in-the-Blank Constitution," op-ed, *New York Times*, April 14, 2010, p. A27.

This process converted the Court, according to Claus and Kay, into "the most powerful sitting lawmaker in the nation,"[36] by having used old but renewed means of relief, particularly equitable remedies, to move beyond prohibitory to mandatory relief. This is one of the most striking developments in modern constitutional law, and it produced changes impossible to imagine a few years earlier. As aforementioned, these means were broadly applied in *Brown v. Board of Education of Topeka*, 347 U.S. 483 (1954), where the Supreme Court held that racial segregation in public education was a denial of the "equal protection of the laws," which, under the Fourteenth Amendment, no state was to deny to any person within the state's jurisdiction. The Court needed to answer various questions to find segregation unconstitutional, such as whether the ruling should order that African American children "forthwith be admitted to schools of their choice" or whether the court should "permit an effective gradual adjustment" to systems.[37] Eventually, these inquiries led the Supreme Court, in May 1954, to declare racial segregation incompatible with the Fourteenth Amendment. It issued the final ruling in the case in May 1955, two and a half years after the initial argument.[38]

In effect, in *Brown*, the Supreme Court changed the meaning of the Fourteenth Amendment. Chief Justice Warren said:

> In approaching this problem we cannot turn the clock back to 1868 when the Amendment was adopted, or even to 1896 when *Plessy v. Ferguson* was written. We must consider public education in the light of its full development and its present place in American life throughout the Nation. Only in this way can it be determined if segregation in public schools deprives these plaintiffs of the equal protection of the laws.

This assertion led Chief Justice Warren to conclude:

> [I]n the field of public education the doctrine of "separate but equal" has no place. Separate educational facilities are inherently unequal. Therefore, we hold that the plaintiffs, and others similarly situated from whom the actions

36 See Laurence Claus and Richard S. Kay, *U.S. National Report*, p. 20. On the different stages in the process of law regarding those clauses, see *id.*, pp. 13–14. The authors argue that "the law of liberty and equality in America is now, in large measure, ultimately created and shaped by the Supreme Court," p. 14.

37 *Brown v. Bd. of Educ.*, 345 U.S. 972, 972 (1953). See Laurence Claus and Richard S. Kay, *U.S. National Report*, p. 26 (footnote 89).

38 *Brown v. Bd. of Educ.*, 345 U.S. 972, 972 (1953). See Laurence Claus and Richard S. Kay, *U.S. National Report*, p. 27 (footnote 91).

> have been brought are by reason of the segregation complained of, deprived of the equal protection of the laws guaranteed by the Fourteenth Amendment.

In other contexts, particularly in France, where the Constitution does not make a declaration of fundamental rights, the role of the Constitutional Council during the past decades must be highlighted, beginning with the important decision adopted on July 16, 1971, concerning freedom of association.[39] In that case, the Constitutional Council accepted the positive legal value of the Preamble to the 1958 Constitution with all its consequences,[40] which conformed with what Louis Favoreu called the *bloc de constitutionnalité.*[41]

Consequently, regarding the particular law establishing a procedure to control the acquisition of legal capacity by association, the Constitutional Council considered it against the Constitution,[42] arguing that the Preamble to the 1946 Constitution referred to the "fundamental principles recognized by the laws of the Republic," among which the principle of liberty of association was to be included. The Council, in accordance with such principle, considered that associations were to be constituted freely and able to develop their activities with the only condition of filing a declaration before the Administration, that was not submitted to a previous authorization by either administrative or judicial authorities. Thus, the Constitutional Council decided that fundamental constitutional principles were included not only in the Preamble of the 1958 Constitution but also in the Preamble of the 1946 Constitution, and through it in the Declaration of Rights of Man and Citizens of 1789. Thus, the limits imposed on associations by the proposed

39 See L. Favoreu and L. Philip, *Les grandes décisions du Conseil Constitutionnel*, Dalloz, Paris 1984, p. 222–237; Bertrand Mathieu, *French National Report*, p. 2.

40 See L. Favoreu, "Rapport général introductif," in *Cours constitutionnelles européenes et droit fondamentaux*, Economica, Presses Universitaires d'Aix-Marseille, 1982, pp. 45–46.

41 See L. Favoreu, "Le principe de Constitutionalité. Essai de definition d'apres la jurisprudence du Conseil Constitutionnel," *Recueil d'Étude en Hommage a Charles Eisenman*, Paris 1977, p. 34. On comparative law, see also Francisco Zúñiga Urbina, "Control de constitucionalidad y sentencia," *Cuadernos del Tribunal Constitucional*, nº 34, Santiago de Chile 2006, pp. 46–68.

42 See the Constitutional Council decision in L. Favoreu and J. Philip, *Les grandes décisions du Conseil Constitutionnel*, Dalloz, Paris 1984, p. 222. See the comments of the July 16, 1971, decisions in J. Rivero, "Note," *L'Actualité Juridique. Droit Administratif*, Paris, 1971, p. 537; J. Rivero, "Principles fondamentaux reconnus par les lois de la République; une nouvelle catégorie constitutionnelle?" *Dalloz 1974*, Chroniques, Paris 1974, p. 265; J. E. Bradsley, "The Constitutional Council and Constitutional Liberties in France," *American Journal of Comparative Law* 20, nº 3 (1972), p. 43; B. Nicholas, "Fundamental Rights and Judicial Review in France," *Public Law*, 1978, p. 83.

bill establishing prior judicial control of the Declaration were considered unconstitutional. In this way, according to Jean Rivero:

> The liberty of association, which is not expressly established either in the Declaration or by the particularly needed principles of our times, but which is only recognized by a Statute of 1 July 1901, has been recognized by the Constitutional Council decision, as having a constitutional character, not only as a principle, but in relation to the modalities of its exercise.[43]

This sort of adaptation of the French Constitution was also developed by the Constitutional Council in the well-known *Nationalization* case in 1982, which applied the article concerning the right of property in the Declaration of the Rights of Man and Citizen of 1789 and declared the right to property as having constitutional force. In its decision of January 16, 1982,[44] even though the article of the 1789 Declaration concerning property rights was considered obsolete, and so its interpretation could not result in a completely different sense from the one defined in 1789,[45] the Constitutional Council stated:

> Taking into account that if it is true that after 1789 and up to the present, the aims and conditions of the exercise of the right to property have undergone an evolution characterized both, by a notable extension of its application to new individual fields and by limits imposed by general interests, the principles themselves expressed in the Declaration of Rights of Man have complete constitutional value, particularly regarding the fundamental character of the right to property, the conservation of which constitutes one of the aims of political society, and located on the same rank as liberty, security and resistance to oppression, and also regarding the guarantees given to the holders of that right and the prerogatives of public power.[46]

In this way, the Constitutional Council not only created a constitutional right by giving the 1789 Declaration constitutional rank and value but also

43 See J. Rivero, "Les garanties constitutionnelles des droits de l'homme en droit français," in *IX Journées Juridiques Franco-Latino Américaines*, Bayonne, May 21–23, 1976 (mimeo), p. 11.

44 See L. Favoreu and L. Philip, *Les grandes décisions du Conseil Constitutionnel*, Dalloz, Paris 1984, pp. 525–562.

45 See L. Favoreu, *Le contrôle juridictionnel des lois et sa légitimité. Développements récents en Europe Occidentale*, Association Internationale des Sciences Juridiques, Colloque d'Uppsala 1984 (mimeo), p. 32.

46 See L. Favoreu and L. Philip, *Les grandes décisions du Conseil Constitutionnel*, Dalloz, Paris 1984, p. 526; L. Favoreu, "Les décisions du Conseil Constitutionnel dans l'affaire des nationalisations," *Revue du Droit Public et de la Science Politique en France et à l'Étranger* 98, nº 2, Paris 1982, p. 406.

adapted the "sacred" right to property established two hundred years earlier to the limitable right of our times, thus allowing the Council to declare unconstitutional certain articles in the Nationalization statute regarding the banking sector and industries of strategic importance (especially in electronics and communications).

The role of constitutional courts in adapting the Constitution to guarantee fundamental rights not expressly established in the Constitution, even in the absence of open constitutional clauses like the Ninth Amendment to the U.S. Constitution, has been commonly accepted, mainly because of the principle of progressiveness in the protection of fundamental rights.[47]

In Switzerland, for instance, before the 1999 constitutional reform was sanctioned, which included an extended declaration of fundamental rights, the Federal Supreme Court interpreted the previous 1874 Constitution, which included only a few fundamental rights, as allowing for very important unwritten fundamental rights, including the guarantee of property (1960);[48] freedom of expression (1961);[49] the right to personal freedom within the meaning of a right to physical and mental integrity (1963);[50] freedom of language (1965);[51] the right to existence and care, including a minimum of governmental assistance in case of need (1995);[52] freedom of assembly and freedom of expression, which encompass the right to hold public demonstrations (1970);[53] and the freedom to demonstrate.[54] Also, before the 1999 constitutional reform, the Federal Supreme Court recognized the freedom to elect and vote as a constitutional right;[55] most important, it enforced the right of women to participate in the Landsgemeinde (assembly of the citizens as the highest legislative body) of the Canton Appenzell-

47 See Pedro Nikken, *La protección internacional de los derechos humanos: Su desarrollo progresivo*, Instituto Interamericano de Derechos Humanos, Ed. Civitas, Madrid 1987; Mónica Pinto, "El principio *pro homine*: Criterio hermenéutico y pautas para la regulación de los derechos humanos," in *La aplicación de los tratados sobre derechos Humanos por los tribunales locales*, Centro de Estudios Legales y Sociales, Buenos Aires 1997, p. 163.

48 See Supreme Court, in ZBl 62/1961, 69, 72; Tobias Jaag, *Swiss National Report*, p. 11 (footnote 49).

49 See BGE 87 I 114, 117; Tobias Jaag, *Swiss National Report*, p. 11 (footnote 51).

50 See BGE 89 I 92, 97 ff.; Tobias Jaag, *Swiss National Report*, p. 11 (footnote 56).

51 See BGE 91 I 480, 485 ff. This includes the right to use one's native language. See Tobias Jaag, *Swiss National Report*, p. 12 (footnote 59).

52 See BGE 121 I 367, 370 ff.; Tobias Jaag, *Swiss National Report*, p. 12 (footnote 61).

53 See BGE 96 I 219, 223 ff.; Tobias Jaag, *Swiss National Report*, p. 11 (footnote 52).

54 See BGE 100 Ia 392, 400 ff.; Tobias Jaag, *Swiss National Report*, p. 11 (footnote 53).

55 *Cf.* BGE 121 I 138, 141 ff.; Tobias Jaag, *Swiss National Report*, p. 12 (footnote 64).

Innerrhoden,[56] where the Cantonal Constitution provided that only men could participate in such an assembly. All these rights were later included in the 1999 Constitution.

In Germany, the Federal Constitutional Tribunal has also developed an important process of interpreting the constitution to protect fundamental rights. Ines Härtel refers to a 2008 decision adopted by the Federal Constitutional Tribunal regarding the searches of computers. in which the Tribunal created a "new" basic right on the "warranty of confidentiality and integrity in information technology systems." In this case, in the course of the judicial review process of a provision of a North Rhine–Westphalia law regarding the change of the statute by the Federal Office for the Protection of the Constitution, the Tribunal ruled on the protection of general personal rights provided in article 2, section 1, in conjunction with article 1, section 1, of the Constitution,[57] in particular within the tension between liberty and security that affects the handling of personal data and information.

In Poland, the Constitutional Tribunal has developed judicial activism regarding the expansion of human rights, particularly after 1989, with the fall of the country's totalitarian system and the need to build the structures of a democratic state of law. The Constitutional Tribunal was pushed to interpret the standards of rights and freedoms not directly expressed in the Constitution, and to complement existing constitutional provisions, according to the new democratic values and system. Consequently, the Tribunal derived such fundamental rights as the right to the protection of human life before birth,[58] the right to trial,[59] the right to privacy,[60] ban on retroactivity,[61] the rule of protection of duly acquired rights,[62] the protection

[56] See BGE 116 Ia 359 ff.; Tobias Jaag, *Swiss National Report*, p. 13 (footnote 66).

[57] See BVerfG, Reference nº 1 BvR 370/07 from February 27, 2008, available at http://www.bverfg.de/entscheidungen/rs20080227_1bvr037007.html; I. Härtel, *German National Report*, p. 12.

[58] See Decision of May 28, 1997, K 26/96, OTK ZU 1997/2/19; Marek Safjan, *Polish National Report*, p. 9 (footnote 22).

[59] See Decision of January 7, 1992, K 8/91, OTK ZU 1992, part 1, pp. 76–84; of June 27, 1995, K4/94, OTK 1993, part 2, pp. 297–310; Marek Safjan, *Polish National Report*, p. 9 (footnote 23).

[60] See Decision of June 24, 1997, K21797, OTK ZU 1997/12/23; Marek Safjan, *Polish National Report*, p. 9 (footnote 24).

[61] See Decision of August 22, 1990, K7/90, OTK 1990, pp. 42–58; Marek Safjan, *Polish National Report*, p. 9 (footnote 25).

[62] See Decision of February 25, 1992 K3/9, OTK 1992, part 1, item 1; Marek Safjan, *Polish National Report*, p. 9 (footnote 26).

of business and legal security,[63] and the principle of proportionality, for instance in the imposition of sanctions.[64]

Also in Poland, the Court has been charged with giving specific content to programmatic clauses established in the Constitution, particularly during the transformation from an authoritarian socialist State to one of democratic rule of law. In this process, the broad catalog of general rules established in the Constitution related to social and economic rights, and the definition of the economic system as a "social market economy" (article 20 of the Constitution) were developed by the Constitutional Court. That is why, regarding these rules, Judge Marek Safjan said, that "if these rules are not to remain a pure ideology and constitutional decorum, expressing the 'wishful thinking' attitude of the authors of the Constitution, the Constitutional Court by turning rules into norms, and seeking at least a minimal normative content in the so-called program norms," has exercised "an increasingly stronger influence on the directions of state policy in these dimensions."[65] For such purpose, the Court following the superior values in the Constitution, has filled in these concepts, pinpointing and determining their boundaries. As Judge Safjan explains:

> It is characteristic for each Constitution to employ a large number of "open" norms having undefined (fuzzy) normative scope, expressing fundamental legal values and creating "axiology of the Constitution." This search for a normative content hidden in the general, undefined constitutional expressions, as well as decoding other – more precise and concrete – norms out of them, setting limits to the application of rules and establishing a special "hierarchy" between the colliding rules and values – is inscribed into the nature of interpretation of the Constitution and is closely connected with the essence of the function of each constitutional court.[66]

63 See Decision of July 15, 1996, K5/96, OTK ZU 1996, part 2, pp. 16–28; Marek Safjan, *Polish National Report*, p. 9 (footnote 28).

64 See Decision of April 26, 1995, K11/94, OTK 1995, part 1, item 12; Marek Safjan, *Polish National Report*, p. 9 (footnote 29).

65 See Marek Safjan, *Polish National Report*, p. 12. On decisions establishing positive normative content from the so-called program norms, see, e.g., National Health Fund of January 7, 2004, K14703, OTK ZU 2004/1A/1; the protection of consumer (biofuels) of April 21, 2004, K33/03, OTK ZU 2004/4A/31; the protection of tenants judgments of January 12, 2001, P11/98, OTK ZU2000/1/3; and April 19, 2005, K 4/05, OTK ZU 2005/4A/37; and the social market economy of January 29, 2007, P5/05,2007/1A/1. See Marek Safjan, *Polish National Report*, p. 12 (footnote 37).

66 See Marek Safjan, *Polish National Report*, p. 7.

With respect to the principle of proportionality, the Constitutional Court of Croatia also has developed this principle, determining that the State must draft legislation related to individual rights and liberties, including in their regulation, appropriate and proportional solutions in the scope of their limitations. The 1990 Constitution refers only to the proportionality principle in article 17 on the restriction of rights and freedoms during a state of emergency, without establishing it as a clear general principle of Croatian Constitutional Law. Consequently, during regular or normal circumstances, article 16 applies, which states only that rights and freedoms can be restricted by law only "to protect freedoms and rights of others, public order, public morality and health."[67] Because the legislators had displayed what was considered political immoderateness by disproportionately restricting rights and freedoms, the Constitutional Court gradually started to apply the proportionality principle in all matters, clearly indicating to legislators the limitations that they could impose on rights and freedoms to protect the general well-being of individuals and their communities.[68]

In Greece, the Council of State, which rules on matters of judicial review, has explicitly recognized the constitutional rank of the proportionality principle as a corollary of rule of law.[69] In contrast, since 1998, the Council of State has construed the constitutional principle of gender equality to allow positive measures that aim to establish true equality between men and women.[70] After a long debate between constitutional scholars and the courts, the Council of State ultimately followed the *Areios Pagos* court by extending the scope of a statutory provision to groups of persons who had been unconstitutionally excluded. In addition, especially since 1993, the Council of State has derived the principle of sustainable development from the Greek Constitution's environmental clauses (article 24) and in connection with European Union law. On this basis, the Council of State has emphasized that the sole constitutionally permissible form of economic development is sustainable development that incorporates the needs of future generations.

67 In the 2000 constitutional amendment, the principle was also incorporated in article 17: "Every restriction of freedoms or rights shall be proportional to the nature of the necessity for restriction in each individual case."

68 See Sanja Barić and Petar Bačić, *Croatian National Report*, pp. 23 ff.

69 See Council of State Judgment nº 2112/1984, *ToS* 1985, 63 (64); Julia Iliopoulos-Strangas and Stylianos-Ioannis G. Koutnatzis, *Greek National Report*, p. 14.

70 See Council of State (Full Bench) Judgment nº 1933/1998, *ToS* 1998, 792 (793). After the 2001 amendments, the Constitution explicitly allows the "adoption of positive measures for promoting equality between men and women" (art. 116, sec. 2). See Julia Iliopoulos-Strangas and Stylianos-Ioannis G. Koutnatzis, *Greek National Report*, p. 16 (footnote 123).

With the 2001 constitutional amendments, the Greek Constitution explicitly established the principle of sustainable development (article 24.1.1)[71]

Regarding the same matter of constitutional courts mutating constitution provisions on fundamental rights, in Portugal, the Constitutional Tribunal, in Decision No. 474/95, established that, although the wording of article 33 of the Constitution prohibited, at that time, only extradition for crimes for which the death penalty was legally possible, the principles of the Constitution also prohibited extradition for crimes punishable by life imprisonment. Furthermore, the Court's ruling provides the keystone for the interpretation of the conditions that must be fulfilled to allow for extradition of persons charged with crimes for which a sentence of death or life imprisonment is possible.[72] The consequence of this mutation was an amendment to the Constitution introduced in 1997 on the wording of article 33.4 of the Constitution, concerning extradition for crimes punishable under the applicant state's law by a sentence or security measure which deprives or restricts freedom in perpetuity or for an undefined duration.

In India, the Supreme Court has introduced important changes in the Constitution, particularly by expanding the scope of fundamental rights. For instance, article 21 of the Constitution establishes, "No person shall be deprived of his life or personal liberty except according to procedure established by law." The Supreme Court ruled in 1970, reversing a previous position, that the expression "procedure established by law" in the article refers to a procedure that must be "right, just and fair." Thus, the Court gave itself the authority to judge whether a procedure laid down by the Legislator conformed to the principles of natural justice,[73] which is especially remarkable because the constituent assembly, after a long debate, had expressly rejected the due process clause.[74]

In contrast, regarding the right to life under article 21 of the Indian Constitution, the Supreme Court has interpreted it to include the right to

[71] See Julia Iliopoulos-Strangas and Stylianos-Ioannis G. Koutnatzis, *Greek National Report*, p. 22.

[72] See Ruling nº 384/05, summary of which can be found in *Bulletin on Constitutional Case-Law*, Venice Commission, Edition 2005, vol. 2, pp. 269–271, in Joaquim de Sousa Ribeiro and Esperança Mealha, *Portuguese National Report*, pp. 9–10.

[73] *Maneka Gandhi v. Union of India*, AIR 1879 SC 597. See Surya Deva, *Indian National Report*, p. 4 (footnote 24).

[74] See Surya Deva, *Indian National Report*, p. 4.

health,[75] the right to livelihood,[76] the right to free and compulsory education up to fourteen years of age,[77] the right to an unpolluted environment[78] and to clean drinking water,[79] the right to shelter,[80] the right to privacy,[81] the right to legal aid,[82] the right to a speedy trial,[83] and various rights of persons under trial (convicts and prisoners).[84] The Court extended the meaning of *life* by, among other things, reading nonjusticiable directive principles of State policy into fundamental rights. As Surya Deva affirmed, the effect of this judicial extension of fundamental rights had a direct bearing on the power of judicial review: the more fundamental rights are recognized, the broader would be the scope for judicial review.[85]

In the Slovak Republic, the Constitutional Court has played an important role in mutating and complementing the Constitution to guarantee the protection of fundamental rights. This has happened, for instance, on matters of the right to personal freedom and physical integrity, particularly regarding the extension of the duration of pretrial detentions without the basis of a

75 See *Parmanand Kataria v. Union of India*, AIR 1989 SC 2039; *Paschim Banga Khet Mazdoor Samity v. State of West Bengal*, (1996) 4 SCC 37; Surya Deva, *Indian National Report*, p. 5 (footnote 28).

76 See *Olga Tellis v. Bombay Municipal Corporation*, AIR 1986 SC 180; *DTC Corporation v. DTC Mazdoor Congress*, AIR 1991 SC 101. In *id.*, p. 5 (footnote 29).

77 See *Unni Krishnan v. State of AP*, (1993) 1 SCC 645. In *id., p.* 5 (footnote 30).

78 See, e.g., *Indian Council for Enviro Legal Action v. Union of India*, (1996) 3 SCC 212; *M C Mehta v. Union of India*, (1996) 6 SCC 750; *Vellore Citizens Welfare Forum v. Union of India*, (1996) 5 SCC 647; *Narmada Bachao Andolan v. Union of India* (2000) 10 SCC 664. In *id.*, p. 5 (footnote 31).

79 See *A P Pollution Control Board II v. M V Nayudu*, (2001) 2 SCC 62. In *id.*, p. 5 (footnote 33).

80 See *Gauri Shankar v. Union of India*, (1994) 6 SCC 349. In *id.*, p. 5 (footnote 32).

81 See *Kharak Singh v. State of UP*, AIR 1963 SC 1295; *Govind v. State of MP*, AIR 1975 SC 1378; *R Raj Gopal v. State of Tamil Nadu*, (1994) 6 SCC 632; *PUCL v. Union of India*, AIR 1997 SC 568; *'X' v. Hospital Z*, (1998) 8 SCC 296. In *id.*, p. 5 (footnote 34).

82 See *M H Hoskot v. State of Maharashtra* AIR 1978 SC 1548; *Hussainara Khatoon v. State of Bihar* AIR 1979 SC 1369; *Khatri v. State of Bihar* AIR 1981 SC 928; *Suk Das v. Union Territory of Arunachal Pradesh* AIR 1986 SC 991. In *id.*, p. 5 (footnote 35).

83 See *Hussainara Khatoon (I) to (VI) v. Home Secretary, Bihar* (1980) 1 SCC 81; *Kadra Pahadiya v. State of Bihar* AIR 1982 SC 1167; *Common Cause v. Union of India* (1996) 4 SCC 33 and (1996) 6 SCC 775; *Rajdeo Sharma v. State of Bihar* (1998) 7 SCC 507 and (1999) 7 SCC 604. In *id.*, p. 5 (footnote 36).

84 See *Sunil Batra v. Delhi Administration* AIR 1978 SC 1675; *Prem Shankar v. Delhi Administration* AIR 1980 SC 1535; *Munna v. State of UP* AIR 1982 SC 806; *Sheela Barse v. Union of India* AIR 1986 SC 1773. In *id.*, p. 5 (footnote 37).

85 See Surya Deva, *Indian National Report*, p. 5.

decision of the court,[86] and on matters of the right to enter and leave the territory of the Slovak Republic freely, which is guaranteed in the Constitution. In the latter case, the Court interpreted this right in such a way that it deduced an obligation of State bodies to actively participate in its protection. According to the Court, the constitutional provision means not only that State bodies are not allowed to create obstacles to the free return of a citizen to the territory of the Slovak Republic but also that State bodies are obliged to actively help citizens to return to the territory. Consequently, the bodies of the Slovak Republic (e.g., the Ministry of Foreign Affairs) have an obligation to help citizens to return to Slovak Republic when they have been kept abroad against their will, even if that obligation is not enumerated in the law and State bodies did not have the explicit requirement to do so.[87]

Of course, all these constitutional mutations are considered legitimate because they follow the basic principle of the progressive protection of human rights. On the contrary, they represent also a case of the pathology of judicial review when courts make such mutations to reduce the scope of protection of fundamental rights, as in Venezuela, where the Constitutional Chamber of the Supreme Tribunal of Justice, in Decision No. 1.939 of December 18, 2008,[88] ignored the decisions of the Inter-American Court on Human Rights by declaring that its rulings condemning the Venezuelan State for violations of human rights are unenforceable in Venezuela. This also occurred with the decision of the Chamber issued on August 5, 2008, in the case of the former judges of the First Court on Contentious Administrative Jurisdiction who were illegitimately dismissed without any sort of judicial guarantees (*Apitz Barbera et al. [First Court on Contentious Administrative Matters] v. Venezuela*[89]). In its decision, the Constitutional Chamber accused the Inter-American Court on Human Rights of usurping the power of the Supreme Tribunal.[90] This decision contradicted article 31 of the

86 See decisions I. ÚS 6/02, I. ÚS 100/04, II. ÚS 111/08, II. ÚS 8/96; Ján Svák and Lucia Berdisová, *Slovak National Report*, pp. 12–13.

87 See Decision nº II. ÚS 8/96; Ján Svák and Lucia Berdisová, *Slovak National Report*, pp. 12.

88 See *Gustavo Álvarez Arias et al.* In fact, the case can be identified as "*Venezuelan Government vs. Inter-American Court on Human Rights.*" See http://www.tsj.gov.ve/decisiones/scon/Diciembre/1939-181208-2008-08-1572.html. See the comments in Allan R. Brewer-Carías, *Reforma constitucional y fraude a la Constitución (1999–2009)*, Academia de Ciencias Políticas y Sociales, Caracas 2009, pp. 253 ff.

89 See.http://www.adc-sidh.org/images/files/apitzbarberaingles.pdf. Judgment of August 5, 2008 (*(Preliminary Objection, Merits, Reparations and Costs)*

90 The issue had been affirmed by the Constitutional Chamber in its known Decision nº 1.942 of July 15, 2003, in which, when referring to the International Courts, the Chamber stated that, in Venezuela, "above the Supreme Court of Justice and according to article 7 of the Constitution,

Constitution, which established the right of access to international protection in matters of human rights, with the State being obligated to carry out the decisions of such international bodies. But the Constitutional Chamber did not stop there. In an evident usurpation of powers, it requested that "the National Executive . . . proceed to denounce the Convention, in view of the evident usurpation of functions in which the Inter American Court on Human Rights has incurred into with the ruling object of this decision." With this, the Venezuelan State continued in its process of separating from the American Convention on Human Rights and avoiding the jurisdiction of the Inter-American Court on Human Rights, using the Supreme Tribunal for this purpose.

Another case in which the Constitutional Chamber of the Supreme Tribunal of Venezuela changed constitutional provisions affecting fundamental rights is refer to the political right to participation by means of referendum, established in article 72 of the 1999 Constitution as a political right of the people to revoke or repeal the mandates of all popular elected offices. The petition for such a referendum must derive from popular initiative, and the mandate is considered revoked when "a number of electors equal or higher than those who elected the official, vote in favour of the revocation."[91] Nevertheless, in a clearly unconstitutional way, the Constitutional Chamber, in Decision No. 2750 of October 21, 2003,[92] abstractly interpreting article 72 of the Constitution, endorsed a resolution of the National Electoral Council (Resolution No. 030925-465 of September 25, 2003) and decided against the Constitution by adding to the provision that the revocation of the mandate can proceed only if votes to revoke, even if greater than those cast for the election, "do not result to be lower than the number of electors that voted against the revocation." As to the revoked

there is no jurisdictional body, unless stated otherwise by the Constitution or the law, and even in this last possible case, any decision contradicting the Venezuelan constitutional order, lacks of application in the country." See "Impugnación de artículos del Código Penal, Leyes de desacato," *Revista de Derecho Público*, nº 93–96, Editorial Jurídica Venezolana, Caracas 2003, pp. 136 ff.

91 This was ratified by the Constitutional Chamber in several decisions: Decision nº 2750 of October 21, 2003, case: *Carlos Enrique Herrera Mendoza (Interpretación del artículo 72 de la Constitución* (Exp. 03-1989), *Revista de Derecho Público*, nº 93–96, Editorial Jurídica Venezolana, Caracas 2003; and Decision nº 1139 of June 5, 2002, case: *Sergio Omar Calderón Duque and William Dávila Barrios*, *Revista de Derecho Público*, nº 89–92, Editorial Jurídica Venezolana, Caracas 2002, p. 171. The same criterion was followed in Decision nº 137 of February 13, 2003, case: *Freddy Lepage Scribani et al.* (Exp. 03-0287).

92 See Carlos E. Herrera Mendoza, *Interpretación del artículo 72 de la Constitución, Revista de Derecho Público*, nº 93–96, Editorial Jurídica Venezolana, Caracas 2003.

public official, the Chamber considered that, "if the option of his permanence obtains more votes in the referendum, he should remain in office." In this way, the Chamber illegitimately changed the nature of the revocation referendum, turning it into a "ratifying" referendum of mandates.[93]

The position of the Venezuelan Supreme Tribunal on the Constitution contradicts the general one of constitutional courts: they cannot substitute for the constituent power by deducing concepts in a way that goes against what is written in the Constitution, nor can they interpret the Constitution in a way so as to arrive at concepts that could be contrary to the constitutional text and its fundamental values. As Jorge Carpizo has pointed out:

> [C]onstitutional courts cannot usurp the functions of the Constituent Power, and consequently, they cannot create provisions or principles that could not be referred to the Constitution; they can deduct implicit principles from those expressly included, like human dignity, liberty, equality, juridical security, social justice, Welfare State.[94]

In the same sense, as Sandra Morelli has pointed out, constitutional courts cannot be "above the Constitution," and they cannot "appropriate the Constitution for themselves, in an abusive way," such as by invading the field of the Legislator or of the Constituent Power. The contrary would open the door to "irresponsible judicial totalitarianism."[95]

93 This mutation had a precise purpose in 2004: to avoid revocation of the mandate of the President of the Republic (Hugo Chávez). He had been elected in August 2000 with 3,757,744 votes, so a greater number of votes in a revocation referendum twould have been enough to revoke his mandate. The number of votes in favor of the revocation of the mandate of the President of the Republic, cast in the August 15, 2004 revocation referendum, was 3,989,008, reason for which his mandate could be considered constitutionally revoked. Nonetheless, the National Electoral Council, because more votes were cast against his revocation of the President mandate, on August 27, 2004 decided instead to "ratify" the President of the Republic in his position until the culmination of the constitutional term in January 2007. See *El Nacional*, Caracas, 08-28-2004, pp. A-1 and A-2. See the comments in Allan R. Brewer-Carías, "La Sala Constitucional vs. El derecho ciudadano a la revocatoria de mandatos populares o de cómo un referendo revocatorio fue inconstitucionalmente convertido en un 'referendo ratificatorio,'" in *Crónica sobre la "in"justicia constitucional: La Sala Constitucional y el autoritarismo en Venezuela*, Colección Instituto de Derecho Público, Universidad Central de Venezuela, nº 2, Editorial Jurídica Venezolana, Caracas 2007, pp. 350 ff.

94 See Jorge Carpizo, *El Tribunal Constitucional y sus límites*, Grijesly Ed., Lima 2009, pp. 56, 68.

95 See Sandra Morelli, *La Corte Constitucional: Un papel por definir*, Academia Colombiana de Jurisprudencia, 2002; *Colombian National Report II*, p. 3.

2. *The Mutation of the Constitution on Institutional Matters*

But constitutional mutations by constitutional courts have not occurred only in the field of fundamental rights; they have also occurred with respect to other key constitutional matters, including the organization and functioning of the State.

For instance, the German Federal Constitutional Tribunal also issued a decision mutating the Constitution, in the case *AWACS-Urteil* on July 12, 1994.[96] The Tribunal reviewed the constitutionality of the deployment, in peacetime, of missions of German Armed Forces to foreign countries. The decision referred to the modalities surrounding the deployment, and the Tribunal concluded that the deployment of troops to foreign countries required the consent of the legislative branch. Although this assertion is reasonable – the Tribunal considered it "a requirement that derives directly from the Constitution" – the truth is that it was not expressly established in the Constitution, and the Legislator had sanctioned no legislative development on the matter. In this case, the Tribunal not only mutated the Constitution but even issued a detailed substitute legislation (provisional measures) contained in the decision, ordering the Legislator and the Executive to proceed according to it until a statute was adopted to establish in a more detailed way "the formal participation of the Legislator in the adoption of decisions related with the use of German troops in military missions."[97]

In Austria, the Constitutional Court has also filled in the fundamental principles of the Constitution, which has had substantial influence on the interpretation of Austrian constitutional law.[98] The most important example is the principle of *Rechtsstaat* (rule of law), from which various concepts have been derived, including the principle of legality and, from it, the principle of clarity, which obliges the legislator to provide clear and detailed provisions, the principle of comprehensibility of legislative acts,[99] and the

96 See BVferG, July 12, 1994, BVeffGE 90, 585–603; Christian Behrendt, *Le judge constitutionnel, un législateur-cadre positif. Un analyse comparative en droit francais, belge et allemande*, Bruylant, Brussels 2006, pp. 352–356; I. Härtel, *German National Report*, p. 20.

97 See BVferG, July 12, 1994, BVeffGE 90, 286 (390), in Christian Behrendt, *Le judge constitutionnel, un législateur-cadre positif. Un analyse comparative en droit francais, belge et allemande*, Bruylant, Brussels 2006, p. 354.

98 See Konrad Lachmayer, *Austrian National Report*, p. 8.

99 See VfSlg 12.420/1990, in Konrad Lachmayer, *Austrian National Report*, p. 8 (footnote 24).

principle of effective legal protection,[100] which obliges Parliament to provide sufficient and adequate legal protection to individuals. Through these interpretations, the Court created new constitutional limitations on Parliament, which had to adapt its legislation to the Court's new standards.

In the same line, the Austrian Court has sometimes even created a new constitutional framework for Parliament to follow when enacting legislation in areas not expressly provided for in the Constitution, such as the privatization process. In four main judgments,[101] the Court established an obligatory framework for privatizing state functions exercised by specific organizations, thus intervening in the legislative function and governmental policy and defining the functions and tasks of the State itself. The Court derived the rules from different provisions of the Constitution, requiring, for instance, the application in all privatization processes of the principles of rationality, efficiency, and legality, as well as the principle of the hierarchical structure of Public Administration. In contrast, according to these rules, the State is only authorized to privatize singular tasks, not an entire area of State functions; and in any case, the State has to provide effective control mechanisms with regard to private organizations performing the tasks of State authorities. Finally, the Court defined core areas of State functions that cannot be privatized at all, including foreign affairs, internal affairs, jurisdiction (judicial system), and criminal law. In this way, the Court created a new understanding of the Constitution and imposed it on all State authorities.[102]

Also regarding the limits of privatization, the Greek Council of State has held that the principles of popular sovereignty and separation of powers do not allow conferring police powers to privatize legal entities.[103]

In the Slovak Republic, where the Constitutional Court has the exceptional attribution of rendering abstract interpretations of the Constitution in cases of disputes between two State bodies with different interpretations of a constitutional provision, the Court has issued important decisions that have

[100] See VfSlg 11.196/1986; Konrad Lachmayer, *Austrian National Report*, p. 8 (footnote 25).

[101] See "Austro Control" decision VfSlg 14.473/1996, "Bundeswertpapieraufsicht" (Federal Bond Authority) decision VfSlg 16.400/2001, "E-Control" decision VfSlg 16.995/2003, "Zivildienst-GmbH" (Compulsory Community Service Ltd) decision VfSlg 17.341/2004; Konrad Lachmayer, *Austrian National Report*, p. 11 (footnote 31).

[102] See Konrad Lachmayer, *Austrian National Report*, p. 11.

[103] See Council of State (Full Bench) Judgment nº 1934/1998, *ToS* 1998, 598 (602–603) (concerning enforcement of no-parking zones); Julia Iliopoulos-Strangas and Stylianos-Ioannis G. Koutnatzis, *Greek National Report*, p. 16 (footnote 125).

mutated and complemented the Constitution. This has happened, for instance, regarding the position and authority of the President of the Republic within the general organization of the State. In the original text of the Constitution of the Slovak Republic, inspired by the classical parliamentary form of the government, the President had the relatively weak position of a *porvoir neuter*. It was the Constitutional Court that directly strengthened the President's position through interpretation of the Constitution, affirming in 1993 that, "even if the Government of the Slovak Republic ("government") is the highest executive body (art. 108), the constitutional position of the President of Slovak Republic is in fact dominant towards the constitutional position of the government."[104] The question debated was whether the President had the right or the constitutional obligation to appoint members of the government on the basis of a motion by the Prime Minister. The Court added that, "to create inner balance within the executive power, the Constitution of the Slovak Republic assigns the President of the Slovak Republic only the obligation to deal with the motion of the Prime Minister, it is not his obligation to comply with it.[105] This decision of the Court had serious consequences for the constitutional system of the Slovak Republic, as it strengthened the position of the President, and made the Court, as mentioned by Ján Svák and Lucia Berdisová, "the direct creator of the constitutional system of the Slovak Republic."[106]

This constitutional mutation was latter reaffirmed in the matter of the competence to appoint the Chief of the General Staff of the Army, which a law had vested in the government. Nonetheless, with article 102 of the Constitution establishing the competence of the President to appoint and recall "higher state officials," the Court interpreted "higher state official" in deciding that there is no "obstacle that could keep the President from the execution of his competence towards Chief of the General Staff of the army as a higher state official."[107]This decision, issued in connection with the direct interpretation of the Constitution by the Court, is considered to have "de facto transformed classical parliamentary form of government into some

104 See Decision nº I. ÚS 39/93; Ján Svák and Lucia Berdisová, *Slovak National Report*, p. 4.

105 *Id.*

106 *Id.*

107 See Decision nº PL. ÚS 32/95; Ján Svák and Lucia Berdisová, *Slovak National Report*, p. 5.

kind of semi-presidential form, and yet without the change of the normative text of the Constitution."[108]

In Canada, where the Supreme Court also has the exceptional power to issue reference judgments at the request of public officials and entities of the State, among the most important Supreme Court decisions on constitutional matters are those in which the Court has created and declared constitutional rules. In particular, in the 1981 *Patriation Reference*,[109] the Court laid down the basic rules governing the patriation of Canada's Constitution from the United Kingdom; and in the 1998 *Quebec Secession Reference*,[110] the Supreme Court dealt with the possible secession of Quebec from Canada. These two cases were decided at the request of the federal government, which has statutory powers to refer questions of law, including those involving the constitutionality of legislation, directly to the Supreme Court of Canada.[111] In the decisions, the Supreme Court laid down some basic rules for guiding constitutional change and warned of potential constitutional crises that could arise from arguably unconstitutional acts, such as an attempt by the federal government to change the powers of the provincial legislatures without their consent or a similarly unilateral decision by the Quebec legislature to declare its sovereignty and secession from Canada.

IV. THE PROBLEM OF ILLEGITIMATE MUTATIONS OF THE CONSTITUTION

If constitutions are superior laws that support the validity of all the legal order, one of the institutional solutions to ensure their enforcement is the existence of a constitutional court,that must act as its guardian, with powers to annul unconstitutional State acts or to declare their unconstitutionality.

In democracies, these courts have always been the main institutional guarantee of freedom and of the rule of law. As such guardian, and as it in any rule-of-law system, the submission of the constitutional court to a constitution is absolute, not subject to discussion,[112] because it would be

[108] *Id.*

[109] [1981] 1 S.C.R. 753, in Kent Roach, *Canadian National Report*, p. 9.

[110] [1998] 2 S.C.R. 217, in Kent Roach, *Canadian National Report*, p. 9.

[111] See Kent Roach, *Canadian National Report*, p. 9.

[112] See Néstor Pedro Sagües, *La interpretación judicial de la Constitución*, LexisNexis, Buenos Aires 2006, p. 32. In article 204 of the Portuguese Constitution, it is expressly set forth that "in matters brought before them for decision, the courts shall not apply any rules that contravene the provisions of this Constitution or the principles contained there."

inconceivable that the constitutional judge can violate the Constitution that he or she is called on to apply. As a matter of principle, it is possible to imagine that other bodies of the State could violate the Constitution (e.g., Parliament), but not its guardian. For such purpose and to ensure that this does not occur, a constitutional court must have absolute independence and autonomy, because on the contrary, a constitutional court subject to the will of the political power, becomes the most atrocious instrument of authoritarianism instead of the guardian of the Constitution. Thus, in the hands of judges subject to political power, the best constitutional justice system is a dead letter for individuals and an instrument for defrauding the Constitution.

Unfortunately, the latter is what has been occurring in Venezuela since 2000. The Constitutional Chamber of the Supreme Tribunal, far from acting within the expressed constitutional attributions, has been adopting decisions that in some cases contain unconstitutional interpretations of the constitution,[113] not only about its own powers of judicial review but also about substantive matters. It has changed or modified constitutional provisions, in many cases to legitimize and support the progressive building of the authoritarian State. That is to say, it has distorted the content of the Constitution, through illegitimate and fraudulent "mutation," which in some cases the people have rejected through referendum.[114]

One of the most important instruments for accomplishing these mutations of the Constitution is the already-mentioned creation of a recourse for abstract interpretation of the Constitution, in which case constitutional interpretations is not made deciding a particular case or controversy or deciding other means of judicial review, but abstractly.

This has happened in many cases of autonomous requests for interpretation filed at the request of the same national executive through the

113 See Allan R. Brewer-Carías, "*Quis Custodiet Ipsos Custodes*: De la interpretación constitucional a la inconstitucionalidad de la interpretación," in *VIII Congreso Nacional de derecho Constitucional, Perú*, Fondo Editorial 2005, Colegio de Abogados de Arequipa, Arequipa, September 2005, pp. 463–489; and Brewer-Carías, *Revista de Derecho Público*, nº 105, Editorial Jurídica Venezolana, Caracas 2006, pp. 7–27. See also Allan R. Brewer-Carías, *Crónica sobre la "in"justicia constitucional: La Sala Constitucional y el autoritarismo en Venezuela*, Editorial Jurídica Venezolana, Caracas 2007; Brewer-Carías, *Reforma constitucional y fraude a la Constitución*, Academia de Ciencias Políticas y Sociales, Caracas 2009.

114 As mentioned, constitutional mutation occurs when the content of a constitutional standard is modified in such a way that, even when the standard maintains its content, it receives a different meaning. See Néstor Pedro Sagües, *La interpretación judicial de la Constitución*, LexisNexis, Buenos Aires 2006, pp. 56–59, 80–81, 165 ff.

attorney general for the purpose of strengthening authoritarianism, the most notorious of which have being the following:

First, regarding article 6 of the Constitution that establishes the fundamental principles of republican government, in an immutable way, expressly including the democratic, elective, and alternate character of the government; principles that have been incorporated in Venezuelan constitutions since 1830. In particular, the principle of alternation in government, as pointed out by the Electoral Chamber of the Supreme Tribunal of Justice in Decision No. 51 of March 18, 2002,[115] implies "the successive exercise of a position by different persons, belonging or not to the same party," conceived to face the desire to remain in power. Nevertheless, in Decision No. 53 of February 3, 2009, the Constitutional Chamber confused "alternate government" with "elective government" to conclude that the principle of alternation implies only "the periodic possibility to choose government officials or representatives." The result was not only to mutate the Constitution, eliminating the principle of alternating government, but to allow a referendum that took place on February 15, 2009, for the people to vote for a "constitutional amendment" to allow for continuous reelection for elective positions. The 2009 amendment was approved in the referendum, and the Constitution was then formally changed to eliminate the principle of alternate government, which by the way was conceived as unmodifiabale in article 6 of the Constitution.[116]

Second, article 67 of the 1999 Constitution expressly establishes that "the financing of political associations with Government funds will not be allowed," a provision that in 1999 radically changed the previous regime of public financing of political parties.[117] This express constitutional prohibition regarding public financing of political parties was also one of the

[115] See Allan R. Brewer-Carías, "El juez constitucional vs. la alternabilidad republicana (La reelección continua e indefinida)," *Revista de Derecho Público*, nº 117, Editorial Jurídica Venezolana, Caracas 2009, pp. 205–211.

[116] *Id.*

[117] As was established in article 230 of the Organic Law of Suffrage and Political Participation of 1998. See Allan R. Brewer-Carías, "Consideraciones sobre el financiamiento de los partidos políticos en Venezuela," in *Financiamiento y democratización interna de partidos políticos: Memoria del IV Curso Anual Interamericano de Elecciones*, San José, Costa Rica, 1991, pp. 121–139; Brewer-Carías, "Regulación jurídica de los partidos políticos en Venezuela," in *Estudios sobre el Estado constitucional (2005–2006)*, Cuadernos de la Cátedra Fundacional Allan R. Brewer Carías de Derecho Público, Universidad Católica del Táchira, nº 9, Editorial Jurídica Venezolana. Caracas, 2007, pp. 655–686.

matters referred to in the 2007 proposed constitutional reform,[118] which sought to modify article 67 to provide that "the State will be able to finance electoral activities." As already mentioned, the 2007 constitutional reform proposal was rejected by popular vote in a referendum of December 2, 2007;[119] but the Constitutional Chamber of the Supreme Court of Justice, in Decision No. 780 of May 8, 2008, also illegitimately mutated the Constitution, contrary to the popular will. The Chamber ruled that the constitutional prohibition only "limit[ed] the possibility to provide resources for the internal expenses of the different forms of political associations, but...said limitation is not extensive to the electoral campaign, as a fundamental stage of the electoral process." That is, the Constitutional Chamber, again, usurped the constituent power, substituted itself for the people, and reformed the provision, thus expressly allowing for government financing of the electoral activities of the political parties and associations, contrary to what the Constitution provides for.

Finally, the decision of the Constitutional Chamber to modify article 203 of the Constitution must be mentioned, as here the Chamber mutated an important constitutional rule of procedure for the approval of organic laws. Article 203 of the Constitution, in effect, defines the various types of organic law[120] and establishes in general terms that, to reform an organic law, a special quorum of two-thirds of the votes of members of the National Assembly is required. The Constitutional Chamber, in Decision No. 34 of January 26, 2004,[121] ruled that such a special quorum was not necessary to initiate the discussion of organic law drafts to reform existing organic laws that have such denomination in the Constitution, thus illegitimately changing a constitutional procedural condition regarding the approval of statutes.

[118] See *Proyecto de exposición de motivos para la reforma constitucional, Presidencia de la República, Proyecto Reforma Constitucional: Propuesta del presidente Hugo Chávez Agosto 2007; Proyecto de Reforma Constitucional, Prepared by the President of the Bolivarian Republic of Venezuela, Hugo Chávez Frías*, Editorial Atenea, Caracas, August 2007, p. 19.

[119] See Allan R. Brewer-Carías, "La proyectada reforma constitucional de 2007, rechazada por el poder constituyente originario," in *Anuario de Derecho Público 2007*, Universidad Monteavila, Caracas 2008, pp. 17-65.

[120] According to article 203, "organic laws" are those qualitied as such in the text of the Constitution itself, as well as those enacted for the purpose of organizing the branches of government, or for the regulation of constitutioonal rights, or which serve as normative framework of other statutes.

[121] See *Vestalia Araujo* case, interpretation of article 203 of the Constitution, at http://www.tsj.gov.ve/decisiones/scon/Enero/34-260104-03-2109%20.htm. See also Daniela Urosa Maggi, *Venezuelan National Report*, p. 14.

Constitutional mutations have also occurred in other countries through judicial decisions, particularly on matters of presidential reelections, which in Latin American constitutional history has always provoked political conflicts because of the traditional general prohibition on reelection. Sometimes, the prohibition has been embodied in provisions considered immutable, as was the case in Honduras, where attempts by former President Manuel Zelaya in 2009 to change the constitutional prohibition on reelection by means of a constitutional assembly provoked one of the most bitter political conflicts in the region in the past decades.[122]

A similar constitutional provision prohibiting the continuous reelection of the President of the Republic is also established in article 147 of the Constitution of Nicaragua, which nonetheless was "reformed" by the Supreme Court of the country in Decision No. 504 of October 19, 2009, when ruling on an amparo action filed against a decision of the Supreme Electoral Council, in which the Council rejected a request to apply the principle to equality to all public officials on matters of election. In the case, no specific candidacy was involved, and the decision consisted in a rejection of the petition due to the lack of attributions of the Supreme Electoral Council to decide on such matter. In the decision, nonetheless, the Supreme Court, incomprehensibly declared article 147 of the Constitution "inapplicable," mutating in an illegitimate way the Constitution, by eliminating from its text the entrenched prohibition on reelection.[123]

[122] See Allan R. Brewer-Carías, "Reforma constitucional, asamblea nacional constituyente y control judicial contencioso administrativo: El caso de Honduras (2009) y el precedente venezolano (1999)," *Revista Aragonesa de Administración Pública*, nº 34 (June 2009), Gobierno de Aragón, Zaragoza 2009, pp. 481–529. In 2010, the Constitution of Honduras was changed in order to establish the possibility of the reelection of the President of the Republic.

[123] See Sergio J. Cuarezma Terán and Francisco Enríquez Cabistán, *Nicaragua National Report*, p. 43.

Chapter 3

CONSTITUTIONAL COURTS' INTERFERENCE WITH THE LEGISLATOR ON EXISTING LEGISLATION

Leaving aside the relation between constitutional courts and the constituent power, the most important and common role of constitutional courts has been developed with respect to legislation, controlling its submission to the Constitution. This role is performed by the courts, not only acting as the traditional "negative" Legislator but also as a jurisdictional organ of the State designed to complement or assist legislative organs in their main function of establishing legal rules.

This role has been assumed by the courts since the initial conception of the diffuse system of judicial review in the United States, deciding not to apply statutes when considered contrary to the Constitution, thus giving preference to the latter; or in the concentrated system of judicial review, which has extended throughout the world during the last century, in which constitutional courts have the power to annul unconstitutional statutes. In all systems, in accomplishing their functions, constitutional courts have always, in some way, assisted the Legislator. At the beginning, in a limited manner, they provided only for the nullity or inapplicability of statutes declared contrary to a Constitution; subsequently, they broadly interpreted the Constitution, and the statutes in conformity with it, giving directives or guidelines to the Legislator to correct the legislative defects.

I. CONSTITUTIONAL COURTS' INTERPRETATION OF STATUTES IN HARMONY WITH THE CONSTITUTION

During the past decades, given the increasing role of constitutional courts not only as the guarantors of the supremacy of a constitution but also as its supreme interpreter through decisions with binding effects on courts, public officials, and citizens, courts have move beyond their initial role as negative legislators, ruled by the traditional unconstitutionality and invalidity-nullity dichotomy.[1] In that trend, their powers have progressively extended, and courts have assumed a more active role interpreting constitutions and statutes, in order not only to annul or not to apply them when unconstitutional but also to preserve the Legislator's actions and the statutes it has enacted, thus interpreting them in harmony with the Constitution.

Thus, when a statute can be interpreted accordingly or contrary to the constitution, courts often make efforts to preserve its validity by choosing to interpret it in harmony with the Constitution and by rejecting interpretations that could result in the statute being declared unconstitutional. This is a general principle currently applied in comparative law.

This role of courts has been a classical principle in the U.S. Supreme Court judicial review doctrine, formulated by Justice Brandeis:

> When the validity of an act of Congress is drawn in question, and even, if a serious doubt of constitutionality is raised, it is a cardinal principle that this Court will first ascertain whether a construction of the statute is fairly possible by which the question may be avoided.[2]

This approach to judicial review, followed in all countries, responds to the principle of conservation or preservation of legislation (norm preservation) when issued by the democratically elected representative body of the State, whose legislative acts are covered by their presumption of constitutionality.[3] This principle has led to two lines of action: (1) by overestimating the presumption, in which the validity of the legislation is assumed until a decision is adopted, and (2) by preserving the piece of legislation by interpreting it according to the Constitution.

In the first case, in Greece, for example, courts traditionally have failed to meaningfully and consistently scrutinize the constitutionality of legislation,

1 See F. Fernández Segado, *Spanish National Report*, pp. 8 ff.

2 See *Ashwander v. TVA*, 297 U.S. 288, 346–48 (1936). The principle was first formulated in *Crowell v. Benson*, 285 U.S. 22, 62 (1932). See "Notes. Supreme Court Interpretation of Statutes to avoid constitutional decision," *Columbia Law Review*, Vol. 53, nº 5, New York, May 1953, pp. 633–651.

3 This presumption implies the following (1) the protection of the statutes, as well as of the functions of the Legislator and its independence; (2) in case of doubt, the unconstitutionality must be rejected; (3) if two criteria exist regarding the interpretation of a statute, the one in harmony with the Constitution must be chosen; (4) when two interpretations, one contrary to the Constitution and the other according to it, the latter must be chosen. See Iván Escobar Forns, "Las sentencias constitucionales y sus efectos en Nicaragua," in *Anuario Iberoamericano de Justicia Constitucional*, Centro de Estudios Políticos y Constitucionales, nº 12, 2008, Madrid 2008, pp. 105–106. See also I. Härtel, *German National Report*, p. 6.

instead emphasizing the need to respect legislative prerogatives and considering the mere existence of legislation that restricts constitutional rights a sufficient basis to uphold its constitutionality.[4]

In the second case, it has been the practice of constitutional courts in all judicial review systems to issue so-called interpretative decisions, which the Constitutional Tribunal of Spain has defined as those

> that reject an unconstitutionality action, that is to say, that declare the constitutionality of the challenged statutory provision, provided that it be interpreted in the sense that the Constitutional Tribunal considered according to the Constitution, or not to be interpreted in the sense that it is considered not according.[5]

Of course, in this regard, interpretative decisions are those that interpret statutes in harmony with the Constitution to preserve their enforcement and to avoid declaring them contrary to the Constitution, a notion that cannot be applied when the courts interpret the Constitution according to a statute to also avoid the declaration of the statute's unconstitutionality. As has been indicated for Greece, if it is true that to avoid reaching a holding of unconstitutionality, Greek courts have regularly interpreted statutory law as conforming to the Constitution, in so doing, "they have occasionally interpreted the Constitution to be in accordance with statutory law rather than conversely or they have exceeded the permissible limits of interpretation to avoid reaching a judgment of unconstitutionality." This refers to the case in which the Council of State construed the statutorily required "permission" of the Orthodox Church for the construction of religious sites of other denominations – against the wording of the statutory law in force at the time – to be a mere nonbinding opinion for the executive branch.[6] On the basis of this interpretation, Julia Iliopoulos-Strangas and Stylianos-Ioannis G. Koutnatzis state that the Council of State found no violation of religious freedom according to the Greek Constitution and the European Convention on Human Rights. In construing statutory legislation

4 See Julia Iliopoulos-Strangas and Stylianos-Ioannis G. Koutnatzis, *Greek National Report*, p. 12.

5 See Decision STC 5/1981, February 13, 1981, FJ 6 in Francisco Javier Díaz Revorio, *Las sentencias interpretativas del Tribunal Constitucional*, Lex Nova, Valladolid 2001, p. 67; José Julio Fernández Rodríguez, *La justicia constitucional europea ante el Siglo XXI*, Tecnos, Madrid 2007, p. 129.

6 See Council of State (Full Bench) Judgment nº 1444/1991, nº *V* 1991, 626 (627); Julia Iliopoulos-Strangas and Stylianos-Ioannis G. Koutnatzis, *Greek National Report*, p. 13 (footnote 94).

contrary to its wording, however, the Council of State substituted its own formulation for that of Parliament, arguably engaging in positive legislation.[7]

In any case, the technique to interpret statutes in harmony or in conformity with the Constitution to preserve their validity has been also applied in cases of the control of "conventionality" of statutes, regarding their conformity with international treaties. With respect to the Netherlands, J. Uzman, T. Barkhuysen, and M. L. van Emmerik stated:

> [T]he courts generally assume that unless Parliament expressly deviates from its international obligations, it must clearly have intended any provision in its Act to be consistent with a given treaty. This assumption is the basis for the courts' usual practice to interpret national law as far as possible in a way consistent with the rights laid down in conventions such as the ECtHR. And it is this practice that has given rise to a few of the most celebrated but also deeply notorious (some might even say activist) Supreme Court judgments.[8]

The technique, in principle, cannot be considered invasive regarding the attributions of the Legislator, and on the contrary, being conceived to help the Legislator, its purpose is to preserve its normative products and, in a certain way, from a practical point of view, to avoid unnecessary legislative vacuums that result from the declaration of a statute as invalid or null.[9] In any case, this judicial review technique of interpretative decisions in which the unconstitutionality of a statute is rejected has helped mold constitutional courts into important constitutional institutions that assist and cooperate with the legislator in its legislative functions.

Constitutional courts have widely used these sorts of interpretative decisions.[10] In Italy, for instance, the Constitutional Court has disregarded the interpretation proposed by the *a quo* judge in the remittal ordinance regarding the unconstitutionality of a legal provision and instead has recommended a different interpretation of the same provision, one that is compatible with the Constitution. In other words, "with the interpretative

7 See Julia Iliopoulos-Strangas and Stylianos-Ioannis G. Koutnatzis, *Greek National Report*, p. 13.

8 See J. Uzman, T. Barkhuysen, and M. L. van Emmerik, *Dutch National Report*, pp. 8, 24, 32, 37.

9 See this assertion regarding the Italian and Spanish judicial review practice in Francisco Javier Díaz Revorio, *Las sentencias interpretativas del Tribunal Constitucional*, Lex Nova, Valladolid 2001, p. 92; F. Fernández Segado, *Spanish National Report*, p. 5.

10 See Francisco Javier Díaz Revorio, *Las sentencias interpretativas del Tribunal Constitucional*, Lex Nova, Valladolid 2001, pp. 59 ff.; F. Fernández Segado, *Spanish National Report*, p. 25 ff.; I. Härtel, *German National Report*, pp. 6–7.

decision of rejection, the question raised is declared groundless, on condition that one interprets the provision challenged in the sense indicated in it."[11] The Court's decision imposes on the *a quo* judge a negative obligation in that he or she is obliged to not insist on attributing to the provision the meaning disregarded by the Court.

Nonetheless, as interpretation is a delicate function, many times accomplished on the border between constitutionality and unconstitutionality, constitutional courts have also established limits or self-restraint regarding interpretative decisions with respect to the wording of the text to be interpreted and the intention of the Legislator when sanctioning the law.[12] In this regard, for instance, the Spanish Constitutional Tribunal has summarized the scope of interpretative decisions in decision STC 235/2007 of November 7, 2007, as follows:

> a) The effectiveness of the norms preservation principle must not ignore or configure the clear text of legal provisions, due to the fact that the Tribunal cannot reconstruct provisions against their evident sense in order to conclude that such reconstruction is the constitutional norm;
>
> b) The interpretation accordingly cannot be a contra legem interpretation, the contrary would imply to disfigure and manipulate the legal provisions; and
>
> c) It is not the attribution of the Tribunal to reconstruct a norm that is explicit in the legal provision, and, consequently, to create a new norm and the assumption by the Constitutional Tribunal of a function of Positive Legislator that institutionally it does not have.[13]

It must also be mentioned that the technique of interpreting the law in harmony with the Constitution to avoid a declaration of unconstitutionality has also been applied in France, by means of *a priori* judicial review, which has been traditionally exercised by the Constitutional Council. The technique is used to consider whether the Legislator has respected the Constitution in interpreting the law according to it.[14] In these cases, the Constitutional Council has a double task: on the one hand, it interprets the statute according to the Constitution; on the other hand, it addresses a directive to the

[11] See Gianpaolo Parodi, *Italian National Report*, p. 3.

[12] See BVerfGE, 69,1 (55); 49, 148 (157), in I. Härtel, *German National Report*, p. 6 (footnote 33).

[13] See Francisco Fernández Segado, *Spanish National Report*, p. 34.

[14] E.g., Decisions 2000-435 DC, 2001-454 DC, 2007-547 DC, in Bertrand Mathieu, *French National Report*, p. 13.

Legislator on the conditions of the exercise of its attributions and, eventually, a directive to the authorities who must apply the law on how they must perform their duties.[15]

As Lóránt Csink, József Petrétei, and Péter Tilk highlighted in referring to Hungary, by setting constitutional requirements regarding the law, the Constitutional Court necessarily gives a narrow interpretation of the norm, thus reducing the possible constitutional meanings. In these cases, the Court does not annul the challenged law but modifies its meaning, and in some cases, it creates a new norm – one that may result in a Court order "to neglect significant parts of the norm," even contradicting "the will of the legislator."[16] In these cases, the Court chooses one possible interpretation from the alternatives, not necessarily the same one the Legislator thought of; that is, the Court interprets the law extensively by determining a requirement that totally alters the effect of the law or gives a new statement that was not originally in the norm, thus creating a new norm.[17] The Constitutional Court's decision establishing new content for a provision is the result of a constitutional interpretation in order to make the law constitutional.[18]

Regarding all these functions of constitutional courts in interpreting statutes in harmony with the Constitution, their interference with the Legislator, and their legislative functions regarding existing and in-force legislation, they can be studied through two courses of action: by complementing legislative functions as provisional Legislators or adding rules to existing Legislation through interpretative decisions and by interfering with the temporal effects of existing legislation.

15 See Bertrand Mathieu, *French National Report*, p. 13.

16 See Decision 48/1993 (VII.2) and Decision 52/1995 (IX.15), in Lóránt Csink, József Petrétei, and Péter Tilk, *Hungarian National Report*, p. 4 (footnote 10).

17 See Decision 41/1998 (X.2), Decision 60/1994 (XII.24), and Decision 22/1997 (IV.25), in Lóránt Csink, József Petrétei, and Péter Tilk, *Hungarian National Report*, p. 4 (footnote 12).

18 See Lóránt Csink, József Petrétei, and Péter Tilk, *Hungarian National Report*, p. 4.

II. CONSTITUTIONAL COURTS COMPLEMENTING THE LEGISLATOR BY ADDING NEW RULES (AND NEW MEANING) TO THE EXISTING LEGISLATIVE PROVISION

Through interpretation, constitutional courts frequently create new legislative rules by altering meaning or adding what is considered lacking in the provision so that it is in harmony with the Constitution.

These additive decisions have been extensively studied particularly in Italy, where it is possible to find the widest variety of decisions issued by the Constitutional Court in declaring unconstitutional a statutory provision. They have been widely studied, analyzed, and classified under the general category of "manipulative" decisions. As Gianpaolo Parodi has explained in the Italian National Report, these decisions of acceptance of unconstitutionality, despite leaving the text of the provision unaltered, transform its normative meaning, at times reducing and at other times extending its sphere of application, not without, especially in the second case, introducing a new norm into the legal system or creating new norms. In this regard, one speaks of manipulative (or manipulating) decisions, and among them, the typically additive and substitutive decisions.[19]

The difference between interpretative decisions and manipulative decisions has also been established by Parodi as follows:

> The first of the two, indeed, preferably makes reference to the subject of the ruling: a norm obtainable in an interpretative way from a legislative statement, rather than a provision, or one of its segments (in this sense, the notion fits both the interpretative decisions of acceptance in a strict sense, and the "non textual" decisions of partial acceptance); the notion of manipulative decision usually throws light on a peculiar effect of the ruling: of alteration and, precisely, manipulation of the meaning *prima facie* of the provision contested, which, on the textual plane remains unaltered.[20]

Within the additive decisions (*sentenze additive*), it is possible to distinguish additive decisions of principle, because the principles formulated in the Court's decision are established to guide "both the legislator, in the necessary normative activity subsequent to the ruling, aimed at remedying the unconstitutional omission; and ordinary judges, so that, while waiting for

[19] See Gianpaolo Parodi, *Italian National Report*, p. 6.

[20] See Gianpaolo Parodi, *Italian National Report*, pp. 6–7.

the legislative intervention, they find, with integration of law, a solution for the controversies submitted to them."[21]

In these cases, as pointed out by the Italian Constitutional Court in 1991, although a declaration of constitutional illegitimacy of a legislative omission leaves to the Legislator its undeniable competence to discipline the matter, even retroactively, through general legislation, "it gives a principle to which the ordinary judge is able to make reference to place a remedy in the meantime to the omission at the time of identification of the rule for the concrete case."[22]

In many cases, through additive decisions, constitutional courts establish that the challenged provision is lacking something for it to be in accordance with the Constitution; deciding that, from that moment on, the provision must be applied as if that something is not missing. As the Constitutional Tribunal of Peru has said, by means of additive decisions:

> [T]he unconstitutionality of a provision or of part of it is declared, in which the needed part for it to result in harmony with the Constitution has been omitted (in the part in which the provision does not establish that). In such cases, the whole provision is declared unconstitutional, but only its omission, so after the declaration of its unconstitutionality it will be obligatory to include within it the omitted aspect.[23]

These decisions, frequently issued to guarantee the right to equality and to nondiscrimination,[24] eventually transform an unconstitutional provision into a constitutional one by adding to the norm what is lacking, or even by substituting something into the provision. In other words, without affecting the challenged provision, they extend or expand its normative content by establishing that such content must include something that is not expressly

21 See Gianpaolo Parodi, *Italian National Report*, p. 10.

22 See Decision nº 295/1991, in Gianpaolo Parodi, *Italian National Report*, p. 10.

23 See Decision of January 3, 2003 (Exp. nº 0010-2002A1-TC), in Fernán Altuve Febres, *Peruvian National Report II*, p. 13.

24 See Francisco Javier Díaz Revorio, *Las sentencias interpretativas del Tribunal Constitucional*, Lex Nova, Valladolid 2001, pp. 183, 186, 203, 204, 274, 299, 300; José Julio Fernández Rodríguez, *La inconstitucionalidad por omisión: Teoría general. Derecho comparado. El caso español*, Civitas, Madrid 1998, pp. 232 ff.; Joaquin Brage Camazano, "Interpretación constitucional, declaraciones de inconstitutionalidad y arsenal sentenciador (Un suscinto inventario de algunas sentencias 'atípicas')," in Eduardo Ferrer Mac-Gregor (coord.), Interpreación Constitucional, Ed. Porrúa, Vol. I, México 2005, pp. 192 ff.; Joaquim de Sousa Ribeiro and Esperança Mealha, *Portuguese National Report*, p. 8.

established in its text.[25] Although these decisions, in a certain way, change the scope of legislative rules regardless of any amended wording, as mentioned by Joaquim de Sousa Ribeiro, "the Court's ruling does not put up a norm *ex nihilo*. Those decisions only put forward a solution imposed by the Constitution provisions and principles by extending a rule already chosen by the legislator."[26]

Of course, the additive rulings as expressed by the Italian Constitutional Court cannot imply a discretional appraisal regarding the challenged provision, in that the Constitutional Court cannot intervene when it is a matter of choosing between a plurality of solutions, all of which are admissible – in that case, the discretion corresponds only to the Legislator.[27] However, they cannot refer to matters that must exclusively be regulated by the Legislator, such as criminal matters.[28]

One example of these additive decisions is one issued by the Constitutional Court of Italy in 1969 regarding the constitutionality of article 313.3 of the Criminal Code, in which the prosecution for insults against the Constitutional Court itself was subjected to previous authorization from the Ministry of Justice and Grace. The Court considered that such authorization contradicted the independence of the Court, arguing that the provision was unconstitutional, deducting that the authorization was to be given by the same Court,[29] and forcing the provision – according to Díaz Revorio – to say something that it was not capable of saying and even eliminating the part of it considered incompatible with the independence of the Court.[30] Another decision of this sort of the Italian Constitutional Court was issued in 1989

25 See Francisco Javier Díaz Revorio, *Las sentencias interpretativas del Tribunal Constitucional*, Lex Nova, Valladolid 2001, pp. 28, 32, 33, 45, 97,146, 165, 167, 292.

26 See Joaquim de Sousa Ribeiro and Esperança Mealha, *Portuguese National Report*, p. 9.

27 See Decision Nos. 109 of April 22, 1986, and125 of January 27, 1988, in Francisco Javier Díaz Revorio, *Las sentencias interpretativas del Tribunal Constitucional*, Lex Nova, Valladolid 2001, p. 273 (footnote 142); Francisco Fernández Segado, "Algunas reflexiones generales en torno a los efectos de las sentencias de inconstitucionalidad y a la relatividad de ciertas fórmulas estereotipadas vinculadas a ellas," in *Anuario Iberoamericano de Justicia Constitucional*, Centro de Estudios Políticos y Constitucionales, nº 12, 2008, Madrid 2008, p. 164–165.

28 See Patricia Popelier, *Belgian National Report*, pp. 13–14; Iván Escobar Forns, "Las sentencias constitucionales y sus efectos en Nicaragua," in *Anuario Iberoamericano de Justicia Constitucional*, Centro de Estudios Políticos y Constitucionales, nº 12, 2008, Madrid 2008, pp. 110.

29 See Decision nº 15, February 12, 1969, in Francisco Javier Díaz Revorio, *Las sentencias interpretativas del Tribunal Constitucional*, Lex Nova, Valladolid 2001, pp. 151–152.

30 See Francisco Javier Díaz Revorio, *Las sentencias interpretativas del Tribunal Constitucional*, Lex Nova, Valladolid 2001, p. 152.

regarding a provision of the Criminal Code that sanctioned those refusing to serve in the military because of conscience with prison terms of two to four years. The Constitutional Court, asked to review the provision, ruled that the sanction was contrary to the constitutional right to equality because the same Criminal Code established a sanction of only six months to two years in a similar situation for those who were called to serve in the military but refused to serve without motives or because of nonserious motives. The consequence was a declaration of unconstitutionality of the provision "in the part in which the minimal sanction is established in two years instead of six months, and in the part in which the maximal sanction is established in four years instead of two years."[31] The result was that the Constitutional Court substituted the sanction of two to four years with another one of six months to two years.

In Germany, one of the typical additive decisions adopted by the Federal Constitutional Court is one regarding the Political Parties Law, which lowered the parties' required threshold of votes with regard to the reimbursement of election campaign costs from 2.5 percent to 0.5 percent.[32]

In Spain, an example of additive or substitutive decision is the one issued by the Constitutional Tribunal in 1988 when deciding on the constitutionality of article 7.4 of the Inter-Territorial Compensation Fund established for financing projects of the Autonomous Communities of the State, which established that, in some cases, the decision regarding the project proposals needed approval "of the Government Council of the Autonomous Communities." The Tribunal considered that this was unconstitutional, because to determine which organ of the Autonomous Communities was to intervene in the approval was a matter corresponding to their own autonomy, and the Court ruled that the reference to the Government Councils must be understood as a reference to the Autonomous Communities, without specific reference to any of their organs.[33]

Another example from the Spanish Constitutional Tribunal is the decision issued in 1993 regarding the benefit of Social Security pensions to the "daughters and sisters" of a holder of a retirement pension, which the Tribunal considered unconstitutional because, contrary to the constitutional

[31] See Decision nº 409 of July 6, 1989, in Francisco Javier Díaz Revorio, *Las sentencias interpretativas del Tribunal Constitucional*, Lex Nova, Valladolid 2001, p. 153.

[32] See BVerfGE 24, 300 (342 f.), in I. Härtel, *German National Report*, p. 19.

[33] See decision STC 183/1988, October 13, 1988, in Francisco Javier Díaz Revorio, *Las sentencias interpretativas del Tribunal Constitucional*, Lex Nova, Valladolid 2001, pp. 154–155.

guarantee of equality, it excluded "sons and brothers" from the benefit, extending the benefits to the latter.[34] In the same sense is a 1992 decision of the Constitutional Tribunal regarding the Urban Tenants Law, whose article 58.1 established that upon the death of a tenant, his spouse could subrogate in his rights and duties. The Court considered that the absence in the provision of any reference to those living *more uxorio* in a marital-like relationship with the deceased tenant was contrary to the right to equality and thus unconstitutional; the result was that the provision was also to be applied to them.[35] Regarding all these cases, as mentioned by F. Fernández Segado, it is possible to consider the Spanish Constitutional Tribunal as a "real positive legislator."[36]

In Portugal, additive decisions have been issued by the Constitutional Tribunal in applying the principle of equality in the sense that, if a norm grants favors to certain groups of persons while excluding or omitting others in violation of an equal protection clause, the exclusion or omission is considered unconstitutional. If the Court has no power to bring about an equal solution for the excluded group, in what has been considered rare cases, the Court's ruling, by itself, has made possible the inclusion of certain groups under the scope of rules that omitted or excluded them. For instance, as pointed out by Sousa Ribeiro, in Ruling No. 449/87, the Court held unconstitutional a norm that established different allowances for a widower and widow in case of death caused by work accident. Furthermore, it stated that the only solution that would comply with the Constitution would be one that granted equal treatment to both, meaning that the favor granted to the widow should be extended to the widower. In addition, in Ruling No. 359/91, the Court considered and ruled on a request from the Ombudsman for not only a successive abstract review of the rules laid down by the Civil Code concerning the transmission of the position of the tenant in the event of divorce when interpreted as not applicable to *de facto* unions, even if the couple in question had underage children, but also a review of the "unconstitutionality by omission of a legislative measure which expressly states that those rules are applicable, with the necessary adaptations, to *de*

34 See Decision STC 3/1993, January 14, 1993, in Francisco Javier Díaz Revorio, *Las sentencias interpretativas del Tribunal Constitucional*, Lex Nova, Valladolid 2001, pp. 177, 274; F. Fernández Segado, *Spanish National Report*, p. 42.

35 See Decision STC 222/1992, December 11, 1992, in Francisco Javier Díaz Revorio, *Las sentencias interpretativas del Tribunal Constitucional*, Lex Nova, Valladolid 2001, pp. 181, 182, 275; F. Fernández Segado, *Spanish National Report*, p. 41.

36 See F. Fernández Segado, *Spanish National Report*, p. 48.

facto unions of couples with underage children." In this decision, the Court issued a declaration with generally binding force of the unconstitutionality of that interpretation for breaching the principle of nondiscrimination against children born outside wedlock, but it did not find unconstitutionality by omission. As a result of the Court's decision, the rules of the Civil Code were thereafter understood as including such *de facto* unions.[37] According to Sousa Ribeiro, such decisions can be considered additive decisions, as their implementation changes the scope of legislative rules regardless of any amendment to the wording of such rules.[38]

Also in Greece, regarding violations of the constitutional equality principle due to the unconstitutional exclusion of persons or groups from a State benefit or the preferential treatment of one person or group at the expense of another, in exercising the diffuse method of judicial review, civil courts have regularly extended preferential treatment to remedy a violation of the equality principle – regardless of whether the discriminatory legislation accords preferential treatment as a general rule or exceptionally.[39] The extension to judges, of legislation concerning remuneration of higher public servants[40] is usually considered a common manifestation of this jurisprudence. Ordinary administrative courts have generally followed the same approach, invoking in their reasoning the European Court of Justice's case law on the principle of equal pay for male and female workers for equal work or work of equal value.[41] More recently, the Council of State has aligned its jurisprudence with that of the Areios Pagos Court, also extending preferential treatment in cases of violation of the constitutional equality principle, as in cases of gender discrimination in social security legislation.[42]

37 See Joaquim de Sousa Ribeiro and Esperança Mealha, *Portuguese National Report*, p. 8.

38 See Joaquim de Sousa Ribeiro and Esperança Mealha, *Portuguese National Report*, p. 9.

39 See, e.g., Areios Pagos Judgment Nos. 3/1990, *NoV* 1990, 1313 (1314); 7/1995 (Full Bench), *EErgD* 1996, 494 (495); 1578/2008, *EErgD* 2009, 180 ff.; Julia Iliopoulos-Strangas and Stylianos-Ioannis G. Koutnatzis, *Greek National Report*, p. 18 (footnote 140).

40 See, e.g., Areios Pagos Judgment nº 40/1990, *EEN* 1990, 579 ff. (579); Julia Iliopoulos-Strangas and Stylianos-Ioannis G. Koutnatzis, *Greek National Report*, p. 18 (footnote 144).

41 See, e.g., Athens Administrative Court of First Instance Judgment Nos. 10391/1990, *DiDik* 1991, 1309 (1309–1310); 3151/1992, *DiDik* 1993, 350 (351). See also Athens Administrative Court of Appeals Judgment nº 3717/1992, *DiDik* 1993, 138 (138–139); Julia Iliopoulos-Strangas and Stylianos-Ioannis G. Koutnatzis, *Greek National Report*, p. 19 (footnote 146).

42 See, e.g., Council of State Judgment Nos. 1467/2004 (Full Bench), *Arm* 2004, 1049 (1050); 3088/2007 (Full Bench), *DtA* 2009, 540 (541); see also Council of State Judgment nº 2180/2004 (Full Bench), *NoV* 2005, 173 (174–175) (extending to pilots remuneration provisions for the cabin crew). See Julia Iliopoulos-Strangas and Stylianos-Ioannis G. Koutnatzis, *Greek National Report*, p. 19 (footnote 148).

Accordingly, as affirmed by Julia Iliopoulos-Strangas and Stylianos-Ioannis G. Koutnatzis, "in extending the applicability of discriminatory, and thus unconstitutional, legislation, Greek courts exercise legislative power in a positive sense."[43]

In a similar way, in South Africa, the Constitutional Court, referring to a 1991 statute (reformed in 1996) that assigned the spouse of a permanent resident in the country the right to automatically obtain a residence permit, considered it discriminatory and unconstitutional because it did not include foreigners in homosexual relationships. The Court complemented the text to include after the word *spouse* the phrase "or the same sex partner in a stable condition."[44]

In Canada, it is also possible to find similar additive judicial review decisions, also on matters of family law and regarding the right to equality, thus supported by constitutional values, in which the Court may read in or add words to legislation to cure a constitutional defect. A famous example is the decision issued by the Supreme Court in *Vriend v. Alberta*, where the Court, though considering Alberta's human rights code unconstitutional because it violated equality rights by failing to protect gays and lesbians from discrimination, decided to add or read into the provision the inclusion of sexual orientation as a prohibited grounds of discrimination rather than striking down the legislation.[45] A similar use of the power was the decision of the Ontario Court of Appeal to strike down the definition of marriage as a union of a man and a woman and to substitute the gender-neutral concept of a union between persons to allow for same-sex marriages, considering that religious views about marriage could not justify excluding same-sex couples from the civil institution of marriage.[46] Although such remedies are not used in a routine fashion to cure all constitutional defects, they, according to Kent Roach, "amount to judicial amendments or additions to legislation."[47]

In Poland, the Constitutional Tribunal has developed these kinds of judgments, which are not directly established in the Constitution or in the

[43] See Julia Iliopoulos-Strangas and Stylianos-Ioannis G. Koutnatzis, *Greek National Report*, p. 19.

[44] See Iván Escobar Fornos, "Las sentencias constitucionales y sus efectos en Nicaragua," in *Anuario Iberoamericano de Justicia Constitucional*, Centro de Estudios Políticos y Constitucionales, nº 12, 2008, Madrid 2008, pp. 111–112.

[45] See *Vriend v. Alberta* [1998] 1 S.C.R. 493; Kent Roach, *Canadian National Report*, pp. 6, 14 (footnotes 5 and 27).

[46] See *Halpern v. Ontario* (2003) 65 O.R. (3d) 161 (C.A.); Kent Roach, *Canadian National Report*, pp. 7, 14 (footnotes 6 and 29).

[47] See Kent Roach, *Canadian National Report*, p. 7.

governing statute. As mentioned by Marek Safjan, "the Tribunal adopts one of the following formulas: 'provision X complies with the Constitution under the condition that it will be understood in the following way . . . ', or 'provision X understood as follows . . . complies with the Constitution' or 'provision X understood in the following way . . . does not comply with the Constitution. . . '. The so called partial judgments usually go further because they directly determine the normative elements included in the provision, which do not comply with a hierarchically higher act (e.g. 'provision X up to an extent in which it envisages that . . . does not comply with the Constitution')."[48] As an example of these decisions,[49] which have been compared with laparoscopic surgery versus an invasive operation, is the case on interpreting the Civil Code to regulate the liability of the State for damage inflicted to an individual by public functionaries.[50] Issuing an interpretative judgment, and therefore avoiding derogation of a Civil Code provision, the Tribunal established a totally new regime of *ex delicto* liability for damages of the State, on the basis of an objective premise of illegality and eliminating the fault of the functionary as a premise of public authority liability.[51]

In Hungary, additive decisions can also be found as a consequence of the Constitutional Court's decisions declaring partial nullity of laws, called mosaic annulment. In this regard, Lóránt Csink, Józef Petrétei, and Péter Tilk point out that the Court has always tried to annul the least possible from the law, that is, only to annul what is necessary to restore constitutionality. For this purpose, as they argued, partial annulment pushed the Court far from negative legislation, as the text that remained in force after the annulment often had a different and sometimes contradictory meaning from the one before constitutional review. This has been the case, for instance, when some words have been annulled, with the result of expanding the scope of grantees of a tax law, either in the field of substantive law[52] or in the field of

48 See Marek Safjan, *Polish National Report*, pp. 13–14.

49 The Polish Supreme Court has opposed this practice of the Constitutional Tribunal, arguing that the process of interpretation is strictly connected with the process of application of a given norm, not with the procedure of its evaluation from the point of view of its conformity with a hierarchically higher act. See Marek Safjan, *Polish National Report*, p. 14.

50 See decision of the Constitutional Tribunal of December 4, 2001, in the case SK18/00, OTK ZU 2001/8/256, in Marek Safjan, *Polish National Report*, p. 14 (footnote 43).

51 See Marek Safjan, *Polish National Report*, pp. 14, 15.

52 See Decision 87/2008 (VI.18). The decision found it discriminatory that only one group of contributors enjoyed tax preferences. The Court annulled the regulation in a way that the preference would also pertain to the members of the other group; Lóránt Csink, Józef Petrétei and Péter Tilk, *Hungarian National Report*, p. 5 (footnote 18).

procedure law;[53] when certain texts of a law restrain a fundamental right concerning the publicity of declarations of properties of local government deputies;[54] and when the competence to determine compensation in matters of criminal law was removed from the minister of justice to the courts, just annulling some words of the Criminal Procedure Code.[55] Another case refers to a decision declaring unconstitutional a comma in a sentence containing an enumeration because it resulted in a different meaning of the sentence, a meaning that was not in conformity with the Constitution.[56]

In the Czech Republic, the Constitutional Court has issued interpretative decisions that read text differently or add sense to constitutional provisions. A typical example, mentioned by Zdenek Kühn, is the judgment in the *Clearance of Defense Counsel* case of January 28, 2004, regarding a law mandating that, in criminal cases in which classified information might be discussed, the defense attorneys are subject to a security clearance. As a result, no defense attorney was available for the defendant in the criminal case before the district court, and the defendant was effectively denied of his or her right to legal aid. Therefore, the district court petitioned the Constitutional Court to annul the law if it included also the "defense attorneys" among those who were subject to a security clearance. The Court rejected this reading of the law and found, against its clear wording, that defense attorneys in criminal proceedings are not subject to this type of clearance. Aware of the controversial nature of its reasoning, the Court added the second part to its verdict, creating a new exception to the clear wording of the law. Hence, the verdict of the judgment includes two parts:

> I. The petition is rejected.
>
> II. Clearance of defense attorney in criminal proceedings for purposes of access to classified information through a security clearance by the National Security Office is inconsistent with Art. 37 par. 3, Art. 38 par. 2, and Art. 40

53 See Decision 73/2009 (VII.10). The Court found it unconstitutional that the law did not grant the possibility of reducing or releasing tax liabilities of individuals. Such a possibility is the result of mosaic annulment. See Lóránt Csink, Józef Petrétei, and Péter Tilk, *Hungarian National Report*, p. 5 (footnote 19).

54 See Decision 83/2008 (VI.13). The decree of the local government allowed only Hungarian citizens to check the declarations and only after certifying their identity. These texts have been annulled. See Lóránt Csink, Józef Petrétei, and Péter Tilk, *Hungarian National Report*, p. 5 (footnote 20).

55 See Decision 66/1991 (XII.21) See in Lóránt Csink, Józef Petrétei, and Péter Tilk, *Hungarian National Report*, p. 5.

56 See Decision 16/1999. (VI.11), in Lóránt Csink, Józef Petrétei, and Péter Tilk, *Hungarian National Report*, p. 5.

> par. 3 of the Charter of Fundamental Rights and Freedoms and with Art. 6 par. 3 let. c) of the Convention on Protection of Human Rights and Fundamental Freedoms.[57]

In this case, the Constitutional Court explained why it included the second part based on the principle of the primacy of constitutionally consistent interpretation over unconstitutional interpretations, adding that "for these reasons, in these proceedings on review of norms, given a negative verdict with interpretative arguments, the Constitutional Court placed the fundamental constitutional principle, arising from a number of significant grounds, in the verdict section of the judgment."[58]

In another case, the *Permanent Residence Case* of 1994, the Constitutional Court annulled the requirement that the Czech citizens who were allowed to claim restitution of their property have permanent residence in the Czech Republic. The Court found the requirement discriminatory and annulled the rule that set the deadline for claiming restitution. The law thus lost much of its clarity because the effect of annulling the deadline was doubtful. The problem was explained in the Court's reasoning:

> However, if the consequences of legalizing this unconstitutional condition are to be repaired, it is not only necessary to cancel the condition itself, but …it is also necessary to ensure that the new wording of . . . the Act [after annulment] can realistically be brought to life. This can be achieved only by opening the period . . . for exercising a claim before the court *for those citizens for whom the condition of permanent residence in the country* has heretofore made impossible the exercise of their right to issuance of a thing.[59]

However, in that case, as explained by in Zdenek Kühn, it was far from clear what the annulment of the deadline effectively meant. In any case, the answer to the law's interpretation could have been found not in the law's text but in the Court's justification of its judgment. Only in referring to the Court's judgment did it become clear that the deadline was newly opened only for those who were prohibited to do so under the earlier version of the

[57] See Decision Pl. ÚS 41/02 of January 28, 2004, published as N. 98/2004 Sb. See http://angl.concourt.cz/angl_verze/doc/p-41-02.php; Zdenek Kühn, *Czech National Report*, p. 9 (footnote 41).

[58] See Zdenek Kühn, *Czech National Report*. p. 9.

[59] See Decision Pl. ÚS 3/94 of July 12, 1994, published in Czech as 164/1994 Sb. See http://angl.concourt.cz/angl_verze/doc/p-3-94.php; Zdenek Kühn, *Czech National Report*, p. 10 (footnote 47).

law (those citizens who had no permanent residence in the Czech Republic) and when the period of time commenced.[60]

The Constitutional Court of Croatia has also developed additive decisions, creating policies by way of strengthening the rule of law and protection of human rights. An important case highlighted by Sanja Barić and Petar Bačić is the one referred to the annulment in 1998 of some provisions of the Pension Adjustment Act, in which the Court considered unconstitutional the fact that, since 1993, the Government ceased to adjust pensions according to increased inflation and cost of living, even though it continued to do so with wages. The result was that during four years (1993–1997) wages increased twice as much as pensions (the average pension was half the average wage), which meant that the standard of living for retired persons was half the one corresponding to the average working population. Therefore, the Constitutional Court ruled that "this legal arrangement…changed the social status of retired persons to such an extent that it created social inequality of citizens" and that the contested provisions "contravene[d] with basic constitutional provisions of article 3 of the Constitution of the Republic of Croatia, which guarantee equality, social justice, and the rule of law; and with article 5 of the Constitution, which states that laws are to be in conformity with the Constitution."[61] As a consequence of the Court decision, retired persons were to receive the unpaid pensions for the period 1993–1997, and six years later, the Croatian Parliament sanctioned the Law on the Enforcement of the Constitutional Court's Ruling, dated May 12, 1998.[62]

In many countries, these decisions have been considered invasive regarding legislative attributions because, through them, the Constitutional Court, by interpretation, proceeds to supplant the Legislator, affecting at length the system of separation of powers. They have also been considered judicial decisions adding a *quid novi* that transforms the negative into positive, so that a Tribunal converts itself from a judge of the constitutionality of statutes into a constitutional "cleaner" of the same, thus

[60] See Zdenek Kühn, *Czech National Report*, pp. 8–9.

[61] See Decision nº U-I-283/1997. of May 12, 1998; Sanja Barić and Petar Bačić, *Croatian National Report*, p. 15.

[62] See Decision on the Promulgation of the Law on the Enforcement of the Constitutional Court's Ruling, dated May 12, 1998, Official Gazette "*Narodne novine*," nº 105/2004; Sanja Barić and Petar Bačić, *Croatian National Report*, p. 15 (footnote 30).

invading the sphere of other branches and adding legislative norms, or positive legislation.[63]

In some way, a similar position is found in the Netherlands regarding the control of conventionality of statutes. The Supreme Court ruled in 1980, in the *Illegitimate Child Case*, that Article 959 of the Civil Procedure Code was to be interpreted in the light of Articles 8 and 14 of the European Convention, to ignore the difference established regarding the procedural treatment between cases concerning the custody of legitimate and illegitimate children, thus allowing the relatives of an orphan born out of wedlock to appeal a decision of the local magistrate withholding custody, which the Civil Procedure Code granted only to legally recognized kin.[64] On the basis of the interpretation already adopted by the European Court of Human Rights regarding the Convention, the Supreme Court accepted the right to appeal for relatives of children born outside of marriage. The same approach was followed in the 1982 *Parental Veto on Underage Marriage Case*, where the Supreme Court spontaneously introduced the duty for parents to justify their decision not to let their underage children enter marriage.[65] Where refusing their consent would be evidently unreasonable, the courts were allowed to substitute the parents' withheld permission, ignoring Article 1:36 (2) of the Civil Code, which prohibited the courts from allowing a marriage where one of the parents objected to it. Again, this judgment was backed up by several decisions of the European Commission on Human Rights,[66] which eventually led to the adoption of more self-restraint on matters of control of conventionality, in the sense that the Court more recently recognized that it was not empowered to set aside national provisions for their inconsistency with Convention law, purely on the basis

[63] See the opinions of M. A. García Martínez, F. Rubio Llorente, G. Silvestri, T. Ancora, and G. Zagrebelsky, in Francisco Javier Díaz Revorio, *Las sentencias interpretativas del Tribunal Constitucional*, Lex Nova, Valladolid 2001, p. 254 (footnotes 70–76).

[64] See Supreme Court judgment of 18 January 1980, *NJ* 1980/463 (*Illegitimate Child*); Jerfi Uzman; Tom Barkhuysen and Michiel L. van Emmerik, *Dutch National Report*, p. 14 (footnote 37).

[65] See Supreme Court judgment of 4 June 1982, *NJ* 1983/32 (*Parental Veto on Underage Marriage*); Jerfi Uzman, Tom Barkhuysen, & Michiel L. van Emmerik, *Dutch National Report*, p. 14 (footnote 39).

[66] See Jerfi Uzman, Tom Barkhuysen and Michiel L. van Emmerik, *Dutch National Report*, p. 14.

of its own interpretation of the Convention but only on the prevailing interpretation offered by the European Court.[67]

Also in the area of family law, in the Netherlands, the Supreme Court has developed its own ability to regulate certain areas of the law by means of the exercise of its power of judicial review of "conventionality" of statutes. In effect, in the *Spring Cases*,[68] the Court considered the provisions of Dutch law that stated that when a child was born to unmarried parents or parents who had never been married before or did not have any intention of doing so in the near future, such parents could exercise no parental authority at all, being able to only obtain shared guardianship; the Court found that this violated Articles 8 and 14 of the European Convention. From that decision, the Court set aside certain provisions of the Civil Code and interpreted others so that they might be read consistently with the Convention, and it eventually elaborately tried to regulate the conditions under which a request for joint parental authority was to be granted by the courts; it devoted an entire page in the case reports to describe the conditions and provide lower courts with a "manual" for how to work through such difficult cases.[69]

In Latin America, a typical additive and substitutive decision can be found in Peru, in the decision adopted by the Constitutional Tribunal in 1997 regarding article 337 of the Civil Code, where, for purposes of a spouse seeking divorce, it "understood that the term '*sevicia*' [extreme cruelty] must be substituted by the phrase 'physical and physiological violence, that is, not only referred to physical cruelty."[70] In Costa Rica, the Constitutional Chamber of the Supreme Court has issued additive decisions on matters of citizenship, as when interpreting that, when article 14.4 of the Constitution establishes that when foreign women marry Costa Ricans, they are Costa Ricans by naturalization if they lost their nationality, the word *woman* must be read as *person* to include men, thus overcoming the discrimination that results from the word "woman" regarding foreign men married to a Costa Rican females. The Court said:

67 See Supreme Court judgment of 19 October 1990, *NJ* 1992/129 (*Gay Marriage*); Supreme Court judgment of 10 August 2001, *NJ* 2002/278 (*Duty of Support*); Jerfi Uzman; Tom Barkhuysen and Michiel L. van Emmerik, *Dutch National Report*, p. 16 (footnote 46).

68 See Joint Supreme Court decisions of 21 March 1986, *NJ* 1986/585–588 (*Spring Decisions*); Jerfi Uzman; Tom Barkhuysen and Michiel L. van Emmerik, *Dutch National Report*, p. 15 (footnote 43) and p. 24.

69 See Jerfi Uzman; Tom Barkhuysen and Michiel L. van Emmerik, *Dutch National Report*, p. 24.

70 See Decision of April 29, 1997 (Exp. nº 0018-1996-1-TC), in Fernán Altuve Febres, *Peruvian National Report II*, pp. 14–15.

> In order to avoid inequalities and future discriminations that could come from the application of the Constitution, exercising the attributions the Constitution assigns the Chamber, it is resolved that when statutes uses the terms "men" or "women," they must be understood as synonymous to the word "person," eliminating all possible "legal" discrimination because of gender; a correction that must be applied by all public officials when requested to take any decision that would require to apply provisions in which such terms are used.[71]

In another case, the Constitutional Chamber of the Supreme Court of Costa Rica, interpreting the Currency Law, considered the matter of the essential contents of contracting freedom and concluded in relation to contractual obligations established in foreign currencies that the exchange rate to be applicable in case of payment in national currency, to avoid the violation of property rights, must be the market rate, that is, the effective commercial value of the foreign currency at the moment of payment, and not the official rate, as indicated in article 6 of the Currency Law. Consequently, the Court established how the provision of the Currency Law was to be read.[72]

In Venezuela, a few examples of additive decisions issued by the Constitutional Chamber can be identified. One of them pertains to a provision of the Organic Law of the Attorney General of the Republic (article 90), in which it is established, in judicial process in which the Republic is a party, the need for consent from the Attorney General regarding the bail to be requested to lift some precautionary measures. In Decision No. 1104 of May 23, 2006, the Chamber declared the partial nullity of this provision because it violated the right to defense and due process, and it established a new wording for the challenged provision, in the sense that the bail must be approved by the corresponding judge and not the Attorney General.[73] Another example is the Organic Law of Public Defense, an institution established in the Constitution as part of the judicial system. Nonetheless, article 3 of the Law specified that the Public Defense Service was to depend on the Public Defender's office, which was considered unconstitutional and annulled by the Chamber, which established in Decision No. 163 of February 28, 2008, that the provision was to be read in

71 See Decision Voto 3435-92, in Rubén Hernández Valle, *Costa Rican National Report*, p. 38.

72 See Decision Voto 3495-92, in Rubén Hernández Valle, *Costa Rican National Report*, p. 39.

73 See Decision nº 1104 of May 23, 2006, *Carlos Brender* case; http://www.tsj.gov.ve/decisiones/scon/Mayo/1104-230506-02-1688.htm. See also Daniela Urosa Maggi, *Venezuelan National Report*, p. 27.

the sense of attaching the Service to the Supreme Tribunal of Justice, not to the Peoples' Defender Office.[74] In addition, in the same decision, the Chamber annulled *ex officio* the provisions establishing the attribution of the Peoples' Defender to appoint the Head of the Public Defense Service, providing for another regime of appointment by the Supreme Tribunal; and it annulled the provision establishing the approval by the People's Defender of the Budget of the Public Defense Service, changing the wording of the Law to attribute that function to the Supreme Tribunal.[75]

This technique of additive rulings on matters of judicial review can also be identified in countries with a diffuse system of judicial review, like Argentina, where the Supreme Court has issued additive decisions on monetary matters. In the *Massa* case,[76] regarding the compulsory conversion of foreign currency into pesos through various emergency legal provisions, the Court ruled that the regime did not violate property rights recognized in the Constitution providing that a conversion of 1.40 pesos to one U.S. dollar be ensured, with a stabilization coefficient and an annual interest rate of 4 percent. This was a judicial addition to the legal emergency regime to avoid it being declared unconstitutional.[77] In human rights cases, the Supreme Court has also issued additive rulings, like in the *Portillo* Case (1989), where the Court was required to rule on the constitutionality of mandatory military service. The petitioner claimed that, to the extent that military service might require the killing of another individual, it affected the petitioner's deep religious beliefs in violation of the free exercise of religion clause of the Constitution. The Court held that, in peacetime, compliance with military service as established by Congress violated such a clause, but it still required the petitioner to serve time in alternative civil service, thus redefining the

[74] See Decision nº 163 of February 28, 2008, *Ciro Ramón Araujo* case. See http://www.tsj.gov.ve/decisiones/scon/Febrero/163-280208-07-0124.htm. See also Daniela Urosa Maggi, *Venezuelan National Report*, pp. 27–28.

[75] *Id.*, p. 28.

[76] See Fallos 329:5913 (2006); Alejandra Rodríguez Galán and Alfredo Mauricio Vítolo, *Argentinean National Report I*, p. 17 (footnote 71). See also the *Bustos* case, Fallos 327:4495 (2004). *Id.*, p. 17 (footnote 70).

[77] See Néstor P. Sagües, "Los efectos de las sentencias constitucionales en el derecho argentino," in *Anuario Iberoamericano de Justicia Constitucional*, Centro de Estudios Políticos y Constitucionales, nº 12, 2008, Madrid 2008, p. 339; Néstor Pedro Sagües, *Argentinean National Report II*, p. 19.

concept of "national defense" despite the fact that Congress did not provide for such an alternative.[78]

Even in France, where the judicial review system until 2009 was reduced to the *a priori* review of legislation not yet in force, the Constitutional Council has exercise its attributions, adding provisions to the reviewed statute and modifying the scope of application of the law. For example, in Decision 82-141 DC of July 27, 1982 regarding the control of constitutionality of the draft statute on TV communications (*communications audiovisielle*), the Council extended the scope of the right to response, interpreting the phrase "without lucrative purpose" to establish the titleholder of the right. As mentioned by Bertrand Mathieu, in this case, the Council has said what the law is, instead of the Legislator, which established the right to response in television communications only to a category of persons. By eliminating those restrictions, the Council extended the scope of the right, substituting itself for the will of the Legislator. The Constitutional Council considered that the Constitution established such right of response without it being reserved to some persons.[79]

III. CONSTITUTIONAL COURTS COMPLEMENTING LEGISLATIVE FUNCTIONS BY INTERFERING WITH THE TEMPORAL EFFECTS OF LEGISLATION

One of the most common interferences of the Constitutional Courts regarding legislative functions is the power of the Courts to determine the temporal effects of legislation enacted by the Legislator. In general terms, in comparative law, three different situations can be distinguished: first are cases in which the Constitutional Court determines when an annulled legislation will cease to have effects at some point in the future; second are cases in which the Constitutional Court, by assigning retroactive or nonretroactive effects to its decisions, determines the date on which legislation ceases to have effects; third are cases in which the Constitutional Court, when declaring null an unconstitutional statute, decides to bring back previously repealed legislation.

[78] See Fallos 312:496 (1989); Alejandra Rodríguez Galán and Alfredo Mauricio Vítolo, *Argentinean National Report I*, p. 15 (footnote 63).

[79] See Bertrand Mathieu, *French National Report*, p. 16. See the decision in http://www.conseil-constitutionnel.fr/conseil-constitutionnel/francais/les-decisions/depuis-1958/decisions-par-date/1982/82-141-dc/decision-n-82-141-dc-du-27-juillet-1982.7998.html.

The matter, for instance, has been expressly regulated in the Constitution of the Republic of South Africa of 1996, which provides the following:

Article 172. Powers of courts in constitutional matters.

1. When deciding a constitutional matter within its power, a court:
   a) must declare that any law or conduct that is inconsistent with the Constitution is invalid to the extent of its inconsistency; and
   b) may make any order that is just and equitable, including
      i. an order limiting the retrospective effect of the declaration of invalidity; and
      ii. an order suspending the declaration of invalidity for any period and on any conditions, to allow the competent authority to correct the defect.

1. *The Power of the Constitutional Court to Determine When Annulled Legislation Will Cease to Have Effects: Postponing the Effect of the Court's Ruling*

The first of the cases in which constitutional courts interfere with the legislative function, by modulating the temporal effects of its decision declaring unconstitutional or null a statute, is when the Court establishes *vacatio sentenciae*, determining when annulled legislation will cease to have effects by postponing the beginning of the effects of its own decision and thus extending the application of the invalidated statute.

In principle, it is a general rule in systems of judicial review in which the constitutional courts have power to annul unconstitutional statutes,[80] as was, for instance, established since the beginning in the 1920 Austrian Constitution (article 140.3), that the Constitutional Court's decisions must be published in an Official Journal. This means, that in principle, as the Court's decisions have *erga omnes* effects as products of the negative legislator, the judicial review decision annulling a statute begins to have effects since the date of its publication, unless the Court establishes another date to avoid legislative vacuums, giving time to the Legislator to enact a new legislation

[80] Although in some countries like Portugal, "The Court has never postponed the effects of its ruling by safeguarding effects produced after the declaration of unconstitutionality (and according to the prevailing opinion on this subject the effects of annulment could not be postponed)." See Joaquim de Sousa Ribeiro and Esperança Mealha, *Portuguese National Report*, p. 6.

to replace the annulled one. In the Austrian Constitution, the Court can postpone the effects of its decision for a term of up to six months, and in the constitutional reform of 1992 this was extended to eighteen months (art. 140.5).[81] In these cases of extending the beginning of the effects of the Court's decisions, the annulled statute remains in force until the extinction of the term or the intervention of the Legislator by enacting a statute to replace the annulled one. Consequently, as the Court has the power to extend the effects of an annulled statute, it can be said that, since the beginning of the concentrated system of judicial review in Europe, the Austrian Constitutional Court was "a corrective jurisdictional legislator and not only a simple negative jurisdictional legislator."[82]

In Greece, article 100.4, para. 2, of the Constitution, provides that the Supreme Special Court invalidates unconstitutional statutory provisions "as of the date of publication of the respective judgment, or as of the date specified in the ruling," thus implicitly recognizing that the Supreme Special Court can establish a different date for the beginning of the effects of the invalidation of the unconstitutional statute.[83]

This also occurs in Belgium, where the Constitutional Court (formerly the Arbitration Court), according to its Organic Law (article 8.2), has the power to provisionally maintain the effects of an invalidated statutory provision – in this case, not for a specific period of time but for the time the Court determines.[84] This term has been established in different ways according to the Court appreciation of facts, for instance, as referred to by Christian Behrendt, to the publication of the Court decision in the *Moniteur*, to the end of the academic year, to the end of the fiscal year, and to the nomination of

81 See Francisco Javier Díaz Revorio, *Las sentencias interpretativas del Tribunal Constitucional*, Lex Nova, Valladolid 2001, p. 266; Francisco Fernández Segado, "Algunas reflexiones generales en torno a los efectos de las sentencias de inconstitutionalidad y a la relatividad de ciertas fórmulas estereotipadas vinculadas a ellas," in *Anuario Iberoamericano de Justicia Constitucional*, nº 12, 2008, Centro de Estudios Políticos y Constitucionales, Madrid 2008, pp. 174, 188.

82 See Otto Pfersmann, "Preface," in Christian Behrendt, *Le judge constitutionnel, un législateur-cadre positif. Un analyse comparative en droit francais, belge et allemande*, Bruylant, Brussels 2006, p. xxxiii; Konrad Lachmayer, *Austrian National Report*, p. 7.

83 See Julia Iliopoulos-Strangas and Stylianos-Ioannis G. Koutnatzis, *Greek National Report*, p. 20 (footnote 152).

84 See Christian Behrendt, *Le judge constitutionnel, un législateur-cadre positif. Un analyse comparative en droit francais, belge et allemande*, Bruylant, Brussels 2006, p. 87, 230, 235, 286, 309; P. Popelier, *Belgian National Report*, pp. 4–7.

the Officials of an organ of the State.[85] In such cases, the effects of the annulled provision cease automatically, thus creating a legislative vacuum, which the Legislator is compelled to fill. This was the case of a 2002 statute modifying the rules for the publication of the *Moniteur* and establishing its exclusive electronic publication, reducing the physical (paper) publication for public consultation to only three copies. Because of the discriminatory character of the reform, impeding the access of some citizens to the Official Journal, the Court in 2004 declared invalid the statute but provided that it was to continue to have effects (*delai d'abrogation*) until July 31, 2005, imposing on the Legislator the obligation to determine alternative rules to overcome the inequalities.[86] That is why, in some cases, the Constitutional Court has determined that the term during which the unconstitutional statute must remain in force extends up to the moment in which the corresponding Legislator issues a new legislation on the matter.[87]

In the Czech Republic, the Constitutional Court has postponed the effects of a decision issued in 2000 to offer the legislature time to enact a new law that would enact a mechanism for just terms in rent.[88] Nonetheless, the most celebrated example is the case of the annulment of the law on judicial review of administrative acts, which did not fit the requirements of the Czech Constitution and, above all, the European Convention of Human Rights. The Constitutional Court repeatedly urged the legislature to enact a new and constitutionally consistent law. Finally, as mentioned by Zdenek Kühn, the Court lost its patience and annulled all of part 5 of the Code of Civil Procedure related to administrative judiciary. It noted that the law as a whole suffered serious constitutional deficits, even though there were many provisions that would be included in a new law, stating:

> After taking into account all calls made by the Court to both the legislature and the executive branch, and after considering the current state of work on the reform of administrative judiciary, the Court decided to delay the effects

85 See Christian Behrendt, *Le judge constitutionnel, un législateur-cadre positif. Un analyse comparative en droit francais, belge et allemande*, Bruylant, Brussels 2006, p. 236.

86 See CA arrêt 106/2004, June 16, 2004. See also the references in Christian Behrendt, *Le judge constitutionnel, un législateur-cadre positif. Un analyse comparative en droit francais, belge et allemande*, Bruylant, Brussels 2006, pp. 313–320.

87 Arrêt 45/2004; Christian Behrendt, *Le judge constitutionnel, un législateur-cadre positif. Un analyse comparative en droit francais, belge et allemande*, Bruylant, Brussels 2006, p. 87, 235, 309–321.

88 See judgment of June 21, 2000, Pl. ÚS 3/2000, *Rent Control I*, published as nº 231/2000 Sb.; Zdenek Kühn, *Czech National Report*, p. 12 (footnote 57).

> of its judgment until December 31, 2002. As it would take some time before enacting the law and its entering into force, it is clear that it is the task for this legislature to enact a new law.[89]

Eventually, the legislature, which delayed the enactment of the new law on administrative judiciary for almost ten years, enacted a new law.

In France, the constitutional law No. 2008-724 of July 23, 2008 reforming article 62 of the Constitution on the judicial review system established that in the case of statutory provisions declared unconstitutional according to article 61-1 (exception of unconstitutionality), the decision has effect since its publication, as the Constitutional Council is authorized to fix another ulterior date. In Croatia, to avoid legal uncertainties occurring in the period between the adoption and publication of a repeal decision by the Constitutional Court, article 55.2 of the 2002 Constitutional Act on the Constitutional Court states:

> The repealed law or other regulation, or their repealed separate provisions, shall lose legal force on the day of publication of the Constitutional Court decision in the Official Gazette Narodne novine, unless the Constitutional Court sets another term.[90]

The same general principle has been applied in Germany, although without such a clear provision as those in Belgium, France, or Croatia. Article 35 of the Federal Constitutional Court of Germany only establishes regarding the execution of its decision that, in individual cases, the Court can establish how such execution will take place. Given this provision, it can be considered usual practice for the Federal Constitutional Court to establish a term for its decision to by applied, which is fixed according to different rules, for instance, a precise date or a particular fact like the end of the legislative term.[91] One recent case, highlighted by I. Härtel, concerns the inheritance tax statutory provision.[92] In some aspects the provision was unconstitutional, but the Tribunal did not annul it but referred it to the

[89] See the judgment of June 27, 2001, Pl. ÚS 16/99, *Part Five of the Code of Civil Procedure – Administrative Judiciary*, published as nº 276/2001 Sb.; Zdenek Kühn, *Czech National Report*, p. 14 (footnote 63) (the Court was referring to the fact of parliamentary elections, which were due in June 2002).

[90] See Sanja Barić and Petar Bačić, *Croatian National Report*, p. 17.

[91] See BVferG, May 22, 1963 (Electoral Circuits), in Christian Behrendt, *Le judge constitutionnel, un législateur-cadre positif. Un analyse comparative en droit francais, belge et allemande*, Bruylant, Brussels 2006, pp. 299–300. See BVferG, November 7, 2006 (Inheritance Tax); I. Härtel, *German National Report*, p. 7.

[92] See BVerfG, court order from 2006-11-7, reference number: 1 BvL 10/02; I. Härtel, *German Report*, pp. 7–8.

Legislator to reform it in conformity with the Constitution, thus maintaining the applicability of the unconstitutional statute until a new legislative regulation could be established. As I. Härtel said: "The continuing implementation was seen as necessary to prevent a situation of legal uncertainty during the interim period, especially affecting, and potentially complicating, the regulations regarding succession of property during a transferor's lifetime. The *BVerfG* has therefore, as a kind of 'emergency legislator,' created a law-like condition (*Steiner*, ZEV 2007, 120 (121)); it has 'invented' a new decision type (*Schlaich/Korioth*, Das Bundesverfassungsgericht, 7th ed. 2007, margin number 395)."[93]

In Italy, the Constitution clearly establishes that when the Constitutional Court declares unconstitutional a statutory provision, it ceases in its effects the day after its publication (article 136, Constitution), which implies that the Constitutional Court cannot postpone the annulment effects or extend the application of the annulled provision.[94] Nonetheless, it is possible to identify in the jurisprudence important cases of deferring the effects in time of a declaration of unconstitutionality. As mentioned by Gianpaolo Parodi, "in these cases, the Court declared the unconstitutional character of legislative provisions by the state successive to the constitutional law no. 3/2001 and detrimental to the new regional attributions, explaining that the state discipline censured would not have ceased to find application until the arrangement and the coming into force of the new regional regulations and setting aside the administrative procedures in progress and founded on the first, even if not yet exhausted, to avoid that, due to the situation of normative void determined by the ruling of acceptance, the guarantee of constitutional rights might result compromised."[95]

In Canada, the Supreme Court has also developed innovative remedies of delaying or suspending the declaration of invalidity for periods of six to eighteen months to provide legislatures an opportunity to enact new constitutional legislation so that there are no lacunae in the legal regime. It was first used in the case *Manitoba Language Reference*, where in the Province of Manitoba all laws were unconstitutional because they had not

[93] See I. Härtel, *German National Report*, p. 8.

[94] In the 1997 proposed reform of the Constitution, which was not approved, one of the reforms aimed to allow the Constitutional Court to postpone the effects of annulment for up to one year. See Francisco Javier Díaz Revorio, *Las sentencias interpretativas del Tribunal Constitucional*, Lex Nova, Valladolid 2001, p. 125 (footnote 166).

[95] On the subject of education, see Const. C., Judgment Nos. 370/2003; 13 and 423/2004. See also Gianpaolo Parodi, *Italian National Report*, p. 13.

been translated into French. The Court delayed the declaration of invalidity under s. 52(1) of the Constitution Act (which says that laws inconsistent with the Constitution are of no force and effect) and justified the use of a suspended declaration of invalidity on the basis that the immediate striking down of all of Manitoba's laws would offend the rule of law. The practical effect of this decision, however, was that Manitoba translated all of its laws over a period of time supervised by the court.[96] Since that time, as mentioned by Kent Roach, "the use of suspended declarations of invalidity has increased, though the Court formally maintains that the remedy should only be used in cases where an immediate declaration of invalidity will threaten the rule of law or public safety or deprive people of benefits simply because the benefit has been extended in an unconstitutionally under inclusive manner."[97] Kent Roach also mentions that the South African Constitution follows the Canadian example and specifically provides for suspended declarations of invalidity (article 172). It must be noted, that, although it may have that practical effect, the suspended declaration of invalidity is not a mandatory order that the legislature enact new legislation. The legislature is legally free to do nothing. In such an event, the court's declaration of invalidity takes effect once the period of delay has expired.[98]

In Brazil, in contrast, in the 2006 Law No. 11.417 developing the provision of article 103-B of the Constitution, when regulating the institution known as *súmula vinculante* and establishing the general principle of the immediate effects of the decisions of the Federal Supreme Tribunal, it authorizes the Tribunal to decide for the effects to start in another moment, taking into account legal security reasons or exceptional public interest.[99] The same sort of regulation is found in article 190.3 of the Polish Constitution, where regarding the decisions of the Constitutional Tribunal, after establishing that they shall take effect from the day of its publication, it authorizes the Constitutional Tribunal to specify another date for the end of the binding force of a normative act, a period that may not exceed eighteen

96 See *Manitoba Language Reference* [1985] 1 S.C.R. 721; Kent Roach, *Canadian National Report*, p. 7 (footnote 8).

97 See *Schachter v. Canada* [1992] 2 S.C.R. 679; Kent Roach, *Canadian National Report*, p. 8 (footnote 9).

98 See Kent Roach, *Canadian National Report*, p. 8.

99 See Jairo Gilberto Schäfer and Vânia Hack de Almeida, "O controle de constitutionalidade no dereitto brasileiro e a possibilidade de modular os efeitos da decisão de inconstitutionalidade," in *Anuario Iberoamericano de Justicia Constitucional*, nº 12, 2008, Centro de Estudios Políticos y Constitucionales, Madrid 2008, p. 384.

months for a statute or twelve months for any other normative act.[100] As has been said by Marek Safjan, "no other organ, except for the constitutional court, may order application of norms declared unconstitutional, which is paradoxical considering that the fundamental role of any constitutional court is to eliminate unconstitutional statutes and not to let them remain in force."[101]

In Spain, the Organic Law on the Constitutional Tribunal has no express provision on this matter, as the Tribunal ruled in Decision 45/1989 that it could not postpone the beginning of the effects of its nullity decision "due to the fact that the Organic Law does not empower the Tribunal, in a different way to what occurs in another system, to postpone or put off the moment of the effectiveness of the nullity."[102] Nonetheless, in subsequent decisions, the Constitutional Tribunal, without legal support, has assumed the power to postpone the beginning of the effects of its nullity decisions, as was the case of the Law 6/1992 establishing the territorial area of the Santoja y Noja Marsh, considered unconstitutional because it interfered with the competencies of the Autonomous Communities. To avoid any lack of protection regarding the environment, the Tribunal postponed the effects of its annulment up to the moment that the corresponding Autonomous Community exercised its legislative attributions.[103] Although the power the Tribunal assumed was proposed to be incorporated in the 2007 reform of the Organic Law, it was not passed, evidence of the role of the Tribunal as positive legislator on matters of judicial review.[104]

Something similar is accepted in Mexico, where the Supreme Court is empowered to postpone the effects of a decision annulling a statute according to its evaluation of the effects of the legislative vacuum produced by the annulment. No maximum term is established in these cases.[105] In Peru, the Constitutional Tribunal applied *vacatio sentenciae* when annulling

100 See Marek Safjan, *Polish National Report*, p. 4 (footnote 13).

101 *Id.*, p. 6.

102 See STC 45/1989, February 20, 1989, in F. Fernández Segado, *Spanish National Report*, pp. 16–17.

103 See STC 195/1998, October 1, 1998, in F. Fernández Segado, *Spanish National Report*, p. 18.

104 See the critic of F. Fernández Segado, *Spanish National Report*, pp. 13, 17.

105 See Tesis Jurisprudencial P./J 11/2001, in SJFG, Vol. XIV, Sept. 2001, p. 1008. See the reference in Héctor Fix Zamudio and Eduardo Ferrer Mac-Gregor, *Las sentencias de los Tribunales Constitucionales*, Ed. Porrúa, Mexico City 2009, p. 69; and "Las sentencias de los tribunales constitucionales en el ordenamiento mexicano," in *Anuario Iberoamericano de Justicia Constitucional*, nº 12, 2008, Centro de Estudios Políticos y Constitucionales, Madrid 2008, pp. 247–248.

in 2002 the Fujimori Government's antiterrorist laws, "to allow the democratic legislator in a short and reasonable delay," to issue legislation on procedural matters that could rationally allow for retrials in cases of those already condemned for treason.[106] In Colombia, the Constitutional Court has often postponed the effects of its decisions annulling statutes.[107]

Finally, it must be mentioned that this possibility of postponing the date on which the effects of a decision begin has also been applied in countries with a diffuse system of judicial review, as in Argentina, where the Supreme Court, to avoid chaotic consequences from the immediate application of its declaration of unconstitutionality of a statutory provision, postponed the beginning of the effects for one year after the decision was published.[108] In other cases, the Supreme Court has clearly ruled for future cases, expanding the scope of protection of the declaratory judgments (*acción declarativa de certeza*), regulated by Article 322 of the National Code of Federal Civil and Commercial Procedure. For instance, in the *Rios* case, decided in 1987, a statute provision providing that only political parties could present candidates to federal elections was challenged because it violated the right to elect and be elected for public office. Even though at the time of the decision the election had passed, the Supreme Court accepted the case, to establish precedent that settles the matter for future cases, thus reaffirming its role as final interpreter of the Constitution and its pretense to expand the effect of its rulings beyond the case being heard.[109]

In the same trend, in the Netherlands, regarding the control of conventionality of statutes, the Supreme Court has postponed the effects of some of its decisions, "true prospective" ones, when the Court does not apply its new interpretation in the case at hand but postpones it.[110]

[106] See Domingo García Belaúnde and Gerardo Eto Cruz, "Efectos de las sentencias constitucionales en el Perú," in *Anuario Iberoamericano de Justicia Constitucional*, nº 12, 2008, Centro de Estudios Políticos y Constitucionales, Madrid 2008, pp. 283–284; Francisco Eguiguren and Liliana Salomé, *Peruvian National Report I*, p. 10.

[107] See, e.g., Decision C-221 of 1997; C-700 of 1999; C-442/01; C-500/01; C-737/01; Germán Alfonso López Daza, *Colombian National Report I*, p. 11 (footnote 26).

[108] See *Rosza* case, *Jurisprudencia Argentina*, 2007-III-414, in Néstor P. Sagües, "Los efectos de las sentencias constitucionales en el derecho argentino," in *Anuario Iberoamericano de Justicia Constitucional*, Centro de Estudios Políticos y Constitucionales, nº 12, 2008, Madrid 2008, p. 352.

[109] See Fallos 310:819 (1987); Alejandra Rodríguez Galán and Alfredo Mauricio Vítolo, *Argentinean National Report I*, p. 10.

[110] See Supreme Court judgment of 12 May 1999, *NJ* 2000/170 (*Labour Expenses Deduction*); J. Uzman, T. Barkhuysen, and M.L. van Emmerik, *Dutch National Report*, p. 26 (footnote 79).

2. *The Power of the Constitutional Court to Determine When Annulled Legislation Will Cease to Have Effects: Retroactive or Nonretroactive Effects of Its Own Decisions*

But regarding the effects of the judicial decisions declaring a statute unconstitutional, another aspect of the temporal effects of the annulment is the retroactive or nonretroactive effects given to the Constitutional Court's decisions. The Court can determine the point in the past at which an annulled legislation ceased to have effects.

This Constitutional Court ruling depends on the nature of the judicial review decision, and it varies according to the system adopted in the given country. If the Court decisions are considered declarative by nature, with *ex tunc* or *ab initio* effects, the judicial review decisions declaring the unconstitutionality of statutes have retroactive effects, and the result is that the statute is considered as if it never had produced effects. If the decisions of the Court declaring a statute unconstitutional are considered constitutive, with *ex nunc* or *pro futuro* effects, the judicial review decisions declaring the statute unconstitutional have nonretroactive effects, not affecting the effects produced by the statute up to its annulment. In some countries, a rule has been established in the statute regulating the Constitutional Court, and in others, the decision to opt for a solution corresponds to the Constitutional Court itself when having the power to determine when the effects of the annulled legislation ceased. In any case, any rigidity on the matter has passed.

A. The Possibility of Limiting the Retroactive *Ex Tunc* Effects Regarding Declarative Decisions

In the case of a classical diffuse system of judicial review, as in the United States, the Supreme Court decisions declaring the unconstitutionality of statutes have in principle declarative effects, in the sense of considering the statute null and void, as if "it had never been passed"[111] or had never "been made";[112] that is, they are generally considered to have *ex tunc* or retroactive

[111] See *Norton v. Selby County*, 118 U.S. 425 (1886), p. 442. See the critics to this ruling in J. A. C. Grant, "The Legal Effect of a Ruling That a Statute Is Unconstitutional," *Detroit College of Law Review*, 1978, nº 2, p. 207, in which he said: "An unconstitutional act may give rise to rights. It may impose duties. It may afford protection. It may even create an office. In short, it may not be as inoperative as though it had never been passed." See also Laurence Claus and Richard S. Kay, *U.S. National Report*, p. 21 (footnote 21).

[112] See *Vanhorne's Lessee* v. *Dorrance* case (1795), 2 Dallas 304.

effects. Nonetheless, this initial doctrine has been progressively relaxed, given the possible negative or unjust effects that could be produced by the Court's decisions regarding the effects that the unconstitutional statute has already produced. This was, for instance, specifically highlighted by Justice Clark in *Linkletter v. Walker* (1965), in applying a new constitutional rule to cases previously finalized. The Court said:

> Petitioner contends that our method of resolving those prior cases demonstrates that an absolute rule of retroaction prevails in the area of constitutional adjudication. However, we believe that the constitution neither prohibits nor requires retrospective effect. As Justice Cardozo said, we think the federal constitution has no voice upon the subject. Once the premise is accepted that we are neither required to apply, nor prohibited from applying a decision retrospectively, we must then weigh the merits and demerits in each case by looking to the prior history of the rule in question, its purpose and effect, and whether retrospective operation will further or retard its operation.[113]

Therefore, considering that "the past cannot always be erased by a new judicial decision,"[114] the principle of the retroactive effects of the Supreme Court decisions in constitutional matters has been applied in a relative way. "The questions – said the Supreme Court in *Chicot County Drainage District v. Baxter State Bank* (1940) – are among the most difficult of those that have engaged the attention of courts, state and federal, and it is manifest from numerous decisions that an all-inclusive statement of a principle of absolute retroactive invalidity cannot be justified."[115] The Supreme Court in any case has abandoned the absolute rule[116] and has recognized its authority to give or to deny retroactive effects to its ruling on constitutional issues; the Supreme Courts of the states have done the same during recent decades.

For instance, in criminal matters, the Courts have given full retroactive effects to their rules when they benefit the prosecuted. In particular, they have given retroactive effects to decisions in the field of criminal liability, for example, allowing prisoners on application for *habeas corpus* to secure their release on the grounds that they are held under authority of a statute that, subsequent to their conviction, was held unconstitutional.[117] The Court has

[113] See *Linkletter v. Walker*, 381 U.S. 618 (1965).

[114] See *Chicot County Drainage District v. Baxter State Bank*, 308 U.S. 371 (1940), p. 374.

[115] *Id.*

[116] See Laurence Claus and Richard S. Kay, *U.S. National Report*, p. 21.

[117] See *Ex parte Siebold*, 100 U.S. 371 (1880).

also given retroactive effects to its decisions on constitutional matters, when it considers the rules essential to safeguard against the conviction of innocent persons, such as the requirement that counsel be furnished at the trial (*Gideon v. Wainwright*, 327 U.S. 335, 1963), or when the accused is asked to plead (*Arsenault* v. *Massachusetts*, 393 U.S. 5, 1968), or when it is sought to revoke the probation status of a convicted criminal because of his or her subsequent conduct (*McConnell v. Rhay*, 393 U.S. 2, 1968), as well as the rule requiring proof beyond a reasonable doubt (*Ivan v. City of New York*, 407 U.S. 203, 1972). Its ruling concerning the death penalty has also been made fully retroactive (*Witherspoon v. Illinois*, 391 U.S. 510, 1968).[118]

In other criminal cases, the position of the Court has been to give no retroactive effects to its rulings on constitutional issues when it also benefits the prosecuted. As J. A. C. Grant said, in 1977, the Supreme Court held that any change in the interpretation of the Constitution that has the effect of punishing acts that were not penalized under the earlier interpretation cannot be applied retroactively; as it is stated in *Marks v. United States* (1977), "the notion that persons have a right to fair warning of that conduct which will give rise to criminal penalties, is fundamental to our concept of constitutional liberty."[119]

Therefore, the rule of retroactiveness of the effects of the Court's decisions in criminal cases is not absolute and has been applied by the Court in considering the justice of its application in each case. Consequently, when the decision has not, for instance, affected the "fairness of a trial" but only the rights to privacy of a person, the Court has denied the retroactive effects of its ruling.

It must also be mentioned that, even in cases of rules related to the idea of the type of trial necessary to protect against convicting the innocent, the rules established by the Supreme Court have been made wholly prospective when to give them retroactive effect would impose what the Court considers unreasonable burdens on the government brought about at least in part by its reliance on previous rulings of the Supreme Court. This happened in *De Stefano v. Woods* (392 U.S. 631 (1968)), which established that state criminal trials must be by jury, and in *Adam v. Illinois* (405 U.S. 278 (1972)), which established the right to counsel at the preliminary hearing whose retroactivity the Court said "could seriously disrupt the administration of our criminal laws." In contrast, in civil cases, it has been considered that

[118] See J. A. C. Grant, *loc. cit.*, p. 237.

[119] See *Marks v. United States*, 430 U.S. 188 (1977), p. 191; J. A. C. Grant, *loc. cit.*, 238.

the new rule established in a court decision on constitutional matters cannot disturb property rights or contracts previously made. In this respect, the Supreme Court in *Gelpcke v. Dubuque* (68 U.S. (1 Wall) 175 (1864)) considered that a decision of the Supreme Court of Iowa was to be given prospective effect only:

> The sound and true rule is, that if the contract, when made, was valid by the laws of the state as then expounded . . . and administered in its courts of justice, its validity and. obligation cannot be impaired by any subsequent action of legislation, or decision of its courts altering the construction of the law.

In other countries that have adopted the diffuse system of judicial review, following the U.S. model, as is the case of Argentina, the same modality of mitigating the retroactive effects of the decisions declaring the unconstitutionality of statutes has been adopted.[120]

The same mitigating process regarding the general rule of the retroactive effects of the judicial review decisions has also been developed in countries, like the Netherlands, regarding the control of conventionality of statutes. Departing from the initial general rule of the retroactive effect of the Supreme Court rulings on the matter, since the 1970s, as referred to by J. Uzman, T. Barkhuysen, and M. L. van Emmerik. These have embraced a lawmaking duty, openly discussing the consequences of judicial review decisions and giving in some cases prospective effects –called qualified prospective decisions– when the Court immediately applies its new interpretation or rule but limits the possibilities for other parties than those in the case at hand to appeal to the new rule. An example is the 1981 *Boon v. Van Loon* case, where the Court changed its case law on the ownership of pensions in divorce law[121] but explicitly limited the temporal effect of its new course to the case at hand and future cases. Where the divorce had already been pronounced, no appeal to the new rule would be possible.[122]

However, it must be mentioned that not all countries following the concentrated system of judicial review have adopted the constitutive effects

[120] See *Itzcovich* case, *Jurispudencia Argentina* 2005-II-723, in Néstor P. Sagües, "Los efectos de las sentencias constitucionales en el derecho argentino," in *Anuario Iberoamericano de Justicia Constitucional*, Centro de Estudios Políticos y Constitucionales, nº 12, 2008, Madrid 2008, p. 351.

[121] See Supreme Court judgment of 27 November 1981, *NJ* 1982/503 (*Boon v. Van Loon*); J. Uzman, T. Barkhuysen, and M. L. van Emmerik, *Dutch National Report*, p. 42 (footnote 138).

[122] See J. Uzman, T. Barkhuysen, and M. L. van Emmerik, *Dutch National Report*, pp. 41–42.

of the decision annulling the unconstitutional statute. In Germany, for instance, the proclaimed principle is the contrary one. As a matter of principle, the decisions of the Federal Constitutional Tribunal when annulling a statute have *ex tunc* and *eo ipse* effects, considering that the annulled statute should never have produced legal effects.[123] Nonetheless, in practice the reality is another, and it is not common to find decisions annulling statutes with purely *ex tunc* effects, except if with the *ex tunc* annulment of the statute the situation of conformity with the Constitution is immediately reestablished.[124] In contrast, the Law regulating the functions of the Federal Constitutional Tribunal establishes in article 95.1 the possible *ex tunc* effects on criminal matters, prescribing that "new proceedings may be instituted in accordance with the provisions of the Code of Criminal Procedure against a final conviction based on a rule which has been declared incompatible with the Basic Law or null and void in accordance with Article 78 above or on the interpretation of a rule which the Federal Constitutional Court has declared incompatible with the Basic Law." In article 95.2, it adds that, "in all other respects, subject to the provisions of Article 95 (2) below or a specific statutory provision, final decisions based on a rule declared null and void pursuant to Article 78 above shall remain unaffected."[125]

In Poland, the decisions of the Constitutional Tribunal annulling statutes according to article 190.4 of the Constitution imply, in addition to the ban on application of the unconstitutional norm in the future, an opportunity to modify past decisions issued, for instance, by courts and administrative organs on the basis of the provisions found unconstitutional, before the judgment was passed. Such provision states that the Constitutional Tribunal's decision "shall be a basis for re-opening proceedings, or for quashing the decision or other settlement in a manner and on principles specified in provisions applicable to the given proceedings."[126]

In Portugal, the effects given to the annulment decisions of the Constitutional Tribunal are also retroactive, although article 282.4 of the Constitution limits the retroactivity of the decision when motives of juridical security, equity, or public interests prevent application of the retroactive

123 See I. Härtel, *German National Report*, p. 10.

124 See Francisco Fernández Segado, *Spanish National Report*, pp. 8, 14.

125 Cf. Francisco Fernández Segado, "Algunas reflexiones generales en torno a los efectos de las sentencias de inconstitucionalidad y a la relatividad de ciertas fórmulas estereotipadas vinculadas a ellas," in *Anuario Iberoamericano de Justicia Constitucional*, Centro de Estudios Políticos y Constitucionales, nº 12, 2008, Madrid 2008, pp. 190–191.

126 See Marek Safjan, *Polish National Report*, p. 5.

principle.[127] Also in Brazil, decisions delivered by the Supreme Federal Tribunal applying the concentrated method of judicial review of the constitutionality of laws normally have *ex tunc* or retroactive effects. Nevertheless, as pointed out by Thomas Bustamante, "the Supreme Court may restrict the effects of the pronouncement of unconstitutionality of a law to deliver *ex nunc* or *pro futuro* decisions or even to determine that the pronouncement of unconstitutionality will produce effects only after a deadline to be set by the Court. There are, however, some requirements for delivering such manipulative decisions: (i) there must be reasons of legal certainty or of (ii) exceptional social interest and, apart from that, (iii) the restriction or the exception to the retroactive efficacy of the decision must be established by a vote of at least two thirds of the members of the Court (in its plenary sitting)."[128]

B. The Possibility of Retroactive Effects for *Ex Nunc* Constitutive Decisions

In the concentrated system of judicial review, the initial principle adopted according to Kelsen's thoughts in the Austrian 1920 Constitution was the one of the constitutive effects of the constitutional courts decision annulling a statute, in the sense that its annulment, similar to the effects of the repeal, implied that the statute produced effects up to the moment in which its annulment was established.[129] According to this rule, the statute whose nullity is declared and established is considered, in principle, by the Court as having been valid up to that moment. That is why in these cases the decision of the Court has *ex nunc* and *pro futuro* or prospective effects, in the sense that, in principle, they do not go back to the moment of the enactment of the statute considered unconstitutional, and the effects produced by the annulled

[127] See María Fernanda Palma, "O legislador negativo e o interprete da Constitucão," in *Anuario Iberoamericano de Justicia Constitucional*, Centro de Estudios Políticos y Constitucionales, nº 12, 2008, Madrid 2008, pp. 174, 329; Francisco Fernández Segado, "Algunas reflexiones generales en torno a los efectos de las sentencias de inconstitucionalidad y a la relatividad de ciertas fórmulas esterotipadas vinculadas a ellas," in *Anuario Iberoamericano de Justicia Constitucional*, Centro de Estudios Políticos y Constitucionales, nº 12, 2008, Madrid 2008, p. 174; Iván Escobar Fornos, *Estudios Jurídicos*, Vol. I, Ed. Hispamer, Managua 2007, p. 493; Joaquim de Sousa Ribeiro and Esperança Mealha, *Portuguese National Report*, pp. 6.

[128] See Law nº 9.882 of December 3, 1999: art. 11; and Law nº 9.868 of November 10, 1999: art. 27; in Thomas Bustamante and Evanlida de Godoi Bustamante, *Brazilian National Report*, p. 26.

[129] See Hans Kelsen, "El control de la constitucionalidad de las leyes. Estudio comparado de las constituciones austriaca y americana," in Revista Iberoamericana de Derecho procesal Constitucional, nº 12, Editorisl Porrúa, Mexico 2009, pp.7-8..

statute until annulment are considered valid. The legislative act declared unconstitutional by the Constitutional Court in concentrated systems of judicial review, therefore, are considered a valid act until its annulment by the court, having produced complete effects until the moment when the court annuls it. Only the interested party that initiated a concrete case of judicial review of a legislative act (*Anlassfall*) can benefit from an exemption to the *ex nunc* rule.[130] Nevertheless, only in Austria does the Court have powers to annul statutes or decrees already repealed, that consequently are without formal validity (Art. 139, 4; Art. 140, 4), which, in principle, supposes some retroactive effects of the judicial review and is an exception to the *ex nunc* effects.

Other countries that, though they follow the general principle of nonretroactive effects of annulments, have reached the same practical effects,[131] even when the contrary (nonretroactive effect) is expressly established in the Constitution, as is the case in Italy with article 136 of the Constitution. The Constitutional Court has interpreted this provision in the sense that the declaration of unconstitutionality of a statute makes it inapplicable to all trials pending decision with *res judicata* force, in the same sense as if it were a *ius superveniens.*[132] Nonetheless, regarding cases already decided, particularly in criminal cases, the retroactive effects of the annulment are accepted when a judicial condemnation has been pronounced on the basis of a statute declared unconstitutional, in which case its execution and its criminal effects must cease (Art. 30, Statute No. 87, 1953). Another indirect exception of the *ex nunc* effects of the decision results from the possibility of annulment of statutes already repealed.

In Spain, according to the provisions of the Constitution, the Constitutional Tribunal's declaration of unconstitutionality or declaration of nullity of a statute means its annulment, and the declaration has *ex nunc*, *pro futuro* effects.[133] That is why the Constitution expressly establishes that "the decisions already adopted in judicial proceedings will not lose their *res judicata* value" (article 161.1.a). The Organic Law of the Tribunal also establishes, "The decisions which declare the unconstitutionality of statutes,

130 See Konrad Lachmayer, *Austrian National Report*, pp. 7–8.

131 See Gianpaolo Parodi, *Italian National Report*, p. 13.

132 See Decision nº 3491, 1957. See the reference in F. Rubio Llorente, *La Corte Constitucional italiana*, Universidad Central de Venezuela, Caracas 1966, p. 30.

133 See J. Arosemena Sierra, "El recurso de inconstitucionalidad," in *El Tribunal Constitucional*, Instituto de Estudios Fiscales, Madrid 1981, Vol. I, p. 171.

dispositions or acts with force of law[,] will not allow the review of judicial proceedings ended by decisions with *res judicata* force in which the unconstitutional act would have been applied" (article 40.1). However, as is the general trend in the concentrated system in granting nonretroactive effects to judicial review decisions, the exception to the *ex nunc* effects is established regarding criminal cases, where a limited retroactive effect is allowed and is extended to administrative justice decisions in cases of administrative sanction cases.[134]

A similar situation can be found in Peru, where the general principle established in article 204 of the Constitution and article 89 of the Constitutional Procedural Code is that the decisions annulling statutes have *pro futuro* effects and are not retroactive. Nonetheless, the same provisions of the Code as applied by the Constitutional Tribunal establish that, in taxation cases, the nullity can produce retroactive effects, which can also be determined by the Constitutional Tribunal.[135] Regarding annulment of statutes in criminal matters, the same principle is also applied by interpretation of article 103 of the Constitution (principle of retroactivity of the law), which allows for the exceptional retroactive effects of the laws in criminal matters.[136]

In France, in the constitutional reform sanctioned on matters of judicial review in 2008 (Constitutional Law 2008-724, of July 23, 2008), it was established that the Constitutional Council's decisions declaring unconstitutional a provision according to article 61-1 of the Constitution are considered repealed since the publication of the decision, as the

[134] See Francisco Javier Díaz Revorio, *Las sentencias interpretativas del Tribunal Constitucional*, Ed. Lex Nova, Valladolid 2001, pp. 104–105, 126–127; Francisco Fernández Segado, "Algunas reflexiones generales en torno a los efectos de las sentencias de inconstitucionalidad y a la relatividad de ciertas fórmulas esterotipadas vinculadas a ellas," in *Anuario Iberoamericano de Justicia Constitucional*, Centro de Estudios Políticos y Constitucionales, nº 12, 2008, Madrid 2008, pp. 192–194.

[135] See Decision STC 0041-2004-AI/TC, FJ 70, in Domingo García Belaúnde and Gerardo Eto Cruz, "Efectos de las sentencias constitucionales en el Perú," in *Anuario Iberoamericano de Justicia Constitucional*, Centro de Estudios Políticos y Constitucionales, nº 12, 2008, Madrid 2008, pp. 281–282.

[136] See Decision STC 0019-2005-AI/TC, FJ 52, in Domingo García Belaúnde and Gerardo Eto Cruz, "Efectos de las sentencias constitucionales en el Perú," in *Anuario Iberoamericano de Justicia Constitucional*, Centro de Estudios Políticos y Constitucionales, nº 12, 2008, Madrid 2008, pp. 281–283.

Constitutional Council is authorized to determine when and how the effects that the annulled provision has produced in the past can be affected.[137]

In the case of Croatia, where decisions of the Constitutional Court have *ex nunc* effect, the final judicial decisions for a criminal offense grounded on the legal provision that has been repealed due to its unconstitutionality do not produce legal effects from the day the Constitutional Court's decision takes effect, and the criminal judicial ruling may be changed by the appropriate application of the provisions in renewed criminal proceedings. Regarding noncriminal offence cases, since 2002, the right to demand the issuing of a new individual act or decision is conferred only to those individuals and legal persons who submitted to the Constitutional Court a proposal to review the constitutionality of the provision of a law. In such cases, the request for changing the individual act should be submitted within a term of six months from the publication of the Court's decision.[138] In Serbia, the general principle of the effects of the Constitutional Court decisions when annulling a law are *ex nunc*. Nonetheless, there are some exceptions to the *pro futuro* effects, as decisions can affect individual legal relationships retroactively. As referred to by Boško Tripković, the Court's decision can have retroactive consequences, although not *ex tunc*, in the sense that everyone whose right has been violated by a final or legally binding individual act adopted on the basis of a law determined unconstitutional by a decision of the Constitutional Court is entitled to demand from the competent authority a revision of that individual act. Nevertheless, this right to revision has certain restrictions: first, proposals for revision may be submitted within six months from the day of the publication of the Constitutional Court's decision in the Official Gazette; second, the revision is restricted to acts delivered within two years before the submission of the proposal or initiative for judicial review (Article 60 of the Law on Constitutional Court).[139]

In the Slovak Republic, article 41b of Act No. 38/1993 regulating the Proceedings before the Court states, as mentioned by Ján Svák and Lucia Berdisová, "if a judgment issued in a criminal proceeding based on the regulation that is in inconformity with the Constitution has not been

[137] See Francisco Fernández Segado, "Algunas reflexiones generales en torno a los efectos de las sentencias de inconstitucionalidad y a la relatividad de ciertas fórmulas esterotipadas vinculadas a ellas," in *Anuario Iberoamericano de Justicia Constitucional*, Centro de Estudios Políticos y Constitucionales, nº 12, 2008, Madrid 2008, p. 175.

[138] See Sanja Barić and Petar Bačić, *Croatian National Report*, p. 8.

[139] See Boško Tripković, *Serbian National Report*, p. 17.

executed, then the ruling of the Constitutional Court on inconformity is a reason for a retrial." The valid decisions issued in civil and administrative proceedings remains unaffected, but obligations imposed by such a decision cannot be subject to enforcement.[140]

The legislative provision does not clearly establish the *ex nunc* effects of the Constitutional Court's decision, as this is a matter in which the case law of the Constitutional Court has settled the rules to be applicable. In effect, in one case, the Constitutional Court had to decide whether it would protect legal certainty and thus not allow the retroactive effect of the ruling (decision on *ex nunc* effect) or would protect the principle of constitutionality and so not allow any application of the regulation that is known to be unconstitutional (decision on *ex tunc* effect); being both, the principle of legal certainty and the principle of constitutionality, fundamental principles of rule of law. Finally, the Constitutional Court decided that it would protect the principle of constitutionality because it was inadmissible to apply the principle of legal certainty absolutely, and it decided that the ruling had ex *tunc* substantive effect. This means that a judge of the ordinary court cannot apply a regulation that is in inconformity with the Constitution. The Constitutional Court thus *de facto* set up a doctrine on the substantial effects of the rulings on inconformity between legal regulation, which is not yet deeply developed.[141]

In other countries, the nonretroactive effects of annulment have been expressly established in the Constitutions, without the aforementioned exception, as in the case of Ecuador[142] and Chile.[143]

140 See Ján Svák and Lucia Berdisová, *Slovak National Report*, p. 6. See also Decision III. ÚS 164/07. *Id.*, p. 8.

141 In the opinion of Ján Svák and Lucia Berdisová, the Constitutional Court of the Czech Republic advocates a bit more "sophisticated" doctrine. That is, the court prefers *ex tunc* substantive effects of the rulings on inconformity of legal regulation on the proceedings that are not validly decided only if the *ex nunc* effect would infringe the fundamental rights and freedoms of aggrieved persons. And so a judge of an ordinary court can apply unconstitutional regulation if the fundamental rights and freedoms will not be infringed. See, e.g., decision of the Constitutional Court of the Czech Republic nº IV.ÚS 1777/07 and other decisions mentioned there. See Ján Svák and Lucia Berdisová, *Slovak National Report*, p. 8 (footnote 11).

142 See Hernán Salgado Pesantes, "Los efectos de las sentencias del Tribunal Constitucional del Ecuador," in *Anuario Iberoamericano de Justicia Constitucional*, Centro de Estudios Políticos y Constitucionales, nº 12, 2008, Madrid 2008, p. 362.

143 Art. 94.3. See Humberto Nogueira Alcalá, "La sentencia constitucional en Chile: Aspectos fundamentales sobre su fuerza vinculante," in *Anuario Iberoamericano de Justicia Constitucional*, Centro de Estudios Políticos y Constitucionales, nº 12, 2008, Madrid 2008, p. 297.

In Bolivia, the same principle of the *ex nunc* effects of the Constitutional Tribunal decisions annulling a statute applies but with the exception regarding cases of formal *res judicata* and on criminal matters if the retroactivity affects harms the legal situation of the condemned.[144] In Nicaragua, article 182 of the Constitution assigns retroactive effects to the annulment decisions of statutes by the Supreme Court, although on matters of amparo, the same Constitution produces only *pro futuro* effects.[145]

In many other cases, like in Venezuela, although the general rule in principle has been *ex nunc*, nonretroactive effects of the Constitutional Chamber's decisions annulling statutes, the Law on the Supreme Tribunal expressly leaves to the Constitutional Chamber the power to determine the temporal effects of its judicial review decisions, which depending on the case, can have retroactive effects or not.[146] The same occurs in Brazil, where the Constitution empowers the Federal Constitutional Tribunal to always decide the temporal effects of its decisions and to determine when they begin,[147] and in Costa Rica, where, to sustain legal security, the Law on the Constitutional Jurisdiction empowered the Constitutional Chamber of the Supreme Court to determine the temporal effects of the judicial review decision. In Mexico, the exception to the nonretroactive effects of Supreme Court decisions annulling statutes refers to criminal matters when it benefits the prosecuted.[148]

144 See Decision S.C 1426/2005-R of November 8, 2005, in Pablo Dermisaky Peredo, "Efectos de las sentencias constitucionales en Bolivia," in *Anuario Iberoamericano de Justicia Constitucional*, Centro de Estudios Políticos y Constitucionales, nº 12, 2008, Madrid 2008, p. 86.

145 See Iván Escobar Fornos, "Las sentencias constitucionales y sus efectos en Nicaragua," in *Anuario Iberoamericano de Justicia Constitucional*, Centro de Estudios Políticos y Constitucionales, nº 12, 2008, Madrid 2008, p. 101.

146 See Allan R. Brewer-Carías, "Algunas consideraciones sobre el control jurisdiccional de la constitucionalidad de los actos estatales en el derecho venezolano," *Revista de Administración Pública*, nº 76, Madrid 1975, pp. 419–446; Brewer-Carías, *Justicia constitucional: Procesos y procedimientos constitucionales*, Universidad Nacional Autónoma de México, Mexico City 2007, pp. 343 ff.

147 See Jairo Gilberto Schäfer and Vânia Hack de Almeida, "O controle de constitucionalidade no dereito brasileiro e a possibilitade de modular os effeitos de decisão de inconstitucionalidade," in *Anuario Iberoamericano de Justicia Constitucional*, Centro de Estudios Políticos y Constitucionales, nº 12, 2008, Madrid 2008, pp. 383–384.

148 See Tesis Jurisprudencial P/J. 74/79, in Héctor Fix Zamudio and Eduardo Ferrer Mac-Gregor, *Las sentencias de los Tribunales Constitucionales*, Ed. Porrúa, Mexico City 2009, p. 69; and "Las sentencias de los Tribunales Constitucionales en el ordenamiento mexicano," in *Anuario Iberoamericano de Justicia Constitucional*, Centro de Estudios Políticos y Constitucionales, nº 12, 2008, Madrid 2008, p. 248.

In Colombia, the Law regulating the Judicial Power (article 45) provided that the Constitutional Court decisions have *pro futuro* effects, except if the Court decided the contrary. In addition, article 51 of Law No. 1836 of the Constitutional Court prevented the Court from giving retroactive effects to its decisions, if they were to affect formal *res judicata*,[149] a provision that the Court declared unconstitutional because it limited its functions. The Court argued that, according to the Constitution, the Court is the sole arbiter to determine the effects of its own decisions.[150] Consequently, the Constitutional Court has the powers to determine the temporal effects of its own decisions and, for instance, to give retroactive effects to them, a matter that it has found that not even the Legislator can regulate.

3. *The Power of Constitutional Courts to Revive Repealed Legislation*

As a matter of principle, as Hans Kelsen wrote in 1928, judicial review decisions declaring null a statutory provision adopted by a Constitutional Court do not imply the revival of the former legislation that the annulled statute repeals; that is, they do not reestablish the legislation already repealed.[151] Nonetheless, the contrary principle is the one applied in Portugal, where the declaration of unconstitutionality with general binding force has negative force of law, as it directly annuls the unconstitutional rule, thus producing as a consequence that "the legal provisions which had been amended or repealed by the norm declared unconstitutional are revived from the date on which the decision of the Constitutional Court becomes effective, unless the Constitutional Court determines otherwise (article 282 (1 and 4) of the Constitution."[152] In Belgium, the revival of the repealed legal provisions as a consequence of the annulment of a statute is the general

[149] See Humberto Nogueira Alcalá, "La sentencia constitucional en Chile: Aspectos fundamentales sobre su fuerza vinculante," in *Anuario Iberoamericano de Justicia Constitucional*, Centro de Estudios Políticos y Constitucionales, nº 12, 2008, Madrid 2008, p. 297.

[150] See Decision C-113 of 1993, in Iván Escobar Fornos, "Las sentencias constitucionales y sus efectos en Nicaragua," in *Anuario Iberoamericano de Justicia Constitucional*, Centro de Estudios Políticos y Constitucionales, nº 12, 2008, Madrid 2008, p. 112; and in *Estudios Jurídicos*, Vol. I, Ed. Hispamer, Managua 2007, p. 511.

[151] See Hans Kelsen, *La garantía jurisdiccional de la Constitución (La justicia constitucional)*, Universidad Nacional Autónoma de México, Mexico City 2001, p. 84.

[152] See Joaquim de Sousa Ribeiro and Esperança Mealha, *Portuguese National Report*, pp. 6–7; and Jairo Gilberto Schäfer and Vânia Hack de Almeida, "O controle de constitucionalidade no dereito brasileiro e a possibilitade de modular os effeitos de decisão de inconstitucionalidade," in *Anuario Iberoamericano de Justicia Constitucional*, Centro de Estudios Políticos y Constitucionales, nº 12, 2008, Madrid 2008, p. 377.

rule.[153] In Austria, the annulment of statutes by the Constitutional Court can have the consequence that other statutes previously repealed by the annulled one will restart their validity beginning on the day in which the annulment is effective, unless the Tribunal decides otherwise (Article 140.6).

This is a matter that in other countries has been decided by the Constitutional Tribunal. For instance, in Poland, in a decision concerning pension regulation, the Constitutional Tribunal directly ordered the restoration of the provision that had earlier been in force and did not contain elements considered unconstitutional.[154] In Mexico, the Supreme Tribunal has decided, particularly in electoral matters, that the nullity of a statute implies the revival of the legislation that was in force before the annulled statute was sanctioned. The decision was adopted to avoid a legislative vacuum, which could affect the legal security on the matter.[155] In Costa Rica, the Constitutional Chamber, when annulling statutes on forestry, tenancy, and monetary matters, decided to revive the legislation that the annulled statute had repealed.[156]

IV. THE DEFORMATION OF THE INTERPRETATIVE PRINCIPLE: CONSTITUTIONAL COURTS' REFORMING OF STATUTES AND INTERPRETING THEM WITHOUT INTERPRETING THE CONSTITUTION

Constitutional courts are interpreters of the Constitution, not interpreters of statutes, except when they do so in connection or in contrast with the Constitution. That is, constitutional courts can only interpret statutes when interpreting the Constitution, to declare a statute unconstitutional, to reject its

[153] See Christian Behrendt, *Le judge constitutionnel, un législateur-cadre positif. Un analyse comparative en droit francais, belge et allemande*, Bruylant, Brussels 2006, pp. 280, 281, 436–437.

[154] Decision of 20 December 1999, K 4/99; Marek Safjan, *Polish National Report*, p. 5 (footnote 12).

[155] See Tesis Jurisprudencial P./J. 86/2007, SJFG, Vol. 26, December 2007, p. 778. See the reference in Héctor Fix Zamudio and Eduardo Ferrer Mac-Gregor, *Las sentencias de los Tribunales Constitucionales*, Ed. Porrúa, Mexico City 2009, pp. 63–64, 74; and "Las sentencias de los Tribunales Constituticonales en el ordenamiento mexicano," in *Anuario Iberoamericano de Justicia Constitucional*, Centro de Estudios Políticos y Constitucionales, nº 12, 2008, Madrid 2008, p. 252.

[156] See Iván Escobar Fornos, *Estudios Jurídicos*, Vol. I, Ed. Hispamer, Managua 2007, p. 513; and in "Las sentencias constitucionales y sus efectos en Nicaragua," in *Anuario Iberoamericano de Justicia Constitucional*, Centro de Estudios Políticos y Constitucionales, nº 12, 2008, Madrid 2008, p. 114.

alleged unconstitutionality, or to establish an interpretation of the statute according to or in harmony with the Constitution. That is, when interpreting statutes, the Constitutional Court is always obliged to do so by interpreting the Constitution, as their function is not to interpret statutes in isolation, without any interpretation of the Constitution, as this last task generally corresponds to ordinary courts.

As Iván Escobar Fornos has pointed out, "a constitutional judge cannot interpret or correct a statute unless it is done regarding its constitutionality; corresponding the task of interpreting the law to ordinary courts."[157] In such cases, constitutional ccourts interpret the Constitution and the law, but the sole interpretation of a statute when no interpretation of the Constitution is made is no more that a legislative reform of a statute by the Constitutional Court. As explained by Francisco Díaz Revorio:

> In order for an interpretative decision to be within the functions of the constitutional court, it is necessary that the interpretation, or the normative content that the constitutional court establishes in harmony with the Constitution, be really the consequence of the constitutional requirement, and the result of a "new" provision without constitutional foundation.[158]

In the same sense, it must be emphasized that constitutional courts are not allowed to create law *ex novo* or to reform statutes, even in matters of judicial review. As the Constitutional Tribunal of Bolivia said in 2005, constitutional courts

> only establish the sense and scope of legal provisions, without creating of modifying a new legal text. In this sense, the provision interpreted by the Courts does not constitute itself in a new legal provision, due to the fact that the judicial authority by mean of interpretation does not create different provisions.[159]

In the same sense, the Constitutional Tribunal of Peru has said:

[157] See Iván Escobar Fornos, *Estudios Jurídicos*, Vol. I, Ed. Hispamer, Managua 2007, p. 497; and "Las sentencias constitucionales y sus efectos en Nicaragua," in *Anuario Iberoamericano de Justicia Constitucional*, Centro de Estudios Políticos y Constitucionales, nº 12, 2008, Madrid 2008, pp. 104.

[158] See Francisco Javier Díaz Revorio, *Las sentencias interpretativas del Tribunal Constitucional*, Lex Nova, Valladolid 2001, pp. 296–297.

[159] See Decision S.C 1426/2005-R. of November 8, 2005, in Pablo Dermizaky Peredo, "Efectos de las sentencias constitucionales en Bolivia," in *Anuario Iberoamericano de Justicia Constitucional*, Centro de Estudios Políticos y Constitucionales, nº 12, 2008, Madrid 2008, p. 86.

> [I]n a different way as the Congress that can ex novo create law within the constitutional framework, the interpretative decisions [of the Constitutional Tribunal] can only determine a provision of law from a direct derivation of constitutional provisions as a *secundum constitutionem* interpretation.[160]

Nonetheless, despite these self-imposed limits, in many cases, a clear interference of the constitutional courts regarding legislative functions, surpassing the assistance or cooperative framework, has ended in extending the text of the interpreted statutes far beyond its literal meaning, modifying the intention or purpose of the original legislator, which are the two main limits of interpretative decisions.[161] Consequently, in many cases, interpretative decisions adopted by constitutional courts have hidden decisions of clear normative content;[162] in them, the Constitutional Court assumes a clear role as positive legislator and even denaturalizes the will of the Legislator. This has been noticed, for instance, in Germany[163] and in Spain.

Referring to the Spanish Constitutional Tribunal's practice of interpreting statutes according to the Constitution, Francisco Fernández Segado has highlighted its "abusive and perverted use," as in decision STC101/2008 of July 24, 2008,[164] where the Tribunal decided an action of unconstitutionality of an article of the Regulation of the Senate, reformed in 2007, after the reform of the Organic Law 6/2007 of the Tribunal. In the latter, a new procedure was established for the appointment by the King of the Members of the Constitutional Tribunal (article 16.1), which stated: "The Magistrates proposed by the Senate will be selected among the candidates nominated by the Legislative Assemblies of the Autonomous Communities in the terms provided by the Regulation of the Chamber [Senate]." The statute's provision was binding in that the Senate, in such case, has no discretion in the selection of the four candidates it must select, which ought to be selected among those nominated by the Autonomous Communities. Nonetheless, an

160 See Decision of February 2, 2006. STC 0030-2005; Fernán Altuve Febres, *Peruvian National Report II*, pp. 27–28.

161 See Francisco Fernández Segado, *Spanish National Report*, p. 20.

162 See Francisco Javier Díaz Revorio, *Las sentencias interpretativas del Tribunal Constitucional*, Lex Nova, Valladolid 2001, p. 97.

163 See, e.g., Helmut Simón, "La jurisdicción constitucional," in Benda et al., *Manual de derecho constitucional*, Instituto Vasco de Administración Pública, Marcial Pons, Madrid 1996, pp. 853–854.

164 See Francisco Fernández Segado, "Algunas reflexiones generales en torno a los efectos de las sentencias de inconstitucionalidad y a la relatividad de ciertas fórmulas esterotipadas vinculadas a ellas," in *Anuario Iberoamericano de Justicia Constitucional*, Centro de Estudios Políticos y Constitucionales, nº 12, 2008, Madrid 2008, p. 167.

exception was introduced in the Senate's Regulation (article 184.b) allowing the Senate to choose the candidate only when the said Legislative Assemblies would not propose "enough candidates" (*candidatos suficientes*) in the prescribed term, a condition hardly to be applied because in Spain there are exist seventeen Legislative Assemblies, each of which can propose up to two candidates each (a total of thirty-four candidates).[165] Eventually, when deciding the action of unconstitutionality, the Tribunal dismissed it, changing the unequivocal will expressed by the Legislator, and established that the expression "enough candidates" referred not only to a numerical matter but also to a subjective matter regarding the suitability (*idoneidad*) of the candidates according to their evaluation by the Senate. This allowed the parliamentary groups of the Senate to propose candidates in a way contradicting the provision of article 26.1 of the Organic Law of the Tribunal. That is, through an interpretative decision, the Constitutional Court produced a new norm *contra legem.*[166]

A case of this sort – also a case of the pathology of judicial review – can also be identified in Venezuela. In effect, according to Articles 335 and 336 of the Constitution, the Supreme Tribunal is the "highest and final interpreter" of the Constitution, as its role is to ensure a "uniform interpretation and application" of the Constitution and "the supremacy and effectiveness of constitutional norms and principles." For such purpose, the 1999 Constitution created the Constitutional Chamber within the Supreme Tribunal, as constitutional jurisdiction (Articles 266,1 and 262), with the exclusive powers to annul statutes (Article 334). To implement the concentrated method of judicial review, the Constitution provides for different means or recourse to the courts, including the popular action for unconstitutionality of statutes, which any citizen can file directly before the Constitutional Division.

In addition, as argued herein, the Constitutional Chamber, without any constitutional or legal support, created in Decision 1077 of September 22, 2000,[167] a recourse for the abstract interpretation of the Constitution, through which any citizen, including public Officers and the Attorney General, can fill a petition to obtain from the Supreme Tribunal a

[165] That is why Francisco Fernández Segado considers it a case of "science fiction," in Francisco Fernández Segado, *Spanish National Report*, p. 35.

[166] See the comments in Francisco Fernández Segado, *La justicia constitucional: Una visión de derecho comparado*, Ed. Dykingson, Madrid 2009, Vol. III, pp. 1031 ff.; F. Fernández Segado, *Spanish National Report*, pp. 35–38.

[167] See Decision nº 1,077 of September 22, 2000, *Servio Tulio León Briceño* case, *Revista de Derecho Público*, nº 83, Editorial Jurídica Venezolana, Caracas 2000, pp. 247 ff.

declarative ruling to clarify the content of legal or constitutional provisions. In these cases, the Constitutional Chamber can establish binding interpretations of the Constitution and of a provision of a statute related to the interpretation of the Constitution, but it is not empowered to establish in isolation binding interpretations of statutory provisions without any parallel interpretation of a constitutional provision. That is, a petition of interpretation regarding a particular statute must be filed only before the Politico-Administrative Chamber of the Supreme Tribunal or the other Chambers; it cannot be filed before the Constitutional Chamber. Consequently, the latter cannot issue interpretations of a statute without interpreting the Constitution; if it does, it is illegitimately interpreting the Constitution.

Nonetheless, the latter occurred in Venezuela, with Decision No. 1541 of June 14, 2008 of the Constitutional Chamber.[168] In that case, a petition to interpret article 258 of the Constitution, filed by the Attorney General of the Republic, the Constitutional Chamber without interpreting such provision – which needed no interpretation at all – decided to interpret article 22 of the 1999 Protection and Promotion of the Investment Law, according to the sense that the Attorney General proposed and asked, that is, to deny that such article contained a general open offer of consent given by the Venezuelan State to submit disputes regarding investment to international arbitration. Article 258 of the Constitution, whose "interpretation" was requested, in fact and legally, required no interpretation at all. It states: "The law shall promote arbitration, conciliation, mediation and any other alternative means of dispute resolution." As there is nothing obscure, ambiguous, or inoperative in this provision, it is obvious that the real purpose of the official petition of constitutional interpretation filed by the representative of the Executive was not to obtain a clarifying interpretation of Article 258 of the Constitution, but to obtain an interpretation of Article 22 of the Investment Law so that it would not contain the State's unilateral consent for international arbitration. In particular, the Attorney General requested from the Constitutional Chamber a declaration that "Article 22 of the 'Investment Law' may not be interpreted in the sense that it constitutes the consent of the State to be subjected to international arbitration" and "that Article 22 of the Investment Law does not contain a unilateral arbitration offer, in other words, it does not overrule the absence of an express declaration made in writing by the Venezuelan authorities to submit to

[168] See Decision 1541 of June 14, 2008, in *Official Gazette* nº 39055 of October 17, 2008.

international arbitration, nor has this declaration been made in any bilateral agreement expressly containing such a provision."[169] As was said in the Dissent Vote in the decision, the petition of interpretation eventually had the purpose of obtaining from the Constitutional Chamber a "legal opinion" by means of *a priori* judicial review, which does not exist in Venezuela, thus implying the exercise of a "legislative function" by the Constitutional Chamber.[170]

In another case decided by the same Constitutional Chamber, by means of Decision No. 511 of April 5, 2004,[171] the Court established *ex officio*, that is, without any relation with the particular case at hand, the rules of procedure applicable in the proceedings to be followed by any of the other Chambers of the Supreme Tribunal of Justice when they decide to assume or take over any judicial cause and process from lower courts for their decision (*avocamiento*) at the Supreme Tribunal. In this case, the Chamber did not interpret any constitutional provision, because this exceptional takeover proceeding (*avocamiento*) regarding cases from lower courts is not a constitutional institution and is regulated only in the Organic Law of the Supreme Tribunal. Thus, usurping legislative functions in this case, the Constitutional Court acted as a direct and *ex officio* positive legislator and created rules of procedure without interpreting the Constitution.

Nonetheless, the extreme case of the pathology of judicial review regarding the relation of constitutional courts with the Legislator and its existing legislation occurs when the former proceeds to "reform" pieces of legislation, openly acting as positive legislator. In effect, one of the most elemental principles in constitutional law is that statutes can be reformed only by other statutes, and consequently, only the Legislator's action can reform statutes. The contrary would be an action contrary to the Constitution, whether it is the Executive that pretends to reform acts of Parliament or any other organ of the State different from the Legislator itself.

In this regard, one of the most astonishing decisions issued by the Constitutional Chamber of the Venezuelan Supreme Tribunal of Justice to "reform" statutes was issued in 2007. Here, the Chamber, *ex officio* and in *obiter dictum*, regarding a provision of the Income Tax Law that in the

[169] *Id.*

[170] *Id.*

[171] See Decision nº 511 of April 5, 2004, *Maira Rincón Lugo* case; http://www.tsj.gov.ve/decisiones/scon/Abril/511-050404-04-0418..%20.htm. See also Daniela Urosa Maggi, *Venezuelan National Report*, pp. 18–19.

particular case it was resolving and was not even challenged on unconstitutional grounds, decided to reform that law. In effect, in Decision No. 301 of February 27, 2007,[172] after rejecting a popular action of unconstitutionality filed in 2001 against articles 67, 68, 69, 72, 74, and 79 of the 1999 Income Tax Law,[173] because of the petitioners' lack of standing, instead of sending the file to the general court's Archives, the Chamber proceeded, after deciding the inadmissibility of the action, and without any judicial debate or discussion on the issue, to reform *ex officio* another article of the Law (article 31), which had not even been challenged by petitioners.

The decision provoked bitter protests in public opinion and in the National Assembly, which, in a unanimous resolution, "categorically rejected" the Constitutional Chamber's decision, considering it "unconstitutional, contrary to the social and collective fundamental rights and social ethics," and declared it "without any legal effects." In addition, the National Assembly publicly praised for the disobedience of the Chamber decision, and "exhorted the Venezuelan people and specifically, the tax payers, as well as the National Tax Service (*Seniat*) to continue with the process of tax returns as it is established in the statute."[174] The Vice President of the National Assembly qualified the Chamber decision reforming an article of the Income Tax Law as one in which the Constitutional Jurisdiction "usurped legislative powers."[175] In fact, in this case, the Constitutional Chamber usurped the legislative function by reforming an article of the Tax Law in an *obiter dictum* of a decision in which the Chamber declared inadmissible an action of unconstitutionality filed against other articles of the same Taxation Law.[176]

Many other decisions of the Constitutional Chamber reforming provisions of legislation have been issued during the past decade, for instance on matters of procedural terms applicable in civil procedure trials: the Chamber partially annulled a provision of the Civil Procedural Law and created new

[172] See *Adriana Vigilanza y Carlos A. Vecchio* case, Exp. nº 01-2862; *Gaceta Oficial* nº 38.635 of March 1, 2007, at http://www.tsj.gov.ve/decisiones/scon/Febrero/301-270207-01-2862.htm. See also Daniela Urosa Maggi, *Venezuelan National Report*, pp. 22–23.

[173] See Decree Law nº 307, *Gaceta Oficial* nº 5.390 Extra. of October 22, 1999.

[174] See in *Gaceta Oficial* nº 38.651 March 26, 2007.

[175] Resolution of March 22, 2007; *El Universal*, Caracas March 23, 2007, p. 1–1; *El Nacional*, Caracas, March 23, 2007, p. 4.

[176] See the general comment on this decision in Allan R. Brewer-Carías, "El juez constitucional en Venezuela como legislador positivo de oficio en materia tributaria," *Revista de Derecho Público*, nº 109, Editorial Jurídica Venezolana, Caracas 2007, pp. 193–212.

wording that establishes a different way of counting procedural terms.[177] On the same matters of procedural terms applicable in criminal procedure trials, the Court modified the Criminal Procedure Code to establish a new way of counting the terms but without annulling the provision.[178] On matters of judicial holidays established in the same Civil Procedural Code, the Court partially annulled the specific provision of the Code eliminating one of the two holiday terms established in it, thus usurping the discretional options to be established on the matter in legislation that is attributed to the National Assembly.[179] In other cases, also regarding procedural rules, when deciding a nullity action against provisions of the Rural Land Law, in which the notice to the interested parties to participate in the respective trial was established by a publication in newspapers, the Court reformed the provisions by adding that the notice was also to be delivered personally to interested parties.[180]

In other cases, the Constitutional Chamber of the Supreme Tribunal has "reformed" the Amparo Law, establishing a new procedure to be applied in the amparo proceedings, and the same Organic Law of the Supreme Tribunal establishes a new set of procedural rules to be applied in judicial review, assuming an active role as positive legislator. In effect, in the first two decisions the Constitutional Chamber adopted after its installment in 2000, the Chamber modified, *ex officio*, articles 7 and 8 of the Organic Law on Amparo, redistributing the competencies of the courts, including its own competencies on matter of amparo,[181] that is, to decide the specific action or

177 See Decision nº 80 of February 1, 2001, case *Article 197 of the Civil Procedural Code*; *Revista de Derecho Público*, nº 85–89, Editorial Jurídica Venezolana, Caracas 2001, pp. 90 ff., at http://www.tsj.gov.ve/decisiones/scon/Febrero/80-010201-00-1435%20.htm. See the comments in Allan R. Brewer-Carías, "Los primeros pasos de la Jurisdicción Constitucional como 'legislador positivo' violando la Constitución, y el régimen legal de cómputo de los lapsos procesales," in *Crónica sobre la "in"justicia constitucional: La Sala Constitucional y el autoritarismo en Venezuela*, Colección Instituto de Derecho Público, Universidad Central de Venezuela, nº 2, Editorial Jurídica Venezolana, Caracas 2007, pp. 511 ff. See also Daniela Urosa Maggi, *Venezuelan National Report*, p. 24.

178 See Decision nº 2560 of August 5, 2005, *Article 172 of the Organic Civil Criminal Code* case; http://www.tsj.gov.ve/decisiones/scon/Agosto/2560-050805-03-1309.htm. See also Daniela Urosa Maggi, *Venezuelan National Report*, pp. 21–22.

179 See Decision nº 1264 of June 11, 2002, *Article 201 of the Civil Procedure Code* case; http://www.tsj.gov.ve/decisiones/scon/Junio/1264-110602-00-1281.htm. See also Daniela Urosa Maggi, *Venezuelan National Report*, pp. 24–25.

180 See Decision nº 2855 of November 20, 2002, *Articles 40 and 42 of the Rural Land Law* case; http://www.tsj.gov.ve/decisiones/scon/Noviembre/2855-201102-02-0311..htm. See also Daniela Urosa Maggi, *Venezuelan National Report*, p. 21.

181 See Decision nº 1, *Emery Mata Millán* case, at http://www.tsj.gov.ve/ decisiones/scon/Enero/01-200100-00-002.htm; and Decision nº 2, of January 20, 2000, *Domingo Ramírez Monja* case, at http://www.tsj.gov.ve/decisiones/scon/Enero/02-200100-00-001.htm; *Revista de Derecho*

complaint for the protection of fundamental rights. Since then, such competencies have been ruled by the Chamber's decision, not by what is provided for in the Organic Law. Another notorious case was Decision No. 7 of February 1, 2000,[182] where the Chamber, on the occasion of ruling in a particular case of amparo, also in an *obiter dictum* and *ex officio*, by means of interpreting articles 27 and 49 of the Constitution that establish the oral trial in the amparo proceeding for the protection of fundamental rights and the basic rules of due process, decided to "adapt" the 1988 Amparo Law to the new 1999 Constitution, completely "reforming" the law by establishing a completely new set of rules of procedure that since have been applied in all amparo cases. The ones established in the Amparo Law have not been applied, though that law remains "in effect" without having been annulled or repealed.[183] Without doubt, in this case, the Chamber exceeded its functions as the highest interpreter of the Constitution and openly proceeded as a positive legislator, "reforming" the text of a statute.[184] Consequently, since 2000, on matters of amparo procedure and of distribution of jurisdiction between the different courts, the applicable "law" in Venezuela is decision Nº 7 of 2000 of the Constitutional Chamber of the Supreme Tribunal that "reformed" the 1988 Amparo Law.[185]

Another decision of the Constitutional Chamber reforming statutes has been issued regarding the rules of procedure concerning actions for judicial review of the constitutionality of statutes. The Organic Law on the Supreme Tribunal of Justice was sanctioned by the National Assembly in 2004,

Público, nº 84, Editorial Jurídica Venezolana, Caracas, 2000, pp. 225 ff. and 235 ff. See Daniela Urosa Maggi, *Venezuelan National Report*, p. 12.

182 Case: *José A. Mejía y otros, Revista de Derecho Público*, nº 81, Editorial Jurídica Venezolana, Caracas 2000, pp. 349 ff. See also http://www.tsj.gov.ve/ decisiones/scon/Febrero/07-010200-00-0010.htm; Daniela Urosa Maggi, *Venezuelan National Report*, pp. 4–5.

183 See Daniela Urosa Maggi, *Venezuelan National Report*, p. 5.

184 See the general comment on this decision in Allan R. Brewer-Carías, "El juez constitucional como legislador positivo y la inconstitucional reforma de la Ley Orgánica de Amparo mediante sentencias interpretativas," in Eduardo Ferrer Mac-Gregor y Arturo Zaldívar Lelo de Larrea (coords.), *La ciencia del derecho procesal constitucional: Estudios en homenaje a Héctor Fix-Zamudio en sus cincuenta años como investigador del derecho*, Instituto de Investigaciones Jurídicas, Universidad Nacional Autónoma de México, Mexico City 2008, Vol. V, pp. 63–80.

185 See Humberto Enrique Tercero Bello Tabares, "El procedimiento de Amparo Constitucional, según la sentencia nº 7 dictada por la Sala Constitucional del Tribunal Supremo de Justicia, de fecha 01 de febrero de 2000. Caso *José Amando Mejía Betancourt y José Sánchez Villavicencio*," *Revista de Derecho del Tribunal Supremo de Justicia*, nº 8, Caracas 2003, pp. 139–176; María Elena Toro Dupuy, "El procedimiento de amparo en la jurisprudencia de la Sala Constitucional del Tribunal Supremo de Justicia (Años 2000–2002)," *Revista de Derecho Constitucional*, nº 6, Editorial Sherwood, Caracas 2003, pp. 241–256.

establishing the rules of procedure regarding actions filed before the Court claiming for the nullity of statutes (article 21.9 ff.). In Decision Nº 1645 of August 19, 2004, a few months after the publication of the Organic Law, the Constitutional Chamber, without declaring any statutory provision unconstitutional, in exercising its normative jurisdiction, proceeded to reform the new law and to establish a completely new judicial procedure.[186]

[186] See Decision 1645 of August 19, 2004, *Gregorio Pérez Vargas* case; http://www.tsj.gov.ve/decisiones/scon/Agosto/1645-190804-04-0824.htm. This decision was ratified and complemented with new procedural rules in Decision 1795 of July 19, 2005. *Promotora San Gabriel* case, http://www.tsj.gov.ve/decisiones/scon/Julio/1795-190705-05-0159.htm; Daniela Urosa Maggi, *Venezuelan National Report*, p. 10. See the comments in Allan R. Brewer-Carías, *Ley Orgánica del Tribunal Supremo de Justicia*, Editorial Jurídica Venezolana, Caracas 2004.

Chapter 4

CONSTITUTIONAL COURTS' INTERFERENCE WITH THE LEGISLATOR REGARDING LEGISLATIVE OMISSIONS

As aforementioned, one of the most important contemporary trends in the transformation of judicial review of legislation, particularly in concentrated systems, has been the development of the possibility for constitutional courts to exercise their power to control the constitutionality of statutes, interpreting them according to the Constitution without being obliged to decide on the nullity of the unconstitutional provisions.

The same sort of control is also exercised regarding the constitutionality of the conduct of the Legislator, not related to statutes duly enacted, but regarding the absence of such statutes or the omissions the statutes contain when the Legislator does not comply with its constitutional obligation to legislate on specific matters or when the Legislator has passed legislation it in an incomplete or discriminatory way. It is important to highlight in all these cases that judicial review decisions adopted by constitutional courts are issued completely separate from the need to annul existing statues, as it is impossible in these cases to characterize the constitutional courts as negative legislators. On the contrary, in many of these cases, constitutional courts act openly as positive legislators, often with the possibility to issue declarations of unconstitutionality of certain legal provisions without annulling them. In some ways, this is similar to what occurs in diffuse systems of judicial review, where the courts have no power at all to annul statutes.

Two sorts of legislative omissions can generally be distinguished: absolute and relative omissions.[1] Absolute omissions exist in cases of the absence of

1 See José Julio Fernández Rodríguez, *La inconstitucionalidad por omisión: Teoría general. Derecho comparado. El caso español*, Civitas, Madrid 1998, pp. 33, 114 ff. According to Thomas Bustamante, "While a complete omission takes place when the legislator does not produce any law although there is a genuine constitutional obligation of regulating some

any legislative provision adopted with the purpose of applying the Constitution or executing a constitutional provision, in which case a situation contrary to the Constitution is created. Relative omissions exist when legislation has been enacted but in a partial, incomplete, or defective way from the constitutional point of view. As pointed out by Luís Fernández Revorio, absolute omissions are related to the "silences of the legislator" that create situations contrary to the Constitution; relative omissions are related to the "silences of the statutes," which also create the same unconstitutional situation.[2]

Both sorts of legislative omissions have been subjected to judicial review by constitutional courts, though not uniformly.

I. CONSTITUTIONAL COURTS' FILLING THE GAP OF ABSOLUTE LEGISLATIVE OMISSIONS

Regarding judicial review of absolute legislative omissions, the matter can be decided by the constitutional courts through two judicial means: when deciding a direct action for the unconstitutionality of an omission by the Legislator and when deciding a particular action or complaint for the protection of fundamental rights filed against an omission of the Legislator that prevents the possibility of enforcing such right.

1. *Direct Action against Absolute Legislative Omissions*

The origin of the direct action seeking judicial review of unconstitutional absolute legislative omissions is found in the 1974 Constitution of the former Yugoslavia, which assigned the Constitutional Guaranties Tribunal the power to decide on cases of lack of legislative development of constitutional provisions that impeded the complete execution of the Constitution (article 377).[3]

constitutional issue, a partial omission occurs when the legislative authority regulates a situation in an unconstitutional way because it does not cover situations that should have been included in the statute." See Thomas Bustamante and Evanlida de Godoi Bustamante, *Brazilian National Report*, p. 11.

2 See Francisco Javier Díaz Revorio, *Las sentencias interpretativas del Tribunal Constitucional*, Ed. Lex Nova, Valladolid 2001, p. 171.

3 See José Julio Fernández Rodríguez, *La inconstitucionalidad por omisión: Teoría general. Derecho comparado. El caso español*, Civitas, Madrid 1998, pp. 244–246.

Two years later, and influenced by the former Yugoslavian institution,[4] the direct action against absolute legislative omissions was incorporated in the 1976 Constitution of Portugal. It assigned the Council of the Revolution, as a political organ assisting the President of the Republic, the necessary powers to verify failures of the Legislator to comply with the Constitution by enacting the necessary statutes to implement the provisions of the new Constitution (article 279, Constitution),[5] and particularly in view of changing prerevolutionary legislation and implementing legislative provisions of the Constitution than banned organizations with fascist ideology.[6]

Up to the sanctioning of the 1982 First Revision of the Constitution, which definitively established this "constitutional control of omission," control of absolute omissions was exercised by the then Council of the Revolution in two occasions and basically as a political means of control.[7] In 1977, through *Parecer* 8/1977 of March 3, 1977, the Council "recommended" that the Assembly of the Republic adopt legislative measures to enforce Article 46.4 of the 1976 Constitution regarding organizations with fascist ideology, establishing as the main condition for the exercise of such control, first, that the constitutional norm could not be self-executing (i.e., it could not require implementation to be applied), and second, that the competent body to adopt the legislative measures must have violated its obligation of issuing legislative provisions to a degree that it obstructed the observance of the Constitution by the very party for whom the constitutional obligation was intended.[8]

In a second case, in *Parecer* 11/1977, April 14, 1978, the Council of the Revolution recommended that the competent legislative bodies adopt

4 See Jorge Campinos, "Brevísimas notas sobre a fiscalizacão da constitucionalidade des leis em Portugal," in Giorgo Lombardi (coord.), *Constituzione e giustizia constitutionale nel diritto comparato*, Maggioli, Rimini 1985; and *La Constitution portugaise de 1976 et sa garantie*, Universidad Nacional Autónoma de México, Congreso sobre La Constitución y su Defensa (mimeo), Mexico City, August 1982, p. 42.

5 See generally Jorge Miranda, "L'inconstitutionalité par omisión dans le droit portugais," in *Revue Européene de Droit Public*, Vol. 4, nº 1, 1992, pp. 39 ff.; José Julio Fernández Rodríguez, *La inconstitucionalidad por omisión: Teoría general. Derecho comparado. El caso español*, Civitas, Madrid 1998, pp. 249 ff.

6 See Francisco Javier Díaz Revorio, *Las sentencias interpretativas del Tribunal Constitucional*, Ed. Lex Nova, Valladolid 2001, pp. 257–260.

7 See M. Gonzalo, "Portugal; El Consejo de la Revolución, su Comisión Constitucional y los Tribunales ordinarios como órganos de control de la constitucionalidad," in *Boletín de Jurisprudencia Constitucional*, Cortes Generales, 8, Madrid 1981, pp. 630, 640.

8 See José Julio Fernández Rodríguez, *La inconstitucionalidad por omisión: Teoría general. Derecho comparado. El caso español*, Civitas, Madrid 1998, pp. 265–266.

legislative measures to guarantee the applicability of Article 53 of the Constitution to domestic servants, conferring to those workers the right to rest and to recreation by limiting the length of the workday and establishing the weekly rest period as well as periodic paid holidays. On this second occasion, the essential contribution of the decision was the extensive interpretation of the Constitutional Commission regarding the initiative to request control of the omission.[9]

Following these previous experiences on judicial review, the 1982 Constitution created the Constitutional Tribunal and established its power to exercise judicial review of legislative omissions regarding the enactment of provisions necessary to make enforceable constitutional mandates (article 283). The standing to sue in these cases was given to the President of the Republic or the Ombudsman at the national level, and to the Presidents of the Regional Assemblies in cases of violation of the rights of the autonomous regions. The decisions of the Tribunal in these cases are only of declarative character and with nonbinding effects, so the Court "cannot substitute itself for the legislator by creating the missing rules nor can it urge them to act by indicating the timing for or the content of such action."[10] In these cases of judicial decisions on legislative omissions, the Tribunal can only inform the competent legislative organ of its findings.

The Portuguese Constitutional Tribunal issued only seven important decisions exercising this judicial review mean of control of legislative omissions.[11] Its first decision was Decision No. 182/1989 of February 1, 1989, on the noncompliance of article 35.4 of the Constitution on the use of computers and the prohibition of third-party access to files containing personal data, given the lack of a legislative measure defining personal data.[12] Another case was Decision No. 474/2002, on the noncompliance of article 59.1-e of the Constitution, given the omission of legislative measures needed to provide social benefits for Public Administration workers who involuntarily found themselves unemployed.[13] In both cases, although the Legislator is not constitutionally obliged to initiate any legislative procedure,

9 See José Julio Fernández Rodríguez, *La inconstitucionalidad por omisión: Teoría general. Derecho comparado. El caso español*, Civitas, Madrid 1998, pp. 265–266.

10 See Joaquim de Sousa Ribeiro and Esperança Mealha, *Portuguese National Report*, pp. 10–11.

11 See Joaquim de Sousa Ribeiro and Esperança Mealha, *Portuguese National Report*, p. 10.

12 See José Julio Fernández Rodríguez, *La inconstitucionalidad por omisión: Teoría general. Derecho comparado. El caso español*, Civitas, Madrid 1998, pp. 268–269; Joaquim de Sousa Ribeiro and Esperança Mealha, *Portuguese National Report*, p. 10.

13 See Joaquim de Sousa Ribeiro and Esperança Mealha, *Portuguese National Report*, p. 10.

the result of the Tribunal's decision was the sanctioning of the needed legislation (Law 10/91 and Law 11/2008).[14]

After the Portuguese constitutional experience, the direct action for judicial review of absolute unconstitutional legislative omissions has been established in only some other countries, mainly in Latin America, including Brazil, Ecuador, and Venezuela.

The first country to follow the Portuguese trends on the matter was Brazil, where judicial review of absolute legislative omissions through a direct action was incorporated in the 1988 Constitution (Articles 102.I.a and 103), which gave power to the Federal Supreme Tribunal to decide the actions filed against the unconstitutionality of legislative omissions, thus impeding the enforcement of a constitutional provision. In this case, also, the action can be filed only by a limited number of State officials or organs, namely the President of the Republic, the Board of the Federal Senate, and the Board of the House of Representatives, and the Board of a Legislative Assembly of a State.

The ruling of the Tribunal declaring unconstitutional a legislative omission to enforce a provision of the Constitution does so without annulling any act and without issuing a direct order to Congress. The Tribunal only must inform the competent organ for it to adopt the necessary measures. In this sense, in a case of an action intended to establish that the value of the minimum wage was unconstitutional because it could not meet the basic needs of a person, the Supreme Federal Tribunal held that, while deciding on these omissive actions, "the Supreme Court can do no more than notify the competent legislative body which should have enacted a normative act, in order to make this body of the Republic aware of the unconstitutionality and to enable it to regulate the matter required by the Constitution, without the interference of the Judiciary."[15] Consequently, the judicial decision in these cases is also declarative, without *erga omnes* and binding effects.[16]

[14] See Joaquim de Sousa Ribeiro and Esperança Mealha, *Portuguese National Report*, pp. 10–11.

[15] See STF, ADI 1439-MC, Rel. Min. Celso de Mello, DJ de 30-5-2003, in Thomas Bustamante and Evanlida de Godoi Bustamante, *Brazilian National Report*, p. 12.

[16] See Marcia Rodrígues Machado, "Inconstitutionalidade por omissão," *Revista da Procuradoria Greal de São Paulo*, nº 30, 1988, pp. 41 ff.; Héctor Fix Zamudio and Eduardo Ferrer Mac-Gregor, *Las sentencias de los Tribunales Constitucionales*, Ed. Porrúa, Mexico City 2009, pp. 38–39; José Julio Fernández Rodríguez, *La inconstitucionalidad por omisión: Teoría general. Derecho comparado. El caso español*, Civitas, Madrid 1998, pp. 285; Marcelo Figuereido, *Brazilian National Report II*, p. 3.

In contrast, in many cases, the Federal Supreme Court has stipulated a deadline for the omission to be filled and has established the self-applicability of the constitutional rule in the event the deadline expired.[17] For instance, in the action filed by the Mato Grosso State Legislature against the unconstitutionality of the omission by the National Congress in drafting the federal supplementary law referred to by Section 4 of Article 18 of the Constitution –related to the creation, merger, consolidation, and subdivision of Municipalities– the Tribunal stipulated a deadline of eighteen months for it to take all the legislative steps necessary to comply with the constitutional provision.[18]

Another Latin American country that has adopted the system of judicial review of absolute legislative omissions is Venezuela, which, in article 336.7 of the 1999 Constitution has empowered the Constitutional Chamber of the Supreme Tribunal of Justice to declare the unconstitutionality of municipal, state, or national legislative organ omissions, when they failed to issue indispensable rules or measures to guarantee the enforcement of the Constitution, or when they issued them in an incomplete way; and to establish the terms, and if necessary, the guidelines for their correction.

This provision gave extended judicial power to the Constitutional Chamber of the Supreme Tribunal, as Constitutional Jurisdiction, to control "legislative silence and legislative abnormal functioning,"[19] surpassing the trends of the Portuguese and Brazilian antecedents, first, by not limiting the standing to file the action to high public officials but configuring it as an *actio popularis*, and second, by granting express powers to the Court to establish the terms and, if necessary, the guidelines for the correction of the omission.

In many cases, the Constitutional Chamber has been asked to rule on omissions of the National Assembly in sanctioning statutes that it is obliged to enact within a fixed term established in the 1999 Constitution – for instance, the Organic Law on Municipal Power was due to be sanctioned within two years following the approval of the Constitution. Even though the Chamber issued two decisions in the case,[20] the National Assembly failed to

[17] See Marcelo Figuereido, *Brazilian National Report II*, p. 4.

[18] See ADI 3682/MT, May 9, 2007, in Thomas Bustamante and Evanlida de Godoi Bustamante, *Brazilian National Report*, p. 12; Marcelo Figuereido, *Brazilian National Report II*, p. 7.

[19] See decision of the Political-Administrative Chamber nº 1819 of August 8, 2000, case: *Rene Molina v. Comisión Legislativa Nacional*.

[20] See decisions of the Constitutional Chamber nº 1347 of May 27, 2003; nº 3118 of October 6, 2003 *Revista de Derecho Público*, nº 93–96, Editorial Jurídica Venezolana, Caracas 2003, pp.

adjust the statute until 2005.[21] In these cases, as it is the general situation regarding constitutional control of legislative omissions, the Constitutional Chamber had not itself became a positive legislator and abstained from deciding in place of the legislative body, that is, it had not legislated itself. Nonetheless, according to the Constitution, the Constitutional Chamber always has the power when declaring the unconstitutionality of a legislative omission "to establish the terms" of the statute to be sanctioned "and[,] if necessary, the guidelines" for the correction of the legislative omissions. That is why, in other cases, the Constitutional Chamber has issued provisional legislation filling the existing vacuum on, for instance, tax matters related to the distribution of competencies between the National and the State level of governments. It occurred when deciding a conflict between the national Law on Tax Stamps and the Ordinance on Tax Stamps of the Metropolitan District of Caracas, by resolving in Decision No. 978 of April 2003[22] to establish the legal regime as strictly applicable on the matter pending the issue of the national legislation on the coordination of tax competencies (article 164.4 of the Constitution).

In addition, in Venezuela, the Constitutional Chamber has been asked to decide not only cases of absolute omissions of the National Assembly to enact statutes that it had the constitutional obligation to sanction, but also other nonnormative acts that the National Assembly must adopt. This was the case, for instance, of the appointment of the members of the National Electoral Council, which the National Assembly must do by a majority of two-thirds of the representatives following a complex procedure involving civil society and citizen participation.[23] In 2004, the National Assembly, after completing almost all the steps of the procedure, failed to appoint the Members of the National Electoral Council, because the official party did not have the necessary votes to appoint its candidates (two-thirds) without any

108 ff. and 527 ff.; and nº 1043 of May 31, 2004, *Revista de Derecho Público*, nº 97–98, Editorial Jurídica Venezolana, Caracas 2004, pp. 270 ff. and 409 ff.

21 The Organic Law was published in *Official Gazette* nº 38327 of December 2, 2005. See the reference in Allan R. Brewer-Carías et al., *Ley Orgánica del Poder Público Municipal*, Editorial Jurídica Venezolana, Caracas 2005, p. 17.

22 Decision nº 978 of April 30, 2003, *Banco Bolívar* case; http://www.tsj.gov.ve/decisiones/scon/Abril/978-300403-01-1535%20.htm. See also Daniela Urosa Maggi, *Venezuelan National Report*, pp. 17–18.

23 See Allan R. Brewer-Carías, "La participación ciudadana en la designación de los titulares de los órganos no electos de los Poderes Públicos en Venezuela y sus vicisitudes políticas," *Revista Iberoamericana de Derecho Público y Administrativo*, Vol. 5, nº 5,2005, San José, Costa Rica 2005, pp. 76–95.

compromise with the opposition parties. In the face of the omission of the National Assembly, a citizen requested that the Constitutional Chamber control the unconstitutionality of the omission and sought a decision of the Constitutional Chamber compelling the National Assembly to accomplish its constitutional duty, which no other organ of the State could assume. Instead, what the petitioner obtained from a Constitutional Chamber of the Supreme Tribunal, packed with Magistrates completely controlled by the Executive, was the direct appointment of the members of the National Electoral Council by the Constitutional Court itself, without complying with the requirements and conditions established in the Constitution. Without doubt, in this case, the Constitutional Court usurped the National Assembly's exclusive powers; acted as positive Legislator and in violation of the Constitution; and through its decision, guaranteed the complete control of the Electoral branch of government by the National Executive.[24]

In other countries, like Costa Rica, the Law on Constitutional Jurisdiction assigns the Constitutional Chamber of the Supreme Court the power to decide actions of unconstitutionality "against the inertia, the omissions and the abstentions of public authorities" (article 73.f).[25]

More recently, in the 2008 Constitution of Ecuador, the direct action for judicial review of legislative omissions was expressly established (article 436.10), assigning the Constitutional Court the power to "declare the unconstitutionality in which the institutions of the State or public authorities incurred because of omissions in complying total or partially the mandates contained in constitutional provisions, within the terms established in the Constitution or in the term considered reasonable by the Constitutional Court." The same provision empowers the Constitutional Court provisionally to "issue the omitted provision or to execute the omitted act according to the law," once the term has elapsed and the omission persists. It is unique in comparative law that constitutional power, even provisional, is given to the Constitutional Court to substitute for the Legislator.

[24] See Decisions Nos. 2073 of August 4, 2003 (case: *Hermánn Escarrá Malaver y oros*) and 2341 of August 25, 2003 (case: *Hermánn Escarrá M. y otros*), in Allan R. Brewer-Carías, "El secuestro del Poder Electoral y la confiscación del derecho a la participación política mediante el referendo revocatorio presidencial: Venezuela 2000–2004," in *Boletín Mexicano de Derecho Comparado*, Instituto de Investigaciones Jurídicas, Universidad Nacional Autónoma de México, nº 112. Mexico City, January–April 2005, pp. 11–73.

[25] See José Julio Fernández Rodríguez, *La inconstitucionalidad por omisión: Teoría general. Derecho comparado. El caso español*, Civitas, Madrid 1998, pp. 300–302.

In Hungary, article 49 of the 1989 Amendment of the Constitution establishes that the Constitutional Court *ex officio* or on anyone's petition can decide on the unconstitutionality of legislative omissions when a legislative organ has failed to fulfill its legislative tasks, instructing the organ that committed the omission to set a deadline to fulfill its task. The Hungarian Constitutional Court has interpreted this competence expansively and has practiced it not only in the cases of unconstitutional failures of fulfillment of legislative obligations resulting from particular legal authorization, but also when the Legislator failed to establish a statute necessary for the emergence of a fundamental right, designated in the Constitution.[26] As mentioned by Lóránt Csink, Józef Petrétei, and Péter Tilk, in exercising this attribution, the Constitutional Court establishes not only the unconstitutionality of the omission of legislation – for instance, by making it impossible for the exercise of a fundamental right – but also the contents of the rules to be sanctioned, which the Legislator must respect.[27]

Regarding Croatia, where the Constitutional Court has powers to proceed *ex officio* on matters of control of constitutionality, the 2002 constitutional reform empowered the Court to adopt reports about any kind of unconstitutionality (and illegality) it has observed and to send them to the Croatian Parliament. Until November 2009, it had adopted six reports addressing important issues that emerged in practice, such as the right to reasonable duration of a trial and the unconstitutionality of regulations on parking fees.[28]

In Bolivia, even in the absence of constitutional or legal provisions, the Constitutional Tribunal created its own power to exercise judicial review control on Legislative omissions. In Decision S.C. 0066/2005 of September 22, 2005, the Court, after verifying its own powers of judicial review, argued

26 An example of such a case is Decision 37/1992 (VI.10). Under Article 61, section (4), of the Constitution, a majority of two-thirds of the votes by the members of Parliament present is required to pass an Act on the supervision of public radio, television, and the public news agency, as well as on the appointment of the directors thereof, on the licensing of commercial radio and television, and on the prevention of monopolies in the media sector. However, until 1996, Parliament failed to adopt a comprehensive Act on radio and television. Likewise, under Article 68, section (5), of the Constitution, a majority of two-thirds of the votes by members of Parliament present is required to pass an Act on the rights of national and ethnic minorities. Decision 35/1992 (VI.10) established an unconstitutional omission as the representation of national and ethnic minorities had not been regulated to the extent and in the manner required by the Constitution; Lóránt Csink, Józef Petrétei, and Péter Tilk, *Hungarian National Report*, p. 5 (footnote 18).

27 See Lóránt Csink, Józef Petrétei, and Péter Tilk, *Hungarian National Report*, pp. 5–6.

28 See Sanja Barić and Petar Bačić, *Croatian National Report*, pp. 12–13.

that, "when the Legislator does not develop a constitutional provision in a particular and precise way, or it develops the provision in a deficient or incomplete way turning the constitutional mandate inefficient, or impossible to be applied because of such omission or deficiency, the Constitutional Tribunal has the attribution to judge the constitutionality of such acts, providing for the Legislator to develop the constitutional provision as imposed by the Constitution."[29] In the case of the National Congress's failure to appoint the members of the Supreme Court of Justice, the Constitutional Tribunal of Bolivia issued a decision in 2004 ruling on the unconstitutionality of the Executive's provisional appointment of the magistrates. To avoid creating a more severe situation of unconstitutionality, the Tribunal postponed the effects of its decision for a term of sixty days, exhorting the Legislator to perform its duties but without usurping its functions.[30]

In other cases, also without a specific means of judicial review to control absolute legislative omissions, the constitutional courts have developed judicial control through other general means of judicial review, as in the case of Mexico, but only by means of the recourse for the solution of constitutional controversies between constitutional organs of the State. Nonetheless, this thesis was abandoned in 2006, in a decision resolving a constitutional controversy in which the Court considered inappropriate such judicial review to control legislative omissions.[31]

[29] See Pablo Dermizaky Peredo, "Efectos de las sentencias constitucionales en Bolivia," in *Anuario Iberoamericano de Justicia Constitucional*, Centro de Estudios Políticos y Constitucionales, nº 12, 2008, Madrid 2008, p. 79.

[30] See Decision S.C. 0129/2004-R, of November 10, 2004, in Pablo Dermizary Peredo, "Efectos de las sentencias constitucionales en Bolivia," in *Anuario Iberoamericano de Justicia Constitucional*, nº 12, 2008, Centro de Estudios Políticos y Constitucionales, Madrid 2008, p. 78.

[31] See Decision 56/2006, in Héctor Fix Zamudio and Eduardo Ferrer Mac-Gregor, *Las sentencias de los Tribunales Constitucionales*, Ed. Porrúa, Mexico City 2009, pp. 71, 72; and "Las sentencias de los tribunales constitucionales en el ordenamiento mexicano," in *Anuario Iberoamericano de Justicia Constitucional*, nº 12, 2008, Centro de Estudios Políticos y Constitucionales, Madrid 2008, pp. 252. See also Eduardo Ferrer Mac-Gregor, "La Corte Suprema di Giustizia del Messico quale Tribunale constituzionale," in Luca Mezetti (coord.), *Sistemi e modelli di giustizia costitutionale*, Cedam, Padua 2009, p. 618.

2. *The Protection of Fundamental Rights against Absolute Legislative Omissions by Means of Actions or Complaints for Their Protection*

The other means for controlling unconstitutional legislative omissions are specific actions or complaints for the protection of fundamental rights that can be filed against the harms or threats that such omissions can cause. This is the case, for example, in many Latin American countries, where amparo actions are filed against omissions of the Legislator or for specific actions for the protection of fundamental rights that have been established.[32] Therefore, in some countries, at least theoretically, it is possible to file amparo actions to protect fundamental rights against legislative omission when such omissions prevent the effective enforcement of a fundamental right.[33]

In particular, mention must be made of the important writ of injunction (*mandado de injunção*) in Brazil, established in Article 5.LXXI, of the Constitution, which is to be "granted whenever the lack of regulatory provision makes the exercise of constitutional rights and liberties, as well as rights inherent in nationality, sovereign status and citizenship, unfeasible." According to the Federal Supreme Tribunal, the writ of injunction does not authorize the Tribunal to fill the gap left by the legislative omission, so the Tribunal cannot enact a normative rule;[34] its function is limited to declaring the delay to develop the normative rule and to notify the Legislator, and the decision has only *inter partes* effects.

In the first writ of injunction decided in 1989, the Tribunal considered that the action attempts to obtain from the Judiciary a declaration of unconstitutionality of an omission in regulating a right, with a view to notify the entity responsible for that regulation to take action.[35] However, there are cases in which the Tribunal has given a broader scope to this procedural remedy. In Case 283 of 1991, the Tribunal recognized a state of negligence

[32] On the amparo proceedings against authorities' omissions in Latin American countries, see particularly Allan R. Brewer-Carías, *Constitutional Protection of Human Rights in Latin America: A Comparative Study of Amparo Proceeding*, Cambridge University Press, New York 2009, pp. 324 ff.

[33] In Venezuela, amparo actions have been filed against omissions of the Legislator regarding certain administrative acts. See Allan R. Brewer-Carías, *La justicia constitucional: Procesos y procedimientos constitucionales*, Universidad Nacional Autónoma de México, Mexico City 2007, pp. 153 ff.

[34] See Decision STF 168/RS, Reporting Justice J. Ministro Pertence, DJU, on April 20 1990, in Marcelo Figuereido, *Brazilian National Report II*, p. 4.

[35] STF, MI 107-QO, Rel. Min. Moreira Alves, DJ de 21-09-1990; Thomas Bustamante and Evanlida de Godoi Bustamante, *Brazilian National Report*, p. 17.

of Congress in regulating provisions established by the Temporary Provisions of the Constitution related to compensation for the victims of abuses committed by the military dictatorship via Secret Acts of the Ministry of Defense, which banned a large number of people from exercising certain economic activities. Because the Temporary Provisions required the passing of a federal statute to regulate such compensation, the victims could not exert their constitutional rights. In the face of this specific situation, the Supreme Federal Tribunal not only ruled that there was an unconstitutional omission but also established a deadline of forty-five days for Congress to pass the statute. The Tribunal determined, moreover, that if parliamentary negligence remained after that deadline, the applicant would be automatically entitled to claim compensation according to the general rules of the Civil Code.[36]

In another relevant case, the Constitution guaranteed a tax privilege to certain social institutions, excluding them from taxation by contributions to the social security, "as long as these entities complied with the conditions established in law" (article 197.5). The Constitution left to the ordinary legislator the task to establish the conditions to be complied to claim immunity from the contributions. Accordingly, the Federal Government understood that such entities could claim no fiscal immunity until Congress passed a law listing such conditions. The Supreme Federal Tribunal, after holding that there was an unjustifiable legislative omission, fixed a deadline of six months for Congress to pass a law eliminating that omission. Furthermore, it determined that, if no law was passed before that deadline, the claimant would be automatically entitled to claim the fiscal benefit.[37]

It must also be mentioned that, in some cases, the Brazilian Federal Supfreme Tribunal has supplied the missing rule through analogy until the Legislator can enact legislation. This was the case in the application of social security rules regarding special pension in the private sector to civil servants working at the Health Department of the public sector (MI 721/DF, March 8, 2007) and in the application to the provisions of a statute (Law 7.783/1989) that governs the right to strike in the private sector (MI 670/ES, October 25, 2007) to civil servants of a State.[38]

[36] STF, MI 283, Rel. Min. Sepúlveda Pertence, DJ de 14-11-1991; Thomas Bustamante and Evanlida de Godoi Bustamante, *Brazilian National Report*, p. 17.

[37] STF, MI 232, Rel. Min. Moreira Alves, DJ de 27-03-1992; Thomas Bustamante and Evanlida de Godoi Bustamante, *Brazilian National Report*, pp. 17–18.

[38] See Marcelo Figuereido, *Brazilian National Report II*, p. 6–7; Thomas Bustamante and Evanlida de Godoi Bustamante, *Brazilian National Report*, p. 19; Luis Roberto Barroso et al., "Notas sobre a questão do legislador positivo," *Brazilian National Report III*, pp. 28 ff., 32.

The same general approach of the constitutional court complementing the Legislator, particularly on matters of protecting fundamental rights, can be found in other countries. For example, in Argentina, the Supreme Court's ruling in the *Badaro* cases concerned automatic adjustment of pensions. In effect, because the Constitution provides for "mobile" pensions (article 14 *bis*), in *Badaro I*,[39] the Supreme Court considered that Congress's inaction with respect to the increase of pensions, which had been seriously reduced as a result of high inflation, violated the constitutional mandate. Therefore, the Court urged Congress to pass legislation within a reasonable time to solve that problem. The Court emphasized that it is not only a power but also a duty of Congress to give effect to the constitutional guarantee of pension mobility, for which it must legislate and adopt measures to guarantee the full enjoyment of the right. Eventually, in view of the lack of action by Congress, in *Badaro II*,[40] the Court, in reurging Congress to enact legislation, resolved to grant the petitioner's request and adopted criteria for readjusting pensions until Congress decided to act.[41]

In another important case, regarding the environment, the Supreme Court in *Mendoza*,[42] decided a complaint filed by a group of neighbors of a settlement known as Villa Inflamable – located on the outskirts of Buenos Aires – against the National Government, the province of Buenos Aires, the government of the City of Buenos Aires, and forty-four private companies, alleging damages caused by multiple diseases that their children and themselves had suffered as a result of the pollution of the water basin Matanza-Riachuelo." In two landmark rulings, the first in 2006 and the other in 2008, the Court ordered the defendants to present an environmental recovery program, entrusted the Matanza-Riachuelo Basin Authority in its implementation, and established detailed court-monitored guidelines on compliance to avoid interprovincial conflicts, all of them matters traditionally within the realm of legislatures and the executive of both federal and provincial levels.[43]

39 Fallos 329:3089 (2006); Alejandra Rodríguez Galán and Alfredo Mauricio Vítolo, *Argentinean National Report I*, p. 16 (footnote 68).

40 Fallos 330:4866 (2007); Alejandra Rodríguez Galán and Alfredo Mauricio Vítolo, *Argentinean National Report I*, p. 17 (footnote 69).

41 See also Néstor Pedro Sagüés, *Argentinean National Report II*, pp. 12–13.

42 Fallos 329:2316 (2006) and Fallos 331:1622 (2008); Alejandra Rodríguez Galán and Alfredo Mauricio Vítolo, *Argentinean National Report I*, p. 17 (footnote 72).

43 See Alejandra Rodríguez Galán and Alfredo Mauricio Vítolo, *Argentinean National Report I*, p. 17.

In Germany, with respect to a complaint for constitutional protection of fundamental rights (*Verfassungsbeschwerde*),[44] the decision of the Constitutional Federal Tribunal No. 26/1969 of January 29, 1969, regarding article 6.5 of the Constitution, which establishes that the law must ensure for children born outside of marriage the same conditions of children born to married parents, in their physical, spiritual, and social development. The Federal Constitutional Tribunal considered that article 1712 of the Civil Code was insufficient regarding the constitutional provision and exhorted the Legislator to reform it according to the conditions set forth in article 6.5 of the Constitution before the end of the legislative term (Autumn 1969), which in fact occurred on August 19, 1969, with the promulgation of the reform.[45] Regarding this decision, Ines Härtel has reported the following:

> The BVerfG has already admonished the Legislator several times to fulfill explicit constitutional obligations through law. The constitutional obligations mentioned are oftentimes those which can only rely on weak forces in society in their realization; an example would be the task of the Legislator to create equal conditions between illegitimate and legitimate children in their physical and emotional development and consequently in their social standing (BVerfGE 8, 210 (216); 17, 148 (155); 25, 167 (173-188)) The respective decision states: "If the Legislator does not accomplish the order assigned to him by Constitution in Art. 6 Sec. 5 GG to reform Illegitimacy Law . . . until the ending of the current (fifth) legislative period of the Bundestag, it is the will of the Constitution to realize as much as possible of the Legislation.[46]

In India, an important case regarding ragging (bullying) at universities must be mentioned. In the exercise of its power under Articles 32 and 142 of the Constitution, in 2001, the Supreme Court decided on public interest litigation initiated in 1998 by Vishwa Jagriti Mission, a spiritual organization, seeking to curb the menace of ragging in educational institutions.[47] The Court, deciding in favor of the protection of fundamental rights, issued several guidelines, not only defining ragging but also

44 See generally Francisco Fernández Segado, "El control de las omisiones legislativas por el Bundesverfassungsgericht," *Revista de Derecho*, nº 4, Universidad Católica del Uruguay, Konrad Adenauer Stiftung, Montevideo 2009, pp. 137–186.

45 See José Julio Fernández Rodríguez, *La inconstitucionalidad por omisión: Teoría general. Derecho comparado. El caso español*, Civitas, Madrid 1998, pp. 313–315.

46 See I. Härtel, *German National Report*, p. 19.

47 *Vishwa Jagriti Mission v. Central Government* AIR 2001 SC 2793; Surya Deva, *Indian National Report*, p. 9 (footnote 58).

contemplating possible causes of ragging, prescribing detailed steps to curb this practice, and outlining diverse modes of punishment that educational authorities could take. The Court also ruled that "failure to prevent ragging shall be construed as an act of negligence in maintaining discipline in the institution," and said, if "an institution fails to curb ragging, the UGC/Funding Agency may consider stoppage of financial assistance to such an institution till such time as it achieves the same." Because ragging continued to be reported in the media, the Indian Supreme Court engaged in its fight to curb ragging, directly appointing, in November 2006, a Committee to suggest remedial measures to tackle the problem of ragging in educational institutions. In May 2007, the Supreme Court ordered that several recommendations of the Committee be implemented without any further lapse of time, establishing, among other things, that "punishment to be meted out has to be exemplary and justifiably harsh to act as a deterrent against recurrence of such incidents."[48] The Court did not leave the task of monitoring the guidelines to the executive branch of the government, ruling that the "Committee constituted pursuant to the order of this Court shall continue to monitor the functioning of the anti-ragging committees and the squads to be formed. They shall also monitor the implementation of the recommendations to which reference has been made above." In 2007, the Supreme Court gave further directions while dealing with specific instances of ragging in two colleges that were investigated by the Raghavan Committee;[49] and in 2009, in *University of Kerala v. Council of Principals of Colleges of Kerala*,[50] it directed all state governments as well as universities to act in accordance with the guidelines formulated by the Committee, considering ragging as a human rights abuse and thus expressly justifying the Court's exercise of power under Article 32 of the Constitution.[51]

In a similar trend, and through judicial means progressively developed for the protection of fundamental rights, the U.S. Supreme Court has filled the gap of legislative omissions, particularly in issuing equitable remedies, like

48 See *University of Kerala v. Council of Principals of Colleges of Kerala*, order dated 16 May 2007; Surya Deva, *Indian National Report*, p. 10 (footnote 61).

49 See J. Venkatesan, "SC Issues Guidelines to Check Ragging," *The Hindu*, May 9, 2009, http://www.thehindu.com/2009/05/09/stories/2009050957401 00.htm; Surya Deva, *Indian National Report*, p. 10 (footnote 62).

50 See *University of Kerala v. Council of Principals of Colleges of Kerala*, order dated 11 February 2009, para. 2; Surya Deva, *Indian National Report*, p. 10 (footnote 63).

51 See Surya Deva, *Indian National Report*, p. 10.

injunctions,[52] through which a court of equity can adjudicate extraordinary relief to an aggrieved party, consisting of an order by the court commanding the defendant or injuring party to do something or to refrain from doing something.[53] These are called coercive remedies because they are backed by the contempt power, or the power of the court to directly sanction a disobedient defendant. Although they are not conceived of as only for the protection of constitutional rights, but for the protection of any right, they have been specifically effective for the protection constitutional rights, particularly preventive injunctions, which are designed to avoid future harm to a party by prohibiting or mandating certain behavior by another party (mandatory injunctions or prohibitory injunctions), and structural injunctions. The latter were developed by the courts after *Brown v. Board of Education* (347 U.S. 483 (1954); 349 U.S. 294 (1955)), in which the Supreme Court declared the dual school system discriminatory, using injunction as an instrument of reform, by means of which the courts in certain cases undertake the supervision over institutional State policies and practices to prevent discrimination. As described by Owen S. Fiss:

> Brown gave the injunction a special prominence. School desegregation became one of the prime litigative chores of courts in the period of 1954–1955, and in these cases the typical remedy was the injunction. School desegregation not only gave the injunction a greater currency, it also presented the injunction with new challenges, in terms of both the enormity and the kinds of tasks it was assigned. The injunction was to be used to restructure the educational systems throughout the nation. The impact of Brown on our remedial jurisprudence – giving primacy to the injunction – was not confined to schools desegregation. It also extended to civil rights cases in general, and beyond civil rights to litigation involving electoral reappointments, mental hospitals, prisons, trade practices, and the environment. Having desegregated the schools of Alabama, it was only natural for Judge Johnson to try to reform the mental hospitals and then the prisons of the state in the name of human rights – the right to treatment or to be free from cruel and unusual punishment – and to attempt this Herculean feat through injunction. And he was not alone. The same logic was manifest in actions of other judges, North and South.[54]

52 See Allan R. Brewer-Carías, *Constitutional Protection of Human Rights in Latin America*, Cambridge University Press, New York 2009, pp. 69 ff.

53 See William Tabb and Elaine W. Shoben, *Remedies*, Thomson West, St. Paul MN 2005, p. 13.

54 See Owen M. Fiss, *The Civil Rights Injunctions*, Indiana University Press, Bloomington 1978, pp. 4–5; Owen M. Fiss and Doug Rendelman, *Injunctions*, Foundation Press, Mineola – New York 1984, pp. 33–34. Thus, structural injunctions can be considered a modern constitutional

In effect, deciding these equitable remedies for the protection of fundamental rights, the Supreme Court in the United States has also created complementary judicial legislation, for instance invoking the Fourth, Fifth, and Sixth Amendments to the Constitution, regarding the conditions for lawful search and arrest in connection with investigation and prosecution of crime. The Court's decisions have resulted in a substantial and relatively complex body of law controlling police behavior, which allows courts to reverse the convictions of defendants who have not been treated in accordance with the judicially produced rules. In contrast, law enforcement agencies interested in securing convictions have an interest in compliance, so police departments have adopted procedures and trained their personnel to follow the rules.[55]

On matters of racial segregation in public education, declared contrary to the equal protection clause set forth in the Fourteenth Amendment, the Supreme Court rulings in *Brown v. Board of Education* required the courts to be involved in the process of administering desegregation plans, which became clear three years later in *Swann v. Charlotte-Mecklenburg Board of Education*,[56] where the Supreme Court approved a detailed decree issued by a district court, based on the recommendation of an expert in educational administration, containing measures like "the design of oddly shaped attendance zones, the pairing or clustering of black and white schools to permit a more reasonable racial balance, compulsory transportation of students to schools outside their neighborhoods, reassignment of teachers and other personnel to reduce the racial character of individual schools and requiring that new schools be constructed in locations that would not contribute to the persistence of segregation."[57] As mentioned by Laurence Claus and Richard S. Kay, the following twenty years witnessed numerous instances of federal judges attempting to reconcile the constitutional imperative with the practical realities of operating a school system, a task often made more difficult by passive or active resistance from local authorities. The practical and political questions associated with managing a

law instrument specifically developed for the protection of human rights, particularly in state institutions; an instrument that has been considered "an implicit part of the Constitutional guarantee of protecting individual rights from inappropriate government action." See William M. Tabb and Elaine W. Shoben, *Remedies*, Thomson West, St. Paul MN 2005, pp. 87–88.

55 See also Laurence Claus and Richard S. Kay, *U.S. National Report*, p. 23.

56 See *Swann v. Charlotte-Mecklenburg Bd. of Educ.*, 402 U.S. 1 (1971); Laurence Claus and Richard S. Kay, *U.S. National Report*, p. 30 (footnote 101).

57 *Id.* at 19–25. See Laurence Claus and Richard S. Kay, *U.S. National Report*, p. 30 (footnote 102).

desegregation regime returned regularly to the Supreme Court, whose judgments, from that point on, were largely concerned with defining limits to the broad judicial mandate sketched out in *Brown* and other decisions. The kinds of issues involved were illustrated by the Supreme Court's 1995 judgment in *Missouri v. Jenkins*,[58] one of its last significant statements on the remedial authority of federal courts in desegregation cases. The district court, in that case, had found that unconstitutional segregation had reduced the quality of the education offered in the affected schools. Over a ten-year period, the district court judge had, consequently, ordered that class size be reduced, that full-time kindergarten be instituted, that summer programs be expanded, that before- and after-school tutoring be provided, and that an early childhood development program be established. The district court also ordered a major capital improvement program and salary increases for teachers and other school employees.[59]

A similar situation occurred in the United States on matters related to the operation of prisons, based on the provision of the Eighth Amendment's prohibition of cruel and unusual punishment, and resulted in long-term supervision of numerous institutions. In litigation challenging the constitutionality of aspects of the Arkansas correctional institutions, federal judges ordered through structural injunctions, among other things, the closing of institutions, the maximum number of inmates in a particular facility and in individual cells, detailed procedures for determining disciplinary violations, and limits on the punishments administered. They required the employment of full-time psychiatrists or psychologists, affirmative action to recruit more minority personnel, and mandatory training of employees to improve race relations in the prisons. The practice of using armed inmates as "trusty" guards was prohibited. Inmates were to be provided with educational opportunities and a fair procedure for filing grievances. The courts retained jurisdiction for more than ten years.[60] Mental hospitals have been the subject of similar decrees,[61] and in somewhat more

58 See *Missouri v. Jenkins*, 515 U.S. 70 (1995). See Laurence Claus and Richard S. Kay, *U.S. National Report*, p. 31 (footnote 104).

59 *Id.* at 74–80. Laurence Claus and Richard S. Kay, *U.S. National Report*, p. 31.

60 See *Hutto v. Finney*, 437 U.S. 678 (1978); Laurence Claus and Richard S. Kay, *U.S. National Report*, p. 32 (footnote 107).

61 See *Wyatt v. Stickney*, 344 F. Supp. 373 (1972). See Laurence Claus and Richard S. Kay, *U.S. National Report*, p. 32 (footnote 108).

contained proceedings, so has the process of apportioning legislative representation.[62]

In Canada, similar to the Latin American amparo proceeding for the protection of constitutional rights, article 24.1 of the Charter establishes the right of anyone, when the rights or freedoms guaranteed by the Charter have been infringed or denied, "to apply to a court of competent jurisdiction to obtain such remedy as the court considers appropriate and just." According to that provision, the courts have the power to issue a wide variety of remedies where they find that the rights of individuals have been violated, including declarations and injunctions requiring the government to take positive actions to comply with the Constitution and to remedy the effects of past constitutional violations. In a leading case related to minority language, the court also issued structural injunctions or interdicts requiring the government, in particular, to provide instruction and facilities. In Canada, the Constitution Act of 1867 provided that both French and English be used in the legislatures and courts of Canada and Quebec, and the provincial constitutions, such as the Manitoba Act of 1870, provided similar rights. In 1985, the Supreme Court confronted a law that purported to abolish the bilingualism obligations of Manitoba, where the French-speaking population had become a minority. Nonetheless, the Court decided that the unilingual laws were unconstitutional but held that immediate invalidation of most of Manitoba's laws was not appropriate because it would produce a legal vacuum that would threaten the rule of law. The Court then decided that it would give the unilingual laws temporary validity for the period of time that was necessary to translate them into French; it retained jurisdiction over the case for a number of years and, during that time, heard various motions concerning the extent of the constitutional obligations for bilingualism.[63] The Court's actions in this regard have been considered a form of remedial activism, somewhat similar to the American and Indian experience of courts maintaining jurisdiction over public institutions such as schools and prisons in the 1970s and 1980s to ensure that they satisfied constitutional standards.[64]

However, legislative omissions have also given rise in Canada to important acts of judicial activism on matters of criminal justice, given the absence of

[62] See *Branch v. Smith*, 538 U.S. 254 (2003); Laurence Claus and Richard S. Kay, *U.S. National Report*, p. 32 (footnote 109).

[63] *Reference re Manitoba Language Rights* [1985] 1 S.C.R. 721; [1985] 2 S.C.R. 347; [1990] 3 S.C.R. 1417n; [1992] 1 S.C.R. 212. See Kent Roach, *Canadian National Report*, p. 18 (footnote 48).

[64] See Kent Roach, *Canadian National Report*, p. 18.

legislative response to enact statutory standards for speedy trials and the prosecutor's disclosure of evidence to the accused. In 1993, however, the Court acted decisively by holding that the Charter requires pretrial disclosure to the accused of all relevant evidence held by the prosecutor,[65] and it held that the right to a trial in a reasonable time would be violated by pretrial delays of more than a year.[66] Another example would be the Supreme Court's decision that holds that it will generally violate the Charter to extradite a person to face the death penalty.[67] Although framed in negative terms that would potentially prevent extradition, the practical effect of the decision is to require the government to take positive steps to seek assurances from states that they will not seek or impose the death penalty on a person extradited from Canada.[68]

In a certain way, in the United Kingdom, where the basic principle is that the court does not substitute itself for the legislature, it is also possible to identify important activities developed by the courts on matters of constitutional review regarding the protection of human rights, by issuing decisions with guidelines that supplement the jurisdiction of the Legislator or the administration. For example, referring to cases of the judges making the law in areas where there was inadequate previous precedent or statute, John Bell mentioned the case regarding the sterilization of intellectually handicapped adults, in which the House of Lords laid down principles that would govern the approval of such cases;[69] and the case decided in *Airedale NHS Trust v. Bland*[70] regarding the situation of a man who was in a permanent vegetative state and being fed through a tube. In the latter case, the House of Lords decided the circumstances, establishing policies on medical treatment for doctors could lawfully accede to the wishes of the man's parents that the feeding stop and that he be allowed to die. That is, in such cases, judicial decisions have provided rules for future application in the absence of any authoritative pronouncement by government.

65 See *R. v. Stinchcombe* [1991] 3 S.C.R. 326; Kent Roach, *Canadian National Report*, p. 11 (footnote 18).

66 See *R. v. Askov* [1990] 2 S.C.R. 1199; Kent Roach, *Canadian National Report*, p. 12 (footnote 19).

67 See *United States v. Burns and Rafay* [2001] 1 S.C.R; Kent Roach, *Canadian National Report*, p. 12 (footnote 21).

68 See Kent Roach, *Canadian National Report*, p. 12.

69 See *Re F (Mental Patient: Sterilisation)* [1990] 2 AC 173; John Bell, *British National Report*, p. 7 (footnote 33).

70 See [1993] 1 All ER 821; John Bell, *British National Report*, p. 7.

In the Czech Republic, the Constitutional Court has filled the gap resulting from the Legislator's omission. The best and most controversial example mentioned by Zdenek Kühn is the one provided by the rent-control saga. In effect, in 2000, the Constitutional Court found unconstitutional rent control as practiced by Czech law, and it annulled the decree of the Ministry of Finance that regulated rent increases in apartment houses. The Court delayed the annulment to offer the legislature time to enact a new law with a mechanism to put rents to just terms, but the legislature declined to deal with the issue. The Court continued to annul decrees that dealt with the issue, and it used more and more compelling arguments to urge the legislature to enact a proper law.[71] In 2006, finally, the Court again criticized the legislative "activity, or rather, inactivity," which resulted in "freezing of controlled rent, which further deepens the violation of property rights of the owners of those apartments to which rent control applied. . . . By not passing them, the legislative assembly evoked an unconstitutional situation."[72] That is why the Constitutional Court rejected the petition but at the same time gave a rather unique verdict No. 1, according to which "[t]he long-term inactivity of the Parliament of the Czech Republic, consisting of failure to pass a special legal regulation defining cases in which a landlord is entitled to unilaterally increase rent, payment for services relating to use of an apartment, and to change other conditions of a lease agreement, is unconstitutional and violates" a number of constitutional rights.[73] The unique verdict was accompanied by a similarly unique reasoning in which the Court directed general courts to increase rents themselves, instead of entirely passive legislature; that is, the Court ordered general courts to make the law instead of the legislature. In this regard, the Court openly held that it must deviate from its role of negative legislator, expressing the following:

> Based on these facts [legislative inactivity], the Constitutional Court, in its role of protector of constitutionality, cannot limit its function to the mere position of a "negative" legislator, and must, in the framework of a balance of the individual branches of power characteristic of a law-based state founded on respect for the rights and freedoms of man and of citizens . . . , create space for the preservation of the fundamental rights and freedoms.

71 See decision of November 20, 2002, Pl. ÚS 8/02, *Rent Control II*, published as nº 528/2002 Sb.; and see decision of March 19, 2003, Pl. ÚS 2/03, *Rent Control III*, published as nº 84/2003 Sb; Zdenek Kühn, *Czech National Report*, p. 14 (footnote 58).

72 See decision of February 28, 2006, Pl. ÚS 20/05, *Rent Control IV*, at http://angl.concourt.cz/angl_verze/doc/p-20-05.php; Zdenek Kühn, *Czech National Report*, p. 13 (footnote 59).

73 *Id.*

> Therefore, the general courts, even despite the absence of the envisaged specific regulations, must decide to increase rent, depending on local conditions, so as to prevent the abovementioned discrimination. In view of the fact that such cases will involve the finding and application of simple law, which is not a matter for the Constitutional Court, . . . the Constitutional Court refrains from offering a specific decision-making procedure and thereby replacing the mission of the general courts. It merely states that it is necessary to refrain from arbitrariness; a decision must be based on rational arguments and thorough weighing of all the circumstances of a case, the application of natural principles and the customs of civic life, the conclusions of legal learning and settled, constitutionally consistent court practice.[74]

The Constitutional Court, in addition, clearly explained in its decision its role in cases of absolute omissions by the Legislator, expressing the following:

> As a consequence of the inactivity of the legislative assembly it can evoke an unconstitutional situation, if the legislature is required to pass certain regulations, does not do so, and thereby interferes in a right protected by the law and by the constitution. . . . [W]e can conclude that under certain conditions the consequences of a gap (a missing legal regulation) are unconstitutional, in particular when the legislature decides that it will regulate a particular area, states that intention in law, but does not pass the envisaged regulations. The same conclusion applies to the case where Parliament passed the declared regulations, but they were annulled because they did not meet constitutional criteria, and the legislature did not pass a constitutional replacement, although the Constitutional Court gave it a sufficient period of time to do so.
>
> The relationship between the legislative and judicial branches arises from the separation of powers in the state, as established in the Constitution. A material analysis necessarily leads us to conclude that this separation is not a purpose in and of itself, but pursues a higher purpose. From its very beginnings it was subjected by the constitutional framers to an idea based above all on service to the citizen and to society. Every power has a tendency to concentration, growth and corruption; absolute power to an uncontrollable corruption. If one of the branches of power exceeds its constitutional framework, its authority, or, on the contrary, does not fulfill its tasks and thus prevents the proper functioning of another branch (in the adjudicated case, of the judicial branch), the control mechanism of checks and balances, which is built into the system of separation of powers, must come into play. . . . [G]eneral courts err if they refuse to provide protection

[74] *Id.*

to the rights of those who have turned to them with a demand for justice, if they deny their complaints merely with a formalistic reasoning and reference to the inactivity of the legislature (the non-existence of the relevant legal regulations), after the Constitutional Court, as protector of constitutionality and review thereof, opened the way for them through its decisions. The Constitutional Court has repeatedly declared the unequal position of one group of owners of rental apartments and buildings to be discriminatory and unconstitutional, and the long-term inactivity of the Parliament of the CR to be incompatible with the requirements of a law-based state. The Constitutional Court, by the will of the constitutional framers, is responsible for the maintenance of the constitutional order in the Czech Republic, and therefore it does not intend to abandon this obligation, it calls on the general courts to fulfill their obligations.[75]

Finally, the case of the Constitutional Court of Colombia must be mentioned, particularly regarding a new constitutional situation that the Court has created to decide specific actions of *tutela* (*amparo*) for the protection of fundamental rights filed by displaced persons within Colombia due to the situation of violence suffered for years, particularly in rural areas and specifically on the occasion of deciding on the factual lack of enforcement of the *tutela* rulings. In such cases of massive violations of human rights, the Court has created what it has called an *estado de cosas inconstitucionales* (factual state of unconstitutionality), which it has used to substitute itself for the ordinary judges, the Legislator, and the Administration in the definition and coordination of public policies, a power that the Constitutional Court has exercised *ex officio*. This was referred to, among other decisions, in Decision No. 007 of January 26, 2009, where the Court ruled on the "[c]oordination with the territorial entities of public policies of attention to the displaced population" and ordered a series of public actions to be executed by a variety of public administration entities.[76] In Decision No. T-025/04, the Court specified the conditions required to declared a factual state of unconstitutionality, such as "(i) the massive and widespread infringement of various constitutional rights affecting a significant number of people; (ii) the prolonged omission of the authorities in the fulfillment of its obligation to guarantee the rights; the adoption of unconstitutional practices, such as incorporating the action of *tutela* as part of the procedure to ensure the violated right; ... (iv) the failure to issue legislative, administrative, or budgetary measures to avoid infringement of Rights; (v) the existence of a social problem whose solution compromises

[75] See Zdenek Kühn, *Czech National Report*, p. 14.

[76] See Sandra Morelli, *Colombian National Report II*, p. 5.

the involvement of several entities, requires the adoption of complex and coordinated actions[,] and demands level of resources requiring important additional budgetary effort; (vi) if all people affected by the same problem would resort to the *tutela* for the protection of their rights, there would be greater judicial congestion."[77]

With these sorts of decisions, as mentioned by Sandra Morelli, the Constitutional Court has "abandoned its role as guarantor of fundamental constitutional rights of an individual in a particular case, to assume another role, that of formulating or contributing to formulate public policies, adding its implementation, and monitoring its implementation to guarantee the satisfaction of needs of displaced populations according to available resources and subject to compliance of procedural requirements that the same Court assumed the role to regulate."[78] This, of course, has nothing to do with the role of the constitutional judge in taking over responsibilities of the legislature and the public administration and in ordering specific actions to public entities and public officials. Sandra Morelli has considered this a "historical betrayal that the Colombian Constitutional Court undertakes, when instead of protecting each displaced individual that had filed action of *tutela* regarding their fundamental rights, even by way of guarantee of the right to equality, ventures into the strange category of the factual state of unconstitutionality and via the general way, without any need to bring an action of *tutela*, assumes the role of supreme administrative authority."[79]

II. CONSTITUTIONAL COURTS' FILLING THE GAP OF RELATIVE LEGISLATIVE OMISSIONS

Apart from the aforementioned cases of specific judicial review to ensure judicial review of *absolute* legislative omissions, judicial review of relative legislative omissions has been extensively developed in the past decades in all democratic countries, particularly in cases in which the matter is not the absence of legislation but the existence of poor, deficient, or inadequate regulation according to the constitutional provisions.[80] This can lead to the

77 *Id.*, p. 8.

78 *Id.*, p. 10.

79 *Id.*, p. 11.

80 See Francisco Javier Díaz Revorio, *Las sentencias interpretativas del Tribunal Constitucional*, Ed. Lex Nova, Valladolid 2001, pp. 293, 294; Héctor Fix Zamudio and Eduardo Ferrer Mac-Gregor, *Las sentencias de los Tribunales Constitucionales*, Ed. Porrúa, Mexico City 2009, pp. 34, 37, 71; Víctor Bazan, "Jurisdicción constitucional local y corrección de las omisiones inconstitucionales relativas," *Revista Iberoamericana de Derecho Procesal Constitucional*, nº 2,

evaluation of the omission and the declaration of the unconstitutionality of the provision containing the omission, as commonly happens in countries with a diffuse system of judicial review.

But in countries with a concentrated system of judicial review, although constitutional courts have the power to annul statutes considered unconstitutional, including those that omit fundamental aspects imposed by the Constitution, in cases of relative legislative omissions being considered unconstitutional, the constitutional courts have also developed the practice of declaring the omission unconstitutional without annulling the provision. In the decisions, the courts send to the Legislator guidelines or instructions to correct the unconstitutionality, thus orienting the Legislator's future activities.[81]

Of course, in all these cases, the purpose of the constitutional courts' controlling the unconstitutionality of relative legislative omissions is not to allow the courts to create new legislative provision; that is, the purpose is not to usurp the Legislator's functions.[82] Nonetheless, in many cases, the result of these judicial decisions has been the encroachment of legislative attributions when orienting or instructing the Legislative body as to how it must fill the omission to make it conform with the Constitution.[83]

1. *Constitutional Courts and Equality Rights: Deciding on the Unconstitutionality of Statutes without Declaring Their Nullity*

As in countries with a diffuse system of judicial review, in countries with a concentrated system of judicial review, constitutional courts have also declared statutory provisions unconstitutional but without annulling them. Instead, in these cases, constitutional courts have limited their activity to declaring unconstitutional the challenged provision only regarding the part that is not in accord with the Constitution. Instead of annulling the provision, in some cases, the courts referred to the Legislator for it to produce the

Instituto Iberoamericano de Derecho Procesal Constitucional, Editorial Porrúa, Mexico City 2004, pp. 189 ff.

81 See José Julio Fernández Rodríguez, *La inconstitucionalidad por omisión: Teoría general. Derecho comparado. El caso español*, Civitas, Madrid 1998, pp. 227 ff.

82 See Héctor Fix Zamudio and Eduardo Ferrer Mac-Gregor, *Las sentencias de los Tribunales Constitucionales*, Ed. Porrúa, Mexico City 2009, p. 34.

83 *Id.*, pp. 36–37; 75, 88.

needed legislation,[84] and in others cases, the constitutional court issued directives, guidelines, recommendations, and even orders to the Legislator to correct the unconstitutional legislative omissions. In all these cases, the constitutional court assists and collaborates with the Legislator.

An important note is that, in almost all the cases of relative legislative omissions that are declared unconstitutional but not annulled, the protection of fundamental constitutional rights have always been involved, particularly the right to equality and nondiscrimination.[85]

In concentrated systems of judicial review, the ability of constitutional courts to declare a legal provision unconstitutional without annulling it has been expressly established in the legislation governing the constitutional court's functions, as in Germany, where in 1970 the reform of the Law related to the Federal Constitutional Tribunal (BVerfG) established a specific function of the Tribunal in specific cases: to give preference to the constitutional interpretation of a statute and to "declare a law to be compatible or *incompatible* with the Basic Law," without the need to declare the provision "to be null and void" (article 31.2).[86] A similar reform was proposed in 2005 in Spain in relation to the Organic Law of the Constitutional Tribunal that established the contrary principle: "when a [Constitutional Tribunal's] decision declares the unconstitutionality of a provision, it must in addition declare the nullity of the challenged provisions."[87] The reform of the Law was not approved in Spain,[88] which did not prevent the Constitutional Tribunal from overcoming the rigidity of the dichotomy and issuing decisions of unconstitutionality without nullity.

An important case resolved by the Spanish Constitutional Tribunal was Decision No. 116/1987, regarding Law 37/1984 of October 22, 1984, which

84 See Christian Behrendt, *Le judge constitutionnel, un législateur-cadre positif. Un analyse comparative en droit francais, belge et allemande*, Bruylant, Brussels 2006, p. 124.

85 See F. Fernández Segado, *Spanish National Report*, pp. 9, 25, 39–42. P. Popelier has pointed out that, in Belgium, "the principle of equality and non discrimination constitutes the reference norm in more than 85% of the decisions adopted by the Constitutional Courts." See P. Popelier, *Belgian National Report*, p. 3.

86 See Christian Behrendt, *Le judge constitutionnel, un législateur-cadre positif. Un analyse comparative en droit francais, belge et allemande*, Bruylant, Brussels 2006, p. 93; See I. Härtel, *German National Report*, pp. 7–9; Francisco Javier Díaz Revorio, *Las sentencias interpretativas del Tribunal Constitucional*, Ed. Lex Nova, Valladolid 2001, p. 260; F. Fernandez Segado, *Spanish National Report*, p. 6.

87 See Francisco Javier Díaz Revorio, *Las sentencias interpretativas del Tribunal Constitucional*, Ed. Lex Nova, Valladolid 2001, p. 301.

88 See F. Fernández Segado, *Spanish National Report*, p. 6

established social rights and benefits to military and police officers for services accomplished during the Civil War, excluding professional military who enrolled in the Armed Forces after 1936. Because of that exclusion, the Constitutional Tribunal considered the Law contrary to the principle of equality, annulled the exclusion, and extended the application of the provision to those who had been excluded.[89] Another important decision was Decision No. 45/1989, where the Constitutional Tribunal found unconstitutional a provision of Law 48/1985 on Income Tax that made the joint tax return for family members compulsory, which implied heavier tax obligations for a person integrated in a family group than for a person with the same income but not part of a family group.[90] The Constitutional Tribunal in this case considered the issue of the dichotomy unconstitutionality-nullity, arguing that, although the text of article 40.1 of the Tribunal's Law was contradictory, it was not necessary for that dichotomy to be applied, particularly in cases of judicial review of an omission, in which case "the nullity as an strictly negative measure[] is manifestly incapable of reordering the Income Tax regime in a way compatible with the Constitution." The Tribunal concluded that it was for the Legislator, "according to the decision, to make the needed modifications or adaptations of the legal regime, according to its normative powers."[91] As Francisco Fernández Segado has pointed out:

> with the decision 45/1989, the Tribunal not only moved away from the legal text, giving birth to decisions of unconstitutionality without nullity, situating itself in the wake of the BVerfG [German Federal Constitutional Tribunal], but in addition categorically breached the binomial unconstitutionality/ nullity characteristic of the vision of the constitutional judge as "negative legislator."[92]

The same technique has been applied in Nicaragua, where the Supreme Court, in a decision recognizing the unconstitutionality of articles 225 and 228 of the Civil Code prohibiting and restricting cases of paternity inquiry, decided not to annul the articles and maintained them with effects pending

89 See F. Fernández Segado, *Spanish National Report*, p. 10.

90 See STC 45/1989, of February 20, 1989, para. 11.; F. Fernández Segado, *Spanish National Report*, p. 12.

91 *Id.* See also STC 13/1992, February 6, 1992, fund. jur. 17; STC 16/1996, February 1, 1996 fund. jur. 8; and STC 68/1996, April 18, 1996, fund. jur. 14, in F. Fernandez Segado, *Spanish National Report*, pp. 12–13.

92 See F. Fernández Segado, *Spanish National Report*, p. 12.

new legislation to be approved by Congress, in order to avoid graver problems that a legal vacuum could produce.[93]

In Switzerland, where judicial review of cantonal laws is allowed, the Federal Court has also decided cases in relative legislative omissions but has refused to assume the role of legislator. In the *Hegetschweiler* case,[94] on the appeal of a married couple, the Supreme Court concluded that a cantonal regulation related to income and property taxes for married couples was unconstitutional because married couples owed higher taxes than unmarried couples who lived together in the same household and had similar financial means; this was considered a breach of the equal treatment precept (Article 8.1, Constitution). The subject matter of the appeal for an abstract control of norms was a new rule that represented an improvement over the previous legal situation. As mentioned by Tobias Jaag, if the Supreme Court had annulled the contested rule, the former rule would have again entered into effect, unless the Court had established a substitute rule. The Supreme Court rejected the appeal and limited itself to stating that the contested rule was not in full conformity with the Constitution; in this manner, the cantonal legislator was asked to remedy the unconstitutional situation. For the couple who appealed, the outcome was most dissatisfactory.[95]

In another case issued in 1986, the Supreme Court found that a cantonal regulation imposing a lower retirement age for women than for men was in breach of the constitutional right to equal treatment of women and men. The Supreme Court, however, left it at that, reasoning that the cantonal legislator needed time to establish the constitutional status.[96] In the same sense, the Supreme Court protected the complaint of a federal official that a rule permitting only women, not men, to take early retirement after thirty-five years of service violated the right to equal treatment of women and men. The Court did not view itself as having competence, however, to issue a correct rule; the petition of the federal official for permission to take early retirement was therefore rejected.[97] In a similar case relating to the equal treatment of

93 See decisions of November 22, 1957, B.J. p. 18730 (1873?), and of June 16, 1986, B.J. p. 105; Iván Escobar Fornos, "Las sentencias constitucionales y sus efectos en Nicaragua," in *Anuario Iberoamericano de Justicia Constitucional*, Centro de Estudios Políticos y Constitucionales, nº 12, 2008, Madrid 2008, p. 102.

94 See BGE 110 Ia 7; Tobias Jaag, *Swiss National Report*, p. 8 (footnote 37).

95 See Tobias Jaag, *Swiss National Report*, p. 8.

96 See Supreme Court in ZBl 87/1986, 482 ff.; Tobias Jaag, *Swiss National Report*, p. 9 (footnote 40).

97 See BGE 109 Ib 86, 88 ff.; Tobias Jaag, *Swiss National Report*, p. 9 (footnote 41).

boys and girls during school lessons, the Court explicitly held: "it would, however, be out of the question for the Supreme Court, on its own initiative, to create a rule in lieu of the cantonal legislator."[98]

In general terms, the main result of constitutional courts exercising judicial review powers regarding statutes with unconstitutional provisions has been the assumption by constitutional courts of a new role as aides to the Legislator; they direct requests, recommendations, and instructions for the legislative organ to issue additional legislation to surpass the constitutional doubts that result from the relative legislative omission.[99]

Even in countries like Switzerland, where there is no judicial review of federal legislation but only regarding cantonal legislation, this does not preclude the Federal Supreme Court from criticizing a federal legislative rule, thereby signaling to the legislators that an amendment of the law is required.[100] For instance, during the past years, several cantonal voting systems have been held unconstitutional because they did not guarantee equal treatment of the voters (equal right to vote). In these cases, the Supreme Court contented itself with declaring that the voting systems were unconstitutional and asking the cantonal legislators to amend the rule that was objected to.[101]

These instruction or directives sent by constitutional courts to the Legislator are in some cases nonbinding recommendations and in other cases obligatory.[102]

2. *Constitutional Courts' Issuing Nonbinding Directives to the Legislator*

In general terms, regarding noncompulsory judicial recommendations – known as exhortative decisions, delegate decisions, or *sentenze indiritzzo*

[98] See Supreme Court, in ZBl 86/1985, 492, 495; Tobias Jaag, *Swiss National Report*, p. 9 (footnote 42).

[99] See Héctor Fix Zamudio and Eduardo Ferrer Mac-Gregor, *Las sentencias de los Tribunales Constitucionales*, Ed. Porrúa, Mexico City 2009, pp. 39, 89.

[100] See BGE 103 Ia 53, 55; Tobias Jaag, *Swiss National Report*, p. 7 (footnote 29).

[101] See BGE 131 I 74, p. 84 ff.; 129 I p. 185, 205 ff.; Tobias Jaag, *Swiss National Report*, p. 7 (footnote 44, 45).

[102] In this sense, Christian Behrendt, in analyzing the situation in Germany, Belgium, and France, distinguishes between what he calls permissive, not binding interferences or *lignes directives*, and the enabling obligatory interferences, or injunctions. See Christian Behrendt, *Le judge constitutionnel, un législateur-cadre positif. Un analyse comparative en droit francais, belge et allemande*, Bruylant, Brussels 2006, pp. 253 ff.

in Italy[103]– the Constitutional Court declares the unconstitutionality of a provision but does not introduce the norm to be applied through interpretation, leaving this task to the Legislator. In Italy, these decisions are also called "principles' additive decisions,"[104] such as Decision No. 171 of 1996, issued by the Constitutional Court to declare unconstitutional a provision of the Law regulating the right to strike in public services. The provision did not provide for previous notice and a reasonable term in strikes of lawyers and advocates.[105]

In other cases, the instruction directed to the Legislator can be conditional with respect to the constitutional court. In Italy, for instance, when dealing with an unconstitutional statute, the Constitutional Court can recommend that the Legislator introduce legislation to eliminate the constitutional doubts. Through the *doppia pronuncia* formula, if the Legislator fails to execute the recommendations of the Court, in a second decision, the Court can declare unconstitutional the impugned statute.[106]

This sort of exhortative judicial review is also accepted in Germany, where it is called "appellate decisions."[107] Here, the Federal Constitutional Tribunal in cases of unconstitutional statutes can issue "an admonition to the Legislator," which contains legislative directives "addressed to the Legislator which can be of norm-requesting as well as norm-demanding nature still considered constitutional, in its impacts and effects, to improve or alternatively replace it,"[108] for which purpose it must give the Legislator a term to do so. Once the term is exhausted, the provision becomes unconstitutional, and the Tribunal must rule on the matter. An example of this type of decision is one issued by the Federal Constitutional Tribunal regarding a survivor's pension. A statute provided that a widow would

[103] See L. Pegoraro, *La Corte e il Parlamento. Sentenze-indirizzo e attivitá legislativa*, Cedam, Padua 1987, pp. 3 ff.; Francisco Javier Díaz Revorio, *Las sentencias interpretativas del Tribunal Constitucional*, Ed. Lex Nova, Valladolid 2001, p. 268; Néstor Pedro Sagües, *Argentinean National Report II*, pp. 4–7.

[104] Francisco Javier Díaz Revorio, *Las sentencias interpretativas del Tribunal Constitucional*, Ed. Lex Nova, Valladolid 2001, pp. 279–284, 305.

[105] See A. Vespaziani, "Una sentenza additiva di principio reguardo allo 'sciopero' degli avvocati," in *Giurisprudenza costitutionalle*, 1996, Vol. IV, pp. 2718 ff. Francisco Javier Díaz Revorio, *Las sentencias interpretativas del Tribunal Constitucional*, Ed. Lex Nova, Valladolid 2001, pp. 281–282 (footnote 164).

[106] See Iván Escobar Fornos, *Estudios Jurídicos*, Vol. I, Ed. Hispamer, Managua 2007, p. 504.

[107] See Francisco Javier Díaz Revorio, *Las sentencias interpretativas del Tribunal Constitucional*, Ed. Lex Nova, Valladolid 2001, pp. 264; Iván Escobar Fornos, *Estudios Jurídicos*, Vol. I, Ed. Hispamer, Managua 2007, p. 505.

[108] See I. Härtel, *German National Report*, pp. 17–18.

always obtain the pension of her late husband, but the widower would obtain his wife's pension in case of her death only if she had primarily provided for the family and earned the family income before or if she had been a public official. The Federal Constitutional Court found that the provision was in process of becoming unconstitutional because of social changes that have taken place particularly on the role of women in the family, asking the Legislator to issue according to its powers to legislate the necessary provisions to prevent the unconstitutionality.[109]

In other cases, the Federal Constitutional Tribunal has limited itself to issue directives to the Legislator but leaving the Legislator to make the political decision. This was the case of the decision issued regarding a statute of March 18, 1965, on the reimbursement of electoral expenses of political parties. The Tribunal also developed some conditions to be followed only if the Legislator decided to implement the reimbursement system.[110]

In France, the Constitutional Council has also issued directives to the Legislator, which even without normative direct effects can establish a framework for future legislative action.[111] They have persuasive effect only because the Constitutional Council always is able to exercise review of the constitutionality of a subsequent law.

A similar technique, called signalizations, has been applied in Poland, through which the Constitutional Tribunal directs the Legislator's attention to problems of general nature.[112]

In Belgium,[113] the Constitutional Court has also applied this technique. In particular, in a 1982 case referring to regional taxation legislation on environmental matters, as to the definition of *pollutant payer*, the former Court of Arbitration issued directives to the regional Legislators establishing the conditions under which *pollutant payer* was not in conformity with the

[109] See BVerfGE 39, 169 ff.; I. Härtel, *German National Report*, pp. 18; Francisco Javier Díaz Revorio, *Las sentencias interpretativas del Tribunal Constitucional*, Ed. Lex Nova, Valladolid 2001, pp. 265 (footnote 115).

[110] See BVerfG, decision of July 19, 1966, BVerfGE 20, 56 (114–115), in Christian Behrendt, *Le judge constitutionnel, un législateur-cadre positif. Un analyse comparative en droit francais, belge et allemande*, Bruylant, Brussels 2006, pp. 176–179, 185 ff.

[111] See Decision 83-164 DC; Bertrand Mathieu, *French National Report*, p. 10.

[112] See, e.g., signalization concerning protection of tenants of June 29, 2005, OTK ZU 2005/6A/77; Marek Safjan, *Polish National Report*, p. 16 (footnote 45).

[113] See P. Popelier, *Belgian National Report*, p. 8.

Constitution's principle of equality.[114] Also in an interesting decision issued by the same former Court of Arbitration in 2004, on the taxation regime for donations to nonprofit associations established in a federal law, the Court sent directives to a regional Legislator that was different from the one that had incurred in an unconstitutionality, that is, to the regional legislator that the Court considered competent to issue legislation on the matter.[115]

In Serbia, Article 105 of the Law on the Constitutional Court empowers the Constitutional Court to give its opinion or to point out the need to adopt or revise laws, or to implement other measures relevant for the protection of constitutionality and legality, which are used to put some pressure on the National Assembly to bring laws for implementation of constitutional provisions or to correct existing unconstitutional rules. In these cases, the court can act *ex officio*, but the opinions do not have binding force. The most important notifications and opinions issued by the Court were connected to noncompliance with deadlines stipulated in constitutional laws for the enforcement of the Constitution.[116]

In the Czech Republic, the Constitutional Court in some cases has also provided a detailed analysis of the law that will fit the constitutional test of the Court after the original law has been annulled.[117] Nonetheless, those guidelines are not binding, and practice shows that the Legislator frequently does not follow the Court's reasoning.[118]

In France, the Constitutional Council – which until 2009 could only review statutes' constitutionality before they were promulgated by the National Assembly – has necessarily issued decisions that have interfered with the legislative function.[119] Consequently, on many occasions, the Council has issued decisions containing nonobligatory directives to the Legislator to sufficiently correct the draft legislation submitted. One example of such a decision on economic matters is the one adopted in 1982 on the occasion of

[114] See CA arrêt 79/93 of November 9, 1993, in Christian Behrendt, *Le judge constitutionnel, un législateur-cadre positif. Un analyse comparative en droit francais, belge et allemande*, Bruylant, Brussels 2006, pp. 175–176, 191 ff.

[115] See CA arrêt 45/2004 of March 17, 2004, in Christian Behrendt, *Le judge constitutionnel, un législateur-cadre positif. Un analyse comparative en droit francais, belge et allemande*, Bruylant, Brussels 2006, pp. 175–176, 230–237.

[116] See Boško Tripković, *Serbian National Report*, pp. 9–10.

[117] See Decision *Anonymous Witness* of October 12, 1994, Pl. ÚS 4/94, at http://angl.concourt.cz/angl_verze/doc/p-4-94.php; Zdenek Kühn, *Czech National Report*, p. 12 (footnote 53).

[118] See Zdenek Kühn, *Czech National Report*, p. 12.

[119] See Bertrand Mathieu, *French National Report*, p. 6.

the control exercised by the Constitutional Council regarding the Nationalization Law, particularly referring to the provisions on compensation regarding the nationalized enterprise stocks. The Council argued that it was necessary for the Legislation to be approved to take into account the corresponding compensation and the phenomenon of monetary depreciation.[120]

On institutional matters, in another decision in 2000, the Constitutional Council issued directives to the Legislator when reviewing a statute on election age. The statute lowered the age to be elected in European elections for non-French candidates to eighteen years but kept the age of twenty-three years for French citizens. The Council expressed that if the Legislator was to reduce the age to be elected, it must do so for all candidates.[121]

In Mexico, in the first decision the Supreme Court adopted to resolve a direct action of a statute's unconstitutionality (37/2001), in addition to declaring the provision unconstitutional, the Court exhorted the Legislator to legislate on the matter, fixing a term of ninety days to do so.[122]

In countries with diffuse systems of judicial review, exhortative rulings have also been issued by Supreme Courts. This is the case in Argentina, in the *Verbitsky* case, where the Supreme Court decided a collective *habeas corpus* petition, without declaring unconstitutional any legal provision of the Province of Buenos Aires. It then exhorted authorities to sanction new legal provisions to take care of the overcrowding and dreadful situation in the penitentiary system.[123] Another important case was *Rosza*, where the Supreme Court, after declaring unconstitutional a decision of the Judiciary Council of the Nation regarding the provisional appointment of judges, exhorted the Congress and the executive to enact a new "constitutionally

[120] See Decision 132 DC of January 16, 1982 (*GD*. n° 31. Loi de nationalization), in Christian Behrendt, *Le judge constitutionnel, un législateur-cadre positif. Un analyse comparative en droit francais, belge et allemande*, Bruylant, Brussels 2006, pp. 173–175.

[121] See CC, Decision 426 DC of March 30, 2000, in Christian Behrendt, *Le judge constitutionnel, un législateur-cadre positif. Un analyse comparative en droit francais, belge et allemande*, Bruylant, Brussels 2006, pp. 176.

[122] See Héctor Fix Zamudio and Eduardo Ferrer Mac-Gregor, "Las sentencias de los tribunales constitucionales en el ordenamiento mexicano," in *Anuario Iberoamericano de Justicia Constitucional*, n° 12, 2008, Centro de Estudios Políticos y Constitucionales, Madrid 2008, p. 252.

[123] See CSIJ, Fallos 328:1146, in Néstor P. Sagües, "Los efectos de las sentencias constitucionales en el derecho argentino," in *Anuario Iberoamericano de Justicia Constitucional*, Centro de Estudios Políticos y Constitucionales, n° 12, 2008, Madrid 2008, p. 340; Néstor Pedro Sagües, *Argentinean National Report II*, pp. 7–11.

valid" regime, provided guidelines for the new regime to follow, and granted Congress one year to implement the new system.[124]

In other cases, the Argentinean Supreme Tribunal, after declaring the unconstitutionality of some statutory provisions, has issued guidelines to Congress for future legislation that indicate the constitutional path that Congress should take on certain affairs. Moreover, in some decisions, it has changed the clear legislative intent – through judicial interpretation – to make the law adequate with the Court's interpretation of the Constitution. These actions show the Court's increasing involvement in realms previously left to the political branches of government. For instance, in the cases *Castillo*[125] and *Aquino* (2004),[126] the Supreme Court declared unconstitutional the Labor Risks Law (Law 24.557), particularly its procedural contents (a matter constitutionally reserved to provincial legislation) and the limits of compensation for labor injuries. The Court found that its provisions denied workers their right to complete restitution. In addition, the Court's rulings demanded congressional action to modify the system in accordance with Court-established guidelines.

In *Vizzoti*, the Supreme Court ruled that the limits to the base salary used to calculate termination compensation provided for in the Employment Law were unreasonable, in light of the constitutional obligation to protect workers against unjustified firings. The Court then provided Congress with guidelines for valid limits, indicating that "the Court's decision does not entail undue interference with congressional powers, nor a violation of the separation of powers, being only the duly exercise of the constitutionally-mandated judicial review over laws and governmental action."[127] In other cases of judicial review of conventionality, regarding the American

[124] Decision of May 23, 2007, *Jurisprudencia Argentina*, 2007-III-414, in Néstor P. Sagües, "Los efectos de las sentencias constitucionales en el derecho argentino," in *Anuario Iberoamericano de Justicia Constitucional*, Centro de Estudios Políticos y Constitucionales, nº 12, 2008, Madrid 2008, p. 341. See also Néstor Pedro Sagües, *Argentinean National Report II*, pp. 11–12. See also Fallos 330:2361 (2007), in Alejandra Rodríguez Galán and Alfredo Mauricio Vítolo, *Argentinean National Report I*, p. 13.

[125] See Fallos 327:3610 (2004); Alejandra Rodríguez Galán and Alfredo Mauricio Vítolo, *Argentinean National Report I*, p. 13.

[126] See Fallos 327:3753 (2004); Alejandra Rodríguez Galán and Alfredo Mauricio Vítolo, *Argentinean National Report I*, p. 13.

[127] See Fallos 327:3677 (2004); Alejandra Rodríguez Galán and Alfredo Mauricio Vítolo, *Argentinean National Report I*, p. 13; Néstor Pedro Sagües, *Argentinean National Report II*, p. 20.

Convention of Human Rights, as in the *Cantos* case (2003),[128] the Argentinean Supreme Court demanded that Congress pass legislation to comply with the binding rulings of the Inter-American Court of Human Rights.

In Colombia, the Constitutional Court has also assumed similar exhortative powers with respect to Congress. After declaring unconstitutional a few articles of Law 600 of 2000 (Articles 382–389) on *habeas corpus*, the Court exhorted Congress to legislate on the matter according to the criteria established in the ruling, and it gave Congress a term in which it needed to legislate.[129]

A similar position has been adopted by the Supreme Court of the Netherlands, despite the ban on judicial review of statutes' constitutionality established in Article 120 of the Constitution. In the 1989 *Harmonization Act* case, the Supreme Court, though maintaining that it was clearly not entitled to review whether an Act of Parliament was compatible with legal principles, made it clear that – had it been allowed to do so – it would have ruled that the 1988 Harmonization Act violated the principle of legal certainty. The Court thus gave the legislature some "expert advice," and the latter, taking the hint, eventually changed the law. As mentioned by J. Uzman, T. Barkhuysen, and M. L. van Emmerik, "the ban on judicial review of legislation then does not prevent the judiciary to engage in a dialogue with the legislature, be it that such occasions remain rare."[130]

In some cases, this dialogue has led the Supreme Court, as in the *Labour Expenses Deduction* case,[131] to rule that it would not – for the time being – intervene because doing so would entail choosing from different policy options. The Court made clear that it might think otherwise if the legislature knowingly persisted in its unlawful course.[132] But in no case can these judicial decisions consist of the Supreme Court giving orders to Parliament to produce legislation by means of injunctions, even if the legislative

[128] See Fallos 326:2968 (2003); Alejandra Rodríguez Galán and Alfredo Mauricio Vítolo, *Argentinean National Report I*, p. 15 (footnote 60).

[129] See Germán Alfonso López Daza, *Colombian National Report I*, p. 11.

[130] See J. Uzman, T. Barkhuysen, and M. L. van Emmerik, *Dutch National Report*, p. 6.

[131] See Supreme Court judgment of 12 May 1999, *NJ* 2000/170 (*Labour Expenses Deduction*). See J. Uzman, T. Barkhuysen, and M. L. van Emmerik, *Dutch National Report*, p. 26 (footnote 79).

[132] See J. Uzman, T. Barkhuysen, and M. L. van Emmerik, *Dutch National Report*, p. 42.

omission renders the legislation incompatible with the European Union law.[133]

3. *Constitutional Courts' Issuing Binding Orders and Directives to the Legislator*

In contrast, in many other cases of judicial review, particularly those referring to relative legislative omissions, constitutional courts have progressively assumed a more positive role regarding the Legislator, issuing not only directives, but also orders or instructions, for the Legislator to reform or correct pieces of legislation in the sense indicated by the Court. This has transformed constitutional courts into a sort of auxiliary Legislator, imposing on the Legislator certain tasks and establishing a precise term for their performance.

This judicial review technique has been used in Germany, where the Federal Constitutional Tribunal, in many cases, after having determined the incompatibility of a legal provision with the Constitution, without declaring its nullity, declares the obligation of the Legislator to resolve the unconstitutional condition and to improve or abolish the law.[134] An early example of this sort of injunctive decision regarding the Legislator was adopted in 1981 with respect to a provision of the Civil Code (Article 1579) that established the regime of alimony, specifically the possibility of it reduction or suppression for equitable reasons and in particular, the exceptions to the reduction based on the impossibility for the holder of the pension to carry on remunerative work due to the attention to be given to the child the former spouse had. This exception was challenged in a particular judicial case that reached the Tribunal, which found that, though motivated by educational and family reasons, the rigidity of the provision prevented the courts from adjusting it to individual circumstances, violating article 2.1 of the Constitution (individual freedom). Consequently, the Tribunal decided that "the Legislator must establish a new regime taking into account the principle of proportionality. The Legislator is free to decide whether to adopt an additional provision or to modify the second part of article 1579."[135]

133 See Supreme Court judgment of 21 March 2003, *NJ* 2003/691 (*State v. Waterpakt*); J. Uzman, T. Barkhuysen, and M. L. van Emmerik, *Dutch National Report*, p. 38.

134 See I. Härtel, *German National Report*, p. 9.

135 See BVerfG, decision of July 14, 1981, BVerfGE 57, 381, in Christian Behrendt, *Le judge constitutionnel, un législateur-cadre positif. Un analyse comparative en droit francais, belge et allemande*, Bruylant, Brussels 2006, pp. 263–268.

In another case, on professional conflicts of interest as contrary to the fundamental right of everyone to choose his or her profession, the Tribunal also issued orders to the Legislator but without leaving it any alternative. The Tribunal found a specific legal conflict of interest (preventing tax counsels from exercising commercial activities) unconstitutional in certain situations, concluding that, "[f]ollowing the principle of proportionality, the Legislator must establish transitory dispositions for the cases in which to immediately end commercial activities could signify a heavy burden. It is for the Legislator to fix the content of these transitory provisions."[136] Another classic example is the Federal Constitutional Tribunal decision in a case of reimbursement for electoral expenses in the electoral campaign of 1969, in which article 18 of the Political Parties Law was considered contrary to article 38 of the Constitution, which guaranteed the equality of candidates in elections. The Constitutional Tribunal ordered the Legislator to substitute the provision declared unconstitutional by issuing another according to the Constitution; it even indicated to the Legislator what not to do to avoid aggravating the unconstitutional inequalities.[137]

Other important cases in which the Federal Constitutional Tribunal has established "legislative programmes" in certain decisions include the *Numerus-Clausus* decision,[138] the decision concerning professors,[139] the decision on abortion, and the decision on alternative civilian service.[140] For instance, in the *Numerus-Clausus* decision and the decision concerning professors, the Tribunal structured the basic rights as participation rights, which guarantee state services, and deducted from this a limitation of university places, and instruction to the Legislator on how to arrange the *Numerus-Clausus*.[141]

A similar sort of decision of the Constitutional Court can be found in Belgium, one of the most illustrative cases being the one related to the electoral constituency of Bruxelles-Hal-Vilvorde Province, in which in a

[136] See BVerfG, decision of February 15, 1967, BVerfGE 21, 183, in Christian Behrendt, *Le judge constitutionnel, un législateur-cadre positif. Un analyse comparative en droit francais, belge et allemande*, Bruylant, Brussels 2006, pp. 259–262.

[137] See BVerfG, decision of March 9, 1976, BVerfGE 41, 414, in Christian Behrendt, *Le judge constitutionnel, un législateur-cadre positif. Un analyse comparative en droit francais, belge et allemande*, Bruylant, Brussels 2006, pp. 275–278.

[138] See BVerfGE 33, 303; I. Härtel, *German National Report*, p. 14 (footnote 89).

[139] See BVerfGE 35, 79; I. Härtel, *German National Report*, p. 14 (footnote 90).

[140] See BVerfGE 48, 127; I. Härtel, *German National Report*, p. 14 (footnote 91).

[141] See I. Härtel, *German National Report*, p. 15.

decision issued in 2003, after finding that the enlargement of the constituency coincided with the one of the Province, the Constitutional Court urged the Legislator to put an end to the unconstitutionality found, establishing in the case a term for the Legislature to do so.[142]

This last technique of issuing orders to the Legislator that impose a term or deadline for it to take the necessary legislative action has been developed in many countries, reinforcing the character of constitutional courts as direct collaborators of the Legislators. In Germany, this technique is considered the general rule in the Federal Constitutional Tribunal's decisions containing injunctions to the Legislator, whether those injunctions establish a fixed date, or the occurrence of a fact not yet determined, a reasonable term, or in the near future.[143] The power of the Tribunal has been deducted from article 35 of the Law regulating its functions (BVerfG),[144] which states that "in its decision the Federal Constitutional Tribunal may state by whom it is to be executed; in individual instances it may also specify the method of execution." According to I. Härtel, "the setting of a deadline is meant to provide a form of pressure against the Legislator and thereby serve the enactment of justice found by the BVerfG."[145] In a recent case on inheritance tax, the Federal Constitutional Court declared unconstitutional the current capital-transfer tax and fixed a deadline of December 31, 2008, for the Legislator to restore a legal condition in conformity with the Constitution.[146] The unconstitutional statute, which had been considered valid until said resolution, therefore maintained validity for more than another year, which was justified by the Tribunal, which pointed out that, in the case of a violation of the principle of equity (Art. 3.1 Constitution) several possibilities for correcting the unconstitutional condition are available to the Legislator, so that the regulation under review is not annulled but simply declared incompatible with the Constitution.[147] Another classical example of these decisions is one issued by the Federal Constitutional Tribunal in 1998 on an individual's freedom to exercise a particular

[142] See CA nº 73/2003 du 26 mai 2003, in P. Popelier, *Belgian National Report*, p. 4.

[143] See I. Härtel, *German National Report*, pp. 7–8; Christian Behrendt, *Le judge constitutionnel, un législateur-cadre positif. Un analyse comparative en droit francais, belge et allemande*, Bruylant, Brussels 2006, pp. 288 ff.

[144] See I. Härtel, *German National Report*, p. 9.

[145] *Id.*, p. 9.

[146] BVerfG, court order from 2006-11-7, reference number: 1 BvL 10/02. I. Härtel, *German National Report*, p. 7.

[147] I. Härtel, *German National Report*, p. 8.

profession, where it considered a provision of a statute contrary to article 12.1 of the Constitution. The Tribunal argued, "Nonetheless, the violation of the Constitution does not lead to the annulment of the provision due to the fact that the Legislator has various possibilities to put an end to the declared unconstitutionality," thus limiting the Tribunal "only to verify[ing] the incompatibility of the unconstitutional provision with article 12,1 of the Constitution." The Tribunal also indicated, "The Legislator is oblige[d] to replace the questioned provision with a regulation in harmony with the Constitution before January 1, 2001."[148]

In a similar sense, in Austria, the Constitutional Court has the power to issue such guidelines for the Legislator that establish the rules to be applied in future legislation. One of the most important decisions of the Constitutional Court, as summarized by Ulrich Zellenberg[149] and referred to by Konrad Lachmayer, relates to the creation of self-governing corporations that exist besides local, municipal self-government, playing an important role in Austrian administration. In a series of decisions, the Constitutional Court established the conditions that the Legislator must meet to create such self-governing bodies, particularly in the field of social insurance. In decision VfSlg 8215/1977, the *Salzburger Jägerschaft* (Salzburg Hunting Association) case, the Court ruled on the requirements with which the Legislator must comply to establish self-governing corporations; it provided rules ensuring state-supervision over administrative affairs and within the autonomous sphere of competencies. In decision VfSlg 8644/1979, the Constitutional Court added the need to provide for a democratic way of nominating the officials of the self-governing corporation. In VfSlg 17.023/2003, the Constitutional Court subjected the action of the self-governing corporation to the principle of efficiency. In decision VfSlg 17.869/2006, the Austrian Constitutional Court restricted the self-governing bodies to enact regulations only with regard to persons within their sphere of competence; that is, they must not address persons who are not its members.[150]

148 BVerfG, decision of November 10, 1998, BVerfGE 99, 202, in Christian Behrendt, *Le judge constitutionnel, un législateur-cadre positif. Un analyse comparative en droit francais, belge et allemande*, Bruylant, Brussels 2006, p. 295.

149 Ulrich Zellenberg, "Self-Government and Democratic Legitimacy," Vol. 3, *ICL-Journal* 2/2009, 123 (http://www.icl-journal.com); Konrad Lachmayer, *Austrian National Report*, p. 10 (footnote 28).

150 See Konrad Lachmayer, *Austrian National Report*, p. 10.

In Croatia, the Constitutional Court also instructed the Legislator in general terms as to how to enact legislation, particularly on matters of the restriction of human rights. This was the case in Decision No. U-I-673/1996, of April 21, 1999, which repealed several provisions of the Law on Compensation for Property Expropriated during the Yugoslav Communist Rule.[151] In that case, as mentioned by Sanja Barić and Petar Bačić, the Court found that some restrictions to the right to dispose of property were disproportionate to the goal the Law attempted to achieve and contradicted the constitutional provisions on the restriction of human rights and freedoms. The Court seized the opportunity to instruct the legislators on future practice by emphasizing that any limitation of human rights and freedoms, be it necessary and Constitution based, represented "an exceptional state, because it does not abide by the general rules regarding constitutional rights and freedoms." The Constitutional Court decided: "Because of this, not only must these restrictions be based on the Constitution, but they also have to be proportional to the target goal and purpose of the law. In other words, this goal and purpose must be achieved with as little interference in the constitutional rights of citizens as possible (if the restrictions can be gradated, of course)."[152]

In France, given the traditional *a priori* judicial review of legislation exercised by the Constitutional Council, one of the most important means to ensure the enforcement of the Council's decisions are the directives called *réserves d'interprétation* or *réserves d'application.* By means of these directives, the Council establishes the conditions for the law to be enforced and applied, and the directives are aimed at the administrative authorities who must issue the regulations of the law and to the judges who must apply the law.[153]

Finally, in Colombia, the Constitutional Court has also ruled on the unconstitutionality of relative omissions by the Legislator and has exhorted Congress to sanction the corresponding statute. This was, for example, the case of the decision of the Constitutional Court issued when reviewing article 430 of the Labor Code, which prohibits strikes in public services. The Court in Decision No. C-473/94 reviewed the omission of the Legislator

[151] See Decision and Resolution of the Constitutional Court, nº U-I-673/1996, dated April 21, 1999, Official Gazette "*Narodne novine*," 39/1999; Decision U-I-902/1999, of January 25, 2000, Official Gazette "*Narodne novine*," 14/2000; Sanja Barić and Petar Bačić, *Croatian National Report*, p. 24 (footnote 65).

[152] See Sanja Barić and Petar Bačić, *Croatian National Report*, p. 25.

[153] See Bertrand Mathieu, *French National Report*, p. 10.

regarding the sanctioning of the legislation concerning the right to strike in essential public services, and "exhort[ed] Congress to legislate in a reasonable term" the corresponding legislation on the matter in accordance with the Constitution.[154]

III. CONSTITUTIONAL COURTS AS PROVISIONAL LEGISLATORS

In many other cases, in addition to constitutional courts issuing orders for the Legislator to enact legislation in a specific way and on a fixed or determined date, which occurs particularly on matters of legislative omissions, constitutional courts have also assumed the role of being provisional Legislators by including in their decisions provisional measures or regulations to be applied in the specific matter considered unconstitutional, until the Legislator sanctions the statute it is obliged to produce. In these cases, the court immediately stops the application of the unconstitutional provision, but to avoid the vacuum that annulment can create, the court temporarily establishes certain rules to be applied until new legislation is enacted.[155] Constitutional courts, in these cases, in some way act as "substitute legislators," not to usurp their functions but to preserve their legislative freedom.[156]

This technique has also been applied in Germany, on the basis of an extensive interpretation of the same article 35 of the Federal Constitutional Tribunal's Law, from which the Tribunal deducted that it has the power to enact general rules to be applied pending the sanctioning by the Legislator of the legislation on the matter in harmony with the Constitution. In these cases, the Tribunal has assumed an "auxiliary" legislative power, acting as a "parliamentary reparation enterprise" and "eroding the separation of powers."[157]

[154] See Germán Alfonso López Daza, *Colombian National Report I*, p. 10; Mónica Liliana Ibagón, "Control jurisdiccional de las omisiones legislativas en Colombia," in Juan Vega Gómez and Edgar Corzo Sosa, *Instrumentos de tutela y justicia constitucional: Memoria del VII Congreso Iberoamericano de Derecho Constitucional*, Universidad Nacional Autónoma de México, Mexico City 2002, pp. 322–323.

[155] See Christian Behrendt, *Le judge constitutionnel, un législateur-cadre positif. Un analyse comparative en droit francais, belge et allemande*, Bruylant, Brussels 2006, pp. 333 ff.

[156] See Otto Bachof, "Nuevas reflexiones sobre la jurisdicción constitucional entre derecho y política," in *Boletín Mexicano de Derecho Comparado*, XIX, nº 57, Mexico City 1986, pp. 848–849.

[157] See the references to the opinions of W. Abendroth, H.-P. Scheider, and R. Lamprech works in Christian Behrendt, *Le judge constitutionnel, un législateur-cadre positif. Un analyse*

The most important and interesting case ruled by the Federal Constitutional Tribunal in this regard has been the one rendered in 1975, referring to the reform of the Criminal Code regarding the partial decriminalization of abortion.[158] The Tribunal found unconstitutional the provision (Article 218a of the Criminal Code) requiring the Legislator to establish more precise rules; it further found that, "[i]n the interest of the clarity of law (*Rechtsklareit*), it seems suitable, according to article 35 of the Federal Constitutional Tribunal Law, to establish a provisory regulation that must be applicable until the new provisions would be enacted by the Legislator." The result was the inclusion in the Tribunal's decision of a detailed "provisional legislation" on the matter, which was immediately applicable and did not fix any precise date for the Legislator to act.[159] Fifteen years later, in 1992, a new statute was approved regarding help to pregnant women and to families, which was challenged because it was contrary to article 1 of the Constitution, which guarantees human dignity. In 1993, the Federal Constitutional Tribunal issued a new decision on the matter of abortion,[160] finding much of the reform contrary to the Constitution and establishing itself, in an extremely detailed way, as "real legislator" on all the rules applicable to abortion in the country.[161] Of course, the Tribunal based its decision on article 35 of the Law, which has been considered insufficient to support this sort of detailed substitutive legislation.[162]

In Switzerland, the Supreme Court has also provided for rules to fill the gap due to legislative omissions concerning enforcement of constitutional rights. For instance, regarding the proceedings on the detention of foreigners, the Supreme Court concluded that the Swiss legal system did not sufficiently protect the right of asylum seekers to protection of their freedom. After

comparative en droit francais, belge et allemande, Bruylant, Brussels 2006, p. 341 (footnotes 309 and 310).

158 BVerfG, decision of February 25, 1975, BVerfGE 39, 1, (68), in Christian Behrendt, *Le judge constitutionnel, un législateur-cadre positif. Un analyse comparative en droit francais, belge et allemande*, Bruylant, Brussels 2006, pp. 342 ff.; I. Härtel, *German National Report*, p. 14.

159 *Id.*

160 BVerfG, decision of May 28, 1993 (*Schwangerrschaftsabbruch II*), February 25, 1975, BVerfGE 88, 203, in Christian Behrendt, *Le judge constitutionnel, un législateur-cadre positif. Un analyse comparative en droit francais, belge et allemande*, Bruylant, Brussels 2006, pp. 346 ff.

161 See the whole text of the regulation in Christian Behrendt, *Le judge constitutionnel, un législateur-cadre positif. Un analyse comparative en droit francais, belge et allemande*, Bruylant, Brussels 2006, pp. 348–351 ff.

162 See the references in Christian Behrendt, *Le judge constitutionnel, un législateur-cadre positif. Un analyse comparative en droit francais, belge et allemande*, Bruylant, Brussels 2006, p. 352.

mentioning that the Legislator must act immediately, it ruled that it was "not prevented from establishing principles, for a transitional period until the effective date of a new rule of law, such that at least . . . the right to freedom pursuant to Article 5 clause 1 of the EHRC will be guaranteed to a sufficient extent."[163] On matters of expropriation, because the respective Law was tailored to the classic case of the compulsory deprivation of property, it does not establish the rules regarding limitations on property that are tantamount to an expropriation (quasi expropriation), and it has developed the conditions and modalities of these forms of expropriation.[164] Even today, the Supreme Court case law in these areas continues to play the role of legislative rules.[165]

In other cases, also mentioned by Tobias Jaag, the Supreme Court has also filled the gap produced by other relative legislative omissions. For instance, in deviation from the Planning and Construction Law of the Canton of Zurich, the Federal Supreme Court approved a zone for public buildings outside of the construction zone to enable sports facilities to be erected. The Court held the legislative rule to be manifestly incomplete to the extent that, contrary to its meaning, it failed to make distinctions that "according to all reason . . . were to be drawn."[166] For the introduction of the *numerus clausus* at universities, the Supreme Court, in the absence of a legislative rule, formulated strict requirements.[167] For telephone monitoring within the scope of criminal investigations, the Supreme Court likewise developed rules by requiring that affected persons be notified and providing for exceptions from this requirement.[168]

In India, and as a consequence of deciding direct actions for the protection of fundamental rights established in article 32 of the Constitution, the Supreme Court has assumed the role of provisional legislator on matters related to police arrest and detention. Surya Deva summarized the case as follows. In August 1986, a nongovernmental organization (NGO) addressed a letter to the Chief Justice of India drawing his attention to certain deaths reported in police lockups and custody. The letter, along with some other similar letters, was treated as a writ petition under Article 32 of the

163 See BGE 123 II 193, 201 ff.; Tobias Jaag, *Swiss National Report*, p. 1 (footnote 57).

164 See BGE 91 I 329 ff. (substantive expropriation); BGE 94 I 286 ff. (appropriation of rights of neighbors); Tobias Jaag, *Swiss National Report*, p. 16 (footnote 89).

165 For instance, a decision issued in 2008, on compensation based on aircraft noise: BGE 134 II 49 ff. and 145 ff.; Tobias Jaag, *Swiss National Report*, p. 16 (footnote 90).

166 See BGE 108 Ia 295, 297; Tobias Jaag, *Swiss National Report*, p. 17 (footnote 91).

167 See BGE 121 I 22 ff.; Tobias Jaag, *Swiss National Report*, p. 17 (footnote 92).

168 See BGE 109 Ia 273, 298 ff.; Tobias Jaag, *Swiss National Report*, p. 17 (footnote 92).

Constitution, for which purpose the Supreme Court issued notices to all state governments and to the Law Commission, with a request to make suitable suggestions. After making reference to constitutional and statutory provisions and international conventions, the Supreme Court, in *D K Basu v. State of West Bengal*,[169] issued eleven requirements, as follows:

> We, therefore, consider it appropriate to issue the following requirements to be followed in all cases of arrest or detention till legal provisions are made in that behalf as preventive measures:
>
> 1. The police personnel carrying out the arrest and handling the interrogation of the arrestee should bear accurate, visible and clear identification and name tags with their designations. The particulars of all such personnel who handle interrogation of the arrestee must be recorded in a register.
> 2. That the police officer carrying out the arrest of the arrestee shall prepare a memo of arrest at the time of arrest and such memo shall be attested by one witness, who may either be a member of the family of the arrestee or a respectable person of the locality from where the arrest is made. It shall be countersigned by the arrestee and shall contain the time and date of arrest.
> 3. A person who has been arrested or detained . . . shall be entitled to have one friend or relative or other person known to him or having an interest in his welfare being informed, as soon as practicable, that he has been arrested and is being detained at the particular place. . . .
> 4. The time, place of arrest, and venue of custody of an arrestee must be notified by the police where the next friend or relative of the arrestee lives outside the district or town through the Legal Aid Organization in the district, and the police station of the area concerned, telegraphically, within a period of 8 to 12 hours after arrest.
> 5. The person arrested must be made of aware of this right to have someone informed of his arrest or detention as soon as he is put under arrest or is detained. . . .
> 8. The arrestee should be subject to medical examination by a trained doctor every 48 hours during his detention in custody. . . .
> 9. Copies of all the documents . . . should be sent to the Magistrate for his record.
> 10. The arrestee must be permitted to meet his lawyer during interrogation, though not throughout the interrogation.[170]

[169] See (1997) 1 SCC 416; Surya Deva, *Indian National Report*, pp. 6–7.

[170] *Id.*

The Court observed that these requirements, which flow from Articles 21 and 22 of the Constitution, must be complied with by all government agencies and that any breach will render the concerned official liable for departmental action, as well as for contempt of court. Even though the requirements were seemingly intended to be a temporary stop-gap arrangement, they continue to be the main rules applicable to dealing with details of arrest and detention.

Another important decision in this same line regarding the protection of human rights was the one adopted in the *Vishaka v. State of Rajasthan* case,[171] on matters of sexual harassment of women at the workplace. The Supreme Court decided on petitions filed before it by social activists and nongovernmental organizations for the enforcement of the rights of working women under Articles 14, 19, and 21 of the Constitution (the right to equality, the right to carry on any profession or trade, and the right to life and liberty, respectively). The Supreme Court, though acknowledging that the primary responsibility for protecting these rights of working women lies with the legislature and executive, in cases of sexual harassment that resulted in the violation of fundamental rights of women workers, found that "an effective redressal requires that some guidelines should be laid down for the protection of these rights *to fill the legislative vacuum*" and consequently, it not only laid down a detailed definition of sexual harassment but also imposed a duty on the employer or other responsible persons in workplaces or other institutions "to prevent or deter the commission of acts of sexual harassment and to provide the procedures for the resolution, settlement or prosecution of acts of sexual harassment by taking all steps required." The Court also issued guidelines covering several different aspects, including taking preventive steps, initiating criminal proceedings under the criminal law, taking disciplinary action, establishing a complaint mechanism, and spreading awareness of the guidelines. The Supreme Court concluded by directing that "the above guidelines and norms would be strictly observed in all work places for the preservation and enforcement of the right to gender equality of the working women. These directions would be binding and enforceable in law until suitable legislation is enacted to occupy the field," having been extended to be applied in nonstate entities such as private companies.[172]

[171] See AIR 1997 SC 3011; Surya Deva, *Indian National Report*, p. 8 (footnote 49).

[172] *Id.*, p. 9.

In these sorts of judicial review decisions, where the constitutional courts issue provisional regulations by interpreting the Constitution, it is possible to mention one decision issued by the Federal Supreme Tribunal of Brazil, through a *súmula vinculante* in which the Tribunal, after adopting a few decisions regarding the prohibition of nepotism in the Judiciary, concluded that, for the implementation of such practice, no formal law needed to be sanctioned because it can be deducted from the principles contained in article 37 of the Constitution. The Tribunal declared that the practice of nepotism (i.e., the appointment of a spouse, partner, or parent of the director or chief executive) in any of the branches of government of the Union, the States, the federal District, and the Municipalities violates the Constitution.[173] Another important case for the Brazilian Federal Supreme Tribunal was the decision adopted when analyzing the constitutionality of the demarcation of indigenous people's land in the area of Raposa Serra do Sol, in Roraima State. After many discussions and political conflicts, the Tribunal decided to sustain the constitutionality of the demarcation made by the Federal Union, but it determined for the demarcation of indigenous peoples' land a detailed set of rules establishing the conditions to always be met in all future demarcation process; this resulted in a decision with *erga omnes* effects.[174]

In Venezuela, it is possible to find cases where the Constitutional Chamber of the Supreme Tribunal of Justice, in the absence of corresponding statutes, has issued decisions containing legislation. In Decision No. 1682 of August 15, 2005, answering a recourse of interpretation of article 77 of the Constitution, the Constitutional Chamber, in exercising its normative jurisdiction, established that the *de facto* stable relations between men and women have the same effects as marriage. The Constitutional Chambers established that the decision applied to all of the legal regime regarding such *de facto* stable relations and determined the civil effects of marriage applicable to them, including matters of pensions, use of partner's name,

173 See *Súmula Vinculante* nº 13, STF, *DJ* 1º.set.2006, ADC 12 MC/DF, Rel. Min. Carlos Britto; Luis Roberto Barroso et al., "Notas sobre a questão do legislador positivo," *Brazilian National Report III*, pp. 33–37.

174 See STF, *DJ* 25.set.2009, Pet 3388/RR, Rel. Min. Carlos Britto; Luis Roberto Barroso et al., "Notas sobre a questão do Legislador Positivo," *Brazilian National Report III*, pp. 43–46.

economic regime, and succession rights, thereby completely substituting itself for the Legislator.[175]

In another case, the Constitutional Chamber has also legislated, this time *ex officio*, and in a decision issued in an amparo proceeding regarding the process of in vitro fertilization. In Decision No. 1456 of July 27, 2006, in effect, the Chamber also exercised its normative jurisdiction to determine *ex officio* the legislative provisions on the matter, including rules on parenthood, assisted reproduction, nonconsensual fertilization, retributive donation, surrogate mothers, and rules on succession.[176] In this case, the Chamber not only acted as positive legislator in establishing all the provisions applicable in case of in vitro fertilization or assisted reproduction, but also ordered the application of the new rules to the particular case involved in the decision, thus giving retroactive effects to the legislative provisions it created, in violation of article 24 of the Constitution, which prohibits the retroactivity of laws.

In all these cases of judicial means established or developed for controlling legislative omissions, it is always important to have in mind the warning given by Justice Cardozo about this problem: "[L]egislative inaction – or the inability of groups to win the necessary votes to pass desired legislation – may lead to attempts to have the judiciary accomplish by judicial review what the legislature has refused to do."[177]

[175] See Decision 1682 of July 15, 2005, *Carmela Manpieri, Interpretation of article 77 of the Constitution* case; http://www.tsj.gov.ve/decisiones/scon/Julio/1682-150705-04-3301.htm. See also Daniela Urosa Maggi, *Venezuelan National Report*, p. 19.

[176] See Decision nº 1456 of July 27, 2006, *Yamilex Núñez de Godoy* case; http://www.tsj.gov.ve/decisiones/scon/Julio/1456-270706-05-1471.htm. See also Daniela Urosa Maggi, *Venezuelan National Report*, pp. 19–20.

[177] See Christopher Wolfe, *The Rise of Modern Judicial Review. From Constitutional Interpretation to Judge-Made Law*, Basic Books, New York 1986, p. 238; *La transformación de la interpretación constitucional*, Civitas, Madrid 1991, p. 325.

Chapter 5

CONSTITUTIONAL COURTS AS LEGISLATORS ON MATTERS OF JUDICIAL REVIEW

One particular aspect in which it is possible to identify interferences of constitutional courts in the legislative function is precisely in matters of legislation on judicial review, particularly in countries with concentrated systems of judicial review, in which not only constitutional courts have created rules of procedure in spite of the existence of a special statute establishing them, but also they have assumed new powers of judicial review and created new actions that can be filed before the courts.

I. CONSTITUTIONAL COURTS CREATING THEIR OWN JUDICIAL REVIEW POWERS

1. *The Judge-Made Law Regarding the Diffuse System of Judicial Review*

In the diffuse, or decentralized, system of judicial review, being a power attributed to all courts, judicial review has always been deduced from the principle of the supremacy of the Constitution and of the duty of the courts to discard statutes contrary to the Constitution, always preferring the latter. Such power of the courts, consequently, does not need an express provision in the Constitution that instructs courts to give preference to the Constitution. As Chief Justice Marshall definitively stated in *Marbury v. Madison* (1 Cranch 137 (1803)):

> Those who apply the rule to particular cases, must of necessity expound and interpret that rule . . . so, if a law be in opposition to the constitution . . . the court must determine which of these conflicting rules governs the case: This is the very essence of judicial duty. If then, the courts are to regard the constitution, and the constitution is superior to any ordinary act of the legislature, the constitution, and not such ordinary act, must govern the case to which they both apply.

Consequently, because of this essential link between supremacy of the Constitution and judicial review, in the United States, judicial review was a creation of the courts – this was also the case in Norway (1820);[1] in Greece (1897);[2] and in Argentina, a few decades later, where judicial review was also a creation of the respective Supreme of High Court, based on the principles of supremacy of the Constitution and judicial duty in applying the law.

In Argentina, the first case in which judicial review was exercised for a federal statute was the *Sojo* case (1887), concerning the unconstitutionality of a law that tried to extend the original jurisdiction of the Supreme Court,[3] similar to *Marbury v. Madison*. In Argentina, the Supreme Court has also developed in case law the contours of its judicial review powers, including binding effects –what has been called an "Argentinean *stare decisis*" effect[4] – and in some cases of protection of collective rights, *erga omnes* effects.[5]

2. *The Extension of Judicial Review Powers to Ensure the Protection of Fundamental Rights*

But most important, particularly regarding the protection of fundamental rights and liberties, constitutional courts in many Latin American countries, in their character of supreme interpreter of the Constitution, in the absence of legislation, have created the action of amparo as a special judicial means for the protection of fundamental rights. This was the case also in Argentina, where, in the 1950s, when constitutional rights, other than physical and personal freedom protected by the *habeas corpus* action, were protected only through ordinary judicial means, the courts found that *habeas corpus* could not be used for such purpose. That is why, for instance, in 1933, the Supreme Court of the Nation in the *Bertotto* case[6] rejected the application of

1 See Eivind Smith, *Norway National Report*, p. 1.

2 See Julia Iliopoulos-Strangas and Stylianos-Ioannis G. Koutnatzis, *Greek National Report*, p. 2.

3 See H. Quiroga Lavié, *Derecho constitucional*, Buenos Aires 1978, p. 481. Before 1863, the first Supreme Court decisions were adopted in constitutional matters but referred to provincial and executive acts.

4 See Néstor P. Sagües, "Los efectos de las sentencias constitucionales en el derecho argentino," in *Anuario Iberoamericano de Justicia Constitucional*, Centro de Estudios Políticos y Constitucionales, nº 12, 2008, Madrid 2008, p. 347.

5 See *Halabi* case, Fallos 332: (2009); Alejandra Rodríguez Galán and Alfredo Mauricio Vítolo, *Argentinean National Report I*, p. 12.

6 See the references to the *Bertotto* case in Joaquín Brage Camazano, *La jurisdicción constitucional de la libertad (Teoría general, Argentina, México, Corte Interamericana de*

the *habeas corpus* proceeding to obtain judicial protection of other constitutional rights. This situation radically changed in 1957 as a result of the decision of the *Angel Siri* case, where the petitioner requested amparo for the protection of his freedom of press and his right to work (because of the closing of the newspaper, *Mercedes*, which he directed in the province of Buenos Aires). This case eventually led the Supreme Court, in a decision of December 27, 1957, to admit the action of amparo, because it found that the courts needed to protect all constitutional rights, even in the absence of a statutory regulation on such action.[7] This important decision was followed by another, the *Samuel Kot* case, of October 5, 1958, where the Supreme Court extended the scope of the amparo proceeding to include the protection of constitutional rights against individuals, not only against authorities.[8] In 1958, the amparo action was regulated in a federal statute, and in the 1994 constitutional reform, it was incorporated in the Constitution (article 43). Nonetheless, before the constitutional reform took place recognizing collective rights like the right to a clean environment and consumers' rights, the Supreme Courts in *Verbitsky* (2005) and *Halabi* (2009) introduced another important reform to the *habeas corpus* and amparo proceeding by recognizing collective protection and class actions.[9] In particular, for class actions, the Supreme Court developed the main rules concerning new class actions, explaining how the courts must act in face of legislative silence on the matter and defining their character, standing conditions, and requirements for representation.[10]

Derechos Humanos), Editorial Porrúa, Instituto Mexicano de Derecho Procesal Constitucional, Mexico City 2005, p. 66.

7 See the reference to the *Siri* case in José Luis Lazzarini, *El juicio de amparo*, La Ley, Buenos Aires, 1987, pp. 26 ff., 373 ff.; Alí Joaquín Salgado, *Juicio de amparo y acción de inconstitucionalidad*, Ed. Astrea, Buenos Aires, 1987, p. 5; Néstor Pedro Sagües, *Derecho procesal constitucional: Acción de amparo*, Vol. 3, 2nd ed., Editorial Astrea, Buenos Aires, 1988, pp. 9 ff. See also Alejandra Rodríguez Galán and Alfredo Mauricio Vítolo, *Argentinean National Report I*, p. 7; Néstor Pedro Sagües, *Argentinean National Report II*, pp. 13–14.

8 See the references to the *Samuel Kot Ltd.* case of September 5, 1958, in S. V. Linares Quintana, *Acción de amparo*, Buenos Aires, 1960, p. 25; José Luis Lazzarini, *El juicio de amparo*, La Ley, Buenos Aires, 1987, pp. 243 ff.; Alí Joaquín Salgado, *Juicio de amparo y acción de inconstitucionalidad*, Ed. Astrea, Buenos Aires, 1987, p. 6.; Susana Albanese, *Garantías judiciales: Algunos requisitos del debido proceso legal en el derecho internacional de los derechos humanos*, Ediar S. A. Editora, Comercial, Industrial y Financiera, Buenos Aires, 2000; Augusto M. Morillo et al., *El amparo: Régimen procesal*, 3rd ed., Librería Editora Platense SRL, La Plata 1998, 430 pp.; Néstor Pedro Sagües, *Derecho procesal constitucional*, Vol. 3, *Acción de amparo*, 2nd ed., Editorial Astrea, Buenos Aires, 1988.

9 See *Verbitsky* case, Fallos 328:1146 (2005); and *Halabi* case, Fallos 332:(2009); Alejandra Rodríguez Galán and Alfredo Mauricio Vítolo, *Argentinean National Report I*, p. 9.

10 See Néstor Pedro Sagües, *Argentinean National Report II*, pp. 14–19.

In India, the most important remedy used for judicial review is that established in articles 32 and 226 of the Constitution to enforce fundamental rights, which provides that the Supreme Court shall have the power for such purpose to issue directions or orders or writs, including writs in the nature of *habeas corpus*, mandamus, prohibition, *quo warranto*, and certiorari, whichever may be appropriate. The Court has interpreted this remedial provision widely so as to liberalize the standing requirements,[11] thus enabling the courts to entertain voices (including in the form of judicial review petitions) from a larger populace, and on occasion even from civil society organizations, which has approached the Court for the enforcement of collective or diffused rights. This has given rise to what is called public interest litigation (PIL) in India, which has led to the Court's expansive interpretation of fundamental rights and matters related to them; thus, it has led to the courts acting as legislators.[12]

In 1999, the Dominican Republic was still the only Latin American country without a constitutional provision establishing the amparo, a situation that did not impede the Supreme Court of Justice from allowing it, applying for that purpose the American Convention on Human Rights. That occurred in a decision of February 24, 1999, in the *Productos Avon S.A.* case, when the Supreme Court, on the basis of the American Convention on Human Rights, admitted the amparo recourse for the protection of constitutional rights, assigned the power to decide on amparo matters to the courts of first instance,[13] and established the general procedural rules for the proceeding. Later, the amparo action was regulated in a statute (2006), and in the constitutional reform of 2009, it was incorporated in the Constitution (article 72). In these cases, the principle of prevalence of human rights declared in the Constitution led the Supreme Courts to create this specific judicial mean of protection, so it was extended in all Latin America.[14]

The Courts, nonetheless, can interpret the judicial review powers attributed to them in the Constitution and adapt their implementation or expand their

[11] See *S P Gupta v. Union of India* AIR 1982 SC 149; *PUDR v. Union of India* AIR 1982 SC 1473; *Bandhua Mukti Morcha v. Union of India* (1984) 3 SCC 161; Surya Deva, *Indian National Report*, p. 2.

[12] See Surya Deva, *Indian National Report*, pp. 2, 4–5.

[13] See Samuel Arias Arzeno, "El amparo en la República Dominicana: Su evolución jurisprudencial," *Revista Estudios Jurídicos*, Vol. XI, nº 3, Ediciones Capeldom, 2002.

[14] See Allan R. Brewer-Carías, *Constitutional Protection of Human Rights in Latin America: A Comparative Study on Amparo Proceeding*, Cambridge University Press, New York 2009, p. 68.

scope, as has occurred in Brazil with the *mandado de injunçào*, to effectively control the relative omissions of the Legislator. In Brazil this can be found in a leading case deciding on the application to civil servants of the rules of strike in the private sector.[15] This has led Luís Roberto Barroso to say that, because of this change in its jurisprudence, the Federal Supreme Tribunal, with constitutional authorization, "has given a step, a long step, in the sense of acting as positive legislator."[16]

In the Slovak Republic, the constitutional complaint for the protection for fundamental rights, given the delay established for the entry in force of the constitutional amendment of article 127 establishing the complaint (December 31, 201), was "created" by the Court despite the previous means of protection repealed as of July 1, 2001. As it has been summarized by Ján Svák and Lucia Berdisová, from July 1, 2001, until December 31, 2001, there did not exist a national means by which natural or legal persons could have pleaded the infringement of their fundamental rights and freedoms before the Constitutional Court. The Constitutional Court filled this vacuum of protection with extensive interpretation of article 124 of the Constitution, which states that "the Constitutional Court shall be an independent judicial authority vested with the mandate to protect constitutionality." The Court deduced from this article that it does have the competence to deal with individual motions by natural persons and legal persons that are pleading infringement of their constitutional rights (no matter how they were called – petition or complaint) even in the period of time from July 1, 2001, until December 31, 2001.[17] The Constitutional Court argued:

> The Constitutional Court is according to art. 124 of the Constitution the judicial authority for protection of constitutionality. This article constitutes the competence of the Constitutional Court to protect mainly fundamental rights and freedoms guaranteed by the Constitution. The Constitutional Court is led by this imperative even after the nullification of the paragraphs about petition (from July 1, 2001) until the entry into force of art. 127 of the Constitution (January 1, 2002) and so it is entitled and obliged to provide individual protection of fundamental rights and freedoms while the court also relies on art. 1 of the Constitution, which states that Slovak Republic is the state governed by the rule of law. That is why fundamental rights and

[15] See STF, DJ 31.out.2008, MI 708/DF, Rel. Min. Gilmar Mendes; Luis Roberto Barroso et al., "Notas sobre a questão do legislador positivo," *Brazilian National Report III*, pp. 28–33.

[16] See Luis Roberto Barroso et al., "Notas sobre a questão do Legislador Positivo," *Brazilian National Report III*, p. 33.

[17] See Ján Svák and Lucia Berdisová, *Slovak National Report*, p. 9.

freedoms cannot be even temporarily deprived of judicial protection as to art. 124 of the Constitution in connection with other articles that guarantee fundamental rights and freedoms.[18]

The Constitutional Court thus acted as if the institute of petition had been repealed not from July 1, 2001, but from January 1, 2002.

In Venezuela, the Constitutional Chamber, in Decision No. 656 of June 30, 2000, admitted the direct amparo action for the protection of diffuse and collective rights and interests established in the Constitution[19] and established the standing conditions for the filing of the action in Decision No. 1395 of November 21, 2000.[20] It ruled a year later on the rules of procedure to be applicable in such cases in Decision No. 1571 of August 22, 2001.[21]

3. *The Need for the Express Provision in the Constitution of Judicial Review Powers of the Constitutional Jurisdiction and Its Deviation*

Particularly in concentrated systems of judicial review, the idea of the supremacy of the constitution and the duty of the courts to say which law is applicable in a particular case[22] has a limitation: the power to judge the unconstitutionality of legislative acts and other state acts of similar rank or value is reserved to a supreme court of justice or to a constitutional court or tribunal. Thus, in the concentrated system of judicial review, all courts have the power only to act as a constitutional judge and to decide on the constitutionality of other norms applicable to the case, regarding acts other

18 Decision of the Constitutional Court nº III. ÚS 117/01. The Court similarly justifies its decision in III. ÚS 124/01: In the period of time from July 1, 2001, to December 31, 2001, the competence of the Constitutional Court was founded on the art. 124 in connection with art. 1 of the Constitution and it was so "in order to provide protection of constitutionality including protection of guaranteed fundamental rights and freedoms of natural persons and legal persons." See also II. ÚS 80/01, III. ÚS 100/01, III. ÚS 116/01; Ján Svák and Lucia Berdisová, *Slovak National Report*, p. 9 (footnote 14).

19 See Decision nº 656 of June 30, 2000, *Dilia Parra Guillen (Peoples' Defender)* case, at http://www.tsj.gov.ve/decisiones/scon/Junio/656-300600-00-1728%20.htm. See also Daniela Urosa Maggi, *Venezuelan National Report*, p. 11.

20 See Decision nº 1395 of November 21, 2000, *William Dávila* case, *Revista de Derecho Público*, nº 84, Editorial Jurídica Venezolana, Caracas, 2000, pp. 330 ff.; Daniela Urosa Maggi, *Venezuelan National Report*, p. 12.

21 See Decision nº 1571 of August 22, 2001, *Asodeviprilara* case; http://www.tsj.gov.ve/decisiones/scon/Agosto/1571-220801-01-1274%20.htm; Daniela Urosa Maggi, *Venezuelan National Report*, p. 12.

22 See W. K. Geck, "Judicial Review of Statutes: A Comparative Survey of Present Institutions and Practices," *Cornell Law Quarterly*, 51, 1966, p. 278.

than statutes or acts adopted in direct execution of the Constitution.[23] Consequently, the concentrated system of judicial review, based also on the supremacy of the Constitution, when reserving constitutional justice functions regarding certain state acts to a constitutional jurisdiction, cannot be developed by deduction through the work of the supreme court decisions, as happened in many countries with the diffuse system of judicial review.

On the contrary, of course, because of the limits that the system imposes on the duty and power of all judges to say which law is applicable in the cases they are to decide, only when prescribed *expressis verbis* through constitutional regulations is it possible to establish the concentrated system of judicial review. The Constitution, as the supreme law of the land, is the only text that can establish limits on the general power and duty of all courts to say which is the law applicable in a particular case and to assign that power and duty in certain cases regarding certain state acts to a specific constitutional body, whether the supreme court of justice or a constitutional court or tribunal.

Therefore, the concentrated system of judicial review must be established and regulated expressly in the Constitution,[24] as constitutional courts are always constitutional bodies, that is, state organs expressly created and regulated in the Constitution, whether they be the supreme court of justice of a given country or a specially created constitutional court, tribunal, or council.

The consequence of the express character of the system of judicial review is that, in principle, on the one hand, only the Constitution can determine the judicial review powers of constitutional courts not being allowed to create without constitutional support different means of judicial review; and on the other hand, only the legislation issued by the Legislator can develop the rules of procedure and the way constitutional courts can exercise their powers of judicial review.

23 See Manuel García Pelayo, "El 'Status' del Tribunal Constitucional," *Revista Española de Derecho Constitucional*, 1, Madrid 1981, p. 19; Eduardo García de Enterría, *La Constitución como norma y el Tribunal Constitucional*, Madrid 1981, p. 65. In particular, in concentrated systems, the tribunals or courts empowered with administrative justice functions can always act as constitutional judge regarding administrative acts. See C. Frank, *Les fonctions juridictionnelles du Conseil d'Etat dans l'ordre constitutionnel*, Paris 1974.

24 See Allan R. Brewer-Carías, *Judicial Review in Comparative Law*, Cambridge University Press, Cambridge 1989, pp. 185 ff.; Jorge Carpizo, *El Tribunal Constitucional y sus límites*, Grijley Ed., Lima 2009, p. 41.

The practice in many countries, nonetheless, has been different – sometimes they adapt their own judicial review powers, and other times they create them.

As aforementioned, one of the main characteristics of the concentrated judicial review system is that the constitutional court exclusively can make constitutional attributions on matters of judicial review of legislation. Such power can only be given to specific constitutional organs by means of a constitutional provision. Consequently, contrary to the diffuse method of judicial review, the concentrated judicial review powers of the constitutional courts cannot be created by the courts themselves, that is, they cannot be the product of judge-made law. That is why in all constitutional systems where a concentrated system of judicial review has been established, it is the Constitution that creates or regulates the constitutional jurisdiction attributing to a specific constitutional court the power of judicial review regarding legislation; the courts are not allowed themselves to create new judicial review powers not attributed to them in the Constitution.

But constitutional courts, in some cases, have extended or adapted their constitutional powers. For instance, they created the technique of exercising judicial review in declaring statutes unconstitutional but without annulling them, as well as the technique of extending the application of the unconstitutional statute for a term and issuing directives to the Legislator for it to legislate in harmony with the Constitution. This technique was developed in Germany, as mentioned by I. Härtel, "without statutory authorization, in fact *contra legem*, as the BVerfG assumed until 1970 the compelling connection between the unconstitutionality and the invalidity of a norm."[25] In the reform of the Federal Constitutional Tribunal Law sanctioned in 1970, the Legislator officially recognized the judge-made law (Articles 31, 79), thereby allowing the Tribunal to declare a provision unconstitutional without annulling it, a matter that still is discussed.[26] That is why – referring to the decision of the Federal Constitutional Tribunal on the

25 See I. Härtel, *German National Report*, p. 8; Francisco Fernández Segado, "Algunas reflexiones generales en torno a los efectos de las sentencias de inconstitucionalidad y a la relatividad de ciertas fórmulas esterotipadas vinculadas a ellas," in *Anuario Iberoamericano de Justicia Constitucional*, Centro de Estudios Políticos y Constitucionales, nº 12, 2008, Madrid 2008, p. 162.

26 See Christian Behrendt, *Le judge constitutionnel, un législateur-cadre positif. Un analyse comparative en droit francais, belge et allemande*, Bruylant, Brussels 2006, pp. 93, 94; F. Fernández Segado, *Spanish National Report*, p. 6.

inheritance tax case,[27] where the Tribunal declared unconstitutional the current capital-transfer tax and fixed a deadline of December 31, 2008, for the Legislator to restore a legal condition in conformity with the Constitution – Härtel also pointed out, "The BVerfG has therefore as a kind of 'emergency Legislator' created a law-like condition; it has 'invented' a new decision type."[28] The same can be said regarding the powers that the Federal Constitutional Tribunal has assumed, for example, issuing provisional legislative rules and measures with substitute legislation as a consequence of the declaration of unconstitutionality of certain provisions. The Constitutional Court in these cases, through judge-made law, has assumed a role that principally corresponds to the Legislator.[29]

In Spain, the same process of judge-made law has been developed by the Constitutional Tribunal, which can declare provisions unconstitutional without annulling them, despite a provision to the contrary in the Organic Law of the Constitutional Tribunal, which states: "[W]hen the decision declares the unconstitutionality, it will also declare the nullity of the challenged provisions" (article 39.1). Spain's Constitutional Tribunal also tried to legitimate this *contra legem* procedural technique in the draft reform of its Organic Law in 2005, which was not sanctioned as drafted.[30]

But in other cases, constitutional courts have created their own judicial review powers not established in the Constitution. As aforementioned, in concentrated systems of judicial review, constitutional courts as Constitutional Jurisdiction cannot exist and cannot exercise their functions of judicial review of legislation without an express constitutional provision that establishes them. That is, as a matter of principle, in democratic regimes governed by the rule of law and the principle of separation of powers, all the powers of constitutional courts must be expressly provided for in the Constitution or in the law as prescribed in the Constitution. Therefore, within the concentrated system of judicial review, it is not possible for the constitutional court to create its own judicial review powers or to expand

27 BVerfG, court order from 2006-11-7, reference number: 1 BvL 10/02. See I. Härtel, *German National Report*, p. 8.

28 See I. Härtel, quoting Steiner, *ZEV* 2007, 120 (121) and Schlaich/Korioth, *Das Bundesverfassungsgericht*, 7th ed. 2007, margin number 395, *German National Report*, p. 9.

29 See Christian Behrendt, *Le judge constitutionnel, un législateur-cadre positif. Un analyse comparative en droit francais, belge et allemande*, Bruylant, Brussels 2006, p. 354.

30 See F. Fernández Segado, *Spanish National Report*, p. 6, 11.

those established in the Constitution.[31] Constitutional courts are an exception regarding the general power of the courts to apply and guarantee the supremacy of the Constitution, being the Constituent Power the one that in order to preserve the Constitution, can exclude or restrict ordinary courts from that task. Being then an exception, and because of the assignment to a constitutional court of the monopoly of Constitutional Jurisdiction, it must be expressly created in the Constitution with expressly established powers.

Nonetheless, in some countries, it is possible to find a deformation of this principle, as in Venezuela,[32] where the Constitutional Chamber of the Supreme Tribunal of Justice, despite the powers established in article 336 of the Constitution, has created new powers of judicial review not envisaged in the Constitution. In particular, without any constitutional or legal support, the Constitutional Chamber of the Supreme Tribunal created in 2000 a recourse for the abstract interpretation of the Constitution, based on the interpretation of its Article 335, which grants the Supreme Tribunal the character of "superior and final interpreter of the Constitution."[33] Although in the Constitution the only recourse of interpretation established is the recourse of interpretation of statutes that can be filed before the various Chambers of the Supreme Tribunal, and only in cases expressly provided for in each statute (Article 266.6), the Constitutional Chamber created this recourse, providing as the only condition for standing that the petitioner must invoke an actual, legitimate, and juridical interest in the interpretation that is needed regarding his or her particular and specific situation. For such purpose, the Constitutional Chamber has held that the petition must always point to "the obscurity, the ambiguity or contradiction between

[31] See, e.g., Francisco Eguiguren and Liliana Salomé, *Peruvian National Report I*, p. 17; Sanja Barić and Petar Bačić, *Croatian National Report*, p. 3.

[32] See Allan R. Brewer-Carías, "La ilegítima mutación de la constitución por el juez constitucional: La inconstitucional ampliación y modificación de su propia competencia en materia de control de constitucionalidad," in *Libro Homenaje a Josefina Calcaño de Temeltas*, Fundación de Estudios de Derecho Administrativo (FUNEDA), Caracas 2009, pp. 319–362.

[33] The recourse was created by Decision nº 1077 of September 22, 2000, *Servio Tulio León* case; *Revista de Derecho Público*, nº 83, Editorial Jurídica Venezolana, Caracas 2000, pp. 247 ff. The procedural rules regarding the recourse were established in decision of the same Constitutional Chamber, nº 1415 of November 22, 2000, *Freddy Rangel Rojas* case. See the comments to these decisions in Allan R. Brewer-Carías, "*Quis Custodiet Ipsos Custodes*: De la interpretación constitucional a la inconstitucionalidad de la interpretación," in *VIII Congreso Nacional de derecho Constitucional, Perú*, Fondo Editorial 2005, Colegio de Abogados de Arequipa, Arequipa, September 2005, pp. 463–489; *Revista de Derecho Público*, nº 105, Editorial Jurídica Venezolana, Caracas 2006, pp. 7–27; Allan R. Brewer-Carías, "Le recours d'interprétation abstrait de la Constitution au Vénézuéla," in *Renouvau du droit constitutionnel: Mélanges en l'honneur de Louis Favoreu*, Dalloz, Paris 2007, pp. 61–70.

constitutional provisions," and the decisions of the Chamber have *erga omnes* and *ex nunc* effects.[34] This sort of recourse seeking the abstract interpretation of statutes gives the Constitutional Court powers to issue bindings "opinions," which generally are not related to a specific case or controversy, which in general terms is considered a function outside the scope of constitutional courts.

To create this recourse, the Chamber based its decision on Article 26 of the Constitution, which establishes the people's right to have access to justice, considering therefore that "citizens do not require a statutory provision establishing the recourse for constitutional interpretation, to file it." On the basis of that argument, the Chamber found that no constitutional or legal provision was necessary to allow the development of such recourse.[35] Three years later, the National Assembly sanctioned the Organic Law of the Supreme Tribunal, which regulated the general means for judicial review, as it was the will of the Legislator to exclude from the powers of the Constitutional Chamber the ability to decide on recourses of abstract interpretation of the Constitution. Nonetheless, the Constitutional Chamber has continued to develop the regulation of the recourse in subsequent decisions, for the purpose of issuing declarative ruling of mere certainty on the scope and content of a constitutional provision.[36]

This extraordinary interpretive power, though theoretically an excellent judicial means for the interpretation of the Constitution, unfortunately has been extensively abused by the Constitutional Chamber to distort important constitutional provisions, to interpret them in a way contrary to the text, or to justify constitutional solutions according to the will of the Executive, because the initiative to file many recourses has been in the hands of the Attorney General. This was the case, for instance, with the various Constitutional Chamber's decisions regarding the consultative and repeal

[34] Of the Constitutional Chamber, see Decision nº 1309 of June 19, 2001, case: *Hermann Escarráa*, and Decision nº 1684 November 4, 2008, case: *Carlos Eduardo Giménez Colmenárez*, *Revista de Derecho Público*, nº 116, Editorial Jurídica Venezolana, Caracas 2008, pp. 66 ff

[35] See Decision nº 1077 of the Constitutional Chamber of September 22, 2000, case: *Servio Tulio León Briceño*, *Revista de Derecho Público*, nº 83, Caracas, 2000, pp. 247 ff. This criterion was ratified later in decision nº 1347, dated September 11, 2000, *Revista de Derecho Público*, nº 84, Editorial Jurídica Venezolana, Caracas 2000, pp. 264 ff.

[36] See, e.g., Decision nº 1347 of the Constitutional Chamber, dated November 9, 2000, *Revista de Derecho Público*, nº 84, Editorial Jurídica Venezolana, Caracas 2000, pp. 264 ff.; Decision nº 2651 of October 2003 (case: *Ricardo Delgado (Interpretación artículo 174 de la Constitución))*, *Revista de Derecho Público*, nº 93-96, Editorial Jurídica Venezolana, Caracas 2003, pp. 327 ff.

referenda between 2002 and 2004, where the Chamber confiscated and distorted the people's constitutional right to political participation.[37] One of the last notoriously politically motivated decisions of the Constitutional Chamber that has been issued using these powers was in answering a petition filed by the Attorney General, not for the purpose of interpreting the Constitution but for the purpose of interpreting a decision of the Inter-American Court of Human Rights that condemned the Venezuelan State for violations of due process rights and judicial guarantees of various superior judges who were illegally dismissed.[38] The result of this process before the Supreme Court was that by means of Decision No. 1.939 of December 18, 2008, the Constitutional Chamber did not "interpret" anything, particularly because judicial decisions are not to be interpreted but to be applied, but just considered the international Court decision was unenforceable in Venezuela, recommending the Executive to denounce the American Convention on Human Rights.[39]

In another case, the Constitutional Chamber created a judicial review power expanding the scope of an existing provision of the Constitution, as it has happened regarding the general power of review the Constitution grants the Constitutional Chamber regarding final decisions adopted by the courts on matters of amparo proceedings and in cases when the diffuse method of judicial review is applied (article 336.10). Even though the express scope of this discretional power of review regarding judicial decisions issued by inferior courts granted to the Constitutional Chamber is precise, the Chamber has modified the Constitution and has assumed, first, powers of review

[37] See Decision Nos. 1139 of June 5, 2002, *Sergio Omar Calderón Duque y William Dávila Barrios* case; nº 137 of February 13, 2003, *Freddy Lepage y otros* case; nº 2750 of October 21, 2003, *Carlos E. Herrera Mendoza* case; nº 2432 of August 29, 2003, *Luis Franceschi y otros* case; and nº 2404 of August 28, 2003, *Exssel Alí Betancourt Orozco, Interpretación del artículo 72 de la Constitución* case. See the comments on these decisions in Allan R. Brewer-Carías, *La Sala Constitucional versus el estado democrático de derecho: El secuestro del poder electoral y de la Sala Electoral del Tribunal Supremo y la confiscación del derecho a la participación política*, Los Libros de El Nacional, Colección Ares, Caracas 2004.

[38] See decision of the Inter-American Court of Human Rights of August 5, 2008, *Apitz Barbera y otros ("Corte Primera de lo Contencioso Administrativo") vs. Venezuela* case, at http://www.corteidh.or.cr. Excepción Preliminar, Fondo, Reparaciones y Costas, Serie C nº 182.

[39] Decision nº 1.939 of December 18, 2008, *Attorney General Office* case, at http://www.tsj.gov.ve/decisiones/scon/Diciembre/1939-181208-2008-08-1572.html. See the comment on this decision in Allan R. Brewer-Carías, "La interrelación entre los Tribunales Constitucionales de América Latina y la Corte Interamericana de Derechos Humanos, y la cuestión de la inejecutabilidad de sus decisiones en Venezuela," in *Anuario Iberoamericano de Justicia Constitucional*, Centro de Estudios Políticos y Constitucionales, nº 13, Madrid 2009, pp. 99–136. See also Daniela Urosa Maggi, *Venezuelan National Report*, pp. 7–8.

regarding any judicial decision in which a court departs from the interpretation given to a constitutional provision by the same Constitutional Chamber or regarding which the Chamber considers that constitutional principles have been violated by the judicial decision; and second, powers of review on the same grounds of decisions issued by other Chambers of the Supreme Tribunal, consequently assuming a *de facto* superior hierarchy in the Judiciary that the Constitution has not conferred on it.[40] Three years later, the Organic Law of the Supreme Tribunal was sanctioned (2004), and this modification of the Constitution was not included by the National Assembly, a fact that did not prevent the Constitutional Chamber, through a new decision issued the same year, 2004,[41] to insist that the rule it established in 2001, despite the provisions of the Organic Law, was to continue to apply.

Another judicial review power that the Constitutional Chamber has assumed without any constitutional support is the incidental concentrated means of judicial review, which is found in countries where a concentrated system of judicial review is established exclusively – this is nonexistent in countries adopting a mixed system of judicial review where the concentrated method is combined with the diffuse method, as happens in many Latin American countries. Nonetheless, despite Venezuela having a mixed system of judicial review, the Constitutional Chamber in a clearly contradictory way has created the possibility of this incidental means of judicial review for the Constitutional Chamber to decide on the annulment of an unconstitutional statute, which is completely contradictory with the diffuse judicial review powers of all courts.[42]

[40] See Decision nº 93 of February 6, 2001, *Corpoturismo* case, *Revista de Derecho Público*, nº 85–88, Editorial Jurídica Venezolana, Caracas 2001, pp. 406 ff., at http://www.tsj.gov.ve/decisiones/scon/Febrero/93-060201-00-1529%20.htm. See also Daniela Urosa Maggi, *Venezuelan National Report*, p. 6.

[41] See Decision nº 1992 of September 8, 2004, *Peter Hofle* case; http://www.tsj.gov.ve/decisiones/scon/Septiembre/1992-080904-03-2332%20.htm. See also Daniela Urosa Maggi, *Venezuelan National Report*, p. 7.

[42] See Decision 2588 of December 11, 2001, *Yrene Martínez* case, in http://www.tsj.gov.ve/decisiones/scon/Diciembre/2588-111201-01-1096.htm; Decision 806 of April 24, 2002, *Sintracemento* case (annulment of article 43 of the Organic Law of the Supreme Tribunal), at http://www.tsj.gov.ve/decisiones/scon/Abril/806-240402-00-3049.htm; Daniela Urosa Maggi, *Venezuelan National Report*, p. 9.

II. CONSTITUTIONAL COURTS CREATING PROCEDURAL RULES ON JUDICIAL REVIEW PROCESSES

One of the specific matters in which judicial review of legislative omissions has taken place has been in the cases where constitutional courts have created rules of procedures for the exercise of their constitutional attributions when those have not been established in the legislation regulating their functions. For such purpose, constitutional courts, such as the Constitutional Tribunal of Peru, have claimed to have procedural autonomy in exercising their extended powers to develop and complement their decisions, but the procedural rules applicable in the judicial review process are not expressly regulated in statutes.[43] Nonetheless, the Constitutional Tribunal of Peru has established some limits to its procedural autonomy; its exercise cannot expand judicial review powers of the Tribunal that are not expressly established in the Constitution.[44]

In Germany, the same principle of procedural autonomy (*Verfahrensautonomie*) has been used to explain the powers developed by the Federal Constitutional Tribunal to complement procedural rules of judicial review. This was the case, for instance, with the application of article 35 of the Law of the Federal Constitutional Tribunal, which establishes that the Court can establish how such execution will take place. On the basis of this provision, for instance, the Federal Constitutional Court established a term for its decision to be applied, which is fixed according to different rules, for instance, a precise date like the end of the legislative term.

In other cases, judicial interference on legislative matters related to rules of procedures on matters of judicial review has been more intense. For instance, in Colombia, the Constitutional Court has assumed the exclusive competency to establish the effects of its own decisions, considering unconstitutional and annulling the provisions of the Law (Decree 2,067 of 1991) regulating its organization an functions in which the Legislator established rules regarding such effects (Articles 21 and 22).[45]

In Venezuela, the Constitutional Chamber of the Supreme Tribunal of Justice, in the absence of legislative rules, has established procedural rules, according to the authorization provided in article 19 of its Organic Law to

[43] See Resolution of the Constitutional Tribunal, Exp. nº 0020-2005-AI/TC, FJ 2; Francisco Eguiguren and Liliana Salomé, *Peruvian National Report I*, p. 14; Fernán Altuve-Febres, *Peruvian National Report II*, pp. 22–23.

[44] See Francisco Eguiguren and Liliana Salomé, *Peruvian National Report I*, p. 17.

[45] See Decision C-113/93; Germán Alfonso López Daza, *Colombian National Report I*, p. 9.

establish a more convenient procedure for accomplishing its constitutional justice functions, "provided that they have legal basis." Consequently, in these cases, it has invoked its normative jurisdiction to establish the procedural rules for judicial review when not regulated in statutes. This has happened, precisely, on matters of judicial review regarding absolute legislative omission and the *habeas data* proceeding.

Regarding judicial review of absolute omissions, though established in the Constitution (article 336.7), its procedure was not regulated in the 2004 Organic Law of the Supreme Tribunal; consequently, the Constitutional Chamber in Decision No. 1556 of July 9, 2002, established the regulation on the matter to be applied until the National Assembly approved the statute establishing the procedural rules.[46]

Regarding the procedural rules on matters of *habeas data* – through which any person can have access to information about him- or herself gathered in official or private registries; has the right to know the use and purpose of such information; and has the right to ask for its updating, rectification, or destruction when erroneous or in cases where it illegitimately affects those rights[47] – in 2001, the Constitutional Chamber assumed exclusive jurisdiction to decide direct *habeas data* actions.[48] The Chamber ruled that it would establish the corresponding procedure for the exercise of its functions: in 2003, in Decision No. 2551 of November 24, 2003,[49] the Chamber based its ruling on the provision of Article 102 of the Law of the Supreme Court of Justice of 1976, which authorized the Supreme Court to establish the rules of procedure in all those cases not expressly regulated by the Legislator. In 2004, the new Organic Law of the Supreme Tribunal was sanctioned, repealing the former 1976 Organic Law of the Supreme Court without providing specific rules of procedure for the *habeas data* action. Thus, the Constitutional Chamber proceeded to modify its previous ruling and reformed the rules of procedure applicable to the *habeas data* actions in

46 See Decision nº 1556 of July 9, 2002, *Alfonzo Albornoz and Gloria de Vicentini* case, at http://www.tsj.gov.ve/decisiones/scon/Julio/1556-090702-01-2337%20.htm. See also Daniela Urosa Maggi, *Venezuelan National Report*, pp. 10–11.

47 See Allan R. Brewer-Carías, *La Constitución de 1999: Derecho constitucional venezolano*, Editorial Jurídica Venezolana, Caracas 2004, Vol. II, pp. 759 ff.

48 See Decision nº 332 of March 14, 2001, *Insaca* case; http://www.tsj.gov.ve/decisiones/scon/Marzo/332-140301-00-1797%20.htm. See also Daniela Urosa Maggi, *Venezuelan National Report*, p. 12.

49 Case: *Jaime Ojeda Ortiz*; http://www.tsj.gov.ve/decisiones/scon/Septiembre/2551-240903-03-0980.htm. See also Daniela Urosa Maggi, *Venezuelan National Report*, p. 13.

Decision No. 1511 of November 9, 2009.[50] The foundation for this decision was the immediate applicability of article 27 of the Constitution establishing the amparo proceeding and the attribution to the Chamber of guaranteeing and interpreting the Constitution. The Court reasoned that it had acted "in order to fill the existing vacuum existing in relation to this highly innovative constitutional action of habeas data."[51]

50 See *Mercedes Josefina Ramírez, Acción de Habeas Data* case; http://www.tsj.gov.ve/decisiones/scon/Noviembre/1511-91109-2009-09-0369.html See in Daniela Urosa Maggi, *Venezuelan National Report*, p. 13.

51 See Allan R. Brewer-Carías, El proceso constitucional de las acciones de habeas data en Venezuela: las sentencias de la Sala Constitucional como fuente del Derecho Procesal Constitucional," in Eduardo Andrés Velandia Canosa (coord.), *Homenaje al Maestro Héctor Fix Zamudio. Derecho Procesal Constitucional. Memorias del Primer Congreso Colombiano de Derecho Procesal Constitucional* Mayo 26, 27 y 28 de 2010, Bogotá 2010, pp. 289–295.

FINAL REMARKS

From all of what I have said, and after analyzing the role of constitutional courts as positive legislators in comparative law – leaving aside the cases for the pathology of judicial review that are directed not to reinforcing democratic principles and evolution but to dismantling democracy using in an illegitimate way a democratic tool[1] – it is possible to deduce the following two conclusions.

First, as noted at the beginning of this study, there is no longer a sharp distinction between two models of judicial review. In the contemporary world there is the experience of judicial review systems in a transformation, convergence, and mixture that was not possible to envision one hundred years ago, when the confrontation between the diffuse and concentrated methods of judicial review began to be imagined.

Second, the clear and simple system of the concentrated judicial review model, based on the binomial unconstitutionality-invalidity, or unconstitutionality-nullity, exercised by a Constitutional Court as a negative legislator, is nowadays difficult to defend.[2]

In fact, contemporary constitutional comparative law shows the existence of constitutional courts that have progressively assumed roles that decades ago corresponded only to the Constituent Power or to the Legislator; in some

1 On Venezuela, see Allan R. Brewer-Carías, *Dismantling Democracy in Venezuela: The Chávez Authoritarian Experiment*, Cambridge University Press, New York, 2010.

2 The model, as defined by Judge Marek Safjan, in the *Polish National Report*, was characterized as follows: "It is not the competence of the constitutional court to make laws or to bring into the legal order any normative elements, which have not been established before under an appropriate legislative procedure; therefore, the constitutional court may not replace the legislator in this process. The constitutional review is based on a coherent structure of a hierarchical legal system and the constitutional court has to operate within this order, drawing its own competence from the constitutional legislator. Judgments passed by the constitutional court cannot contain anything that has not been already proclaimed by the supreme norm laid down in the Constitution whereas the role of the constitutional review will always be limited to the application of law – although placed at the highest level of the normative hierarchy – and cannot involve creation of norms." See Marek Safjan, *Polish National Report*, p. 1.

cases, they have discovered and deduced constitutional rules, particularly on matters of human rights not expressively enshrined in the Constitution and that could not be considered to have been the intention of an ancient and original Constituent Power. In other cases, constitutional courts have progressively been performing legislative functions, complementing the Legislator in its role of lawmaker and, in many cases, filling the gaps resulting from legislative omissions, sending guidelines and orders to the Legislator, and even issuing provisional legislation.

Nonetheless, the important results of a comparative law approach to the subject of constitutional courts as positive legislators are the common trends that can be found in all countries and in all legal systems; trends that are more numerous and important than the possible essential and exceptional differences, which confirms the importance of comparative law. That is why, in matters of judicial review, constitutional courts in many countries – to develop their own competencies and exercise their powers to control the constitutionality of statutes, to protect fundamental rights, and to ensure the supremacy of the Constitution – have progressively begun to study and analyze similar work developed in other Courts and in other countries, thus enriching their rulings.

Today, it is common to find in constitutional courts' decisions constant references to decisions issued on similar matters or cases by other constitutional courts. So it can be said that, in general, there is no aversion to using foreign law to interpret, when applicable, the Constitution. On matters of fundamental rights, for instance, the process of the internationalization of the constitutionalization of such rights in the way it has occurred during the past sixty years has resulted in a globalization process regarding the general applicable regime, which is indistinctively used to control the constitutionality or the conventionality of statutes, producing uniform principles of constitutional law never seen before.

Consequently, on the matter of judicial review, it is simply incomprehensible to pretend that the judicial solutions in a given country – on matters of the right to equality and nondiscrimination, or the right to privacy or due process, or the right not to be subject to torture – could be considered an endemic matter exclusively to a particular country, and that in the interpretation of the Constitution of the country, it is impossible to rely on judicial solutions to the same problems in other countries. This is at least a general trend that, with the exception of some judges and scholars in the United States, is possible to identify in comparative law, as a subject like the one studied in this General Report demonstrates. Consequently, in general terms, for a public comparative law scholar, it is incomprehensible that nominees to the U.S. Supreme Court have the almost-inevitable duty to express in their confirmation hearings before the Senate, for example, that "American Law does not permit the use of foreign law or international law to interpret the Constitution," and this a "given" question regarding which "[t]here is no debate."[3] A different matter is the possible use of foreign law in the U.S. universities for academic purposes. Regarding this assertion, Justice Ruth Bader Ginsburg has said that she "frankly [doesn't] understand all the brouhaha lately from Congress and even from some of my colleagues about referring to foreign law," explaining that the controversy was based in the misunderstanding that citing a foreign precedent means the court considers itself bound by foreign law as opposed to merely being influenced by such power as its reasoning holds. That is why she formulated the following question: "Why shouldn't we look to the wisdom of a judge from abroad with at least as much ease as we would read a law review article written by a professor?"[4]

And this is precisely what is now common in all constitutional jurisdictions all over the world: constitutional courts commonly consider that, with respect to foreign law, when they have to decide on the same matter and on the basis of the same principles, in the same way that they would study the matter through others authors' opinions and analysis from books and articles, they can also rely on courts' decisions from other countries, which can be useful because those courts dealt not only with a theoretical proposition, but also with a specific solution already applied to resolve a particular case.

3 Judge Sonia Sotomayor, at the confirmation hearing before the Senate, on July 15, 2009. See "Sotomayor on the Issues," *New York Times*, July 16, 2009, p. A18.

4 See Adam Liptak, "Ginsburg Shares Views on Influence of Foreign Law on Her Court, and Vice Versa," in *New York Times*, April 12, 2009, p. 14.

PART TWO

NATIONAL REPORTS

For the purpose of the general report I wrote for the *XVIII International Congress of Comparative Law*, organized by the International Academy of Comparative and held in Washington, D.C, in July 2010, on the subject of *Constitutional Courts as Positive Legislators*, I received national reports and papers for the following countries: Argentina, Australia, Austria, Belgium, Brazil, Canada, Colombia, Costa Rica, Croatia, Czech Republic, France, Germany, Greece, Hungary, India, Italy, Mexico, Netherlands, Nicaragua, Norway, Peru, Poland, Portugal, Serbia, Slovakia, Spain, Sweden, Switzerland, United Kingdom, United States, and Venezuela.

Only those national reports written in the official languages of the Academy and that were authorized by their authors to be published in this book, are here published.*

* See the complete list of the national reports and papers received in the Apendix.

ARGENTINA

CONSTITUTIONAL COURTS AS POSITIVE LEGISLATORS

Alejandra Rodríguez Galán
Professor, Universidad de Buenos Aires
Board Member, Asociación Argentina de Derecho Comparado
argalan@gmail.com

Alfredo Mauricio Vítolo
Professor, Universidad de Buenos Aires
Board Member, Asociación Argentina de Derecho Comparado
avitolo@derecho.uba.ar

The Argentine Constitution was enacted in 1853, and the country's founding fathers drafted it essentially along the lines of the American Constitution. Like its model, it provides for a strict separation of powers between the three branches of government, the Executive, Legislative, and Judiciary. In the matter at stake, it vests the legislative power of the Nation in a bicameral Congress,[1] and it grants to the Judiciary, formed by a Supreme Court and those inferior tribunals as Congress may establish,[2] the power to "to hear and decide all cases arising under the Constitution and the laws of the Nation."[3] On the basis of this clause, it has been held that courts are not allowed to render any decision or opinion outside the boundaries of a specific case.

According to the Constitution, the Argentine Supreme Court has limited original jurisdiction in cases involving the Provinces, foreign ministers, and

1 Argentine Constitution, Section 44.

2 *Id.*, Section 108.

3 *Id.*, Section 116.

other diplomats, whereas its appellate jurisdiction is regulated by law within the constitutional boundaries of federal jurisdiction.[4]

Since its inception in 1862, the Argentine Supreme Court, following U.S. Supreme Court Justice John Marshall's reasoning in *Marbury v. Madison*,[5] has adopted the American model of judicial review, according to which all courts, federal or provincial and of all levels, have the right to declare an act of Congress, or an action of the Executive, unconstitutional and therefore inapplicable in the case at stake.[6]

One of the oldest Argentine acts still in effect, Law 48, enacted in 1863, sets down the requirements for access to Supreme Court's review. A more recent reform to the National Procedural Code in 1990 grants the Supreme Court the ultimate discretionary decision as to whether or not to hear a case.[7]

Do Argentine courts legislate? Such question poses a dilemma that goes beyond the countermajoritarian difficulty. There is no doubt that when a judge decides a case, the decision, by confronting the action being judged with the law, gives some room for the judicial creation of – at least – rules of individual application by means of construction or by filling in the gaps in the statute being considered.

To the extent that Argentine judges have the power to annul (with *inter parte* effects) unconstitutional laws, they behave as negative legislators – though in a much more limited role that that of European constitutional courts – and exercise political power, as their decision is imposed on the will of the political branches of government, which has prompted some scholars to consider that judicial review in Argentina is, essentially, political.[8]

However, in our opinion, equating this judicial role of the Argentine courts with the congressional power to make the law with general effect applicable to everyone, in the absence of a clear constitutional mandate in that sense; that is to say, that Argentine courts (or even the Argentine Supreme Court) are positive legislators, is somewhat different.

[4] *Id.*, Section 117.

[5] 5 U.S. 137 (1803).

[6] *Ramón Ríos*, Fallos 1:32 (1863); *Domingo Mendoza*, Fallos 3:131 (1865); *Sojo*, Fallos 32:120 (1887); *Di Mascio*, Fallos 311:2478 (1988), J. Belluscio, concurring. On judicial review in Argentina, in general, see Juan V. Sola, *El control judicial de constitucionalidad*, Abeledo Perrot, Buenos Aires, 2001; Alberto B. Bianchi, *Control judicial de constitucionalidad*, 2nd ed., Abaco, Buenos Aires, 2002; Carlos S. Fayt, J., *Supremacía constitucional e independencia de los jueces*, Depalma, Buenos Aires, 1994.

[7] National Code of Federal Civil and Commercial Procedure, Section 280.

[8] Alfonso Santiago (h.), *Los modelos institucionales de la Corte Suprema*, in *Función política de la Corte Suprema*, Abaco-Austral, Buenos Aires, 2000.

It should be pointed out that, in Argentina, judicial decisions, in principle, have only *inter parte* effects, as no constitutionally mandated *stare decisis* principle exists. Judges in Argentina do not consider themselves bound to follow the Supreme Court's precedent.[9] As a consequence, law schools in Argentina do not generally train prospective lawyers to identify the holding and various dicta of a case. However, Argentine courts, in deciding cases, tend to follow the reasoning of other tribunals (even of their same level) in similar cases, and particularly those decisions of the Supreme Court, as a support tool – not as a mandatory rule – together with other sources of law, to interpret legal and constitutional provisions. Nowadays, it is almost impossible to find a judicial decision in Argentina that does not cite other cases in support of its ruling. Distinguishing is also customary. It can be said, using common law terms, that Argentine courts, in general, consider other courts' decisions pure dicta.

Notwithstanding the lack of a binding effect of judicial decisions over other cases, the Argentine Supreme Court (whose members – as well as the whole federal judiciary – are tenured for life), since its early decisions, has leaned toward establishing a *de facto stare decisis* rule as regards its interpretation of the Constitution and of federal laws, thus aiming to provide litigants with some degree of certainty as to how the law will be interpreted, a requirement the Court finds embedded in the due process clause of the Argentine Constitution. In *García Aguilera*, a case decided in 1870, barely eight years after the court's establishment, the Supreme Court held in a since oft-repeated statement that "lower courts are required to adjust their proceedings and decisions to those of the Supreme Court in similar cases."[10] Moreover, the Supreme Court frequently denies its discretionary review (equivalent to the U.S. denial of certiorari) in those cases that deal with long-established matters, unless the petitioner raises new arguments; it revokes – considering them without sufficient basis – those decisions that contradict prior Supreme Court rulings without giving new reasons to distinguish the ruling. However, the Supreme Court has not considered itself obligated to this principle and has not hesitated in overruling its prior precedent without giving much reason or solely because of a change in the Court's majority.

By this power, the Argentine Supreme Court, through its original and appellate jurisdiction (both ordinary and extraordinary), has risen to become

[9] See generally Santiago Legarre and Julio César Rivera (h.), "Naturaleza y dimensiones del "*stare decisis*," *La Ley* 2005-F, 850; Alberto B. Bianchi, "De la obligatoriedad de los fallos de la Corte Suprema (una reflexión sobre la aplicación del stare decisis)," *El Derecho*, Serie Especial de Derecho Constitucional, Buenos Aires, 2000/2001, p. 335.

[10] Fallos 9:53 (1870).

the final interpreter of the Constitution in all cases that come before it for review. Although the Argentine Supreme Court's powers are formally different from those of European constitutional courts, as one of the most prominent Argentine constitutional law scholars has said: "the Supreme Court is frequently called 'Court of Constitutional Guaranties' since it has been granted the power to defend the Constitution in its entirety, but essentially in those parts where it touches the intimate essence of the human dignity, of its freedom, of its rights."[11]

In interpreting the Constitution and defining its role vis-à-vis the other branches of government, the Supreme Court in its different compositions has traditionally navigated between being overly activist and exercising self-restraint on constitutional matters. This swinging path is due to the frequent change in the composition of the Court and its perceived independence from the national Executive, an unfortunately frequent situation since the mid-1940s, given the political instability of the country.

Since the mid-twentieth century, and particularly after the return to democracy in 1983, in most matters, the Argentine Supreme Court has adopted an activist role. The increase of the judicial review power over matters previously considered political questions; the judicial recognition of certain constitutionally guaranteed procedural safeguards in the absence of implementing legislation; the expansion of standing to sue on constitutional matters (which was helped by the constitutional reform of 1994); and a living-constitution approach to constitutional interpretation, particularly in light of the international treaties on human rights, among other issues, have made the Judiciary, and specifically the Supreme Court, a key player in the political arena, not only through the declaration of unconstitutionality of laws and executive actions but also through prompting or restraining the enactment of legislation in several matters and indicating the path Congress should take regarding the regulation of certain affairs. Moreover, in recent years, the Supreme Court has strengthened its powers by accepting *sua sponte* constitutional review and by pretending to expand the effect of its decisions beyond the scope of the case being decided. When the matter at stake is of interest to the Supreme Court, it is ready to forget its long-established precedent that constitutional review should be the last resort and applicable only if the case cannot be solved on other grounds.[12]

11 Germán J. Bidart Campos, *La Corte Suprema, Tribunal de garantías constitucionales*, 13.

12 See Alberto B. Bianchi, *Una Corte liberal: La Corte de Alfonsín*, Abaco, Buenos Aires, 2007.

Chief Justice Lorenzetti, in his concurring opinion in *Itzcovich,*[13] in dictum, provided some guidelines as to when a law will be declared unconstitutional, to "contribute to judicial certainty": "It is necessary to differentiate among three different possibilities: 'constitutional interpretation' [*interpretación adaptativa*], 'subsequent unconstitutionality' [*inconstitucionalidad sobreviniente*] and the disqualification of the law as a result of its effects." He explained that, to the extent that constitutional interpretation consists in ascribing a meaning to a rule, when it comes to indefinite legal concepts, there are ways to interpret the rule considering the historical and social condition without having to expel the rule from the legal system, indicating that only exceptionally should the Court declare the law unconstitutional. That dictum reaffirmed the Chief Justice's view of the Supreme Court as acting as a truly Constitutional Court, as negative legislator, and with the final word as to the proper interpretation of legislative action.

I. REDUCTION OF THE SCOPE OF THE POLITICAL QUESTIONS DOCTRINE

The political-questions doctrine was expounded for the first time by the Supreme Court in 1893 in *Cullen v. Llerena.*[14] In the decision, the Court, in refusing to hear a case concerning the scope of Congress's lawmaking power, held: "It is a basic rule of our public law that each of the high powers that constitute the government of the Nation has the right to apply and interpret the Constitution when it exercises the powers that it grants to each of them," a rule that has been followed many times since. Traditionally, the Court has resorted to this doctrine to exercise its self-restraint when dealing with politically sensitive matters.[15] However, this extremely deferential view regarding the powers of the different branches of government seems to have changed in recent years.

In 1986, contrary to prior settled rulings that considered the matter nonjusticiable,[16] a unanimous Court recognized in dictum that the decision of provincial legislatures in impeachment process may be subject to judicial

[13] Fallos: 328:566 (2005).

[14] September 7, 1893, in Fallos 53:431 (1893).

[15] Julio Oyhanarte, "El caso Bonfante y la autolimitación de los jueces," *El Derecho,* Buenos Aires, nº 57, pp. 805 ff.

[16] *Joaquín Castellanos,* Fallos 136:147 (1922).

review if the decision violated the individual's right to due process of law[17] – that dictum was, less than six months later, elevated to holding in *Magín Suárez*,[18] and later in *Nicosia*, it was extended to cover the impeachment process of federal judges.[19]

In 1999, the Court decided in *Fayt*[20] that it was empowered to decide on the constitutionality of a constitutional amendment, thus overruling prior case law in which it had held that such matters were outside the realm of judicial review.[21]

More recently, the Supreme Court expanded even further its powers over the other branches of government when it held that it had the right to review the constitutionality of congressional decisions in exercising its role as judge of the elections, returns, and qualifications of its own members,[22] and even of internal congressional proceedings within Congress's lawmaking process.[23]

II. RECOGNITION OF PROCEDURAL GUARANTEES IN THE ABSENCE OF LEGISLATION

The Argentine Constitution, being one of the oldest in the world, and like most of its time, does not provide for specific procedural guarantees, other than general references to the individual's right to due process of law, leaving the implementing details to Congress and – because Argentina is a federal country – to provincial legislatures.

However, in 1957, in *Siri*,[24] the Supreme Court created – in the absence of legislation – the *acción de amparo*, a summary constitutional proceeding for any judge to review the validity of governmental action that allegedly violates constitutional rights, whenever the resort to ordinary proceedings would prove useless. In its decision, which one year later was expanded to cover violations of constitutional rights by private parties,[25] the Supreme Court held that "individual guarantees exist and protect individuals solely by

17 *Graffigna Latino*, Fallos 308:961 (1986).

18 Fallos 308:2609 (1986).

19 Fallos 316:2940 (1993).

20 Fallos 322:1609 (1999).

21 *Soria de Guerrero*, Fallos 256:556 (1963).

22 Argentine Constitution, Section 64; *Bussi*, Fallos 324:3358 (2001); *Patti*, Fallos 331:549 (2008).

23 *Binotti*, Fallos 330:2222 (2007); *Halabi*, Fallos 332: 111: (2009).

24 Fallos 239:459 (1957).

25 *Samuel Kot S.R.L.*, Fallos 241:291 (1958).

reason of them being established in the Constitution, without regard to implementing legislation." These two cases prompted the government (at such time a *de facto* one) to enact legislation essentially along the guidelines developed by the Supreme Court.[26] Nonetheless, the act tried to limit amparo jurisdiction by declaring it inadmissible in the event that the petitioner demands the declaration of the unconstitutionality of an act of Congress or of a presidential decree.

The Supreme Court in 1990 declared such disposition unconstitutional,[27] and in 1994, the *acción de amparo* was granted express constitutional status,[28] following along the lines of the Court's guidelines. Since then, it has become the main avenue for the activism of courts, and especially of the Supreme Court.

In *Comunidad Indígena Eben Ezer c. Provincia de Salta*,[29] decided in 2008, the Supreme Court revoked a provincial High Court ruling that denied an amparo claim by a native community to prevent the sale of lands in which its members had traditionally lived and worked. Plaintiff had stated that the community's own survival depended on the natural resources that existed in those areas, the lands of which were deeply bonded to their traditions, customs, and rituals, and which values the members of the native community transmit from generation to generation. The provincial High Court's denial had been based in the fact that the claim was time barred at the time of its filing.

According to the Supreme Court's criteria, Salta's ruling was incompatible with the judicial duty – by means of amparo jurisdiction – to give "immediate protection to those human rights included in the National Constitution," which indicates that, when laws, decrees, or local rules are clearly contrary to those rights (as in the case at stake, the time-barring provision), "the existence of the rule should not result in an obstacle to the immediate re-establishment of the affected liberty." The Court considered that this ruling should lead the way to future rulings concerning the scope of the right to judicial protection as defined by the American Convention on Human Rights.

26 Law 16,986.

27 *Peralta*, Fallos 313:1513 (1990).

28 Argentine Constitution, Section 43.

29 Fallos 331:2119 (2008).

III. STANDING

Constitutional standing is the aptitude or capacity required to access to constitutional jurisdiction. In the Argentine system, in principle, the individual entitled to urge judicial review must prove actual injury, as courts are prevented from rendering advisory opinions or acting outside the boundaries of a specific case.[30] The Supreme Court has always stated that a petition demanding the unconstitutionality of a particular act or statute without actual injury (the so-called *acción abstracta de inconstitucionalidad*) falls outside the sphere of judicial power.[31]

The constitutional reform of 1994 has expressly recognized some "new" rights, such as the right to a clean environment[32] and consumers' rights.[33] As regards those rights, any form of discrimination, and those other rights of general public interest (*derechos de incidencia colectiva*), the Constitution expanded amparo standing beyond the injured party to the Federal Ombudsman (*Defensor del Pueblo*) and to nongovernmental organizations.

This constitutionally mandated expansion of standing has served the Supreme Court in expanding it even further through its rulings, notwithstanding the absence of legislation.

Prior to the constitutional amendment, in *Ekmekdjián c. Sofovich*,[34] the Supreme Court recognized the petitioner's standing to require from a television station the exercise of the right to reply, recognized in article 14.1 of the American Convention on Human Rights, to anyone "injured by inaccurate or offensive statements or ideas," against a defamatory statement made by a guest against the Virgin Mary in a television show, considering that there is sufficient "actual injury" to allow standing if the contested statements offend the substantive beliefs of petitioner, even if not made directly against the offended person.

When individual freedom is at stake, the Habeas Corpus Act, expressly recognized by the Constitution in the new article 43, allows any person –

[30] Argentine Constitution, Section 116: "The Supreme Court and the lower courts of the Nation are empowered to hear and decide all cases arising under the Constitution and the laws of the Nation." See generally Juan V. Sola, *Derecho constitucional*, LexisNexis, Buenos Aires, 2006, chaps. 10–11.

[31] *Polino*, Fallos: 317:335 (1994); *Mosquera*, Fallos 326:1007 (2003).

[32] Argentine Constitution, Section 41.

[33] *Id.*, Section 42.

[34] Fallos 315:1492 (1992).

besides the affected person – to file a *habeas corpus* petition on behalf of any individual who has been illegally deprived of his or her freedom.

In *Verbitsky*,[35] the Supreme Court expanded *habeas corpus* standing by admitting for the first time a pluri-individual corrective *habeas corpus* writ petitioned by a nongovernmental organization in favor of all inmates of federal prisons, extending the individuality requirement that has traditionally characterized this writ.

In *Halabi*,[36] the Supreme Court extended amparo standing under section 43 of the Constitution to those situations in which the matter at stake is not a collective good, because individual rights clearly divisible have been encumbered, but a sole, unique, and continuous event has affected a large number of individuals and thus is identified as a homogeneous event. The Court considered, that besides the individual damage, which differs in each case, the claimants' motives are the same for all potential plaintiffs. In the Court's reasoning, the existence of the same factual and legal scenario makes it reasonable to conduct only one judicial process with expansive effects of its decision. The Court, however, has not established the rules or provided guidelines for this new type of judicially created class action.

IV. *ACCIÓN DECLARATIVA DE CERTEZA* (DECLARATORY JUDGMENTS) AS A DIRECT FORM OF EXERCISE OF CONSTITUTIONAL REVIEW

The Supreme Court in several recent decisions has expanded the scope of declaratory judgments (*acción declarativa de certeza*), broadly construing the cases-or-controversies constitutional requirement to assert jurisdiction. The proceeding, regulated by section 322 of the National Code of Federal Civil and Commercial Procedure,[37] has been established as a tool to protect a substantial, concrete, and defined interest, with limited *inter parte* effects.

Although traditionally the Supreme Court has required that the petitioner proves that the challenged action affects a legitimate direct interest of the

[35] Fallos 328:1146 (2005).

[36] *Halabi*, Fallos 332: 111: (2009).

[37] National Code of Federal Civil and Commercial Procedure, Section 322: "It may be presented an action that intends to obtain a merely declarative ruling, in order to urge to stop a state of uncertainty concerning the existence, reach or manners of a legal relationship, in the case that the lack of certainty could result in an actual attack or damage to the plaintiff provided there is no legal alternative to immediately put an end to such uncertainty."

petitioner and that the activity has sufficient concretion,[38] a criteria similar to the ripeness requirement set out by the U.S. Supreme Court, recent decisions show that, in those cases where highly controversial matters are at stake, it is open to relax the standard to allow the Court to have its saying.

In *Rios*,[39] decided in 1987, a case in which the petitioner challenged the constitutionality of an act providing that only political parties can present candidates to federal elections, considering such requirement an unreasonable regulation of the right to elect and be elected for public office, the Supreme Court accepted hearing the case even though the election had passed to establish precedent that settle the matter for future cases, reaffirming its role as final interpreter of the Constitution and its pretense to expand the effect of its rulings beyond the case being heard.

More recently, in *Halabi*,[40] the Court accepted to hear a case in which the constitutionality of Law 25,873 and its implementing decree authorizing judicial monitoring of phone calls and Internet traffic were questioned on the grounds of vagueness contrary to privacy rights recognized in the Argentine Constitution, despite the fact that the entry into force of the law had been suspended and, therefore, no actual injury existed.

V. *SUA SPONTE* CONSTITUTIONAL REVIEW

The Supreme Court traditionally (and despite some scattered dissents) refused to rule on the constitutionality of a law unless there was a clear petition of the parties in that sense.[41] This requirement was considered a cornerstone in the separation-of-powers doctrine, to avoid the courts – being essentially countermajoritarian – becoming a superpower controlling their own decisions on other government branches' actions.

However, in 2001, the Court accepted *sua sponte* constitutional review. In *Mill de Pereyra*,[42] and later in *Banco Comercial Finanzas*,[43] the Supreme Court considered such type of review not only acceptable but also constitutionally required, following Marshall's reasoning in *Marbury* that courts must conform their decisions to the Constitution.

38 *Provincia de Santiago del Estero c/ Nación Argentina*, Fallos 307:1379 (1985); *Elyen S. A. c. La Pampa*, Fallos 328:502 (2005).

39 Fallos 310:819 (1987).

40 *Halabi*, Fallos 332: 111 (2009).

41 *Ganadera Los Lagos*, Fallos 190:142 (1941).

42 Fallos 324:3219 (2001).

43 Fallos 327:3117 (2004).

The possibility to declare *sua sponte* (though always within the boundaries of a case brought to the Court's attention) the unconstitutionality of laws and executive actions has contributed – particularly when coupled with the other new mechanisms already discussed – to strengthening the courts' powers vis-à-vis Congress and the Executive.

VI. *ERGA OMNES* EFFECT OF JUDICIAL DECISIONS

As indicated already, the Argentine system of judicial review entrusts all judges, federal and provincial,[44] of whatever level, to control the constitutionality of laws and governmental action. To the extent that they resolve "cases," judicial decisions only have *inter parte* effects, despite their value as an auxiliary or secondary source for future decisions.

However, after the constitutional amendment of 1994 that expanded standing in those cases affecting rights of general public interest, scholars have debated the effects of decisions in such cases.

In *Halabi*,[45] the Supreme Court tried to give a final word on the matter and indicated for the first time that its decision in these types of cases should have *erga omnes* effect. However, it gave only slim reasons for its holding: "There is a legal and factual homogeneity in the matter at stake that makes it reasonable to render a single judgment with an expansive effect of the decision." The importance of the holding would have required a more reasoned judgment, particularly because it potentially affects the right of defense and the due process of law of those other individuals who were not party to the case. What would have happened if the Court's decision, contrary to the current outcome, ruled in favor of the act's validity? Should that have barred other injured party's claims?

VII. ACTIVIST JURISPRUDENCE

In the past few years, Supreme Court decisions have intended to include some matters in the legislative agenda or, in other cases, to indicate the constitutional path that Congress should take regarding certain affairs. Moreover, in some decisions, the Court has changed the clear legislative intent, – through judicial interpretation – to square the law with the Court's interpretation of the Constitution. These actions show the Court's increasing

[44] Even though provincial judges do not apply federal law, they are bound to apply the Constitution, which is directly enforceable against the provinces, and to uphold its supremacy.

[45] *Halabi*, Fallos 332: 111: (2009).

involvement in realms previously left to the political branches of government.

1. *"Educating" Congress*

This new activist role of the Supreme Court is clear in different areas of the law.

(a) In 2004, in the cases *Castillo*[46] and *Aquino*,[47] the Supreme Court declared the unconstitutionality of the Labor Risks Law, Law 24,557, as regards its procedural contents (a matter constitutionally reserved to provincial legislation) and the limits of indemnification for labor injuries, considering that its provisions deny workers their right to a complete restitution.

These cases, by invalidating the system created by law, even though with *inter partes* effects, implied a *de facto* annulment of the challenged legislation. In addition, the Court's rulings demanded congressional action to modify the system in accordance with court-established guidelines.

(b) In *Vizzoti*,[48] the Supreme Court ruled that the limits to the base salary used to calculate termination compensation provided for in the Employment Law were unreasonable, in light of the constitutional obligation to protect workers against unjustified firings.[49]

The Court then provided Congress with guidelines as to valid limits, indicating that "the Court's decision does not entail undue interference with congressional powers, nor a violation of the separation of powers, being only the duly exercise of the constitutionally-mandated judicial review over laws and governmental action."

(c) In *Rosza*, decided in 2007,[50] the Supreme Court, in declaring the unconstitutionality of the regime concerning the appointment of interim federal judges, urged Congress to enact a new "constitutionally valid" regime, providing the guidelines that said new regime should follow, and granting Congress one year to implement the new system.

(d) The Constitution provides that Supreme Court's appellate jurisdiction be exercised in accordance with the rules and exceptions

46 Fallos, 327:3610 (2004).

47 Fallos: 327:3753 (2004).

48 Fallos 327:3677 (2004).

49 Argentine Constitution, Section 14 *bis*.

50 Fallos 330:2361 (2007).

provided for by Congress.[51] Following such rule, Congress has enacted legislation providing that all cases ordering the government to pay social security benefits must be appealed to the Supreme Court, which actually delays payment to elderly people. In *Itzcovich*,[52] the Court declared that the appeal procedure has become unconstitutional in that it affects the petitioner's right to a speedy trial. The Court emphasized that reasonableness requires that a law continue to be coherent with the Constitution throughout the period of its enforcement:

> When a rule frustrates or detracts the purposes of the law in which it is inserted, so as to conflict with constitutional principles, it is the justices' duty to desist from such rule and stop its enforcement in order to guarantee the Constitution's supremacy, as this is the moderating function of the Judiciary Power and one of the main guarantees against potential abuse by the government.

Shortly after the ruling, Law 26,025 was passed and modifications introduced to the system to comply with the decision.

2. *Reconciling Internal Legislation with Human Rights Treaties by Means of Interpretation*

In several cases, the Supreme Court has resorted to an "integrationist" interpretation to reconcile local legislation with human rights treaties.

In 1992, in *Ekmekdjián c. Sofovich*,[53] the Supreme Court recognized that international treaties have precedence over internal legislation. The constitutional amendment of 1994 ratified this principle and even gave to a series of enumerated international documents "constitutional hierarchy."[54] Since then, the Court has held that constitutional review includes confronting internal laws and regulations with international conventions, and that it has the power to declare such laws "unconventional."[55]

Among those documents, the Constitution gave constitutional status to the American Convention on Human Rights, which, among other rights,

51 Argentine Constitution, Section 117.

52 Fallos: 328:566 (2005).

53 Fallos 315:1492 (1992).

54 Argentine Constitution, Section 75.22.

55 *Mazzeo*, Fallos 330: 3248 (2007).

establishes the right of any person accused of a criminal offense to appeal the judgment to a higher court.[56]

The Argentine criminal legal system provided, for those cases tried before a three-judge panel in oral proceedings, only a limited review of the judgment before the Corte Nacional de Casación Penal. In *Casal*,[57] decided in 2005, the Supreme Court held that the only way to square the requirement established in the Convention with the Argentine criminal legal system, was to interpret section 456 of the Criminal Procedural Code as permitting an ample review of the prior ruling.

In a similar path, in 2006, in *Cantos*,[58] the Court demanded that Congress pass legislation to comply with the binding rulings of the Inter-American Court on Human Rights.

3. *Amending Political Will and Rewriting Statutes*

In another set of cases, the Supreme Court ruling not only invalidated legislation but also replaced the unconstitutional rule with a different one.

(a) The Argentine Constitution recognizes the right to marriage. In regulating such right, Congress established that divorce did not entail the right to a new marriage, a clause whose constitutionality was upheld several times. However, in 1986, the Supreme Court applied a "dynamic" – living constitution – approach, and in *Sejean*,[59] it considered that changes to societal perception requires giving a new scope to the right to human dignity, which led to the unconstitutionality of the statute that had been in force for almost a century. This decision was the prelude to a reform of the law of civil marriage, which new law, following the Supreme Court decision, admitted the possibility of a subsequent marriage.[60]

(b) In *Portillo*,[61] decided three years later, the Court was required to rule on the constitutionality of mandatory military service. The petitioner claimed that, to the extent that military service might require the killing of other individuals, it affected the petitioner's deep religious beliefs in

56 American Convention on Human Rights, Art. 8.2.h.

57 Fallos, 328:3399 (2005).

58 Fallos 326:2968 (2003).

59 Fallos 308:2268 (1986).

60 In a similar case, at the time this report was written, a local court in the city of Buenos Aires had resolved (decision not final) that a Civil Code provision defining marriage as the union of a man and a woman is unconstitutional, as it violates the equal protection clause of the Constitution.

61 Fallos 312:496 (1989).

violation of the free exercise of religion clause of the Constitution. The Court held that, in peacetime, compliance with military service as established by Congress violated such clause, but notwithstanding, it required the petitioner to serve his time doing alternative civil service, redefining the concept of national defense despite the fact that Congress did not provide for such an alternative.

(c) The Supreme Court has as well reinterpreted political will when it needed to square the law with new realities.

In *Petric*,[62] decided in 1998, it reinterpreted the scope of the right to reply recognized by the American Convention on Human Rights. Despite that the Convention recognized such right against statements made through a "legally regulated medium of communication," the Court expanded its scope to statements made through the press (which in Argentina is not and cannot be legally regulated).

(d) The Supreme Court, through its decisions, has also lessened the effects of certain legislative political choices that, in the Court's opinion, alter fundamental rights.[63] In *Milone*,[64] the Court mitigated the effects of a law concerning labor accidents that allowed labor insurance companies to pay the indemnification in monthly installments throughout the life of the individual. By declaring the mechanism unconstitutional, it obliged the insurance company to pay the indemnification in single, lump-sum payment.

(e) The Court's ruling in the *Badaro* cases, concerning automatic adjustment of pensions ratifies this criterion. The Constitution provides for "mobile" pensions.[65] In *Badaro I*,[66] the Court considered that Congress's inaction regarding the increase of pensions, in light of them having been seriously reduced as a result of high inflation, was a violation of the constitutional mandate, and therefore it urged Congress to pass legislation within a reasonable time to solve the problem.

The Court emphasized that it is not only a power but also a duty of Congress to give effect to the constitutional guarantee of pension mobility, for which it must legislate and adopt measures to guarantee the full enjoyment of the right.

62 Fallos 321:885 (1998).

63 The Argentine Constitution provides that Congress has the power to regulate constitutional rights without altering them (Argentine Constitution, Sections 14 and 28).

64 Fallos 327:4607 (2004).

65 Argentine Constitution, Section 14 *bis*.

66 Fallos 329:3089 (2006).

In view of the lack of action by Congress, in *Badaro II*,[67] the Court, while reurging Congress to enact legislation, resolved to grant the petitioner's request and adopted a criteria for readjusting pensions until Congress decides to act.

(f) The financial crisis of the last months of 2001 gave occasion to numerous active rulings; *Bustos*[68] and *Massa*[69] are probably the most significant ones. In those cases, petitioners sought the unconstitutionality of Executive Emergency Decrees 1570/01 and 214/02, which required the conversion of all dollar-denominated debts into peso ones, thus establishing an inflation-adjustment mechanism. The Court, in upholding the constitutionality of the Decrees, provided for an additional interest in favor of the petitioner, which Congress had not envisaged. In *Bustos*, moreover, Justice Zaffaroni's dictum proposed a complex, multitier mechanism to restore deposits in a clear attempt to reformulate the legislative intent.

(g) The Court's activist approach is shown as well in matters concerning the environment. In *Mendoza*,[70] the Supreme Court, in exercise of its original jurisdiction, received a complaint filed by a group of neighbors of a settlement known as Villa Inflamable, located in the outskirts of Buenos Aires, against the National Government, the Province of Buenos Aires, the government of the City of Buenos Aires, and forty-four private companies, alleging damages caused by multiple diseases that their children and themselves had suffered as a result of the pollution of the river basin Matanza-Riachuelo. In two landmark rulings, the first in 2006 and the other in 2008, the Court ordered the defendants to present an environmental recovery program, entrusted the Matanza-Riachuelo Basin Authority with its implementation, and established detailed court-monitored guidelines as regards compliance to avoid interprovincial conflicts, all of them matters traditionally within the realm of legislatures and the Executive of both federal and provincial levels.

67 Fallos 330:4866 (2007).

68 Fallos 327:4495 (2004).

69 Fallos 329:5913 (2006).

70 Fallos 329:2316 (2006); Fallos 331:1622 (2008).

VIII. CONCLUSION

After this analysis, we cannot but concur with Jorge Vanossi's words:

> We believe our Supreme Court, has appropriately defined its role when it has characterized itself in a triple condition: as a court of constitutional guarantees, as final interpreter of the Constitution, and as palladium of freedom.[71]

In a nutshell, although not reaching to government by the Judiciary or to acting as positive Legislators, in Argentina, the famous *Marbury* quote "it is emphatically the province and duty of the judicial department to say what the law is" is a reality.

[71] Jorge R. Vanossi, *Teoría Constitucional*, 2d ed., Ed. Depalma, Buenos Aires 2000, Vol. II, pp. 371–399.

AUSTRALIA

INTERPRETATION AND REVIEW

Cheryl Saunders
Professor, University of Melbourne
c.saunders@unimelb.edu.au

I. FRAMEWORK

1. *Authority for Review*

Constitutional review, in the sense of judicial review of the actions of all organs of State, including the legislature on grounds of constitutionality, is an established feature of Australian constitutional arrangements. Review was assumed by the framers of the Constitution either as a consequence of the status of the Constitution as an act of the Imperial Parliament or as a necessary incident of federation or both.[1] It was accepted with equanimity by the first Commonwealth Attorney General, charged with the responsibility of introducing the legislation to establish the High Court.[2] That Court entertained a range of constitutional disputes in the first year of its establishment,[3] and within five years, it had invalidated laws of both the Commonwealth and some State Parliaments,[4] consistent with Quick and Garran's expectation that it would be a "guardian of the Constitution"

1 See the sources cited in James A. Thomson, "Constitutional Authority for Judicial Review: A Contribution from the Framers of the Constitution" in Gregory Craven (ed.), *The Convention Debates 1890–1898, Commentaries, Indices and Guide* (Sydney, Legal Books, 1986), 173, esp. 186.

2 Commonwealth, House of Representatives, *Parliamentary Debates*, 18 March 1965.

3 Including *D'Emden v. Pedder* (1904) 1 CLR 91; *Peterswald v. Bartley* (1904) 1 CLR 497; *Deakin v. Webb* (1904) 1 CLR 585.

4 Including *Deakin v. Webb* (State); *R v. Barger* (1908) 6 CLR 41 (Commonwealth).

against "encroachments" from both spheres.[5] In 1951, a Justice of the High Court described "the principle of *Marbury v. Madison*" as "axiomatic" in Australia.[6] The description has become de rigueur,[7] and it unquestionably reflects Australian practice.

It is occasionally noted, nevertheless, that the Constitution does not explicitly provide for review.[8] Review of legislation on grounds of constitutionality also jars with one strand of the Australian constitutional inheritance,[9] although it is entirely compatible with the other. Neither of these points should be overstated. Although it is somewhat odd that jurisdiction in matters "arising under this Constitution, or involving its interpretation" was relegated to a list of matters that the Parliament "may" confer on the High Court,[10] there is plenty of evidence, in both the text of the Constitution and relevant extrinsic sources, that constitutional review was intended.[11] The tension between responsible government and constitutional review is a somewhat more complex point, drawing on a symbiotic mix of the tradition of parliamentary sovereignty and what often is claimed to be a greater degree of public confidence in the institutions of elected government in a system of this kind.[12] But parliamentary sovereignty was never a feature of Australian constitutional arrangements, and arguments that elected institutions in a unitary system can be trusted to respect constitutional principles adequately do not automatically transfer to a federal constitutional setting.

Ironically, the view that federal constitutional compliance can be left to elected central institutions is more persuasive in the United States, with its system of checks and balances, including the more effective institutional

[5] J. Quick and R.R. Garran, *Annotated Constitution of the Australian Commonwealth* (Sydney, Angus & Robertson, 1901), 725.

[6] *Australian Communist Party v. Commonwealth (Communist Party* case) (1951) 83 CLR 1, 262 per Fullagar J (noting also the status of the Constitution as an "instrument emanating from a superior authority").

[7] *Attorney-General (WA) v. Marquet* (2003) 217 CLR 545, 570 per Gleeson CJ, Gummow, Hayne, and Heydon JJ; *Behrooz v. Secretary, Department of Immigration, and Multicultural and Indigenous Affairs* (2004) 219 CLR 486, 525 per Kirby J; see also *Singh v. Commonwealth* (2004) 222 CLR 322, 330 per Gleeson CJ.

[8] Thomson, *op. cit.*

[9] Stephen Gageler, "Foundations of Australian Federalism and the Role of Judicial Review" (1987) 17 *Federal Law Review* 162.

[10] The jurisdiction has been conferred: Judiciary Act 1903 (Cth) s. 30(a).

[11] Textual indications can be found in covering clause 5 and sections 74 and 76(i). See generally Thomson, *op. cit.*

[12] Gageler, *op. cit.*, 169 ff.

representation of the States in central organs of government.[13] It has provided no deterrent to the exercise of constitutional review in Australia, where the High Court is recognized as the ultimate interpreter of the Constitution, there is no developed doctrine of deference and compliance with orders of a Court is regarded as integral to the rule of law.[14] Nevertheless, the perceived tension between responsible government and constitutional review helps explain the Australian approach to constitutional interpretation, which is examined more closely in the following part.

2. *Jurisdiction*

As in most common law legal systems that accept constitutional review, the form of review in Australia is diffuse, in the sense that the review function is not assigned to a specialist constitutional court.[15] Diffuse review has two consequences that are relevant for the present purposes. The first is that a court that interprets and applies the constitution typically has jurisdiction to apply other legal norms as well. In particular, the Australian High Court can apply any other Australian legal norms, including either Commonwealth or State legislation or the Australian common law, which gives it maximum flexibility to avoid the unnecessary application of constitutional norms, if it intends to do so.[16] The second is that constitutional review is not the province of a single court but may be carried out by other courts within the legal hierarchy that possess the necessary jurisdiction.

The Commonwealth Constitution created a distinction between federal and State jurisdiction. There are nine heads of federal jurisdiction, five of which are conferred directly on the High Court in its original jurisdiction, leaving the remaining four to be conferred on the Court at Parliament's discretion.[17] Although the constitutional review jurisdiction is in the latter group, the jurisdiction in section 75 to deal with matters in which specified remedies are sought against "an officer of the Commonwealth" effectively protects the constitutional review jurisdiction of the High Court as long as the

13 Herbert Wechsler, "The Political Safeguards of Federalism" (1954) 54 *Columbia Law Review* 543; and see discussion in Gageler, *op. cit.*, at 193 ff.

14 See generally Murray Gleeson, "Courts and the Rule of Law" in Cheryl Saunders and Katy Leroy, *The Rule of Law* (Sydney, Federation Press, 2003).

15 For distinctions between diffuse and concentrated review, see Cheryl Saunders, "The Interesting Times of Louis Favoreu" (2007) 5 *International Journal of Constitutional Law* 1, 11 ff.

16 For a classic illustration of such an approach, see the reasons of Gleeson CJ in *Al-Kateb v. Godwin* (2004) 219 CLR 562, 571 ff.

17 The first group is in s. 75 and the second in s. 76.

Constitution is accepted as part of the law to be applied.[18] All of the heads of jurisdiction in sections 75 and 76 can be conferred as federal jurisdiction on State courts or on other federal courts.[19]

Even in the absence of federal jurisdiction, State courts had their own State jurisdiction to apply the Constitution, which was made binding on them in clause 5.[20] In the exercise of this jurisdiction, the Supreme Court of Victoria dealt with a constitutional dispute in 1902, before the High Court was established.[21] After the establishment of the High Court, however, the Commonwealth Parliament removed from the State courts power to exercise State jurisdiction in areas also covered by federal jurisdiction and replaced it with federal jurisdiction, in large part to control appeals to the Privy Council.[22] There is now no extant State jurisdiction "arising under" the Commonwealth Constitution or "involving its interpretation,"[23] but the Federal Court and State courts at all levels have express federal jurisdiction to carry out constitutional review.[24]

Under section 73 of the Constitution, the High Court also has broad appellate jurisdiction from both federal and courts, which it exercises only when it is prepared to grant special leave.[25] Constitutional disputes can thus go directly to the High Court or reach it in its capacity as the final court of appeal. Supporting legislation adds further flexibility to these arrangements. The High Court may deal with a matter lodged in its original jurisdiction if it considers it appropriate to do so; if not, it may remit the matter to an appropriate lower court.[26] Alternatively, a constitutional question that begins

18 See also s. 75(iii) and (iv). For acknowledgement of the point in the text, see *Plaintiff S157/2002 v. Commonwealth* (2003) 211 CLR 476, 482–3 per Gleeson CJ; 505 ff. per Gaudron, McHugh, Gummow, Kirby and Hayne JJ.

19 S. 77 (i), (iii).

20 *Lorenzo v. Carey* (1921) 29 CLR 243, 255 per Higgins J; see also Quick and Garran, *op. cit.*, 791.

21 *In re the Income Tax Acts (No 4) Wollaston's Case* (1902) 28 VLR 357.

22 *Minister of State for the Army v. Parbury Henty & Co Pty Ltd* (1945) 70 CLR 459, 505 per Dixon J. The mechanism used draws on the constitutional power in s. 77(ii) to define the extent to which the jurisdiction of any federal court is exclusive of that of State courts: Judiciary Act 1903 s. 39.

23 *Felton v. Mulligan* (1971) 124 CLR 367, 373 per Barwick CJ.

24 See Australian Law Reform Commission, *The Judicial Power of the Commonwealth: A Review of the Judiciary Act 1903 and Related Legislation*, Report nº 92, 2001, ch. 12 http://www.austrlii.edu.au/au/other/alc/publications/reports/92/ (9 April 2009).

25 Judiciary Act 1903 (Cth) s. 35 and 35AA (for appeals from State and Territory courts), s. 35A (for special leave criteria).

26 Judiciary Act 1903 (Cth) s. 44.

in a lower court must be removed into the High Court on the application of an Attorney General and may be so removed, at the discretion of the Court, on the application of another party.[27] A legislative requirement for notice to be given to all Attorneys General when a constitutional question is raised in any court, before the court proceeds in the cause, is effective in alerting governments to the need to intervene or seek removal, but it is also a cause of delay, prompting recommendations from the Australian Law Reform Commission to streamline the procedure.[28]

3. *Concrete Review*

Constitutional review in Australia also is concrete rather than abstract. Again, this is consistent with the common law preference for determining the applicable law in a factual setting that frames a legal dispute, typically involving two or more parties in an adversarial relationship to each other.[29] In Australia's case, however, a requirement for concrete review is given constitutional force by the framework for the strict separation of judicial power, understood to preclude federal courts from exercising any power that is not "federal judicial power" within the meaning of the Constitution.[30] As defined, federal judicial power has largely subsumed the requirements of justiciability.[31] The justiciability of an issue is occasionally queried, though increasingly rarely, and there is no developed political question doctrine.

A. Advisory Opinions

Some forms of abstract review are precluded by the value of judicial independence that underlies the separation of judicial power[32] and by the definition of judicial power itself, including the requirement for a decision to be binding.[33] In addition, more stringent limitations have been derived,

[27] Judiciary Act 1903 (Cth) s. 40.

[28] ALRC, Report nº 92, *op. cit.*, Recommendation 13-1.

[29] But see the reference procedure in Canada: Supreme Court Act 1985, s. 53, upheld most recently in *Reference Re Secession of Quebec* [1998] 2 SCR 217.

[30] *R v. Kirby; ex parte Boilermakers' Society of Australia* (1956) 94 CLR 254.

[31] *Thomas v. Mowbray* (2007) 233 CLR 307, 354 per Gummow and Crennan JJ. As this passage also suggests, there is a distinct but limited category of issues that are not justiciable because they are held to be entrusted by the Constitution to one of the other branches of government.

[32] *Hilton v. Wells* (1985) 157 CLR 57, per Mason and Deane JJ; an example is suggested by *Wilson v. Minister for Torres Strait Island Affairs* (1996) 189 CLR 1.

[33] *Brandy v. Human Rights and Equal Opportunity Commission* (1995) 183 CLR 245.

however improbably,[34] from the word *matter*, which prefaces all the heads of federal jurisdiction and appears elsewhere in the Judicature chapter of the Constitution.[35] In 1921, the High Court held, in effect, that the Parliament could not confer on a court jurisdiction to give advisory opinions even when such opinions were confined to the validity of enacted legislation and when the determination of the court was "final and conclusive."[36] Under such an arrangement, there was no "matter" within the meaning of the Constitution, because there was no "immediate right, duty or liability to be established by the determination of the Court," which would be obliged to make a "declaration of the law divorced from any attempt to administer that law."[37] There have since been occasional proposals to amend the Constitution to enable the High Court to give advice on constitutional questions. One passed both Houses of the Parliament, but none has advanced to the referendum stage,[38] and formal change seems unlikely.

The principal argument in favor of allowing such opinions is the convenience of being able to determine the constitutional validity of legislation before action is taken pursuant to it. One reason change has come to be regarded as less pressing is that potential inconvenience has been diminished by the development of forms of legal action that have been used successfully to bring questions about the validity of new legislation before the Court in the absence of a full-blown dispute, without contravening the requirement for a "matter."[39] The most important of these is a challenge to the validity of Commonwealth legislation after it is enacted but before

[34] Quick and Garran described the term as "the widest word to embrace every possible kind of judicial procedure that could arise" within the heads of federal jurisdiction: *op. cit.*, 765. For recognition that judicial power and federal judicial power are not coextensive, see *Kable v. Director of Public Prosecutions (NSW)* (1996) 189 CLR 51, 136, per Gummow J.

[35] Including s. 73. It is settled that a decision from which an appeal is taken under s. 73 also must "finally determine the parties rights and obligations": *Mellifont v. Attorney-General (Qld)* (1991) 173 CLR 289, 300.

[36] A determination was expressed to be final and conclusive; the court construed this to require "an authoritative declaration of the law": *In re Judiciary and Navigation Acts (Advisory Opinions* case) (1921) 29 CLR 257.

[37] *Id.*

[38] Constitution Alteration (Advisory Jurisdiction of the High Court) 1983; for details of all proposals, see Henry Burmester, "Limitations on Federal Adjudication" in Brian Opeskin and Fiona Wheeler (eds.), *The Australian Federal Judicial System* (Melbourne, MUP, 2000) 227, 242–244.

[39] This does not assist with one other purpose for which advisory opinions have been proposed: to advise on compliance with procedural requirements of the Constitution, including the prerequisites for a double dissolution under s. 57: Burmester, *op. cit.*, 242.

proclamation, brought on behalf of one or more plaintiff States.[40] Questions about the validity of Commonwealth legislation dealing with pharmaceutical benefits,[41] marriage,[42] and corporations[43] were resolved early in this way. More generally, a declaration of invalidity of an Act of the Commonwealth or a State Parliament can be sought by an individual plaintiff whose legal interests are "or in the immediate future probably will be" affected by the legislation in question.[44] Attorneys General may also seek declarations in relation to the validity of legislation enacted in their own jurisdiction.[45]

B. Declarations of Incompatibility

Nevertheless, the narrowness of the distinctions drawn between actions that are sufficiently concrete and those that are not,[46] coupled with some disagreement within the Court about exactly what constitutes a matter, makes it difficult to predict with any certainty on which side of the line some actions may fall.[47] The uncertainty has practical significance for any attempt on the part of the Commonwealth to introduce a legislative bill of rights modeled on the Human Rights Act of 1998 (United Kingdom) in a form that preserves the final supremacy of the Parliament on human rights questions but encourages "dialogue" on rights between courts and the elected branches.[48] One of several constitutional difficulties that such a measure

40 But see Cowen and Zines, noting that these actions are "exceptional": Z. Cowen and L. Zines, *Federal Jurisdiction in Australia* (Sydney, Federation Press, OUP, 3rd ed. 2002), 16.

41 *Attorney-General (Vict); ex rel Dale v. Commonwealth (Pharmaceutical Benefits* case) (1945) 71 CLR 237.

42 *Attorney-General (Vic) v. Commonwealth (Marriage Act* case) (1962) 107 CLR 529.

43 *New South Wales v. Commonwealth (Incorporation* case) (1990) 160 CLR 482.

44 *Toowoomba Foundry Pty Ltd v. Commonwealth* (1945) 71 CLR 545, 570 per Latham CJ; see also *Croome v. Tasmania* (1997) 191 CLR 119. But see *Bass v. Permanent Trustee* (1999) 198 CLR 334, 356, requiring the action to be "based on facts, found or agreed."

45 For example, *Attorney-General (NSW); Ex rel MacKellar v. Commonwealth* (1977) 139 CLR 527; but see *In re McBain; Australian Catholic Bishops' Conference* (2002).

46 Compare *Mellifont v. Attorney-General (Queensland)* (1991) 173 CLR 289 with *Director of Public Prosecutions (SA) v. B* (1998) 194 CLR 566 and *North Ganalanja Aboriginal Corporation v. Queensland* (1996) 185 CLR 595; see generally Burmester, *op. cit.*, 238–242.

47 For analysis of the complexity of the jurisprudence, see Christos Mantziaris and Leighton McDonald, "Federal Judicial Review Jurisdiction after *Griffith University v. Tang*" (2006) 17 *Public Law Review* 22, 30.

48 A declaration of incompatibility, in terms of the Human Rights Act 1998 (UK) s. 4; a declaration of inconsistent interpretation in terms of the Charter of Human Rights and Responsibilities Act 2006 (Vic).

would face[49] is whether a declaration by a court that challenged legislation is incompatible with protected rights but does not affect either the validity of the legislation or the rights of the parties is consistent with the separation of powers under the Commonwealth Constitution and in particular with the requirement for a matter.

A purposive approach to the application of the Constitution to a relatively novel arrangement of this kind would favor validity. Although the declaration itself would not determine any "right, duty or liability," at least between the parties, it would arise out of a concrete dispute and would involve the application of human rights norms to legislation in a factual setting, and it would prevent no threat to judicial independence.[50] It is a reflection on the apprehension engendered by the technicality of the High Court's approach to the definition of federal judicial power that much of the commentary on this issue is devoted to ingenious arguments about how a matter might be constructed from an obligation of the Attorney General to respond in writing to a declaration and that there is considerable pessimism about the outcome, in any event.[51]

4. *Standing*

The Australian rules of standing reflect tension between two views. One, which historically has been dominant, is that the primary role of courts is to protect the "legal rights of individuals" at the instance of the individuals concerned,[52] leaving public rights to be enforced at the instance of representatives of the public.[53] The second is that everyone has an interest in the observance of the law generally and compliance with the Constitution

49 Others include the validity of any provision requiring the Courts to interpret legislation consistently with human rights and the extent to which such legislation could be applied to the States.

50 Geoffrey Lindell, "The Statutory Protection of Rights and Parliamentary Sovereignty: Guidance from the United Kingdom?" (2006) 17 *Public Law Review* 188, 204.

51 See Michael McHugh, "A Human Rights Act, the Court and the Constitution" and the references there cited: Presentation given at the Australian Human Rights Commission, 5 March 2009, http://hreoc.gov.au/letstalkaboutrigts/events/McHugh_2009.html (viewed 15 April 2009); cf. Lindell, *op. cit.*

52 *Bateman's Bay Local Aboriginal Council v. Aboriginal Community Benefit Fund Pty Ltd* (1998) 914 CLR 247, 275–277, per McHugh J.

53 *Re McBain; ex parte Australian Catholic Bishops Conference* (2002) 209 CLR 372, [8], per Gleeson CJ.

particularly, which justifies the standing of individuals or groups with a sufficient interest to prosecute an action effectively and responsibly.[54]

Consistently with the former view, Australian law is generous in its recognition of the standing of the Attorneys General of the Commonwealth and the States. To this end, it has adapted the traditional common law right of an Attorney General to take legal action in the public interest to the more demanding conditions of a federal political system.[55] Attorneys General may initiate action to uphold the Commonwealth Constitution against a law of any jurisdiction, including their own.[56] Their statutory rights to intervene in constitutional cases and to require removal of constitutional proceedings into the High Court complement this general rule.[57]

The standing of individuals is more restrictive. Standing to seek a declaration or an injunction to enforce public rights under the general law requires a "special interest in the subject matter of the action,"[58] and for the moment, at least, the test appears to extend to complaints about constitutional breach. The test is liberally applied, but it must be satisfied if the point is raised; and standing sometimes is denied.[59] It presently is unclear whether a taxpayer has standing to challenge unconstitutional expenditure[60] or a voter to challenge unconstitutional electoral laws,[61] although Members of Parliament have been accorded standing for the former purpose.[62] The basis on which the Court is prepared to grant individuals leave to intervene

54 Cf. the interest-based grievance and enforcement approaches to standing identified by Peter Cane and Leighton McDonald, *Principles of Administrative Law* (Oxford, OUP 2008), 186.

55 *Attorney-General (Vict); ex rel Dale v. Commonwealth (Pharmaceutical Benefits* case) (1945) 71 CLR 237, 272 per Dixon J; *Truth About Motorways v. Macquarie* (2000) 200 CLR 591, 628 per Gummow J; cf. *Victoria v. Commonwealth and Hayden (AAP* case) (1975) 134 CLR 338, 387, per Stephen J.

56 *Id.*, 630. But see the following observation prompted by the unusual circumstances in *In re McBain*, in which the Commonwealth Attorney sought to intervene to uphold the validity of a State statute: "the Attorney-General . . . cannot have a roving commission to initiate litigation to disrupt settled outcomes in earlier cases, so as to rid the law reports of what are considered unsatisfactory decisions respecting constitutional law": at 76, per Gaudron and Gummow JJ (concluding that in this instance there was no matter).

57 Judiciary Act 1903 (Cth) s 78A, 40(1); see also s. 78B. The intervention rates are high: Enid Campbell, "Intervention in Constitutional Cases" (1998) 9 *Public Law Review* 255, 256. On the right to intervene, see *K-Generation Pty Ltd v. Liquor Licensing Court* [2009] HCA 4 [155].

58 *Australian Conservation Foundation v. Commonwealth* (198) 146 CLR 493, 530.

59 Cane and McDonald, *op. cit.*, 192.

60 *Victoria v. Commonwealth and Hayden (AAP* case) (1975) 134 CLR, 387–388, per Stephen J.

61 *Attorney-General (Cth); ex rel McKinlay v. Commonwealth* (1975) 135 CLR 1, 26, per Barwick CJ, even though the defendant Commonwealth had not argued that the plaintiffs lacked standing: at 16.

62 *Combet v. Commonwealth* (2005) 224 CLR 494, 557.

or to appear as *amici curiae* parallels the standing requirements. The former must show a sufficient interest. An *amicus* applicant must show that it will "assist the Court in a way that the Court would not otherwise have been assisted."[63] A would-be complainant who lacks standing may seek a fiat from an Attorney General to mount a relator action in reliance on the Attorney's authority, but compliance lies entirely within the Attorney's discretion.[64]

There are signs of change, driven in part by evolving attitudes toward the role of citizens in a democracy but also by skepticism about the efficacy of leaving the enforcement of public rights to the office of Attorney General, which in Australia is filled by an elected Member of Parliament who also is a Minister and typically is a member of the Cabinet.[65] Restrictive standing rules also sit uneasily with the protected jurisdiction against officers of the Commonwealth under section 75(v); one of the remedies, prohibition, has no particular standing requirements, and rights of action under section 75(v) have become integral to the Australian conception of the rule of law.[66] The direction of change is suggested most obviously by the progressive relaxation of the special interest test;[67] some relaxation of the circumstances in which submissions of amici may be accepted;[68] and a tendency on the part of some members of the Court to probe the history and logic of the standing rules, emphasizing the significance of section 75(v).[69] The Court has also held that the Constitution itself does not impose distinct standing requirements, so that Parliament may expand the right to take legal action, at least in relation to the enforcement of its own legislation.[70] In contrast, recommendations by the Australian Law Reform Commission to formally

63 *Levy v. Victoria* (1997) 189 CLR 579, 604 per Brennan CJ; cf. Kirby J, 650.

64 Christopher Maxwell, "In the Line of Fire: Re McBain and the Role of the Attorney-General as a Party" (2002) 13 *Public Law Review* 283 287; see also Cheryl Saunders and Paul Rabbat, "Relator Actions: Practice in Australia and New Zealand" (2002) 13 *Public Law Review* 292–295.

65 For contrast with the role of Attorney-General in the United Kingdom, see *Bateman's Bay Local Aboriginal Council v. Aboriginal Community Benefit Fund Pty Ltd* (1998) 914 CLR 247, 262.

66 *Bodruddaza v. MIMA* (2007) 228 CLR 651, 668, referring to the impact of s. 75(v) generally.

67 *Bateman's Bay Local Aboriginal Council v. Aboriginal Community Benefit Fund Pty Ltd* (1998) 914 CLR 247, 265–267 and the cases there cited.

68 *Wurridjal v. Commonwealth of Australia* [2009] HCA 2 [260] ff. per Kirby J.

69 E.g., in *Bodruddaza*, 668; also *Combet v. Commonwealth* (2005) 224 CLR 494, 557 per McHugh J.

70 *Truth About Motorways v. Macquarie* (2000) 200 CLR 591, 611 per Gaudron J, 637 per Gummow J, 659 per Kirby J, 670 per Callinan J. For a warning that in some cases standing is necessary to constitute a justiciable controversy, see, e.g., Gaudron J at 211–212.

relax the rules of standing have not been accepted,[71] and there is room for concern that relaxation might encounter constitutional difficulties after all, from the requirement for a matter with which the rules of standing are necessarily linked.[72]

II. APPROACH

The Commonwealth Constitution has been molded by judicial interpretation for more than one hundred years. The interpretive approach of the High Court exhibits tensions that are familiar in other constitutional systems: between constitutional development by means of judicial review as opposed to formal textual change; between principles applied to the interpretation of other legal texts and recognition of the distinctive demands of an instrument with the higher status, expected longevity and generality of expression of a Constitution; between the intentions of the makers of the Constitution and the concerns of later generations; between the responsibility of courts to uphold the Constitution and of elected institutions to take action in the public interest. In Australia's case, these tensions are exacerbated by cultural differences between the two constitutional traditions on which the Australian constitutional system draws, which requires a delicate balancing act on the part of the courts and, to a lesser degree, by the original status of the Constitution as a British Act of Parliament.[73]

Famously, the product of these tensions in Australia is an approach to constitutional interpretation generally described as legalism. Legalism has no precise limits, however, and its application often is a matter of degree.[74] This section begins by sketching five phases of constitutional interpretation during which Australian legalism has waxed and waned. The following section examines more closely the techniques of legalism and its principal Australian competitor, for which I have used the terminology of realism, though without conviction, as will be seen. The final section outlines the

71 ALRC, *Beyond the Door-keeper: Standing to Sue for Public Remedies* (Report nº 78 1996).

72 *Croome v. Tasmania* (1997) 191 CLR 119, 133 per Gaudron, McHugh, and Gummow JJ. It is clear, however, that in this respect a matter is broader than cases and controversies under Article III of the Constitution of the United States; see *Truth About Motorways v. Macquarie* (2000) 200 CLR 591, [112]][119], per Gummow J.

73 In their contemporary commentary, for example, Quick and Garran drew attention to the relevant provisions of the Interpretation Act 1889 (UK): J. Quick and R. R. Garran, *Annotated Constitution of the Australian Commonwealth* (Melbourne, Angus & Robertson, 1901), 792.

74 For a detailed and perceptive analysis, see Leslie Zines, *The High Court and the Constitution* (Sydney, Federation Press, 2008), chap. 17.

extent to which legalism enables the meaning of the Constitution to evolve over time.

1. *Phases*

Any attempt to divide the interpretive history of a constitution into phases must necessarily be rough. Phases are dictated by a combination of circumstances and people. It is rare for either to signal a sharp change from one interpretive style to another. In any phase, moreover, there are likely to be outliers on the court who threaten the validity of generalizations. These caveats should be kept in mind for the purposes of the following account.

A. 1903–1920

The first decade or so after the establishment of the High Court was dominated by two federalism-related problems for which the Constitution made no specific provision.[75] The first was the extent to which the legislation of the respective spheres of government could apply to institutions of the others, a question that first arose in the context of State taxation of Commonwealth officers[76] but that soon arose in reciprocal form, in relation to the application of Commonwealth industrial relations legislation to State employees.[77] The second problem concerned the dividing line between listed Commonwealth powers and the unexpressed residue of power left to the States, particularly when the scope of the former was ambiguous and a wider interpretation interfered with a settled area of State activity.[78]

The first High Court comprised three justices, all of whom had been framers of the Constitution and two of whom had been leaders of the Conventions of 1891 and 1897–98, respectively.[79] Their answer to these problems was that, in general,[80] each sphere of government is immune from

75 For other important constitutional questions raised in this period, see Geoffrey Sawer, *Australian Federal Politics and Law 1901–1929* (Melbourne, MUP, 1956).

76 *D'Emden v. Pedder* (1904) 1 CLR 91.

77 *Federated Amalgamated Government Railway and Tramway Service Association v. New South Wales Railway Traffic Employees Association (Railway Servants'* case) (1906) 4 CLR 488.

78 As in *Huddart, Parker & Co Pty Ltd v. Moorehead* (1908) 8 CLR 330.

79 Samuel Griffith (CJ; Convention of 1891); Edmund Barton (Convention of 1897–98; also first Prime Minister); Richard O'Connor.

80 For exceptions that ultimately assisted to undermine the doctrines, see, e.g., *Attorney-General (NSW) v. Collector of Customs* (*Steel Rails* case) (1908) 5 CLR 818; *Farey v. Burvett* (1916) 21 CLR 433.

legislation of the other, under a doctrine of immunity of instrumentalities, and Commonwealth powers should be interpreted where possible so as not to affect powers deemed to be left by the Constitution to the States under a doctrine of reserved powers. In developing both doctrines, the Court relied on conceptions of the type of federation established by the Constitution. It drew also on decisions of the Supreme Court of the United States on "analogous questions," pointing to the similarity between the two Constitutions.[81] In 1906, two additional Justices were added to the Court[82] who also had been framers of the Constitution but who took a different view of both implications doctrines. In 1920, their views prevailed.[83]

B. 1920–1944

A second, distinct interpretive phase began in 1920, shortly after the end of the First World War. The movement toward Australian independence was under way. A sense of Australian nationhood had been encouraged by the experience of the war and in particular by the disaster of the Gallipoli campaign, which remains a symbol for Australian national sentiment. Looking back at this time fifty years later, admittedly with the benefit of hindsight, Justice Windeyer remarked on the "growing realization that Australians were now one people and Australia one country."[84]

The event that marks the beginning of this period with such certainty was the decision in the *Engineers'* case, which repudiated the immunities doctrines and instituted a new approach to constitutional interpretation generally and to the treatment of Commonwealth legislative powers in particular.[85] The Constitution was to be interpreted "naturally in the light of the circumstances in which it was made, with knowledge of the combined fabric of the common law, and the statute law which preceded it."[86] Implications not referable to constitutional text or common law principle

81 E.g., *D'Emden v. Pedder* (1904) 1 CLR 91, per Griffith CJ. The influential cases included *McCulloch v. Maryland* (1819) 4 Wheat 316, and, in due course, *Collector v. Day* (1871) 11 Wall 113.

82 Isaac Isaacs and Henry Bournes Higgins.

83 See generally Leslie Zines, *The High Court and the Constitution* (Sydney, Federation Press, 5th ed. 2008), 1–9.

84 *Victoria v. Commonwealth* (1971) 122 CLR 353, 396. On the interaction between judicial hindsight and historical understanding, see *Wacando v. Commonwealth* (1981) 148 CLR 1, 22, cited in Henry Burmester, "Justice Windeyer and the Constitution" (1987) 17 *Federal Law Review* 65, 77.

85 *Amalgamated Society of Engineers v. Adelaide Steamship Co Ltd* (1920) 28 CLR 129.

86 *Id.*

were precluded. The interpretive approach of the Privy Council was to be preferred to that of the Supreme Court of the United States. The latter were distinguished by reference to responsible government and the indivisibility of the Crown, as "two cardinal features" of the Australian political system.[87] The potential for "extravagant use of granted powers" was a matter for the political process and not relevant to the deliberations of a court. It followed that Commonwealth powers should be given full effect, according to their terms; that in most cases Commonwealth law could bind State institutions; but that State law normally would not bind the Commonwealth because Commonwealth law was supreme, under section 109.

There is room for argument about when this period ends. The year 1944 marks the approach of the end of the Second World War, during which the Court upheld the validity of a scheme whereby the Commonwealth unilaterally took over State powers to impose income tax, in a classic application of *Engineers'* case methodology, including denial of the relevance of "alleged abuse of power" to the judicial, as opposed to the political process.[88] More important, however, Owen Dixon returned to active service on the High Court that year, which marks the beginning of a largely unbroken period of twenty years of his intellectual domination of the Court.[89]

C. 1944–1981

Dixon was a puisne Justice of the High Court for the first eight years of this period and Chief Justice from 1952 to 1964. Under his influence, a form of Australian legalism that most closely approached what he described as the "strict logic and the high technique of the common law" reached its zenith.[90] Dixon's form of legalism required judges to make their "best endeavour to apply an external standard . . . found in a body of positive knowledge" and not "deliberately to abandon" a legal principle "in the name of justice or of

87 On one view, both are irrelevant in this context; but see Gageler, *op. cit.*, 182.

88 *South Australia v. Commonwealth* (*First Uniform Tax* case) (1942) 65 CLR 373 per Latham CJ. Cases decided in this period also laid down the ground rules for Commonwealth constitutional supremacy and for a broad understanding of the Commonwealth grants power: see *Clyde Engineering v. Cowburn* (1926) 37 CLR 466; *Hume v. Palmer* (1926) 38 CLR 441; *Victoria v. Commonwealth* (1926) 38 CLR 399.

89 Dixon was appointed to the High Court in 1929 but held a range of other positions during the war, and from 1942 to 1944, he was Australian Minister in Washington. Early signs of his interpretive approach, which was influential from the outset, can be seen in, for example, *West v. Commissioner of Taxation (NSW)* (1937) 56 CLR 657.

90 Owen Dixon, "Concerning Judicial Method" (1956) 29 *Australian Law Journal* 468, 469.

…social convenience."[91] In contrast, it also assumed that the law would be "developed . . . adapted . . . and . . . improved" by the "enlightened application of modes of reasoning traditionally respected in the courts."[92]

In a telling demonstration of the use to which high technique could be put, Dixon had earlier noted, with apparent ingenuousness, that "[s]ince *Engineers'* . . . a notion seems to have gained currency that . . . no implications can be made," adding that "of all instruments a written Constitution seems the last to which" such a "method of construction" can be applied.[93] On his watch, implications returned, not only to justify limitations on the power of the Commonwealth to enact a law "which discriminates against States, or . . . which places a particular disability or burden on them"[94] but also in the form of an inference from chapter 3 of the Constitution, which precludes the conferral of nonjudicial power on a federal court.[95] Both doctrines rely on foundational principles of the Constitution, which would now be explained in terms of structure[96] (but in reality require some reference to principles outside the text.[97];.

Legalism continued as the dominant interpretive mode after Garfield Barwick succeeded Dixon as Chief Justice in 1964. Its application was often stylized and artificial, however, and in key areas, the legal tests by which it was claimed validity could objectively be determined became increasingly less convincing, thus producing some arbitrary results.[98] The election of a Labor government in 1972, after more than twenty years in opposition, also produced three years of turbulent politics during which the Court faced a range of novel constitutional questions about the institutions of government,

91 *Ibid.*, 471–472.

92 *Ibid.*

93 *West v. Commissioner of Taxation (NSW)* (1937) 56 CLR 657.

94 *Melbourne Corporation v. Commonwealth* (*State Banking* case) (1947) 74 CLR 31, per Dixon J.

95 *R v. Kirby; ex parte Boilermakers' Society of Australia* (*Boilermakers'* case) (1956) 94 CLR 254.

96 Cheryl Saunders, "Constitutional Structure and Australian Federalism" in Peter Cane (ed.), *Centenary Essays for the High Court of Australia* (Sydney, LexisNexis/Butterworths 2004), 174.

97 See Windeyer in TPT case: 123 CLR 392

98 The areas most affected were the meaning of duties of excise under s. 90 and scope of the absolute freedom of trade, commerce and intercourse among the States in s. 92: see Mason, *op. cit.*, 156–157; also David Jackson, "The Role of the Chief Justice: A View from the Bar" in Cheryl Saunders (ed.), *Courts of Final Jurisdiction* (Sydney, Federation Press, 1996), 21, 22.

including the electoral rules,[99] which were not so readily resolved by old formulas and that assisted in laying the ground for the next phase.

D. 1981–1998

The period 1981–1998 was dominated by two changes in the context in which the Court operates. The first was the countdown to formal independence, effected by the Australia Acts in 1986, leaving the High Court as the final court of appeal in all questions of Australian law. Coupled with the Court's discretion to choose the cases that it would hear following the introduction of a special leave requirement in 1984, this gave the Court the opportunity to exercise what one of Australia's most senior advocates described as "the traditional functions of an ultimate appellate court . . . to declare the law on particular matters, and to remedy significant miscarriages of justice."[100] The second was the phenomenon of internationalization and globalization, accelerated by the collapse of communism in Europe in 1989. One manifestation in Australia was a dramatic increase in the international arrangements to which Australia was a party,[101] many, though not all of which, were implemented into domestic law,[102] and some of which came before the Court in one way or another.[103]

There was a discernible shift in the interpretive method of the High Court during this period. In part, this was attributable to changes in tone and style, which were evident under all three of the Chief Justices who held office in these years but were particularly marked during the chief justiceship of Anthony Mason, from 1987 to 1995.[104] In a major speech made shortly after taking office as Chief Justice, Mason noted that the Court had departed from strict formalism, acknowledged its lawmaking role, and argued that courts had a responsibility to develop the law with "an eye to the justice of a rule and to the fairness and practical efficacy of its operation."[105] As a corollary,

[99] The story is told in Geoffrey Sawer, *Federation under Strain* (Carlton, MUP 1977).

[100] Jackson, *op. cit.*, 22.

[101] The Senate Legal and Constitutional Affairs Committee estimated in 1995 that more than three hundred treaties had been concluded in the previous decade: *Trick or Treaty? Commonwealth Power to Make and Implement Treaties* (November 1995), para. 2.6.

[102] For example, the ICCPR, which came into force for Australia in November 1980; Australia accepted the competence of the Human Rights Committee from January 1993.

[103] For example, *Koowarta v. Bjelke-Petersen* (1982) 153 CLR 168; *Commonwealth v. Tasmania (Tasmania Dam* case) (1983) 158 CLR 1; *Mabo v. Queensland* (1989) 166 CLR 186.

[104] The others were William Gibbs (1981–87) and Gerard Brennan (1995–98).

[105] Mason, *op. cit.*, 158.

the style of judicial reasoning should assist understanding of judgments so that law is not "an esoteric mystery, administered by a priestly class."[106]

In some respects, there were substantive changes in the methodology of the Court as well. Most obviously, during this phase, the Court was prepared to look at substance rather than form,[107] to supplement textual analysis with consideration of purpose,[108] and to sacrifice what sometimes was illusory objectivity to the more subjective demands of proportionality.[109] Some of the touchstones for validity developed in the previous phase were abandoned in consequence, and the meaning of a group of constitutional provisions dealing with "legal and social unity" was reconceived.[110] Second, the Court displayed greater boldness in what Dixon had described as "reasoning from the more fundamental of settled legal principles to new conclusions."[111] The most controversial cases in this category found some protection for liberty and due process in the constitutional separation of judicial power[112] and, in a more novel development still, implied a guarantee of freedom of political communication from the third pillar of principle on which the Constitution rests: representative and responsible government.[113] Third, in at least one case, *Mabo (No. 2)*, the Court abandoned settled legal principle for reasons that were primarily connected with justice and contemporary standards of decency in Australia and elsewhere.[114]

How far the substantive changes to the methodology of the Court during this phase fall outside the boundaries of Australian legalism is a matter of consideration in the following part. In any event, both the methodological shift and some of the highest-profile cases caused considerable controversy and greater-than-usual friction with the elected branches of government. In a notable softening of new doctrine toward the end of this phase, the

[106] *Ibid.*

[107] *Hematite Petroleum Pty Ltd v. Victoria* (1983) 151 CLR 599.

[108] *Cole v. Whitfield* (1988) 165 CLR 360.

[109] *Castlemaine Tooheys Ltd v. South Australia* (1990) 169 CLR 436.

[110] S. 92 and 117 in particular; to a lesser extent, s. 90. The quotation is from *Street v. Queensland Bar Association* (1989) 168 CLR 461 per Brennan J. See generally Cheryl Saunders, "Australian Economic Union," in A. Mullins and C. Saunders (eds.), *Economic Union in Federal Systems*, (Sydney, Federation Press, 1994) 1.

[111] Dixon, "Concerning Judicial Method," *op. cit.*, 472.

[112] *Chu Kheng Lim v. Minister for Immigration, Local Government and Ethnic Affairs* (1992) 176 CLR 1; *Kable v. Director of Public Prosecutions* (1996) 189 CLR 51.

[113] In particular *Australian Capital Television Pty Ltd v. Commonwealth* (1992) 177 CLR 106; *Theophanous v. Herald and Weekly Times Ltd* (1994) 182 CLR 104; *Lange v. Australian Broadcasting Corporation* (1997) 189 CLR 520.

[114] *Mabo v. Queensland (No 2)* (1992) 175 CLR 1 per Brennan J.

constitutional guarantee of freedom of political communication was tied more closely to the "text and structure" of the Constitution,[115] heralding a return to a more overt form of legalism over the final decade.

E. 1998 to the Present

The first part of this phase was marked by continuing tension between the courts and executive government over judicial decisions on indigenous rights. Other sources of tension emerged later, from legislation and Executive action designed to discourage and manage onshore applications for refugee status, which included ouster of the jurisdiction of courts, and from the tightening of security legislation in November 2001 following the attacks in New York in 2001 and the bomb attacks in Bali in 2002. To the extent that this is a consistent theme of this period, it might be deemed to begin a year or so earlier, following the decision in *Wik* that native title can coexist with pastoral leases.[116] But the appointment in 1998 of a new Chief Justice, who from the outset identified both judicial independence and judicial restraint as attributes of the rule of law, makes this an equally convenient starting point.[117] Gleeson retired in 2008 and was succeeded by Robert French; it is too early to tell, however, whether this will make a substantive difference to the methodology of the Court, and for the moment, this phase should be considered as continuing.

As a generalization, the characteristics of the court's interpretive method during this phase have been greater recourse to sometimes highly technical legal argument; reliance on legal criteria for decision making, supported by historical analysis; a consequential repudiation of the relevance of other considerations; and a corresponding tendency to downplay the extent of judicial choice. Legalism has been reaffirmed as the Court's guiding methodology.[118]

On closer examination, however, it is clear that the clock has not entirely been turned back to the legalism of the third phase, itself a compound of

[115] *Lange v. Australian Broadcasting Corporation* (1997) 189 CLR 520.

[116] *Wik Peoples v. Queensland* (1996) 187 CLR 1.

[117] E.g., Murray Gleeson in "The Role of the Judge and Becoming a Judge," Speech to the National Orientation Judicial Programme 16 August 1998; "The Future State of the Judicature," speech to the Third Annual Colloquium of the Judicial Conference of Australia, 11 September 1998, http://www.hcourt.gov.au?publications_05_2.html#MurrayGleeson (viewed 20 April 2009).

[118] Murray Gleeson, "Judicial Legitimacy," Speech to the Australian Bar Association Conference, July 2000, http://www.hcourt.gov.au?publications_05_2.html#MurrayGleeson (viewed 20 April 2009).

different approaches.[119] The high technique of the earlier phase is less evident. In contrast, many of the developments in constitutional doctrine in the wake of 1986 remain in place, though sometimes in a modified form.[120] In addition, the Court in this phase has had creative challenges and opportunities of its own, which make repudiation of extralegal considerations implausible. Most obviously, it inherited the task of adapting the Constitution to the realities of the new relationship between Australia and the United Kingdom.[121] The conclusion to which this process led, that all Australian law is derived from Australian sources, in what W. M. C. Gummow has described as a "multi-planar structure," has also been productive of considerable "doctrinal development" in ways that are characteristic of the new legalism.[122]

2. *Legalism and Realism*

A. Legalism

On the occasion of his swearing in as Chief Justice in 1952, Owen Dixon affirmed his commitment to "strict and complete legalism."[123] That commitment was echoed by two of his predecessors, whose periods as Chief Justice spanned most of following fifty-five years.[124] Legalism is widely accepted as the orthodox methodology for constitutional adjudication in Australia.

It is difficult to pinpoint the outer parameters of Australian legalism, however. This is partly because it is not applied consistently, so exceptions to most generalizations can readily be found. More important, however, it is because it has been applied by different judges in different contexts over time. At its core is insistence that courts resolve questions before them by reference to standards drawn from a body of existing law, not to standards

[119] Michael McHugh, "The Constitutional Jurisprudence of the High Court: 1989–2004" (2008) 30 *Sydney Law Review* 5.

[120] See the substitution of a test of reasonable necessity for the more overtly proportional requirement of appropriate and adapted to determine compliance with s. 92 in *Betfair Pty Ltd v. Western Australia* [2008] HCA 11 [101], [102]. On subsequent developments in relation to the freedom of political communication, see Zines, *op. cit.*, 535 ff.

[121] *Sue v. Hill* (1999) 199 CLR 462; *Singh v. Commonwealth* (2004) 222 CLR 322; *Joosse v. Australian Securities and Investment Commission* (1998) 159 ALR 260.

[122] W. M. C. Gummow, *Change and Continuity* (Oxford, OUP, 1999), 77.

[123] *Swearing in of Sir Owen Dixon as Chief Justice* (1952) 85 CLR xi, xiv.

[124] Garfield Barwick (1964–81), Murray Gleeson (1998–2008).

that are "subjective or personal" to a judge.[125] Appropriate external standards most obviously are found in constitutional and statutory text and precedent, but at least for the most famous advocate of legalism, the sources from which court might properly derive assistance are somewhat wider, including "fundamental . . . settled legal principles."[126]

Beyond this core requirement, itself somewhat fluid, methodological approaches with claims to the mantle of legalism can be ranged along a spectrum. At one end, the spectrum shades into formalism and textualism. Approaches at the other end draw on the very considerable variety of analytical options authorized by the "strict logic" and "high technique" of the common law, understood also as including the embellishments of equity, with its preference of "substance to form."[127] In this mode, legalism lends itself to considerable development of the law to achieve just and workable outcomes, though without acknowledgement of choices consciously or unconsciously made. At least in its application to constitutional questions, legalism also can accept that considerations on the basis of which a court acts are susceptible to characterization as political and that implications are necessary to constitutional construction.[128] High technique often enables an inconvenient line of authority to be circumvented,[129] but a precedent may also be expressly repudiated, at least where it involves a "fundamental error in constitutional principle" with significance that spreads beyond the immediate case.[130]

B. Realism

By contrast, the approach of the Court in the period immediately before and for a decade after the enactment of the Australia Acts has sometimes been described as realism.[131] This is understandable, insofar as the Court did

125 Dixon, "Concerning Judicial Method," *op. cit.*, 471.

126 At 472. For reliance on principle, see the *State Banking* case, per Dixon J.

127 Gummow, *Change and Continuity, op. cit*, 74.

128 *State Banking* case, per Dixon J.

129 For example, in the *Boilermakers'* case.

130 *Commonwealth v. Cigamatic Pty Ltd (In Liq)* (1962) 108 CLR 372; see also the treatment in *Victoria v. Commonwealth (Second Uniform Tax* case) (1957) 99 CLR 575 of the interpretation of the power incidental to the power to impose taxation in the *First Uniform Tax* case. For limits to overruling of a precedent, see the treatment of the meaning of s. 96 in the *Second Uniform Tax* case.

131 Jason L. Pierce, *Inside the Mason Court Revolution* (Durham, NC, Carolina Academic Press, 2006) 25; see also Anthony Mason, "The Role of the Judge at the Turn of the Century," Fifth

not accept that "distinctively *legal* rules and reasons . . . justify a unique result in most cases" and was prepared to identify the considerations by reference to which choices were made.[132] These considerations ranged beyond legal and constitutional principle[133] to aspects of contemporary context[134] and, occasionally, community values.[135] Perception of a qualitative difference in the methodology of the Court during this period also is encouraged by extrajudicial observations of some of its leading members, including the deliberate rejection of legal formalism by Chief Justice Mason himself.[136]

However, the distinctiveness of this phase in the interpretive method of the High Court should not be overstated. Consideration of external factors that are not legal in character, involving at least implicit acknowledgement of judicial discretion, is not unknown in other phases of the history of the Court, although it occurred more regularly during this time.[137] As important, by the 1980s, the Court was too much the heir to the Australian tradition of constitutional interpretation to stray far enough from the genuine influence of constitutional text, structure, and authority to deserve classification as realist,[138] if by that is meant an approach to adjudication in which "judges respond primarily to the stimulus of the facts of the case, rather than to legal rules and reasons."[139] It would be more accurate to describe this phase as one in which the Court accepted that the range of its options were bounded by

Annual Oration in Judicial Administration 1993, in Anthony Mason and Geoffrey Lindell, *The Mason Papers* (Sydney, Federation Press 2007), 44, 55.

132 Brian Leiter, "American Legal Realism" in W. Edmundson and M. Golding (eds.), *The Blackwell Guide to Philosophy of Law and Legal Theory* (Oxford, Blackwell, 2003), referring to the formalist approach to adjudication, which was repudiated by the American realists.

133 See, e.g., the analysis of *Western Australia v. Commonwealth* (*First Territories Representation* case) in Zines, *op. cit.*, 639–642.

134 See Zines, *op. cit.*, 631–632, in relation to consideration of the international context in *Commonwealth v. Tasmania* (*Tasmanian Dam* case) (1983) 158 CLR 1.

135 *Onus v. Alcoa* (1981) 149 CLR 27 per Stephen J; *Minister of State for Immigration and Ethnic Affairs v. Ah Hin Teoh*. Neither of these is a constitutional case.

136 Mason, "Future Directions in Australian Law," *op. cit.*, 155 ff.; see also the somewhat more cautious remarks in Anthony Mason, "The Role of a Constitutional Court in a Federation: A Comparison of the Australian and United States Experience" (1986) 16 *Federal Law Review* 1, 28.

137 Zines, *op. cit.*, 618–628; see also *New South Wales v. Commonwealth* (*Work Choices* case) (2006) 229 CLR, 1, 79: "it is essential to recognise the fundamental and far-reaching legal, social, and economic changes in the place now occupied by the corporation."

138 Anthony Mason, "Trends in Constitutional Interpretation" (1995) 18 *University of New South Wales Law Journal* 237, 245: "the Constitution is our paramount law, and interpretation requires that we give effect to its language and heed what it says."

139 Leiter, *op. cit.*, describing the core claim of realism.

law but that, within those boundaries, there was often room for choice, the bases for the exercise of which should be acknowledged. In some areas it undoubtedly perceived the boundaries as lying further apart than its predecessors or successors would have been prepared to do, although it is far from clear that the overall outcome of the constitutional decisions at this time is a radical departure from a norm.[140]

C. Realistic Legalism

It is generally assumed that the advantage of legalism in Australia is that it shields courts from the perception that constitutional review entrenches on spheres of policy making and lawmaking properly left to the elected branches of government.[141] This assumption may have additional force in a constitutional system in which the combination of a culture of parliamentary sovereignty with an entrenched constitution places additional pressures on constitutional review. If the assumption is correct, it follows that the political attacks on the High Court from 1996 are attributable, at least in part, to the change in its interpretive method.

Although there is something to be said for this chain of reasoning, the reality is more complex. The culture of parliamentary sovereignty that accompanies responsible government and the constraints of a Constitution that is superior law initially were reconciled with each other on the basis of a federation being the only conceivable form of government that would bring the entire continent together; of an entrenched constitution being necessary for federation; and of constitutional review being necessary to resolve disputes about the federal framework. For almost eighty years thereafter, federal questions dominated Australian constitutional law. Even the conclusion that federal courts cannot exercise nonjudicial power was explained in 1956 as a concomitant of a federal form of government.[142] Consistent with this understanding of the purpose and effect of the Constitution, Dixon's commitment to legalism in 1952 was justified as "the only way to maintain the confidence of all parties in Federal conflicts."[143] Although it seems obvious with hindsight that legalism was likely to be

[140] Michael McHugh, "The Constitutional Jurisprudence of the High Court," *op. cit.*

[141] The Hon. Daryl Williams, "The Role of the Attorney-General" (2002) 13 PLR 252, 259 and the sources there cited.

[142] *Boilermakers'* case, 267–268, 276.

[143] (1952) 85 CLR xiv.

useful for the same reason in relation to other "great conflicts,"[144] at the time, almost all of these were federalism related. Even the highly sensitive issue of the validity of Commonwealth legislation outlawing the Communist Party of Australia in the early years of the Cold War presented itself as a question about the federal division of power. The equanimity with which the Court's conclusion of invalidity was met by the government has been attributed to the "neutral conceptions" of the Court.[145]

Against this background, the interpretive phase that spanned the 1980s and much of the 1990s courted controversy for at least three reasons. Most obviously, by exposing the reasoning of the Court more explicitly, it prompted questions about the legitimacy of the judicial role. Equally important, however, it revealed ways in which those parts of the Constitution that distribute functions between the institutions of Commonwealth government might also operate as a constraint on power, with no particular federalism rationale but with rights-protecting effect. Understanding of the first three chapters of the Constitution was transformed during this period as a result. In addition, as Australian constitutional jurisprudence expanded beyond questions of federalism the Court become involved in issues that were more easily understood, on which passions sometimes ran high, and that were more readily perceived as "political."[146] The potential for controversy over constitutional questions was heightened by some of the decisions of the Court in other areas, most obviously those concerning native title.[147]

Criticism of the High Court on the grounds of judicial activism has been stemmed in the past decade. This can be attributed both to the reversion of the Court to a more legalistic style of reasoning and to its renewed emphasis on the federal character of the Constitution, in the course of which any suggestion that the separation of powers might provide protection for liberty has almost entirely disappeared.[148] It is not surprising that the variety and

[144] *Ibid.*

[145] Williams, *op. cit.*, 258.

[146] Cf. Barwick CJ in 1976: "we have no Bill of Rights and that means that our work is strictly legal work," in Address to the National Press Club (1976) 50 *Australian Law Journal* 433, 434, quoted in Williams, *op. cit.*, 259.

[147] See also *Dietrich v. The Queen* (1992) 177 CLR 292; and see generally McHugh, "The Constitutional Jurisprudence of the High Court," *op. cit.*

[148] *Al-Kateb v. Godwin* (2004) 219 CLR 562, *Fardon v. Attorney-General (Qld)* (2004) 223 CLR 575; *Thomas v. Mowbray* [2007] HCA 33; cf. *Chu Kheng Lim v. Minister for Immigration, Local Government and Ethnic Affairs* (1992) 176 CLR 1; *Kable v. Director of Public Prosecutions* (1996) 189 CLR 51. See generally Zines, *op. cit.*, 282 ff.

flow of constitutional litigation has been stemmed as well. But the Court has been exposed instead to criticism on other grounds: the impracticality of some of its decisions,[149] the often convoluted nature of its reasons,[150] outcomes that unnecessarily offend human rights standards,[151] and its failure to give effect to meaningful constraints on Commonwealth power in general and Commonwealth executive power in particular.[152]

In the light of this experience, it is tempting to suggest that the way forward lies in an amalgam of the approaches of the past twenty years, which combines greater openness in judicial reasoning with somewhat greater restraint in the development of the law while recognizing that the Constitution is an instrument that provides a framework not only for the federation but also for institutional checks and balances through which power is controlled and rights can receive a modicum of protection.

3. *Interpretation and Change*[153]

A. An Instrument of Government

Any version of legalism enables some adaptation of the Constitution to contemporary circumstances. A constitution that is written in relatively general terms has a degree of natural flexibility. In addition, it has been accepted from the outset that the character of the Constitution "as an instrument of government meant to endure" must be taken into account in the interpretative process.[154] In a reflection on the influence of the battle over interpretive method during the first twenty years after federation, it is generally assumed that this aphorism requires the Court always to "lean to the broader interpretation" of a constitutional expression unless there are clear indications that it should not.[155] This approach has had its principal

[149] One decision much criticized on this ground is *Re Wakim; Ex parte McNally* (1999) 198 CLR 511: see, e.g., Zines, *op. cit.*, 616; cf. Cheryl Saunders, "Administrative Law and Relations between Governments: Australia and Europe Compared" (2000) 28 *Federal Law Review* 263.

[150] An extreme example is *R v. Hughes* (2000) 202 CLR 535.

[151] E.g., *Al-Kateb v. Godwin* (2004) 219 CLR 562.

[152] *New South Wales v. Commonwealth* (*Work Choices* case) (2006) 229 CLR, 1; *Combet v. Commonwealth* (2005) 224 CLR 494.

[153] See generally Leslie Zines, "Dead Hands or Living Tree? Stability and Change in Constitutional Law" (2004) 25 *Adelaide Law Review* 3.

[154] *Australian National Airways Pty Ltd v. Commonwealth* (1945) 79 CLR 29, 81 per Dixon J; see also *Jumbunna Coalmine, No Liability v. Victorian Coal Miners' Association* (1908) 6 CLR 309, 367, per O'Connor J.

[155] *Jumbunna*, *op. cit.*

impact on the scope of the heads of legislative power allocated to the Commonwealth and accounts for at least part of the expansion of Commonwealth power since the decision in *Engineers*. Its relevance to the interpretation of the few express guarantees in the Constitution is much less clear and its application to them has been mixed.[156] By definition, it has no application at all to constitutional implications.

Nevertheless, the longevity of a deeply entrenched constitution places an essentially text-based interpretive method under pressure, as the conditions in which the constitution operates change over time.[157] In Australia, this has been further alleviated in at least two ways.

First, principles of statutory interpretation focus not only on the text but also on the context and, sometimes, the purpose of an instrument. In the application of these principles to the very particular case of the Australian Constitution, moreover, context is understood to include what often is described as the structure of the Constitution, which in some instances goes beyond the structure of the instrument itself to the core elements of the principles of government for which it provides.[158] Using the concept of structure, implications have been drawn from parts of the Constitution establishing the various institutions of government, so as to provide a deeper level of protection for the institutions themselves, on which Australian constitutionalism in turn depends.[159]

Second, Australian doctrine draws a distinction between the connotation and the denotation of constitutional terms, assisted by the generality with which they often are expressed.[160] The connotation refers to the core meaning and is fixed at the date of the enactment of the Constitution in 1900.[161] The denotation is apt to pick up subsequent developments, as long

156 Compare, e.g., *Attorney-General (Vic); ex Rel Black v. Commonwealth (DOGS* case) (1981) 146 CLR 599 (s. 116: freedom of religion) and *Street v. Queensland Bar Association* (1989) 168 CLR 461; see generally Zines, *The High Court and the Constitution, op. cit.*, 30.

157 Jeremy Kirk, "Constitutional Interpretation and a Theory of Evolutionary Originalism" (1999) 27 *Federal Law Review* 323.

158 Cheryl Saunders, "Constitutional Structure and Australian Federalism" in Peter Cane (ed.), *Centenary Essays for the High Court of Australia* (Sydney, Butterworths 2004), 174; cf. *McGinty v. Western Australia* (1996) 186 CLR 140, 184, per Dawson J.

159 See, e.g., *Austin v. Commonwealth* (2003) 215 CLR 185 (federalism); *Plaintiff S157/2002 v. Commonwealth* (2003) 211 CLR 476 (judicial independence and the rule of law); *Lange v. ABC* (1997) 189 CLR 520 (representative democracy).

160 *Re Professional Engineers' Association* (1959) 197 CLR 208, 267 per Windeyer J. See generally Zines, *The High Court and the Constitution, op. cit.*, 25–27.

161 Cf. *Grain Pool of WA v. Commonwealth* (2000) 202 CLR 479 per Kirby J.

as they also satisfy the core.[162] Views may differ on where the boundary between the two lies in relation to particular terms, as the much-debated example of whether the Commonwealth's marriage power extends to same-sex marriage shows.[163] Nevertheless, this reasoning has played a role in extending the coverage of Commonwealth power to aviation,[164] new forms of intellectual property,[165] a wider range of industrial disputes,[166] and radio and television broadcasting.[167]

The distinction between connotation and denotation sometimes also is used to explain how, by 1999, the United Kingdom had become a "foreign power" for the purposes of section 44(i) of the Constitution, precluding Australians with British citizenship from election to the Commonwealth Parliament.[168] In addition, however, the willingness of the High Court to conceive of the Constitution as an instrument that contained within it the seeds of a Constitution for an independent Australia provided a platform for the many adjustments that have had to be made, ranging from reconception of the authority for the Constitution to construction of a constitutional framework for the exercise of the external sovereignty of Australia and revision of constitutional provisions relating to the scope of the Australian community.

B. Relevance of the Framers

The origin of Australian legalism in the techniques of statutory interpretation makes the meaning of the Constitution at the time of the

[162] For the philosophical derivation of this distinction and reference to other forms in which it appears, see Jeffrey Goldsworthy, "Originalism in Constitutional Interpretation" (1997) 25 *Federal Law Review* 31.

[163] *Re Wakim* (1999) 198 CLR 511 per McHugh J; *Grain Pool, op. cit.*, per Kirby J. For analysis, see Kris Walker, "The Same-Sex Marriage Debate in Australia" (2007) 11 *International Journal of Human Rights* 109.

[164] For the purposes of both the trade and commerce power (s. 51(i)) and the guarantee of the freedom of trade and commerce among the States (s. 92): see, e.g., *R v. Burgess* (1936) 55 CLR 608. On the inclusion of aviation in the scope of the defense power (s. 51(vi)), see Goldsworthy, *op. cit.*, 33.

[165] *Grain Pool, op. cit.*; but see *Davis v. Commonwealth* (1988) 166 CLR 79, 96, in relation to the scope of the power over trade marks: s. 51(xviii).

[166] S. 51(xxxv).

[167] S. 51(v); *R v. Brislan; ex p. Williams* (1935) 166 CLR 262; *Jones v. Commonwealth (No 2)* (1965) 112 CLR 206.

[168] *Eastman's* case, *op. cit.*, per McHugh J, explaining the outcome in *Sue v. Hill* (1999) 199 CLR 462; cf. Anthony Mason, "Trends in Constitutional Interpretation" (1995) 18 *University of New South Wales Law Journal* 237, 242.

enactment a key consideration in resolving disputes. It is not surprising in these circumstances that, when originalism emerged as an influential approach to constitutional interpretation during the 1980s in the United States,[169] it attracted some attention in Australia, particularly as divisions over interpretive method emerged in the course of the 1990s. The temptation to understand the Australian interpretive method through the lens of originalism was further encouraged when the High Court decided, in 1988, that historical sources, including the record of debate at the two Conventions, could be taken into account in constitutional interpretation "for the purpose of identifying the contemporary meaning of the language used."[170]

Originalism comes in a variety of forms. For one of its most famous exponents, Antonin Scalia, it depends not on the intent of the drafters of the Constitution but on more general understanding of constitutional meaning at the time of the founding.[171] The Australian approach to determination of the meaning of constitutional terms in 1900 is much the same, insofar as it seeks, not always consistently, to avoid reliance on the subjective intention of the framers of the Constitution.

Even so, Australian legalism is not originalism, and all but one of the present Justices are legalist, rather than originalist, in their approach.[172] The original meaning of constitutional terms is only one of the considerations taken into account in drawing meaning from the text and structure of the Constitution, albeit an important one.[173] The starting point is the Constitution itself, interpreted with the aid of the multiple techniques of legalism, which offer a degree of flexibility and from time to time enable the Constitution to be "read in a new light."[174] Constitutional interpretation in accordance with the tenets of legalism also requires consideration of more than one hundred years of constitutional doctrine. Much of that, moreover, has been settled in the light of constitutional experience elsewhere. Insofar as originalism

169 See, e.g., Robert Bork, "The Constitution, Original Intent and Economic Rights" (1986) 23 *San Diego Law Review* 823; Antonin Scalia 'Originalism: The Lesser Evil" (1989) 57 *The University of Cincinnati Law Review*, 849.

170 *Cole v. Whitfield* (1988) 165 Commonwealth Law Reports, 360.

171 Antonin Scalia and Kevin J. Ring, *Scalia Dissents* (Washington, DC, Regnery Publishing, 2004) 8.

172 The occasional exception is Heydon J: see, e.g., *Forge v. Australian Securities and Investment Commission* [2006] HCA 44 [250]; *Roach v. Electoral Commissioner* [2007] HCA 43 [181]; *Wong v. Commonwealth of Australia* [2009] HCA 3.

173 *SGH Limited v. Commissioner of Taxation* (2002) 210 CLR 51 [44] per Gummow J; *Singh v. Commonwealth* (2004) 222 CLR 322 [21] ff. per Gleeson CJ.

174 *Victoria v. Commonwealth* (1971) 122 CLR 353, 396, per Windeyer J.

precludes reference to foreign legal sources that could not have been taken into account when the Constitution was made, it is inconsistent with Australian practice, which has accepted the relevance of the experience of other jurisdictions in resolving Australian constitutional problems since the Constitution came into effect.[175] Even the most thoughtful analyses of the extent to which Australian interpretive method might be able to be understood in terms of originalism have found it necessary to qualify the latter as "moderate,"[176] "evolutionary,"[177] or "faint-hearted."[178] In the circumstances, legalism remains a more accurate label, however vulnerable to criticism it may be.

III. SOURCES

1. *Precedent*

Apart from the Constitution itself, the principal source on which Australian courts draw in resolving constitutional disputes is earlier decisions of courts in the Australian court hierarchy. The High Court has been at the apex of that hierarchy for most constitutional questions since federation,[179] and it now has unquestioned authority. Decisions of the High Court are binding on all other Australian courts and generally are followed by the High Court itself, subject to what is said here.

There are presently seven Justices of the High Court. The quorum for a Full Court is two Justices, but a typical minimum is three and in practice at least five Justices are likely to sit on significant cases. All seven Justices generally sit *en banc* for constitutional cases of any degree of importance, whether in the original jurisdiction of the Court or on appeal. It is relatively unusual for the Court to sit with an equal number of Justices, but where this occurs and where the Court is evenly divided, the decision of the Court below is affirmed, in the case of an appeal. If such a situation occurs when the Court is sitting in its original jurisdiction, the decision of the Chief

175 But see the reasons of Heydon J in *Forge*, *Roach*, and *Wong*.

176 Goldsworthy, *op. cit.*

177 Jeremy Kirk, "Constitutional Interpretation and a Theory of Evolutionary Originalism" (1999) 27 *Federal Law Review* 323.

178 *Eastman's* case, per McHugh J [140], quoting Antonin Scalia, who describes his own originalism in the same terms: "The Role of a Constitutional Court in a Democratic Society" (1995) 2 *Judicial Review* 141, 142.

179 Constitution s. 74.

Justice prevails.[180] Although these rules ensure that there is an outcome in such cases, the decisions themselves are not regarded as binding precedents in the High Court.[181]

The High Court normally follows its own decisions, in the interests of "continuity and consistency."[182] It has always maintained the authority to depart from them for sufficient reason, however, and from time to time, it has done so.[183] The Court may be more ready to overrule itself in constitutional than other cases, because of the inability of Parliament to alter a constitutional rule.[184] The considerations that it takes into account in exercising this discretion include the magnitude of the perceived error, the extent to which the challenged precedent has become embedded in the jurisprudence by subsequent decisions of the Court, the practical steps taken in reliance on the challenged precedent, and the degree of inconvenience that overruling would cause.[185] In the past, the Court has declined to hear argument about whether an earlier case was wrongly decided;[186] its right to do so has been contested by individual Justices, however, and it may be that future courts will not take the same view.[187]

2. *Extrinsic Materials*

The High Court has always taken history into account and, indeed, its interpretive method obliges it to do so.[188] Nevertheless, until relatively recently, the Court precluded itself from examining a range of historical

[180] Judiciary Act 1903 s. 23 (2)(a), (b).

[181] *Tasmania v. Victoria* (1935) 52 CLR 157 per Dixon J. For a more recent example, in which this rule was unsuccessfully contested, see the treatment of *Gould v. Brown* (1998) 193 CLR 346 in *Re Wakim* (1999) 198 CLR 511, per Gummow and Hayne JJ.

[182] *R v. Commonwealth Court of Conciliation and Arbitration (Brisbane Tramways* case) (1914) 18 CLR 54, per Barton J.

[183] Examples are given by Aickin J in *Queensland v. Commonwealth* (*Second Territories Representation* case) (1977) 139 CLR 585.

[184] *Perpetual Executors & Trustees Association of Australia Ltd v. Federal Commissioner of Taxation* (1949) 77 CLR 493, per Latham CJ.

[185] *Commonwealth v. Hospital Contribution Fund* (1982) 150 CLR 49 per Gibbs CJ. See also *Second Territories Representation* case, per Stephen J; cf. *Esso Australia Resources v. Commissioner of Taxation* (1999) 201 CLR 49 [164] per Callinan J.

[186] *Evda Nominees v. Victoria* (1984) 154 CLR 311.

[187] In *Evda Nominees* by Deane J, and on numerous subsequent occasions by Kirby J: e.g., *XYZ v. Commonwealth* [2006] HCA 25 [80], and the other cases there cited. In *XYZ*, the joint judgment noted that it is "unnecessary to embark on the question of what is involved in the statement," in *Evda Nominees.*

[188] *Amalgamated Society of Engineers v. Adelaide Steamship Co Ltd* (1920) 28 CLR 129.

sources for the purpose. It was accepted that in constitutional cases the Court might draw historical inferences from successive drafts of the Constitution before it came into effect.[189] The Court was unable, however, formally to take into account the record of debates of the Constitutional Conventions and other, comparable, extrinsic material.[190] In consequence, after those who had been involved in framing the Constitution left the Court, many of its historical conclusions necessarily were based on assumptions about historical fact; on earlier judicial decisions drawing historical conclusions; or on those historical materials that were acceptable in the Court, including, somewhat surprisingly, Quick and Garran.[191] In 1988, however, in the course of a complete revision of the understanding of the guarantee of freedom of interstate trade, commerce, and intercourse in section 92, the Court accepted that historical sources were admissible and made extensive use of them.[192] Reference to historical sources, including the Convention Debates, is now a frequent practice.

The question of the source from which the High Court derives any nonlegal information on which its reasoning is based is not confined to history but arises in relation to other forms of information as well: social, economic, and commercial data; political facts; and community values. In many cases, information is received under a somewhat generous doctrine of judicial notice as a matter of "general public knowledge."[193] In general, however, the Court lacks developed procedures whereby such information can formally be presented to it and handled in a way that is consistent with the adversarial process.[194] In part, this may be the consequence of assumptions about the extent to which such information is relevant when decisions are made on legal criteria alone. In this respect, it is notable that,

[189] *Tasmania v. Commonwealth* (1904) 1 CLR 329, 333, per Griffiths J, in argument, although the point also is put into practice in the reasons of the Court.

[190] John Waugh notes that the availability of this material made Australia a "constitutional laboratory": "Lawyers, Historians and Federation History" in Robert French, Geoffrey Lindell, and Cheryl Saunders (eds.), *Reflections on the Australian Constitution* (Sydney, Federation Press, 2003), 25, 26.

[191] J. Quick and R. R. Garran, *Annotated Constitution of the Australian Commonwealth* (Sydney, Angus & Robertson 1901). For the use made of this source, see Helen Irving, "The Framers' Vision of the High Court" in Peter Cane (ed.), *Centenary Essays for the High Court of Australia* (Sydney, LexisNexis Butterworths, 2004), 17, 34.

[192] *Cole v. Whitfield* (1988) 165 CLR 360. Occasional references can be found in earlier cases from the 1970s: Carl McCamish, "The Use of Historical Materials in Interpreting the Commonwealth Constitution" (1996) 70 *Australian Law Journal* 638, 654.

[193] *Stenhouse v. Coleman* (1944) 69 CLR 457, per Dixon J.

[194] For discussion of some cases in which this difficulty has been manifest, see *Thomas v. Mowbray* (2007) HCA 33 [527–529], per Callinan J.

even during the period when the Court most explicitly took nonlegal considerations into account, there was no corresponding change to its procedures.[195] Consistent with its position as an apex court, procedures in the High Court in any event are designed to avoid the trial of facts as far as possible, even when they are ordinary facts that could arise between the parties in proceedings in original jurisdiction.[196]

The issue arises in an acute form when a fact is a constitutional fact on which the validity of a challenged law depends. Such a fact is not necessarily an ordinary fact in issue between the parties and thus automatically subject to the rules of evidence.[197] However, it may be contested by the party claiming invalidity. The difficulty of dealing with material of this kind is compounded in one particular context in which it is likely to arise: a challenge to the validity of security legislation, where the constitutional fact is the existence of a threat to security that provides the necessary link between the legislation and the power on which it relies. The Court must be satisfied of the existence of such a fact and will not rely on assurances by the executive branch.[198] In contrast, the latter may be unwilling to lead evidence, at least in public.[199] Final resolution of how such facts should be determined so far has been avoided either by reliance on an extended doctrine of judicial notice or other "rational considerations"[200] or by resolving the case on another ground.[201] A more extended analysis of the problem in a recent case, in which it was suggested that the rules of evidence do not apply to the determination of constitutional facts but that the information should be made available to all parties in a manner that enables them to present evidence if they wish to do so, is likely to frame future consideration of the issue.[202]

[195] John Doyle, "Implications of Judicial Law-Making" in Cheryl Saunders (ed.), *Courts of Final Jurisdiction* (Sydney, Federation Press, 1996) 84, 97–98.

[196] See in particular the effect of a case stated or a demurrer: Kenneth Hayne, "High Court Rules 2004," *Introductory Remarks at Seminars for the Legal Profession* October–November 2004, http://www.hcourt.gov.au/speeches/haynej_04nov04.html (viewed 1 May 2009).

[197] For the distinction, see *Thomas v. Mowbray* (2007) HCA 33 [614] per Heydon J.

[198] *Thomas v. Mowbray* [225]–[226] and the cases there cited, per Kirby J.

[199] George Winterton, "The *Communist Party* case" in H. P. Lee and George Winterton (eds.), *Australian Constitutional Landmarks* (Cambridge, CUP, 2003, 108, 124.

[200] *Marcus Clark & Co Ltd v. The Commonwealth* (1952) 87 CLR 177, 227 per McTiernan J.

[201] *Australian Communist Party v. Commonwealth* (1951) 83 CLR 1; *Thomas v. Mowbray* (2007) HCA 33.

[202] *Thomas v. Mowbray* (2007) HCA 33 [636]–[639] per Heydon J.

3. *Foreign Law*

The High Court has always referred relatively freely to the law of other jurisdictions in dealing with questions of both constitutional and nonconstitutional law. Although statistics are incomplete, it is clear that the frequency has varied from an extremely high proportion of foreign-to-Australia citations in the first decade to gradually declining proportions thereafter.[203] A study in 2000 suggested that the decline came to an end around 1950, after which the proportion has remained more or less steady, at around 25 percent.[204] Preliminary results from a new, more comprehensive study covering the decade from 1998 suggest that the proportion of constitutional cases and of majority judgments in which foreign law is cited is well more than 50 percent.[205] These statistics do not indicate how the foreign authority is used or whether it has been accepted or rejected. Anecdotally, treatment is mixed. Anecdotally, also, citations of foreign law appear across a wide range of constitutional issues, including federalism, separation of judicial power, and political rights.[206]

The practice itself is not controversial in Australia. This is unsurprising in relation to the years immediately following federation, given the reliance on foreign models in the drafting of the Constitution.[207] References to British authorities also are unsurprising in the decades before independence, when the decisions of the Privy Council were binding and offered a conduit through which constitutional experience elsewhere was brought to bear on comparable Australian constitutional questions.

But neither of these factors explains the prevalence of references to decisions of the Supreme Court of the United States handed down after the Australian Constitution was enacted, which continued throughout the twentieth century. And reference to British and Canadian authority persisted throughout the period when a distinctive Australian common law began to emerge and as appeals to the Privy Council were severed. In 1986, the

203 Brian Opeskin, "Constitutional Law in a Global Era" in French, Lindell, and Saunders, *op. cit.*, 171, 184.

204 The study in fact shows a decline to 10 percent at the beginning of the 1980s; this is such a deviation from the pattern, however, that it is likely to be the consequence of the sampling technique.

205 Results not yet published but available from the author.

206 For one qualitative study, see Cheryl Saunders, "The Use and Misuse of Comparative Constitutional Law" (2006) 13 *Indiana Journal of Global Legal Studies* 37.

207 See also the annotations in Quick and Garran, *op. cit.*, which outlines the foreign practices to which each section of the Constitution is referable and identifies some of the foreign authorities that might assist in understanding them.

relevance of British decisions in Australia was formally considered by the High Court in terms that are significant for present purposes. Independence meant that statements in British decisions "should no longer be seen as binding on Australian courts." Nevertheless:

> The history of this country and of the common law makes it inevitable and desirable that the courts of this country will continue to obtain assistance and guidance from the learning and reasoning of United Kingdom courts just as Australian courts benefit from the learning and reasoning of other great common law courts [but] the precedents of other legal systems are not binding and are useful only to the degree of the persuasiveness of their reasoning.[208]

The range of jurisdictions to which the High Court is most likely to refer is relatively narrow: the United Kingdom, the United States, Canada, New Zealand, India, South Africa, and Ireland.[209] The use that it makes of such authority is broadly comparable to that of other common law courts that follow the same practice. Foreign law generally is used for the purposes that Emeritus Justice Laurie Ackermann of South Africa once suggested: "seeking information, guidance, stimulation, clarification, or even enlightenment[,] . . . keeping the judicial mind open to new ideas."[210] It is always a secondary consideration, especially if there is an Australian authority in point. Obvious legal and structural differences between Australia and other jurisdictions typically are taken into account, although subtler differences may be missed.

In Australia, as elsewhere, there is some potential for the practice of referring to the law of other jurisdictions to become caught up in the debate on judicial activism. This has been largely avoided so far, not least because references to foreign law have always been considered compatible with Australian legalism.[211] The practice is presently under pressure from various quarters, however, which in time may affect the extent and manner of its use. These include the perception of the growing distinctiveness of the Australian legal and constitutional system and the palpable, if so far limited, influence in Australia of the United States debate on originalism, with its implications for the use of foreign law. The present picture is further confused by some

[208] *Cook v. Cook* (1986) 162 CLR 376.

[209] Opeskin, *op. cit.*, 186.

[210] Laurie H. Ackermann, "Constitutional Comparativism in South Africa: A Response to Sir Basil Markesinis and Jorg Fedtke" (2005) 80 *Tulane Law Review* 169, 183.

[211] Dixon, "Concerning Judicial Method," *op. cit.*, 470–471; see also the use made of foreign authorities by Dixon J in *Melbourne Corporation v. Commonwealth* (1947) 74 CLR 31.

acerbic exchanges within the High Court about the relevance of international law to constitutional interpretation, to which the Court takes a quite different approach.

4. *International Law*

Australia adheres to a distinctively dualist theory of the relationship between domestic and international law, which derives from its common law foundations.[212] International law is not part of the domestic legal system; treaties must be transformed by statute to affect rights and interests under Australian law, and there is uncertainty about whether customary international law also is subject to transformation.[213] The rule has historical roots but draws its contemporary rationale from the separation of powers, under a Constitution that leaves the authority to make and ratify treaties with the executive alone.[214]

Even without a specific act of transformation, international law may indirectly affect Australian law in a variety of ways.[215] It may have an influence on the development of the common law,[216] although caution is required to ensure that judicial decision is not a substitute for parliamentary enactment.[217] It may be taken into account in interpreting legislation, although there is some inconsistency in judicial pronouncements about whether the legislation need be enacted to implement the treaty and the extent of the ambiguity that must first be found.[218] There is authority that a treaty to which Australia is a party may give rise to a procedural legitimate expectation that administrators will act in conformity with it, so that a person

212 Ironically, early drafts of the Constitution would have given treaties direct effect. It is generally assumed that this was an oversight, and the offending provision was removed in 1897: Hilary Charlesworth, Madelaine Chiam, Devika Howell, and George Williams, "Deep Anxieties: Australia and the International Legal Order" (2003) 25 *Sydney Law Review* 423.

213 *Nulyarimma v. Thompson* (1999) 165 ALR 621; Andrew D Mitchell, "Genocide, Human Rights Implementation and the Relationship between International and Domestic Law: *Nulyarimma v. Thomson*" (2000) 24 *Melbourne University Law Review* 15. For a critique of the dichotomy between incorporation and transformation in the Australian context, see Kristen Walker, "Treaties and the Internationalisation of Australian Law" in Cheryl Saunders (ed.), *Courts of Final Jurisdiction* (Sydney, Federation Press, 1996), 204.

214 *Simsek v. McPhee* (1982) 148 CLR 636.

215 For a comprehensive summary see Charlesworth et al., *op. cit.*

216 *Mabo v. Queensland* (nº 2) (1992) 175 CLR 1 per Brennan J.

217 *Minister of State for Immigration v. Teoh* (1995) 183 CLR 273, drawing an analogy between derivative development of the common law by reference to statute and to international law.

218 Compare *Teoh's* case with *Plaintiff S157/2002 v. Commonwealth* (2003) 211 CLR 476 per Gleeson CJ [29].

affected by the decision is entitled to be given notice if that is not the case.[219] This authority has been eroded by subsequent cases, however, and the principle must now be regarded as unsettled.[220]

As a general rule, international law is not used as an aid in constitutional interpretation. This was established by earlier decisions of the High Court, when it was still accurate to describe international law as "a law for the intercourse of States with one another and not a law for individuals."[221] The view that international human rights law should be taken into account in cases where the meaning or application of the Constitution is unclear was pressed strongly by one member of the Court, Michael Kirby, during the Court's recent interpretive phase.[222] In the absence of constitutional rights, such arguments typically are directed to restriction of the scope or application of Commonwealth heads of legislative power.[223] Thus, in *Kartinyeri*, Justice Kirby held that the answer to the question of whether the power to make laws with respect to the "people of any race for whom it is deemed necessary to make special laws" could be used to discriminate against an indigenous group should be answered in the negative, in the face of both customary international law and treaty.[224]

In this as in other cases, the remaining Justices remained unpersuaded of the applicability of international law. The resulting, sometimes hostile, exchanges reveal a range of reasons. There is no proper analogy between the use of international law for the purposes of constitutional interpretation and the principle of statutory construction because the former operates as a constraint on power that Parliament cannot overcome. Most current rules of international law postdate the making of the Constitution; to take them into account in interpreting the Constitution would be to amend the Constitution without using the formal alteration procedure; in any event, international law is too voluminous to be practically useful for this purpose; moreover,

[219] *Teoh* [36].

[220] In particular, *Re Minister for Immigration and Multicultural Affairs; ex parte Lam* (2003) 214 CLR 1.

[221] *Polites v. Commonwealth* (1945) 70 CLR 60, per Starke J.

[222] *Newcrest Mining (WA) Ltd v. Commonwealth* (1997) 190 CLR 513. The issue had been raised just before his appointment to the Court in 1996 in the particularly stark context of the *Stolen Generations* case: *Kruger v. Commonwealth* (1997) 190 CLR 1.

[223] But see *Al-Kateb v. Godwin*, where the meaning of the separation of judicial power also was in issue: (2004) 219 CLR 562.

[224] *Kartinyeri v. Commonwealth* (1998) 195 CLR 337.

Australia is not necessarily represented on the committees by which some of the international instruments are interpreted and applied.[225]

Some of these points might also be made about the use of foreign law, and occasionally the two are run together.[226] Generally, however, they are distinguished, a phenomenon that might be explained in a variety of ways. References to foreign law present no challenge to the separation of executive and legislative power. Unlike international treaties to which Australia is a party, foreign law has no claim to be binding and represents only a source of ideas that "attracts adherence as opposed to obliging it."[227] References to foreign law have long since been established as a component of the high technique of legalism. International law is not only a relative newcomer; Justice Kirby linked it to a different approach to constitutional interpretation that recognized the Constitution as a "living force."[228] International law represents a new source of restrictions on Commonwealth heads of power, unsupported by the text or structure of the Constitution. It thus presents a new challenge to the plenary character of Commonwealth power that was settled in *Engineers*.[229]

Nevertheless, there is some evidence in Australia of the interpenetration of international and domestic law, even in the constitutional context. Most notably, international law has been a medium for the dramatic expansion of Commonwealth power vis-à-vis the States, when the external affairs power in section 51(xxix) of the Constitution was interpreted to authorize Commonwealth legislation to implement any international agreements to which Australia is a party.[230] The extent to which the legislation gives effect

[225] *Al-Kateb v. Godwin* (2004) 219 CLR 562 [66] ff., per McHugh J. The latter point is made by Heydon J in *Roach v. Electoral Commissioner* (2007) HCA 43 [181].

[226] See, e.g., the reasons of Heydon J in *Roach* at [181], but see Kirby J in *Al-Kateb v. Godwin* at [155] ff. Cf. the reasons of McHugh J in *Al-Kateb v. Godwin*, apparently distinguishing the usage of the two: [51] ff.

[227] Patrick Glenn, "Persuasive Authority" (1987) 32 *McGill Law Review* 261, 263. The exchange in *Al-Kateb* between McHugh and Kirby JJ about whether international law represents rules or principles may reflect this distinction.

[228] The approach is outlined in Michael Kirby, "Constitutional Interpretation and Original Intent: A Form of Ancestor Worship" (2000) 24 *Melbourne University Law Review* 1. The quotation is from one of the framers of the Constitution, Andrew Inglis Clark, *Studies in Australian Constitutional Law* (Melbourne 1901).

[229] The point may underlie the observations in Zines, *The High Court and the Constitution, op. cit.*, 32.

[230] *Commonwealth v. Tasmania* (*Tasmanian Dam* case) (1983) 158 CLR 1. The Court will not consider whether the treaty itself is valid in international law: *Horta v. Commonwealth* (1994) 181 CLR 183.

to such an agreement in turn became a measure of validity.[231] Very occasionally, international law is raised in relation to other constitutional questions as well. In *XYZ*, the extent to which international law recognizes the extraterritorial jurisdiction of states was considered in rejecting a challenge to the validity of Commonwealth legislation criminalizing sexual acts with persons younger than sixteen, outside Australia, on the part of Australian citizens or residents.[232] In *Bradley*, Chief Justice Gleeson referred to international law sources, among others, to demonstrate the "fundamental importance" of judicial independence.[233] These are minor instances, however. For the foreseeable future, more extensive use of international law in constitutional interpretation is likely to be inhibited by a combination of the content of the Constitution and the prevailing interpretive approach.

BIBLIOGRAPHY

Australian Law Reform Commission, *Beyond the Door-Keeper: Standing to Sue for Public Remedies* (Report No. 78, 1996).

Australian Law Reform Commission, *The Judicial Power of the Commonwealth* (Report No. 92, 2001)

COWEN, Z., and L. ZINES. *Federal Jurisdiction in Australia*, 3rd ed. Sydney: Federation Press, Oxford University Press, 2002.

GALLIGAN, BRIAN. *A Federal Republic: Australia's Constitutional System of Government*. Cambridge: Cambridge University Press, 1995.

GALLIGAN, BRIAN. *Politics of the High Court: A Study of the Judicial Branch of Government in Australia.* St. Lucia: University of Queensland Press, 1987.

GUMMOW, W. M. C. *Change and Continuity*. Oxford: Oxford University Press, 1999.

OPESKIN, BRIAN, and FIONA WHEELER, eds. *The Australian Federal Judicial System*. Melbourne: Melbourne University Press, 2000.

PATAPAN, HAIG. *Judging Democracy: The New Politics of the High Court of Australia.* Cambridge: Cambridge University Press, 2000.

PIERCE, JASON L. *Inside the Mason Court Revolution: The High Court of Australia Transformed.* Durham, NC: Carolina Academic Press, 2006.

[231] *Tasmanian Dam* case, at 259, per Deane J; see generally Zines, *The High Court and the Constitution, op. cit.*, 392.

[232] *XYZ v. Commonwealth* (2006) HCA 25 [5] ff. per Gleeson CJ.

[233] *North Australian Legal Aid v. Bradley* (2004) 218 CLR 146 [3]. The sources were the Universal Declaration of the Independence of Justice and the Beijing Statement of Principles of the Independence of the Judiciary in the Lawasia Region.

SAUNDERS, CHERYL, ed. *Courts of Final Jurisdiction*. Sydney: Federation Press, 1996.

SAWER, GEOFFREY. *Australian Federal Politics and Law*, 2 vols. Melbourne: Melbourne University Press, 1956.

SCALIA, ANTONIN. *A Matter of Interpretation.* Princeton, NJ: Princeton University Press, 1998.

Senate Legal and Constitutional Affairs Committee. *Trick or Treaty? Commonwealth Power to Make and Implement Treaties*. Senate of Australia, November 1995.

ZINES, LESLIE. *The High Court and the Constitution.* Sydney: Federation Press, 2008).

AUSTRIA

CONSTITUTIONAL COURTS AS POSITIVE LEGISLATORS

Konrad Lachmayer
Researcher and lecturer, Faculty of Law, University of Vienna
konrad.lachmayer@univie.ac.at

I. INTRODUCTION: CONSTITUTIONAL JUSTICE IN AUSTRIA

The Austrian Constitution was enacted in 1920 and, regarding its process of origin, was mainly influenced by Hans Kelsen, who especially focused on the creation of a Constitutional Court (Verfassungsgerichtshof). The Constitutional Court is a centralized body that has the function of controlling the constitutionality of various acts of the state, including judicial review of legislation. The competences of the court have been continually extended over the past ninety years, which has substantially improved the access to constitutional justice. However, the Constitutional Court was designed as a kind of "negative legislator"; its function is to control and to declare legislative and administrative acts void when they are deemed to be unconstitutional or in breach of fundamental rights.

The developments of the past three decades clearly show that the Court is willing to become more active by using different possibilities to extend its competences toward taking a more active role in constitutional interpretation. This contribution shall analyze the different ways of transforming constitutional law through jurisdiction.

Since 1925, article 138, paragraph 2, of the Austrian Constitution has enabled the Austrian Constitutional Court to act as a "positive legislator." Although the practical relevance of the provision is not very significant, it clearly gives positive powers to the court in a sensitive area: the division of competences between the Federation and the States (*Länder*). The provision[1] reads as follows: "The Constitutional Court furthermore determines at the application of the Federal Government or a state Government whether a legislative or executive act is part of the competence of the Federation or the States." This means that the Constitutional Court has the final say on the question of whether the ultimate authority belongs to the Federation or the States (*Länder*). It is important to know that, in the Austrian concept of a federal state, concurring competences do not exist, only a strict separation of powers. The judgment of the Constitutional Court,[2] pronounced within its competence in article 138, paragraph 2, of the Austrian Constitution, is understood to be an authentic interpretation of the constitution, meaning that the Constitutional Court is enacting constitutional law. This is the sole example of an explicit competence of the Constitutional Court in its function as a positive legislator. All the other aspects, which shall be discussed here, are not explicit in the same way but show important developments of the legal culture and interpretation of the Constitutional Court.

II. BRIEF DESCRIPTION OF THE JUDICIAL REVIEW METHOD APPLIED IN AUSTRIA

1. *Introduction*[3]

The competence of the Constitutional Court to decide on questions of the relation between the Federation and the States (*Länder*), which is part of the federal principle of the Austrian Constitution, was important in the conceptual design of the Court. Over the past thirty years, issues concerning fundamental human rights have become more and more important in the daily work of the Court. Today, procedures dealing with violations of human rights are the main task of the Constitutional Court.

1 The Austrian Constitution is not codified in one constitutional act but in various constitutional acts and constitutional provisions. However, the main document of the Austrian Constitution is the Federal Constitutional Act of 1920, as amended in 1929. This act is referred to as the Austrian Constitution in this report. See Anna Gamper, "Introduction to the Study of the Law of the Austrian Federal Constitution," Vol. 2, *ICL-Journal* 2/2008, 92 (http://www.icl-journal.com).

2 Although the decisions of ordinary courts are called judgments, in the Austrian legal language, the decisions of the Constitutional Court are called *Erkenntnis* (cognition). The judges of the constitutional court do not decide; they cognize (*erkennen*); see Art. 137–145 Austrian Constitution "The Constitutional Court cognize . . ."

3 See in general Manfred Stelzer, *An Introduction to Austrian Constitutional Law* (2nd edn., Vienna LexisNexis 2009).

From an organizational perspective, it should be mentioned that the Austrian Constitutional Court consists of a president, a vice president, and twelve additional judges.[4] The judges are appointed by the Federal President of the Austrian Republic on proposal by the federal government (president, vice president, six judges) and by Parliament (the other six judges).[5] The Court decides by majority vote; the President usually has no vote.[6] Concurring or dissenting opinions are not permitted.

The Constitutional Court is one of three supreme courts in the Austrian system of legal protection. The other highest courts are the Administrative Court (Verwaltungsgerichtshof) and the Supreme Court (Oberster Gerichtshof, which deals with civil and criminal cases). The Constitutional Court is the only court empowered to declare legislative acts unconstitutional and to nullify them. However, the other supreme courts have the jurisdiction to interpret the legislation according to the constitution (*verfassungskonforme Interpretation*). If the courts have doubts on the constitutionality of a statute (Act of Parliament) or a general administrative act, they are obliged to file an application to the Constitutional Court.[7] The consequence of this concept is that individuals cannot file a complaint to the Constitutional Court if ordinary courts are competent to decide. The concept of *Verfassungsbeschwerde* (constitutional complaint) is not realized in the Austrian system of constitutional justice.

The concepts of separation of powers and legal protection in Austria separate administrative matters from civil and criminal matters. Legal protection within administrative criminal matters can be obtained before administrative bodies and finally before the Administrative Court and the Constitutional Court (with regard to human rights violations). In civil and criminal matters,[8] the individual seeks legal protection before the ordinary courts and finally before the Supreme Court. Thus, the individual cannot apply to the Constitutional Court when doubting the constitutionality of a legislative act. The Supreme Court itself regularly applies to the Constitutional Court. However, a significant lack of legal protection exists within the Austrian constitutional system, because individuals have no

4 See Ronald Faber, "The Austrian Constitutional Court – An Overview," Vol. 2, *ICL-Journal* 1/2008, 49 (http://www.icl-journal.com).

5 Art. 147 Austrian Constitution.

6 See Sec. 31 Constitutional Court Act.

7 See Art. 89 Austrian Constitution.

8 An important reservation has to be made. Some relevant aspects of criminal and civil matters are part of the administrative matters. Thus, only the core elements of civil and criminal matters are reserved for ordinary courts.

possibility to access constitutional justice in this area. A legislative attempt to solve these problems of legal protection failed in 2008 for political reasons.[9]

2. *Access to Constitutional Justice*

The typical (and most common) access to constitutional justice is a constitutional complaint after the completion of an administrative procedure. The most important access to constitutional justice is provided by article 144 of the Austrian Constitution,[10] according to which every person has the possibility to obtain a constitutional review on normative decisions by administrative authorities. In such case, the appellant claims the infringement of a fundamental right or the unconstitutionality of a legislative act on which an administrative decision is based. The complaint can be filed only if all other legal remedies have been exhausted.

In 1975, access to constitutional justice was broadened.[11] An individual person can now directly apply to the Constitutional Court to have a legislative act declared unconstitutional (*Individualantrag*).[12] This option is only subsidiary to the existing ways of access to constitutional justice.[13] The requirements for such a direct application are very strict in that the statute has a direct and actual effect on the (legal) rights of the individual concerned.[14] In addition, article 140 of the Austrian Constitution demands that there is no other legal remedy to reasonably obtain legal protection. Thus, because individuals can appeal to administrative authorities or ordinary courts, it is not permitted to call on the Constitutional Court directly. The Constitutional Court examines these requirements quite strictly. This is the reason the number of cases launched by individuals before the Constitutional Court is very limited.

9 On reform plans, see Ronald Faber, "The Austrian Constitutional Court – An Overview," Vol. 2, *ICL-Journal* 1/2008, 49 (52); on the constitutional reform of 2008, see Harald Eberhard and Konrad Lachmayer, "Constitutional Reform 2008 in Austria: Analysis and Perspectives," Vol. 2, *ICL-Journal* 2/2008, 112 (118) (http://www.icl-journal.com).

10 Regarding the fragmented structure of the Austrian Constitution, see Harald Eberhard and Konrad Lachmayer, "Constitutional Reform 2008 in Austria: Analysis and Perspectives," (2008) 2 *ICL-Journal* 112–23 (http://www.icl-journal.com).

11 Other possibilities regarding election or financial disputes are not mentioned in detail here. See Art. 141 Austrian Constitution; Art. 137 Austrian Constitution.

12 See Art. 140 Austrian Constitution.

13 Art. 140 para. 1 of the Austrian Constitution does not offer a general possibility to appeal against a legislative act.

14 VfSlg 8009/1977.

After World War II (i.e., in the so-called Second Republic), the Constitutional Court broadened access to its jurisdiction with regard to more informal acts of law enforcement (*Faktische Amtshandlungen*),[15] such as (disproportionate) police controls or (violent) acts of administrative authorities. In the constitutional amendment of 1975, this possibility of access to constitutional justice was codified in article 144 of the Austrian Constitution.[16] The workload became so considerable that the competence to deal with these acts of law enforcement was transferred to Independent Administrative Tribunals (*Unabhängige Verwaltungssenate*) established at the end of the 1980s.[17] However, access to constitutional justice is guaranteed, as there is a possibility to file a complaint against the decision of the Independent Administrative Tribunal before the Constitutional Court.

As of 2008, the competences of both the Supreme Administrative Court as and as the Constitutional Court in Asylum have been severely restrained: asylum seekers can no longer apply to the Administrative Court but only to the so-called Asylum Court. Moreover, the Constitutional Court can dismiss claims of asylum seekers without examining the merits of the complaint.

In the context of separation of powers, the so-called abstract judicial review of statutes (*Abstrakte Normenkontrolle*) should also be mentioned. One third of the Members of Parliament or governments of the States (*Länder*) can apply directly to the Constitutional Court for review of the accordance of federal statutes with the Constitution.[18]

From the perspective of individuals, only the administrative procedure ensures appropriate access to constitutional justice. Existing problems of legal protection in administrative procedures relate to the possibilities of obtaining legal protection. Only specific acts of administrative authorities can be subject to an administrative procedure. An important compensation of the deficits of access to constitutional justice is state liability for damages caused by unlawful acts of the administration.[19] Regarding civil and criminal matters, access to constitutional justice is, as mentioned earlier, restricted because the respective court itself has to apply to the Constitutional Court. Moreover, the financial burden is much higher than in ordinary court proceedings. Thus, Austrian constitutional law does not provide for general access to constitutional justice (*Allgemeine Rechtswegegarantie*).

15 See Bernd-Christian Funk, *Der verfahrensfreie Verwaltungsakt* (Springer, Vienna 1975).

16 See Constitutional Amendment 1975, Federal Law Gazette (Bundesgesetzblatt) nº 302.

17 See Constitutional Amendment 1988, Federal Law Gazette (Bundesgesetzblatt) nº 685.

18 Art. 140 Austrian Constitution.

19 See Art. 23 Austrian Constitution and the Authority Liability Act.

Finally, the Constitutional Court itself has *ex officio* the possibility to start a judicial review procedure within its competence to review administrative decisions regarding violations of human rights. If the Constitutional Court doubts the conformity of an Act of Parliament with the Constitution, or of specific ordinances that must be applied by the Constitutional Court when reviewing administrative decisions, it has to interrupt the procedure and start a review of the legislative act. After deciding the constitutionality of the Act of Parliament, the Constitutional Court can continue the review of the administrative decision. If the Constitutional Court annuls the Act of Parliament, the administrative decision is also regarded as unconstitutional because it usually violates the principle of legality.

The Constitutional Court cannot take over cases from lower courts or administrative bodies.

III. JUDICIAL QUESTIONS ON MATTER OF JUDICIAL REVIEW

1. *Judicial Decisions on Judicial Review*

If an individual files a complaint at ordinary courts, courts can apply to the Constitutional Court (concrete judicial review); alternatively, Parliament or the government of a State initiates an abstract judicial review. In such cases, the Constitutional Court has jurisdiction to review all the laws enacted by Parliament, including legislative acts of federal Parliament as well as of State Parliaments (*Landtage*). Moreover, the Constitutional Court can review the Austrian Constitution itself. The Constitution can be reviewed with regard to a violation of the basic principles of the Constitution,[20] notably the principle of democracy, the federal state, the rule of law, separation of powers, or the general system of human rights.[21] Moreover, the Constitutional Court can review general ordinances of the government and of the administration and is furthermore authorized to review administrative decisions with regard to the violation of human rights.

The Constitutional Court is entitled not only to interpret the Constitution but also to nullify acts of Parliament and administration. Moreover, the Court can declare that statutes that are not in force anymore were unconstitutional while they were in force. From a constitutional perspective, the Court is

[20] VfSlg 16.327/2001; see also Eberhard/Lachmayer, 2 *ICL-Journal* 2/2008, 115.

[21] Anna Gamper, "Die Rolle der Bauprinzipien in der Judikatur des österreichischen Verfassungsgerichtshofes," 55 *Jahrbuch Öffentliches Recht* 2007, 537; Anna Gamper, Vol. 2, *ICL-Journal* 2/2008, 96 (http://www.icl-journal.com).

entitled neither to reform legislation nor to substitute for the legislator or to substitute for the policy making of the government. The factual and legal influence of the Constitutional Court, however, extends far beyond the constitutional framework of the Court. Concrete cases mentioned here exemplify the increasing influence of the Court, especially over the past thirty years.

2. *Effects of Judicial Decisions on Constitutional Matters*

The legal effects of judicial decisions depend on the procedure before the Constitutional Court. If the Court decides on administrative decisions, the effect is restricted to the parties (*inter partes* effect). In the tradition of continental jurisdiction, neither *stare decisis* nor a system of precedents is known. The general, *erga omnes* effects apply to decisions of the Constitutional Court with regard to the annulment of legislative acts or general administrative ordinances.

The Constitutional Court has a large margin of appreciation with regard to the time-related effect of the annulment of statutes. The time dimension of annulment of legislative acts (statutes) is of highest importance. In general, the Constitution (article 140, paragraph 5, of the Austrian Constitution) determines that the annulment takes effect at the end of the day on which the judgment is officially published. Therefore, judgment usually has *ex nunc* effects. However, there are important exceptions and other options. The Constitutional Court itself can decide that the judgment has other (than *ex nunc*) effects. This competence of the Court has an important impact on the political relevance of judgments. The large margin of appreciation of the Constitutional Court implies important powers of the Court to influence legislation and its effect on pending cases. The range of options includes *pro futuro* effects as well as retroactive effects.

The first and most important possibility is that the Constitutional Court can postpone the effects of its own judgment. The deadline may be up to eighteen months (article 140, paragraph 5, of the Austrian Constitution). The purpose of this suspension is to give Parliament the possibility to react to the change of circumstances. However, within this period, nobody can file a complaint challenging the constitutionality of this legislative act because of *res iudicata*, as the Constitutional Court has already decided on the annulment of the statute. Thus, persons affected by the statute lose their legal protection position and their respective rights. The decision on postponing the effects of the judgment is, as mentioned before, up to the court alone. As time is precious, eighteen months can prove a very long period, causing many political, economic, or technical side effects. Thus, the power of the

Constitutional Court is extremely important in this respect. Interestingly enough, it is common for the Constitutional Court not to state reasons why the effects are suspended or why the time limit has a specific duration.

Besides these *pro futuro* effects of the judgment, the Constitutional Court also has the possibility to accord retroactive effects to its judgments. As mentioned, the general concept of the Constitution provides *ex nunc* effect, but with one important exception, the so-called *Anlassfall* (the concrete case that initiated the judicial review of the legislative act). Because the effect of the annulment is *ex nunc*, the individual who filed the complaint would not benefit from the judgment. That is why the Constitution exempts the *Anlassfall* from the general *ex nunc* effects.

Moreover, the Constitutional Court started to extend the exception for the *Anlassfall* to further cases. The Constitutional Court distinguishes between cases benefitting from the annulment of the statutes and those that do not. In conclusion, the effects of the judgment of the Constitutional Court range from an entire *ex nunc* effect to a *pro futuro* effect.

IV. IMPORTANT DEVELOPMENTS AND DECISIONS OF THE CONSTITUTIONAL COURT

1. *Developing the Contents of the Fundamental Principles of the Austrian Constitution*

The fundamental principles of the Austrian Constitution form the core of Austrian constitutional law (the constitution within constitutional law). These principles are – more or less – explicitly mentioned in the Austrian Constitution. It has been up to the Constitutional Court to fill them with specific contents. Thus, the Austrian Constitutional Court has had major influence on the interpretation of Austrian constitutional law beyond judicial self-restraint.

The most famous example of interpretation relates to the principle of *Rechtsstaat* (rule of law).[22] Various concepts were derived from the *Rechtsstaat* principle: the principle of legality, which is, *inter alia*, established in article 18 of the Austrian Constitution, is regarded as the cornerstone of *Rechtsstaat*. The Constitutional Court also developed the principle of clarity, which obliges the legislator to provide clear and detailed

[22] Stelzer, 9–11.

provisions.[23] Moreover, the Constitutional Court established a principle of comprehensibility of legislative acts.[24] In addition to these dimensions of the principle of legality, the Austrian Constitutional Court established the principle of effective legal protection,[25] which obliges Parliament to provide sufficient and adequate legal protection to individuals.

The most remarkable judgment, however, results from a procedure dating from 2001.[26] For the first time, the Austrian Constitutional Court declared constitutional law itself as unconstitutional and annulled a constitutional provision. The reason for this judgment was the ongoing policy of the Austrian legislator to (indirectly) legitimize unconstitutional provisions, which had been annulled by the Constitutional Court, by creating new constitutional provisions mirroring the former unconstitutional provisions. In the 2001 case, the Constitutional Court declared void a constitutional provision excluding parts of the Public Procurement Act from its compliance with the constitution. Thus, the scope of review by the Constitutional Court was limited to the basic principles of the Constitution. The Constitutional Court held that the democracy principle and the *Rechtsstaat* principle were violated by exempting constitutional compliance with a significant aspect of legislation (public procurement) in a general manner.

By and large, the Austrian Constitutional Court used the *Rechtsstaat* principle for other purposes than interpreting the Constitution. The Constitutional Court refined (from a positive perspective) or manipulated (from a negative viewpoint) the Constitution to create new limitations on Parliament. Parliament had to adapt its legislation to the new standards of the Court. However, the judgments cannot be understood as a substitution for governmental policy making or as a general substitution for the legislator.

2. *Concrete Guidelines for the Legislator*

The judgments of the Constitutional Court on self-governing bodies may serve as a further example. Besides the local self-government of municipalities, the so-called nonterritorial self-government plays an important role in Austrian administration.[27] The Austrian Federal Economic

23 Stelzer, 49.

24 VfSlg 12.420/1990.

25 VfSlg 11.196/1986.

26 VfSlg 16.327/2001.

27 Harald Eberhard, "Focus: Self-Government in Austria," Vol. 3, *ICL Journal* 2/2009, 120 (http://www.icl-journal.com).

Chamber and the Austrian Chamber of Labor serve as significant examples. The judgment VfSlg 17.023/2003 dealt with the Austrian self-governing bodies of public social insurance. The body concerned was the central holding, which encompasses all self-governing bodies of social insurance.

Zellenberg summarized the development of the case law as follows:

According to the Constitutional Court's decision VfSlg 8215/1977 on the Salzburger Jägerschaft (Salzburg Hunting Association), the legislator is free to establish self-governing corporations provided it meets three constitutional requirements: The law must be in conformity to the *Sachlichkeitsgebot* (i.e., it must be based on objective grounds), state supervision over the self-governing corporations on their administrative affairs must be ensured and finally, within their autonomous sphere of competences, in which their bodies are not subject to directives of the state, they are to be charged with the provision of only those public tasks which lie in the exclusive or predominant interest of their members and which are suitable to be performed by them in collective action. In later decisions, such as VfSlg 8644/1979, the Constitutional Court added as a fourth requirement the necessity of a democratic way of appointing the officials of the self-governing corporation. In VfSlg 17.023/2003 the Constitutional Court not only confirmed the older decisions, but also went two important steps further: First, it held that a self-governing corporation must also act in conformity with the principle of efficiency, regarded as but one aspect of the Sachlichkeitsgebot by the Court.[28]

Second, the Austrian Constitutional Court refined the margin of appreciation with regard to the system of internal democratic legitimation of these bodies.

In the judgment VfSlg 17.869/2006, the Austrian Constitutional Court went even further.[29] The Court restricted the self-governing bodies to enact regulations only with regard to persons within the sphere of competence of those self-governing bodies. A legislative act related to self-governing bodies must not address persons who are not members of that self-governing body. This restrictive criterion was justified by the necessity of democratic legitimation, and in this respect, it changed the case law of the Court.

[28] Ulrich Zellenberg, "Self-Government and Democratic Legitimacy," Vol. 3, *ICL-Journal* 2/2009, 123 (http://www.icl-journal.com).

[29] Erich Pürgy, "Self-Government in Austria – Range of the Own Sphere of Competence," Vol. 3, *ICL-Journal* 2/2009, 126 (http://www.icl-journal.com).

The issue of nonterritorial self-governing bodies was not regulated in the Austrian Constitution in substance. The constitutional amendment of 2008[30] changed the situation and integrated the case law of the Austrian Constitutional Court. With its case law on self-governing bodies, the Court created new constitutional criteria for the establishment of self-governing bodies in Austria. This case law limited parliamentary legislation on the one hand but also gave the Parliament a positive guideline for the establishment of such bodies on the other hand. The Constitutional Court, therefore, had a significant impact on the reform of legislation, the Austrian Constitution included.

3. *Creating Constitutional Systems*

The Constitutional Court expanded its role. The Court did not stop at developing only specific guidelines but created constitutional systems that Parliament has to consider within its legislation. Important examples are the judgments on privatization delivered over the past twenty years. In four main judgments,[31] an obligatory framework for privatization of state functions exercised by specific organizations was developed by the Constitutional Court. This framework is derived from different provisions of the Austrian Constitution. The framework of the Court includes requirements such as rationality, efficiency, and legality. Moreover, the Austrian Constitutional Court developed the principle of the hierarchal structure of administration, demanding from Parliament further requirements regarding privatization acts. Thus, the state is only authorized to privatize singular tasks, not an entire area of state functions. Moreover, the state has to provide effective control mechanisms with regard to private organizations that perform tasks of state authorities.

Finally, the court defined core areas of state functions that cannot be privatized at all. These core areas include foreign affairs, internal affairs, jurisdiction (judicial system), and criminal law. By defining such core areas of the Austrian state, the Constitutional Court intervened in the legislative and governmental policy to define the functions and tasks of the state itself. The Austrian Constitution does not refer to such tasks at all. By establishing such restrictions, the Constitutional Court created a new understanding of the

30 See Constitutional Amendment 2008, Federal Law Gazette (Bundesgesetzblatt) nº 2.

31 "Austro Control" Judgment VfSlg 14.473/1996, "Bundeswertpapieraufsicht" (Federal Bond Authority) Judgment VfSlg 16.400/2001, "E-Control" Judgment VfSlg 16.995/2003, "Zivildienst-GmbH" (Compulsory Community Service Ltd) Judgment VfSlg 17.341/2004.

Constitution that is shaped in a concept with static elements. In its four judgments, the Court started to extend even these core areas. The Court discovered sensitive areas of fundamental rights, which are also part of these core areas.

The Constitutional Court has based this system on the idea of democratic legitimacy, which reflects a specific understanding of a state and state functions. In a similar manner, the German Constitutional Court,[32] in its recent judgment on the Lisbon Treaty,[33] introduced restrictions on ongoing European integration.

This example of interpretation of the Constitution shows that constitutional systems arise out of the jurisdiction of the Constitutional Court in a way that influences and limits Parliament in its decision-making process; it also demonstrates that the Constitutional Court is increasingly involved in the policy-making process as an important political actor.

4. *Principle of Equality*

The most notorious and active role of the Constitutional Court is mirrored in its focus on the principle of equality (equal protection clause). The core understanding of the principle of equality reflects the protection of all citizens' rights to be treated equally before the law, without discrimination on the grounds of birth, sex, estate, class, or religion (article 7 of the Austrian Constitution).

The Constitutional Court did not restrict itself to question equal treatment or discrimination in concrete cases, but it developed, on the basis of article 7 of the Austrian Constitution, a general test of reasonability for the legislator.[34] This general test of reasonability is an important tool of the Constitutional Court for gaining influence over the policy-making process in Parliament. Although the test of reasonability is a tool that the Court does not often use, the legal possibility of interfering in the political process is important. The possibility of the government justifying the reasonability of a legislative act remains under the scrutiny of the Court. As a counterprinciple to the general test of reasonability, the Court also accepts a margin of

[32] See German Constitutional Court (BverfG), Judgment of 30 June 2009, 2 BvE 2/08, 2 BvE 5/08, 2 BvR 1010/08, 2 BvR 1022/08, 2 BvR 1259/08, and 2 BvR 182/09.

[33] See Katharina Pabel, "The Judgment on the Mandatory Civil Service: The Influence of the Fundamental Rights on the Discussion about Outsourcing," Vol. 4, *ICL–Journal* 2/2010 (http://www.icl-journal.com).

[34] Stelzer, *Introduction* 100; see also Magdalena Pöschl, *Gleichheit vor dem Gesetz* (Springer, Vienna 2008) 264–79.

appreciation for the political dimension within legislation. However, it is up to the Court to argue either way: control or margin, reasonable justification or illegitimate arbitrariness.

This understanding of the principle of equality opens up the broadest margin of appreciation for the Constitutional Court itself. It allows the Court to notify its own political views, which have to be considered by the government *pro futuro*.

V. CONCLUSION – OPENING UP CONSTITUTIONAL POTENTIALS AND VALUE-BASED JUDGMENTS

The dynamic of the Constitutional Court and its move toward a more active court is a phenomenon of the past thirty years. The influence of the European Convention on Human Rights[35] and Austria's accession to the European Union[36] should not be underestimated, although the examples described herein do not deal with this specific area. The influence of the European Courts (European Court of Human Rights and European Court of Justice) has also led to a more value-based approach of the Constitutional Court. The general approach of the Constitutional Court demonstrates a shift toward a more active court, not be compared with the developments in the case law of the German Constitutional Court. For example, the Constitutional Court still has not addressed important questions of counterterrorism measures. However, the influence of the Constitutional Court on constitutional law and ordinary law is significant. In various ways, the Constitutional Court has established its role as an important player in the policy-making process in Austria.

[35] See Philipp Cede, "Some Aspects of the Case Law of the Austrian Constitutional Court on Art. 6 ECHR," Vol. 3, *ICL–Journal* 1/2009, 27 (http://www.icl-journal.com).

[36] Albert Posch, "Community Law and Austrian Constitutional Law," Vol. 2, *ICL-Journal* 4/2008, 272 (http://www.icl-journal); Harald Eberhard, "Austria: The Role of the 'Länder' in a 'Centralized Federal State,'" in Panara and De Becker (eds.), *The Role of the Regions in the European Governance* (Routledge Cavendish, Oxford 2010).

BELGIUM

THE BELGIAN CONSTITUTIONAL COURT AS POSITIVE LEGISLATOR: IN SEARCH OF A BALANCE BETWEEN RIGHTS' PROTECTION AND RESPECT FOR ACTS OF PARLIAMENT

Patricia Popelier
Professor, University of Antwerp,
Research Group Government and Law
Patricia.popelier@ua.ac.be

INTRODUCTION

Constitutional review of Acts of Parliament in Belgium is assigned to a special Constitutional Court. The reason for the Court's establishment in 1983 lays in the emergence of the Belgian federal state, which implied the coexistence of federal laws and state laws. Originally, the Court was called the Court of Arbitration to emphasize its limited competences; until 1988, its only mandate was to supervise the division of powers between the federation and the federated entities (called regions and communities). Gradually, the Court evolved into a full Constitutional Court.[1] Crucial to this evolution was the 1988 assignment to the Court of the competence to review the compatibility of statutes to the equality and nondiscrimination clause as laid down in the articles 10 and 11 of the Belgian Constitution.[2] The Court accepts that these articles can be combined with rights laid down in

1 These statutes are called federal laws, decrees, and ordonnances. Decrees are enacted by the communities and regions; the Brussels Region enacts ordonnances.

2 For an overview, see P. Popelier, *Procederen voor het Grondwettelijk Hof*, Anvers, Intersentia, 2008, 426 p.; M. Rigaux and B. Renauld, *La Cour constitutionnelle*, Brussels, Bruylant, 2008, 330 p.

constitutional or international provisions and unwritten legal principles, such as the principle of legal certainty. The legislator has confirmed this extensive interpretation of the Court's competences in 2003. Since then, the Court has power to review statutes against the provisions that allocate competences to the federal state, the regions, and the communities; against all articles in title II of the constitution (on fundamental rights, including articles 10 and 11); and against the articles 170, 172, and 191 of the Constitution (rights concerning taxes and equal protection of foreigners on Belgian territory). In 2007, the former Court of Arbitration was renamed the Constitutional Court.[3]

In this report, I discuss the different ways in which the Constitutional Court interferes with the normative activity of the legislator. I start by identifying the different ways in which the Court adopts an active role determining constitutional outlines (section I). The focus of this report, however, is on the way the Court deals with legislative lacunae. After giving an overview of the Court's case law (section II), I outline the constitutional framework (or its absence) (section III). Finally, I analyze the consequences of the Court's finding of a legislative lacuna (section IV).

I. THE IMPACT OF THE CONSTITUTIONAL COURT ON CONSTITUTIONAL RELATIONS

Undoubtedly, the establishment of the Constitutional Court has profoundly influenced the positions of other constitutional actors. First, it has encroached on the position of existing courts, not in the least on the Court of Cassation (Supreme Court), which had been the only court able to impose on other courts the interpretation of legal and constitutional provisions.[4] Further, by interpreting the provisions that allocate competences to the federal state, the regions, and the communities, the Constitutional Court redefines the balance among these levels of government.

A recent illustration is the case of the Flemish care insurance.[5] The Constitutional Court confirmed that the Flemish community has the power to organize care insurance, insuring all inhabitants of Flanders (older than

[3] In this report, we use Constitutional Court (CC), unless we refer to a decision dated before 8 May 2007; in that case, we use Court of Arbitration (CA).

[4] See the report of a conference organized to reconcile the three highest courts, A. Arts, I. Verougstraete, and R. Andersen et al. (eds.), *Les rapports entre la Cour d'arbitrage, le Pouvoir judiciaire et le Conseil d'État*, Bruges, La Charte, 2006.

[5] CA n° 33/2001, 13 March 2001; CA n° 8/2003, 22 January 2003; CA n° 51/2006, 19 April 2006; CC n° 11/2009, 21 January 2009.

twenty-five years) against special care needs, in line with the Flemish (exclusive) competence of organizing care. However, the Belgian Constitutional Court stated that care policies can also be regarded as federal competences, thereby suggesting the possibility of parallel or even concurrent competences, whereas the constitution envisaged a strict system of exclusive powers.[6]

The telecommunications case provides for another recent illustration.[7] The Constitutional Court invokes the principle of proportionality to modernize the distribution of powers in this domain. According to the Court, the convergence of the sectors of radio and television diffusion on the one hand and telecommunications on the other hand leads to a "despecialization" of infrastructure and resources and to the creation of new services, which no longer respond to classical definitions of diffusion and telecommunications. Despite this evolution, the law provides for a distribution of powers along the lines of these classical definitions. Because of the technological convergence, especially concerning the common use of certain infrastructures for transmission, the distribution of powers laid down by law according to the Constitutional Court compels for cooperation between the federal authorities and the communities. Although the constitution provides for a dual federalism based on exclusive powers, the Constitutional Court in this way reinforces cooperative federalism.

In this report, the focus is on the impact of the Constitutional Court on the legislator. The Court's power to submit Acts of Parliament to constitutional review is important in itself: as statutes are not inviolable, the legislator is no longer sovereign. Moreover, the Constitutional Court is a negative legislator because it has the power to annul statutes: removing *erga omnes* a statute from the legal order comes down to a legislative act.[8]

The assessment of the Court as a negative legislator, however, does not seize the complete impact of the Constitutional Court on the legislator and on political relations. When reviewing statutes to the constitution, the Court fulfils a creative task by completing abstract constitutional concepts. Even when maintaining the statute, the Court's role is a creative one, as constitutional review implies the interpretation of both the statute and the

6 See J. Velaers and J. Vanpraet, "De materiële en territoriale bevoegdheidsverdeling inzake sociale zekerhei en sociale bijstand," I, *TBP* 2008, 344–345, and II, *TBP* 2009, 215–216. See also B. Cantillon, P. Popelier, and N. Mussche (eds.), *The social welfare state*, Antwerp-Cambridge, Intersentia, 2010.

7 CA n° 132/2004, 14 July 2004; CA n° 128/2005, 13 July 2005; CA n° 163/2006, 8 November 2006.

8 The legislator admitted this; see *Compte Rendu* Senate 28 April 1983, p. 1839.

constitution. To declare a statute in conformity with the Constitution, the court sometimes departs from the interpretation envisaged by the legislator or established in the case law of the ordinary courts.

For example, the Constitutional Court interpreted the words "incite to discrimination, hate or violence" in the Anti-Discrimination Act in such a way that the intention to incite to discriminatory, hateful, or violent conduct should be demonstrated.[9] As noted by Sottiaux, this is a strict interpretation that was not intended by the legislator and moreover runs counter to the case law of the Court of Cassation.[10]

The Constitutional Court has clearly become an important actor in the constitutional setting. According to Favoreu, a monist parliamentary system in which the executive is the emanation of Parliament needs a constitutional judge as counterweight because the opposition has become too weak to fulfill the role.[11] Indeed, in Belgium, Parliament is no longer the center of gravity in the political debate. Moreover, the emancipated citizen takes up a critical role regarding the laws that affect him. The result is made visible in statistics: in 85 percent of the decisions pronounced by the Constitutional Court, the principle of equality and nondiscrimination has been invoked.[12] The equality test ultimately comes down to an evaluation of the reasonableness of the statute.[13] By doing so, the Constitutional Court compels the legislator to justify its acts in line with modern concepts of democracy.

Nevertheless, especially when executing the equality and proportionality test, the line between legal control and discretionary power is subtle. In general, the Court adopts a reserved attitude. However, in exceptional cases, it pronounces a decision with disturbing political consequences.

The most illustrative example concerns the electoral district of Brussels-Halle-Vilvorde. A Flemish political majority demands the division of the district into the bilingual district of Brussels, on the one hand, and the Flemish district of Flemish-Brabant (including Louvain, Halle, and

9 CA nº 157/2004, 6 October 2004.

10 S. Sottiaux, "Grondwetsconforme interpretatie. Garantie of aantasting van de scheiding der machten?" in A. Alen and S. Sottiaux (eds.), *Leuvense Staatsrechtelijke Standpunten 2*, Bruges, Die Keure, 2010, nº 58.

11 L. Favoreu, *Les Cours Constitutionnelles*, 3d ed., Paris, Presses Universitaires de France 1996, p. 14.

12 For more concrete data, see P. Popelier, "Constitutionele toetsing van wetgeving in België," *RegelMaat* 2006, 121–122.

13 I have elaborated on this in P. Popelier, "The role of the Belgian Constitutional Court in the Legislative Process," 26 *Statute Law Review* 1 (2005) 32–39.

Vilvorde), on the other hand. In a decision from 1994, the Constitutional Court declared that this electoral district is in conformity with the Constitution, although it exceeds the borders of linguistic and regional territories, referring to the need for a balance between the linguistic communities.[14] After the enlargement of the electoral districts into provincial districts, the Court disapproved of the maintenance of the electoral district Brussels-Halle-Vilvorde,[15] although it would have been reasonable to use the same argument of balance to uphold the electoral district. The court did not annul the act but instead gave the legislator an injunction to revise the regulation within a certain time frame. This decision has given urgency to a dossier that had been on the political agenda for some decades. It contributed to the fall of the federal government, which resulted in a political crisis of which the traces are still tangible today.

In the *Brussels-Halle-Vilvorde* case, the Constitutional Court gave the legislator an injunction to legislate. This is an example of the way the Constitutional Court interferes with the normative activity of the legislator. The most remarkable hypothesis of such interference occurs when the Constitutional Court declares a legislative omission unconstitutional. This will be analyzed in the next section.

II. LEGISLATIVE OMISSIONS IN THE CASE LAW OF THE CONSTITUTIONAL COURT

When the Constitutional Court decides on an existing statute, it may in an indirect way interfere with the normative activity of the legislator. For example, the annulment of a statute may cause a legal gap or an incoherency that compels the legislator to act. Sometimes the Court takes these effects into account. For example, it may accept that the unconstitutional provision maintains its effects during a certain period of time. During this period, the legislator may legislate to remedy the unconstitutional act.

For example, in Case N° 11/2005, the Court stated that to prevent legal uncertainty caused by the retroactive effect of the annulment (especially with regard to persons who filed for a permit relying on the legislation that has been annulled) and to enable the legislator to adopt new legislation, there was cause for the maintenance of the effects of the annulled provisions until

[14] CA n° 90/94, 22 December 1994.

[15] CA n° 73/2003, 26 May 2003.

December 31, 2005.[16] The Special Act on the Constitutional Court gives the Constitutional Court such power.

Another hypothesis consists of the maintenance of the statute despite its unconstitutional character, combined with the warning that if, after expiration of a certain term, the unconstitutional act is submitted to the Court once more, it will pronounce the proper consequences.[17]

This was the case in a decision concerning traffic regulations.[18] The Court noted that the concerned provision does not meet constitutional requirements resulting from the legality principle in penal law.[19] However, it took into account the fact that the consequences of a declaration of unconstitutionality would jeopardize a multitude of prosecutions brought into action and would render impossible any prosecution on the basis of this act, at the cost of failing to achieve the legislator's objective to reduce the number of traffic deaths by 33 percent by 2006 and by 50 percent by 2010, as recommended by the European Commission. The Court concluded that the Act was in conformity with the constitution. However, in its motives, it included a reservation requiring the legislator to insert in the statute criteria for the division of infractions into categories.

Sometimes the Court confirms that a statute in itself is in conformity with the constitution while declaring at the same time the absence of a statue unconstitutional when it provides for an analogous regulation for a comparable category of persons. The first decision in this respect dates to 1996.

The decision concerned a provision that provided for access to the Council of State to annul an administrative act, excluding acts even of an administrative nature enacted by a legislative assembly. According to the Court, the fact that no request for annulment of an administrative act of a legislative assembly is provided for is contrary to the equality principle laid down in articles 10 and 11 of the Belgian Constitution. Nevertheless, the preliminary question was rejected because the discrimination originated not

16 CA nº 11/2005, 19 January 2005, B.8. For comparable decisions, see, e.g., CA nº 10/93, 11 February 1993, CA nº 66/98, 10 June 1998, CA nº 45/2004, 17 March 2004, CA nº 114/2004, 30 June 2004, CA nº 163/2006, 8 November 2006.

17 E.g., CA nº 56/93, 8 July 1993, nº 53/93, 1 July 1993, nº 27/2005, 2 February 2005. See the case law analyzed in P. Popelier, "De beoordeling door het Arbitragehof van het ontbreken van een wettelijke regeling," *Rechtskundig Weekblad* 1996–1997, 1250. See also A. Alen, "Ongrondwettige lacunes in de wetgeving volgens de rechtspraak van het Arbitragehof," in *Liber Amicorum Roger Blanpain*, Bruges, La Charte, 1998, 656.

18 CA nº 27/2005, 2 February 2005.

19 B.8.

from the Act on the Council of State but from the absence of a comparable statute concerning legislative assemblies.[20] The legislator revised the Act on the Council of State, including the power to annul administrative acts enacted by legislative assemblies and concerning public procurement and personnel. In another decision, the Constitutional Court discerned another discrimination because the power to annul administrative acts of legislative assemblies related to individual acts, to the exclusion of normative acts. Here again, the Court observed that the discrimination did not originate from the Act as such but instead from the omission of the legislator to organize a procedure allowing to contest the legality of a normative act.[21]

More often, the Constitutional Court concludes that an unconstitutional gap finds its origin in the statue challenged before the Court. In these cases, the Court considers that the statute is unconstitutional insofar as it does not apply to a certain category of persons. This is a declaration of unconstitutionality or a modulated annulment with respect to what has not been regulated in the Act.

1. *Some Examples*

Article 12*bis*, section 4, paragraph 3, of the Belgian Nationality Code violates articles 10 and 11 of the Belgian Constitution insofar as it does not allow for the extension of the term for appeal during judicial holidays.[22]

The last paragraph of article 57, section 2, of the 1976 Statute concerning public centers for social care violates article 22 of the Constitution but only insofar as the provision does not guarantee that parents have the same access to the center where their child receives material aid.[23]

The 1985 Act violates articles 10 and 11 of the Belgian Constitution insofar as it, while granting an allowance to full-time employees in the case of a six-month parental leave, does not grant the same allowance to employees combining offices to a total of 100 percent.[24]

The annulment of the Act insofar as it is not applicable to a certain category of persons is often combined with the maintenance of the effects

20 CA nº 31/96, 15 May 1996.

21 CA nº 89/2004, 19 May 2004.

22 CA nº 52/2004, 24 March 2004.

23 CA nº 131/2005, 19 July 2005.

24 CC nº 63/2009, 25 March 2009.

of the Act during a limited period of time, to enable the legislator to remedy the unconstitutional gap.[25]

In exceptional cases, the Constitutional Court annuls the complete provision. In these cases, the Court will always maintain the effects of the annulled provision, precisely because the statute is not unconstitutional as such but only insofar as it is not applicable to a certain category.

For example, in Case No. 49/2001 the Court expressly took into account that the annulment was motivated solely by the absence of a certain procedure, and it therefore maintained the effects of the provision until June 30, 2001.[26]

Finally, the Court sometimes extends the scope of a statute without the intervention of the legislator. This is the case when the Court annuls a provision that expressly excludes a certain category of persons.

2. *Two Examples*

In Case No. 157/2004, the Court considered that, in the Anti-Discrimination Act, the legislator had opted for a system of protection against discrimination requiring objective and reasonable justification in the case of differences in treatment. In this system, it did not find it pertinent to exclude certain motives for discrimination from the Act's scope. Therefore, it annulled the provision, limiting the motives for discrimination to which the Act applied.[27]

Constitutional and international provisions provide for the protection of a journalist's information sources. The Court annulled the provision in an Act that excluded certain persons from this protection, notably those persons who engage in journalist activities but not on a regular basis or not as independent or paid employees.[28]

Even more remarkable is a recent evolution in the case law of both the Constitutional Court and the Court of Cassation, according to which the ordinary courts under certain conditions are entitled to remedy an unconstitutional gap. I discuss this case law in section IV because it relates to the consequences of the Constitutional Court's interference.

25 This is, however, not always the case; e.g., CA n° 123/2006, 18 July 2006.

26 CA n° 49/2001, 18 April 2001.

27 CA n° 157/2004, 6 October 2004.

28 CA n° 91/2006, 7 June 2006.

In the cases cited here, the Constitutional Court not only decides on the challenged Act but also has a positive impact on the legislator's activity, as it determines the content of legislative acts that have not yet been enacted. The intensity of this impact, however, varies. In some cases, the Court gives a mere injunction to the legislator without declaring the act or an omission unconstitutional;[29] in other cases, the Court does declare the act or the omission unconstitutional. The sensitive nature of a case appears to incite the Court to adopt a more reserved attitude.[30] Also in matters that the Constitution explicitly assigns to the legislative power, the Court stresses that only the legislative power, including Parliament, is able to remedy a legislative omission. However, the case law does not provide for clear criterions for the Court's line of conduct.

A final observation concerns the inadequacy of the terms provided for the legislator to revise a statute. In general, the term provided to the legislator is an average of eight or nine months, with a minimum of three months[31] and a maximum of twelve months. In cases that call for a profound revision of the statute, the term is often too short to allow for careful preparation.[32]

III. LEGAL FRAMEWORK

When establishing the Belgian Constitutional Court, the legislator only envisaged the review of existing law. According to the Special Act on the Constitutional Court, the Court passes judgment on the request for annulment of a statute[33] and, if well founded, will annul the statute or a part of it.[34] The Special Act on the Constitutional Court also provides for preliminary questions concerning the conformity of a statute with the

[29] E.g., CA n° 134/2003, 8 October 2003.

[30] E.g., CA n° 134/2003, 8 October 2003; see V. Verlinden, "Lacunes in de wetgeving: wat doet het Arbitragehof?" *Rechtskundig Weekblad* 2003–2004, 1021.

[31] CA n° 154/2004, 22 September 2004. The new legislation was enacted ten months after the decision and seven months after expiration of the term.

[32] As I have observed in P. Popelier, "Rechtsbescherming tegen discriminerende wetgeving, de rol van het Arbitragehof en de mogelijkheid tot rechtsherstel door de rechter en wetgever," *Rechtskundig Weekblad* 2006–07, 261; P. Popelier, *Procederen voor het Grondwettelijk Hof*, Antwerp, Intersentia, 2008, 372–373.

[33] Art. 1 Special Law on the Constitutional Court.

[34] Art. 8 Special Law on the Constitutional Court.

Constitution.[35] The preliminary question must even indicate which provisions of the statute are being submitted to constitutional review.[36]

Nevertheless, the decisions of the Constitutional Court are not always limited to statutes already enacted but sometimes have an impact on legislation that has not yet been produced. In his comparative study, Behrendt reveals that recently the Belgian Constitutional Court has been in many ways even more active in this respect than the interventionist German Bundesverfassungsgericht.[37]

In his doctoral thesis, Behrendt uses the term *interference* (*interférence*) to indicate the repercussions of the Constitutional Court's decision on the legislator's future lawmaking activity.[38] According to the author, the Court's injunction comes down to the empowerment of the legislator to produce certain well-defined laws. Yet the legislator has this power anyway, as the Constitution explicitly confers the power to legislate to the legislator. The question is rather whether the Constitutional Court may restrict the discretionary power of the Court with an injunction to make a specific law. Neither the constitution nor the Special Act on the Constitutional Court gives the Constitutional Court this power. As I have already noted, the legislator did not even envisage the hypothesis of an appeal against a legislative omission. For this reason, the Constitutional Court rejects the request for annulment of a legislative vacuum or annulment of the implicit refusal to enact a specific law.[39] Nevertheless, the Court does judge the absence of a legislative measure provided the request is put in the form of a challenge against an existing statute. Therefore, some authors plead for the insertion of an explicit provision that gives the Court the power to interfere with the legislator's legislative activity.[40]

35 Art. 142 Constitution and Art. 26, para. 1, Special Law on the Constitutional Court.

36 Art. 27, § 2, Special Law on the Constitutional Court.

37 See C. Behrendt, *Le juge constitutionnel, un législateur-cadre positif*, Brussels-Paris, Larcier-LGDJ, 2006, 537 p.

38 C. Behrendt, *Le juge constitutionnel, un législateur-cadre positif*, Brussels-Paris, Larcier-LGDJ, 2006, pp..7 and 101–103.

39 E.g., CA n° 10/1992, 13 February 1992, CA n° 87/2000, 5 July 2000, CA n° 131/2006, 28 July 2006.

40 See A. Alen, "Ongrondwettige lacunes in de wetgeving volgens de rechtspraak van het Arbitragehof," in *Liber Amicorum Roger Blanpain*, Bruges, La Charte, 1998, 668–669, P. Popelier, "De rechtspraak van het Arbitragehof over lacunes in de wetgeving," in A. Alen (ed.), *Twintig jaar Arbitragehof*, Anvers, Kluwer, 2005; H. Simonart, "Observations," *J.T.* 1997, 5.

IV. CONSEQUENCES OF THE FINDING THAT A LEGISLATIVE LACUNA IS CONTRARY TO THE CONSTITUTION

The question rises as to what avail the absence of a legislative measure is being challenged. After all, the annulment of a statute "in as far" as it does not contain a certain measure maintains the statute as it is. In principle,[41] the direct consequences of such an annulment are nonexistent. The same is true for a declaration of nonconformity of a legislative omission. The judge who referred the question is bound to apply the statute as it is, because in principle, the judge is not allowed to complete the statute without intervention of the legislator.[42] The injunction is directed toward the legislator. However, the legislator does not always respond to the Court's judgments. Although, especially at the federal level, the legislator has improved the procedure for the canalization of the Court's case law, the judgments often remain without legislative response.[43] Even in the case of legislative intervention, the judgment of the Constitutional Court may easily turn out to be a Pyrrhic victory for those who have started procedures.

For citizens, it is difficult to comprehend that under the rule of law the Court, while confirming that a legislative omission is unconstitutional, is incapable of imposing redress. In practice, the courts try to find a compromise. Five arguments explain why the request for annulment of a legislative omission or a preliminary question concerning a legislative omission can be useful.

1. The court may give an extensive interpretation, according to which the statute applies to a category of persons which according to the established or literal interpretation would be excluded.[44]

2. The motivation for bringing action before the Court may be of a political nature, intended to seek the Court's aid to activate the legislator.

[41] There are some exceptions, as when the Court annuls the entire provision and an older, more profitable version revives; see CA n° 137/2006, 14 September 2006. Another hypothesis is that the statute is unconstitutional insofar as it does not give room for the application of a principle of good administration; e.g., CA n° 127/2003, 1 October 2003. A more elaborate analysis can be found in P. Popelier, "Rechtsbescherming tegen discriminerende wetgeving," *Rechtskundig Weekblad* 2006–07, 251.

[42] Council of State (CoS) Wijnen, n° 112.229, 4 November 2002, CoS Veulemans, n° 133.116, 25 June 2004, Cass. 18 September 2003 (n° C.010535.N.), Cass. 10 June 2005 (n° C.020624.N.).

[43] See A. Goris, K. Muylle, and M. Van der Hulst, "Twintig jaar Arbitragehof v. wetgever: van wantrouwen naar dialoog," in A. Alen, *Twintig jaar Arbitragehof*, Antwerp, Kluwer, 2005, 46–73.

[44] See, e.g., CA n° 24/97, 30 April 1997.

3. The judgment that a legislative omission is contrary to the Constitution may entail a claim for compensation. The Court of Cassation has confirmed the liability of the Belgian State for faulty acts and omissions of the legislator.[45] However, in most cases, it will be difficult to prove causality between fault and damages or to prove the extent of the damages. Difficulties rise especially when the omission is contrary to the equality principle, considering the discretionary power of the legislator to remedy the discrimination. Moreover, the Constitutional Court usually combines an annulment with the maintenance of the legal effects of the statute for a certain period of time. In that case, the Belgian State is not liable for damages resulting from the legislative omission during that period.

4. It appears from the case law that ordinary courts, after having referred a preliminary question to the Constitutional Court, complete the statute without waiting for legislative intervention. So, among other examples,[46] in several cases, the Labor Courts imposed their proper rules for calculating the term of notice for part-time employees.[47] In doing so, they ignored that the Constitutional Court, when declaring unconstitutional the omission of a specific regulation on notice for part-time employees, specifically noted that it belongs to the legislator's discretionary power to decide which particular rules should be adopted.[48] Judicial decisions displaying this kind of activism, however, risk being squashed by the Court of Cassation.

5. Recently, the Court of Cassation and the Constitutional Court have under certain conditions acknowledged the power of judges to remedy an unconstitutional omission by completing the statute.[49]

45 Cass. 28 September 2006, *Rechtskundig Weekblad* 2006–07, 213. See, inter alia, P. Popelier, *Procederen voor het Grondwettelijk Hof*, Antwerp, Intersentia, 2008, 400–404; M. F. Rigaux, "Eloge de la modestie publique," *Chroniques de Droit Public* 2007, 187–201; A. Van Oevelen, "De aansprakelijkheid van de Staat, de Gewesten en de Gemeenschappen voor onrechtmatige wetgeving," *Tijdschrift voor Wetgeving* 2006, 400–416.

46 For another illustration, see Court of Appeal Antwerp 25 November 1997, *Rechtskundig Weekblad* 1998–99, 1496. See also L. Dehin and P. Henry, "Droit d'appel de l'inculpé renvoyé devant les jurisdictions correctionnelles: une précision et une gestion," *La revue de jurisprudence de Liège, Mons et Bruxelles (J.L.M.B)*, 1995, 384 and the report De Leval, "La pertinence de la question préjudicielle et l'usage de la réponse par le juge *a quo*," in *Les relations entre la Cour d'arbirage, le pouvoir judiciaire et le Conseil d'Etat*, Bruges, La Charte, 2006, 269.

47 Labour Court Antwerp 3 April 2000, *R.W.* 2000–01, 911, Labour Court Antwerp 15 March 2004, *Ors* 2004 summarized by A. Vanoppen, Labour Court Brussels 11 April 2008 and 9 January 2009.

48 CA n° 45/99, 20 April 1999.

49 On this evolution, see P. Popelier, "Het Hof van Cassatie over lacunes in de wetgeving: toenadering tot het Grondwettelijk Hof," note sub Cass. 17 January 2008, *Rechtskundig Weekblad* 2008–09, 1186–1189.

In a decision of 31 July 2008, the Constitutional Court stated for the first time that the judge who referred a preliminary question to the Court has the power to fill a legislative gap.[50] The Court, however, stipulated two conditions. First, the judge is only allowed to fill a gap in an existing statute; he or she cannot cure a legislative omission that calls for the enactment of a new law. Second, the terms in which the Constitutional Court has formulated a violation of the constitution must be sufficiently precise and complete.[51]

In Case No. 111/2008, the Constitutional Court stated that a provision in the law violated articles 10 and 11 of the Constitution insofar as it did not provide for a direct appeal to the Court of Cassation against the decision of the Chamber of Accusation reviewing the regularity of the use of specific research methods. In its decision, the Constitutional Court stated that the judge could remedy this gap because the finding was put in sufficiently clear and precise terms to permit the judge to apply the provision in conformity with the Constitution.[52]

After some hesitations,[53] the Court of Cassation followed suit.[54] According to the Court of Cassation, the judge is even obliged to remedy, insofar as possible, any lacuna in the law that, according to the Constitutional Court, constitutes a violation of the constitution.[55]

The Court of Cassation stated that this follows from the Constitutional Court's Decision No. 111/2008 that the statutory provision at stake presents a discriminatory gap. It cited the Constitutional Court's position concerning the possibility of the judge remedying this gap and concluded that, in the absence of legislative intervention, the Court of Cassation can fill the gap on its own accord and admit a direct appeal against the decision of the chamber of accusation concerning the regularity of the use of certain research methods.[56]

50 CC n° 111/2008, 31 July 2008.

51 See, inter alia, CC n° 111/2008, 31 July 2008; CC n° 74/2009, 5 May 2009; CC n° 177/2009; 12 November 2009.

52 CC n° 111/2008, 31 July 2008.

53 Cass. 12 August 2008 (P.08.1065.N).

54 Cass. 2 September 2008 (P.08.1317.N); Cass. 14 October 2008 (P.08.1329.N) *R.W.* 2008–2009, 1184; Cass. 28 October 2008 (P.08.0706.N); Cass. 25 November 2008 (P.07.0345.N). Implicit: Cass. 3 February 2009 (P.07.0988.N).

55 Cass. 3 November 2008 (S. 07.0013.N).

56 Cass. 2 September 2008 (P.08.1317.N).

These courts stipulate the mentioned conditions to prevent ordinary judges from exceeding their powers and taking the place of the legislator. Legislative intervention is necessary as soon as redress implies a political choice. The Court of Cassation clarifies that the judge would violate the principle of separation of powers if he or she were to take the place of the legislator. This would be the case if the lacuna was of such a nature that redress would require either the enactment of a new rule, which should be submitted to a reevaluation of social interests by the legislator, or the modification of several legal provisions.[57]

The Constitutional Court had declared that the 1971 statute on industrial accidents violated articles 10 and 11 of the Constitution insofar as it did not apply to unpaid apprentices who were victims of an industrial accident while operating in a working environment, as prescribed in the educational program. The Court of Cassation noted that the judge could not remedy this lacuna simply by extending the scope of the statute to unpaid apprentices and victims of an industrial accident in the framework of their educational program. To fill this gap, it was necessary to decide who would be designated as employer, obliged under penal law to take out insurance to the benefit of the apprentices concerned. It is not the judge's responsibility to make this choice in the stead of the legislator.[58]

The Constitutional Court derives yet another condition from the legality principle. The judge is not allowed to complete a statute in domains that the Constitution expressly reserves to the legislator to guarantee the consent of Parliament (e.g., in the case of tax matters or penal law).[59]

In Case No. 64/2009, the Constitutional Court annulled two provisions in the Anti-Discrimination Act but only insofar as they do not, among the protected criteria, envisage convictions concerning trade unions (*conviction syndicale*). According to the Court, the conditions for a jurisprudential completion of the gap are met: the gap is situated in the Act challenged before the Court, and the discrimination has been formulated in sufficiently precise and complete terms. The Constitutional Court noted, however, that, although it is the judge who can pronounce judgment concerning a civil claim to apply the Act to discrimination on the ground of convictions concerning trade unions, the legality principle in penal matters prevents this in penal cases. Article 12 of the Constitution states

57 Cass. 3 November 2008 (S. 07.0013.N).

58 Cass. 3 November 2008 (S. 07.0013.N).

59 CC n° 64/2009, 2 April 2009; CC 122/2009, 16 July 2009; CC 123/2009, 16 July 2009.

that "no one can be prosecuted except in the cases provided for by law." As "law" in this provision refers to an Act of Parliament, only the legislator is able to remedy a gap.[60]

Finally, the principle of legal certainty may prevent the application of a jurisprudential extension to facts that date from a period before the decision of the Constitutional Court declaring that the legislative omission is contrary to the Constitution. This restriction follows from a decision of the Court of Cassation. According to this decision, it falls with the ordinary courts to determine the effects in time of preliminary rulings pronounced by the Constitutional Court.[61] The Court of Cassation added that, when determining the effects in time, the judge should take into account the principle of legal certainty and legitimate expectations based on legal provisions. The legal ground for this competence, however, is disputable, because the legislator, though conferring to the Constitutional Court the competence to determine the effects in time of an annulment, has intentionally excluded such competences in the case of preliminary rulings.[62]

CONCLUSIONS

It is clear that the Belgian Constitutional Court interferes with the legislative activity of the legislator. The Constitutional Court has become an important actor in constitutional law. In most cases, the legislator has the final word. The legislator is, however, restricted by the Constitutional Court, which forces him or her to carefully consider and justify any legislative acts.

From the perspective of the principle of separation of powers, the Constitutional Court's activism causes a tension. In this respect, it is striking that, as has been observed already, the case law of the Constitutional Court does not reveal solid criteria or guidelines to deal with unconstitutional acts and omission, which only the legislator is able to remedy. Such criteria for balancing jurisprudential activism, on the one hand, and respect for the

[60] CA n° 64/2009, 2 April 2009. In the same sense, concerning the Brussels and Flemish Anti-Discrimination Acts: CC n° 122/2009, 16 July 2009; CC n° 123/2009, 16 July 2009.

[61] Cass. 20 December 2007, *R.W.* 2007–08, 1369. See E. Dirix, "Rechterlijk overgangsrecht," *Rechtskundig Weekblad* 2008–09, 1757; P. Popelier, "Rechterlijk overgangsrecht revisited. Over een juridisch vacuüm, een prejudicieel arrest en de werking van rechterlijke uitspraken in de tijd," *Rechtskundig Weekblad.* 2007–08, 1371–1374.

[62] An amendment proposed to confer this competence to the Constitutional Court (Amendment n° 47, *Doc. Parl.* Senate 2001–2002, 2-897/4) was rejected: *Doc. Parl.* Senate 2002–2003, 2-897/6, pp. 232–233.

legislature, on the other hand, can nevertheless be drawn from a comparative analysis. Sottiaux discerns the following criteria from a comparative analysis: (1) the Court should opt for a technique permitting to give redress without implying a political choice that the legislator must make, (2) the Court should respect as much as possible the purpose of the Act and the preferences of the legislator, (3) it should take into account the budgetary impact of its decision, and (4) it should consider the philosophy and coherency of the entire Act.[63] Sometimes, the Court takes into account one of these criteria explicitly; in other cases, it applies the criteria without explicit consideration; in rare cases, it seems to exceed the limits of the separation of powers without giving explanation.

For example, the Constitutional Court may decide for the maintenance of the legal effects of an annulled provision if the retroactive effect of the annulment would entail consequences that are "excessive"[64] or contrary to the purpose of the Act.[65] As noted earlier, the Court may decide to maintain the legal effects of an annulled provision to enable the legislator to revise the Act. Also, in the decision already mentioned concerning traffic regulations, the Constitutional Court explicitly referred to the purpose of the Act to declare the Act constitutional, despite the finding that it was in fact contrary to the legality principle in penal cases.[66] Finally, the conditions that must be met for a jurisprudential completion of a statute are stipulated in view of giving redress without implying a political decision.

Nevertheless, in other cases, the decision of the Constitutional Court entails excessive consequences or involves a completion or interpretation of the Act that was not foreseen or wanted by the legislator. The Brussels-Halle-Vilvorde case is an example thereof.[67] The Anti-Discrimination Act case is another illustration: the annulment of the provision excluding discrimination on the ground of political convictions and convictions concerning trade unions extended the scope of the Act in a way that was explicitly not desired by the legislator.[68]

[63] S. Sottiaux, "Grondwetsconforme interpretatie. Garantie of aantasting van de scheiding der machten?" in A. Alen and S. Sottiaux (eds.), *Leuvense Staatsrechtelijke Standpunten 2*, Bruges, Die Keure, 2010.

[64] E.g., CC n° 105/2007, 19 July 2007, CC n° 154/2007, 19 December 2007.

[65] E.g., CA n° 2/92, 15 January 1992.

[66] CA n° 27/2005, 2 February 2005. See *supra* para. II.

[67] See *supra* para. I.

[68] See *supra* para. II. For a critical observation in this regard, see J. Velaers, "Het Arbitragehof en de anti-discriminatiewet," *Tijdschrift voor Bestuurswetenschappen en Publiekrecht* 2004, 603–605.

It is necessary for the Court to balance the protection of the citizen against arbitrary actions and omissions, on the one hand, and respect for the elected legislator, on the other hand. For this reason, the Court should always justify why, instead of annulling a statutory provision or declaring it unconstitutional, as foreseen by the Special Act on the Constitutional Court, it interprets an Act in a way that diverges from the Act's purpose or established case law or why it attaches other consequences to a finding of nonconformity. This would force the Constitutional Court to always consider its responsibility as a positive legislator.

BRAZIL

CONSTITUTIONAL COURTS AS NEGATIVE LEGISLATORS: THE BRAZILIAN CASE*

Thomas Bustamante
Professor, Federal University of Minas Gerais
thomas_bustamante@yahoo.com.br

Evanilda de Godoi Bustamante
Advocate at the Brazilian Bar.
evanildagodoi@ig.com.br

INTRODUCTORY CONSIDERATIONS

One of the main topics proposed for discussion at the eighteenth International Congress of the International Academy of Comparative Law was the legislative role of Constitutional Courts in contemporary democracies. The Brazilian state, like many of those from the Iberic and Latin American tradition, can be characterized as a mixed legal system that attempts to reconcile a model of diffused and *incidenter tantum* judicial review with a concentrated and abstract model in which the Constitutional Court pronounces abstract decisions in direct actions of unconstitutionality. These decisions have *erga omnes* and strictly binding effects.

Before the Constitution of 1988, the Brazilian system of judicial review could be classified as much more akin to the American tradition of judicial review than to the Austrian model developed by Hans Kelsen, which concentrates the jurisdiction on constitutional matters in a single Constitutional Court. Every judge was (and still is) competent to assess a violation of the Constitution by the ordinary laws. The declaration of unconstitutionality was merely a step for the judge to follow in the justification of his or her decision. Even though a dispute over the constitutionality of an Act could eventually reach the higher courts by means of an appeal, there was no warranty that this would ever happen.

Although there was an abstract action for assessing the constitutionality of statutes, the scope of this action was very strict and only the General-Attorney of the Republic (who was at the same time the *Procurador* [Prosecutor] of the Federal Government and the Chief of the Public Ministry) was empowered to bring it before the Supreme Court. In a legal system where the General-Attorney of the Republic was directly subordinated to the President of the Republic and where the Executive Administration was authorized to legislate in place of the Congress in a wide range of areas, as in Brazil was at the time of the military dictatorships of the three decades before the Constitution of 1988, that sort of action was of little utility.[1]

These brief historical considerations help one understand the roots of the current Brazilian system of constitutional jurisdiction. They explain, for instance, the fact that any judge in the country has jurisdiction to decide a constitutional issue.

Nonetheless, the Constitution of 1988, despite that it kept the incidental system of judicial review, was deliberately designed to break down this tradition. The basic Kelsenian ideas that a decision that pronounces unconstitutionality is not declaratory but rather constitutive; that there can be no "unconstitutional" statute in the sense of a null and void piece of legislation but only a statute "contrary to the Constitution" that can be derogated by the Constitutional Courts through a special procedure different from ordinary legislation; and that, as a general rule, the Constitutional Court pronounces *erga omnes* decisions creating a derogatory rule that eliminates a previous norm incompatible with the Constitution (in such a way that the court is a negative legislator), deeply influenced the institutional settings of the Brazilian state and the doctrines about the relationship between the legislative and the judicial branches.

The Constitution of 1988, without naming the Federal Supreme Court a Constitutional Court, placed that court in a special position and established a

1 In the previous Brazilian Constitution, there was no distinction between the General Attorney of the Republic and the General-Advocate of the Union. The separation between the Public Ministry (headed by the former) and the General Advocacy of the Union (headed by the latter) is one of the important changes in the institutional setting of the republic undertaken by the novel Constitution. By means of this distinction, the public interest is differentiated from the interest of the Government, not merely from a rhetorical point of view. The Constitution has created a legal office subordinate to the President, the competence of which is to defend the interests of the Federal Government, and an autonomous office, the competence of which is to protect the rule of law, the public estates, the fundamental legal rights, and other collective or diffuse rights, such as protection of the environment. For a brief comment on the Public Ministry after the Constitution of 1988, see *infra*, note 12.

set of privative competences to exercise judicial review. The court is competent to decide (abstract) actions of unconstitutionality against most statutory provisions, regardless of any specific situations to which they are applied. Such direct actions can be brought before the court by a relatively vast group of entities that represent general sectors of the society.

This concentrated system of judicial review coexists with the historical model of incidental and diffuse constitutional adjudication. The simultaneity of the two traditional models is perhaps the most distinctive feature of the Brazilian system of judicial review.

Even though the judicial ideology that dominates the discourse of the Supreme Court is faithful to Kelsen's image of the Constitutional Court as no more than a negative legislator, our analysis will reveal that there are occasions on which it effectively acts as a positive lawmaking agency, albeit one that is strictly bound to the Constitution and sensitive to its own judicial role. In fact, one can easily agree that the Brazilian Constitution expressly requires the Court to lay down general and abstract norms that sometimes are hierarchically ranked at the same level of ordinary legislation. To justify this assertion, we analyze the Brazilian system of judicial review by separating the incidental and diffuse review from abstract and concentrated review.

I. THE DIFFUSED AND INCIDENTAL SYSTEM OF JUDICIAL REVIEW

The model of incidental and concrete judicial review remains applicable in Brazil and is a central feature of the Brazilian legal tradition. It is a concrete form of judicial review because the unconstitutionality of a norm (no matter where it finds its sources: in a statute, in an international treaty, in an administrative decree, in a conventional norm in a contract, and so on) is argued by one of the parties in the course of an ordinary legal dispute. As opposed to most European countries, which have a Constitutional Court, the judge must decide the constitutional issue him- or herself. The decision as to the (un) constitutionality of the norms is a necessary step that the judge has to take before reaching a conclusion. In addition to being a concrete system of judicial review, the Brazilian system is also one of diffuse judicial review, because the constitutional jurisdiction is spread out through the court system. Every court in Brazil has constitutional jurisdiction. When unconstitutionality is argued before a first-instance judge, there is no need for any special formalities, except to give the other party the chance to counter the arguments advanced for the declaration of unconstitutionality. The Constitutional Court does not have a say on the issue unless the case reaches it by an extraordinary appeal that is admissible only after a final second-instance decision is pronounced.

When unconstitutionality is argued before a court of appeal or any other high court, the constitutional issue can be decided only in a plenary session of the Court. The reporter judge must suspend the judgment of the case until a decision on the constitutional query is achieved by the majority of the full house.[2]

Nevertheless, the rule that establishes this privative competence to the plenary sitting of the courts does not avoid contradictory decisions. The Brazilian judicial system is heavily fragmented, for several reasons. First, Brazil is a federal state, comprising twenty-six States and one autonomous district, where the headquarters of the federal government are situated. Each State has its own courts, and rarely a precedent from a different court of appeal of the same hierarchy is quoted in a state court. Second, there are different and completely autonomous court systems, the competences of which are determined by the subject matters of the cases: there is a Federal Court system (which decides issues of interest of the Federation or of its subsidiaries, such as autarchies, public enterprises, public foundations, federal universities), an Electoral Court system (which has administrative competences to organize the general elections; normative authority to issue general norms supplementing the electoral legislation and jurisdictional competences over a vast range controversies around the application of electoral law – for instance, cases about limits of the freedom of expression, unlawful political advertisements, and abuses of economic power in the elections), a Labor Court system (which decides labor cases and is informed by the principle of the protection of employees against the dominant position of their employers), a Military Court system (which adjudicates mostly on military crimes), and the General State Courts (which have jurisdiction on all remaining subjects, such as civil disputes in general and criminal cases in which the Federation is not a victim or an interested party).

When there is no binding precedent applicable to a case, there is no procedural mechanism enabling a party or a judge to submit the constitutional issue to the Supreme Court before a decision is reached in the ordinary courts. Apart from exceptional cases, which will be dealt with later in this report, the technique of *avocamiento*, which is admitted in some Latin American countries, does not find an equivalent in Brazil. Only final decisions from the ordinary courts can be challenged by an "extraordinary appeal" (*recurso extraordinário*) to the Federal Supreme Court. These

2 *Constituição da República Federativa do Brasil*: art. 97.

extraordinary appeals are admitted to decide constitutional controversies. They can neither reexamine the evidence or any question of fact nor adjudicate on a question of interpretation of infraconstitutional laws. The issue of the unconstitutionality of any statute, international treaty, legislative decree, or administrative resolution that establishes a general norm can be brought before the Supreme Court via a *recurso extraordinário*, although there are some procedural barriers aimed at filtering the number of appeals to the Federal Supreme Court.[3]

The amount of discretion of the court in choosing the appeals it will decide is relatively low. Until relatively recently there was nearly no discretion at all (all cases that fulfill certain procedural requirements were submitted to the court), but a recent constitutional amendment has determined that only cases of general repercussion (*repercussão geral*) can be submitted to the court.[4] The basic idea is that only cases that reflect the status of positive law in a relevant way should be decided by the Court. The main purpose of the appeals to the Supreme Court is not to protect individual situations but to unify the interpretation of valid law. To decide whether an issue is of general repercussion, a judgment of the plenary session of the Federal Supreme Court (which is constituted by eleven Ministers) is necessary. It is in the case

[3] Some of these requisites are established in legislation, such as the need to discuss the constitutionality of a law as an incidental question before the lower courts. It is a burden of the appellant to formulate an argument for the unconstitutionality of the normative act and to ensure that the court explicitly expresses an opinion on the constitutional issues. If the court remains silent after a claim of unconstitutionality is raised by a party, it is up to that party to request a clarifying pronouncement over the constitutionality of the norm within five days of the publication of the decision. A thesis that was not discussed by the lower courts cannot reach the Supreme Court unless that Court leaves the incidental claim of unconstitutionality undecided after being warned by the interested party (see STF: *Súmula 356*). This requisite seems reasonable and is quite accepted by constitutional lawyers, even though it requires some special argumentative techniques that are not always dominated by general practitioners. There are, however, serious problems that refer to requisites that are not established in any law and that do not find any statutory justification. The court creates a filter to diminish the number of cases on which it has to adjudicate. In this sense, there is a chain of precedents ruling that an extraordinary appeal cannot be brought before the Supreme Court to protect the principle of legality (or, in other words, the rule that "no one shall be obliged to do or to refrain from something unless by order of a law" – *Constituição da República Federativa do Brasil*: art. 5, II). This principle contains a prohibition for administrative authorities to create general norms other than in the situations explicitly authorized either by the Constitution or by a statute. The case law of the Supreme Court, however, created a constraint establishing that the violation of the Constitution that leaves the way to an extraordinary appeal must be "direct and frontal," that is, must be assessed merely by comparing the unconstitutional act with the Constitution. There is a judge-made rule stating that "extraordinary appeals are inadmissible to remediate a violation of the principle of legality whenever its verification presupposes to revise the interpretation given by the court of origin to the infra-constitutional legislation" (STF: *Súmula 636*).

[4] *Constituição da República Federativa do Brasil*: art. 103, § 3, with the wording given by the 45th Constitutional Amendment of 30 December 2004.

law of the Court that one will find the criteria for identifying such cases. Nevertheless, once a party demonstrates that his or her case fits the constitutional definition of a case of general repercussion, the party has a constitutional right to see the case decided by the Court.

As a rule, the incidental declaration of the unconstitutionality of a provision or an act neither is strictly binding nor has *erga omnes* effect. According to the wording of the Constitution, for an *incidenter tantum* decision to become universally efficacious, the Federal Senate must pass a resolution derogating the norm.[5] The Federal Supreme Court, when reaching a definitive decision recognizing the unconstitutionality of a legal provision, notifies the Senate, which has discretion as to whether the norm should be formally abrogated. Nonetheless, in spite of this constitutional provision, the Senate still has not passed any resolution eliminating a particular legal provision that has been declared unconstitutional by the Supreme Court. This does not mean, however, that the final decisions of the Supreme Court are not authoritative. Even though as a rule the decisions of the courts have *inter partes* efficacy, constitutional precedents are of fundamental importance in the Brazilian legal system. If we stick to the classification of the institutional force of judicial precedents adopted by one of the authors of this report in a previous writing, who distinguishes three levels of normativity for judicial precedents (precedents "binding in a strong sense," precedents "binding in a weak sense," and precedents "merely persuasive"), we can place this sort of case law in the intermediate category and characterize it at least as "binding in a weak sense."[6]

As we will see later in this report, there is a clear trend of substantially increasing the normative powers of the Supreme Court in the decisions of unconstitutionality, regardless of whether they are pronounced in the course of a legal dispute or in a Direct Action of Unconstitutionality.

Some signs of this trend are the recent constitutional and legislative reforms that augmented the binding character of the decisions of the Court. However, before examining these reforms, we outline some of the aspects of the concentrated system of constitutional review.

5 *Constituição da República Federativa do Brasil*: art. 52, X.

6 See Thomas Bustamante, "Precedent in Brazil" in E. Hondius (ed.), *Precedent and the Law – Reports to the XVIIth Congress of the International Academy of Comparative Law, Utrecht, 16–22 July 2006*, Brussels, Bruylant, 2007, pp. 289–309. A general theory of precedent applicable to the Brazilian legal system can be found in Thomas Bustamante, *Teoria do Precedente: A justificação e a aplicação de regras jurisprudenciais*, São Paulo, Malheiros, forthcoming (2011).

II. THE CONCENTRATED SYSTEM OF JUDICIAL REVIEW

1. *Concentrated Constitutional Jurisdiction by Direct Actions*[7]

The concentrated system of judicial review in Brazil was inspired by the systems from European countries such as Austria, Germany, Spain, Italy, and Portugal. Nevertheless, there are some specific features that distinguish the Brazilian model.

There are four basic types of direct and abstract actions of unconstitutionality in Brazil: the Direct Action of Unconstitutionality (*Ação Direta de Inconstitucionalidade*);[8] the Declaratory Action of Constitutionality of a Federal law or normative act (*Ação Declaratória de Constitucionalidade*);[9] the Direct Action against an Unconstitutional Omission (*Ação Direta de Inconstitucionalidade por Omissão*);[10] and the Claim against the Disrespect to a Fundamental Precept (*Argüição de Descumprimento de Preceito Fundamental*).[11] All these actions have a limited group of authorities or entities that can figure as claimants, which we specify herein. In any direct form of constitutional review, the General Advocate of the Union (*Advogado-Geral da União*) will be heard in defense of the normative act. The General-Attorney of the Republic, in turn, will have a chance to present a *memorandum* when he is not the author of the action.[12]

7 In short, a *direct action* is defined as a form of abstract constitutional review. The constitutionality of the norm is itself the object of the claim, for there is no concrete right considered by the court in the decision. A direct claim of unconstitutionality must not deal with any subjective or concrete situation. Its concern is the general validity of a norm, not its applicability.

8 *Constituição da República Federativa do Brasil*: art. 102, I, "a."

9 *Constituição da República Federativa do Brasil*: art. 102, I, "a."

10 *Constituição da República Federativa do Brasil*: art. 103, § 2.

11 *Constituição da República Federativa do Brasil*: art. 103, § 1.

12 The *Advogado Geral da União* and the *Procurador Geral da República* should not be confused. The former is the head of the General Advocacy of the Union and defends interests of the Union, considered a political entity of the Federation, and of the Federal Government. He is subordinate to the President of the Republic, and his main task is to represent the Union and act as a procurator of the Federal Government. The latter, in turn, is the head of the Public Ministry, which is an autonomous institution – not subordinate to any administrative, legislative or judicial authority – constituted by public prosecutors whose role is to protect the public interest and the rule of law in its broad sense. The Constitution of 1988 places the Public Ministry in a special position in Brazil's institutional design. In addition to having the monopoly of the initiative of criminal procedures in general (apart from some rare exceptions defined in the Criminal Code), this institution is the main body of the Republic when it comes to controlling the legality of the administrative action. For the constitutional definition of the competences of the General-

Let us outline some of the features of these actions.

A. The Direct Action of Unconstitutionality

The Direct Action of Unconstitutionality is the main instrument by which the Supreme Court adjudicates on a general impugnation of the validity of a legal diploma or any particular statutory provision. Any general normative act from a Federal source or a State source can be challenged by a Direct Action of Unconstitutionality (henceforth ADIN, which stands for the *Ação Direta de Inconstitucionalidade*).[13] Among the federal norms are included the normative acts, which internalize the Treaties that the Brazilian Republic celebrates with foreign nations.

There are, however, a few norms left outside the scope of this constitutional action. The Supreme Court, on the basis of a relatively weak argument, has held that legislative acts that have been passed before the promulgation of the Constitution cannot be reviewed by an ADIN. A distinction was drawn between an unconstitutional provision – that is, a provision produced in violation of the Constitution – and an ancient law that was not received by the new Constitution. Even though both of the laws are to be repealed by the Courts, the case law establishes that a collision between a preconstitutional act and the Constitution should be resolved in light of concrete cases, according to the principles of intertemporal law (i.e., according to the principle *lex posterior derogat priori*). Even though the courts (including, of course, the Supreme Court) may depart from laws that were implicitly abrogated by the Constitution (for there has been no reception of these laws), they should do so not on the grounds that such laws

Advocacy of the Union and the institutional functions of the Public Ministry, see *Constituição da República Federativa do Brasil*: art. 131 ff. (for the General-Advocacy of the Union) and art. 129 ff. (for the Public Ministry). For more on the structure and the institutional functions of the Brazilian Public Ministry, see Hugo Nigro Mazzilli, *Regime Jurídico do Ministério Público*, 6th ed. São Paulo: Saraiva, 2007.

13 The Brazilian Federation is formed by the Federal Union, the States, and a large number of Municipalities, which are autonomous entities that have their own governments and their own legislative assemblies. The general view among Brazilian constitutional lawyers is that such entities belong to the Federation. Notwithstanding, the constitutional provision that regulates the ADIN does not include Municipal laws among the acts that can be challenged by this form of direct action. There are pragmatic reasons for that: in 2006, there were 5,564 Municipalities in the Brazilian territory (http://www.culturatura.com.br/brasil/, visited on 10 September 2009). It would be practically impossible for a single court constituted by eleven judges to exert direct constitutional jurisdiction over such a large number of legislative bodies. It is important to note, however, that the fact that the Supreme Court is not competent to adjudicate on ADINs against municipal laws does not eliminate the possibility of analyzing a claim of unconstitutionality of such statutes by means of extraordinary appeal. Most of the unconstitutional municipal laws are, however, repealed by the State Courts instead of the Federal Supreme Court.

are unconstitutional but rather on the assumption that they belong to an old legal system that no longer exists, as a new Constitution necessarily inaugurates a new juristic order.[14] Because of this technicality, a large set of laws enacted before the Constitution of 1988 is immune from direct constitutional review.[15]

Furthermore, apart from the preconstitutional statutes, laws of concrete effects – that is, normative acts "which have a clearly delimitated object and a clear set of addressees" and thus can be considered laws only in a formal sense, for they "do not discipline abstract juridical relations"[16] – cannot be challenged by an ADIN, and nor can any acts that have been already derogated by Congress.[17]

As ruled by the Constitution, the following authorities can legitimately bring an ADIN before the Supreme Court: the President of the Republic, the Governing Boards of the Federal Senate or of the Chamber of Deputies, the Governing Boards of the Legislative Assemblies of the Federal States, the Governors of the States, the General-Attorney of the Republic (*Procurador Geral da República*), the Federal Section of the Brazilian Association of

14 See STF, Rp. 946, Rel. Min. Xavier de Albuquerque, RTJ, 82 (1)/44; Rp. 1012, Rel. Min. Moreira Alves, RTJ, 95 (3)/990. This case law, despite being very old, is constantly renewed by novel decisions of the court. See STF, AI 386.830-AgR-ED-Edv-Agr-Ed, Rel. Min. Celso de Mello, DJ de 4-02-2005.

15 The roots of this jurisprudence lie in a sort of Kelsenian orthodoxy. In his general theory of law and state, Kelsen explains the reception of ancient laws by a novel constitution in this way: "If laws which were introduced under the old constitution 'continue to be valid' under the new constitution, this is possible only because validity has expressly or tacitly been vested in them by the new constitution. . . . The new order 'receives,' i.e.[,] adopts, norms from the old order; this means that the new order gives validity to (puts into force) norms which have the same content of the old order" (Hans Kelsen, *General Theory of Law and State*, Cambridge, MA: Harvard University Press, 1945, p. 117). When Kelsen holds that the new order created by a Constitution provides a new basis for the validity to norms of the old order, he appears to be denying the possibility of a conflict between an ancient law and the new constitution (as the nonreceived norms belong to a different legal order). One should notice, however, that Kelsen is merely providing a theoretical explanation of the creation of a new legal system, not giving any recommendation to the Constitutional Court. We have plenty of reasons to doubt that Kelsen himself would maintain that, in a legal system in which all the laws are submitted to direct forms of judicial review, the old and anachronistic laws that defy the constitution should be excluded from constitutional jurisdiction. We hope that the Court finds a way out of this jurisprudence in the years to come. Meanwhile, a solution to minimize this problem can be provided by recent statutes that regulated the Claim against the Disrespect to a Fundamental Precept, which is a direct action subsidiary to the Direct Action of Unconstitutionality. This solution, however, would not eliminate the problem, as not all constitutional provisions can constitute a parameter for that claim (see subsection 2.1, "c").

16 For a comment on the topic and a detailed analysis of the case law of the Supreme Court, see Gilmar Mendes, Inocêncio M. Coelho and Paulo G. Branco, *Curso de Direito Constitucional*, 2nd ed., São Paulo: Saraiva, 2008, p. 1117.

17 STF, ADI 647, Rel. Min. Moreira Alves, DJ de 27-3-1992, p. 3801.

Advocates (Ordem dos Advogados do Brasil), any Political Party represented in Congress, and any national union or class-representing association.[18]

B. The Declaratory Action of Constitutionality

The Declaratory Action of Constitutionality (henceforth ADC, which stands for *Ação Declaratória de Constitucionalidade*) was not included in the original wording of the Constitution of 1988. It was introduced by the Third Amendment to the Constitution, in 1993. Only federal normative acts can be the object of an ADC, although the same authorities who can bring an ADIN before the Supreme Court are also competent to bring an ADC.[19]

The distinctive feature of the ADC is that its purpose is to demonstrate not the unconstitutionality of a normative act but rather its compatibility with the Constitution. Because every court and every first-instance judge has constitutional jurisdiction, sometimes the lower courts are overwhelmed with identical claims arguing against the constitutionality of a particular statutory provision. In fiscal matters and issues related to State pensions, the number of identical cases contesting the constitutionality of tributes or criteria used by the Government to update state pensions can be alarming. In the year 2008, for instance, 46.94 percent of the new cases submitted to the Supreme Court (i.e., 34,394 of the total of 73,221 cases submitted to the Supreme Court) dealt with fiscal law and administrative law matters.[20]

As established by Federal law, the proponent of the ADC must indicate in the bill of complaint "the existence of relevant judicial controversy over the application of the provision which constitutes the object of the Declaratory Action."[21] The purpose of the action, as summarized by Minister Gilmar Mendes in an academic writing, must be the preservation of the presumption of constitutionality of the legislation, which can be threatened if there are a large number of decisions departing from the norm.[22] It is a burden of the claimant to demonstrate that there is relevant judicial controversy over the constitutionality of the provision by quoting a substantial number of

18 *Constituição da República Federativa do Brasil*: art. 103, I to IX.

19 *Constituição da República Federativa do Brasil*: article 103, with the wording given by the 45th Constitutional Amendment of 30 December 2004.

20 Official Statistical Database of the Federal Supreme Court, available at http://www.stf.jus. br.

21 Law nº 9.868 of 10 November 1999: art. 14, III.

22 Gilmar Mendes, *Jurisdição Constitucional: o controle abstrato de normas no Brasil e na Alemanha*, São Paulo: Saraiva, 1998, pp. 92 ff. The same author also writes about this topic in Gilmar Mendes et al., *op. cit.* (note 16), p. 1130.

contradictory decisions from different judicial bodies.[23] In this sense, the Court has held that the claimant on the ADC must, at the time of filing the claim, demonstrate a relevant proportion of judicial disagreement. This view was justified by a *reductio ad absurdum*: such judicial disagreement must be strong enough to install a state of general lack of legal certainty, for otherwise the anticipatory rulings of unconstitutionality would mischaracterize the jurisdictional nature of the activity of the Supreme Court by turning the Court into an organ of consultation and thereby opening the way to the risk of undermining the balance of powers between the Legislative and the Judicial Branches of Government.[24]

In line with the purpose of increasing the degree of legal certainty and unifying the interpretation of the Constitution, there are some additional powers conferred to the Court. When assessing the procedural requirements of the ADC, the reporter judge may, if not satisfied with the decisions quoted by the claimant, request additional information from any other court or create a commission of experts to analyze evidence on the impact of jurisprudential disagreements in the current state of the law.[25] Furthermore, the Court may, by a collective judgment of the absolute majority of its members (i.e., six of its eleven Ministers), issue restraint orders determining other jurisdictional bodies of the Republic (State Courts, Federal Courts, Labor Courts, Electoral Courts, Military Courts, and first-instance judges) to suspend the judgment of all cases regarding the application of the law or the normative act under discussion.[26]

C. The Direct Action against Unconstitutional Omissions

Although the ADIN challenges a positive norm and is aimed at derogating unconstitutional legislative acts, the Direct Action against an Unconstitutional Omission (Omissive ADIN) deals with the inertia of the lawgiver, that is, an "unconstitutional gap" in the legal system.[27] The Constitution is deprived of its cogency by the lack of a normative act that should have already been passed by Congress.

[23] See the jurisprudential directives stated in these two cases: STF, ADC 1, Rel. Min. Moreira Alves, DJ de 16-05-1995 and STF, MC em ADC 8, Rel. Min. Celso Mello, DJ de 04-04-2003.

[24] STF, MC em ADC 8, Rel. Min. Celso Mello, DJ de 04-04-2003.

[25] Law nº 9.868 of 10 November 1999: art. 20, § 1 and § 2.

[26] Law nº 9.868 of 10 November 1999: art. 21.

[27] Gilmar Mendes et al., *op. cit.* (note 16), p. 1077.

There are, of course, several dilemmas that remain unsolved in the case law. If what characterizes the legislative activity is its continuous and intermittent character, how can one recognize an unconstitutional omission? If the court is prohibited by the democratic principle and by the principle of the rule of law to substitute for the legislator when he or she is negligent in concretizing the Constitution, what kind of efficacy can be attributed to a decision that recognizes an unconstitutional omission? If there is no procedure for coercively executing this decision, how can one expect the decision that recognizes an unconstitutional omission to be authoritative? These questions are still unanswered and probably will remain so for a long time.

The Brazilian doctrine of the unconstitutional omissions follows the pattern of the case law of the German Constitutional Court.[28] In the academic literature, for instance, two types of unconstitutional omissions are recognized: complete and partial omissions. A complete omission takes place when the legislator does not produce any law, despite the fact that there is a genuine constitutional duty to regulate some constitutional issue, whereas a partial omission occurs when the legislative authority regulates a situation in an unconstitutional way because it does not cover a set of situations that should have been included in the statute. The classic case is the concession of a benefit in detriment to the principle of equality. The law is unconstitutional because it fails to cover situations that should have been included in its general hypothesis.[29]

The number of omissive ADINs in Brazil is relatively low, and the number has continued to drop. As the Constitution gets older, a smaller number of matters referred to in its text are left completely unregulated. The trend is for the Court to deal more with partial omissions than with complete omissions.[30]

As it happens with the ADIN, one may bring and omissive ADIN before the Court, not to uphold his or her own right but to protect the juridical order as a whole. The object of the action is the integrity of the legal order, not any specific right.

In general, the Supreme Court's case law on constitutional omissions can be classified as conservative. The court attributes heavy weight to the principle of democracy and to the principle of division of powers. The

[28] A comparative discussion on the topic can be found in Gilmar Mendes, *op. cit.* (note 16), pp. 1177–1204.

[29] Gilmar Mendes et al., *op. cit.* (note 16), p. 1201.

[30] *Id.*

classic idea of a system of checks and balances recommends that one avoid any type of judicial activism when it comes to providing a remedy for unconstitutional omissions. The court seems to incline itself toward the view that, in the case of a complete absence of a regulation required by the Constitution, the Court should declare its unconstitutionality without pronouncing the nullity of any act and without issuing a direct order to Congress. In this sense, the Court has held, in an omissive ADIN that intended to establish that the value of the minimum wage was unconstitutional because it could not satisfy the basic needs of a person, that while deciding omissive ADINs, the Supreme Court can do no more than notify the competent legislative body that should have enacted a normative act, to make that body of the Republic aware of the unconstitutionality and to enable it to regulate the matter required by the Constitution without the interference of the Judiciary.[31]

In case of normative acts within the competence of the Executive, however, the Constitution establishes that the Court should give the administrative authority a deadline of thirty days to eliminate the omission.[32]

As mentioned earlier, one of the difficulties with omissive ADINs is determining when there is an unconstitutional omission. The Court has held that the general rule must be that if the legislative process has already initiated, there can be no unconstitutional omission of the legislator.[33] Nevertheless, more recent decisions hold that if the *intertia deliberandi* is unequivocally characterized and the delay amounts to negligence, the Court may pronounce an unconstitutional omission despite the existence of a bill under discussion.[34] In a leading case in which it was demonstrated that there was a ten-year delay in enacting an act that was expressly required by the Constitution for the creation and redefinition of territorial boundaries of Municipalities, the court held that there had been a breach of the duty to legislate and that the *inertia deliberandi* could be challenged by an omissive ADIN.[35] This recent case is also important because it opened the possibility to set a deadline for Congress to legislate: the Court determined that the lawgiver should enact a statute, within eighteen months of the publication of the decision, to eliminate the omission and to regulate retrospectively the facts that occurred (and the political and administrative acts practiced)

31 STF, ADI 1439-MC, Rel. Min. Celso de Mello, DJ de 30-5-2003.

32 *Constituição da República Federativa do Brasil*, art. 102, § 2.

33 STF, ADI 2.495, Rel. Min. Ilmar Galavão, DJ de 2-8-2002.

34 Gilmar Mendes et al., *op. cit.*, (note 16), p. 1187.

35 STF, ADI 3.682, Rel. Min. Gilmar Mendes, DJ de 06-09-2007.

between the promulgation of the Constitution (or, to be more specific, the Amendment to the Constitution that established the duty to legislate) and the coming into force of the upcoming regulation.[36]

D. The Claim against the Disrespect to a Fundamental Precept

The Claim against the Disrespect to a Fundamental Precept of the Constitution (henceforth ADPF, for *Argüição de Descumprimento de Preceito Fundamental*) is subsidiary to the ADIN and can be brought before the Court by the same entities that can bring the other types of direct action.[37] Even though the ADPF was mentioned in the original wording of the Constitution of 1988 (and not merely introduced by an Amendment to the Constitution, as was the ADC), it was not regulated until the coming into force of a law that was passed in December 1999. Because of its subsidiary character, only when there is no alternative means to protect the fundamental precept against the violation perpetrated by a normative act can it be admitted.[38]

The ADPF is of significant importance because it makes it possible to protect the Constitution against acts that are left outside of the scope of the ADIN. The most obvious cases are Municipal laws and normative acts that were in force before the promulgation of the Constitution.[39] At the time of the coming into force of the statute that regulates the ADPF, there was genuine social pressure for the admittance of a direct action for adjudicating on the constitutionality of preconstitutional and Municipal laws.

Furthermore, the ADPF enabled the Court to assess the validity of acts that have always been excluded from abstract constitutional jurisdiction. Any normative act of a public authority can be challenged by an ADPF, including "interpretative directives" issued by a court of justice.[40] In this sense, the *súmulas* of the Brazilian courts of justice might be submitted to a direct assessment of their constitutionality.[41] A *súmula* (from Latin, *súmmula*) is an

36 *Ibid.*

37 Law nº 9.882 of 3 December 1999: art. 1.

38 Law nº 9.882 of 3 December 1999: art. 4, § 1.

39 Law nº 9.882 of 3 December 1999: art. 1, p. u., I.

40 In this sense, although there is still no case law on this issue, I quote the opinion of Minister Gilmar Mendes in an academic writing, in which he argues that "it seems *out of question*" that a judicial act interpreting the constitution can be the object of an ADPF. See Gilmar Mendes et al., *op. cit.* (note 16), p. 1161.

41 In spite of the fact that the *súmulas* have a relevant degree of bindingness in Brazilian law, when the new statute was passed, the case law of the Supreme Court was settled in the direction that it

abridgment of law that is relatively authoritative because it is enacted by a court of justice to publicize its own case law. Perhaps the closest equivalent to the *súmula* that one can find in foreign law is the Italian *massima*, which can be defined as "a very abstract statement representing the core of meaning of a legal rule, as it is interpreted by the judgment considered."[42] *Súmulas* are edited only after a set of repetitive decisions, and their enactment is preceded by a vote of the full panel of the Court. Nearly all the courts in Brazil have repertories of their *súmulas*, and for obvious reasons, jurists tend to attribute a great deal of authority to them.[43]

Finally, as Minister Gilmar Mendes has recently argued, the ADPF may be used to review administrative acts of regulation (*regulamentos administrativos*) that violate either the principle of due process of law (which establishes that "no one shall be deprived of her liberty or her property without the Due Process of Law")[44] or the principle of formal legality (which establishes that "no one shall be obliged to do or to refrain from something unless by order of a law").[45] In our opinion, however, the ADPF should be applicable to such normative administrative acts only when they are enacted by the Municipal administration, for in the case of Federal laws or laws from the member states of the Federation, these acts are already covered by the ADIN.[46]

An open question for Brazilian constitutional lawyers is, Which constitutional norms can constitute a parameter for and ADPF? What should the Court understand as a "fundamental precept"? In this topic, there is no final answer in legislation or in the case law. It would be recommendable to pass a law establishing a complete list of subjects that can be protected by the ADPF. In the absence of such legislation, however, the Court developed its own directives to define the fundamental character of a constitutional provision. After recognizing that it is "very difficult to delimitate, *a priori*, the fundamental precepts of the Constitution," the Supreme Court held that at least the following group of norms are protected by the ADPF: (1) the

cannot constitute an object of an ADIN, on the grounds that it lacks the general characteristics of a normative act. See STF, ADI 594, Rel. Min. Marco Aurélio, DJ de 15-04-1994.

42 Michele Taruffo, "Precedent in Italy" in E. Hondius (ed.), *Precedent and the Law – Reports to the XVIIth Congress of the International Academy of Comparative Law, Utrecht, 16–22 July 2006*, Brussels, Bruylant, 2007, p. 181.

43 For a short explanation in English of the force of precedents and *súmulas* in Brazilian law, see Thomas Bustamante, *op. cit.* (note 6).

44 *Constituição da República Federativa do Brasil*, art. 5, LIV.

45 *Constituição da República Federativa do Brasil*, art. 5, II.

46 For the Minister's opinion, see Gilmar Mendes et al., *op. cit.* (note 16), p. 1168–1170.

individual rights;[47] (2) those precepts that, by virtue of an explicit constitutional provision, cannot be suppressed by an Amendment to the Constitution and therefore form the immutable core (*cláusulas pétreas*) of such Constitution;[48] and the so-called sensitive principles of federalism,[49] that is, the set of norms that, if disrespected, would authorize the interference of the Union in the competences of the States or the interference of the States in the competences of the Municipalities.[50]

2. *Concentrated Constitutional Review by Concrete Claims*

In addition to the four types of abstract claims of unconstitutionality highlighted already, there are two special writs that are relevant for constitutional jurisdiction. The first one is the Writ of Injunction (*Mandado de Injunção*), which establishes a specific remedy for unconstitutional omissions when such omissions prevent the exercise of a right already established by the Constitution. The second is the Writ of *Mandado de Segurança*, which is an action that can be brought against a public authority (be it a physical person or an administrative body) that by its illegal action keeps one from exercising a legal right.[51]

These two actions, the Writ of Injunction and the *Mandado de Segurança* (when used to challenge a bill under discussion in one of the Houses of Congress), are a form of concentrated, though not abstract, constitutional review. It is concentrated because the jurisdiction is privative to the Supreme Court, but concrete because the writs are used to protect a right of the claimant rather than the general integrity of the legal order.

[47] In the speech of the Reporter Judge, the court refers to the "individual and collective rights" enumerated at art. 5, I–LXXVIII, of the Constitution. An open question is whether social rights and labor rights should be considered fundamental precepts of the Constitution. There are arguments in both directions.

[48] *Constituição de República Federativa do Brasil*: art. 60, § 4. Those principles are those that protect the Federal form of Government, the separation of powers, the freedom of general elections, and fundamental legal rights.

[49] *Constituição de República Federativa do Brasil*: art. 34.

[50] STF, ADPF 33-MC, Rel. Min. Gilmar Mendes, DJ de 06-08-2004.

[51] The writ of *Mandado de Segurança* antedates the Constitution of 1988 by fifty years. It was introduced by the Constitution of 1934, and its main inspiration was the Writ of Mandamus, from the law of the United States. Nevertheless, in spite of the fact that the MS and the Writ of Injunction have similar effects (they both lead to a court order determining or restraining one from a particular action), they can be distinguished because the latter is a remedy within the discretion of the courts, whereas the former is a judicial action in which the courts have no discretion in enforcing the right of the claimant. For more on the *Mandado de Segurança*, see Hely Lopes Meirelles, *Mandado de Segurança*, 30th ed., updated by Arnoldo Wald et al., São Paulo: Malheiros, 2007.

A. *Mandado de Segurança* (When Used to Contest an Act within the Legislative Procedure)

The *Mandado de Segurança* (henceforth MS) is a type of constitutional action that is brought against a public authority to obtain an injunctive relief in the form of a court order restraining such authority from performing a particular act. The MS can be grounded either on a violation of constitutional norms or on a violation of ordinary statutory regulations.[52] In the vast majority of cases, the incidental declaration of unconstitutionality within a MS does not differ from in the rest of the diffuse and incidental forms of judicial review, but in one specific case, it does have a particular feature that transforms it into an instrument of concentrated constitutional review: the proponent of an MS may challenge the production of a general normative act. Any interested party is able to sue the Governing Board of the Federal Senate or the Governing Board of the Chamber of Deputies to prevent the House from passing an unconstitutional act that would affect a liquid right of the claimant.[53] By that procedure, the Supreme Court is empowered to interfere in the legislative process to knock down a bill by exercising a preventive form of constitutional jurisdiction.[54]

[52] Nevertheless, one cannot challenge the general effects of a law by an MS, for its efficacy is limited to the protection of a particular individual right. In this sense, there is an old *Súmula* that has been continuously applied by the court. See STF, *Súmula* 266: "It is inadmissible to challenge a general law by a Mandado de Segurança" (this is not a literal translation; the canonical form of the *súmula* in Portuguese is "Não cabe mandado de segurança contra lei em tese"). This *súmula* does not mean, however, that one cannot deploy constitutional arguments in support of one's rights. As long as there is a liquid right in issue and as long as the effects of the decision do not extend beyond the individual legal relations of the case, the MS can be processed by the courts. The jurisdiction to adjudicate on a MS is determined by the territory over which the body that enacted the act challenged by the writ has authority. In case of an act of Congress, however, there is a constitutional provision attributing that competence to the Federal Supreme Court.

[53] One of the distinctive features of the *Mandado de Segurança* is that it is a special procedure for protecting only liquid rights. A liquid right is understood in the relevant legal statutes (especially Law nº 1.533/1951) as a right that is based on uncontroversial factual circumstances. There can be no controversy over the facts of the case and the claimant must have unequivocal documental evidence. The circumstance of being brought against a bill in discussion by Congress turns the MS into a *sui generis* direct action, as the effects of the decision, instead of being *inter partes*, are generalized and become *erga omnes* once the act is nullified.

[54] For some case law on the admissibility of the *Mandado de Segurança* for preventing an unconstitutional bill from being passed, see STF, MS 20.257, Rel. Min. Moreira Alves, DJ de 8-10-1980; STF, MS-AgRg 21.303, Rel. Min. Octavio Galloti, DJ de 2-8-1991; STF, MS 24.356, Rel. Min. Carlos Velloso, DJ de 12-9-2003, as well as other subsequent decisions quoted in Gilmar Mendes et al., *op. cit.* (note 16), p. 1078.

B. The Writ of Injunction (*Mandado de Injunção*)

The Constitution of 1988 established a large number of rights to be regulated by ordinary legislation. Nevertheless, there is a constitutional provision stating that all fundamental legal rights are "immediately applicable."[55] The constituent lawmaker, to uphold the efficacy of the Constitution, created a new constitutional remedy named Writ of Injunction (*Mandado de Injunção*, henceforth MI). The MI is also a form of concentrated though concrete judicial review. One may bring an MI before the Supreme Court not in defense of the general integrity of the legal order but in defense of one's own rights.

Like the Omissive ADIN, the MI is a constitutional writ whose function is to break down the inertia of the legislator. The writ is admissible whenever the lack of a regulatory infraconstitutional norm "makes it impossible to exercise the civil liberties and fundamental legal rights or the prerogatives related to nationality, sovereignty and citizenship."[56]

The first leading case on the admissibility of the MI was decided merely one year after the promulgation of the Constitution of 1988. In this case (MI 107), the Court held that the efficacy of a decision delivered in an MI is similar to that of an Omissive ADIN: the MI is an action that intends to obtain from the Judiciary a declaration of unconstitutionality of an omission in regulating a right, with a view to notify the entity responsible for that regulation to take action, as with the Omissive ADIN.[57] The Court was very firm in its conviction that it could not act as a positive legislator, in the words of Hans Kelsen.[58] No additive decisions either to integrate or to amend the legislation were allowed.

There are, however, some cases in which the Court gave a broader scope to the procedural remedy of the MI. For example, in MI 283, the Court recognized a state of negligence of Congress in regulating a norm established by the Temporary Provisions of the Constitution.[59] That norm stipulates a duty to provide compensation for the victims of abuses committed by the military dictatorship via secret acts of the Ministry of

55 *Constituição da República Federativa do Brasil*, art. 5, § 1.

56 *Constituição da República Federativa do Brasil*: art. 5, LXXI.

57 STF, MI 107-QO, Rel. Min. Moreira Alves, DJ de 21-09-1990.

58 Hans Kelsen, "La garantie juridictionelle de la constitution (La Justice constitutionnelle)," *Revue du droit public*, 1928, pp. 197–257, also quoted in the General Report of this collective work.

59 *Constituição da República Federativa do Brasil – Ato das Disposições Constitucionais Transitórias* (ADCT): art. 8, § 3.

Defense, which banned a large number of people from exercising certain economic activities. Because the Constitution required the passing of a Federal law to regulate the particulars of such compensation, the victims could not exercise their constitutional rights. In light of this situation, the Supreme Court not only ruled that there was an unconstitutional omission but also established a deadline of forty-five days for Congress to legislate. The Court determined, moreover, that in case the state of parliamentary negligence remained after that deadline, the applicant would be automatically entitled to claim compensation against the Union, in the form of the general rules of the Civil Code.[60]

In another relevant case, the Constitution guaranteed a fiscal privilege to beneficent institutions of social assistance, excluding them from taxation by contributions to the social security, "as long as these entities complied with the conditions established in law."[61] The Constitution has left to the ordinary legislator the task to discipline the conditions with which those entities should comply to claim immunity from the contributions. Nevertheless, the Federal Government understood that such entities could claim no fiscal immunity until Congress passed a law listing such conditions. The Supreme Court, after holding that there was an unjustifiable legislative omission, set a deadline of six months for Congress to pass a law eliminating the omission. Furthermore, it determined that, if no law was passed by that deadline, the claimant would be automatically entitled to claim the fiscal benefit.[62]

In these two cases, the court took a step toward judicial legislation, albeit only with *inter partes* effect. That step, however, was of limited significance. In both cases, the Constitution is very clear about the rights that are protected by its provisions. There is no doubt about the semantic meaning of the constitutional norms, and it is very easy to understand the scope of the right that is determined by the basic norm. The reference to ordinary legislation can mean no more than the assertion the lawmaker may, within a certain margin of appreciation, restrict or extend the protection of such rights. One could even say that the MI was not really needed in those cases, on the grounds that the Constitutional provisions at issue were immediately applicable, despite the fact that the legislator might restrict them.[63]

60 STF, MI 283, Rel. Min. Sepúlveda Pertence, DJ de 14-11-1991.

61 *Constituição da República Federativa do Brasil*, art. 195, § 7.

62 STF, MI 232, Rel. Min. Moreira Alves, DJ de 27-03-1992.

63 In this sense, a prestigious part of the doctrine argues with plausible arguments that the remedy of the MI is unnecessary, as the Constitution establishes that fundamental legal rights are immediately applicable and the methods of constitutional interpretation enable jurists to

C. Additive Decisions and the Writ of Injunction

In some recent decisions, the Supreme Court has made substantial changes in its case law by recognizing the possibility of additive decisions within a Writ of Injunction (MI). In a claim (an MI) filed against the absence of a law regulating strike actions by public servants, the Court overruled in part its leading case (MI 107) concerning the limits of the judicial powers of filling in unconstitutional gaps. The Brazilian Constitution expressly contemplates among the fundamental labor rights the right to strike, and it has a specific provision requiring a Federal law to lay down the particulars of strike actions within the public services. Nevertheless, nearly twenty years after the promulgation of the Constitution, no law had been passed regulating these matters. Although the Government stated that its servants were not allowed to go on strike until a statute fixing the limits and the conditions for exercising this right was enacted, the unions of workers and many leaders of labor organizations interpreted the aforementioned constitutional provision as establishing an unlimited or unconstrained right. In times of tension between the Government and its servants, the situation has reached a level at which serious losses have been suffered by the population. In administrative bodies like the National Institute of Social Security, a multimonth strike has led thousands of pensioners to suffer intolerable delays in receiving their pensions. Administrative claims of new benefits have been suspended, and a large part of the population has been unable to claim benefits like maternity leave or the allowance paid by the Government (in place of salary) to health leave. As the Court held, the absence of a regulation in this issue has led to a "state of nature" that has "serious consequences for the Rule of Law." As Minister Gilmar Mendes expressed in his opinion, to leave the issue unregulated would amount to a sort of "judicial omission" in protecting the Constitution.[64]

In the face of this context, the Supreme Court pronounced the first additive decision – or at least the first admittedly additive decision – in the history of its case law. As opposed to the decisions on the MI 283 and the MI 232 – where it ruled that a constitutional right may be directly applicable despite the possibility of restrictive legislation only if its content can be directly determined by the interpretation of the constitutional text – the Court decided to make positive regulations for a situation that was leading to serious social

establish, in concrete cases, the sphere of applicability such rights. See Luís Roberto Barroso, *O controle de constitucionalidade no direito brasileiro*, São Paulo: Saraiva, 2006, p. 112.

64 STF, MI 670, Rel. Min. Gilmar Mendes, DJ de 31-10-2008.

conflicts. After analyzing in detail the practice of additive decisions in the Italian tradition, the Court made express reference to the works of Portuguese Professor Rui Medeiros, who states that additive decisions integrating legislation or yet regulations adopted by the court are "constitutionally obligatory."[65]

The Court decided thus to analogically apply the ordinary labor laws that regulate strike action in private labor contracts. Until further legislation is passed, public servants are subjected at least to the same rules that apply to ordinary workers as to the abusive forms of strike action.[66]

Nevertheless, one should not overestimate the impact of this new case in the state of the law. Arguments by analogy are a central feature to any legal system, and there is nothing original or particular to developed forms of constitutional review. The sole distinctive feature of this type of case law is that it constitutes an analogical decision with *erga omnes* effects, as it establishes a rule to be generally observed until further legislative acts are passed by Congress.

In spite of the general effect of its analogical decisions, the Court insists that it is acting not as a positive legislator but merely as the "guardian of the Constitution."[67]

III. EFFECTS OF THE JUDICIAL DECISIONS ON CONSTITUTIONAL MATTERS

1. *Inter Partes and Erga Omnes Decisions*

The distinction between *inter partes* and *erga omnes* effects of constitutional decisions provides the key criterion for distinguishing the decisions of constitutional questions in concrete cases (i.e., as an incidental question in a legal dispute) and in abstract constitutional actions (i.e., claims

65 See the opinion of Minister Gilmar Mendes, which is transcribed in Gilmar Mendes et al., *op. cit.* (note 16), pp. 1214–1219. See also, for a more developed account on the doctrine of additive decisions to which the Court adheres, Rui Medeiros, *A Decisão de Inconstitucionalidade*, Lisboa: Universidade Católica Editora, 1999, pp. 301–318. In our opinion, however, the directive suggested here seems to be merely that additive decisions integrating legislation are admitted, whereas additive decisions reforming legislation are not. When a norm is considered constitutionally obligatory, this seems to mean that the norm is determined by the Constitution, and therefore no additive decision is needed.

66 STF, MI 670, Rel. Min. Gilmar Mendes, DJ de 31-10-2008.

67 *Ibid.*

detached from any case of application of the provision challenged by direct actions).

As a rule, decisions of unconstitutionality – including the cases of partial annulment of a legal norm without textual reduction of a statutory provision (*declaração de inconstitucionalidade parcial sem redução de texto*) and the interpretation in accordance with the Constitution (*interpretação conforme à Constituição*) – pronounced in abstract or direct actions are *erga omnes* efficacious and have both a derogatory effect on the unconstitutional provision and a repristinating effect on the legislation that was abrogated by it.[68]

Decisions on abstract constitutional actions do not resolve concrete disputes but eliminate the statutes or the provisions pronounced unconstitutional.

In contrast, decisions of unconstitutionality within a legal dispute have *inter partes* effect and thus lack authority to derogate statutory legislation. Nonetheless, there is an ongoing discussion in the Supreme Court about the possibility of attributing *erga omnes* efficacy to incidental constitutional decisions that the Court might have adopted in concrete constitutional review. In a case in which only four of the eleven Ministers of the Federal Supreme Court delivered their judgments, some Ministers of the Court argued that the system of constitutional review in Brazil has suffered a constitutional mutation. The constitutional provision that requires that a Resolution of the Federal Senate be passed to attribute *erga omnes* efficacy to a final decision of unconstitutionality laid down by the Supreme Court would have lost its juridical relevancy:[69] once the system of judicial review developed in the direction of permitting the Court to lay down a group of binding *súmulas*,[70] there would be no point in requiring a Resolution of the Senate to do something that the Court could do by its own authority.[71] If this

68 "The pronouncement of unconstitutionality in abstract actions, as a result of its repristinating efficacy, implies the reestablishment of the norms derogated by the norm whose constitutionality is challenged by a direct action (RTJ 120/64 – RTJ 194/504-505 – ADI 2.867/ES, *v.g.*). . . . Because the unconstitutional law is invalid (RJT 102671), it does not even have derogatory efficacy" (STF, ADI 2.215-MC/PE, Rel. Min. Celso de Mello, Informativo/*STF* n. 224).

69 *Constituição da República Federativa do Brasil*, art. 52, X.

70 *Constituição da República Federativa do Brasil*, art. 103-A.

71 For a discussion on the supposed constitutional mutation that would undermine art. 52, X, of the Brazilian Constitution, see the Official Bulletin of the Court: *Informativos* n. 454 and 463, available at http://.stf.gov.br.

interpretation prevails, a constitutional mutation implicitly derogating a particular constitutional provision will be explicitly recognized.[72]

2. *Binding and Nonbinding Decisions*

In addition to the distinction between *inter partes* and *erga omnes* decisions, there is another relevant classification in Brazilian law with regard to the efficacy of judicial decisions about the (un)constitutionality of a provision. The Third Amendment to the Brazilian Constitution, from 17 March 1993, established that the decisions of the Federal Supreme Courts in ADINs and ADCs not only have *erga omnes* efficacy but also are binding on all the judicial and administrative bodies of the Federal Union, the States, and the Municipalities.[73]

More recently, another Amendment to the Constitution empowered the Federal Supreme Court to enact, by a decision of two-thirds of its members and after a series of reiterated decisions about a constitutional issue, a special type of *súmulas* with binding efficacy over all the bodies of the Judiciary and all the administrative authorities of the Federal, State, and Municipal Governments. These *súmulas* differ from the ordinary *súmulas* of the Court and are explicitly named *súmulas vinculantes* (binding *súmulas*).[74] The Court may decide to issue these *súmulas* on its own authority, but any of the parties able to bring an ADIN before the Court can also request the promulgation, revision, and annulment of a binding *súmula*.[75] The *súmulas*, as their own *nomen iuris* reveals, are also strictly binding.

Finally, a recent Federal Law attributed binding effects not only to the decisions of the Federal Supreme Court in ADINs, ADCs, and binding *súmulas* but also to any decision in an ADPF.[76]

The key difference between the *erga omnes* and the strictly binding effects of judicial decisions is that the latter means not only that a decision is

[72] For the opinion of Minister Gilmar Mendes, who is among the four judges who have delivered their votes, see Gilmar Mendes et al., *op. cit.* (note 16), pp. 1084–1091. This opinion is particularly interesting because it is an enthusiastic defense of the claim that there has been a derogatory constitutional mutation.

[73] See *Constituição da Repúblida Federativa do Brasil*: art. 102, § 2, with the wording given by the 45th Constitutional Amendment of 30 December 2004.

[74] *Constituição da Repúblida Federativa do Brasil*: art. 103, with the wording given by the 45th Constitutional Amendment of 30 December 2004.

[75] *Constituição da Repúblida Federativa do Brasil*: art. 103, § 2, with the wording given by the 45th Constitutional Amendment of 30 December 2004.

[76] Law nº 9.882 of 3 December 1999: art. 10, § 3.

applicable to all juridical relations but also that there is a constitutional writ to guarantee the efficacy of such decisions. This constitutional writ is named "Complaint to Preserve the Competences of the Federal Supreme Court and the Authority of its Decisions" (henceforth *Reclamação*, for the Portuguese *Reclamação para Preservação da Competência do Supremo Tribunal Federal e Garantia da Autoridade de Suas Decisões*).[77] Any party, in the course of any judicial or administrative dispute, may bring a *Reclamação* before the Federal Supreme Court. The Supreme Court may issue constraint orders and annul any judicial or administrative decision of any body of the Republic.[78] In this case, and only in this case, there is a Brazilian equivalent of the technique of *avvocamiento*.

Here we have another situation in which the Court clearly acts as a positive legislator. In effect, it can be argued that the efficacy of the binding decisions of the Supreme Court – and particularly the efficacy of a binding *súmula* – is equivalent to the general efficacy of the legislation, for these decisions, and especially the binding *súmulas*, establish the final interpretation of the Constitution.[79]

3. *The Scope of the Binding Effects of the Decisions of the Court*

One of the most controversial problems of Brazilian constitutional law is whether it is admissible to challenge, by means of a Reclamação, a judicial decision that violates not only the ruling of a binding decision of the Supreme Court but also its justifying reasons (*fundamentos determinantes*). In a case decided in October 2003, the Federal Supreme Court decided that the writ would be admissible to compel the lower courts to respect not only the concrete order that pronounces the unconstitutionality of a particular

[77] *Constituição da Repúblida Federativa do Brasil*: art. 102, I, "l."

[78] For a brief explanation of the *Reclamações* in Brazilian Law, see Gilmar Mendes, "A reclamação constitucional no Supremo Tribunal Federal" in Marcelo Novelino Camargo, *Leituras Complementares de Direito Constitucional*, Salvador: Jus Podivm, 2nd ed., 2008, pp. 401–435.

[79] In spite of being the final interpretation of the Constitution, the binding decisions of the Federal Supreme Court find a limit, as they cannot bind Congress. The authority of the binding constitutional decisions does not reach Congress because the legislative body is still allowed to enact a new statute with the same wording of the previously annulled on the grounds of its unconstitutionality (STF, Rcl 2.617 AgR, Rel. Min. Cezar Peluso, DJ de 20.05.2005). Even though it is likely that this new text will also be challenged by a direct action of unconstitutionality, it might be the case that a constitutional mutation is recognized and the statute is validated. The writ of *Reclamação* is admitted only if the unconstitutionality of the new statute is pronounced in another binding decision.

provision or establishes that it shall be interpreted in a particular sense but also the motivation, or the *ratio decidendi*, of a binding decision.[80]

Nevertheless, in spite of this decision of the plenary sitting of the Court, there is still an ongoing discussion among its members over the thesis that the binding efficacy of a decision transcends the particular order laid down by the Court and thus encompasses the reasoning or the general principles formulated to justify the conclusions of the Court.[81] There is no objective method for determining the *ratio decidendi* of the decisions of the court in ADINs, ADCs, or ADPFs.

One thing seems to be certain. It is very unlikely that the Court will attribute binding effects to a decision that pronounces the constitutionality of a norm even when the parties offer new reasons that were not submitted to the Court in the previous judgment. If one is able to put forward arguments that were not discussed by Ministers of the Court in a previous case that pronounced the constitutionality of a rule, there is no reason to believe that the rule will be "protected" from a claim of unconstitutionality on grounds not yet analyzed by the Court. The *erga omnes* and binding effects of the decision are thus merely of *prima facie* character. A decision that holds that the law X is compatible with the Constitution for the set of reasons R can always be challenged on the basis of the reason r^1 if that reason does not belong to the set R. To put it more simply, a decision that establishes the constitutionality of a legal provision is valid with a sort of *clausula rebus sic stantibus*, as some social changes and newer juridical understandings of the matter analyzed by the Court in the past might justify a change in the Court's doctrine.[82]

80 STF, RCL 1.987, Rel. Min. Maurício Corrêa, DJ de 21.04.2004.

81 See, e.g., the opinions already delivered in these two *Reclamações*: Rcl 2986, Rel. Min. Celso de Mello (Excerpt from the opinion of the reporter judge published at STF: *Informativo* n. 379, available at http://www.stf.jus. br) and Rcl. 5470, Rel. Min. Gilmar Mendes (excerpt from the opinion of the reporter judge published at STF: *Informativo* n. 496, available at http://www.stf.jus. br). These opinions are in line with the precedent from the Rcl. 1.987, quoted in the previous note. In a recent decision, however, the court has rejected, also by its plenary sitting, the thesis that the justifying reasons of a binding decision would also bind the lower courts and leave way to a *Reclamação*, on the grounds that the argument on which the claimant relied was no more than an *obiter dictum* (STF, Rcl 2475 Agr, Rel. Min. Marco Aurélio, DJ de 01.02.2008). It seems that the court still lacks a proper theory for determining which parts of its judgments are binding and which are nothing but an *obiter dictum*.

82 Gilmar Mendes, *op. cit.* (note 22), p. 284.

4. *Interpretative and Reductive Decisions by the Federal Supreme Court*

In the speeches of the Ministers of the Federal Supreme Court, one can find express and recurrent references to many interpretative and reductive decisions, such as the technique of interpretation in accordance with the Constitution, the pronouncement of partial unconstitutionality without textual reduction, and the pronouncement of partial unconstitutionality with textual reduction. These are all interpretative techniques of infraconstitutional laws. The decisions of the court in these situations have *erga omnes* efficacy and are absolutely binding on lower courts, as long as they are pronounced within the context of an action whose decisions are characterized by these types of effects.

The interpretative decisions of the Federal Supreme Court, when issued in the context of abstract and concentrated constitutional review, are strictly binding on all judicial and administrative bodies.[83]

A pronouncement of partial unconstitutionality with textual reduction is perhaps the most frequent of these methods. If a legislative provision, in the same paragraph or sentence, contemplates two or more alternative hypotheses, it might be the case that only one of them violates the Constitution. The unconstitutionality of the provision is partial because, among the multiple facts covered by the abstract description of the norm, only a few make the norm unconstitutional. A reductive decision is one that "eliminates part of the linguistic-uncontroversial core of the area of application of a norm."[84] A pronouncement of unconstitutionality with textual reduction is thus one that eliminates some expression from the wording of a legal provision. In an abstract formula, the pronouncements of unconstitutionality with textual reduction of a norm can be described thus: if a normative sentence S contemplates, in the conditions of application of the norm N, the facts C^1, C^2, . . ., and C^n; and if C^n is considered to be incompatible with the Constitution, the court may revise the sentence C by eliminating C^n from the set of the conditions of application of N. To quote an example, the Federal Supreme Court pronounced unconstitutionality with textual reduction when a Federal Law regulating the activity of advocacy established that every advocate had "professional immunity" and thus that "speeches and manifestations in the exercise of his professional activities, either in or out of court," did not amount to the crimes of "injury, defamation

83 STF, Rcl 2.143 Agr, Rel. Min. Celso de Mello, DJ de 06.06.1993.

84 Aleksander Peczenik, *The Basis of Legal Justification*, Lund, 1983, p. 51.

or contempt."[85] It was held that this provision was unconstitutional while it immunized lawyers from being persecuted by the crime of contempt. The Court held that if lawyers were excluded from the scope of the criminal provision that punishes contempt of court, the autonomy of the courts and the authority of their decisions would be seriously endangered, and therefore it pronounced the unconstitutionality of the expression "and contempt," albeit keeping in force the rest of the legislative provision.[86] In the same case, many other provisions of the same statute were reduced in the same way, for the Court held that the advocates were immunized to such an extent that the privileges could not find a justifying reason and violated, among others, the principle of equality before the law.[87]

A pronouncement partial of unconstitutionality without textual reduction, in turn, takes place when the legislative provision violates the constitution if interpreted in its literal or ordinary meaning. The court interprets a particular expression of the statute in a restrictive way to eliminate from the abstract norm that can be derived from the wording of the provision any sense that would collide with the Constitution. Instead of a principle of constitutional interpretation, this is considered a principle for the interpretation of the infraconstitutional legislation. Its function is to preserve the presumption of legitimacy of the legislation while avoiding maintaining in force unconstitutional readings of a statute.

Even though some scholars attempt to differentiate the pronouncement of partial unconstitutionality without textual reduction from the interpretation in accordance with the Constitution, from the pragmatic point of view, there is no difference between the two of them. To use a Kelsenian category, we can say that, in both cases, the Court eliminates from the "frame" that defines the possible meanings of a lower-level norm those meanings that would make it incompatible with the constitutional norm that provides the basis of its validity. Whenever it is semantically possible, the Court should interpret an infraconstitutional norm in a way that avoids the annulment of such a norm.

These methods of legal interpretation might, however, represent a threat to the accepted principle that the Court should always act as a negative legislator. When interpreting a statute in accordance with the Constitution, the Court recognizes and reasserts that it is strictly forbidden to extend the scope of a legal provision in such a way that would create a general norm not established by the lawgiver. As the Court defines it, the interpretation in

85 Law nº 8.906 of 4 July 1994: art. 7, § 2.

86 STF, ADI 1.127, Rel. Min. Paulo Brossard, DJ de 29.06.1994.

87 *Ibid.*

accordance with the Constitution is a "technique of constitutional review which can not lead to a particular interpretation that falls outside of the range of hermeneutic possibilities" left by the text as a normative statement.[88] It is inadmissible to apply this interpretative method whenever it is impossible to choose, among the possible meanings of the infraconstitutional norm, one that would eliminate the unconstitutionality. One cannot avoid the pronouncement of unconstitutionality when the meaning of the norm is undisputed.[89]

5. *The Temporal Effects of the Decisions on Constitutional Matters (on Direct Actions of Unconstitutionality)*

In Brazilian law, judges and courts generally consider themselves bound by the principle stated by Justice Marshall in *Marbury v. Madison*: as a rule, unconstitutional laws are null and void and of no effect.[90] The influence of the early decisions from the Supreme Court of the United States over the development of judicial review in Brazil is remarkable, probably because of the influence of the ideas of one of the greatest Brazilian jurists of all times, Rui Barbosa, who was a strong voice in defense of the civil rights in the country and one of the architects of the historical model of constitutional review.[91]

As it was held in a relatively recent case, "the natural order of things" directs itself toward the view that a decision pronouncing the unconstitutionality of a norm is retroactive to the date of the issuance of the norm considered unconstitutional.[92]

Had the lawgiver not passed statutory provisions explicitly authorizing the Supreme Court to lay down manipulative decisions, there would probably still be some resistance from the community of jurists against decisions with merely *ex nunc* or prospective efficacy.

The current law is that decisions delivered in abstract and concentrated forms of judicial review of the constitutionality of laws normally have *ex tunc* or retroactive effects. Nevertheless, the Supreme Court may restrict the

[88] STF, ADI 3.046, Rel. Min. Sepúlveda Pertence, DJ de 28.05.2004.

[89] STF, ADI 1.344-MC, Rel. Min. Moreira Alves, DJ de 19.04.1996.

[90] *Marbury v. Madison*, 5 U.S. (1 Cranch) 137 (1803).

[91] For a historical record of the system of judicial review of the constitutionality of the law in Brazil, with particular emphasis on the works of Rui Barbosa, see Paulo Bonavides, *Curso de Direito Constitucional*, 6th ed., São Paulo: Malheiros, 1996, pp. 267–310.

[92] STF, ADI 2.728, Rel. Min. Marco Aurélio, DJ de 05.10.2007.

effects of the pronouncement of unconstitutionality of a law to deliver *ex nunc* or *pro futuro* decisions or even to determine that the pronouncement of unconstitutionality will produce effects only after a deadline set by the Court. The Court must comply with the following requisites while delivering such manipulative decisions: (1) there must be reasons of legal certainty or of (2) exceptional social interest and, moreover, (3) the restriction or the exception to the retroactive efficacy of the decision must be established by a vote of at least two-thirds of the members of the Court (in its plenary sitting).[93]

There is no doubt, therefore, that manipulative decisions with regard to the temporal efficacy of the pronouncement of unconstitutionality of a law are admitted in the Brazilian legal system. Nevertheless, it is a consensus that the Courts should manipulate the temporal effects of the decision of unconstitutionality not on the basis of purely pragmatic reasons but rather on the basis of strictly juridical reasons.

6. *The Temporal Effects of the Decisions on Constitutional Matters (on Diffuse Decisions on Constitutional Matters)*

In spite of the lack of an express provision authorizing the courts to restrict the retrospective efficacy of the decisions of unconstitutionality in diffused and *incidenter tantum* judicial review, the Supreme Court has broadened the scope of the permission established by article 27 of Law No. 9.868 of 19 November 1999.

As matter of fact, this provision, which authorizes the Court to limit the retrospective efficacy of decisions of unconstitutionality, is remarkably similar to the constitutional provision that, in the Portuguese Republic, authorizes the same measures.[94] The same order of questions that were raised in Portugal is now open to Brazilian debate. The Court decided thus to rely on the doctrinal interpretation dominant in that country. In interpreting the Portuguese constitutional provision, Professor Rui Medeiros claims that the article 282nd (4th) of the Portuguese Constitution applies not only to concentrated constitutional adjudication but also to diffuse judicial decisions of unconstitutionality of statutes.[95]

In consonance with this view, there are some decisions of the Federal Supreme Court admitting decisions pronouncing the unconstitutionality of

93 See Law nº 9.882 of 3 December 1999: art. 11; Law nº 9.868 of 10 November 1999: art. 27.

94 *Constituição da República Portuguesa*, art. 282 n. 4.

95 Rui Medeiros, *A Decisão de Inconstitucionalidade*. Lisboa: Universidade Católica Editora, 1999, pp. 743–744.

laws with purely prospective efficacy even in the diffuse and concrete forms of constitutional jurisdiction.[96] The pronouncement of unconstitutionality *in concreto* can be limited if "another constitutional principle justifies the denial of the application of the principle of nullity," that is, of the general rule that decisions of unconstitutionality have retrospective efficacy.[97]

In some exceptional cases, the Court has even admitted the pronouncement of unconstitutionality without annulment of any concrete acts, on the grounds that the retrospective decision of unconstitutionality would itself violate the constitution to an extent even greater than would the maintenance of the unconstitutional acts (whose effects, in the particular case, could not be undone without serious losses to a large proportion of society).[98]

7. *Constitutional Mutations*

Constitutional mutations are also admitted in the jurisprudence of the Federal Supreme Court. A mutation is understood as a change in the interpretation of a constitutional provision, the meaning of which is altered in spite of the maintenance of the same wording of the Constitution. If it were not for the binding efficacy of some constitutional decisions, there would be nothing special about constitutional mutations to distinguish them from the general practice of overruling. Because of the general effects of such changes, in some very exceptional cases, the Court has applied the technique of prospective overruling to avoid retrospective changes in the law that would cause social instability.[99] The general rule, however, is to avoid this technique and not to apply it unless the parties advance very strong reasons.

IV. CONCLUSION: THE IDEA OF THE NEGATIVE LEGISLATOR

The analysis of the Brazilian case law in this report has shown that the idea that the Supreme Court should act as a negative legislator, and not as a positive lawmaker, is deeply entrenched in the ideology of the Brazilian legal system. We have seen, however, that as a matter of fact there is a significant range of situations in which the Court does act as a positive legislator despite its official discourse. Is this a contradiction? How should we reconstruct the

96 STF, Informativo n. 418, available at http://www.stf.gov.br.

97 STF, HC 82.959/ES, Rel. Min Marco Aurélio, DJ de 01.09.2006 (see, e.g., the opinion of Min. Gilmar Mendes).

98 STF, RE 442.683-8, Rel. Min. Carlos Velloso, DJ de 24.03.2006.

99 Supremo Tribunal Federal, HC 82.959/SP, Rel. Min. Marco Aurélio, DJ de 01.09.2006.

ideal and the factual interpretations of the thesis that courts are negative legislators, with particular reference to the Brazilian Supreme Court?

When the Court expressly asserts that its competences do not authorize it to lay down general norms and thus act as a positive legislator, it makes a normative claim and establishes for itself a general obligation to respect the authority of Congress. This obligation is connected to an ideal aspect of the judicial practice. This aspect can be characterized as a regulative ideal.

The function of the ideal of the negative legislator is the same function of the ideal that there is always a correct answer to any legal dispute. This idea, suggested by Ronald Dworkin in *Law's Empire*, is relevant to legal practice because it amounts to the existence of an interpretative principle that requires judges to justify their decisions in the best possible way, as if there were one single correct answer.[100] It is a duty to judicial authorities that commands them to seek the correct answer and to struggle to justify their decisions in the most rational way within the possibilities allowed by the law.

The ideal of the negative legislator has an analogous function. In effect, it is a theoretical construction closely connected to Hans Kelsen's strong democratic convictions. The judge should adjudicate, and in that sense, concretize the Constitution by individualizing its norms. The idea of a negative legislator is by no means incompatible with the idea that the courts have authority to create concrete norms on the basis of the general norms laid down in the Constitution. The Judiciary has expressly recognized authority to enact interpretative norms to ensure the impartial application of the Constitution.

One could never question, however, that on several occasions, these normative powers have amounted to a (partial) decentralization of the legislative function. Even though the norms produced by the judges are still concrete and individual, when compared with the broad principles incorporated in the Constitution, they still hold a great deal of generality. Kelsen would hardly doubt that. Nevertheless, the ideal of the negative legislator remains plausible. This ideal is a normative claim that establishes that judges should respect the competences of the ordinary legislator and adopt a sort of judicial self-restraint, as long as it is possible to do so. If this is the correct interpretation of the idea that judges are negative legislators, then the Brazilian Federal Supreme Court is strongly committed to this ideal, in spite of its general normative competences.

[100] Ronald Dworkin, 11th ed., *Law's Empire*, Cambridge, MA: Belknap, 2000.

CANADA

THE CANADIAN CONSTITUTIONAL COURTS AS POSITIVE LEGISLATORS

Kent Roach
Professor of Law and Prichard-Wilson Chair in Law and Public Policy, University of Toronto
kent.roach@utoronto.ca

INTRODUCTION

The comparison between the negative and positive roles of constitutional courts provides an interesting perspective on the nature of judicial review and judicial activism in a particular country. Decisions in which courts explicitly require governments to take positive steps either to comply with the Constitution or to provide remedies for constitutional violations are examples of judicial activism in the sense that the unelected judiciary require elected legislatures and governments to act. That said, the more traditional role of judges as negative legislators with powers to invalidate unconstitutional laws and actions may effectively require positive government regulation to be enacted in response. In the modern world, it may not be acceptable for courts acting as a negative legislator to have the final word, and the negative remedies of courts may invoke positive legislative responses from governments. Hence, the distinction between courts acting in a negative or positive fashion may be less clear than when first articulated by Kelsen. This more nuanced understanding of the role of the court as a positive legislator is of particular importance in Canada because of work that has demonstrated frequent legislative replies to Supreme Court of Canada decisions that have simply invalidated legislation as inconsistent with the Canada's constitutional bill of rights, the Canadian Charter of Rights and Freedoms.

This chapter starts with a brief description of the system of judicial review under the Canadian Constitution. Although Canada generally follows the American model of judicial review in the sense that courts of general jurisdiction make constitutional decisions in specific cases, the ability of Canadian governments to refer abstract legal and constitutional questions to the courts on a reference procedure is an important feature of the Canadian system that to some extent echoes some European models of judicial review. The reference procedure is of particular importance for the Court's positive role because it has triggered some of the Court's most important actions as a positive legislator, including its actions in creating and declaring basic rules to govern the patriation of Canada's Constitution from the United Kingdom and the possible secession of Quebec from Canada.

Analytical distinctions are drawn in this section between the Court's role in interpreting rights and its role in crafting remedies for constitutional violations. It will be seen that the Supreme Court of Canada has been more comfortable acknowledging its positive role in providing remedies for constitutional violations. For example, the Court has recognized that some constitutional defects in legislation can be cured by courts' adding to legislation by reading in words rather than by invalidating the legislation. The most famous and controversial use of such powers are in cases in which appellate courts reformulated the laws governing marriage to provide for same-sex marriages. Another remedy, the delayed or suspended declaration of invalidity, explicitly contemplates and encourages positive governmental action as a response to judicial findings that legislation is unconstitutional. As we will see, however, there are some limits to how far Canadian courts will go in requiring governments to take positive actions, even as a remedy for an acknowledged constitutional violation.

The Canadian Constitution provides for a few constitutional rights, mainly relating to minority-language rights, that explicitly require positive government action, but the majority of constitutional rights are framed in negative terms that contemplate restrictions on government actions. Some Charter rights are ambiguous in the sense that that they could have both positive and negative dimensions. As we will see in the second section of this report, however, the Court can be cast in the role of a positive legislator even when it enforces traditional negative rights.

The second section of this country report examines specific instances in which Canadian courts have acted as positive legislators. The section takes a contextual approach that evaluates the role of courts as positive legislators in a variety of areas, including criminal justice, national security, gay rights, political policy, minority-language rights, labor policy, health policy, and socioeconomic rights. Such an approach reveals that the Supreme Court of

Canada is more comfortable with its role as a positive legislator in some contexts than in others. Although the Court enforces negative rights in the criminal justice and national security context, it has acted as a positive legislator in these contexts. Also, the Court's approach has evolved over time. In the first two decades of the Charter, the Court was reluctant to play the role of a positive legislator with respect to labor policy, but this has recently changed. Despite these changes, the Court has remained uncomfortable with playing the role of positive legislator with respect to health-care policy and rights to welfare or social assistance. In the former case, the Court has limited itself to negative remedies that do not necessarily contemplate positive state action, whereas in the latter case, it has simply deferred to the distributive decisions made by Canadian governments.

I. CANADA'S SYSTEM OF JUDICIAL REVIEW

1. *Federalism and the Court as Negative Legislator*

The preamble to Canada's Constitution Act of 1867 recognized that Canada was to have a constitution similar in principle to that of the United Kingdom. This recognized the importance of both parliamentary democracy and the rule of law in Canada. From the start, however, Canada has had a more robust form of judicial review than Britain. The status of the Constitution Act of 1867 as imperial legislation gave that document supremacy over other laws enacted by the federal or provincial legislatures. Judicial review in Canada from 1867 to 1982 focused on enforcement of the division of powers between the two levels of governments. Over the years, the courts invalidated a range of federal and provincial laws in ordinary litigation arising from disputes between individuals and governments. The courts also gave legal opinions on references about whether proposed pieces of legislation were within the legislative competence of the requesting level of governments. Although such reference decisions were technically advisory opinions, they were, consistent with the rule of law, followed by governments. Some judicial decisions enforcing the division of powers were criticized for thwarting federal government action, such as during the Great Depression, and others were lauded for striking down provincial laws that interfered with fundamental freedoms. A judicial decision striking down a law as violating the division of powers meant that, consistent with parliamentary supremacy, the other level of government would have the power to enact the same law. The most relevant point for our purposes is that the courts acted as negative legislators in striking down laws on the basis of infringement of the federal division of powers.

2. *The Canadian Charter of Rights and Freedoms*

In 1982, Canada not only patriated the Constitution Act of 1867 so that it would be subject to domestic amending procedures, but also added a constitutional bill of rights, the Canadian Charter of Rights and Freedoms. (henceforth, the Charter).[1] The Charter was enacted in part because of a concern that the Supreme Court of Canada had not been vigorous enough in its interpretation or enforcement of a statutory bill of rights, the 1960 Canadian Bill of Rights, which applied only to the activities of the federal government. The Charter applies to all level of governments. It protects fundamental freedoms, democratic rights, mobility rights, legal rights, equality rights, and various minority-language rights subject to section 1, which provides that "the Canadian Charter of Rights and Freedoms guarantees the rights and freedoms set out in it subject only to such reasonable limits prescribed by law as can be demonstrably justified in a free and democratic society." Section 33 enables provincial and federal legislatures to enact laws for a renewable five-year period notwithstanding the fundamental freedoms, legal rights, or equality rights in the Charter.

3. *Negative and Positive Rights*

Most of the rights in the Charter, such as the legal right to be secure against unreasonable search and seizure, are framed in negative terms that focus on protecting the individual from state action. Some rights are, however, framed explicitly to contemplate positive government action. For example, the democratic rights contemplate that every citizen will be able to vote in elections at least every five years. Minority-language rights contemplate that governments will provide available services in both French and English and that, where numbers warrant, the government will provide minority-language instruction and educational facilities out of public funds.

Two key rights in the Charter, the fundamental justice or due process right and equality rights, are framed in terms that are somewhat ambiguous as to whether they demand negative restraints or positive actions from governments. For example, section 7 of the Charter provides both that "everyone has the right to life, liberty and security of the person," which by itself could contemplate positive government action, and that they have the right not to be deprived of life, liberty, or security of the person "except in accordance with the principles of fundamental justice." Similarly, the

1 Part I of the *Constitution Act, 1982* being Schedule B of the *Canada Act, 1982* (U.K.) c.11.

equality rights in section 15 of the Charter contemplate equality before and under the law, which may focus on formal inequalities that could be cured by invalidation of laws, but they also contemplate the "equal protection and equal benefit of the law," which may require the equal extension of state benefits.

4. *Charter Litigation*

Charter issues in Canada are decided by ordinary courts in the course of litigation. A person who wishes to challenge the constitutional validity of a statute must notify the appropriate Attorney General, who then can intervene in the case to defend the law. All constitutional cases proceed through normal appeal routes, and the Supreme Court of Canada has discretion to consider appeals in matters of national importance. The Court is composed of nine judges and is the final Court of Appeal for all matters of federal and provincial private and public law, including constitutional issues. Although the Court hears many Charter cases, it is not a constitutional court, and most of the Charter appeals that it hears arise in the course of appeals from criminal cases. The court has recognized a limited form of public interest standing if there is no other way for a directly affected person to challenge the constitutionality of the legislation,[2] and courts have exercised their discretion to decide constitutional issues even when the dispute is otherwise moot on a similar basis.[3] With one exception to be discussed here, the Canadian system is one of diffuse review that departs from the constitutional court tradition of many parts of the world. The practical effect of the Canadian system of judicial remedy is that there is an expectation that the successful litigant will receive an immediate and tangible remedy, even if the courts use the case to articulate more general constitutional norms.

5. *Reference Cases*

An important exception to the general rule that constitutional matters are decided in ordinary litigation is that the federal government has statutory powers to refer questions of law, including those involving the constitutionality of legislation, directly to the Supreme Court of Canada. The provincial governments have similar statutory powers to refer issues to the Court of Appeals in their provinces, with the Supreme Court having the

2 *Canadian Churches v. Canada* [1992] 1 S.C.R. 236.

3 *Borowski v. Canada* [1989] 1 S.C.R. 342.

discretion to hear appeals from such decisions. Unlike in the United States or Australia, the Canadian Constitution has not been interpreted as prohibiting the resolution of constitutional issues except in live cases and controversies. At the same time, the Court's answers in reference cases are technically nonbinding on the government, in the sense that they cannot be interpreted as regular judgments of the court. At the same time, there are broad expectations that, having asked for the Court's constitutional advice, the government will follow it.

The reference procedure can be used by governments to encourage the courts to act as positive legislators. The two most important reference decisions decided by the Supreme Court, the 1981 *Patriation Reference*[4] and the 1998 *Quebec Secession Reference*,[5] arose in circumstances in which the federal government essentially invited the Court to lay down some basic rules to guide constitutional change and to advert potential constitutional crises that could have been caused by arguably unconstitutional acts, such as an attempt by the federal government to change the powers of the provincial legislatures without their consent or a similarly unilateral decision by the Quebec legislature to declare its sovereignty and secession from Canada. In both cases, the Court responded with judgments that could be considered activist both in a jurisprudential sense and in the sense that the judicial decision required governments to take positive action. In the case of the *Patriation Reference*, the positive action was that the federal government would have to obtain substantial provincial consent before changing provincial governments' powers by the enactment of the Charter, and in the case of the *Quebec Secession Reference*, the federal and Quebec governments would have to enter into secession negotiations after a sufficiently decisive vote for sovereignty in Quebec. In both cases, the Court effectively required governments to take positive action in the form of initiating negotiations. At the same time, however, the Court was careful to allow elected governments a considerable degree of freedom in deciding how to resolve negotiations. These cases are significant because they suggest both that Canadian governments in some contexts desire that the Supreme Court act as a positive legislator and that the Court itself sees some limits as to how prescriptive it can be as a positive legislator.

Another high-profile reference was the 2004 *Same Sex Marriage Reference*.[6] In that reference, the federal government asked the Supreme

4 [1981] 1 S.C.R. 753.

5 [1998] 2 S.C.R. 217.

6 [2004] 3 S.C.R. 698.

Court to determine whether proposed legislation recognizing same-sex marriage was (1) within the federal government's powers under the division of powers, was consistent with (2) freedom of religion and (3) equality rights, and (4) was required as a matter of equality rights. The Court answered the first three questions in the affirmative but declined to answer the fourth question because the federal government had already expressed its intent to recognize same-sex marriage and had not appealed lower-court decisions recognizing same-sex marriages. In addition, a number of lower courts had accepted that the prior statutory restrictions on marriage that precluded same-sex marriage constituted an unjustified violation of equality rights. In those cases, the Courts of Appeal had ordered immediate remedies, which meant that there were thousands of same-sex marriages performed in many parts of Canada by the time the Supreme Court heard the reference. The Supreme Court was concerned that a decision might disturb same-sex marriages that had already been performed in a number of provinces. This decision demonstrates how Canadian governments can seek judicial approval of controversial measures before they are enacted. To be sure, the draft legislation was subsequently enacted by the elected Parliament, but it received important support because of the Court's conclusion that it was within the jurisdiction of the federal government and that the legislation did not violate the Charter.

6. *Constitutional Remedies*

The Charter includes a specific provision authorizing courts to grant remedies. Section 24(1) of the Charter provides:

> Anyone whose rights or freedoms, as guaranteed by this Charter, have been infringed or denied may apply to a court of competent jurisdiction to obtain such remedy as the court considers appropriate and just.

This provision applies in cases where individual litigants have established that their rights have or will soon be violated by government action. This provision allows courts to issue a wide variety of remedies in cases where they find that the rights of individuals have been violated. These remedies include declarations and injunctions that require the government to take positive action to comply with the constitution and to remedy the effects of past constitutional violations. The courts have issued structural injunctions or interdicts to require the government to provide minority-language instruction and facilities. In these cases, the court has retained jurisdiction while the government takes steps to provide and, in some cases, build new facilities. The Supreme Court of Canada, in a 5–4 decision, upheld the trial judge's ability to retain jurisdiction and require progress reports from the government with the majority stressing the trial judge's broad remedial discretion under section 24(1) of the Charter and the importance of devising effective remedies. The dissenters argued, however, that the judge's ongoing role was inconsistent with the judicial role and the finality of judicial judgments and was unfair to the governmental defendants.[7] Other countries, including India, South Africa, and the United States, have had somewhat similar experiences with structural injunctions.[8] Canada's limited experience with structural injunctions, however, has been limited to cases involving minority-language rights, which, as already discussed, are framed in explicitly positive terms.

The Charter as part of the Constitution is also enforced through a specific constitutional supremacy clause. Section 52(1) of the Constitution Act of 1982, like the Charter, was added to the Constitution in 1982. It provides the following:

> The Constitution of Canada is the supreme law of Canada, and any law that is inconsistent with the provisions of the Constitution is, to the extent of the inconsistency, of no force and effect.[9]

This provision is framed in negative terms, consistent with both the American *Marbury v. Madison*[10] tradition of judicial review and Canada's tradition of courts striking down laws that were inconsistent with the constitutional division of powers between federal and provincial legislatures. Nevertheless, the courts have applied this supremacy clause in ways that require or provide an opportunity for positive government action.

7. *Positive Alternatives to Judicial Invalidation: Reading In or Judicial Amendments to Legislation*

The Supreme Court has held that the supremacy clause in section 52(1) of the Constitution Act of 1982 does not restrict courts to striking down entirely or partially unconstitutional legislation. Rather, in limited circumstances, where such remedies are consistent with the overall purposes of legislation

[7] *Doucet Boudreau v. Nova Scotia* [2003] 3 S.C.R. 3. All judgments of the Supreme Court of Canada are available in both English and French at http://csc.lexum.umontreal.ca.en/.

[8] Kent Roach and Geoff Budlender, "Mandatory Relief and Supervisory Jurisdiction" (2005) 122 *S. A.L.J.* 325.

[9] Constitution Act, 1982 s. 52(1).

[10] 5 U.S. 1 (1 Cranch) 137 (1803).

and supported by constitutional values, the Court may read in or add words to legislation to cure a constitutional defect. A famous example of the use of the power was the Supreme Court's decision to add or read in protection against discrimination on the basis of sexual orientation to Alberta's human rights code that prohibited discrimination in the private sector rather than strike down the entire legislation because it violated equality rights by failing to protect gays and lesbians from discrimination.[11] The Court in this case cured a legislative omission of protection against discrimination on the basis of sexual orientation by adding those words to the statute. A similar use of the power was the decision of the Ontario Court of Appeal to strike down a definition of marriage as a union of a man and a woman and to substitute the gender-neutral concept of a union between persons to allow for same-sex marriages.[12] Such remedies amount to judicial amendments or additions to legislation.

The reading-in or amendment remedy is not used in a routine fashion to cure all constitutional defects. Indeed, it is used only in cases in which judges are confident that the default remedy of striking down legislation is not necessary because both the overall purposes of the legislation and the values of the Charter support adding words to legislation by reading in and that the striking down the legislation would cause unnecessary work for the legislature. Courts have generally refused to issue reading-in remedies that would fundamentally change legislation. For example, the Court refused to amend unconstitutionally underinclusive legislation that provided leave benefits for parents who adopted children to include parents who gave birth to their children. Such a reading-in remedy would fundamentally change the legislation by adding a much larger group (biological parents) to a benefit scheme that had been provided to a much smaller group (adoptive parents).[13] The calculus was different in the gay rights case because the court simply added the smaller group of gays and lesbians to various benefits that the heterosexual majority already enjoyed.

Canadian courts also will make reference to constitutional values when interpreting legislation. For example, the Court has upheld laws against obscenity[14] and the use of corrective force against children[15] only after

[11] *Vriend v. Alberta* [1998] 1 S.C.R. 493.

[12] *Halpern v. Ontario* (2003) 65 O.R. (3d) 161 (C.A.).

[13] *Schachter v. Canada* [1992] 2 S.C.R. 679.

[14] *R. v. Butler* [1992] 2 S.C.R. 452. See also *R. v. Sharpe* [2001], where the Court read in restrictions on a new child pornography offense as an explicit constitutional remedy but also engaged in less explicit reading down as a technique of statutory interpretation. See Kent Roach, *Constitutional Remedies in Canada* (Aurora: Canada Law Book, 2010), ch. 14.

reinterpreting these laws in a restrictive fashion as a matter of statutory interpretation. One problem with such a "deformation of the interpretative principle"[16] is that courts may not pay the same attention that they do when crafting constitutional remedies to whether they are fundamentally changing the law as the legislator enacted it. In the field of criminal law, especially, this also means that a law as interpreted by the Court in the shadow of constitutional norms and possible constitutional invalidation may bear only slight resemblance to the law as written by the legislature and that attempts to give the public fair notice about what is prohibited. At the same time, the Court has used this robust form of statutory interpretation as a means to update old laws and to bring them into harmony with constitutional norms.[17] Such robust interpretation could also be seen as provisional legislation in the sense that the legislator can always amend the legislation to modify and displace the Court's interpretation. This has not happened in the obscenity or child correction cases, however, because of concerns that rules other than those developed by the courts would be constitutionally suspect and also because of a lack of consensus on such socially divisive issues.

8. *Alternatives to Immediate Invalidation: Delayed Declarations of Invalidity and Reply Legislation*

Another example of judicial creativity in the area of constitutional remedies that can cast the court as a positive legislator is the Court's decision to suspend declarations of invalidity for periods of six to eighteen months to provide legislatures an opportunity to enact new constitutional legislation so that there are no lacunae in the legal regime. This remedy of a suspended declaration of invalidity recognizes that the immediate declaration of invalidity is a blunt remedy in the age of a positive state. It was first used in a case where all of a province's laws were unconstitutional because they had not been translated into French. The Court justified the use of a suspended declaration of invalidity on the basis that the immediate striking down of all of Manitoba's laws would offend the rule of law. The practical effect of this decision, however, was that Manitoba translated all of its laws over a period of time supervised by the Court.[18]

15 *Canadian Foundation for Children v. Canada* [2004] 1 S.C.R. 74.

16 Allan R. Brewer-Carías, "Constitutional Courts as Positive Legislators," in this volume.

17 On the role of courts in updating old statutes, see Guido Calabresi, *A Common Law for the Age of Statutes* (Cambridge, MA: Harvard University Press, 1982).

18 *Manitoba Language Reference* [1985] 1 S.C.R. 721.

Since that time, the use of suspended declarations of invalidity has increased though the Court formally maintains that the remedy should be used only in cases where an immediate declaration of invalidity will threaten the rule of law or public safety or deprive people of benefits simply because the benefit has been extended in an unconstitutionally underinclusive manner.[19] The South African Constitution follows the Canadian example and specifically provides for suspended declarations of invalidity.[20]

Although it may have that practical effect, the suspended declaration of invalidity is not juristically understood as a mandatory order that the legislature enact new legislation. The legislature is legally free to do nothing. In such an event, the Court's declaration of invalidity will take effect once the period of delay has expired. In the vast majority of cases, however, the legislature will enact new legislation before the declaration of invalidity takes effect so that the overall effect of the Court's remedy is to produce new legislation.

Even when the suspended declaration of invalidity is not used, new legislation is frequently enacted as a response to judicial invalidation of legislation. In a seminal 1997 article, Peter Hogg and Allison Bushell examined cases in which the Supreme Court had invalidated laws under the Charter and concluded that in about two-thirds of those cases, new legislation on the topic had been enacted.[21] An updated article similarly concludes that the legislature has responded to judicial invalidation of laws in more than 60 percent of cases.[22] These findings suggest that, even when the Supreme Court acts more traditionally as a negative legislator by striking down unconstitutional legislation, it often stimulates a positive process that results in law reform and the enactment of new legislation.

A slightly different but related alternative to the use of suspended declarations of invalidity is the much rarer use by Canadian courts of prospective rulings. These occur in cases where the Supreme Court explicitly notes that it will provide the government some period of time before its decisions take effect. The Court did this in a case in which it announced that

[19] *Schachter v. Canada* [1992] 2 S.C.R. 679.

[20] South African Constitution s. 172.

[21] Hogg and Bushell, "The Charter Dialogue between Courts and Legislatures" (1997) 35 *Osgoode Hall L.J.* 75.

[22] Peter Hogg, Allison Bushell, and Wade Wright, "Dialogue Re-visited" (2007) 45 *Osgoode Hall L.J* 1. Some have disputed these figures on the basis that about half of reply legislation is not genuine dialogue because the legislature simply repeals the offending legislation or follows suggestions articulated by the Court about the content of constitutional legislation. Christopher Manfredi and James Kelly, "Six Degrees of Dialogue" (1999) 37 *Osgoode Hall L.J.* 513.

it would give the police thirty days to include information about the availability of free legal advice as part of the constitutional right to counsel,[23] and in a case where it declared that a province would, in six months' time, have to provide interpretation services for medically required services.[24] The Court has subsequently noted that such prospective rulings constituted a departure from a traditional understanding of judicial review associated with Blackstone and Dicey that conceives of courts as simply applying the law as it has always existed. The Court declared that the norm remained the traditional idea of immediate and retroactive relief but also acknowledged that it could accept prospective judicial rulings in cases where the Court makes a substantial change in the law, where the government has reasonably relied on the previous law, and where an immediate and retroactive remedy would interfere with valid governmental functions.[25] A particularly difficult factor in a system in which constitutional review is conducted through ordinary litigation is that a prospective ruling may leave a successful litigant without an immediate remedy.[26] In this way, there may be a tension between the Court acting prospectively as a positive legislator and the Court doing justice in the particular case. The Canadian courts attempt to resolve this tension by requiring that its departures from the norm of immediate retroactive relief be justified as fair to all parties concerned.

Summary

Although constitutional litigation in Canada is diffuse[27] – in that it is generally confined to ordinary litigation and annulment of unconstitutional laws is the default remedial position of Canadian courts – there are several features of the Canadian Constitution that contemplate positive action by Canadian courts. A few constitutional rights in Canada, such as the rights of linguistic minorities to education and to bilingual legislation, are framed in explicitly positive terms, and as such, they seem to contemplate that judicial enforcement will require the government to take positive action. Other Canadian constitutional rights, such as rights to due process and equality, are framed in more ambiguous terms but may also require positive action.

23 *R. v. Brydges* [1990] 1 S.C.R. 190.

24 *Eldridge v. British Columbia* [1997] 3 S. C.R 624.

25 *Canada v. Hislop* [2007] 1 S.C.R. 429.

26 Sujit Choudhry and Kent Roach, "Putting the Past Behind Us? Prospective Judicial and Legislative Constitutional Remedies" (2003), 21 *S.C.L.R.* (2d) 205.

27 Allan R. Brewer-Carías, "Constitutional Courts as Positive Legislators," *supra*.

Section 24(1) of the Charter also grants Canadian courts broad remedial discretion to order whatever remedy is appropriate and just in the circumstances, and this power can include court orders that government take positive actions in structural interdict or remedies cases. The Canadian courts have recognized the limits of judicial invalidation as a remedy by frequently delaying such negative remedies to provide the legislature an opportunity to enact new constitutional legislation. Alternatively, the Canadian courts have even more directly acted as positive legislators by curing constitutional deficiencies in laws by reading in and reading down statutory terms in a manner that makes them constitutional and, in a few cases, by issuing rulings only with prospective effect. Judicial amendments of legislation or prospective declaration of new rules are made only when the Court determines that the interaction of statutory purposes and constitutional norms produces a precise result that does not require the Court to choose between a range of constitutionally compliant options. Prospective rulings are rare and made only when the courts determine that they are fair to all parties.

Neither the robust remedial powers of Canadian courts nor their ability to delay or suspend declarations of invalidity have been used in a manner that actually enacts new legislation or requires legislatures to enact new legislation or new rules. Nevertheless, annulment of laws frequently has the indirect effect of requiring the legislator to promulgate new legislation,[28] and in such circumstances, courts act indirectly as positive legislators. Finally, the Canadian Constitution can facilitate the courts' role as a positive legislator by eschewing an American-style case-and-controversy requirement and allowing governments to refer abstract and controversial issues to the courts for judicial guidance. In such settings, Canadian courts have fashioned new constitutional rules to govern constitutional amendments, including processes that would be required with respect to Quebec's possible separation from Canada and those concerning the recognition of same-sex marriage. In short, the Canadian Constitution provides a partial platform for the courts to act as positive legislators. The remainder of this chapter explores the actual experience of courts acting as positive legislators in Canada.

[28] *Ibid.*

II. CANADA'S EXPERIENCE WITH COURTS AS POSITIVE LEGISLATORS

1. *Criminal Justice*

The Supreme Court has decided many cases concerning the exercise of police powers under the Charter. These cases usually have involved challenges to police powers that have not been explicitly authorized by legislation. For example, in a variety of cases, the Court has ruled that warrantless seizure of private material would violate the Charter unless authorized by legislation and in particular by a warrant issued by a judicial official.[29] Taken by themselves, these decisions seem consistent with the courts' traditional role as a negative legislator. At the same time, Parliament has responded to almost all these decisions with laws authorizing judicial warrants and, in some cases, authorizing warrantless searches. A particularly important response to a court decision is the procedure that allows the state to obtain a warrant on reasonable grounds from a judge to seize DNA material. Parliament was effectively required to enact new warrant procedures as a response to judicial decisions holding that warrantless searches were unconstitutional and that evidence obtained through such searches should be excluded from criminal trials. The Canadian experience with search-and-seizure law demonstrates how the enforcement of traditional rights against state interference with the individual and the use of judicial remedies of exclusion of evidence can require the state to take positive remedial action.

Some of the Court's most dramatic acts of judicial activism in the criminal justice area have been a direct response to legislative inertia. Law reform bodies had long called on Parliament to enact statutory standards for speedy trials and disclosure of evidence to the accused by the prosecutor, but these matters of law reform were never a legislative priority. In the early 1990s, however, the Court acted decisively by holding that the Charter requires pretrial disclosure to the accused of all relevant evidence held by the prosecutor[30] and that the right to a trial in a reasonable time in section 11(b) of the Charter would be violated by pretrial delays of more than a year.[31] The latter holding caused controversy after it led to many cases being thrown out

[29] *R. v. Duarte* [1990] 1 S.C.R. 30; *R. v. Wong* [1990] 3 S.C.R. 36; *R. v. Stillman* [1997] 1 S.C.R. 607; *R. v. Feeney* [1997] 2 S.C.R. 13.

[30] *R. v. Stinchcombe* [1991] 3 S.C.R. 326.

[31] *R. v. Askov* [1990] 2 S.C.R. 1199.

in the most congested courts. The negative remedy of stays of proceedings required that governments hired more prosecutors and appointed more judges to ensure that cases in the future could be processed within constitutional speedy-trial standards.[32] Like the search-and-seizure experience, this demonstrates that the Court can assume the role of a positive legislator even when it relies on traditional negative remedies such as exclusion of evidence or stays of proceedings. Another example is the Supreme Court's decision that holds that it will generally violate the Charter to extradite a person to face the death penalty.[33] Although framed in negative terms that would potentially prevent extradition, the practical effect of this decision is to require the government to take positive steps to seek assurances from states that they will not seek or impose the death penalty on a person extradited from Canada.

2. *National Security*

Since September 11, 2001, matters of national security have risen in prominence, and the Court has decided several important cases that have had the effect of causing the government to take positive action. The Court has been particularly active with respect to the use of immigration law as antiterrorism law. A 2002 Supreme Court decision holding that deportation of a noncitizen on national security grounds to a substantial risk of torture would generally violate the Charter[34] and may require the government to take positive actions in the form of obtaining assurances that a noncitizen suspected of involvement with terrorism will not be tortured if returned to his or her country of citizenship.

In *Charkaoui v. Canada I*,[35] the Court held that the nondisclosure of intelligence that was submitted to the court in support of the detention and eventual detention of a noncitizen suspected of being a threat to national security violated the principles of fundamental justice protected under section 7 of the Charter. The Court noted a variety of ways in which secret evidence used by the state could be subject to adversarial challenge. The Court suspended its declaration that the present system was unconstitutional and of no force and effect for a year. Shortly before the year's suspended declaration of invalidity was to expire, Parliament enacted new legislation

32 *R. v. Morin* [1992] 1 S.C.R. 771.

33 *United States of America v. Burns and Rafay* [2001] 1 S.C.R.

34 *Suresh v. Canada* [2002] 1 S.C.R. 3.

35 [2007] 1 S.C.R. 350.

that allowed security-cleared special advocates to have access to and challenge the secret evidence. The government appointed a number of such special advocates. In this way, the Court's ruling resulted in new legislation and the creation of a new party to the immigration law proceedings.[36]

In one lower-court decision, the Court held that a Canadian citizen who had been placed on a United Nations 1,267 list of persons associated with al-Qaeda had been denied his Charter right to return to Canada by the refusal of the Canadian government to issue him an emergency passport that would allow him to return to Canada from Sudan. The judge ordered that the man be escorted by Canadian officials and be returned to a Canadian court room. The government complied with this decision.[37] This decision underlined how Canadian courts can act as positive legislators even in the national security contexts where courts have traditionally deferred to governments.

A final decision, however, suggests that there are some limits as to how far Canadian courts may go with respect to devising positive remedies in the national security context. A lower court held that the Canadian government had breached the constitutional rights of Canadian citizen Omar Khadr when they interrogated him at Guantánamo Bay, where he has been held since he was captured, at fifteen years of age, fighting American forces in Afghanistan. The lower court ordered Canada to take the positive step of requesting Khadr's return to Canada as the only effective remedy for the breach of his rights. It also stressed that Canada had a positive duty to protect a Canadian citizen on the basis of domestic case law that recognizes the special status of children with respect to crime and the need to rehabilitate.[38] On appeal, however, the Supreme Court reversed this remedial order on the basis that it would interfere too much with the foreign-affairs prerogatives of the Canadian government as it conducted diplomacy with the United States.[39] This decision suggests that, although Canadian courts have rejected the American practice of holding that certain political questions are nonjusticiable, they may have introduced a *de facto* political-question doctrine that precludes judicial remedies that require the Canadian

36 See Kent Roach. "*Charkaoui* and Bill C-3: Some Implications for Anti-Terrorism Policy and Dialogue between Courts and Legislators" (2008) 42 *S.C.L.R.* 2d 281, available at http://www.law.utoronto.ca/faculty_content.asp?profile=47&perpage=255&cType=facMembers &itemPath=1/3/4/0/0.

37 *Abdelrazik v. Canada* 2009 FC 580.

38 *Khadr v. Prime Minister* 2009 FC 495 at para. 91 rev'd in part 2010 SCC 3.

39 *Khadr v. Canada* 2010 SCC 3.

government to make specific diplomatic representations.[40] This conclusion has, however, been controversial. In subsequent litigation, a lower court has found that Khadr has still not received an effective remedy and asserted that the judiciary can order Canada to request Khadr's repatriation.[41] This decision, has, however, been stayed pending appeal. Although Supreme Court decisions in the national security context have required the government to enact new legislation providing for a special advocate scheme, the Court has been reluctant to require the Canadian government to make diplomatic representations in a specific case as a remedy for constitutional violations of the rights of a Canadian citizen held by the Americans at Guantánamo.

3. *Gay Rights*

The most visible area of courts acting as positive legislators in Canada has been in litigation over the rights of gays and lesbians, which culminated in the judicial and then legislative recognition of same-sex marriage. As mentioned already, the Supreme Court in 1998 unanimously held that an Alberta law prohibiting discrimination in the private and public sectors violated equality rights under the Charter because of its failure to protect gays and lesbians from discrimination on the grounds of their sexual orientation. The majority of the Court decided that the appropriate remedy was to read sexual orientation into the prohibited grounds of discrimination in the law. This was an active remedy, but the Court justified it on the basis that, short of using the section 33 override, including sexual orientation was the only choice left to the Alberta legislature. Alberta accepted this ruling and did not use the override.[42]

In 1999, the Court decided another significant case that involved a challenge to Ontario family-law legislation that limited the definition of

[40] Kent Roach, "The Supreme Court at the Bar of Politics: The Afghan Detainee and Omar Khadr Cases" (2011) *N.J.C.L.* (forthcoming).

[41] After the 2010 Supreme Court decision, Canada issued a diplomatic note requesting that the United States not use evidence obtained by Canada in his prosecution, but the United States refused to interfere with Khadr's ongoing military commission trial. A lower court subsequent found that Canada had violated Khadr's right to procedural fairness by not allowing him to comment on the adequacy of the diplomatic note before it was issued. The judge stressed that Khadr had not received an effective remedy and that the court could order Canada to request his repatriation if that was the only effective remedy. *Khadr v. Canada* 2010 FC 715. The government has appealed and obtained a stay of this ruling relying on the Supreme Court's unwillingness to order the government to request Khadr's repatriation in *Khadr v. Canada* 2010 SCC 3.

[42] *Vriend v. Alberta* [1998] 1 S.C.R. 493.

spouses to opposite-sex partners. The majority of the Court held that this law was an unjustified violation of equality rights, but instead of changing the definition of spouse in the law, it declared the law invalid subject to a six-month delay to provide the legislature an opportunity to respond.[43] Ontario and many other jurisdictions responded with new laws providing same-sex couples with the same rights and obligations provided to opposite-sex couples. This decision underlines how even negative judicial remedies, when used against the positive state, can require the enactment of new laws that comply with court rulings while they regulate society.

In 2003, the Ontario Court of Appeal held that the traditional definition of marriage was an unjustified violation of equality rights. It concluded that religious views about marriage could not justify excluding same-sex couples from the civil institution of marriage. The Court of Appeal did not defer to the fact that Parliament had, a few years earlier, affirmed its commitment to the traditional definition of marriage even while it included same-sex couples in spousal benefits. It refused to suspend the declaration that the traditional definition of marriage was unconstitutional and issued a mandatory order to ensure that the litigants in the case could promptly marry.[44] This immediately created facts on the ground, namely thousands of same-sex marriages that could not be undone because, even if a legislature had been prepared to use the override, the override could not be used with retroactive force.[45] Similar decisions recognizing same-sex marriages were made in British Columbia and Quebec.

The federal government decided it would not appeal the Ontario or other similar decisions to the Supreme Court. It prepared draft legislation defining marriage as the union of two persons but also recognizing that this civil definition of marriage did not affect the ability of religious institutions to decide whom to marry. The government then decided to refer this bill to the Supreme Court for an advisory opinion about its constitutionality. In its decision on the reference,[46] the Court decided that Parliament had jurisdiction to enact the proposed legislation and that the reference to its jurisdiction over marriage in the 1867 Constitution was not frozen to exclude jurisdiction over same-sex marriage. The Court also held that the recognition of same-sex marriage would not violate the equality rights or the freedom of religion of those opposed to gay marriage. These decisions can be seen as

43 *M v. H.* [1999] 2 S.C.R. 3.

44 *Halpern v. Canada* (2003) 65 O.R.(3d) 161 (C.A.).

45 *Ford v. Quebec* [1988] 2 S.C.R. 712.

46 *Reference re Same Sex Marriage* [2004] 3 S.C.R. 698.

empowering but not necessarily requiring the eventual federal legislation that recognized same-sex marriage. Indeed, the Court refused to answer whether the traditional definition of marriage violated the Charter, noting that the government had indicated its intention to provide for same-sex marriages throughout Canada and that a decision that the traditional definition of marriage did not violate the Charter would throw doubt on acquired rights and binding decisions in the provinces in which same-sex marriage had been recognized. In 2005, Parliament enacted legislation defining marriage as the union of two persons but also providing that this would not affect the ability of religious officials to decide not to conduct marriages contrary to their religious belief.[47]

The rapid development of gay rights in Canada can largely be attributed to the Court's explicit and implicit role as a positive legislator. Without Charter litigation, it is unlikely that Canada would have recognized same-sex marriage in 2005 or that Alberta would have included sexual orientation as a prohibited ground of discrimination in its human rights code. The courts have flexed their remedial muscles both by reading in sexual orientation to Alberta's human rights code and by not suspending a remedy that provided for the immediate recognition of same-sex marriages in Ontario. The use of the reference procedure in relation to the same-sex marriage law also demonstrates how governments may seek judicial approval for controversial legislation and how Canadian courts can provide constitutional foundations for new legislation. At the end of the day, however, the new rules governing same-sex marriage are contained in legislation enacted by Parliament .

4. *Aboriginal and Treaty Rights*

The Court has also asked as a positive legislator in enforcing Aboriginal and treaty rights. The Supreme Court has found that Aboriginal rights require the Crown to consult with the Aboriginal peoples before undertaking actions that affect their rights. The duty to consult is located in the Crown's fiduciary duty toward Aboriginal peoples,[48] as well as treaty rights,[49] and it requires the government to take positive actions to negotiate with Aboriginal people before authorizing actions, such as resource developments, that will adversely affect Aboriginal and treaty rights. At one level, it is undeniable that these cases are an example of judicial creativity that require the state to

47 *Marriage for Civil Purposes Act* S. C. 2005 c.33.

48 *Haida Nation v. British Columbia* [2004] 3 S.C.R. 511.

49 *Mikisew Cree v. Canada* [2005] 3 S.C.R. 388.

take positive action. On another level, however, they are arguably more deferential of the state's interests in development than a more traditional approach taken by courts that have issued interim injunctions to restrain large developments that adversely affect Aboriginal and treaty rights pending litigation of the substantive claims. Chief Justice McLachlin, for example, has asserted that, although government has positive duties to negotiate and accommodate, Aboriginal groups do not have "a veto over what can be done with land pending final proof of the claim . . . what is required is a process of balancing interests, of give and take," and she has contrasted this approach with the "all or nothing situation"[50] in which an injunction either halts development or allows it to go forward. Sometimes court decisions that impose positive procedural obligations on the state can be more deferential to the government's interests than arguably more traditionally negative judicial activity that restrain state activity. This has certainly been true in the Aboriginal rights context, but it may also be the case in much of administrative law.

5. *Political Policy*

The Court has acted as a positive legislator in a number of cases involving the political process. In 1997, the Court considered claims that across-the-board salary reductions for provincially appointed judges violated judicial independence.[51] The Court held that all changes to judicial salaries must go before an independent commission and that the government must justify as rational any decision to reject the recommendations of the independent commission. The rationale for the independent commission was to avoid direct bargaining between judges and government that could, in the Court's view, impair judicial independence. One judge, in a strong dissent, rejected the appeal to unwritten constitutional principles as well as the Court's conclusion that the independent commission process was constitutionally required.[52] Although some jurisdictions had already established independent commissions to hear submissions and make recommendations about judicial salaries, the Court's decision effectively required all jurisdictions to establish such commissions.

In 1993, the Court invalidated prohibitions on the ability of all prisoners to vote in federal elections. This decision required governments to take steps to

[50] *Haida Nation v. British Columbia* [2004] 3 S.C.R. 511 at paras. 48, 14.

[51] *Provincial Judges Reference* [1997] 3 S.C.R. 3.

[52] *Id.* at paras. 296–325 per LaForest J.

allow prisoners to vote. Parliament responded to this decision with a new law prohibiting prisoners serving two years or more from voting. In 2002, the Court invalidated this law.[53] The effect of the decisions was to require governments to take steps to ensure that prisoners could vote in elections. In a 2003 Charter challenge brought by the leader of the Communist Party of Canada, the Court held that a federal election law that extended state benefits only to political parties that ran candidates in fifty ridings or more violated the right to effective representation under section 3 of the Charter.[54] The Court suspended its declaration of invalidity for a twelve-month period to give Parliament an opportunity to develop new constitutionally compliant legislation. New legislation provided benefits to minor parties that ran at least one candidate in an election and were supported by 250 members and four officers of the party.[55] The new rules were clearly prompted by the courts, but their details were developed in the legislative process.

6. *Minority-Language Policy*

The Constitution Act of 1867 provided that both French and English be used in the legislatures and courts of Canada and Quebec and the Manitoba Act of 1870 provided similar rights in the legislatures and courts of Manitoba. In 1985, the Supreme Court confronted a law that purported to abolish the bilingualism obligations of Manitoba. The law had been enacted in 1890 at a time when the French-speaking population of Manitoba had become a minority and the Court faced almost a hundred years of unilingual laws. The Court decided that the unilingual laws were unconstitutional given the clear requirement that laws be enacted in both English and French, but it held that immediate invalidation of most of Manitoba's laws was not appropriate because it would produce a legal vacuum that would threaten the rule of law. The Court then decided that it would give the unilingual laws temporary validity for the period of time that was necessary to translate them into French. The Court retained jurisdiction over the case for a number of years, and during that time, it heard various motions concerning the extent of the constitutional obligations for bilingualism.[56] The Court's actions in this regard can considered a form of remedial activism somewhat similar to the

53 *Sauve v. Canada* [1993] 2 S.C.R. 438 *Sauve v. Canada* [2002] 3 S.C.R. 519.

54 *Figuerora v. Canada* [2003] 1 S.C.R. 912 at para. 37.

55 An Act to amend the Canada Election Act S. C. 2004 c.24.

56 *Reference re Manitoba Language Rights* [1985] 1 S.C.R. 721; [1985] 2 S.C.R. 347; [1990] 3 S.C.R. 1417n; [1992] 1 S.C.R. 212.

American and Indian experience of courts maintaining jurisdiction over public institutions such as schools and prisons in the 1970s and 1980s to ensure that they satisfied constitutional standards. At the same time, however, the Court did not depart in this case from clear obligations under the Manitoba Act of 1870, and its supervision of remedial delay prevented what it considered the more drastic remedy of invalidating most of Manitoba's laws.

Section 23 of the Charter provides rights for minority-language school instruction and minority-language educational facilities where the number of children eligible to receive minority-language instruction in English or French warrants. Section 23 is an explicitly positive right that on its face requires the spending of public funds for minority-language instruction and facilities. The Supreme Court has generally interpreted these rights generously. It has emphasized the important role of not only minority-language instruction but also of minority-language school facilities and school boards in preserving minority-language and cultures.[57] Thus, the right has been interpreted to require the provision of both instruction and facilities.

In a controversial 2003 decision, a 5–4 majority of the Court held that the urgency of preserving minority-language cultures, combined with the delay of a province in constructing Francophone schools and its violation of section 23, justified a trial judge's decision to retain jurisdiction over the case and require the government to report back to the Court and the parties on its progress in building the schools in various parts of the province. Four of the nine judges on the Supreme Court dissented on the basis that such remedial activism violated the separation of powers between the courts and the government and was procedurally unfair to the government. The minority objected to the manner in which the trial judge exercised his remedial discretion and expressed concerns that the trial judge might try to manage the construction of the schools. Even the dissenting judges, however, did not dispute the fact that the court could order injunctive relief against the government as an appropriate and just remedy and could, if necessary, enforce such injunctive relief through the use of the court's contempt powers.[58] This case affirms that structural injunctions as used in the United States, India, and South Africa can also be used to enforce Charter rights in Canada. At the same time, however, such injunctions are rarely used in

[57] *Mahe v. Alberta* [1990] 1 S.C.R. 342; *Arsenault-Cameron v. Prince Edward Island* [2000] 1 S.C.R. 3; *Solski v. Quebec* 2005 SCC 14.

[58] *Doucet–Boudreau v. Nova Scotia* [2003] 3 S.C.R. 3.

Canada and have so far generally been confined to the context of minority-language rights.[59]

7. *Social and Economic Policy*

Although the Court has acted as a positive legislator with respect to elements of political, Aboriginal, and minority-language policies, it has generally not been willing to act as a positive legislator on matters of socioeconomic policy, with the possible exception of some matters of labor and health policy to be discussed here. In particular, the Canadian courts have not impeded significant restructuring and restrictions on social welfare benefits in Canada over the past fifteen years. In 1991, the Court held that there were no obstacles in terms of the constitution or the doctrine of legitimate expectations to prevent the federal government from drastically reducing its transfers to the provinces for social assistance.[60] Two years later, the Court also rejected a claim by a person on social assistance that the federal government had breached its own statutory commitments with respect to minimum levels of social assistance.[61] In 1999, the Court rejected an equality rights challenge to a provision that reduced the survivor benefits of young widowers under a public pension scheme.[62] In 2002, the Supreme Court rejected a Charter challenge to a Quebec scheme that reduced by a third the social assistance benefits of those younger than thirty. Four judges dissented on the basis that the scheme resulted in unjustified age discrimination, and two of them dissented on the basis that section 7 of the Charter included positive obligations to protect rights to life, liberty, and security of the person. The judges who dissented, however, were not prepared to order that the benefits be immediately restored. Instead, they would have suspended the declaration of invalidity for eighteen months to allow the government to devise a wide range of constitutional responses.[63] So far, the Court has not interfered with restrictions on social welfare. Although the existence of the positive state recasts Kelsen's stark dichotomy between the negative and positive role of the state, the Canadian courts have not stood in the way of a significant neoliberal retrenchment of the positive state that provides the poor with social assistance.

59 Kent Roach, *Constitutional Remedies in Canada* (Aurora: Canada Law Book, 2010), ch. 13.

60 *Reference re Canadian Assistance Plan* [1991] 2 S.C.R. 525.

61 *Finlay v. Canada* [1993] 1 S.C.R. 1080.

62 *Law v. Canada* [1999] 1 S.C.R. 497.

63 *Gosselin v. Quebec* [2002] 2 S.C.R. 429.

Canadian courts have been reluctant to impose either *de facto* or *de jure* positive demands on the state's budgets for social and economic standings. Canadian courts have accepted Lon Fuller's arguments that courts as institutions that hear claims between two parties on specific issues are not in a good position to make decisions that allocate between the competing demands on the state's budget.[64] A similar reluctance to interfere with governmental budgeting decisions also explains a unanimous 2004 decision to uphold a law that extinguished some pay equity arrears and postponed for three years pay equity payments awarded to Newfoundland nurses. The Court held that, although the singling out of the pay equity payments for the nurses constituted gender discrimination, it was nevertheless justified under section 1 of the Charter as a reasonable response to the fiscal crisis the province faced and the need for the province to balance the competing demands on the government's budget. The Court recognized that "the provincial government in this case *could* have thrown other claims and priorities to the winds and simply paid the $24 million but in its view, the cuts it would have had to make elsewhere to permit this to happen would have created even greater grief and social disruption. The budget is simply a forum for juggling spending priorities of all types."[65] The deference demonstrated in this decision to the government's distributive choices suggests that Canadian courts are unlikely to assume the role of positive legislator with respect to socioeconomic rights in the foreseeable future. In what follows, I examine two areas – labor and health policy – that seem to be possible exceptions to the Court's deference on socioeconomic matters. I suggest, however, that these exceptions are not really exceptions, because the Court was convinced that it could intervene in these areas without taking on distributive responsibilities that might otherwise be associated with becoming a positive legislator on matters of socioeconomic policy.

8. *Labor Policy*

After initially being deferential in deciding that freedom of association under the Charter did not include the right to strike[66] or the right to bargain collectively,[67] the Court has recently been more active with respect to labor

[64] Lon Fuller, "The Forms and Limits of Adjudication" (1978) 92 *Harv. L. Rev.* 353.

[65] *Newfoundland v. NAPE* [2004] 3 S.C.R. 381 at para. 95.

[66] *Reference re Public Service Employee Relations Act (Alberta)* [1987] 1 S.C.R. 313.

[67] *Professional Institute of the Public Service of Canada v. Northwest Territories (Commissioner)* [1990] 2 S.C.R. 367; *Delisle v. Canada* [2001] 3 S.C.R. 1016.

policy. For example, the Court held that the exclusion of agricultural workers from Ontario's collective-bargaining regime violated freedom of association.[68] An interesting feature of this decision was that, although the Court declared that the categorical exemption of agricultural workers from labor legislation was unconstitutional, it suspended that declaration of invalidity for eighteen months to provide the government with an opportunity to consult and devise a suitable regime tailored to the circumstances of agricultural workers. A conservative government in Ontario enacted new legislation in response to the Court's ruling,[69] but that legislation has been struck down as infringing freedom to association.[70] In reaching this decision, the Court relied on a subsequent Supreme Court of Canada decision that held that the right to collective bargaining was part of freedom of association and was violated by legislation that prohibited bargaining over contracting out and layoffs in the health-care sector.[71] These cases suggest that the court is prepared to require legislatures to enact legislation that provides for the essentials of collective bargaining and that it may find some attempts by legislatures to comply with the positive obligations imposed by the courts to be unconstitutional. Nevertheless, it is noteworthy that in these cases the Court did not prescribe the precise terms of the legislation or the results of the collective-bargaining process. As in the constitutional references, the Court was mainly concerned with the processes of bargaining and was relatively agnostic about the outcomes of the bargaining. These decisions that involved suspended declarations of invalidity for eighteen-month periods suggests that Kelsen's stark distinction between the Court's role as a positive and negative legislator no longer captures the complexity of judicial review in the modern Canadian state. The Court can wield the power of negative remedies while knowing that the legislature will in the era of the positive state have an obligation to enact new legislation. The new legislation will comply with constitutional norms, and if the courts conclude that it does not, they can start the dialogic process of judicial invalidation and legislative reconstruction again. In such a regime, the Court is not forced to choose between being a negative or a positive legislator. It can be both, and it can work in partnership with the legislature.

68 *Dunmore v. Ontario* [2001] 3 S.C.R. 1016.

69 *Agricultural Employees Protection Act* S. O. 2002 c.16.

70 *Fraser v. Ontario* 2008 ONCA 760.

71 *Health Care Services and Support-Facilities Subsector Bargaining Assn v. British Columbia* 2007 SCC 27.

9. *Health-Care Policy*

Health-care policy is one of the most important components of Canada's social and economic policies, and here, as in labor policy, it could be argued that the Court has departed from a pattern of judicial deference and has assumed the role of a positive legislator. The Court's activism with respect to selected components of health-care policy, however, can be explained on the basis of its interventions in health-care policy largely following the traditional model of the Court acting as a negative legislator and being limited to the remedy of legislative invalidation of unconstitutional laws.

It was widely assumed when the Charter was drafted that it would not affect Canada's laws concerning abortion. Canada's 1969 abortion law criminalized abortions unless they were approved by a hospital committee as necessary to protect the life or health of the woman and were performed in hospitals. In 1988, however, the Supreme Court invalidated this abortion law in a 5–2 decision. Four of the judges stressed what they saw as procedural flaws in the law that caused delays in receiving committee approval, uneven standards applied by the committees, and uneven regional availability of abortions.[72] All the judges contemplated that Parliament could justify some restrictions on abortion and that new legislation would likely be forthcoming from Parliament. In this way, the decision seemed to fit into the pattern observed previously of the courts striking down laws, but legislatures were in a position in which they devised new laws that complied with constitutional standards. Parliament attempted to enact a new criminal law restricting abortions, but it was defeated by a tied vote in Canada's appointed Senate, and no government has since attempted to legislative on this divisive social issue. In this case, the Court's decision did not produce a legislative response, and it was consistent with the traditional role of courts as negative legislators.

The Court intervened around the edges of health-care policy in 1997 by holding that the failure to provide sign-language interpreters for deaf patients when they received medically necessary services violated equality rights under the Charter. In the result, the Court issued a declaration but suspended it for a six-month period to allow the government to devise a system to provide the needed interpretation. The Court also was influenced by evidence that the costs of complying with its ruling would not be great.[73] In

72 *R. v. Morgentaler* [1988] 1 S.C.R. 30.

73 *Eldridge v. British Columbia* [1997] 3 S.C.R. 624. For an argument that it underestimated the costs see Christopher Manfredi and Antonia Maioni, "Courts and Health Policy" (2002) 27 *J. Health Policy Law* 211.

2004, the Court overturned lower courts in British Columbia that had held that the government's failure to pay for intensive therapy for autistic children was an unjustified violation of equality rights. The Court held that the parents of autistic children had not been denied equal protection of the law because there was no legal right to all medically required services, only to those that the government chose to include in its Medicare plan. In addition, the Court stressed that the government had decided not to designate those who provided intensive therapy for autistic children as health-care providers who could receive public payments. The Court's decision maximized the ability of governments to determine the scope of health-care services that the public system will pay for.[74] The Court appeared to be influenced by the extensive costs of the therapy requested in this case. The case suggests that the courts may not stand in the way of governmental decisions to define the scope of publicly funded health care in Canada and, as such, is consistent with the thesis that Canadian courts will not act as positive legislators in the realm of distributive socioeconomic policy.

The Supreme Court surprised many who expected continued deference toward the government's determination of health-care policy when in 2005 it invalidated a Quebec law that prohibited private medical insurance for those medically essential services that were covered by Quebec's public health-care system.[75] The majority's judgment did not recognize a positive right to prompt health care but concluded that it was arbitrary and unjustified to restrict private health insurance given wait times for medically necessary procedures. In other words, the decision does not guarantee any particular type of health care, only a freedom to contract for private medical insurance given the delays in the public system. The Court's decision is consistent with its role as a negative legislator because it relied on the simple remedy of striking down legislative restrictions on private health insurance. Courts will likely be less willing to act as a positive legislator if doing so requires them to employ more complex remedies that may be needed to protect persons who must rely on the public health-care system because they cannot afford or are not eligible for private health insurance.[76]

74 *Auton v. British Columbia* [2004] 3 S.C.R. 657.

75 *Chaoulli v. Quebec* [2005] 1 S.C.R. 791.

76 Kent Roach, "The Courts and Medicare: Too Much or Too Little Judicial Activism?" in Flood, Roach and Sossin, eds., *Access to Care Access to Justice* (Toronto: University of Toronto Press, 2005).

CONCLUSION

Canada provides an interesting case study of courts as positive legislators. Most constitutional litigation in Canada is conducted in the course of regular litigation between the state and the individual. Nevertheless, the Canadian courts have developed innovative remedies, such as the delayed or suspended declaration of invalidity, which encourage legislators to enact new and constitutional legislation before the court's negative remedy of invalidating legislation takes effects. This is an explicit recognition of how, in a developed highly regulated society, the Court's traditional role as negative legislator can have the effect of prompting the government to take a variety of positive actions. Indeed, the frequent positive legislative replies that follow from Canadian decisions striking down legislation suggests that Kelsen's stark dichotomy between the negative and the positive role of constitutional courts has become anachronistic in the age of the modern state.

Much Charter litigation in Canada involves attempts by those accused of a crime to obtain negative remedies, such as the exclusion of unconstitutionally obtained evidence or the termination of cases on constitutional grounds. Nevertheless, many of these cases have resulted in governments taking positive actions, ranging from the enactment of new procedures to authorize search and seizures to the investment of more funds in criminal justice to comply with constitutional speedy-trial standards. Even when they appear to act as traditional negative legislators, Canadian courts can prompt a process of positive law reform.

Canadian courts have also ventured more explicitly but more cautiously into the role of positive legislator. This has occurred in some cases in which Canadian governments have taken advantage of their ability to refer to the Court abstract constitutional questions that are not tied to particular cases or controversies. In the course of some famous reference decisions, the Supreme Court of Canada has proclaimed basic standards for constitutional change, including negotiations that would follow a successful vote for Quebec's secession from Canada. The Court has played the role of the positive legislator in these and other cases, but it has generally focused on establishing basic procedural parameters that could result in a wide range of substantive outcomes. It is also significant that elected governments have often invited the Court to develop basic constitutional rules in these areas.

The Canadian courts have also acted as positive legislators in some other contexts. The Court has also enforced positive minority-language rights in an active fashion that has involved courts retaining jurisdiction over the case until governments have taken the positive translation and school construction measures that are necessary to comply with the rights. Even the recognition of basic constitutional rights, such as the right to vote and the right of a citizen to return to Canada, implies a duty on the state to take positive action to ensure compliance. The Supreme Court has read in sexual orientation as a prohibited ground of discrimination in legislation prohibiting discrimination. Lower courts similarly read in the ability of same-sex couples to marry. The willingness of Canadian courts to make up for unconstitutional omissions in the scope of legislation is an important example of positive judicial legislation. At the same time, however, Canadian courts will only add or read in words to legislation in cases where they are satisfied that both the purposes of the statute and the Constitution support the judicial amendment. In cases with a range of constitutional options, Canadian courts will generally not add to legislation but rather will suspend the negative remedy of a declaration of invalidity to give the legislature an opportunity to select among the constitutionally satisfactory options and to enact new legislation. In short, Canadian courts will explicitly act as positive legislators when they conclude that doing so is the only possible response to constitutional infirmities in the positive state.

The Canadian courts are most comfortable in playing a role as positive legislator in contexts in which they can work in partnership with legislatures. For example, judicial invalidation of laws that restrict benefits to minority political parties or collective bargaining clearly contemplated that the legislator would respond with new laws that respected the constitutional standards proclaimed by the Court. Similarly, the Court invalidated national security procedures that allowed detention and deportation on the basis of secret evidence but gave the government a year to develop the details of a regime that would subject the secret evidence to adversarial challenge. The suspended declaration of invalidity pioneered by Canadian courts and subsequently adopted in the South African constitution symbolizes an interaction between negative judicial remedies and positive legislative responses to such decisions, which suggests that Kelsen's dichotomy between negative and positive legislation has become a false choice.

Nevertheless, the distinction between the negative and positive roles of courts continues to have some residual rhetorical appeal in Canada. In particular, it can help explain the general deference of the Canadian judiciary with respect to socioeconomic policy, as well as the few occasions in labor and health policy on which the Court has departed from such deference. With respect to most socioeconomic policy, including rights to subsistence and publicly funded health care, the Canadian courts have run away from suggestions that they should be positive legislators. The Court's caution in this respect reflects considerable uneasiness about explicitly assuming the role of positive legislator with respect to the distribution of limited economic resources. In the few cases in which the Court has intervened, such as in the *Morgentaler* abortion case and the *Chaoulli* case on private health insurance, it has been comforted by the fact that it acted as a negative legislator. In other words, the Court simply struck down state activity that prevented access to abortions or private health insurance. In this sense, Kelsen's distinction between negative and positive judicial roles continues to have influence in Canada. Nevertheless, this influence is in tension with the court's acceptance of its role as a positive legislator in other contexts and the fact that even negative judicial decisions invalidating unconstitutional laws often will result in positive legislative responses.

COLOMBIA

LE JUGE CONSTITUTIONNEL COLOMBIEN, LÉGISLATEUR-CADRE POSITIF: UN GOUVERNEMENT DES JUGES?

German Alfonso Lopez Daza[1]
Professor, Surcolombiana de Neiva University
germanlo@usco.edu.co

INTRODUCTION

Contrairement a la constitution colombienne de 1886 qui autorisait dans certains cas le Président de la République, le Congrès, et la Cour Suprême de Justice à appliquer directement le contenu du texte constitutionnel, le nouveau texte promulgué par l'Assemblée Nationale Constituante de 1991 inclut une liste importante de principes et règles directement applicables par les juges, fonctionnaires administratifs ou litigants en Colombie.

La constitution de 1886 ne prévoyait pas de mécanismes d'application généralisée comme celui de l'exception d'inconstitutionnalité; celle-ci existait mais il était rare que le conseil constitutionnel y ait recours.

Selon le concept traditionnel de l'état de droit, les juges avaient pour mission d'appliquer les règles et principes énoncés par les codes et les lois. La constitution s'exprimait à travers la loi et l'interprétation directe du texte supérieur ne se faisait pas, les niveaux de constitutionnalisation étaient très vagues.

[1] DEA en Institutions et Politiques Publiques à l'Université de Paris I (Sorbonne). Doctorat en Droit constitutionnel á l'Université de Paris II (Panthéon-Assas). Professeur et chercheur à l'Universidad Surcolombiana à Neiva (Colombie). Directeur du Groupe "Nuevas Visiones del Derecho).

La Constitution de 1991 a changé les concepts du constitutionnalisme: elle a imposé la suprématie directe de la constitution[2] et la protection des droits constitutionnels fondamentaux des citoyens en rendant règles et principes directement applicables à tout type de conflits.

Cette dernière décade a connu de nombreux changements au niveau de la théorie des sources du droit (liant l'application directe de la constitution à une nouvelle utilisation des précédents judiciaires), au niveau de l'argumentation juridique et au niveau de la façon d'aborder le problème des sources et l'interprétation du droit.

Le juge constitutionnel se transforme alors en créateur conscient de ses règles constitutionnelles; il n'est plus un simple exécuteur et l'utilisation de la constitution est a la portée de tous les citoyens.

C'est dans ce contexte que cet article a pour objet de présenter quelques décisions judiciaires de la cour constitutionnelle colombienne du point de vue de la sentence manipulatrice ou modulation des sentences. Dans un premier temps, nous ferons une brève description des changements générés par les décisions de la cour constitutionnelle et des affrontements entre les différents pouvoirs publics qui s'ensuivirent. Dans un deuxième temps, on examinera la typologie des sentences manipulatrices du contrôle constitutionnel concluant à une cassure de la traditionnelle séparation des pouvoirs et à une transformation du tribunal constitutionnel en législateur–cadre positif. Finalement, on fera référence à la théorie du concept "gouvernement des juges" élaborée par Edouard Lambert en 1921 et de sa possible application au cas colombien.

I. DYNAMISME DE LA COUR CONSTITUTIONNELLE COLOMBIENNE DANS SON RÔLE DE PROTECTRICE DE LA CONSTITUTION DE 1991.

La jurisprudence colombienne de la Cour Constitutionnelle allant dans le sens de la défense des droits fondamentaux et de la solution de conflits liés aux droits sociaux a créé une attitude de confiance et de respect des citoyens envers la cour constitutionnelle.

[2] La Court Constitutionnel colombienne a exprimé que la Charte Politique de 1991 a un pouvoir obligatoire, c'est-à-dire, elle est directement applicable, principalement dans les cas de protection de droits fondamentaux. Voir les arrêts T-406 de 1992 Magistrat exposant Ciro Angarita Barón, C-479 de 1992 M.E. José Gregorio Hernández Galindo et Alejandro Martínez Caballero, C-543 de 1992 M.E. José Gregorio Hernández Galindo, T-006 de 1992 M.E. Eduardo Cifuentes Muñoz, T-567 de 1992 M.E. Alejandro Martínez Caballero, Fabio Morón Díaz et José Gregorio Hernández.

Celle-ci a pour mission principale de veiller au respect de la suprématie de la constitution grâce aux recours des actions de tutelle et des sentences de constitutionnalité.[3]

Cette tâche confiée à la cour durant ces 18 années de fonctionnement du haut tribunal constitutionnel a débouché sur la création d'une vaste doctrine constitutionnelle jurisprudentielle, base du constitutionnalisme colombien du XXIème siècle.

Les créations jurisprudentielles telles que *l'effet inter partes*, *l'effet inter comunis* ou *erga omnes*, l*a voie de fait*, *l'état de choses inconstitutionel* ou la

[3] L'article 241 de la Constitution colombienne établit les pouvoirs de la Cour constitutionnelle colombienne ainsi: ART. 241 - Une Cour constitutionnelle est confiée à la garde de l'intégrité et la suprématie de la Constitution, dans le cadre strict et précis de cet article. À cette fin, exerce les fonctions suivantes:

1. Décider sur les requêtes en inconstitutionnalité formés par des citoyens contre les actes modifiant la Constitution, quel que soit son origine, que des vices de procédure dans leur formation.
2. Décider, avant le prononcé populaire sur la constitutionnalité de l'appel à un référendum ou d'une assemblée constituante pour modifier la Constitution, que des vices de procédure dans leur formation.
3. Décider sur la constitutionnalité d'un référendum sur les lois et les plébiscites et les référendums à l'échelle nationale. Celui-ci que par des vices de procédure dans son annonce et la mise en œuvre.
4. Décider sur les requêtes en inconstitutionnalité formés par des citoyens contre les lois, tant pour leur contenu et de vices de procédure dans sa formation.
5. Décider sur les requêtes en inconstitutionnalité formés par des citoyens contre la force du droit décrets émis par le gouvernement fondée sur l'article 150, paragraphe 10 et 341 de la Constitution, pour leur contenu ou des erreurs de procédure dans leur formation.
6. Décider sur les excuses à l'article 137 de la Constitution.
7. La décision finale sur la constitutionnalité des décrets législatifs adoptés par le gouvernement fondé sur les articles 212, 213 et 215 de la Constitution. 8. La décision finale sur la constitutionnalité des projets de loi qui ont été contestée par le gouvernement comme inconstitutionnel, et les projets de loi statutaires proposées, tan pour leur contenu et de vices de procédure dans sa formation.
9. D'examen, de la manière prescrite par la loi, les décisions judiciaires se rapportant aux travaux de l'application de droits constitutionnels.
10. La décision finale sur la constitutionnalité des traités internationaux et les lois portant approbation. À cette fin, le gouvernement a renvoyé à la Cour, dans les six jours après la promulgation de la loi. Tout citoyen peut intervenir pour défendre ou contester sa constitutionnalité. Si la Cour déclare la Constitution, le gouvernement peut procéder à un échange de lettres, sinon ils ne seront pas ratifiés. Quand un ou plusieurs dispositions d'un traité multilatéral d'être déclarée inconstitutionnelle par la Cour constitutionnelle, le Président de la République ne peut exprimer son consentement pour la réservation.
11. Pour rédiger son propre règlement.

Paragraphe. Lorsque la Cour trouve des vices de procédure dans la formation de l'acte soumis à son contrôle, elle donnera l'ordre de le rendre à l'autorité dont il prononça à, si possible, modifier le défaut. Remédier au défaut, il se prononcera sur la constitutionnalité de la loi.

protection des droits de 3eme et 2eme génération par la voie de la *connexité*, sont des garanties du respect de *l'Etat Social et Démocratique de Droit* créé par l'Assemblée Nationale Constituante en 1991.

II. JUSTICE CONSTITUTIONNELLE VERSUS POUVOIR EXECUTIF-POUVOIR LEGISLATIF

La Constitution Politique de 1991 a pour vocation la protection des droits essentiels qui, souvent, n'étaient pas respectés (droit à la vie, à la paix, justice sociale, solidarité, droit au travail). Pourtant, elle fait l'objet de nombreuses critiques:

- Depuis son entrée en vigueur, elle n'a pas rempli sa mission de protection[4] durant ces 18 dernières années.
- Il y aurait un manque de cohérence de certains articles, l'absence d'une idéologie bien définie, un corpus trop long, une réglementation excessive.
- Ses 28 réformes

La majorité de la doctrine colombienne et la Cour Constitutionnelle reconnait que la Charte politique n'est qu'une première étape pour atteindre une véritable justice sociale et la protection des doits fondamentaux.[5]

Cette protection est faite par les juges de la République qui ont à leur disposition le recours en *tutela*, et autres voies de recours constitutionnelles comme l'action populaire, habeas corpus.

Les juges colombiens rendent avant tout justice et ne gouvernent pas. Il est possible que dans certains cas de vide juridique ou de loi contraire à la justice, le juge oblige la juridiction administrative colombienne à l'aide de ces nombreux recours qui lui donnent un réel pouvoir sur l'action de l'administration: l'Etat Social de Droit.

Le juge constitutionnel doit d'abord mettre en application les principes et règles,[6] dictés par la cour constitutionnelle et chercher à rendre justice. Ce

[4] Autrement dit, le «fétichisme constitutionnel» a changé au cours des dernières années, lorsque la population a pris conscience que les problèmes sociaux ne sont pas résolus avec le changement de la constitution.

[5] C'est ce qu'a déclaré la Cour constitutionnelle dans l'affaire C-479, 1992 et 1994 T-217.

[6] La Cour constitutionnelle a clairement conceptualisée, la différence entre les principes et les valeurs et la façon dont elles devraient être appliquées dans un État social de droit, la décision T-406 1992 ME Ciro Angarita Barón.

qui l'oblige à s'immiscer, contrairement à la théorie de Montesquieu, dans d'autres domaines que le sien.

Cette ingérence dans d'autres branches du pouvoir a provoqué des affrontements entre celles-ci et la Cour Constitutionnelle., rapportés d'ailleurs par tous les médias et baptisés par les journalistes "*choques de trenes.*" [7] La Cour Constitutionnelle intervient dans les cas suivants:

1- Pour violation des droits fondamentaux dans les sentences de *tutela* prononcées par l'administration publique.

2- Pour faire appliquer la théorie de la *voie de fait* dans les sentences de "tutela" dictées par le Conseil d'Etat, la Cour Suprême de Justice ou Supérieur de la "*Judicatura*."

3- Pour inconstitutionnalité des lois ou décrets affectant de façon directe le pouvoir exécutif.

4- pour inactivité législative, vide juridique ou de lacune normative afin de donner des directives au Congrès de la République.

Les arrêts de la Cour Constitutionnelle d'inconstitutionnalité du Concordat signé par le Saint Siège[8] et la Colombie, de dépénalisation de la consommation d'hallucinogènes à usage personnel,[9] de la légalisation de l'euthanasie,[10] de la protection du droit à l'inviolabilité parlementaire des congressistes,[11] l'inconstitutionnalité de la norme régulatrice du système UPAC,[12] de l'interdiction d'augmentation des salaires des fonctionnaires,[13] de l'interprétation donnée par la jurisprudence du Conseil d'Etat relative à l'action en nullité,[14] de la dépénalisation de l'avortement[15] et plus récemment

7 Sur ce sujet est abondante doctrine colombienne. Voir, entre autres, les articles suivants: "Las Vías de Hecho como generadoras del *Choque de Trenes* en la jurisprudencia constitucional. (1992-2008)," par *Carlos Fernando Gómez García* publiée en http://criteriojuridico.puj.edu.co/; "Tutela contra sentencias de las altas Cortes o choque de vanidades," par Rubén Darío Henao Orozco publiée en http://www.iidpc.org/pdf/ajr6HenaoOrozco.pdf; "'El choque de trenes' o las Contradicciones entre las Altas Cortes del Poder Judicial," en *Crítica Política* Numero146 http://escuelajuridica.org; "El choque de trenes. Sobre los sistemas de interpretación jurídica en Colombia," par Jaime Giraldo Ángel en http://www.tribunales.colpsic.org.co/documentos/Giraldo_CDT.pdf, parmi beaucoup d'autres

8 Arrêt C-027 de 1993 M.E. Simón Rodríguez Rodríguez.

9 Arrêt C-221 de 1994 M.E. Carlos Gaviria Díaz.

10 Arrêt C-239 de 1997 M.E. Carlos Gaviria Díaz.

11 Arrêt SU-047 de 1999 M.E. Carlos Gaviria Díaz y Alejandro Martínez Caballero.

12 Arrêt C-700 de 1999 M.E. José Gregorio Hernández Galindo.

13 Arrêt 1433 de 2000 M.E. Antonio Barrera Carbonell.

14 Arrêt C-426 de 2002 M.E. Rodrigo Escobar Gil.

15 Arrêt C-355 de 2006 M.E. Jaime Araujo Rentería y Clara Inés Vargas.

de celle d'une réforme constitutionnelle pour vice de fond[16] ont déchainé la critique: la Cour Constitutionnelle est trop présente et outrepasse ses compétences. Du fait de son "activité" intense, on l'accuse de "prévaricateur" et on regrette que la Colombie soit devenue un "un gouvernement des juges."

Le contrôle judicaire des lois n'est pas démocratique et la Cour en arrive à définir des politiques publiques. On craint un risque de politisation du pouvoir judiciaire,

Pourtant si l'on considère des aspects du pays comme sa tradition démocratique ininterrompue, sa relative stabilité institutionnelle, son développement de la démocratie participative et son principe de séparation des pouvoirs, tout porte à penser que nous n'avons pas un "gouvernement des juges."

Nous allons examiner cette question à la lumière de la théorie étrangère et il se pourrait que nous arrivions à une conclusion tout différente.

Malgré la connotation péjorative de cette expression, elle désigne sur le plan constitutionnel un contenu théorique très élaboré que nous allons brièvement exposer.

III. LA COUR CONSTITUTIONNELLE COLOMBIENNE-LÉGISLATEUR CADRE POSITIF

On reproche à la Cour Constitutionnelle d'avoir créer un climat d'insécurité juridique.[17] Le contrôle constitutionnel des lois l'a amenée à dicter différentes sentences de constitutionnalité inspirées de la théorie Kelsenienne du législateur–cadre négatif.[18]

16 Arrêt C-588 de 2009 M.P. Gabriel Eduardo Mendoza Martelo.

17 Quelques constitutionnalistes colombien comme Luis Carlos Sáchica et Ivan Vila Casado parmi beaucoup d'autres, critiquant ouvertement la procédure devant la Cour constitutionnelle outrepasser ses limites. Sáchica catalogue comme un «tribunal strabique» parce que l'accuse de regarder la politique avec un œil et avec l'autre fixe son regarde pétrifié dans sa jurisprudence (*Ámbito jurídico*, 15 au 26 mars 2010) Vila Casado pour sa part accusé d'avoir «sauté la clôture» parce qu'elle n'a pas été abrogée pouvoirs en vertu de l'article 241 de la Constitution quand il a déclaré inconstitutionnelle une modification constitutionnelle approuvée par le Congrès colombien, a cause de vice de fond, étant sa compétence des erreurs de procédure ou de forme (*Ámbito jurídico* Septembre 2009).

18 Kelsen propose la création d'un tribunal spécialisé, indépendant des pouvoirs publics traditionnels compte tenu des problèmes à résoudre (la suprématie de la Constitution). Quand il parle de «législateur négatif», il le fait en pensant dans le cas américain et autrichien. Kelsen a déclaré: «un tribunal habilité à annuler des lois, individuellement ou en général, agit comme un législateur négative. *Cit.*, Perez Tremps, Pablo, 1981, *Tribunal constitucional y magistratura.*

Hans Kelsen défendait l'existence des tribunaux constitutionnels,[19] gardiens de la suprématie de la Constitution et de la régularité de la normativité en vigueur. Selon le juriste viennois, une Constitution qui ne prévoit pas de garantie d'annulation d'actes inconstitutionnels n'est pas une Constitution à caractère complètement obligatoire.[20]

Pour lui, le tribunal constitutionnel est un législateur-cadre négatif: le parlement élabore les lois (législateur–cadre positif) et le juge constitutionnel a pour mission de les annuler si celle-ci sont contraires à la Constitution. Ces facultés de libre création par le parlement et d'annulation par la Cour Constitutionnelle sont définies par la Constitution.

La décision prise par le juge constitutionnel n'a pas d'effet rétroactif et son application devient obligatoire à partir de sa publication. Ceci afin de préserver la sécurité juridique du système.

Toutefois, Kelsen impose une restriction très importante: le principe de séparation des pouvoirs selon la tradition de Montesquieu, doit être respecté. Les tribunaux constitutionnels ne peuvent donc pas créer de normes juridiques positives, sous peine d'empiéter sur les compétences du Parlement.

Ce concept de "législateur-cadre négatif" est actuellement dépassé par la doctrine italienne, espagnole et allemande, et celle de leur Cour et tribunal constitutionnels respectifs.[21]

Ce modèle kelsenien de contrôle a pour effet l'application du principe *erga omnes* selon lequel les sentences de constitutionnalité des tribunaux sont applicables à tous.

En cas de norme déclarée inconstitutionnelle. Celle-ci doit être immédiatement supprimée et cette annulation a le même caractère que celui d'une loi nouvelle. Certains essayistes affirment que la demande d'inconstitutionnalité n'est pas à proprement parler une "demande" telle

Madrid. CCE, pp. 6 et suiv. Hans, Kelsen, 1979. *Théorie générale du droit et de l'Etat* (trad. Maynez Garcia). Mexique. UNAM, pp.303 à 334.

19 Cette déclaration qu'il a défendu, se trouve dans une doctrine classique constitutionnelle du début du XXe siècle: *Qui devrait être le défenseur de la constitution*? Dans ce travail, Kelsen fait référence à l'organe dont la fonction est de défendre la constitution contre d'éventuelles violations des normes inférieures. Kelsen et Carl Schmitt se sont affronté ouvertement; Schmitt a défendu la position du chef d'état en tan que défenseur de la constitution et refuse cette fonction dans la Cour Constitutionnelle.

20 Hans Kelsen, "La garantía jurisdiccional de la Constitución," dans: *Escritos sobre democracia y socialismo*. Madrid 1988. Pág. 48.

21 Eliseo Aja, *Las tensiones entre el Tribunal Constitucional y la Europa actual*, Barcelona: Editorial Ariel 1998.

qu'elle est formulée dans la Théorie Générale du Procès en tant que prétention d'un droit subjectif, mais plutôt une "initiative législative negative."[22]

Kelsen propose deux modalités pour les arrêts d'annulation: certains à effet rétroactif et d'autres à effet non rétroactif prévoyant un délai d'application de la norme annulée. Il conçoit également la possibilité qu'un arrêt d'inconstitutionnalité ait un effet rétroactif.[23] Kelsen donne autorité aux juges constitutionnels de différer l'application de ses arrêts ou de décider si les normes sont applicables ou remplaçables. Ces considérations reflètent la difficulté d'unification des arrêts de constitutionnalité prononcés par ces tribunaux.

Cette souplesse dans la fixation de la date des effets des arrêts répond avant tout à la multiplicité des cas examinés: politiques, économiques et surtout sociaux.

Selon la doctrine, cette technique remonte au XIXe siècle et était utilisée par la Cour Suprême des États Unis. Plus tard, au XXe siècle, vers 1925, quelques tribunaux européens (Allemagne, Espagne, Italie) y ont recours afin de nuancer l'effet de leurs arrêts. La Cour Constitutionnelle regroupe ce genre d'arrêts dans la catégorie «modulation des effets des arrêts». La doctrine[24] et la jurisprudence distinguent les procédés d'interprétation manipulatrice, conditionnée, d'intégration, et de substitution.

En Colombie, la Cour Suprême utilise cette technique depuis 1912 et le Conseil d'État depuis 1947 dans les cas d'action d'inconstitutionnalité et d'action en nullité.

La Cour Constitutionnelle y a recours depuis 1991 (Constitution politique de 1991): elle module ou modifie le texte de la norme à réviser et change ainsi l'effet prévu par le législateur. On distingue 7 groupes de sentences.

22 Aníbal, Quiroga León, *Los excesos del Tribunal Constitucional Peruano: a propósito del control concentrado de la constitución*, p. 11.

23 Kelsen, *Ibid.*, p. 149.

24 Voir principalement: Hernán Alejandro, Olano García, "Tipología de nuestras sentencias constitucionales," publié dans la revue *Vniversitas* 2004. Edgar, Solano González, *Sentencias manipulativas e interpretativas*. Tesis de grado. Bogotá: Universidad Externado de Colombia, 2000. Marco Gerardo, Monroy Cabra, *La interpretación constitucional*. Librería del Profesional. Bogotá 2002. Alejandro, Martínez Caballero, "Tipos de sentencias en el control constitucional de las leyes: la experiencia colombiana," dans *Revista Estudios Socio Jurídicos*. Bogotá: Universidad del Rosario volumen 2 numero 1 marzo de 2000, p. 9.

1. *Sentences manipulatrices*

Elles modifient le sens de la loi en réécrivant le texte. Par exemple, la sentence C-948 du 6 novembre 2002, en révision de l'article 3 de la loi 734 de 2002 (code disciplinaire unique) qui disait:

> („,)
>
> (La Procuraduria Générale de la Nation) et le Conseil Supérieur de la Judicatura (sont) compétents (en principe) pour avoir connaissance, seulement à la fin du procès, des fautes reprochées aux fonctionnaires de la branche judiciaire, à l'exception de ceux qui ont une curule constitutionnelle.

La Cour a déclaré les énoncés entre parenthèses inconstitutionnels et le texte en vigueur dit ceci:

> le Conseil Supérieur de la Judicatura est compétent pour avoir connaissance, seulement à la fin du procès, des fautes reprochées aux fonctionnaires de la branche judiciaire, à l'exception de ceux qui ont une curule constitutionnelle.

2. *Sentence substitutive*

Ce sont celles qui transforment le sens du texte de loi et remplacent une partie de celle-ci interprétée comme non conforme à la constitution par la Cour. Par exemple, la sentence C-113/93 qui révise la constitutionnalité des incises deux et quatre de l'article 21 du Décret 2067 de 1991 et l'article 24 du même Décret. Dans le premier, la Cour déclare inconstitutionnelles les incises qui prévoyaient les effets des sentences de la Cour et confirme qu'elle seule a la compétence de fixer les effets de ses arrêts.

3. *Sentences interprétatives ou conditionnées*

Dans ces arrêts, la Cour précise qu'une norme est constitutionnelle seulement si son interprétation est en accord avec celle de la Cour. C'est le cas de l'objection d'inconstitutionnalité de l'article 30 (partiel) du Code du Travail et de l'article 238 (partiel) du Décret-loi 2737 de 1989.

L'arrêt, a déclaré constitutionnel sur ses fondements 31 et 33, l'expression de l'incise 2 de l'article 238 du Décret-loi 2737 de 1989, *"il est interdit de faire travailler les mineurs de moins de 14 ans et les parents ont l'obligation de les scolariser"* sous la condition que la prestation subordonnée aux services rendus par les enfants âgés de moins de quinze (15) ans et de plus de quatorze (14) ans, soit sujette aux conditions prévues dans les conventions 138 "Sur l'âge minimum d'admission à l'emploi" et 182 "Sur l'interdiction des travaux pénibles du travail des enfants" de la OIT.

4. *Sentence additive ou d'intégration*

L'arrêt C-109/1995 la définit ainsi: c'est une modalité qui autorise le juge constitutionnel, en vertu de la norme de la Charte (C.P. article 4), à appliquer directement les normes constitutionnelles sur la législation, afin de palier à son vide juridique normatif ou les imprécisions législatives.

Cet arrêt ajoute à la norme examinée les éléments dont l'absence la rendrait inconstitutionnelle, sentence C-690/96.

Telle est la fonction d'intégration de la doctrine constitutionnelle dont le caractère obligatoire, pour être source de droit, a été reconnu par la Cour. Il ne pouvait en être autrement puisque la Constitution est non seulement un système de sources mais aussi la norme juridique suprême, qui a la faculté d'imposer ses décisions à l'administration colombienne.

Nous illustrons ce cas par la décision C-470 de 1997, pour analyse de la constitutionnalité de l'article 238 du Code Substantiel du travail. La norme disait:

> Art.239.- Interdiction de licencier.
>
> Aucun employé n'en peut être renvoyé sous prétexte de grossesse ou d'allaitement.
>
> On considère que le licenciement est causé par la grossesse ou l'allaitement s'il est réalisé pendant la grossesse ou dans les trois (3) mois suivant l'accouchement et ce sans autorisation des tribunaux concernés.
>
> L'employée renvoyée sans autorisation des tribunaux concernés a droit au paiement d'une indemnité équivalente au salaire de soixante (60) jours en plus des indemnisations et prestations rattachées à ce salaire et au paiement de douze (12) semaines de congés payés définis dans ce chapitre, si ceux-ci n'ont pas été pris.(...)

Qu'a donc décidé la Cour? Elle a déclaré constitutionnel l'article 239 du Code Substantiel du travail, modifié par l'article 35 de la loi 50 de 1990. Le licenciement d'une employée durant sa grossesse ou dans les trois (3) mois suivant l'accouchement sera nul, si celui-ci n'a pas été autorisé par les autorités compétentes, qui ont pour devoir de vérifier si le licenciement n'est pas abusif. Cette décision s'appuie sur le fondement du principe d'égalité (C.P., Art.13) et sur la protection de la maternité dans la Constitution. (C.P.Art 43 et 53).

5. *Sentence de recommandation du législateur.*

Ces sentences de la Cour «recommandent, suggèrent ou exhortent» le législateur à établir une norme pour un domaine bien précis tout tenant compte des paramètres fixés par le tribunal constitutionnel. La sentence C-473/94.MP.Alejandro Martinez Caballero, en révision de l'article 430 du Code Substantiel du travail, qui interdit le droit de grève à tous les employés du secteur public. Selon la sentence de la cour "*exhorter le Congrès à réglementer, dans un certain délai, le droit de grève conformément à la Constitution.*" [25]

6. *Les sentences-lois.*

Dans ce cas, la Cour impose au Congrès de rédiger une loi selon les principes normatifs dictés par elle. La sentence C-620/01 Magistrat exposant Jaime Araújo Rentería qui révise l'article 144 de la Loi 600 de 2000 (Code de procédure pénale).

La Cour a déclaré inconstitutionnels les articles 382, 383, 384, 385, 386, 387, 388 et 389 de la Loi 600 de 2000, à partir du 31 décembre 2002, et a ordonné au Congrès de réguler le droit fondamental de habeas corpus ainsi que les recours et procédures de sa protection dans une loi statutaire qui devra être expédiée avant le 31 décembre 2002. Cependant, il fallut attendre la législature 2004-2005 pour que le Congrès réglemente enfin cet important principe.

Une autre sentence-loi, (C-700/1999) qui déclare inconstitutionnels certains aspects du système financier colombien, entre autres, celui de l'UPAC, et ordonne au Congrès de réglementer selon le contenu e la sentence. Cette fois-ci, le Congrès a expédié la loi 546 le 23 décembre 1999, avant que la sentence d'inconstitutionnalité ne prenne effet (20 juin 2000).

7. *Les sentences à effet différé*

Celles-ci sont applicables dans un temps futur. Par exemple, la sentence C-700/1999 relative au système financier colombien qui a déclaré

[25] Dans quelques arrêts, la Court donne un ordre directement au législateur comte tenu les déficiences dans les fonctions législatives. Ce sont les cas des arrets: C-1433 de 2000 M.E. Antonio Barrera Carbonell dont la Court a exprimé: 1. Déclarer que dans l'article 2 de la loi 547 de 2000 il ya eu une violation d'un devoir juridique fait par le Congrès, qui découle des dispositions de la Constitution identifiés dans le corps de cette décision et, plus précisément, les articles 53 et 150, paragraphe 19, alinea e) et l'article 4 de la loi 4 de 1992.

inconstitutionnels certains articles du Décret 663 de 1993 (Statut organique du système financier) et qui structure le système UPAC, a différé son application au 20 juin 2000.[26]

Il est évident que la modulation des sentences par la Cour a suscité de fortes critiques dans les milieux politiques, économiques et chez certains doctrinaires, la principale étant celle de son "*activisme législatif*" et ingérence dans le pouvoir législatif et politique.

C'est le cas dans le domaine pénal où la sentence C-237 de 1997, après révision des normes du code pénal antérieur, a approuvé l'euthanasie sans donner lieu au Congrès et au gouvernement de participer à un débat.

Il est vrai que le juge constitutionnel s'est substitué au législateur et au pouvoir réglementaire de l'exécutif dans certains cas. Mais l'intervention de la cour peut être justifiée si l'on considère l'inactivité du législateur en Colombie. Ce qui, ajouté au fait que la Cour Constitutionnel a réussi, grâce à son travail, à gagner le respect des citoyens colombiens et surtout celui des secteurs juridique et politique, a enrayé les critiques dont elle faisait l'objet.

IV. CONSTRUCTION THÉORIQUE DU CONCEPT "GOUVERNEMENT DES JUGES"

Cette expression de "gouvernement des juges" vient des États Unis d'Amérique en 1903, le président Theodore Roosevelt s'est opposé au "darwinisme juridique" de la Cour suprême et a critiqué l'intervention législative des juges dans la vie économique. Le président se référait au pouvoir des juges d'écarter la loi et d'en donner une interprétation irresponsable. Il accusait également ces derniers de s'être auto-attribué ce rôle de législateur.

[26] Dans des cas exceptionnels, la Cour constitutionnelle colombienne a accepté de différer le temps les effets de ses décisions d'inconstitutionnalité. Voir notamment l'affaire C-221 1997 ME Alejandro Martínez Caballero, C-700, 1999, ME José Gregorio Hernández Galindo, S.V. de Alfredo Beltrán Sierra et José Gregorio Hernández Galindo. S.V. Vladimiro Naranjo Mesa et Eduardo Cifuentes Muñoz SV Galvis Tafur Alvaro, C-442/01 M.P. Marco Gerardo Monroy Cabra partielle de sauvetage juges Vote Jaime Araujo Renteria, Alfredo Beltrán Sierra, Eduardo Montealegre et Alvaro Tafur Galvis Lynnet; C-500/01 MP Álvaro Galvis Tafur S.P.V. Jaime Araujo Renteria, C-737/01 M.E. Eduardo Montealegre Lynnet S.V. Marco Gerardo Monroy Cabra, SV Jaime Araujo Renteria, Alfredo Beltrán Sierra, Alvaro Tafur Galvis, Clara Inés Vargas Hernández ME C-754/04 Álvaro Galvis Tafur A.V. Jaime Araujo Renteria, S.P.V. et A.V. Espinosa José Manuel Cepeda, Rodrigo Escobar et Rodrigo Gil Yepes Uprimny, SPV Álvaro Galvis Tafur En d'autres occasions en l'absence de tel exception, la Court n'a pas accepté de moduler ces effets; voir les arrêts C-756/02 Affaire C-245/02 et MP M.P. José Manuel Cepeda Espinosa. Sur le même sujet voir l'Auto M.P. 311/01 Jaime Araujo Rentería.

C'est Edouard Lambert[27] qui a repris cette idée pour en faire une théorie applicable à l'Europe, qu'il dénomma “le gouvernement des juges,” et qu'il développa dans son livre *le gouvernement des juges et la lutte contre la législation sociale aux États unis, l'expérience américaine du contrôle judiciaire des lois* publié en 1928.[28]

La principale accusation des critiques et théoriques (v.g. Michel Troper, Otto Pferman, Etienne Picard, etc) est qu'un tribunal composé de membres nommés de façon arbitraire ou par complaisance, jouisse d'un tel pouvoir de décision et ceci sans aucun contrôle.

Selon Lacharrière,[29] il y aurait usurpation du pouvoir du législateur de la part d'une institution sans que la constitution l'y autorise.

Troper,[30] constitutionnaliste français et professeur universitaire de Paris, ajoute qu'il y a contradiction dans le fait que les juges prennent des décisions politiques puisque la fonction de ceux-ci n'est pas de gouverner mais de juger. Ils appliquent les lois mais ne les interprètent pas.

D'après lui,[31] le concept de gouvernement des juges présente quatre caractéristiques:

1) Les juges gouvernent parce qu'ils disposent d'une partie du pouvoir législatif; thèse proposée par Lambert et Kelsen. Ce dernier ajoute que si les juges peuvent rejeter une loi, c'est qu'ils ont également un pouvoir législatif et sont des législateurs-cadres négatifs.
2) Les juges ont le pouvoir d'utiliser des recours ou contrôles de constitutionnalité.
3) Les juges ont la possibilité d'appliquer des principes vagues. Selon Eisenman, disciple de Kelsen, “si le juge peut dicter lui-même les principes applicables, alors le gouvernement des juges se substitue au gouvernement du législateur.” Troper explique que “si les principes sont formulés de façon claire et précise et si le juge est enfermé dans sa propre jurisprudence, alors il n'y a pas gouvernement des juges.”
4) Les juges vont à l'encontre de la volonté du législateur. Troper cite Ardant au sujet de la Cour suprême des États Unis d'Amérique “avec

27 Edouard, Lambert, *Le gouvernement des juges et la lutte contre la législation sociale aux Etats Unis, l'expérience américaine du contrôle judiciaire des lois,* Paris, M.Giard&Cie. 1921, p. 276

28 Il est maintenant possible d'obtenir une réimpression de 2010 publiée par l'éditorial Tecnos Editorial (Madrid).

29 R., Lacharriere, Opinion disidente, publié dans la *Revista Pouvoir* nº 13,1980, dedié au Conseil Constitutionnel Français, pp. 133 135

30 Michel, Troper, “Existe-t-il un concept de gouvernement de juges?,” dans *Gouvernement des juges et démocratie,* Publications de la Sorbonne, Paris, 2001.

31 *Ibid.*, p.26

> cinq votes contre quatre, elle peut mettre en échec l'application votée par les représentants élus de la nation."

Si l'on s'en tient à ces quatre cas, effectivement, la Colombie a bien une Cour constitutionnelle qui exerce "un gouvernement des juges." Elle a bien un rôle de législateur-cadre négatif lorsqu'elle déclare une norme inconstitutionnelle (cas numéro 1).[32]

Cependant la Cour va plus bien au-delà encore grâce aux sentences manipulatrices dont elle dispose. Elle a le pouvoir de donner des ordres au Congrès pour qu'il légifère selon ses recommandations.[33]

La Colombie présente également le cas numéro 2, elle peut réviser certains décrets dans certains cas (surtout si l'état d'exception est déclaré), les lois statutaires (sur les droits fondamentaux), les lois autorisant l'approbation d'accords internationaux et la loi du Plan national de développement du Président.

Non seulement la Cour révise les sentences de *tutela* et rend des décisions de révision de constitutionnalité, mais elle est aussi créatrice de principes de doit, allant au-delà de l'application exclusive des principes contenus dans la constitution.[34]

Le cas numéro 3 se présente aussi en Colombie: La Cour a déjà modifié sa propre jurisprudence quand elle a estimé nécessaire de le faire: sentence SU 047 de 1999 de révision d'une *tutela.*

Le cas numéro 4 existe également en Colombie. Les décisions sont approuvées par une faible majorité (5 contre 4). La sentence C-221 de 1994 sur la dépénalisation de la dose de drogue à usage personnel a été décidée par 5 votes contre 4.

32 Selon l'article 241 de la Constitution Politique de 1991.

33 Voir les affaires C-473/94, C-109/1995, C-477/1999, C-170/2004, C-836/2001, C-620/01, C-700/1999.

34 Sur ce point peut être illustré par le traitement accordé par la Cour constitutionnelle la question de l'avortement. Dans un premier jugement de constitutionnalité (C-133 1994 Antonio Barrera Carbonell), la Haute Cour a déclaré que la peine consacré dans le Code pénal colombien est constitutionnelle. En un second, troisième et quatrième arrêt sur le même sujet (affaire C-013 1997 ME José Gregorio Hernández, C-647 2001 Alfredo Beltrán Sierra et C-198 ME 2002 Clara Inés Vargas), la Cour a confirmé ses précédentes position. Cependant, l'affaire C-355 2006 Jaime Araujo Renteria et Clara Inés Vargas, la Cour a décriminalisé l'avortement dans trois cas particuliers, en faisant valoir que les droits de la mère ne peuvent être sacrifiés pour la protection de la vie enfant à naître. Il est clair d'une nouvelle approche en termes de principes constitutionnels contre les droits reproductifs des femmes. Cette nouvelle interprétation constitutionnelle a été rejetée dans de nombreux conservateurs religieux et les Colombiens qui élèvent l'inviolabilité absolue du droit à la vie.

L'on se demande alors comment les juges peuvent aller contre le travail du législateur. Comment la volonté des représentants démocratiquement élus peut-elle ne pas être respectée par ceux qui n'ont pas été élus?

On pourrait répondre à ces questions en considérant plusieurs points:

- l'attachement profond de la Cour constitutionnelle à l'École de droit libre et le réalisme juridique.
- la jurisprudence des valeurs.
- la transformation de la justice constitutionnelle en en justice redistributive.
- le changement de paradigme juridique colombien.
- le nouveau concept de l'État constitutionnel.
- le nouvel ingrédient de l'État de droit.
- le rôle du juge dans la société

En réponse à ce problème, les États Unis et l'Europe propose la réserve judiciaire: que le tribunal lui-même s'auto-contrôle afin de ne pas s'excéder dans ses interprétations contraires à la loi et de respecter la volonté des pouvoirs publics.

Mais cette autodiscipline semble difficile à appliquer. En attendant de trouver des solutions à cette problématique, le gouvernement continue de préparer une réforme de la justice qui prévoit de diminuer le pouvoir de la Cour constitutionnelle et donc de supprimer le mécanisme par excellence de protection des droits fondamentaux: l'action de *tutela*.

De plus, il faudrait aussi élargir cet exposé et parler d'un nouveau protagoniste de cette dynamique juridico-constitutionnelle: la juridiction administrative et la procédure de l'action populaire qui semblent suivre le même chemin que la *tutela*.

BIBLIOGRAPHIE

AJA, ELISEO. *Las tensiones entre el Tribunal Constitucional y la Europa actual,*Editorial Ariel, Barcelona 1998.

BRUNET, PIERRE. "Le juge constitutionnel est-il un juge comme les autres? Reflexions methodologiques sur la justice constitutionnel," publié dans *La notion de justice constitutionnel,* Dalloz, Paris 2005.

GIRALDO ÁNGEL, JAIME. "El choque de trenes. Sobre los sistemas de interpretación jurídica en Colombia," publié dans http://www.tribunales.colpsic.org.co/documentos/Giraldo_CDT.pdf.

GOMEZ GARCIA, CARLOS FERNANDO. "Las Vías de Hecho como generadoras del *Choque de Trenes* en la jurisprudencia constitucional. (1992-2008)," publié dans http://criteriojuridico.puj.edu.co/.

GUSY, CHRISTOPH. Juge constitutionnel et "gardien de la constitution". Publicado en *La notion de justice constitutionnel,* Dalloz, Paris: 2005.

HENAO OROZCO, RUBÉN DARÍO. "Tutela contra sentencias de las altas Cortes o choque de vanidades," publié dans http://www.iidpc.org/pdf/ajr6HenaoOrozco.pdf.

KELSEN, HANS. *Teoría General del Derecho y del Estado* (trad. de García Maynez), UNAM, México:1979.

------------------- .*¿Quién debe ser el defensor de la constitución?,*Editorial Técnos, Madrid 1995

-------------------. "La garantía jurisdiccional de la Constitución,"dans *Escritos sobre democracia y socialismo,* Madrid 1988, p. 48.

LAMBERT, EDOUARD. *Le gouvernement des juges et la lutte contre la législation sociale aux Etats Unis, l'expérience américaine du contrôle judiciaire des lois,* M.Giard&Cie., Paris 1921.

LACHARRIERE, R. "Opinion disidente," publié dans *Pouvoir,* No. 13, 1980, dediée au Conseil Constitutionnel, pp. 133-135.

LÓPEZ DAZA, GERMÁN ALFONSO. *La justicia constitucional colombiana: ¿un gobierno de los jueces?,* Editorial Universidad Surcolombiana, Neiva 2005.

MARTINEZ CABALLERO, ALEJANDRO. "Tipos de sentencias en el control constitucional de las leyes: la experiencia colombiana," dans *Revista Estudios Socio Jurídicos.* Bogotá, Universidad del Rosario, vol. 2, No. 1, Bogotá 2000, p. 9.

MONROY CABRA, MARCO GERARDO. *La interpretación constitucional,* Librería del Profesional, Bogotá 2002.

OLANO GARCIA, HERNÁN ALEJANDRO, "Tipología de nuestras sentencias constitucionales," *Vniversitas,* Bogotá 2004.

Pérez Tremps, Pablo, *Tribunal Constitucional y Poder Judicial,* Centro de Estudios Constitucionales, Madrid 1985.

QUIROGA LEÓN, ANÍBAL. *Los excesos del Tribunal Constitucional Peruano: a propósito del control concentrado de la constitución,* Lima, p.11.

SAA VELAZCO, ERNESTO. "El gobierno de los jueces," publié dans *La constitución por construir. Balance de una década de cambio institucional,* Centro Editorial Universidad del Rosario, Bogotá 2001.

SOLANO GONZALEZ, EDGAR. *Sentencias manipulativas e interpretativas.* Tesis de grado, Universidad Externado de Colombia, Bogotá 2000.

TROPER, MICHEL. "Existe-t-il un concept de gouvernement de juges?," dans *Gouvernement des juges et démocratie,* Publications de la Sorbonne, Paris 2001.

JURISPRUDENCE

ARRETS DE LA COURT CONSTITUTIONNELLE COLOMBIENNE

-Sentencia T-406 de 1992 M.P. Ciro Angarita Barón

-Sentencia C-479 de 1992 M.P. José Gregorio Hernández Galindo y Alejandro Martínez Caballero

-Sentencia C-543 de 1992 M.P. José Gregorio Hernández Galindo

-Sentencia T-006 de 1992 M.P. Eduardo Cifuentes Muñoz

-Sentencia T-567 de 1992 M.P. Alejandro Martínez Caballero, Fabio Morón Díaz y José Gregorio Hernández.

-Sentencia T-217 de 1994 M.P. Alejandro Martinez Caballero

-Sentencia T-406 de 1992 M.P. Ciro Angarita Barón

-Sentencia C-027 de 1993 M.P. Simón Rodriguez Rodriguez.

-Sentencia C-221 de 1994 M.P. Carlos Gaviria Díaz.

-Sentencia C-239 de 1997 M.P. Carlos Gaviria Díaz.

-Sentencia SU-047 de 1999 M.P. Carlos Gaviria Díaz y Alejandro Martínez Caballero.

-Sentencia C-700 de 1999 M.P. José Gregorio Hernández Galindo.

-Sentencia 1433 de 2000 M.P. Antonio Barrera Carbonell.

-Sentencia C-426 de 2002 M.P. Rodrigo Escobar Gil

-Sentencia C-355 de 2006 M.P. Jaime Araujo Rentería y Clara Inés Vargas.

-Sentencia C-588 de 2009 M.P. Gabriel Eduardo Mendoza Martelo.

-Sentencia C-1433 de 2000 M.P. Dr. Antonio Barrera Carbonell

-Sentencia C-221 de 1997 M.P Alejandro Martínez Caballero

-Sentencia C-700 de 1999, M.P José Gregorio Hernández Galindo A.V. Alfredo Beltrán Sierra y José Gregorio Hernández Galindo. S.V. Vladimiro Naranjo Mesa y Eduardo Cifuentes Muñoz S.V. Álvaro Tafur Galvis;

-Sentencia C-442/01 M.P. Marco Gerardo Monroy Cabra Salvamentos Parciales de Voto de los Magistrados Jaime Araujo Rentería, Alfredo Beltrán Sierra, Eduardo Montealegre Lynnet y Álvaro Tafur Galvis;

-Sentencia C-500/01 M.P. Álvaro Tafur Galvis S.P.V. Jaime Araujo Rentería,

-Sentencia C-737/01 M.P. Eduardo Montealegre Lynnet S.V. Marco Gerardo Monroy Cabra Salvamentos Parciales de Voto de los Magistrados Jaime Araujo Rentería, Alfredo Beltrán Sierra, Álvaro Tafur Galvis, Clara Inés Vargas Hernández

-Sentencia C-754/04 M.P. Álvaro Tafur Galvis A.V. Jaime Araujo Rentería, S.P.V. y A.V. Manuel José Cepeda Espinosa, Rodrigo Escobar Gil y Rodrigo Uprimny Yepes, S.P.V. Álvaro Tafur Galvis

-Sentencias C-756/02 y C-245/02 M.P. M.P. Manuel José Cepeda Espinosa.

-Sentencia C-133 de 1994 M.P. Antonio Barrera Carbonell
-Sentencia C-013 de 1997 M.P. José Gregorio Hernández
-Sentencia C-647 de 2001 M.P. Alfredo Beltrán Sierra
-Sentencia C-198 de 2002 M.P. Clara Inés Vargas
-Sentencia 355 de 2006 M.P.Jaime Araujo Rentería y Clara Inés Vargas,
-Sentencia C-473/94 M.P. Alejandro Martínez Caballero
-Sentencia C-109/1995 M.P. Alejandro Martínez Caballero
-Sentencia C-477/1999 M.P. Carlos Gaviria Díaz
-Sentencia C-836/2001 M.P. Rodrigo Escobar Gil
-Sentencia C-620/01 M.P. Jaime Araujo Rentería
-Sentencia C-700/1999 M.P. José Gregorio Hernández Galindo

AUTOS DE LA COURT CONSTITUCIONNELLE COLOMBIENNE

Auto 311/01 M.P. Jaime Araujo Rentería.

COLOMBIA

THE COLOMBIAN CONSTITUTIONAL COURT: FROM INSTITUTIONAL LEADERSHIP, TO CONCEPTUAL AUDACITY

Sandra Morelli
Colombian Academy of Jurisprudence
Smorellirico99@gmail.com

I. PRELIMINARY CONSIDERATIONS

With regard to the risks and dysfunctions that could have derived from the recognition of the power of control and custody of the supremacy of the Constitution to a judicial body that would be responsible for issuing legal rulings regarding the constitutionality of the law, and whose most paradigmatic exponent was Hans Kelsen,[1] much had to be thought both by authors as well as by statesmen, responsible for its implementation. Put another way, the practice of the constitutional courts, with their excesses and shortcomings, should not surprise us or even result in abandonment of this institutional scheme to make way to schools of thought and political currents that consider the Constitution merely a political decision – yes, a fundamental one, according to Carl Schmit[2] – but, in consequence, dependent on the deciderata of the majority. The control of constitutionality is not, in that perspective, anything more than political power.[3]

1 Hans Kelsen, *Teoría de la constitución*, 1982.

2 *Teoría de la constitución*, Alianza Editorial, 1996.

3 Eduardo, García de Enterría, *La constitución como norma y el Tribunal constitucional*, Editorial Civitas 2006, Allan R. Brewer-Carías, *La justicia constitucional: procesos y procedimientos constitucionales*, Editorial Porrúa, 2007. These texts take into account the new essential elements of the controversy around the type of constitutional review. For a more philosophical point of view, see Hernández, Carlos Miguel, http://www.cepc.es/rap/publicaciones/revistas/3/REPNE_086_194:.pdf.

In the United States, the constituents of Philadelphia in 1787, having not decided on the control of constitutionality, did delve into the intangible character of the Constitution, which without a doubt is assumed to be the fundamental decision of the Federation. This was precisely what made it possible for Supreme Court Justice Marshall, in the case *Marbury v. Madison*, to rule that the Supreme Court was entitled to refrain from applying laws contrary to the constitutional text.

Judge Marshall's ruling was based on the principle of separation of powers, which endowed specific independence to the judicial power and limited the thereto absolute supremacy of the legislative branch to the Constitution, which he did with utmost skill in reasoning, which he exercised for more than three decades on the Court.[4]

It is important to point out that the *Marbury* decision established a distance from the French concept regarding the intangible character of the law, whose prevalence the French justified, and continue to justify, by virtue of the democratic origin of Parliament, source of all legitimacy. This explains why in the postrevolutionary period, the Napoleonic concept of the state posited that the judge should be limited to acting as a mere *bouche de la loi*, and why they chose, afterward, a form of previous constitutional control: a constitutional council that is a part of Parliament.

The foregoing does not mean that it can be ignored that the Conseil Constitutionnel was homologated, in its scope, which is far from timid, to the decisions made by any European constitutional court and more specifically by the German, Italian, or Spanish courts.[5]

The truth is that, today, in the Western world there is a tendency to give prevalence to legal and judicial control exercise by constitutional courts in order to ensure the supremacy of the constitution. The origin of this trend is only indirectly political, so that its legitimacy is not, strictly speaking, democratic. This derives from the position of constitucional courts within the state's institutional context, sometimes wrongly called supraconstitutional,[6] which means that they are above the other powers but not above the constitution and its *autoritas*, thanks to the qualities of the members of such courts and their actions.

4 We cannot ignore the political origin of Judge Marshall, his role in the Constituent Assembly in Philadelphia, his role as Secretary of State, and even his previous direct involvement in the matter, which later would need to be resolved to appoint some justices or not.

5 Louis Favoreau, *Le grandes decisions de Conseil Constitutionnel*, Dalloz, Paris 1975.

6 The case of the Italian doctrine, verbigratia Giuseppe de Vergottini, *Diritto Constituzionale Comparato*, CEDAM, 1990.

Therefore, in recent history, since the advent of the state founded on a basic juridical norm, the Constitution, in force in Colombia and Venezuela since the nineteenth century,[7] we can hardly be surprised by what is happening in a more or less widespread manner as a result of the decisions of courts or of the constitutional tribunals. The control of the supremacy of the Constitution by a judicial body leaves vast spaces open to interpretation and ultimately converts justices into the owners of the Constitution – as said by Pier Paolo Portinaro[8] – which raises two questions. First, Is this appropriation healthy for the constitutional state? As the answer is necessarily negative, the second is, Is there a way to exercise proper control of constitutionality without appropriating abusively the constitution for oneself? In theory, yes.[9]

To state the obvious, particularly for scholars of juridical-constitutional matters, the appropriation of the Constitution by the court is not desirable. This is not because of the decline of the democratic principle as a result of the court invading the sphere of the legislature, and at times other organs, but because it constitutes a noxious concentration of power, whether casual and fragmentary, in connection with a specific decision, that conflicts with the pillars of a constitutional state and opens the door to the irresponsible judicial totalitarianism.[10]

Under the aegis of the peremptoriness of what has been said, and from the perspective of utmost ethical-conceptual communion with the model of control of constitutionality of judicial origin and method, and precisely not to create an irreversible gap among the concept, the idea, the paradigm, and the reality, the academic community continues with the task of honest reflection around those decisions of the Constitutional Court in Colombia, which over nearly two decades of existence of the corporation should not have been issued as they were, since its legitimacy could be undermined. And even many times, with scorn and malice, there are persons who consider that the

[7] Both in Colombia and Venezuela, and without getting into dispute as to which country was the pioneer, as this is irrelevant, the truth is the practice and culture of the supremacy of the constitution, assumed as a joint norm, it existed in these countries since the nineteenth century and was respected, as the civil codes already established that in every case of incompatibility between the constitution and the law, the procedure should be the nonapplicability of the respective law.

[8] *Realismo político*, Editorial Nueva Visión, 20.

[9] Sandra Morelli, *La Corte Constitucional Colombiana: un legislador complementario*, Bogotá, Universidad Externado de Colombia, 2006, see Final considerations.

[10] See Sandra Morelli, *La Corte Constitucional: Un papel por definir*, Best Book of Law, Chamber of the Book, Colombia, 2002, Colombian Academy of Jurisprudence.

power by mandates of efficiency, should be exercised free of controls, all considered superbly illegitimate hurdles.

From this perspective, we will now examine only two decisions of the Colombian Constitutional Court that show a well-established jurisprudential trend, the permanence of which is more or less predictable, to the detriment of the Constitution itself on several of its cardinal points: the separation of powers; the limitation of powers of the constitutional judge; and the substitution, this really one a serious matter, of the absolute nature of human or fundamental rights. This happens when they enter the constitutional legal order of a country by means of statistical tables, through which, when they, acquire the position of a constitutional mandate or of the relevant statutory law, the effectiveness, validity and inviolability of rights becomes a statistical matter, relative and predictable; not of the human being as an individual, endowed with an area of law insurmountable by any sovereign power, but as an imperative to formulate a public policy that in the opinion of the justices of the Court is reasonably and is executed in accordance with the indicators of administrative efficiency.

The other decision that even today cannot be doomed in its real content in the absence of even the text of the decision, even though there is the ruling, or put in a more accurate fashion with the real events, the press release, in what concerns the declared unconstitutionality by which a referendum was called with the intention of making possible a second reelection of President Álvaro Uribe.

II. DISPLACEMENT IN COLOMBIA

One of the biggest problems encountered by the Colombian population in rural areas is forced displacement, which has occurred in recent decades as a result of guerrilla and paramilitary violence.

To the atrocity of the aggression, the victims of violence have been subjected to vexatious situations as a result of the indifference or inefficiency of the state to address their most basic needs, which affects the scope of their fundamental rights. And the law of displaced people, No. 387 of 1997, seems dead letter, as well as the *Acción de Cumplimiento* (Enforcement Action) established in the Constitution and conceived of precisely to enforce the application of the laws.[11]

[11] Article 87 of the Constitution and Law 397 of 1997.

That is why, the actions of *tutela*,[12] in very great numbers, have been the means invoked by these people to ensure that the civil servants of the public administration fulfill their responsibilities.

The Constitutional Court, facing the contempt of its mandates, resorted to a method to obtain the efficacy of the social state of law, which it had previously applied and whose foundation was in what the Court itself already had called the unconstitutional state of affairs.

This situation derives from the concentrated functions in the head of the body responsible for protecting the supremacy of the Constitution, and consequently the guardian of the efficacy of the legal order.

The legal community has made few comments with respect to the unconstitutional state of affairs, and it is surprising that constitutional tribunals like the Peruvian one have appropriated the dossiers for themselves after praising Colombia's conceptual audacity.[13]

1. *What Is the Unconstitutional State of Affairs?*

An Unconstitutional State of Affairs is a legal creation of the Constitutional Court itself, by virtue of which the aforementioned corporation has occasion to exercise the faculty of guarding over the supremacy of the Constitution in a concrete case through the the action of *tutela* of a fundamental right: "Sentence T 025 of 2004 and Procedural decisions 177 of 2005, 218 and 266 of 2006 and 052 of 2008. Coordination of the public policies of attention by the territorial entities to the displaced population thru the territorial entities," of January 26. By this, the Constitutional Court resolved the following:

> First. – TO ORDER THAT via General Secretariat to remit to the Interior and Justice Ministry both the reports sent to the different territorial entities to this Corporation, in response to the Procedural decision 052 of 2008, and the Report of the analysis of answers of the territorial entities to the Procedural decision 052 of 2008, elaborated for the Center of Socio-juridical Investigations of the University of the Andes, with the purpose that the Interior and Justice Ministry, in carrying out its functions, coordinate

12 Defined as, according to the article 86 of the Constitution, the action that every person has to protect his fundamental constitutional rights when are being violated or when there is a menace of violation from an authority, and exceptionally, from an single individual, so that it ceases such conduct and opts for corrective measures, as long as there is no other means of defense, which is why it is considered a subsidiary mechanism.

13 See Exp. nº 3149-2004-ac/tc, Lambayeque, Sentence of the Constitutional Tribunal, Lima, January 20, 2005, Second Chamber of the Constitutional Tribunal.

effectively the policies of attention to the displaced population with the different territorial entities, notwithstanding the coordination competitions that by virtue of the Law 1190 of 2008 correspond to The Presidential agency for the Social Action and the International Cooperation, and to he National Department of Planning, as well as to the National Council for the Integral Attention to the Displaced Population by Violence " CNAIPD..

Second. – TO DETERMINE that, notwithstanding the mechanism of coordination established in the Law 1190 of 2008, from now on the Interior and Justice Minister will have to directly exert, in what corresponds to him according to the reforms introduced to such law, the coordination between the National Government and the territorial entities and the other functions that this entity has under its responsibilities on the subject of forced displacement.

Third. – TO ORDER to the National Council for the Integral Attention of the Displaced population CNAIPD and, therefore, to the heads of the public entities that integrate it, that, in application of the effective norms on material distribution of competitions and the ordained by the sentence T 025 of 2004 and the follow-up Procedural decisions, to collaborate and support the territorial entities in order to pay attention efficiently and efficaciously to the displaced population. In those municipalities that on account of their precarious institutional capacity cannot take care of the displaced population, the entities which composed the aforementioned Council will have to apply the constitutional principle of subsidiarity to guarantee the effective satisfaction of the rights of the displaced population.

Fourth. – TO ORDER the Interior and Justice Minister that (i) he orders that the present Procedural decision be communicated immediately to all territorial entities by the means at his disposal and, later on, (ii) to send to the Constitutional Court, before March 02, 2009, a document in which they indicate the municipalities that require more support in order to pay attention efficiently and efficaciously to the displaced population, indicating why they are high-priority in the matter of forced displacement.

Fifth. – TO ORDER all the departmental governors and district and municipal mayors who, in carrying out their functions, within their respective jurisdiction fulfilled adequately their functions on the subject of attention to the displaced population and collaborate decidedly with the National Government in the definition and execution of mechanisms that will enable to guarantee the effective enjoyment of the rights of the displaced population and to surpass the situation of unconstitutional affairs.

Sixth. – TO ORDER the mayors and governors that the Interior and Justice Minister had considered priority on the subject of attention to the displaced population that, at the latest the April 15, 2009, and later on every year, present a report to the National Council for the Integral Attention of the Displaced population by Violence in which they indicate what commitments they can assume to guarantee the effective enjoyment of the rights of the displaced population, and in case they do not have the budgetary or administrative capacity, to indicate the difficulties that they present to take care of the displaced population, taking in considerations the procedural decisions of the sentence T 025 of 2004 and the subjects enunciated in article 4 of Law 1190 of 2008.

Seventh. – TO ORDER the National Council for the Integral Attention of the Displaced Population by Violence that, before June 1, 2009, to design a policy that will enable to involve and compromise the territorial entities in the overcoming of the situation of unconstitutional affairs and in securing the effective enjoyment of the rights of the displaced population effectively. Said politics will have to be formalized by means of an administrative act.

Eighth. – TO ORDER the responsible authorities to incude the subjecto of the involvement and commitment of the territorial entities in the attention of the displaced population in the audience of rendition of accounts, foreseen in the paragraph as 2 of article 3 of the Law 1190 of 2008, in which the advances on the subject of effective enjoyment of the rights of the displaced population will show up. Ad hoc they will have to take into account the reports ordered in the numeral previous.

Ninth. – TO ORDER the National Council for the Integral Attention of the Displaced Population by Violence that, from the reports sent by the territorial entities as indicated by the Law 1190 of 2008 and the reports ordered in the numeral seventh of the resolutory part of the present providence, to use the legal tools within reach of any of the entities that conform the aforementioned Council to assure the commitment of the territorial entities with the adoption of decisions oriented to assure the effective enjoyment of the rights of the displaced population in their respective territorial span.

Tenth. – TO ORDER the National Council for the Integral Attention of the Displaced Population by Violence that from April 1, 2010, to send, with respect to each high-priority territorial entity, a certificate regarding the sufficiency or insufficiency of the contribution of each one to the overcoming of the situation of unconstitutional affairs. By means of this mechanism the CNAIPD will be able to certify to those territorial entities whose actions contribute to the advancement in the effective enjoyment of the rights of the displaced population and to the overcoming of the difficulties in the institutional capacity and the budgetary effort, and likewise, it will be able to decertify those that delay unwarrantedly in the fulfillment of their responsibilities. The aforementioned certificate (i) will have to be based in objective criteria previously communicated to the high-priority territorial entities, (ii) it will be of public knowledge, (iii) it will indicate the conditions that the respective territorial entity must fulfilled in order to continue receiving resources and in general, the support of the Government regarding the effective enjoyment of the rights of the displaced population and (iv) it will have to be sent with the periodicity that the Council itself determines.

> Eleventh. – TO ORDER the National Council for the Integral Attention of the Displaced Population by Violence, pursuant to the ordered in article 2 of the Law 1190 of 2008, that when soliciting the budgetary information to the territorial entities, it establishes a procedure that will allow to make a fiscal follow-up of the local budgets destined to the programs of attention of the displaced population, disaggregated by sections, accounts, and executers, just as should be done by organizations of the national order.
>
> Twelfth. – TO ORDER the director of the Presidential Agency for Social Action and International Cooperation to the Constitutional Court on the application of the indicators of effective enjoyment of rights of the displaced persons, must contain a chapter disclosing the information distinguishing the situation territorially regarding the situation related to the effective enjoyment of rights.
>
> Thirteenth. – TO COMMUNICATE this Order to the Norwegian Refugee Council to adopt the decisions it deems appropriate to monitor compliance with this Procedural decision. . . .

This procedural decision, that the corporation issued by virtue of the conviction, lacking any constitutional or legal basis, that the breach of a decision of *tutela* or several in the same direction, relating to several subjects but with the same facts, uttered by that court, repeatedly and systematically, and by virtue of the state of unconstitutional affairs that it creates, must replace the judge responsible for reporting and dealing with contempt, and assume the role of permanent supreme administrative authority, to overcome such situation.

In this respect, Sentence T-025/04 asserted:

> Among the factors assessed by the Court to determine whether there exist an unconstitutional state of affairs [include the following: (i) the massive and widespread infringement of various constitutional rights affecting a significant number of people; the prolonged omission of the authorities in the fulfillment of its obligation to guarantee the rights; (iii) the adoption of unconstitutional practices, such as incorporating the action of as part of the procedure to ensure the right violated, (iv) the failure to issue legislative, administrative or budgetary measures to avoid infringement of rights, the existence of a social problem whose solution compromises the involvement of several entities, requires the adoption of complex and coordinated actions and demands [a] level of resources requiring important additional budgetary effort; (vi) if all people affected by the same problem would resort to the action of *tutela* for the protection of their rights, there would be greater judicial congestion.

It also added:

> Several factors confirm the existence of a state of unconstitutional affairs on the situation of the population internally displaced. First of all, the gravity of the situation of infringement of rights faced by the displaced population was expressly recognized by the legislator when defining displaced status, and emphasizing the mass violation of rights. Secondly, another element that confirms the existence an unconstitutional state of affairs in the matter of forced displacement, is the high volume of actions of *tutela* filed by displaced persons to obtain various subsidies and the increase of them. Thirdly, the cumulative cases in the present action of *tutela* confirms that unconstitutional state of affairs and indicate that the violation of rights affects much of the displaced population in many parts of the country and that the authorities have failed to take required corrective measures. Fourth, the continuing violation of those rights is not attributable to a single entity. Fifth, the violation of rights of [internal displaced persons] is based on structural factors set out in paragraph 6 of this Order[,] within which stands out the lack of correspondence between what the rules say and the means to fulfill them, aspect that acquires a special dimension when appraising the inadequate resources facing the evolution of the problem of displacement taking into consideration the magnitude of the problem confronting the institutional capacity to respond timely and effectively to it. In conclusion, the Court would formally declare[] the existence of an unconstitutional state of affairs concerning living conditions of internally displaced populations. Therefore, both the national and the territorial authorities within the orbit of its powers, shall adopt corrective measures to overcome this state of affairs.

It is thus, in consequence, that from the concrete protection of the supremacy of the constitution with respect to fundamental rights, the Court jumps to a general protection of fundamental rights, whose specific guarantee seems to fade into the ocean of rights whose satisfaction it is intended that the State assume. It should be noted that the vast majority of the rights are those of social content, whose satisfaction does not depend, in general, of the action or omission of a unique authority.

So, the Constitutional Court, facing noncompliance with its decisions and the inhuman situation of displaced populations, chooses to make use of each and every one of the provisions of the Constitution, which contains principles, values, duties, obligations, and organic and functional distributions of competence, to try to resolve the unconstitutional state of affairs.

Thus, for example, Sentence T-025/04 mentions the following:

> The authorities are obliged by the means they deem necessary, to correct, the visible social inequalities, to facilitate the inclusion and participation of weak, marginalized and vulnerable sectors of the population in the economic and social life of the nation, and to encourage a gradual improvement in the conditions of existence of the poorest sectors of society.
>
> Two kinds of duties are imposed to the State. On the one hand, it must adopt and implement policies, programs or affirmative actions to achieve true equality of conditions and opportunities among the associates, and in doing so comply with its constitutional obligations of progressively fulfilling the economic, social and cultural rights of the population, implementing what has been termed in constitutional jurisprudence "the Clause for the eradication of the present injustices." And, on the other hand, it should refrain from advancing, promoting, and implementing policies, programs or measures ostensibly regressive, in matters of economic, social and cultural rights, leading clearly and directly to an aggravation of the situation of injustice, exclusion or marginalization which it is intended to correct, without preventing gradual and progressive progress towards the full satisfaction of such rights.

And it adds:

> The adoption of measures in favor of the marginalized groups does not constitute an exclusive competence of the legislature, but itis a mandate for action, aimed at transforming the material conditions which cause or perpetuate exclusion and social injustice. This duty of the state, although it needs to be developed by the law, and it is tied to respective budget appropriations, cannot be indefinitely postponed in the state agenda.

After reading those paragraphs, it is interesting just how the Constitutional Court begins by giving great strength to the constitutional provisions to the extent that it seems that validity and effectiveness where the only characterization of the legal order. But soon afterward, the discourse begins its rapid descent to remember the need to forecast budget allocations for the sake of the constitutional mandates. However, until now, the Court limits itself, as in the past, to remember that the legislature has to adopt measures to ensure that budget allocations in order for the actual situation to be corrected; it does not give an order, and in that sense, it does not invade the sphere of competence of the legislature, which cannot be postponed indefinitely in time. And here, begins to be noticeable the prudent bias that the constitutional judge starts to have in its institutional role..

By declaring what the Court has called an unconstitutional state of affairs, it has abandoned its role as guarantor of the fundamental constitutional rights of an individual in a particular case, in order to assume another different role, that of formulating or contributing to the formulation of public policies and of assuring its implementation and control of its execution. A role that tend to guarantee the satisfaction of needs of displaced populations according to available resources and subject to compliance with procedural requirements that the Court is responsible for organizing.

In the sections transcribed here, which correspond to the ones that the rapporteur of the Court wanted to call attention to, the main core of the fundamental constitutional rights that the Court should protect with actions of *tutela* regarding each individual becomes clear. It is limited to an enumeration of examples, which looks more like a reminder to authorities, something more like a catalog of good conduct that is general and abstract than a constitutional imperative.

The Court, by contrast, focuses all its attention on establishing a framework for coordinated action so that the various authorities at the national and local levels, after formulating an appropriate policy for the reinserted displaced, could proceeds with its implementation to ensure the suitable provision of certain goods and services that are not necessarily in direct relationship with the core of the fundamental rights of the interested people, which led them to initiate actions of *tutela*.

Each and every one of the measures taken by the Court is characterized by reasonableness and relevance but has nothing to do with the role of the Constitutional Judge, who commendably wants to effectively direct all constitutional requirements, including those rights relating to employment and performance, for the sake of reaching the social state of law, which goes beyond the effective protection of fundamental constitutional rights of individuals and takes over responsibilities of the legislature and of the public administration. Obviously, in that capacity, the Constitutional Judge assumes both the budgetary and the administrative actions of the Colombian state in such a way that its simple role is to give peremptory orders that for example, in twenty-four hours health care must be provided to a young displaced person who requires surgery, but without establishing programs to determine the scope of the actual availability of resources,

> By way of insufficient budget appropriation and the failure to correct major weaknesses of institutional capacity, the progressive advance in the satisfaction of the rights of the displaced population has not only been delayed, but has been deteriorating over time in some respects. This decline is, prima facie, contrary to the constitutional mandate to guarantee the effective enjoyment of the rights of all IDPs Therefore, the first duty of the competent authorities is to avoid [such a] practical setback in the aspects relating to the level of protection of the rights of all displaced, where it has been found, and such decline might be the result of the evolution of the problem and of factors beyond the will of the responsible public servants.

And the Court continues:

> Given the current magnitude of the problem of displacement in Colombia, as well as the limited nature of the resources available to the State to meet this goal, one must accept that when designing and implementing a specific public policy to protect the displaced population, the competent authorities should carry out a balancing exercise and establishment of priority areas which will provide timely and effective care to these people Therefore, not always it will be possible to satisfy, in a concomitantly way to the maximum possible level, the benefit-rendering dimensions of all the constitutional rights of all displaced people, given the material constraints and the actual dimensions of the evolution of the phenomenon of displacement.

So the country has pass from an utopian Constitutional Court, which, in the world of benefit rights, tried to transmute its sentences into blank checks – in order to overcome the finite and insufficient resources of the Colombian state[14] – into a seemingly high-rhetoric Constitutional Court, although in reality, a reductionist one, limiting the absolute nature of fundamental rights, to the point that its discourse, the Court deliberately confused them with constitutional rights.

The descent of the Court places it in the role of the friendly companion of the national government, because having assumed the budgetary constraints and institutional underdevelopment, the Court not only transmuted and conflated fundamental rights with other constitutional rights but also replaced them with satisfactory compliance standards.

It is in this way, how the catalog of fundamental rights is guided by a study done by a superb Colombian university, indeed the same as the rapporteur's of the ruling, whose management indicators are to be satisfied.

Consider, then, the historic betrayal of the Colombian Constitutional Court when, instead of protecting each internally displaced person who had filed an action of *tutela* regarding fundamental rights, even by way of guarantee of the right to equality, it ventures into the strange category of the unconstitutional state of affairs, and without any need to bring an action of *tutela*, as stated, acts as a supreme administrative authority:

> There are certain minimum rights of the displaced population to be satisfied in all circumstances by the authorities to IDPs (internally displaced

[14] Sandra Morelli, *La Corte Constitucional: un papel por definir*, *op. cit.*

persons), since on this ground is played the decent livelihoods of people in this situation.

In order to define the minimum level of satisfaction of the constitutional rights of the displaced persons, a distinction should be made between (a) the respect for the essential core of fundamental constitutional rights of the IDPs, and (b) the satisfaction, on the part of the authorities, of certain benefit duties derived from the rights recognized at international and constitutional levels on the head of the IDPs. As refers to the former, it is clear that the authorities can never act in such a way as to injure or threaten the core of fundamental constitutional rights of the displaced persons. To that extent, the IDPs cannot be liable to prosecution by the authorities that attempt, for example, against their personal integrity or their freedom of expression. Regarding the latter, the Chamber notes that most of the rights recognized to IDPs by international norms and the Constitution imposed on the authorities, by the circumstances in which the IDPs find themselves, clear obligations of benefit character, which necessarily involve public expenditure. It is there, in the preservation of basic conditions that allow them to survive with dignity, where it should be drawn a clear boundary between state obligations of imperative and urgent compliance against the displaced population, and those which, although they have to be met, do not have the same priority.

In this case, the Chamber will give two types of orders. Some orders of complete execution, related to the unconstitutional state of affairs and aimed at guaranteeing the rights of all the displaced population, regardless of whether they have come to the tutela to protect their rights. Such orders aim to ensure that the agencies responsible for addressing the displaced people establish, within a reasonable time and within the orbit of its powers, the necessary corrective to overcome the problems of insufficient resources and precarious institutional capacity to implement state policy attention to the displaced population. The simple character commands which will also be conducted in this process are designed to answer specific requests of the actors in the present case of tutela, and result compatible with the line of decisions of the Constitutional Court for the constitutional protection of the rights of the population in situation of displacement.

As for the necessary orders to overcome the massive and continued breach of rights of the IDPs originated in structural factors, the Court will declare the existence of an unconstitutional state of affairs and notified the responsible authorities in the field, to adopt, within the orbit their competences and within a reasonable time, the remedies that are necessary. These orders are aimed to adopt decisions which allow to overcome both the inadequacy of resources, as the weaknesses in the institutional capacity. Since the National Council of Integral Attention to the IDPs is the body responsible for policymaking and to ensure budget allocation for the programs of attention for the displaced population, the Chamber will communicate the unconstitutional state of affairs so that this instance be the one to determine the way to overcome the inefficiency of resources and

> weaknesses in institutional capacity. The National Council for Integral Attention to the Displaced Population should, within a maximum of six months counted from the receipt of the above communication, must complete the actions aimed at ensuring that all displaced persons actually enjoy effectively the minimum protection of their rights.
>
> When the different authorities receive a request from an IDP, in which he claims protection of one of its rights, the competent authority shall: (1) incorporate him in the list of displaced petitioners[;] (2) inform the internally displaced that before the end of 15 days maximum time within which he will receive response to his request[;] (3) inform him within a period of 15 days if the application meets the requirements for processing, and if otherwise, to indicate to him clearly how he can correct it so that it can have access to assistance programs; (4) if the application meets the requirements, but there is no budget availability, will advance the steps necessary to obtain the resources, determine the priorities and the order in which they settled; (5) if the application meets the requirements and there is sufficient budget availability, he will be informed when it will become effective the benefit and the procedure shall continue to receive it effectively. In any case, he should refrain from asking for an injunction ruling to fulfill their legal duties respect of the fundamental rights of the IDPs.
>
> The action of tutela cannot be used to alter the order in which aid is delivered, nor to ignore the rights of other displaced persons who did not resort to an tutela and, are in equality of conditions, pending a response by the entity.[15]

One of the thorniest issues, no doubt, is that the Court may act .The world's constitutional courts have the responsibility to create and preserve their own legitimacy, for which they have to know how to preserve the right balance between public powers and their role as guarantors of constitutional order. So, self-control emerges as the only possibility for this important body not usurping the powers and faculties that correspond to other bodies.

However, the parameters of self-control are closely related to the specific technique of constitutional interpretation. That is why, authors have referred like Javier Pérez Royo in his book *Curso de derecho constitucional*, to the proscription of any *ex officio* action by the constitutional courts, explaining that the justification of the constitutional court is based principally on the characteristics of its own organization and operation, and of the procedure through which it operates. It is a body that cannot intervene automatically but must do so *ex parte* and in a very controlled manner both politically and

[15] T-653010 del 2004.

judicially: its skills are listed and rated; its decisions always refer to individual cases and are therefore timely decisions; the procedure by which the constitutional court obtains information and then processes and determines a sentence severely limits the scope of its decision, as it may adversely restrict legislature but cannot replace it positively; and so on. Using the words of Bergasse in the Constituent Assembly of the French Revolution, we might say that the constitutional court is justified as an institution devoid of any activity against the state's political system and not having any influence over the minds who make or maintain such regime, it has in order to protect all individuals and all rights, a force that, being all-powerful to defend and help, it will be absolutely null as soon as its purpose changes, trying to use it to oppress. Without a doubt, it is its low hazard as an instrument of oppression, where lies the most convincing justification of the constitutional court in a democratic state.[16]

However, the Colombian Constitutional Court, for the sake of overcoming the unconstitutional state of affairs, – an unfortunate expression because things are not unconstitutional or constitutional, they simply are – has made its own functions and responsibilities those of the executive and the legislature, a fact that is reprehensible *per se*. The Constitutional Court must also respect the principle of separation of powers and the exhaustive nature of those powers. In other words, the Constitutional Court is also subject to the Constitution.

However, in the past, the Court had used the same figure to overcome the unconstitutional state of affairs, but at that time, unlike now, it had not lost its orientation regarding for instance the protection of the fundamental constitutional rights of prison inmates.

On this occasion, it usurps competences, infringes on the principle of separation of powers, and stands as a mere body of internal control of the Administration. And this, thanks to the substitution of the traditional decisions by which peremptory orders of *tutela* effective for the protection of fundamental rights within forty-eight hours, provoking contempt, by decisions in which the Court stands as the supreme administrative authority and as such, helps the ordinary administration in the care of the victims of displacement to guarantee respect of the procedures and adequate satisfaction of benefits that state programs have planned.

This new Court has not given up the abusive exercise of its competencies; but it has lost the zeal with which initially it wanted to ensure the

16 Javier Pérez Royo, *Curso de Derecho constitucional*, Marcial Ponds, Madrid 2003, pp. 166–167.

effectiveness of rights, to the point that in good time, it abandon any abusive and fragmentary disposition of any provision of the national budget, but descends into a pragmatism such that if it continues along this path, itsr existence within the states rather than moot, would adversely affect the inviolability of fundamental rights.

What is expected of a court, then? To keep on the path for which it was created, the protection of fundamental rights, it has to venture into the world of benefit rights and ensure the supremacy of the Constitution through the exercise of constitutional control in the abstract.

Informal proceedings to do what other bodies should do, or actually do, disjoint and unbalance the institutional order. The Court appears likely to abuse its power, which makes moot its very existence.

III. THE CONSTITUTIONAL CONTROL OF LAWS.

1. *Warning*

When this report was written, more than two months had passed after the Colombian Constitutional Court informed, in the communiqué transcribed here, of its decision on Law 1,354 of 2009[17] through which a constitutional referendum was called, that would allow the President of the republic to be reelected a second time. At that time the full text of the decision was not yet available, which reveals that the Court did not practice the best procedure, as the unavailability reduces the transparency and credibility of the Court.[18]

However, from the material available, we have made some notes, but it is important to note that they are preliminary. The text of the press release[19] is as follows:

Through which it was decided on the constitutionality of Law 1,354 of 2009, summoning to a constitutional referendum.

1. Text of the law under review:

Law 1,354 of 2009

(September 8)

[17] Law of September 8, 2009. See in *Diario Oficial* nº 47.466 of September 8, 2009

[18] The full text of the decision was later published in 2011. See in http://www.corteconstitucional.gov.co/relatoria/2010/c-141-10.htm.

[19] See *Comunicado* nº 9, February 26, 2010, in http://www.corteconstitucional.com.

Through which a constitutional referendum is submitted to the people for a proposed constitutional reform.

THE CONGRESS OF COLOMBIA DECREES:

Article 1. The 1st paragraph of Article 197 of the Constitution shall be as follows:

"Whoever is elected as President of the Republic for two constitutional terms, may be elected for another term only."

Do you approve the previous statement.

Yes: ( )

No: ( )

Blank ballots: ( )

Article 2. This Law shall be effective as of the date of its promulgation.

2. *Basis of the decision.*

2.1. *Constitutional control: the scope of jurisdiction and parameter of control.*

The exercise of the functions of guarding the integrity and supremacy of the Political Constitution corresponds to the Constitutional Court, making the automatic control of a law by calling a constitutional referendum in accordance with the indicated in paragraph 2 of Article 241 of the Political Constitution.

In addressing the constitutionality of Law 1,354 of 2009, the Constitutional Court points out the extent of its competence, which refers to the study of both the procedure of creation of the legal rule in Congress, as well as the process of legislative citizen initiative. Thus, the regulatory setting for the exercise of constitutional review is made by the constitutional provisions, Law 134 of 1994 (Statutory Law – Mechanisms for Citizen Participation), Law 130 of 1994 (Statutory Law – on political parties and movements) and functional regulatory laws in the legislative process (Law 5 of 1992).

Additionally, the Constitutional Court reiterates its jurisprudence regarding the limits of power to reform the Constitution, insisting that the constituent power derivative has the power to amend the Constitution, not to replace it, so any changes in the identity of the constitutional text involves a competition for excess in the exercise of reform.

2.2. *Democratic principle and forms.*

Among the various elements that make up any democracy is respect for the formal procedures provided for the exercise of mechanisms of citizen participation. For the Constitutional Court, rather than mere rituals, such forms are set up in guarantee of the fundamental rules of representative democracy and participation and are essential components of democratic principles.

2.3. Vices in the processing of the legislative initiative of citizens.

In examining the process of the citizens' initiative that led to the Law 1354 of September 20, the Constitutional Court verified the occurrence of a number of irregularities related to the financing of the campaign for constitutional reform initiative. Such abnormalities, seen together, constitute a serious violation of basic principles of a democratic system, namely: transparency and political pluralism enshrined in Articles 1, 155, 374 [of the] Constitution and Articles 24, 27, 97 and 98 of Law 134 of 1994.

(i) First of all, an outside organization to the initiative – the Association Colombia First – carried on its own deals as a committee of advocates ignoring the statutory mandates of the legislature, and ultimately, the constitutional principles. Since the formation of a promoters Committee itself, the Association was responsible for two fundamental tasks in managing the campaign for the referendum: (i) accounting and (ii) the "management of the funds." Based on such imprecise tasks, the Association Colombia First raised and managed major economic contributions to fund-raising campaign to support a public referendum, resources that were transferred to the Committee of Promoters by mutual agreement. It is evident the existence of unity of management and administrative procedures, between the Committee of Promoters of the legislative initiative of citizens and the Association Colombia First, relevant data when considering the transparency of the process of campaign financing of obtaining public support, and of course, the violation of the Statutory Law of Mechanisms for Participation and the Political Constitution. It was concluded therefore that the Committee of Promoters of the initiative made use of an outside association, that was always controlled, to advance work that according to the law were its own, in particular those relating to campaign financing for collection of leading citizens support of the process of constitutional reform.

(ii) It was also established that during the campaign for the legislative initiative of citizens that led to the Law 1,354 of 2009, the Committee of Advocates spent a lump sum more than six (6) times the amount authorized by the National Electoral Council; to that it might be added that it received individual contributions almost thirty (30) times higher than what is allowed, contributions that were made to a non-authorized organization by the statutory legislature, such as the Association Colombia First. These actions also constitute a violation of the mandates of the Statute Law of Participative Mechanisms (Articles 97 and 98), violated the constitutional principle of transparency, since all the action was intended to circumvent the statutory and constitutional mandates, as well as the constitutional principle of pluralism, allowing it to have disproportionate resources to benefit or favor the proposal to convene a constitutional reform.

2.4. Vices in the legislative process.

(i) These vices that occurred during the citizens' initiative in turn had an implication on the legislative procedure as the proceedings before the Congress of the Republic of the Law 1,354 of 2009 began without attaching certification of the National Registrar of the Civil State provided in Article 27 of the Statute Law on Mechanisms of Participation in compliance with the requirements for the implementation of mechanisms for citizen participation, among others, compliance with global and individual ceilings for funding. The absence of such certification inhibits initiation of the legislative process and vitiates the constitutionality of the entire procedure carried on in Congress.

(ii) A second vice in the legislative process involves the modification of the original text of the draft bill backed by the citizens' initiative supported by 14.59% of the electorate, which took place during the third debate, in the First Permanent Constitutional Committee of the Senate. This change involved the possibility of proposing to the people the second consecutive immediate reelection, while the original text related to a mediate reelection or by interchange periods. The Court considered that with a modification of this magnitude, Congress – constitutionally deprived of legislative initiative on constitutional referenda – exceeded the limitations that the principle of participatory democracy imposes on the legislative function that arises from the citizens' initiative, which is a vice of unconstitutionality of the Law 1,354 of 2009. This introduced a substantial change to the project but failed to turn the principle of identity and of follow up in the legislative process, as it was presented after the debates before the House of Representatives so that the text finally adopted was subjected to only two debates, the one done in the First Commission and in the plenary of the Senate. As a consequence of this, it was not possible to refer the disagreements between the texts approved by each chamber to the Conciliation Commission, internal body that has no power to replace any of the established rules for the implementation of the four debates.

(iii) An analysis of the factual circumstances related to the publication of Decree 4,742 of 2008, by which Congress was convened in extraordinary session, shows that the plenary of the House of Representatives met when the Decree had not yet been published in the Official Journal. In this scenario, the Court concludes that Congress, and specifically the House of Representatives, at 00:05 am on December 17, 2009, had no legal grounds to authorize its meeting in special session. In fact, this support was only present at 18h:20m of December 17, 2009, when it completed the process of elaboration of the Official Journal.

(iv) The Court finds that to the string of irregularities which are unconstitutional vice, is added the Law that five representatives of the Cambio Radical party voted against internal policies underwritten and approved by them This situation tends to ignore Article 108, a norm with direct legal effectiveness mandating that members of the Public

Corporations elected by the same political party or movement will act within them as benches (bancadas). Regardless of the subjective considerations of due process, to be observed, from an objective dimension on the political rationality of Congress, the consequence of direct infringement of the Constitution generates the invalidation of the votes proffered against the express constitutional provision. Thus, a change of party, under the specific conditions and as part of a chain of vices and irregularities that took place cannot be a tool to ignore the Constitution in the terms of not only Article 108, but also of Article 133.

(v) In relation to the potential jurisdictional vices or excesses in the exercise of the power of constitutional reform, the Court recounted the jurisprudential line drawn since 2003 under the name of the theory of substitution, confirming that in light of the jurisprudence of this Corporation, it is not feasible any constitutional reform unfamiliar with structural principles or defining elements of the Constitution of 1991, and the control could be performed even on the very same law that summons them. Regarding the Law 1,353 of 2009, the Court found that it ignores some structural axes of the Political Constitution and the principle of separation of powers and the system of checks and balances, the rule of alternation and preset periods, the right to equality and the general and abstract nature of the laws.

3. Conclusion.

The referred procedural vices, which occurred in the course of the citizen's initiative and during the legislative process that culminated in the promulgation of Law 1,354 of 2009, involve the lack of important constitutional principles and formal procedures required by the Constitution and the law for the holding of a referendum on popular initiative amending the Constitution. It is not, therefore, a matter of mere procedural irregularities but of substantial violations of the democratic principle, one of whose essential components is the respect of the forms provided so that the majority's opinion is known.

4. Decision.

By virtue of the foregoing, the Constitutional Court of the Republic of Colombia, administering justice on behalf of the People and mandated by the Constitution, decides:

To declare UNCONSTITUTIONAL in its entirety, the Law 1354 of 2009, "Through which it calls for a constitutional referendum and thru which it is submitted to the people a proposed constitutional reform."

5. Additional considerations.

The justices Jorge Pretelt and Mauricio González Cuervo saved their votes against the unconstitutionality stated in this Sentence.

Mauricio González Cuervo, President

2. *The Control of the Constitutionality of the Acts Amending the Constitution*

The theory of constituent power is of the utmost importance, because it provide the basis for constitutional mutations without ignoring the imperative of adapting the rules to reality, mutations that can take place without infringement of the institutional order.

The constituent power, as a legal category, is that body that, according to established constitutional procedures and by definition of the very same constituent, is empoweredto reform the Constitution. It is then the derivative constituent.

The primary constituent is actually a sociolopolitical category, whose existence and operation presupposes the rupture of the existing constitutional regime or the creation of a new state by erasing any preexisting constitutional support.

From this perspective, there is nothing more surprising than the national body responsible for monitoring the supremacy of the Constitution and preserving it, in sharp contrast with the provision of article 247 of the Constitution that limit its power to jurge the vices of procedure when from the control of the constitutionality of the laws by means of which it is summoned to a constitutional referendum, it assumes a material control of constitutionality, and it does it raising the issue that the proposed constitutional reform would constitute a substitution of the constitutional system, so that only the primary constituent would be legitimized for such purpose.

There are several surprising aspects of this reasoning of the Constitutional Court, which we refer to herein, but for now, let it suffice to emphasize that the constitutional doctrine that serves as sustenance to the Court, even in evident contradiction with the constitutional mandate, as we explain later, refers to the primary constituent the faculty to reform the constitution.

Because the Congress of the Republic has the power to reform the Constitution, the call for a national constitutional assembly is also provided in the Constitution to such effect. That, along with the legislative initiative and the constitutional referendum, are considered authorized instances in order to select, or validate the constitutional reform process as a whole. As these instances are all established in the Constitution now in force in Colombia, they must be considered a derivative constituent power.

Thus, when evoking the primary constituent to introduce reforms that imply substitution or subrogation of the Constitution, the Colombian Constitutional Court is, on the one hand, severing the powers to reform of the constituted bodies, and, on the other hand, referring to *de facto* powers, extraconstitutional, the mutations in the Constitution.

This is a strange way to preserve and interpret the supremacy of the Constitution, because what was established there was the viability of constitutional revisions and mutations, as long as they respect the procedures established in the Constitution itself.

This time, the Constitutional Court, as long ago did the Supreme Court of Justice, closed the door to constitutional reforms and threw away the key. Thus, it should not be a surprise, facing the imperative of reforms, real or perceived, that we shall be doomed again to the call of extraconstitutional powers, which means nothing else than the rupture the constitutional state of law, with the risks of arbitrariness that this implies and the serious questions about its outcome.

A. Constitutional Control Limited to the Vices of Procedure

To limit constitutional control of the laws by means of which a referendum is summoned to reform the Constitution, to only review mere vices of procedure, far from being a whim of the constituent, picks up historical experiences that the country wanted to surpass and are according to the dictates of the global doctrine on the powers of the constitutional courts regarding reforms to the constitutional texts.

Usually, contemporary constitutions include within their chapters one that refers to their reform. Except for the case of specific and explicit nonmodifiable clauses, in general terms, the constituents understand the right of future generations to adapt the constitutional texts to new social demands and new contexts. This should be done, yes, in accordance with the procedures and by the bodies defined in the Constitution itself, which ensures both institutional legitimacy of the reform and its democratic nature.

This explains why control of constitutionality has to be limited, therefore, to verify that the reform is done in the Chamber and as provided by the Constitution.

Tribunals and constitutional courts can monitor constitutional reforms when the constitutional texts whose supremacy must be preserved do not contain specific nonmodifiable clausesthat would prohibit any possible reforms to the Constitution. Indeed, ontologically, any reform opposes the reformation of the Constitution, so that the constitutional court, to preserve the supremacy of the Constitution, would always declare unconstitutional the reforms of the controlled text.

But beyond this logical and ontological fallacy, the fact is that a court lacking popular legitimacy, but able to freeze the fundamental norm of the State, would have political power and be above the democratic principle. This goes against the philosophy of the constitutional state of law.

Nevertheless, the Colombian Constitutional Court assumed the task of creating a doctrine that, though contrary to the Constitution, gave the Court superiority to it. In this way, because the constitutional jurisprudence prevails over the Constitution – and because the Court's interpretations of the diverse contents were more likely opposite to their true meaning – the Constitutional Court abrogated the power to define when an amendment to the Constitution could be considered constitutionally valid because of its content. If, according to the opinion of the Constitutional Court, the reform concerns a matter that implies substituting for or subrogation of the constitutional text, it is not possible to issue a decision to endorse such reform because the constitutional bodies are incompetent and it relates to procedure.

That doctrine is considered jurisprudence and served as the basis for the declared unconstitutionality of the law that called for a constitutional referendum whereby the President's reelection would be feasible, even for a third term.

Beyond the unresolved questions generated by the fact that the Court iassumes to make a material control of a constitutional reform and endorses the second but not the third term, as if the ontological judgment of reproach is configured on the basis of quantity rather than on the content itself – one reelection yes, a second one no, eight years yes, twelve are unconstitutional – the truth is that the audacity of our Constitutional Court when exerting constitutional control is not limited to usurping the power of the legislator, as can be seen.

B. The Procedural Vices of the Law through Which a Constitutional Referendum Is Summoned

In an all-encompassing perspective of the proceedings, the Constitutional Court exerted its control, starting off regarding the collecting signatures that supports the popular initiative law to summon a referendum to reform the Constitution.

In the process of verifying compliance with binding procedures contained both in the statutory law of mechanisms of participation and in the statutory law that contains the regulations of Congress, a number of digressions were verified, vitiating on grounds of unconstitutionality the discussion procedure of the law.

In harmony with constitutional orthodoxy, these vices by themselves would have excluded the specific law from the legal order without needing to have delved into such areas as commented on here.

Nonetheless, two of the points raised by the Court warrant additional comments: the faculty of Congress to introduce reforms to the law under consideration by means of one legislative initiative and the consequences of the validity of the law violating the Law of Benches (*bancadas*).

a. *The Power of the Congress of the Republic to Amend the Law Presented at the Request of a Popular Initiative*

The thesis raised by the Constitutional Court assumes that the Congress of the Republic is a mere "stone witness" (*convidado de piedra*) in the processing of draft bills of popular initiative. This is not so.

A proper reading of the Constitution requires the conclusion that the faculty granted to a percentage of the electorate to present a legislative initiative – that is, to submit to a draft bill to Congress for consideration – is not different from what the Constitution recognizes as the faculty of any congressman, the government, some jurisdictional bodies, and so on.

In none of the previous cases an argument of this type was even raised. The legislative initiative is the ability to spur Congress to deliberate on any item subject to its consideration, and finally approve it, notwithstanding the reforms that it decided to introduce.

That a percentage of the electorate enjoys the same privilege, cannot lead to confuse the Congress itself with that number of citizens that cannot be homologated to the people themselves.[20]

b. *The Violation of the Law of Benches (*Bancadas*)*

The *Bancadas* Law is intended to strengthen political parties and to contribute to a more orderly and transparent legislative work of Congress. Its transgression involves penalties, but it is debatable that it originates the constitutional invalidity of the statute approved with votes uttered by those who are violating such law.

It draws attention that this thesis was the one supported by the ones who gave a dissent vote once it was discovered that parliamentary approval of the legislative act by means of which it gave legal life to the reelection of

[20] See Sandra Morelli, "El referenddo constitucional," AAVV, Academia Colombiana de Jurisprudencia, 2002.

incumbent president, Álvaro Uribe Vélez, counted on the favorable vote of persons convicted criminally for bribery, typified from the gifts received just to cast their vote for such reform.[21]

The Court, by contrast, rejected the recourse as untimely, as if the claimant could have known the crime before its judicial corroboration and subsequent conviction.

The incoherent position of the Constitutional Court must ve reviewed, in the sense that before the corroboration of a criminal act as cause of a legislative act, it eluded its analysis and thereby abstained to secure the legal consequences that derive from there on; but now, with contempt of law, which at best leads to a disciplinary sanction and loss of investiture for the violators, enlarge the proportions of such digressions until endowing them with the invalidating force of a law. The revision must be made bearing in mind that that when practicing as the constitutional judge the Court must take into account the imperative of preserving the intention of the Legislator. Hence, a decision that fundamentally assumes that the violation of any law by members of Congress entails the violation of the law subject to approval, which when faced with the conviction of congressmen for gifts received to approve the first reelection, opted for a different thesis; does little service to the Colombian democracy and to the principle of separation of powers..

These notes make clear how the Constitutional Court of Colombia, in order to keep of its historical responsibility, has to reflect on its institutional role for the sake of reverting to the one that constitutionally corresponds with it.

[21] "Dissenting opinion," to the Procedural Act 156 of 2008, Magistrate Jaime Araujo Renteria, Reference: Exp. D-5645, Review Application against Sentence C-1040 of October 19, 2005.

COSTA RICA

THE NORMATIVE RESOLUTIONS OF THE CONSTITUTIONAL COURT

Rubén Hernández Valle
Professor, University of Costa Rica
rhernandez@ghp.co.cr

I. TYPOLOGY OF FAVORABLE LEGAL REVIEW RESOLUTIONS

It is possible to individualize an ample typology of favorable resolutions in constitutional proceedings directed to exercise *a posteriori* control over the legal review of the laws: (a) exhortative; (b) simple unconstitutionality; (c) interpretative; (d) inapplicable; and (e) normative. Each category is in turn divided into subcategories, as we will see below.

1. *Favorable Exhortative Resolutions*

Favorable exhortative resolutions are a technique exclusively used when control is exercised over laws. They are characterized by the fact that the constitutional judge, after establishing that a specific legal provision violates the Constitution, instead of declaring its nullity, grants a specific term to the legislators for its amendment instead of just removing the portion thereof that is incompatible with the political Constitution.

In practice, the efficacy of this is doubtful, because parliaments do not always abide by the recommendations of constitutional judges, which led the jurisprudence of the Italian Corte Costituzionale to create the procedural technique of the *doppia pronuncia*. In accordance with this technique, legislators are advised in a first resolution that, should they fail to enforce the recommendations contained within the term granted for the purpose, a second resolution will be issued to declare the unconstitutionality of the challenged provision.

There is then a *doppia pronuncia*, that is, a conditioned dismissal resolution, plus a favorable resolution if the legislators fail to comply with the warning contained in the resolution, because, to a certain extent, the first resolution establishes guidelines and directions to be followed by the Legislator on how to regulate a specific matter in accordance with the constitutional law. In Italy, these judgments have ended up being ironically called *sentenze-delega*.

Another modality is used in Germany and in Austria, where the exhortative judgment provides that, should legislators fail to comply with the Court's mandate within the term fixed in its dispositive or "therefore" portion, then the challenged provision shall be automatically null and void. Therefore, it is an unconstitutionality judgment, the annulling efficacy of which is subject to a condition precedent.

Accordingly, if the condition precedent is not met and the legislators do comply with the exhortation of the constitutional judge, the favorable resolution will not produce annulment effects.

Both modalities of exhortative judgments aim to prevent the qualification of the constitutional judge as a negative legislator and to provide an opportunity to the competent political body to amend within a reasonable term a provision issued by it that violates the Constitution.

The Costa Rican Constitutional Chamber adopted recently a new modality of exhortative judgments. In fact, when resolving an action to declare unconstitutional a provision contained in the Electoral Code that authorized the Supreme Tribunal of Elections to cancel the credentials of congresspeople upon their violation of their duty of probity, an obligation established in the Law of Illicit Enrichment and against Corruption, the jurisprudence of our maximum interpreter of the Constitution established that the regime of immunities of the members of the supreme branches is exclusively regulated in the political Constitution and so cannot be expanded by law. Therefore, said provision of the Electoral Code was declared unconstitutional.

In this same judgment, a term of thirty-six months was granted to the Legislature, in its capacity as the Constitution-amending power, to introduce in the constitutional text the violation of the duty of probity as one of the reasons for the loss of credentials by a congressperson (Vote 11352-10).

This is without doubt a *sui generis* exhortative judgment, because it is not directed to Parliament in the exercise of its legislative duties – for which it is constitutionally and legally empowered – but as the Constitution-amending power, which goes beyond the powers of any Constitutional Court.

A Constitutional Court can and should declare null and void constitutional provisions involving violations in the procedure followed for their issuance, because this is a power of juridical nature. However, an order to the Constitution-amending power to legislate in a specific manner goes beyond the Court's powers. The exercise of the power to amend the Constitution is political in nature, and so it can be exercised in a discretional manner by the legislature, without the interference of any other State body. The opposite would violate the principle of separation of powers, established by article 9 of our Constitution.

2. *Simple Unconstitutionality Resolutions*

In those cases in which the subject matter of the legal review consists of provisions, that is, regulatory texts or acts, the specific purpose of a favorable judgment is to remove such provision from the legal system by means of a declaration of nullity.

In these cases, the unconstitutionality is caused by a conflict between the text of the provision or the act and a constitutional provision or principle.

A. Simple Unconstitutionality Declaration of Partial Nature

The declaration can be partial when it refers to a portion of a text (e.g., an article, a paragraph), or a portion of the act; the other provisions contained in the challenged regulatory text remaining valid.

For example, an unconstitutionality action filed to declare null a specific provision contained in the Civil Code, if admitted, would affect only the validity of the challenged article and not the validity of the other provisions contained in said code.

B. Simple Unconstitutionality Declaration of Full Nature

Full simple unconstitutionality declarations affect the entire regulatory text or act that has been challenged. This occurs, for example, when declaring an entire law unconstitutional as a result of a violation in the procedure of its enactment, because it failed to obtain a qualified majority, or because it was passed without requesting a prior binding opinion. In these cases, the constitutional judge annuls the entire law; in other words, the full regulatory text disappears from the legal system.

3. *Interpretative Resolutions*

Interpretative resolutions, depending on the modality in question, declare both the unconstitutionality of texts and that of the provisions derived from them (Zagrebelsky).

Therefore, there are two modalities of interpretative favorable resolutions that are clearly distinguishable: (1) when the unconstitutionality is caused by an erroneous interpretation or misapplication of a provision in a specific case, and (2) when the challenged text or provision is unconstitutional because of its effects.

A. Unconstitutionality as a Result of Erroneous Interpretation or Misapplication of a Provision in a Specific Case

It occurs frequently that the text of a provision or act that has been challenged as unconstitutional does not violate directly the block of constitutionality. However, its erroneous interpretation or misapplication by the Court or by administrative authorities results in a clear constitutional violation, because the provision derived from this interpretation or application is in open violation of the Constitution, its values, or its principles.

The favorable resolutions in these cases declare not the text of the challenged provision or act unconstitutional but the erroneous interpretation or misapplication of the text by the judicial or administrative authorities.

What happens in legal terms is that new provisions are created by means of the erroneous interpretation or misapplication of a text, different from those contained in the interpreted or applied provision. Those new provisions frequently violate the block of constitutionality.

In these cases, the constitutional judge provides that a specific interpretation or application of a text has created a provision that violates the Constitution, thus declaring unconstitutional the provision resulting from the erroneous interpretation or misapplication.

The text of the provision or act from which the provision that has been declared unconstitutional derives remains unchanged and continues with its normal effects. Accordingly, the Courts and administrative authorities cannot apply the annulled interpretation to this text.

This type of judgment presents a significant problem: is the interpretation given by the constitutional judge binding or not binding for the other administrative and Court bodies, particularly for cassation courts.

In most legal systems, such resolutions do not preclude interpretations different from those given by the constitutional judge, provided that such interpretations are compatible with the Constitution, its principles, and its values. This type of resolution actually prohibits other administrative and Court bodies from interpreting or applying the challenged provisions in a way that may violate the Constitution.

The foregoing alternative is used in those legal systems that tend to respect the classic principle of continental law that Cassation Courts have the last word on the interpretation of the law.

Thus, vesting in a constitutional judge the power to interpret laws that have been submitted to legal review evidently enters into conflict with the cassation tradition, which reserves to Cassation Courts a monopoly on the ultimate interpretation of the law.

In the praxis, there are constant confrontations because Cassation Courts tend to ignore the interpretations of subconstitutional provisions by Constitutional Courts. The result is an interpretative dichotomy between two high courts: one required to look to the protection of legality (Cassation Court) and the other empowered to protect the principle of constitutional supremacy (Constitutional Courts).

Italy, where serious differences arose between the Corte Costituzionale and the Criminal Cassation Court, has elaborated the doctrine of the living law. In accordance with that doctrine, the jurisprudence repeatedly and peacefully applied by regular courts – particularly Cassation Courts – about the interpretation of the laws has to be respected by the Corte Costituzionale, which is inhibited to provide a different interpretation.

This Italian solution presents the inconvenience of eliminating the advantage of the original system: permitting a greater degree of creativity among legal operators, which makes possible new interpretations of subconstitutional legislation, provided that those interpretations are also compatible with the Constitution.

In contrast, the original system presents a great inconvenience that the Italian technique tends to alleviate: it causes legal uncertainty, also forcing the affected party to file new unconstitutionality actions every time that the regular judges provide interpretations different from the one of the Constitutional Court.

The second solution, which is the one applied, for example, by Costa Rican law, establishes the *erga omnes* mandatory nature of the jurisprudence and precedents of the Constitutional Court in such way that its interpretations on the scope of the provisions or acts subject to legal review of legislation are binding and mandatory for all legal operators, with the exception of the Court itself.

This solution presents the inconvenience of precluding creative interpretations from judges and administrative officials, who might correctly try one or several interpretations of the provisions and acts subject to constitutionality control, all of them compatible with the Constitution but different from those of the Constitutional Court.

B. Unconstitutionality as a Result of the Effects of the Challenged Text or Provision

Provisions declare that a text or provision is null and void not because it violates the Constitution directly but because its application modifies unconstitutionally another provision of the legal system or implies an indirect violation of the parameter of the judgment of constitutionality. Accordingly, the application of a null and void provision causes reflectively or indirectly a violation of the Constitution.

In the first hypothesis, we might think of an executive decree that indirectly increases the rate of a specific tax, which is a matter reserved to the law. The unconstitutionality in this case occurs reflectively, because the effects produced by the decree on the law – modifying the original rate established by it – make the decree unconstitutional.

Likewise, challenged provisions sometimes violate indirectly the constitutionality block. For example, if a law establishes that only persons who are members of cooperatives can sell lottery tickets to the public, then such a legal provision would be unconstitutional because of its effects, as it would force lottery vendors to become cooperative members to conduct such commercial activity validly. In other words, such a provision would violate, with its effects, the right to free association that the Constitution guarantees to all citizens.

In brief, in this case, a favorable resolution would declare unconstitutional not a provision or act that has been challenged because it violates directly and immediately the Constitution, its principles, and its values, but its effects, because the enforcement of the provision or act would unconstitutionally modify another provision or violate indirectly the Constitution.

4. *Favorable Resolutions of Inapplicability*

As a final category of favorable unconstitutionality resolutions are those cases in which the Court, without annulling the challenged provision or act, does declare its unenforceability in a specific case.

Favorable unconstitutionality resolutions always produce at least unenforceable effects with regard to the challenging party and the administrative procedures and proceedings suspended as a direct consequence of the admission for processing of the Court action or inquiry, as the case may be, with regard to which the favorable resolution was issued. From a procedural point of view, such distinction is based on the difference between the efficacy and the authority of the resolution.

According to an Italian author, the efficacy consists in "the attitude of the resolution to produce its effects and in the effective production thereof . . . while the authority would be an ulterior and diverse effect of the resolution, a quality of its effects, and precisely its immutability referable to all its effects" (Liebman).

By transferring this scheme to the constitutional procedural scope, the authority of a favorable resolution refers to the subjective aspect of the judgment, and the efficacy is limited to its objective aspect. Consequently, all problems inherent to the relationship of the constitutional process with the *a quo* proceedings, belong to the subjective profile, that is, to the authority of the resolution of the Constitutional Court.

For this reason, the Constitutional Courts and the courts of ordinary jurisdiction are prevented from attaching the *inter partes* efficacy of a favorable unconstitutionality resolution; in other words, as said by an Italian author: "the Court could not violate the guaranties of the constitutional *res judicata* on the subjective plane, that is, for that portion which refers to the relationship between the declaration of unconstitutionality and its effects in the *a quo* proceedings" (D'Amico).

5. *Normative Resolutions*

Normative resolutions are issued by the Constitutional Court and create more conflict in the doctrine and in the jurisprudence, because it is through these procedural instruments that the Constitutional Court may end up replacing Parliament in its function as creator of primary provisions with *erga omnes* efficacy. There are two types of normative resolutions: additive and substitutive.

A. Favorable Additive Resolutions

Favorable additive resolutions are issued in cases of unconstitutionality by omission. Consequently, they declare unconstitutional not the text of the challenged general provision or rule but what the text or provision fails to say or should say.

From a procedural point of view, these resolutions declare unconstitutional a provision "to the extent" that it establishes or fails to establish a right in favor of a single group of persons or against others.

As stated by a Spanish author:

> This situation [violation of the principle of equality by omission] occurs in those cases in which the law, regulating some cases, ignores other substantially analogous, or else, when unjustifiably delimits the scope of application of the discipline in question to gender, race, opinion, religion, etc. In some cases, the Court can resolve the unconstitutionality by interpreting the provision in an ample manner, including then the assumptions or using the tool of analogy. However, it is not an easy issue. The principle of equality does not impose equal treatment, but that the different treatment may be justified, may be reasonable. On the other hand, one of the limits to the interpretative criteria to analogy is that it is not possible to interpret in an ample manner whatever is regulated as an exception. (Ahumada Ruiz)

Consequently, these resolutions declare null and void the challenged resolution "to the extent" that they benefit or damage exclusively specific categories of subjects for reasons that are neither justified nor reasonable, because such exclusion or discrimination implies a clear violation of the principle of equality under the law.

Such resolutions may be issued in cases that issue new regulations protecting rights acquired under the repealed regulations, via the legislative technique of transitory provisions.

In the case of additive resolutions, the Constitutional Courts have two options: to create a resolution for the specific case, extending the benefit to those unlawfully excluded and thus entering the arena of additive resolutions, or to refrain from doing so, letting the lawmaker or the administration, as the case may be, correct the unconstitutional omission.

The jurisprudence of the Italian *Corte Costituzionale* has established that additive resolutions "are only admitted when the adjusting solution should not be the result of discretionary assessment, but the necessary consequence of a judgment of legitimacy, in which the Court actually proceeds to establish a logically necessary expansion, sometimes implicit in the interpretative potentiality of the regulatory context in which the challenged provision is inserted. However, when there is a plurality of solutions, which derive from possible assessments, the intervention of the Court is not admissible, and the respective selection corresponds only to the lawmaker" (Vote 125/88).

A minor variation of this type of resolution is the distributive additive resolution. In this case, the Constitutional Court, by declaring discriminatory the omission of the lawmaker, simultaneously orders that the amount the beneficiaries currently receive be distributed among all those equally entitled. The purpose is to respect the constitutional principle of budgetary balance and to protect the right of the petitioners (Grosso).

However, this presents the inconvenience of substantially decreasing the rights of the original beneficiaries, which does not seem to fall under the powers of Constitutional Courts, as those rights were acquired in good faith under legislation enacted by Parliament in the exercise of its constitutional powers.

B. Favorable Substitutive Resolutions

Favorable substitutive resolutions are characterized by an innovation to the preexisting legal system, as they introduce new provisions with *erga omnes* effects. They may be of two types: those that introduce new provisions and those that make effective resolutions that were repealed by provisions that have been declared unconstitutional.

The technique of the first type is expressed sometimes in the suppression of specific words or paragraphs of a provision or a text, in such a way that the regulatory contents of the original text changes.

This type of resolution should be differentiated from that of partial simple unconstitutionality, which declares the invalidity of a proposition that constitutes by itself a severable precept, even if it is included in a provision that contains other precepts not affected by the declaration of nullity.

The characteristic of the substitutive favorable resolutions, however, is that the constitutional judge assumes the role of a regular lawmaker in that he or she creates legal provisions with *erga omnes* efficacy, which replace those declared unconstitutional, either because the original text acquires another meaning with the words or paragraphs annulled or because the constitutional judge introduces new provisions to replace the ones annulled.

There are several examples of this in the jurisprudence of the Costa Rica Constitutional Chamber. It is worth it to mention at least two relevant cases.

i. A Foreigner Who Marries a Costa Rican Can Become a Citizen through Naturalization

There is a resolution of the Constitutional Chamber that interpreted article 14 (subsection 4) of the Constitution, which provides "The following are Costa Ricans by naturalization: . . . A foreign woman who loses her nationality when marrying a Costa Rican," so that the word *woman* read as *person* to cover *men*, too.

When the provision was issued in 1949, there was a strong cultural imprint in society of gender inequality, thus the trend to protect women, who were generally considered weaker. However, those cultural patterns began to radically change in the 1970s, and now both sexes have the same rights and duties.

The Court said in connection with this matter:

> The mere comparison of the quoted provisions with the challenged provision demonstrates that the benefit granted exclusively to a foreign woman married to a Costa Rican is a discrimination against foreign men married to Costa Rican female citizens, artificially creating a disadvantage by taking away benefits based on gender, thus violating the constitutional and universal spirit of equality and non-discrimination. Note that in this case, the inequality that injures the interests of the petition is not a mere "reasonable and objective" differentiation, but an evidently unjustified, baseless and disproportionate treatment, which is the product of social, cultural, economic and political conditioning factors fortunately overcome, a treatment that currently injures the human dignity of a particular individual, as a specific positive subjective right to equality, and the family unity as an objective social right, from the time it establishes a hateful restriction that violates, by discrimination, the legal and spiritual balance of the family, also protected by the Constitution and by international provisions, and therefore, a subjective right of the injured party. . . . For the purpose of avoiding future inequalities and discriminations that may arise in the application of the fundamental Chart and other legal instruments in force, and in the exercise of the powers vested by the Constitution in this Court, it is resolved that whenever the legislation uses the terms "man" or "woman", they should be understood as synonymous of the word "person", thus eliminating every possible "legal" discrimination based on gender, correction that should be applied by all public officials whenever they receive any claim which resolution requires to apply regulations that use the aforesaid words. (Vote 3435-92)

We are evidently before an evolving interpretation, because in the current world, men and women have the same rights and duties. However, it is clear that the Court made the Constitution say something that was not in its original text.

ii. Freedom of Contract

We find another example of evolving interpretation in a resolution by means of which the Constitutional Court established the essential contents of the freedom of contract and annulled article 6 of the Currency Law, because it violated such freedom, by allowing obligations acquired in foreign currency to be paid in colones at the official exchange rate.

The Court considered that the debtor could comply validly with his or her obligations contracted in foreign currency by paying them in colones but not at the official exchange rate, as established by said provision of the Currency Law, rather at the market exchange rate. Otherwise, there would be lack of equilibrium in the reciprocal obligations between creditor and debtor, with an evident illicit enrichment of the latter.

The Court said the following with regard to this matter:

> However, in paragraph (2) *in fine* of the latter, the debtor is empowered to comply with his obligations contracted in foreign currencies by paying them in colones "at the official exchange rate in force as of the date of payment," an aspect in which the restored provision is also unconstitutional, because it would permit an evident disequilibrium against the creditors, with a manifest violation of Article 45 of the Constitution and the constitutionality criteria to which Consideration XIII supra refers, considering that this official rate does not match – being lower or higher – to the actual commercial value which the owed foreign currency may have on the market as of the date of payment. This would imply, on the one hand, the unlawful expropriation, without indemnity, of the capital of the debtors and, on the other, an unjustified enrichment of the debtors, as has been occurring too frequently in our country. Furthermore, it might even be hypothetically possible that the provision would damage the debtors themselves, should the official rate be fixed at an amount higher than the actual exchange value. Consequently, and in exercise of the powers vested in it by Article 89 of the Law of Constitutional Jurisdiction, the Court opts to order the annulment, by connection or consequence, of the aforesaid final sentence, as the only constitutionally valid solution to maintain the financial equilibrium of contracts; in such way that paragraph (2) of Article 6 of the Currency Law, which effectiveness is re-established in virtue of the declared unconstitutionalities, shall be read as follows: "However, contracts can be entered and obligations can be acquired in foreign currencies, which, at the debtor's options, may be paid in colones." These colones shall be in turn calculated at the effective commercial value of the owed foreign currency at the time of the payment; that is, at their real exchange value, responding to sufficiently objective, verifiable and fair criteria – the latter as to the fairness typical of a contractual relationship, specifically concerning the equivalency in the exchanges and the proportion in the distributions – ; value which should be ultimately appreciated in a reasonable manner and on case by

> case basis by the courts of justice, without resorting to arbitrary or merely subjective criteria, such as a parity established by the legislature, by the government or administratively. In this sense, the rate or value of exchange of the colón that should prevail in any case should not be in function of a measuring unit with regard to other currencies, but in function of the objective and real value, that is, its price as a merchandise, value for which determination it is just necessary to resort to the value actually used in the so-called free market of currencies. (Vote 3495-92)

There is no doubt that this is a resolution that takes into consideration the evolutionary behavior, because when the original provision was approved, the official exchange rate did match the market rate. However, as a result of the massive devaluation suffered by the country's currency at the end of the 1970s and beginning of the 1980s, the official exchange rate became divorced forever from the economic reality, a legal fiction. In this case, the Court changed the original text of the provision again.

The second type, that is, substitutive resolutions that restore the effectiveness of repealed provisions, occurs in those cases in which the annulled regulation causes a gap in the legal system to be filled while lawmakers issue the appropriate substitutive regulation.

The exercise of this power is usually justified by arguing that, otherwise, the regulatory gap left by the declaration of unconstitutionality might cause serious dislocations of social security, justice, or peace.

This type of judgment is usually accompanied by an exhortation, in such way that the lawmaker ultimately issues the appropriate substantive regulation in accordance with the parameters established in the resolution of the Constitutional Court. For this reason, the regulations created by Constitutional Courts by means of favorable substitutive resolutions are transitory in nature.

Additive resolutions – which both create new provisions with *erga omnes* efficacy and restore repealed legislation – are the most daring modality of action of the constitutional judge. To a certain extent, they permit judges to invade the regular legislative function and replace the will of the parliamentary body.

However, their defenders sustain that evident reasons of legal certainty in the specific case justify the exercise of such extraordinary powers of the constitutional judge; if not, certain declarations of unconstitutionality, though safeguarding the principle of constitutional supremacy, would endanger seriously social stability and peace.

II. CRITICAL ANALYSIS OF NORMATIVE RESOLUTIONS

In comparative law there are two well-defined trends concerning the existence of normative resolutions: one sector accepts them without reticence and another strongly rejects them.

1. *The Justification of Normative Resolutions*

For an important sector of the doctrine, which has enjoyed major development in Italy, the creative function of the Constitutional Courts is an unavoidable stage in the evolution of the constitutional jurisdiction. On this order, it has been sustained that Constitutional Courts develop a function of mediation in social and political conflicts, reason for which normative or manipulative resolutions appear as procedural instruments necessary for the development of such ends (Modugno).

According to Modugno, the Italian Corte Costituzionale has assumed, in recent years, the function of mediator and moderator of conflicts that have failed to be resolved by other institutional bodies that are competent for this purpose.

In contrast, the activity of the Court, though jurisdictional in nature, is also necessarily a political activity, in an ample sense. In other terms, each legal conflict is always a conflict of interests, reason for which there is always a political motive in the foundation of each resolution of the Court.

Accordingly, Modugno concludes that the Court is today involved in the development of a positive role, parallel and complementary to the one played by the Parliament. Although there are questions about whether a body that lacks in principle democratic legitimacy may assume such a task, his answer has been ultimately positive.

In fact, Modugno sustains that, if it is assumed that the Court has the authority to interpret systematically the legislative and constitutional provisions, and if unconstitutionality is never a certain datum merely disclosed through Court resolutions but the fruit of a selection (the Court is often required to assess whether there is a risk that one of its resolutions cause an even graver situation of unconstitutionality than the original one), then favorable normative resolutions represent a ductile instrument, adaptable to the various specific situations – as such, they cannot be waived.

In this order of ideas, another great Italian jurist, Vezio Crisafulli, fondly remembered justifying manipulative resolutions by considering that they propitiate the display of the effects of constitutional provisions hindered by the absence of laws. According to Crisafulli, the new discipline that produces the normative resolution is not the result of a Court fantasy, because the Court is prohibited from creating law freely (as lawmakers do), but constitutional judges have to limit themselves to specifying and individualizing a provision already implicit in the system and, therefore, deductible from it by means of the appropriate hermeneutic instruments.

Therefore, normative resolutions are endowed with a self-enforcing capacity. As they are legislation in descriptive terms – not free but induced and deducted – they are *rime obligate* legislation, not true legislation (Crisafulli).

2. *Criticism of Regulatory Resolutions*

Another doctrinal position, based on the premise that Constitutional Courts are rigorously jurisdictional bodies, sustains that it is not possible to admit the category of normative resolutions. If the provisions that are intended to be introduced in the legal system are derivable from the legal system in force, those legal provisions should be introduced only by lawmakers.

Therefore, Constitutional Courts cannot claim the "aristocratic" privilege of individualizing, by themselves, with *erga omnes* efficacy, which new provisions or which provisions derived from the legal system should fill the gaps left by the laws declared null and void.

An Italian author has said on the subject: "There is no Court monopoly that empowers it to declare exclusively the precepts implicit in legislation, not even to define the scope of constitutional rules" (Zagrebelsky). If the provision is present in the system, it is the duty of the judge (of all judges) to make it explicit; if the provision does not exist, it is the duty of the lawmaker (and only the lawmaker) to create it. With its intervention in the first case, the Court violates the scope of jurisdiction of the judges and in the second case, the scope of lawmakers.

This author concludes that if the issue of constitutional legitimacy requires simultaneously the annulment of the challenged law and its replacement by new provisions, the Court should refuse to get involved in creating new provisions, which would ultimately imply the resolution of the controversy with a pure and simple ruling of annulment.

However, when the action to declare unconstitutionality is limited to the additive-discretionary aspect, the Court must reject the issue as a whole, because it is not competent to resolve the matter. In such case, the outcome should be an inadmissibility resolution (Lavagna).

III. REGULATORY RESOLUTIONS AND THE LIMITS TO THE CONSTITUTIONAL JURISDICTION

The legal-formal and political-institutional foundations of the constitutional jurisdiction also determine its limits. Such limits define the boundary line beyond which we find the territory of merely political issues, in which the intromission of the constitutional judge is forbidden.

Therefore, the initial legal problem is to delimit in a precise manner when a matter should be considered political and, therefore, outside the competence of the constitutional jurisdiction.

As a principle, and from the view of constitutional jurisdiction, a matter should be considered political when there is no constitutional provision or principle that can be used as a parameter of validity for the challenged provision or act.

Paradoxically, it was Kelsen who established the theoretical foundations that provide legal foundation to the idea that there should not be any gaps in constitutional law.

As a necessary excursus, let's remember that it was actually the Viennese jurist who qualified constitutional jurisdiction as negative legislation, thus permitting the conclusion of the logical-juridical impossibility that the constitutional judge may replace the will of the lawmaker by means of so-called normative or manipulative resolutions.

In contrast, and going back to the guiding thread of our discourse, the Kelsenian theory of the legal pyramid assumes the existence of the principle of legal regularity, according to which there should be correspondence and conformity between the lowest and the highest level of the legal system. This principle should be logically met in all strata of the legal system, which are immediately or indirectly subordinate to the Constitution, because each is a stage of the process of creation and enforcement of law in the modern State.

This principle, taken to its ultimate consequences, leads to the impossibility of having gaps in constitutional law, because the infraconstitutional provisions should always entail, by logical-juridical requirements, the existence of at least a constitutional principle that gives them juridical foundation.

This thesis gives foundation to the powers of Constitutional Courts to issue normative resolutions, which, in certain modalities thereof, allow judges to act just as regular lawmakers do, that is, to issue resolutions with *erga omnes* efficacy.

For example, when the Constitutional Courts declare unconstitutionality and establish in the same resolution the provision that will fill the normative gap left by the one that has been removed from the legal system, or when, for the same reasons, they restore the effectiveness of a repealed law, it is evident in both cases that they are exercising a typical regular legislative function, not a jurisdictional function.

However, there is a substantial difference between the political decision and the judicial resolutions, because whereas the former looks toward the future, the latter looks to the past. In other terms, "a political decision is characterized by being argued and arguable based on the purposes sought, while a Court decision can only achieve general acceptance, that is, legitimacy, if based on premises that already enjoy such acceptance" (De Otto).

In contrast, and as a principle, the Constitution is not a normative system that disciplines political conflicts in an all-comprehensive manner. Rather, the Constitution is a framework, inside which there are ample spaces that are constitutionally irrelevant, gaps in constitutional law.

Likewise, the incorporation of substantive provisions to the Constitution should be compatible with political pluralism, because the lawmaker is not just a mere executor of the Constitution but a State body who acts with discretionary power inside the framework fixed by it, reason for which the free actions of the legislature often need to enunciate such precepts that authorize it to have an ample spectrum of diverse political interpretations.

For this reason, the powers of the Constitutional Courts to define the scope of constitutional provisions, principles, and values find a specific and insurmountable limit in the principle of political pluralism. In the application of this principle, the lawmaker can develop the Constitution in different manners, provided that all of them are compatible with its *ratio*. Therefore, the constitutional judge cannot assess the political discretionary power of the lawmaker to choose one or another option; but he or she can and should ensure that such selection does not violate the limits of the legal discretionary power.

On this order, a Spanish jurist established in a very lucid manner that "the lawmaker is not an executor of the Constitution, but rather a power that acts inside its framework and this free action requires in many cases (although obviously not in all) that the enunciation of such constitutional precepts may permit a wide bundle of diverse interpretations. Not 'legal' interpretations, but political interpretations; in other words, different ways to understand the constitutional text, which enunciations have to be built, therefore, with concepts of high abstraction value" (Rubio Llorente).

The problem of the limits to the constitutional jurisdiction, through the prism of political issues, may also be analyzed from the point of view of the characters of the case. In fact, every constitutional issue is, without a doubt, a conflict of interests or powers that should be resolved as a legal controversy, in other words, by means of applying a rule that is assumed to be independent of the material relationships. Consequently, the existence of a constitutional jurisdiction means that the political-constitutional subjects have agreed to leave the resolution of their disputes to an independent instance through the application of legal provisions. Consequently, the limits to the constitutional jurisdiction coincide with the limits to the matter regulated by constitutional law.

However, the activity of the courts of justice is not creation, but interpretation of the law. Therefore, the constitutional judge cannot replace the will of the lawmaker, because constitutional interpretation, though conditioned by evident political components, is always legal interpretation. Accordingly, the limits to the constitutional jurisdiction are closely related to the limits to constitutional interpretation.

From this point of view, Constitutional Courts are a type of neutral power, the activity of which is limited to support the effectiveness of the respective constitutional system, which implies that they cannot change it or, even less, prevent its amendment.

Consequently, the constitutional jurisdiction is not only unable to prevent a constitutional amendment but also is in charge of guaranteeing that such amendment may be conducted in accordance with the procedures established in the Constitution.

It must be remembered that, in any case, the popular sovereignty, as a question of fact, should be supported on the notion of political consensus (Aragón).

Consequently, constitutions regulate in a juridical manner the changes of consensus that occur in the underlying civil society. For this reason, the changes of consensus, that is, the mutations of the material contents of the Constitution, can be achieved only by means of the procedures for constitutional amendment, because such function corresponds to the people, as holder of the popular sovereignty by means of conventions or constituent assemblies, and not to Constitutional Courts, which are appointed bodies, the legitimacy of which derives directly from the constitutional text itself.

The limit to the interpretative power of the Constitutional Courts is an element of the rationalizing function of the Constitution. Although this function does admit the possibility of a constitutional change by means of interpretation, it is also true that it excludes the violation of the Constitution by deviation from the text in a specific text and the amendment of the material contents of the Constitution by means of interpretation. As a German jurist said: "Where the interpreter prevails over the Constitution, it is no longer interpreting it but changing or violating it" (Hesse).

Consequently, the North American principle of the living Constitution has to be understood as a legal update of the constitutional text in accordance with the coordinates of time and space, not as the modification of its material contents, which is a function of political nature and, therefore, different from the legal function of Constitutional Courts of specifying the contents of constitutional provisions, principles, and values.

In conclusion, the limits to the interpretative power of the Constitution are established by the condition of appointed bodies of the Constitutional Courts, which prevent them from amending the Constitution by means of procedures other than those expressly authorized for the purpose by the constituent assembly.

Therefore, normative resolutions are admissible only to the extent that they develop principles and values contained in the Constitution. However, when they fill the gap left by the lawmaker, by means of imposing a new provision not derivable from the Constitution or restoring the effectiveness of repealed provisions, it is evident that, in such hypotheses, the respective Constitutional Courts are replacing Parliament in their genuine political role of creating provisions with *erga omnes* effects. Consequently, such normative resolutions are spurious, because they imply a subversion of the constitutional order, as the judiciary is assuming the role of the legislature, which, in democratic systems of government, is granted only to Parliament.

BIBLIOGRAPHY

AHUMADA RUIZ, MARÍA DE LOS ANGELES, "El control de constitucionalidad de las omisiones legislativas", en *Revista del Centro de Estudios Constitucionales*, N°, Madrid, 1989

ARAGÓN REYES, MANUEL, *Constitución y democracia*, Madrid, 1989

CRISAFULLI, V., *Lezioni di diritto costituzionale*, II, Padova, 1984

DE OTTO, IGNACIO, *Lecciones de Derecho Constitucional*, Oviedo, 1982

GROSSO, E., *Sentenze costituzionali di spesa "che non costino"*, Torino, 1991

HESSE, KONRAD, "La interpretación constitucional" en *Escritos de Derecho Constitucional*, Madrid, 1983

KELSEN, HANS, *La jurisdicción constitucional*, México, 1964

LAVAGNA, C., "Sulle sentenze "additive" della Corte costituzionale," in *Giur. it.*, 1969, IV, 151.

MODUGNO, F., *L'invalidità della legge*, I e II, Milano, 1970

RUBIO LLORENTE, FRANCISCO, "Los problemas de la interpretación constitucional en la jurisprudencia del Tribunal Constitucional español" en *La Forma del Poder*, Madrid, 1993

ZAGREBELSKY, G, *La giustizia costituzionale*, Bologna, 1988

CROATIA

CONSTITUTIONAL COURTS AS POSITIVE LEGISLATORS

Sanja Barić, S.J.D.,
Assistant Professor of Constitutional Law, University of Rijeka
sanja.baric@pravri.hr

Petar Bačić, S.J.D.,
Assistant of Constitutional Law, University of Split

I. THE CONSTITUTIONAL COURT OF THE REPUBLIC OF CROATIA: COMPOSITION, COMPETENCES, AND PROCEEDINGS

1. *Introduction*

Croatia had its Constitutional Court when it still formed part of the former Socialist Federal Republic of Yugoslavia. Constitutional Courts were established both on the federal level and as federal units. The Croatian Constitutional Court had been established by the 1963 Constitution, and it was retained by the later 1974 Constitution. Its primary competence was abstract norm control, and it examined the constitutionality and legality of self-governing general acts. Given the socialist ideology on the supremacy of the elected assembly, if the Court found a law to be contrary to the Constitution, it could not repeal the law. It could only declare its inconformity, and the Assembly would have six months to enact new legislation. It was not competent to decide on the constitutionality and legality of individual acts. The first democratic Constitution of the Republic of Croatia (hereinafter, the Constitution), promulgated on December 22, 1990, in its Basic Provisions, article 3, states, "[F]reedom, equal rights, national equality, commitment to peace, social justice, respect for human rights, inviolability of ownership, conservation of nature and the human environment, the rule of law, and a democratic multiparty system are the highest values of the constitutional order of the Republic of Croatia." The whole system of the Republic of Croatia has been organized accordingly, including the constitutional position of the Constitutional Court.

The Constitutional Court of the Republic of Croatia (hereinafter, the Constitutional Court, or CC) was constituted on December 5, 1991, and after the judges took their oath before the President of the Republic, it started to function on December 7, 1991. The constitutional position of the Constitutional Court follows the Kelsenian, continental European tradition, as it is designed as an intermediate branch that controls all three branches of government (legislative, executive and judicial). It neither is placed above them in a hierarchy nor is part of them in an organizational or functional way. The Constitutional Act on the Constitutional Court of September 24, 1999,[1] added a substantial number of procedural provisions to cure shortcomings in and vagueness of the previous 1991 Act.[2] After constitutional revisions of 2000[3] and 2001,[4] revision of the Constitutional Act on the Constitutional Court took place on March 15, 2002.[5] Finally, the Consolidated Version of the Constitutional Act on the Constitutional Court of the Republic of Croatia was published on March 18, 2002 (hereinafter, the Constitutional Act, or CACC).[6] Apart from linguistic harmonization with the Constitution, the 2002 revision incorporated important alterations regarding, for example, active legitimation of abstract review, protection of human rights and fundamental freedoms, and introduction of new competences for the Constitutional Court. These are pointed out in relevant subchapters. It also expressly regulated important safeguards of the Court's independency (CACC, article 2): "The Constitutional Court shall be independent of all state bodies, and shall independently distribute the assets approved in the state budget for the functioning of the activities of the Constitutional Court, in accordance with its annual budget and the law." The internal organization of the Constitutional Court is regulated by the Rules of

[1] Official Gazette, "*Narodne novine,*" nº 99/1999. It suffices to say that the former Constitutional Act had forty-seven articles, and the 1999 one consisted of ninety-six.

[2] Official Gazette, "*Narodne novine,*" nº 13/1991.

[3] Official Gazette, "*Narodne novine,*" nº 113/2000 (primarly for the purpose of reduction of presidential powers).

[4] Official Gazette, "*Narodne novine,*" nº 28/2001 (abolishment of the Upper Chamber of the Parliament).

[5] Official Gazette, "*Narodne novine,*" nº 29/2002.

[6] Official Gazette, "*Narodne novine,*" nº 49/2002.

Procedure of the Constitutional Court of the Republic of Croatia. The President of the Constitutional Court is in charge of application of the Rules, whereas the Rules are interpreted by the Court itself.

2. *Composition and Terms of Duty*

Originally, the Constitutional Court consisted of eleven judges appointed by the House of Representatives (Lower Chamber of the Parliament) by absolute majority of votes on the recommendation of the House of Counties (Upper Chamber of the Parliament) for a period of eight years. After the latest constitutional revision and abolishment of the Upper Chamber, the Court consists of thirteen judges appointed by the Croatian Parliament (as a unicameral Parliament) by absolute majority vote. Because a constitutional revision requires a two-thirds majority of votes from members of Parliament (MP), strong arguments have been raised in recent years that the majority for election of the CC judges should also be a two-thirds majority.

A lack of provisions on the renewability of term was interpreted as creating no obstacles for reelection. The judge of the Court may be a person who is Croatian citizen; who graduated as a lawyer and has at least fifteen years of experience in the legal profession (twelve years for doctors of legal science, added by the 1999 Constitutional Act); and who is distinguished by scientific, expert, or public work. The 2002 revision introduced elaborate provisions on election. The procedure for electing a judge of the Constitutional Court is now instituted by the Committee of the Croatian Parliament competent for the Constitution (hereinafter, Competent Committee). The Committee publishes an invitation in the Official Gazette, *Narodne novine*, to judicial institutions, law faculties, the chamber of attorneys, legal associations, political parties, and other legal persons and individuals to propose candidates for the election of one or more judges of the CC. An individual may even propose him- or herself as a candidate. After expiration of the term, the Competent Committee performs a public interview with each candidates who complies with the conditions and, on the basis of presented data and interviews, composes a short list of candidates. As a rule the short list includes more candidates than the number of judges of the Constitutional Court who will be elected. The Competent Committee then submits to the Croatian Parliament, together with its proposal, the list of all the candidates who comply with conditions, as well as the reasons the Committee gave a particular candidate priority over other candidates. The MPs vote for each proposed candidate individually, and a candidate is considered elected judge of the CC if he or she receives a majority vote of the total number of representatives in the Croatian Parliament. The Court appoints its President from among its judges for a period of four years by a secret ballot.

The constitutional judges cannot hold any other public or professional office, but the Constitutional Act specifies that they may continue academic (scientific and educational) activities on a part-time basis, as well as, to a lesser extent, memberships in lawyers', humanitarian, cultural, sport, and other similar associations. The current president of the Constitutional Court, Dr. Jasna Omejec, is a university professor, and the first president, Dr. Jadranko Crnić, was also president of the Croatian Red Cross. A judge may not belong to any political party. Needless to say, several of the current judges were, before their appointment, publicly well-known members of political parties.

The provisions on the termination of judges' duties are typical: judges may be relieved of duty before the expiration of the period for which they were appointed, on their own request, if they are sentenced to prison or if they become incapacitated. If a judge of the Constitutional Court requests to be relieved of office and if the Croatian Parliament does not decide on the request within three months, the office of judge of the Constitutional Court terminates by force of the Constitutional Act three months after the request was made. Proceedings to determine permanent incapacity of a judge to perform his or her duties are performed by the Court itself. The President of the Court (or three judges if the President has requested dismissal) initiates this procedure, although the decision is rendered by the majority of all judges.

3. *Competences of the Constitutional Court*

As a matter of principle, the Constitutional Court guarantees compliance with, and application of, the Constitution of the Republic of Croatia and bases its work solely on provisions of the Constitution and the Constitutional Act. Thus, the Constitutional Court has following competences:

- Decides on the conformity of laws with the Constitution
- Decides on the conformity of other regulations with the Constitution and laws
- May decide on constitutionality of laws and constitutionality of laws and other regulations that have lost their legal force, provided that, from the moment they lose legal force until the submission of a request or a proposal to institute the proceedings, not more than one year has passed (added by constitutional revision in 2000)

- Decides on constitutional complaints against the individual decisions of governmental bodies, bodies of local and regional self-government, and legal entities with public authority, when those decisions violate human rights and fundamental freedoms, as well as the right to local and regional self-government guaranteed by the Constitution of the Republic of Croatia
- Observes the realization of constitutionality and legality and notifies the Croatian Parliament on the instances of unconstitutionality and illegality observed thereto (added by constitutional revision in 2000)
- Decides on jurisdictional disputes among the legislative, executive, and judicial branches
- Decides, in conformity with the Constitution, on the impeachment of the President of the Republic
- Supervises the constitutionality of the programs and activities of political parties and may, in conformity with the Constitution, ban their work
- Supervises the constitutionality and legality of elections and national referenda and decides on the electoral disputes that are not within the jurisdiction of courts
- Performs other duties specified by the Constitution (e.g., the President of the Republic takes a solemn oath before the President of the Constitutional Court).

The first three competences are, in reality, abstract and concrete judicial review, whereas the fourth is concretized in the right to direct constitutional complaint by private individuals to the Constitutional Court. The right to application includes a right to initiate constitutional legal proceedings and a right to obtain a decision on the disputed act.

4. *Proceedings of the Constitutional Court*

The 1999 Constitutional Act introduced a chapter, "Procedure before the Constitutional Court – General Provisions," in which the previously existing provisions in other chapters were combined with the new ones. It includes provision on the form of application addressed to the Court, references to judges acting as reporters in particular cases, expenses of the proceedings, and so on. Other details are regulated by the Court's own Rules of Procedure.

The operation of the Constitutional Court is public, and its sessions are, in principle, accessible to members of the press. Permission of the President of the Constitutional Court is required for television transmission and radio broadcasting from the Constitutional Court. All decisions and important rulings passed in the proceedings for reviewing the constitutionality of laws and the constitutionality and legality of other regulations, as well as decisions and rulings related to the protection of human rights and fundamental freedoms guaranteed by the Constitution, are published in the Official Gazette of the Republic of Croatia, *Narodne novine*.

In most of the cases, the Court decides at sessions. However, it may hold a prior consultative session if needed, or it may hold a public hearing. Everyone is required to present to the Constitutional Court, on its request, documents and information needed in proceedings. As of the 2002 revision, if repeated requests have not been complied with, the Constitutional Court can order that the documents be seized.

The Court renders decisions (on the merits of the case) and rulings (in all other cases) by the majority vote of all judges, unless otherwise stipulated in the Act (e.g., a decision on constitutional complaint is made unanimously in the committee of six judges). Decisions and rulings must contain issue, holding, and reasoning. Separate opinions are allowed, as is the publishing of dissents. Several authoritative dissents have been presented in recent years.[7]

The very important 1999 revision was the inclusion of a time limit of one year, within which the Constitutional Court needs to render its decision in abstract and concrete review, and in proceedings related to constitutional complaint. The unreasonably long duration of proceedings has increasingly become a problem in constitutional adjudication. This is especially relevant in view of Croatia's participation in the Council of Europe and the fact it ratified the European Convention on Human Rights, on October 17, 1997 (see more *infra* I.7.).

Another significant novelty as of 1999 was that the Constitutional Court does not suspend its proceedings if the disputed act becomes noneffective or is altered and brought in compliance with the Constitution and/or law during the constitutional adjudication. This is exactly the opposite solution to the provision of the 1991 Constitutional Act, which, for example, enabled the prolongation of the well-known Pension Adjustment Case (see *infra* II.1.).[8] Namely, by enacting new legislation, Parliament was in position to prevent the CC from rendering the final decision on constitutionality. Of course, the

7 Ruling U-I-2788/2003, Official Gazette, *"Narodne novine,"* nº 6/2005 (on the notion of *vacatio legis*). The dissent was a year later adopted as a majority view.

8 Ruling and Decision U-I-283/1997, Official Gazette, *"Narodne novine,"* nº 27/1998, 67/1998 and 161/1998.

case would be suspended if the proponent dropped it or if the requirements for the conducting of proceedings ceased to exist.

5. *Abstract Review*

The Constitutional Court is empowered to perform only the successive constitutional review; it does not have any authority to participate in enacting laws or other regulations, nor can it seize such authority *a priori*. Moreover, the Court does not give advisory opinions (which should not be confused with the notion of abstract review) and does not sanction legislative omissions. The latter view has been expressly adopted in the Court's current practice, but the nonbinding reasoning of its decisions would point out the need of legislative action in certain direction.[9] Thus, the practice of reading in the law (or regulation) present in some Western countries (e.g., United States, Canada, Italy) did not develop in Croatia, but the possibility of remedying the unreasonable omissions arguably exists through the mandatory annulment of regulations that violate human rights and fundamental freedoms or that unjustifiably put some individuals, groups, or organizations in a more favorable position (see *infra* I.8). Similarly, the Court rightly finds itself incompetent to decide in the case of alleged inconsistency among two norms of the same level (two ordinary laws).[10] However, there is an obvious inadequacy[11] in the Court's practice regarding its acceptance of jurisdiction in cases of alleged inconsistency of domestic laws and international agreements, and rejection of jurisdiction in cases of alleged inconsistency among domestic ordinary and organic laws. Namely, both jurisdictions have not been *expressis verbis*, listed neither in the Constitution nor in the Constitutional Act. However, article 140 of the Constitution clearly states that international agreements have greater legal force than domestic laws. Similarly, by interpreting article 82 (special procedure for enactment of organic laws), the Court clearly pronounced that organic laws have higher legal force than ordinary laws.[12] Organic laws are thus perceived in both a material and a procedural sense as having higher legal effect, but unlike Spain or France, the Court did not develop any indirect way of effectively honoring their proclaimed position.

9 E.g., see Decision U-VII-54/1993, Official Gazette, *"Narodne novine,"* n° 51/1994.

10 E.g., Rulings U-I-94/1992, U-I-94/1992, U-II-137/1995.

11 For an elaborate critique, see in Sanja Barić, ORGANSKI ZAKONI I USTAVNI SUD REPUBLIKE HRVATSKE U USPOREDNOPRAVNOJ PERSPEKTIVI, in *Liber Amicorum in honorem dr. sc. Jadranko Crnić (1928.-2008.), Novi Informator*, 2009, pp. 251–283.

12 E.g., Decision U-I-774/2000, Official Gazette, *"Narodne novine,"* n° 1/2001.

It is also worth mentioning that the Constitutional Court is not competent to decide on conformity of international agreements with the Constitution. Although there were interesting arguments raised as to the unconstitutionality of concordats with the Holy See in view of constitutional provisions on the equality of religion, the Court had no choice but to dismiss the case.[13] There is a proposal from certain experts, politicians, and the Court itself that its jurisdiction should encompass an *a priori* decision on the constitutionality of international agreements. The proposal states that the proclamation of inconsistency of an international agreement with the Constitution would prevent its ratification.

There are two types of abstract review: review of request (the proceedings are instituted by the very petition of enumerated bodies) and review of proposal (anyone can suggest a review, but the motion is subject to previous examination by the Court as to whether allegations give sufficient rise to doubting the constitutionality or legality of a disputed act).

The review can be requested by the President of the Republic, the Government of the Republic (for the examination of conformity of a regulation with the Constitution and law), the ombudsman (in matters regarding the rights of citizens in front of public administration and bodies with public authorities), and the representative bodies of the units of local and regional self-government (in matters concerning the organization, competence, or financing of units of local and regional self-government). In the latter case, the Court will decide on using an emergency procedure within a term of thirty days after the request was filed. Furthermore, the active legitimation is by the 1999 Constitutional Act conferred on one-fifth of members of Croatian Parliament (previously the whole Parliament, or one-third of MPs), and on parliamentary committees. This change should be evaluated in light of forthcoming parliamentary elections and estimations of who will constitute the future government. Namely, after nine years in power and the death of the first president, Dr. Franjo Tudjman, the ruling HDZ party (Croatian Democratic Union party) rightly expected to lose both presidential and parliamentary elections in 2000.

Finally, the Constitutional Court can proceed *ex officio* if it considers necessary to examine a particular piece of legislation or regulation. Although in some instances it might be reasonable for it to act *proprio motu*, the Court cautiously avoids this power, showing generally a considerable measure of deference. The Court established standards connected with this authorization, having in mind its implicit obligation to decide on legal, not

[13] Ruling U-I-2788/2003, Official Gazette "*Narodne novine,*" nº 6/2005.

political, matters. It has acted *proprio motu* only in cases where matters regarding the Constitutional Court itself have been obviously unconstitutionally regulated by an act other than the CACC.[14]

6. *Concrete Review*

Before 2002, when the issue of constitutionality and legality arose in proceedings before courts, the Supreme Court was the only body empowered to seize the Constitutional Court after being notified by the relevant court of justice. Now any court of justice is allowed to present a request for review of constitutionality or legality to the Constitutional Court. If it is a matter of doubting the constitutionality of a law, a referring court will stop the original proceedings until a final decision of the Constitutional Court is made, whereas in cases of suspect regulations or bylaws, the referring court will directly apply the law and continue its proceedings. In both cases, the Supreme Court will be informed of the requests by the Constitutional Court itself. When the court of justice by the final judgment has refused to apply the regulation because of its unconstitutionality or illegality, but the Constitutional Court finds that such unconstitutionality or illegality does not exist, everyone whose right has been violated may request a change of the final judgment of the court during the term of one year from the publication of the Constitutional Court decision.

7. *Effects of the Constitutional Court's Decision*

The decision and rulings of the Constitutional Court are final and enforceable. They are obligatory – every individual or legal person is bound to obey them. All bodies of the central government and the local and regional self-government, within their constitutional and legal jurisdiction, execute the decisions and the rulings of the Constitutional Court. However, the central liability for ensuring the execution of the CC's decisions lies with the Government of the Republic of Croatia. In addition, the Court designs the manner of enforcement, and it may require any other body to follow its order.

The Constitutional Court shall repeal a law, or its part, if it finds it to be unconstitutional. The repealed law, or repealed legal provision, becomes ineffective *ex nunc* – that is, from the day of the decision's publication in the official gazette (or later if the Court decided so). In the case of the

14 Decision U-I-39/2002, Official Gazette "*Narodne novine,*" n° 10/2002.

examination of constitutionality or legality of regulation or bylaw, the Court may either repeal (*ex nunc*) or annul (*ex tunc*) the unconstitutional and/or illegal act. The Constitutional Court may annul a regulation, or its separate provisions, taking into account all the circumstances important for the protection of constitutionality and legality, and especially bearing in mind how seriously it violates the Constitution or the law, as well as the interest of legal security,

- If it violates the human rights and fundamental freedoms guaranteed by the Constitution (articles 21–69 of the Constitution)
- If, without grounds, it places some individuals, groups, or associations in a more or a less privileged position

When the CC establishes unconstitutionality or illegality in reviewing the constitutionality of a law, or the constitutionality and legality of another regulation, or some provisions that are no longer in legal force, it renders a declaratory decision.

Article 52 of the CACC (introduced in 1999) enables further examination of already-examined legal acts. This is possible only in the case of acts previously found to comply with the Constitution and laws. At the same time, it leaves the door open to the dynamic interpretation of the Constitution, especially to the new meaning that particular human rights could acquire.

Apart from its effect on the examined general norm, the decision of the Constitutional Court brings about other legal effects in relation to individual acts issued on the basis of the impugned norm. In principle, proceedings before the Constitutional Court do not stop the enforcement of individual acts, including those issued on the basis of the law or regulation whose constitutionality, or legality, is being examined. If the enforcement could lead to irreparable or hardly reparable consequences, the Court may temporarily suspend the enforcement until its final decision, provided that this is not contrary to the public interest and does not create greater damage to a third party. The final sentence for a criminal offense grounded on a legal provision that has been repealed because of its unconstitutionality does not produce legal effects from the day the CC's decision takes effect, and the criminal sentence may be changed by the appropriate application of the provisions on renewing criminal proceedings. It is particularly worth mentioning the 2002 revision of provisions related to the right to demand the issue of a new individual act in all other, noncriminal, offense cases. Under the previous CACC provisions, individual legal acts issued on the basis of a repealed law, or a repealed or annulled regulation, could have been changed by the issuing authority on the proposal of anyone to whom the individual acts referred.[15] As of 2002, in the case of repealed laws and regulations, this right is conferred only to those individuals and legal persons who submitted to the Constitutional Court a proposal to review the constitutionality of the provision of a law or the constitutionality and legality of the provision of another regulation, and from whom the Constitutional Court accepted the proposal and repealed the provision of the law. In contrast, in case of annulment of a regulation, the right to request new proceedings remains with anyone. In both cases, the request to change the individual act should be submitted within six months from the publication of the CC's decision. Limiting the right to request the change of an individual act based on a repealed general norm was a strange interpretation of the old Latin legal maxim *iura vigilantibus scripta sunt* (rights are written and/or granted only to those who watch over their rights), criticized by constitutional experts at the time. Its perverse effects have recently been particularly obvious. In confronting the effects of the economic crisis, the Croatian Parliament introduced in July 2009 the so-called crisis tax. The law was immediately impugned before the CC by the request of the President of the Republic. However, because the general public was informed of possible reimbursements for overpaid tax, in the case that the tax was found unconstitutional, reimbursements would be granted only to those who formally proposed the review of constitutionality themselves. In the subsequent four months, the Constitutional Court was overwhelmed by more than eighty thousand proposals for constitutionality review submitted by individual and legal persons. The Constitutional Court rendered its final decision on November 17, 2009, upholding the law and rejecting all allegations of its unconstitutionality.

8. *Constitutional Complaint*

Approximately 70 of 147 articles of the Croatian Constitution directly or indirectly contain provisions on human rights and freedoms. The protection of the constitutionally guaranteed rights and freedoms received a meaningful tool with the institution of constitutional complaint. As mentioned in the introduction, this remedy did not exist before 1991.

The right to lodge a constitutional complaint is guaranteed to anyone who deems that his or her constitutional rights and freedoms have been violated

15 Within six months of the Constitutional Court decision, and only if between the delivery of individual act and the institution of proceedings before the Constitutional Court did not elapse more than one (repealed law or regulation) or two (annulled regulation) years.

by an individual act of a state body, a body of local and regional self-government, or a legal person with public authority, which can decide about his or her rights and obligations, or about suspicion or accusation for a criminal act, or his or her right to local and regional self-government guaranteed by the Constitution. A complaint has to be filed within thirty days from the delivery of the impugned decision. The additional requirement is the exhaustion of all other legal available legal remedies.[16]

The long duration of judicial proceedings in general has been an issue in Croatia for a number of years. After its accession to the Council of Europe, and consequently to the European Convention on Human Rights, the criticism became more apparent, translating in a number of applications to the Strasbourg court on the grounds of articles 6 and 13 of the European Convention. In an attempt to provide an effective remedy in such cases, the 1999 Constitutional Act introduced the following solution: individuals were allowed to directly approach the Constitutional Court if it was completely clear that the impugned act, or the unreasonable prolongation of its issuance, violates constitutional rights and freedoms and that the rejection of constitutional examination could create grave and irreparable consequences. The provision was revised again in 2002 to empower the CC to initiate proceedings in response to a constitutional complaint even before all legal remedies have been exhausted in cases when the court of justice did not decide within a reasonable time on the rights and obligations of the party, or on the suspicion or accusation of committing a criminal offence, or in cases when the disputed individual act grossly violates constitutional rights and it is completely clear that grave and irreparable consequences may arise for the applicant if proceedings are not initiated. Thus, the unreasonable duration of trial was expressly proclaimed as a right in itself, regardless of the impact of the duration of trial on other constitutional rights (as in the 1999 Constitutional Act). If the decision is passed to adopt the constitutional complaint for not deciding in a reasonable time, the Constitutional Court determines a deadline for the competent court of justice by which that court should pass the act meritoriously, with a decision as to the applicant's rights and obligations, or the suspicions or accusation of a criminal offense. Moreover, when finding a breach of the right to trial in a reasonable time, the Constitutional Court has to determine appropriate compensation for the violation of this particular right. The latter solution has been criticized because it obliges the Court to allocate compensation: it is not a possibility

[16] It is prescribed that two of extraordinary legal remedies should be exhausted: a judicial review of administrative decision and a revision of the Supreme Court of Croatia.

but a duty. By the beginning of 2005, more than 60 percent of all constitutional complaints (which themselves form an almost 80 percent of the Court's total workload) were alleging unreasonable duration of proceedings, which in turn extremely burdened the Constitutional Court.[17] In 2005, Croatian Parliament enacted the new Law on Courts,[18] narrowing the actual jurisdiction of the Constitutional Court. Namely, the Court remained the final guarantor of the right to trial in a reasonable time, but it is now competent to decide only in a final stage, in relation to duration of proceedings before the Supreme Court. The right to reasonable duration is protected hierarchically within the judicial structure: the immediately higher-level court is competent to decide on duration of proceedings before the immediately lower-level court. A solution adopted relieves the pressure on the Constitutional Court, but not without serious criticism that lies beyond the scope of this report.[19]

As a novelty in the procedural matters, the 1999 Constitutional Act provides that a committee of three judges can reject a complaint for procedural reasons. As of 2002, decision on merits is rendered unanimously by a committee of six judges. Lacking unanimity, or if the committee believes there is broader significance in the matter of the particular constitutional complaint, it may bring the case before the session of the full Court.

As mentioned in previous section, the proceedings before the Constitutional Court do not *per se* stop the enforcement of individual acts, but if the enforcement could lead to irreparable or hardly reparable consequences, the Court may temporarily suspend the enforcement until its final decision, provided that this is not contrary to the public interest and does not create greater damage to a third party.

The Constitutional Court is not a court of full jurisdiction. Thus, in the proceedings following the constitutional complaint it may, besides the ruling on rejecting the complaint, make a decision by which the constitutional

17 There was even a constitutional complaint brought against the Constitutional Court itself, based on the provision of the CACC that in principle sets a period of one year for CC's decision. Because the particular constitutional complaint was not decided in a one-year period, the complainant asked the Court to render a final ruling. The Court rejected the complaint, demonstrating that the right to trial in a reasonable time does not apply to Constitutional Court's proceedings. Ruling U-IIIA-1871/2002, Official Gazette *"Narodne novine,"* nº 49/2003.

18 *Zakon o sudovima*, Official Gazette *"Narodne novine,"* nº 150/2005.

19 To mention only few: it is seriously doubted whether a law that is not a Constitutional Act can actually curtail in such a manner the Constitutional Court's jurisdiction; the provisions of 2005 Law on Courts are insufficiently clear as to the procedure; the practical efficiency of a hierarchical review is unlikely, and so on.

complaint is adopted and the case returned for a renewed procedure to the authority by whose decision the constitutional right had been violated. In exceptional cases, damages or some other compensation may be ordered. In any case, the Court cannot replace the impugned act with a new one. The Court acts as the interpreter of the Constitution, the authority of which – irrespective of all hierarchy – must be followed. The Court in its repealing decision states which constitutional rights or freedoms have been violated and in what way. The authority whose act is repealed is obliged to issue another act instead of the repealed one, and in doing so, it is bound by the legal position of the Court on the violation of the constitutionally guaranteed rights and freedoms of the complainant. Thus, the Constitutional Court decision has the immanent force of precedent.

9. *Other Competences*

A. Jurisdictional Disputes

The Constitutional Court resolves jurisdictional disputes among the legislative, executive, and judicial authorities, both in positive (two or more authorities take action to decide on the same matter) and negative (the seized authority refuses to take action as it deems the matter as falling outside its competence) disputes.

B. Impeachment of the President of the Republic

Under article 104 of the Constitution, the President of the Republic of Croatia is impeachable for any violation of the Constitution he or she has committed in the performance of duties. Proceeding for the impeachment of the President of the Republic may be instituted by the Croatian Parliament by a two-thirds majority vote. The Constitutional Court decides by two-thirds majority of all judges. The decision is to be reached within thirty days. If the Court sustains the impeachment, the President's duties cease immediately by force of the Constitution.

C. Supervision of the Constitutionality of Programs and Activities of Political Parties

The freedom of political activity is guaranteed. Nevertheless, a party that, by its program or actions, threatens the democratic constitutional order, independence, unity, or territorial integrity by use of force and violence will not be allowed to operate. The Court may ban its work on the application of the President of the Republic, the Croatian Parliament, the Government, the Supreme Court of the Republic of Croatia, the body authorized for registering parties, and the Attorney General of the Republic of Croatia.

D. Control of the Constitutionality and Legality of the Elections and the National Referendum and the Electoral Disputes

The Constitutional Court has numerous and significant competences in connection with elections. Institution of proceedings for examination of allegedly unlawful or unconstitutional activities during elections may be requested by any political party, any candidate, a minimum of one hundred voters, or a minimum of 5 percent of the voters in a constituency. If the Court finds violation, it shall inform the public through media and, if necessary, warn the competent authorities. Furthermore, if the violation influenced or could have influenced the results of the elections, the Court shall annul all or some electoral actions that preceded the violation.

The Constitutional Court also decides in the last instance on complaints against the decrees of the Electoral Committee of the Republic. The Constitutional Act details this, but the most important detail is that the decision in an electoral dispute excludes the right to constitutional complaint for the same alleged violation.

The rules on proceedings in electoral disputes apply, accordingly, to the supervision of national referendum. The constitutional revision of 2000 introduced a popular initiative in the Croatian constitutional order. Now, 10 percent of voters can demand a national referendum on any issue that can be put to referendum by Parliament. At the request of the Croatian Parliament, the Constitutional Court is competent to establish whether the question proposed to be put to referendum is in accordance with the Constitution and whether the requirements for popular initiative, set by the Constitution, have been met. The Court decides within a term of thirty days.

E. Constitutional Court Procedures of Appeal

After the 2000 parliamentary elections, the left-center coalition revised the Constitution twice in a less than six months. In the 2001 constitutional revision, the Upper Chamber of the Parliament was abolished. Its competency to decide on appeals against decisions to relieve a judge of office and on disciplinary responsibilities of a judge transferred to the Constitutional Court. Details are regulated by the 2002 CACC. A judge may appeal to the Constitutional Court against the decision to relieve him or her of office or against the decision of the National Judicial Council on disciplinary responsibility, within a term of fifteen days after the disputed decision is delivered. The decision is made by majority vote in a council of the Constitutional Court composed of six judges. If the appeal is adopted as grounded, the matter returns to the National Judicial Council for renewed proceedings, and that body is bound by the legal opinion of the Constitutional Court as to the violation of the appellant's constitutional rights expressed in the repeal decision. The Constitutional Court decision or ruling on the appeals of judges excludes the right of appellants to lodge a constitutional complaint.

Furthermore, even candidates in the procedure for appointing judges may seek protection before the Constitutional Court. The procedure is the same as in a regular constitutional complaint. Thus, a candidate may lodge a constitutional complaint against the decision of the National Judicial Council about appointing judges after he or she has exhausted all legal remedies before the Administrative Court of the Republic of Croatia (through a request grounded on the special provisions of the Administrative Lawsuits Act on the protection of constitutionally guaranteed human rights and freedoms).

F. Monitoring the Execution of Constitutionality and Legality, and Supervisory Control over Passing Regulations for Executing the Constitution, Laws, and Other Regulations

The 2000 constitutional revision introduced two new competences to the Constitutional Court. In monitoring the execution of constitutionality and legality, in full session, the Court adopts reports about any kind of unconstitutionality and illegality it has observed and sends them to Parliament. Up to November 2009, it had adopted six reports addressing important issues that emerged in practice (e.g., right to reasonable duration of a trial, unconstitutionality of regulations on parking payment).

The other competence is supervisory control over the passing of regulations to execute the Constitution, laws, and other regulations. If the Constitutional Court finds that the competent body has not passed a regulation to execute provisions of the Constitution, laws, and other regulations, and was obliged to pass such a regulation, it informs the Government of the Republic of Croatia. If it is the Government of the Republic of Croatia that has not passed a regulation for executing provisions of the Constitution, laws, and other regulations, then Parliament will be informed. Until now, the Court did not act on this competence, and on two occasions, when requested by private individuals, it rightly declined its competence.

II. JUDICIAL ACTIVISM IN CONSTITUTIONAL REVIEW DECISIONS OF THE CONSTITUTIONAL COURT OF THE REPUBLIC OF CROATIA

According to the data at our disposal and a limited insight into the Constitutional Court's normative strategy and practice, we have arrived at the conclusion that the following forms of judicial activism are discernable in the performance (case law) of the CC so far: judicial activism in terms of the conflict with the legislative branch as a typical factor in the process of the political decision making; methodological activism; procedural activism; and substantial activism that reflects the regard for the preservation of the democratic process as opposed to mere political decision making; and a tendency toward the protection of human rights.[20]

We define each of these types of judicial activism and review them separately. However, before classifying types of judicial activism, we list several facts on the performance of the CC that are available at the Court's official Web site. Up to December 31, 2007, the Constitutional Court had received 39,471 cases, of which 32,146 had been settled. The presenters were mostly individuals and legal persons (94 percent of cases). Constitutional complaints (designation U-III) far exceeded any other kind of complaints – they accounted for 28,844 cases, or 82 percent. There were 3,306 (9.3 percent) applications (requests and proposals) for constitutional review of legislative acts with the force of law (designation U-I). There were 2,327 (6 percent) applications for constitutionality and legality review of other regulations (designation U-II). There were 579 (1.7 percent) cases of electoral disputes and constitutionality and legality review of elections (designation U-VIIA), which are not within the jurisdiction of the courts.[21]

According to the data, approximately 97 percent of cases pertained to the constitutional complaints settlement and the constitutional review of laws and other regulations. This state of affairs confirms that the constitutional adjudication process is essential to guarantee constitutionality and protection of human rights, and the Constitutional Court of the Republic of Croatia is a good example.

[20] Aaviksoo B., JUDICIAL ACTIVISM IN CONSTITUTIONAL REVIEW DECISIONS OF THE SUPREME COURT OF ESTONIA, Juridica International, nº II, 2007, pp. 60–69, and classifications that we use to define the types of activism of the Croatian Constitutional Court are available at http://www.juridica.ee/print_article_en. php?document=en/international/2007/2/132527.ART.0.pub.php.

[21] See table PRIMLJENI/RIJEŠENI PREDMETI U RAZDOBLJU OD 1990. DO 31. 12. 2007, at http://www.usud.hr/uploads/PRIMLJENI-RIJESENI%20PREDMETI-020708.pdf.

Of the total number of cases pertaining to constitutional review (3,306), 99 percent were proposals to start the constitutionality assessment procedure brought forward by individuals and legal persons. The other 1 percent were requests brought forward by authorized presenters (e.g., Parliament members, representative bodies of the units of local and regional self-government, courts, people's ombudsman). The CC had settled 86 percent of the cases. In 262 cases, the Court had repealed the law or certain provisions of the law. According to information from Petar Klarić, the former president of the Constitutional Court (2003–7): "The percentage of repealing decisions is decreasing. It dropped from approximately 10% during the first five years to 3.35% for the period from 2001 to 2005."[22] These statistics also mostly refer to 2,327 cases pertaining to constitutionality and legality reviews of other regulations.

In addition to those statistics, Klarić mentioned the following in his speech celebrating the fifteenth anniversary of the Court: "In addition to evolving towards greater judicial activism by way of constitutional interpretation, the performance of the Constitutional Court is characterized by the application of an adequate degree of judicial self-restraint, which is especially applied to borderline issues of interference in politics and interest relations."[23] We are primarily interested in which type of activism this evaluation refers to.

1. *Judicial Activism versus the Legislative Branch*

According to methodology proposed by S. I. Smithey and J. Ishiyama, the level of judicial activism in every state that exercises constitutional review can be arrived at by dividing the total number of repealed laws by the total number of applications, that is, opportunities that the court had to review the constitutionality of laws.[24] In this way, the authors determined the classical definition of judicial activism, according to which the Court exercises judicial activism when its decisions are in conflict with the decisions of the government.[25] From December 22, 1990, to December 31, 2007, the CC received 3,306 requests and proposals to review the constitutionality of laws. Of those, 2,840 cases had settled, and in 262 cases, the CC had decided to

[22] Klarić, P., GOVOR ZA 15. GODIŠNJICU USTAVNOG SUDA, available at http://www.usud.hr.

[23] Klarić P., *op. cit.*, p. 7 (judicial activism and judicial self-restraint underlined by P. B. & S. B.).

[24] See Smithey I. S. and Ishiyama J., JUDICIAL ACTIVISM IN POST-COMMUNIST POLITICS, *Law & Society Review*, issue 36, n° 4, 2002, pp. 719–742.

[25] See Aaviksoo B., *op. cit.*, p. 61.

repeal the law or some of its provisions. According to the proposed model of analysis, the CC exercised judicial activism in 9.2 percent of cases pertaining to laws' constitutionality review.

Reviewing the relationship between the Constitutional Court and the legislative branch from a "functional and pragmatic" point of view, then president of the Court Smiljko Sokol (1999–2003) concluded that "most of the cases concerning the constitutional review, especially repealing decisions . . . have political connotations. The restriction of the parliament's sovereignty is justified by the aim to ensure the protection of implementation and advancement of the rule of law. Even more so, it calls for a certain level of activism."[26] It is useful to compare the percentage of the so-called repeal decisions with similar statistics from other courts. For example, in the first forty years (up to 1991), the German Constitutional Court repealed approximately 200 laws and another 223 regulations. In terms of percentages, judges on the German Constitutional Court had exercised their power to review the constitutionality on 20 percent of all federal laws and had repealed 4.6 percent of laws.[27] The Spanish Constitutional Tribunal received 143 applications to review the constitutionality of laws from 1981 to 1990. Judges on the Spanish Constitutional Tribunal reviewed 101 laws, of which 53, or 52 percent, were found unconstitutional.[28]

In 1992, Nikola Filipović, a judge on the Croatian Constitutional Court, said, "The Constitutional Court is, after all, an institution that applies the law, but creates no policies." Jadranko Crnić, former president of the Court (1991–1999), was of the same opinion for a long time.[29] Nevertheless, during his presidency, the Constitutional Court adopted a decision (Decision No. U-I-283/1997, May 12, 1998) that objectively reflected one of its most significant attempts to create policies by strengthening the rule of law and protecting human rights. Provisions of articles 1–4 and 6 of the Pension

26 Sokol S., USTAVNI SUD REPUBLIKE HRVATSKE U ZAŠTITI I PROMICANJU VLADAVINE PRAVA, Collected papers of Zagreb Law Faculty, vol. 51, nº 6, 2001, p. 1164.

27 Constitutional Court Act (Bundesverfassungsgerichtsgesetz), adopted on March 12, 1951, allowed for the Federal Constitutional Court, which was stipulated by the Basic Law (1949), to start functioning. See Kommers D.P., THE CONSTITUTIONAL JURISPRUDENCE OF THE FEDERAL REPUBLIC OF GERMANY (2nd ed.), Duke University Press, Durham, NC, 1997, p. 9. See also Stone Sweet A., GOVERNING WITH JUDGES – CONSTITUTIONAL POLITICS IN EUROPE, OUP, Oxford, 2000, pp. 63–73.

28 See data on German, Spanish, Italian, and French constitutional courts in Stone Sweet A., *op. cit.*, pp. 63–73. Also see Podolnjak R., IZBOR SUDACA USTAVNOG SUDA REPUBLIKE HRVATSKE U KOMPARATIVNOJ PERSPEKTIVI, Collected papers of Zagreb Law Faculty, nº 1, 2007, p. 547.

29 "We are basically partial to that view"; see Crnić J., VLADAVINA USTAVA, Informator, Zagreb, 1994, p. 14.

Adjustment Act (Law on Adjustment of Pensions and Other Allowances from the Pension and Disability Fund and Administration of Funds of the Pension and Disability Fund) were repealed by this decision.

The decision pertained to the Government and Parliament's actions, which the Court had found unconstitutional even before the decision became effective. In 1993, the Government of the Republic of Croatia ceased to adjust pensions according to increases in inflation and cost of living (or following the principle of wage movements), even though it continued to do so with wages. According to the facts determined during the proceedings, the result was that wages increased twice as much as pensions from July 1993 to December 1997; that is, in 1997, the average pension was half of the average wage, which means that the standard of living for retired persons (pensioners) was half the standard of the working population with average incomes. Therefore, the Constitutional Court ruled that "this legal arrangement . . . changed the social status of retired persons to such an extent that it created social inequality of citizens," which is why it found the contested provisions to "contravene . . . basic constitutional provisions of article 3 of the Constitution of the Republic of Croatia, which guarantee[s] equality, social justice, and the rule of law; and with article 5 of the Constitution, which states that laws are to be in conformity with the Constitution." On May 12, 1998, all the aforementioned Pension Adjustment Act provisions were repealed by Decision No. U-I-283/1997. Furthermore, retired persons were to receive the unpaid pensions for the period 1993–97.

The legislative and executive branches turned out to be very "hostile" toward the Constitutional Court and its decision. Vladimir Šeks, one of the leading politicians of the ruling party and vice president of Parliament, announced the adoption of a law that would restrict the Constitutional Court's activism. At the same time, Zlatko Mateša, then prime minister, questioned the state's debt to pensioners by saying that the state would go bankrupt if it were to repay the debt. Renowned international jurists commented on the decision as well. Stephen Holmes claimed that the ruling proved that "there is still an ongoing war between the state and the society" in some postcommunist countries of Europe. Lech Garlicki compared the decision to a similar one of the Polish Court, saying that it represented "a serious warning to the government."[30]

[30] "In 1991, the government of Poland did a similar thing as the Croatian government in 1993. The Parliament adopted the law that decreased the rates of pension adjustment on the basis of inflation. The Constitutional Court of Poland decided to allow it, but not retroactively. The Court decided that the law would only be applied to 'future' pensioners. Since this government measure was retroactive, the debt had to be repaid. However, the government announced

The correct response of the legislative branch did not occurr until six years later, when Parliament adopted the Decision on the Promulgation of the Law on the Enforcement of the Constitutional Court's Ruling, dated May 12, 1998.[31] In the meantime, complex issues in the relationship between the CC and Parliament had emerged. One of the most prominent issues was that of the impact of the Court's decisions, that is, legal effects of the review of the constitutionality of abstract laws, as well as the attitude of the legislative branch toward the repealing of "its" laws. The issue was actually about whether the Court could perform the role of the guardian of constitutionality and legality without first being regulated in detail and without prior prescribing of conditions and outcomes of its decisions.[32] The adoption of the 2002 Constitutional Act on the Constitutional Court of the Republic of Croatia played a significant part in laying down the rules of the game in the relationship between the two institutions. To avoid legal uncertainties occurring in the period between the adoption and the publication of a repeal decision, the Constitutional Act also states, "The repealed law or other regulation, or their repealed separate provisions, shall lose legal force on the day of publication of the Constitutional Court decision in the Official Gazette *Narodne novine*, unless the Constitutional Court sets another term."[33]

bankruptcy should the state be forced to repay. In addition, for the Constitutional Court decision to be implemented, the parliament had to adopt a separate provision. It took them five years to do so. In 1997, a sort of a compensation act was adopted, but the pensioners still have not been compensated entirely. This means that the Court's decision has not been fully implemented. Both the Court and the Government have been severely criticized. The finance minister resigned. Pensioners will probably receive compensation in the form of vouchers upon the completion of privatization. When will that be? No one knows." See ULOGA USTAVNOG SUDA RH U "RATU IZMEĐU DRŽAVE I DRUŠTVA"' (29/9/98), Voice of America, at http//www.voa.gov/miscl/croatia/penzi.html. See also Sadurski W., RIGHTS BEFORE COURTS, Springer, Dordrecht, 2005, p. 191.

31 See Decision on the Promulgation of the Law on the Enforcement of the Constitutional Court's Ruling dated May 12, 1998, Official Gazette *"Narodne novine,"* n° 105/2004.

32 S. Sokol is right to emphasize the importance of two major issues when it comes to establishing the Constitutional Court's constitutional part in relation to three branches of government: "Firstly, there has to be a legal, constitutional and actual assurance of the Court's organizational and functional independence in the interaction between the Court and the Government. Secondly, national authorities must apply and implement the Court's decisions regardless of their interests and attitude towards individual decisions. If the Constitutional Court decisions are disregarded or partially implemented in order to meet the authorities' needs, the Constitutional Court, which has no means of coercion at its disposal, will not be able to fulfill its constitutional role." Sokol S., ODNOS USTAVNOG SUDA I TIJELA SUDBENE VLASTI, Collected papers of Zagreb Law Faculty, vol. 50, n° 1–2/2000, p. 57.

33 Article 55, paragraph 2 of THE CONSTITUTIONAL ACT ON THE CONSTITUTIONAL COURT, Official Gazette *"Narodne novine,"* n° 49/2002. See Crnić J., KOMENTAR

However, it is important to emphasize that, in this case, the Constitutional Court's activism is intertwined with the definition of a social welfare state that has not been made concrete either by constitution makers or by legislators, which leads us to the second type of judicial activism of the Constitutional Court of the Republic of Croatia.[34]

2. *Methodological Activism of the Constitutional Court – The Interpretation and Power of the Legal Argument*

It is possible to determine the degree of judicial activism by a critical insight into methodology and argumentation in connection with constitutional interpretation. Judicial activism is actually determined with regard to legal argumentation. According to some authors, the issue concerns the argumentation that is only partially based on constitutional documents; for others, the argumentation is different from the constitution makers' original intent; and for others, it is about arguments that arise from nonlegal, historical, traditional, ambiguous or abstract principles, and so on.[35] Methodological activism is thus seen as a form of activism that does not end in the so-called negative legislation exercised by the Court; rather, it acts as a complement to existing standards. In other words, it serves the purpose of shaping circumstances so as to adjust them to the Constitution and the legislators' positive decisions.[36]

Adhering to the attitude that the Constitutional Court "cannot exercise its fundamental constitutional authority of constitutionality and legality review and protection of rights guaranteed by the constitution without the interpretation of first of all constitutional and also legal provisions," S. Sokol, as the President of the Court, often emphasized its "activist approach

USTAVNOG ZAKONA O USTAVNOM SUDU REPUBLIKE HRVATSKE, *Narodne novine*, Zagreb, 2002, pp. 137–144.

34 S. Rodin claims that certain constitutional concepts, such as the constitutional concept of a social state (article 1 of the Constitution), are not "self-explanatory and they demand additional interpretation." However, the Constitutional Court has so far done the most in the concretization, that is to say, the definition of this concept, which is clear from the aforementioned decision. Rodin S., USTAVNI SUD DEFINIRA SOCIJALNU DRŽAVU, Revija za socijalnu politiku, vol. 5, nº 2, 1998, p. 4, available at http://www.rsp.hr/ojs2/index.php/rsp/article/view/338/342.

35 See Aaviksoo B., *op. cit.*, p. 61.

36 The case *Numerus Clausus I Case (1972) 33 BverfGE 303* before the German Federal Constitutional Court is well known in the field of comparative constitutional law. This case initiated the Court's judicial intervention in the enrolment policy, which had been exclusive until then. The policy of student admission had been monopolized by German universities (*numerus clausus*). See Kommers D. P., THE CONSTITUTIONAL JURISPRUDENCE OF THE FEDERAL REPUBLIC OF GERMANY, Durham, NC, Duke University Press, 1997, p. 282.

to constitutional interpretation."[37] In doing so, Sokol did not advocate unlimited activism in the laws' constitutionality review. He is rather of the opinion that there should be a "certain level" of activism so as to protect and promote the rule of law:

> Basically, the doctrine of judicial self-restraint should not be applied in the protection and promotion of the rule of law. On the other hand, the application of the doctrine is necessary when it comes to actual political questions, for example, the conflict of interests between two national authorities that does not affect the field of human rights or constitutionally determined autonomy of civil society institutions.[38]

The Constitutional Court has gradually developed its interpretational capacity toward methodological activism through its decisions. Among several important decisions, the decision to repeal a number of provisions of the Law on the State Judicial Council was the most important.[39] This institution had long been just an extension of the ruling party, openly ignoring the Constitutional Court's decisions. Furthermore, its actions had damaged the remaining bits of the Judiciary's reputation.[40]

In Decision U-I-659/1994, the Constitutional Court further elaborated its attitude on the rule of law, which is "the highest value of Croatia's constitutional order and as such contains, *inter alia*, the issue on the general characteristics which the laws should have to be in congruity with the rule of law," deciding in the process that "this is the most important issue for review of the constitutionality of the disputed Law" (subparagraph 10). Furthermore, the Constitutional Court believes that the rule of law is "more than mere requirement for acting in keeping with the law: it embraces the

[37] Sokol S., USTAVNA INTERPRETACIJA USTAVNOG SUDA U KONTROLI USTAVNOSTI ZAKONA, in USTAVNI SUD U ZAŠTITI LJUDSKIH PRAVA (ed. Crnić J. & Filipović N.), Organizator, Zagreb, 2000, p. 17.

[38] *Ibid.*, p. 21.

[39] Law on the State Judicial Council, Official Gazette *"Narodne novine,"* n° 58/93, 49/99. The Constitutional Court repealed the following provisions: provision of article 9, paragraph 5, which reads: "and the State Judicial Council"; provision of article 16, paragraph 5; provisions of article 18; provisions of article 23, paragraphs 1–4; provision of article 29, paragraph 1; provisions of article 37, paragraphs 1–2; provisions of article 37, paragraph 3, which reads: "the Croatian Parliament, House of Counties proposal." Official Gazette *"Narodne novine,"* n° 31/2000, March 22, 2000.

[40] See Uzelac A., AMENDMENTS TO THE LAW ON COURTS AND LAW ON THE STATE JUDICIAL COUNCIL – ELEMENTS OF THE REFORM OF THE ORGANIZATIONAL JUDICIAL LEGISLATION, in CROATIAN JUDICIARY: LESSONS AND PERSPECTIVES, Croatian Helsinki Committee for Human Rights and Netherlands Helsinki Committee, Zagreb, 2002, pp. 37–79.

requirements that concern the contents of the laws . . . the rule of law is not just the rule of laws, but also the rule by rights which – in addition to the requirements regarding the constitutionality and legality, as the most important principles of every regulated legal order – also contains additional requirements, concerning laws themselves and their content" (subparagraph 11). Subparagraph 12 of the decision represents "a strong message to the legislators and other constitutional authorities"[41] concerning the position and role of the rule of law in Croatia's constitutional and democratic order: "In that sense, the Court particularly points out that, within the legal order founded on the rule of law, laws must be general and equal for all, and legal consequences must be unambiguous for all those to whom the law is applied. In addition, the Court points out that legal consequences must be adequate to the legitimate expectations of parties involved in every specific case where the law is directly applied to them."

By the Constitutional Court Decision and Ruling Nos. U-I-659/1994, U-I-146/1996, U-I-228/1996, U-I-508/1996, and U-I-589/1999, dated March 15, 2000, the judges on the CC had significantly expanded constitution makers' definition of the rule of law as a fundamental value. To that effect, subparagraph 11 of the aforementioned decision testifies to an increase in "liberal interpretation of the constitution" and an activist approach that encourages the consolidation of the rule of law and democracy in the Republic of Croatia.[42] Nevertheless, that "more liberal and broader use of the constitutional interpretation" as a source of "increased activism" has been gradually reduced with "a certain level of judicial self-restraint," which definitely had something to do with an increased number of constitutional complaints submitted by many Croatian citizens who felt that their rights were not adequately protected by the regular judiciary.[43]

41 See Bačić A., VLADAVINA PRAVA I INSTITUCIJE KONTROLE USTAVNOSTI ZAKONA, in USTAVNI SUD U ZAŠTITI LJUDSKIH PRAVA, Organizator, Zagreb, 2000, p. 53.

42 See Sokol S., USTAVNA INTERPRETACIJA USTAVNOG SUDA U KONTROLI USTAVNOSTI ZAKONA, in USTAVNI SUD U ZAŠTITI LJUDSKIH PRAVA (ed. Crnić J. & Filipović N.), Organizator, Zagreb, 2000, p. 24; More on the decision is in Sokol S., USTAVNI SUD REPUBLIKE HRVATSKE U ZAŠTITI I PROMICANJU VLADAVINE PRAVA, Collected papers of Zagreb Faculty of Law, 6/2001, pp. 1170–1171; Bačić A., VLADAVINA PRAVA I INSTITUCIJE KONTROLE USTAVNOSTI ZAKONA, in USTAVNI SUD U ZAŠTITI LJUDSKIH PRAVA, Organizator, Zagreb, 2000, p. 54; Rodin S., THE CONSTITUTIONAL COURT AND SEPARATION OF POWERS IN THE REPUBLIC OF CROATIA, in CROATIAN JUDICIARY: LESSONS AND PERSPECTIVES, Croatian Helsinki Committee for Human Rights and Netherlands Helsinki Committee, Zagreb, 2002, pp. 205–218.

43 Quotes from P. Klarić's speech marking the Constitutional Court's 15th anniversary. See Klarić P., GOVOR ZA 15. GODIŠNJICU USTAVNOG SUDA, p. 7, available at: http://www.usud.hr/.

3. *Procedural Activism – Precedence of Form over Content*

Procedural approach determines judicial activism according to procedural criteria rather than merit (substance). This form of activism exists when Constitutional Court judges ignore procedural limitations or see them as a means to broaden possibilities for their intervention. One of the most important procedural limitations is the political-question doctrine, together with some other doctrines (e.g., court-access doctrine, dispute doctrine).

The political-question doctrine originated in the United States. American judges apply it in cases of deciding whether a matter is appropriate for judicial review (matters not appropriate for review traditionally includes foreign policy, national security, and organization of government).[44] The judges referred to the doctrine (actually to lack of jurisdiction and unjusticiability) whenever they wanted to refrain from intervening in politics. Constitutional courts of Germany and Austria, which served as main models for the Croatian constitutional adjudication, have developed a "considerable influence on the political process." Moreover, the German Constitutional Court has developed "the assertive 'champion of democracy' doctrine and did not hesitate to fight consistently for its political influence."[45]

The Croatian Constitutional Court, for different reasons, has not displayed that kind of assertiveness. It has, however, made the political-question doctrine relative by defending the rule-of-law principle. It is possible to deduce this from the rule-of-law principle itself. In other words, constitutionality control that curbs *a priori* the impossibility of questioning certain issues because they represent discretionary authority of the legislative and executive branches speaks in defense of this principle.

Nevertheless, the political-question doctrine has influenced significantly the Constitutional Court of the Republic of Croatia since its inception. It was

[44] B. Smerdel defines the political-question doctrine as a doctrine according to which "the Court is to refrain from intervening in political matters and remain strictly within the bounds of the application of the law area. In reality, intervention is unavoidable because all the Supreme Court decisions of any importance have a significant political impact, as seen in the Court's rulings on the demarcation of jurisdiction between federal authorities and state governments; racial equality, death penalty, or on the relationship between the executive and legislative branches." See Smerdel B. and Sokol S., USTAVNO PRAVO, Zagreb, 1995, p. 102. According to BLACK'S LAW DICTIONARY, the political-question doctrine is the judicial principle that a court should refuse to decide an issue involving the exercise of discretionary power by the legislative or executive branch of government; or the political question is a question that a court will not consider because it involves the exercise of discretionary power by the executive or executive branch of government. Political question is also referred to as nonjusticiable question. See BLACK'S LAW DICTIONARY (8th ed.), 2004, p. 1197.

[45] See Smerdel B. and Sokol S., USTAVNO PRAVO, Faculty of Law, Zagreb, 2006, p. 201.

especially evident in the constitutional review of the President's well-known 1991 "wartime decrees."[46] Legal reviewers tried to prove that a certain form of procedural activism had been applied; that is, that constitutional judges had disregarded procedural limitations of article 17 (derogative clause) of the Constitution. M. Matulović thus concluded that the CC's position on ending the proceedings in aforementioned case was "completely untenable":

> Firstly, it is not in accordance with the provision of the article 17, paragraph 1[,] of the Constitution that states: "During a state of war or an immediate threat to the independence and unity of the Republic, or in the event of some natural disaster, individual freedoms and rights guaranteed by the Constitution may be restricted. This shall be decided by the Croatian Parliament by a two-thirds majority of all representatives or, if the Croatian Parliament is unable to meet, at the proposal of the Government and upon the counter-signature of the Prime Minister, by the President of the Republic." The Parliament was obviously able to meet because it was in session when the President made these provisions. Secondly, the attitude of the Constitutional Court, according to which when human rights are restricted due to exceptional circumstances, the onset of these circumstances is not to be previously determined by a separate decision, is not in

[46] During that period, the Constitutional Court had stopped the constitutional review of the following decrees with statutory force: (1) decree on internal affairs during state of emergency or imminent threat to independence and unity of the Republic of Croatia (Official Gazette "*Narodne novine,*" nº 55/91); (2) decree on offenses against public order during state of emergency or imminent threat to independence and unity of the Republic of Croatia (Official Gazette "*Narodne novine,*" nº 55/91); (3) decree on public gatherings during state of emergency or imminent threat to independence and unity of the Republic of Croatia (Official Gazette "*Narodne novine,*" nº 55/91); (4) decree on protection against fire during state of emergency or imminent threat to independence and unity of the Republic of Croatia (Official Gazette "*Narodne novine,*" nº 55/91); (5) decree on identity cards during state of emergency or imminent threat to independence and unity of the Republic of Croatia (Official Gazette "*Narodne novine,*" nº 55/91); (6) decree on reporting of residence during state of emergency or imminent threat to independence and unity of the Republic of Croatia (Official Gazette "*Narodne novine,*" nº 55/91); (7) decree on armories during state of emergency or imminent threat to independence and unity of the Republic of Croatia (Official Gazette "*Narodne novine,*" nº 55/91); (8) decree on education, cultural affairs, and sport during state of emergency or imminent threat to independence and unity of the Republic of Croatia (Official Gazette "*Narodne novine,*" nº 55/91); (9) decree on science and research activities during state of emergency or imminent threat to independence and unity of the Republic of Croatia (Official Gazette "*Narodne novine,*" nº 55/91); (10) decree on gun control during state of emergency or imminent threat to independence and unity of the Republic of Croatia (Official Gazette "*Narodne novine,*" nº 55/91); (11) decree on providing of information during state of emergency or imminent threat to independence and unity of the Republic of Croatia (Official Gazette "*Narodne novine,*" nº 57/91); (12) decree on implementation of sanctions for criminal acts, economic offenses, and misdemeanors during state of emergency or imminent threat to independence and unity of the Republic of Croatia (Official Gazette "*Narodne novine,*" nº 55/91); (13) decree on rights of war invalids and members of their families (Official Gazette "*Narodne novine,*" nº 57/91).

> accordance with article 4 of the International Pact on Civil and Political Rights. The Constitutional Court's attitude is an example of inappropriate approach to the interpretation of constitutional provisions on the restriction of human rights in case of immediate public threat. In addition, this attitude reaffirms the fact that national courts play a minor role in their effort to protect human rights during state of emergency.[47]

Broad interpretation of *ius standi* provisions in the CACC (1999) represents the opposite type of procedural activism. Abiding by the principles of equality and the rule of law, judges dismissed the grammatical interpretation of the Constitution (article 125) and the Constitutional Act (article 62) by choosing to maintain the view that "constitutional complaint presenters can be not only citizens (individuals), but all legal persons as well ("everyone" – see article 28, paragraph 1 of the CACC)."[48]

4. *Substantial Activism – Support for Democracy and Constitutional Rights*

Substantial (real) activism, of all forms of contemporary activism, has the largest following. Even though it is sometimes hard to distinguish different forms of activism, substantial activism is primarily detected through legal and political analyses of decision contents, and less through the nature of interpretation or through exceeding procedural limitations. The following statement is an attempt at defining substantial activism: "Judicial activism or substantive policy-making involves the interference by the court in directing social processes in areas where it lacks so-to-say privilege of policy-making."[49] There are two areas of special interest for the development of judicial activism: preservation of the democratic order and protection of human rights.

The relationship between judicial activism and democratic order has been particularly analyzed by John H. Ely, in the framework of the modern American theory of judicial review. According to Ely, the meaning of constitutional adjudication must be found in strengthening the process of political representation, removing obstacles to political change, or facilitating

47 Matulović M., LJUDSKA PRAVA – UVOD U TEORIJU LJUDSKIH PRAVA, Hrvatsko filozofsko društvo, Zagreb, 1996, p. 465.

48 See Crnić J., USTAVNA TUŽBA, doctoral dissertation, Zagreb, 1999, p. 159. Aforementioned provision is now Article 128 of the Constitution, and Article 62, paragraph 1, of the Constitutional Act on the Constitutional Court (2002).

49 See Aaviksoo B., *op. cit.*, p. 63.

the representation of minorities.[50] For example, the Federal Constitutional Court of Germany has significantly added to the notion of democracy as one of the fundamental principles of the Republic of Germany (besides federalism, separation of powers, and the rule of law). Because the 1949 German Basic Law does not define the notion of democracy, the Constitutional Court has set the frame for the German constitutional democracy by way of deciding on parliamentary democracy, elections, voting, and political parties.[51]

Therefore, there are Constitutional Court decisions that, despite representing a repeal of the legislators' choices, actually contribute to the preservation of democracy. This fact allows for and represents a solid vindication of the conclusion that the constitutional adjudication is one of the fundamental preconditions of democracy. Such is, for example, Decision No. U-I-177/2002, dated April 20, 2006, by which the Constitutional Court repealed one of the articles of the Act on Amendments of the Law on Referendums and Other Forms of Personal Participation in the Performance of State Powers and Local and Regional Self Governance (NN 92/01).[52] According to the Constitutional Court's opinion, the provision of the said law, which prescribes the possibility of evaluating the referendum issue,[53] is not in accordance with the provisions of article 86, paragraphs 1 and 2 of the Constitution, which specify issues eligible for referendums and result in the conclusion that "the issue of referendums is entirely determined by the Constitution and it falls into the category of the so-called constitutional reserves." Besides that, the legislators were not authorized to prescribe the Constitutional Court's jurisdiction (which is solely prescribed by the Constitution and the CACC), thereby violating article 128 of the Constitution (subparagraph 3 and 4 of the decision). In the said case, the

[50] Hart J. E., DEMOCRACY AND DISTRUST (14th ed.), Harvard University Press, Cambridge, MA, 2001, p. 268.

[51] Kommers D. P., THE CONSTITUTIONAL JURISPRUDENCE OF THE FEDERAL REPUBLIC OF GERMANY, Duke University Press, Durham, NC, 1997, pp. 166–238 (especially chapter 5 on political representation and democracy).

[52] Decision nº U-I-177/2002, dated April 20, 2006, Official Gazette *"Narodne novine,"* nº 58/2006.

[53] This pertains to article 8(h) of the Amendments of the Law on Referendums and Other Forms of Personal Participation in the Performance of State Powers and Local and Regional Self-Governance (Official Gazette *"Narodne novine,"* nº 92/2001): "Upon a demand for a referendum, the Parliament is free to request that the issue be assessed by the Constitutional Court within 30 days. If the Constitutional Court determines that the issue is not in conformity with the Constitution and the law, the referendum will not be held." Official Gazette *"Narodne novine,"* nº 92/2001, October 24, 2001.

Constitutional Court protected the citizens' right to decide via referenda as "the basic form of direct democracy."[54]

Decision No. U-III/2678/2006, dated April 4, 2007, by which the Constitutional Court repealed the Administrative Court's ruling, influenced the process of strengthening the political representation and recognizing political minorities' legitimate rights.[55] The Constitutional Court stated that the interpretation of the Local and Regional Self-Government Act included in the Administrative Court's contested ruling was wrong because it had been founded on "formalist interpretation of authorized legal provisions and rules of procedure," in which process this court "did not take into account the legal purpose of representative body meetings at the request of one third of all its members," and that is the protection of a multiparty democratic system and a representative minority (subparagraph 7 of the decision). The Constitutional Court judges pointed out the necessity to remove all those measures that the parliamentary majority used to restrict the parliamentary minority's rights in the democratic process by emphasizing that the representative minority had been given special protection by the legislators.

In addition to the protection of democracy, the Constitutional Court's activism is most evident in the protection of human rights. Constitutional courts in many European countries (e.g., Austria, Czech Republic, Hungary, Germany, Slovenia, Spain) have jurisdiction over the protection of human rights. According to article 128 of the Croatian Constitution, the Constitutional Court is also obligated to protect these rights. The court has the right to "decide on constitutional complaints against the individual decisions of governmental bodies, bodies of local and regional self-government and legal entities with public authority, when these decisions violate human rights and fundamental freedoms, as well as the right to local and regional self-government guaranteed by the Constitution of the Republic of Croatia."

The protection of human rights by deciding on constitutional complaints is, as a rule, of subsidiary nature, as a constitutional complaint may be lodged only after every possible legal remedy against violation of the constitutional rights has been exhausted (see *supra* I.8).[56] However,

[54] According to Sokol S.; see Smerdel B. and Sokol S., USTAVNO PRAVO, Zagreb, 2006, p. 219.

[55] The Decision n° U-III/2678/2006 dating April 4, 2007; Official Gazette *"Narodne novine,"* n° 42/2007.

[56] It should also be mentioned that the CACC allows for exceptions to this rule in article 63. See Constitutional Act on the Constitutional Court of the Republic of Croatia, Official Gazette *"Narodne novine,"* n° 49/02 (consolidated text).

constitutional complaint has become a very significant instrument in the Croatian Constitutional Court's activism. The former president of the court, S. Sokol, also admits to this. Just before his term ended in 2003, Sokol stated that "for a long time, the Court in practice developed a kind of interpretative activism . . . in order to protect human rights and uphold the rule of law more completely."[57]

In the period 1990–2007, the Constitutional Court received 28,000 constitutional complaints, representing 82 percent of all applications received by the CC; it adopted 4.18 percent of the constitutional complaints. The number of constitutional complaints was on the rise, year after year. For example, in 1991, the CC received 25 constitutional complaints, whereas in 2007, the number reached 4,175 complaints. A sudden increase in number of complaints occurred in 2000.[58] However, the constitutional complaint option created certain difficulties from the start:

> Since its inception, the Constitutional Court has been in a tight spot, trying to fulfill two demands: firstly, for trying to offer a broad and comprehensive legal protection based on extensive interpretations of constitutional provisions on constitutional rights, but at the risk of crossing given constitutional boundaries and thus jeopardizing its relationship with other government bodies, especially the Supreme Court; and secondly, for trying to employ a more restrictive interpretation that ensures an additional protection of basic constitutional rights, together with maintaining the Constitutional Court's privileged position with regard to the judiciary.[59]

In our search for the decisions that illustrate the Constitutional Court's substantial activism in the protection of constitutional rights, we must point to the decisions relating to the principle of proportionality, a general legal principle of Croatia's constitutional order. According to this principle, the state must regulate individual rights and liberties through appropriate and proportional means.[60] The 1990 Constitution of the Republic of Croatia

[57] Sokol S., USTAVNI SUD REPUBLIKE HRVATSKE U ZAŠTITI I PROMICANJU VLADAVINE PRAVA, in USTAV KAO JAMAC NAČELA PRAVNE DRŽAVE (ed. Crnić J. and Filipović N.), Organizator, Zagreb, 2002, p. 26.

[58] According to P. Klarić, the former president of the Constitutional Court, "this increase should be attributed in part to the rise of constitutional complaints logded against County Courts decisions, which occurred in 1999. . . . The result was not only the Constitutional Court overload and its transformation into the highest ranking regular court, but also a disturbance in jurisdiction of the Constitutional and Supreme Court." See Klarić P., *op. cit.*, p. 6.

[59] Belajec V., USTAVNE OSNOVE ZA PODNOŠENJE USTAVNE TUŽBE, in USTAVNI SUD U ZAŠTITI LJUDSKIH PRAVA (ed. Crnić J. and Filipović N.), Organizator, Zagreb, 2000, p. 100.

[60] See Smerdel B & Sokol S., USTAVNO PRAVO, Faculty of Law, Zagreb, 2006, p. 58.

refers to the proportionality principle in article 17, which tackled the problem of restrictions on rights and freedoms during a state of emergency.[61] However, at the time of the original constitutional document, the principle of proportionality was not "clearly indicated as a general principle of our Constitutional Law."[62] During regular (normal) circumstances, the 1990 Constitution required the application of article 16, according to which the rights and freedoms could be restricted by "law [only] in order to protect freedoms and rights of others, public order, public morality and health."[63] Article 83 of the Constitution stated that such laws must be adopted by a majority vote of all Parliament representatives.[64] Because the legislators had displayed political immoderateness by disproportionately restricting rights and freedoms, the Constitutional Court had gradually started developing a form of the proportionality principle that would give a clear indication to the

61 See article 17 of the CONSTITUTION OF THE REPUBLIC OF CROATIA (1990): "(1) During a state of war or an immediate threat to the independence and unity of the State, or in the event of severe natural disasters, individual freedoms and rights guaranteed by the Constitution may be restricted. This shall be decided by the Croatian Parliament by a two-thirds majority of all members or, if the Croatian Parliament is unable to meet, at the proposal of the Government and upon the counter-signature of the Prime Minister, by the President of the Republic. (2) The extent of such restrictions shall be adequate to the nature of the danger, and may not result in the inequality of persons in respect of race, color, gender, language, religion, national or social origin. (3) Not even in the case of an immediate threat to the existence of the State may restrictions be imposed on the application of the provisions of this Constitution concerning the right to life, prohibition of torture, cruel or degrading treatment or punishment, on the legal definitions of penal offenses and punishments, or on freedom of thought, conscience and religion."

62 See Rodin S., NAČELO PROPORCIONALNOSTI – PORIJEKLO, USTAVNO UTEMELJENJE I PRIMJENA, Collected papers of the Zagreb Faculty of Law, 1–2/2000, p. 45.

63 See article 16 of the CONSTITUTION OF THE REPUBLIC OF CROATIA, which was amended in 2000. The present version states: "(1) Freedoms and rights may only be restricted by law in order to protect freedoms and rights of others, public order, public morality and health. (2) <u>Every restriction of freedoms or rights shall be proportional to the nature of the necessity for restriction in each individual case</u>" (underlined by P. B. & S. B.).

64 See the 1990 CONSTITUTION OF THE REPUBLIC OF CROATIA, article 83: "(1) Laws which regulate national rights shall be passed by the Chamber of Deputies by a two-thirds majority vote of all representatives. (2) Laws which elaborate the constitutionally freedoms and the rights of man and citizen, the electoral system, the organization, responsibilities and operation of government bodies and the organization and the organization of local self-government and administration shall be passed by the Chamber of Deputies by a majority vote of all representatives." After constitutional changes that occurred in 2000, these issues were transferred to article 82 which states: "(1) Laws (organic laws) which regulate the rights of national minorities shall be passed by the Croatian Parliament by a two-thirds majority vote of all representatives. (2) Laws (organic laws) which elaborate the constitutionally defined human rights and fundamental freedoms, the electoral system, the organization, authority and operation of government bodies and the organization and authority of local and regional self-government shall be passed by the Croatian Parliament by a majority vote of all representatives."

legislators of what are necessary limitations on rights and freedoms to protect the well-being of individuals and their communities.

Substantial activism of the Constitutional Court has been developing gradually. It emerged in the Court's decisions during the presidency of J. Crnić, and it assumed definitive shape during the presidency of S. Sokol. One of the earlier examples is the Decision and Resolution No. U-I-673/1996, of April 21, 1999, by which several provisions of the Law on Compensation for Property Expropriated during the Yugoslav Communist Rule had been repealed.[65] With regard to the issue of the tenants' legal right of preemption, which emerged during the constitutional review of the law, by repealing article 29, paragraph 1, of the said law, the Constitutional Court decided that "the legal pre-emptive right may restrict the right to dispose of the property, but this restriction must be in accordance with the goal for which it was included in the Law on Compensation." Furthermore, it stated that the legislators could have protected the original owners' interests by applying milder means than those provided in the contested law (i.e., open-ended, or nonlimited, right of preemption). Besides having been disproportionate to the goal attempted to be achieved by the law, these restrictions also contradicted the constitutional provisions on the restriction of human rights and freedoms. The Constitutional Court seized the opportunity to instruct the legislators on future practice by emphasizing the fact that any limitation of human rights and freedoms, be it necessary and Constitution based, represents "an exceptional state, because it does not abide by the general rules regarding constitutional rights and freedoms." The CC decided: "Because of this, not only must these restrictions be based on the Constitution, but they also have to be proportional to the target goal and purpose of the law. In other words, this goal and purpose must be achieved with as little interference in the constitutional rights of citizens as possible (if the restrictions can be gradated, of course)."

The Constitutional Court continued to explain the principle of proportionality further with the January 11, 2000, Decision No. U-I-1156/1999, by which article 8, paragraph 1, of the Law on Limitation of Use of Tobacco Products was repealed, stating: "in the situation when the Constitution explicitly obliges the application of the requirement of proportionality (proportionality test) in states of emergency, this Court deems that condition to be even more valid during the time of 'regular state' in the

[65] See Decision and Resolution of the Constitutional Court, nº U-I-673/1996, dated April 21, 1999 (Official Gazette *"Narodne novine,"* 39/1999) and Decision U-I-902/1999, dated January 25 2000 (Official Gazette *"Narodne novine,"* 14/2000).

country."[66] The following Constitutional Court's Decision No. U-I-902/1999, dated January 25, 2000, by which the CC repealed certain provisions of the Law on Institutions of Higher Education, defined the absolutely guaranteed intrinsic purpose of university autonomy with regard to the broader purpose of said autonomy. This purpose can be limited insofar as the legislators prove that "the public interest in the restriction of the university autonomy is stronger than the university's interest that the autonomy be realized."[67]

Despite high expectations, the adoption of the so-called new constitutional complaints settlement technology in 2000, according to which the Constitutional Court decides only in cases of violation of constitutional rights, did not relieve the civic pressure on the Court.[68] This new practice of the CC provoked a discussion on the possible consequential refusal of constitutional protection of certain rights.[69] But the fact remains that the Constitutional Court, by working actively to protect fundamental rights, added to its own activism. The Constitutional Court imposed certain decision-making parameters on the legislators by establishing strict control of rationality and by balancing out of legislative regulation of certain issues

[66] See Decision U-I-1156/2000, dated January 11, 2000 (Official Gazette *"Narodne novine,"* 14/2000), by which the Court repealed article 8, paragraph 1, of the Law on Limitation of Use of Tobacco Products (Official Gazette *"Narodne novine,"* 128/1999).

[67] See Decision U-I-902/1999, dated January 25, 2000 (Official Gazette *"Narodne novine,"* 14/2000).

[68] See Sokol S., USTAVNI SUD REPUBLIKE HRVATSKE U ZAŠTITI I PROMICANJU VLADAVINE PRAVA, in USTAV KAO JAMAC NAČELA PRAVNE DRŽAVE (ed. Crnić J. and Filipović N.), Organizator, Zagreb, 2002, p. 26. According to data, the increase in constitutional complaints continued even after 2000. See table PRIMLJENI/RIJEŠENI PREDMETI U RAZDOBLJU OD 1990. DO 31. 12. 2007, available at http://www.usud.hr/uploads/PRIMLJENI-RIJESENI%20PREDMETI-020708.pdf.

[69] On controversies generated by the new practice of the Constitutional Court, which limited the admissibility of constitutional complaints to constitutional rights, see S. Rodin's review that basically states the following: "Despite some vague wording, and even conceptual mistakes, the Constitutional Court's new practice concerning the criteria required for a constitutional complaint to be admissible is similar to solutions accepted in some other legal systems, namely Germany. It is directed towards a clearer differentiation between the jurisdiction of the Constitutional Court and that regular courts, and towards the decrease of the Constitutional Court's workload. This practice serves to stimulate regular courts to take responsibility for the primary protection of human rights and give some guarantee that severe violations of these rights will be adequately addressed by the Constitutional Court, which is now unburdened by numerous unsubstantial petitions." See Rodin S., TEMELJNA PRAVA I DOPUŠTENOST USTAVNE TUŽBE, u USTAVNI SUD U ZAŠTITI LJUDSKIH PRAVA (ed. Crnić J. and Filipović N.), Organizator, Zagreb, 2000, p. 221. N. Gavella poses the same question with regard to the constitutional protection of ownership rights. See Gavella N., NEKA RAZMIŠLJANJA U POVODU USKRATE USTAVNOSUDSKE ZAŠTITE VLASNIŠTVA, *Informator*, nº 4815, 2000. See S. Rodin's answer in the previously cited text.

(e.g., preemption rights,[70] freedom of enterprise and ownership,[71] university autonomy[72]). In the beginning of that process, the legislators were limited only by the Constitution. But the Constitutional Court's decisions determined the legislators' future formal and legal practice by a more rational and more balanced approach. The Constitutional Court's decision in itself authorizes the Court's intervention in case of a lack of political commitment to resolve certain issues in new ways.[73] This practice of the Constitutional Court of the Republic of Croatia certainly deserves to be designated as substantial activism.

III. CONCLUSIONS ON THE ACTIVISM OF THE CONSTITUTIONAL COURT OF THE REPUBLIC OF CROATIA

The legal and constitutional development of the Republic of Croatia and a gradual stabilization of state institutions from 1990 until the present day are, in a special way, reflected in the theory and practice of constitutional adjudication. The development of constitutional jurisprudence in Croatia can be compared with the state of affairs in other so-called new democracies. The tendency of constitutional courts to build up their reputation and position in political systems is a common characteristic of new democracies. However, since 1989, each of these institutions has developed judicial activism using its own methods. Some constitutional courts had been immediately labeled "activist" (e.g., Polish, Hungarian, and Czech courts).[74] Others have developed activism gradually in accordance with somewhat difficult conditions of preserving proclaimed democratic principles and

[70] See Decision and Ruling U-I-673/1996, dated April 21, 1999 (Official Gazette *"Narodne novine,"* 39/1999) and Decision U-I-902/1999, dated January 25, 2000 (Official Gazette *"Narodne novine,"* 14/2000).

[71] See Decision and Ruling U-I-1156/2000, dated January 11, 2000 (Official Gazette *"Narodne novine,"* 14/2000), by which the Court repealed article 8, paragraph 1, of the Law on Limitation of Use of Tobacco Products (Official Gazette *"Narodne novine,"* nº 128/1999).

[72] See Decision U-I-902/1999, dated January 25, 2000 (Official Gazette *"Narodne novine," 14/2000*), by which the Court repealed certain provisions of the Law on Institutions of Higher Education.

[73] See Canon B.S., A FRAMEWORK FOR THE ANALYSIS OF JUDICIAL ACTIVISM, in Haplern S. S. and Lamb C. M. (ed.), SUPREME COURT ACTIVISM AND RESTRAINT, Lexington, 1982, p. 385.

[74] See items in Sadurski W. (ed.), CONSTITUTIONAL JUSTICE, EAST AND WEST: DEMOCRATIC LEGITIMACY AND CONSTITUTIONAL COURTS IN POST-COMMUNIST EUROPE IN A COMPARATIVE PERSPECTIVE, Kluwer Law International, The Hague, 2002.

institutions. The Republic of Croatia, that is, its Constitutional Court, falls into that category. Being that the concept of constitutional adjudication existed under the socialist regime in Croatia, the Constitutional Court possibly had, at least in theory, a chance to show that it did not hold a subordinate position vis-à-vis the legislative branch. However, the Constitutional Court's judges did not show a particular inclination toward activism. In performing their most important duties (e.g., protecting human rights, controlling the legislative and executive branches), they gradually arrived at activism. The judges had always been more tactically rather than strategically oriented. This inference is corroborated by the following objective and subjective indicators.

First, the judges themselves have shown awareness of the Constitutional Court's activist practice. According to P. Klarić, the former president of the Court, the performance of this institution "is characterized by the application of an adequate level of judicial self-restraint, which is especially applied to borderline issues of interference in political interests . . . in addition to evolving towards greater judicial activism by way of constitutional interpretation."[75]

Second, under direct and indirect influence of the Constitutional Court, the Parliament amended article 4 of the Constitution on separation of powers, article 16 of the Constitution on the proportionality principle, article 29 of the Constitution on the right to a fair trial, and the Constitutional Act on the Constitutional Court (that broadened the Court's jurisdiction especially with regard to maintaining a reasonable duration of court proceedings concerning basic human rights).[76]

Finally, the existence of judicial activism in Croatia is confirmed by comparative researches into constitutional jurisprudence of former socialist countries. We cited S. I. Smithey and J. Ishiyama's research as an example and their measurement of the degree of judicial activism in postcommunist politics. Starting with the analysis of different variables (authority to overturn legislation, amount of repealed laws, the Constitutional Court's independence and power of constitutional authorities, existence of constitutional declaration of rights and freedoms, federalization, regionalization, existence of competition between parliamentary parties, and public opinion on constitutional jurisprudence vis-à-vis other branches of government), we end with a summary of certain values. This research definitely has some flaws, like the one-sided analysis of Croatian issues, as

[75] See Klarić P., *op. cit.*, p. 8.

[76] *Ibid.*

well as the propensity for behaviorist rather than institutional interpretations ("it is political context, rather than the institutional design, that provides insight into the process of judicial activism").[77] However, the research notes some aspects of constitutional and judicial review in Croatia.[78] This is all indication, albeit limited indication, that we need to infer that judicial activism is not a "political myth" in Croatia and other former socialist countries.[79]

Regarding the performance of the Constitutional Court, we wish to make clear the uncontroversial fact that constitutional adjudication in the period 1990–2008 has proved a positive and constructive factor of constitutional democracy in Croatia. This assessment did not result from a previously set approach to or quality of explicit judicial activism that characterized some other constitutional courts in former socialist countries. It resulted even less from strict self-restraint, or passive defense of its constitutional role. It is, in fact, safe to say that this undoubtedly active institution (when it comes to receiving and processing cases) has taken an activist approach only on occasion.[80]

77 Smithey I. S. and Ishiyama J., JUDICIAL ACTIVISM IN POST-COMMUNIST POLITICS, *Law & Society Review*, issue 36, nº 4, 2002, p. 738.

78 In the said research, the position of the Constitutional Court of the Republic of Croatia is considered by Smithey and Ishiyama to be within the framework of constituent components evaluation. By attaching a separate set of values to each component (1. Can judicial decisions be overturned? 2. Presence of *a priori* review? 3. How long is the judges' term of office compared to other political actors? 4. How many actors are involved in selection of judges? 5. Who establishes court proceedings? 6. What conditions must be met for judicial removal?) the final result (judicial power score) is obtained according to the formula: 1 + 2 + 3 + 4 + 5 + 6: 6. The authors give Croatia 0.47 points. The order of results is this (from the lowest to highest): 0, 31, Slovakia; 0,39, Estonia; 0.39, Mongolia; 0.42, Russia; 0.45, Belarus; 0.47, Croatia; 0.50, Azerbaijan; 0.53, Ukraine; 0.56, Czech Republic; 0.56, Slovenia; 0.56, Georgia; 0.58, Hungary; 0.58, Latvia; 0.61, Macedonia; 0.70, Lithuania; 0.70, Bulgaria; 0.72, Moldova; 0.83, Armenia; 0.95, Romania. A more complete analysis includes Czech Republic, Estonia, Georgia, Latvia, Lithuania, Moldova, Russia, and Slovakia. See Smithey I. S. and Ishiyama J., *op. cit.*, p. 731.

79 It is one of the legitimate theses in the debate on the separation of powers, the relationship between the branches of government, and, of course, judicial activism. According to this thesis, irresponsible judges and their decisions concerning the constitutionality review of laws can harm the democratic process. Kermit Roosevelt, in his book THE MYTH OF JUDICIAL ACTIVISM: MAKING SENSE OF SUPREME COURT DECISIONS, Yale University Press, New Haven, CT, 2006, p. 262, focuses on a certain cultural myth about judicial activism, according to which irresponsible judges and some of their decisions do a lot of damage to the democratic system of government. Critics emphasize that Roosevelt is more inclined to the preservation of the democratic decision-making process than to the preservation of freedom. See Sandefur T., THE WOLVES AND SHEEP OF CONSTITUTIONAL LAW: A REVIEW ESSAY ON KERMIT ROOSEVELT'S THE MYTH OF JUDICIAL ACTIVISM, Program for Judicial Awareness, Working Paper 06-004, at http://ssrn.com/abstract=954029.

80 It is useful to remember that judicial activism can go both in positive and in negative directions. In the former case, constitutional judges make decisions concerning moves made by other

This kind of moderate judicial activism is justified by and associated with two influential sets of factors. The first set includes a number of different domestic circumstances, within and without the Constitutional Court itself: wartime circumstances, during which national political leaders expected no contestation of the principle of the unity of state power from other institutions; initial unquestionable authority of the head of state and the uncritical position taken by the judges; gradual adjustment of judges to new values such as the rule of law, separation of powers, and the antimajority power of constitutional review; a search for a more adequate normative tool that would help elaborate constitutional independence and coordination; and constitutional judges having distorted views of constitutional patriotism. The second set of factors is associated with the type and nature of constitutional review in Croatia. These factors are also arguments that dismiss antimajority objections to the existing type of constitutional review. The contribution assessment of the Croatian Constitutional Court, which is the representative of the European type of concentrated constitutionality control, is primarily influenced by structural provisions and rules of procedure. There are several limitations imposed on the CC and its judges: (1) the procedure for electing judges, which is considerably affected by political authorities, although it also affects the representation of the Court; (2) term of office and occasional changes in the setup of the Court, which reflect a change of political majority; (3) the Court's decisions are open for public review and can be amended by constitutional changes; (4) the Court is not equipped with a mechanism for carrying out of its decisions; (5) the decisions are reached by the interpretation and application of the text of the Constitution instead of political argumentation. Concerning the political authorities, the CC is limited because directly shaping policies is not permitted.

The Constitutional Court's determination to protect basic human rights is the strongest justification for occasional displays of activism in its practice. Constitutional adjudication ensures a just and continuous representation of the democratic political process by subjecting political branches of the government to constitutionality control. This argument provides us with the following conclusion: as long as the Constitutional Court protects and consolidates basic human rights of Croatian citizens, constitutional adjudication, together with all its powers, will have democratic legitimacy.

constitutional bodies on the basis of constitutional provisions and autonomous expertise. In the latter case, their decisions are more or less the result of political or some other kind of pressure, or their decisions are deliberately biased and discriminate in favor of certain political or ideological views. See Cerar M., SLOVENIA'S CONSTITUTIONAL COURT WITHIN SEPARATION OF POWER, in Sadurski W., *op. cit.*, p. 216.

We believe that we have successfully proved that, in the process of winning and preserving democratic legitimacy, significant contribution has been given by the aforementioned occurrences of judicial activism and interpretations of the Constitution that inspire its active defense and unhesitating constitutional interference in the legislative process.

CZECH REPUBLIC

CZECH CONSTITUTIONAL COURT AS POSITIVE LEGISLATOR?

Zdenek Kühn
Associate Professor of Jurisprudence, Charles University Law School
Judge of the Supreme Administrative Court of the Czech Republic
Praha
Zdenek.kuhn@nssoud.cz

The Czech idea of the constitutional tribunal is closely associated with the concept of the constitutional court as a negative legislator. The idea goes back to the early 1920s, to the teaching of normativist school of law that influenced the creation of the first Czechoslovak Constitutional Court of 1920. The idea of the Court as a negative legislator is controlling nowadays as well; it has found its way into all major textbooks in the field.[1]

In this report, I first outline the history of the constitutional courts on the Czech territory. I also explain the power held by the current Czech Constitutional Court. The second part describes constitutional complaints and their potential to modify the conception of the Court as negative legislator. Then I proceed with analyzing interpretative decisions in abstract constitutional review, which accounts for the situation when the Court does not annul the law but rather provides its interpretation, which is constitutional. The fourth and fifth sections deal with several types of cases in which the constitutional court serves as a real negative legislator. First, I analyze several positive aspects of decisions annulling laws. Then I discuss one of the most controversial issues – the constitutional court's lawmaking activity in the area of unconstitutional gaps in the legal order. In the sixth

1 For instance, a leading Czech book on legal theory describes the Constitutional Court at work through the lens of the Kelsenian negative legislator. J. Boguszak, J. Čapek, A. Gerloch, *Teorie práva* [Legal Theory], Eurolex Bohemia, Prague 2001.

section, I raise the question of what happens to the text of the law if the last amendment to that law is annulled by the Court. Is it possible that the Court will revive the earlier version of that law through its annulment, or will it produce – as a genuine negative legislator – only a gap in the legal system? Finally, I offer the Court's own self-perceptions and provide some conclusions.

I. THE HISTORY AND THE POWERS OF THE CZECH CONSTITUTIONAL COURT

The Czech Republic enjoys one of the oldest traditions of the Kelsenian centralized constitutional review in the world. Czechoslovakia was the first country in the world that incorporated in its Constitution provisions on a constitutional court. The Czechoslovak Constitutional Court antedates its Austrian Constitutional Court based on the Austrian Constitution of 1920.[2] Its establishment was the result of the revolutionary atmosphere after World War I. As in Austria, in Czechoslovakia, the Constitutional Court was a brainchild of the normativists, namely Franz Weyr, a close collaborator of Hans Kelsen. Therefore the normativist idea of the constitutional tribunal as a negative legislator stood in the very origins of Czech constitutionalism.[3]

Although the Court was not entirely insignificant, it suffered from serious setbacks. The initial impetus to review a statute had to be given by either a chamber of Parliament, the Supreme Court, or the Supreme Administrative Court. The high courts, however, did not have the power in relation to a pending case, but *in abstracto*, through the Court acting *en banc*.[4] Another major problem was that the statute could not be reviewed if it had been promulgated more than three years before the motion to annul the law.[5] In addition, after the terms of the justices appointed in 1921 expired in 1931, the legislature delayed several years (until 1938) before appointing new justices. It was generally understood that the reason for that was the hesitance of the legislature to appoint the body that would exercise control over the legislature's own law. The new justices were appointed only a few months before the collapse of Czechoslovakia (German occupation in March

2 Stanley L. Paulson, On Hans Kelsen's Role in the Formation of the Austrian Constitution, in Werner Krawietz, Robert S. Summers, Ota Weinberger, Georg Henrik von Wright, The Reasonable as Rational? On Legal Argumentation and Justification. *Festschrift* for Aulius Aarnio, Duncker & Humblot, Berlin 2000, 385–395, at 390.

3 František Weyr.

4 See the decision of the Supreme Administrative Court, Boh.adm. 1097/22, 1757/22.

5 Art. 12 of the Constitutional Court Act of 1920.

1939) and thus did not have time to finish important cases pending before the court.[6] During the era of communism (1948–89), the very idea of a constitutional court was virtually impossible.[7] A new constitutional court was created in 1992, but it functioned for only several months and died out with the dissolution of Czechoslovakia on January 1, 1993.

Ultimately, the Czech Constitutional Court (CCC) was created in 1993. Its agenda and overall design is inspired by the German model of the constitutional court. The most important power of the CCC is to decide on issues of constitutionality of acts of Parliament. This issue can be brought to the CCC by the President or a group of either forty-one Deputies or seventeen Senators (*in abstracto*, i.e., without basis in any real-life case);[8] by any court of general jurisdiction, if that court opines that the law applicable to the pending case is unconstitutional; or by an individual litigant who has exhausted all remedies before general courts. Another important power of the CCC, and its most frequent activity, is deciding on constitutional complaints of individual litigants after they have exhausted all available remedies, including proceedings before ordinary courts. We will see that it is the constitutional complaint and the Court's friendly attitude toward complainants that is one of the factors able to reshape the Court's status of a negative legislator.

The Court's remaining competences (e.g., jurisdictional disputes between state bodies and self-governing regions, constitutionality of international treaties, impeachment) are very rarely, if ever, applied in practice. Unlike its

6 As a result of the restrictive conditions for the initiation of constitutional review, few statutes were ever struck down. Therefore, some scholars dealing with the issue preferred the diffuse system of constitutional review. Eventually, they proposed broadening the Constitutional Court's powers, improving the system for the selection of justices (e.g., the elimination of the role of political parties, or the limitation of eligibility to be a justice only to professors or former judges of the supreme courts) and increasing the number of subjects who would be entitled to initiate proceedings before that Court. Jaroslav Krejčí, *Principy soudcovského zkoumání zákonů v. právu československém* [The principles of judicial review of law in the Czechoslovak law], Nákladem vydavatelství časopisu Moderní stat, Prague 1932. None of these reforms was ever realized.

7 Although during the era of the so-called Prague Spring of 1968 there were strong arguments in favor of renewal of a constitutional court as a sort of reaction to Stalinist crimes of the 1950s (see J. Pelikán (ed.), *The Czechoslovak Political Trials, 1950–1954: The Suppressed Report of the Dubček Government's Commission of Inquiry 1968*, London: MacDonald 1971, at 281) and even a constitutional law on the establishment of the constitutional court was enacted in 1968, this initiative was dropped after the Soviet invasion, and the reform proposal was never realized during the communist era.

8 The number of parliamentary referrals between the fall 1993 and the end of 2004 was close to ten annually; of the laws challenged, every third law was either totally or partially annulled. See the Web site of the CCC, http://www.concourt.cz (visited 1 July 2009).

short-lived federal predecessor (the Constitutional Court of Czechoslovakia), the CCC does not have the power to provide generally binding interpretation of the Constitution that would have no connection to either abstract constitutional review or constitutional complaint. Thus, the Court's interpretation of the constitution is always incidental, serving to justify a decision in a pending case.

The Court's internal structure is different from its German and Spanish counterparts. The Court's fifteen justices decide *en banc* mostly issues of abstract review of constitutionality of laws, whereas ordinary constitutional complaints against decisions of public authorities (including general courts) are always decided by chambers of three justices (there are four chambers of the Court). Only if the chamber decides to deviate from the Court's jurisprudence is the case referred to *en banc* proceedings.[9]

II. CONSTITUTIONAL COMPLAINTS AGAINST DECISIONS OF GENERAL COURTS

1. One often overlooked phenomenon is the extent to which constitutional courts are able to reshape the law by deciding on constitutional complaints. The necessary condition for the effective quasi-legislative function in this field, however, seems to be the power of the constitutional tribunal to review decisions of general courts for the constitutionality of their interpretation of the law (as opposed to controlling whether interpreted law is unconstitutional). This is a novelty when compared with Kelsen's idea of a constitutional tribunal. Kelsen did not envision a constitutional tribunal that would intrude into individual cases decided by ordinary judges. Individual cases should have been within the exclusive competence of ordinary judges in Kelsen's view, and constitutional justices were empowered solely to determine the constitutionality of general norms, not of individual judicial decisions.[10]

2. The Kelsenian model of the constitutional tribunal that shall not interfere with judgments of the general courts is more or less followed in

[9] For more detail, see the basic English description available at the Court's Web site, http://www.concourt.cz.

[10] It is nicely explained in a short description of Kelsen's model of constitutional judiciary, as implemented in 1920 in both Austria and Czechoslovakia; see Hans Kelsen, "Judicial Review of Legislation: A Comparative Study of the Austrian and the American Constitution," 4 *The Journal of Politics* 183–200 (1942).

today's Austria.[11] However, the Czech Republic opted for a different model. Following the German version of the centralized constitutional judiciary,[12] the CCC exercises judicial review of the constitutionality both of general rules and of individual decisions, including the judgments of general law courts. The fact that the constitutional court can directly interfere with decisions of general courts is one of the defining features of the Czech Court.[13] In contrast, in most of postcommunist Europe,[14] one might find only very indirect interactions between the constitutional and ordinary judiciaries. Most constitutional tribunals in Eastern Europe have no power to quash the judgment of the general court for that judgment's unconstitutional interpretation of law unless the law itself is unconstitutional.

In 2008, of 3,250 cases brought before the CCC, 3,208 were constitutional complaints.[15] It is true that only about 6 percent or 7 percent of constitutional complaints will be actually decided by the Court, and the rest would be

[11] On the difference between Austrian and German constitutional courts, see D. Merten, Aktuelle Probleme der Verfassungsgerichtsbarkeit in der Bundesrepublik Deutschland und in Österreich, in Festschrift E. Melichar, 107–123; C. Grewe, "Vergleich zwischen den Interpretationsmethoden europäischer Verfassungsgerichte und des Europäischen Gerichtshofes für Menschenrechte" 58 *Zeitschrift für ausländisches öffentliches Recht und Völkerrecht* 459, at 462 (2001). In English, see Herbert Hausmaninger, *The Austrian Legal System* (2nd ed.), Kluwer Law International 2000, 147–148.

[12] See § 13 para. 8a of the law on Federal Constitutional Court, Art. 93 para. 1 (4a) and (4b) of the Basic Law. The system in Spain is similar (Art. 43 ff. of the organic law on the Constitutional Tribunal). In postcommunist Europe, this model is much less popular. Besides the Czech Republic (and since 2002, Slovakia), it seems to exist only in Slovenia (Art. 21 para. 1 (6) of the Act on the Constitutional Court of the Republic of Slovenia, Uradni list [Official Gazette] n° 15/1994, accessible in English at the Web site of the Slovenian Constitutional Court, http://www.us-rs.si (visited on May 16, 2003)) and Croatia (Art. 127 para. 1 of the Constitution of Croatia, Art. 62 ff. of the Constitutional Act on the Constitutional Court of the Republic of Croatia, Narodne novine [Official Gazette] n. 49/02 of May 3, 2009, accessible in English at http://www.usud.hr/, visited on May 16, 2009).

[13] I have elsewhere argued that the fact that CCC regularly reviews constitutionality of ordinary court decisions has substantial potential to influence the postcommunist ideology of judicial decision making. See Z. Kühn, "Worlds Apart: Western and Central European Judicial Culture at the Onset of the European Enlargement," 52 *American Journal of Comparative Law* 531 (2004). Also Procházka highlighted that the CCC, because of its procedure on constitutional complaints and the review of judicial decisions, is the most judicial constitutional tribunal in Central Europe. R. Procházka, *Mission Accomplished: On Founding Constitutional Adjudication in Central Europe*. CEU Press, Budapest, New York 2002, at 166.

[14] Cf., e.g., Art. 1 of the Act n° XXXII of 1989 on the Constitutional Court of Hungary or Art. 79 para. 1 and Art. 191 para. 1 point 6 of the 1997 Constitution of Poland, cf. generally also Procházka, *supra*, note 13.

[15] See the Web site of the CCC, http://www.concourt.cz (visited August 16, 2009).

dismissed as apparently unjustified; however, this number is substantially higher than in Germany, Spain, or the United States.[16]

3. One might plausibly argue that lawmaking activity of the Court through constitutional complaints brings nothing more than the truism that any interpretative activity entails not only interpretation but also formation of something new. It is, of course, true. However, what makes the jurisprudence of the CCC unique if compared with most judgments of ordinary courts is its much broader scope and the open-ended character of constitutional provisions applied by the CCC.

The lawmaking nature of the case law relating to constitutional complaints is further highlighted by the fact that the CCC generally follows activist German methodology, according to which, for example, the German Federal Constitutional Court emphasized that constitutional law is "an objective value order,"[17] espoused the theory that constitutional law "radiates" throughout the legal order.[18] The Czech Constitutional Court made a systematic attempt to transplant into the national legal order major German constitutional doctrines, including the doctrines of the radiation of constitutional law throughout the legal system (*Ausstrahlungswirkung*),[19] which characterizes mainstream German tendencies in respect to the third-party effect of basic rights. According to this doctrine, "[a]s far as the

[16] In 2005, the German Federal Constitutional Court decided about 2.5 percent of the entire body of constitutional complaints on their merits (see http://www.bverfg.de/organisation/gb2005/A-IV-1.html, visited 1 January 2008); the Spanish Constitutional Tribunal decided in 2001 approximately 3.5 percent cases (http://www.tribunalconstitucional.es/TRIBUNAL.htm, visited 22 July 2009); the U.S. Supreme Court decides approximately 80–100 cases per year, that is, 1.5 percent of its entire workload (http://www.supremecourtus.gov). This number seems to be declining in the United States; cf. E. A. Hartnett, "Questioning Certiorari: Some Reflections Seventy-Five Years after the Judges' Bill," 100 *Columbia L. Rev.* 1643 (2000). The fact that the CCC decided on merit 183 cases in 2004, which made up to 6.7 percent of all constitutional complaints in 2004, keeps this figure steadily above 5 percent (V. Šimíček, Ústavní stížnost [Constitutional Complaint], 3rd ed., Prague, Linde 2005, p. 91), can be partly explained by the initial phase of the interactions between general courts and the CCC. The German Federal Constitutional Court was also more assertive in its first period vis-à-vis general courts. In the 1950s and the early 1960s, it decided on merit 4–5 percent of all constitutional complaints, and that number declined to 3 percent in the late 1960s and 1970s. See Ch. von Starck (hrsg.) Bundesverfassungsgericht und Grundgesetz: Festgabe aus Anlass des 25 jährigen Bestehens des Bundesverfassungsgerichts. Tübingen: J. C. B. Mohr (Paul Siebeck) 1976, pp. 405 ff.

[17] BVerfGE 7, 198 (Lüth).

[18] On this point in English, see Robert Alexy, *A Theory of Constitutional Rights* (J. Rivers trans.), Oxford 2002, 350 ff. (explaining the "substantive fundamentality" of the constitution in this way: "constitutional rights and constitutional rights norms are substantively fundamental, because they incorporate decisions about the basic normative structure of state and society").

[19] Cf. e.g., BVerfGE 7, 198 (206), "*Lüth*" and the decision of the Czech Constitutional Court published in Coll. of CCC decision vol. 12, p. 97 (III. ÚS 139/98).

position of the judge is concerned, radiating effect establishes a duty to take account of the influence of constitutional rights on private law norms when interpreting them."[20] The radiation of basic rights throughout the legal system[21] means that many cases, though governed *prima facie* by "simple," that is, nonconstitutional law only, have constitutional dimensions, so that to decide them properly, the provisions of simple law must be interpreted and applied in a manner that takes into account and balances conflicting constitutional rights.[22] This brings the CCC as a court with power to say ultimately what the law is in virtually any case.

For instance, when applying provisions of the Czech Civil Code concerning defamation and slander, judges must take into account the freedom of speech and counterbalance it against the rights of personal honor. To ignore this constitutional dimension of the application of ordinary law (i.e., the conflict of basic rights in horizontal relations) would lead to a one-sided jurisprudence, completely undermining free speech by private means. Facing an apparent inclination by the ordinary courts to proceed in precisely this way,[23] we might well think of it as yet another doctrinal remnant of the communist era. Although communist case law dealt with defamation and

[20] Alexy, *supra* note 18, 355–356. Recently, the German Federal Constitutional Court expanded this doctrine into the area of the law of contracts, which marked yet another step in the constitutionalization of private law. E.g., BVerfGE 89, 214. Cf. Peer Zumbansen, "The Law of Contracts," in: Mathias Reimann, Reinhard Zimmerman (eds.), *The Oxford Handbook of Comparative Law*, Oxford 2006.

[21] The CCC directed ordinary courts that "one of the functions of the Constitution, and especially of the constitutional system of basic rights and freedoms, is its 'radiation' throughout the legal order. The sense of the Constitution rests not only in ordering basic rights and freedoms, as well as institutional mechanism and process of making legitimate state decisions, not only in a direct effect of the Constitution and its position as the source of law, but also in a duty of state and public bodies to interpret and apply law considering the protection of basic rights and freedoms. In this case it means the duty of the law courts to interpret particular provisions of the civil procedure code from the viewpoint of the sense and purpose of constitutionally guaranteed basic rights and freedoms." The judgment III. ÚS 139/98 published in Coll. of CCC decisions vol. 12, p. 97.

[22] See, e.g., BVerfGE 18, 85, *passim* (1964) or BVerfGE 80, 137, at 155 (1989), referring to ordinary nonconstitutional law as *einfaches Recht*, literally translated as "simple" law. The Czech Constitutional Court took this concept from its German counterpart. Cf., e.g., the judgment of the CCC III. ÚS 224/98, Coll. of CCC decisions, vol. 15, p. 17. The concept of ordinary law rests on the differences between constitutional and nonconstitutional law. The former implies balancing and difficult evaluative reasoning on the basis of constitutional values, which is not the case of the latter unless it has the constitutional dimension – then balancing is realized through the application of constitutional principles and rights based on the principle of radiation.

[23] Cf. as a typical example judgment of the CCC of 15 March 2005, I. ÚS 367/03, Coll. of CCC decisions, vol. 36, p. 605 (*Rejžek v. Vondráčková*), translated at http://angl.concourt.cz/angl_verze/doc/1-367-03.php.

slander, and accorded even private individuals a certain area of freedom from outside intrusion, it almost completely disregarded freedoms of speech and the press. The CCC has changed this interpretation (law in action), with little change on the formal level by the legislature (law in books).

The CCC often bases its reasoning on abstract clauses such as the rule of law, or the right to a fair trial or human dignity, thus creating a complex set of dynamic constitutional propositions that extend far beyond the strict reading of the constitutional texts.[24] The significance of such reasoning is far reaching, not restricted only to the field of constitutional law but touching even the long-standing conceptions of law, judicial decision making, and so on. M. Taruffo has rightly mentioned that this character of constitutional courts is, in fact, a worldwide phenomenon, fundamentally changing the very core of continental culture.[25] Facing this perspective, the content of the law is ultimately defined by the constitutional court. In fact, this type of activist interpretative methodology of constitutional courts moved the CCC far from being solely a negative legislator.

4. The very nature of the constitutional court's power over ordinary courts' judgments tells us that this activity can be effective only if ordinary courts generally respect the constitutional rulings, so that, rather than the constitutional court being obliged to expend its limited judicial resources on repeatedly deciding the same issue (which will inevitably be the case if ordinary courts fail to respect its decisions), each new holding would concern a novel and significant issue. Even if a constitutional tribunal is not hampered in its work by being denied the competence to intervene into adjudication by ordinary courts, which is the case of the CCC, it still does not have the actual capacity to police all conceivable constitutional defects contained in ordinary court decisions. After all, constitutional courts do not have dozens of judges sitting in numerous senates, as is the custom for the supreme court in European judicial systems, but at most, fifteen (the Czech Republic) or sixteen (Germany) justices, who cannot possibly process the same number of cases that the supreme courts do. Therefore, however, the continental constitutional judiciaries have not been endowed with a

24 For an excellent analysis of the interpretative technique of the Central European constitutional courts, see Procházka, supra note 13,, 203–263.

25 Michel Taruffo, Institutional Factors Influencing Precedents, in MacCormick D. N., Summers R. S. (eds.), *Interpreting Precedents: A Comparative Study*, Aldershot: Dartmouth 1997, 437, at 450. Cf. also the new final chapter in the second edition of John Henry Merryman, *The Civil Law Tradition*, Stanford, CA, Stanford University Press 1985.

certiorari like power; in fact, various substitutes are being developed to serve the same needs.[26]

A necessary supplement to this is the obligation of judges of general courts to follow the case law of the CCC. In fact, the CCC describes the issue of binding force of its decisions as a *conditio sine qua non* of its existence.[27] Despite some original controversy,[28] it seems to be generally accepted that the constitutional interpretation is binding for all courts.[29]

5. There are several nice examples of a rather unimportant difference between interpretation consistent with the constitution, on the one hand, and a formal annulment of the law by the CCC, on the other hand. Sometimes ordinary courts evinced unwillingness or, at best, an inability to follow constitutional doctrines despite the Constitutional Court's repeated attempts to specify the constitutional limits of statutory construction. On several occasions, there have been repeated constitutional complaints objecting to the ordinary courts' defiance of prior rulings in similar cases. In such cases, the CCC has been compelled to annul the statute at issue and to caution the legislature that, to avert the danger that a statute is applied in an unconstitutional manner, it must be drafted in more precise terms.[30]

26 On this aspect in Germany, see Werner Heun, Access to the German Federal Constitutional Court, in Ralf Rogowski, Thomas Gawron (eds.), *Constitutional Courts in Comparison. The U.S. Supreme Court and the German Federal Constitutional Court*, Berghahn Books, New York, Oxford 2002, 125–156.

27 The case n° III. ÚS 425/97, published in the Collection of cases of the CCC vol. 10, p. 285, English translation of this decision can be found at http://www.concourt.cz.

28 Cf. Z. Kühn, "Making Constitutionalism Horizontal: Three Different Central European Strategies" in Andras Sajó, Renata Uitz (eds.), *The Constitution in Private Relations: Expanding Constitutionalism*, Eleven International Publishing, Utrecht 2005, 217–240. For the analysis of the controversy, see article of Justice of the CCC, Pavel Holländer, "The Role of the Constitutional Court for the Application of the Constitution in Case Decisions of Ordinary Courts" 86 (4) *Archiv für Rechts- und Sozialphilosophie* 537, at 542 (2000). The Justice, now the Deputy President of the CCC, claims that if the judgments of the CCC were not binding, "the decisions of the Constitutional Court would become useless. The Constitutional Court would be forced to a conclusion which is absurd and intolerable: it would not rely on the possibility of constitutionally consistent interpretation, but it would instead leave the principle of judicial self-restraint and in case of any however tiny possibility of unconstitutional construction would annul the statute."

29 See, e.g., the judgment of the Supreme Administrative Court of May 30, 2007, 1 Afs 125/2006-63.

30 For instance, the annulment of Art. 250f of the Czech Civil Procedure Code, allowing an ordinary court to decide a case *in camera* and without first consulting the parties' views on the use of this procedure. Although if this discretion were interpreted carefully, the provision would withstand constitutional review, one of the Constitutional Court's senates referred the matter to be decided by the plenum because the provision was "as a matter of fact unconstitutional" and the unconstitutionality could not be eliminated by the Constitutional Court's interpretative

Occasionally, the Court has concluded that a constitutionally conforming construction, though possible, is unlikely to be achieved in the judicial practice and, therefore, has annulled the statute without attempting to lay down for the ordinary courts a constitutionally conforming interpretation.[31]

III. INTERPRETATIVE DECISIONS IN ABSTRACT CONSTITUTIONAL REVIEW: "SOFT CONSTITUTIONAL REVIEW"

1. One of the most interesting examples of positive legislating by constitutional courts is interpreting law in a constitutional way in the course of abstract review proceedings. In contrast with deciding constitutional complaints, which is often closely connected to the fact scenario of a real-life case before the Constitutional Court, deciding issues of abstract review is, *per se*, much more general. It must be emphasized that the CCC treats cases of both the so-called abstract control of norms (proceedings initiated by a group of parliamentarians or the President with no connection to any real-life case whatsoever) and concrete control of norms (proceedings initiated by a general court in deciding a real-life case) in the same fashion. This means that facts of the case related to proceedings before the general court are not decisive and that the CCC decides the issue in purely abstract way.

2. It is here where the rule of the interpretation of the law consistent with the Constitution is very important. It can be seen as a prerequisite to any rational system of judicial review. This rule promotes the efficient practice of judicial review as it eliminates, in the greater number of cases, the need to nullify statutes. In this sense, it might moderate relations between the constitutional court and the legislature. However, it might also strengthen the power of the constitutional court: as a leading expert on comparative constitutionalism noted, "[C]onstitutional tribunals have more of a chance to provide lasting and unsupervised determinations of the law by interpreting the law rather than voiding it."[32] Some have even dubbed this (rightly in my opinion) "soft constitutional judicial review."[33]

decisions. See decision Pl. ÚS 18/96 published as nº 269/1996 Sb., ÚS 6, 109 (1996). For another example, see Procházka, supra note 30,, at 160.

31 The decision Pl. ÚS 25/97 published as nº 159/1998 Sb., *The Residence of Aliens Case*.

32 A. Sajó, "Constitutional Adjudication in Light of Discourse Theory" 17 *Cardozo Law Review* 1193, at 1208 (1995).

33 Martin Shapiro and Alec Stone Sweet, *On Law, Politics and Judicialization*, Oxford University Press, Oxford 2002, at 156.

"Theoretically every statutory provision might be applied wrongly, i.e.[,] in conflict with the Constitution," said the CCC. "However, the circumstances that a statute might possibly be read in an unconstitutional manner cannot *per se* provide grounds for annulling it."[34] If a statute can be construed in several ways, of which some are unconstitutional and at least one is constitutional, the CCC would avoid annulment.[35] It is the duty of the ordinary courts, the Court highlighted, to apply the statute in a constitutionally permissible way.[36]

As we have seen, the CCC has the efficient tool to control general courts and their obedience to the CCC's jurisprudence. Moreover, the CCC has the possibility of the second guess. It can monitor how the law is applied by general courts via constitutional complaints. If the interpretation provided in the earlier constitutional judgment proves impossible because of unwillingness, or more often inability to be applied by general judges, the CCC always has the power to annul the law.[37]

3. In those countries where constitutional courts cannot review the constitutionality of lower-court decisions, this rule is much more problematic, as the constitutional court has no obvious means to sanction the disregard by ordinary courts of their own constitutionally conforming interpretation of the law. Therefore, for instance, the Hungarian Constitutional Court found a sort of solution in the Italian concept of living law, which aims to overcome a similar problem relating to the model of constitutional review in Italy. The Italian Constitutional Court also lacks the power to adjudicate constitutional complaints. It has been quite active in issuing constitutionally conforming interpretations, and it pioneered the

[34] The judgment Pl. ÚS 8/98, published also as n° 300/1998 Sb., *Tax Proceedings Law Case*.

[35] The U.S. Supreme Court developed this rather commonsense rule a long time ago. As the Supreme Court, per the first Justice Harlan, declared already in 1884, "if there were room for two constructions, both equally obvious and reasonable, the court must, in deference to the legislature of the State, assume that it did not overlook the provisions of the Constitution, and designed the act of 1871 to take effect. Our duty, therefore, is to adopt that construction which, without doing violence to the fair meaning of the words used, brings the statute into harmony with the provisions of the Constitution." *Grenada County Supervisors v. Brogden*, 112 U.S. 261, 268–269 (1884). Similarly, this rule is firmly established in Germany, where it is referred to as the principle of the constitutionally conforming interpretation (*Verfassungskonforme Auslegung*). See P. Sachs (ed.), *Grundgesetz: Kommentar*, Beck, München 1996, 61–62. The Federal Constitutional Court held that "if a rule allows several readings, but only one reading leads to a constitutionally permissible construction, the reading consistent with the Basic law is obligatory." BVerfGE 49, 148 (157). In Germany, the first decision that established this doctrine was perhaps BVerfGE 2, 266 (282), quoted in Sachs, at 61, note 61.

[36] The judgment Pl. ÚS 48/95, published also as n° 121/1996 Sb.

[37] Cf. the text related to footnotes 30 and 31 supra.

concept of interpretive decisions. It uses the threat of subsequent annulment of the living law, the term for interpretations that ordinary courts insist on in the face of their own constitutionally conforming interpretation, to sanction its interpretive decisions.[38] The Hungarian Constitutional Court proclaimed that the law will be reviewed as it is interpreted by law courts and will be annulled even if another plausible interpretation, consistent with the constitution, exists.[39] The concept of living law is, of course, controversial and open to theoretical doubt because the legislature, which passed the law susceptible to the constitutionally conforming interpretation, is in this way punished for the behavior of ordinary courts.[40]

4. The positive nature of interpretative judgments of the CCC is sometimes emphasized by another feature. The statement of the Court's judgment (verdict) in which the petition to annul the law is rejected usually consists of one simple sentence: "The petition is rejected." All the remaining parts together with constitutional interpretation, is to be found in the Court's justification, which follows the verdict. Recently, however, given the occasional defiance by the general courts and other public bodies of its interpretational rulings, the CCC started to incorporate the decisive part of its constitutional interpretation into the verdict. It must be said that, in the Czech Republic, the verdict of the Court's judgment is taken as formally binding; therefore, its wording deserves a special attention.

Let us take as a typical example the judgment in *Clearance of Defence Counsel* case of January 28, 2004. In this case, the law mandated that in criminal cases where classified information might be discussed, the defense attorneys are subject to a security clearance. As a result, no defense attorney was available for the defendant in the criminal case before the district court, and the defendant was effectively denied of his right to legal aid. Therefore, the district court petitioned the CCC to annul the law if it used also the defense attorneys among those who were subject to a security clearance. The CCC rejected this reading of the law and found against its clear wording that defense attorneys in criminal proceedings are not subject to this type of clearance. Being aware of the controversial nature of its reasoning, the CCC

38 See, e.g., E. Cheli, F. Donati, Methods and Criteria of Judgment on the Question of Rights to Freedom in Italy, in D. Beatty (ed.), *Human Rights and Judicial Review: A Comparative Perspective*, Kluwer 1994.

39 See the Hungarian Constitutional Court case on Legal Guardians and the Family Act, decision nº 57/1991 of November 8, 1991, per Lábady, J., and the foreword to this decision in László Sólyom, Georg Brunner, *Constitutional Judiciary in a New Democracy: The Hungarian Constitutional Court*, University of Michigan Press, Ann Arbor 2000, at 171.

40 See the dissenting opinion in the Hungarian case, *id.*

added the second part to its verdict. This part is a positive rule that effectively created a new exception to the clear wording of the law. Hence, the verdict of the judgment includes two parts:

I. The petition is rejected.

II. Clearance of defense attorney in criminal proceedings for purposes of access to classified information through a security clearance by the National Security Office is inconsistent with Art. 37 par. 3, Art. 38 par. 2, and Art. 40 par. 3 of the Charter of Fundamental Rights and Freedoms and with Art. 6 par. 3 let. c) of the Convention on Protection of Human Rights and Fundamental Freedoms.[41]

The CCC explained the reasons it included the second part. After it highlighted the principle of the primacy of constitutionally consistent interpretation over unconstitutional interpretations, it added that, "[f]or these reasons, in these proceedings on review of norms, *given a negative verdict with interpretative arguments*, the CCC placed the fundamental constitutional principle, arising from a number of significant grounds, in the verdict section of the judgment" (emphasis added).

The CCC decided to use the second part possibly because the reviewed law had meanwhile lost its validity and been replaced by a new law, with similar wording. The constitutional principle highlighted at the beginning of the judgment has been, therefore, applicable to both laws. The judgment of the CCC viewed against the backdrop of such a verdict is far from being a negative legislator. The second part of the verdict provides in a formalized way (different from mere justification found in the opinion of the Court) a specific enacted rule. The practice is criticized for not having basis in the law, for elevating the Court to the status of the legislature, and for excessively formalizing precedential features of the Court's jurisprudence.[42]

5. The CCC, however, continues occasionally to use this type of statement. I fail to see any consistent use in this matter, though. In a majority of cases, the CCC also has reinterpreted the text of the law but has not included a new rule in its verdict. Thus, a new rule shall be interpreted from the opinion. A nice example is *Shifting the Burden of Proof Case*. The rule subject to review was about the burden of proof in discrimination cases, according to

41 The judgment Pl. ÚS 41/02 of January 28, 2004, published as n° 98/2004 Sb., quoted according to an English translation found at http://angl.concourt.cz/angl_verze/doc/p-41-02.php (I modified some words to fit the text here).

42 See Z. Kühn, M. Bobek, R. Polčák, *Judikatura a právní argumentace* [Case law and legal argumentation], Auditorium, Prague 2006.

which the facts asserted about the claim that the party was directly or indirectly discriminated against on the grounds elaborated by EU law were considered by the court as proven in labor matters, unless the contrary was to be found in the proceedings. The CCC clarified that it is not enough to assert the facts; one must "also prove[] that one was not treated in the usual, non-disadvantaging manner" (paragraph 73). The CCC pointed out that the formulation of the contested rule requires an interpretation that is virtually a borderline case in which one can still, by interpretation of the statutory text, and concluded that it is precisely as a result of this interpretation that the contested provision could be considered constitutional. Therefore it would be extremely desirable for the legislature to consider whether it cannot conduct the transposition of the cited EC Council directives for the target audience of the relevant procedural norms in a somewhat clearer manner" (paragraph 78).[43]

IV. POSITIVE ASPECT OF NEGATIVE DECISIONS OF THE COURT

1. It is the judgment that annuls the law that inspired Kelsen to call the constitutional court a negative legislator. Kelsen meant by this first that the norm can be eliminated only by another norm.[44] Second, what is specific for the constitutional court is that the court can issue a generally binding norm that is, however, of purely negative nature. It is able to eliminate another norm from the legal system; however, it is not able to establish a new norm of a specific content.[45] In a way, this argument is obviously right. At the same time, it fails to account for a simple fact that a negative decision to annul the norm usually entails something positive as well.

2. For instance, the judgment that annuls the exception to the rule is not only about annulling the exception but also about expanding the impact of the original rule to which the exception used to exist. In other words, given the judgment of the CCC, the original exception to the rule is no longer applicable. The example is the case that annulled the exception according to which some administrative fines were not subject to judicial review. The judgment was obviously about the derogation of the norm (negative

[43] See the judgment Pl. U.S. 37/04 decided on April 26, 2006, available in English at http://angl.concourt.cz/angl_verze/doc/p-37-04.php, *Shifting the Burden of Proof Case*.

[44] "To annul a norm means to deprive an act, whose subjective meaning is a norm, of the objective meaning of a norm` and this means to terminate the validity of one norm by another norm." Hans Kelsen, *Pure Theory of Law*, 2nd ed., Peter Smith, Gloucester 1989, at 268.

[45] See Hans Kelsen, *General Theory of Law and State*, 1945, 271–272.

legislator). However, the judgment can be also explained as implying a new rule according to which all administrative fines (including those that used to be excluded) are subject to judicial review.[46]

3. Sometimes, a positive aspect of the decision annulling the law is not clear because the law, after losing part of its text to annulment, is unclear. Then the law should be interpreted with respect to the judgment of the constitutional court and its reasoning. One of the most striking examples is the 1994 case in which the CCC annulled the requirement that Czech citizens who were allowed to claim the restitution for their property have permanent residence in the Czech Republic. The CCC found the requirement discriminatory and annulled the rule that set the deadline to claim the restitution. The law thus lost much of its clarity because the effect of annulling the deadline was doubtful. The problem was explained in the Court's reasoning:

However, if the consequences of legalizing this unconstitutional condition are to be repaired, it is not only necessary to cancel the condition itself, but ... it is also necessary to ensure that the new wording of . . . of the Act [after annulment] can realistically be brought to life. This can be achieved only by opening the period . . . for exercising a claim before the court *for those citizens for whom the condition of permanent residence in the country* has heretofore made impossible the exercise of their right to issuance of a thing.[47]

However, it was far from clear what the annulment of the deadline effectively meant in the *Permanent Residence Case*. It was possible that it would be open for anyone to bring a new restitution claim anytime. Moreover, as to the text of the law, there were serious doubts about the deadline for the new claimants, especially when a new period was supposed to commence for them. The answer to the law's interpretation was possibly found not in the law's text but in the Court's justification of its judgment. Only referring to the Court's judgment did it become clear that the deadline was newly opened only for those who were prohibited to do so under the earlier version of the law (those citizens who had no permanent residence in the Czech Republic) and when the period of time commenced. Interestingly, the judgment was criticized by dissenting justices who argued that the Court

46 See the judgment Pl.ÚS 28/98 of November 23, 1999, published as 2/2000 Sb. [Official Gazette].

47 See the judgment Pl.ÚS 3/94 of July 12, 1994, *Permanent Residence case*, available in English at http://angl.concourt.cz/angl_verze/doc/p-3-94.php, published in Czech as 164/1994 Sb. (emphasis added).

went far beyond its powers and effectively did what the legislature should have done – created a new deadline for the claimants with no residence. The dissenting justices argued that it was up to the Court to annul the condition of the permanent residence but that it was up to the legislature to enact a new deadline that would give time to bring a new claim for those who were deprived of doing so by the earlier version of the law.[48] In this way, the dissenters effectively applied the theory of the constitutional court as a negative legislator, a theory that mattered little to those who were in the Court's majority.

4. Exceptionally, the CCC pronounces a verdict in which it both annuls the law and states a binding interpretation of the law. The situation is somewhat similar to the one described in connection with interpretative decisions in abstract constitutional review.[49] Here, however, the rule is annulled and the CCC is even closer to the position of positive legislator than in the example provided in the *Permanent Residence Case*;[50] unlike that case where the interpretation of the law had to be inferred from the Court's reasoning, in this case, the binding interpretation is included directly in the verdict. The most interesting example is the *Custody Regulation Case*, whose statement of the judgment consists of the following two parts:

> 1. The provision of § 242 par. 2 of Act no. 141/1961 Coll. is annulled as of the day this judgment is promulgated in the Collection of Laws.
> 2. Under Art. 5 par. 4 of the Convention for the Protection of Human Rights and Fundamental Freedoms it is necessary that an accused be heard by a court before a decision is made concerning his complaint against a decision by the Public Prosecutor to extend custody.[51]

Here, the first part of the verdict involves derogation (hence negative legislator); the second part, however, involves a positive statement of the rule. The CCC explained that it included the positive statement of the rule to explain a "correct" interpretation of the law after the annulment:

The importance of emphasizing substantial grounds arises in those cases where, even after annulling a statutory provision that is inconsistent with the constitutional order, the ordinary law framework for the adjudicated issue is

[48] See the dissenting opinions as published in Coll. CCC decisions vol. 1, 279 (1994) – in Czech only.

[49] See the text related to footnotes 41 ff. above.

[50] See footnote 47.

[51] Cf., e.g., the judgment of March 22, 2005, Pl. U.S. 45/04, *Custody Regulation case* (English translation available at http://angl.concourt.cz/angl_verze/doc/pl-45-04.php).

not clear. This applies particularly in a case where, even after annulling the statutory framework, bodies of state power could apply the law inconsistently with the principles, which led to the annulment of the statutory provision in question. Therefore, the Constitutional Court included in the verdict of its judgment the constitutional principle (or the interpretive arguments for it) that arises from a set of substantial grounds leading to the decision on the petition to annul the statutory provision.[52]

V. UNCONSTITUTIONAL GAPS IN THE LEGAL SYSTEM: PROVIDING CONSTITUTIONAL REMEDIES OR JUDICIAL SUBSTITUTION FOR THE LEGISLATOR?

1. The best example of the CCC acting as negative legislator is a line of decisions annulling laws where such annulments created actual gaps in the system of law. It is usually the case that the CCC annuls an entire rule, a large body of the law, or sometimes entire statute (instead of annulling the exception to the rule, as has been discussed here). The gap consequently calls for legislative enactment. Here, one might argue, the CCC serves as a genuine negative legislator, as it obviously has no power to fill the gap itself. Still, there are several possibilities for redressing the situation. Those possibilities (or at least some of them) question the very concept of the constitutional court acting as negative legislator.

2. First, a question is, To what extent can decisions of the CCC annulling the law provide guidelines to the legislature about how a new law should be framed? Sometimes, the CCC provides a detailed analysis of the law that will fit the constitutional test of the Court after the original law has been annulled.[53] The CCC is not very consistent in using such legislative guidelines, however. More recently, such legislative guidelines have been increasingly criticized by some influential justices as against the very core of the Court's function as negative legislator. For instance, in 2006, Chief Justice Pavel Rychetský argued in his dissenting opinion:

> Solely in passing I would recall that I have long espoused the view that, as the Constitutional Court is a "negative legislator," it does not possess the power to make broad considerations de lege ferenda; in no case do I consider that they qualify as part of the "supporting grounds" of the decision

[52] *Id.*

[53] See, e.g., the judgment of October 12, 1994, Pl. ÚS 4/94, *Anonymous Witness case* (English translation available at http://angl.concourt.cz/angl_verze/doc/p-4-94.php).

to which can be attached generally binding effects, in the sense of Art. 89 Par. 2 of the Constitution.[54]

It is plausible that such legislative guidelines do not really make the Court a positive legislator because only few Czech scholars would argue that such guidelines strictly bind the legislature.[55] Moreover, what is also visible from the practice is that the legislature frequently does not obey the Court's reasoning.

3. If the legislature enacts the statute against the previous judgments of the Court, then the sanction is logical – another annulment of the statute.[56] However, the question remains as to whether there are other remedies for the Court if the legislature does not fill the gap created by the Court's annulment. The best and most controversial example is the one provided by the rent-control saga.

In 2000, the CCC found rent control under Czech law unconstitutional, and it annulled the decree of the Ministry of Finance that regulated the increase in rent in apartment houses. The CCC delayed the annulment to offer the legislature time to enact a new law that would establish a mechanism to place rents at just terms.[57] The legislature declined to deal with the issue, however. The CCC continued to annul the decrees that dealt with the issue, using more and more compelling arguments urging the legislature to enact a proper law.[58] In 2006, finally, the CCC again criticized the legislative "activity, or rather, inactivity," which resulted in "freezing of controlled rent, which further deepens the violation of property rights of the owners of those apartments to which rent control applied. . . . By not passing them, the legislative assembly evoked an unconstitutional situation."[59] That

[54] See the dissenting opinion of Chief Justice to the judgment of July 11, 2006, Pl. ÚS 18/06, *Removal of Chief Judge case* (English translation available at http://angl.concourt.cz/angl_verze/doc/p-18-06.php).

[55] In my own papers, I argued that the entire Court's reasoning is an important factor for the legislature to take into account when drafting a new law (and a rational legislature will use them). See Z. Kühn, "Je Parlament ČR vázán odůvodněním nálezů Ústavního soudu ČR?" [Is the Parliament bound by the justification of the judgments by the Constitutional Court?] *Právník* vol. 139, 2000, nº 8, 721 ff. Most Czech lawyers are even less willing to argue that the legislature has the legal duty to take into account the Court's reasoning.

[56] A good example is the case quoted in footnote 54 (here, the legislature enacted the possibility to dismiss the presiding judge of the court by the executive branch despite the fact that the CCC condemned such a possibility in its earlier judgment).

[57] See the judgment of June 21, 2000, Pl. ÚS 3/2000, *Rent Control I*, published as nº 231/2000 Sb.

[58] See the judgment of November 20, 2002, Pl. ÚS 8/02, *Rent Control II*, published as nº 528/2002 Sb.; the judgment of March 19, 2003, Pl. ÚS 2/03, *Rent Control III*, published as nº 84/2003 Sb.

[59] See the judgment of February 28, 2006, Pl. ÚS 20/05, *Rent Control IV*, available in English at http://angl.concourt.cz/angl_verze/doc/p-20-05.php.

is why the CCC rejected the petition. But it gave a rather unique verdict, according to which "[t]he long-term inactivity of the Parliament of the Czech Republic, consisting of failure to pass a special legal regulation defining cases in which a landlord is entitled to unilaterally increase rent, payment for services relating to use of an apartment, and to change other conditions of a lease agreement, is unconstitutional and violates" a number of constitutional rights.[60]

The unique verdict is accompanied by a similarly unique reasoning. First, the CCC directed general courts to increase rents themselves, instead of entirely passive legislature. In other words, the CCC ordered general courts to make the law instead of the legislature. The CCC openly held that it must deviate from its role of negative legislator:

> Based on these facts [legislative inactivity], the Constitutional Court, in its role of protector of constitutionality, *cannot limit its function to the mere position of a "negative" legislator*, and must, in the framework of a balance of the individual branches of power characteristic of a law-based state founded on respect for the rights and freedoms of man and of citizens . . . create space for the preservation of the fundamental rights and freedoms. Therefore, the general courts, even despite the absence of the envisaged specific regulations, must decide to increase rent, depending on local conditions, so as to prevent the abovementioned discrimination. In view of the fact that such cases will involve the finding and application of simple law, which is not a matter for the Constitutional Court, . . . the Constitutional Court refrains from offering a specific decision-making procedure and thereby replacing the mission of the general courts. It merely states that it is necessary to refrain from arbitrariness; a decision must be based on rational arguments and thorough weighing of all the circumstances of a case, the application of natural principles and the customs of civic life, the conclusions of legal learning and settled, constitutionally consistent court practice.[61]

This part of the judgment contributed to a strong criticism of the CCC made by some politicians who understand this as overstretching the Court's role. Many regular judges do not seem to be happy with this opinion either. I must repeat, however, that the CCC has its weapon against disobedient judges – a constitutional complaint against unconstitutional judgments.

Second, the CC explained why it used a unique verdict, which had no precedent in earlier case law. Here, the CCC was highly critical of what it

60 *Id.*, the verdict I.

61 *Id.* (emphasis added).

alleged was continuing disrespect of the legislature to its case law. The CCC agreed with the claim that there is "unconstitutional gap in legislation consisting of the fact that the envisaged legal regulations have not yet been passed." I provide a longer quote from this very important judgment:

> As a consequence of the inactivity of the legislative assembly it can evoke an unconstitutional situation, if the legislature is required to pass certain regulations, does not do so, and thereby interferes in a right protected by the law and by the constitution. . . . [W]e can conclude that under certain conditions the consequences of a gap (a missing legal regulation) are unconstitutional, in particular when the legislature decides that it will regulate a particular area, states that intention in law, but does not pass the envisaged regulations. The same conclusion applies to the case where Parliament passed the declared regulations, but they were annulled because they did not meet constitutional criteria, and the legislature did not pass a constitutional replacement, although the Constitutional Court gave it a sufficient period of time to do so.. . .
>
> The relationship between the legislative and judicial branches arises from the separation of powers in the state, as established in the Constitution. A material analysis necessarily leads us to conclude that this separation is not a purpose in and of itself, but pursues a higher purpose. From its very beginnings it was subjected by the constitutional framers to an idea based above all on service to the citizen and to society. Every power has a tendency to concentration, growth and corruption; absolute power to an uncontrollable corruption. If one of the branches of power exceeds its constitutional framework, its authority, or, on the contrary, does not fulfill its tasks and thus prevents the proper functioning of another branch (in the adjudicated case, of the judicial branch), the control mechanism of checks and balances, which is built into the system of separation of powers, must come into play. . . . [G]eneral courts err if they refuse to provide protection to the rights of those who have turned to them with a demand for justice, if they deny their complaints merely with a formalistic reasoning and reference to the inactivity of the legislature (the non-existence of the relevant legal regulations), after the Constitutional Court, as protector of constitutionality and review thereof, opened the way for them through its decisions. The Constitutional Court has repeatedly declared the unequal position of one group of owners of rental apartments and buildings to be discriminatory and unconstitutional, and the long-term inactivity of the Parliament of the CR to be incompatible with the requirements of a law-based state. The Constitutional Court, by the will of the constitutional framers, is responsible for the maintenance of the constitutional order in the

> Czech Republic, and therefore it does not intend to abandon this obligation, it calls on the general courts to fulfill their obligations.[62]

4. Interestingly, there was another option that involved annulling the entire law regulating rents (and thus pressing the legislature to enact a new regulation), but the Court avoided this controversial option. In some other cases, however, the CCC did not hesitate to annul the entire law dealing with some specific problem if the problem rested on the fact that not one specific rule, but the entire law, be modified. The CCC, being solely a negative legislator, uses annulment of the law as a sort of weapon of mass destruction, thus creating the gap in the entire branch of law, which forces the legislature to enact a new law. One important condition, however, is to delay the effects of the judgment so the legislature has the actual chance to prepare and enact a new regulation. In deciding whether to delay effects of its judgments, the Court enjoys a complete discretion.

The most celebrated example of this type is the case of annulling the law on judicial review of administrative acts. Because administrative judiciary as existed in the 1990s did not fit the requirements of the Czech Constitution and, above all, the European Convention of Human Rights, the CCC repeatedly urged the legislature to enact a new and constitutionally consistent law. Finally, the CCC lost its patience and annulled all of part 5 of the Code of Civil Procedure, related to administrative judiciary. It noted that the law as a whole suffered serious constitutional deficits, even though there were a lot of provisions that would be included in a new law as well:

> After taking into account all calls made by the CCC to both the legislature and the executive branch, and after considering the current state of work on the reform of administrative judiciary, the CCC decided to delay the effects of its judgment until December 31, 2002. As it would take some time before enacting the law and its entering into force, it is clear that it is the task for this legislature to enact a new law.[63]

The legislature, which delayed enacting the new law on administrative judiciary for almost ten years, finally went on and enacted a new law. It mattered that, without enacting a new law on the administrative judiciary, there would have been no recourse to administrative courts since January 1,

[62] *Id.*

[63] See the judgment of June 27, 2001, Pl. ÚS 16/99, *Part Five of the Code of Civil Procedure – Administrative Judiciary*, published as n° 276/2001 Sb. (the Court was referring to the fact of parliamentary elections, which were due to occur in June 2002).

2003, because the earlier law had been annulled by the CCC with effects starting on that day.

5. The last possibility for enforcing the judgments of the CCC against the legislature, which remained passive and did not comply with constitutional decisions, has been recently articulated by the CCC. It is the duty of the government to pay damages to those who were harmed by an unconstitutional gap in the legal order, despite repeated decisions of the CCC that urged the legislature to fill the gap. The case also relates to the rent-control saga.[64] This opinion has been criticized by a dissenting justice as having no counterpart in Europe. The accountability of the state for not following earlier constitutional judgments shall be political, the justices claimed, not legal through payment of damages.[65]

VI. THE CZECH CONSTITUTIONAL COURT ACTING OPENLY AS POSITIVE LEGISLATOR – CASES OF CONSTITUTIONALITY OF AMENDMENTS TO THE LAW

1. The judgment of the CCC does invalidate the unconstitutional statute *ex nunc*.[66] This contrasts the Czech system of constitutional review with those systems in which the constitutional court declares unconstitutional and null the statutory rule from the very beginning of its existence (e.g., Germany). It also means that the Court's derogation of the statutory norm is technically comparable to the legislative derogation.[67]

2. One of the most intriguing questions is, What happens to the law if only the amendment (derogation or modification) to that law is annulled? The Court was able for a long time to avoid such a question, as it always claimed that, if the law were amended and the content of the law questioned, then it is not the amendment but the law as amended that is subject to constitutional review. This claim fits the pattern established by Kelsen, according to whom the law's amendment does not have a permanent legal existence. Quite the contrary, at the moment the rule amends the law, its normative life dies out,

[64] The statement of the plenum of the CCC of April 28, 2009, Pl. ÚS-st 27/09, published as 136/2009 Sb.

[65] See *id.*, dissenting opinion of Justice Holländer.

[66] See Articles 70–71 of the Czech Constitutional Court Act of 1993, available in English at http://www.concourt.cz.

[67] In this, the Czech system is also consistent with the Kelsen's teachings. See notes 44 and 45 above and the the accompanying text.

as it has no other independent normative purpose.[68] This effectively means that, if the law as amended is annulled as unconstitutional, the result is the gap in the law and not the revival of the earlier text of the same law.

3. However, recently the issue became much more complicated when the CCC started to annul some amendments not for their substance (which would be impossible under the Court's jurisprudence) but for the unconstitutional procedure that led to their enactment. Such an annulment begs the question, What is the result of the annulment – a revival of the earlier text of the law or the regular situation (i.e., the gap in the system that is created)? The answers to this question differ.

4. The first answer relies on the concept of negative legislator. In 2002, the CCC explained that it is of the of the opinion that the annulment of the contested unconstitutional rule may not revive an already-repealed law. The CCC, while exercising constitutional review of norms, acts as a so-called negative legislator, empowered only to derogate the law found unconstitutional. That is why annulment of the contested enactment may also result solely in its elimination from the legal order of the Czech Republic, not the effective establishment of a new rule in the form of the revival of an already-repealed enactment. The opposite view would likely lead to the creation of serious legal uncertainty and overstepping of the constitutionally mandated competences of the CCC. Thus, revival of the repealed or amended legal rule through the decision of the CCC is possible only if the constitutional law had required such (see, e.g., article 140, paragraph 6 of the Constitution of Austria).[69]

5. More recently, the CCC seems to modify its case law. In its 2004 case, the CCC held that the annulment of derogatory clause of the law "revives the state of affairs established by [the earlier law]." The CCC noted that "this fact could result in a considerable amount of legal uncertainty." That is why the CCC has decided to delay the coming into effect of the annulment of the contested provisions until the end of the calendar year (over nine months), to allow Parliament a sufficiently long period of time to adopt a new proper legal rule.[70] This case is now controlling in the Court's jurisprudence.

[68] H. Kelsen, Derogation, in *Essays in Jurisprudence in Honor of Roscoe Pound* (R. Newman ed.), Bobbs-Merrill 1962.

[69] See the judgment of February 12, 2002, Pl. ÚS 21/01, *The power of the Senate to take part in legislative proceedings*, published as n° 95/2002 Sb., Part VII.2.

[70] See the judgment of March 9, 2004, Pl. ÚS 2/02, *Transformation of rights to use land case*, published as n° 278/2004 Sb.

VII. COURT'S SELF-PERCEPTIONS AND CONCLUSIONS

Despite all the examples mentioned above, the idea of the constitutional court acting merely as negative legislator remains a sort of continuing narrative in the Court's own jurisprudence. While being repeatedly highlighted in its own case law, this idea serves as an important factor in legitimizing the Court's decision making. In dissenting opinions, however, the same idea can be used to repeatedly criticize the Court's majority for overstepping the proper boundaries of the Court's legitimate role.

The easiest example of the use of negative-legislator rhetoric is explaining the actual role of the Court to the parties that demand from the Court something beyond its powers, such as the expansion of an enacted rule of the law.[71] A more interesting, and a typical example of the legitimizing rhetoric, is a classical delineation of the Court's powers vis-à-vis the legislature that results in the Court's self-restraint. The CCC typically refers to the negative legislator when it refuses to annul the law. For instance, while reviewing the law on the residence of aliens, the CCC noted that the criticism against the law by the referring court was the lack of detailed regulation and the vagueness of the regulation. Such an issue is not within the competences of the CCC, however. The CCC "fulfills the function of negative legislator[;] it is empowered to annul unconstitutional laws and their specific provisions. The CCC is not empowered to replace annulled laws by new laws, i.e.[,] to fill gaps in the legal order by its own law making activity."[72] Similarly, the CCC noted in another case that, if a constitutional interpretation of the norm in question is possible, "it is not desirable for the CCC, as a body for the protection of constitutionality and also as a negative legislator, to further widen the alleged constitutional gap through its derogative intervention."[73] The meaning of the negative-legislator rhetoric is again clear – it is to show the limits of the CCC powers and to suggest that those limits are to some extent possibly overcome by interpretative judgments of the Court.

Quite often, the term *negative legislator* is used without any clear sense, just to highlight the discretion of the legislature empowered by political considerations, and much more limited Constitutional Court, obliged to

[71] Here the CCC simply asserts that it is not within its competence to do anything like this, explaining its role as negative legislator. See procedural decision of December 12, 1997, II.ÚS 74/97, unpublished, available at http://nalus. usoud.cz.

[72] See the judgment of May 12, 2009, Pl. ÚS 10/08, *Detention of Aliens case*, published as nº 229/2009 Sb., para. 98.

[73] The judgment 28 March 2006, Pl. ÚS 42/03, *Protection of Apartment Lease case*, published as nº 280/2006 Sb., para. 62.

judge the issues of constitutionality. For instance, the Court refused to deal with the issue that courts (civil or administrative) should deal with expropriation cases. It highlighted the broad area enjoyed by the legislature in deciding how to apply various legal doctrines in particular circumstances. The CCC rejected the arguments that the logic of the Constitution requires administrative judges, not general judges, to deal with issues of expropriation and just compensation. The CCC is solely a negative legislator that is obliged to control constitutionality of the law rather than its doctrinal purity. Here, the use of the concept of negative legislator is of purely rhetorical nature, with no clear juridical meaning.[74]

In contrast, in many other examples, the concept of negative legislator is a welcome tool for dissenting justices to criticize the majority for overstepping the Court's proper boundaries.[75] In this way, the concept serves to guard the Court from going too much beyond its role.

Thus, it can be fairly said that the concept of the Court acting as negative legislator is common. It dominates legal discourse, the Court's own self-perception, and the expectations of political actors. The continuous assertive jurisprudence of the Court, however, steadily undermines this concept. We have seen that the Court is able to make new law through hundreds of constitutional complaints, which are decided on merits. This role is further highlighted by open-ended provisions of the Constitution that are used to specify the content of the interpreted law. Even more important, the Court makes the law through its interpretative decisions in abstract constitutional review. Here, the Court does not annul the law but directs the ordinary courts and all public bodies to use just one interpretation that is consistent with the Constitution. Even if the Court annuls the law, its annulment usually has some positive aspects, so it is hard to talk only about a negative legislator. Last but not least, if the Court creates a gap by its annulment, it continues to develop several techniques that provide incentives for the legislature to enact a new law. At least in one instance the Court mandated that ordinary courts fill the gap in the law instead of the inactive legislature. To what extent these attempts of the Court that touch the limits of the division of powers would be successful remains to be seen.

74 See the judgment of April 7, 2009, Pl. ÚS 26/08, *Expropriation Law and Civil Courts case*, published as nº 171/2009 Sb., para. 28.

75 For a very interesting example, see the text accompanying the footnote 48.

FRANCE

LE CONSEIL CONSTITUTIONNEL "LEGISLATEUR POSITIF" OU LA QUESTION DES INTERVENTIONS DU JUGE CONSTITUTIONNEL FRANÇAIS DANS L'EXERCICE DE LA FONCTION LEGISLATIVE

Bertrand Mathieu
Professeur à l'Ecole de droit de la Sorbonne – Université Paris I
Directeur du Centre de recherche de droit constitutionnel
prb.mathieu@orange.fr

En se prononçant sur les effets dans le temps ou la portée matérielle d'une invalidation de la loi, en fixant par voie de directives la manière dont une loi doit être interprétée, appliquée, ou en fixant un cadre à l'intervention du législateur *ad futuram,*[1] le juge constitutionnel intervient dans la perfection de l'œuvre législative.

Le terme de «législateur positif» renvoie à cette intervention.

Notre propos n'est pas ici de prendre position sur la question de la fonction normative du juge et son articulation avec la fonction normative du législateur et de l'autorité gouvernementale d'un point de vue théorique. Alors même que la distinction entre le pouvoir juridictionnel et le pouvoir politique nous semble devoir être l'axe majeur de la répartition des pouvoirs,[2],nous estimions qu'il existe entre la fonction législative et la fonction juridictionnelle une différence de nature que «l'appétit» des organes juridictionnels tend à brouiller. En réalité, la relative faiblesse des organes

1 C. Behrendt, *Le juge constitutionnel, un législateur-cadre positif*, Bruylant, LGDJ, 2006, p. 1 et 2.

2 *Cf.* P. Ardant et B. Mathieu, *Institutions politiques et droit constitutionnel*, LGDJ, 2009.

législatifs, les pathologies de la loi,[3] la crise de la légitimité politique, et donc démocratique, la place acquise par les droits fondamentaux, la perméabilité entre les ordres juridiques, tant nationaux que supra juridiques, nourrissent la constitution de l'empire juridictionnel.

Il n'en reste pas moins que l'idée de séparation absolue des fonctions ne résiste pas à la réalité et que la question est celle de la mesure.

Au delà de ces observations assez triviales et au deçà d'une position doctrinale dogmatique, l'objet de cette étude est de décrire la manière dont, en France, le Conseil constitutionnel intervient dans l'exercice de la fonction législative à l'occasion du jugement porté sur la constitutionnalité de la loi.

Cette analyse de la jurisprudence d'un juge, généralement et traditionnellement respectueux de la volonté du législateur, montre cependant que ce type de contrôle génère, par nature, une intervention, parfois profonde dans l'exercice de la fonction législative.

I TITRE LIMINAIRE: ELÉMENTS D'ANALYSES SUR LE CONTRÔLE DE CONSTITUTIONNALITÉ EN FRANCE

Le contrôle de constitutionnalité en France est le long aboutissement d'une évolution qui s'est opérée dans un contexte de départ particulièrement défavorable. Marqué par la méfiance contre les juges, alors que les Parlements d'Ancien régime avaient freiné les réformes susceptibles de faire évoluer la monarchie, le droit constitutionnel français n'a jamais accordé au juge une place équivalente à celle occupée par les titulaires des autres fonctions de l'Etat. La naissance, le développement, la reconnaissance[4] d'un pouvoir juridictionnel s'est opérée, sous la V° République, à l'encontre du texte constitutionnel qui ne voit dans la justice qu'une autorité. Par ailleurs, la création du Conseil constitutionnel en 1958 visait essentiellement à créer une instance permettant de protéger le domaine de compétence du gouvernement contre d'éventuels empiètements du législateur. Si la Constitution de la V République s'est attachée à remettre en cause la souveraineté parlementaire, c'est plus sur le terrain institutionnel que sur le terrain juridictionnel que cette opération a été conçue. Pas plus que la IV République (1946-1958) n'était parvenue à mettre en place un véritable contrôle de constitutionnalité, la V° République ne tire pas vraiment les leçons de Carré de Malberg et du mouvement révisionniste qui se manifeste

[3] *Cf.* B. Mathieu, *La loi*, Dalloz, 2010.

[4] Par le Conseil constitutionnel, notamment décision 80-119 DC.

à la fin de la III° République (1875-1940). Selon le professeur strasbourgeois il serait nécessaire qu'il soit procédé à une révision constitutionnelle qui transforme la Constitution «en un corps de règles statutaires qui comprendrait, sur toutes les matières que l'organe constituant entend se réserver à lui même, tous les principes qui lieront le législateur et borneront ses compétences. Alors il y aurait place pour un contrôle juridictionnel consistant à confronter les lois avec les textes constitutionnels et destiné à imposer au législateur le respect de l'ordre juridique supérieur établi par la Constitution ».[5] Or dans la Constitution de 1958, ni catalogue de droits fondamentaux, ni véritable juridiction constitutionnelle. Seulement une volonté, dans le Préambule de la constitution, d'inscrire les nouvelles institutions dans la tradition républicaine française en rappelant la Déclaration des droits de l'homme de 1789 et le Préambule de la Constitution de 1946 qui s'était attaché lui même à compléter les droits inaliénables et sacrés de 1789 par des droits économiques et sociaux nécessaires aux temps nouveaux tout en rappelant la place des lois de la République, c'est à dire essentiellement l'acquis républicain de la III° République. Si la souveraineté du Parlement est contestée par la prééminence du pouvoir gouvernemental et plus spécifiquement par la fonction éminente du Président de la République, il est encore inconcevable que la loi, expression de la volonté générale, soit soumise au contrôle du juge. Serviteur de la loi, le Conseil d'Etat considère qu'il ne peut en contrôler la validité. Issue d'une jurisprudence de la III° République, pourtant expressément élaborée dans le contexte du droit public de l'époque, la théorie de la loi écran, qui interdit toute contestation d'un acte réglementaire qui conduirait à apprécier la constitutionnalité de la loi qui le fonde est reprise à leur compte par les juridictions judiciaires. C'est le Conseil constitutionnel qui prend l'initiative du changement en intégrant les textes visés dans le Préambule de 1946 et relatifs à ce que l'on appelle aujourd'hui les droits et libertés fondamentaux, au sein des nomes de référence du contrôle de constitutionnalité de la loi. La célèbre décision de 1971 «Liberté d'association», préparée antérieurement ainsi que nous l'ont appris la lecture des délibérations du Conseil constitutionnel,[6] constitue le premier acte de cette «saga». Le deuxième acte, qui offre aux acteurs politiques l'accès à ce nouvel outil, c'est la réforme de la Constitution opérée en 1974 à l'initiative du Président Giscard d'Estaing. Elle permet à soixante députés ou à soixante sénateurs, c'est à dire à l'opposition, de saisir le

[5] *La loi expression de la volonté générale*, rééd. Dalloz, 1984.

[6] *Les Grandes délibérations du Conseil constitutionnel*, Dalloz, 2009.

Conseil constitutionnel. C'est l'acte voté par le Parlement, non encore rendu parfait par la promulgation par le Président de la République, qui est contrôlé par le Conseil constitutionnel. La censure par le Conseil constitutionnel de la loi, ou de l'une de ses dispositions, fait obstacle à son insertion dans l'ordonnancement juridique. Cependant la fonction du Conseil ne peut être analysée comme un simple pouvoir d'empêcher. En effet le Conseil peut interpréter telle ou telle disposition afin de justifier de sa constitutionnalité mise en cause par les saisissants, il peut décider que telle disposition de la loi est séparable, alors son inconstitutionnalité n'entraine pas celle de l'ensemble du texte législatif ou, au contraire inséparable, sa censure entrainera alors celle de l'ensemble de la loi… Plus que de savoir si le Conseil constitutionnel opère comme participant au travail législatif, constitue une troisième chambre, intervenant après le Sénat ou l'Assemblée nationale, ou exerce une véritable fonction de juge, questions qui restent assez théoriques, il convient simplement de noter que le Conseil participe à l'interprétation de la loi, à la fixation de son sens, voir détermine partiellement les conditions dans lesquelles elle devra être mise en œuvre.

Il n'en reste pas moins que la loi publiée restait pour l'essentiel incontestable (sauf à ce que le Conseil constitutionnel s'en saisisse à l'occasion d'une loi en modifiant le champ d'application). Ce sont en réalité les exigences du droit international, et plus particulièrement du droit de l'Union européenne et du droit de la Convention européenne des droits de l'homme qui vont conduire la Cour de cassation, puis avec retard le Conseil d'Etat à écarter l'application de la loi inconventionnelle. Cette jurisprudence est construite sur un fondement constitutionnel, l'article 55 de la Constitution, qui prévoit que « les traités ou accords régulièrement ratifiés ou approuvés ont, dès leur publication, une autorité supérieure à celle des lois …» et à l'invitation implicite du Conseil constitutionnel qui s'estime incompétent pour apprécier la conventionalité de la loi dans le cadre du contrôle de constitutionnalité. Les masques tombent: le juge peut juger la loi. Les rôles sont répartis: au Conseil constitutionnel le contrôle de la constitutionnalité de la loi, dans le cadre d'un contrôle abstrait, a priori et sur saisine politique, au juge ordinaire, judiciaire ou administratif, le contrôle de la conventionalité de la loi en vigueur à l'occasion de son application et dans le cadre d'un contentieux. Reste que la constitutionnalité de la loi ne peut être appréciée à l'occasion de son application, alors que le contrôle de constitutionnalité présente de nombreux angles morts, tenant notamment au fait que de nombreuses dispositions législatives antérieures à 1974 sont encore en vigueur et que, même postérieurement à cette date, le contrôle a priori n'est pas systématique. Les cartes n'étaient pas jouées d'avance, de simples évolutions jurisprudentielles pouvaient transformer le paysage, soit que le Conseil constitutionnel revienne sur sa jurisprudence de 1975 et se saisisse, au moins partiellement, du contrôle de conventionalité, soit que les juges judiciaires et administratifs rompent avec la jurisprudence de « la loi écran » et reprennent la main s'agissant du contrôle de conventionalité. Aucune de ces lignes n'ayant bougé, le contrôle du respect des droits et libertés fondamentaux s'opère essentiellement par la voie du contrôle de conventionalité, s'agissant tout du moins des très nombreuses dispositions législatives que le Conseil constitutionnel n'a pas eu à examiner. Il existe alors un paradoxe français à ce que à l'affirmation, largement théorique ou platonique, de la prééminence constitutionnelle corresponde une impotence juridictionnelle des normes constitutionnelles. Au surplus, le Conseil constitutionnel reconnaît dans une décision de 2006 (2006-540 DC), qui précise une jurisprudence établie en 2004 (2004-496 DC), l'existence de principes inhérents à l'identité constitutionnelle de la France. Ces principes, par définition, ne peuvent être protégés dans le cadre d'un contrôle de conventionalité. A cette situation aussi contestable sur le terrain de l'Etat de droit, les justiciables ne pouvant faire valoir les droits qu'ils tiennent de la Constitution, que sur celui du rapport entre les ordres juridiques, l'articulation entre les droits européens et le droit constitutionnel tendant à s'organiser de fait dans une logique hiérarchique bénéficiant aux premiers, deux réponses pouvaient être apportées. La première consistait à permettre un contrôle de constitutionnalité diffus, opéré par les juges ordinaires, mais ainsi qu'il a été relevé ces derniers se sont refusés à « franchir le Rubicon ». Au surplus l'instauration d'un contrôle diffus était susceptible de poser des problèmes de sécurité juridique dans un système juridictionnel caractérisé par l'existence de deux ordres de juridiction séparés et indépendants l'un de l'autre. La seconde solution consistait à confier au Conseil constitutionnel un contrôle concentré de la constitutionnalité de la loi, concret et à l'occasion d'un litige, l'hypothèse d'une saisine directe par les citoyens n'ayant pas été sérieusement envisagée. Ce projet a fait l'objet d'une première tentative de réalisation à l'initiative du Président du Conseil constitutionnel de l'époque, ancien Garde des sceaux et proche du Président Mitterrand, Robert Badinter. L'instauration d'une nouvelle procédure appelée « exception d'inconstitutionnalité » qui permettait à chaque justiciable de soulever la question de l'inconstitutionnalité d'une disposition législative devant un juge à l'occasion d'un procès, cette question étant en définitive jugée par le Conseil constitutionnel a fait l'objet d'un projet de loi constitutionnel en 1993 qui n'a pas été adopté du fait de l'hostilité du Parlement, et notamment du Sénat, et faute d'une véritable volonté politique du Président Mitterrand de le porter à nouveau.[7] C'est à l'occasion de l'élection présidentielle de 2007 que la question est à nouveau au cœur du débat politique. L'ensemble des grands partis politiques inscrivent le contrôle de la constitutionalité de la loi a posteriori dans leur projet. Elu, le Président Sarkozy engage une procédure visant à une réforme importante de la Constitution, crée à cette fin un Comité de réflexion présidé par l'ancien Premier Ministre, Edouard Balladur, et introduit cette question au titre de celle qui devront être examinées par le Comité. Les propositions du Comité retiennent l'instauration d'une procédure d'exception d'inconstitutionnalité (appelée aussi question préjudicielle de constitutionnalité). Après quelques hésitations, le Président Sarkozy décide d'inscrire cette nouvelle procédure dans le projet de loi constitutionnelle qui est adopté le 27 juillet 2008. Une loi organique du 10 décembre 2009 fixe les conditions d'application des dispositions constitutionnelles relatives à cette importante réforme qui entre en vigueur le 1 mars 2010.

Dans ses grandes lignes, la procédure est la suivante, à l'occasion d'un litige devant n'importe quelle juridiction, un justiciable peut invoquer la violation par une disposition législative qui lui est appliquée des droits et libertés que lui reconnaît la Constitution. Cette question, qui prime sur une éventuelle question de conventionnalité, d'ou l'intitulé retenu de « question prioritaire de constitutionnalité, arrête alors le déroulement du procès le juge doit se prononcer sans délai sur le point de savoir disposition n'a pas été déjà déclarée conforme à la Constitution, sauf changement de circonstances, et si la question n'est pas dépourvue de caractère sérieux. Si ces conditions sont remplies, la question, selon un mécanisme de double filtre, est transmise au Conseil d'Etat ou à la Cour de cassation, selon l'ordre juridictionnel intéréssé, qui se prononce dans un délai de trois mois sur le point de savoir si la question est sérieuse ou nouvelle et dans l'affirmative la transmet au Conseil constitutionnel, si ce dernier juge la disposition contraire à la Constitution, il en prononcera l'abrogation en disposant de la compétence d'en aménager les effets dans le temps.

Il est évident que cette nouvelle procédure offre au Conseil constitutionnel de nouveaux instruments d'intervention quant à la portée de son examen de constitutionnalité.

D'une part, si le contrôle de constitutionnalité est considéré comme un contrôle objectif, ainsi qu'il ressort des travaux parlementaires

[7] *Cf.* R. Badinter, *Constitutions*, Dalloz, 2010, n°1.

préparatoires,[8] ce contrôle sera opéré à l'occasion de l'application de la loi, in concreto, ce qui peut influer sur son sens et sa portée. A l'appui de cette remarque doit être pris en considération un élément important qui tient au fait que tant le juge saisi que le Conseil constitutionnel devront prendre en compte des changements de circonstances, qui pourront être de fait, pour apprécier la possibilité d'examiner à nouveau la constitutionnalité d'une disposition déjà et antérieurement déclarée conforme à la Constitution par le Conseil constitutionnel. D'autre part un nouveau dialogue, voire une nouvelle concurrence, vont s'instaurer entre les juges ordinaires et le Conseil constitutionnel, notamment, en ce qui concerne la fonction d'interprétation, non seulement de la Constituions, mais aussi de la loi.[9] La question de l'autorité reconnues à ces interprétations devra nécessairement être posée au delà de la portée d'autorité de chose jugée, traditionnellement et de manière restrictive, reconnue aux décisions du Conseil constitutionnel.[10] Enfin, le Conseil constitutionnel sera très probablement conduit dans certaines hypothèses à déclarer la dispositions contestée conforme à la Constitution sous réserve de directives d'interprétation ou d'application, dont il use déjà dans le cadre du contrôle a priori, qui prendront une autre portée alors que la loi est contrôlée à l'occasion de son application. Ce sont ces directives ou réserves qui constituent probablement l'arme essentielle du Conseil constitutionnel entendu comme législateur positif.

S'agissant de la question prioritaire de constitutionnalité ces éléments relèvent très largement de la prospective à l'heure ou ces lignes sont écrites, ils ne peuvent cependant être ignorés.

L'intervention du Conseil constitutionnel dans la fonction législative n'est qu'indirecte. Il convient d'abord de fixer les conditions générales de cette intervention, avant d'analyser plus précisément l'une des techniques employées par le Conseil constitutionnel, qui constitue une intervention plus directe dans l'exercice de la fonction législative, à savoir les réserves d'interprétation.

[8] *Cf.* B. Mathieu, "La question de constitutionnalité, une nouvelle voie de droit," *La Semaine juridique*, 2009, n°52, p. 54.

[9] *Cf.* G. Zagrebelsky, *Le droit vivant*, Constituions, Dalloz, 2010, n°1.

[10] *Cf.* M.Disant, *L'autorité de la chose interprétée par le Conseil constitutionnel*, LGDJ, 2010.

II. LES INTERACTIONS ENTRE LA FONCTION JURIDICTIONNELLE DU CONSEIL CONSTITUTIONNEL ET LA FONCTION LÉGISLATIVE

C'est par une analyse réflexive de ses fonctions que le Conseil constitutionnel fixe les principes qui régissent sa relation avec le législateur et avec la fonction législative.

Ce souci de distinguer la fonction juridictionnelle de la fonction législative n'interdit cependant pas au Conseil d'intervenir dans la fonction législative selon des modalités qui sont consubstantielles à l'exercice même de la fonction du juge au regard de la norme qu'il contrôle et qui résultent également du moment où il intervient et de la place spécifique qui est la sienne au regard du processus législatif.

1. *Les principes cadres*

La grille d'analyse qui permet de mesurer le pouvoir d'intervention du Conseil constitutionnel peut être établie à partir de trois formules, édictées par le Conseil lui même qui légitiment et définissent à la fois les caractères de son intervention:

> -«La loi est l'expression de la volonté générale dans le respect de la Constitution» (décis. 85-197 DC)

Cette formulation met symboliquement fin à la souveraineté de la loi. Corrigeant la formule selon laquelle «la loi est l'expression de la volonté générale», qui pouvait fonder la reconnaissance de cette souveraineté, elle légitime l'intervention du Conseil constitutionnel.

> -«Le Conseil constitutionnel ne dispose pas d'un pouvoir d'appréciation et de décision de même nature que celui du Parlement» (décis. 92-316 DC, 94-341 DC, 96-377 DC, 2000-433 DC…)

Cette affirmation, selon laquelle ne Conseil constitutionnel ne peut de substituer sa propre appréciation à celle du législateur établit la séparation fondamentale qui existe entre la fonction politique du législateur et la fonction juridictionnelle du Conseil. Elle justifie la réserve du Conseil qui n'est pas légitime à déterminer parmi les solutions possibles celle qui doit être choisie, il ne lui appartient que de censurer parmi ces solutions celles qui violent la Constitution». En ce sens lors de sa délibération du 27 juillet 1982, le Conseil manifeste sa volonté de ne pas s'immiscer de façon trop intrusive dans la fonction normative du parlement.[11]

-«Le législateur ne peut transférer à des autorités réglementaires ou juridictionnelles des compétences que la Constitution lui a confié» (décis. 2006-540 DC).

Cette formulation renvoie au principe de séparation des pouvoirs. Plus précisément elle s'inscrit en contre point de certaines théories, comme la théorie réaliste de l'interprétation,[12] qui conduisent à justifier la faculté du juge de donner son sens à la norme législative. En revanche, ce principe peut justifier l'intervention du Conseil constitutionnel qui, au moyen de directives ou de réserves, d'application ou d'interprétation, vise à prolonger en quelque sorte la volonté du législateur, de telle manière que la Constitution ne soit pas violée à l'occasion de l'application de la loi.

2. *De quelques modalités d'intervention médiates du Conseil constitutionnel*

On relèvera ici un certain nombre de mécanismes qui conduisent le Conseil à exercer une incidence sur la substance même de la loi, voire de la Constitution, non à la suite d'une intervention qui a cet objet, mais par un effet quasi mécanique qui tient à l'exercice même de son office.

- Les incidences sur la fabrication de la loi

L'existence d'un contrôle de constitutionnalité a priori a nécessairement des incidences, en amont, sur le processus de fabrication de la loi, ainsi que l'a relevé le Président de la République dans son discours devant le Conseil constitutionnel le 1 mars 2010. Ce phénomène ne peut qu'être renforcé par la mise en œuvre du contrôle de constitutionnalité a posteriori.

- Les incidences sur les révisions constitutionnelles

Une décision du Conseil constitutionnel peut induire indirectement une modification de la Constitution. Il en est d'abord ainsi s'agissant de l'adaptation de la Constituions aux traités européens. Ces traités (par

11 *Les Grandes délibérations du Conseil constitutionnel*, p. 348.

12 Cf les analyses magistrales de Michel Troper au soutien de cette théorie.

exemple ceux de Maastricht, d'Amsterdam, de Lisbonne, le Traité portant Constitution pour l'Europe) sont soumis au Conseil constitutionnel essentiellement pour qu'il détermine la portée de la révision constitutionnelle nécessaire pour permettre l'adoption d'une loi autorisant la ratification du traité. Sans que la révision ne soit induite par la décision du Conseil, le pouvoir gouvernemental peut également surmonter l'obstacle que représente une censure du Conseil constitutionnel en faisant adopter par le Parlement réuni en Congrès (mais il pourrait aussi être fait appel au Peuple par référendum) une modification de la Constitution permettant au législateur d'adopter à nouveau de telles dispositions. Cette procédure heureusement dénommée par le Doyen Vedel «lit de justice» traduit la suprématie du pouvoir constituant sur le juge fut-il constituant, alors qu'il n'existe pas en France de possibilités pour le juge constitutionnel de faire obstacle à une révision constitutionnel au nom de principes substantiels. Le lit de justice vise à écarter ou à prévenir une censure du juge constitutionnel. C'est ainsi que la modification des dispositions constitutionnelles relatives au droit d'asile a permis au législateur de reprendre des dispositions législatives relatives à la mise en œuvre des accords de Schengen précédemment censurées par le Conseil constitutionnel comme contraire à l'état du droit constitutionnel (Loi constitutionnelle n°93-1256 du 25 novembre 1993 faisant suite à la décision 93-325 DC). C'est également ainsi que des dispositions législatives relatives à la parité hommes-femmes pour certaines élections politiques (82-146 DC) d'abord censurées par la Conseil constitutionnel ont pu être reprises après révision de la Constitution (loi constitutionnelle n° 99-569 DC du 8 juillet 1999), que des lois expérimentales, dont l'existence avait été encadrée par le Conseil, ont pu être adoptée à la suite d'une révision constitutionnelle C'est également pour contourner une jurisprudence du Conseil constitutionnel (décis. 2006-533 DC) que la loi constitutionnelle du n°2008-724 du 23 juillet 2008 a permis que la loi favorise l'égal accès des femmes et des hommes aux responsabilités professionnelles et sociales. C'est en revanche pour étendre la portée d'une jurisprudence relative aux lois expérimentales (93-322 DC) que leur existence a été reconnue par le constituant (loi constitutionnelle 2003-276 du 28 mars 2003).

- La question de la séparabilité des dispositions inconstitutionnelles

Lorsqu'il relève l'inconstitutionnalité d'une disposition législative, dans le cadre du contrôle a priori, le Conseil constitutionnel détermine la portée de cette inconstitutionnalité, soit qu'il considère que cette disposition est inséparable de l'ensemble de la loi, la loi est alors déclarée contraire à la

Constitution dans son ensemble, soit qu'il considère la disposition comme inséparable d'autres dispositions de la loi, soit qu'il considère la disposition comme séparable des autres dispositions de la loi, auxquels cas, la déclaration d'inconstitutionnalité sera partielle. Ce qui implique que le Conseil se prononce sur la cohérence interne de la loi. A sa sortie de l'examen du Conseil la loi pourra donc être promulguée dans une rédaction autre que celle adoptée par le législateur (cf. décis. 71-44 DC, 75-76 DC, 93-322 DC, 2004-496 DC…).

- Les conséquences tirées de l'inconstitutionnalité relevée

Le Conseil constitutionnel a jugé que devaient être maintenues dans l'ordonnancement juridique des dispositions qu'il a jugées inconstitutionnelles. Dans cette hypothèse le Conseil constitutionnel se prononce en faveur de l'inconstitutionnalité d'une disposition législative inscrite dans la loi qui est soumise à son examen. Mais il ne tire pas les conséquences de cette analyse, en jugeant que néanmoins la disposition dont il s'agit ne doit pas être séparée de l'ensemble législatif dans lequel elle est insérée. Ainsi la loi sera promulguée avec certaines dispositions qui ont été jugées inconstitutionnelles. La sanction de cette inconstitutionnalité est alors suspendue, ou différée, jusqu'à ce que le législateur prenne les dispositions qui permettent d'y mettre un terme.

Plusieurs raisons peuvent justifier une telle pratique. D'abord le Conseil a pu juger qu'une sanction de la disposition inconstitutionnelle pourrait engendrer une violation, implicitement jugée plus grave, d'une autre exigence constitutionnelle. Tel est le cas lorsque le Conseil constitutionnel se refuse à censurer une disposition législative relative à un mode de scrutin pour les élections régionales estimant qu'une telle invalidation engendrerait une violation de l'objectif constitutionnel d'égalité entre les hommes et les femmes (décis. 2003-468 DC*)*. Cette absence de censure peut aussi tenir au fait que l'invalidation de la loi engendrerait une violation d'un intérêt général constitutionnel (décis. 2005-528 DC). S'agissant de l'espèce où une censure aurait engendré une violation des obligations communautaires de la France (qui constituent une exigence constitutionnelle), le Conseil reporte les effets de la déclaration d'inconstitutionnalité afin que puisse être respectée l'obligation de transposition d'une directive européenne (décis. 2008-564 DC). Le procédé se rapproche de celui opéré par le Conseil d'Etat qui depuis une date relativement récente accepte de différer dans le temps les effets d'une annulation prononcée (CE 11 mai 2004, Association AC !). Dans le même sens, la faculté offerte au Conseil constitutionnel de régler les effets dans le temps de l'abrogation d'une disposition législative dans le cadre du contrôle de constitutionnalité a posteriori se rapproche du mécanisme retenu par le Conseil d'Etat. En effet l'article 62 de la Constitution, tel que modifié par la loi constitutionnelle du 27 juillet 2008, permet au Conseil constitutionnel, dans le cadre du contrôle a posteriori opéré par la question prioritaire de constitutionnalité, soit de reporter les effets dans le temps de cette abrogation pour des motifs qui tiennent en fait à des considérations de sécurité juridique, soit, au contraire, de donner à l'abrogation prononcée un certain effet rétroactif afin de faire bénéficier le justiciable qui est à l'origine de cette question des effets de l'abrogation de la disposition législative contestée.

D'autre part, la censure peut ne pas être prononcée car le législateur a pu ne pas respecter des exigences nouvelles et complexes. Dans cette hypothèse, pour des raisons de fait, le Conseil pardonne au législateur une faute jugée, en l'état, compréhensible, en lui laissant la faculté de s'amender dans l'avenir. Ce n'est pas alors la censure qui est reportée dans le temps, car la disposition législative entre en vigueur sans conditions particulières, mais c'est la sanction du comportement du législateur qui est reportée. Tel a été le cas de la loi de finances adoptées immédiatement après une réforme profonde de la loi organique relative aux lois de finances (décis. 97-395 DC et 2005-528 DC, cf. également 2005-530 DC à propos d'une loi de financement de la sécurité sociale). Ainsi le Conseil peut ne pas censurer une disposition qu'il juge cependant inconstitutionnelle en invitant le législateur à mettre un terme dans l'avenir à une telle pratique. Dans cette hypothèse, le Conseil se place en quelque sorte à un rang para-constitutionnel en délivrant une autorisation provisoire de non respect d'une exigence constitutionnelle.

La réserve du Conseil constitutionnel peut également se manifester par un usage restreint de son contrôle. Il est ainsi s'agissant du contrôle de dispositions législatives relatives au découpage des circonscriptions électorales. Par exemple, dans la décision 2010-602 DC, le Conseil constitutionnel rappelle la règle constitutionnelle selon laquelle « l'Assemblée nationale, désignée au suffrage universel direct, doit être élue sur des bases essentiellement démographiques selon une répartition des sièges de députés et une délimitation des circonscriptions législatives respectant au mieux l'égalité devant le suffrage ». Il estime en l'espèce que le découpage n'est pas contraire à la Constitution alors que les motifs d'intérêt général invoqués par le législateur pour justifier la délimitation de certaines circonscriptions présentent «un caractère discutable (cf. dans le même sens décis. 86-218 DC et 2003-475 DC). Comme le relève A.

Levade,[13] le Conseil se borne à prononcer une décision de « non inconstitutionnalité manifeste».

Le Conseil peut également jouer le rôle d'un législateur subsidiaire en précisant les conséquences d'une censure qu'il prononce sur d'autres dispositions législatives et sur leur application dans le temps (décis. 2008-568 DC).

- L'outil de la proportionnalité

Le contrôle de proportionnalité peut constituer une ingérence directe dans la fonction législative. Le principe de proportionnalité peut être utilisé de manière différente par le Conseil constitutionnel. Dans le premier cas, il veille à ce que la norme édictée respecte l'ensemble des exigences constitutionnelles qui s'imposent au législateur. Ces exigences étant le plus souvent contradictoires (respect de la vie privée c. liberté d'information des journalistes; liberté individuelle c. exigence de sécurité…), la Conseil vérifie que la conciliation opérée par le législateur ne soit pas manifestement disproportionnée au détriment de l'un des principes en cause. Le Conseil ne se substitue pas au législateur pour déterminer quelle solution doit être retenue, mais il fixe des seuils, un plancher et un plafond, qui délimitent la marge de manouvre du législateur. Lorsque cette conciliation ne peut être opérée in abstracto et a priori, le Conseil renvoie au juge de l'application de la loi le soin de l'opérer[14] (cf. 94-352DC, s'agissant mesures de police nécessitant la conciliation de la protection de l'ordre public et des libertés individuelles). Dans un second cas le principe de proportionnalité constitue une exigence constitutionnelle expresse, il est consubstantiellement lié à tel ou tel principe constitutionnel. Il en est ainsi s'agissant du principe d'égalité (art1 DDHC), de liberté (art. 4 DDHC), de la propriété (art. 17 DDHC), de la nécessité des peines (Art. 8 DDHC)…Dans toutes ces hypothèses la référence au principe de proportionnalité ne constitue que l'une des facettes de l'opération classique consistant à confronter une règle législative à un principe constitutionnel. Il existe cependant une autre hypothèse dans laquelle le Conseil constitutionnel se réfère au principe de proportionnalité pour apprécier la cohérence interne de la loi. Dans cette hypothèse, le Conseil vérifie que les moyens retenus ne sont pas manifestement disproportionnés aux objectifs fixés. C'est alors une à une intervention plus

13 *La semaine juridique*, éd. Gale, 2010, n°11-274.

14 *Cf.* A. Viala, Viala A. *Les réserves d'interprétation dans la jurisprudence du Conseil constitutionnel*, LGDJ, 1999, p 171.

directe dans l'opération même de fabrication de la loi que se livre le Conseil constitutionnel (cf. décision 93-331 DC, 94-341 DC et 2000-439 DC).[15] Cette manière de procéder est particulièrement marquée dans la décision 2009-599 DC. Le Conseil constitutionnel censure le dispositif retenu par le législateur concernant la taxe carbone en invoquant essentiellement deux arguments. Le premier tenant à la violation du principe d'égalité est classique, le second nous intéresse plus directement ici. Il considère en effet qu'à partir du moment où une très grande partie des activités émettrices de gaz à effet de serre et de dioxyde de carbone ne seront pas soumises à la contribution, la loi va à l'encontre de l'objectif de lutte contre le réchauffement climatique. Le Conseil opère alors un examen, non seulement de la conformité de la loi à des exigences inscrites dans la Constitution, mais aussi de la cohérence interne de la loi. Ce faisant le juge constitutionnel, comme le font d'ailleurs ses homologues étrangers, pénètre plus profondément au cœur même de la décision politique. L'analyse du Conseil constitutionnel devient alors plus sujette à la critique politique ou, comme en l'espèce, à une critique portant sur la validité de l'analyse économique à laquelle le Conseil se réfère pour opérer ce contrôle de cohérence de la loi.

III. ANALYSE D'UNE MODALITÉ SPÉCIFIQUE D'INTERVENTION DU CONSEIL CONSTITUTIONNEL: LES RÉSERVES D'INTERPRÉTATION

Après quelques remarques générales sur la nature et le champ d'application des réserves d'interprétation, qui constituent des interventions assumées dans l'exercice de la fonction législative ou dans le prolongement de l'acte législatif, il conviendra d'identifier les destinataires de ces réserves avant de s'essayer à quelques éléments de typologie.[16]

1. *Eléments de définition et champ d'application*

Les réserves d'interprétation constituent un ensemble d'instruments par lequel le Conseil constitutionnel cadre et encadre les conditions de mise en œuvre de la loi, il complète ainsi l'intervention du législateur. Soit le Conseil estime que le degré d'imprécision est tel qu'il ne peut intervenir pour

15 Sur cette technique, *cf.* B. Mathieu et M. Verpeaux, *Contentieux constitutionnel des droits fondamentaux*, LGDJ 2002.

16 Sur cette question, outre les références bibliographiques déjà citées, *cf.* Di Manno T. *Le juge constitutionnel et la technique des décisions interprétatives en France et en Italie*, Economica, 1997.

combler l'incertitude. La censure de la loi tient alors à l'incompétence négative du législateur. C'est à dire que le législateur est resté en deçà de sa compétence et qu'ainsi il renvoie aux autorités administratives ou au juge l'exercice des compétences que la Constitution lui a confiées (cf. *supra*). Soit le Conseil estime que la marge d'imprécision n'est pas suffisante pour prononcer l'invalidation du texte. Dans cette hypothèse, le Conseil va recourir à des réserves d'interprétation, ou d'application, adressées soit à l'autorité chargée de prendre les mesures réglementaires d'application, soit aux juges chargés de mettre en œuvre la loi. La réserve d'interprétation précise le sens qui devra être donné à la loi, la réserve d'application s'attache en quelque sorte aux prolongements de la loi, au contenu des dispositions normatives nécessaires à sa mise en œuvre effective. Mais de telles directives peuvent s'adresser au législateur lui même (cf. décis. 83-164 DC). Elles n'ont pas d'effet normatif direct mais encadrent l'action ultérieure du législateur. Dans cette hypothèse, on peut considérer comme l'analyse G. Behrendt, que « le juge constitutionnel indique au législateur comment une loi peut être rédigée, produit une norme juridique qui habilite ce dernier à édicter une loi conformément à l'interférence émise ».[17] Il n'en reste pas moins, comme le note lui même cet auteur, que cette « interférence » n'a qu'un caractère persuasif. Il n'en reste pas moins que le Conseil, saisi d'une loi ultérieure, dispose des moyens d'en sanctionner la violation.

La fonction normative de ces réserves tient à l'autorité qui leur est reconnue, notamment par les juges d'application de la loi qui auront à se prononcer, soit quant à l'interprétation de loi, soit quant à la validité des actes administratifs d'application de la loi. Le recours, à la fois par la doctrine et par le juge constitutionnel lui même, au concept d'autorité de chose jugée s'avère à la fois efficace et trop restreint. Efficace, en ce que le Conseil insère en général ses réserves dans le dispositif de la décision (ce qu'il a fait très tôt, cf. par exemple décis. 68-35 DC), les faisant ainsi bénéficier de l'autorité reconnue à des décisions qui, au titre de l'article 62 al 2 de la Constitution, «s'imposent aux pouvoirs publics et à toutes les autorités administratives et juridictionnelles». Restreint, en ce que cette interprétation ne vaut que pour la disposition considérée et ne s'impose pas de manière générale au titre de l'autorité de chose interprétée. La réussite de la nouvelle procédure de contrôle a priori devra conduire à de nouvelles réflexions sur cette question, pour des raisons, tenant notamment à la sécurité juridique et à la cohérence de l'interprétation du texte constitutionnel par les différentes juridictions (cf. supra).

17 Ouvrage précité.

La réserve peut également se manifester formellement avec une plus ou moins grande intensité. Parfois le Conseil pose une *stricte* réserve d'interprétation. Tel est le cas s'agissant de la décision 98-411 dans laquelle le Conseil précise qu'il appartiendra au juge de faire application de dispositions du code pénal (non référenciées dans la loi examinée) aux termes desquelles il n'y a pas de crimes ou de délits sans intention de le commettre.

La réserve d'interprétation se distingue de la réserve d'application par le fait qu'elle se suffit par elle même sans qu'il soit nécessaire de confier aux autorités chargées d'appliquer la loi une mission de vigilance. Il en est ainsi lorsque le conseil précise que la possibilité offerte par la loi au propriétaire de s'opposer à la pratique de la chasse sur ses biens ne saurait faire l'objet d'une demande de justification (décis. 2000-434 DC).

Le recours à ces réserves d'application est particulièrement marquant s'agissant de la procédure des ordonnances de l'article 38 C, c'est à dire de l'adoption par le gouvernement de dispositions relevant du domaine de compétence du législateur sur habilitation de ce dernier. le Conseil contrôle alors la loi d'habilitation et encadre l'intervention de l'autorité réglementaire. Par ailleurs, il s'adresse également au juge administratif chargé le cas échéant de contrôler la régularité de ces ordonnances (décis. 95-370 DC).[18]

Le recours à ces réserves d'interprétation traduit souvent la volonté du Conseil de ne pas établir un conflit frontal avec le législateur en prononçant une déclaration d'inconstitutionnalité. En ce sens également, le Conseil peut sembler se montrer respectueux de la volonté du législateur en jouant en quelque sorte le rôle d'un auxiliaire afin que ce qui est déterminé comme l'expression de sa volonté soit respecté par les autorités qui auront la mission d'appliquer la loi. Comme le relève A. Viala,[19] il s'agit de « faire en sorte que l'opposabilité de la Constitution ne s'évapore pas au fur et à mesure que l'on descend dans la hiérarchie normative, mais qu'elle garde intacte, au contraire, toute sa vitalité et toute sa force à l'égard des autorités infra législatives au cours de l'application de la loi ».

Cependant, le Conseil se refuse à intervenir trop directement dans le processus d'application de la loi. Il considère, en effet que la conformité de la loi à la Constitution ne peut être appréciée au regard de l'application qui pourrait en être faite (décis. 83-162 DC, 84-176 DC, 2001-451 DC). C'est en

18 *Cf.* B. Mathieu, Les rôles respectifs du Parlement, du Président de la République et du Conseil Constitutionnel dans l'édiction des ordonnances de l'article 38, *Revue française de droit administratif*, 1987, p. 700.

19 *Op. cit.* p. 95.

fait à un jeu d'équilibriste que se livre le Conseil constitutionnel entre sa volonté de respecter les compétences des autorités administratives et juridictionnelles chargées de l'application de la loi et son souci de veiller à ce que soit respectée la Constitution à l'occasion de l'application de la loi, lorsque se dessine le risque d'une interprétation de la loi contraire à la Constitution. La première de cette préoccupation se manifeste dans certains des délibérés du Conseil. Ainsi lors de sa séance du 10 novembre 1982, le rapporteur rappelle que le Conseil constitutionnel n'est pas une Cour suprême et qu'il doit respecter les ordres judiciaires et administratifs.[20] De même le Conseil a pu considérer que si deux interprétations sont également possibles, la disposition législative ainsi frappée d'ambigüité doit être invalidée comme manifestant le non respect par le législateur de ses compétences constitutionnelles. (décis. 85-191 DC).

Cette analyse s'insère parfaitement dans le cadre du contrôle a priori, alors que le Conseil peut encadrer l'application de la loi mais non la déterminer. En revanche, dans le cadre de la question prioritaire de constitutionnalité, le Conseil sera le plus souvent confronté à une manifestation de l'inconstitutionnalité de la loi révélée à l'occasion de son application.

N'est probablement pas sans lien avec cette dernière observation le fait que le Conseil constitutionnel se refuse de procéder à une interprétation « gratuite » de la loi déférée. Il considère, en effet qu'il ne lui appartient de procéder à l'interprétation du texte qui lui est déféré que dans la mesure où cette interprétation est nécessaire à l'appréciation de sa constitutionnalité (décis 91-298 DC et 2009- 590 DC). Comme le relève F. Luchaire,[21] « si aucune des différentes interprétations possibles ne rend la loi contraire à la Constitution, le Conseil constitutionnel n' pas à choisir l'une d'entre elles. Cette remarque prend une signification particulière dans le cadre de la procédure du contrôle a posteriori (question prioritaire de constitutionnalité) à l'occasion de laquelle les requérants pourraient être tentés de saisir le Conseil constitutionnel, pas tant pour lui faire déclarer telle ou telle disposition législative inconstitutionnelle, mais pour surmonter une interprétation de la loi par le juge judiciaire ou administratif contraire à leurs intérêts et, donc, pour obtenir une interprétation favorable. On imagine en effet mal que le Conseil puisse, dans tous les cas, déclarer la disposition législative soumise à son examen conforme à la Constitution sans prendre parti sur l'interprétation qui doit être retenue.

20 *Les Grandes délibérations du Conseil constitutionnel,* Dalloz, 2009, p. 345.

21 *La portée constitutionnelle des droits et libertés*, Economica, 1987, p. 40.

2. *Les destinataires des réserves d'interprétation*

Les directives d'application s'adressent essentiellement aux autorités administratives et juridictionnelles en général (2000-433 DC). Elles peuvent viser, plus précisément, une autorité particulière. Il en est ainsi des autorités administratives indépendantes, par exemple, la Commission des opérations de bourse (décis 2001-452 DC), ou la Commission nationale des comptes de campagne (89-271 DC). Dans cette dernière hypothèse, la directive constitue à la fois une interprétation de la loi et une directive d'application adressée à la dite autorité. Elles peuvent également être adressées à des organes parlementaires. Il en est ainsi lorsque, s'agissant d'un règlement parlementaire, le Conseil précise qu'il appartiendra à la conférence des présidents de veiller au respect du droit d'amendement des parlementaires (décis. 2005-526 DC). Elles peuvent également s'adresser à des assemblées territoriales (2007-559 DC). Ces directives peuvent aussi être adressées aux autorités chargées de prendre des décisions individuelles. Il appartient ainsi aux chefs d'établissements scolaires de fonder leurs décisions de recrutement sur la capacité des intéréssés à satisfaire les besoins de l'établissement (2003-471 DC). La directive peut plus spécifiquement s'adresser aux «autorités compétentes de la Cour des comptes» (décis. 2005-519 DC) ou au Conseil supérieur de la magistrature (décis. 2003-466 DC). Le Conseil peut aussi inviter les autorités compétentes, sans le faire directement lui même, à compléter la loi afin que son application soit conforme à la Constitution. Tel est le cas lorsque le Conseil précise qu'en l'absence de précision sur l 'élément moral de l'infraction, il appartient au juge de faire application de certaines dispositions du code pénal (décis. 99-411 DC).

Les directives d'interprétation peuvent s'adresser au législateur. Elles portent alors essentiellement sur l'interprétation de la contrainte constitutionnelle et interviennent en amont.

La réserve peut constituer un simple avertissement pour l'avenir alors même que la constitutionnalité de la loi examinée n'est pas en cause. C'est ainsi, qu'après avoir relevé que le maintien de *France telecom* dans le secteur public était conforme à la Constitution, le Conseil ajoute, par un *obiter dictum*, que l'abandon ne pourrait résulter que d'une loi. C'est ainsi une invite au législateur à ne pas déléguer sa compétence et une interdiction faite au gouvernement d'intervenir en la matière qui sont opérés (décis. 96-380 DC). Il en est de même lorsque le Conseil précise que la loi est conforme à la Constitution car elle ne vise pas à édicter telle règle dont il précise qu'elle eut été contraire au principe d'égalité (87-235 DC).

A l'inverse le Conseil a pu déterminer la portée d'une déclaration d'inconstitutionnalité qu'il prononce en interprétant les dispositions maintenues de manière à ce qu'elles produisent les effets souhaités par le législateur (décis. 568 DC). C'est alors la volonté du législateur que le Conseil vise à préserver, alors qu'il annule la lettre de la loi.

L'efficacité de ces directives est cependant réelle du fait que le Conseil pourra être conduit à opérer un contrôle à double détente[22], soit que le texte censuré sera à nouveau déféré, soit que la censure trouve à frapper une disposition législative ultérieure affectée du même vice. Le Conseil peut ainsi se référer, même implicitement, à des directives d'interprétation fixées dans des décisions antérieures, (cf. décis. 473 DC, 506 DC et 567 DC, 2007-559 DC).

3. *La portée des réserves d'interprétation: essai de typologie*

- L'exclusion d'une interprétation inconstitutionnelle: le postulat du respect de la Constitution par le législateur

L'une des techniques qui permet de sauver la loi est de postuler que le législateur est censé avoir voulu respecter la Constitution et donc d'en déduire une interprétation conforme qui s'imposera à l'occasion de l'application de la loi (décis. 2000-435 DC, 2001-454 DC, 2007-547 DC). C'est un raisonnement qui est expressément ou implicitement le support de la plupart des directives édictées par le Conseil constitutionnel. La formule qui exprime le plus clairement ce raisonnement est celle qui consiste à affirmer que la disposition législative examinée «n'a pas pour objet et ne saurait avoir pour effet de ...» (décis. 2004-490 DC, 2007-547 DC). Le Conseil se livre alors à un «coup double» il interprète la loi conformément à la Constitution et adresse au législateur une directive relative aux conditions d'exercice de sa compétence, et le cas échéant, une directive sur la manière dont la loi devra être appliquée aux autorités qui en sont chargées

La réserve peut avoir, et dans ce sens, pour objet d'exclure l'une des interprétations possibles. Ainsi, par exemple, le Conseil a considéré que le législateur n'a pu vouloir empécher les réfugiés de bénéficier du droit d'asile reconnu par la Convention de Genève (décis. 86-216 DC). Dans cette hypothèse, dite d'interprétation neutralisante,[23] le Conseil ne retient pas parmi les interprétations possibles de la loi, ouvertes par le législateur, celle qui est conforme à la Constitution. Il considère que le législateur n'a pu vouloir violer la Constitution, cette « présomption d'innocence » le conduit

[22] Selon l'expression de G. Drago, *Contentieux constitutionnel français*, 2° ed. PUF, p. 412.

[23] Selon la formule d'A. Viala.

en quelque sorte à compléter la loi pour la rendre conforme à ce qu'il postule être la volonté du législateur. Ainsi le Conseil précise le sens qu'il convient de donner à des dispositions du règlement de l'Assemblée nationale et précise que ce n'est qu'en ce que ces dispositions doivent être interprétées comme ne faisant pas obstacle aux prérogatives du gouvernement qu'elles sont conformes à la Constitution (cf. décis 92-314 DC, 95-368 DC, 2004-403 DC). Il peut également déterminer la seule interprétation conforme à la Constitution. Il considère alors que «toute autre interprétation méconnaitrait les exigences constitutionnelles» (97-389 DC).

- L'argument de la maladresse du législateur

Le Conseil peut aussi intervenir comme correcteur des maladresses du législateur. Dans cette hypothèse, la recherche de la volonté du législateur n'est pas formelle, le Conseil réécrit la loi afin de la rendre conforme à l'intention réelle du législateur. Il peut ainsi «trouver» dans la loi des éléments qui pouvaient en paraître exclu du fait d'une maladresse rédactionnelle (décis. 87-235 DC). Le Conseil fait alors plus œuvre de commentateur que de censeur. Il peut également en ce sens être conduit à se référer à la logique du texte pour interpréter l'une de ses dispositions (décis. 2000-436 DC, cf. eglt. décis. 86-217 DC, 92-307 DC, 93-325 DC, 2004-490 DC). Il peut également être conduit à se référer aux travaux préparatoires (2000-436 DC, 2001-448 DC, 2005-512 DC) ou aux dispositions d'une directive communautaire (décis. 2006-540 DC) que le législateur est ainsi présumé avoir voulu respecter. De manière habile, mais constructive, le Conseil se glisse en quelque sorte dans ce qu'il estime être la volonté du législateur pour estimer que l'indépendance conférée par la loi à un organisme implique une intention du législateur quant à sa composition (décis. 86-217 DC).

- La tentation de la réécriture

Cependant la frontière est parfois mince qui sépare ce travail rédactionnel de celui qui tend à opérer une réécriture plus substantielle de la loi. L'un des exemples les plus flagrants en ce sens est l'intervention du Conseil relative à la loi sur le pacte civil de solidarité (décis. 99-419 DC). Dans la décision qui se rapporte à ce texte, le Conseil, notamment, redéfinit le texte comme établissant un contrat portant communauté de vie, notamment et implicitement, sur le plan sexuel, ce qui ne ressortissait évidemment ni du texte voté ni des débats. Au delà de réécriture de nombreuses dispositions de ce texte, qui peut alors difficilement être lu sans la décision qui s'y rapporte, le Conseil tranche là ou le législateur ne l'avait pas clairement fait sur la nature même de ce contrat. Cette définition ne conditionne pas tant la constitutionnalité du texte qu'elle répond à une exigence de sécurité juridique présupposé qui permet au Conseil lui même de donner un sens aux diverses dispositions dont il devra contrôler la constitutionnalité. De même c'est sous couvert du respect de la volonté du législateur que le Conseil modifie le champ d'application de la loi en précisant que la référence faite au respect du droit d'auteur doit s'entendre compte tenu du contexte dans lequel elle s'insère et qu'elle vise donc aussi les droits voisins du droit d'auteur (2006-540 DC).

La correction de la loi peut viser seulement à la compléter, à en combler une insuffisance. Il en ainsi lorsque le Conseil précise ce que l'Etat devrait faire si telle recette transférée aux départements venait à diminuer (décis. 2003-489 DC).

Les réserves relatives à l'application de la loi par le juge, ou l'autorité administrative, constituent autant des directives qui leur sont adressées que des compléments apportés à la loi. C'est ainsi que s'agissant d'une disposition législative relative à un préjudice indemnisable, le Conseil précise que le juge pourra allouer une indemnité complémentaire (à celle prévue par la loi) et précise les éléments qui devront être pris en compte. (décis. 98-403 DC). La formulation peut être très précise. Ainsi s'agissant de dispositions législatives relatives à des contrôles d'identité, le Conseil précise «il appartient aux autorités juridictionnelles et administratives de veiller à les *(les précautions prévues par le législateur)* respecter intégralement, ainsi qu'aux tribunaux compétents de censurer, de réprimer, les cas échéant, les illégalités qui seraient commises et de pourvoir éventuellement à la réparation des conséquences dommageables» (décis. 80-127 DC). La directive peut être formulée en termes très généraux, il en est ainsi lorsque le Conseil précise que le pouvoir réglementaire devra appliquer la loi «de manière à respecter le principe de la liberté d'association» (décis. 2000-434 DC) ou à ne pas mettre en cause le onzième alinéa du Préambule de 1946 (objectif du droit à la santé et au travail, décis. 86-225 DC et 2004-504 DC), ou à respecter le droit de chacun de mener une vie familiale normale (2003-467 DC). Aussi largement, mais de manière différente, le Conseil constitutionnel précise qu'il appartiendra au Conseil d'Etat de vérifier l'existence et le caractère suffisant du motif d'intérêt général en cause (2004-490 DC).

Le Conseil peut aussi utiliser toute la palette des directives à sa disposition. Ainsi dans la décision 89-260 DC, il complète la norme législative relative aux sanctions contre les auteurs de délits boursiers en précisant que, dans l'hypothèse d'un cumul de sanctions financières et pénales, le montant global des sanctions prononcées ne devra pas dépasser le montant le plus élevé des sanctions encourues. Puis il demande aux autorités administratives et juridictionnelles compétentes de veiller au respect de cette exigence dans la mise en œuvre de ces dispositions.

- La modification du champ d'application de la loi

La réserve d'interprétation peut opérer clairement une modification du champ d'application de la loi. C'est ainsi que dans la décision 82-141 DC relative à une loi sur communication audiovisuelle, le Conseil élargit le champ du droit de réponse en retranchant les termes « sans but lucratif » utilisés pour définir les titulaires de ce droit. Le délibéré relatif à cette décision montre que cette intervention du Conseil quant à la substance même de la loi a fait l'objet d'un vrai débat.[24] En réalité dans une telle hypothèse le Conseil dit la loi à la place du législateur. En effet, en l'espèce, le législateur n'a entendu établir un droit de réponse dans le cadre de la communication audiovisuelle qu'à certaines catégories de personnes, le Conseil élargit le champ des personnes concernées en supprimant les imitations apportées. Il n'est alors pas seulement fait obstacle à la volonté du législateur pour des motifs constitutionnels, mais à la décision du législateur est substituée une autre décision. Il est difficile de considérer que le législateur a voulu ce qu'il a exclu. La décision du Conseil ne peut alors se justifier que pour autant que deux conditions soient en l'espèce remplies: la Constitution exige un droit de réponse et ce droit de réponse ne doit pas être réservé à certains titulaires. En effet, si seul le principe d'égalité est en cause, le législateur aurait pu préférer ne pas attribuer de droit de réponse, et dans ce cas, c'est la déclaration de non conformité qui renvoie la décision au législateur qui est la plus respectueuse de sa compétence. De la même manière, sous couvert d'une réserve d'interprétation, le Conseil censure le caractère limitatif du préjudice indemnisable en cas de réquisition de logement (décis 98-403 DC). On peut, en l'espèce, estimer que le droit à réparation constituant une exigence constitutionnelle, le législateur ne disposait pas d'autres alternatives. Dans le même sens, afin que soit respecté le principe d'égalité de traitement des candidats dans les concours de la fonction publique, le Conseil constitutionnel impose que la faculté, instaurée par la loi, de consultation des dossiers individuels des candidats, soit en fait comprise comme une obligation (décis. 76-67 DC). Le raisonnement est le même s'agissant des conditions d'attribution du statut civil coutumier à un enfant (décis. 99-410

24 *Les Grandes délibérations du Conseil constitutionnel*, précité, p. 348.

DC). En ce sens également la décision (2005-528 DC) par laquelle le Conseil précise, alors que la loi ne le fait pas, que la régularisation de la situation d'un enfant entré en France dans la cadre du regroupement lui ouvre droit aux prestations familiales. Le Conseil juge également qu'une disposition législative doit s'entendre comme s'appliquant sous réserve du respect de l'ensemble des stipulations d'une convention, alors que la loi ne vise qu'un article de cette convention (décis. 93-325 DC).

Il s'agit en fait d'une correction de la loi. La même logique se retrouve dans la décision 89-257 DC. La disposition législative examinée prévoit qu'un syndicat peut introduire une action en justice en faveur d'un salarié à condition d'avertir ce dernier par une lettre recommandée avec accusé de réception. Le Conseil ajoute à la loi en précisant que la lettre doit contenir toute précision utile sur la nature et l'objet de l'action exercée, la portée de l'acceptation et le droit de mettre un terme à tout moment à cette action. Dans cette hypothèse, le Conseil ne se borne pas à préciser la manière dont la loi devra être appliquée, il modifie le sens de la règle posée. De manière très directe alors que le législateur avait souhaité imposer des quotas par sexes dans la composition des recrutements de la fonction publique, le Conseil enlève le venin de la loi en précisant, à l'encontre de la volonté exprimée par le législateur, que la considération du sexe ne devra pas prévaloir sur celle tenant aux capacités (décis. 2006-533DC). Il en est de même lorsque le Conseil précise que la priorité instituée par le législateur en faveur des étudiants boursiers ne joue qu'à aptitudes égales (décis. 2003-471 DC). Ou encore, lorsque le Conseil précise qu'une disposition écartant la responsabilité pénale et civile de certaines personnes dans certaines hypothèses ne saurait avoir pour effet d'engager leur responsabilité dans d'autres cas (2004-496 DC). De même que le délit d'aide au séjour irrégulier des étrangers en France commis en bande organisée ne saurait concerner les organismes humanitaires d'aide aux étrangers (décis. 2004-492 DC).

- La paralyse de l'application de la loi

Le procédé des réserves d'interprétation peut également avoir pour effet, ou pour objet, d'infléchir la volonté du législateur. Tel est le cas dans la décision 93-323 DC par laquelle le Conseil ne censure pas de nouvelles modalités de contrôle d'identité, visant en fait à mettre fin à une jurisprudence de la Cour de cassation, tout en subordonnant la constitutionnalité de la loi au respect d'un certain nombre de conditions qu'elle ne contient pas et qu'il énumère, ces conditions se rapprochant de celles exigées par la Cour de cassation et auxquelles le législateur entendait justement faire obstacle.

Le Conseil a même été jusqu'à poser des conditions à l'application de la loi qui la rendent partiellement inapplicable. Tel a été le cas s'agissant de l'utilisation des tests génétiques dans le cadre du regroupent familial (décis. 2007-557 DC). A tel point que, dans cette hypothèse, le gouvernement a renoncé à prendre les mesures réglementaires d'application nécessaires à l'effectivité des normes législatives. Dans le même sens, et s'agissant de dispositions législatives controversées permettant sous le nom de « détention de sureté » de maintenir un détenu dangereux en système fermé à l'issue de sa peine, le Conseil (décis.2008-562 DC) a fermé la voie de l'application rétroactive de cette disposition et a conditionné le prononcé d'une telle rétention à l'existence de soins médicaux durant la peine de privation de liberté, ce qui, en l'état n'est presque jamais le cas.

4. *Eléments statistiques sommaires*

La présentation par le Conseil constitutionnel, sur son site internet (http://www.conseil-constitutionnel.fr/) de l'ensemble des réserves d'interprétation renforce incontestablement l'autorité de ces réserves. Ces réserves voient également leur caractère normatif implicitement affirmé. Ce catalogue des réserves s'inscrit également dans un souci de sécurité juridique alors que les justiciables peuvent dorénavant invoquer devant toute juridiction et à l'occasion de tout litige l'inconstitutionnalité de la loi. Il permet incidemment de disposer d'une vue globale de ces réserves. De 1984 à 2008 sur 390 décisions, rendues dans le cadre de l'examen de constitutionnalité des lois, 87 décisions sur les 390 rendues contiennent des réserves d'interprétation. Ce chiffre est cependant trompeur alors qu'une même décision peut contenir jusqu'à 12 réserves d'interprétation. Il est ainsi de la décision 99-419 DC relative à la loi sur le pacte civil de solidarité, ce qui traduit le travail de réécriture de la loi auquel s'est livré le Conseil constitutionnel (cf. également décis. 2003-490 DC, loi organique portant statut d'autonomie de la Polynésie française). Mais, nombreuses sont les décisions qui contiennent 9 réserves (par exemple 93-325 DC, 2001-448 DC, 2003-467 DC, 2007-547 DC). Alors que de 1984 à 1998 sur 240 décisions rendues, 30 contiennent des réserves d'interprétation, de 1999 à 2008, sur 167 décisions rendues, 57 contiennent des réserves d'interprétation. Le recours aux réserves d'interprétation s'est donc, globalement, accentué au fur et à mesure de la multiplication des saisines.

1984	3
1985	0
1986	3
1987	2
1988	0
1989	1
1990	0
1991	2
1992	3
1993	3
1994	3
1995	2
1996	6
1997	1
1998	1
1999	6
2000	5
2001	5
2002	3
2003	8
2004	10
2005	6
2006	4
2007	6
2008	4

On peut également relever que la fréquence des réserves varie en fonction des domaines d'intervention du législateur. C'est ainsi que les réserves sont les plus nombreuses s'agissant des textes intéressant l'ordre public et le droit pénal (14 décisions), le droit des collectivités territoriales (12 décisions), les finances publiques (11 décisions), le droit des étrangers (7 décisions), la justice (4 décisions).

EN GUISE DE CONCLUSION

Il convient de replacer la question ici traitée dans une vision plus générale de l'exercice par le Conseil constitutionnel français de sa fonction de juge constitutionnel. De ce point de vue, l'analyse qui vient d'être exposée pourrait conduire à fausser le jugement de qui n'est pas familier de la jurisprudence du Conseil constitutionnel. La manière dont la question est posée et le sujet traité peut déformer la perspective. En effet il s'est agi ici de s'essayer à expliciter la palette des moyens dont le Conseil dispose pour intervenir sur le contenu de la loi et les conditions de son application, au travers d'un certain nombre d'exemples dont la liste ne peut d'ailleurs être considérée comme exhaustive. Sans que le rôle joué par ces instruments doivent être minimisé, il convient de noter que, de manière générale, le Conseil constitutionnel se montre assez respectueux de la volonté du législateur, comme en témoigne, par exemple, la place occupée dans sa jurisprudence par la référence à l'intérêt général,[25] probablement plus que d'autres juridictions constitutionnelles ou européennes. Mais c'est d'un autre sujet qu'il s'agit.

[25] *Cf.* B. Mathieu, M. Verpeaux, *L'intérêt général, norme constitutionnelle*, Dalloz, 2007.

GERMANY

CONSTITUTIONAL COURTS AS POSITIVE LEGISLATORS

Ines Härtel,
Professor, University of Bochum
LS-Haertel@rub.de

The Court responsible for the review of constitutional questions in the Federal Republic of Germany is the Bundesverfassungsgericht (BVerfG), situated in Karlsruhe. It is mentioned in article 92 of the German Constitution, called Grundgesetz (Basic Law – GG). Article 93 GG contains the catalog of jurisdiction, and Article 94 GG regulates its composition. The Bundesverfassungsgericht consists of federal judges and other members; the members of the Bundesverfassungsgericht are elected half by Parliament (Bundestag) and half by the Bundesrat (German Federal Council). The judges are not allowed to be members of the Bundestag, the Bundesrat, the government, or corresponding institutions at the Federal-State level.

As a court, the Bundesverfassungsgericht is part of the judiciary, but nevertheless the Constitutional Legislator grants the Bundesverfassungsgericht an accentuated position.[1] It is mentioned in Article 92 GG as prior to all other courts, and Article 93 f. GG comprehends further detailed specifications. The main function of the Bundesverfassungsgericht is to ensure and to enforce Constitutional Law against the bodies of sovereign power. In literature, the Bundesverfassungsgericht is called Hüter der Verfassung (guardian of the Constitution).[2]

1 Vollmeyer, DÖV 2009, 55 ff.; Komorowski/Bechtel, Politische Vierteljahresschrift, Sonderheft 36 (2006), 282–305; Steiner, NJW 2001, 1919 ff.

2 The expression is due to Carl Schmitt, Der Hüter der Verfassung, 1929; Scholz, APuZ (B 37-38/2001); Ossenbühl, in Scholz/Bandura (eds.), 2001, 33–53; Schulze-Fielitz, AöR 1997, 121 ff.

Beyond this, the Bundesverfassungsgericht is a constitutional body like the Bundestag, the Bundesrat, and the Federal Government.[3] Therefore, the Bundesverfassungsgericht has autonomy to create bylaw, it is not seated by a ministry, it is not under supervision, and it establishes its budget on its own.[4]

Because of its specific position, critical voices have arisen in the literature. In their opinion, the Bundesverfassungsgericht interpreted its jurisdiction by itself and thus broke the mold of the prevalent system of "checks and balances in a democracy."[5]

I. JUDICIAL MEANS FOR JUDICIAL REVIEW

1. *Civil Rights Injunctions*

The German Basic Law offers natural persons the right to take legal action to review the constitutionality of statutes or judgments. The so-called Verfassungsbeschwerde (Constitutional Complaint) is regulated in Article 93, Sec. 1, N° 4a GG, Sec. 13 N° 8a, 90ff BVerfGG (Law of the Bundesverfassungsgericht). It is the rightful proceeding to review measures of public authority and to declare constitutional violations. Everybody is able to take legal action, but before doing so, he or she has to deplete the legal process. The Bundesverfassungsgericht only reviews specific violations of the German Basic Law; it is no body of superrevision and therefore does not review a false interpretation or application of a statute. The content of the judgment is regulated in Sec. 95 BVerfGG. The Bundesverfassungsgericht asserts which articles of the German Basic Law have been violated and, if necessary, annuls the judgment. If the Verfassungsbeschwerde against a statute is successful, the Bundesverfassungsgericht annuls it; in some cases, the Bundesverfassungsgericht declares only the unconstitutional character of the statute.

3 Jahrbuch des öffentlichen Rechts der Gegenwart 6 (1957), pp. 144 ff.; Scholz, APuZ (B 37-38/2001).

4 Schlaich/Korioth, Das Bundesverfassungsgericht, 7th ed. 2007, margin number 29; Voßkuhle, in v. Mangoldt/Klein/Starck, Grundgesetz-Kommentar, vol. 3, 5th ed. 2005, Art. 93 margin number 30.

5 Höffe, Der Staat 38 (1999), 171 (179).

2. *Direct Actions to Control the Constitutionality of Statutes*

The German Basic Law (GG) in connection with the Bundesverfassungsgerichtsgesetz (BVerfGG) provides several possibilities of direct action to control the constitutionality of statutes. Besides the already-mentioned Verfassungsbeschwerde there are Abstract Judicial Review and Concrete Judicial Review, which form the meeting point between the Bundesverfassungsgericht and the Legislator.[6] They are regarded as gateways for the expansion of the Bundesverfassungsgericht's political power.[7] Abstract Judicial Review is a form of action to review the constitutionality of Federal Law or State Law or to review the conformity of State Law with Federal Law without it being the subject matter of a concrete proceeding. Abstract Judicial Review is regulated in Article 93, Sec. 1, N° 2/2a GG, Sec. 13 N° 6/6a, 76ff BVerfGG. The Federal Government, the State Government, or one-third of the members of Parliament are authorized to make an application to the Bundesverfassungsgericht. Abstract Judicial Review allows the broadest of reviews of a statute possible. The review takes place detached from any particular case and refers to the compatibility of the statute with the complete German Basic Law.[8]

Concrete Judicial Review is also regulated in the German Basic Law. In this proceeding, the Bundesverfassungsgericht reviews the constitutionality of a statute submitted by a German court. The Court must be convinced of the unconstitutional character of the statute and clarification of the matter must be relevant to the case. Judicial review is conducted on the basis of the concrete legal proceeding. Concrete Judicial Review is regulated in Article 100, Sec. 1 GG iVm, Sec. 13 N° 11. 80ff BVerfGG.

In its decision, the BVerfG declares whether a norm is constitutional. If so, the BVerfG declares the norm to be constitutional. In the case of unconstitutionality, however, the BVerfG has evolved different methods to deal with unconstitutionality. The BVerfG can basically declare a norm invalid that is not compatible with the Basic Law, Sec. 78 S. 1 BVerfGG. To forestall the declaration of invalidity, which is in some cases connected to extensive consequences, the BVerfG has developed alternatives of gradation that avoid annulment but still leave the Court with a certain influence on

6 Landfried, Bundesverfassungsgericht und Gesetzgeber, 1984, p. 47.

7 Holtfort, in Däubler/Küsel (eds.), Verfassungsgericht und Politik. Kritische Beiträge zu problematischen Urteilen, 1979, p. 193.

8 Blasberg, Verfassungsgerichte als Ersatzgesetzgeber, 2003, p. 11.

Legislation.[9] The statute can be declared partially invalid, incompatible, still compatible, or compatible if interpreted in conformity with the Constitution. Alternatively, the BVerfG sets the Legislator vague or exact provisions for a reform, with or without deadline, transitional period, or transitional arrangement.[10]

3. *Direct Actions to Control the Constitutionality of Legislative Omissions*

The Constitution stipulates a mandate of regulation to the Legislator in some passages (e.g., Article 4, Sec. 3 S. 2, 29 Sec. 7 S. 2, 38 Sec. 3). These provisions are the basis for Constitution-complementing subconstitutional statutes.[11] If the Legislator does not carry out the duty of regulation, the question arises as to how much the BVerfG can obligate the bodies of legislation to fulfill their tasks or can respectively fill the gap itself.[12] This can be carried out only within the limits of procedural conditions dictated by the BVerfG; a judicial review fails, however, in absence of a reviewable norm. One could, at best, think of either a Verfassungsbeschwerde or an Organstreitverfahren (a constitutional dispute between bodies of the state);[13] a violation of the Law through legislative omission in a federal body or single citizen is, however, to be assumed only rarely.[14] Should a proceeding be necessary, the BVerfG is left with the possibility of declaring the unconstitutionality of omission and thereby indirectly requiring the Legislator to set a standard.[15]

9 Siedler, Gesetzgeber und Bundesverfassungsgericht, 1999, p. 91.

10 Voßkuhle, in v. Mangoldt/Klein/Starck, Grundgesetz-Kommentar, vol. 3, 5th ed. 2005, Art. 93 margin numbers 46 ff.; Graßhof, in Umbach/Clemens/Dollinger (eds.), Bundesverfassungsgerichtsgesetz-Kommentar, 2nd ed. 2005, § 78 margin numbers 19 ff.; Löwer, in Isensee/Kirchhof (eds.), Handbuch des Staatsrechts, 3rd ed. 2005, § 70 margin numbers 115 and 120 ff.

11 Gusy, Parlamentarischer Gesetzgeber und Bundesverfassungsgericht, 1985, p. 150.

12 Grzeszick; in Maunz/Dürig, Grundgesetz-Kommentar, 53rd ed. 2009, Art. 20, margin number 56; Gusy, Parlamentarischer Gesetzgeber und Bundesverfassungsgericht, 1985, p. 151; Möstl, DÖV 1998, 1029 ff.

13 Blasberg, Verfassungsgerichte als Ersatzgesetzgeber, 2003, p. 138; Benda/Klein, Verfassungsprozeßrecht, 2nd ed. 2001, margin number 496.

14 Schlaich/Korioth, Das Bundesverfassungsgericht, 7th ed. 2007, margin number 229; Cremer, Freiheitsgrundrechte, 2003, pp. 137 ff.

15 Graßhof, in Umbach/Clemens/Dollinger (eds.), Bundesverfassungsgerichtsgesetz-Kommentar, 2nd ed. 2005, § 78 margin number 84; Gusy, Parlamentarischer Gesetzgeber und Bundesverfassungsgericht, 1985, pp. 152 f.; Schlaich/Korioth, Das Bundesverfassungsgericht, 7th ed. 2007, margin numbers 408 f.

4. *Ex Officio Powers of Constitutional Judges and of the Constitutional Court or Tribunals*

Article 20, Sec. 3 GG, principally determines an obligation of jurisdictional power to justice and law. It could be concluded from this that no maneuvering room is granted to jurisdiction.[16] In contrast to the Government, however, jurisdiction is designed to work "close to Law."[17] The Legislator creates abstractly general regulations through statutes that encounter a multitude of different facts and circumstances of cases and thus are in need of interpretation by the judge.[18]

The central point is thus judicial decision making.[19] Precisely through this and through the judicial constitutive role contained in law, a certain amount of state control is granted to the judiciary. In terms of the Constitution, a tension consequently arises between the precept of democracy of Article 20, Sec. 2 GG, and the principle of judicial independency with sole responsibility of Article 92, 97 Sec. 2, 98 Sec. 2 GG.[20]

Among the different branches of jurisdiction (Article 92, 95 Sec. 1 GG), constitutional jurisdiction takes an exceptional position; the BVerfG is a court autonomous and independent of all constitutional institutions and at the same time a constitutional institution that has to fulfill a multitude of official and constitutionally defined tasks.[21]

5. *Authority of the Supreme Court of Constitutional Courts to Remove and Take Over Cases from Lower Courts (Avocamiento)*

The Bundesverfassungsgericht is not comparable to the Supreme Court; that is, it reviews only specific constitutional law, not, for example, the expedience of a court's considerations.[22] The BVerfG has commented: "The

16 Grigoleit, Bundesverfassungsgericht und deutsche Frage, 2004, § 2 p. 44; Scholz, APuZ (B 37-38/2001); in Badura/Scholz (eds.), Verfassungsgerichtsbarkeit und Gesetzgebung, p. 23.

17 Mahrenholz, in Badura/Scholz (eds.), Verfassungsgerichtsbarkeit und Gesetzgebung, p. 23.

18 Kirchhof, NJW 1986, 2275; Stern, Das Staatsrecht der Bundesrepublik Deutschland, vol. 2, 1980, p. 894.

19 Grigoleit, Bundesverfassungsgericht und deutsche Frage, 2004, § 2 p. 44; Steiner, NJW 2001, 2919 ff.

20 Stein, Politische Bildung in den Achtzigerjahren 1983, p. 36 (38); Grigoleit, Bundesverfassungsgericht und deutsche Frage, 2004, § 2 p. 44. Leibholz, in Das Bundesverfassungsgericht, 1963, p. 61 (65 f.); Höffe, Der Staat 38 (1999), 171 ff.

21 Jahrbuch des öffentlichen Rechts der Gegenwart 6 (1957), pp. 144 ff.; Stern, Das Staatsrecht der Bundesrepublik Deutschland, vol. 2, 1980, pp. 341 ff.; Roellecke, in Isensee/Kirchhof (eds.) Handbuch des Staatsrechts, 3rd ed. 2005, § 67 margin numbers 15 ff.

22 BVerfGE 18, 85 (92).

arrangement of the proceeding, the declaration and consideration of the statement of facts, the interpretation of Subconstitutional Law and its application in individual cases are exclusively concerns of the courts generally in charge and excluded from the BVerfG's review."[23]

The BVerfG has the competence, in Verfassungsbeschwerde proceedings, to annul valid decisions of courts of all jurisdictional branches; it thereby automatically intervenes in the independency of said courts.[24] The BVerfG does not control whether the findings are rightful according to subconstitutional law; rather, it observes whether failures in interpretation occurred, which are based on a fundamentally incorrect opinion about the sense of a basic right, especially about the extent of its protection, and that are also in their tangible dimension relevant to the given case.[25]

II. JUDICIAL DECISIONS ON JUDICIAL REVIEW

The BVerfG dealt with a total of 175,880 pending cases between September 7, 1952, and December 31, 2008. Of those, 3,573 were concerned with abstract and specific judicial review (2.03 percent), and 169,592 cases, or 96.42 percent, were constitutional complaints.[26] These numbers, on the one hand, illustrate the dominance of judicial review processes; on the other hand, they show the extent of work accomplished by the BVerfG and the professionalism acquired during the given time.

1. *Constitutional Interpretation*

In the process of constitutional interpretation, the judges of the BVerfG have the ability to recognize the spheres of responsibility, allotted to specific powers by Basic Law.[27] The interpretation of a statute in conformity with the Constitution implicates the obligation to choose from among different interpretations of the law the one that provides the statute with constancy under the Basic Law.[28] A maximum of constancy under the Basic Law is

23 BVerfGE 18, 85 (92).

24 Schlaich/Korioth, Das Bundesverfassungsgericht, 7th ed. 2007, margin number 502.

25 BVerfGE 18, 85 (93); 102, 347 (362).

26 Information available at http://www.bverfg.de/organisation/gb2008/A-I-1.html.

27 Stein, Politische Bildung in den Achtzigerjahren 1983, p. 36 (41).

28 Blasberg, Verfassungsgerichte als Ersatzgesetzgeber, 2003, pp. 39 ff.; Leibholz, in Das Bundesverfassungsgericht, 1963, p. 61 (77); Stein, Politische Bildung in den Achtzigerjahren 1983, p. 36 (44).

sustained through this procedure.[29] This procedure of norm preservation is further affirmed by the respect shown to the authority of the immediately democratically legitimated Legislator.[30] In the Federal Republic of Germany, the final decision about the constitutional interpretation of a statute lies with the BVerfG; other specialized courts are nevertheless required to perform constitutional interpretations by themselves.[31] In the opinion of the BVerfG, a presumption already points to the compatibility of a statute with the Basic Law and therefore principally prefers the constitutional interpretation of said statute.[32] The constraints of a constitutional interpretation of a statute are basically, also from the BVerfG's point of view, the wording and the Legislator's discernable intention.[33] Problems in constitutional interpretation occur when the Legislator's intention is reversed into its opposite.[34] What deserves particular mention here is the possibility of a constitutional interpretation of the Strafprozessordnung (code of criminal procedure) regulations regarding custody toward a reading, clearly contradicting the exact wording, that in the case of suspicion of severe criminal offense conditional discharge can be granted.[35] In this case, the statute can no longer be applied without taking constitutional jurisdiction into consideration; publishers feel compelled to indicate said jurisdiction by the BVerfG in respective passages.[36] Attention has to be paid furthermore to the risk of constitutional interpretation becoming a panacea for deficient legislation.[37]

2. *Declaration of the Unconstitutional Character of Statutes (Declaration of Incompatibility)*

The declaration of unconstitutionality and the declaration of incompatibility have taken over a place next to the annulment of a norm in

[29] BVerfGE 9, 200; 33, 70.

[30] Bethge, Jura 2009, 18 (21); Blasberg, Verfassungsgerichte als Ersatzgesetzgeber, 2003, pp. 40 f.; Simon, EuGRZ 1974, 85 (86); Schultze-Fielitz, in Dreier (ed.), Grundgesetz-Kommentar, vol. 2, 2nd ed. 2006, Art. 20 Rn 87.

[31] Bettermann, Die verfassungskonforme Auslegung, 1986, p. 32; Schlaich/Korioth, Das Bundesverfassungsgericht, 7th ed. 2007, margin number 32.

[32] BVerfGE 2, 266 (282); Blasberg, Verfassungsgerichte als Ersatzgesetzgeber, 2003, p. 42.

[33] BVerfGE 69, 1 (55); 49, 148 (157).

[34] Starck, Das Bundesverfassungsgericht im politischen Prozeß der Bundesrepublik, 1976, p. 27.

[35] BVerfGE 19, 342 (352).

[36] Take note of footnote to § 116 StPO (Strafprozessordnung) in "Schönfelder – Deutsche Gesetze."

[37] Blasberg, Verfassungsgerichte als Ersatzgesetzgeber, 2003, p. 56.

the practice of the BVerfG.[38] Within the framework of legislation, this process has caused alterations as to two aspects: Sec. 31, Sec. 2 S. 2.3 BVerfG requires a statute to be either declared compatible or incompatible with the Basic Law or to be annulled; Sec. 79, Sec. 1 BverfGG, regulates the consequences of penalties that are based on "a norm declared incompatible with the Basic Law or annulled according to §78 BVerfGG." The Legislator has thereby approved that the justice refrains from annulment in specific cases.[39] This decision takes effect either in situations where annulment with ex tunc effects would result in a condition even further abstracted from constitutional regularity than the given one,[40] or when the principle of equality is violated. In the latter case, various possibilities to correct the said violation exist in principle, and the BVerfG cedes the right of decision to the Legislator to either abolish privileges or to enhance them on persons wrongly disregarded.[41]

A case of considerable importance, recently adjudged by the BVerfG, has been the resolution on inheritance tax.[42] In this resolution, the BVerfG declared the current capital transfer tax as unconstitutional and fixed a deadline of December 31, 2008, for the Legislator to restore a legal condition in conformity with the Constitution.[43] The (unconstitutional) statute, which had been considered valid until the resolution, was to remain valid for more than a year. The BVerfG justifies this procedure according to prevailing jurisdiction by pointing to the fact that, in the case of violation of the principle of equity (Article 3, Sec. 1GG) several possibilities of correction of said unconstitutional condition are available to the Legislator, so that the regulation, which is to be examined, is not annulled but simply declared incompatible with Article 3, Sec. 1 GG. The declaration of incompatibility basically entails the fact that the affected norms are no longer applicable in an extent resulting from the general tenor.[44] In the given case, the BVerfG found it necessary to exceptionally allow the continuing implementation of

38 Concerning this issue, compare Blasberg, Verfassungsgerichte als Ersatzgesetzgeber, 2003, pp. 97 ff.; Gusy, Parlamentarischer Gesetzgeber und Bundesverfassungsgericht, 1985, pp. 188 ff; Schlaich/Korioth, Das Bundesverfassungsgericht, 7th ed. 2007, margin numbers 394 ff.

39 Gusy, Parlamentarischer Gesetzgeber und Bundesverfassungsgericht, 1985, pp. 188 ff.

40 BVerfG 83, 130 (154), steady jurisdiction.

41 BVerfGE 101 397 (409); Bethge, Jura 2009, 18 (21).

42 BVerfG, court order from 2006-11-7, reference number: 1 BvL 10/02; concerning this issue compare Seer, ZEV 2007, 101 ff.; Balle/Gress, BB 2007, 2660 ff.

43 BVerfG, court order from 2006-11-7, reference number: 1 BvL 10/02, guiding principle 2.

44 Heusch, in Umbach/Clemens/Dollinger (eds.), 2nd ed. 2005, § 31 margin number 82; Graßhof, in Umbach/Clemens/Dollinger (eds.), 2nd ed. 2005, § 78 margin number 59.

the current inheritance-tax law until a new legislative regulation was established. The continuing implementation was considered necessary to prevent a situation of legal uncertainty during the interim, especially affecting and potentially complicating the regulations regarding succession of property during a transferor's lifetime. The BVerfG has therefore, as a kind of "emergency Legislator," created a lawlike condition;[45] it has "invented" a new decision type.[46]

This whole procedure happened without statutory authorization, in fact contra legem, as the BVerfG assumed until 1970 the compelling connection between the unconstitutionality and the invalidity of a norm.[47] The necessity of said decision type can be explained on the basis of the considerations alleged about the decision concerning the Poor Law.[48]

A legal regulation favoring Group A over Group B does not per se violate the principle of equity of Article 3, Sec. 1 GG. The general principle of equity is special in comparison to other civil rights and liberties, insofar as it does not outright except specific state actions but forbids the treatment of one group of addressees to be different from the treatment of another group, where no differences of such nature or severity exist between both groups that unequal treatment is justified.[49] Because either the preferential treatment of the one group is unconstitutional or the disregard of the other group, compliance with Article 3 Sec. 1 GG can be reached either by abolishing the preference or by expanding the preferential treatment on both group. Hence there is no unambiguous consequence.[50] An annulment can therefore not be declared by the BVerfG given insufficient norm substance.

After having determined incompatibility, the BVerfG declares the obligation of the Legislator to resolve the unconstitutional condition. The law is not ex tunc declared invalid; responsibility resides with the Legislator to either improve or abolish the law.[51] The decision toward a declaration of incompatibility induces the eligible binding force of Sec. 31, Sec. 2 S. 1 BVerfGG; it also prevents any further execution of the norm that has been

45 Steiner, ZEV 2007, 120 (121).

46 Schlaich/Korioth, Das Bundesverfassungsgericht, 7th ed. 2007, margin number 395.

47 Benda/Klein, Verfassungsprozeßrecht, 2nd ed. 2001, margin number 1244.

48 BVerfGE 33, 349.

49 BVerfGE 62, 256 (274); 82, 126 (146).

50 Schlaich/Korioth, Das Bundesverfassungsgericht, 7th ed. 2007, margin number 402.

51 Hein, Die Unvereinbarkeitserklärung verfassungswidriger Gesetze durch das Bundesverfassungsgericht, 1988, pp. 168 ff.

declared unconstitutional.[52] Until the Legislator takes action, the norm is usually not applicable unless the BVerfG explicitly enables temporary application. It has done so in the already-mentioned resolution regarding inheritance law to prevent legal uncertainty.

The BVerfG has furthermore proceeded to fix a definite deadline for the Legislator to take necessary action. The given amount of time is assessed rather pragmatically: the greater are the difficulties that the Legislator has to overcome, the more time is to be granted to the Legislator.[53] Sec. 35 BVerfGG is considered the legal basis for setting a deadline. This article authorizes the BVerfG to determine the enforcer of the decision and, in individual cases, to regulate the manner of the enforcement. The deadline is meant to pressure the Legislator and thereby serve the enactment of justice found by the BVerfG.[54] In most cases, however, the setting of a deadline by a Constitutional Court is regarded as dispensable.[55]

3. *Annulment (Complete or Partial) of Unconstitutional Statutes*

Annulment of a statute through the BVerfG is enabled by Secs. 78, 82 Sec. 1 and 95 Sec. 3 BVerfGG, given the case that the statute is incompatible with the Basic Law. The effects of this direction are occasionally disputed. Annulment theory assumes annulment of a statute incompatible with the Basic Law to be *ex tunc* and *eo ipse* (without further constitutive action).[56] This is justified by the argument of substantive justice, whereupon an unconstitutional statute should never have developed legal effect.[57] Other voices, however, argue in support of invalidity from the date of constitutional decision by the BVerfG and refer, in doing so, to the certainty of the law.[58] The BVerfG itself argues in support of annulment theory, the

52 Bethge, Jura 2009, 18 (21).

53 BVerfGE 102, 192 (223).

54 Pohle, Die Verfassungswidrigerklärung von Gesetzen, 1979, p. 157.

55 Blasberg, Verfassungsgerichte als Ersatzgesetzgeber, 2003, p. 135; Hein, Die Unvereinbarerklärung verfassungswidriger Gesetze durch das Bundesverfassungsgericht, 1988, p. 173.

56 Schlaich/Korioth, Das Bundesverfassungsgericht, 7th ed. 2007, margin number 379; Ipsen, Die Rechtfolgen der Verfassungswidrigkeit von Norm und Einzelakt, 1980, pp. 69 ff.

57 Siedler, Gesetzgeber und Bundesverfassungsgericht, 1999, p. 92.

58 Birk, BayVBl. 1981, 673 (674); Schneider, Die Funktion der Normenkontrolle und des richterlichen Prüfungsrechts im Rahmen der Rechtsfolgenbestimmung verfassungswidriger Gesetze, 1988, p. 80.

effects of which are restricted by the regulations of Sec. 79 BVerfGG among others.[59]

A distinction has to be drawn between different forms of annulment:

- Quantitative (partial) annulment either refers to a statute as a whole or to single regulations.
- Complete annulment refers to only part of a statute, which is by itself constitutional and is declared void in connection with the annulment of the unconstitutional part.[60]

Ultimately, there is a partial annulment without reduction of the standard text; quantitative annulment refers to the text. However, the BVerfG occasionally declares a norm void not referring to parts of the text or single words but to particular case configurations not separately indicated in the standard text.[61] The wording of the statute remains unchanged thereby, whereas one particular way of application is considered incompatible with the Basic Law.[62] The BVerfG recently decreed the invalidity of single norms in the much-noted case on the Sales Promotion Funds Law. This proceeding dealt with the question of whether the levy raised by companies of the agricultural and food sector on the basis of the Sales Promotion Funds Law is compatible with the Basic Law, especially its requirements regarding the collection of a nontax contribution. Its revenue accrues to a sales promotion fund that is meant to promote sales and liquidation of products from the respective industries. Sec. 2 of the Sales Promotion Funds Law reads as follows: "The sales promotion fund is to centrally promote distribution and liquidation of products from the German agriculture and food industry by means of opening up and maintaining domestic and foreign markets using modern approaches with simultaneous consideration of concerns expressed by consumer, animal, and environment protection. In doing so it is meant to work towards an improvement of product quality and safety as well as an improvement in the market orientation of products."

The Bundesverfassungsgericht determined the unconstitutionality of the contribution arranged as a special levy referring to Sec. 10 AbsFondsG (Sales Promotion Funds Law) resulting in the invalidity of Sec. 2, Sec. 1, up to Sec. 4 S. 1; Sec. 6, Sec. 10, Sec. 1 up to Sec. 8; Secs. 11 and 12 AbsFondsG. Responsibility for the funding of the public sales promotion

59 Siedler, Gesetzgeber und Bundesverfassungsgericht, 1999, pp. 92 f.

60 Gusy, Parlamentarischer Gesetzgeber und Bundesverfassungsgericht, 1985, pp. 184 ff.

61 Sachs, DVBl. 1979, 390; Siedler, Gesetzgeber und Bundesverfassungsgericht, 1999, pp. 95 ff.

62 Schlaich/Korioth, Das Bundesverfassungsgericht, 7th ed. 2007, margin number 386.

should not fall to the German agriculture and food industry. This would mean a curtailment of the individual businesses' entrepreneurial freedom. The central promotion campaigns could also be seen as a curtailment of one's own entrepreneurial advertising budget. There were insufficient indications for an added value of state-organized promotion in comparison with private-sector promotion.

The invalidity of the regulation regarding the contribution in Sec. 10 AbsFondsG entails the invalidity of further regulations of the statute mentioned, as they would become meaningless from the BVerfG's point of view, with the abandonment of the contribution as a financing instrument for an agricultural promotion network. Part of the statute, however, is still preserved by the BVerfG's being considered useful in the execution of settlement functions: the regulation regarding the foundation of the sales promotion fund as a legally responsible public body and provisions regarding the respective bodies and finances; provisions regarding supervision by the Federal Ministry of Food, Agriculture and Consumer Protection; the investigative competence of the Federal Audit Office; the provision regarding tax exemption; the regulation according to which the sales promotion fund of the Federal Agency for Agriculture is to refund personnel and material costs for the previous collection of contributions.

The BVerfG timed the announcement of the decision at the beginning of the periods significant in the main proceeding: July 1, 2002. This is a difference from the *ex tunc* effect, which basically dates to the point of issue of the norm. The present case is a matter of unconstitutionality because of a change of conditions and circumstances: The Sales Promotion Fund Law had already been reviewed in 1990 and considered constitutional by the BVerfG.[63] It later determined, however, that although the presence of disadvantages to be averted in intracommunity competition could still be accepted in a reasonable way in 1990, the situation of the German agriculture and food industry had developed to its advantage since then. In cases of unconstitutionality, because of a change in conditions, a later date for the beginning of the *ex tunc* effect than the point of issue of the norm can thus come into consideration.[64]

[63] BVerfG, 2 BvL 54/06 from 2009-2-3, available at http://www.bverfg.de/entscheidungen/ls20090203_2bvl005406.html.

[64] BVerfGE 82, 159 ff.

4. *Influencing the Constitution*

A Constitution is never at a standstill.[65] The BVerfG is also called on to take part in the constitutional change through its jurisdiction, insofar as said jurisdiction can feature creative potential.[66] Rudolf Smend once stated: "The Basic Law virtually applies in the way the BVerfG interprets it."[67]

A more recent decision by the BVerfG regarding the online searches of computers confirms this statement.[68] In this decision, the BVerfG further developed the dogmatics of basic rights regarding the protection of general personal rights in Article 2, Sec. 1 GG, in conjunction with Article 1, Sec. 1 GG.[69] Regarding the background of this decision, it should be mentioned that it deals with the tension between liberty and security, the shift from industrial to informational society, and the entailed necessary sensitivity regarding the handling of personal data and information.[70] The BVerfG assumed an invalidity of the provisions of North Rhine–Westphalian Law regarding the change of the statute by the Federal Office for the Protection of the Constitution.[71] The subject of the annulled regulation is the search of a computer using so-called Trojans to access hard-drive and main memory while the computer is online.[72]

In the course of its review, the Bundesverfassungsgericht created a "new" basic right to the guarantee of confidentiality and integrity in information technology systems. The BVerfG saw a necessity for this basic right in the constantly increasing importance of information technology. The more recent developments of information technology led to an omnipresence of information technology systems, resulting in the fact that their usage had become of crucial importance to the lifestyle of many citizens.[73]

This specification of the general personal rights protects from intrusions into information technology systems, as far as this protection is not already

[65] Löwer, in Isensee/Kirchhof (eds.), Handbuch des Staatsrechts, vol. 3, 3rd ed. 2005, § 70 margin number 114.

[66] Leibholz, in Das Bundesverfassungsgericht, 1963, p. 61 (62).

[67] Hesse, JZ 1995, 265 (266 ff.); Wieland, in Dreier (ed.), Grundgesetz-Kommentar, vol. 3, 2nd ed. 2008, Art. 93 margin number 31.

[68] Smend, in Das Bundesverfassungsgericht, 1963, p. 24.

[69] BVerfG, reference number: 1 BvR 370/07 from 2008-2-27, available at http://www.bverfg.de/entscheidungen/rs20080227_1bvr037007.html.

[70] Concerning this issue compare Härtel, NdsVBl. 2008, 276 ff.

[71] Härtel, NdsVBl. 2008, 276 (277).

[72] Härtel, NdsVBl. 2008, 276 (277).

[73] BVerfG, reference number: 1 BvR 370/07 from 2008-2-27, section number 171.

guaranteed by other basic rights (e.g., Article 10, Article 13 GG in particular) or the basic right to informational self-determination (Grundrecht auf informationelle Selbstbestimmung).

In the course of this procedure, the BVerfG not only confines itself to the content-related expansion of the allgemeines Persönlichkeitsrecht (general right of personality), it also contributes to the dogmatics of basic rights by determining concrete causes for intrusion and specific confines: a palpable danger for an outstandingly important object of legal protection has to be present first of all.[74] The BVerfG demands, furthermore, that any hidden infiltration into an information technology system is strictly to occur under reservation of judicial writ and that the statute that enables such intrusion has to cover precautionary measures to protect the core areas of private life.[75]

5. *Decisions Including Legislative Structures*

The Federal Constitutional Court is to supervise whether the Legislator orients itself toward the decisions on values of the Constitution; it cannot principally dictate which possibilities of application under consideration the Legislator is to take.[76] Constitutional review is thus confined to the observance of ultimate limits, and transgression is discernable only in cases of evidence.[77]

The BVerfG allows the Legislator sufficient flexibility of prognosis especially in economic, social, and sociopolitical areas.[78] The Constitutional Court is required to "secure the space of free policy-making guaranteed by the Constitution to other constitutional bodies."[79] For these reasons, the Bundesverfassungsgericht has always refused to judge school systems in terms of pedagogy or to review aims of educational policy and pedagogy or didactic issues regarding their constitutionality.[80]

Decisions become problematic when they meet areas of constitutional law that are expressions of immediate political decision, as was the case, for

74 BVerfG, reference number: 1 BvR 370/07 from 2008-2-27, guiding principle 2.

75 BVerfG, reference number: 1 BvR 370/07 from 2008-2-27, guiding principle 3.

76 Leibholz, in Das Bundesverfassungsgericht, 1963, p. 61 (76).

77 Concerning this issue, compare, among others, BVerfGE 9, 337; 23, 24 f.; 27, 283; 53, 195 ff.

78 BVerfGE 25, 12 f.; 38, 61.

79 BVerfGE 36, 16.

80 Concerning this issue, compare BVerfGE 34, 181 ff; 45, 141 ff; 53, 195 ff.

example, in the decisions regarding the Basic Treaty,[81] or alternatively in decisions concerning officials.[82]

According to the Basic Law, the BVerfG owns all authority of decision making in such cases; therefore, it cannot, like the Supreme Court, for example, refer to the political-question doctrine, according to which certain matters are entrusted to political bodies by law or the Constitution and are thereby not subject to jurisdiction.[83]

It remains questionable as to how far the BVerfG is allowed to provide the Legislator with judicial guidelines and to make demands on legislative actions in terms of an appeal.

Is the BVerfG allowed to compile legislative programs and thereby prescribe how the Legislator is to conduct its functions? To answer this question further, differentiation has to be made. The BVerfG is indeed allowed to compile certain guidelines for legislation in order to specify comprehensive constitutional norms; these are meant to provide mere "impulses" only.[84] Such decisions concern tax legislation,[85] as well as regulations regarding broadcasting corporations.[86]

Moreover, appellative decisions by the BVerfG are allowed in which the Court simply calls on the Legislator to take legislative action.[87] This kind of decision leaves the arrangement of the specific task to the Legislator and thereby does not curtail its freedom of legal arrangement.[88]

Already in the 1970s, however, the BVerfG departed from this line as it determined legislative programs in certain decisions and involved matters in the binding force, which were meant to be regulated in the future. Notable examples are the Numerus-Clausus decision,[89] the decision concerning professors,[90] the decision on abortion, and the decision on alternative civilian

81 BVerfGE 36, 1.

82 BVerfGE 3, 58; 6, 132.

83 Schlaich/Korioth, Das Bundesverfassungsgericht, 7th ed. 2007, margin number 493; Blasberg, Verfassungsgerichte als Ersatzgesetzgeber, 2003, p. 6; Stein, Politische Bildung in den Achtzigerjahren 1983, p. 36 (44); Stern, Das Staatsrecht der Bundesrepublik Deutschland, vol. 2, 1980, pp. 961 f.; Leibholz, in Das Bundesverfassungsgericht, 1963, pp. 61 (67 f.).

84 BVerfGE 7, 205.

85 BVerfGE 6, 76 f. (The Bundesverfassungsgericht pointed out here, that the splitting in the income tax law would not violate Art. 6 Sec. 1 GG).

86 BVerfGE 12, 260 ff.; 57, 259 guiding principle 2.

87 Benda/Klein, Verfassungsprozeßrecht, 2nd ed. 2001, margin numbers 1279 ff.

88 Stein, Politische Bildung in den Achtzigerjahren 1983, p. 36 (45).

89 BVerfGE 33, 303.

90 BVerfGE 35, 79.

service.[91] In the Numerus-Clausus decision and the decision concerning professors, the BVerfG structured the basic rights as participation rights, which guarantee state services. It deduces from this a limitation of university places, instructs the Legislator on how to arrange the Numerus-Clausus.[92] In the context of the decision concerning abortion, the BVerfG considered the Legislator responsible for determining an absolute threat of punishment in the case of abortion to protect the system of values of the Basic Law. The Court has thus abandoned the liberty-securing effect of basic rights and made them the basis of liberty-depriving measures. Furthermore, it has dictated the Fristenlösung, a modified abortion law, to the Legislator.

The BVerfG more frequently has outlined specific provisions to the Legislator: most often in the form of an *obiter dictum*, which does not participate in the legal effect of the decision but is with wise foresight taken into account by the Legislator.[93] This was the case in the BVerfG's decision regarding the Non-Smokers Protection Act (Nichtraucherschutzgesetz) of the states of Berlin and Baden-Württemberg.[94] Both statutes included certain exemption clauses declaring smoking permissible in completely separate side rooms, provided that the rooms were clearly indicated as smoking rooms and that concerns of protecting nonsmokers were not affected by them.

The BVerfG regarded this regulation as not compatible with the Constitution insofar as the exemption clauses did not embrace certain small gastronomies sites relying on beverage sales (corner pubs) that were, in particular, heavily impaired by the smoking ban.

More important for the present discussion is, however, that the BVerfG determined in a hypothesis, to be qualified as an obiter dictum, that the Legislator, according to the scope to be allowed to it, would rightly be able to give priority to health protection over impaired liberty rights, particularly the professional freedom of proprietors and the smokers' freedom of conduct, and consequently impose a strict ban on smoking in gastronomies sites.[95] In cases of such regulations, no exemption clause was needed for small-scale businesses, as outstandingly important matters of common welfare justified an absolute ban.

91 BVerfGE 48, 127.

92 Stein, Politische Bildung in den Achtzigerjahren 1983, p. 36 (45).

93 Scholz, in Karpen (ed.), Der Richter als Ersatzgesetzgeber, 2002, p. 15 (24).

94 BVerfG, 1 BvR 3262/07 from 2008-7-30, available at http://www.bverfg.de/entscheidungen/rs20080730_1bvr326207.html.

95 Concerning this issue, compare Gröschner, ZG 2008, 400 ff.

The dissenting opinions of the judges Bryde and Masing suggest that the BVerfG dared to take a step toward the role of a surrogate Legislator in this case. According to Masing, the deliberations on the constitutionality of a strict smoking ban are neither necessary for constitutional review of the provisions under attack nor fundamental for the reasoning of the Senate. Such a concept was not politically enforced in any federal state, so that no cause was given for such an *obiter dictum*. If the Senate conducted detailed reasoning on this matter anyhow, this would display an improper intrusion into legislative politics. Bryde, as well, cannot completely support the Senate's decision; regarding the absolute ban on smoking, he remarks that the Bundesverfassungsgericht was not to demand coherency that no democratic Legislator is able to achieve. If the Legislator was forced by such political conditions into an all-or-nothing decision that is allowing it, in theory, a radical, hardly politically enforceable solution but meanwhile using exemptions and defects to annul the achieved progress, this would endanger the reformability of politics.

6. *Additive Decisions Reforming Legislation*

Given the accelerated change of social conditions and the limited options for reaction of the Legislator, as well as the abstract wording of many norms, the adjustment of established right to changing circumstances belongs to the duties of the judiciary.[96]

Oftentimes, the BVerfG sets down its own transitional arrangements.[97] In doing so, the BVerfG assumes that Sec. 35 BVerfGG gives legitimization to achieve the given task in the most appropriate, rapid, convenient, simple, and effective manner.[98]

Regarding commuter tax relief, the BVerfG declared the established regulation of the Einkommensteuergesetz (income tax law) incompatible with Article 3, Sec. 1 GG.[99] The Legislator decided on the basis of the budgetary position to grant commuter tax relief only after traveling twenty-one kilometers. A transitional but definite and consistent arrangement is needed from the point of view of the BVerfG for the time period until a new legal regulation is decided on to continuously handle the fiscal mass

96 BVerfG 96, 394.

97 Blasberg, Verfassungsgerichte als Ersatzgesetzgeber, 2003, pp. 182 f.

98 BVerfG 6, 300 (304).

99 BVerfG, 2 BvL 1/07 from 2008-12-9, section number (1–91), available at http://www.bverfg.de/entscheidungen/ls20081209_2bvl000107.html.

proceedings to preserve the functionality of fiscal authority. This arrangement is meant to decide on allowances of expenditures on journeys between home and the workplace, as well as journeys to one's family home. The precept of not applying the regulations declared incompatible of Sec. 9, Sec. 2 S. 1 and S. 2 Einkommensteuergesetz, after the point of decision of the Bundesverfassungsgericht and to suspend pending cases would otherwise lead to indefensible delays, especially in the implementation of income tax proceedings, thus putting unacceptable strain on taxpayers. Only a generalized solution could be considered a temporary transitional arrangement from the BVerfG's point of view. It fixed the standard rate for travel allowances at 0.30 euro per kilometer traveled. Until a final, retroactively effective legal transition arrangement and reform is issued, Sec. 9, Sec. 2 S. 2 EstG, is to be applied according to orders by the BVerfG, with the stipulation that factual limitation on "increased" allowances "from km 21 travelled" is omitted.

7. *Admonitory Decisions*

To prevent the effects of annulment, the BVerfG occasionally makes issues an admonition to the Legislator.[100] Therein it commits the Legislator to monitor the norm, "currently still" or "currently still, as judged from the momentary state of knowledge and experience," considered constitutional, in its impacts and effects, to improve or alternatively replace it.[101]

These admonitions thus contain legislation directives addressed to the Legislator that can be of norm-requesting and norm-demanding nature.[102] Such admonitory decisions are often made in complex regulatory areas in which a great scope of assessment is assigned to the Legislator. Regulations that are oftentimes affected, apart from that, are those that are subject to a certain change in conditions. The stock of standards is not affected by such an admonitory decision. The standard is not invalid or incompatible with the

[100] Schlaich/Korioth, Das Bundesverfassungsgericht, 7th ed. 2007, margin number 431; Benda/Klein, Verfassungsprozeßrecht, 2nd ed. 2001, margin number 1281; Löwer, in Isensee/Kirchhof (eds.), Handbuch des Staatsrechts, vol. 3, 3rd ed. 2005, § 70 margin number 124.

[101] Benda/Klein, Verfassungsprozeßrecht, 2nd ed. 2001, margin number 1279; Graßhof, in Umbach/Clemens/Dollinger (eds.) Bundesverfassungsgerichtsgesetz-Kommentar, 2nd ed. 2005, § 78 margin number 10.

[102] Bethge, Jura 2009, 18 (24).

Constitution; it is rather (still) valid from the constitutional point of view.[103] The admonition is nevertheless part of the binding force and thus commits the Legislator. This type of decision is, just as the declaration of incompatibility, not legally settled.[104] The decision regarding a survivor's pension can be viewed as a typical example of an admonitory decision.[105] The decisive clauses provided that a widow would always obtain the pension of her late husband; the widower, however, should obtain his wife's pension in case of her death if she had primarily provided for the family and earned the family income before or if she had been an official. The BVerfG remarks in this decision: The arrangement regarding the survivor's pension was not accessible for short-term solution attempts because of its importance for broad sections of the population and its significant financial consequences, and it had, on the contrary, to be initiated in the long term with all due prudence and on an at least fairly secured ground. This reform task, however, could be accomplished only by the Legislator. Therefore, sufficient time had to be granted to it, during which it was still allowed to manage with standardization and generalization.

The BVerfG, however, would see reasons for constitutional objection if the Legislator refrained in the future from striving intensely for a more appropriate solution, which would avert the movement toward the unconstitutionality of the current regulation's effect. A constitutional obligation for the Legislator could therefore be derived from the situation at this point, to provide a reform, which would eliminate the possibility of violation of Article 3, Sec. 2 and 3 GG, for the future. Extensive and time-consuming spadework was necessary to clear the way for such an arrangement regarding the mentioned difficulties. The BVerfG, however, assumes that the reform should be enacted until the end of the legislative period after the next to come.[106] The appeal, therefore, leaves sufficient scope for the Legislator while clearly spelling out that another judicial review could lead to invalidation.

[103] Voßkuhle, in v. Mangoldt/Klein/Starck, Grundgesetz-Kommentar, vol. 3, 5th ed. 2005, Art. 93, margin number 51; Löwer, in Isensee/Kirchhof (eds.), Handbuch des Staatsrechts, vol. 3, 3rd ed. 2005, § 70 margin number 125.

[104] Siedler, Gesetzgeber und Bundesverfassungsgericht, 1999, p. 177.

[105] BVerfGE 39, 169 ff.

[106] BVerfGE 39, 169 (194).

8. *Judicial Replacement of the Legislator*

What remains questionable is whether the judge can replace the Legislator. If the BVerfG decides in the cases of so-called collisions of norms on the compatibility of nation- or statewide norms with the Constitution, or if it decides whether a regulation of international law is a constituent of federal law, such a judicial decision has legal force at the same time as the effect that the Federal Minister of Justice is to publish the wording of the decision like a statute in the Law Gazette.[107] Insofar as "judicial force intrudes the sphere of legislation."[108] The same applies in those cases in which the BVerfG adjourns the enactment of a statute through a provisional order or adjusts the enactment of a statute to the conditions created either by the adjournment or by the decision according to Sec. 35 BVerfGG.[109] The traditional system of checks and balances, however, is no longer applied in its pure form in modern constitutional states; in fact, a lot of barely preventable intersections often occur.[110]

The BVerfG has already admonished the Legislator several times to fulfill explicit constitutional obligations through law. The constitutional obligations mentioned are oftentimes those that can rely only on weak forces in society in their realization; an example is the task of the Legislator to create equal conditions between illegitimate and legitimate children in their physical and emotional development, and consequently in their social standing.[111] The respective decision states: "If the Legislator does not accomplish the order assigned to him by Constitution in Art. 6 Sec. 5 GG to reform Illegitimacy Law . . . until the ending of the current [fifth] legislative period of the Bundestag, it is the will of the Constitution to realize as much as possible of the Legislation."

The decision of the Federal Constitutional Court regarding the Political Parties Act can also be named in this context, in which it practically lowered the parties' required threshold of votes with regard to the reimbursement of election campaign costs from 2.5 percent to 0.5 percent.[112]

107 Maunz, in Maunz/Dürig, Grundgesetz-Kommentar, 53rd ed. 2009, Art. 93 margin number 47; Leibholz, in Das Bundesverfassungsgericht, 1963, p. 61 (78).

108 BVerfGE 1, 396 (409).

109 Leibholz, in Das Bundesverfassungsgericht, 1963, p. 61 (78 f.).

110 Roellecke, in Isensee/Kirchhof (eds.), Handbuch des Staatsrechts, vol. 3, 3rd ed. 2005, § 67 margin numbers 44 f.; Leibholz, in Das Bundesverfassungsgericht, 1963, p. 61 (79).

111 BVerfGE 8, 210 (216); 17, 148 (155); 25, 167 (173–188).

112 BVerfGE 24, 300 (342 f.); Arndt, in Vogel/Simon/Podlech (eds.), Die Freiheit des Anderen, Festschrift für Hirsch, 1981, S. 423 (427).

Further examples include the second sit-in blockade decision and its quasi-legislative change of Sec. 240 Strafgesetzbuch (penal code);[113] the judicature, reaching up to the settlement of even executive details regarding abortion;[114] and the fundamental decision regarding deployment abroad of the Bundeswehr (the federal armed forces), which the BVerfG attached not only to contractual provisions of international law but also to a preceding parliamentary poll, necessary for every deployment.[115] Regarding the abortion issue, it must be mentioned that the current legislature did not see itself in the position to arrange a constitutional settlement on which consensus might be obtained. Consequently, the BVerfG was assigned the issue and has solved the problem fundamentally and to overall satisfaction.[116] During the out-of-are deployments, the foregoing violation of the constitutional balance of powers came about: consent of the Bundestag to every particular deployment of the Bundeswehr abroad is indeed not constitutionally dictated; executive authority decides on its own, after a ratification of contracts of international law has taken place, if and in how far soldiers are to be deployed.[117]

9. *Judicial Replacement of the Government in Policy Making Processes*

An anticipatory effect of constitutional jurisdiction on political decision making is occasionally assumed in Germany.[118] Politics have increasingly based their legislative projects on opinions and experts' hearings, which include valid decisions of the BVerfG, decision tendencies, and *obiter dicta* in their statements.[119]

[113] BVerfGE 92, 1 ff.

[114] BVerfGE 88, 203 ff; Starck, JZ 1993, 816 ff; Lerche, in Heinze (ed.), Festschrift Gitter, 1998, pp. 509–517.

[115] BVerfGE 90, 286 ff.

[116] Scholz, in Karpen (ed.), Der Richter als Ersatzgesetzgeber, 2002, p. 15 (20); Stein, Politische Bildung in den Achtzigerjahren 1983, 36 ff; Steiner, NJW 2001, 2919–2924.

[117] Roellecke, Der Staat 34 (1995), 415–428; Scholz, in Karpen (ed.), Der Richter als Ersatzgesetzgeber, 2002, p. 15 (20); Vollkommer, in Schilken (ed.), Festschrift Gerhardt, 2004, pp. 1023–1041.

[118] Landfried, Bundesverfassungsgericht und Gesetzgeber, 1984, p. 52; v. Beyme, Das politische System der Bundesrepublik Deutschland, p. 370; Hesse, Verfassungsrechtsprechung im historischen Wandel, JZ 1995, 265 (268); Starck, Das Bundesverfassungsgericht im politischen Prozeß der Bundesrepublik, 1976, p. 16.

[119] Scholz, APuZ (B 37-38/2001); Landfried, Bundesverfassungsgericht und Gesetzgeber, 1984, p. 52.

Nevertheless, a connection to politics is needed in a constitutional state to forestall a decline into abuse of rights and power. The constitutional state and political consciousness are in a state of interdependent relativity and assertion. The resolutions passed by the BVerfG are however no political arrangements of issues or political decisions. The Basic Law has resolved that political questions of law should be decided not by power but on a juridical level. Constitutional jurisdiction can thus also be characterized as political jurisdiction.[120] The essential subject of regulation of constitutional law is thus the political process.[121] Constitutional jurisdiction is, however, liable to the allocation of competences, which means that it is not to become a force of political power or policy forming. These responsibilities reside with Government and Parliament.[122]

III. EFFECTS OF JUDICIAL DECISIONS ON CONSTITUTIONAL MATTERS

The central standard regarding the effects of decisions is Sec. 31 BVerfGG, which regulates the effect of decisions in relation to other authorities and to the citizens.

In cases of rejection of norms by the BVerfG, the question arises as to whether an interdiction to reissue a norm exists.[123] The two Senates of the BVerfG disagree on this point: the first Senate assumes that a norm-rejecting decision would not prevent the Legislator from passing a coextensive or at least content-similar reform, but the second Senate refers to Sec. 31, Sec. 1 BVerfGG, and assumes a binding force of the decision with primary reasons for all constitutional bodies of the Federation insofar that a Federal statute of same content cannot be reenacted.[124] Ultimately, an interdiction of the reiteration of a norm is to be rejected regarding the regulation of Sec. 95 Sec. 1 S. 2 BVerfGG, which allows the BVerfG to decree an interdiction of the reiteration of a norm, and for the reason that such rejection offers better

120 Concerning this issue, compare Leibholz, in Das Bundesverfassungsgericht, 1963, p. 61 (64 f.); Gusy, Parlamentarischer Gesetzgeber und Bundesverfassungsgericht, 1985, pp. 41 ff.; Stein, Politische Bildung in den Achtzigerjahren 1983, p. 36 (40); Schlaich/Korioth, Das Bundesverfassungsgericht, 7th ed. 2007, margin numbers 505 ff., 530 ff., 548 ff.

121 Starck, Das Bundesverfassungsgericht im politischen Prozeß der Bundesrepublik, 1976, p. 7.

122 Stein, Politische Bildung in den Achtzigerjahren 1983, p. 36 (41).

123 Löwer, in Isensee/Kirchhof (eds.), Handbuch des Staatsrechts, vol. 3, 3rd ed. 2005, § 70 margin number 105.

124 Heusch, in Umbach/Clemens/Dollinger (eds.), Bundesverfassungsgerichtsgesetz-Kommentar, 2nd ed. 2005, § 31 margin number 64.

possibilities for taking into consideration changing conditions and circumstances.[125]

Sec. 31, Sec. 2 S. 1 BVerfGG, decrees that the decisions of the BVerfG on the compatibility or incompatibility of a statute with the Constitution, including the declaration of invalidity, have legal force. These jurisdictional decisions with legal force are published by the Federal Ministry of Justice in the Law Gazette, Sec. 31, Sec. 2 S. 3 BVerfGG. This publishing leads to legal clarity and the liability of constitutional decisions on statutes not only toward governmental bodies, as it is the case through Sec. 31, Sec. 1 BVerfGG, but also toward all citizens.[126] Legal force thereby achieves a validity *inter et erga omnes*.[127] Especially in cases of budgetary-relevant decisions, the BVerfG has passed on to the practice of settling for a declaration of incompatibility and not decreeing invalidity with the consequence of an *ex tunc* effect; the Legislator is usually obliged to a *pro futuro* revision.[128] Principally, the declaration of invalidity develops *ex tunc* effect and comes into effect *ipso iure*.[129] The BVerfGG does not contain explicit regulations on the legal force of constitutional decisions. Jurisdiction and legal doctrine, however, assume that the BVerfG's decisions accrue in legal force.[130] Issues of judicial review become formally effective; their nonappealability comes into effect with the issuing of the decision.[131] Regarding the subjective, tangible legal force, the characteristics of constitutional procedural law become effective; legal force can, in principle, become effective only among the parties involved.[132]

125 Bethge, in Maunz/Schmidt-Bleibtreu/Bethge (eds.), Bundesverfassungsgerichtsgesetz-Kommentar, 30th supplemental set 2009, margin numbers 71 f.; Schlaich/Korioth, Das Bundesverfassungsgericht, 7th ed. 2007, margin number 484.

126 Schlaich/Korioth, Das Bundesverfassungsgericht, 7th ed. 2007, margin number 496; Heusch, in Umbach/Clemens/Dollinger (eds.), Bundesverfassungsgerichtsgesetz-Kommentar, 2nd ed. 2005, § 31 margin number 87.

127 Benda/Klein, Verfassungsprozeßrecht, 2nd ed. 2001, margin number 1313; Löwer, in Isensee/Kirchhof (eds.), Handbuch des Staatsrechts, vol. 3, 3rd ed. 2005, § 70 margin number 113; Heusch, in Umbach/Clemens/Dollinger (eds.), Bundesverfassungsgerichtsgesetz-Kommentar, 2nd ed. 2005, § 31 margin number 80.

128 Köppe, in van Ooyen/Möllers (eds.), Das Bundesverfassungsgericht im politischen System, 2006, p. 435 (446).

129 Löwer, in Isensee/Kirchhof (eds.), Handbuch des Staatsrechts, vol. 3, 3rd ed. 2005, § 70 margin number 113; Benda/Klein, Verfassungsprozeßrecht, 2nd ed. 2001, margin number 1251 f.

130 BVerfGE 20, 56 (86 f.); 69, 92 (103); Löwer, in Isensee/Kirchhof (eds.), Handbuch des Staatsrechts, vol. 3, 3rd ed. 2005, § 70 margin number 103; Schlaich/Korioth, Das Bundesverfassungsgericht, 7th ed. 2007, margin number 440 ff.

131 BVerfGE 1, 89 ff.

132 Concerning this issue compare Löwer, in Isensee/Kirchhof (eds.), Handbuch des Staatsrechts, vol. 3, 3rd ed. 2005, § 70 margin number 103.

BELGIUM, FRANCE, GERMANY

L'ACTIVITÉ DU JUGE CONSTITUTIONNNEL COMME LÉGISLATEUR-CADRE POSITIF

Christian Behrendt[*]
Professor, University of Liege
christian.behrendt@ulg.ac.be

INTRODUCTION

1.– La présente contribution vise à rendre compte des principaux éléments d'un projet de recherche que nous avons pu mener à terme récemment[1] et qui nous a valu le grand honneur de recevoir le *Prix de thèse du Groupement européen du droit public.* [2]

2.– Le contrôle de la constitutionnalité des lois, dans sa forme "européenne,"[3] concentrée dans les mains d'une juridiction constitutionnelle spécialisée, a déjà fait l'objet de très nombreux travaux et études. Ce n'est pas

* L'auteur est diplômé des universités d'Oxford (Magister Juris, 2001), de Paris I Panthéon-Sorbonne (Docteur en droit, 2005) et de Yale (LL.M., 2006)

1 Thèse de doctorat soutenue en 2005 à l'Université de Paris I Panthéon-Sorbonne, sous la direction des professeurs Otto Pfersmann (Paris I) et Jean-Claude Scholsem (Liège), et parue en 2006 aux éditions Bruylant (Bruxelles) et LGDJ (Paris), sous le titre "*Le juge constitutionnel, un législateur-cadre positif*" (537 pages, ISBN 2-8027-2146-1). Nous tenons à exprimer toute notre gratitude à nos deux directeurs, qui, par leurs judicieux conseils, ont substantiellement amélioré la qualité de nos modestes travaux.

2 Ainsi que le *Prix de thèse du Conseil constitutionnel français.* En raison de cette dernière distinction, le texte de la présente contribution a déjà été publié aux *Cahiers du Conseil constitutionnel* (n° 20, pages 161 à 168).

3 Par opposition à sa forme "américaine." Pour une comparaison entre les modèles européen et américain de justice constitutionnelle, voy. notamment L. Favoreu, "Modèle américain et modèle européen de justice constitutionnelle," *Annuaire international de Justice constitutionnelle*, 4 (1988), 51—66, G. Nolte, "European and US constitutionalism: comparing essential elements," in *European and US Constitutionalism*, Cambridge, Cambridge University Press, 2005, 3—20, et M. Rosenfeld, "Constitutional adjudication in Europe and the United States: paradoxes and contrasts," in *même ouvrage*, 197—238.

l'objet ici de les répertorier; leur nombre est à ce point important que même une bibliographie sélective, limitée aux ordres juridiques belge, français et allemand, dépasse aisément plusieurs milliers de contributions.[4]

En analysant le concept du 'contrôle de la constitutionnalité des lois', la doctrine s'est ainsi intéressée à la différence qui existe entre la non-conformité *totale* et *partielle* d'une norme législative, elle a analysé le problème des *effets dans le temps* d'une invalidation, qui peut opérer *ex nunc* ou *ex tunc*, et elle a examiné la question de savoir si une norme législative, lorsqu'elle est invalidée, est ou non *séparable* du texte dont elle faisait partie. Par ailleurs, il a été relevé que la constatation formelle qu'une norme législative est contraire à la Constitution ne signifie pas nécessairement que cette norme peut être invalidée.[5] Là où l'invalidation est possible, la doctrine a décrit les tensions qui existent entre une disparition *ab initio* de la norme et le principe de *confiance légitime*.[6] Enfin, elle a abordé le problème de la *protection juridictionnelle provisoire*, c'est-à-dire le régime juridique applicable entre le moment où l'application d'une norme législative est *suspendue* et le moment où la décision *finale* qui statue sur sa constitutionnalité intervient.[7] Bref, la doctrine a réalisé des progrès tout à fait substantiels dans le domaine du contrôle de la constitutionnalité des lois.

3.– Mais malgré toutes ces avancées, l'intégralité des travaux que nous venons d'évoquer partent du présupposé que les décisions du juge constitutionnel pourraient seulement avoir un effet sur des normes législatives *déjà existantes*: ainsi, quand la doctrine évoque la distinction entre non-conformité partielle et totale, elle examine des normes législatives *existantes*; quand elle examine si une disposition législative est séparable d'une autre, elle compare deux normes *existantes*; quand elle disserte sur les effets dans le temps d'une annulation, elle recherche en définitive la date à

4 Pour un premier aperçu, voy. la bibliographie de nos recherches doctorales; même si celle-ci n'a aucune prétention à l'exhaustivité.

5 Ce problème est omniprésent en Belgique, où la Cour d'arbitrage, saisie par voie préjudicielle, ne dispose pas de la possibilité d'annuler une norme législative qui est incompatible avec la Constitution; elle peut seulement en *constater* l'inconstitutionnalité. Aussi paradoxal que cela puisse paraître, la procédure préjudicielle, telle qu'elle est actuellement organisée, *permet donc expressément* la survivance de normes dont l'inconstitutionnalité est pourtant formellement établie par une décision de justice rendue en dernier ressort.

6 L'une des manières de concilier ces deux concepts est de permettre au juge constitutionnel de déterminer *une date* à partir de laquelle sa décision déploie ses effets, afin de ne pas remettre en cause des situations juridiques existantes. Une telle possibilité existe notamment en Belgique, grâce au second alinéa de l'article 8 de la loi spéciale sur la Cour d'arbitrage du 6 janvier 1989 (*Moniteur belge*, 7 janvier).

7 Pour la Belgique, voy. notamment G. Rosoux, "Leçons de l'éphémère. (…) La Cour d'arbitrage et la suspension," *Revue belge de droit constitutionnel*, 2003, 13–68.

laquelle une norme *existante* cesse d'avoir des effets en droit; enfin, quand elle fait référence au mécanisme de la protection constitutionnelle *ad interim*, elle évoque la possibilité de suspendre l'application d'une norme législative *existante*.

4.– Or – et c'est en ce sens qu'il convient de dépasser la théorie orthodoxe du contentieux constitutionnel – l'effet des décisions du juge constitutionnel ne se limite *pas* nécessairement aux normes législatives qui ont déjà été édictées mais peut aussi opérer *ad futurum*, c'est-à-dire peut avoir une incidence sur l'adoption ou le contenu de normes législatives que le Pouvoir législatif *n'a pas encore produites*. C'est précisément à ce problème que sont consacrées nos recherches.

5.– Il peut à première vue paraître insolite de consacrer un travail scientifique à une telle problématique: est-il bien sérieux d'examiner l'effet de décisions du juge constitutionnel sur des normes qui *n'existent pas encore*? S'agit-il vraiment d'une étude de droit constitutionnel *positif*? À cette question, on peut clairement répondre par l'affirmative et de très nombreuses décisions du juge constitutionnel français, belge et allemand permettent de démontrer ce point. Si, dans le cadre du présent exposé – qui se veut un résumé – nous ne pouvons les présenter dans leur intégralité, nous voudrions néanmoins en reproduire *deux*, l'une en provenance du juge constitutionnel français, l'autre de la Cour d'arbitrage belge.[8] Elles démontrent clairement que la juridiction constitutionnelle, lorsqu'elle opère un contrôle de conformité d'une norme législative existante, peut par ailleurs exercer une influence juridique *sur la production et le contenu de normes législatives futures*.

C'est ainsi qu'on peut lire dans une décision du Conseil constitutionnel français, rendue en 1983:

> "Considérant que l'article 89 [de la loi soumise au Conseil] permet à certains agents de l'administration des impôts (...) de procéder (...) à (...) des perquisitions et des saisies pour la recherche des infractions en matière d'impôts directs et de taxes sur le chiffre d'affaires (...);
>
> Considérant que, selon les (...) auteurs de la saisine, l'article 89 est rédigé de façon imprécise et générale en ce qui concerne la nature des infractions poursuivies et les pouvoirs qu'il confère aux agents de l'administration des impôts; qu'en outre, il laisse les perquisitions qu'il prévoit à la discrétion de fonctionnaires qui peuvent y procéder alors même qu'il n'existe aucun indice

8 Pour le surplus, nous nous permettons de renvoyer aux 2e et 3e parties de notre thèse, et spécialement aux *listes récapitulatives* qui reprennent l'intégralité des décisions ainsi recensées (ces listes figurent aux nos 151 et 275 de l'ouvrage).

d'infraction; que, par suite, ils estiment ces dispositions contraires à la liberté individuelle dont l'article 66 de la Constitution confie la garde à l'autorité judiciaire; (…)

Considérant que, quelles que soient les garanties dont les dispositions de l'article 89 entourent les opérations qu'elles visent, *ces dispositions ne précisent pas l'acception du terme infraction qui peut être entendu en plusieurs sens et ne limitent donc pas clairement le domaine ouvert aux investigations en question; qu'elles n'assignent pas de façon explicite au juge ayant le pouvoir d'autoriser les investigations des agents de l'administration la mission de vérifier, de façon concrète, le bien-fondé de la demande qui lui est soumise; qu'elles passent sous silence les possibilités d'intervention et de contrôle de l'autorité judiciaire dans le déroulement des opérations autorisées; qu'enfin, elles n'interdisent pas une interprétation selon laquelle seules les visites effectuées dans des locaux servant exclusivement à l'habitation devraient être spécialement autorisées par le juge, de telle sorte que à contrario, les visites opérées dans d'autres locaux pourraient donner lieu à des autorisations générales*;

Considérant qu'ainsi, *pour faire pleinement droit* de façon expresse tant aux exigences de la liberté individuelle et de l'inviolabilité du domicile qu'à celles de la lutte contre la fraude fiscale, les dispositions de l'article 89 *auraient dû être assorties de prescriptions et de précisions interdisant toute interprétation ou toute pratique abusive* et *ne sauraient dès lors, en l'état, être déclarées conformes à la Constitution.*" [9]

Dans un arrêt du 19 janvier 2005, le juge constitutionnel belge relève que:

"le législateur (…) a méconnu le principe d'égalité en établissant deux catégories de procédures dont l'une ne comporte pas de garanties de consultation et d'impartialité suffisantes.

Le moyen est fondé (…).

Pour éviter l'insécurité juridique qui naîtrait du caractère rétroactif de l'annulation, notamment à l'égard des personnes qui ont introduit une demande de permis en se fiant à la réglementation critiquée, et **afin de permettre au législateur (…) d'adopter une nouvelle réglementation**, il convient, en application de l'article 8, alinéa 2, de la loi spéciale du 6 janvier 1989 sur la Cour d'arbitrage, de maintenir les effets des dispositions annulées jusqu'au 31 décembre 2005."[10]

[9] Conseil constitutionnel (ci-après: CC), décision 164 DC du 29 décembre 1983 (*Grandes décisions du Conseil constitutionnel*, n° 34, *Perquisitions fiscales*), *Rec.*, 72–73. C'est nous qui soulignons.

[10] Cour d'arbitrage (ci-après: CA), arrêt 11/2005 du 19 janvier 2005, considérants B.5.5., alinéa 2, B.6. et B.8. C'est nous qui soulignons.

6.– Dans ces deux illustrations, on peut observer que la décision du juge constitutionnel a non seulement une incidence sur la norme *qui lui est soumise* mais exerce également un effet sur *l'activité future* du législateur, puisqu'elle *prédétermine*, du moins partiellement, le contenu de normes législatives que celui-ci n'a pas encore édictées.[11] Nous pouvons par ailleurs constater que *l'intensité* de l'effet n'est pas identique dans les deux décisions: alors que la première ne crée, à proprement parler, aucune obligation de légiférer, tel est bien le cas dans la seconde.

7.– À partir de ces constatations, nous pouvons formuler quatre questions principales: Si l'on accepte l'idée que le juge constitutionnel exerce un « effet directeur » sur l'activité future du législateur, comment cet effet peut-il être décrit en termes *normatifs*? (I) Une fois cette description effectuée, comment ses différentes manifestations, à intensité variable, peuvent-elles être *classifiées* ? (II) Ensuite, quelle est l'*importance* de l'effet directeur dans les trois pays analysés? En d'autres termes, combien de jugements du juge constitutionnel français, belge et allemand correspondent à chaque degré d'intensité? (III) Enfin, après avoir *décrit*, *classifié* et *quantifié* le recours à la technique de l'effet directeur, comment cette utilisation peut-elle être *évaluée*? Peut-on affirmer qu'elle constitue une inéluctable conséquence de la normativité, méconnue jusque dans un passé récent, de la Constitution ou convient-il de la considérer comme une ingérence *indue* des juridictions constitutionnelles dans le processus législatif, processus qui doit demeurer réservé aux Assemblées démocratiquement élues? (IV) Les développements qui suivent visent à présenter les principales réponses à ces questions, sans préjudice, bien entendu, d'un certain nombre de remarques complémentaires qui peuvent être trouvées ailleurs.[12]

I. LA NOTION D'"INTERFÉRENCE"

8.– Dans les deux illustrations que nous venons de présenter, nous avons pu relever que les décisions du Conseil constitutionnel et de la Cour d'arbitrage avaient un effet sur le contenu de dispositions qui n'ont pas encore été produites. Nous désignerons par le terme "*interférence*" cette *incidence d'une décision d'une juridiction constitutionnelle sur l'activité normative future d'un organe législatif*; dans les deux décisions précitées, le

[11] Il nous importe beaucoup de souligner le caractère exclusivement *juridique* de notre étude. L'incidence *juridique* des décisions du juge constitutionnel sur l'activité du législateur doit être soigneusement distinguée de leur incidence simplement *factuelle*, ou *politique*, qui est étrangère à notre champ d'investigation (sur ce point, voy. les nos 5 et 6 de l'ouvrage).

[12] Nous indiquerons en note les passages de l'ouvrage qui y sont spécifiquement consacrés.

juge constitutionnel *interfère* donc –au sens technique– avec l'activité normative du législateur.[13]

La notion d'interférence, dans l'acception que nous venons de lui donner, constitue le *concept-clef* de notre travail: nos travaux portent sur *l'interférence du juge constitutionnel*[14] *avec l'activité normative du législateur*. Ce problème est analysé dans trois pays, à savoir en Belgique, en France et en Allemagne.

9.– Après avoir introduit la notion d'interférence en tant que telle, il convient de l'articuler dans le cadre d'une théorie générale du droit. Dès lors que notre perception du droit est fondée sur le *positivisme juridique,*[15] il échet de fournir une description de la notion d'interférence à l'aide des outils conceptuels que nous offre *cette* théorie.

10.– Disons-le d'emblée: la notion d'interférence peut être décrite comme une *habilitation* (en allemand: *Ermächtigung;* en anglais: *empowerment*). En effet, selon la *Théorie pure du droit* de Hans Kensen,

> dans le cadre d'un ordre juridique, "habiliter" signifie conférer un pouvoir juridique, c'est-à-dire la faculté de créer du droit.[16]

Le droit étant constitué de normes juridiques, l'*habilitation* désigne donc *l'action de conférer à un organe la faculté de produire des normes*

13 La notion d'"interférence," telle que nous venons de l'employer ici, constitue une notion *purement technique*, créée spécialement pour l'occasion, *dont la portée s'écarte des significations courantes*. La même observation vaut pour le verbe « interférer ». La création de ces notions est cependant indispensable parce que nous ne pouvons nous baser sur aucune notion préexistante qui serait en mesure de refléter fidèlement le phénomène en question. Pour plus de détails sur ce point, voy. les nos 7 et 101-103 de l'ouvrage.

14 L'expression "juge constitutionnel" ne vise naturellement pas un magistrat constitutionnel, personne physique, mais a été choisie par commodité de langage pour désigner la jurisprudence de la juridiction constitutionnelle.

15 Cette précision n'est pas vaine, comme l'observe fort opportunément Lucien François (L. François, *Le cap des tempêtes, Essai de microscopie du droit*, Bruxelles et Paris, Bruylant et LGDJ, 2001, 57, note 27): bien trop peu d'auteurs prennent la peine d'indiquer, lorsqu'ils procèdent à l'analyse d'un concept juridique, la *théorie du droit sur laquelle ils se fondent*; or, cette précision est essentielle dans la mesure où il n'existe pas une *seule et unique* théorie du droit, mais *plusieurs théories concurrentes*, comme par exemple celles du positivisme, du jusnaturalisme, du réalisme (cette théorie étant notamment soutenue par le professeur italien Ricardo Guastini et le professeur français Michel Troper) et du dworkinisme (d'après le philosophe du droit américain Ronald Dworkin; cette dernière théorie étant particulièrement influente dans le monde anglophone).

16 H. Kelsen, *Théorie pure du droit*, 2e édition, traduction Ch. Eisenmann, Paris, Dalloz, 1962, 161. Texte original (*Reine Rechtslehre*, 2e édition, Vienne, Deuticke, 1960, 123): ["Sofern « ermächtigen » innerhalb einer Rechtsordnung soviel bedeutet wie eine Rechtsmacht, das heißt, die Fähigkeit verleihen, Recht zu erzeugen (…)"].

juridiques, en déterminant les conditions de validité de ces normes. Or, puisque l'habilitation permet la production de normes juridiques et qu'une norme juridique ne peut exister qu'en vertu d'une autre norme juridique,[17] une habilitation constitue *elle-même* une norme juridique.

Le juge constitutionnel qui interfère avec l'activité normative du législateur, en lui indiquant comment une loi peut être rédigée, produit donc une *norme juridique* qui habilite ce dernier à édicter une loi conformément à l'interférence émise. La notion d'*interférence* peut dès lors être définie comme *l'habilitation qui confère à son destinataire le pouvoir de produire à l'avenir* [18] *des normes dotées d'un certain contenu*, étant entendu que, dans le cadre de notre recherche, l'*auteur* de la norme d'habilitation est le juge constitutionnel et que son *destinataire* est le législateur.

II. LA CLASSIFICATION DES INTERFÉRENCES

11.– Le "moule commun" des interférences étant dégagé, il convient de partir à la recherche de critères qui nous permettent de procéder à une subdivision du concept d'"interférence," afin de répartir les interférences en plusieurs *catégories*.

12.– Pour trouver ce critère de division, il suffit de poursuivre la lecture de la *Théorie pure du droit* de Hans Kelsen. En exposant le concept d'habilitation, le professeur de Vienne relève:

> Il n'est pas superflu de souligner qu'il n'y a aucune nécessité à ce que, lorsqu'un individu est habilité à une conduite déterminée, il soit pour autant obligé à cette conduite. Mais il est naturellement possible, et il se rencontre fréquemment en fait qu'un individu ou un ensemble d'individus soient, en même temps qu'habilités, juridiquement obligés de faire usage de cette habilitation, c'est-à-dire que l'action à laquelle le sujet est habilité par l'ordre

[17] Voy. H. Kelsen, *Théorie pure du droit*, 2e édition, traduction Ch. Eisenmann, *ouvrage précité*, 256: "La validité d'une norme ne peut avoir d'autre fondement qu'une autre norme". Texte original: ["Der Geltungsgrund einer Norm kann nur eine andere Norm sein"] (*Reine Rechtslehre*, 2e édition, *ouvrage précité*, 196). Cette idée était déjà présente dans la première édition de la *Reine Rechtslehre* de 1934: voy. les pages 65, 72 et 82–83 (Leipzig et Vienne, Deuticke, 1934).

[18] On pourrait nous reprocher le caractère superfétatoire des mots "à l'avenir," en affirmant qu'une habilitation est nécessairement accordée pour l'avenir. Pour ceux qui estiment que ce point va de soi, ces mots peuvent effectivement être omis. Nous avons cependant pour notre part moins de certitudes: une habilitation ne pourrait-elle jamais être dotée d'une portée rétroactive ?

juridique soit en même temps prescrite, c'est-à-dire érigée en contenu d'une obligation.[19]

On le voit, Kelsen distingue deux cas de figure: dans l'un, l'organe auquel l'habilitation est accordée est en même temps destinataire d'une obligation juridique qui lui impose de faire usage de cette habilitation, dans l'autre, cette obligation fait défaut. Nous avons déjà précédemment relevé que toute interférence constitue techniquement une habilitation. Ceci nous permet d'appliquer la distinction mise en avant par Kelsen à la notion d'interférence.

La *summa divisio* de nos recherches peut dès lors s'énoncer comme suit: l'interférence est-elle ou non assortie d'un caractère contraignant ? Autrement dit: l'habilitation qu'accorde le juge constitutionnel au législateur est-elle ou non accompagnée d'une *obligation juridique* qui vise à mettre en œuvre cette habilitation ? On voit ainsi apparaître deux catégories d'interférences, selon que l'habilitation accordée par le juge constitutionnel au législateur est ou non accompagnée d'une *obligation juridique* qui lui impose d'en faire usage

13.– La première catégorie comprend les interférences qui ont un caractère simplement *permissif*. Le législateur est habilité à produire des normes législatives dotées d'un certain contenu, sans pour autant y être obligé. Ces interférences seront appelées *lignes directrices*.

14.– Le second groupe comprend les habilitations dont la mise en œuvre est sanctionnée par une obligation juridique. Le législateur est non seulement habilité à produire des normes législatives futures, mais une norme juridique lui impose par ailleurs de faire usage de cette habilitation. Les énoncés du juge constitutionnel ont par conséquent un caractère *obligatoire*. Ces interférences seront dénommées *injonctions*.[20]

19 H. Kelsen, *Théorie pure du droit*, 2e édition, traduction Ch. Eisenmann, *ouvrage précité*, 161-162. Texte original (*Reine Rechtslehre*, *ouvrage précité*, 123): ["Da Normen nicht nur ein bestimmtes Verhalten gebieten (oder verbieten), sondern auch zu einem bestimmten Verhalten ermächtigen können, ist es nicht überflüssig, hervorzuheben, daß, wenn ein Individuum zu einem bestimmten Verhalten ermächtigt ist, es damit zu disem Verhalten nicht ver-pflichtet sein muß. (…) Aber man kann rechtlich verpflichtet sein, von einer Ermächtigung Gebrauch zu machen; eine Handlung, zu der ein Individuum von der Rechtsordnung ermächtigt ist, kann zugleich geboten, das heißt: zum Inhalt seiner Pflicht gemacht sein."] On remarquera que les mots "et il se rencontre fréquemment en fait" qui figurent dans la traduction d'Eisenmann font défaut dans le texte original de Kelsen. Traduire, c'est déjà interpreter.

20 Tout comme les termes *interférence* et *ligne directrice*, cette appellation est purement conventionnelle, mais il faut bien disposer d'une terminologie.

15.– À l'intérieur de ces deux grandes catégories d'interférences, des classifications *supplémentaires*, plus fines, peuvent encore être opérées. L'on se permettra toutefois de ne pas les étudier dans le cadre du présent exposé.[21]

* * *

16.– Cette division des interférences – qui, sans exemples concrets, peut paraître assez abstraite – est illustrée par de nombreuses décisions au cours des seconde et troisième parties de notre travail, l'une consacrée aux lignes directrices (seconde partie) et l'autre aux injonctions (troisième partie). C'est à cet examen de jurisprudence constitutionnelle, qui comprend, en termes de volume, près de deux tiers de notre thèse et passe en revue une centaine de décisions du Conseil constitutionnel, de la Cour d'arbitrage et du *Bundesverfassungsgericht* allemand, que nous nous permettons de renvoyer le lecteur intéressé.

III. L'IMPORTANCE QUANTITATIVE DES INTERFÉRENCES

17.– Après avoir décrit et classifié les différentes manifestations des interférences, il échet de savoir *combien* de décisions du juge constitutionnel français, belge et allemand correspondent à chaque degré d'intensité. Il s'agit en d'autres termes de déterminer l'*importance quantitative* des interférences dans notre champ de recherche. Afin de fidèlement refléter la réalité, nous devons analyser séparément l'importance des *lignes directrices* et des *injonctions*.

18.– Avant de réaliser ces opérations, une observation générale doit encore être émise. Loin de représenter une simple opération de comptage, l'évaluation quantitative de la présence des interférences dans la jurisprudence constitutionnelle française, belge et allemande constitue une tâche malaisée. Bien que nous disposions d'un "moule théorique commun" auquel tous les énoncés du juge constitutionnel peuvent être confrontés,[22] une catégorisation binaire des décisions selon qu'elles contiennent ou non une interférence –en quelque sorte une division en décisions "blanches" et "noires"– est souvent difficile à réaliser en pratique. Cette difficulté est avant tout générée par la *diversité de la formulation* des énoncés du juge constitutionnel, diversité qu'aucune théorie ne permet d'englober

[21] Sur ce point, voy., dans l'ouvrage, les nos 96 et 101—103 (présentation générale), 132—138 (subdivision des lignes directrices) et 199-210 (subdivision des injonctions).

[22] Voy. ci-dessus, nos 8—10.

complètement. Si la doctrine constitutionnelle n'est pas en mesure de fournir une théorie qui puisse "travailler toute seule", c'est-à-dire identifier d'une manière mécanique, sur la base de critères objectifs, les décisions qui nous intéressent, c'est parce que les différents types de décision

> ne constituent pas des catégories claires, étanches et cloisonnées. Il advient qu'ils se superposent et que telle ou telle décision d'une cour constitutionnelle ne puisse être classée parfaitement dans une seule catégorie. Il est également difficile, en droit comparé, d'identifier clairement le profil caractéristique de chaque type de décision et les rapports étroits qu'il peut présenter avec d'autres profils ou catégories. [23]

L'observation du professeur Fernández Rodríguez peut se résumer en quatre mots: *le "gris" subsistera toujours*. Ce constat préliminaire ne doit cependant pas conduire à l'inertie scientifique: ce n'est pas parce qu'une analyse ne peut être effectuée avec une précision parfaite qu'elle doit être complètement abandonnée. Si tel était le cas, le genre humain ne réaliserait probablement *plus aucune* recherche portant sur des faits observables. À l'instar des peintres qui dessinent des cercles sans jamais atteindre le cercle parfait, nos travaux visent donc à proposer des classifications qui demeurent tout aussi indigentes.

1. *L'importance des lignes directrices*

19.– Sur la base d'une lecture *exhaustive* des décisions du juge constitutionnel français[24] et belge,[25] et sur la base d'une *sélection* des décisions du juge constitutionnel allemande,[26] les constatations suivantes peuvent être émises (une statistique complète, qui comprend les références précises de toutes les lignes directrices que nous avons pu recenser, peut être trouvée au numéro 151 de l'ouvrage).

[23] J.J. Fernández Rodríguez, "Typologie des dispositifs des décisions des cours constitutionnelles," *Revue belge de droit constitutionnel*, 1998, 335.

[24] En France, ont été prises en compte toutes les décisions pertinentes rendues jusqu'au 1er juillet 2005 inclus, soit:
- toutes les décisions pertinentes de la série DC jusqu'au numéro 515 inclus,
- toutes les décisions de la série L jusqu'au numéro 200 inclus ainsi que
- l'unique décision de la série LP (1 LP).

[25] En Belgique, ont été prises en compte toutes les décisions rendues jusqu'au 1er juillet 2005 inclus, soit jusqu'à l'arrêt 118/2005 inclus.

[26] Le volume total de la jurisprudence du *Bundesverfassungsgericht* dépasse les 47.000 pages, de sorte qu'un dépouillement intégral de ses décisions nous était matériellement impossible.

19.1– La première observation tient en ce que le nombre de lignes directrices est nettement plus élevé en France qu'en Belgique ou en Allemagne. Alors que 75 cas peuvent être relevés dans les décisions du juge constitutionnel français, on n'en dénombre que 34 dans les arrêts de son homologue belge et 6 dans les jugements de son collègue d'outre-Rhin. À première vue, ce résultat peut étonner: ne s'accorde-t-on pas à dire que le juge constitutionnel français fait généralement preuve d'une plus grande prudence à l'égard du législateur que le juge constitutionnel allemand ? [27]

Or, la contradiction n'est qu'apparente: plus un juge constitutionnel adopte une attitude respectueuse vis-à-vis du Pouvoir législatif, plus il aura recours, lorsqu'il interfère avec l'activité normative du législateur, à des interférences *non* obligatoires, c'est-à-dire à des lignes directrices. À l'inverse, plus un juge constitutionnel développe une jurisprudence interventionniste, plus il émettra des interférences *obligatoires*, c'est-à-dire des injonctions. Considérés sous cet angle, le nombre élevé d'interférences *non* obligatoires en France et leur faible quantité en Allemagne ne peuvent surprendre.[28]

19.2– La deuxième constatation qui ressort de notre recherche est que l'utilisation des lignes directrices *progresse* en France: plus de la moitié d'entre elles (43 sur 75) ont été émises au cours des quinze dernières années (1990-2005).[29] Aucune augmentation significative ne peut en revanche être constatée dans les deux autres pays.

2. *L'importance des injonctions*

20.– Au niveau des interférences *obligatoires*, les résultats sont sensiblement différents (une statistique exhaustive de toutes ces décisions peut être trouvée au n° 275 de l'ouvrage). Trois observations générales peuvent être formulées.

20.1– La première consiste à signaler que le nombre des injonctions est nettement plus élevé en Allemagne qu'en Belgique ou en France. Si 60 cas

27 Voy. notamment M. Fromont, *La justice constitutionnelle dans le monde*, Paris, Dalloz, 1996, 134, L. Favoreu, "La constitutionnalisation de l'ordre juridique. Considérations générales," *Revue belge de droit constitutionnel*, 1998, 235–236, J.J. Fernández Rodríguez, "Typologie des dispositifs des décisions des cours constitutionnelles," *Revue belge de droit constitutionnel*, 345–346, E. Zoller, *Droit constitutionnel*, 2e édition, Paris, PUF, 1999, 177–179 et 280.

28 La retenue du Conseil constitutionnel suppose en effet une parcimonie d'*injonctions*, non un faible nombre de *lignes directrices*. De même, le rôle pionnier du juge constitutionnel allemand est établi par un grand nombre d'*injonctions*, non par une multitude de *lignes directrices*. C'est donc la statistique relative aux *injonctions* (voy. ci-après) qui permet seule d'apprécier la pertinence des thèses susmentionnées.

29 Par rapport à une activité totale du Conseil de 46 années (1959–2005).

peuvent être relevés au sein de la jurisprudence du juge constitutionnel allemand, on n'en dénombre que 20 dans les arrêts de la Cour d'arbitrage et six dans les décisions du Conseil constitutionnel. Ce résultat est parfaitement conforme à nos attentes: le juge constitutionnel allemand est beaucoup plus interventionniste que ses homologues français et belge, et les présentes statistiques confirment cette impression par des chiffres concrets (même si l'on ne doit pas oublier que le *Bundesverfassungsgericht* existe depuis *plus longtemps* que ses homologues belge et français).

20.2– La deuxième remarque tient en ce que la technique des injonctions de légiférer constitue un phénomène juridique *assez ancien*: le premier cas observable en Allemagne date de juin 1958,[30] soit d'une époque où le Conseil constitutionnel français n'était pas encore né. Ce serait donc commettre une grave erreur de jugement que de mettre en cause le caractère *durable* du phénomène et d'affirmer qu'il s'agit d'un simple "effet de mode," avec toute la connotation éphémère que cette qualification implique.

20.3– Enfin, la troisième observation tient en ce que l'utilisation des injonctions – spécialement de celles assorties d'un délai pour légiférer – progresse de manière significative *en Belgique*: alors qu'on dénombre dix cas pour toute la période de 1985 à 2003 (soit dix-huit années), on en compte six pour la seule année 2004. Pendant l'année 2005, quatre cas supplémentaires doivent être mentionnés.[31] Aucune augmentation notable, dans un passé récent, ne peut en revanche être constatée dans les deux autres pays, même si l'on peut relever en Allemagne une légère augmentation de la fréquence des injonctions depuis les années soixante-dix.

* * *

21.– À l'issue de la présente section consacrée à l'importance quantitative des interférences, on peut par ailleurs émettre une observation générale, qui est valable à la fois pour les lignes directrices et pour les injonctions.

L'ordre juridique français est doté d'une Cour constitutionnelle qui effectue un contrôle *général* et *a priori* de constitutionnalité des normes législatives. L'ordre juridique allemand possède un système de contrôle *général* et *a posteriori*. L'ordre juridique belge connaît quant à lui un mécanisme *spécialisé* et *a posteriori*. Or, ont peut clairement établir que les

30 Décision du 11 juin 1958, *BVerfGE* 8, 1 (28).

31 Au 1er juillet 2005, date de la clôture de nos recherches. Il s'agit des arrêts CA, 11/2005 du 19 janvier 2005 (exposé au n° 5 de la présente contribution), 29/2005 du 9 février 2005, 62/2005 du 23 mars 2005 et 101/2005 du 1er juin 2005.

interférences, qu'elles soient ou non pourvues d'une force obligatoire, sont présentes *dans chacun de ces trois États*, malgré les différences – sensibles – relatives à la mise en œuvre du contrôle de constitutionnalité. En d'autres termes, les interférences sont observables *tant* dans la jurisprudence d'une Cour constitutionnelle à compétence générale *que* dans celle d'une "cour constitutionnelle à compétence limitée," [32] et *tant* dans les décisions rendues dans un contrôle *a priori que* dans celles prononcées *a posteriori*. Ceci permet d'affirmer que l'articulation *ratione materieœ* et *ratione temporis* du contrôle de la constitutionnalité des normes législatives est *sans incidence* sur l'existence d'injonctions du juge constitutionnel dans l'activité normative du législateur. Cette conclusion est substantielle, dans la mesure où elle apporte un élément supplémentaire au 'socle commun' du contentieux de constitutionnalité, dont les *éléments constitutifs communs* sont en train d'être dégagés.[33]

IV. LE RECOURS À LA TECHNIQUE DES INTERFÉRENCES: UNE TENTATIVE D'ÉVALUATION

22. – Après avoir décrit, classifié et quantifié les différentes manifestations des interférences dans les trois pays de notre champ de recherche, une dernière question subsiste: comment faut-il, *évaluer* leur utilisation par la Cour d'arbitrage, le Conseil constitutionnel et le *Bundesverfassungsgericht* ? À cet égard, nos travaux semblent permettre trois constatations majeures.

23. – La première, de loin la plus importante, constitue la véritable 'thèse' de notre travail: le juge constitutionnel *interfère réellement* – au sens technique du terme – avec l'activité normative du Pouvoir législatif, en lui *permettant* la production de dispositions législatives (lignes directrices) ou en lui *prescrivant* une telle production (injonctions). Comme le permet en effet d'établir l'examen des décisions du juge constitutionnel français, belge et allemand auquel nous nous sommes livré,[34] ces 'interférences' peuvent être *concrètement observées* dans la jurisprudence constitutionnelle de nos pays de référence. Techniquement, elles constituent des *habilitations de production normative* par lesquelles le juge constitutionnel indique au

[32] CA, arrêt 32 du 29 janvier 1987, considérant B.b.8.1.

[33] En langue française, voy. notamment L. Favoreu, *Les Cours constitutionnelles*, 3e édition, Paris, PUF, Collection "Que sais-je ?" (n° 2293), 1996, 127 pages, M. Fromont, *La justice constitutionnelle dans le monde*, Paris, Dalloz, 1996, 140 pages, et J. Pini, *Recherches sur le contentieux de constitutionnalité*, thèse (Aix-Marseille III, 1997), non publiée, 453 pages dactylographiées.

[34] Voy. les 2e et 3e parties de l'ouvrage.

législateur *quel contenu les dispositions futures devront avoir pour être conformes au prescrit constitutionnel.*

24.– Le second constat se situe sur un autre plan, celui de la philosophie politique: loin d'*enlever* au législateur un pouvoir de décision, les interférences ont précisément pour effet de le lui *restituer*. Lorsque le juge constitutionnel interfère avec l'activité normative du législateur, cela témoigne, aussi paradoxal que cela puisse paraître, d'une forme d'auto-limitation (*self restraint*) du magistrat constitutionnel: le Pouvoir législatif est amené à élaborer *lui-même* une réglementation *et d'en porter la responsabilité politique*. Si l'on part de la maxime que, dans un État démocratique, les décisions de principe doivent être prises par des Assemblées parle-mentaires, élues au suffrage universel, le fait de les conduire à *effectivement exercer* ce pouvoir ne constitue pas une manifestation d'un "gouvernement des juges" mais *prévient justement une érosion du Pouvoir législatif.* Que les décisions des Assemblées soient soumises à l'*appréciation de l'électeur* va de soi: il s'agit là de l'essence du parlementarisme. C'est précisément pour cette raison que *l'abandon des prérogatives parlementaires ne peut être admis* et doit, le cas échéant, être combattu par le juge constitutionnel.[35] La doctrine allemande a été attentive à cette facette particulière du contentieux constitutionnel dès les années soixante-dix[36] et la même idée peut être retrouvée dans les écrits constitutionnels italiens[37] et français.[38]

[35] Même la formulation d'une *obligation de légiférer* est conforme à cet objectif.

[36] W. Rupp-von Brünneck, "Verfassungsgerichtsbarkeit und gesetzgebende Gewalt, Wechselseitiges Verhältnis zwischen Verfassungsgericht und Parlament," *Archiv des öffentlichen Rechts*, 102 (1977), 20, et A. Gerontas, "Die Appellentscheidungen, Sondervotumsappelle und die bloße Unvereinbarkeitsfestellung als Ausdruck der funktionnellen Grenzen der Verfassungsgerichtsbarkeit," *Deutsches Verwaltungsblatt*, 1982, 486.

[37] A. Pizzorusso, "Les sentences de la Cour constitutionnelle et la couverture financière des lois," *Annuaire international de Justice constitutionnelle*, 4 (1988), 496:

"l'adoption, par les juges constitutionnels, de solutions techniques comme celles qui consistent en l'emploi de types de décisions diversement intermédiaires, entre celles d'admission et celles de rejet, ne constitue pas, contrairement à ce que certains semblent penser, une prévarication à l'égard des autres pouvoirs de l'État, mais *constitue bien une forme d'autolimitation de la Cour constitutionnelle* tendant à éviter les difficultés excessives engendrées par l'annulation de lois entières ou de dispositions de lois contenant des éléments d'inconstitutionnalité."

C'est nous qui soulignons.

[38] Th. di Manno, Le juge constitutionnel et la technique des décisions 'interprétatives' en France et en Italie, thèse (Aix-Marseille III, 1996), Aix-en-Provence et Paris, PUAM et Economica, 1997, 18, et A. Viala, Les réserves d'interprétation dans la jurisprudence du Conseil constitutionnel, thèse (Montpellier I, 1998), Paris, LGDJ, 1999, 288.

25.– Le troisième et dernier constat concerne plus spécifiquement les interférences *obligatoires*, c'est-à-dire les *injonctions*. Si l'on excepte les six décisions du Conseil constitutionnel français qui relèvent de cette catégorie,[39] il s'agit là d'un phénomène *exclusivement belge et allemand*. Or, la comparaison entre ces deux pays débouche sur des résultats inattendus: si le juge constitutionnel allemand a la réputation d'être particulièrement interventionniste – interventionnisme dont l'arrêt *IVG II*[40] constitue sans doute la dernière avancée – la Cour d'arbitrage belge semble, ces dernières années, avoir amorcé une politique à bien des égards *plus active encore*. Ce 'surplus' d'activisme du juge constitutionnel belge se manifeste de quatre façons différentes.

25.1– Le premier indice qui permet de conclure à une intensité plus *grande* des interventions du juge constitutionnel belge tient en le simple *nombre* d'injonctions qui sont adressées au législateur. Si le juge constitutionnel allemand a, en chiffres absolus, émis davantage d'injonctions que son homologue belge,[41] ce dernier utilise depuis peu cette technique d'une manière véritablement *immodérée* et dépasse, *proportionnellement à la même période*, de loin l'activité du premier.[42]

25.2– La seconde manière par laquelle se traduit la plus grande intensité des injonctions du juge constitutionnel belge a trait à la *durée des délais* que la Cour d'arbitrage et le *Bundesverfassungsgericht* accordent au législateur pour mettre fin à une inconstitutionnalité:[43] alors que la Cour de Karlsruhe accorde en moyenne 21 mois au Pouvoir législatif pour apporter les corrections nécessaires, la Cour de Bruxelles exige en moyenne une réaction dans les neuf mois.[44]

25.3– Troisièmement, l'intensité des injonctions émises par le *Bundesverfassungsgericht* et la Cour d'arbitrage diffère en raison de la *qualité même* des délais qui sont accordés au législateur: alors que le juge

39 Il s'agit des décisions 111 DC du 30 décembre 1979 (*Rec.*, 40), 138 DC du 25 février 1982 (*Rec.*, 44), 410 DC du 15 mars 1999 (considérant 17), 431 DC du 6 juillet 2000 (considérant 11), 447 du 18 juillet 2001 (considérants 14–15) et 468 DC du 3 avril 2003 (considérants 26–28). Sur ce point, voy. aussi le n° 275 de l'ouvrage.

40 Commenté au n° 269 de l'ouvrage.

41 Soixante injonctions en Allemagne, par rapport à vingt en Belgique. Ce résultat ne peut toutefois étonner: la première décision de la Cour allemande (*BVerfGE* 1, 1) date de 1951, alors que le premier arrêt de la Cour d'arbitrage (arrêt 1) n'intervient que 34 ans plus tard, en 1985.

42 Pour une statistique précise, voy. les tableaux présentés au n° 275 de l'ouvrage.

43 Pour une statistique précise sur la longueur des délais dans les deux pays, voy. les tableaux présentés au n° 278 de l'ouvrage.

44 Voy. le n° 279.1 de l'ouvrage.

constitutionnel allemand a principalement recours au mécanisme – plutôt modéré – des délais *de sollicitation*, son homologue belge utilise en règle la catégorie – nettement plus énergique – des délais *d'abrogation* .[45] Ce n'est que dans des circonstances exceptionnelles, quand ce second mécanisme de délais risque de véritablement compromettre *la pérennité du système parlementaire*, que la Cour d'arbitrage assortit, elle aussi, ses injonctions d'un délai de sollicitation.[46] L'utilisation presque systématique des délais d'abrogation est cependant *dangereuse* et peut exposer l'ordre juridique belge à des problèmes essentiels de fonctionnement. Une illustration patente en est l'arrêt 106/2004 de la Cour d'arbitrage du 16 juin 2004, relative à la procédure de publication des textes législatifs et réglementaires, auquel le législateur ne donne suite qu'*in extremis*, à 48 heures de l'expiration du délai imparti.[47]

25.4 – Il existe encore un quatrième aspect qui démontre la plus grande intensité des injonctions du juge constitutionnel belge: contrairement à son homologue de Karlsruhe, la Cour de Bruxelles n'assortit pas ses interférences de *mesures provisoires.*[48] Or, c'est précisément l'*absence* de telles mesures qui traduit une intensité *plus grande* des interventions du juge

45 Cette distinction, essentielle, entre délais de sollicitation et d'abrogation peut être résumée comme suit. Lorsqu'il a recours à un délai de ***sollicitation***, le juge constitutionnel indique au législateur le moment pour lequel celui-ci doit avoir produit la norme *destinée à faire disparaître l'inconstitutionnalité* (par exemple pour le 30 juin 2006). En revanche, lorsqu'il formule un délai ***d'abrogation***, il indique au législateur le laps de temps au cours duquel la norme *déclarée inconstitutionnelle* peut encore être appliquée (il énonce par exemple que telle norme législative *peut encore être appliquée* jusqu'au 30 juin 2006). Le délai de sollicitation prend donc comme point de référence la norme que le législateur *doit produire* (la 'nouvelle' norme), tandis que le délai d'abrogation prend comme point de référence la norme qui doit *être remplacée* (l''ancienne' norme). Les deux formes de délais ont des effets substantiellement différents: contrairement au dépassement d'un délai de sollicitation, le dépassement d'un délai d'abrogation *crée automatiquement un vide juridique*. Pour de plus amples développements sur la distinction entre délais de sollicitation et d'abrogation, voy. les nos 225 et suivants de l'ouvrage.

46 Voy. CA, arrêt 73/2003 du 26 mai 2003, analysé aux nos 256–261 de l'ouvrage.

47 Par l'arrêt 106/2004 (commenté au n° 249 de l'ouvrage), la Cour d'arbitrage a en effet annulé, *avec effet au 1er août 2005*, les articles 474 et 475 de la loi-programme du 24 décembre 2002, qui réglaient la procédure de publication des textes officiels au *Moniteur belge*. Or, à défaut d'une nouvelle intervention législative avant cette date, *plus aucune loi, aucun arrêté – et d'ailleurs aucun arrêt de la Cour d'arbitrage – n'aurait pu être légalement publié et, dès lors, être opposé aux citoyens*. La réaction législative, la loi du 20 juillet 2005, ne fut publiée au *Moniteur* que le 29 juillet, soit à deux jours de l'expiration du délai. Pour le dire clairement: la Cour d'arbitrage a joué avec le feu. En effet, le remède tout à fait classique, à savoir une *loi rétroactive*, votée postérieurement à l'expiration du délai, prenant cours au dernier jour utile pour agir (31 juillet 2005), aurait été inopérant en l'espèce: cette loi sur la publication des lois *aurait également dû être publiée au Moniteur*, ce qui aurait été impossible, faute de base légale, après l'expiration du délai. On ne peut qu'espérer que la hardiesse dont le juge constitutionnel a fait montre dans cette affaire fasse à l'avenir place à des décisions plus modérées.

48 Sur cette notion, voy. les nos 264–272 de l'ouvrage.

constitutionnel: l'édiction de mesures provisoires conduit en effet à *alléger* le caractère contraignant de l'injonction.[49]

CONCLUSIONS

26. – Nos travaux permettent d'établir que le juge constitutionnel interfère avec l'activité normative du législateur et exerce de la sorte une activité "*positive,*" au sens kelsénien du terme.[50] Ces interférences peuvent être lourdes de conséquences et confèrent à la juridiction constitutionnelle une responsabilité de tout premier rang dans la *direction normative de l'État.*[51] Faut-il pour autant conclure que le juge constitutionnel "en fait trop" ?[52] Sommes-nous passés de "l'irrigation du droit par le juge constitutionnel"[53] à "l'oligarchie dans la démocratie"?[54]

Il nous semble que non. Si des excès dans la jurisprudence constitutionnelle peuvent être pointés du doigt[55], un élément essentiel du débat ne doit pas être perdu de vue: c'est que le juge constitutionnel *n'a pas le dernier mot.* Le constituant peut en effet à tout moment modifier les normes de référence du juge constitutionnel et ainsi neutraliser sa jurisprudente.[56]

49 Voy. sur ce point, voy. le n° 318.2 de l'ouvrage.

50 Pour plus de détails sur ce point, voy. les nos 321–331 de l'ouvrage.

51 Voy. notamment les décisions de justice constitutionnelle sur l'*interruption volontaire de grossesse*, problème auquel les trois Cours de notre champ de recherche ont été confrontées: voy.

- en France, CC, décisions 54 DC du 15 janvier 1975 *[IVG I]* et 446 DC du 27 juin 2001 *[IVG II]*,
- en Belgique, CA, arrêts 32/90 du 24 octobre 1990 et 39/91 du 19 décembre 1991, et
- en Allemagne, BVerfG, arrêts du 25 février 1975 *[IVG I]* (*BVerfGE*, 39, 1, examiné au n° 268 de l'ouvrage à paraître) et du 28 mai 1993 *[IVG II]* (*BVerfGE*, 88, 203, examiné au n° 269).

52 Ph. Blachèr, "Le Conseil constitutionnel en fait-il trop ?," *Pouvoirs*, 105 (2003), 17-28, ici 27: "en se situant sur le seul terrain du droit, il est possible de soutenir que le Conseil constitutionnel 'en fait trop'"

53 N. Molfessis, "L'irrigation du droit par les décisions du Conseil constitutionnel," *Pouvoirs*, 105 (2003), 89–101.

54 W. Brohm, "Die Funktion des BVerfG – Oligarchie in der Demokratie ?," *Neue juristische Wochenschrift*, 2001, 1–10; voy. aussi P. Martens, "Les cours constitutionnelles: des oligarchies illégitimes ?," in *La République des juges*, Actes du colloque organisé par le Jeune Barreau de Liège le 7 février 1997, 53–72.

55 Voy. avant la décision *IVG II* de la Cour constitutionnelle allemande, présentée au n° 269 de l'ouvrage.

56 Voy. notamment L. Favoreu, "La légitimité du Conseil tient à ce qu'il n'a pas le dernier mot," *Le Figaro*, 27 août 1993, 5, et, "Le Parlement constituant et le juge constitutionnel," *Mélanges en l'honneur de Pierre Avril*, Paris, Montchrestien, 2001, 238.

Une certaine vigilance à l'égard de juges qui ont le pouvoir d'invalider des textes votés par des Assemblées démocratiquement élues, alors qu'ils ne puisent eux-mêmes leur légitimité dans aucune élection, est certes de mise.[57] Mais il convient de se garder de conclusions extrêmes: si l'intervention de plus en plus marquée de la justice constitutionnelle soulève des interrogations, elle semble toujours préférable à l'*absence pure et simple* d'une telle instance, absence qui transformerait à nouveau le texte constitutionnel en un "recueil de bons conseils à l'usage du législateur,"[58] dépourvu de normativité. Le juge constitutionnel Paul Martens a parfaitement résumé cette situation en soulignant que:

> "la démocratie ne peut tolérer que des pouvoirs s'exercent à l'abri des juges pas plus qu'elle ne peut admettre que des juges ne se justifient que devant leur conscience." [59]

27.– La réussite du difficile acte de balance entre le *'trop peu'* d'une cour constitutionnelle chétive et le *'trop'* d'un véritable législateur prétorien[60] *n'est pas assurée d'avance*. Tel un satellite[61], le juge constitutionnel *peut glisser de son orbite*, vers le bas ou vers le haut, et exposer de la sorte son ordre juridique à de graves dangers.

Comment l'aider à rester sur la bonne trajectoire ? À notre sens, l'un des moyens privilégiés pour assurer l'indispensable équilibre de la justice constitutionnelle tient en l'*étude attentive de ses décisions*. Rares sont les domaines où le rôle de la *doctrine*, argumentée et indépendante, dépouillée des contingences politiques du moment, peut être d'une aussi grande utilité. Si nos travaux, dont nous mesurons par ailleurs les limites, peuvent fournir une modeste contribution à ce débat, ils ont déjà pleinement atteint leur objectif.

57 M. Verdussen, *Les douze juges, La légitimité de la Cour constitutionnelle*, Bruxelles, Labor, 2004, 51–56.

58 Ch. Eisenmann, *La justice constitutionnelle et la Haute Cour constitutionnelle d'Autriche*, thèse (Paris, 1928), Paris, LGDJ, 1928, 22.

59 P. Martens, "De quelques contrôles juridictionnels sur les acteurs politiques," *Revue de Droit de l'Université Libre de Bruxelles*, 16 (1997), 318.

60 A. Söllner, "Der Richter als Ersatzgesetzgeber," *Zeitschrift für Gesetzgebung*, 10 (1995), 1–16. Spécifiquement sur le contexte allemand, voy. aussi le délicieux article, éminemment polémique, de R. Lamprecht, "Oligarchie in Karlsruhe: Über die Erosion der Gewaltenteilung," *Neue juristische Wochenschrift*, 1994, 3272-3274.

61 J. Rivero, "Fin d'un absolutisme," *Pouvoirs*, 13 (réédition 1991), 5.

GREECE

CONSTITUTIONAL COURTS AS POSITIVE LEGISLATORS

Julia Iliopoulos-Strangas
Professor of Constitutional Law,
University of Athens, Law School
juliostr@law.uoa.gr

Stylianos-Ioannis G. Koutnatzis
Ph.D. in Constitutional Law (Freie Universität Berlin),
LL.M. (Harvard), LL.B. (Athens).

In international comparison, Greek courts recognized the judicial power to review the constitutionality of legislation very early on the basis of constitutional supremacy. However, from the late nineteenth century to the late twentieth century, Greek courts generally deferred to the political branches of government, and in practice, they have rarely challenged legislative or executive acts on constitutional grounds. Situated between the American and the European models, constitutional adjudication in Greece eludes neat definition in terms of both the system of review and its concrete application by the courts. Following an overview on the system of judicial review in Greek constitutional law (see section I),[1] this report examines its concrete application. It focuses on the development of the interplay between judicial self-restraint and judicial activism, in addition to positive legislation through judicial review of the constitutionality of legislation and its limits (see section II).

[1] The present report generally follows the English translation of the Greek Constitution of 1975 (as revised in 1986, 2001, and 2008) [abbreviated: Const.] by Xenophon Paparrigopoulos and Stavroula Vasilouni, which is available online at http://www.parliament.gr [3 March 2010].

I. THE SYSTEM OF JUDICIAL REVIEW

1. *Judicial Organization*

The Greek judicial system is divided into functionally different subsystems, each with its own high court. The courts are divided into administrative, civil, and criminal courts (Art. 93 § 1 Const.).[2] The Areios Pagos Court (Άρειος Πάγος) sits at the apex of all civil and criminal courts; the Council of State (Συμβούλιο της Επικρατείας), modeled on the French Conseil d'État, functions primarily as the supreme administrative court (Art. 95 Const.).[3] The Constitution also provides for a third high court,[4] the Court of Audit (Ελεγκτικό Συνέδριο), to which no lower courts correspond, and which has comparatively limited judicial responsibilities.[5] In addition, the current 1975 Constitution established a Supreme Special Court (Ανώτατο Ειδικό Δικαστήριο) charged with a number of responsibilities of a constitutional nature, namely the adjudication of electoral disputes; the settlement of jurisdictional conflicts between the courts and the administrative authorities, or between different judicial jurisdictions; the interpretation of a statutory provision or an assessment of its constitutionality when conflicting judgments are issued among the high courts of different jurisdictions; and the designation of rules of international law as generally acknowledged (Art. 100, § 1 Const.).[6] The Supreme Special Court is

[2] Although justice is administered by three hierarchies of courts (administrative, civil, and criminal), the same judges regularly alternate between civil and criminal courts. See, e.g., K. D. Kerameus, Judicial Organization and Civil Procedure, *in* K. D. Kerameus & Ph. J. Kozyris (eds.), *Introduction to Greek Law* (3rd revised ed., Alphen aan den Rijn 2008), 341–378 (342–344). On the Greek high courts, see, in general, N. K. Klamaris, Die Funktion und die Rolle der obersten Gerichtshöfe Griechenlands, *in* E. Schilken et al. (eds.), *Festschrift für Hans Friedhelm Gaul zum 70. Geburtstag*, Bielefeld 1997, 289–299.

[3] According to Art. 95 Const., the Council of State's jurisdiction "pertains mainly to a) the annulment upon petition of enforceable acts of the administrative authorities for excess of power or violation of the law, b) the reversal upon petition of final judgments of ordinary administrative courts, as specified by law, c) the trial of substantive administrative disputes submitted thereto as provided by the Constitution and the statutes, d) the elaboration of all decrees of a general regulatory nature."

[4] The Constitution additionally appoints specialized high courts for adjudicating suits against magistrates for faulty wrongful judgment (Art. 99), criminal offences of Cabinet members or undersecretaries committed during the discharge of their duties (Art. 86), and based on 2001 amendments, disputes concerning remunerations and pensions of magistrates (Art. 88 § 2).

[5] Being primarily an institution charged with auditing government expenditures, the judicial function of the Court of Audit is limited to disputes concerning pensions and the liability of civil or military servants (Art. 98 Const.).

[6] For more information on the Supreme Special Court's jurisdiction, see, e.g., J. Iliopoulos-Strangas, Les décisions de la Cour spéciale suprême grecque et leur mise en œuvre, *in* Cour

composed of the presidents and judges of Greece's high courts, who exercise this role along with their other judicial duties and, in some procedures, with two law professors.[7] Although the high court presidents serve in the Supreme Special Court *ex officio*, all other members of the Court are chosen by lot for two-year terms (Art. 100, § 2 Const.).

2. *Control of Legislative and Executive Acts*

A. Origins and Development of Judicial Review throughout Greece's Constitutional History

Greece's 1827 Constitution, adopted during the last stages of the Greek Independence War, included a set of rudimentary provisions that appointed the judiciary as guardian of the Constitution.[8] In contrast, the Constitutions of 1844 and 1864 did not include explicit provisions in this regard. Initially, the Areios Pagos dispelled the notion of judicial review of the constitutionality of legislation, emphasizing that the courts are merely required to apply legislation and pronounce judgment on this basis and are not authorized to fault a statute or strike it down on the grounds that the sovereign Parliament had no power to enact it.[9] However, after groundbreaking rulings at the lower level,[10] the Areios Pagos changed course.[11] According to a seminal Areios Pagos ruling handed down in 1897,

Constitutionnelle d'Andorre (ed.), *Colloque de justice constitutionnelle de la Principauté d'Andorre*, Andorra 2007, 75–91 (80–83).

[7] Art. 100 § 2 Const. requires the inclusion of law professors on the bench when the Supreme Special Court adjudicates conflicts between the courts and the administrative authorities or between different jurisdictions or controversies on the interpretation or constitutionality of a statutory provision.

[8] See Art. 143 *alinea* a of the 1827 Constitution (guaranteeing constitutional supremacy to ordinary legislation); Resolution of the National Assembly on the Ratification of the 1827 Constitution, §§ A–B (describing the legislature, the Governor, and the judiciary as guardians of the Constitution and explicitly prohibiting unconstitutional legislative and executive action); see also G. Kassimatis, *Constitutional Adjudication*, Athens-Komotini 1999, 43–44 Fn. 40 [in Greek].

[9] See Areios Pagos judgment n° 198/1847, Collection of Areios Pagos Judgments in Civil Cases, Athens 1847, 765 (771) [in Greek] (adding that "the contrary system would result in the impropriety of subordinating the parliamentary statute under the judicial power, while the judiciary should be subordinate to the statute, applying it exactly, rather than faulting it").

[10] See Athens Court of Appeals judgment nos. 1710/1892, *Themis* 1892–1893, 5; 1847/1893, *Themis* 1892–1893, 615; Athens Court of First Instance judgment n° 3504/1892, *Themis* 1892–1893, 474.

[11] For an insightful analysis of the origins of constitutional review in Greece, see Ph. Vegleris, La Constitution, la Loi et les Tribunaux en Grèce, *in Annales de la Faculté de Droit de Liège*,

"when . . . a statutory provision contravenes the Constitution, modifying through an ordinary statute a fundamental provision of the Constitution, the court is entitled not to apply this [statutory] provision in the matter that it is adjudicating".[12] In view of this, since the late nineteenth century, judicial review of the constitutionality of legislation has traditionally rested on the Greek Constitution's rigid character and its position as the supreme law of the land.[13] Though less detailed, the Areios Pagos's reasoning is generally similar to the U.S. Supreme Court's reasoning in the seminal *Marbury v. Madison* decision,[14] although no direct influence has been identified.[15] Similarly, Greece's subsequent Constitutions of 1911 and 1952 – in contrast to the short-lived Constitution of 1927[16] – included no explicit provisions on judicial review of the constitutionality of legislation. However, the Areios Pagos, as well as the Council of State, since its first ruling after its establishment in 1929,[17] has continued to recognize the judicial power to refrain from applying unconstitutional legislation on a regular basis. As a result, judicial review of legislation gradually developed into a constitutional custom.

B. Judicial Review under the Greek Constitution of 1975

a. *Constitutional Basis of Judicial Review*

The 1975 Constitution, which was enacted after the restoration of democracy in Greece in the wake of a seven-year military dictatorship and

Liège/Hague 1967, 439–478 (445–455); Y. Drossos, *An Essay on Greek Constitutional Theory*, Athens-Komotini 1996, 181–200 [in Greek].

12 See Areios Pagos judgment nº 23/1897, *Themis* 1898, 329 (concerning the expropriation of land at Lake Kopaida).

13 On the concept of constitution in the Greek legal system, see generally J. Iliopoulos-Strangas & E. Prevedourou, Greece – Le droit de l'Union européenne et les Constitutions nationales, *in* British Institute of International and Comparative Law (ed.), *F.I.D.E., XX. Congress London 30 October–2 November 2002, Volume II: Reports and Conclusions*, London 2003, 259–366 (262–263).

14 5 U.S. 137 (1803).

15 See also A. Manitakis, *Greek Constitutional Law, Volume I: Fundamental Concepts*, Athens-Thessaloniki 2004, 461 [in Greek].

16 Art. 5 of the 1927 Constitution, providing that "judicial power is vested in independent courts subject only to the law," included an "interpretative clause" stipulating that "the true sense of this provision is that the courts have the duty not to apply statutes, if their contents are contrary to the constitution."

17 See Council of State judgment nº 1/1929, *Themis* 1929, 361.

that remains in force today,[18] added explicit provisions on judicial review of legislation pertaining to constitutional norms. The Constitution states that "the courts shall be bound not to apply a law with content that is contrary to the Constitution" (Art. 93, § 4). Additionally, the Constitution stipulates that "in no case whatsoever shall [judges] be obliged to comply with provisions enacted in violation of the Constitution" (Art. 87, § 2).

b. *Substantive and Procedural Constitutional Claims*

The wording of Art. 93, § 4, of the Constitution not only establishes an explicit constitutional foundation for judicial review of the constitutionality of legislation but, in accordance with long-standing judicial practice under previous Greek Constitutions, also provides a basis for differentiating between substantive and procedural claims of unconstitutionality. Accordingly, in contrast to substantive claims, no judicial review of statutory legislation is generally available to allege a violation of constitutional provisions on legislative procedure,[19] which is regarded as parliamentary *interna corporis*.[20] Greek courts tend to construe the *interna corporis* concept broadly. For instance, they exclude from judicial review of legislation provisions that refer to the lawmaking authority of the legislative body as such. One such example is Art. 72, § 1, of the Constitution, which lists several legislative matters, including bills and proposals that implement the Constitution in the exercise and protection of individual rights that should be debated and voted on in Parliament's plenum instead of its committees and sections.[21]

[18] Although the constitutional amendments of 1986 and 2008 had no bearing on judicial review of legislation, the 2001 amendments limited the judicial review power of the high court panels. See *infra* in the text (section I.B.2.d.).

[19] For an exception, see Art. 73 § 2 *alinea* c Const. (providing that "the insertion of provisions pertaining to pensions in bills introduced to regulate other matters, is not permitted under penalty of nullity").

[20] Parliamentary *interna corporis* is usually called internal formal constitutionality to distinguish it from external formal unconstitutionality, which is limited to the external attributes of statutes (i.e., promulgation by the President of the Republic and publication in the *Government Gazette*) and is subject to judicial review. See, e.g., K. Mavrias, *Constitutional Law* (4th ed., Athens-Komotini 2005), 318 [in Greek].

[21] See, e.g., Council of State judgment nos. 903/1981 (Full Bench), *To Syntagma* (=ToS) 1981, 701 (703) and 2185/1994, *Nomiko Vima* (=NoV) 1985, 922 (923) (denying judicial review of compliance with Art. 72 § 1 Const.). For a critical perspective, see, e.g., P. Dagtoglou, Judicial Review of Constitutionality of Laws, *European Review of Public Law/Revue européenne de droit publique* (=ERPL/REDP) 1989, 309–327 (314).

c. *Primary Features of Judicial Review*

The Greek system of judicial review has remained largely unchanged since the introduction of the judicial review power in the late nineteenth century. Accordingly, Greek courts generally follow a diffuse, incidental, and concrete system of review.[22] Generally speaking, all courts (civil, criminal, and administrative) of all levels are charged with the control of the constitutionality of statutes to the extent necessary for adjudicating a particular case. In the first place, the courts are required to respond to a claim of unconstitutionality put forward by a litigant, provided that he or she has standing. Moreover, the courts' constitutional obligation extends to reviewing the unconstitutionality of legislation *ex officio*, as well.[23] However, the Council of State has tended to consider judicial review *ex officio* as optional rather than obligatory for the courts.[24] In so doing, it has arguably failed to distinguish between the general obligation to review the unconstitutionality of legislation *ex officio* and the exceptional obligation to provide grounds for this review only when a litigant puts forth a claim of unconstitutionality or when the review results in a finding of unconstitutionality.[25]

Lacking a constitutional jurisdiction as such, structural (organizational) controversies among State organs are not subject to judicial resolution. Further, the Greek Constitution does not provide for a review of the constitutionality of statutes on an abstract basis (either before or after their

[22] See, in general, E. Spiliotopoulos, Judicial Review of Legislative Acts in Greece, *Temple Law Quarterly* 1983, 463–502; A. Manitakis, Fondement et légitimité du contrôle juridictionnel des lois en Grèce, *RIDC* 1988, 39–55; W. Skouris, Constitutional Disputes and Judicial Review in Greece, *in* Ch. Landfried (ed.), *Constitutional Review and Legislation. An International Comparison*, Baden-Baden 1988, 177–200; Dagtoglou, *supra* note 21, 309–327; J. Iliopoulos-Strangas and G. Leventis, Der Schutz der sozialen Grundrechte in der Rechtsordnung Griechenlands, *in* J. Iliopoulos-Strangas (ed.), *Soziale Grundrechte in Europa nach Lissabon – Eine rechtsvergleichende Untersuchung der nationalen Rechtsordnungen und des europäischen Rechts*, Baden-Baden/Athens/Brussels/Vienna 2010, 249–323 (294–297); Ph. Spyropoulos and Th. Fortsakis, *Constitutional Law in Greece*, Alphen aan den Rijn 2009, 206–207; S. I. Koutnatzis, Grundlagen und Grundzüge staatlichen Verfassungsrechts: Griechenland, *in* A.v. Bogdandy et al. (eds.), *Handbuch Ius Publicum Europaeum*, Volume I, Heidelberg 2007, 151–215 (186–188).

[23] See, e.g., Iliopoulos-Strangas and Leventis, *supra* 22, 295; see also A. Manitakis, Incidental Control of the (Un)constitutionality of Statutes and Judge's (Self)-Constraints, *ToS* 2006, 403–429 (426–427) [in Greek] (emphasizing that the *ex officio* control of the unconstitutionality of statutes requires that the procedural requirements of admissibility and standing are met).

[24] See, e.g., Council of State judgment n° 3195/2000, *Dikaiomata tou Anthropou* (=DtA) 2002, 1199 (1199).

[25] For a convincing critique, see K. Yannakopoulos, Reviewing the (Un)constitutionality of Statutes Ex Officio, *DtA* 2002, 1175–1193 (1177 et seq.) [in Greek].

entry into force), irrespective of a specific case.[26] By the same token, unlike Germany's constitutional complaint (*Verfassungsbeschwerde*), Greece's constitutional system offers no direct action to rule on the constitutionality of statutes. In addition, as a general matter,[27] no judicial remedies are available to directly challenge the legislature's failure to fulfill its constitutional obligations (e.g., in cases in which it does not implement the Constitution's social rights guarantees).[28] However, provided that the exercise of legislative duties is clearly constitutionally required, the state liability norms[29] offer an indirect means to compel the legislature to fulfill its constitutional duties. Although state liability for legislative acts had long been a controversial issue in Greece[30] – as it was recognized only exceptionally (e.g., in cases of property rights violations), in recent years, most scholars[31] and the courts[32] have increasingly recognized state liability, even in cases of legislative inaction.

Consistent with the formulation of Art. 93, § 4, of the Constitution, a statutory provision found by a court to be unconstitutional cannot be applied in a specific case before the court. Some scholars argue that the establishment of unconstitutionality cannot serve to help reinstate an older law, unless Parliament clearly links the abolition of the law with its replacement by new provisions.[33] According to this approach, the revival of the previous legal regime would undermine the Constitution's institutional balance, thus making the courts a positive legislator that competes with

[26] Exceptionally, the Court of Audit is charged with issuing advisory opinions concerning bills on pensions or on the recognition of service for granting the right to a pension (Art. 98 § 1 d Const.), which encompasses *inter alia* constitutional considerations.

[27] But see the Council of State's far-reaching jurisprudence on environmental matters; on this issue, see *infra* section II.B.2. of this report.

[28] See generally D. Tsatsos, *Constitutional Law – Fundamental Rights: General Part*, Athens-Komotini 1988, 212 [in Greek] (arguing for political rather than legal remedies in cases of legislative inaction); but see Iliopoulos-Strangas and Leventis, *supra* 22, 296–297 (countering that the constitutional provisions on judicial review of the constitutionality of legislation do not differentiate between acts and omissions of the legislature).

[29] The basic provision for state liability for unlawful damage caused by public servants in the Greek legal system is Art. 105 of the Introductory Law to the Civil Code.

[30] See in detail P. Pavlopoulos, *The State's Civil Liability*, Volume II.A., Athens-Komotini 1989, 142 et seq., 152 et seq. [in Greek].

[31] See, e.g., P. Dagtoglou, *General Administrative Law* [updated by P.-M. Efstratiou] (5th ed., Athens-Komotini 2004) 1014 et seq. [in Greek]; J. Iliopoulos-Strangas, La responsabilité de l'Etat en tant que legislateur, *RHDI* 1998, 311–336 (321 et seq.).

[32] Cf., e.g., Areios Pagos judgment n° 13/1992 (Full Bench), *Elliniki Dikaiossini* (=EllDni) 1992, 1432 (1432–1433); Athens Administrative Court of Appeals judgment n° 2174/1991, *Dioikitiki Diki* (=DiDik) 1991, 1141 et seq.

[33] See Dagtoglou, *supra* note 21, 319–320.

Parliament in lawmaking. However, the existence of a statutory gap, following a ruling of unconstitutionality, can fail to meet constitutional requirements. Therefore, the courts can revive the previous legal regime or apply legislative provisions with similar content.[34] In any event, the courts normally have no power to strike down a statutory provision found to be unconstitutional. Rather, unconstitutional provisions remain generally valid and can be applied in future cases.

d. *Means of Concentration of Review*

Despite adopting a diffuse approach to judicial review as a matter of principle, in fact, the availability of legal remedies against judicial decisions,[35] the lower courts' standard practice of following the pronouncements of the high courts, and the constitutionally based option for individuals to directly challenge executive acts before the Council of State,[36] have resulted in a substantial concentration of judicial review. Consequently, some scholars consider the Council of State as Greece's constitutional court par excellence.[37]

In addition, however, as a matter of principle, the diffuse system of judicial review had no exceptions under the previous Greek Constitutions, the 1975 Constitution directly qualified this approach to foster legal certainty and consistency. On condition that high courts of different jurisdictions have issued conflicting judgments on the substantive unconstitutionality (or interpretation) of a statutory provision, the Constitution provides a conflict-

[34] See Iliopoulos-Strangas, *supra* notes 87–89; see also Ch. Tsiliotis, An Overview of the Application of the Greek System of Control of the Constitutionality of Statutes in Light of the Discussion on the Establishment of a Constitutional Court in Greece – Quo vadis?, *ToS* 2006, 1117–1156 (1144) [in Greek].

[35] Apart from appeals initiated by the litigants themselves, Greek procedural law provides the so-called revision in favor of the law, which may be initiated by the Public Prosecutor of the Areios Pagos in civil and criminal cases and by the Minister in charge or the General Commissioner of State in administrative cases; see respectively Code of Civil Procedure, Art. 557; Code of Criminal Procedure, Art. 505 § 2; Presidential Decree nº 18/1989, Art. 53 § 5.

[36] See *infra* note 78 and accompanying text.

[37] Cf., e.g., E. Venizelos, The Particularities of the Greek System of Judicial Control of the Constitutionality of Legislation: A Factor of Intensive or Limited Scrutiny? *in* E. Venizelos (ed.), *The Interpretation of the Constitution and the Limits of Judicial Review of the Constitutionality of Legislation*, Athens-Komotini 1994, 13–32 (15–18) [in Greek]; A. Manitakis, *The Establishment of a Constitutional Court*, Athens-Thessaloniki 2008, 30 [in Greek]; for an illustrating comparison between the Greek Council of State and the U.S. Supreme Court, see G. Gerapetritis, Balance of Powers and Judicial Interventionism: Comparative Thoughts on the Function of the Greek Council of State and the United States Supreme Court, *in Jubilee Book for the Council of State – 75 Years*, Athens-Thessaloniki 2004, 197–227 [in Greek].

resolution mechanism. The Constitution requires Greece's high courts – the Council of State, Areios Pagos, and Court of Audit – to refer issues of unconstitutionality (or interpretation) of this statutory provision to the Supreme Special Court,[38] which is charged with settling the conflict (Art. 100, § 1, Const.).[39] In the meantime, any judicial proceedings that depend on the outcome of the Supreme Special Court's consideration of the matter are suspended.[40] The Constitution explicitly provides that the Supreme Special Court's judgments are irrevocable (Art. 100, § 4, *alinea* a Const.), thus preventing all forms of subsequent appeal to the Supreme Special Court and all other judicial or nonjudicial bodies. The Supreme Special Court declares unconstitutional statutory provisions to be invalid *erga omnes* (i.e., not only inapplicable) as of the date of publication of the respective judgment (*ex nunc*) or as of the date specified in the ruling (Art. 100, § 4, *alinea* b Const.). In light of this, the Supreme Special Court assumes the duties of a negative legislator,[41] thus prompting constitutional scholars to call it a quasi-constitutional court.[42] Nevertheless, the Supreme Special Court adopted a strict approach regarding admissibility, requiring the high courts of different jurisdictions to directly apply the same statutory provision to establish the Supreme Special Court's conflict-resolving power.[43] Although the Supreme Special Court has relaxed this requirement in recent years,[44] the high courts of each jurisdiction, as expected, have been applying different sets of statutes. As a result, rarely is the requirement of a previous jurisdictional conflict met to establish the Supreme Special Court's jurisdiction.

38 Provided that the conflicting judgments requirement is met, ordinary legislation gives every individual with standing (as well as public officials, such as the Minister of Justice and the Public Prosecutor of the Areios Pagos) the right to bring a motion to the Supreme Special Court (see Act nº 345/1976 [Supreme Special Court Code], Art. 48).

39 For details on this procedure, see P. Dagtoglou, Die Verfassungsgerichtsbarkeit in Griechenland, *in* Ch. Starck & A. Weber (eds.), *Verfassungsgerichtsbarkeit in Westeuropa* (2nd ed., Baden-Baden 2007), 289–311; Iliopoulos-Strangas, *supra* note 6,,75–91.

40 See Act nº 345/1976 [Supreme Special Court Code], Art. 50 § 3.

41 Consistent with this, Act nº 345/1976 [Supreme Special Court Code] requires in Art. 21 § 2 the publication of the Supreme Special Court's judgments in a special issue of the *Government Gazette*.

42 Cf., e.g., Dagtoglou, *supra* note 39, 292; see also Iliopoulos-Strangas, *supra* note, 79: "Cour … plutôt … de compétences constitutionnelles que constitutionnelle."

43 For an overview, see C. Bacoyannis, The Supreme Special Court Institution – 20 Years in Retrospect, *in 20 Years 1975 Constitution*, Athens-Komotini 1998, 311–337 (321–322) [in Greek].

44 Cf. Supreme Special Court Judgment nº 27/1999, *ToS* 2000, 150 (152–153) (finding it sufficient that a high court judgment indirectly construes the same statutory provision as another high court). See also P. Pararas, The Interpretative Extension of the Supreme Special Court's Jurisdiction, *ToS* 2000, 145–150 [in Greek].

Consequently, the invalidation of a parliamentary statute following a Supreme Special Court ruling has occurred only in exceptional circumstances.[45] In addition, the Supreme Special Court's power does not extend to conflicts between high courts based on the interpretation of a constitutional (versus statutory) provision.[46] Despite these caveats, in view of the Supreme Special Court's jurisdiction in constitutional matters, Greece's judicial review system under the 1975 Constitution reflects a mixture of both diffuse and concentrated elements. Accordingly, despite the usual classification of the Greek system as following the American model of judicial review,[47] the Greek system does not neatly fit the traditional definition of the American or the European system of constitutional adjudication.[48]

Greece's 2001 constitutional revision raised an additional, and quite controversial, qualification of the diffuse system of judicial review. When high court panels (i.e., sections of the Council of State, the Areios Pagos, or the Court of Audit) find a statutory provision unconstitutional, they are bound to refer the issue to the respective plenum (Art. 100, § 5, *alinea* a Const.). The only exception to this obligation is when the issue of the provision's constitutionality has been adjudicated by a previous decision of the plenum or of the Supreme Special Court (Art. 100, § 5, *alinea* b Const.). As a result, high court panels have less power to exercise judicial review of the constitutionality of legislation than lower courts, the latter having no obligation to refer the adjudication of a claim of unconstitutionality to another body.[49] In practice, however, high court plenums generally follow the high court panel's position on the issue of constitutionality.[50] As for the

45 For examples of invalidation of parliamentary statutes ordered by the Supreme Special Court, see Iliopoulos-Strangas and Leventis, *supra* note 22, 264.

46 See Supreme Special Court judgment n° 38/1989, *DiDik* 1990, 274 (274–275) as opposed to the Supreme Special Court's earlier case law that accepted its power to resolve controversies on interpretations of constitutional provisions, see judgment n° 16/1983, *Epitheorissi Ergatikou Dikaiou* (=EErgD) 1984, 249 (250).

47 See, e.g., Manitakis, *supra* note 15, 460–462.

48 See also Kassimatis, *supra* note 8, 39.

49 For a critical perspective, see, e.g., P. Pararas, The Control of Constitutionality of Legislation at the Target of the Revision, *DtA* 2001, 75–81 [in Greek]; S. Vlachopoulos, The Control of Constitutionality of Legislation by High Court Sections, *DtA* 2001, 83–97 [in Greek]; for a defense of the amendment's rationale see E. Venizelos, *The "Acquis" of the Constitutional Revision*, Athens-Komotini 2002, 363–367 [in Greek].

50 For empirical data on the first years of application of the revised Art. 100 § 5 Const., see Aik. Sakellaropoulou, The Control of Constitutionality of Legislation under Art. 100 § 5 Const. Procedural Organisation of Control or Limitation of Diffuse Control?, *in* A. Manitakis & A. Fotiadou (eds.), *The Constitutional Court in a System of Incidental Control of Constitutionality of Legislation*, Athens-Thessaloniki 2008, 23–46 (39–42) [in Greek] (pointing out that the

consequences of the plenum's holding of unconstitutionality, the Constitution does not empower high court plenums to strike down parliamentary statutes. The latter power rests exclusively with the Supreme Special Court. Accordingly, a high court plenum's finding of unconstitutionality results in the statute being inapplicable in the specific case pending before the court but will remain in the books and could apply in future cases.[51]

e. *The Proposal to Establish a Constitutional Court*

The constitutional documents of 1968 and 1973, drafted by the military dictatorship that ruled Greece from 1967 to 1974, provided the legal underpinnings for the establishment of a so-called Constitutional Court. However, the documents conferred on the Constitutional Court limited functions that essentially never entered into force. More recently, following proposals in the mid-1990s, the conservative government party proposed a constitutional court in 2005.[52] Important specifics of the proposal, such as the selection method of constitutional court judges, remained largely vague. In general, if this constitutional court were to have been established, all courts of all jurisdictions and levels would have retained the power to review the constitutionality of all legislation. At the same time, however, the courts would have been required to initially refer any issue of unconstitutionality of statutes to the high court plenum of their jurisdiction. In addition, the amendment would have required the high court plenums to refer questions of unconstitutionality of statutes to a constitutional court that would have replaced the Supreme Special Court currently provided in Art. 100 of the Constitution. As a result, if this proposed constitutional amendment had been enacted, the constitutional court would have become the sole Greek court authorized to declare a statutory provision unconstitutional and thus inapplicable. Accordingly, the proposal would have created an extensive concentration of the review system.

Council of State's plenum has followed the panel's opinion of unconstitutionality in twenty-two out of twenty-five cases adjudicated under the revised Art. 100 § 5 Const. until March 2007); see also M. Pikramenos, The Control of Constitutionality of Legislation under Art. 100 § 5 Const. and the Problem of the Constitutional Court, *in* X. Contiades (ed.), *Five Years after the 2001 Constitutional Revision*, Volume 2, Athens-Komotini 2006, 775–811 (808–809) [in Greek].

51 See, e.g., Mavrias, *supra* note 20, 324.

52 The text of the proposal has been published *in ToS* 2006, 823–845 (841–843) [in Greek].

Although the government's proposed constitutional amendment did not garner the necessary bipartisan support to pass,[53] it generated considerable debate in Greece over the system of judicial review. In an advisory opinion, the Council of State took a unanimous position against the reform proposal, arguing that it would negatively affect the rule of law and undermine the protection of fundamental rights.[54] Constitutional scholars voiced a wider spectrum of views on this proposal. Several scholars argued in favor of establishing a constitutional court, citing gaps and inconsistencies in the existing judicial review system[55] and putting forward comparative law arguments.[56] In contrast, other scholars focused on potential jurisdictional conflicts, uncertainties and delays that would result from implementing this reform.[57] Regarding the scope of the reform, some scholars painstakingly emphasized that the establishment of a constitutional court would not have ended the diffuse judicial review system but merely modified its application mainly in its margins,[58] whereas others viewed the proposal as a radical change to the existing judicial review system.[59] Accordingly, some scholars argued that the diffuse system is so deeply ingrained in Greece's

[53] On the complicated constitutional amendment process, see Art. 110 §§ 2–6 Const. (mandating passage of the amendment proposal in two consecutive legislative periods with a qualified majority at least in one of these periods and requiring the lapse of five years between amendments).

[54] See Council of State opinion nos. 5/2006, *NoV* 2006, 1154 and 4/2007, *Armenopoulos* (=Arm) 2007, 1395; see also opinion n° 6/2000, available at Enossi Dikastikon Leitourgon tou Symvouliou tis Epikrateias (ed.), *The Revision of the Constitution and the Council of State*, Athens-Komotini 2001, 27–53 (48) [in Greek].

[55] See, e.g., E. Venizelos, The Establishment of a Constitutional Court in the Context of the Greek System of Judicial Review of the Constitutionality of Legislation, *in* E. Venizelos and K. Chryssogonos, *The Problem of Constitutional Adjudication in Greece*, Athens-Komotini 2006, 11–47 (29–35) [in Greek]. For an important earlier contribution, see Kassimatis, *supra* note 8, 115–120 (120) (arguing that the introduction of a distinct constitutional jurisdiction is a "historical necessity").

[56] For an extensive comparative overview, see K. Chryssogonos, Present and Future of Constitutional Adjudication in Greece, *in* Venizelos and Chryssogonos (eds.), *supra* note 55, 49–125 (64–102) [in Greek]; but see V. Ferreres Comella, The European model of constitutional review of legislation: Toward decentralization?, *International Journal of Constitutional Law* 2004, 461–491 (470 et seq.) (highlighting internal and external pressures to decentralize constitutional review).

[57] See especially Manitakis, *supra* note 50, 5–53; see also K. Menoudakos, The Constitutional Court in a System of Incidental Judicial Review of the Constitutionality of Legislation, *in* Manitakis & Fotiadou, *supra* note 50, 3–12 (6–11) [in Greek].

[58] See, e.g., Venizelos, *supra* note 55, 32.

[59] See, e.g., Manitakis, *supra* note 37, 12–13; see also A. Rantos, The Revision Proposal to Establish a Constitutional Court in Greece, in Manitakis & Fotiadou, *supra* note 50, 13–22 (21) [in Greek].

constitutional tradition that it is part of the nonamendable[60] principles of rule of law and separation of powers of the Greek Constitution – more particularly, the constitutionally entrenched right of each litigant to demand a review of the constitutionality of legislation in the course of litigating cases.[61] The significant prevalence of the concentrated model of judicial review in modern constitutional systems counters this last assumption.[62]

Nevertheless, reflecting a comparative paradox, critical observers of Greece's political and legal developments reasonably considered the proposal to establish a distinct constitutional court as the government's attempt to silence criticism of the legislative and executive branches on constitutional grounds. Accordingly, the proposal to establish a constitutional court seemed to emanate from substantive perceptions of judicial overreaching.[63] Regardless of the validity of the notion that the proposed constitutional court would in fact be predisposed to provide justification and legitimacy to the political branches of government,[64] its implementation would have established, through the double-reference procedure, two additional judicial filters to enable holdings of unconstitutionality. Conversely, it would have left untouched the judicial power to uphold the constitutionality of legislation,[65] thus constitutionalizing an onerous presumption of constitutionality of statutes. In contrast, the proposal largely failed to address the systemic deficits of constitutional

60 According to Art. 110 § 1 Const. "the provisions of the Constitution shall be subject to revision with the exception of those which determine the form of government as a Parliamentary Republic and those of Art. 2 § 1 [human dignity], 4 §§ 1, 4 and 7 [equality before the law, eligibility of Greek citizens only for public service, nonrecognition of titles of nobility or distinction], 5 §§ 1 and 3 [right of all persons to develop their personality, personal liberty], 13 § 1 [freedom of religious conscience], and 26 [separation of powers]."

61 See especially Manitakis, *supra* note 37, 15–19, 113–115; see also Ph. Spyropoulos, *Introduction to Constitutional Law*, Athens 2006, 148 [in Greek]; G. Tassopoulos, The Constitutional Position of the Judiciary in our Political System, in D. Tsatsos et al. (eds.), *The New Constitution*, Athens-Komotini 2001, 357–384 (371–372, 375–377) [in Greek].

62 See also Chryssogonos, *supra* note 56, 111–113.

63 See, e.g., Manitakis, *supra* note 37, 33; G. Tassopoulos, *Institutional Checks and Balances and the Revision of the Constitution*, Athens-Thessaloniki 2007, 182 [in Greek]; Cf. in this light the jurisprudence on the equality principle and environmental protection, *infra* section II.B.

64 See emphatically Manitakis, *supra* note 37, 15, 36, 44, 109; but see D. Tsatsos, Towards a Greek Polity of Judges? Why I Ultimately Disagree with the Establishment of a Constitutional Court, *in* D. Tsatsos (ed.), The Revision of the Constitution, Athens 2006, 37–48 (42) [in Greek] (arguing against the establishment of a Constitutional Court to avoid considerably limiting the primacy of political decisions).

65 On this inconsistency, see critically Chryssogonos, *supra* note 56, 110; Ch. Yeraris, Reform or Development of the Supreme Special Court, in Manitakis and Fotiadou, *supra* note 50, 121–133 [in Greek].

adjudication in Greece, such as the unavailability of a direct constitutional complaint,[66] an abstract review procedure,[67] and the lack of a judicial avenue to address procedural constitutional claims[68] and disputes of an organizational nature (e.g., conflicts between State organs).[69]

f. *Control of Conventionality*

Although the Greek Constitution has no explicit provision for the control of conventionality of statutes, Greek courts consider the supralegislative status of international treaties based on Art. 28, § 1, of the Constitution[70] as sufficient basis to control conventionality,[71] if the treaty in question is self-executing. The quintessential example of a self-executing treaty is the European Convention on Human Rights (ECHR);[72] however, scholars disagree on whether the control of conventionality can occur *ex officio*[73] or

[66] See also Tsiliotis, *supra* note 34, 1155–1156.

[67] For establishing an abstract review procedure on both a repressive and preventive basis, see Venizelos, *supra* note 50, 33–34; see also St. Matthias, The Constitutional Court, *in* Manitakis and Fotiadou, *supra* note 50, 109–119 (114–115) [in Greek]; Yeraris, *supra* note 65, 131 (both suggesting in essence the introduction of a preventive review of an abstract nature).

[68] See, e.g., Kassimatis, *supra* note 8, 118 (arguing in favour of this review).

[69] See also N. Alivizatos, Do We Need a Constitutional Court? (1992), in N. Alivizatos (ed.), The Uncertain Modernisation and the Opaque Constitutional Amendment, Athens 2001, 54–65 (64) [in Greek]; Chryssogonos, *supra* note 56, 50–51, 101, 120 (identifying in this respect a serious deficit in Greece's judicial protection system and arguing in favour of judicial power to adjudicate such controversies); but see E. Venizelos, *Courses in Constitutional Law* (2nd ed., Athens-Komotini 2008), 266 [in Greek] (suggesting that the adjudication of structural constitutional disputes would undermine judicial authority).

[70] According to Art. 28 § 1 Const. "the generally recognized rules of international law, as well as international conventions as of the time they are ratified by statute and become operative according to their respective conditions, shall be an integral part of domestic Greek law and shall prevail over any contrary provision of the law."

[71] On control of conventionality, see, e.g., I. Ö. Kaboğlu and S. I. Koutnatzis, The Reception Process in Greece and Turkey, *in* Helen Keller and Alec Stone Sweet (eds.), *A Europe of Rights – The Impact of the ECHR on National Legal Systems*, Oxford/New York 2008, 451–529 (464–466) with further references.

[72] See, e.g., Ph. Vegleris, Statut de la Convention des droits de l'homme dans le droit grec, *in Mélanges dédiés à Robert Pelloux*, Lyon 1980, 299–318 (303); D. Briolas, L'application de la Convention Européenne des Droits de l'Homme dans l'ordre juridique des États contractants: Théorie et pratique helléniques, *in* J. Iliopoulos-Strangas (ed.), *Grundrechtsschutz im europäischen Raum/La protection des droits de l'homme dans le cadre européen*, Baden-Baden 1993, 82–116 (87, 90); St. Perrakis, Le juge grec et la Cour de Strasbourg, *in* P. Tavernier (ed.), *Quelle Europe pour les droits de l'homme?*, Brussels 1996, 171–187 (175).

[73] See G. Papadimitriou, The Internationalization and Communitization of Judicial Protection, *NoV* 44 (1996), 569–576 (571) [in Greek]; K. Chryssogonos, *The Incorporation of the European Convention on Human Rights in the Greek Legal Order*, Athens-Komotini 2001, 225 [in Greek].

only after a corresponding claim of a litigant.[74] Similar to the control of constitutionality, if Greek courts have found that a statutory provision is inconsistent with international law, the provision cannot be applied in the pending case. However, unconventional legislation remains in effect and thus can be applied on a future occasion.

Despite this general convergence, some differences remain between the courts' control of constitutionality and conventionality of statutes. First, in contrast to the control of constitutionality, when Greece's high courts reach conflicting judgments on the compatibility of a statute with international human rights law, there is no conflict-resolving mechanism to which courts or parties can turn.[75] Consequently, different supreme courts may hold varying doctrinal positions on the interpretation of international human rights treaties. Similarly, the obligatory reference to the respective high court plenum does not apply to cases of statutes found to be inconsistent with the ECHR[76] or another international human rights treaty that has been incorporated into Greek domestic law. In fact, some scholars predict that, in the future, the control of conventionality will outweigh the control of constitutionality, thereby permitting high court panels to evade the obligatory reference procedure.[77]

g. *Control of Executive Acts*

In terms of judicial review of executive acts, Greek administrative courts review the constitutionality and legality of administrative actions,[78] including both individual and general measures (i.e., in the terminology of Greek administrative law, individual and normative administrative acts). Although the courts generally exercise judicial review of statutes on an incidental basis and do not apply unconstitutional (or unconventional) statutes, but leave

74 See, e.g., Briolas, *supra* note 72, 94.

75 Cf. also Supreme Special Court judgment nº 29/1999, *EllDni* 2000, 1565–1566 (no jurisdiction in the case of conflicting judgments on the compatibility of a Greek statute with European community law).

76 Cf. Council of State judgment nº 372/2005, *DtA* 2005, 1329 (1341).

77 See F. Arnaoutoglou, Grèce: Le Conseil d'Etat, *in* J. Iliopoulos-Strangas (ed.), *Cours suprêmes nationales et cours européennes: concurrence ou collaboration?*, Athens-Brussels, 2007, 179–185 (184–185).

78 See, in general, E. Spiliotopoulos, Le contrôle juridictionnel de l'action administrative, *in* E. Spiliotopoulos & A. Makrydimitris (eds.), *L'Administration Publique en Grèce*, Athens-Komotini 2001, 123–140; P.-M. Efstratiou, Die gerichtliche Kontrolle administrativer Entscheidungen im griechischen Bau-, Umwelt- und Wirtschaftsverwaltungsrecht, *in* J. Schwarze & E. Schmidt-Aßmann (eds.), *Das Ausmaß der gerichtlichen Kontrolle im Wirtschaftsverwaltungs- und Umweltrecht*, Baden-Baden 1992, 111–202 (116 et seq.).

them in force, the Greek Constitution establishes (in addition to incidental review of executive acts) the direct jurisdiction of the Council of State "to annul[] upon petition enforceable acts of the administrative authorities for excess of power or violation of the law" (Art. 95, § 1, *alinea* a Const.). Contrary to judicial review of statutory legislation, judicial review of executive acts extends not only to positive actions but also to executive organs' omissions despite their obligation to act. Nonetheless, judicial review of executive omissions cannot result in the courts' taking over the role of an executive body and enacting an executive act.[79] Rather, administrative courts refer such cases to the competent executive agency so that the latter can carry out the required action.

Recent Council of State decisions have tended to qualify the usual dichotomy between judicial review of legislative and executive acts. Thus, responding to the political branches' occasional tendency to enact planning regulations of an individual nature per statute to bypass direct judicial review, the Council of State has emphasized that this practice is constitutionally permissible only exceptionally and subject to judicial scrutiny.[80] Furthermore, in a 2008 preliminary ruling, a Council of State section ruled that courts could directly challenge legislative acts that include individual measures (i.e., planning regulations that do not require for their implementation executive acts).[81] It remains to be seen whether the Council of State's plenary session will side with this approach, which would significantly modify Greece's judicial review system.

In addition, concerning decrees of a general regulatory nature (i.e., presidential decrees), the Greek Constitution provides for their review from the Council of State before their enactment on an abstract basis (Art. 95, § 1, *alinea* d, Const.). Although the findings of this preventive review are neither legally binding nor limited to constitutional considerations, the executive branch consistently adheres to them as a matter of practice and modifies the decrees before enacting them on the basis of the Council of State's recommendations.

[79] See, e.g., Iliopoulos-Strangas and Leventis, *supra* note 22, 298.

[80] Council of State (Full Bench) judgment n° 1847/2008, *ToS* 2008, 708 (715–716).

[81] Council of State judgment n° 391/2008, *Efimerida Dioikitikou Dikaiou* (=EfimDD) 2008, 184 et seq.

h. *Control of Constitutional Amendments*

Constitutional scholars disagree as to whether Art. 93, § 4, of the Constitution –the predominant constitutional source of judicial review in Greece– encompasses judicial review of constitutional amendments. However, in effect, most scholars agree that courts are authorized to monitor both compliance with substantive amendment limits enumerated in Art. 110, § 1, of the Constitution,[82] and adherence to the amendment procedure provided in Art. 110, §§ 2–6, of the Constitution.[83] The amendment provision as such (Art. 110 Const.) as well as Art. 1, § 3, of the Constitution, which stipulates that "[all powers] shall be exercised as specified by the Constitution" amount to an adequate constitutional basis for this approach in conjunction with the Constitution's rigid character and the general constitutional provisions on judicial review of the constitutionality of legislation (Art. 87, § 2, and Art. 93, § 4).[84] Greek courts have affirmed their power to engage in judicial review of constitutional amendments without specifying the exact constitutional basis or engaging in any meaningful scrutiny of constitutional amendments.[85]

II. THE APPLICATION OF JUDICIAL REVIEW

From a formal perspective, most scholars agree that judicial decisions –with the sole exception of Supreme Special Court decisions that strike down a parliamentary statute (Art. 100, § 4, *alinea* 2 Const.)[86]– do not constitute a source of law in Greece.[87] Accordingly, Greek courts' decisions in constitutional matters generally have no force of precedent and their legal effect is limited *inter partes*. As a matter of constitutional law, the same court in a future occasion, along with other courts and the political branches of the State, have no obligation to follow a previous judicial interpretation of the Constitution.

82 See *supra* note 60.

83 See *supra* note 53.

84 See, e.g., Tassopoulos, *supra* note 63, 199–202 with further references; but see Manitakis, *supra* note 15, 330 (suggesting that judicial review is limited to the substantive amendment limits and does not encompass compliance with the amendment procedure).

85 For an example of judicial review of the constitutional amendment procedure, see Supreme Special Court judgment n° 11/2003, *DtA* 2009, 553 (555–556).

86 See *supra* section I.B.2.d.

87 See, e.g., Spyropoulos & Fortsakis, *supra* note 22, 78; but see E. Spiliotopoulos, *Greek Administrative Law*, Athens-Brussels 2004, Nr. 64, who considers the Council of State's administrative law decisions as sources of law.

Ingrained in a civil law tradition, Greek judges have long adopted a deferential approach to the legislative and executive branches of government, regularly privileging parliamentary sovereignty over fundamental rights and scrupulously protecting state interests at every cost.[88] However, in recent years, Greek courts have increasingly played a vital role in fleshing out and developing constitutional standards. The following section briefly summarizes Greek courts' application of judicial review of the constitutionality of legislation and describes manifestations of both judicial restraint and judicial activism (see section A). Following this, we examine aspects in the application of judicial review of the constitutionality of legislation that involves the exercise of a legislative function in a positive respect or the judicial encroachment on legislative and executive prerogatives (see section B)..

1. *The Development of Constitutional Jurisprudence*

A. The Greek Courts' Deferential Tradition

Despite Greece's comparatively early recognition of judicial review of legislation as a matter of principle, traditionally Greek courts have failed to meaningfully and consistently scrutinize the constitutionality of legislation. Rather, emphasizing the need to respect legislative prerogatives, the courts have typically considered the mere existence of legislation that restricts constitutional rights as a sufficient basis to uphold its constitutionality. Accordingly, Greek courts have long operated on the basis of a substantive presumption of constitutionality of statutes and have extended this presumption far beyond a procedural assumption of validity until a judicial pronouncement is made.[89] Consequently, they have considerably overestimated the presumption's legal importance.[90] Consistent with this,

88 See, e.g., N. Alivizatos, The Presidency, Parliament and the Courts in the 1980s, *in* R. Clogg (ed.), *Greece 1981–89. The Populist Decade*, London 1993, 65–77 (71) (pointing out that the Greek judge acts "more as an agent of the state than as an independent arbitrator"); see also K. Yannakopoulos, Rights in the Council of State's Case Law, in M. Tsapogas and D. Christopoulos (eds.), *Rights in Greece 1953–2003*, Athens 2004, 439–468 (456) [in Greek].

89 For arguments in this vein, see, e.g., Yannakopoulos, supra note 24, 1181–1184 and Fn. 12.

90 On the presumption of constitutionality, see generally Venizelos, *supra* note 69, 258–259; for a critical perspective, see, e.g., N. Alivizatos, The "Presumption of Constitutionality of Statutes" – Interpretive Indication or Political Call?, *in* Aristoteleio Panepistimio Thessalonikis (ed.), *Essays in Honour of Aristovoulos Manessis*, Volume 1, Thessaloniki 1994, 63–76 (71–75) [in Greek]; G. Tassopoulos, The Role of the Judge in Reviewing the Constitutionality of Legislation: Self-Restraint or Activism?, *in 20 Years 1975 Constitution, supra* note 43, 339–386 (355–362) [in Greek]; Ph. Spyropoulos, Die Vermutung der Verfassungsmäßigkeit der Gesetze und die

Greek courts have regularly failed to use the proportionality test to resolve cases that pit a rights-based claim against a public-interest justification for the infringement of that right. For instance, during the 1950s and 1960s, when the Greek courts exceptionally cited the ECHR, they tended to cite the limitation clauses in Arts. 8–11, § 2, of the ECHR[91] to assert that legislative and administrative measures were not inconsistent with the ECHR, but they failed to engage in a necessity review of these measures.[92] The courts' deferential position to the political branches of government persisted throughout most of the 1970s and 1980s.

To avoid reaching a holding of unconstitutionality, Greek courts have regularly interpreted statutory law as conforming to the Constitution.[93] In so doing, however, they have occasionally interpreted the Constitution to be in accordance with statutory law rather than conversely, or they have exceeded the permissible limits of interpretation to avoid reaching a judgment of unconstitutionality. For instance, the Council of State construed the statutorily required permission of the Orthodox Church for the construction of religious sites of other denominations –against the wording of the statutory law in force at the time– to be a mere nonbinding opinion for the executive branch.[94] On the basis of this interpretation, the Council of State found no violation of religious freedom according to the Greek Constitution and the ECHR. In construing statutory legislation contrary to its wording, however, the Council of State substituted its own formulation for that of the Parliament, thus arguably engaging in positive legislation.

verfassungskonforme Gesetzesauslegung, *in* G. Kassimatis & M. Stolleis (eds.), *Verfassungsgeschichte und Staatsrechtslehre. Griechisch-deutsche Wechselwirkungen*, Frankfurt am Main 2001, 283–290 (287–290).

91 Arts. 8–11 § 2 ECHR lists legitimate grounds for restricting the right to respect for private and family life, freedom of thought, conscience and religion, freedom of expression and freedom of assembly and association, provided these restrictions are "necessary in a democratic society."

92 See, e.g., the Council of State (Full Bench) judgment n° 607/1967, *Epitheorissi Dimossiou Dikaiou & Dioikitikou Dikaiou* (=EDDD) 1967, 183–184 (exclusion of citizens from working in a public transportation company because of their possible political allegiances); see also the Council of State (Full Bench) judgment n° 575/1966, *EDDD* 1966, 311–312 (justification of civil mobilisation by reference to Art. 4 § 3 c ECHR).

93 For an overview, see, e.g., Ph. Doris, Statutory Interpretation with Reference to Constitutional Provisions in the Civil Courts' Case Law, *EllDni* 1991, 1188–1198 [in Greek]; K. Chryssogonos, Statutory Interpretation in Conformity with the Constitution in the Council of State's Case Law, *ToS* 1994, 223–279 [in Greek] both with further references.

94 See Council of State (Full Bench) judgment n° 1444/1991, *NoV* 1991, 626 (627).

B. Phases in the Judicial Implementation of the 1975 Constitution

In terms of the interplay between judicial restraint and judicial activism, the implementation of the Greek Constitution of 1975 can be viewed in four phases.[95]

In the initial phase, in the first years after the 1975 Constitution was in force, the judicial implementation of the Constitution oscillated between traditional and new elements. In most cases, the courts made no use of the new Constitution's potential to conscientiously and comprehensively protect fundamental rights. For instance, the courts narrowly construed the "right of a person to a prior hearing" before administrative actions or measures,[96] despite the unqualified wording of Art. 20, § 2, of the Constitution; they derived no justiciable obligation from Art. 22, § 4, of the Constitution, providing that "the State shall care for the social security of the working people";[97] and they avoided a broad interpretation of Art. 22, § 2, of the Constitution, which guarantees labor's collective bargaining.[98] Nonetheless, on some occasions, for instance, in cases involving the freedom of expression[99] and press[100] and the constitutional protection of the environment,[101] the Council of State relativized its customary deferential position in exercising judicial review of the constitutionality of legislation.

The second period of the Constitution's judicial implementation coincided with the socialist government's ascendancy to power, from 1981 to 1989. During this eight-year period, the relationship between the State's political

95 For further analysis, see also Koutnatzis, *supra* note 22, 171–176.

96 See, e.g., Council of State judgment nos. 1905/1977, *ToS* 1977, 455 (456–457) and 3417/1998, *ToS* 1979, 110 (111).

97 See, e.g., K. Kremalis, Der Verfassungsschutz des Rechts auf Sozialversicherung der Arbeitnehmer nach der griechischen Rechtsprechung, *in* F. Ruland et al. (eds.), *Verfassung, Theorie und Praxis des Sozialstaats. Festschrift für Hans F. Zacher zum 70. Geburtstag*, Heidelberg 1998, 441–455.

98 See, e.g., Council of State (Full Bench) judgment nº 632/1978, *ToS* 1978, 178 (180–181); Areios Pagos (Full Bench) judgment nº 626/1980, *ToS* 1981, 110 (111–112).

99 Cf., e.g., Council of State judgment nº 2209/1977, *ToS* 1977, 636 (637) (emphasizing that limitations of the military personnel's freedom of expression should not abrogate the "core" of the freedom of expression).

100 See, e.g., Council of State (Full Bench) judgment nº 903/1981, *ToS* 1981, 701 (704–705) (holding that the statutory delegation for the executive branch to determine the minimum allowed price of newspapers violates the Constitution's freedom of press guarantee).

101 See, e.g., the Council of State (Full Bench) judgment nº 811/1977, *ToS* 1977, 442 (445) (directly deducing from Art. 24 Const. the executive branch's obligation to consider environmental aspects in the weighing of interests).

and judicial branches was intensely debated.[102] As a matter of principle, the courts adopted a deferential approach, recognizing the legislative and executive branches' need for significant leeway.[103] Accordingly, the courts have upheld the constitutionality of controversial statutes, such as the reform of university legislation;[104] the state broadcasting monopoly;[105] and the assignment of the management of the Greek Orthodox monasteries' property to a State institution, which was widely perceived as the State's confiscation of the church's property.[106] In 1984, for the first time, the Council of State explicitly recognized the constitutional stature of the proportionality principle as a corollary of the rule of law principle.[107] Nevertheless, at least to the late 1980s, the Greek courts typically failed to thoroughly scrutinize the constitutionality of legislative and executive acts on the basis of proportionality considerations.[108] Instead, they regularly upheld limitations of constitutional rights on the nebulous grounds of public interest, even when they could have cited specific constitutional provisions as a source of limitations.[109]

Despite the general reluctance, toward the end of the 1980s, Greek courts began setting clear limits on the political branches of government on specific domains of state action. Most notably, the courts began to more carefully scrutinize the constitutionality of state measures that negatively affected the environment. For instance, in 1988, the Council of State started considering

102 See, e.g., N. Androulakis, "The State of the Judges – A Nonexistent Spectre," *NoB* 1985, 1505–1515 [in Greek]; M.P. Stathopoulos, Reviewing the Constitutionality of Laws: Democracy between the Scylla of Authoritarianism or Populism and the Charybdis of Aristocratism, *ERPL/REDP* 1991, 87–123.

103 Cf. Alivizatos, *supra* note 88, 72: "The traditional self-restraint of the civil law judges ultimately prevailed over their political inclinations."

104 Cf. Supreme Special Court judgment nº 30/1985, *ToS* 1985, 182 (186 et seq.); Council of State (Full Bench) judgment nº 2923/1987, *ToS* 1987, 747 (749).

105 Cf. Council of State (Full Bench) judgment nº 5040/1987, *ToS* 1987, 727 (728–729).

106 Cf. Council of State judgment nº 5057/1987, *NoV* 1988, 801 (802 et seq.); but see the European Court of Human Rights judgment of 9 December 1994, Serie A, Nr. 301 A – *Holy Monasteries / Greece* (finding a violation of Art. 6 § 1 ECHR [right to a fair trial] and Art. 1 of the Additional Protocol of the ECHR [protection of possessions]).

107 Council of State judgment nº 2112/1984, *ToS* 1985, 63 (64).

108 See also G. Gerapetritis, *Proportionality in Administrative Law*, Athens-Komotini 1997, 108 et seq. (123–124) (arguing that the proportionality principle is adequately subsumed within Greek administrative law).

109 See, e.g., the Council of State (Full Bench) judgment nos. 400/1986, *ToS* 1986, 433 (436–437); 1094/1987, *ToS* 1987, 279 (281 et seq.). For a criticism, see, e.g., P. Dagtoglou, Public Interest and Constitution, *ToS* 1986, 425–433 [in Greek]; P. Pavlopoulos, Judicial Control of the Constitutionality of Legislation or Judicial Control of the Legality of the Constitution?, *NoV* 1988, 13–35 (29 et seq.) [in Greek].

the existing status of urban planning regulations to be constitutionally entrenched.[110] Accordingly, planning regulations changes can be made only if they do not diminish the protection of the natural and settled environments. Moreover, on the basis of the constitutional protection of the environment, the Council of State began upholding rigorous limitations on constitutional property rights even without compensation.[111]

In the third stage, from the late 1980s to the late 1990s, the Council of State, most notably, its fifth section, further developed and refined its environmental jurisprudence.[112] In cases of conflict between environmental concerns and other constitutionally protected interests, the Council of State effectively accorded priority to environmental protection.[113] In contrast, in other areas, the courts maintained their customarily deferential approach, reacting reluctantly to the claim of unconstitutionality. For instance, in accordance with their traditional position, Greek courts reduced the constitutional protection of property rights to the rights *in rem*[114] and generally upheld the constitutionality of statutes retroactively abrogating claims, even when the claims had been recognized by final judicial decisions.[115] Similarly, while exercising its nonjudicial duty of providing expert opinion on presidential decrees (Art. 95, § 1, *alinea* d, Const.), the Council of State adopted a deferential approach vis-à-vis the privatization of public enterprises of vital importance for the common good.[116]

All in all, while effectively maintaining a balance between a restrained and an activist posture, during this period, the courts failed to adequately explain

110 See Council of State (Full Bench) judgment n° 10/1988, *ToS* 1988, 117 (120–121); see also in detail *infra*, section II.B.2.a. of this present report.

111 See *infra* note 158 and accompanying text.

112 For an overview, see, e.g., Iliopoulos-Strangas & Leventis, *supra* note 22, 276–277; K. Chryssogonos and X. Contiades, Der Beitrag Griechenlands zur europäischen Rechtskultur: der verfassungsrechtliche Umweltschutz, *Jahrbuch des öffentlichen Rechts - neue Folge* 2003, 21–41 (27 et seq.); I. K. Karakostas, *Greek and European Environmental Law*, Athens-Brussels 2008, 71 et seq.; G. Papadimitriou/M. Florou, Environmental Law in Greece, *in* N. S. J. Koeman (ed.), *Environmental Law in Europe*, The Hague/London/Boston 1999, 293–319 (298 et seq.); N. Papaspyrou, A Farewell to Judicial Passivity: The Environmental Jurisprudence of the Greek Council of State, *Journal of Modern Greek Studies* 1999, 63–84.

113 See, in detail, section II.B.2. of this present report.

114 See, e.g., the Council of State judgment n° 2705/1991, *EDDD* 1992, 456 and the Areios Pagos judgment n° 363/1995, *ToS* 1996, 1050.

115 See, e.g., the Council of State judgment n° 1272/1994, *DiDik* 1994, 1151–1152 and the Areios Pagos judgment n° 345/1994, *NoV* 1995, 246–247.

116 On this issue, see, e.g., Th. Antoniou, The Constitutional Restrictions of Privatisation, *RHDI* 1998, 277–289; Th. Fortsakis, Le secteur public: contenu, limites, privatisations, *in* *L'Administration Publique en Grèce*, *supra* note 78, 141–163 (149 et seq.) both with further references.

the differences in the breadth and depth of judicial review in different constitutional domains. In addition, although the Greek courts gradually, but not consistently, subjected legislative and executive actions to more rigorous scrutiny, this greater scrutiny did not always correspond to a coherent proportionality review. Rather, when the Greek courts did apply a proportionality test, they tended to scrutinize the appropriateness and necessity of state action. In contrast, they typically avoided engaging in cost-benefit balancing. Consistent with this, most constitutional scholars considered such balancing equivalent to a scrutiny of the wisdom, rather than the constitutionality, of state actions.[117]

The fourth period in the development of Greece's constitutional jurisprudence, from the late 1990s to the present, has led to a certain alignment of judicial review standards. Partly influenced by international human rights law, the Greek courts have qualified the preferential treatment of the State as a litigant[118] and have struck down the statutory ban of compulsory enforcement of judicial decisions against the State[119] and the detention of individuals for failure to pay a debt owed to the State,[120] thus abandoning several traditional assumptions. Similarly, regarding the scope of property rights, after initially conferring protection on all possessions based on Art. 1 of the ECHR's Additional Protocol,[121] Greek courts have begun broadly interpreting the property clause of the Greek Constitution (Art. 17) to encompass not only *in rem* rights but also *in personam* rights.[122] Moreover, the courts have explored new dimensions in interpreting constitutional guarantees, thus considerably extending their scope. For instance, since 1998, the Council of State has construed the constitutional principle of gender equality to allow positive measures that aim to establish

[117] Cf. K. Chryssogonos, *Individual and Social Rights* (3rd ed., Athens 2006), 90 et seq. [in Greek] with further references.

[118] Cf. Council of State (Full Bench) judgment nos. 2808/2002, *ToS* 2003, 164 et seq.; 1780/2006, *ToS* 2006, 953 et seq. (954); Areios Pagos (Full Bench) judgment nº 12/2002, *ToS* 2002, 316–317.

[119] Cf. Areios Pagos (Full Bench) judgment nº 21/2001, *ToS* 2002, 106 et seq. Since the 2001 constitutional amendments, Art. 94 § 4 *alinea* 3 Const. explicitly provides that "judicial decisions are subject to compulsory enforcement also against the public sector, local government agencies and public law legal persons, as specified by law."

[120] Cf. Council of State (Full Bench) judgment nº 250/2008, *ToS* 2008, 235 et seq.; Supreme Special Court judgment nº 1/2010.

[121] See Areios Pagos (Full Bench) judgment nº 40/1998, *NoV* 1999, 752 (753).

[122] See Areios Pagos (Full Bench) judgment nº 6/2007, *NoV* 2007, 1613 (1616, 1617).

an actual equality between men and women.[123] After a long debate between constitutional scholars and the courts, the Council of State ultimately followed the Areios Pagos by extending the application scope of a statutory provision to groups of persons unconstitutionally excluded.[124] Regarding the limits of privatization, the Council of State has held that the principles of popular sovereignty and separation of powers do not allow conferring police powers to private legal entities.[125] Relying on the separation of powers principle (Art. 26, Const.) in connection with the equality principle (Art. 4, § 1, Const.) and the right to legal protection (Art. 20, § 1, Const.), the Council of State identified a general constitutional ban on the abrogation of claims ruled on in final judicial decisions.[126] Overcoming earlier doubts, the Greek courts have also recognized the constitutional status of the principle of the protection of legitimate expectation,[127] thus setting considerable limits on the legislature. Arguably, in finding that not only the compulsory but also the optional inclusion of religious affiliation in identity cards violates the constitutionally guaranteed right to religious freedom (Art. 13), the Council of State issued a broad constitutional ruling that was unnecessary to adjudicating the case.[128] However, the Council of State has recently qualified some of its environmental jurisprudence.[129] Although the particulars of the Council of State's doctrinal approach are questionable,[130] this development has effectively helped harmonize judicial review standards across different substantive areas of constitutional law.

Since its 2001 amendments, the Greek Constitution explicitly provides that "[r]estrictions of any kind which . . . may be imposed upon [the rights of the human being] . . . should respect the principle of proportionality" (Art. 25, §

[123] See Council of State (Full Bench) judgment n° 1933/1998, *ToS* 1998, 792 (793). After the 2001 amendments the Constitution explicitly allows the "adoption of positive measures for promoting equality between men and women" (Art. 116 § 2 Const.).

[124] On this issue, see in detail, *infra*, section II.B.1. of this report.

[125] See Council of State (Full Bench) judgment n° 1934/1998, *ToS* 1998, 598 (602–603) (concerning enforcement of no-parking zones).

[126] Cf. Council of State (Full Bench) judgment n° 542/1999, *ToS* 1999, 340 (342–343).

[127] See Council of State judgment n° 1508/2002, *DtA* 2003 (Special Issue), 354 (357). See also the contributions *in* Rule of Law and Legitimate Expectation, *DtA* 2003 (Special Issue), 11 et seq.; P. Mouzouraki, Le principe de confiance légitime en droit administratif hellénique, *Revue française de droit administratif* 2005, 143–152.

[128] See Council of State judgment n° 2283/2001, *ToS* 2001, 1026 (1041); Cf. J. Iliopoulos-Strangas, Religious Affiliation and Identity Cards: Constitutional Aspects, *Typos tis Kiriakis*, 2 September 2001, 11 [in Greek].

[129] See, in detail, section II.B.2. of this report.

[130] Cf. Th. Antoniou, Balancing as a Method of Interpretation in the Council of State's Case Law, *in Jubilee Book for the Council of State*, *supra* note 37, 969–981 [in Greek].

1). Thus, the Greek Constitution establishes the proportionality principle as an explicit boundary with which all limitations on rights should comply. Subsequently, Greek courts have tended to scrutinize not only the appropriateness and necessity of state measures but also the proportionality *stricto sensu* between rights-based claims and public-interest justifications for the infringement of those rights.[131] However, the Council of State has limited itself to striking down only state measures that are obviously inappropriate or disproportional.[132] Accordingly, judicial reluctance to fully enforce the Constitution's fundamental rights guarantees partly persists. Against the backdrop of the rule-exception relation between fundamental rights and their limitations, it is doubtful whether this approach can pass constitutional muster.[133]

2. *Positive Legislation through Constitutional Adjudication*

Though generally stressing the limits of judicial review, on some occasions, the Greek courts have engaged in policy making, thus exercising legislative functions of a positive nature while reviewing legislation. Apart from construing statutory law to conform with the Constitution,[134] the most prominent examples of this jurisprudential approach concern the extension of preferential treatment in cases of violation of the constitutional equality principle (see section 1) and the constitutional protection of the environment (see section 2).

A. Extension of Preferential Treatment in Equality Principle Cases

The most common violations of the constitutional equality principle involve the unconstitutional exclusion of persons or groups from a state benefit, or the preferential treatment of one person or group at the expense of another. In reacting to the judicial pronouncement of unconstitutionality, the legislative and executive branches of government generally have several policy options. First, they can extend the state benefit or the preferential treatment to the persons or groups that have been judged unconstitutionally

131 See, e.g., Areios Pagos judgment (Full Bench) nº 43/2005, *NoV* 2005, 1587 et seq.

132 See, e.g., Council of State (Full Bench) judgment nº 990/2004, *DtA* 2005, 834 (854 et seq.).

133 On the proportionality principle as a mechanism to implement this rule-exception relation, see S. I. Koutnatzis, The Contribution of the Proportionality Principle in Realizing the Rule-Exception Relation Between Fundamental Rights and Their Limitations, *in Essays in Honour of Loukas Theocharopoulos and Dimitra Kontogiorga-Theocharopoulou* 2010 [in Greek].

134 See *supra* note 94 and accompanying text.

excluded. Second, they can abolish the state benefit or the preferential treatment accorded to the persons or groups unconstitutionally privileged. Third, they can choose one of several possible intermediate solutions located between extending the state benefit or preferential treatment to all similarly situated persons or abolishing them altogether. Indeed, achieving constitutional equality requires the political branches of government to accord equal rights and benefits to all persons or groups, provided that they are situated in similar circumstances. Whether equality is realized at a low, middle, or high level is, as a general matter, constitutionally irrelevant. Accordingly, in keeping with Greek courts' traditionally deferential attitude, one would expect them to merely declare a differential treatment unconstitutional without encroaching on the legislative prerogative to decide how to remedy the inequality.[135]

Consistent with this, several constitutional scholars[136] have refused to extend the applicability of a discriminatory provision citing the separation of powers principle and the Constitution's budgetary constraints.[137] Other scholars have adopted a differentiated approach based on whether discriminatory legislation provides a state benefit as a matter of rule or as an exception.[138] Thus, they suggest extending preferential treatment to the group that legislation unfairly exempts and thus discriminates against. However, if existing legislation grants preferential treatment to a group on an exceptional basis, these scholars argue that an extension of the preferential treatment to all negatively affected groups would overstep the bounds of the judicial role. Although some scholars counter this last point by arguing that the Constitution requires courts, as State organs, to extend the applicability of unconstitutional legislation to restore constitutional equality and comprehensively protect fundamental rights,[139] this position appears to be a minority view in the scholarly debate.

135 For the following analysis, see, in detail, Iliopoulos-Strangas and Leventis, *supra* note 22, 309–310.

136 See, e.g., Ph. Vegleris, Le conseil d'état et l'examen de la constitutionnalité des lois en Grèce, *in Studi in onore di Silvio Lessona*, Volume II, Bologna 1961, 597–655 (635–640); P. Dagtoglou, *Constitutional Law – Individual Rights* (2nd ed., Athens-Komotini 2005), 1205–1209 (1209), 1464–1466 [in Greek].

137 See, e.g., Art. 80 § 1 Const. (providing that "no salary, pension, subsidy or remuneration should be entered in the State budget or granted, unless it is provided for by statute concerning the organization or other special statute").

138 See, e.g., A. Manessis, The Constitutional Equality Principle and its Application by the Courts, *Ephimeris Ellinon Nomikon* (=EEN) 1958, 445–455 (449–450) [in Greek]; see also Th. Antoniou, *Equality before and through the Law*, Athens-Komotini 1998, 204 et seq. [in Greek].

139 See, e.g., Ch. Anthopoulos, *The Issue of the Functional Obligation of Fundamental Rights*, Thessaloniki 1993, 135 et seq. (139–141) [in Greek].

For several decades, Greek courts have failed to adopt a consistent approach on this issue. On the one hand, the civil courts have regularly extended preferential treatment provided by unconstitutional legislation to remedy a violation of the equality principle – regardless of whether the discriminatory legislation accords preferential treatment as a general rule or exceptionally.[140] In so doing, civil courts basically ignore the Constitution's budgetary provisions.[141] Rather, to justify the judicial extension of unconstitutional legislation, civil courts have relied on a general set of constitutional provisions that form the basis for judicial review of the constitutionality of legislation[142] and that impose on all Greeks the fundamental duty of "respect towards the Constitution and the laws concurrent thereto."[143] The extension to judges of legislation concerning remuneration of higher public servants[144] is usually seen as a common manifestation of this jurisprudence.[145]

Ordinary administrative courts have generally followed the same approach, additionally invoking in their reasoning the European Court of Justice's (ECJ) case law on the principle of equal pay for male and female workers for equal work or work of equal value (Art. 141, EC-Treaty [Art. 157 of the Treaty on the Functioning of the European Union]).[146]

In contrast, the Council of State had traditionally adopted a differentiated approach. Since the 1950s, it had extended a generally applicable

[140] See, e.g., Areios Pagos judgment nos. 3/1990, *NoV* 1990, 1313 (1314); 7/1995 (Full Bench), *EErgD* 1996, 494 (495); 1578/2008, *EErgD* 2009, 180 et seq.

[141] See *supra* note 137.

[142] Art. 87 § 2 and 93 § 4 Const.

[143] Art. 120 § 2 Const.

[144] See, e.g., Areios Pagos judgment nº 40/1990, *EEN* 1990, 579 et seq. (579).

[145] On such occasions, however, the courts have occasionally tended to justify the extension of preferential treatment based on Art. 88 § 2 Const. (providing that "the remuneration of magistrates shall be commensurate with their office"). In reaction to this jurisprudence, the 2001 constitutional amendments established a special court – composed by a majority of law professors and barristers – charged with adjudicating disputes concerning the range of remunerations and pensions of magistrates provided that the resolution of the relevant legal issues may affect the salary, pension, or fiscal status of a wider circle of persons (Art. 88 § 2 Const.). However, it the meantime, this special court effectively followed the previous approach, not hesitating to extend the preferential treatment. See, e.g., the special court's judgment nº 1/2005, *EfimDD* 2006, 28 (28–29); see also its judgment nº 13/2006, *ToS* 2007, 95 (105) (finding that the violation of the equality principle establishes the state's liability for unlawful damage).

[146] See, e.g., Athens Administrative Court of First Instance judgment nos. 10391/1990, *DiDik* 1991, 1309 (1309–1310); 3151/1992, *DiDik* 1993, 350 (351); see also Athens Administrative Court of Appeals judgment nº 3717/1992, *DiDik* 1993, 138 (138–139).

preferential treatment to encompass possible exceptions.[147] However, citing its noninterference with legislative prerogatives, the Council of State had hesitated to adopt this approach on a general basis in cases that require extending a provision that is applicable only exceptionally. Nonetheless, most differential treatment cases between persons or groups do not fit in the rule-exception model. Either no distinction between rule and exception is possible, or such a distinction requires a considerable amount of empirical research, which is beyond the purview of the judiciary's role and competence. Consistent with this, in recent years, the Council of State has increasingly abandoned its rule-exception jurisprudence. Rather, it has aligned its jurisprudence with that of the Areios Pagos, generally extending preferential treatment in cases of violation of the constitutional equality principle, for instance, in cases of gender discrimination in social security legislation.[148] In the recent Council of State jurisprudence, it remains unclear whether it is possible to extend the applicability of a provision with a clearly exceptional character.[149] If this is not the case, the Council of State generally extends preferential treatment to the persons or groups unfairly excluded or discriminated against.

Accordingly, in extending the applicability of discriminatory, and thus unconstitutional, legislation, Greek courts exercise legislative power in a positive sense.[150] Among the several policy options that could remedy an unconstitutional situation, the courts favor extending rather than abolishing preferential treatment, or finding a middle-ground solution. Certainly, failing to extend preferential treatment would carry a significant risk. Considering the long-standing inertia of Greece's legislative and executive authorities to promptly and effectively comply with unconstitutionality decrees, it appears that a different approach would run the risk of rendering the verdict of unconstitutionality an empty shell. Nevertheless, the possible maintenance of an unconstitutional situation and judicial encroachment among the political branches of government through extending the preferential treatment is not an either-or proposition. Thus, the courts could consider using a range of

[147] See, e.g., Council of State judgment n° 1519/1995, *NoV* 1996, 1051 (1052).

[148] See, e.g., Council of State judgment nos. 1467/2004 (Full Bench), *Arm* 2004, 1049 (1050); 3088/2007 (Full Bench), *DtA* 2009, 540 (541); see also Council of State judgment n° 2180/2004 (Full Bench), *NoV* 2005, 173 (174–175) (extending to pilots legislation concerning remuneration provisions of cabin crew).

[149] See on this issue the Council of State judgment n° 3324/2000 (Full Bench), *DtA* 2004, 225 (228–229).

[150] N. Alivizatos, The Judge as Legislator, *in* Alivizatos (ed.), *supra* note 69, 76–85 (84) [in Greek]; see also Manitakis, *supra* note 37, 95 (considering as the most flagrant example of positive legislation the cases on the remuneration of magistrates).

approaches practiced in comparative constitutional adjudication, such as setting a deadline for the legislature to react to the unconstitutionality holding[151] and extending preferential treatment only if the legislature has failed to meet the deadline. Although there is no explicit constitutional basis for such an approach,[152] it furthers the goal of restoring constitutional equality while effectively limiting, to the extent possible, judicial interference with legislative prerogatives.

B. The Council of State's Environmental Jurisprudence

The Council of State's intensive jurisprudence on constitutional protection of the environment has been subject to considerable debate in Greece, giving rise to separation-of-powers concerns. The original formulation of Art. 24, § 1, of the Constitution provided the State's duty to protect the natural and cultural environment and to adopt special preventive and repressive measures for the preservation of the environment – without conferring a subjective right on individuals.[153] Nonetheless, from early on, the Council of State has closely scrutinized the constitutionality of state measures that adversely affect the environment. Accordingly, some scholars have hailed this environmental jurisprudence as Greece's contribution to European legal culture.[154] To effectively respond to environmental concerns, Greece's Council of State has tended to develop a distinct environmental doctrine that differs from its general approach in several respects.

First, in contrast to its general reluctance in the direct judicial implementation of constitutional guarantees that require the intervention of

[151] See, e.g., from the jurisprudence of the German Federal Constitutional Court, *Entscheidungen des Bundesverfassungsgerichts*, Volume 94, 241 (266); Volume 100, 104 (136–137).

[152] However, the wording of Art. 100 § 4 *alinea* 2 Const., providing that the Supreme Special Court invalidates unconstitutional statutory provisions "as of the date of publication of the respective judgment, or as of the date specified in the ruling," implicitly recognizes that the Supreme Special Court can order the invalidation of an unconstitutional statute *pro futuro*. In spite of that, Act n° 345/1976 [Supreme Special Court Code] provides in Art. 51 § 4 merely the possibility to invalidate a parliamentary statute on a retroactive basis.

[153] After the 2001 constitutional amendments, Art. 24 § 1 Const. provides that the protection of the natural and cultural environment constitutes not only "a duty of the State," but also "a right of every person."

[154] Chryssogonos and Contiades, *supra* note 112,; see also J. Iliopoulos-Strangas [cooperation: S. Koutnatzis], Impulse aus dem griechischen Verfassungsrecht für den europäischen Grundrechtsschutz, *in* P. J. Tettinger and K. Stern (eds.), *Kölner Gemeinschaftskommentar zur Europäischen Grundrechte-Charta*, Munich 2006, 31–54 (45).

the legislature,[155] the Council of State considers Art. 24, § 1, of the Constitution as a fundamental right that establishes a cause of action against the State, even if the legislature has taken no initiative to implement the abstract constitutional guarantee.[156] Similarly, the Council of State has deemed the executive branch to be directly responsible for ensuring the adequate protection of cultural sites even in cases of legislative inaction.[157] Moreover, on several occasions, the Council of State has effectively upheld rigorous limitations on property rights, even without compensation to further environmental considerations.[158] Regarding the constitutional requirements for transfer of development rights as a compensation for development restrictions, the Council of State has indicated in *obiter dicta* the detailed contents a new bill would need to pass judicial scrutiny, thus arguably engaging in positive legislation.[159] Although we cannot exhaustively present the Council of State's far-reaching environmental jurisprudence, this report focuses on two aspects of particular interest from the perspective of judicial priority setting: (1) the constitutional protection of the existing status of legislative protection and (2) the constitutional principle of sustainable development and its implications.

a. *Constitutional Entrenchment of the Current Status of Environmental Protection*

In regard to most social rights, the Council of State has generally refused to recognize a constitutional mandate to maintain the existing status of social protection.[160] Rather, it has emphasized the power of the State's legislative

[155] The Council of State has also pointed out (see judgment nº 400/1986, *ToS* 1986, 433 (436)) that Art. 21 § 3 Const., which provides that "the State shall care for the health of citizens," establishes the State's direct constitutional obligation to take positive measures to protect public health and at the same time recognizes an individual right to demand the realization of this obligation. However, this far-reaching pronouncement has remained rare and has had no following in subsequent jurisprudential developments.

[156] See, e.g., Council of State judgment nos. 2281/1992 (Full Bench), *ToS* 1992, 593 (596); 55/1993 (Full Bench), *Arm* 1993, 175 (175); 2818/1997, *Arm* 1997, 1072 (1075).

[157] See, e.g., Council of State judgment nos. 3146/1986 (Full Bench), *ToS* 1987, 146 (147); 2182/1994, *Nomos kai Physsi* (=No&Ph) 1995, 523 (524–525).

[158] See, e.g., Council of State judgment nº 3521/1992 (Full Bench), *NoV* 1993, 792 (793); for an overview, see generally Y. Drossos, *Constitutional Limitations of Property and Compensation*, Athens 1997, 188 et seq. [in Greek]; G. Sioutis, Art. 24 § 1 [Commentary], *in* G. Kassimatis and K. Mavrias (eds.), *The Interpretation of the Constitution*, Athens-Komotini, 2003, nos. 47 et seq. [in Greek].

[159] On this issue, see Papaspyrou, *supra* note 112, 70–71.

[160] For an analysis, see, in detail, Iliopoulos-Strangas & Leventis, *supra* note 22, 314–318; see also Koutnatzis, *supra* note 22, 189–190.

and executive branches to reallocate resources as they see fit, even at the cost of decreasing social benefits.[161] In contrast, the Council of State regularly derives from the Constitution absolute protection of the existing status of urban planning regulations. As a result, the Constitution prohibits the legislative and executive branches from implementing land-use planning measures that would negatively affect urban planning conditions (e.g., by reducing public green spaces or unbuilt areas) and allows only those modifications aimed to improve existing environmental conditions.[162] In the course of this jurisprudence, the Council of State has regularly accorded priority to environmental protection vis-à-vis competing constitutionally protected rights or interests, even when a compelling constitutional justification to this effect is lacking. Eventually, this dichotomy – in terms of the standards of constitutional scrutiny between the protection of the environment and other constitutionally protected rights and interests – has prompted the Council of State to advance the laudable goal of environmental protection by exercising functions that are usually preserved in the State's political branches. Although it has formally set limits on the legislature, by lopsidedly prioritizing environmental concerns, the Council of State's environmental jurisprudence has not avoided substantively engaging in judicial priority setting. Thus, this jurisprudence has been seen as encroaching on the legislature's prerogatives to set public policy. Against this backdrop, since the late 1990s, the Council of State has generally qualified its high prioritization of environmental concerns. Albeit rather reluctantly and inconsistently, the Council of State has derived a certain constitutional guarantee of the existing legislative status of protection from other constitutional social guarantees as well,[163] such as the State's

161 See, e.g., concerning the constitutional protection of social security (Art. 22 § 5 Const.), Council of State judgment nos. 241/1989, *Epitheorissi Dikaiou Koinonikis Asfalissis* (=EDKA) 1989, 479 (479); 2973/1991, *ToS* 1991, 399 (400). See also Council of State (Full Bench) judgment nos. 3096/2001, *ToS* 2002, 124 and 3100/2001, *NoV* 2002, 235 (upholding the merger of social security institutions). However, since the late 1980s, the Council of State has consistently stressed the public law character of compulsory insurance, ruling out any private initiative in this field; the leading cases are judgments nos. 139/1987, *EErgD* 1987, 509–510 and 5024/1987 (Full Bench), *EDKA* 1988, 234–235; see also the Full Bench judgments nos. 3096/2001, *ToS* 2002, 124 and 3100/2001, *NoV* 2002, 235.

162 See, e.g., Council of State judgment nos. 10/1988 (Full Bench), *ToS* 1988, 117 (120–121); 106/1991 (Full Bench), *ToS* 1991, 146 (150–151); 646/1995, *ToS* 1996, 530 (532); 2002/2003 (Full Bench), *NoV* 2003, 2150 (2151–2152).

163 Regarding family protection, see, e.g., Council of State judgment nos. 1674/1998 (6th Section), *DiDik* 1998, 961 (962); 2409/1998 (Grand Chamber), *DiDik* 1999, 444 (445). It should be noted, however, that the Council of State (Full Bench) and the Supreme Special Court have addressed the same case without taking a position as to whether the existing status of family protection – provided through statutory law – enjoys some degree of constitutional protection.

obligation to protect the family[164] and to care for the social security of working people.[165]

Indeed, the harmonization of the standards of scrutiny seems necessary to safeguard the Constitution's normative unity[166] and to dispel criticism of the Council of State for prioritizing environmental considerations at the expense of other constitutional rights or interests. In addition, most constitutional scholars rightly limit the scope of constitutional protection to the essential features of the status quo rather than including all its particulars. To avoid excessively impairing the legislative and executive branches' power to set their own policy priorities, democracy and separation-of-powers considerations merely prohibit arbitrary interference with the status quo or the elimination of statutory protection. Additionally, most constitutional scholars argue for transitional arrangements to mitigate the substantial and unpredictable consequences of statutory modifications. Accordingly, most scholars rightly argue merely for certain protections of the status quo with respect to all constitutionally protected social rights.[167]

b. *The Principle of Sustainable Development*

In addition, especially since 1993, the Council of State has derived from the Greek Constitution's environmental clauses (Art. 24) in connection with European Community law the principle of sustainable development. On this basis, the Council of State has emphasized that the sole constitutionally permissible form of economic development is sustainable development that incorporates the needs of future generations. The courts are developing sustainable development requirements on a case-by-case basis. Accordingly, the judiciary has barred the implementation of several public works projects

See Council of State judgment nº 2944/2000, *ToS* 2001, 1356 et seq.; Supreme Special Court judgment nº 3/2001, *DtA* 2002, 107 et seq. Regarding social security, see, e.g., Council of State judgment nº 1479/1997 (Full Bench), *DiDik* 1997, 876 (877) (pointing out that "the social security institution is not impaired in its entirety").

164 According to Art. 21 § 1 Const.: "The family, being the cornerstone of the preservation and the advancement of the Nation [along with marriage, motherhood and childhood], shall be under the protection of the State."

165 According to Art. 22 § 5 Const.: "The State shall care for the social security of the working people, as specified by law."

166 See also G. Katrougalos, *Constitution, Law and Rights in the Welfare State . . . and Beyond,* Athens 1998, 165.

167 See, e.g., Iliopoulos-Strangas and Leventis, *supra* note 22,314-315, 317-318 and Fn. 253 with further references; but cf. P. Pararas, The Freedom to Work and the Right to Work in Art. 22 § 1 Const., *ToS* 1979, 259-280 (271–274) [in Greek] (arguing in favor of absolute protection of the existing legislative status quo of all social rights).

that would have threatened the environment.[168] Similarly, at the procedural level, in contrast to its general standing doctrine, the Council of State has adopted the ecological-neighbor construction principle, thus conferring on a wide range of persons and legal entities the power to bring an action against administrative activities and omissions that damage environmental goods.[169] However, in this respect as well, the Council of State has recently qualified the prioritization of environmental concerns. Although with the 2001 constitutional amendments the Greek Constitution explicitly refers to the principle of sustainable development,[170] the Council of State identifies a violation of this principle only when environmental damage is irreversible or obviously disproportional vis-à-vis the anticipated benefit of a project.[171] Similarly, in recent years, the Council of State has more strictly construed the procedural requirements to bring an action on environmental issues.[172] It remains an open question whether consistency could have been restored in the standards of constitutional scrutiny without conveying the impression that constitutional protection is limited to the lowest common denominator of substantive and procedural constitutional requirements.

III. FINAL REMARKS

In summary, Greek courts have recognized constitutional supremacy as the basis for judicial review of the constitutionality of legislation since the late nineteenth century. The Greek system of judicial review is diffuse and incidental as a matter of principle. However, it provides several factual and legal avenues for concentrating judicial review power in the high courts plenums and the Supreme Special Court. In several respects, however, constitutional adjudication in Greece is deficient. Structural constitutional law and procedural violations of constitutional guarantees remain by and

168 See, e.g., Council of State judgment nos. 53/1993, *No§Ph* 1994, 290 (292); 2759/2994, *ToS* 1995, 167 (172).

169 See in detail, G. Sioutis, *The Legal Interest in the Annulment Petition*, Athens-Komotini 1998, 261, 266 et seq., 272 et seq. [in Greek] with further references; Cf. also Ph. Spyropoulos, Standing to Raise Constitutional Issues, *RHDI* 2002, 233–240 (235).

170 According to Art. 24 § 1 *alinea* 2 Const., "the State is bound to adopt special preventive or repressive measures for the preservation of the environment in the context of the principle of sustainable development."

171 See Council of State judgment nos. 613/2002 (Full Bench), *NoV* 2002, 1972 (1973–1974); 3478/2000 (Full Bench), *NoV* 2002, 195 (197–198); in a similar sense see also judgment n° 1672/2005 (Full Bench), *EfimDD* 2006, 50–51 (requiring consideration of alternative means that would avoid or limit environmental damage instead of a categorical approach that would prohibit environmental damage *a priori*).

172 On this issue, see Sioutis, *supra* note 111, n° 39 with further references from the case law.

large beyond the purview of judicial review. Neither an abstract review of the constitutionality of a statute nor a direct constitutional complaint avenue or a judicial remedy for the legislature's failure to fulfill its constitutional obligations is generally available. In spite of this, the recent discussion on the possible establishment of a constitutional court in Greece arguably stemmed from the political branches' unease with politically disturbing judicial rulings handed down in the existing system. In contrast, the proposal to establish a constitutional court largely failed to address the existing systemic deficits of constitutional adjudication.

Despite recognizing their power to review and rule on the constitutionality of legislation, in exercising this power, Greek courts have long maintained a deferential attitude to the political branches of government. In fact, they have seemed to consider the mere existence of a legislative limitation a sufficient basis to uphold its constitutionality, without reviewing its necessity and proportionality in light of the least restrictive alternatives. In recent years, the courts and constitutional scholars have pursued constitutional considerations more often. However, vestiges of the courts' long-standing deference remain. In addition, the standards of constitutional scrutiny remain partly inconsistent among different domains of constitutional law. Most typically, the courts have extended the applicability of preferential treatment to groups of persons discriminated against and have prioritized environmental considerations over other constitutionally entrenched rights or interests. In these respects, the courts have become engaged in priority setting, thus exercising quintessentially legislative functions. On other occasions, paradoxically enough, the courts' reluctance to declare a holding of unconstitutionality results in the courts' usurping legislative functions to construe statutory law contrary to its wording, simply so it can pass constitutional muster.

All in all, in light of Greece's previous experiences of failing to act on the axiom of constitutional supremacy, judicial empowerment in reviewing the constitutionality of statutes is a positive development. Nevertheless, despite recent steps in this direction, much remains to ensure a uniform and consistent application of constitutional rules, notwithstanding the predispositions of the individual judges. At the end of the day, the judiciary fulfills its constitutional role neither when it avoids declaring a statute as unconstitutional at all costs nor when it imposes its own policy preferences without sufficient constitutional basis. Admittedly, in reviewing the constitutionality of statutes, the constitutional rule of law and the effective protection of fundamental rights typically clash with the political branches' prerogatives to set priorities and policy goals and to determine the budget allocation as corollaries of the democratic principle. Certainly, against this background, it is sometimes a Herculean task for the judiciary to strike the constitutionally appropriate balance. Intellectual consistency and honesty should be paramount considerations in this quest – irrespective of whether judicial activity in the case at hand more appropriately qualifies as negative or as positive legislation.

HUNGARY

CONSTITUTIONAL COURT AS POSITIVE LEGISLATOR

Lóránt Csink,
Lecurer, Károli University, Budapest
lorant.csink@kim.gov.hu

József Petrétei,
Professor, University of Pécs
pepe@ajk.pte.hu

Péter Tilk,
Lecturer, University of Pécs
tilk@ajk.pte.hu

I. ANTECEDENTS OF CONSTITUTIONAL ADJUDICATION

Before the political transition, no institution could emerge for the protection of the Constitution, given the nature of the ancien régime. However, the general refusal of constitutional jurisdiction was not unanimous in legal literature; from the mid-960s, several authors have suggested setting up an institution to grant remedies for any violation of the Constitution. In the history of Hungarian public law, there has been no institution performing the classical functions of constitutional jurisprudence. The Constitution of 1949, a break from the traditions of European and Hungarian constitutional development, terminated the public institutions performing similar functions to a constitutional court (e.g., Canvassing Court, Administrative Court).

The revolution of 1956 eliminated the former organizations of dictatorship, but it had no time to create the conditions of constitutionalism. Within the frameworks of the political system, the constitutional revision of 1972 emphasized the necessity of the protection of the Constitution, and the idea of a parliamentary committee arose, controlling constitutionalism.[1] However, politicians had found the institution suspicious until the middle of the 1980s, when the idea of establishing an organ, formally separate from Parliament, emerged to institutionalize "efficient" protection of the Constitution. This organ was the Constitutional Council. The adoption of the law in 1983 was a new and significant step toward fostering constitutional protection, even though it could not act as real protector in the political atmosphere. First, because the majority of its members were elected by, and responsible to the Parliament, which could recall them any time. Second, because the Council was not about to clarify legal arguments, its members from the field of law were in the minority.

The Constitutional Council cannot be considered a constitutional court, not even in regard to its competences. Although it had the right to control laws, it was not about to annul them in case of unconstitutionality. The Council only contributed to the interpretation of the Constitution, and the pertaining law did not grant *actio popularis* (i.e., the right to initiate *ex post* review for everyone).

Although in the late 1980s the idea of strengthening the Council emerged, in 1989, it was finally replaced by a brand new institution of Hungarian public law: the Constitutional Court.

II. THE ESTABLISHMENT OF THE CONSTITUTIONAL COURT

The foundation of the constitutional and statutory regulations on the Constitutional Court (hereinafter "the Court") took place at the political transition (Act XXXI of 1989, on the amendment of the Constitution, and Act XXXII of 1989, on the Constitutional Court, hereinafter ACC).[2] Their regulations are the results of the compromise of the opposing powers. These Acts can be interpreted only by taking into consideration the special circumstances of a country in transition. The current regulations are imperfect in some ways, because of the quick legislation, the establishment of other institutions protecting rights, and the inconsistent amendments, but their merit lies in the establishment of the Court itself and the determination of its efficient and abstract competences.

1 Bibó, István: Válogatott tanulmányok 1935–1979. (Selected Studies 1935–1979). Magvető, Budapest, 1990, p. 164.

2 See further details at Kilényi, Géza: Ungarn schreitet in Richtung Rechtsstaatlichkeit (Hungary Steps Forward to the Direction of Rule of Law). EuGRZ 1989/23–24, pp. 513–518.

The Court, as an individual body, was first institutionalized by Act I of 1989 in Hungarian public law. According to the Constitution, the president and the ten members of the Court would be elected and recalled by Parliament. The competence of the Court would include both the constitutional review of laws and other competences determined by law. Within the framework of *ex post* review, the Court was in charge of annulling all unconstitutional laws, except for statutes whose application could have only been suspended.

The concept of the regulation seemed to contain only the basic provisions, saying that the details would be set in a separate statute. In the spring of 1989, the legislator was finished with the draft on the execution of the Constitution. The draft, although it was not adopted, contained the detailed provisions for the operation, procedure, and construction of the Court, clearly representing the conceived model of constitutional jurisdiction under the Parliament, as a preliminary structure of separation of powers. The Court they had in mind was more than the Constitutional Council but much less than the Court of our times. However, the Court's competence was extremely large in the draft; it included functions of canvassing boards, the dissolution of parties operating unconstitutionally, and so on. In contrast, most of the competences could have been initiated by officials indicated in the statute.[3]

Such a theory of the Court was accepted only as a starting point at the trilateral political negotiations (National Roundtable). During the Roundtable talks, the need of constitutional adjudication always arose in connection with the expanse of constitution making. Only toward the end of the negotiations was it realized that a materially new Constitution had been born, one that was worth protecting even with constitutional adjudication.

The new draft of ACC, with a close connection to the draft on the text of the Constitution, became a significant part of the agreement on 18 September 1989. The participants of the National Roundtable agreed on a constitutional court having effective competences and several functions. As part of the agreement, anyone became entitled to initiate the Court's procedure. Also did the Roundtable accord on the first five judges of the Court.[4] The ACC was adopted by the last Parliament of the ancien régime on 19 October 1989, just after the Constitution. According to the summarized

3 Holló, András: Az alkotmányvédelem kialakulása Magyarországon. (The Foundation of Constitutional Protection in Hungary). Bíbor, Budapest, 1997.

4 Bozóki, András (ed.): A rendszerváltás forgatókönyve (Scenario of the Transition). Magvető, Budapest, 1999, pp. 399–447.

opinion of the judicial committee of Parliament, this statute "proved to be the most humble one with the least emotions and contradictions among the four basic statutes of the transition." As for the Parliamentary Records, nobody expressed their opinion during the general debate, and the detailed debate was practically about nothing else but the residence of the Court.[5]

The cause of the large competences being established proved that the opposition of the governing Communist Party (Hungarian Socialist Labour's Party, HSLP) feared that HSLP would gain the majority in Parliament, even in free elections. The unpredictable results of an election also led the representatives of HSLP to strengthen the Court, which could be an obstacle for the new power. Therefore, the Court received the right to annul statutes, even though HSLP had not been willing to grant it earlier. The point was that the Court could annul laws only on lower levels and that statutes can only be subjects of review. But the final version included the possibility of the annulment of statutes, too.

The above-mentioned Act I of 1989 only declared the necessity of the creation of the Court, but its concerning provisions did not come into force. However, after the adoption of the Act on the amendment of the Constitution, the following Act adopted was the ACC, which highlights the significance and importance of the Court during the transition. The ACC, like other laws with a rush adoption, was modified several times, but the significant competences remained unchanged.

Consequently, during the political transition, the Court was free to create its own place in the constitutional order, including not only its political role and importance but also its legal character. In the stream of the political transition, the creators of the Court had no clear vision on the functions of constitutional courts, nor did they clarify what role the Hungarian Court should play. From the beginning, the Court has performed its functions to solve the constitutional problem, even if it has **had** to give up its classical function of negative legislation.

III. THE LEGAL CHARACTER OF THE DECISIONS OF THE COURT

In the Hungarian legal system, the decisions of the Court are sources of law in many aspects.

[5] Kukorelli, István (ed.): Alkotmánytan I (Constitutional Studies I). Osiris, Budapest, 2003, pp. 387–388.

First, the decisions of the Court declaring unconstitutionality result in the annulment of the law in question, which is effective for everyone (*erga omnes*). So the annulment leads to the derogation of laws; therefore, the decisions of the Court become sources of law. The Court's decision on the annulment is negative legislation. Although the decision, generally, contains no new norm, its legal effect is that the particular law terminates, and that law cannot regulate everyday relations any longer.

Second, decisions of the Court are sources of law in the sense that ordinary courts and other judicial bodies have to make their verdicts directly referring to the Court's decisions, as they are binding on everyone.

Third, the legal principles expounded in the decisions of the Court determine the constitutional meaning and content of other legal regulations. And the obligatory legal principles being set in the holdings of the Court's decision often include positive regulations.[6]

IV. THE MANIFESTATION OF POSITIVE LEGISLATION

1. *Constitutional Requirement*

During *ex post* constitutional review of a particular law, the Court, by interpreting the Constitution, might set the constitutional requirements the law has to meet.[7] In these cases, the Court defines the scope of constitutional interpretation; the examined law is constitutional in all the senses that meet the constitutional requirements.[8] The reason can be found in the tolerance of the legal system: if any law has both a constitutional and an unconstitutional interpretation, the Court will indicate the interpretation that makes the law conform to the Constitution.

Setting constitutional requirements involves the constitutional interpretation of the law in question. However, it is not law interpretation but the definition of all possible interpretations that are in accordance with the Constitution. In other words, the examined law is constitutional if it fulfills the requirements the Court has set. As long as the defined requirement is originally in the norm, the constitutional requirement keeps its original function of interpretation.[9] By setting such requirements, the Court

6 See examples at judge László Sólyom's concurring to Ruling 42/1998 (X. 2).

7 Sólyom, László: Az alkotmánybíráskodás kezdetei Magyarországon. (The Dawn of Constitutional Adjudication in Hungary). Osiris, Budapest, 2001, pp. 364–372.

8 Decision 38/1993 (VI. 11.)

9 Sólyom, *op. cit.*, p. 367.

necessarily gives a narrow interpretation of the norm and reduces the possible meanings to the constitutional ones. In these cases, the Court does not annul the challenged law but can modify its meaning and, in some cases, create a new norm. Determining constitutional requirements may result in the following:

- The Court orders to neglect significant parts of the norm, contradictory to the will of the legislator.[10]
- The Court chooses one possible interpretation from the alternatives, not necessarily the same one the legislator thought of.[11]
- The Court interprets the law extensively, by determining a requirement that totally alters the effect of the law.
- The Court gives a new statement that was not originally in the norm (i.e., it creates a new norm).[12] The constitutional requirement establishing new content is practically a constitutional interpretation, within the frames of the posterior review. In these cases, the new content that makes the law constitutional derives directly from the Constitution; the Court finds it necessary to set the requirements the jurisdiction should meet.

In most cases, constitutional requirements concern the judiciary; ordinary courts are obliged to interpret laws in accordance with the constitutional requirement. However, in each case, the Court establishes constitutional requirements together with the annulment of the challenged law, as there remains nothing to interpret, and the determination of the possible constitutional regulations concerns the legislator, as it is the positive instruction for a future regulation.[13]

The normative content of the Court's decisions also effect the preparation of drafts, which the legislator is obliged to consider; otherwise, the adopted law will easily be found unconstitutional and be annulled. The Court stated that, not affecting the competence and responsibility of the legislator, the interpretation of the Constitution could obligatorily define certain elements that are essential in a democratic state.[14] Simultaneously, the Court reckoned that *ex post* constitutional review is not to examine the political, social, or economical effects of the challenged law; it focuses only on the

10 See Decision 48/1993 (VII. 2.) and Decision 52/1995 (IX. 15.)

11 "Whenever the Court respects only one meaning of the law as constitutional, it modifies the law; it keeps the law in force in a way the legislator did not want to" Sólyom, *op. cit.*, p367.

12 See Decision 41/1998 (X. 2.), Decision 60/1994 (XII. 24.) and Decision 22/1997 (IV. 25.)

13 Sólyom, *op. cit.*, p. 370.

14 Decision 52/1997 (X. 14.)

constitutionality of the provisions of the law.[15] The concept of the legislator and the reasoning of the challenged law can be subjects of constitutional review only if they affect the text of the law.[16] The Court neither esteems the political concept of the law nor suggests other possibilities. Its decision on the constitutionality of the norm only means that, besides some other possible solutions, the examined one is constitutional.[17]

2. *Mosaic Annulment*

According to the ministerial reasoning of the ACC, the petitioner of the constitutional review may initiate the full or partial annulment of the unconstitutional law. Theoretically, this could mean that the full annulment of the unconstitutional law is the general principle, but the Court has refused such a solution. The Court has always aspired to tolerate the legal system and to annul the least from the law – nothing more than necessary for the restoration of constitutionality. For this purpose, the Court annulled not only paragraphs and sections but also certain texts within the section (mosaic annulment). However, this pushed the Court far from negative legislation, as the text remained in force after the annulment often had a different, and sometimes contradictory, meaning to the one before constitutional review.

For instance, mosaic annulment resulted in the expanse of the scope of grantees of a tax law, either in the field of substantive law (Decision 87/2008 [VI.18]),[18] or in the field of procedure law (Decision 73/2009 [VII. 10]).[19] Typically, the Court applies mosaic annulment when certain texts of a law restrain a fundamental right (e.g., Decision 83/2008 [VI. 13], concerning the publicity of declarations of properties of local government deputies).[20] Decision 66/1991 (XII. 21) proved the most that mosaic annulment is a tool of positive legislation. The decision found it unconstitutional that criminal law compensations are determined by the minister of justice; therefore, it

15 Decision 15/1993 (III. 12.)

16 Decision 28/1991 (VI. 3.)

17 Sólyom, *op. cit.*, p. 732.

18 The decision found it discriminatory that only one specific group of medicine contributors enjoyed tax preferences. The Court annulled the regulation in a way that the preference would also pertain to the members of the other group.

19 The Court found it unconstitutional that the law did not grant the possibility for the reduction or the release of tax liabilities of individuals. As a result of mosaic annulment such a possibility is given.

20 The decree of the local government allowed only Hungarian citizens to check the declarations, and only after certifying their identity. These texts have been annulled.

annulled some words of the Criminal Procedure Code in a way that removed the competence from the minister to the courts. Simultaneously, Decision 51/2009 (IV. 29) on the constitutionality of property registers annulled some elements of two provisions of the law, and as a result, a third provision remained in force that was contradictory to the original meaning.

Finally, it is noteworthy that, in one case, the comma in a sentence was found unconstitutional. Decision 16/1999 (VI. 11) annulled the comma in an enumeration because it resulted in a different meaning of the sentence, a meaning that is in conformity with the Constitution.

3. *Role of the Court in the Examination of Omissions*

According to Art. 49. of the ACC, if the Court establishes *ex officio* or on anyone's petition that a legislative organ failed to fulfill its legislative tasks issuing from its lawful authority, thereby bringing about unconstitutionality, it sets a deadline and instructs the organ that committed the omission to fulfill its task.

The Court interpreted this competence expansively and practiced it not only in the cases of unconstitutional failures of fulfillment of legislative obligations resulting from particular legal authorization but also when the legislator failed to establish a statute necessary for the emergence of a fundamental right, designated in the Constitution.[21] In this competence, the Court not only establishes the omission of legislation but also bears reference to what the contents of the norm to be adopted should be. In such cases, the unconstitutional situation is caused by the very lack of a provision with a specific content (typically making it impossible to exercise one of the fundamental rights); that is why it is necessary for the Court to set, in the holdings of the decision, positive requirements for the legislator with respect to how to regulate certain issues.[22] For instance, the Court stated that the

[21] An example for such a case is Decision 37/1992 (VI. 10.). Under Article 61 section (4) of the Constitution, a majority of two-thirds of the votes by the Members of Parliament present is required to pass an Act on the supervision of public radio, television, and the public news agency, as well as on the appointment of the directors thereof, on the licensing of commercial radio and television, and on the prevention of monopolies in the media sector. However, until 1996, the Parliament failed to adopt a comprehensive Act on radio and television. Likewise, under Article 68 section (5) of the Constitution, a majority of two-thirds of the votes by the Members of Parliament present is required to pass an Act on the rights of national and ethnic minorities. Decision 35/1992 (VI. 10.) established an unconstitutional omission as the representation of national and ethnic minorities had not been regulated to the extent and in the manner required by the Constitution.

[22] Sólyom, *op. cit.*, p. 370.

judicial review of public administration decisions should be regulated in a way that courts could judge the merits of the decision (Decision 32/1990 (XII. 22]). Seldom does the Court establish the norm to be adopted in the holding of its decision, but in the reasoning, it often determines the elements with which the norm would be constitutional, that is, the elements the Court "wishes to see" in future legislation.

The activism of the Court has also been revealed in exercising the competence related to omissions: first because the Court expanded its competence to several kinds of omissions; second, it obliges the legislator to adopt a norm in accordance with the positive rulings the Court has set; and last but not least, because the competence can also be practiced *ex officio*.

4. *Interpretation of the Constitution*

When interpreting the Constitution, the Court makes no law, even though it is positive legislation in a sense that it determines the direction of future legislation. Therefore, in this competence, the Court defines not the law but the principles beyond it.

With the ACC, the duty of the Court is the interpretation of the provisions of the Constitution on the request of officials indicated therein. The interpretation of the Constitution, however, is not limited to this competence (Decision 36/1992), as during *ex post* review in each case, the disclosure of the meaning of the related constitutional provision is necessary. The competence of interpreting the Constitution set forth in the ACC adds to this in that it also provides for the abstract interpretation of the Constitution. Even though the ACC indicates as task of the Court that it "interpret certain provisions of the Constitution," the practice of the Court reveals the meaning of certain provisions not in themselves but with regard to the system of the Constitution in its entirety.

The sense of the provisions of the Constitution pertaining to fundamental rights comes into light in the continuous interpretations in which the Court focuses both on the particular case and on its former interpretations. The Court keeps on forming the thesis of its previous interpretations. The Court may stress various elements of the same provision during the different interpretations, but they must be free from contradictions: the posterior interpretations must regard the previous ones.[23] The Court is not the sole organ entitled to interpret the Constitution, but its interpretation is different

[23] Decision 36/1992 (VI. 10.).

from the others, as it has an *erga omnes* effect (i.e., it is binding on everyone). The interpretative adjudication clarified the nature and the subjects of fundamental rights. In addition, the Court developed the content of particular fundamental rights and defined certain parts of them as separate fundamental rights (e.g. the right to self-determination from human dignity). The constitutional jurisdiction has led to the enlargement of the list of fundamental rights, it has determined their contents and restrictions, and it has differentiated between constitutional and fundamental rights. Such an activity was extremely important, as the rights in the Constitution are rather general declarations than legal regulations; because of their briefness, they are not very accurate, so they essentially need constitutional adjudication.

In the early phase of its operations, the Court declared that it did not undertake to answer hypothetic constitutional questions, and in several decisions, it took into consideration how abstract the question imposed should be. On the one hand, the Court, interpreting its competence narrowly, requires necessary closeness between the statement of facts and the related provision of the Constitution, and it provides interpretation of the Constitution only for the solution of a "particular constitutional problem" (Decision 31/1990).[24] It is noteworthy that sometimes the petitions of the highest public authorities do not fulfill this requirement.[25]

At the same time, however, the Court also demands certain distance; it requires that the issue not be closely related to the case, and that the decision not become factual (Decision 36/1992),[26] because the Court is not a counsel but the judge of Parliament (Decision 16/1991).

The Court interpreted its competence restrictively also from the aspect that it did not wish to overtake the law interpretation competence of other organs, especially of ordinary courts. Therefore, it adjudges petitions related to the abstract interpretation of the Constitution only if the constitutional problem directly derives, without the inclusion of another law, from the Constitution.

24 The Court refused to make a statement about the possibility to raise the interest rates of housing loan, because it would have meant the interpretation of the "constitutional provision in some abstract way unrelated to any individual problem, or that there is a possibility for unbound interpretation."

25 E.g., the petition of the President of the Supreme Court [Ruling 538/G/2006 (2009)] or the petition of the ombudsman [Ruling 1169/G/2007 (2009)].

26 On this, the Court did not interpret whether the petition for the dismissal of the director of the public radio may be considered the violation of freedom of press; it could have given, therefore, statement of fact answer for the dispute of the prime minister and the President of the Republic.

In the early years of the operation of the Court, petitions regarding preventive Constitution interpretation were typical.[27] The interpretation of the Constitution was requested of the Court during disputes between political concepts (Decision 21/1990),[28] or when the petitioners wished to prevent possible attacks (Decision 63/1992, Decision 74/1992).[29] However, some petitions arose, and later these became typical, which involved the Court in an already-existing constitutional debate (Decision 48/1991, Decision 8/1992, Decision 36/1992),[30] and even later the Court accepted a petition filed after the closure of the case underlying the basis of the constitutional law dispute (Decision 47/2007).[31]

[27] Sólyom, *op. cit.*, pp. 310–311.

[28] In the subject of compensation, in connection with which the Court pointed out that regarding compensation no difference shall be made with regard to the subject of property.

[29] The former requested the interpretation of the Court regarding the possibility of transforming the structure of the army and the latter regarding the possibility of measuring the denominational affiliation of the population.

[30] In connection with the circumstances, the President of Republic is entitled to reject the appointment petitions.

[31] The President of the Republic requested the interpretation of the Court regarding whether he shall comply with the honoring petitions; even though he has already complied with the objected petitions before filing the petition. The Court qualified the issue as "individual constitutional problem," without giving details.

INDIA

CONSTITUTIONAL COURTS AS POSITIVE LEGISLATORS: THE INDIAN EXPERIENCE

Surya Deva[*]
Visiting Research Fellow, University of New South Wales, and Associate Professor, School of Law, City University of Hong Kong
suryad@cityu.edu.hk

INTRODUCTION

This National Report for India seeks to review the way in which the courts in India have employed and expanded the power of judicial review and in that process ended up legislating on many occasions. It first highlights how the Indian constitutional courts have not only vigorously guarded their power of judicial review but also have self-empowered themselves through a series of decisions. It then shows, with the help of a few illustrative cases, the extent to which the Indian courts have acted as positive legislators. The chapter concludes with a brief critique of this trend.

At the outset, it should be noted that, unlike some other countries,[1] in India there are no separate courts to deal exclusively with constitutional issues. Under the Indian Constitution, the power to interpret the Constitution and entertain judicial review petitions is exercised by the Supreme Court and the High Courts. In this report, therefore, the term *constitutional courts* refers to the Supreme Court and the High Courts taken together. Nevertheless, considering that the Supreme Court has the final say on constitutional

* Visiting Research Fellow, University of New South Wales. BA (Hons.), LLB, LLM (Delhi); PhD (Sydney). Formerly, Assistant Professor, National Law Institute University, Bhopal; Lecturer, Faculty of Law, University of Delhi, Delhi

1 For example, Austria, France, Germany, Russia, and South Africa have separate constitutional courts.

interpretations and on judicial review petitions,[2] the report will primarily focus on the constitutional jurisprudence of the Supreme Court.

I. JUDICIAL REVIEW: CONSTITUTIONAL PROVISIONS AND JUDICIAL INTERPRETATION

The Indian Constitution envisages "the judiciary as a bastion of rights and justice."[3] The Constitution has made extensive provisions regarding the appointment, tenure, salaries, retirement age, and removal of the judges to secure the independence of judiciary.[4] An independent judiciary armed with the power of judicial review was the constitutional device chosen to protect people's human rights, to preserve the rule of law, and to safeguard the sanctity of the Constitution.[5] It is not, therefore, incorrect to say that the judiciary is the "logical, primary custodian" of the Constitution.[6]

1. *Judicial Review: The Provisions*

The Indian Constitution does not expressly grant the courts the power to review the decisions of the other two wings of the government: legislature and executive. As noted by Professor Mahendra P. Singh, this power is implied in the constitutional scheme:

> Judicial review in India is based on the assumption that the Constitution is the supreme law of the land, and all governmental organs, which owe their origin to the Constitution and derive their powers from its provisions, must function within the framework of the Constitution, and must not do anything which is inconsistent with the provisions of the Constitution.[7]

[2] Mahendra P. Singh, *V N Shukla's Constitution of India*, 11th ed. (Lucknow: Eastern Book Co., 2008), 488 (hereinafter Singh, *Shukla's Constitution of India*).

[3] Granville Austin, *The Indian Constitution: Cornerstone of a Nation* (Oxford: Clarendon Press, 1966), 175 (hereinafter Austin, *Cornerstone of a Nation*).

[4] Constitution of India 1950, arts. 121, 124, 125, 146, 211, 217, 218, 221, and 229. See also M. P. Singh, "Securing the Independence of the Judiciary: The Indian Experience" (2000) 10 *Indiana International & Comparative Law Review* 245; Austin, *Cornerstone of a Nation*, above n 3, 176–83.

[5] Mahendra Pal Singh & Surya Deva, "The Constitution of India: Symbol of Unity in Diversity" (2005) 53 *Jahrbuch des Offentlichen Rechts der Gegenwart* [Yearbook of Public Law, Germany] 649, 671.

[6] Granville Austin, "The Supreme Court and the Struggle for Custody of the Constitution" in Kirpal et al. (eds.), *Supreme but Not Infallible – Essays in Honour of the Supreme Court of India* (New Delhi: Oxford University Press, 2000), 13.

[7] Singh, *Shukla's Constitution of India*, above n 2, A53–A54.

One may, though, find a provision in the Constitution that prohibits the state from making any law in contravention of fundamental rights enumerated in Part III of the Constitution.[8] This provision empowers the courts to judge the constitutional validity of laws[9] vis-à-vis fundamental rights. However, even in the absence of this provision, the courts would have had the power to test the constitutional validity of a law on the ground it violated fundamental rights.[10]

The remedy to enforce fundamental rights is guaranteed by Articles 32 and 226 of the Constitution. Article 32, which in itself is a fundamental right, provides that the Supreme Court shall have the power "to issue directions or orders or writs, including writs in the nature of habeas corpus, mandamus, prohibition, quo warranto, and certiorari, which ever may be appropriate, for the enforcement" of fundamental rights. The Court has interpreted this remedial provision widely so as to liberalize the *locus standi* requirements[11] and to develop epistolary jurisdiction.[12] The wide ambit of Article 32 has been employed by the Supreme Court to issue a range of orders and directions – for example, to order the payment of compensation, to enforce labor laws, to issue directions for the adoption of children by foreigners, to preserve ecological balance, to protect working women from sexual harassment, and to control pollution of the river Ganges.[13]

Article 226 confers a similar power on the High Court to issue writs. There are, however, three notable differences. First, unlike Article 32, Article 226 is not a fundamental right. Second, the writ issuing power of the High Courts is constrained by territorial limitation, in that they cannot issue writs to any person or authority outside their territorial jurisdiction.[14] Third, whereas the power under Article 32 can be exercised only for the enforcement of

8 Article 13(2) reads: "The State shall not make any law which takes away or abridges the rights conferred by this Part and any law made in contravention of this clause shall, to the extent of the contravention, be void."

9 The term *law* is defined expansively to include "any ordinance, order, by-law, rule, regulation, notification, custom or usage having in the territory of India the force of law." Constitution of India 1950, art. 13(3)(a). See Singh, *Shukla's Constitution of India*, above n 2, 42–43.

10 *A K Gopalan v. State of Madras* AIR 1950 SC 27.

11 *S P Gupta v. Union of India* AIR 1982 SC 149; *PUDR v. Union of India* AIR 1982 SC 1473; *Bandhua Mukti Morcha v. Union of India* (1984) 3 SCC 161.

12 *Sunil Batra v. Delhi Administration* AIR 1980 SC 1579; *Dr Upendra Baxi v. State of UP* (1982) 2 SCC 308; *Mohan Law Sharma v. State of UP* (1989) 2 SCC 600. See generally Surya Deva, "Public Interest Litigation in India: A Critical Review" (2009) 28 *Civil Justice Quarterly* 19, 24.

13 See Singh, *Shukla's Constitution of India*, above n 2, 322–23.

14 Constitution of India, art. 226(1). See Singh, *Shukla's Constitution of India*, above n 2, 620–21.

fundamental rights, the power under Article 226 extends to issue orders and/or writs for "any other purposes" as well.

In addition to the writ jurisdiction, the Indian Constitution confers wide original and appellate jurisdiction on the Supreme Court. Under Article 131, the Supreme Court has the original (and exclusive) jurisdiction to entertain disputes that may arise between the government of India and one or more states or between two or more states. An appeal also lies to the Supreme Court from any judgment, order, or final order of a High Court if the High Court certifies that "the case involves a substantial question of law as to the interpretation of the Constitution."[15] The Constitution also has special provisions that confer appellate jurisdiction on the Supreme Court in criminal and civil matters decided by the High Courts.[16] However, Article 136 confers a wide discretion on the Supreme Court to "grant special leave to appeal from any judgment, decree, determination, sentence or order in any cause of matter passed or made by any court or tribunal." Last but not least, the Constitution confers on the Supreme Court a residuary power to pass any decree or make any order as is necessary to do complete justice in any matter pending before it.[17]

As far as the High Courts are concerned, they have, as mentioned already, quite wide writ issuing power, though only within their respective territories. In addition, the High Courts have the power to transfer cases from subordinate courts to themselves if the case involves a substantial question of law as to the interpretation of the Constitution.[18] Where cases involving "the same or substantially the same questions of law" are pending before the Supreme Court and one or more High Courts (or before two or more High Courts), and if the Supreme Court is satisfied that such questions are substantial questions of general importance, it can transfer such cases to itself for disposal.[19] Both provisions of the Indian Constitution are underpinned by the same rationale, that is, to ensure consistent interpretation on constitutional issues or other important questions of law.

Before we move to review the judgments that have strengthened the power of judicial review, it is useful to note some constitutional provisions that indirectly support this power. Article 141 of the Indian Constitution provides that the "law declared by the Supreme Court shall be binding on all courts

15 Constitution of India, art. 132.

16 *Id.*, Constitution of India, arts 133 and 134.

17 *Id.*, art. 142.

18 *Id.*, art. 228.

19 *Id.*, art. 139-A.

within the territories of India."[20] Even though this provision expressly mentions only courts, all state agencies and officials are bound by the Supreme Court rulings. The Constitution further mandates that all civil and judicial authorities act in aid of the Supreme Court.[21] Finally, both the Supreme Court and the High Courts are courts of record and possess the power to punish for their contempt.[22]

2. *Judicial Review: The Interpretation*

If one looks at the case law, the power of judicial review can hardly be considered implicit. The power not only has been made explicit by the courts in their numerous decisions but also has extended and has been strengthened to the extent that it is almost impossible to take away or curtail the power of judicial review, even by constitutional amendment. The judiciary can test the validity not only of laws and executive actions but also of constitutional amendments. On many occasions, the Supreme Court has even given directions to the other organs of the state to follow the constitutional mandate. An attempt is made here to take readers through a quick tour of some significant judgments, which collectively have allowed the constitutional courts in India to assert to their authority to levels perhaps inconceivable to many constitutional law scholars.

First, in the late 1970s, the Supreme Court ruled, reversing its previous position, that the expression "procedure established by law" in Article 21 of the Constitution[23] means a procedure that is "right, just and fair" – thus giving itself the authority to judge whether the procedure laid down by the legislature conformed to the principles of natural justice.[24] This is especially remarkable because the Constituent Assembly had expressly rejected the due process clause after a long debate.[25]

Second, starting around the same time, the Court began to liberalize the *locus standi* requirements for filing writ petitions for violations of

20 Even the guidelines issued by the Supreme Court will amount to law declared under this provision. *Vishaka v. State of Rajasthan* AIR 1997 SC 3011.

21 Constitution of India, art. 144.

22 *Id.*, arts. 129 and 215.

23 Article 21 reads: "No person shall be deprived of his life or personal liberty except according to procedure established by law."

24 *Maneka Gandhi v. Union of India* AIR 1879 SC 597. See T. R. Andhyarujina, "The Evolution of Due Process of Law and the Supreme Court" in Kirpal (eds.), *Supreme but not Infallible*' above n 6, 193; Singh, *Shukla's Constitution of India*, above n 3, 199–204.

25 Austin, *Cornerstone of a Nation*, above n 3, 101–06.

fundamental rights.[26] This enabled the courts to entertain voices (including in the form of judicial review petitions) from a larger populace, on occasion even from civil society organizations that approached them to enforce collective or diffused rights. But more important, the liberalization of *locus standi*, coupled with an expansive interpretation of fundamental rights noted here, provided the roots for the evolution of public interest litigation (PIL) in India. The development of PIL jurisprudence had a direct relation with courts acting as legislators because most instances of judicial legislation, as we will see in the next section, arose out of PIL cases.

Third, the Supreme Court has also expanded the scope of fundamental rights, in particular of the right to life under Article 21 of the Constitution.[27] For example, the right to life has been interpreted to include the right to health;[28] livelihood;[29] free and compulsory education up to the age of fourteen years;[30] an unpolluted environment;[31] shelter;[32] clean drinking water;[33] privacy;[34] legal aid;[35] a speedy trial;[36] and various rights of

[26] See Ashok H. Desai and S. Muralidhar, "Public Interest Litigation: Potential and Problems" in Kirpal et al (eds.), *Supreme but not Infallible*' above n 6, 159, 162–67; S P Sathe, *Judicial Activism in India – Transgressing Borders and Enforcing Limits* (New Delhi: Oxford University Press, 2002), 201–09; Justice P. N. Bhagwati, "Judicial Activism and Public Interest Litigation" (1985) 23 *Columbia Journal of Transnational Law* 561.

[27] See M. P. Jain, "The Supreme Court and Fundamental Rights" in S. K. Verma and Kusum (eds.), *Fifty Years of the Supreme Court of India – Its Grasp and Reach* (New Delhi: Oxford University Press, 2000), 1, 22–37, 51–52; Sathe, above n 26, 209–29; Singh, *Shukla's Constitution of India*, above n 2, 192–96.

[28] *Parmanand Kataria v. Union of India* AIR 1989 SC 2039; *Paschim Banga Khet Mazdoor Samity v. State of West Bengal* (1996) 4 SCC 37.

[29] *Olga Tellis v. Bombay Municipal Corporation* AIR 1986 SC 180; *DTC Corporation v. DTC Mazdoor Congress* AIR 1991 SC 101.

[30] *Unni Krishnan v. State of AP* (1993) 1 SCC 645.

[31] See, e.g., *Indian Council for Enviro Legal Action v. Union of India* (1996) 3 SCC 212; *M C Mehta v. Union of India* (1996) 6 SCC 750; *Vellore Citizens Welfare Forum v. Union of India* (1996) 5 SCC 647; *Narmada Bachao Andolan v. Union of India* (2000) 10 SCC 664.

[32] *Gauri Shankar v. Union of India* (1994) 6 SCC 349.

[33] *A P Pollution Control Board II v. M V Nayudu* (2001) 2 SCC 62.

[34] *Kharak Singh v. State of UP* AIR 1963 SC 1295; *Govind v. State of MP* AIR 1975 SC 1378; *R Raj Gopal v. State of Tamil Nadu* (1994) 6 SCC 632; *PUCL v. Union of India* AIR 1997 SC 568; *'X' v. Hospital Z* (1998) 8 SCC 296.

[35] *M H Hoskot v. State of Maharashtra* AIR 1978 SC 1548; *Hussainara Khatoon v. State of Bihar* AIR 1979 SC 1369; *Khatri v. State of Bihar* AIR 1981 SC 928; *Suk Das v. Union Territory of Arunachal Pradesh* AIR 1986 SC 991.

[36] *Hussainara Khatoon (I) to (VI) v. Home Secretary, Bihar* (1980) 1 SCC 81; *Kadra Pahadiya v. State of Bihar* AIR 1982 SC 1167; *Common Cause v. Union of India* (1996) 4 SCC 33 and (1996) 6 SCC 775; *Rajdeo Sharma v. State of Bihar* (1998) 7 SCC 507 and (1999) 7 SCC 604.

undertrials, convicts, and prisoners.[37] This extension of the meaning of *life* has been achieved, among other things, by reading nonjusticiable directive principles of state policy into fundamental rights.[38] The effect of this judicial extension of fundamental rights had a direct bearing on the power of judicial review: the more fundamental rights are recognized, the broader is the scope of judicial review.

Fourth, the Indian Supreme Court in *Kesvananda Bharti v. State of Kerala* read an implied limitation on the power of Parliament to amend the Constitution;[39] the Court has held that Parliament cannot amend the basic features or basic structure of the Constitution.[40] Furthermore, there is no complete or exhaustive list of the basic features – the courts decide these features as and when necessary.

Fifth, applying the basic features doctrine laid down in *Kesvananda Bharti*, the Supreme Court declared that judicial review is a basic feature of the Constitution.[41] So, the power of judicial review cannot be excluded, even by constitutional amendment.

Sixth, through judicial interpretation, the Supreme Court held that the power of the President of India to appoint judges of the Supreme Court and the High Courts is not unfettered and that the term *consultation* in Articles 124(2) and 217(1) means "concurrence."[42] According to this interpretation, the process of the appointment of judges is initiated by the Chief Justice of India after consultation with a certain number judges of the Supreme Court and/or High Courts.[43] Because the recommendation of the Chief Justice of India is generally binding on the President, the higher judiciary in India has become, by and large, a self-appointed judiciary.

37 *Sunil Batra v. Delhi Administration* AIR 1978 SC 1675; *Prem Shankar v. Delhi Administration* AIR 1980 SC 1535; *Munna v. State of UP* AIR 1982 SC 806; *Sheela Barse v. Union of India* AIR 1986 SC 1773.

38 Part IV of the Constitution (Articles 36–51) enumerates the directive principles of state policy. Article 37 provides that these principles, though fundamental in the governance of the country, shall not be enforceable in any court.

39 Article 368 of the Constitution places no substantive limitations on the power of the parliament to amend the Constitution.

40 AIR 1973 SC 1461. See Raju Ramachandran, "The Supreme Court and the Basic Structure Doctrine" in Kirpal et al. (eds.), *Supreme but Not Infallible* above n 6, 107.

41 *Waman Rao v. Union of India* AIR 1981 SC 271; *S P Sampath Kumar v. Union of India* AIR 1987 SC 386; *L Chandra Kumar v. Union of India* AIR 1997 SC 1125.

42 *S C Advocates on Record Association* v. *Union of India* (1993) 4 SCC 441; *In re Presidential Reference*, AIR 1999 SC 1.

43 Singh, *Shukla's Constitution of India*, above n 2, 473, 607–08.

II. JUDICIARY BECOMING LEGISLATOR: SOME EXAMPLES

A combined effect of all the court decisions reviewed in the previous section is that, over the years, the Indian Supreme Court has established itself as probably the most powerful (perhaps untouchable) court in any democracy. A few example decisions further support this conclusion. In particular, the decisions demonstrate the extent to which the Apex Court has stepped in the shoes of the legislature.

1. *Guidelines for Police Arrest and Detention:* D K Basu v. State of West Bengal[44]

In August 1986, a nongovernmental organization (NGO) addressed a letter to the Chief Justice of India to draw his attention to certain deaths reported in police lockups and custody.[45] The letter, along with other similar letters, was treated as a writ petition under Article 32. The Supreme Court issued notices to all state governments, and to the Law Commission, with a request to make suitable suggestions.[46]

After making reference to constitutional and statutory provisions and international conventions, the Supreme Court issued 11 requirements as follows:

> We, therefore, consider it appropriate to issue the following requirements to be followed in all cases of arrest or detention till legal provisions are made in that behalf as preventive measures:
>
> (1) The police personnel carrying out the arrest and handling the interrogation of the arrestee should bear accurate, visible and clear identification and name tags with their designations. The particulars of all such personnel who handle interrogation of the arrestee must be recorded in a register.
>
> (2) That the police officer carrying out the arrest of the arrestee shall prepare a memo of arrest at the time of arrest and such memo shall be attested by one witness, who may either be a member of the family of the arrestee or a respectable person of the locality from where the arrest is made. It shall be countersigned by the arrestee and shall contain the time and date of arrest.

44 (1997) 1 SCC 416.

45 *Id.*, 422, para. 1.

46 *Id.*, 423, para. 4.

> (3) A person who has been arrested or detained . . . shall be entitled to have one friend or relative or other person known to him or having an interest in his welfare being informed, a soon as practicable, that he has been arrested and is being detained at the particular place. . . .
>
> (4) The time, place of arrest and venue of custody of an arrestee must be notified by the police where the next friend or relative of the arrestee lives outside the district or town through the Legal Aid Organisation in the district and the police station of the area concerned telegraphically within a period of 8 to 12 hours after arrest.
>
> (5) The person arrested must be made of aware of this right to have someone informed of his arrest or detention as soon as he is put under arrest or is detained. . . .
>
> (8) The arrestee should be subject to medical examination by a trained doctor every 48 hours during his detention in custody. . . .
>
> (9) Copies of all the documents . . . should be sent to the Illaqa Magistrate for his record.
>
> (10) The arrestee must be permitted to meet his lawyer during interrogation, though not throughout the interrogation.[47]

The Court observed that these requirements, which flow from Articles 21 and 2(2) of the Constitution, must be complied with by all government agencies and that any breach will render the concerned official liable for department action and for contempt of court.[48]

It is apparent from the requirements formulated by the Supreme Court that these were aimed to complement and/or supplement the existing regulatory framework related to arrest and detention. It is interesting that the requirements look more like subordinate or delegated legislation (e.g., regulations drafted by the executive agency) than proper legislation, for they deal with minute details concerning arrest and detention. The requirements were seemingly intended to be a temporary stop-gap arrangement, but they are still in force thirteen years after their proclamation.

[47] *Id.*, 435–36, para. 35 (emphasis in original). For a critique, see Surya Deva, "Arresting the Arresters' Power to Arrest" (1999) 3:1 *Legal Spectrum* 5.

[48] *Id.*, 436–37, paras. 36 and 37.

2. *Sexual Harassment of Women at Workplace:* Vishaka v. State of Rajasthan[49]

Certain social activists and NGOs filed a petition in Supreme Court under Article 32 for the enforcement of the rights of working women under Articles 14, 19, and 21 – that is, the right to equality, the right to carry on any profession or trade, and the right to life and liberty, respectively.[50]

The Supreme Court acknowledged that, although the primary responsibility for protecting the rights of working women lies with the legislature and executive, it could not decide not to act. The Court observed: "When, however, instances of sexual harassment resulting in violation of fundamental rights of women workers under Arts. 14, 19 and 21 are brought before us for redress under Art 32, an effective redressal requires that some guidelines should be laid down for the protection of these rights *to fill the legislative vacuum*."[51] It is clear that the Supreme Court was conscious of entering the domain of the legislature, which is why it offered multiple justifications for its decision to fill the legislative vacuum.[52] It also noted in the judgment, by way of caution, that the government of India had given its consent to the guidelines.[53]

The Court laid down a detailed definition of sexual harassment in the following terms:

> [S]exual harassment includes such unwelcome sexually determined behaviour (Whether directly or by implication) as:
>
> a) Physical contact and advances;
>
> b) a demand or request for sexual favours;
>
> c) sexually coloured remarks;

49 AIR 1997 SC 3011.

50 The immediate incident that triggered this petition was a brutal gang rape of a social worker. *Id*, 3012, para. 2.

51 *Id.*, 3013, para. 3 (emphasis added). It is interesting to note that in an article published before this judgment was delivered, I had tried to explain judicial activism by a theory of vacuum filling. Surya Deva, "Who Will Judge the Judges? A Critical Purview of Judicial Activism" (1997) 1 *Delhi University Law Journal* 30, 31.

52 "Thus, the power of this Court under Art. 32 for enforcement of the fundamental rights and the executive power of the union have to meet the challenge to protect the working women from sexual harassment and to make their fundamental rights meaningful. Governance of the society by the rule of law mandates this requirement as logical concomitant of the constitutional scheme." *Id.*, 3014, para. 8.

53 *Id.*, 3014, para. 9.

> d) showing pornography;
>
> e) any other unwelcome physical, verbal or non-verbal conduct of sexual nature.
>
> Where any of these acts is committed in circumstances whereunder the victim of such conduct has a reasonable apprehension that in relation to the victim's employment or work whether she is drawing salary, or honorarium or voluntary, whether in Government, public or private enterprise such conduct can be humiliating and may constitute a health and safety problem. It is discriminatory for instance when the woman has reasonable grounds to believe that her objection would disadvantage her in connection with her employment or work including recruiting or promotion or when it creates a hostile work environment. Adverse consequences might by visited if the victim does not consent to the conduct in question or raises any objection thereto.[54]

In light of this definition, the Supreme Court imposed a duty on the employer or other responsible persons in workplaces or other institutions "to prevent or deter the commission of acts of sexual harassment and to provide the procedures for the resolution, settlement or prosecution of acts of sexual harassment by taking all steps required."[55] The Court also issued guidelines covering several different aspects (e.g., taking preventives steps, initiating criminal proceedings under the criminal law, taking disciplinary action, establishing a complaint mechanism, and spreading awareness of the guidelines).[56]

The Supreme Court concluded by directing that "the above guidelines and norms would be strictly observed in all work places for the preservation and enforcement of the right to gender equality of the working women. These directions would be binding and enforceable in law until suitable legislation is enacted to occupy the field."[57]

One important implication of this judgment lies in the fact that the Court extended the protection of the right against sexual harassment under Article 21 against nonstate actors such as private companies.

54 *Id.*, 3016, para. 16.

55 *Id.*, 3016, para. 16.

56 *Id.*, 3016–17, para. 16.

57 *Id.*, 3017.

3. *Ragging Menace at Universities*

To curb the menace of ragging (or bullying) in educational institutions, Vishwa Jagriti Mission, a spiritual organization, filed a PIL in the Supreme Court in 1998 seeking direction from the Court. In exercise of its power under Articles 32 and 142 of the Constitution, the Supreme Court issued several guidelines in 2001.[58] The Court not only offered a definition of ragging but also contemplated possible causes of ragging, prescribed detailed steps to curb the practice, and laid down diverse modes of punishment that educational authorities can take. Moreover, the Apex Court outlined various consequences that would follow for not being able to stop ragging. For example, a "[f]ailure to prevent ragging shall be construed as an act of negligence in maintaining discipline in the institution on the part of the management, the principal and the persons in authority of the institution. Similar responsibility shall be liable to be fixed on hostel wardens [and/or] superintendent[s]."[59] Going one step further, the Court ruled that if "an institution fails to curb ragging, the UGC/Funding Agency [University Grants Commission] may consider stoppage of financial assistance to such an institution till such time as it achieves the same. An [*sic*] University may consider disaffiliating a college or institution failing to curb ragging."[60]

Despite these wide-ranging guidelines, the media continued to report instances of ragging. That kept the Indian Supreme Court engaged in its fight to curb ragging. In November 2006, the Court appointed a Committee under the chairmanship of Mr. R. K. Raghavan, the ex-director of the Central Bureau of Investigation (CBI), to suggest remedial measures to tackle the problem of ragging in educational institutions. In its May 2007 order, the Supreme Court ordered that several recommendations of the Committee be implemented without any further lapse of time.[61] It is useful to look at some of these directions.

> 1. The punishment to be meted out has to be exemplary and justifiably harsh to act as a deterrent against recurrence of such incidents.
>
> 2. Every single incident of ragging where the victim or his parent and/or guardian or the head of institution is not satisfied with the institutional arrangement for action, a First Information Report must be filed without

[58] Vishwa Jagriti Mission *v. Central Government* AIR 2001 SC 2793.

[59] *Id.*, 2795.

[60] *Id.*, 2796.

[61] *University of Kerala v. Council of Principals of Colleges of Kerala*, order dated 16 May 2007.

> exception by the institutional authorities with the local police authorities. Any failure on the part of the institutional authority or negligence or deliberate delay in lodging the FIR [First Information Report] with the local police shall be construed as an act of culpable negligence on the part of the institutional authority. If any victim or his parent and/or guardian of ragging intends to file FIR directly with the police, that will not absolve the institutional authority from the requirement of filing the FIR.

The Court did not leave the task of monitoring the guidelines to the executive branch of the government. Therefore, it ruled that that the "Committee constituted pursuant to the order of this Court shall continue to monitor the functioning of the anti-ragging committees and the squads to be formed. [It] shall also monitor the implementation of the recommendations to which reference has been made above." The Supreme Court gave further directions in dealing with specific instances of ragging in two colleges that were investigated by the Raghavan Committee.[62]

In its order of 11 February 2009, the Supreme Court made extensive reference to the two reports of the Raghavan Committee,[63] differentiated "ragging" from "introduction,"[64] provided a historical account of ragging in societies other than India,[65] and directed all state governments and universities to act in accordance with the guidelines formulated by the Committee.[66] The Court also stated that ragging is a human rights abuse,[67] thus expressly justifying the Court's exercise of power under Article 32 – something that was not visible in earlier judgments on ragging.

Noting that some ragging incidents had surfaced despite earlier court orders and measures undertaken by the government agencies, the Court on 8 May 2009 ordered that certain recommendations of the Raghavan Committee are implemented with immediate effect.[68] Recommendations included direction to establish an Anti-Ragging Committee and an Anti-Ragging Squad in every academic institution and a Monitoring Cell on

62 J. Venkatesan, "SC Issues Guidelines to Check Ragging," *The Hindu*, 9 May 2009, http://www.thehindu.com/2009/05/09/stories/200905095740100.htm.

63 *University of Kerala v. Council of Principals of Colleges of Kerala*, Arising out of SLP(C) 24295 of 2004, order dated 11 February 2009, para. 2.

64 *Id.*, para. 4–6.

65 *Id.*, paras. 13, 14, and 22–25.

66 *Id.*, para. 26.

67 *Id.*, paras. 8 and 12.

68 *University of Kerala v. Council, Principals' Colleges, Kerala*, Civil Appeal n° 887 of 2009, order dated 08 May 2009, para. 1.

Ragging at university and state levels.[69] In addition, a helpline at the national level was to be put in place.[70] The Supreme Court acknowledged the limitation of guidelines formulation and, therefore, focused its attention on the implementation of the guidelines, including prescribing penal consequences. It observed:

> Such regulations shall have to be enforced strictly, and penal consequences for the heads of the institutions/administration of the institution who do not take timely steps in the prevention of ragging and punishing those who rag. In addition to penal consequences, departmental enquiries be initiated against such heads institutions/members of the administration/faculty members/non-teaching staff, who display an apathetic or insensitive attitude towards complaints of ragging.[71]

One may note that the Supreme Court is trying not only to legislate specific details normally seen in secondary legislation but also to ensure the implementation of such judicial legislation by giving specific directions and monitoring compliance. By doing so, the Court, in a way, is becoming an all-in-one governance agency – performing legislative, executive, and judicial functions.

CONCLUSION

On the basis of the review here of the constitutional provisions and judicial pronouncements, several conclusions can be drawn as to how the Indian courts have exercised their power of judicial review to act as positive legislators. First, most instances of judicial legislation have arisen in PIL, a discourse that the courts developed primarily to protect the human rights of disadvantaged sections of society. This PIL grounding has enabled Indian courts to communicate and engage with people through representative NGOs or social activists – a position and privilege that the judges and courts do not normally enjoy in a democracy.

Second, although the phenomenon of legislative gaps is not unique to India, it is quite clear that courts have been seemingly more than willing to fill those gaps than their counterparts in other common law jurisdictions. It also seems that the Indian legislature has, by and large, not tried to assert its

69 *Id.*, para. 1 (iii)/(vi)/(vii).

70 *Id.*, para. 1 (x).

71 *Id.*, para. 4.

authority in areas where such gaps were visible or pointed out by the judiciary – thus leaving a power vacuum to be filled in by the judiciary.

Third, it is apparent that the courts in India have been much more than positive legislators; they not only have legislated but also have acted as an executive branch by monitoring the implementation of the guidelines or recommendations they have issued. They have done so while adjudicating disputes, thus combining legislative, executive, and judicial powers on many occasions. It is paradoxical that the courts have tried to justify this infringement of the doctrine of separation of powers on the ground of protecting constitutionalism and upholding the rule of law.

Fourth, it is arguable that this all-encompassing ambit of the power of judicial review in India will have adverse implications for the Indian constitutional scheme. For instance, the routine judicial usurpation of legislative or executive functions might make the other two government wings less rather than more responsive. It is also doubtful whether the courts will be able to achieve those objectives that the legislature or the executive is more suitable and/or capable of pursuing. The only consolation is that the higher judiciary is not totally unaware of these concerns.

ITALY

THE ITALIAN CONSTITUTIONAL COURT AS POSITIVE LEGISLATOR

Giampaolo Parodi
Professor of Comparative Public Law,
Law Faculty, University of Pavia
giampaolo.parodi@unipv.it

1. A study of cases on the – manipulative, additive, integrative, "creative" – decisions by which the Italian Constitutional Court, in the current jurisprudential practice, poses as a positive legislator requires certain introductory remarks on the typology of the constitutional decisions and, before that, some outlines of the model of control of constitutionality operating in Italy, with particular regard to the proceeding in an incidental way.

Although, especially on the morrow of the constitutional revision of 2001 that reformed the Italian regional system, the procedure in the direct way – on state appeal, for control of regional laws; on regional initiative, for control of the legislative acts of the State and other Regions (art. 127 of the Constitution) – recorded a considerable quantitative increase, on these pages, it is opportune to limit oneself to judgment in an incidental manner (*incidenter* proceeding).

Indeed, the latter makes up the seat of control of the constitutionality of laws in a general way – any legislative act may be its subject, and any constitutional provision may make up the parameter – and in that context, the typology of constitutional decisions was historically and overridingly elaborated, starting from the interpretative and manipulative ones (and likewise monitory, or of address, with which the Court directs warnings to the legislator, in an almost advisory key).

2. On the basis of the classification criteria habitually followed in studies of Italian and comparative constitutional justice, control of constitutionality

in an incidental way presents a series of elements which determine the ascribing to the group of "mixed" systems, that is, characterized as much by typical connotations of the centralized European, continental model as by elements exactly of the widespread syndicate (judicial review of legislation).

The syndicate of constitutionality in an incidental way entrusted to the Constitutional Court and presents itself as a centralized control of widespread initiative, according to an effective definition now recurrent, which intends to underline, on the one hand, the monopoly of the Court as to the judgment on laws in its full extension through the possible declaratory judgment of their unconstitutional character, and on the other hand, the establishment entrusted to the initiative of any judge, in the presence of conditions of proposability of the relevance and of the not-manifest groundlessness (the question of constitutional illegitimacy cannot be clearly unfounded).

One is dealing, wishing to highlight certain qualifying characteristics, of a control, or judgment that it is: (a) successive (not preventive), having as subject laws and equivalent acts already in force, and general (not specific) in that it is susceptible to being promoted to scrutinize any flaw of constitutionality; (b) incidental (not principal), resolution of the question of constitutionality being necessary for the continuation or definition of a separate common judgment (the main judgment, or *a quo* judgment); (c) concrete (not abstract), what appears necessitated by the connection between the main and incidental judgment and the requisite of relevance, in the terms described further on; (d) jurisdictional (not political, despite the political nature that the evaluations of the judge sometimes present and the inevitable incidence, more or less accentuated, of the constitutional decisions in the sphere of political organs); (e) in part "of objective law," in that (perhaps overridingly) directed at guaranteeing, according to the original logic of centralized control, the internal coherence of the legal system and in part "of subjective law," in that directed at avoiding that the application of unconstitutional laws harms protected subjective positions of individuals, that which appears coherent with the incidental nature of the mechanism; (f) unwillingness of the *a quo* judge and of the parties to the *a quo* judgment; (g) to unnecessary parties even though possible, the constitution in incidental judgment before the Court being a right of the parties in the principal judgment, whose missing exercise does not however determine needs of integration of the debate (apart from the obligation, which rests on the referring judge, of notification to the same of the order of remittal).

As regards the declaration of unconstitutional character, one is dealing with a decision (a) provided with general efficacy (*erga omnes*) and (b) limitedly retroactive, in terms that are necessary to specify more clearly.

3. It is necessary to propose some mention of the *di merito* decisions of the Italian Constitutional Court, by which a question is declared founded or not.

To this category is necessary to ascribe – among those declaring the question unfounded, alongside the decisions of rejection – the numerous orders of manifest groundlessness, which, though directed at censuring the lack of a condition of admissibility of the question and succinctly motivated, tackle the question of constitutional legitimacy, declaring it, precisely, clearly unfounded. This happens both in the presence of an unfounded question *ictu oculi*, because of an erroneous interpretative assumption, because of the erroneous reconstruction of the legislative framework or, again, the impossibility of having repercussions on ambits reserved to the discretionary power of the legislator; both when the Court finds itself faced with a question identical to another already declared unfounded, or – not in full harmony with the evident favor for the remittal of the *quaestio* resulting from art. 1 of const. law 1/1948 and art. 23 of law 87/1953 – in the presence of questions simply analogue to others already previously declared unfounded.

With respect to the decision of rejection, which declares the question raised unfounded, the literature emphasizes how this has as subject not already a provision or a norm deduced in an interpretative way from a legislative statement but the question of constitutional legitimacy in that. Indeed, although decisions of acceptance declare the unconstitutional character of a provision or a norm, decisions of rejection limit themselves to declaring the question of constitutional legitimacy groundless, proposed in an incidental or principal way.

From art. 136, para. 1, of the Constitution, one traditionally infers, arguing *a contrario*, the efficacy only *inter partes* of the decision of rejection, however put in doubt by those who prefer to configure the decision as pending not on the *quaestio* or on the provision or the norm denounced, but on the "regulatory situation" (Ruggeri). According to the trend that is by far most prevalent – both in the literature and in the jurisprudence – the decision of rejection produces an effect of a preclusive type limited to the *a quo* judgment, under the scope of which the same question declared unfounded may not be proposed again or sent back to the Court.

Interpretative decisions of rejection have taken on great importance, and more generally, the decision-making techniques – ever more frequently used – directed at promoting the interpretation of the law in compliance with the Constitution, or constitutionally orientated, by common judges.

The decision-making technique typically directed at stimulating the interpretative adjustment of the legislative provisions to the Constitution is the so-called interpretative decision of rejection. Such a decision declares, typically, the question raised by the *a quo* judge unfounded "in accordance with which in motivation" (from the most recent decisions No. 379 and 403/2007; No. 2, 10, 165, 211 and 308/2008; No. 276/2009). Precisely, with the interpretative decision of rejection, the Court disregards the interpretation proposed in the remittal ordinance – implying but not explicitly declaring its unconstitutional character – and it recommends a different interpretation of the same provision, compatible with the Constitution. In other words, with the interpretative decision of rejection, the question raised is declared groundless, on the condition that one interprets the provision challenged in the sense indicated in the decision of the constitutional judge.

With respect to effectiveness, it is necessary to distinguish. With regard to the *a quo* judge, such a ruling – besides producing the preclusive effect typical of the decisions of rejection – is binding on interpretative grounds. In the past, there have been cases in the literature of authoritative voices (Crisafulli) in favor of the thesis that obliges the judge referring to the (adjusting) interpretation formulated in the motivation; however, the prevailing opinion is that, from an interpretative decision of rejection, there derives not a positive obligation but a negative obligation, in observance of which the *a quo* judge is simply obliged to not insist on attributing to the provision the meaning disregarded by the Court. With regard to the judges different from the one who promoted the constitutional judgment concluded with the interpretative ruling of rejection, the latter has an effectiveness that is merely persuasive, unlike in Germany, where the *verfassungskonforme Auslegung* of the federal constitutional court has general effectiveness. In contrast, faced with a jurisprudence that is reluctant to adopt the adjusting indication suggested with the interpretative decision of rejection, the Court always has at its disposal the instrument of the decision of acceptance to remove, with effectiveness *erga omnes*, the unconstitutional living law.

According to the general lines normally followed by constitutional jurisprudence, faced with a living law, the Court abstains from its own adjusting initiatives: it refers to that to reject questions raised on the stock of interpretations diverging from the consolidated orientation; it declares it unconstitutional if one is dealing with a living law contrary to the Constitution. Rarely, in the presence of a unconstitutional living norm, does the Court, instead of declaring the unconstitutional character, invite the *a quo* judge to disregard it and to interpret the provision in a way that complies with the Constitution (yet again recently, in Judgment 91/2004, the Court clarified that "in the presence of a consolidated jurisprudential orientation that has acquired the characteristics of a 'living law,' the evaluation of whether or not to abide by such an orientation is a mere faculty of the remitting judge").

Recently, however, this general line has tolerated some derogation, there being no lack of cases, at times conflictual, of interpretative decisions of rejection directed at recommending to the ordinary judge an interpretation other than that living, or however having established itself in the jurisprudence of the Corte di cassazione (Supreme Court), even in the presence of an explicit and reiterated refusal of the latter to adhere to the interpretation deemed by the constitutional judge in compliance with the Constitution, but by the Corte di cassazione not practicable (exemplary is the outcome resulting from the Cass. Pen., Sez. Un., 17-05-2004, No. 23016 and, later, in Const. Court, Judgment 299/2005, which, after a long conflict on interpretative grounds, acknowledged the living law contrary to the Constitution and declared its unconstitutional character).

Probably one is dealing with a reflection of the ever more marked tendency of the Constitutional Court to maintain as much as possible on the grounds of common jurisdiction the work of adjustment of the legislative system to constitutional principles, in the framework of an ever more accentuated development of the elements of the judicial review of legislation within our system of concentrated control of constitutionality. According to the Court, "any possible residual uncertainties of reading are destined to dissolve once that pre-eminent, hermeneutic canon has been adopted, where the principle of constitutional supremacy that forces the interpreter to opt, among the many solutions abstractly possible, for that which makes the provision comply with the Constitution" (Judgment 198/2003). This trend is evident also in an analysis of the numerous procedural decisions of manifest inadmissibility; in the most recent jurisprudence, in fact, such decisions are, generally speaking, preferred, as a function of stimulating the constitutionally orientated interpretation, to the same interpretative decisions of rejection (among the interpretative decisions of rejection in recent jurisprudence, see Const. Court, Judgments 198 and 233/2003).

4. For decisions of acceptance, it is necessary first to state some notions about the effects of a decision of unconstitutional character. The question of the effectiveness of the declaration of unconstitutional character in accordance with art. 136 of the Constitution and 30 Law 87/1953 has invariably superimposed, as happened in the context of other judicial systems, that, relative to the declarative, or rather constitutive, nature of the decisions of acceptance and concerning the invalidity or the annullability of the unconstitutional law. The prevalent literature has come out in favor of the thesis of annullability of the provision declared unconstitutional – though not unanimously – even on the basis of the consideration, borrowed from

Kelsen, that "an invalidity that cannot be ascertained if not by one organ, through a particular procedure to the exclusion of every other, is solved . . . in a form of annullability, and not of nullity" (Crisafulli).

It has also been pointed out that the value at least partially constitutive of the declaration of unconstitutional character should be deduced directly from art. 136 of the Constitution, which, envisaging the cessation of effectiveness of a law declared unconstitutional, "presupposes that, prior to the decision, the law itself had such effectiveness" (Pierandrei). In contrast, the cessation of effectiveness *ex* art. 136 "is not . . . a removal of the 'effects' already produced: it is the 'deprivation' (that the law is to suffer) of that capacity to produce effects and that, consequently, no longer allows the very same law to be able to 'continue' to regulate (or to impose the discipline of) certain situations" (Politi). The declaration of unconstitutional character constitutes an element of the case in point delineated by art. 136 of the Constitution and by art. 30 of Law 87/1953, so that the loss of effectiveness and the obligation of nonapplication, even retroactively, of the law declared unconstitutional intervenes not directly as a result of the ruling of the Court but as a consequence of the ascertainment contained in the ruling of acceptance, respectively *ope constitutionis* and *ope legis* (Zagrebelsky).

The question as to the declarative or better constitutive nature of the decision of acceptance has received an articulated response, on the basis of which the decision of acceptance would combine elements of declarative type and elements of constitutive type, presenting itself, according to a first setting out, as a ruling of "constitutive ascertainment" (Pierandrei, Pizzorusso). Later, this reconstructive hypothesis was clarified, attributing to the decision of unconstitutional character a declarative value of the invalidity (as a relation of antinomy between the censured provision and the Constitution) and constitutive, instead, of the ineffectiveness (Guastini, Modugno). This decision in effect raises, *ex novo*, a generalized and ratified obligation, formerly nonexistent, of disapplication of the provision, or norm, struck down by the ruling.

For its part, the Court particularly emphasized the differences between the premises of the abrogation and the declaratory judgment of unconstitutional character – the latter implying the invalidity of the legislative provision in question – to configure the ruling of acceptance as a decision of annulment (cf. Const. Court Judgments 127/1966; 58/1967 and 49/1970).

In addition, with regard to the organs of application, annulment by the Constitutional Court has effects also with regard to the legislator, subjected to the obligation of the constitutional decision. The constitutional jurisprudence has indeed clarified that the decisions of acceptance have as addressee not only those who are called on to apply the law but also the legislator, for whom it is "estopped to pursue and reach, directly or indirectly, outcomes corresponding to those already deemed detrimental of the Constitution" (Judgment 223/1983; see also Judgment 922/1988).

The decision of unconstitutional character as a decision of annulment, having effectiveness *erga omnes* under the scope of a model concentrated on control of constitutionality, opposes the disapplication of the unconstitutional law, having effectiveness *inter partes* and particularly of the judicial review of legislation.

With respect to the question relative to the limits of effectiveness *ex tunc* of the decision of acceptance – which, as is habitually said, does not affect the "exhausted relations" – it is to be solved through "the interpretation and application of ordinary law, under the scope of the competence of the jurisdictional organs" (Const. Court, Judgment 127/1966; in accordance with Const. Court, Judgment 49/1970). The events and the institutions of procedural and substantial order that may bring about the exhaustion or intangibility of a situation or a legal relationship, precluding any contestation in an irrevocable way, are numerous; among others, the becoming final of judicial decisions; the procedural preclusions; the prescription.

The limit of exhausted relations does not operate in relation to penal decisions of condemnation, in the terms of art. 30, fourth and final paragraph, of Law 87/1953.

5. With respect to the typology of the decisions of unconstitutional character, it is necessary first to make reference to the simple decisions of acceptance (*accoglimento*) and the interpretative decisions of acceptance.

The jurisprudence has delineated a much higher number of case studies than that which appeared imaginable at the time of the coming into force of the Constitutional Court, consolidating – alongside the decision of simple acceptance, the declarative of the constitutional illegitimacy of a provision (of a legislative statement) – models of decisions of "partial" unconstitutional character, aimed at censuring at times segments of legislative provisions, at others normative meaning contrary to the Constitution, identified among those jointly or alternatively expressed by the provision contested.

A first variant is that of the interpretative decisions of acceptance, with which the Court declares the unconstitutional character of one of the norms alternatively, or separately, expressed by a provision.

The literature has spotlighted both the structural and the functional affinities that bring together interpretative decisions of acceptance and interpretative decisions of rejection, as well as the differences. In the latter respect, in the interpretative decision of rejection, the unconstitutional interpretation remains in the shadow; on the contrary, in interpretative acceptance, the interpretation in accordance with the Constitution remains in the shadow; furthermore, the effectiveness *erga omnes* specific to the decisions of acceptance makes the outcome of promotion of the interpretation in accordance with the Constitution more certain.

According to a scheme followed especially in the initial period of activity of the Court, but occasionally reproposed even in recent times, in applying the principle of conservation of normative documents and that of the "least repercussive solution" (Zagrebelsky), the Court exercises its function of guidance with regard to the interpreters first pronouncing, as long as there is no consolidated "living" unconstitutional interpretation, an interpretative decision of rejection; and second, once the poor jurisprudential outcome of the adjusting interpretation recommended with the first decision has been ascertained, pronouncing, under the logic of the "double ruling," an interpretative decision of acceptance or, possibly, a pure and simple decision of acceptance (exemplary – and always recalled in this respect – the age-old matter of art. 2 T.U.L.P.S. (Consolidated Act of Public Security), subject first to an interpretative decision of rejection, No. 8/1956, and later, having verified the persistence of an application *contra constitutionem*, to an interpretative decision of acceptance, No. 26/1961).

6. With respect to the main subject of this contribution, namely manipulative decisions, the conviction is widespread that certain decisions of acceptance, despite leaving unaltered the text of the provision declared unconstitutional, transform the normative meaning by reducing or extending the sphere of application, not without introducing a new norm into the legal system or creating new norms. In this regard, one speaks of manipulative (or manipulating) decisions, into which typically enter – according to the prevalent literature – additive and substitutive decisions, as well as, according to a more extensive classifying option, the rulings of partial acceptance: both the nontextual ones (which leave unaltered the text of the provision subject to judgment) and the textual decisions of partial acceptance (declared unconstitutional but limited to certain words), should there derive a mutation of the legislative provision able to change the meaning. owever, theoretical reasons to consider manipulative the same interpretative decisions of acceptance are not totally lacking.

The notions of interpretative decision and manipulative decision are in part different. The former preferably makes reference to the subject of the ruling: a norm obtainable in an interpretative way from a legislative statement rather than a provision or one of its segments (in this sense, the notion fits both the interpretative decisions of acceptance in a strict sense and the nontextual decisions of partial acceptance); the notion of manipulative decision usually throws light on a peculiar effect of the ruling: of alteration and, precisely, manipulation of the meaning *prima facie* of the provision contested, which, on the textual plane (apart from the case recalled above of certain "textual" decisions of partial acceptance) remains unaltered.

In the category of manipulative decisions are interpretative decisions (or decisions of nontextual partial acceptance), which declare unconstitutional one of the norms jointly (or cumulatively) expressed by the provision denounced or – as in the German literature with regard to decisions of partial invalidity of the BVerfG – reduce the sphere of application (*Anwendungsbereich*) of the provision affected by partial constitutional illegitimacy.[1]

In these hypotheses, the Constitutional Court does not move from the premise – on which the diverse technique of judgment of the interpretative decision of acceptance as strictly understood is founded – of a multiplicity of possible alternative interpretations, to strike down one of the statutes separately expressed by the provision denounced.[2] The interpretative decision of partial acceptance is manipulative in the limits in which it reduces the normative meaning, or, better, the sphere of applicability, of the legislative ruling, by leaving the text unchanged.[3]

The decisions of partial acceptance (not just on norms or normative meanings but on provisions or segments of a provision) do not have a manipulative effect if the provision or a part of the legislative provision declared unconstitutional (according to the formula art. X of law Y is constitutionally illegitimate in the words ABC) correspond to a self-sufficient norm, isolable from the other normative meanings expressed by the contested provision, and likewise the legislative text that remains, in its normative meaning, is autonomous. One is dealing, in these cases, with a

1 In the most recent jurisprudence, cf., *ex plurimis*, Const. C., judgment no. 148, 149,185, 239, 360/2003; no. 135, 186, 223, 334, 335 and 339/2004; 199/2005; no 379 and 403/2007; no 2, 10, 165, 211 and 308/2008; 276/2009.

2 Strictly speaking, the premise of the interpretative decision of partial acceptance is the attribution to the provision contested of a certain normative meaning, albeit complex. For instance, "If a, b, or c, then X," meaning that results partially unconstitutional, limitedly to a case in point – for instance, c – to which one applies the consequence or the legal qualification envisaged (in the example proposed, X). There is no hermeneutic alternative, nor a doubt about the applicability of the provision in question in case c. One moves, on the contrary, from the assumption that it applies to the case c, to pass to declaring the provision unconstitutional just in the part in which it reincludes such a case in point.

3 See, e.g., *ex plurimis*, Const. C., judgment no. 356/1991; n. 238 and no. 311/1996.

decision provided with the usual "caducatory" effects with regard to a legislative provision or one of its segments.[4]

The manipulative nature of the decision of partial textual acceptance is evident whenever it provokes a mutation of the provision denounced, by altering or, at times, inverting the sense (e.g., a declarative decision of the unconstitutional character of a provision limited to a negation or to a clause of exclusion inserted in it).[5]

Concerning the question of the effectiveness of the manipulative constitutional decisions – in particular of the additive and substitutive decisions, often qualified as normative or creative – they make explicit norms (of legislative type, already implicit in the system) legitimately impose themselves with effectiveness *erga omnes* on subjects of the legal system, because the ruling of the Constitutional Court, in its additional profile, results constitutionally imposed "with obliged rhymes."[6]

According to a different, more up-to-date reconstruction,[7] one distinguishes between an "ablatory" profile and an additive (or substitutive) profile of the additive (or substitutive) decision, to recognize only for the first binding effectiveness *erga omnes*, and to the second the value of mere, though authoritative, proposal, aimed at the interpreters, of integration of the law made incomplete by the "ablatory" part of the ruling. [8]

In the most recent literature, the trend is widespread to consider the additive judgments not yet – as in the traditional perspective – declarative of the unconstitutional character of the legislator's omissions[9] rather than declarative of the unconstitutional character of implicit norms (or living

4 See, e.g., Const. C., judgment no. 424/1995.

5 See, e.g., Const. C., judgment no. 340/1992. More recently, Const. Court, judgment no. 390/2004.

6 Crisafulli, *Lezioni di diritto costituzionale, op. cit.*, 408.

7 For a review of the apparent logical foundation of traditional literature, see esp. Lavagna, *Sulle sentenze "additive" della Corte costituzionale*, in *Giur. it.*, 1969, IV, 151, in *id.*, *Ricerche sul sistema normativo*, Milan, 1984, 669 ss.

8 Cf. Picardi, *Le sentenze "integrative" della Corte costituzionale*, in *Scritti in onore di Costantino Mortati*, Milan, 1977, 597 ss.; Zagrebelsky, *La giustizia costituzionale, op. cit.*, 301.

9 On legislative omissions as subject of the additives and their classification Cf. Mortati, *Appunti per un studio sui rimedi giurisdizionali contro i comportamenti omissivi del legislatore*, in *Foro it.*, 1970, V, 153 ss.; Delfino, *Omissioni legislative e Corte costituzionale (delle sentenze costituzionali c.d. creative)*, in *Studi in onore di G. Chiarelli*, II, Milan, 1974, 911 ss.; Silvestri, *Le sentenze normative della Corte costituzionale*, in *Scritti in onore di Vezio Crisafulli*, I, Padova, 1985, 778; Grosso, *Sentenze costituzionali di spesa "che non costino,"* Turin, 1991, 22 ss.; Parodi, *La decisione additiva a dispositivo generico*, Turin, 1996, 122 ss.

rules) of exclusion,[10] inferable in an interpretative way of the provision of law censured, in the part in which it does not envisage something.[11] More precisely, according to the doctrinal orientation, the additive decision consists of two profiles: an ablatory (or caducatory) profile; and an additive (or integrative) profile. Of the two, only the first is considered binding *erga omnes*, because it coincides with the declaratory judgment of unconstitutionality of an exclusive norm implicit in the provision contested; the second is deemed merely persuasive effectiveness, in that it suggests, authoritatively, the direction in which the organ orient itself in the application when called to integrate the law made incomplete by the ablatory intervention imputable to the binding part of the decision. In light of such a reconstruction, the overridingly explicit function of additive decisions is that they orient the integrative activity of the organs of the application: integration of lacunae provoked by the constitutional decision, or to those preexisting lacunae in the case one understands the additive decision as pending on omissions of the legislator.[12]

In the category of decisions having additive dispositives , we can distinguish between traditional additives, characterized by a precise dispositive; additive with indeterminate dispositive; additive of principle; and additive of generic dispositive.

6.1. Traditional additive decisions aim to integrate the legislative rules and regulations through the introduction of a legal norm – previously nonexistent or ineffective – suitable to receive immediate application and enforcement by the lower judges without any need of a discretionary judgement .[13]

6.2. As for the second, one deals with rulings that presuppose an integration of the legal system imposed by the Constitution but indicated in the dispositive in indeterminate terms, so as to leave to the organs of

10 In this sense, Paladin, Corte costituzionale e principio generale d'eguaglianza: aprile 1979-dicembre 1983, in *Scritti in onore di Vezio Crisafulli, op. cit.*, 636; Elia, *Le sentenze additive e la più recente giurisprudenza della Corte costituzionale (ottobre 1981-luglio 1985)*, ivi, 302 ss.

11 Pugiotto, *Dottrina del diritto vivente e ridefinizione delle sentenze additive*, in *Giur. cost.*, 1992, 3695 ss.

12 According to Elia, *Le sentenze additive e la più recente giurisprudenza della Corte costituzionale (ottobre 1981-luglio 1985)*, *op. cit.*, 307 ss., 323 ss., the ruling of an additive decision usually presupposes renouncement of a an interpretative decision of rejection, aimed at recommending an adjusting interpretation of extensive type.

13 In the recent jurisprudence, Cf. Const. C., judgment no. 169, 211, 253, 262, 275, 345, 371 and 350/2003; no. 35, 98, 113, 206, 222, 245, 253 and 367/2004; no. 1, 11, 12, 77, 79, 88, 89, 158, 165, 201, 245, 254, 269, 270, 321, 329, 339 and 401/2007; no. 50, 51, 63, 70, 94, 142, 143, 144, 160, 167, 168, 181, 278, 323, 336, 387 and 400/2008; no. 11, 19, 28, 75, 86, 87, 124, 151, 173, 177, 183, 207, 232, 247, 273, 294, 317, 333 and 339/2009.

application a margin of interpretative discretionality. Additive decisions with indeterminate dispositive do not postulate the unavailability of a solution univocally inferable from the constitution, but they are characterized by a greater vagueness than the "self-applicative"[14] dispositive. Naturally, the vagueness of the dispositive, preordained to confer on the judge a power to make concrete the same dispositive, may also characterize substitutive decisions and of partial acceptance.

6.3. In the most recent constitutional jurisprudence, especially starting from the end of the 1980s, there is a newer type of decisive instrument: additive decision of principle. At times, reference is made to this variant of the additive ruling by means of further denominations: *declarative decision*, *additive of mechanism*, *additive with generic dispositive*. One deals with rulings characterized by a generic formulation that are indeterminate of the dispositive, which limits itself to declaring the unconstitutional character of the provisions contested in the part in which they do not envisage a mechanism, a criterion, or a normative solution – among the many that may legitimately, and therefore indifferently, be hypothesized – of adjustment, equalization, updating, and the like. Despite the additive structure of the dispositive, such decisions do not introduce – to take up a reconstruction of the additive decisions still supported by some credit – precise or self-applicative norms to the legal system, nor do they suggest that jurisdictional organs called on to give a follow up to the constitutional decision integrative solutions univocally inferable from the constitution or from the legislative system.[15]

An explicit and fundamental premise of generic additive dispositives is the concurrence of a plurality of solutions suitable to fill in or overcome the unconstitutional lacuna, among which, by express recognition of the Court, only the legislator is competent to choose. The decision-making technique

[14] The dispositives of interest here include indeed terms and locutions ascribable to the category of the juridical, or legislative concepts, which the German jurist qualifies as indeterminate (*unbestimmte Rechtsbegriffe, unbestimmte Gesetzesbegriffe*), formulated thus with the aim of attributing to the organs of application a particularly accentuated discretionality in order of their concretization. See, e.g., Const. C., judgment no. 218/1994, which declared a provision of the law no. 135/1990 on the subject of the fight against AIDS unconstitutional, "in the part in which it does not envisage sanitary ascertainments of the absence of seropositivity to infection from HIV as a condition for the expletion of activities that involve risks for the health of third parties." But one could also mention the well-known judgment no. 27/1975, on the subject of voluntary interruption of pregnancy; judgment no. 303/1996, on the subject of adoption and judgment no. 239/1998, on the subject of war pensions. More recently, judgment no. 151/2009, on artificial insemination.

[15] Cf. Parodi, *La sentenza additiva a dispositivo generico, op. cit.*, 112 ss.; *Id.*, *Le sentenze additive di princìpio, op. cit.*, 160 ss.

that one is dealing with allows the Court to avoid, in such a situation, recourse to the defeatist solution, and inspired by excessive self-restraint, of the decision of inadmissibility of the question, in the presence of an additive *petitum* that does not appear "with obliged rhyme."[16] At the origin of additive decisions of principle, there is the need to avoid or limit undesired practical consequences, especially of a financial order, but not only, which with the ruling of "traditional" additive decisions could produce themselves immediately. These decisions are also presented as more respectful of the sphere reserved to the discretion of the legislator, even though, frequently, they are adopted to promote the direct application of constitutional principles indicated in them by the jurisdictional organs.[17]

Decisions with a generic dispositive are said to be additive of principle because principles are formulated in them to guide both the legislator, in the necessary normative activity subsequent to the ruling to remedy the unconstitutional omission, and ordinary judges, so that, while waiting for the legislative intervention, they find, with integration of law, a solution for the controversies submitted to them. This is theorized in a particularly perspicuous way in the decision of the Constitutional Court No. 295/1991, in the following terms of general importance: "the declaration of constitutional illegitimacy of a legislative omission – such as that recognised in the hypothesis of missing anticipation, by the regulating statute of a constitutionally guaranteed right, of a mechanism suitable to ensure the effectiveness of this – while it leaves to the legislator, recognising the undeniable competence, of introducing and disciplining even retroactively such a through general legislation, it gives a principle to which the ordinary judge is able to make reference to place a remedy in the meantime to the omission at the time of identification of the rule for the concrete case."

One is dealing with decisions characterized by a dual function: on the one hand, to steer the legislator in fulfillment of the obligation of reform deriving from the constitutional parameters applied and specified by the decision of

16 The inadmissibility of the question is still the solution adopted in the presence of requests for extraneous additive interventions, for their "openly creative character," to the powers of the Court, and coming into the discretionality of the legislator, as one reads in Const. C., judgment no. 382/2004; in an analogous sense, judgment no. 175/2004, which censured the "abnormality" of the request formulated by the judge *a quo*. Cf. also Const. C., judgment no. 2, 33, 332/2003; ord. no. 76/2003; ord. no. 83, 112, 145, 185, 199, 225, 233, 249, 333 and 381/2007; judgment no. 202, 240, 251, 325, 376 and 431/2008; ord. no. 31, 58, 116, 177, 186, 270, 293, 299, 316, 333, 379, 406 and 421/2008.

17 This refers to the substitution of the legislator by the jurisdictional organs favored by the decision-making technique that Bartole deals with, *I requisiti dei procedimenti giurisdizionali e il loro utilizzo nella giurisprudenza costituzionale*, in *Giur. cost.*, 1999, 199.

the Court; on the other hand, to await the intervention of the legislator and to guide ordinary judges called on to fill the unconstitutional lacunae in defining the concrete controversies submitted to them.[18]

Along with this category of additive decisions of principle, explicitly or implicitly addressed by both the legislator and the judges, one should note that the additive decision of principle is explicitly or implicitly directed only at the legislator. If, indeed, in the cases recalled here, the jurisprudential follow-up of the additive decisions of principle often has difficulties and uncertainties, in other cases, the successive practice with decisions having generic dispositives has highlighted a substantial incapacity to express applicative solutions in accordance with the principles indicated by the Court.[19] In these cases, and in those where the same additive decision of principle is addressed only to the legislator,[20] the ruling appears as a merely declarative decision of the unconstitutional character of legislative omissions, not fully in line with art. 136 of the Constitution or art. 30 of Law No. 87/1953, which postulate the annulment of a legislative norm as a normal or necessary effect of a declaration of unconstitutional character.[21] Then there is no lack of decision that, with regard to its receivers, does not contain any indications.[22] However, it is easy to notice that development of a jurisprudential follow-up in accordance with the principles formulated by the decision – awaiting the necessary legislative intervention, considered nonfungible – depends essentially on the concrete possibility of filling the (axiological[23]) lacuna censured by the Court and on the choices of the interpreter faced with the legislative omission declared unconstitutional, with

18 Cf. Const. C., judgment nos. 560/1987; 406 and 497/1988; 420 and 421 /1991; 88/1992; 288/1994; 284/1995; 143/1997. Judgment no. 179/1999 and 160/2008 can also be assimilated to these.

19 Cf. Const. C., judgment nos. 204 and 232/1992; 243/1993; 376/1994; 171/1996; 280/2005. Judgment nos. 201 and 339/2007; 1/2008 could also be assimilated to these.

20 Cf. Const. C., judgment nos. 390/2000; 185 and 417/1998; 309/1999; 243/1993; 277/1991. Lastly, Const. C., judgment nos. 196/2004; 219/2005.

21 In this sense, Celotto, *Corte costituzionale e legislatore. Riflessioni sugli interventi normativi volti a limitare l'efficacia nel tempo di decisioni di incostituzionalità*, in Modugno (edited by), *Trasformazioni della funzione legislativa, I, I "vincoli" alla funzione legislativa*, Milan, 1999, 160 ss.; *Id.*, *Impresa artigiana: indebito contributivo e interessi*, in *Mass. Giur. lav.*, 1999, 303 ss.

22 See, e.g., Const. C., judgment nos. 26 and 61/1999.

23 Cf. G. Parodi, *Lacune e norme inespresse nella giurisprudenza costituzionale*, in Comanducci, Guastini (edited by), *Struttura e dinamica dei sistemi giuridici*, Turin, 1996, 87 ss.

regard to the direct applicability of the constitutional principles from time to time relevant.[24]

With respect to the effectiveness of additive decisions of principles with regard to the legislator, some attach a binding value to the decision that sets out a "principle of living constitutional law";[25] others attach binding effectiveness to them in consideration of the nature of decision of acceptance.[26] There are those who doubt the legally binding nature of the rulings in question with regard to the legislator and assimilate their effectiveness to that of the other constitutional decisions with exhortative significance, even in the case of the additives of principle or invitations addressed to the legislator strengthened by the circumstance of being formulated "in a decision qualified as being of acceptance, rather than in a decision qualified as of inadmissibility."[27] In this regard, the practice of the past twenty years has shown a legislative follow-on not always well timed but generally adequate in the fulfillment of the obligations deriving from the decisions.

The typology of manipulative constitutional decisions also includes substitutive decisions, which declare a legislative provision unconstitutional, in the part in which it envisages something, rather than something different. At times, the statute or its fragment indicated in substitution is formulated between inverted paragraphs, as if one were dealing with a fragment destined to take the place of that declared unconstitutional: in this case one

24 On the jurisprudential follow-up to additives of principle Cf., lastly, Lamarque, *Il seguito giudiziario delle decisioni della Corte Costituzionale*, *op. cit.*, 217 ss.

25 Zagrebelsky, *Problemi in ordine ai costi delle sentenze costituzionali*, in *Le sentenze della Corte Costituzionale e l'art. 81, u.c., della Costituzione*, Milan, 1993, 150.

26 According to Anzon, *Nuove tecniche decisorie della Corte Costituzionale*, in *Giur. cost.*, 1992, 3213, if the legislator disregards the indications contained in the additive decision of principles "would violate the precept of the immediate and general binding effectiveness, as per art. 136."

27 Pizzorusso, *Corte costituzionale: un nuovo tipo di sentenza?*, in *CorG*, 1993, 773 s. On the admonitions and the auspices addressed to the legislator, Cf. Pegoraro, *La Corte e il parlamento. Sentenze-indirizzo e attività legislativa*, Padua, 1987. In the most recent jurisprudence, the auspice of a new discipline of the subject is formulated in the decisions of rejection nos. 71, 346 and 264/2003. A real and true admonition of the legislator is contained in the decision 310/2003, in which, even though recognising the groundlessness of the censures prospected, one states, on the theme of suspension of the executive procedure for the release of immovables, that such a procedure "cannot be paralysed indefinitely with a series of pure and simple extensions, beyond a reasonable limit of tolerability." This admonition was reiterated in the successive judgment no. 155/2004, in which one states that, should the legislative choices "follow still further the logic adopted up until now, they could not subtract themselves from the proposed censures of constitutional illegitimacy . . ., also in consideration of the *vulnus* that the protraction of the extensions cause to the principle of the reasonable duration of the proceedings to the coherence of the legal system."

sometimes speaks of "textual" substitutive decisions.[28] Other times, the substitutive ruling formulates the norm destined to take the place of that declared unconstitutional, without the insertion of new fragments in the text of the provision declared constitutionally illegitimate.[29] The trend is to reconstruct this type of decision as the combination of a decision of partial acceptance and an additive.

7. Some space must be dedicated to the modulation of the temporal effects of the decision of unconstitutional character. Of particular importance for the purposes of this contribution is the practice, recently reproposed after fifteen years of almost total abeyance, of the modulation of the temporal effects of the declaratory statement of unconstitutional character.

The Italian system of control of constitutionality does not expressly envisage the possibility of limiting or modulating the effects over time of the declaration of unconstitutional character. In the Constituent Assembly, one set aside the proposal of borrowing from the Austrian system the instrument of *Fristsetzung*;[30] and in more recent times, the hypothesis of introducing into the Italian Constitution a solution inspired by the Austrian model, matured in the parliamentary commission for constitutional reforms set up by the constitutional Law No. 1 of 1997, has not had, with the entire project of revision, any follow-on.[31]

In the jurisprudential seat, nonetheless, techniques of decision aimed to limit normal effects of ascertaining unconstitutional character have been widely experimented with and assigned to many functions. First is to prevent the caducatory effects of the decision from being retroactive before the unconstitutional character supervenes, whenever this unconstitutional character is not originary. Second is to avoid the undesired consequences of the declaratory judgment of unconstitutional character (e.g., legislative voids, compromising the necessary guarantee of constitutional rights, residual disciplines even farther from the Constitution, new or higher financial burdens for the state or other public bodies). Third is to declare the unconstitutional character of an omission of the legislator without invading the sphere reserved to the discretion of the latter.

28 See, e.g., Const. C., judgment nos. 215/1987; 440/1988; 27/2005.

29 See, e.g.,, among the best known, Const. C., judgment no. 15/1969, which declared the constitutional illegitimacy of art. 313, third co., c.p., "in the limits in which it attributes the power to give authorisation to proceed for the crime of contempt of the Constitutional Court to the Minister of Justice instead of to the Court itself." More recently, Const. C., judgment no. 104 and 301/2003; no. 204, 224, 281 and 426/2004; 222/2005.

30 Cf. *supra*, para. 1.

31 Cf. *infra*, para. 4.

Thus, one can distinguish, on the one hand, the declaration of constitutional illegitimacy that supervened in the true sense and is aimed to prevent the caducatory effects of the decision from being retroactive unjustifiably before the illegitimacy supervened, and on the other hand, the nonretroactive or partially retroactive decision of acceptance that is dictated by worries of a practical nature.[32] In both cases, at issue are declaratory judgments of unconstitutional character – remitting to the concept of constitutional illegitimacy that supervened or successive more or less explicitly according to the greater or smaller properties of such a qualification – with an indication, in the dispositive, of the nonretroactive or limited retroactive character of the effects of the decision (the declaration of unconstitutional character that supervened may also include the specification of *dies a quo*, of the moment starting from which the effects will be produced).

Decisions of the second type, declarative of the unconstitutional character that supervened "in an improper sense," respond to the logic of the dual ruling. Indeed, they may be preceded by admonitory (or exhortative) decisions of precarious rejection[33] or by decisions of inadmissibility, also with a more or less accentuated admonitory importance.

In the most recent jurisprudence, there are important cases of limitation and deferment of the effects in time of the declaration of unconstitutional character, not properly evocative of the figure of the supervened unconstitutional character. In these cases, the Court declared the unconstitutional character of legislative provisions by the state successive to constitutional Law No. 3/2001 and detrimental to the new regional attributions, explaining that the state discipline censured would not have ceased to find application until the arrangement and the coming into force of the new regional regulations and setting aside the administrative procedures in progress and founded on the first, even if not yet exhausted, to avoid that, due to the situation of normative void determined by the ruling of acceptance, the guarantee of constitutional rights might be compromised.[34]

[32] For all, Cf. Romboli, *Il giudizio di costituzionalità delle leggi in via incidentale*, in *Id.* (ed.), *Aggiornamenti in tema di processo costituzionale*, Turin, 1999, 188 ss.

[33] Paradigmatic the jurisprudential event of the legislative exclusion of publicity of the hearings before tax commissions, concluded with the judgment of the Constitutional Court no. 50 of 1989.

[34] Cf. Const. C., judgment nos. 370/2003; 13 and 423/2004, on the subject of education. Cf. also Const. C., judgment nos. 16 and 49/2004. A little after is judgment no. 426/2004, extraneous to the regional subject, but explicitly directed at limiting its own effects over time.

Beside the techniques of judgment specifically aimed to contain the effects of the ascertainment of unconstitutional character, the practice of the Constitutional Court also knows models of decision aimed to delay a decision of acceptance through procedural rulings of as dilatory type (in the German literature, one writes of *Entscheideungsverzögerung*) or by means of precarious decisions of rejection (analogous to the so-called *Appellentscheidungen* of the German BVerfG), declarative of the provisional constitutionality of the contested discipline. In these rulings, the illegitimacy of the norm is only overshadowed, not expressly stated; at times, more or less explicitly, one alludes to a future illegitimacy, about to show itself but not yet supervened (the discipline contested, one reads in the decisions of the BVerfG, is "still in accordance with the constitution").

BIBLIOGRAPHY

ANZON, A., "Nuove tecniche decisorie della Corte costituzionale," in *Giur. cost.*, 1992

BARTOLE, S., "I requisiti dei procedimenti giurisdizionali e il loro utilizzo nella giurisprudenza costituzionale," in *Giur. cost.*, 1999

CELOTTO, A., *"Corte costituzionale e legislatore. Riflessioni sugli interventi normativi volti a limitare l'efficacacia nel tempo di decisioni di incostituzionalità,"* in Modugno, F. (ed.), *Trasformazioni della funzione legislativa, I, I "vincoli" alla funzione legislativa*, Milano, 1999

CRISAFULLI, V., *Lezioni di diritto costituzionale*, II, Padova, 1984

DELFINO, F., "Omissioni legislative e Corte costituzionale (delle sentenze costituzionali c.d. creative)," in *Studi in onore di G. Chiarelli*, II, Milano, 1974

ELIA, L., *"Le sentenze additive e la più recente giurisprudenza della Corte costituzionale (ottobre 81-luglio 1985),"* in *Scritti in onore di Vezio Crisafulli*, Padova, 1985

GROSSO, E., *Sentenze costituzionali di spesa "che non costino"*, Torino, 1991

GUASTINI, R., *Dalle fonti alle norme*, Torino, 1992

GUASTINI, R., *Teoria e dogmatica delle fonti*, Milano, 1998, 508 ss.

LAMARQUE, E., "Il seguito giudiziario delle decisioni della Corte costituzionale," in Malfatti, E., Romboli, R., Rossi, E (eds.), *Il giudizio sulle leggi e la sua "diffusione"*, Torino, 2002.

LAVAGNA, C., "Sulle sentenze "additive" della Corte costituzionale," in *Giur. it.*, 1969, IV, 151; and in Id., *Ricerche sul sistema normativo*, Milano, 1984

MODUGNO, F., *L'invalidità della legge*, I e II, Milano, 1970

MODUGNO, F., "Validità (diritto costituzionale)," in *Enciclopedia del diritto*, XLVI, Milano, 1994.

MORTATI, C., "Appunti per un studio sui rimedi giurisdizionali contro i comportamenti omissivi del legislatore," in *Foro it.*, 1970

PALADIN, L., *"Corte costituzionale e princìpio generale d'eguaglianza: aprile 1979-dicembre 1983,"* in *Scritti in onore di Vezio Crisafulli*, Padova, 1985

PARODI, G., "Lacune e norme inespresse nella giurisprudenza costituzionale," in Comanducci, P., Guastini, R. (ed.), *Struttura e dinamica dei sistemi giuridici*, Torino, 1996

PARODI, G., *La sentenza additiva a dispositivo generico*, Torino, 1996

PARODI, G., *"Le sentenze additive di principio,"* in "Foro italiano", 1998

PEGORARO, L, *La Corte e il parlamento. Sentenze-indirizzo e attività legislativa*, Padova, 1987

PICARDI, N., *Le sentenze «integrative» della Corte Costituzionale.* in *Scritti in onore di Costantino Mortati,* Milano, 1977

PIERANDREI, F., "Corte costituzionale," in *Enc. dir.*, X, 1962

PINARDI, R., *La Corte, i giudici ed il legislatore. Il problema degli effetti temporali delle sentenze d'incostituzionalità*, Milano, 1993

PIZZORUSSO, A., "Art. 136," in *Comm. Cost. Branca, Art. 134-139*, Bologna-Roma, 1981

PIZZORUSSO, A., "Corte costituzionale: un nuovo "tipo" di sentenza?," in *CorG*, 1993

POLITI, F., *Gli effetti nel tempo delle sentenze di accoglimento della Corte costituzionale (Contributo ad una teoria dell'invalidità costituzionale della legge)*, Padova, 1997

PUGIOTTO, A., *Sindacato di costituzionalità e diritto vivente. Genesi, uso, implicazioni*, Milano, 1994

PUGIOTTO, A., "Dottrina del diritto vivente e ridefinizione delle sentenze additive," in *Giur. cost.*, 1992

ROMBOLI, R., "Il giudizio di costituzionalità delle leggi in via incidentale," in *Id.* (ed.), *Aggiornamenti in tema di processo costituzionale*, Torino, 1999.

RUGGERI, A., *Le attività "conseguenziali" nei rapporti fra la Corte costituzionale e il legislatore (premesse metodico-dogmatiche ad una teoria giuridica)*, Milano, 1988

RUGGERI, A., *Storia di un "falso". L'efficacia inter partes delle sentenze di rigetto della Corte costituzionale*, Milano, 1990

SILVESTRI, G., *Le sentenze normative della Corte costituzionale*, in *Scritti in onore di Vezio Crisafulli*, I, Padova, 1985

ZAGREBELSKY, G, *La giustizia costituzionale*, Bologna, 1988

ZAGREBELSKY, G., *"Problemi in ordine ai costi delle sentenze costituzionali,"* in *Le sentenze della Corte costituzionale e l'art. 81, u.c., della Costituzione*, Milano, 1993

MEXICO

THE MEXICAN SUPREME COURT AS POSITIVE LEGISLATOR

Eduardo Ferrer Mac-Gregor*
Professor and member of the Legal Research Institute,
Universidad Nacional Autónoma de México (UNAM)
Judge Ad Hoc of the Interamerican Court of Human Rights
eferrerm@servidor.unam.mx

INTRODUCTION

From a material point of view, the Mexican Supreme Court of Justice of the Nation (hereinafter, SC) has evolved from an appeals court into a constitutional court, specifically since the constitutional reform of December 31, 1994. From that date, its composition decreased from twenty-six to eleven Justices, and it was empowered to pronounce the invalidity of norms with future *erga omnes* effects through two mechanisms: the abstract unconstitutionality cause of action and constitutional controversies.

These powers are exclusive to the SC. As such, the best doctrine has considered it a real constitutional court, although it still presides over matters inherent to a legality court, as it is at the top of the federal judicial branch. Because of its dual duties (constitutional and legal), it has been deemed that the system controlling constitutionality in Mexico has a mixed nature, to the extent that it has European or centralized control features and some aspects of the diffuse or American system, as the SC also presides over amparo

* *Editor in Chief of* Revista Iberoamericana de Derecho Procesal Constitucional

proceedings[1] (on review),[2] in which it may declare only the inapplicability of an unconstitutional norm to a specific case.

The full exercise of these constitutional powers has led the SC to evolve the type of decisions it issues. In this manner, it has left behind the conceptualization of the famous Viennese jurist Kelsen because it has ceased to be a simple negative legislator, having progressed to what may be considered a true positive legislator in line with certain evolving constitutional court trends.[3]

To justify the foregoing, I herein briefly analyze the SC as a constitutional court, as well as the effects of its decisions and, specifically, the cases that allow us to observe its active and law-creating role.

I. THE SUPREME COURT AS A CONSTITUTIONAL COURT

1. *Brief Background*

The oldest background on the SC is found in the Real Audience of Mexico, established on November 29, 1527, as the highest judicial instance at the time of New Spain (1521–1821).

During the time of the fight for independence (1810–21), there operated what has been considered the first federal court: the Supreme Court of Justice of Mexican America, located in Ario de Rosales, Michoacán (1815).

However, the SC was formally regulated by the first Constitution in force in the independent Mexico. The Federal Constitution of the United Mexican States, enacted on October 4, 1824, organized the judicial branch in its article 123, which bestowed said power on the Supreme Court of Justice.

Subsequently, centralist constitutional codes (the Seven Laws of 1836 and the Organic Bases of the Mexican Republic of 1843) also regulated the SC.

Commencing with the enactment of the Federal Constitution dated February 5, 1857, the SC obtained constitutional control powers defined

1 Under Mexican law, *amparo* literally means "shelter" and is legally defined as providing the complainant with shelter and protection of the Federal Justice System as the result of a favorable amparo proceeding. The amparo proceeding challenges the constitutionality of the act of a governmental authority, thereby forestalling the enforceability of the authority's act if the amparo court rules in the complainant's favor.

2 The SC can act as a court of appeals when a first judgment is challenged and it regards the constitutionality of laws or other general rules, or when it comes to a very important case, using a sort of certiorari power.

3 Cf. FERRER MAC-GREGOR, Eduardo (coord.), *Crónica de tribunales constitucionales en Iberoamérica*, Buenos Aires/Madrid, Marcial Pons, 2009.

through the amparo proceedings. This instrument over the course of the late nineteenth century evolved the particular nature that it has today, which was defined in the Federal Constitution of 1917 in force.

2. *Constitutional Evolution*

For the purposes here, the two most important constitutional judicial reforms, and specifically those regarding the SC transformation into a constitutional court, took place in the years 1987 and 1994.

(1) The purpose of the constitutional reform dated August 29, 1987, was to turn the Court into a specialized court of a constitutional nature, as expressly set forth in the reform's statutory purpose. In this manner, the mere legality control previously presided over by the SC transferred to the Collegiate Circuit Courts.

(2) Six years later, the most important constitutional judicial reform of the past years appeared. The reform of December 31, 1994, encompassed a total of twenty-seven substantive articles and twelve transitory provisions. The relevance of the same is divided into two fundamental aspects: the SC's organic composition (reduced from twenty-six members to eleven) and the creation of a complete constitutional control system, which considerably approaches the European constitutional courts.

3. *Powers*

A. Constitutional Control.

The SC presides essentially over three constitutional control instruments: (1) the abstract unconstitutionality cause of action, (2) constitutional controversies (jurisdictional or power conflicts between State bodies and branches), and (3) amparo proceedings.

(a) *Abstract unconstitutionality cause of action.* This power is exclusive to the SC by means of the unconstitutionality cause of action, a mechanism regulated by article 105, section II, of the Federal Constitution.

Those entitled to file the action are 33 percent of the members of (federal or state) legislative bodies; the Attorney General of the Republic; political parties; and the Human Rights Commissions (ombudsmen), whether at the National or State level.

As I mention herein, a supramajority vote is necessary to declare generally effective invalidity, that is to say, when eight (of eleven) votes are obtained. Should there be a simple majority (five, six, or seven votes), the action is held nonjusticiable (dismissed) and the action has no effect (*improcedente*). This supramajority requirement has been criticized by doctrinaires, and there exist proposals to withdraw it.

(b) *Specific control*. This takes place through two instruments: constitutional controversies and amparo proceedings. Unlike the abstract unconstitutionality cause of action, to have standing to sue in these proceedings, the plaintiff must have suffered some specific affectation of legal or legitimate interests; otherwise, the constitutional suit is inadmissible.

(i) *Constitutional controversies* (jurisdictional or power conflicts). Article 105, section I, provides eleven subsections that may be classified in three categories: (1) conflicts between different legal orders due to the legality or constitutionality of a general norm or an act (e.g., the Federation and a State and the Federal District, the Federation and a State); (2) conflicts between bodies of different legal orders due to the legality or constitutionality of general norms or of acts (e.g., the Executive Branch and the Congress of the Union); and (3) conflicts between bodies of the same legal order due to the constitutionality of general norms or of acts (e.g., between two branches of a state, between a state and a municipality of the same state).[4]

This constitutional process is exclusive to the SC. Resolutions may produce future general effects with the same supramajority vote requirement of eight justices. However, unlike the unconstitutionality cause of action, if there exists a relative majority, the resolution of the constitutional controversies produces *inter partes* effects.

(ii) *Amparo proceedings*. Regulated by constitutional articles 103 and 107, this is the most deeply rooted constitutional control mechanism in Mexico, not only because it has a centenarian tradition but also because it represented the sole effective constitutional protection mechanism up to the oft-cited 1994 constitutional reform.

One of its characteristics is that decisions pronounced in amparo proceedings provide protection only *inter partes*; that is, the challenged law is inapplicable to a specific case and to the amparo plaintiff (*quejoso*), although it is still valid for anyone else. Nevertheless, in December 2010, the Congress of the Union approved a constitutional amendment which allows a general declaration of unconstitutionality with *erga omnes* effects solely in the so called "Amparo against laws". In this case, when an indirect amparo trial deals for the second time with the unconstitutionality of a general norm,

[4] Cf. COSSÍO DÍAZ, José Ramón, "Artículo 105 constitucional," in FERRER MAC-GREGOR, Eduardo (coord.), 5th ed., Mexico City, Porrúa, 2006, Volume II, pp. 957–999, at p. 982.

the Supreme Court will inform the authoritative legislative body. If the problem persists for 90 calendar days, the Supreme Court will issue (if approved by at least 8 votes) the general declaration of unconstitutionality, in which the Court will determine its reach and the conditions in terms of the statutory law.

B. Other Jurisdiction and Powers

In addition to those three constitutional powers, the SC has other special constitutional jurisdiction as well as multiple jurisdictions of different kinds that are more like those of an appeals court, thus distancing itself as a constitutional court. Among the most important powers are the investigation procedure of the SC, which allows the SC to investigate possible serious individual rights violations, regulated by the second paragraph of article 97 of the Mexican Constitution; the power of preemption to preside over those amparo proceedings that originally correspond to Collegiate Circuit Courts or to Unitary Circuit Courts on appeal of ordinary trials in which the Federation is a party and when it is warranted due to the interest and relevance of the matter; the resolution of contradiction between precedents and of jurisdictional conflicts between Collegiate Circuit Courts; the presiding over of determined administrative claims remedies; and deciding on the removal of authorities as a result of violation of amparo decisions.

II. THE SUPREME COURT AS A POSITIVE LEGISLATOR

The nullification of a law is essentially produced by applying the norms of the Constitution. Free creation which is a characteristic of legislation is virtually absent in a nullification. While the legislator is not bound by the Constitution except in regards to procedure and only exceptionally in regards to the contents of laws that they shall enact – and this, only by general principles or directions – the activity of the negative legislator, that is, constitutional jurisdictional activity, to the contrary, is absolutely determined by the Constitution. Specifically for this reason, its duties are similar to those of any other court in general, and said duties mainly constitute application of the Law and, only to a lesser extent, creation of Law. Therefore, its duties are truly jurisdictional.[5]

[5] KELSEN, Hans, "La garantía jurisdiccional de la Constitución (la justicia constitucional)," *Revista Iberoamericana de Derecho Procesal Constitucional*, Mexico City, nº 10, July–December 2008, pp. 3–46, at p. 25.

The conception of the famous jurist Hans Kelsen was such that when he wrote the preliminary draft of the Constitution of Austria of 1920, he created for the first time a specialized constitutional regulatory control body: the Constitutional Court. This Court narrowed its duties to constitutionality analysis and, in the applicable case, proceeded to declare invalid the norm challenged.

As I illustrate herein, the tasks of the modern constitutional courts have surpassed the sole nullification of laws. Constitutional justice challenges are increasingly complex and need a much more participative intervention by constitutional judges. Thus, they have advanced into territory that, for Kelsen, was unthinkable and probably undesirable. Along these lines, problems of unconstitutionality incite the creative role of the constitutional judge, who must bring into action all the legal tools within his or her reach, combined with sensitivity, prudence, and self-control.

I hereafter discuss my ideas on the decisions issued by the SC acting as a Constitutional Court, and I then reflect on complex cases in which the constitutional response has gone beyond a simple negative legislator.

To determine the effects and contents of constitutional decisions issued by the SC (and to comment on exceptional cases), it is necessary to distinguish between the three constitutional control mechanisms, as each has different characteristics.

1. *Amparo Proceedings (Specific Effects)*

Beginning with the 1847 Constitution, the rulings issued by the Supreme Court of Justice in amparo matters have been limited to protection in a specific case, in compliance with the traditional principle of relativity of decisions. I deem that this situation must be overcome to include the general declaration of unconstitutionality, at least in the "amparo against laws" sector.

This has caused the result that "favorable"[6] amparo constitutional decisions are limited to solely protecting the petitioner, even though their effects, unlike other constitutional proceedings, are retroactive to the time the violation was committed (*ex tunc*), in compliance with article 80 of the Amparo Law: "The purpose of a decision granting amparo is that of restoring to the petitioner full entitlement of the individual right violated,

[6] The original Spanish uses the words *estimatoria* and *desestimatoria* to denote those decisions that have been upheld and those decisions that have been overruled, respectively. For the purpose of clarity and emphasis, I use *favorable* and *unfavorable* as approximations to those.

reestablishing the state of things as they were before the violation, when the act challenged is positive in nature; and if act is negative in nature, the effect of the amparo shall be to obligate the challenged authority to act so as to respect the right in question and to itself comply with what the right demands."

As a matter of fact, the Amparo Law provides that the effects of decisions under this constitutional right are retroactive; however, SC jurisprudence has advanced to also granting future or *ex nunc* effects to favorable *amparo* decisions and not only retroactive or *ex tunc* effects. This advancement is meaningful because it breaks the authority's practice of reapplying the same provision that had been the object of protection, thereby preventing the petitioner from bearing the burden of lodging new amparo proceedings against future application of similar acts of the authority. In keeping with the *res judicata* principle, the temporary effects of a favorable decision consist not only of restoring the petitioner's rights to the state in which they were found before contravention of their fundamental rights took place, by acting backward by destroying application of the act that resulted in the amparo proceeding lodged, but also of the application acts that, in the applicable case, have arisen during the integration of the proceeding – but said effects also act forward, which implies that the effect of the amparo is to prevent the norm that has been declared unconstitutional from being subsequently applied to the petitioner or offended party.[7]

In jurisprudential terms, the limited specific effects of amparo decisions have been broadening in such a manner that, in determined cases, protection has been extended to individuals other than the amparo petitioner. This happens, for instance, when the effects are extended to the petitioner's codefendants, which without filing the corresponding constitutional action, if the procedural record proves that there exists necessary joinder of defendants between said codefendants or that the situation of the joint defendants is identical, similar or common to that of the individual who did lodge the amparo proceedings, as the effects of the aforementioned joinder of defendants are produced only within the corresponding proceeding; thus, they may be transferred to the constitutional proceeding.[8]

Regarding the binding effects of jurisprudence, it should be highlighted that administrative authorities are not yet bound to apply them in the grounds

[7] Cf. the following jurisprudence theses: *GSJF*, 8th Epoch, Plenary, April–June 1989; *SJFG*, Plenary, Volume IV, November 1996, p. 135; and *SJFG*, Plenary, Volume X, November 1999, p. 19.

[8] Cf. P.J.9/96, *SJFG*, Plenary, Volume III, February 1996, p. 78.

and reason for their resolutions (this aspect should be changed in the future). However, the Federal Court of Tax and Administrative Justice, though a formally administrative body, performs materially jurisdictional duties and is obligated to apply jurisprudence declaring a law unconstitutional. The latter does not imply a pronouncement of a constitutional nature because it is restricted to the application of the jurisprudence; that is, it should only verify the appropriateness of its application to the specific case, as inferred from the criteria upheld in jurisprudential theses 2a./J. 38/2002 and P./J. 38/2002.[9]

In addition to the foregoing jurisprudence, it must be pointed out that the Second Chamber of the SC established its criterion, also of jurisprudential nature, stating that, even though the administrative authorities are not bound to apply jurisprudence declaring a law unconstitutional, they must comply with decisions issued by the Federal Court of Tax and Administrative Justice that declare a resolution null and void on the basis of such type of jurisprudence.[10]

The obligatory nature of jurisprudence declaring a law unconstitutional has a wider scope if one abides by the principle of amendment of defects in the complaint contained in article 76 *bis*, section I, of the Amparo Law. The purpose of the amendment of defects in the complaint is to efficiently control the constitutionality of the laws so that the Constitution prevails as the Supreme Law, which does not imply avoiding the appropriateness of amparo proceedings, as expressed in the jurisprudential thesis P./J. 7/2006 of the Plenary Court.[11] Therefore, the amendment of the complaint applies to questions of legal merits once the amparo proceeding is appropriate regarding the law or act challenged.

The amendment of the complaint on such terms is appropriate and is not hindered by a claim against the first or subsequent application acts of the laws that have been declared unconstitutional by jurisprudence of the Highest Court, as learned from jurisprudence P./J. 8/2006.[12] The foregoing does not mean that the causes of inappropriateness derived from the express or tacit consent of the law referred to by sections XI and XII of article 73 of the Amparo Law are invalid. This is so because, if these causes take place, they shall operate to the extent permitted by law; however, the dismissal of the proceedings regarding the application acts is not admissible but, instead

9 2nd./J. 38/2002, *SGFG*, Ninth Epoch, Volume. XV, May 2002, p. 175; and P./J. 38/2002, *SJFG*, Ninth Epoch, Volume XVI, August 2002, p. 5.

10 2a./J. 89/2004, *SJFG*, Ninth Epoch, Volume XX, July 2004, p. 281.

11 T. XXIII, Plenary, *SGFJ*, February 2006, p. 7.

12 T. XXIII, Ninth Epoch, *SJFG*, February 2006, p. 9.

in regard to the acts, the amparo shall be appropriately granted if said acts are grounded in any law that has been declared unconstitutional by jurisprudence. It should be taken into consideration that, on the terms of article 80 of the aforementioned law, amparo has restitution with nonretroactive effects; therefore, the granting of the amparo may not include prior acts but only present and future acts, as specified in the resolution issued by the Plenary Court upon resolving jurisprudential thesis 54/2004-PL.[13] The benefit of the amendment of complaint defects is applicable not only to direct amparo proceedings but also to indirect amparo proceedings, at the trial or review stages, as determined by plenary jurisprudence P./J. 6/2006.[14]

The expansive strength of jurisprudence is made clear with the Plenary's determination to create jurisprudence in generic or thematic matters, which implies their mandatory application by Federal Judicial Branch judges and courts in amparo proceedings for all the cases encompassed by the same or analogous cases even though different legal norms are involved (but have identical or similar content). The preceding is set forth in plenary jurisprudence P./J. 104/2007.[15]

Using as a point of departure the greater strength of jurisprudence by establishing general or thematic jurisprudence, the jurisprudential thesis established by the Plenary Session of the Highest Court acquires special relevance. This precedent states that, what is important for setting jurisprudence by reiteration, is that there is a common criterion applicable to various cases even though the specific circumstances of the analyzed norms vary (e.g., enforceability, issuing authorities, article number). Thus, the possibility of establishing thematic jurisprudence eases and expedites the definition of jurisprudential guidelines that must be obligatorily applied, because, regardless of whether the cases are identical, there may be defined therein the criterion that reestablishes constitutional order to similar cases, thereby increasing its effectiveness.[16]

Last, it is important to emphasize that in some decisions that grant amparo, directly related to unjust treatment under the norm, it has been determined that their effect is to recognize the petitioner's incorrectly denied right. The preceding makes evident the broadening of the protective mantle.[17]

13 Decision published in the *SJFG*, Ninth Epoch, Volume XXIII, February 2006.

14 T XXIII, Ninth Epoch, *SJFG*, February 2006, p. 7.

15 T. XXVI, Ninth Epoch, *SJFG*, December 2007, p. 14.

16 Thesis P. XVI/94, published in the *GSJF*, Eighth Epoch, 77, May 1994, p. 38.

17 Thesis P. 93/2009, CT. 61/2009, *SJFG*, XXX, Ninth Epoch, August 2009, p. 175.

Aside from these jurisprudential criteria, which in some way attempt to broaden the efficacy of favorable amparo decisions for the effects of time and personal scope, it is recommendable that the constitutional and legal reforms that have been submitted since 2001 to the Congress of the Union be approved. Specifically, the draft of the constitutional reform and the new Amparo Law, which among its relevant aspects are the following: surpassing the individual effect of amparo decisions through a general statement of unconstitutionality in cases of amparo proceedings against laws; the substitution of the antiquated concept of legal standing that is still being applied in this area by a broader legitimation concept, defined as legitimate interest; the extension of the scope of protection to those human rights provided for in international treaties duly incorporated into the Mexican system; the restriction of the so-called *amparo para efectos* so as to avoid unnecessary returns to lower courts as a result of violations of form; and progress toward new conceptions of what constitutes an authority so that an amparo is appropriate, overcoming a formalistic criteria, as there exists a clear comparative law trend toward horizontal protection of fundamental rights (*drittwirkung*).

2. *Abstract Unconstitutionality Cause of Action against General Norms (Laws and International Treaties) and Constitutional Controversies (*Erga Omnes *Effect)*

The subject of the effects of constitutional decisions attains greater dynamism when it deals with abstract unconstitutionality cause of actions and constitutional controversies referred to in sections I and II of constitutional article 105. This is so because the decisions issued in the constitutional proceedings may be generally applicable, that is, *erga omnes*, in those predicates established in the same Constitution and its regulatory law. This means that, in those cases of supramajority favorable decisions (voting by at least eight of the eleven Justices who make up the full SC bench), it is sometimes necessary to attenuate the effects of the ruling. In these instances, the constitutional control body has flexible powers to determine the date and application conditions of the constitutional decisions, as it is necessary to mitigate the possible negative effects of the legislative vacuum produced by nullification of the legal norm, the text of which has been declared unconstitutional. Hence, the SC possesses broad powers to determine the effects and other conditions of enforceability of the favorable decisions it issues, as article 41, section IV, of the Regulatory Law referring to the contents that should be expressed in the decisions states as a requirement that a decision must demarcate "The scope and effect of the decision, precisely expressing, if applicable, the bodies obligated to abide by the decision, the general norms or acts regarding which it applies and all of those elements necessary for its full effect within the corresponding scope."[18]

This broad power granted to the SC enables it to determine in each case the scope and effect of favorable decisions, especially when a supramajority vote is obtained so as to declare invalidity in general terms, extending the effects of the decision to others norms whose validity depends on the very norm invalidated, regardless of whether the norm in question has an identical or lesser hierarchy as the challenged norm. The interdependency relationship existing between the norms determines, because of the same invalidating defect, their contraposition with the prevailing constitutional order.[19] Moreover, recently, on the basis of these broad powers, not only have the normative portions directly affected by unconstitutionality been declared invalid but also invalidity has been extended to all the challenged normative system. The preceding is the result of considering the challenged provision as a piece of an integrated normative system in which each part is indissolubly logically related to the whole and, as such, the expulsion of only one of the relevant portions of the system would result in the disconfiguration or redesign of the system. This, in turn, leads to necessarily establishing the revival of the norms in force before those that were declared invalid.[20]

An example of the preceding is unconstitutionality cause of action 47/2006 and actions joined thereto, which determined the validity of transitory articles 3 and 5 of Decree 419, which respectively extended the legislative mandate of the Deputies of the Sixty-second Congressional Legislature for the State of Chiapas and of the present Town Council members. This declaration of invalidity had the effect that the aforementioned legislators and Town Council members concluded their term in office as foreseen before the issuance of the challenged Decree 419. Consequently, the new election of deputies and constitutional and municipal town councils was done in conformity with the legislation in force, before the later reform; that is, the enforceability of the norms previously enforceable was revived.[21]

[18] By interpreting this precept and its constitutional powers by issuing the favorable decisions, the Supreme Tribunal has established jurisprudential thesis P./J. 84/2007, *SJFG*, volume XXVI, December 2007, p. 777.

[19] Cf. P./J. 32/2006, *SJFG*, volume XXIII, February 2006, p. 1169.

[20] Cf. P/J. 85/2007 and 86/2007, *SJFG*, volume XXVI, December 2007, pp. 849 and 778, respectively.

[21] The reasons posed to revive the aforementioned regulation are substantially the following: "The revival of electoral legislation that has not yet been reformed, has the purpose of providing the

In a similar case, the SC determined that all provisions contained in Decrees 353, 354, and 355, published in the Official Gazette of the State of Colima on August 31, 2008, including the transitory articles regulating the decrees' entry into force, were unconstitutional. The High Court, taking into account that the decrees reformed the Electoral Code of the State of Colima and the State Electoral Challenge System Law, subject area wherein the paramount principle is certainty, determined that the subsequent elections process in the State of Colima would be governed by the laws before Decrees 353 and 354 that had been declared invalid. However, the Court clarified that the aforementioned revival would take effect only for the following electoral process, as it would be necessary to issue new legislation for future elections. Furthermore, it determined that the revived legislation could not be reformed during the electoral proceeding, as is provided for in article 105, section II, penultimate paragraph, of the Federal Constitution.[22]

It is convenient to remember Kelsen's thoughts regarding the revival of norms:

> It is possible, in this regard, to think of another means: to empower the Constitutional Court to stipulate – jointly with the resolution that annuls the general norm – that the general norms that regulated the subject prior to the annulled law may enter into effect. Then it would be prudent to entrust to the selfsame Court the decision in which case this power to re-establish the previous legal situation should be used. It would be lamentable if the Constitution made the reappearance of this previous state an imperative general rule whenever general norms are annulled. . . . The power thus conferred on the Constitutional Court to make norms positively enforceable would greatly accentuate the legislative nature of its duties, furthermore it would only encompass the norms which had been made enforceable, previously, by the common legislator.[23]

The Supreme Court's previously described broad powers are also related to the principle of *iura novit curia* governing the two relevant constitutional proceedings, to the extent that the SC when issuing its rulings should correct

voters, political parties and the organizations that participate in the election with legal certainty, pursuant to the principle of certainty that rules this subject and which impedes that, due to the pending proximity of the renewal of the of the bodies of popular representation, the transcendental regulations which shall regulate this form of access by citizens to public power be unknown, as for example, amongst other, the terms related to the preparation of the elections." Cf. A.I. 47/2006 and its accumulated 49/2006, 50/2006 and 51/2006, dated December 7, 2006.

22 Cf. A.I. 107/2008 and its accumulated 108/2008 and 109/2008, dated November 20, 2008.

23 KELSER, HANS, "La garantía jurisdiccional de la Constitución (la justicia constitucional)," *op. cit.*, p. 37.

the errors that it observes upon citing the invoked provisions and amend the grounds for invalidity expressed in the complaint. It may also base a declaration of unconstitutionality on any constitutional provision without necessarily invoking the provision in question, except in the case of electoral unconstitutionality causes of action (article 71 of the regulatory law).[24]

Another relevant aspect in these two constitutional proceedings is the binding character of the reasoning contained in the grounds that form the basis for the decision, if these are approved by at least eight justices of the SC. The *ratio decidendi* is binding on all the national courts, whether federal or state, on the terms of article 43 of the Regulatory Law, and because this provision does not makes a distinction between favorable or appropriate decisions and unfavorable decisions or denials, it should be understood that it applies to both types of rulings. It makes reference to the reasons containing the *thema decidendum* and not to *obiter dictum*, that is, an element isolated from the argumentative discourse – these are so frequent in our world that occasionally they materialize in jurisprudential thesis, when they should not be obligatorily binding because they are not part of the principal argument.[25]

That is why it is important, in order to determine the effects and effectiveness of constitutional decisions in those proceedings, to distinguish between the decisions of acceptance (*acogimiento*) or non-supramajority invalidating decision from those that are characterized as supramajority invalidating decisions. The first are those decisions that, even though there is a majority vote, do not meet the necessary constitutional and legal requirement to be fully effective. This distinction even includes different consequences if they are unconstitutionality causes of actions or constitutional controversies. This supramajority voting requirement lacks practical sense, considering that, at times, the plenary of our Highest Court convenes without all of its members (the quorum necessary is eight), so that on occasion a unanimous vote is necessary or it would suffice for one or two minority votes would prevail over the majority, thus causing the ruling's lack of generally enforceability. It is desirable to do away with this requirement in the future, as it has no reason to exist in such complex and technical questions such as allegations of the unconstitutionality of general provisions.

24 Cf. P./J. 6/2003, *SJFG*, volume XX, September 2004, p. 437.

25 Cf. 1st./J.2/2004, *SJFG*, volume XIX, March 2004, p. 130.

This may become an obstacle to real effectivity, as has been demonstrated by events in other constitutional courts in comparative law.[26]

Some doctrinal sectors have deemed that conditioning constitutional control on a minority is inappropriate for courts. And, as frequently expressed, this cannot be justified as protection of the presumed constitutionality of laws, as the preceding derives its existential justification from other aspects that are no applicable to the body entrusted with the definitive interpretation of the Constitution, if there exist a simple majority that finds unconstitutional the challenged norm (which implies in reality that no conforming interpretation is possible). This characteristic of supramajority voting to declare invalid challenged general norms has been broadly criticized and described by an author as "the greatest defect of the Mexican Federal unconstitutionality cause of action."[27]

Non-supramajority favorable decisions in cases of an abstract cause of action challenging the constitutionality of a law imply that, despite the existence of a simple majority (five, six, or seven votes)[28] that admit the constitutional claim and deem unconstitutional the challenged norm, they do not produce the norm's nullity or its expulsion from the legal order because the eight-vote requirement for a general decision of unconstitutionality is not satisfied. In this situation, the Plenary Court, confronted with this insurmountable procedural obstacle, should unfavorably rule on the cause of action and order the matter filed, as provided for in the second paragraph of article 72 of the applicable Regulatory Law and expressly make said declaration in the grounds for decision pertaining to the ruling. In the decision, reference should be made only to the lack of supramajority vote, and the considerations of the majority should not become part of the ruling; however, in the applicable case, they may be incorporated as non-

26 Few constitutional courts set forth supramajority voting as a requirement to invest constitutional decisions with general effectivity. One of the most representative examples of the futility of this requirement is found in Peru, where the Court of Constitutional Rights (1979) and the Constitutional Court (1993) faced serious operational problems due to the high percentage of required votes. The new Constitutional Procedural Code, in force since December 1, 2004, retains supramajority voting but with fewer requirements. Regarding this legislation, see ABAD YUPANQUI, Samuel B., DANOS ORDÓÑEZ, Jorge, EGUIGUREN PRAELI, Francisco J., GARCÍA BELAUNDE, Domingo, MONROY GÁLVEZ, Juan, and ORE GUARDIA, Arsenio, *Código Procesal Constitucional. Estudio introductorio, exposición de motivos, dictámenes e índice analítico*, 2nd ed., Lima, Palestra, 2005.

27 BRAGE CAMAZANO, Joaquín, *La acción abstracta de inconstitucionalidad*, Mexico City, UNAM, 2005, p. 347; especially on this topic, see his criticisms to the presumed constitutionality of the law, pp. 347–352.

28 If the necessary quorum for the Plenary is at least eight Supreme Court justices, the non-supramajority could be only five, six, or seven.

supramajority votes. The SC itself has interpreted the phenomenon of the non-supramajority decision in the following manner:

> If there exists a majority, but there are less than eight votes finding the norm unconstitutional, then there shall be a plenary declaration of the impossibility (non-subsistence) to decide the action and there will be no holding issued neither in regards to the constitutionality which is implicitly reached, since the validity of the challenged norm is respected by applying a technical rule protecting the respective presumption that the legislative body obeyed the Constitution. That this was the result reached due to the lack of a supramajority vote is reflected by the absence of legal arguments by the Supreme Court supporting and strengthening the expression of the legislature. In accordance to the judicial system, it is also logical that in the eventuality of an unfavorable declaration on the unconstitutionality cause of action, even though there does not exist a pronouncement by the Supreme Court on a related subject, the Justices in the non-supramajority and the minority votes may draft votes giving the arguments which support the said opinion.[29]

This resolution does not imply a declaration of the constitutionality of the challenged norm, as it does not resolve the constitutional controversy because of a procedural impediment that is indispensable and necessary to nullify the challenged provision and so expel it from the legal order. Therefore, the ruling really produces similar effects to a proceeding dismissal, leaving unadjudicated the merits of the matter as a result of an insurmountable procedural obstacle leading to the dismissal of the constitutional cause of action.[30]

In contrast, when the favorable non-supramajority decision is the result of a constitutional controversy proceeding, the action will not be dismissed as in the preceding case but the decision is binding only between the parties.[31] In general, the reach of the effects of constitutional controversies is subordinated to the categorical relations existing between the plaintiff and the defendant.[32] The decision is only generally enforceable – *erga omnes* – if it is a challenge to generally applicable provisions (not acts) and if the constitutional controversy sentence was approved by a majority of at least

29 Sixth whereas clause of the decision of the unconstitutionality cause of action 10/2000, decided on January 29 and 30, 2002.

30 Cf. P./J. 15/2002, *SJFG*, vol. XV, February 2002, p. 419.

31 Cf. P. 14/3007, as well as jurisprudential thesis P.J.72/96 and P.J. 108/2001, *SJFG*, volume XXV, May, 2007, p. 1533; *SJFG*, volume IV, November 1996, p. 249; *SJFG*, volume XIV, September 2001, p. 1024.

32 Cf. P.J. 9/1999, *SJFG*, volume IX, April 1999, p. 281.

eight votes and is a controversy involving States or municipalities that have been challenged by the Federal Government, or of municipalities challenged by the States, or in those cases referred to in clauses (c), (h) and (k) of section I of constitutional article 105.[33]

In regards to the temporal effects of decisions on both abstract unconstitutionality causes of action and constitutional controversies, two general rules are provided. The first rule consists of leaving up to the Supreme Court's discretion the setting of the date that the decision will enter into force,[34] which on many occasions is the day following publication of the final decision in the *Federal Official Gazette*. This delay of the temporal enforceability of rulings allows the SC the flexibility to consider the particularities of each case and, by this means, mitigate the possible consequences of the legislative vacuum produced by the expulsion of the general provision declared unconstitutional. A maximum term for this delay is not provided for as in Austria, where it may never exceed eighteen months after the publication of constitutional ruling.

In contrast, following the criterion that normally governs challenges to general norms pursuant to the European system, the effects of the ruling are future (*ex nunc*), and it may have retroactive effect only in criminal cases benefitting the accused (*ex tunc*).[35] However, the SC has sustained that, regardless of subject matter, it may stipulate extraordinarily that the declaration of invalidity becomes effective from the date on which the complaint is presented, if due to suspension of the challenged acts things have remained in the state in which they were at the moment the controversy was presented or from the moment in which the precautionary measure was conceded, if the aforementioned concession occurred after the complaint was presented.[36]

Although the previously referenced retroactivity is exceptionally decreed, it should be stated that in Latin American legal orders and jurisprudences a moderate retroactivity is accepted. The original Austrian conception of effects into the future has undergone important exceptions, to the degree that frequently European constitutional courts (e.g., Austria, Germany, Italy,

[33] These sections establish: "c) The Executive Branch and the Congress of the Union; the former and any of the Chambers of the latter or in its case the Permanent Commission, whether as federal institutions or of the Federal District; . . . h) Two branches of the same State, regarding the constitutionality of their acts or general provisions; . . . k) two Federal District governmental bodies regarding the constitutionality of their acts or general norms."

[34] Cf. P. /J. 11/2001, *SJFG*, volume XIV, September 2001, p. 1098.

[35] Cf. P./J. 74/97, *SJFG*, volume VI, September 1997, p. 548.

[36] Cf. P./J. 71/2006, p. 1377, *SJFG*, volume XXIII, May 2006, p. 1377.

Spain) allow certain retroactive effects (*ex tunc*) in their constitutionality rulings. This means that the typical rights-creating decisions (which imply invalidity of the norm) inherent to decisions of unconstitutionality of general provision are substituted for in some instances by declaratory decisions (nullification), which imply granting retroactive effects. This also occurs in the North American system, in which rulings exceptionally may have future effects, as occurs with the decisions issued by the Supreme Court of the United States from the second half of the past century in determined cases.

3. *Legislative Omissions*

Another topic that warrants comment is legislative omissions. At the federal level, there does not exist any specific cause of action to challenge legislative omissions; therefore, the challenges are channeled through three existing constitutional control mechanisms. The jurisprudential criterion in effect is that the remedies of amparo proceedings[37] and the abstract unconstitutionality cause of action[38] are inappropriate to challenge this type of unconstitutionality. Nevertheless, the constitutional controversy has been jurisprudentially accepted as means to challenge legislative omissions.[39] Using as a point of departure the premise that legislative bodies have powers or authority that may either be facultative or obligatory in keeping with the principle of the functional division of the branches of government,[40] four distinct types of legislative omissions have been differentiated: (1) absolute in jurisdiction that must be exercised obligatorily, when the legislative body has the obligation or mandate to issue a determined law and has not done so; (2) relative to jurisdiction that must be exercised obligatorily when the legislative body has the obligation or mandate to issue a determined law but does so incompletely or deficiently; (3) absolute in jurisdiction that may be exercised at will when the legislative body decides not to act because it does not have any mandate or obligation imposed on it; and (4) relative in legislative jurisdiction, but when it issues the law, it does so incompletely or deficiently.[41]

37 Cf. P. CLXVIII/97*SJFG*, volume VI, December 1997, p. 180.

38 Cf. P./J. 16/2002 and P./J. 23/2005, *SJFG*, volume XV, March 2002, p. 995; and *SJFG*, volume XXI, May 2005, p. 781.

39 Cf. P./J. 82/99, *SJFG*, volume X, August 1999, p. 568.

40 Cf. P./J. 10/2006, *SJFG*, volume XXIII, February 2005, p. 1528.

41 P./J. 11/2005, *SJFG*, volume XXIII, February 2006, p. 1527.

This concept rests on the comparative law trend accepting challenges to the unconstitutionality of legislative omissions as either relative or absolute in nature.[42] Nonetheless, this criterion was modified beginning with the constitutional controversies resolved on October 15, 2007,[43] related to the challenge to the federal legislature's failure to issue the norms establishing the legal conditions so that indigenous towns and communities may purchase, operate, and manage communications media. A majority of five votes against four determined the inappropriateness of a constitutional controversy to challenge legislative omissions.

Without prejudice to the foregoing, recently the Plenary Supreme Court declared a legal basis for the constitutional controversy filed against the legislative omission of the State Congress of Jalisco. The controversy consisted of challenging the lack of regulation for voluntary retirement of the State Supreme Court of Justice Magistrates, and as a consequence of the preceding, it was decided that the Jalisco state legislature would legislate in the following ordinary congressional session period to correct the noted defect.[44] Similarly, a decision was issued in a different controversy on a closely related topic, declaring its appropriateness, as we shall see here.

The previous comments show that the SC has had to preside over diverse proceedings in which legislative omissions were challenged, without following a uniform jurisprudential line in this regard. Furthermore, it should be said in analyzing these matters that some of the SC's members have doubted precisely whether the High Court has sufficient powers to resolve these matters, so as to exhort the legislator to act and even to issue guidelines to the legislative bodies. These vacillations make evident that there exist specific subject matters and areas in which the SC has not fully exercised its role of Constitutional Court and where it has been overly cautious, precisely by not transforming itself into a positive legislator. Notwithstanding the preceding, there are voices inside the Court that opine otherwise.

In effect, on April 22, 2010, the Supreme Court resolved constitutional controversy 25/2008, which alleged lack of retirement regulation, provided for by article 61 of the Political Constitution of Jalisco, in favor of the magistrates and judges who were forced to retire or did so voluntarily. With a six-vote majority, it declared that a legal basis existed for the allegations and the state congress was granted a term to issue the corresponding norm.

42 Cf. P./J. 12/2006, 13/2006 and 14/2006, *SJFG*, volume XXIII, February 2006, pp. 1532, 1365 and 1250, respectively.

43 Constitutional Controversy 59/2006 and other forty-four controversies with identical themes.

44 Cf. decision made May 10, 2010, issued in Constitutional Controversy 49/2008.

The minority considered that the rights of retiring judges and magistrates should be protected during the time that the legislative omission persisted, and to this end, the minority based its considerations precisely on the possibility that the SC acting as a Constitutional Court should adopt a more protective solution, and as such it held:

> From this perspective, it seems to us that within the effects possible for this Supreme Court to establish in its ruling when it observes that a legislative omission produces unconstitutionality, is the possibility of making applicable, within the scope of a determined federal entity, a different legislation – existing or repealed, federal or from any other state – temporarily, until the state legislature remedies the respective omission, if the preceding is necessary to reestablish the infringed constitutional order and avoid consummation of the consequences of the violation.
>
> All constitutional courts have a law-creating function, acting at the constitutional level, above federal and state ordinances, so that derived from article 41 of the regulatory law, it is possible for this Supreme Court to reconstruct through judicial decisions portions of the legal order.
>
> This may be done by establishing guidelines that must be obeyed by judicial officials in the absence of legislation remedying the unconstitutional omission or, whenever it is more convenient, by remitting to other legal ordinances, including those that have been repealed or that belong to other partial ordinances. However, the preceding does not imply substituting the legislative function, since it is a transitional measure that, for the purpose of giving full effect to a favorable decision, fills a vacuum by applying a valid alternative, subject to the legislature's acting in full use of its power, only being limited by the text of the Constitution.
>
> The preceding does not presuppose invading the sphere of the state legislator because the constitutional court does not operate at the federal level but instead at the constitutional, total or national level, which empowers it to act, on the terms of the selfsame article 41 of the regulatory law "in its corresponding scope," so as to ensure the effects of its rulings.[45]

The preceding makes patent that at least four Justices are convinced that the SC act as more than a simple negative legislator, adopting such measures as those proposed. Although it is still a minority position, it does indicate the level of deliberation present in the Highest Mexican Court.

[45] Concurring votes formulated by Justices Arturo Zaldívar Lelo de Larrea, Olga María Sánchez Cordero de García Villegas, José Ramón Cossío Díaz, and Guillermo I. Ortiz Mayagoitia in the decision issued by the Plenary Court in Constitutional Controversy 25/2008, presented by the Judicial Branch of the State of Jalisco.

CONCLUSIONS

(1) The SC, as the limiting body of the Federal Judicial Branch, is based on a solid historical background; however, since February 5, 1857, it started to have constitutional control powers, specifically amparo proceedings, which began profiling its new role.

(2) The SC has ceased being only an appeals court to materially become a constitutional court. This has been the trend observed through various constitutional reforms, in which the intention of the constitutional congress has been expressed, particularly in the relevant 1994 constitutional reforms.

(3) The constitutional court nature of the SC is observed both in its organic structure and in the fact that it has powers over amparo proceedings, and it concentrates two constitutional rights, the abstract unconstitutionality cause of action (against general norms) and constitutional controversies, in which the SC may declare norms invalid, with future *erga omnes* effects.

(4) The accurate exercise of the aforementioned powers has positioned the SC as the body that guarantees the rule of the Constitution in our country, which, given the increasingly complex and demanding nature of conflicts brought under its jurisdiction, has had to use the techniques and tools of other Constitutional Courts in comparative law, such as interpretation according to the Constitution, weighing, new constitutional pleading trends, and of course the modalities and effects of its resolution, which are increasingly complex.

(5) Constitutional decisions issued in amparo proceedings have traditionally been effectively limited to the petitioner. However, jurisdictional practice reflects an expansive strength derived from jurisprudence declaring a law unconstitutional, which has mainly arisen by upholding the following criteria:

(a) The obligatory nature of jurisprudence application not only by all jurisdictional bodies under the Federal Judicial Branch but also by the Federal Court of Tax and Administrative Justice, which, though constituted as a formally administrative body, performs materially jurisdictional duties.

(b) The obligation of administrative authorities to comply with the decisions issued by the Federal Court of Tax and Administrative Justice, which pronounce the nullification of a resolution or an act challenged on the basis of the jurisprudence that determines that the law on which said resolution or act is unconstitutional.

(c) The amendment of defects in the complaint if dealing with the second or subsequent application acts under the law that was jurisprudentially declared unconstitutional. The latter does not imply evading questions of the inappropriateness of amparo proceedings but only preventing that procedural technical issues hinder the rule of the higher constitutional order.

(d) The formulation of thematic jurisprudence applicable to analogous cases even when the specific circumstances of the norms or cases analyzed vary, which exclusively binds judges and court, pertaining to the Federal Judicial Branch, not those courts under a separate Branch, as the jurisprudence cannot grant them the constitutional control jurisdiction that they lack.

(6) Contrary to amparo proceedings, the decisions issued in unconstitutionality causes of action and constitutional controversies may have general, or *erga omnes*, effects in the predicates established in the Constitution and its regulatory law, provided that a supramajority of eight votes (of eleven) exists, as mandated by the Constitution. Furthermore, the SC has broad powers to determine the effects and other conditions of enforceability for the favorable decisions that it issues.

(7) In using the previously mentioned powers, the SC has extended the effects of the declaration of invalidity to other norms for which validity depends on the very norm invalidated, given the interdependency existing between the norms; likewise, it has extended the declaration of invalidity to all of the challenged normative system, as it deems that an integrated and indissolubly normative system has been composed; when this has occurred, it has even decreed the revival of the norms in force prior to those that were declared invalid.

(8) Another relevant aspect of the decisions issued in unconstitutionality causes of action and constitutional controversies consists of the jurisprudentially binding nature of the *ratio decidendi*, that is, the reasoning contained in the grounds that form the basis of the grounds for the decision, if these are approved by at least eight of the eleven justices of the SC. This binding effect includes favorable and unfavorable decisions that meet the aforementioned supramajority voting requirement.

(9) The prior examples confirm the SC's increasing activity as a constitutional court, conscious of its law-creating function.

(10) Contrary to the SC trend observed in unconstitutionality causes of action and constitutional controversies, and even in amparo proceedings, broadening the scope of application, modalities, and effects of its rulings, in the subject area of legislative omission, it has been doubtful and inconsistent. Here, I have observed changes in criterion and vacillations regarding the scope of the Supreme Court's powers; however, this has not been an impediment to issuance of important opinions related to the progressive and constitutional nature of the Highest Court.

NETHERLANDS

THE DUTCH SUPREME COURT: A RELUCTANT POSITIVE LEGISLATOR?

Jerfi Uzman,
Ph.D Candidate at Leyden University.
j.uzman@law.leidenuniv.nl

Tom Barkhuysen,
Professor of Constitutional and Administrative Law , Leyden University and a practising member of the Amsterdam Bar (Stibbe).

Michiel L. van Emmerik,
Associate Professor of Constitutional and Administrative Law, Leyden University and Deputy Judge at the Amsterdam District Court.

INTRODUCTION

With respect to constitutional fundamental rights review by the judiciary, the Netherlands has always been a bit of a stranger in Europe. Comparatists usually describe the way judicial review of statutes in Europe is shaped as different from the American system, where the Supreme Court has basically empowered itself to review the constitutionality of statutory laws.[1] The authority to strike down legislation in the New World is therefore exercised by the judiciary at large, and it is the highest appellate court that ultimately decides on the matter.[2] By contrast, the European tradition is closely connected to the existence of Kelsenian constitutional courts specialized in reviewing the constitutionality of statutes and executive action.[3] Such courts

1 *Marbury v. Madison*, 5 U.S. (1 Cranch) 137 (1803).

2 Tushnet 2006, pp. 1242–1244.

3 See, e.g., Von Beyme 1988, pp. 24–25.

notably exist in, for instance, Germany, Italy, Austria, Spain, and Belgium but also in the relatively younger liberal democracies like Poland and the Czech Republic. Constitutional courts almost by definition engage in a critical dialogue with the national legislature. When Hans Kelsen famously described constitutional courts as negative legislators, he was referring to their power to annul acts of the legislature.[4]

It is at this point that the Dutch differ from most of their European neighbors. Their legal system does not involve concentrated review by a specialized constitutional court. This is largely because judicial review of primary legislation is traditionally prohibited pursuant to Article 120 of the Dutch Constitution. It is clear from the outset that this ban on judicial review reduces the need for a specialized court. One would be mistaken, however, to conclude that there is no such thing as judicial fundamental rights review in the Netherlands. Quite the contrary, Dutch courts usually subject executive action and occasionally Acts of Parliament to rigorous fundamental rights review in a way that Mark Tushnet would probably describe as "strong judicial review."[5] This kind of review is dispersed in the sense that it is carried out by any court in the country. They do so on the basis of another provision in the Dutch Constitution, Article 94. It contains the duty to set aside any kind of regulation – be it statutory or not – if the application of these regulations conflicts with provisions of treaty law that "bind all persons," which means that they have direct effect or contain – as one might say – judicially manageable standards.[6] Statutes can therefore be reviewed by the judiciary for their consistency with written provisions of international law. The gradual growth of human rights treaty systems, such as the International Covenant on Civil and Political Rights (ICCPR) and, even more notably, the European Convention on Human Rights and Fundamental Freedoms (ECHR), has resulted in an increasingly self-conscious attitude of the courts toward parliamentary legislation. This is strengthened by the fact that the Dutch courts are obliged to ensure the effective application of European Union law – which also contains fundamental rights – in the domestic legal order as a matter of EU law itself.[7] They must therefore carefully examine whether national law is compatible with the law of the European Union and, if necessary, either construe

4 Kelsen 1945, pp. 268–269.

5 See Tushnet 2008.

6 On judicially manageable standards, see Fallon 2006, pp. 1274–1332.

7 European Court of Justice (ECJ) judgments of 5 February 1963, Case 26/62 (*Van Gend & Loos*); 15 July 1964, Case 6/64 (*Costa v. E.N.E.L.*).

national law consistently with EU law or set it aside if such an interpretation proves impossible under national constitutional law.[8]

In this contribution, we describe the way the Dutch courts have – in a sometimes rigorous, sometimes cautious, and sometimes downright activist way – engaged in rights review of parliamentary legislation. As we will note, the case law of the highest courts shows a tendency to assume a positive lawmaking role in a limited number of cases. Yet simultaneously the courts have gradually adopted a cautious doctrine to draw a line between, what they consider, acceptable and illegitimate judicial lawmaking. Although, as we have observed, it is not a constitutional court, our account will focus on a specific court, called the Hoge Raad (literally "High Council"). It is usually referred to as the Supreme Court of the Netherlands. As the highest court in civil, criminal, and taxation cases, it ultimately rules on the lawfulness and interpretation of statutory law in a majority of cases. However, the Court has limited jurisdiction over the administrative courts. This particular field of law has its own highest courts (most notably the Administrative Jurisdiction Division of the Council of State) that carry out a similar lawmaking role.[9] For the sake of clarity, we generally limit our account here to the case law of the Supreme Court. The highest administrative courts usually follow a comparable approach and use similar terminology when it comes to their constitutional position with regard to judicial lawmaking.[10]

Before starting our account of the lawmaking role of the courts in civil liberties adjudication, we will touch on the way in which fundamental rights are protected in the Dutch domestic legal order by virtue of international law. This subject will be more extensively discussed by our colleague Evert Alkema in his national report with regard to the incorporation of public

[8] This duty for national courts is consistently underlined by the ECJ, as in the *Colson & Kamann* case (ECJ 10 April 1984, C-14/83, *Jur.* 1984, p. 1891). For further reading, see Craig & de Búrca 2008, pp. 305–376; Claes 2006; Arnull, Dashwood, Ross, and Wyatt 2000, pp. 60–83; Van Gerven 2000, pp. 501–536.

[9] The others being the Central Appeals Court (Centrale Raad van Beroep) and the Industrial Appeals Tribunal (College van Beroep voor het Bedrijfsleven). For a brief account of the Dutch judicial organization, see Kraan 2004, p. 635.

[10] See, e.g., two relatively recent judgments of the Administrative Jurisdiction Division of the Council of State on suffrage: ABRvS 29 October 2003, *JB* 2004/3 (*Suffrage for Mentally Handicapped*); ABRvS 21 November 2006, *JB* 2004/308 (*Eman & Sevinger*). An interesting example of the administrative courts engaging in positive legislating provides their case law on the reasonable time requirements in judicial decisions. Departing from the clear text of the statute in question, it formulated clear rules on the basis of Art. 13 of the European Convention. See ABRvS 4 June 2008, *AB* 2008/229. Moreover see (in Dutch) De Poorter and Van Roosmalen 2009, pp. 219–227.

international law in the Dutch legal order.[11] Before we do, it is noteworthy to underline that the position of national courts in the structure of European Union law is very different from their position under the European Convention on Human Rights and the other human rights treaties. We touch only briefly on the subject of EU law and focus mainly on the human rights treaties. After discussing the international law framework, we proceed with a discussion of the leading cases with regard to the lawmaking powers of the courts. To that end, we analyze some of the more activist judgments of the Supreme Court in which it has tried to judicially reform legislation on the basis of international fundamental rights review. We also attempt to offer some flavor of the dialogue in which the Court has sometimes tried to manipulate or guide the legislature in a certain direction. From that perspective, we moreover deal briefly with some of the reactions offered by legal scholarship. We then cover some of the more procedural aspects of the lawmaking role of the courts, such as the means and effects of judicial review of legislation. This entails a brief account of the current legal actions open to individuals challenging the validity of statutes and the specific injunctions the courts are allowed – or expressly not allowed – to issue in such cases. We end this contribution by summarizing briefly the different issues we encountered, thereby dealing explicitly with the questions posed by the general reporter.

I. THE BAN ON JUDICIAL CONSTITUTIONALITY REVIEW AND ITS SCOPE

1. *Article 120 of the Dutch Constitution*

A convenient starting point for a debate on rights review in the Netherlands might be that the Netherlands does have a written constitutional document, which –like in Germany– is literally called the Basic Law (*Grondwet*) but is usually translated as the "Constitution." It is a relatively sober document outlining the system of government. The first chapter is devoted to civil liberties and social rights. Chapter 6 includes some provisions on the administration of justice. As we have already mentioned, the traditional cornerstone concerning the constitutional position of the courts in the Netherlands is Article 120 of the Constitution, which reads:

[11] To be published in the International Academy of Comparative Law, IACL series.

> The constitutionality of Acts of Parliament and treaties shall not be reviewed by the courts.[12]

The message this provision contains is threefold. First and foremost, there is to be no judicial review of the constitutionality of statutes.[13] This means that there is no role for the courts to play when it comes to deciding either whether a certain statutory provision is in breach with the Constitution or whether the legislative process followed the correct procedural rules.[14] Such matters are to be left to the legislature, which in the Netherlands is composed of both the government (i.e., the Queen and the Cabinet) and the First and Second Chambers of Parliament, or the States General, as it is properly called.[15] We henceforth use the terms *Parliament* and *legislature* interchangeably.

The term *constitutionality* in Article 120 is to be interpreted broadly. The courts assume that they are banned not only from determining the unconstitutionality of statutes but also from declaring them incompatible with the Kingdom Charter[16] or general principles of law.[17] They might occasionally refuse to apply a certain statute by reference to the fact that such an application violates a legal principle.[18] However, they can do so only where there are exceptional circumstances that the legislature did not

12 As derived from the jointly published translation of the Ministries of Foreign Affairs and the Interior (2002). A copy of this translation can be found at http://www.minbzk.nl/english/. There is currently a bill pending in Parliament to amend Art. 120. This so-called Halsema proposal aims to allow the courts to review statutes for their consistency with most of the civil liberties mentioned in the Constitution. See Heringa and Kiiver 2009, p. 165.

13 When using the term *statutes*, we refer to primary legislation, enacted by the national legislature, which – according to Art. 81 of the Constitution – is composed of Parliament and the government.

14 Supreme Court judgment of 27 January 1961 (*Van den Bergh*). The courts consider themselves banned from interfering in the legislative process on the basis of procedural constitutional requirements as well. See Supreme Court judgment of 19 November 1999, *NJ* 2000/160 (*City of Tegelen v. Province of Limburg*).

15 Cf. Art. 81 of the Constitution. For further research, see Heringa & Kiiver 2009, pp. 103–107, *supra* note 13.

16 The Kingdom of the Netherlands is more or less structured in a way between a federation and a confederation of states (the Netherlands, the Netherlands Antilles, and Aruba). They are united by the Crown and a constitution for the federation called the Charter for the Kingdom of the Netherlands, or the Kingdom Charter (Statuut). It is relatively concise, however, compared with the constitutions of the three member states. Unquestionably, the Charter takes precedence over the national constitutions, but in reality, those constitutions are far more relevant in practice. Charter review is therefore quite rare.

17 Supreme Court judgment of 14 April 1989, *NJ* 1989/469 (*Harmonisation Act*).

18 See, e.g., the Supreme Court judgment of 9 June 1989, *AB* 1989/412 (*Short-Term Volunteers*).

expressly consider at the time of passing the act. In such cases, the refusal to apply the law does not in itself affect the binding nature of the Act in question. The courts then assume that Parliament would most probably have wanted them to ignore the statute. This was, for instance, the case in 1989, when a group of short-term civil servants were promised a pension benefit that, at the end of the day, the administration was not prepared to award. In the *Short-Term Volunteers* case, the government argued that the pensions of civil servants were carefully regulated by parliamentary legislation. As the Act in question had not incorporated the promise, the denial of the benefit was a matter of parliamentary legislation, and the courts were not allowed to have a say on the matter.[19] The Court decided differently and allowed the appeal. It considered that Parliament had not deliberately refused to meet its obligations and that the Court was thus in a position to disapply the statute in question.

Even if no such situation arises, the courts are not prevented from expressing their views on the issue put before them. In the 1989 *Harmonisation Act* judgment – its landmark case on Article 120 – the Supreme Court maintained that it was clearly not entitled to review whether an Act of Parliament was compatible with legal principles, but it made it painfully clear that – had it been allowed to do so – it would have ruled that the 1988 Harmonisation Act violated the principle of legal certainty. The court thus gave the legislature some piece of what might properly be called expert advice and the latter, taking the hint, eventually changed the law. The ban on judicial review of legislation then does not prevent the judiciary to engage in a dialogue with the legislature, be it that such occasions remain rare.

Second, the prohibition against primary legislation review that Article 120 imposes on the courts is a narrow exception to the general rule that the courts are in fact competent to test any provision for its consistency with rules of higher law including general legal principles.[20] Courts may therefore decide on the constitutionality of ministerial decrees and administrative, provincial, or municipal regulations. The competence to do so was already established in 1864 by the Supreme Court.[21] A third message to be read in Article 120 of the Constitution is that the courts may not review written international law

19 *Id.*

20 See the Supreme Court judgment of 16 May 1986, *NJ* 1987/251 (*State v. Society for Agricultural Aviation*).

21 Supreme Court judgment of 6 March 1864, *W* 2646 (*Pothuys*). For further reading on the subject, see Kortmann and Bovend'Eert 2000, pp. 134–135.

for its compatibility with the Dutch Constitution. This effectively means that, in the Dutch legal order, treaties take precedence over any kind of national law, including the constitution itself. Article 120 is complemented by Article 94 of the Constitution, which basically states that any law (including the Constitution itself) that is incompatible with justiciable provisions of treaties is not to be applied. Quite apart from Article 120, the Courts also consider themselves banned from deciding on the constitutionality of European Union law. The Supreme Court has completely accepted the absolute supremacy of EU law over national law, emphasizing that the effect of EU law in the Dutch legal order is a matter of the Community rather than the national Constitution.[22] As we will see, this has great consequences for the role of the courts.

2. *Summary*

The conclusion of this brief introduction to Article 120 of the Constitution may be that – as a general rule – it formally bans the courts from reviewing whether Acts of Parliament are compatible with higher law, with the notable exception of self-executing treaty provisions. Sometimes the courts do express their views on the constitutionality of primary legislation and consider themselves entitled to refrain from applying unconstitutional legislation on the basis that Parliament would not have wanted them to apply it in view of exceptional circumstances in a particular case. They are moreover empowered to review any other piece of legislation for its constitutionality and may review Acts of Parliament for their compliance with written provisions of international law to the extent that the provisions provide judicially manageable standards for review. This has practically led to a situation in which international human rights law (most notably the ECHR) has taken over the role as the most important civil rights charter for the Netherlands. Judicial review – whether of legislation or of executive action – is primarily focused on the European Convention, the International Covenant, and some other human rights treaties. As we limit our discussion here to judicial review of parliamentary legislation, we from now on focus primarily on the role of the courts in reviewing on the basis of these treaties. We therefore proceed with a discussion of the constitutional framework for the implementation of international law.

[22] Supreme Court judgment of 2 November 2004, *NJ* 2005/80.

II. ENFORCING INTERNATIONAL HUMAN RIGHTS LAW

1. *Introduction: Monism and Article 94 of the Constitution*

The Dutch are widely known to have a friendly constitutional climate for international law. As we said earlier, international law takes precedence even over the Constitution itself. This friendly climate essentially originates from the traditionally rather monist approach of the Dutch legal profession. As early as 1919, the Supreme Court expressed its opinion that international law as such is automatically applicable in the domestic legal order. There is thus no need for any kind of conversion to norms of national law.[23] Not only are treaty provisions as such accepted as valid law as a matter of customary law, but they are also recognized to be of a higher order. Accordingly, the courts generally assume that, unless Parliament expressly deviates from its international obligations, it must clearly have intended any provision in its Act to be consistent with a given treaty. This assumption is the basis for the courts' usual practice to interpret national law as far as possible in a way consistent with the rights laid down in conventions such as the ECHR. And it is this practice that has given rise to a few of the most celebrated but also deeply notorious (some might even say "activist") Supreme Court judgments. On such occasions, it may well read in the statute some highly detailed rules that have little to do with either the text of the statute in question or its legislative history.[24]

To turn back to the supremacy rule, should Parliament legislate expressly against the text and the prevailing interpretation of a treaty, the treaty irrefutably takes precedence over the conflicting statute. This has arguably always been the case, but from 1953, there has been a clear provision in the Dutch Constitution empowering the courts to disapply the statute in question. This provision is currently laid down in Article 94 of the Constitution, which reads as follows:

> Statutory regulations in force within the Kingdom shall not be applicable if such application is in conflict with provisions of treaties that are binding on all persons or of resolutions by international institutions.

[23] Supreme Court judgment of 3 March 1919, *NJ* 1919, p. 371 (*Treaty of Aachen*). For a further discussion, see Zwaak 2001, pp. 597–599.

[24] See, e.g., the two Supreme Court judgments of 21 March 1986, *NJ* 1986/585 and *NJ* 1986/588 (*Spring Judgments*) on parental authority. See further the judgment of 27 May 2005, 2005/485 (*Parental Authority II*). We discuss these cases at length further on.

The key question, which is ultimately for the courts to decide on, is what exactly constitutes a provision of a treaty "that binds all persons." The importance of the answer to this question lies in the fact that the courts may not disapply the national statute if it only conflicts with provisions of international law that do not fit this description. According to Article 93, a treaty binds all persons when it is proclaimed and insofar as it contains provisions that may by their very nature be eligible to bind all persons. This shifts the issue to only what kind of provision would be "eligible to bind all persons.".

2. *"Eligible to Bind all Persons" and Judicial Lawmaking*

In the current case law of both the Supreme Court and the highest administrative courts, this requirement comes down to two questions.[25] First, whether the contracting state parties have expressly agreed on the nature of the treaty provision. This is seldom the case, however. The courts therefore usually convert the question into a matter of justiciability. Does the text of the provision provide the courts with judicially manageable standards to decide the case? In the words of the Supreme Court in its 1986 landmark judgment concerning a major railway strike: "Does the provision require the legislature to legislate on a certain subject or is it by its very nature eligible to function as 'objective law' without further ado?"[26] The real question thus becomes whether the courts are able to derive from the provision some clues as to how to decide cases without having to engage in extensive judicial lawmaking. This brings us near the heart of our subject in this report, because if the courts decide wrongly on this issue, they might end up having to decide the case by reading into the treaty detailed rules that the treaty itself is really unable to yield. And they may then be legislating rather than judging the case, which makes them vulnerable to charges of judicial activism. The key criterion (whether the treaty provision textually provides a sufficient degree of manageable standards) therefore theoretically serves as a preliminary question for the courts to solve to keep them away from political territory.

What complicates matters, however, is that the decision of whether a particular treaty provision is likely to bind all persons is generally a yes-or-no decision. Once the courts consider a provision self-executing (which we, for

25 See, e.g., the Supreme Court judgment of 30 May 1986, *NJ* 1986/688 (*Railway Strike*); Judicial division of the Council of State, judgment of 15 September 2004, *AB* 2005/12.

26 *Ibid.*

the sake of simplicity, use interchangeably for the phrase "binding on all persons"), they consider themselves bound by such a ruling in further cases. Both the circumstances and the context of a specific case are therefore irrelevant when it comes to the question of the self-executing nature of the treaty provision. Deciding whether the provision is self-executing is much like deciding whether a patient is pregnant. She either is or is not, but that has little to do with the circumstances. Yet this may confront the courts with a dilemma, because although the text might produce a clear outcome in one case, it might equally fail to do so in the next. Phrased differently: the text might yield some clear standards, but those standards might prove insufficient in a particular national context. A clear example is furnished by the principle of nondiscrimination, as laid down, for instance, in Articles 26 ICCPR and 14 ECHR. These provisions provide the applicant with a relatively clear right, so it is usually equally clear for the government what it must or may not do. The question whether a given statute constitutes unlawful discrimination might sometimes pose a challenge to the courts, but usually not one they cannot handle by using a balancing test. The text of the provisions may therefore be considered self-executing. Having met this challenge, however, the court might then face the equally difficult task of providing a remedy for the violation. In some cases, there might be several different outcomes of the case, each of which could be equally lawful.

Suppose that the court holds that the exclusion of a certain group of people from a tax exemption is unjustified. Because it is clear what the government should not have done – exclude people from a benefit granted to others – the treaty provisions give the courts relatively clear guidance as to whether there is a violation. They are therefore binding on all persons. However, just disapplying the statute would either not provide the applicants with a remedy or would take the courts in political territory because it would grant a benefit to a large group of people where the legislature might just as lawfully have denied it to anyone. After all, the principle of nondiscrimination only requires that both groups are treated the same, not that they both have the tax benefit. In such cases, the binding-on-all-persons requirement itself does not prevent the courts from having to engage in positive lawmaking.

This dilemma raised some discussion in legal literature on the question whether the decision to mark a provision as self-executing ought to be contextual (depending on the characteristics of a given case) or dichotomic by nature. The Supreme Court has never been very explicit on the subject. Several authors concluded from the earlier-mentioned judgment in the 1986 *Railway Strike* case that, as it was either the agreement between the contracting parties or the text of the treaty provision that was decisive, it must logically follow that the nature of the case in question was not a relevant factor in the decision as to whether the treaty was self-executing. In its own view, the Supreme Court took a dichotomic approach.[27] Others maintained quite the opposite. In a case in 1984, the Supreme Court, for the first time in its history, explicitly acknowledged that it had a lawmaking role to play.[28] But it pointed out that this lawmaking role would have been outstretched had it accepted the claim of an applicant who felt discriminated against and invoked the nondiscrimination clause of paragraph 26 of the ICCPR to acquire a right to Dutch citizenship. The Court made it clear that it would have to choose between different outcomes, each of which was equally consistent with the nondiscrimination requirement of Article 26. Because that would involve a choice the Court took to be essentially political by nature, it granted that the going practice of the government constituted a different treatment between men and women, but it refused to rule on the question of whether that constituted a violation of Article 26. Most scholars then concluded that the Court had meant to say that Article 26 was not self-executing in that particular case as it had otherwise refused judgment, which the courts are not allowed to do under Article 13 of the General Provisions Act of 1829.[29]

Meanwhile, the general feeling has turned to the dichotomic view. It is important to note in this respect that the Supreme Court itself seems to have abandoned its practice of refusing to rule on the question of whether there is a violation. It is still reluctant to provide a remedy (other than an informal declaration of incompatibility) in cases where that would involve political decision making, but it does deal with the argument of complainants that the statute in question is incompatible with fundamental human rights law.[30] And so it reviews statutory legislation on the basis of treaty law – thereby implying that the treaty is self-executing – even in cases where the remedy remains a political issue. The Court moreover confirmed its new course in its Yearly Report of 1995–96.

To sum up, fundamental rights review in the Netherlands primarily relies on international human rights documents, such as the ECHR and the ICCPR. These treaties automatically have legal effect in the Dutch legal order. Courts may, on the basis of Article 94 of the Constitution, review Acts of

27 Fleuren 2004.

28 Supreme Court judgment of 12 October 1984, *NJ* 1985/230 (*Dutch Citizenship*).

29 See, e.g., Brouwer 1992, p. 279.

30 The landmark case in this respect is the *Labour Expenses Deduction* judgment in 1999. See Supreme Court judgment of 12 May 1999, *BNB* 1999/271. This judgment reappears frequently in this report.

Parliament for their compliance with Convention rights if the treaty is proclaimed and insofar as the individual provisions are self-executing. A provision either is considered self-executing at all times or is not. The key criterion is whether the treaty provision textually provides a sufficient degree of manageable standards for the courts to decide the case on. The binding-all-persons requirement therefore theoretically serves as a preliminary question to be solved by the courts to keep them from having to decide among several political outcomes. However, because the specific constitutional characteristics of a given case do not play a role in deciding the issue of whether a particular treaty provision is self-executing, the courts may frequently confront a provision that in itself may provide some clear standards but that may nonetheless force the court to engage in positive lawmaking in certain specific situations. These days, the courts are aware of this dilemma, and they have tried to cope with it in a careful manner. Before we turn to the case law of the Supreme Court and its reception by legal scholarship, let us first say something about the historical reception and current position of European human rights law in the Netherlands, as they are closely connected to the way the Dutch courts carry out their lawmaking role.

3. *The Increasing Role of the European Convention in National Case Law*

Although the Netherlands has usually lived up to its relatively monist tradition, it does not follow that the European Convention was always given the full weight in practice it ought to have had on a purely formal basis. As we have said before, with the introduction in 1953 of the current Article 94 of the Constitution, it became common ground that treaty law clearly takes precedence over any kind of legislation. Only a year later, on 31 August 1954, the Kingdom of the Netherlands joined the ECHR; yet for nearly thirty years, the courts remained reluctant to apply the Convention, let alone disapply legislation violating it.[31] Until the 1980s, the judiciary was so cautious that there was hardly one case in which the Supreme Court found a violation of a Convention right.[32] If a Convention right was involved, the Court either would try to refer to a comparable right in Dutch law or would deny the self-executing nature of the Convention right. It was also common practice to interpret Convention (or indeed Covenant) rights in such a way

31 What might have played a role, though, was that the Convention was initially rarely invoked before the courts.

32 The notable exception being a judgment of the Supreme Court of 23 April 1974, *NJ* 1974/272.

that they had either a very narrow scope or a very broad limitation clause.[33] Conflicts between national legislation and human rights treaty law thus seemed very rare in the 1960s and 1970s. This led E. A. Alkema to conclude in 1980 that the courts had played only a limited role in the implementation of the ECHR.[34] However, things started to change rapidly soon after Alkema reached this conclusion, and already in 1988 the story sounded different.[35] After a remarkable decision of the Maastricht District Court in 1977, disapplying a provision of the 1935 Road Traffic Act because it violated Article 8 of the ECHR, an era began in which the courts overcame their initial reluctance within a few years.[36]

The Supreme Court was no exception. In 1980, it ruled that Article 959 of the Civil Procedure Code was to be interpreted in the light of Articles 8 and 14 of the European Convention. The legislature had knowingly established a difference in procedural treatment between cases concerning the custody of legitimate and illegitimate children. In the latter case, it was impossible for relatives of an illegitimate orphan to appeal against a decision of the local magistrate withholding custody. The Civil Procedure Code granted a right to appeal only to legally recognized kin and the legislature had always explicitly taken the view that there was no kinship between illegitimate children and family members of the parents.[37] The Court considered the views on the justification of this different treatment of legitimate and illegitimate children considerably changed. This was reflected in the case law of the European Court of Human Rights, notably in its 1979 *Marckx* judgment.[38] This judgment thus served as an argument to replace legislative history as the appropriate method of interpretation. The Supreme Court might have made law in the sense that it created a right to appeal for relatives of illegitimate children. But it is clear that the Court's understanding of the word *kinship* was rooted firmly in the case law of the European Court interpreting the Convention, which, as we know, takes a clear precedence over national law. The same story applied when in 1982 the Supreme Court spontaneously introduced the duty for parents to justify their decision not to

[33] Van Dijk 1988a, pp. 640–641.

[34] Alkema 1980, pp. 182–183.

[35] See Van Dijk 1988a, pp. 641–649.

[36] Maastricht District Court, judgment of 14 November 1977, *Netherlands Yearbook of International Law* 1978, p. 293. For further reading, see Van Dijk 1988a, p. 641; Myjer 1980, pp. 21–29.

[37] Supreme Court judgment of 18 January 1980, *NJ* 1980/463 (*Illegitimate Child*).

[38] ECtHR 13 June 1979, *Publ.* Series A, 13, pp. 14–20 (*Marckx v. Belgium*).

let their underage children enter marriage.[39] Where refusing their consent would be evidently unreasonable, the courts were allowed to substitute the parents' withheld permission, ignoring Article 1:36(2) of the Civil Code, which prohibited the courts from allowing a marriage in which one of the parents objected to it. Again, this judgment was backed up by several decisions of the European Commission on Human Rights.

Halfway through the 1980s, the Court's case law was at its peak in terms of self-consciousness. In 1984, it actually went one step further when it explicitly ordered the District Courts to set aside Section 1:161(1) of the Civil Code, thereby fundamentally interfering in Dutch family law. This provision requires the courts when allowing a divorce to appoint both a guardian and a supervising guardian, consequently implying that parental authority ends with the divorce. On the basis of Article 8 of the Convention, the Court maintained that it should be possible for the courts to leave (joint) parental authority intact when such a course would be in the best interest of the child in question. In such cases, the District Court had to set aside Section 1:161(1), thus effectively allowing for dual custody.[40] What was remarkable about this case –which, incidentally, is called the *Dual Custody* case– was that this time the Supreme Court had no clear mandate from either the European Court or the Commission when it held that the application of Section 1:161(1) of the Civil Code violated the Convention. A more marginal and abstract review by the Court –leading to a different outcome– would probably have sufficed.[41] Furthermore, the case showed that the Court was prepared to make full use of its power under Article 94 of the Constitution to ignore an Act of Parliament to issue relief based on the violation of the Convention.[42] The Dutch judiciary evidently was no longer reluctant but appeared to be downright eager to apply Convention law. Some years later, in 1986, the Court issued its famous – or infamous – so-called

39 Supreme Court judgment of 4 June 1982, *NJ* 1983/32 (*Parental Veto on Underage Marriage*). See also Supreme Court judgment of 20 December 1985, *NJ* 1987/54.

40 Supreme Court judgment of 4 May 1984, *NJ* 1985/510 (*Dual Custody*).

41 For some discussion on this issue, see (in Dutch) Alkema's Case Note under *NJ* 1985/510, and De Vet 1985, pp. 218–222. In English, see Van Dijk 1988a, p. 644.

42 This was not the only case in which the Supreme Court was prepared to go that far. See, e.g., its judgments of 1 July 1983, *NJ* 1980/463 (*Insanity Act*); of 22 June 1988, *NJ* 1988/955 (*Additional Tax Claim*); of 24 November 2000, *NJ* 2001/376 (*Matos v. Dutch Antilles*) and of 16 November 2001, *NJ* 2002/469 (*Pig Farming Reform Act*). Especially the lower courts have reacted rather enthusiastically to this development. See the judgment of the District Court of Amsterdam dated 14 January 1992, *NJ* 1992/401; District Court of Maastricht, judgment of 11 February 1993, *NJ* 1993/728; District Court of Amsterdam, judgment of 28 November 1995, *NJ* 1996/564; and Leeuwarden Court of Appeal 5 February 2003, *NJ* 2003/352.

Spring decisions.[43] They showed that the Court had not only overcome its reluctance to apply the Convention; it had also developed a rather more self-conscious attitude toward legislation and its own ability to regulate certain areas of law such as family law. The decisions will be elaborated on in the next section, and we consequently leave it at this for the moment.

The 1980s are usually regarded as the high-water mark in the Supreme Court's case law concerning fundamental rights review. They showed some of what few have called the more activist judgments of the Court. But they marked the beginning of a slow retreat as well. In some cases, by contrast, it exercised considerable restraint. For instance, in the *Dual Custody* case we mentioned previously, the Court categorically refused to engage in judicial lawmaking (or rather in a positive sense in any case) and was prepared only to set aside the impugned statutory provision.[44] The same year, 1984, witnessed the *Citizenship* case, where the Court refused to remedy an alleged violation of Article 26 of the International Covenant because there were several ways of dealing with the unequal treatment (if there was indeed a difference in treatment) and choosing would mean encroaching on the policy prerogative of the legislature.[45] We already touched on this judgment because it has led most authors to believe that the Court had applied the self-executing argument of Article 94 of the Constitution as an instrument to avoid entering into political territory. From the 1990s onward, the Court explicitly recognized that it was not empowered to set aside national provisions for their inconsistency with Convention law, purely on the basis of its own interpretation of the Convention. In other words, it considered itself unable to offer claimants a broader understanding of the European Convention than the prevailing interpretation offered by the European Court.[46] Accordingly, judicial lawmaking without a clear mandate by the European Court of Human Rights remains a phenomenon of the previous century.[47]

43 Joint Supreme Court decisions of 21 March 1986, *NJ* 1986/585–588 (*Spring Decisions*).

44 *Supra* note 40.

45 *Supra* note 28.

46 Supreme Court judgment of 19 October 1990, *NJ* 1992/129 (*Gay Marriage*); Supreme Court judgment of 10 August 2001, *NJ* 2002/278 (*Duty of Support*).

47 This was also clearly illustrated by the recent *Post-Salduz and Panovits* case, where the Court, on the basis of Art. 6 of the Convention, introduced the duty for police authorities to provide suspected criminals access to an attorney if they so choose (Supreme Court judgment of 30 June 2009, *NJ* 2009/349). Introducing this requirement was backed, however, by two judgments of the European Court, ECtHR 27 November 2008, *appl.* 36391/02 (*Salduz v. Turkey*), and ECtHR 11 December 2008, *appl.* 4268/04 (*Panovits v. Cyprus*).

4. *Concluding Remarks*

Together with the – as some might say – highly activist *Spring* decisions, this case law created a difficult legacy, both for the Court itself and for legal scholarship. It did confirm that the Supreme Court considered itself competent to assume a lawmaking role – certainly in a negative sense but sometimes even in a positive sense. But it raised questions as to what extent the Court was allowed to play such a role and what ought to be its obligations toward the victims of human rights violations. These questions are discussed in the next section. What may be concluded from the current one is that, although the judiciary was reluctant at first to apply the human rights treaties, it gradually overcame its cold feet. The 1980s constituted a phase wherein the Dutch courts accepted the human rights treaties, particularly the European Convention, as a judicially enforceable Bill of Rights for the Netherlands.[48] Of course, the 1983 Constitution already provided a civil rights charter, but because of the ban on judicial review and its broad limitation clauses, it had only a limited role to play, except perhaps for the political branches. The European Convention provided the courts with an enforceable equivalent.

To some extent, this came as a real novelty to them. For decades, the relationship between the courts and Parliament had largely been shaped by the existence of Article 120 of the Constitution, prohibiting the courts from reviewing any Act of Parliament. For all its particularities and exceptions, that provision constituted a bright-line rule for the courts to rely on. Never before had they been confronted with the difficulties concerning the boundaries of their role with respect to the prerogatives of the legislature. Not to such an extent as they were confronted with in the 1980s and the years to follow in any case. Their approach to this new question was initially not unequivocal or clear. Legal arguments concerning the positioning of the courts, the Supreme Court in particular, and Parliament scattered among several already-existing doctrines. The Court and legal scholarship for instance tried to cope with some of the constitutional difficulties by using Article 94's self-executing requirement in a somewhat dexterous manner. They also tried to fit in the Supreme Court's new role in the discussions about its lawmaking role in general, which primarily took place in the fields of civil and criminal law, but certainly not in constitutional law.[49] This

48 Van Dijk 1988a, p. 649.

49 This was observed by Alkema in his article (in Dutch), Alkema 2000, pp. 1053–1058. See also De Lange 1991.

attracted the attention of constitutional scholars to the debate on the lawmaking powers of the judiciary. And it is that debate to which we, too, now turn our attention.

III. THE LAWMAKING ROLE OF THE COURTS

1. *Introduction*

As we have observed, fundamental rights review of parliamentary legislation in the Netherlands is highly dispersed in the sense that it is carried out largely by ordinary courts on the basis of international human rights law. This means that the constitutional position of courts engaging in fundamental rights review is essentially not different from that of the courts in general. Having a separate constitutional court to decide on the constitutionality of statutes and their consequences might produce a separate set of rules regarding the proper boundaries for such a court. This is because it is not hierarchically subordinate to other courts, nor can it, strictly speaking, subject other courts to its general jurisdiction. That is definitely not the case in the Netherlands, where constitutional review in the sense of rights review takes place only within the general judicial framework. The rules that govern the boundaries of ordinary statutory interpretation therefore apply equally to fundamental rights adjudication.

A general characteristic of a civil law system is the lack of a doctrine of judicial precedent. The Dutch are no exception in this regard. Here, the concept of *res judicata* traditionally has a rather narrow meaning: it prevents the same parties from litigating the same case over again. Moreover, what the Court has dictated in its judgment, either on points of law or on points of fact, is lawfully binding, but theoretically only on the parties before it.[50] The Dutch legal system officially does not recognize a doctrine of *stare decisis*, where courts are bound by their own precedents or the precedents of higher courts.[51] In practice, however, the reasoning of the Supreme Court is generally followed by lower courts and sometimes – on a voluntary basis – even by the highest administrative courts.[52] As the Supreme Court has the power to reverse decisions of the ordinary courts, there seems little point for the latter to do otherwise. Following the case law of the Supreme Court is

[50] Van Hooijdonck & Eijsvoogel 2009, p. 39.

[51] See Loth 2009, p. 278.

[52] *Ibid.*

thus largely a matter of pragmatism besides the more fundamental reason of equality.[53] The Supreme Court also considers itself to some extent bound by its own case law and frequently refers to it. In practice, therefore, the Court's case law may be regarded as a source of law.[54] However, that does not alter the fact that the Court operates in a civil law system, where the separation of powers traditionally places some weight on the fact that it is the duty of the legislature to make the law and that of the courts to apply it.[55] And although this principle has, on the whole, never been applied very strictly in the Netherlands, it is certainly not an open-and-shut case that the courts have a lawmaking role to play. There is, then, a slight tension between Dutch constitutional theory, on the one hand – more or less repudiating a lawmaking role for the courts – and current legal practice, on the other hand.

In this section, we first describe the case law of the Supreme Court on its supposed lawmaking function. We then turn to the justifications and the critique legal scholarship has offered in reaction to this case law. Finally, we discuss some of the proposals that have recently been put forward to facilitate the Court's lawmaking function.

2. *Defining the Process of Lawmaking*

It has often been said that the courts have always assumed a lawmaking role, even from the outset.[56] The legal process simply is inconceivable without some judicial lawmaking. Until the 1980s, the Dutch Supreme Court never actually said that it had a duty to do so, but clearly it had always been forced to interpret the law. However, according to one prominent author, the Court was not likely to engage in lawmaking before 1960.[57] That raises the question of what the term *lawmaking* actually means. When former president Martens of the Supreme Court spoke of lawmaking as intrinsic to judging a case in his remarkable farewell speech for the Court, he evidently used it in a different way from the prominent author we mentioned just now. Martens evidently used a broader notion of what constituted judicial lawmaking than the other author, whose use of the term came closer to what one might call judicial activism.

[53] That is even more true of the administrative courts, whose judgments are not under review by the Supreme Court. When administrative courts follow the Supreme Court's case law, they do so on an entirely voluntary basis, mainly to serve the coherence of the law in general.

[54] *Supra* note 51. Moreover, see Koopmans 1999, pp. 124–125.

[55] *Ibid.*

[56] See, e.g., a contribution by former Supreme Court president Martens 2000, p. 747.

[57] Schoordijk 1988, pp. 8–9.

Lawmaking in the spirit of Hans Kelsen is indeed intrinsic to the judicial process. The courts create law just by interpreting a statute and applying it to an individual case.[58] In that view, any interpretation means creating law, no matter how close the court sticks to the literal wording of the provision in question. However, such lawmaking is hardly something to get excited about. True as the description in legal-theoretical terms may be, such a definition is far too broad to distinguish between legitimate and illegitimate lawmaking. One may, however, also speak of lawmaking when the court deviates from the literal wording of a legislative text to fill a legal gap. In this sense, it is perfectly possible for the court to remain firmly within the boundaries of the system and the objectives (teleology) of the statute, but then again, it might not.[59] Where that is the case, the court would have to assume a clearly political role. In such cases, the Court, rather than the legislature, gives direction to society.[60]

3. *The Case Law of the Supreme Court Concerning its Lawmaking Role*

Since the beginning of the twentieth century, the Dutch Supreme Court has increasingly assumed that it may not only apply the law but develop it as well.[61] In 1959, in *Quint v. Te Poel*, it explicitly ruled that where an Act of Parliament leaves a legal vacuum, the answer must lie within the existing statutory system.[62] The Court thus firmly implied that it was obviously empowered to fill the gap. Moreover, it marked a clear boundary between what the court understood to be legitimate lawmaking in the sense of developing the law on the basis of existing law and illegitimate lawmaking. That boundary was to be comprised by the existing statutory system.

As we have already implied, the Court has explicitly recognized its lawmaking role in the 1980s. In the *Citizenship* case of 1984, it mentioned a lawmaking duty for the courts but quickly added that making policy decisions clearly exceeded this duty.[63] Several authors have since noted that

58 See Kelsen 1934/1992, p. 68.

59 This is what the German legal literature calls *Gesetzesimmanente Rechtsfortbildung*, as opposed to *Gesetzesübersteigende Rechtsfortbildung*, where the courts exceed such boundaries. See Larenz 1991, pp. 366–367.

60 For an example of this use of the term *lawmaking*, see Stolker 1993, p. 57. See further Bell 1985, p. 6.

61 See, e.g., its landmark case on the interpretation of torts: *Lindenbaum v. Cohen*, Supreme Court judgment of 31 January 1919, *NJ* 1919, p. 161.

62 Supreme Court judgment of 30 January 1959, *NJ* 1959/548 (*Quint v. Te Poel*).

63 *Supra* note 28.

when the Court speaks of lawmaking, it nearly always does so in a negative way – refusing to accept a specific interpretation or remedy because that would outstretch its judicial role.[64] When it does feel that it may fill a gap, it hardly ever argues why lawmaking in a particular case is justified. This is clearly illustrated by two cases we have already mentioned. In the *Citizenship* case of 1984, it ruled that the limitations of its lawmaking duty would not allow it to remedy a violation of Article 26 of the International Covenant, whereas in the *Spring Decisions* of 1986, it made no reference whatsoever to its lawmaking duty to justify its rather consequential judgment.[65]

After the Supreme Court openly coined its own lawmaking duty in 1984, the legislature quickly followed suit. In 1988, it adopted the proposed Bill for a revised Judicial Organisation Act, in which a new Article 101a (currently Article 81) included specifically as the duties of the Supreme Court, to "secure the uniformity of the law and advance the development of the law."[66] With the development of the law, Parliament clearly recognized a lawmaking duty for the courts.[67] However, the question remains as to what constitutes development of the law and what exceeds mere development and turns into (illegitimate) lawmaking.

A. The *Dual Custody* Case: Distinguishing Positive from Negative Lawmaking

In its 1984 judgment on dual custody, the Supreme Court followed the line of reasoning it had already set out in the 1959 *Quint v. Te Poel* case and applied it for the first time to fundamental rights review. As we have seen before, this case concerned the applicability of Section 1:161(1) of the Civil Code, which required the courts to appoint one guardian when granting a

64 See, e.g., Kortmann 2005, p. 250 (in Dutch).

65 Admittedly, the Advocate General had extensively gone into the matter. See the Supreme Court judgments of 12 October 1984, *NJ* 1985/230 (*Dutch Citizenship*), and of 21 March 1986, *NJ* 1986/585-588 (*Spring Judgments*).

66 Act of 1827 concerning the Judicial Organization, *Stb.* 1827, 20, most recently amended on 11 December 2008, *Stb.* 2009, 8.

67 Koopmans 1999, p. 131; Martens 2000, p. 747. Recognition of the lawmaking duty of the courts moreover appeared in some correspondence between the Minister for Justice and the Second Chamber of Parliament in 1989 (after the adoption of the Bill), where the minister mentioned three duties of the Supreme Court: securing the uniform application of the law, leading the development of the law, and providing individuals with adequate legal protection. He marked the first two elements as a "the lawmaking duty" (*Kamerstukken II* 1988/89, 21 206, nº 2, p. 42).

divorce.[68] In a case before the District Court of Amsterdam, the parents of six-year-old Ingolf requested joint custody after the divorce. The District Court refused the request, arguing that its duty pursuant to Section 1:161(1) to appoint one guardian clearly ruled out the possibility of appointing two. Appealing the decision, the parents invoked Article 8 of the ECHR. However, the Supreme Court agreed with the District Court. It argued that the legal system did not allow joint guardianship, not even on the basis of Article 8 of the Convention. This interpretation of Article 1:161(1) of the Civil Code would outstretch the judicial function, as it would engage the Court in positive legislating. It considered that introducing dual custody would not easily fit into the existing statutory system. It did not explain why that was the case, nor had the Advocate General done so (he had actually argued the opposite), but there it was. Yet the Court managed to find a solution. The justices pointed out that Article 94 may not have allowed them to positively engage in judicial rule making, but it did give them the power to set aside certain provisions of the Civil Code on the ground that their application would violate the Convention. Considering that ignoring Section 1:161(1) would leave parental authority – on the basis of Article 1:161(4) of the Civil Code – intact, it subsequently ordered the District Court to inquire whether joint responsibility for both parents would serve the child's best interest.[69]

What the *Dual Custody* case shows remarkably well is that the Court made a crucial distinction between its power (based on Article 94) to set aside the Civil Code and its lack of power to settle the issue by promulgating its own, more convenient, rules if those rules were incompatible with the existing statutory scheme. Ignoring one statutory provision to apply another hardly qualifies as doing justice to this statutory scheme but evidently the Court took Article 94 of the Constitution for a clear mandate to deviate from that scheme so long as it stayed on the negative side by just ignoring a provision.

B. The *Dutch Citizenship* Case: Avoiding Policy Decisions

The 1984 *Citizenship* judgment, in which the Court explicitly recognized its lawmaking duty, added a new dimension to this. In this case, the Court confronted a claim of an illegal immigrant who, during his stay in the Netherlands, had married a Dutch woman. Because his stay in the Netherlands was illegal and because he had built up quite a remarkable

68 *Supra* note 62.

69 Supreme Court judgment of 4 May 1984, *NJ* 1985/510 (*Dual Custody*).

criminal record, he was asked to leave. The applicant then informed the authorities of his wish to acquire Dutch nationality. He relied on Article 8 of the Nationality Act, granting the foreign wife of a Dutch husband the right to acquire Dutch nationality by informing the authorities of her wish. However, the provision obviously applied only to women, not men. The applicant argued that Article 8 violated paragraph 26 of the International Covenant and had therefore to be interpreted in such a way that men, too, had the right to acquire Dutch nationality. The Court did not accept the argument. It even refused to review whether the Act violated the Covenant because, had it found a violation, it would not have been able to remedy the situation. Unlike in the *Dual Custody* case, setting aside the statute would clearly not benefit the claimant because the provision was positively phrased. It did not deny the applicant a right, just awarded it underinclusively to women. Setting aside the statute would only deprive women of their privileged position; however, women in general were not party to the case.

The question thus became whether the Court was allowed to read in the words "and men" to the provision, thereby widening its scope. Under the *Quint v. Te Poel* reasoning, the issue would have been whether such reading in would contradict the statutory scheme. It might have, but the Court did not go into that. Instead, it argued that widening the scope to include men would not be the only lawful solution. Article 26 of the ICCPR merely prohibited unequal treatment, and to abrogate the right for women was just as lawful as extending the right to men. This was a matter of policy and to choose between the two would be to encroach on the political prerogative of Parliament. And so the Court left open the question of whether the statutory provision violated Article 26 of the Covenant and turned down the applicant's claim. It thereby added to its discourse a new ground to abstain from issuing a remedy: it was not prepared to choose between different policy outcomes. What might also have played a role, though, is the fact that at the time of the judgment, a new statutory scheme had already been introduced in Parliament.

The *Citizenship* judgment has received some criticism for its perceived overspill of judicial restraint.[70] It is striking, therefore, that the Court delivered two judgments that are widely considered among its most activist only a year later.[71]

70 See Van Dijk 1988b, pp. 199–202.

71 *Supra* note 43.

C. The *Spring* Decisions: Judicial Activism or Prudent Lawmaking?

On September 21, 1984, a child was born from two parents. That was not unusual. Indeed, nature will not have it any other way, at least not for the time being. What was so special about this case was that the parents were not married at the time of birth, nor had they ever been married or had any intention of doing so in the near future. They were happily living together and saw no need for marriage. That had been quite unusual for decades, but in the 1970s and 1980s, more and more people in the Netherlands decided not to marry. Under Dutch law, such parents could exercise no parental authority at all. They could only obtain shared guardianship. The Court held that this distinction violated Articles 8 and 14 of the European Convention. What followed was an obscure mixture of setting aside certain provisions of the Civil Code and extensively interpreting others so that they might read consistently with the Convention. The Court thus elaborately tried to regulate the conditions under which a request for joint parental authority was to be granted by the courts. The Court devoted an entire page in the case reports to describe these conditions. It did not elaborate on the question as to what authorized the Court to issue such regulations. They were not formally proclaimed but were mentioned as part of the interpretation of the Civil Code. What the Court effectively did was provide lower courts with a manual for how to work through such difficult cases by using their combined powers to set aside and reinterpret national law in a uniform and Convention-proof manner. It probably considered it necessary to do so in the interest of legal certainty. However, as one author wrote: "This is legislation rather than judgment."[72] The question may well be asked whether such an extensive interpretation suited the contemporary statutory scheme. It probably did not. To that extent, the judgment did not seem to meet the criterion of the 1959 *Quint v. Te Poel* judgment. Moreover, many political policy issues were involved here. The question might equally be asked why the Court did not make reference to the criterion it had set out in its *Citizenship* judgment just one year earlier.

D. After the High-Water Mark: A Slow Retreat to Judicial Restraint

After the 1980s, the Supreme Court began its slow retreat to an attitude of greater judicial restraint. It increasingly refused to review Acts of Parliament on the basis of the argument that it was not in a position to offer a remedy. In

[72] Alkema in his Case Note under the judgment in *NJ* 1986/588.

a vast number of cases, it followed the reasoning it had already followed in the *Citizenship* judgment.[73] The *Spring* decisions had fundamentally changed Dutch family law, but they remained exceptions in the fundamental rights case law of the Court. What changed, though, was that the Court sometimes applied the *Citizenship* reasoning even in cases where it might have had the opportunity to set aside a provision on the basis of Article 94 of the Constitution. The sharp contrast it had introduced in the *Dual Custody* case, when it said that it could not add something to the law but was able to set it aside (effectively reaching the same outcome), might not have been abandoned, but it was certainly blurred to some extent. The Court may have taken in some of the critique of Advocate General Moltmaker in the *Spring* cases. He argued that the difference between filling a gap and setting aside a provision is of a formal rather than of a substantive nature.[74] For Moltmaker, there existed no clear distinction between negative and positive lawmaking.

Whenever setting aside a statute would have rather undesirable consequences, either because that would create a legal gap or otherwise, the Court would abstain from doing so. In the 1998 *Car Expenses Deduction* case, for instance, the Court refrained from setting aside a provision of the Income Tax Act of 1964, because even though it would have solved the relevant inequality, it would instantly have introduced another inequality.[75] In another case concerning court levies, its motive not to set aside the statutory provision probably resulted from fear of the financial consequences for public expenditure.[76] Incidentally, the Court even applied the *Citizenship* reasoning to cases where setting aside the statute would have been an appropriate remedy. Thus, in a 1997 case concerning the possibility of two women adopting a child, it refused to review whether Article 1:227 of the Civil Code – which effectively excluded same-sex couples from adopting a child – violated Articles 8 and 14 of the European Convention.[77] It followed the reasoning of the Advocate General, who had argued that there were several possible policy outcomes, and because setting aside the statute would lead to one of them, by doing so, the Court would make a political choice, which of course would not do.

[73] See, e.g., the Supreme Court judgments of 16 November 1990, *NJ* 1991/475 (*Paternity*), and 8 July 1994, *NJ* 1995/30 (*Expert Witness*).

[74] See para. 6.1.3 of the Advocate General's conclusion.

[75] Supreme Court judgment of 15 July 1998, *BNB* 1998/293 (*Car Expenses Deduction*).

[76] Supreme Court judgment of 30 September 1992, *BNB* 1993/30 (*Court Fees*). Fear of a heavy burden also played a role in the Supreme Court judgment of 28 May 2004, *NJ* 2006/430 (*Probationay Release*).

[77] Supreme Court judgment of 5 September 1997, *NJ* 1998/686 (*Double Mothers*).

E. Toward a New Model: The 1999 *Labor Expenses Deduction* Judgment

In the 1990s, several scholars expressed their uneasiness with regard to the abstaining practice.[78] Some of the questions that arose were whether Article 94 of the Constitution allowed such a move and how abstaining had to be considered from the perspective of effective legal protection of fundamental rights. The Court eventually responded with a landmark judgment in 1999, which addressed both questions by introducing a new model composed of elements of some of the cases we have just discussed.[79]

The case itself concerned a technicality regarding the tax deduction for those with relatively high labor costs as compared to those with standard labor costs. We do not discuss the facts of the case here. What matters is that the Court was confronted with a relatively clear inequality between the two groups in Article 37 of the Income Tax Act of 1964. It explicitly considered this provision in violation of Articles 14 and 1 of the European Convention's First Protocol. The Court then proceeded to the question whether it was in a position to remove the inequality. It eventually concluded that it was not. But in doing so, it merged some of different lines of reasoning of its previous case law, adding to that a few drops of the concern articulated by legal scholarship.

For the very first time, the Court connected its supposed lawmaking duty to the principle of effective legal protection. It implied that it was obviously under a duty to provide adequate protection and started off by stressing that to set aside the impugned provision was not a sound option, as this would not benefit the claimant. As was the case in the *Citizenship* judgment, Article 37 of the Income Tax Act was positively framed in the sense that it allowed a deduction for an underinclusively phrased group. The Court thus considered that setting aside the provision would not, on its own accord, create a right to the deduction for the discriminated group. This is important because what the Court appears to have implied is that if setting aside the statute had been a suitable remedy for the applicant, it would have done so – even if that had ultimately led to only one of several possible outcomes. As in the *Dual Custody* case, the Court would then take Article 94 of the Constitution for a clear mandate to act. The Court may therefore have dismissed its cautious attitude in the 1997 *Same-Sex Parents* case, where it refused to set aside the

[78] See, e.g., De Wet 2008, pp. 241–242.

[79] Supreme Court judgment of 12 May 1999, *NJ* 2000/170 (*Labour Expenses Deduction*).

statutory provision on the basis that there were other legitimate policy outcomes as well.[80]

The Court then proceeded to examine in what way it could possibly provide a remedy, given that setting aside the statute on the basis of Article 94 was of no use. It considered that there was a legal gap concerning the question of whether the applicant had a right to the deduction. It could either fill this gap on its own initiative or leave the matter for the legislature. The answer to the question of which course to take, according to the Court, depended on the outcome of a balancing test involving the principle of effective legal protection and some desirable judicial restraint "in the current constitutional structure." The Court finally gave some clues as to how such balancing should take place, using its earlier case law as a catalog of topoi. From its *Quint v. Te Poel* reasoning, it derived that if the existing statutory scheme provided clues for deciding the case, it would fill the gap.[81] If, however, there were different policy outcomes to choose from, choosing between them would – for the time being – be a matter best left for the political branches.[82] This consideration led some authors to carefully try and compare it to the political question doctrine of the U.S. Supreme Court.[83]

The Court did, uncharacteristically, explain why it was not prepared to interfere in the legislative process when there were different policy outcomes to choose from. It stressed that the courts had to observe some "desirable judicial restraint" and that it had only limited possibilities for engaging in a quasi-legislative process.[84] Its explanation was, of course, primarily intended for the ears of those who had been critical of the Court's restrained attitude in years leading up to the judgment. To that end, the Court added one other remark. As we have seen, the Court had taken the view that if such a situation arose where there were different policy outcomes to choose from, it would, for the time being, leave the matter for the legislature to decide. It then explicitly stressed that the outcome of its balancing test might be different if the legislature was familiar with the inconsistency and chose to

[80] *Supra* note 77.

[81] See also the Supreme Court judgment of 17 August 1998, *BNB* 1999/123 (*Commercial Registration Number Plates*).

[82] This is basically the *Dutch Citizenship* line of reasoning (*supra* note 28).

[83] Unfortunately, only in Dutch, see Bovend'Eert 2009, p. 151; De Werd 2004, pp. 69–126.

[84] Already in 1993, a study showed that the reasons for the Court to refrain from positive lawmaking (or as the study called it, "engaging in politics in the sense of giving direction to society") were primarily of a rather practical nature; it basically boiled down to the question of whether the Court would be able to regulate in issue in society. See (in Dutch) Stolker 1993, *supra* note 60, and for a revised version, see Uzman and Stolker 2009, pp. 475–496.

ignore it. What the Court said, in fact, was that it assumed itself competent to engage in lawmaking even where that meant making policy decisions, but it had to wait for the legislature to act first. Yet if Parliament deliberately maintained the incompatible regulation, the Court would not hesitate to do whatever it thought Parliament evidently might or in any case should have done.

There is a remarkable paradox here with the approach taken by the Court in its case law concerning the ban on judicial review of the constitutionality of statutes as laid down in Article 120 of the Constitution. In its celebrated *Harmonisation Act* judgment of 1989, the Court had ruled that it may not declare statutory provisions void for their lack of consistency with either the Constitution or legal principles.[85] But as we have seen, it made an exception for cases where Parliament could not have known about the inconsistency. It then implicitly assumed that Parliament would have wanted it not to apply the incompatible provision. This approach appears to deviate from the *Labour Expenses Deduction* approach, where the Court considered itself competent to legislate if Parliament had knowingly failed to do so.

The difference between the two approaches lies in the nature of the review undertaken by the Court. With respect to Article 120 of the Constitution, the Court has to observe the fact that the question of whether a statute is constitutional is ultimately for Parliament to decide. The Dutch version of parliamentary sovereignty (as far as it exists) therefore fundamentally differs from that of the United Kingdom where, as Dicey phrased it, "Parliament has the right to make or unmake any law whatever."[86] The Dutch Parliament may certainly not make or unmake any law whatsoever. Its powers are limited by the Constitution. However, Article 120 reserves for Parliament the right to have the ultimate say on the question of whether it has overstepped such limitations. So the Courts may not only safely assume that it is Parliament's desire to legislate in conformity with the Constitution; they must respect the fiction even when it is clear that Parliament has actually no such intention at all. The situation is different with regard to treaty law. Here the same assumption applies: the legislator aims to legislate in compliance with its international obligations, but the question of whether it has actually done so is ultimately a matter for the courts to decide. Article 94 of the Constitution makes that painfully clear. If Parliament therefore knowingly ignores its obligation to legislate consistently with, for instance, the European Convention, the courts must intervene and ultimately issue a

85 *Supra* note 17.

86 Dicey 1885/1959, pp. 3–4.

remedy. The relationship between the Supreme Court and the legislature is then much more one between equals than the relationship with regard to constitutional review, where Parliament has the authoritative say.

In the case at hand, the *Labour Expenses Deduction* case, the Court developed a line of reasoning it had already put in practice some years earlier. In another tax decision, concerning commercial registration plates, the Court had been willing to grant the victims of an unequal treatment the benefit they had been denied by the legislature.[87] Of course, there was no clear obligation for Parliament to grant these car owners the impugned benefit. It could equally have decided to abolish the entire scheme. There were then two choices. And yet the Court felt that it was entitled to choose the first option without leaving the matter to Parliament. There were two reasons for this. First of all, the government had actually warned Parliament that its amendment would most probably violate the Convention. Parliament had not in any way contradicted this statement but had nevertheless passed the bill amended. It was therefore painfully clear that Parliament had knowingly legislated inconsistently with the Convention. Moreover, granting the aggrieved car owners the benefit was exactly what the government had proposed to do in the first place. It therefore fit in neatly with the existing statutory scheme and thus met the important criterion of the 1959 *Quint v. Te Poel* case.

In contrast, it has become clear that the Court is not likely to assume that the legislature has consciously left a violation intact. After the 1997 *Number Plates* judgment, the Court has never actually considered filling a gap when there were policy choices to make. Quite the contrary, when confronted with the alleged sluggishness of the legislature in amending the law in a few cases where the Court had declared the Act incompatible with Convention rights, it explicitly accepted the argument of the government that it had tried to amend the law with all deliberate speed.[88] In the same judgments, it has also ruled that, when remedying the inconsistency, Parliament may freely choose to change the law only for the future in the sense that it need not necessarily enact its amendments with retroactive effect.[89]

[87] *Supra* note 81. This was a case in 1997, but already in 1990 the Court had mentioned its readiness to issue a remedy if Parliament did not take up the matter after the Court had expressed its concerns. See the Supreme Court judgment of 31 January 1990, *NJ* 1990/403 (*Unreasonable Delay*).

[88] Supreme Court judgments of 24 January 2001, *BNB* 2001/291, and 14 June 2002, *BNB* 2002/289 (*Labor Expenses Deduction II*).

[89] *Ibid.*

The 1999 *Labour Expenses Deduction* judgment basically sums up the Court's attitude to positive and negative lawmaking in fundamental rights cases. It is clear that the Court recognizes its duty to provide effective redress to claimants who successfully invoke human rights treaties. Moreover, it has developed a kind of step-by-step plan to decide on the nature of the redress:

1. It will always try to interpret any indefinite provision consistently with the treaty provision in question.

2. It will try to provide redress by means of negative lawmaking: it examines whether setting aside the impugned provision might settle the case. Only if that is not the case does the question arise as to whether the Court may engage in positive lawmaking by using its interpretative mandate.

3. As a matter of principle, it considers itself empowered to do so when there is a clear alternative that agrees with the existing statutory scheme.

4. It should leave the matter for Parliament to resolve when there are policy decisions at stake. The Court will then not easily encroach on the political prerogative of Parliament.

5. But it is – at least theoretically – prepared to do so when Parliament evidently has no intention of putting things right within a reasonable period of time.

The Court generally complies with its own framework, and it may therefore be said that it usually exercises judicial constraint when it comes to positive lawmaking in the sense of issuing regulations on the basis of its duty to interpret the law. There is one notable exception, however, to this general rule. And we turn our attention briefly to that exception.

F. The Exception to the Rule: European Union Law

Where a statute violates European Union law rather than the European Convention on human rights or one of the other human rights treaties, the Supreme Court does not consider it possible to leave the matter for the legislature. The basic assumption for the Supreme Court is that Articles 93 and 94 of the Constitution – regulating the effects of international law in the domestic legal order – do not apply to European Union law. As early as 1963, the European Court of Justice (ECJ) ruled in its landmark cases *Van Gend & Loos and Costa v. E.N.E.L.* that the European legal order is fundamentally monistic, meaning that Community law is both of direct effect and superior to any kind of national law (including national constitutions) on its own accord.[90] The Dutch Supreme Court has never challenged this claim, and in 2004, it even accepted it explicitly.[91] This effectively means that it is ultimately the law of the EU itself that, in the view of the Supreme Court, determines the extent to which Community law affects the Dutch legal order. To that end, the European Court of Justice has derived some stringent rules concerning the effective legal protection of Community law by the national courts from the EC Treaty. Although the ECJ has consistently ruled that the effects of an inconsistency between national and Community law are a matter for national courts to deal with, it has simultaneously laid down some minimum guidelines to secure the uniform and effective application of Community law throughout the Union.[92] National courts are required to interpret national law as far as possible in conformity with Community law.[93] Were such an interpretation, according to the national rules of adjudication, to prove impossible, then the national court in question would be obliged to set aside the national rule.[94] The ECJ has underlined that any national rule that handicaps the possibilities of courts to secure the uniform and effective execution of Community law must be put aside as well.[95] Mitigating the undesired consequences of the application of Community law can be considered only by the ECJ itself.[96] Last but not least, the ECJ takes a relatively straightforward approach to remedies in discrimination cases. In such cases, the national courts have to extend the more favorable rule to the aggrieved party as well.[97] The ECJ does not consider such an extension to be any kind of policy decision but a logical outcome of applying the principle of nondiscrimination to a given case, thereby deviating considerably from the approach usually adopted by the Dutch Supreme Court.

The Supreme Court has faithfully carried out its duties under Community law in this respect. A recent example taken from the field of taxation might

[90] *Supra* note 7.

[91] Supreme Court judgment of 2 November 2004, *NJ* 2005/80 (*Compulsory Break*).

[92] See, e.g., ECJ judgments of 27 March 1980, Case 61/79 (*Denkavit*); of 30 April 1998, C-37-38/96 (*Sodiprem*); of 16 January 2003, C-265/01 (*Pansard*); and of 6 March 2007, C-292/04 (*Meilicke*).

[93] *Supra* note 8.

[94] See, *inter alia*, ECJ judgments of 15 July 1964, Case 6/64 (*Costa v. E.N.E.L.*), and of 9 March 1978, Case 106/77 (*Simmenthal*).

[95] See, e.g., the *Simmenthal* judgment, *supra* note 94.

[96] ECJ judgments of 17 May 1990, C-262/88 (*Barber v. Guardian*); 1 April 2008, C-267/06 (*Tadao Maruko*).

[97] See, *inter alia*, ECJ judgments of 27 June 1990, C-33/89 (*Kowalska*), and of 26 January 1999, C-18/95 (*Terhoeve*).

illustrate this. In the *Ilhan* case, the Court determined that Article 1 of the Car and Motorcycle Taxation Act constituted a violation of Articles 43 and 55 of the EC Treaty.[98] It considered that modifying – and consequently interpreting the statutory provision consistently with Community law – would outstretch its lawmaking duties, as the existing statutory scheme and its legislative history did not yield any particular way forward. However, it refused to consider leaving the matter for Parliament, as it surely would have done, had it concerned a case under a human rights treaty. Instead, it decided to set aside the Act at large, thereby effectively annulling the entire tax measure.[99] To provide the required redress, the Court thus fell back on to its classical role of a Kelsenian negative legislator.

4. *Reactions of "La doctrine" after 1999*

As we have seen, there has always been a considerable debate on the question of whether the courts have a lawmaking role to play and, if so, how far this role might be stretched. This has traditionally been a debate among civil lawyers interested in methods of interpretation. But as the role of the courts with respect to fundamental rights review changed and increased in the 1980s, the lawmaking powers of the ordinary courts clearly became a matter of constitutional law. This presented constitutional scholars with the basic question of whether the traditional doctrines on the role of the courts were adequate in the field of fundamental rights review.[100] However, such was the general consensus among civil lawyers now that the courts were under a clear duty to develop and shape the law that there was also from the very outset among constitutional scholars a tendency to agree on the basic fact that the courts had a considerable lawmaking role to play.[101] Dutch constitutional doctrine has therefore never been very fundamentally critical of the courts acting as a positive legislator. What is more, the term *positive legislator* would hardly be used at all.

Consensus somewhat eroded in 2005 as a Nijmegen law professor questioned the lawmaking duty of the courts.[102] He argued that this so-called

[98] Supreme Court judgment of 14 November 2008, *BNB* 2009/3 (*Ilhan*).

[99] The Judicial division of the Council of State seems to take a less rigorous stand. In the *Eman & Sevinger* case, it did invoke the limits of its lawmaking duties in a case concerning EU law, *supra* note 10.

[100] See, *inter alia*, the authors mentioned in footnote 49.

[101] This attitude was expressed in 2000 by the parting president of the Supreme Court Martens in his farewell speech (*supra* note 56).

[102] Kortmann 2005.

lawmaking duty was an invention by the Supreme Court itself, the creation of which was to a large extent itself a piece of lawmaking without any basis in written law.[103] However, he was not the only one critical of the Supreme Court's attitude. At the other end of the spectrum, there had already been scholars arguing that the Court's attitude toward individual victims was possibly too restrained to provide effective legal redress.[104] In short, the debate was renewed.

Today legal scholarship can roughly be divided into three categories. First, there are those who are of the opinion that there is no legal basis whatsoever for the courts to engage in lawmaking.[105] Courts decide cases, and in the process of doing that, they might find and apply the law, but they certainly do not go about creating it. Second, probably the vast majority of scholars argue that there is a role for the courts with respect to judicial lawmaking, but it is equally clear that it should primarily be Parliament that enacts the law.[106] They generally assume that Article 81 of the Judicial Organisation Act provides a clear basis for the courts to develop – and thus shape – the law, even if that means engaging in an activity close to legislating. They expressly reject the argument that the Supreme Court may never engage in lawmaking because it lacks the appropriate democratic legitimacy. Most of them assume that the courts do not derive their legitimacy no from any democratic principle but from the rule of law.[107] However, this group lacks coherence in the sense that, although most scholars agree that the courts have a lawmaking role to play when reviewing legislation, they differ on the extent of the lawmaking duty. The basic question here is whether the courts may encroach on the policy prerogative of the legislature. There are those who think the courts clearly incompetent to do so.[108] They consequently disagree with the stance the Supreme Court has taken in its *Labour Expenses Deduction* judgment, when it abstained from lawmaking but warned that it might in the future decide otherwise if Parliament remained inactive.[109] Others maintain that, although it is usually improper for the courts to engage

[103] *Ibid.*

[104] Van Dijk 1988b; Martens 2000; Barkhuysen and Van Emmerik 2006, p. 63.

[105] *Supra* note 102. Moreover, see Schutte 2009, pp. 676–680.

[106] See, e.g., Koopmans 1999, p. 134; Martens 2000, p. 751; Brenninkmeijer 2001, p. 26; De Werd 2004, p. 120.

[107] See the authors mentioned in the previous footnote. Critically, however, see Bovend'Eert 2009, pp. 142–143.

[108] Most recently, see, e.g., Bovend'Eert 2009, p. 143 (see the previous footnote).

[109] See the previous section.

in politically sensitive issues, it may nonetheless be necessary for them to do so to provide effective redress.[110]

Apart from this difference in opinion, the common denominator of this second group is that it regards lawmaking by the courts as possible but clearly the exception. It is, first of all, a spin-off of deciding individual cases and, in the case of fundamental rights review, something necessary but abnormal. Setting aside statutory law and subsequently formulating guidelines for society is the core business not of the courts but of Parliament.[111] They stress, in other words, the primacy of Parliament in policy making and legislating.[112] There is, however, a third group of authors who appear to argue for a more sweeping understanding of the lawmaking role of the courts. For such authors, the courts – especially the Supreme Court – and the legislature are "partners in the business of the law."[113] Building firmly on the civilian tradition, they argue that Parliament is not able to anticipate every sudden change of direction society takes. Therefore, judge-made law is "an absolute must," its contribution to the development of the law indispensable, and it should be regarded not as the exception but as the rule.[114] Looking after the parties of the case at hand is not the only primary duty of the courts: they have an equally important duty toward the development of the law in general. However, one may wonder whether such scholars are still addressing the same subject. As we have seen, there is some disagreement about the extent to which the term *lawmaking* ought to be used. The civil law approach is very much directed toward the filling of legal gaps the legislature is simply unable to fill. That situation substantially differs from what concerns constitutional scholars most, that is, when the courts must set aside a clear statutory provision that nevertheless fails to produce an appropriate remedy for the case at hand. Still, the Dutch debate on the lawmaking powers of the courts is very much fashioned by the existence of this group. As we will see in the next section, their efforts seem to have influenced the Supreme Court as well as the legislature, and reforms are under way to adapt the Court's position in the legal system to its lawmaking role.

[110] Notably, see Martens 2000, p. 751; moreover, Happé 1999, p. 43; Adams 2009, p. 1098.

[111] See the outline drawn up by Bovend'Eert 2009, pp. 140–142.

[112] See also Adams 2009, p. 1098.

[113] See, e.g., Vranken 2006, pp. 8–9.

[114] *Ibid.*

IV. MEANS AND EFFECTS OF JUDICIAL REVIEW

1. *Introduction*

In this section, we offer a brief outline of the way in which dialogue among the courts, the parties of the individual case, and the legislature is shaped. Particular topics include the specific procedures to attain a remedy for a human rights violation (including legislative omissions), specific injunctions concerning unlawful legislation, and the effects of decisions concerning rights review. Moreover, we turn our attention briefly to the specific techniques the Supreme Court occasionally applies to mitigate the consequences of its lawmaking activities.

2. *Procedures Available to Enforce Fundamental Rights Law*

As we have said before, the Netherlands does not have a constitutional court. Consequently, there are no specific procedures for claimants to complain about infringements of fundamental rights. No *recurso de amparo, habeas corpus, or Verfassungsbeschwerde* exist in the Dutch legal order. As we have noted before, this does not mean that the courts have no role to play when confronted with violations of (international) human rights. As long as the right in question is laid down in a self-executing treaty provision, the courts may review legislation for its consistency with such rights both in a direct and an indirect way.

The power for the ordinary and administrative courts to review legislative rules for their consistency with higher laws was already established in 1864.[115] As we have discussed, rules of international law automatically take precedence over national rules and are therefore recognized as higher law in the Dutch legal order. Should the courts conclude that national provisions are inconsistent with treaty law, then, as we have seen, they must either interpret the provision in conformity with the treaty or, if that is impossible, set aside the national provision on the basis of Article 94 of the Constitution. The courts then apply either remaining national law or the norm of the treaty provision itself. This may ultimately lead to a remedy by way of granting the requested permit after all, awarding damages, or acquitting on criminal charges, whatever the case may be. It is important, however, to stress that Article 94 of the Constitution does not empower the courts to declare statutes

[115] Supreme Court judgment of 6 March 1864, *W* 2646 (*Pothuys*), *supra* note 21.

void. It requires the courts only to set aside individual provisions in individual cases.

Direct review of legislation is also a possibility, if it does not happen often with regard to statutes. The bulk of both positive and negative legislating by the courts with regard to primary law takes place in procedures of indirect review. But having said that, it is certainly possible to start civil proceedings against the State for unlawfully enacting a statute. In a landmark judgment of the Supreme Court, *Pocketbooks II,* the Court ruled that Article 1401 of the Civil Code (currently Article 6:162), which concerns a general tort, was generally applicable to the legislative function of the government.[116] Although successful appeals concerning the unlawfulness of primary legislation remain scarce, it is by no means impossible that the Supreme Court one day accept this kind of claim. In the 2001 (first) *Pig Farming Reform Act* judgment, the Court was in any case prepared to review whether some of the Bill's provisions constituted an unlawful act in the framework of Article 6.162 of the Civil Code, rendering the State liable for damages.[117]

3. *Remedies for Fundamental Rights Violations*

The difficult question, however, is not whether the courts may accept a claim concerning the lawful enactment and application of an Act of Parliament, but rather what remedies they may issue when they conclude the Act to be inconsistent with international law.[118] Perhaps the least difficult remedy in this particular respect is the power of the civil courts to award damages for unlawful legislation. This may certainly be an option.[119] Another available remedy concerns the power of the courts to issue a declaratory judgment to the effect that the enacted bill is unlawful, where the unlawfulness may, of course, arise from incompatibility with international treaty law. Such declarations may be made by all ordinary courts whether low or Supreme, and as we will see in the next section, they can formally bind only the parties in the case at hand. In practice, however, the binding force of such declarations is rather substantive. The courts may also issue an injunction to the effect that the government may not apply to the impugned

[116] Supreme Court judgment of 24 January 1969, *NJ* 1969/316 (*Pocketbooks II*).

[117] Supreme Court judgment of 16 November 2001, *NJ* 2002/469 (*Pig Farming Reform Act*). Moreover, see Supreme Court judgment of 14 April 2000, *NJ* 2000/713 (*Kooren Maritiem v. State*).

[118] Cf. Schutgens 2009, pp. 36–39.

[119] See, *inter alia*, the *Pig Farming Reform Act* judgment, *supra* note 117.

Act. This is called *buitenwerkingstelling* (rendering inapplicable). Like declaratory judgments and other decisions by the regular courts, this kind of injunction formally only binds the parties before the court.[120] However, it is possible for interest groups, for example, to claim that the government be ordered not to apply the statute in question in any case.[121] Third parties may therefore profit from such a judgment in the sense that applying the statutory provision in their cases would constitute another unlawful Act toward the original claimant.

However, there are also injunctions that the courts consider themselves prohibited from applying. The courts do not have the power to annul Acts of Parliament or indeed any other kind of legislation. An injunction formally compelling the State to withdraw a particular piece of legislation – no matter how unlawful it is – cannot be issued.[122] Such an order would be tantamount to quashing the provision, to which the courts have no constitutional power.

Another injunction the courts consider themselves not empowered to issue concerns the order to Parliament (or indeed any other legislator) to produce legislation where the inconsistency with higher law is a question of legislative omission rather than an express act.[123] In its landmark judgment on this matter, the Supreme Court explicitly ruled that it could not issue such an order, even though the omission rendered the legislation incompatible with EC law and therefore unlawful.[124] The Court ruled that the question of whether the State should meet its international obligations and, if so, in what manner – was a political decision for Parliament. Furthermore, the question whether there ought to be legislation and, if so, what should be its content equally was a political matter on which the courts should have nothing to say.[125] There is a curious paradox here, because the Supreme Court considers itself incompetent to order the legislature to enact or withdraw legislation because that would be a political matter, but it also considers itself, as a matter of last resort, empowered to carry out its lawmaking duty to the extent that it issues positive legislation.[126] Moreover, the Court has had no objection

[120] See Supreme Court judgment of 1 July 1983, *NJ* 1984/360 (*LSV*). Moreover, see Schutgens 2009, pp. 78 ff.

[121] *Ibid.*

[122] Supreme Court judgment of 1 October 2004, *NJ* 2004/679 (*Fauna-Protection v. Province of Friesland*).

[123] Supreme Court judgment of 21 March 2003, *NJ* 2003/691 (*State v. Waterpakt*).

[124] *Ibid.*

[125] *Ibid.*

[126] Cf. Boogaard 2008, pp. 478–483.

against warning the legislature that it might in the future carry out this duty if Parliament stayed inactive for too long a period. However, according to the Court, there is a clear difference between setting aside a statute (and extensively interpreting it) and an order to Parliament to the effect that it should produce legislation. The difference is that the latter has a generally binding effect because the future legislation will, of course, have such an effect, whereas the effects of both setting aside the statute and interpreting it are, at least on a formal basis, limited to the parties at hand.

4. *Effects of Judgments*

We now describe briefly the effects that court decisions regarding the interpretation of statutory law usually have. Such effects may have two dimensions. The first dimension concerns their binding nature. Do judgments of the courts, those of the Supreme Court in particular, bind the legislature, the government, and other courts? We deal here mainly with the distinction between effects *erga omnes* and *inter partes*, as well as the concept of *res judicata* in Dutch law. The second dimension relates to the temporal effects of courts' decisions. We outline those effects in the next section and try to give some impression of how the Supreme Court tries to mitigate the farther-reaching consequences of its judgments.

The first question is whether Supreme Court decisions concerning the lawfulness and the interpretation of statutory law in the light of fundamental rights have general (*erga omnes*) effects. The simple answer is that they do not. First of all, the judicial system contains several columns that are not necessarily hierarchically subordinate to each other. The lack of any constitutional court having ultimate authority in that respect is clearly felt here. Moreover, as we have already outlined, the Dutch court system does not include a rule of judicial precedent.[127] This means that the decisions of any court, including the Supreme Court, theoretically bind only the parties before it. Even within the ordinary judiciary, there is no formal obligation to follow Supreme Court precedents.[128] As we also remarked earlier, the practical effects of court decisions are not as meager as they look at first sight, but quite the contrary. In the interests of equality and legal certainty, the courts generally observe one another's decisions, particularly within the column of the ordinary courts, where the lower courts are bound by judgments of the Supreme Court. Even the administrative courts and the

[127] *Supra* note 51. Moreover, see (in Dutch) Bovend'Eert 2006, pp. 157–177.

[128] See Schutgens 2009, p. 221.

Supreme Court usually try to respect each other's judgments, be it on a voluntary basis. There is, then, a relatively strong general effect. It has recently been argued that the Supreme Court has established this substantive approach in a judge-made rule, partly by using its doctrine on *res judicata*.[129]

To start with, the Court may reverse the decisions of the lower courts in its own columns, namely the civil, criminal, and tax divisions. If those courts do not observe the judgments of the Supreme Court, the Supreme Court will regularly make use of its power to do so. Problems arise primarily with respect to administrative law. Neither the Supreme Court nor the highest administrative courts exercise any true jurisdiction over each other. Therefore, neither is forced to follow any case law of the other. In a series of judgments in 2004 and 2005, however, the Supreme Court considered itself bound by a ruling of the highest administrative courts to the extent that such a ruling determines the inapplicability of a legislative provision because of its inconsistency with higher law.[130] It did not matter whether the parties before the Supreme Court had been involved in the administrative procedure. Third parties were equally bound to this ruling of the administrative courts. Things may be different if the administrative court decides to declare the legislative provision consistent with higher law. In that case, third parties – which had not been litigating in the administrative procedure – would not be bound to that ruling in that they are allowed to bring an action in the civil court system.[131]

The question remains, of course, as to whether there is a similar rule compelling the administrative courts to give effect to the judgments of the Supreme Court. Although pleaded for by some scholars, there has not yet been any case law in that direction.[132] However, one might argue that Supreme Court judgments generally bind the organs of the legal entity that is party to the proceedings. If the complaint about the unlawfulness of a legislative Act is brought forward in a direct action against the State, any organ of the state – including the administrative courts – should consider itself bound by a ruling of the Court. This argument does not apply, however, to the many cases in which a complaint against a statutory provision occurs indirectly in the course of proceedings before the ordinary

[129] *Ibid.*, p. 222.

[130] Supreme Court judgments of 18 February 2005, *NJ* 2005/283 (*Aujeszky*), and 11 October 2005, *NJB* 2005, pp. 2106–2107 (*Territorial Order Nijmegen*). See also Schutgens 2009, pp. 222–235.

[131] Supreme Court judgment of 17 December 2004, *NJ* 2005/152 (*OZB v. State*).

[132] See, e.g., Schutgens 2009, p. 234.

courts. In contrast, as we have said before, the administrative courts usually try to observe the rulings of the Supreme Court, irrespective of whether they consider themselves bound to them. It is therefore to be expected that they will comply with a ruling concerning the unlawfulness of legislation.

5. *Mitigating the Temporal Effects of Judgments*

The other dimension concerns the temporal effects of Supreme Court judgments. Such judgments usually have retrospective effect in the sense that the courts have traditionally always assumed that any interpretation regarding the law they might arrive at is part of the law itself.[133] In this rather old-fashioned view, it is not the court shaping the law but rather finding the correct interpretation of the law as rightfully intended by the legislature.[134] The Supreme Court was never very clear, however, about the classic temporal effects of its judgments. In the older case law, it assumed that its new interpretation had retrospective effect.[135] As we have shown in the previous section, the Court's view of its own role as well as that of legal scholarship has changed over the years and from the 1970s onward, the Court has increasingly become more willing to mitigate the temporal effects of its judgments.[136] As the Court embraced a lawmaking duty, it became possible to openly discuss the consequences of judicial overruling. The last few decades have therefore provided some examples of judicial prospective overruling. Legal literature distinguishes true prospective overruling from qualified prospective overruling.[137] One may speak of the true variant if the Court does not apply its new interpretation in the case at hand but postpones it to some time in the future. One uses the term *qualified* prospective overruling when the Court immediately applies its new interpretation or rule but limits the possibilities for other parties than those in the case at hand, to appeal to the new rule. An example of the latter provides the 1981 *Boon v. Van Loon* judgment, where the Court changed its case law on the ownership of pensions in divorce law.[138] Here the Court explicitly limited the temporal effect of its new course to the case at hand and future cases. Where the

[133] See Supreme Court judgment of 22 June 1883, *W* 4924 (*Jansen v. Heiting*). See moreover Scholten 1974, p. 137.

[134] See Polak 1984, pp. 229–230. For criminal law, see Rozemond 1998, pp. 246–268.

[135] See the *Jansen v. Heiting* case, *supra* note 133.

[136] For a historical overview of the changing attitude of the Court, see Polak 1984, pp. 231–244.

[137] Polak 1984.

[138] Supreme Court judgment of 27 November 1981, *NJ* 1982/503 (*Boon v. Van Loon*).

divorce had already been pronounced, no appeal to the new rule would be possible.

As a clear example of the first option (true prospective overruling) might serve the classic case law concerning the *Labour Expenses Deduction*, we have elaborately discussed in the previous section.[139] Here, the Court ruled that it would not – for the time being – intervene because doing so would entail choosing from different policy options. But it made it clear that it might think otherwise if the legislature knowingly persisted in its unlawful course. It remained therefore open for the Court to overrule its 1999 judgment in the future on the basis that it had informed Parliament of the unlawful nature of the provision in question. In the follow-up of this case, it moreover explicitly ruled that Parliament was not obliged to add retroactive effect to its subsequent amendments of the impugned Income Tax Act.[140] This judgment also shows, however, that the Court is usually not prepared to fix a certain date before which the existing legislation should be amended. As far as we know, the Court has not yet done so anyway.[141]

A mixture of both options can be found in a similar decision of the Supreme Court in a case in which it ruled that the policy to exclude ministers' official cars from income tax violated the principle of equal treatment.[142] However, it temporarily limited the possibilities of third parties to invoke the case in their own dealings with the tax authorities. It ruled that, as long as the unequal treatment concerned a small privileged group and the government was unaware of the legal principle at stake, it would not allow complaints as long as it could be said that the tax inspector was unaware that he was treating taxpayers unequally. The Court effectively said that the government should immediately quit the impugned practice, but it refused to accept the argument for the sake of the claimants in the case at hand.

These examples show that the Court occasionally eases some of the pain of extensively interpreting or setting aside a statute by prospective overruling. It has even explicitly recognized so in a recommendation it made to the government in 1991 on questions about lifting the ban on judicial

139 *Supra* note 79.

140 Supreme Court judgment of 14 June 2002, *BNB* 2002/289 (*Labour Expenses Deduction II*).

141 None of the other courts has ever fixed a specific date, but one of the three highest administrative courts, the Central Court of Appeal in social security matters, did retrospectively consider once that time was up as it overruled an earlier judgment to effectively give the government some time. See, e.g., its judgment of 7 December 1988, *AB* 1989/10 (*General Widows and Orphans Act*).

142 Supreme Court judgment of 5 February 1997, *BNB* 1997/160 (*Ministers' Official Cars*).

constitutional review by amending Article 120 of the Constitution.[143] It effectively pleaded for such an amendment and argued that the fear for infringements on the principle of legal certainty might be dispelled by pointing at the possible ways of mitigating judgments that could pose a threat to legal certainty.

6. *Judicial Reforms*

In a recent report by members of the Supreme Court itself, concerns were expressed about the way in which the Court was forced to carry out its lawmaking duty.[144] First of all, the commission responsible for the report emphasized the crucial role the Supreme Court had to play in the administration of justice and the development and, consequently, the creation of the law. It argued that the Court is currently flooded with cases that, from the perspectives of either legal protection of citizens or the development of the law, were of little importance. More important, however, the commission also drew attention to the fact that the Court was partly unable to fulfill its lawmaking duties because important cases might not necessarily reach the court or, if they do, reach it only after a lengthy period of time. The commission suggested two remedies. First of all, it pointed to an already-existing instrument, which it thought would be worth using more extensively, which concerns cassation in the interest of the law *(cassatie in het belang der wet*). The Procurator General at the Supreme Court may, under Article 78(6) of the Judicial Organisation Act, appeal to the Supreme Court on behalf of the government where both parties in the case are unable to do so and he is of the opinion that there is a need for a clear judgment by the Court. The judgment of the Supreme Court in such a case cannot affect the legal position of both parties in the case at hand, but it can provide clarity. Second, the commission pleaded for experimenting with a limited preliminary question procedure. This would allow a relatively speedy clarification of legal issues where there is massive uncertainty among the courts and the legal profession. Meanwhile, the Minister for Justice has expressed his endorsement of the proposals and has announced plans to

143 The recommendation of 31 October 1991 was published in *NJCM Bulletin* 1992, pp. 243–259.

144 This is the Hammerstein report: *Versterking van de cassatierechtspraak* (Strengthening cassation), The Hague, 2008. See in http://www.rechtspraak.nl/Gerechten/HogeRaad/Over+de+Hoge+Raad/Publicaties/Summary+of+the+Report+of+the+Hammerstein+Committee+Improving+cassation+procedure.htm.

establish a limited preliminary procedure in cases of mass claims.[145] It remains to be seen how this development will affect the lawmaking role of the Supreme Court in due time. The reforms envisaged show, however, that both the Supreme Court itself and the responsible cabinet ministers openly acknowledge the positive lawmaking role of the Supreme Court.

SUMMARY

In the introduction to this contribution, we promised to briefly summarize our findings, thereby attending to the questions posed by the general reporter. In the course of our analyses, we touched on three main themes. As a preliminary point of order, we gave a brief account of how fundamental rights review takes place in the Dutch legal system. The Constitution contains a bill of rights but also bans the courts from reviewing parliamentary legislation on the basis of the Constitution. Fundamental rights review thus mainly takes place on the basis of international human rights law.

With regard to the *judicial means for judicial review*, it should be emphasized from the outset that the Netherlands does not have a specialized constitutional court. Fundamental rights review is both highly dispersed and general in the sense that any court is empowered to review Acts of Parliament for their consistency with self-executing provisions of treaty law in the course of general statutory interpretation. This means that there are no specific constitutional complaints available to victims of fundamental rights violations, such as the *recurso de amparo*. Constitutional issues may be raised in any kind of judicial procedure, but it should be noted that Article 120 of the Dutch Constitution prohibits the courts from reviewing the constitutionality of parliamentary legislation. With regard to violations of either the Constitution or any other provision containing fundamental rights, victims of violations may file a regular complaint in the civil courts on the basis of a general tort (Article 6:162 of the Civil Code). Consequently, no specific civil rights injunctions exist. Civil remedies typically include the award of damages and a formal declaration of the unlawful nature concerning the enactment or application of the statute in question. When courts consider a particular remedy outside the scope of their respective lawmaking duty, they may also issue a declaration to the extent that the statute in question is inconsistent with a fundamental right or liberty and leave it at that (besides awarding the victim the costs of the proceedings).

[145] *Parliamentary Reports of the Second Chamber* 2007/2008, 29, 279, nº 69.

Such declarations have no binding effect on the government, except when the State is party to the case at hand. However, the government generally recognizes the authority of the highest courts in legal matters and thus considers itself under a moral obligation to change the law. Although the courts may appeal to the legislature to enact legislation, they do not have any power to order either the government or the legislature to do so.

As a point of reference, we have chosen to offer an account of the role of the Supreme Court. The members of the Court do not have any *ex officio* powers, nor does the Court have an express power to remove and take over cases from lower courts or tribunals. As we have seen, however, the Procurator General at the Supreme Court does have the power to institute proceedings at the Supreme Court if a case is decided by lower courts and the parties are no longer in a position to appeal to the Supreme Court. Debates on the lawmaking duties and powers of the Court have resulted in proposals for a more ambitious use of this instrument. Such proposals have moreover resulted in an experiment to establish a preliminary question procedure in a limited number of cases to centralize and quicken the process of judicial lawmaking in the interest of uniformity and legal certainty.

We have furthermore elaborated on the Supreme Court's case law on judicial review and judicial lawmaking. As we have observed, the Court may, on the basis of Article 94 of the Constitution (or on the basis of EU law), set aside statutory provisions. Annulment is, at least theoretically, not possible, as the Court's decisions bind only the parties of the case. However, courts are allowed to declare the inconsistent nature of statutes, and such declarations issued by the Supreme Court come very close to an annulment in practice. Our account particularly showed that the Court is usually prepared to provide victims of human rights violations redress if such redress means setting aside the statute. Using its interpretative authority to alter and reform legislation is entirely another matter. Although the Court considers itself competent to play a modest lawmaking role, it is prepared to play that role only where it is not required to engage in political decision making. This means that it will fill a legal gap on the basis of international human rights law only if there is just one legitimate outcome of the case or if a specific outcome fits neatly in the existing statutory scheme. If these requirements are not met, the Court will abstain both from judicial lawmaking and from accepting the claim. However, it does consider itself competent to overrule such a demonstration of restraint if it believes the legislature to be negligent. It thus only abstains for the time being.

This connects closely with our last point, concerning the effects of judicial decisions of the Supreme Court. As we have observed, the Court's philosophy – from a purely theoretical standpoint – has always been that its case law is not a formal source of law. It binds only the parties before it. In practice, however, the judgments of the Court clearly have a binding nature, at the very least for the lower courts in its judicial columns (taxation, criminal, and civil law). Again, on a purely formal basis, the judgments of the Court have only *ex tunc* or retrospective effects. This follows from the Court's traditional approach that it finds, rather than creates, the law. However, in recent times, the Court has adopted a more flexible view by using its practice to abstain in certain cases to provide the legislature with a limited period of time to remedy a particular violation. Some authors have attached the label of "prospective overruling" to this approach. However, the Court's practice still shows that it is very reluctant to really enforce such a conditional overruling. Furthermore, the *Labour Expenses Deduction* case shows that the Court does not consider it necessary for the legislature to regulate the retroactive effects of a judicially declared violation.

The general impression the Dutch Supreme Court gives is that of a very prudent Court, exercising considerable restraint, at least when it comes to the question of remedies. It should be noted, however, that the Court does leave open the possibility of judicial lawmaking if it deems it necessary for an effective protection of fundamental rights. Moreover, the case law concerning fundamental rights and judicial lawmaking shows largely that the legislature usually pays a great deal of respect to fundamental rights. Most cases reaching the Court concern relatively minor breaches of fundamental rights provisions. The restraint the Court shows may therefore be considered somewhat justified. Apparently, the Dutch legislative process includes some mechanisms to ensure a reasonable degree of consistency, at least with internationally accepted human rights norms. Such mechanisms are certainly worth looking into. But that's another story.

BIBLIOGRAPHY

ADAMS, M., "Toekomstmuziek bij de Hoge Raad: waarom geen jaarverslagen à la Française?" [Future plans of the Supreme Court: Why not yearly reports *à la Française?*), *NJB,* 2009, p. 1098.

ALKEMA, E. A., "The Application of Internationally Guaranteed Human Rights in the Municipal Legal Order," in Kalshoven, F., et al. (eds.), *Essays on the Development of the International Legal Order*, Alphen a/d Rijn: Kluwer Academic, 1980, pp. 181–198.

ALKEMA, E. A., "Gedifferentieerde rechtsvinding door de rechter in veranderende staatkundige verhoudingen" (Distinctive judicial interpretation in a changing constitutional setup), *Nederlands Juristenblad*, 2000, pp. 1053–1058.

ARNULL, A., DASHWOOD, A., ROSS, M., and WYATT, D., *Wyatt & Dashwood's European Union Law,* London: Sweet & Maxwell, 2000.

BARKHUYSEN, T., and VAN EMMERIK, M. L., "Rechtsherstel bij schending van het EVRM in Nederland en Straatsburg," *NJCM Bulletin*, 2006, pp. 39–64.

BELL, J., *Policy Arguments in Judicial Judgments*, Oxford: Clarendon Press, 1985.

BOOGAARD, G., "Verhullend bevelen – Wetgevingsbevelen en de rol van de Nederlandse rechter" (Cloaked commands – Legislative orders and the role of the Dutch courts), *Tijdschrift voor Bestuurswetenschappen,* 2008, pp. 478–483.

BOVEND'EERT, P. P. T., "Rechterlijke (on)gehoorzaamheid ten opzichte van precedenten. *Stare decisis* in de jurisprudentie van de U.S. Supreme Court," in De Groot-Van Leeuwen, L. E., et al. (eds.), *De ongehoorzame rechter,* Deventer: Kluwer, 2006, pp. 157–177.

BOVEND'EERT, P. P. T., "Wetgever, rechter en rechtsvorming: 'Partners in the business of law?'" *Rechtsgeleerd Magazijn Themis*, 2009, pp. 145–153.

BRENNINKMEIJER, A. F. M., "De rechtgever" (The law giver), *Nederlands Juristenblad*, 2001, pp. 1191–1201.

BROUWER, J. G., *Verdragsrecht in Nederland* (Treaty Law in the Netherlands), Zwolle: W. E. J. Tjeenk Willink, 1992.

CLAES, M., *The National Courts Mandate in the European Constitution*, Oxford: Hart, 2006.

CRAIG, P., and de BÚRCA, G., *EU Law,* Oxford: Oxford University Press, 2008.

DE VET, M. P. J. M., "Gezagsvoorziening na (echt)scheiding in Europees perspectief," *Nederlands Juristenblad*, 1985, pp. 218–222.

DE LANGE, R., *Publiekrechtelijke rechtsvinding* ('Legal Interpretation in Public Law'), Zwolle: W.E.J. Tjeenk Willink, 1991.

DE POORTER, J., and VAN ROOSMALEN, M., "Motivering van rechtsvormende uitspraken door de Afdeling Bestuursrechtspraak" (Reasoning in lawmaking judgments of the Administrative Law Division of the Council of State), *Nederlands Tijdschrift Bestuursrecht*, 2009, pp. 219–227.

DE WERD, M., "De constitutionele taak van de rechter" (The constitutional duty of the courts), in Bovend'Eert, P. P. T., et al. (eds.), *Grenzen aan de rechtspraak?* (Limitations to justice?), Deventer: Kluwer, 2004, pp. 69–126.

DE WET, E., "The reception process in the Netherlands and Belgium," in Keller, H., and Stone Sweet, A. (eds.), *A Europe of Rights – The Impact of the ECHR on National Legal Systems*, Oxford: Oxford University Press, 2008, pp. 229–309.

DICEY, A. V., *Introduction to the Study of the Law of the Constitution*, 10th ed., London: MacMillan, 1885/1959.

FALLON, R. H., "Judicially manageable standards and constitutional meaning," *Harvard Law Review*, 2006, pp. 1274–1332.

FLEUREN, J. W. A., *Een ieder verbindende bepalingen van verdragen* (Self-executing provisions of treaties), The Hague: Boom Juridische Uitgevers, 2004.

HAPPÉ, R. H., *Schuivende Machten* (Shifting powers), Deventer: Kluwer, 1999.

HERINGA, A. W., and Kiiver, Ph., *Constitutions Compared*, Antwerp: Intersentia 2009.

KELSEN, H., *General Theory of Law and State*, Cambridge, MA: Harvard University Press, 1945.

KELSEN, H., *Introduction to the Problems of Legal Theory (Paulson ed., 1992),* Oxford: Clarendon Press, 1934/1992.

KOOPMANS, T., "Nabeschouwing," in Wiarda, G. J., *Drie typen van rechtsvinding* (Three types of finding the law), Deventer: W. E. J. Tjeenk Willink, 1999, pp. 117–150.

KORTMANN, C. A. J. M., "De rechtsvormende taak van de Hoge Raad" (The lawmaking duty of the Supreme Court), *Trema*, 2005, p. 250.

KORTMANN, C. A. J. M., and BOVEND'EERT, P.P.T., *Dutch Constitutional Law*, The Hague: Kluwer, 2000.

KRAAN, K., "The Kingdom of the Netherlands," in Prakke, L., & Kortmann, C., *Constitutional law of 15 EU member states*, Deventer: Kluwer, 2004, pp. 590–650.

LARENZ, K., *Methodenlehre der Rechtswissenschaft* (Principles of legal method), Berlin: Springer Verlag, 1991.

LOTH, M., "Courts in quest of legitimacy," in Huls, N., et al. (eds.), *The Legitimacy of Highest Courts Rulings*, The Hague: T. M. C. Asser Press, 2009, pp. 267–288.

MARTENS, S. K., "De grenzen van de rechtsvormende taak van de rechter" (The limitations of the lawmaking duty of the courts), *Nederlands Juristenblad*, 2000, p. 747.

MYJER, E., "Tekenen van een Hollandse Springe?" (Signs of a Dutch spring?), *NJCM Bulletin*, 1980, pp. 21–29.

POLAK, M. V., "Algemene beginselen van rechterlijk overgangsrecht" (General principles of judicial transitional law), *Rechtsgeleerd Magazijn Themis*, 1984, pp. 228–260.

ROZEMOND, K., *Strafvorderlijke rechtsvinding* (Law finding and criminal procedure), Deventer: Gouda Quint, 1998.

SCHOLTEN, P., *Asser-Scholten (Algemeen deel)*, Zwolle: W. E. J. Tjeenk Willink, 1974.

SCHOORDIJK, H. C. F., "Hoe vat(te) de Burgerlijke kamer van de Hoge Raad zijn rechtsvormende taak op?" (How does or did the Civil Chamber of the Supreme Court conceive its lawmaking duty?), in Baardman (ed.), *De plaats van de Hoge Raad in het staatsbestel* (The constitutional position of the Supreme Court), Zwolle: W. E. J. Tjeenk Willink, 1988, pp. 3–30.

SCHUTGENS, R. J. B., *Onrechtmatige wetgeving* (Unlawful legislation), Deventer: Kluwer, 2009.

SCHUTTE, C. B., "De 'rechtsvormende taak' van de rechter. Een kritische noot" (The "lawmaking duty" of the courts – A critical remark), *Ars Aequi*, 2009, pp. 676–680.

STOLKER, C. J. J. M., "De politieke rol van de burgerlijke rechter" (The political role of the civil courts), in Rood, M. (ed.), *Rechters en politiek* (Judges and politics), Zwolle: W. E. J. Tjeenk Willink, 1993, pp. 53–85.

TUSHNET, M., "Comparative constitutional law," in Reimann, M., and Zimmermann, R., *The Oxford Handbook of Comparative Law*, Oxford: Oxford University Press, 2006, pp. 1225–1257.

TUSHNET, M., *Weak Courts, Strong Rights – Judicial Review and Social Welfare Rights in Comparative Constitutional Law*, Princeton, NJ: Princeton University Press, 2008.

UZMAN, J., and STOLKER, C., "De politieke rol van de (burgerlijke) rechter *revisited*" (The political role of the (civil) courts revisited), in Barkhuysen, T., Van Emmerik, M. L., and Loof, J. P. (eds.), *Geschakeld recht*, Deventer: Kluwer, 2009, pp. 475–496.

VAN DIJK, P., "Domestic status of human rights treaties and the attitude of the judiciary: The Dutch case," in Nowak, M., Streurer, D., and Tretter, H., *Progress in the Spirit of Human Rights* (FS Felix Ermacora), Strasbourg: Engel Verlag, 1988a, pp. 631–650.

VAN DIJK, P., "De houding van de Hoge Raad jegens de verdragen inzake de rechten van de mens" (The attitude of the Supreme Court towards human tights treaties), in B. Baardman (ed.), *De plaats van de Hoge Raad in het staatsbestel* (The constitutional position of the Supreme Court), Zwolle: W. E. J. Tjeenk Willink, 1988, pp. 173–209.

VAN GERVEN, W., "Of rights, remedies and procedures," *Common Market Law Review*, 2000, pp. 501–536.

VAN HOOIJDONCK, M., and EIJSVOOGEL, P. V., *Litigation in the Netherlands – Civil Procedure, Arbitration and Administrative Litigation*, The Hague: Kluwer Law International, 2009.

VON BEYME, K., "The Genesis of Constitutional Review in Parliamentary Systems," in Landfried, C. (ed.), *Constitutional Review and Legislation – An International Comparison*, Baden-Baden: Nomos, 1988, pp. 21–38.

VRANKEN, J. B. M., *Exploring the Jurist's Frame of Mind: Constraints and Preconceptions in Civil Law Argumentation*, Deventer: Kluwer Law International, 2006.

ZWAAK, L., "The Netherlands," in Blackburn, R., and Polakiewicz, J. (eds.), *Fundamental Rights in Europe*, Oxford: Oxford University Press, 2001, pp. 595–624.

NORWAY

CONSTITUTIONAL COURTS AS POSITIVE LEGISLATORS

Eivind Smith
Professor, University of Oslo
eivind.smith@jus.uio.no

I. ON THE ORIGINS OF THE NORWEGIAN SYSTEM OF JUDICIAL REVIEW

The Norwegian system of judicial review of the constitutionality of legislative norms is the second oldest in the world. With no explicit basis in the Constitution of 1814, which is still in force and therefore the second oldest still in existence in the world as well,[1] it has emerged through court practice since around 1820. Furthermore, it should be noted that the final decisions (i.e., mainly those of the single Supreme Court) were systematically respected (if not always loved) by the other constituted powers.

After nearly two hundred years, it seems therefore safe to affirm that the power of judicial review of ordinary legislation does not have a firm basis in article 88 of the Constitution, read in conjunction with constant institutional practice: according to this provision, the Supreme Court "pronounces judgment in the final instance." This goes not only for "traditional" legal matters like penal and civil law. Even constitutional law falls within the scope of judicial review.

From 1814 onward, the opinions (reasoning) on point of facts and law on which the verdicts of the Supreme Court were based were kept secret. For a

1 A translation into English of the updated text is found at http://www.stortinget.no/en/In-English/About-the-Storting/The-Constitution/The-Constitution/ (consulted in the fall of 2010).

number of reasons, including political concern about controversial cases of judicial review, this situation caused rising unrest in Parliament, which – notwithstanding resistance from the executive – fought through legislation (adopted in 1863) forcing the Court judges to vote individually while stating their reasons in public.

Shortly afterward (1866), the first case came in which the opinion of then president of the Court (Peder Lasson, speaking for the majority) clearly exposed the doctrinal basis of judicial review on which this part of the activities of the judiciary (namely the Supreme Court itself) were based.[2] In this way, Lasson could be regarded as the Norwegian John Marshall, in the opinion of the U.S. Chief Justice in the famous 1803 case *Marbury v. Madison*.[3]

However, the verdict in the *Wedel Jarlsberg* case cannot properly be qualified as Norway's *Marbury v. Madison*: at that time (1866), judicial review had quite simply been exercised for some forty-five years. This qualification may be justified also by reference to the fact that sometimes vivid public debate over the institution of judicial review broke out (e.g., during the 1840s), well before the professional secrecy of the Court's opinions was abolished.

Why did the Norwegian judiciary (under the leadership of the new Supreme Court) start using the Constitution as positive law almost from the beginning of the constitutional epoch? No single explanation seems on offer. A combination of factual elements may help us further.

Such elements include the Constitution's character as the founding document of the modern State of Norway, in this way somewhat similar to the character of the constitution of the United States. Moreover, it contained in itself the declaration of independence of the new state (and still does; see article 1) and functioned for many years as a *prima* bulwark against tentative acts of the Kings of Sweden and Norway to change the constitutional system in a direction giving himself more power. In combination, such factors even contributed largely to establishing a highly symbolic status for the Constitution of 1814.

Even the fact that the title given to the Constitution (*Grunnlov*, or "Basic Law") invites to regarding it as a law (a statute, a *gesetz*) like others to be applied by the judiciary, albeit with a higher dignity than ordinary statutes, as with the existence of a clause (article 94) maintaining "the currently

2 Judgment of 1 November 1866, reported in UfL VI (1866) p. 165 (Wedel Jarlsberg).

3 5 U.S. (1 Cranch) 137 (1803).

applicable laws of the State" (from the times of the absolute monarchy) in force insofar as "they do not conflict with this Constitution," thus inviting the judiciary to exercise a kind of judicial review.

In quite another direction, there has never been a formal career system for judges in Norway, unlike in so many other European countries. As a matter of fact, most members of the Supreme Court throughout history have not previously performed a substantial career in lower instances. Instead, they have been appointed directly from other professions to sit on that Court. Notably, the presence of former (or sometimes even active) politicians was quite frequent until recently, thus ensuring the Supreme Court a less technical character than we so often find in systems with career judges (in the formal sense). It seems more than likely that this has helped pave the way toward developing an active jurisprudence in the field of constitutional law.[4]

II. ON THE CHARACTER OF THE NORWEGIAN SYSTEM OF JUDICIAL REVIEW

The Norway judiciary is headed by a single supreme court. However, this is not the outcome of a transplant from one-headed judicial systems like those found in countries of common law inspiration (like the United States). To the contrary, national history suffices for explaining this part of the Norwegian legal system. Quite simply, it is inherited from the system that developed under the (at least formally) absolute Danish-Norwegian monarchy that the Constitution of 1814 brought to an end.[5] Later on, no one has ever managed to get on the political agenda questions like whether to

4 On the On the history, character and practice of the Norwegian system of judicial review (in a comparative context) in English, see, for instance, my contributions in *Festskrift til Fredrik Sterzel* (Uppsala: Iustus Förlag, 1999) pp. 289–305 ("On the formation and development of constitutional jurisdiction in a democratic society") and in E. Smith (ed.), *The Constitution as an instrument of change* (Stockholm: SNS Förlag, 2003) pp. 11–18 ("The Constitution as an instrument of change: Introduction") and pp. 171–187 ("Courts and the Parliament: The Norwegian system of judicial review of legislation"). See also the Norwegian contributions in E. Smith (ed.), *Constitutional justice under old constitutions* (The Hague: Kluwer Law International, 1995). I have written more extensively on these issues in Norwegian; see, for example, my *Hoyesterett og folkestyret. Provingsretten overfor lover* [The Supreme Court and the democracy: Judicial review of legislation] (Oslo: Universitetsforlaget, 1993) and my general treatise on Norwegian constitutional law in a comparative perspective (*Konstitusjonelt demokrati* [Constitutional democracy], Bergen: Fagbokforlaget, 2009). In French, more information and food for thought may be found in, for example, a number of my contributions in *Annuaire International de Justice Constitutionnelle* (Paris: Economica) from the past twenty-five years.

5 As far as Norway is concerned – in Denmark, the absolute monarchy lasted until the Constitution of 1849.

add a system of administrative courts or even a specialized constitutional court.

The main characters of the review system may be summarized in the following way:

a) The Norwegian system of judicial review belongs to the family of American systems as opposed to the European model characterized by the existence of a specialized constitutional courts.

b) Review takes place in any case where constitutional norms intervene and must be addressed to determine the solution of the relevant case.

c) The review system is decentralized or diffuse in the sense that every court (and every judge) asked to decide on a case where constitutional issues are involved is empowered (and bound) to act as a constitutional judge.

d) Review may take place in cases of any field of law (civil, administrative, penal).

e) Review operates only in individual cases (*in concreto*).

f) Review takes places only *ex post*, that is, after the contested provision has been set in force and has given rise to problems of a constitutional kind.

g) Verdicts have formal effect only *inter partes*, entailing, for instance, the nonapplication of unconstitutional norms to the parties in the case.

h) In other words, the contested provision cannot be declared null and void with effect *erga omnes*.

To (some of) these elements (a–h), some modifications ought to be added:

a) Belonging to a family of legal institutions does not necessarily imply that the family members behave (functions) the same way.

b) This means that the courts have the power and the obligation to take even the Constitution into account as positive law.

c) In the last instance, constitutional questions of some importance or complexity will normally be brought up to the Supreme Court by way of appeal (see art. 88 of the Constitution).

d) No supplement needed.

e) It goes without saying that more than one party may act together in court.

f) Of course, *ex post* verdicts may functions as precedents, thus contributing to the determination of the outcome of future cases. More important in our context, however, the opinions of the court may give authoritative guidance regarding the appreciation of constitutional questions that it is still not necessary (or possible for procedural reasons) to decide on, in a way close to *ex ante* review.

g) Even if the formal effect is limited to the parties to the case, the effectiveness of declarations of unconstitutionality (or formal application of the subconstitutional norm as construed to not enter into conflict with the constitution) in the Norwegian system is likely to come close to that following decisions with formal effect *erga omnes*; as a matter of fact, Norwegian public authorities have always conformed to court verdicts (even) when based on constitutional norms.

h) No supplement to the remarks *ad* g). is needed.

Read together, the preceding remarks explain why the Norwegian system of judicial review emerged so early in our constitutional history and why it – by far – remains the most active and prominent one among those now operating (at least in principle) in the Scandinavian countries.

At the same time, however, the American character of the system of judicial review, in combination with the civil law character of the Norwegian legal system, tends to limit the possibilities for the judiciary, namely the Supreme Court, to act as a positive legislator. We now turn to this question.

III. THE SUPREME COURT OF NORWAY AS A POSITIVE LEGISLATOR?

As already pointed out, the Norwegian system of judicial review of the constitutionality of legislation has no explicit basis in the text of the Constitution. Nevertheless, its existence as part of the constitutional system is commonly accepted.[6] As a part of the constitutional setup, it may simply be explained as the outcome of a most reasonable interpretation of art. 88 of the Constitution read in the light of nearly two centuries of jurisprudence.[7]

From what has just been said, it follows that the Constitution contains no clauses on the specific powers of the judiciary in constitutional matters. As a matter of fact, the same goes for ordinary legislation.

Together, these two observations entail a third one. In Norway, the judiciary's role as a constitutional judge must be exercised according to the ordinary mechanism of procedural law. This includes penal procedure, but the norms regarding civil procedure would normally be of the greatest practical importance. By the same token, it becomes clear that the

6 It goes without saying that some do not like it, and that the way it is actually used sometimes opens up criticism on political and other grounds.

7 See further my *Konstitusjonelt demokrati* [Constitutional democracy] (Bergen, 2009: Fagbokforlaget) chapters III.6 and VII.6.

possibilities of the Supreme Court to act as positive legislator are most limited indeed.

As already pointed out, the basic structure of the system implies that the judiciary has to limit itself to reviewing the law applicable in individual cases. Under certain conditions, however, this cannot possibly be done without reviewing the relevant legal norm as such. That would be the situation when the party (or parties) to the case can claim to be in a legal or factual situation considerably different from the typical one for which the contested norm has been adopted. In this way, the conclusion would have some sort of *erga omnes* effect, not in theory but in practice, as it appears in the bisecular tradition of Norway.

A recent example may explain this observation. In the spring of 2010, the Supreme Court had to consider a case involving the nonretroactivity clause in article 97 of the Constitution.[8] Two cases raised by three shipowners were combined in the proceedings of the Supreme Court on a question regarding retroactivity on a fiscal reform and with huge effects for the state budget. The outcome (unconstitutionality) would have to be directly applied to all the other shipowners in a similar situation, even if they never had to go to court. In this way, it was the fate of the statutory norm rather that its application on individual parties (shipowners) that was at stake.

However, this does not really mean that the judiciary departs from its main role as negative legislator (in the sense of Kelsen). Having recourse to one or the other of the different techniques available under ordinary procedural law, it can hardly avoid stopping or redirecting the course of the contested legal norm due to unconstitutionality (or to avoid having to conclude in such a way). In this way, it could hardly avoid contributing to forming the future legal system by specifying certain limits that cannot be overcome without constitutional amendment (or – more practically – by choosing a different legislative road to a similar goal). But this is hardly different from any other function as a negative legislator.

In addition to the concrete character of judicial review in the Norwegian system within a civil law system, the tradition of relatively modest (or legal positivist or – in the positive sense – moderately activist) style of constitutional interpretation of the Supreme Court of Norway contributes in the same direction. In the next turn, the underlying pattern regarding the prevailing Scandinavian concept of democracy tends to induce a somewhat

[8] Rt. 2010 p. 143 (*rederiskatt*).

exaggerated respect not only for Parliament as an institution but even for individual pieces of legislation.

By the way, don't forget that Norway is a unitary state in a way that forces the Supreme Court to oppose not first and foremost the legislation of federated entities, as most often in the United States, for instance. Its foremost opposite entity really is the legislative branch of government at the national level itself.

In recent years only, this respect may appear as being challenged (even) from within the judiciary itself – probably not least under the influences of international human rights, as quite actively applied by the Norwegian Supreme Court. We may be heading up a phase where judicial review of the constitutionality of legislation regains a degree of self-confidence on behalf of the judiciary, a degree that seems already to have been achieved in the field of review against international treaty-based human rights standards.

But there is little that makes us believe that the basic character of the review as one of negative legislation will completely disappear. The main exception seems to be the presence, for a number of years already, of a number of cases where the opinions of (members of) the Supreme Court engage questions about the constitutionality of given legislative provisions that have not yet been raised in formal proceedings but may appear in later cases. Insofar as such statements are shared by the (majority of) the Court, we are faced with a kind of positive legislation – "if the law is framed like X, it might not pass the text of constitutionality."

By far the best-known instance in this category in the jurisprudence of the Supreme Court of Norway is the judgment reported in *Norsk Retstidende* (Rt.) 1980 p. 455 (Hoaas). In a case directly regarding other issues, the Court (in the words of the first voting judge, speaking for a unanimous Court) took the opportunity to state that, if a case regarding the constitutionality of a legislative provision making the specialized Labour Court the last instance in a broad category of labor law affairs should be brought to the cognizance of the Court, that provision "might contradict Article 88 of the Constitution" (my translation).

The Supreme Court never got an opportunity to decide on that issue. Quite simply, the signal was understood and the statute changed correspondingly.

More than an example of the Supreme Court acting as positive legislator, however, the 1980 Hoaas case represents a (rather tiny) category of cases where the Supreme Court has exercised a kind of *de facto* review *ex ante* within a system formally allowing review *ex post* only. Admittedly, thus, it is a modest example of positive legislation.

As an element of appreciation of the system of judicial review in existence in Norway, it may nevertheless be worthwhile mentioning that, even if boasting of being one of the world's two most ancient systems of judicial review, many relative newcomers (constitution systems and courts) have decidedly established themselves as wider reaching – and, in a certain sense, more daring – than the Norwegian system of judicial review as it appears close to two centuries later.

By the same token, we may easily leave aside some of the most acute elements of the likely follow-up discussions about the phenomena referred to, at least since Edouard Lambert's famous book of the 1920s, as a "gouvernement des juges.".

POLAND

THE CONSTITUTIONAL COURT AS A POSITIVE LEGISLATOR

Marek Safjan
Professor, University of Warsaw
Geraldine.Daviet@curia.europa.eu

I. PRELIMINARY REMARKS

It is more than evident that the constitutional court – in the European system – has a considerable impact on the legislative process. The classic separation of powers, based on Montesquieu's model, cannot be considered sufficient to describe the reality or – more accurately – the infrastructure of the modern state of law. Owing to the channeled system of constitutional review, the constitutional court cannot be directly classified as one of the legislative or judicial organs, however broadly understood. Nonetheless, the Kelsenian conception of constitutional justice involves a distinct division between the legislative power and prerogatives of the constitutional court:[1] in this perspective, the constitutional court does introduce some changes to the legislative system, but it acts only as a negative legislator. It is not the competence of the constitutional court to make laws or to bring into the legal

1 Cf. H. Kelsen, Istota i rozwój sądownictwa konstytucyjnego (Wesen und Entwicklung der Staatsgerichtsbarkeit; *The Essence and the Development of the Constitutional Justice*), Warsaw 2009, published by Biuro Trybunału Konstytucyjnego (translation by B. Banaszkiewicz). In Kelsen's opinion "The institution of constitutional jurisprudence not only does not contradict the principle of separation of powers, but – on the contrary – it confirms it" (p. 40) and further a negative legislator, i.e. the constitutional court, "is in its operation essentially determined by the constitution, and it is in this very moment that its function is the same as the function of the courts in general: it involves mostly application of law and – in this sense – effective exercise of the judicial power. . . . The structure of this organ is not determined by any other rules than those which apply to the organization of courts or, generally, to the organs exercising executive power."

order any normative elements, which have not been established before under an appropriate legislative procedure; therefore, the constitutional court may not replace the legislator in this process. Constitutional review is based on a coherent structure of a hierarchical legal system, and the constitutional court has to operate within that order, drawing its own competence from the constitutional legislator. Judgments passed by the constitutional court cannot contain anything that has not been already proclaimed by the supreme norm laid down in the Constitution, whereas the role of the constitutional review is always limited to the application of law – although placed at the highest level of the normative hierarchy – and cannot involve creation of norms.

This apparently clear and simple model of constitutional review, strictly determining the position of the constitutional court, seems difficult to defend, as proved by the long-established, nearly hundred-year tradition of constitutional justice in Europe. The model loses its coherence in two dimensions: first, in the area of the court's competence to create this normative sphere that, in turn, creates the model of constitutional review (i.e., the very constitutional norm). Second, the conception lacks coherence from the point of view of the constitutional court's prerogatives with regard to the norms that are subject to review (i.e., the statutes). In both dimensions, there are elements that require revision of our ideas concerning the position of the constitutional court, which is formally regarded – as postulated by the Kelsenian model – as an organ with a competence of a negative legislator only.[2]

My analysis attempts to identify which factors play a role in revising our idea of the constitutional justice. I also try to establish whether the modern tendencies are an involuntary and dangerous deformation of the function of constitutional justice or – the contrary – may be treated as an inevitable consequence of the adopted model of constitutionality of law and the stimulating mechanisms, as inscribed into the "nature" of this organ.[3]

2 Such an approach is still considered obligatory in all official documents of the Polish Constitutional Tribunal, cf. e.g. the position presented in "Informacja o istotnych problemach wynikających zdzialalności i orzecznictwa Trybunału Konstytucyjnego" (Information on important problems arising from the activity and jurisprudence of the Constitutional Tribunal) in 2008, Warszawa 2009, p. 15: "The constitutional principle of separation of powers excludes, in consequence, participation of the Constitutional Tribunal in the exercise of legislative power and imposes a self-restraining approach when evaluating petitions and complaints questioning the normative solutions adopted by the legislator." See also judgment of 19 July 2007, K11/ 06.

3 In the Polish literature this issue has been long discussed, cf., e.g., R.Hauser, J. Trzcinski, *Prawotwórcze znaczenie orzeczeń Trybunału Konstytucyjnego w orzecznictwie Naczelnego Sądu Administracyjnego* (Lawmaking judgments of the Constitutional Court in the jurisprudence of Supreme Administrative Court), LexisNexis 2008. K. Gonera, E. Łętowska,

II. WHAT IS THE FUNCTION OF THE COURT AS A POSITIVE LEGISLATOR?

The opinion that the modern constitutional court more and more often performs legislative functions, replacing the legislator in its role of the lawmaker, is quite frequent in the doctrine of constitutional justice. It also entails a more general conclusion: that of a gradual transformation of parliamentary democracy in the judicial democracy or – even – in the "judicial government."[4] Without going into detail, it is worth reflecting how – theoretically – the constitutional court takes over the prerogatives of a positive legislator. Most generally, we should assume that the role of a positive legislator implies the creation of new normative content in relation to the existing legal state: either with respect to the very model (i.e., the constitutional norm) or to the statutes (lower-rank legislation) that undergo constitutional review. Although the methods and mechanisms of positive impact may vary substantially, they usually remain somewhat concealed, never being openly proclaimed or clearly expressed in a legal solution, as doing so would transgress the boundaries of the ethos and ideology of constitutional justice.

The first section of this report presents the indirect, positive impact connected with the conception of the constitutional court as a negative legislator; the second section looks at the positive influence, having a different form, much more profound than just the positive reflex of a negative ruling. In the last section, I attempt to evaluate these tendencies.

III. INDIRECT POSITIVE IMPACT – EFFECTS OF NEGATIVE LEGISLATION

The opinion that the constitutional court – when declaring a normative act unconstitutional – exerts a direct impact on the existing legal order is certainly banal. *A posteriori* review may be exercised in many ways, and the procedures adopted in this respect in various systems differ substantially.

"Wieloaspektowość następstw stwierdzania niekonstytucyjności (Multiple aspects of effects of the judgment on unconstitutionality of legal provisions)" *Państwo i Prawo* 2008, nº 5, p. 20 ff. See also L. Garlicki, Ewolucja ustrojowej roli i kompetencji polskiego Trybunału Konstytucyjnego. ed. M. Zubik, Warszawa 2006, Konstytucyjnego; M. Safjan, "Skutki prawne orzeczeń Trybunału Konstytucyjnego," *Państwo i Prawo* 2003, nº 3.

4 See Alec Stone Sweet, *Governing with judges: Constitutional politics in Europe*, Oxford University Press 2000; M. Davies, "Government of Judges: An Historical Review," *American Journal of Comparative Law* 1987, nº 35, pp. 559 ff; O. Wiklund (ed.), *Judicial Discretion in European Perspective*, Kluwer Law International 2004.

The Polish model – like some others in Europe – envisages a procedure initiated both under the so-called abstract review (i.e., not connected with a concrete case) by a constitutionally defined group of legitimized bodies[5] and (as in the case of concrete review) a procedure initiated through an individual application to the Constitutional Tribunal[6] or through a question of law submitted by a court in a case pending.[7] In the last two cases, the question of unconstitutionality is connected with concrete court proceedings: either closed with a final judgment (individual petition) or still pending. The type of review procedure, however, is not important for the character of the judgment passed by the constitutional court. In both categories, the ruling is always abstract: it contains an *in abstracto* evaluation of constitutionality of a legal norm. In the Polish model, the judgments passed by the Constitutional Tribunal always refer to the law, not to the facts (the Tribunal's verdict expresses its evaluation of the law, not of a given court's decision).

If a normative act is declared unconstitutional, its provisions that were questioned by the Tribunal become void, and, consequently, eliminated from the legal system. However, the negative effects of such a decision cannot be reduced to this simple statement, because the impact exerted by a judgment declaring unconstitutionality of an act is far more complicated. A negative decision not only eliminates a legal norm from the system (negative effect) but also – and not infrequently – makes an impact on other provisions of law by modifying their present meaning (positive effect).

5 Art. 191.1. The following may make application to the Constitutional Tribunal regarding matters specified in Article 188: (1) the President of the Republic, the Marshal of the Sejm, the Marshal of the Senate, the Prime Minister, 50 Deputies, 30 Senators, the First President of the Supreme Court, the President of the Chief Administrative Court, the Public Prosecutor-General, the President of the Supreme Chamber of Control and the Commissioner for Citizens' Rights, (2) the National Council of the Judiciary, to the extent specified in Article 186, para. 2; (3) the constitutive organs of units of local self-government; (4) the national organs of trade unions as well as the national authorities of employers' organizations and occupational organizations; (5) churches and religious organizations; (6) the subjects referred to in Article 79 to the extent specified therein. 2. The subjects referred to in para. 1 subparas. 3–5 may make such application if the normative act relates to matters relevant to the scope of their activity.

6 Art. 79.1: In accordance with principles specified by statute, everyone whose constitutional freedoms or rights have been infringed shall have the right to appeal to the Constitutional Tribunal for its judgment on the conformity to the Constitution of a statute or another normative act upon which basis a court or organ of public administration has made a final decision on his freedoms or rights or on his obligations specified in the Constitution. 79.2: The provisions of para. 1 above shall not relate to the rights specified in Article 56.

7 Art. 193: Any court may refer a question of law to the Constitutional Tribunal as to the conformity of a normative act to the Constitution, ratified international agreements or statute, if the answer to such question of law will determine an issue currently before such court.

First, no provision acts in a legal vacuum. Therefore, elimination of a constitutional provision does not necessarily create a loophole in an area of law that was previously governed by the unconstitutional provision, but it fills this loophole by enlarging the scope of other provisions. It is, therefore, nothing else but a (positive) amendment to the content of a legal norm; what is more, the amendment affects a different norm than the one that was reviewed and eliminated. Thus, elimination of, for example, a special law (*lex specialis*) by its very nature increases (positive effect) the scope of application of a general law (*lex generalis*), which is expressed in the well-known formula *lex specialis derogat lege generali.*[8]

Second, to the extent in which there are retroactive consequences of a constitutional court judgment, the impact of the negative legislator will – by its nature – imply not only a simple elimination of a provision *pro futuro*, that is, a ban on application of the unconstitutional norm in the future, but also an opportunity to modify the legal status (legal relations), which is an essentially legislative function, in the past. In the Polish system, the scope of influence of retroactive effects is controversial. Likewise, Polish law does not differ between simple incompliance with the Constitution and invalidity of norms, as is the case especially in the German system. The express wording of the Constitution, however, states clearly that retroactive application of norms may undermine the decisions issued earlier (before the judgment was passed) by the public authority (i.e., courts and administrative organs) on the basis of the provisions found unconstitutional.[9] This creates a context of legal fiction, which assumes that when a given (court or administrative) decision was issued, the provision of law (which was only later declared unconstitutional) was not in force. As a result, a given legal situation can be evaluated according to different criteria (i.e., without taking

8 We can quote here numerous examples, for example, elimination of a provision regulating statutory limitation of claims for specific relationships, which may lead to an application of a general norm (in different wording) in the scope of statutory limitation (cf. judgment of 1st September 2006 related to art. 442 of the Civil Code SK 14/05, OTK ZU 2006/8 A/97); elimination of a provision reducing compensation may lead to an application of a general law concerning compensation (see judgment of 23 September 2003 related to art. 160 Code of Administrative Procedure K 20/02, OTK ZU 2003/7A/76).

9 Cf. art. 190, para. 4: A judgment of the Constitutional Tribunal on the nonconformity with the Constitution, an international agreement or statute, of a normative act on the basis of which a legally effective judgment of a court, a final administrative decision or settlement of other matters was issued, shall be a basis for reopening proceedings or for quashing the decision or other settlement in a manner and on principles specified in provisions applicable to the given proceedings.

into account the unconstitutional provision), and a new decision may be issued in the case in question (positive effect).[10]

Third, it is possible – at least theoretically – to consider effects of a negative decision by the constitutional court, whereby the former provisions, which were later replaced with new ones, come back into force and are then declared unconstitutional.[11] This would imply filling a loophole not with other currently binding provisions of law (e.g., general norms; see section 1), but with the norms earlier derogated by the same legislator. Assuming that such a hypothesis is correct would mean that the consequences of a constitutional judgment are par excellence positive, they enter the area of legislative prerogative because they bring back to life the norms that the positive legislator wished to eliminate from the system. Although this variant is rejected by most of the Polish doctrine, it cannot be totally abandoned because it was applied in at least one of the judgments of the Polish Constitutional Tribunal.[12]

Fourth, the Polish system has a specific legal mechanism connected with declaration of constitutional unconformity of a normative act; it essentially consists in the possibility of adjournment of the effective date of a judgment passed by the Constitutional Tribunal.[13] This means that an unconstitutional normative act is eliminated from the system only after the period specified in the judgment lapses (the period however may not exceed eighteen months), not – which is a rule – from the date of the judgment publication in the Official Gazette of the Republic of Poland.[14] This solution may be seen as a

[10] In the Polish system, the scope of application of art. 190, para. 4, is broad and concerns all judgments, not only convictions but also civil judgments and administrative decisions.

[11] Cf., *inter alia*, R. Hauser, J. Trzciński, *op. cit.*, p. 102, and following P. Radziewicz, "Restoration of a legal provision in result of a judgment passed by the Constitutional Tribunal," *Przegląd Sejmowy* 2005, nº 3, p. 121 ff.

[12] Cf. judgment of 20 December 1999, K 4/99 concerning pension regulations. In this judgment, the Constitutional Tribunal directly ordered restoration of the provision that had been in force and did not contain elements considered unconstitutional. In the opinion of the Constitutional Tribunal, declaration of material related to the content of the provision incompliance with the Constitution makes the provision void. In consequence, the amended provisions have to be quoted in the wording they had up to the date of promulgation of the amending provisions declared unconstitutional.

[13] Cf. art. 190 (3) of the Constitution. A judgment of the Constitutional Tribunal shall take effect from the day of its publication; however, the Constitutional Tribunal may specify another date for the end of the binding force of a normative act. Such time period may not exceed eighteen months in relation to a statute or twelve months in relation to any other normative act. Where a judgment has financial consequences not provided for in the Budget, the Constitutional Tribunal shall specify date for the end of the binding force of the normative act concerned, after seeking the opinion of the Council of Ministers.

[14] Cf. art. 190. (1) Judgments of the Constitutional Tribunal shall be of universally binding application and shall be final. (2) Judgments of the Constitutional Tribunal regarding matters

mechanism investing the Constitutional Tribunal with the function of positive legislator. Unlike in the case of a typical judgment, the constitutional court orders to apply certain provisions (positive effect), which were in this case declared unconstitutional, by setting a date until which the questioned normative act may temporarily remain in force. No other organ, except for the constitutional court, may order application of norms declared unconstitutional, which is paradoxical, considering that the fundamental role of any constitutional court is to eliminate unconstitutional statutes and not to let them remain in force. Such solution raises doubts when applied in practice and is considered controversial; however, it is also difficult to deny the grounds that justify its validity. The main argument is the prevention of negative consequences for the legal system, which might occur if the provisions declared unconstitutional immediately lost their binding force (e.g., if the loophole created after derogation of unconstitutional provisions was filled with other provisions), which would generate yet greater nonconformity with the Constitution than further (prolonged) application of the provisions of the questioned normative act.[15] Irrespective of the correctness of such a solution, the consequences caused by the postponement of a judgment undoubtedly resemble the function of a positive rather than a negative legislator.

To recapitulate the analysis of the possible consequences of the most typical judgments of constitutional courts, such as those declaring unconstitutionality of a normative act, we should note that it is not always easy to draw the boundaries between the functions of the constitutional court as a positive or negative legislator. This phenomenon is not at all new, and it essentially corresponds with the pure Kelsenian model, or, even, is quite a natural consequence of introduction of this model – provided we do not forget the banal truth that the laws do not operate in isolation; therefore, a legal norm decoded from the system is always an effect of application of inferential rules taking into account the relations between different provisions of law, often originating from different normative acts. It is therefore quite obvious that elimination of one element from a complex legal

specified in Article 188 shall be required to be immediately published in the official publication in which the original normative act was promulgated. If a normative act has not been promulgated, then the judgment shall be published in the Official Gazette of the Republic of Poland, *Monitor Polski*.

15 Cf., e.g., the judgment related to parking fees in cities, of 10 December 2002, P6/02, OTK ZU2002/7A/91. The provisions establishing parking fees were found unconstitutional, but their immediate expiration could have caused total chaos in the capital city because of drivers who would not have to pay any parking fees. The Constitutional Tribunal decided to defer the effective date of the judgment, giving the legislator a chance to pass new regulations.

structure changes this structure in its different segments and may influence the content of the legal norm, which is ultimately decoded from the system.

In the next section, I look at the mechanisms in constitutional jurisprudence that exert a much greater impact on legislation and, in some cases, make it even possible to change the content of normative acts.

IV. DIRECT FORMS OF IMPACT EXERTED BY THE CONSTITUTIONAL COURTS VERSUS NORMATIVE ACTS

1. *Interpretation of the Constitution*

As was mentioned earlier, in constitutional jurisprudence, we may observe the positive impact on the normative acts either in relation to the constitutional model (constitutional norm that is the basis of review) or in relation to a norm that is subject to constitutional review.

The first situation (impact on the content of the constitutional norm) is strongly associated with a phenomenon defined in the European literature as judicial activism. This mechanism consists of open and creative interpretation of constitutional norms, especially those that have the form of the so-called fundamental rules and general constitutional clauses. It is characteristic for each Constitution to employ a large number of open norms having undefined (fuzzy) normative scope, expressing fundamental legal values, and creating axiology of the Constitution. This search for a normative content hidden in the general, undefined constitutional expressions, as well as decoding other – more precise and concrete – norms out of them, setting limits to the application of rules and establishing a special hierarchy between the colliding rules and values – is inscribed into the nature of interpretation of the Constitution and is closely connected with the essence of the function of each constitutional court.[16] This process is widely described in the contemporary legal literature, and here readers can be referred to some well-known titles.[17] Against the phenomenon of judicial activism or creativism,

16 Cf. Christopher F. Zurn, *Deliberative Democracy and the Institutions of Judicial Review*, Cambridge University Press 2007, p. 264 ("If however, any organ with the power of constitutional review is introduced into the system and if the protection – elaboration dynamics is unavoidable, then the authorized constitutional review organ will be ineluctably involved with the generation of general and prospective constitutionals norms, and thereby undermine the classical conception of the separation of powers.")

17 See, foremost, R. Dworkin, Biorąc prawa poważnie (Taking the laws seriously), Warsaw 1998; R. Alexy, *The Argument for Injustice: A reply to legal positivism*, Oxford University Press 2004, J. Rawls, *Teoria sprawiedliwości*, Warsaw 1994.

there appears a thesis of a living constitution, which – being subject to the dynamic interpretation of the constitutional court – evolutionally changes its content, adapting its rules and values to the changing social context, in an attempt to meet the new challenges and expectations but also to face the threats posed to a man by the contemporary world and to absorb the new phenomena and needs generated by the development of mechanisms governing the society or by the constant development of science and technology. The constitution exists, therefore, through creative constitutional jurisprudence, which gradually and evolutionally shapes its content, ensuring stability of the rules expressed therein.[18] One of the important – though often neglected – arguments supporting judicial activism is the pursuit of what is sometimes called normativization of the constitution, and consists in drawing – from open, generally formulated rules – concrete normative content, without which the constitution would be merely an act of purely ideological proclamation, nontranslatable into concrete rights, freedoms but also duties (obligations). Radiating of the constitution and constitutionalization of the legal system by decoding concrete content from the axiology expressed by the rules and clauses, however, inevitably invests judges with prerogatives, which bring their activity closer to the creational functions of law.[19] This short study is not able to answer the question about the character and nature of the process of decoding the content from undefined constitutional norms. This answer could vary, considering the difference of the research perspective: in a purely formal analysis, we are always confined to mere explanation indicating the boundaries of judicial interpretation, which remain in this perspective only a process of application of norms, not their creation. In the theoretical, philosophical, and sociological analysis, the constitutional court lays down norms, which it decodes from the rules and

[18] It would be difficult to assume that this thesis is commonly accepted; cf., e.g., fundamental opposition against the interpretative assumption so formulated by the Judge Antonin Scalia: "A change occurred in the last half of the [twentieth] century, and I am sorry to say that my Court was responsible for it. It was my Court that invented the notion of a 'living Constitution.' Beginning with the Cruel and Unusual Punishment Clause of our Eighth Amendment, we developed the doctrine that the meaning of the Constitution could change over time, to comport with 'the evolving standards of decency that mark the progress of a maturing society'" (see *Mullahs of the West: Judges as moral arbiters*, Warsaw, August 24, 2009, lecture delivered by invitation of the Commissioner for Citizens' Rights.

[19] This is concisely described in an essay by Màuro Cappelletti: "And judges do not make those choices through any powers of mystical divination: the law is not revealed to them, but decided by them. If judges are the mouths of the law, they are also – to some inevitable extent – the writers of the script" (cf. "Some Thoughts on Judicial Law-Making," in Mélanges *en l'honneur d'Imre Zajtay, Mohr*, Tübingen 1982, p. 100. See also E. McWhinney, *Supreme Courts and Judicial Law-Making: Constitutional Tribunals and Constitutional Review*, Dordrecht 1986, pp. 89 ff.

values included in the undefined constitutional expressions. However, if we do not want to lose this process in the essay devoted to the function of the constitutional court as a positive legislator, it should be included in this analysis.

The Polish constitutional court is characterized by quite a large scope of judicial activism. In the first period of the Tribunal's activity, especially after 1989, the scope of activism was determined by a given historical context connected with the fall of a totalitarian system and a necessity to rebuild the structures of a democratic state of law.[20] The fundamental political transformation, in the period when adequate constitutional norms were still missing,[21] practically pushed the constitutional court toward substantial creativity, which consisted in decoding the standards of rights and freedoms – which were not directly expressed in the constitutional norms – from the axiology of a new democratic system. The judgments that laid down such standards in fact complemented the existing constitution, and the rules formulated in the judgments of the Constitutional Tribunal were later anchored in express provisions of the new Constitution. The key role was that of the rule of democratic state of law, introduced shortly after the fall of the communist system. From that rule, the justices derived, among other things, such fundamental rules as the right to the protection of human life before birth,[22] the right to trial,[23] the right to the protection of privacy,[24] the ban on retroaction,[25] the rule of protection of duly acquired rights,[26] rules of so-called decent legislation,[27] protection of business in course and legal

20 See especially W. Sadurski, *Rights before Courts: A Study of Constitutional Courts in Post-communist States of Central and Eastern Europe*, Springer 2005.

21 From 1989 to 1997 (when the new Constitution came into force), to a large extent the provisions of the old, communist Constitution were still binding, only partly amended by the new Constitution, which introduced, among other things, the democratic rule of law.

22 Cf. judgment of 28 May 1997, K 26/96,OTK ZU 1997/2/19.

23 Cf., e.g., judgment of 7 January 1992K8/91, OTK ZU 1992, part I, pp. 76–84; of 27 June 1995 K4/94, OTK 1993, part II, pp. 297–310

24 Cf. judgment of 24 June 1997, K21797,OTK ZU 1997/12/23.

25 Cf., e.g., judgment of 22 August 1990 K7/90, OTK 1990, pp. 42–58 (concerning pension benefits to employees).

26 Cf. judgment of 25 February 1992 K3/9, OTK 1992, part 1, item 1 (concerning acquisition of the property of the Communist Party)

27 This rule, also in the light of the present Constitution, is not expressed directly and is based solely on constitutional jurisprudence. The constitutional court has derived from this rule – among other things – an order for legal provisions to be clear and understandable; cf., e.g., judgment of 15 December 2008 P57/07, OTK ZU 2008/10A/178.

security,[28] and principle of proportionality.[29] Most of these rules belong to the canon of universal democratic values, adopted expressly in the constitutions of most democratic states. However, we are justified to pose a question as to whether the constitutional court was authorized to create these rules and to introduce them to the system on the basis of a general and templatelike constitutional norm, which expresses the principle of the democratic state of law. From the historical perspective, the process of system transformation, within which creativity of constitutional court and its pro-democratic determination was a factor that substantially determined the pace and direction of the changes, I have no doubt that the social and political revolution justified such an attitude of the constitutional court. Nonetheless, the answer to such a question may be different if we look at this phenomenon unemotionally and analyze acceptable limits of judicial interpretation, which clearly transforms into the creation of norms of constitutional importance. Can relativization of these limits be justified, taking into account the historical aspect, political context and aspirations of the society? At this moment, we may well put forward this question but have to leave it without a definite answer.

In the period that followed proclamation of the new Constitution, the significance of the rule of democratic state of law decreased. Many of the rules decoded by the judgments from the democratic state of law were directly included in the Constitution. Although the scale and direction of judicial activism changed, the nature of the phenomenon of creation of norms of constitutional significance did not. Under the binding constitution, the role of the key principle – which is the basis for creative pursuit of judicial perfection, like in the jurisprudence of other constitutional courts, especially the Federal Constitutional Court of Germany – is performed by the rule of the protection of inviolable human dignity.[30] This rule was recently applied in the judgment on unacceptable use of certain preventive

[28] Cf. judgment of 15 July 1996, K5/96, OTK ZU 1996, part II, pp. 16–28 (concerning customs duties). Jurisprudence based on this rule a precise order to pass new tax solutions no later than one month before the commencement of fiscal year, as citizens should not be surprised during the fiscal year with changes not envisaged earlier by the tax regulations.

[29] Cf., e.g., judgment of 26 April 1995 K11/94, OTK 1995, part I, item 12 (formula of proportionality adopted in the jurisprudence was *de facto* incorporated in the text of the Constitution of 1997).

[30] Cf., *inter alia*, F. Rymarz, *Zasada ochrony przyrodzonej i niezbywalnej godności człowieka w orzecznictwie Trybunału Konstytucyjnego* (The principle of the human dignity in the jurisprudence of the constitutional jurisprudence), Przegląd Sadowy 2003, n° 6, pp. 3–22; K. Complak (ed.), *Godność człowieka jako kategoria prawna* (The human dignity as the legal notion*)*, Warsaw 2001.

measures in the combat against terrorism,[31] and earlier it was the basis for eviction of an illegal tenant.[32] Another example is a judgment in which the constitutional court found significant normative content in the rule of protection of the common good. This principle was one of the grounds to declare unconstitutional the solutions adopted in the national health system, due to a lack of transparent rules of availability of medical services offered by the system of public health care.[33] In the process of decoding rules (and – *de facto* – their creation) and finding a new normative content, the quality of the argumentative process applied by the constitutional court becomes increasingly important. Growing expectations with respect to the quality of the arguments used by the court not only are a test for the correctness of the judgments but also pose real limits to judicial arbitrariness.

In the process of decoding the rules of the system, the constitutional court essentially avoids adopting a way of interpretation that would lead to imposing a certain vision in the sphere of social and economic policies, which in turn would direct the activities of Parliament and government toward some specific legal solutions. It is pretty evident, however, that a modern European state, member of the European Union, has strongly determined directions of social and economic solutions, in which the fundamental rules of the system and the protection of fundamental rights clearly overlap with specific solutions in the social, economic, or fiscal sphere.[34] In such a perspective, all solutions of social or economic nature adopted in the system may acquire a constitutional dimension and push the constitutional courts (like the European Court of Justice[35]) to look for

[31] Cf. judgment on prohibition of preventive shooting down a passenger aircraft with innocent passengers aboard dated 30 September 2008 K44/07, OTK ZU 2008/7A/126.

[32] Cf. judgment on eviction of 14 December 2007 K 26/05, OTK ZU2007/11A/153

[33] Cf. judgment of 7 January 2004 K14/03, OTK ZU 2004/1A/1.

[34] Cf. such provisions as art. 20 of the Constitution (a social market economy – based on freedom of economic activity; private ownership; and solidarity, dialogue, and cooperation between social partners – shall be the basis of the economic system of the Republic of Poland), concerning social security of a retired employee:

Art. 67: A citizen shall have the right to social security whenever incapacitated for work by reason of sickness or invalidism as well as having attained retirement age. The scope and forms of social security shall be specified by statute.

Art. 76: Public authorities shall protect consumers, customers, hirers, or lessees against activities threatening their health, privacy and safety, as well as against dishonest market practices. The scope of such protection shall be specified by statute.

[35] In jurisprudence of the European Court of Justice, this tendency is clear, especially with regard to a broadly understood rule prohibiting discrimination, whose application in judicial practice leads to considerable interference with the sphere of social solutions in Member States (e.g., with regard to employment contract); cf. application of nondiscrimination rule in the European law, e.g. C. McHugo, *Positive Action and Race Discrimination: Challenges for the European Court*

concrete, more detailed answers in the rules, such as prohibition of all discrimination, protection of social rights, or the rule of economic freedom.[36] These tendencies may be enhanced by the fact that a broad catalog of general rules related to social and economic rights and defining the economic system as a system realizing the rule of social market economy (art. 20 of the Constitution) are introduced to the constitution. Against the background of such constitutional constellation, it is difficult not to avoid confusion of the creative and interpretative function and inevitable tendency shown by the constitutional court to enter – creatively – the sphere of program conceptions that not so long ago were reserved to the prerogatives of the positive legislator. If these rules are not to remain a pure ideology and constitutional decorum, expressing the wishful thinking attitude of the authors of the Constitution, the constitutional court by turning rules into norms, and seeking at least a minimal normative content in the so-called program norms,[37] will at the same time exert an increasingly stronger influence on the directions of state policy in these dimensions.

To conclude, we can say that the modern constitutional court transforms into a positive legislator first and foremost in the process of interpreting general and undefined constitutional norms. However banal is the thesis that the interpretative attempts – always anticipating the application of law (not only *clara* but *omnia sunt interpretanda*) and seeking concrete normative content – are getting closer to the process of lawmaking, in the case of interpretation of constitutional norms, the area left to the discretion of the constitutional judge is far greater. This occurs especially when the process of interpretation of rules is inevitably connected with so-called moral choices, where certain values, which are not directly expressed in the system or moral preferences of the judges themselves, become reference points. In Poland, as

of Justice, Firenze 2005; D. Martin, *Egalité et non-discrimination dans la jurisprudence communautaire: Étude critique à la lumière d'une approche comparatiste*, Brussels 2006, pp. 588 ff.

[36] Application of these general rules in the European law is associated with a usually creative, lawmaking role of the European Court of Justice. See, e.g., J. P. Puissochet, "Des Traités et des Juges: La Fonction de la Jurisprudence dans l'élaboration du droit communautaire," in *Problèmes d'interprétation à la mémoire de Constaninos N. Kakouris*, Brussels, Bruylan 2003, pp. 303 ff. P. S. Weatherill, *The Constitutional Competence of the EU to Deliver Social Justice*, ERCE 2006, nº 2, p. 135.

[37] Such attempts to decode positive normative content from the so-called program norms are made by jurisprudence; cf., e.g., judgment concerning the law on National Health Fund of 7 January 2004, K14703, OTK ZU 2004/1A/1; protection of consumer (biofuels) of 21 April 2004 K33/03, OTK ZU 2004/4A/31; protection of tenants' judgments of 12 January 2001 P11/98, OTK ZU2000/1/3, and of 19 April 2005, K 4/05, OTK ZU 2005/4A/37; social market economy of 29 January 2007 P5/05, 2007/1A/1.

in many other countries, the most typical case is the judgment on admissibility of abortion on so-called social grounds,[38] where the field of choice was placed on the top of the system, touching the fundamental notions related to the definition of a person on the one hand and those of human autonomy and privacy on the other hand.

Now, we discuss another form of the impact exerted by the constitutional court on the content of law – the subject of constitutional review.

2. *Interpretation of laws: Interpretative rulings*

Many European constitutional courts apply in their practice not only the classical judgments declaring unconstitutionality of a normative act but also other forms of rulings, which are inconsistently defined as interpretative, conditional, or partial judgments (the latter review a norm only up to a certain extent).[39] It is quite difficult here to talk about precise classifications or definitions, as these terms have not been defined and, what is more, they are not envisaged by the constitutional norms, whereas different meanings are ascribed to them. Their common denominator is a situation in which the act under review remains in force but with a modified normative content. This way we can reach our goal, which is to restore the constitutional character of the norm under review, without strong interference with the legal order, which always and inevitably entails direct declaration of unconformity with an act placed on a higher hierarchical level.

The Polish constitutional practice has also developed another kind of judgment, which is not directly envisaged by the Constitution or by the Constitutional Tribunal Act. In its most typical form, the Tribunal adopts one of the following formulas: "provision X complies with the Constitution under the condition that it will be understood in the following way" or "provision X understood as follows . . . complies with the Constitution" or "provision X understood in the following way . . . does not comply with the Constitution." So-called partial judgments usually go further because they directly determine the normative elements included in the provision, which

[38] Cf. judgment on constitutionality of the law on abortion.

[39] Polish literature in this field is relatively broad; cf., e.g., A. Mączyński, *O tak zwanych wyrokach interpretacyjnych Trybunału Konstytucyjnego/Konstytucyjnego/Teoria i praktyka wykładni prawa* (So-called interpretative judgments of the constitutional court, in Theory and the practice of the law interpretation), ed. P. Winczorek, Warsaw 2006; J. Trzciński, "Orzeczenia interpretacyjne Trybunału Konstytucyjnego" (Interpretative judgments of the constitutional courts), *PiP* 2002, nº 1; A. Józefowicz, "Orzeczenia interpretacyjne Trybunału Konstytucyjnego" (Interpretative judgments of the constitutional courts), *PiP* 1999, nº 11.

do not comply with a hierarchically higher act (e.g., "provision X up to an extent in which it envisages that . . . does not comply with the Constitution").

In all the cases mentioned here, the review norm remains in the system, which means that the content of the provision is changed (positive effect) without the need for direct legislative interference. In this way, the constitutional court – metaphorically speaking – takes a shortcut, skipping the legislative stage, which typically involves replacement of the defective norm with a norm that is structured correctly by the legislator. There is no doubt that the constitutional court acts in this case as a positive legislator.

However, the problem is not free from fundamental controversies, which have been expressed in the literature and have even become a source of conflict between the Supreme Court and the Constitutional Tribunal.[40] The Supreme Court, opposing this practice of the Constitutional Tribunal, argues that the process of interpretation is strictly connected with the process of application of a given norm, and not with the procedure of its evaluation from the point of view of its conformity with a hierarchically higher act. Interpretation of law is the competence of universal courts. Therefore, the view according to which a binding norm cannot be interpreted in a given way breaks into the prerogatives of the courts and can even limit their independence, whereby the courts are subordinate only to the Constitution and to the statutes.[41] Counterarguments stress the essence of the prerogative of the Constitutional Court, which, when analyzing constitutionality of a norm, cannot be restrained in its right to interfere with the legal order in a narrower scope (interpretative judgment), if it can do so in a much broader scope (*argumentum a maiori ad minus*). Elimination of a concrete normative meaning of a norm (and consequently, elimination of one or more possible meanings of a given norm) may be compared to laparoscopic surgery versus an operation that always leaves a scar (i.e., an open wound). The wound is a loophole in the legal system and usually complicated consequences with regard to the retroactive effects of a norm definitely eliminated from the system, which could have been avoided by accepting an interpretative judgment.[42] This problem is clearly illustrated by the fundamental conflict

[40] Cf., e.g., the speech delivered by the President of the Constitutional Tribunal at the General Assembly of the Constitutional Tribunal in 2003.

[41] Cf. art. 178 of the Constitution: judges, within the exercise of their office, shall be independent and subject only to the Constitution and statutes.

[42] Generally, the effects of an interpretative judgment may be more complicated. It seems, for example, that in this case it is also possible to undermine judgments and decisions passed earlier on the basis of an erroneous, unconstitutional interpretation of a given provision (art. 190(4) quoted earlier applies). It is also different in the case of partial judgments, which eliminate a fragment of a reviewed normative act.

between the two court instances, which arose in connection with an interpretative judgment related to an important provision of the Civil Code regulating the liability of the State for the damage inflicted to an individual by public functionaries.[43] Issuing an interpretative judgment, and therefore avoiding derogation of a Civil Code provision, the Tribunal established a totally new regime of *ex delicto* liability for damages of the State, on the basis of an objective premise of illegality and eliminating the fault of the functionary as a premise of public authority liability. This interpretation, though in compliance with a norm of the new Constitution (art. 77(1)),[44] essentially opposed the interpretation adopted for nearly forty years in the court practice, especially in the practice of the Supreme Court. The latter interpretation was consistent about the fact that the fault of the direct culprit (functionary) is a necessary premise of the liability. This system did not allow for maintaining any longer the State liability based on the premise of fault, but this does not mean that the line adopted by the Constitutional Tribunal was right. Perhaps it would have been right to declare, instead of the interpretative judgment, full unconstitutionality of the provision of the Civil Code under review and to leave it to the legislator to write a positive new norm of great importance for the interest of an individual and for realization of the legal guarantees expressed in the Constitution. This issue is subject of polemics in the literature, whereby it seems that interpretative judgments should not be treated as a method of changing a well-established and stable line adopted in the judgments by universal courts. The subject of review and evaluation of constitutionality should be a norm understood in a way that results from the present court practice. The constitutional court would aspire to a role that never belonged to it if it was trying to reverse – by means of interpretative judgments – the established tendencies in the judicial practice, even if in effect we would obtain such an interpretation of a norm in the court practice that could not be made compliant with the Constitution. In such a situation, there is no other way out than to apply an instrument of review going further, that is, a judgment declaring a norm entirely unconstitutional (we have to accept that an unambiguous court interpretation excludes in consequence the search for other meanings of the norm). In the judgment of the Constitutional Tribunal discussed earlier, the atypical character of the situation consisted in the fact that the earlier, long-standing court interpretation lost its validity when the new Constitution entered into

[43] Cf. judgment of the Constitutional Tribunal of 4 December 2001 in the case SK18/00, OTK ZU 2001/8/256.

[44] Art. 77 of the Constitution: Everyone shall have the right to compensation for any harm done to him by any action of an organ of public authority contrary to law.

force. It is justified to propose the so-called secondary constitutionality of a norm, that is, a provision that originally conformed to the Constitution and became unconstitutional after the Constitution was changed. Such was the case of interpretation adopted in the judgments related to the necessity of the premise of fault for the liability for damages caused by the functionary in the light of the previous provisions of the Constitution. We can accept that, since 1997, the directive of interpretation of law in compliance with the Constitution led to a fundamental reform of this interpretation, which the Constitutional Tribunal has done in its judgment, creating a *de facto* new norm on the state's liability in the Civil Code.

3. *Signalization*

A specific form of the impact exerted by the constitutional court on the legislator is so-called signalization, which contains concrete proposals with regard to a domain, in which the practice clearly showed the need for urgent legislative intervention. Signalization is not a normative project, nor is it a binding opinion of the Constitutional Tribunal, and it is not directly connected with a given case that is subject of the proceedings. It directs the legislator's attention to the problems of general nature, which cannot be presented on the grounds of the constitutional court when deciding about a concrete case.[45] The opinions about the purpose and usefulness of signalization are not unanimous. Can the constitutional court express – by means of signalization – a wider content than the one presented so far? An answer to this question is not unambiguous. On the one hand, there is little point in claiming that it would repeat the content earlier expressed in the judgments; on the other hand, if we adopt a different opinion, it is easy to transgress a boundary, beyond which there are only automatic, positive proposals of legislative character, which may provoke accusations of political involvement of the court. Correctly structured signalization should always operate with unique certain parameters of future solutions resulting from constitutional regulations, and never ready-made normative solutions, if we want to respect the principle according to which the constitutional court must never replace the legislator in the choice of economic or social policies. As we mentioned earlier, it is difficult to apply this assumption in practice because certain constitutional criteria open up a broad area of freedom of

[45] Cf., e.g., signalization concerning protection of tenants of 29 June 2005, OTK ZU 2005/6A/77 and constitutional status of junior judges (court officers before formal appointment to the post of judge) of 30 October 2006 OTK ZU 2006/9A/146.

evaluation. In my opinion, signalization should be treated as an instrument of an extraordinary character. Although I am not entirely certain about its usefulness either, I would see it only with regard to such cases in which unconstitutionality of legal solutions in a certain domain results from legislative loopholes and therefore is a consequence of what is defined as legislative omission. The Constitutional Tribunal in Poland, like most constitutional courts, cannot declare a legislative omission in its judgment, and therefore it has no measures to force the legislator to fill the normative loophole.[46]

CONCLUSIONS

The modern constitutional court, with its complex legal instrumentarium of impact on the legal system, becomes an increasingly active actor in the field of legislative activity. Parallel to the process of constitutionalization of the legal system is a process of serious narrowing of the area of legislative freedom on the side of legislative bodies. The capacity of the Kelsenian *Grundnorm* being a point of reference for the hierarchic review of law is considerably enlarged, because the new constitutional norm has entered spheres that it has never entered before in the traditional constitutions of the nineteenth century and the beginning of the twentieth century. A special role in this respect is played by human rights, which are strongly supported not only in the system of constitutional norms but also on the level of international acts, which most often have direct application in the national legal order and are hierarchically placed above internal law. From this point of view, the principle of equal treatment has gained great popularity. Broadly understood, this principle may justify extensive interference of the constitutional court in the legal system and sometimes may have a form of express orders directed to the legislator to shape the legal relations in a

46 Only the Hungarian constitutional court has such a prerogative. The constitutional court may find unconstitutional a provision showing, for example, legislative omissions. Unconstitutionality results from a lack of some specific element, such as arbitrary omission by the legislator of a certain category of entities, which might benefit from given legislative preferences. See also, among others, judgment of 3 December 1996, K 25/95, of 9 October 2001 Sk8/00, of 16 November 2004, P 19/03. There exists, however, a specific solution in the Polish law that allows the universal court to treat legislative omission as a premise for universal liability for compensation by a public authority. Legislative omission may be treated as manifestation of so-called normative lawlessness, and thus constitute a premise for compensation liability of the State pursuant to an express provision of the Civil Code; cf. art. 417. See also L. Bosek, *Odpowiedzialność państwa za bezprawność legislacyjna* (State liability for illegal normative acts), Warszawa 2007.

concrete way.[47] In the contemporary, more integrated Europe, which is building a homogenous system of legal standards, in many domains, the role of the courts grows more and more strong, especially that of supranational courts (e.g., European Court of Human Rights, European Court of Justice), in positive definition of what is the necessary component of the binding law. Toward EU member states, the European Court of Justice plays a role of a specific constitutional court of the European Union, and its judgments adopted especially in the prejudicial proceedings and concerning interpretation of the European law become an automatic source of obligation for the national legislator to such an extent, in which they decode from the European norm the necessary elements, that they must be taken into account by the national legislator in the process of implementation of EU rules.[48] Naturally, this function of the ECJ may be effectively exercised only in cooperation with national court instances, especially those of higher level (i.e., with the supreme courts but also universal courts, which play a role of the European Community courts). Therefore, we must not neglect the fact that, in modern times, it is not only the process of constitutionalization but also that of Europeanization of law that defines the boundaries within which the positive legislator can move and determine the direction of adopted legal solutions. Apart from the interpretative directive ordering the interpretation of law in compliance with the constitutional norm, there is a directive on interpretation in accordance with the European law (an interpretation friendly to European law, a consequence of a widely adopted rule of community law being supreme to the national laws).[49] The consequences drawn here are sometimes quite far reaching. The national court, denying

[47] Cf. M. Safjan, "Efekt horyzontalny praw podstawowych w prawie prywatnym: autonomia woli a zasada równego traktowania" (Horizontal effects of the fundamental rights: the contractual freedom and the principle of the equal treatment), *Kwartalnik Prawa Prywatnego* 2009, n° 2, pp. 297 ff.

[48] Cf. broad literature on quasi-legislative activity of ECJ, among others, L. Burgorgue-Larsen, "Les juges face à la charte. De la prudence à l'audace," in *Face à la charte des droits fondamentaux de l'Union Européenne* (sous la direction L. Burgorgue-Larsen), Brussels Brylant, pp. 4 ff.; M. Vranken, "Role of the advocate general in the law-making process of the European Community," *Anglo-American Law Review* 1996, n° 1, pp. 39 ff.; M. Cappelletti, "Some Thoughts on Judicial Law-Making," in *Mélanges en l'honneur d'Imre Zajtay*, Tübingen 1982, p. 97; Ole Due, "The Law-making Role of the European Court of Justice Considered in Particular from the Perspective of Individual and Undertakings," *Nordic Journal of International Law* 1994, vol. 63, pp. 123 ff. Cf., e.g., characteristic text of Karen J. Alter and Laurence R. Helfer, "International Courts Have in Their DNA the Capacity to Be Expansionist Lawmakers (Nature or Nurture? Judicial Law Making in the European Court of Justice and the Andean Tribunal of Justice)," *Northwestern Law, Public Law and Legal Theory Series* n° 09-16, 2009, p. 24.

[49] Cf. especially judgment of 11 May 2005, K18/04, OTK ZU 2005, 4A/37; judgment of 17 July 2007 P16/06, OTK ZU 2007/7A/79.

application of a national norm that is contradictory to European law or interpreting creatively a national norm in the spirit of a European norm *de facto*, applies in the legal system a new, previously nonexistent norm, thus becoming in a way a positive legislator on the level of a specific case. The process of hierarchical review of law, together with all its consequences, is being systematically dispersed and decentralized in comparison to the Kelsenian model. In effect, we note that never before have the courts of continental Europe exerted such a strong impact on shaping the positive law as at the present level of European integration.

Returning to my original question of whether we face real judicial government, which, having abandoned the traditional function of the arbiter and administrator of justice, actually aspires to governing, we may give this question a partially positive answer unless we equal the exercise of power mostly with the legislative competences as it probably is in the structure of the state of law. However, we cannot, at the same time neglect, at least potential threats to the model of a democratic state in which the will of the representatives of the nation should have a decisive role. The judges invested with ever-greater power have to accept ensuing responsibility for the future of our democratic systems. It must be accompanied by the sense of self-restraint and humbleness toward the society that entrusts them with such a broad scope of power. This, however, is a topic for quite a different essay.

PORTUGAL

CONSTITUTIONAL COURTS AS POSITIVE LEGISLATORS

Joaquim de Sousa Ribero
Professor, University of Coimbra
ribeiro@fd.uc.pt

Esperança Mealha,
emealha@tribconstitucional.pt

I. BRIEF DESCRIPTION OF THE JUDICIAL REVIEW METHOD APPLIED IN PORTUGAL

The most important aspect of the Portuguese system of control of the constitutionality of legal norms is the fact that, according to Article 204 of Portuguese Constitution, "in matters brought before them for decision, the courts shall not apply any rules that contravene the provisions of this Constitution or the principles contained there."

Every court (judicial, administrative, and fiscal) is vested with jurisdiction to review complaints involving violation of the Constitution. Moreover, every single judge is, in itself, a sort of constitutional court, as he or she must control the constitutionality of the rules that are applicable to the matters that are brought before the judge. If the judge thinks that those rules contravene the provisions of the Constitution, then he or she must refuse to apply them. However, the decisions in constitutional issues of other courts are not definitive, as there is always the possibility to appeal to the Constitutional Court.

The Constitutional Court is the only authority vested with ultimate jurisdiction to review of constitutionality, so that Article 221 of the Portuguese Constitution states: "The Constitutional Court is the court that has the specific power to administer justice in matters involving questions of legal and constitutional nature."

It must be mentioned that Portugal does not have mechanisms like the German *Verfassunsgsbeschwerde* or the Spanish *recurso de amparo*. Thus, the Portuguese Constitutional Court – as well as all other Portuguese courts, which are vested with the power of judicial review of legislation, being their decisions subject to appeal to the Constitutional Court – controls only the constitutionality of legal norms, not the concrete decisions involving alleged violations of the Constitution. For instance, it does not control the constitutionality of decisions of other courts *qua tale*, but only the constitutionality of the legal norms (or one interpretation of them) applied, or in which the application is denied on the grounds of its unconstitutionality – in those decisions. The Portuguese system of judicial review is based on a pure control of legal norms, even if the Court has a broad concept of legal norm when it defines its own competence of control.

It must also be emphasized that there are two main mechanisms of control: concrete and abstract. The concrete control is based on two main types of appeals: those against decisions refusing to apply a legal rule on the ground of unconstitutionality and those against decisions applying a legal rule, the constitutionality of which was challenged during the proceedings. The abstract control, in contrast, includes the anticipatory review of constitutionality and the general (or *ex post*) review of constitutionality, in which the requests can be submitted to the Court by several entities, such as the President of the Republic, the President of the Assembly of the Republic, the Prime Minister, the Ombudsman, the Attorney-General, or one-tenth of the Deputies of the Assembly of the Republic.

1. *The Preemptive Control*

The Portuguese Constitution has, indeed, a special provision for preemptive control of any laws, with no exception. According to Article 278, paragraph 1, of the Constitution of Portuguese Republic, the President of the Republic may request the Constitutional Court to undertake an anticipatory review of the constitutionality of any provision of an international treaty that has been submitted to the President for ratification, or of an instrument sent to the President for promulgation as a law (from the Parliament) or a decree law (from the Government), or of an international agreement in which the decree-giving approval has been presented for the signature of the President. And, according to Article 279, paragraph 1, if the Constitutional Court rules that a provision of a decree or international agreement is unconstitutional, the instrument must be vetoed by the President of the Republic or the

Minister for the Republic, as the case may be, and shall be returned to the organ that approved it. The decree may not be signed or promulgated unless the organ that approved it deletes the provision ruled to be unconstitutional or, as appropriate, confirms it by a majority of two-thirds of the Deputies present, provided that the majority exceeds an absolute majority of the Deputies entitled to vote.

2. *The Abstract Review and the Concrete Review of Legislation*

The main instrument of control of constitutionality of laws is sequential or remedial, which covers either abstract review or concrete review of legislation. From a statistic point of view, concrete control is, largely, the main instrument of control of the constitutionality of legal limits to human rights. In this field, the Constitutional Court has jurisdiction to hear appeals against any of the following court decisions:

(a) Decisions refusing to apply a legal rule on the ground of unconstitutionality (on this case, the appeal is mandatory to the Attorney)

(b) Decisions applying a legal rule, the constitutionality of which was challenged during the proceedings.

3. *The Enforceability and Implementation of Decisions of the Constitutional Court*

The enforceability of the Constitutional Court's decisions must be considered differently than concrete and abstract control.

(a) As far as concrete control is concerned, the implementation of the decisions of the Court depends solely – totally – on the attitude adopted by the courts that have taken the decisions submitted to Constitutional Court. The Court does not have the power to ensure *ex officio* that its decisions are well applied by other courts. This includes all decisions of the Constitutional Court. And the citizens, it must be said again, do not have direct access to the Court to protect their own rights. A citizen must file a complaint in other courts and then, through the mechanism of the appeal, obtain access to the Constitutional Court.

It must be said that there is a high level of general compliance from other courts with the Constitutional Court decisions. It is difficult to measure this level of compliance, but some empirical studies have shown that it is high.

(b) Considering the abstract control, the effect of constitutional decisions is quite effective.

In prior review cases, when the Court pronounces a rule unconstitutional, the President of the Republic is obliged to veto the text in question and return it to the body that passed it, whereupon the latter must abide by the Court's decision.

If the text is altered by the body that passed it and the rule or rules that were deemed unconstitutional are removed, or, in the case of the Assembly of the Republic, despite the ruling that it is unconstitutional, the text is confirmed by a qualified two-thirds majority (Article 279 of the Constitution), the President of the Republic is then able to enact or sign it. This does not prevent the Constitutional Court from holding that such rules are unconstitutional later on, as part of other forms of reviewing constitutionality.

At the same time, if the text is reformulated and the alterations are not just limited to the removal of the rules that the Constitutional Court has judged unconstitutional, the President of the Republic, as appropriate, can request a new prior review of any of the rules it contains (Article 279(3) of the Constitution).

In successive abstract review cases, the Constitutional Court decides whether each rule that is submitted to it is (totally or partially) unconstitutional or is not unconstitutional.

In the event that the Constitutional Court concludes that one or more rules that it has been asked to review are unconstitutional, its decision possesses generally binding force. This means that the rule is eliminated from the legal system and can no longer be applied, be it by the courts, the public administration, or private individuals.

II. POWERS OF THE CONSTITUTIONAL COURT

1. *Portuguese Constitutional Court as a Negative Legislator*

The constitutionality review system established in the Portuguese Constitution is, as stated before, a mix of the concentrated method of judicial review (European model) and the decentralized or diffuse method of judicial review (American model).[1]

1 The Portuguese mixed system deviates significantly from the European model of concentrated judicial review – see André Alen/Michel Melchior, "The relations between the Constitutional Courts and the other national courts, including the interference in this area of the action of European courts, General Report," *Conference of European Constitutional Courts, XIIth*

The starting point in explaining the role of the Portuguese Constitutional Court is that it is entrusted with a control function with a negative nature, not participating in the active lawmaking decision or ordering another authority to act. The Court's power is to ascertain and declare whether the norm is in accordance with, or in contravention of, the provisions and principles of the Constitution. That means it possesses a cassation function and restricts itself to annul norms that do not comply with the Constitution.

But ahead of such premise, the Constitutional Court plays a role not entirely defensive but also a role in the creation of the legal order, even if we cannot regard its decisions as constituting a genuine source of law. In its position of supreme interpreter of the Constitution, the Court makes explicit the principles and mandates implicit in the Constitution and specifies the meaning of broad constitutional principles, such as equality, proportionality, and due process of law; it also establishes a way to interpret and harmonize precepts in the Constitution that may appear to be in conflict with or even unrelated to each other.

Although the Court cannot act as substitute for the legislator or for the government in policy making, the constitutional case law has a positive impact in providing general criteria and guidance for the acts of public powers and lower courts, namely an effective influence in the lawmaking process.

In conclusion, the Portuguese constitutional system cannot be fully understood if it does not include the *acquis* formed by the constitutional case law[2]

2. *Powers of the Court and Effects of Constitutional Review Decisions*

As a court, the Constitutional Court shares characteristics common to all courts, namely its decisions are binding on every other authority. But unlike other courts, the Constitutional Court plays a specific role in the constitutional system, and its composition and responsibilities are laid down directly by the Constitution itself (article 223). Besides its leading role as guardian or ultimate guarantor of the Constitution, it has unique powers in

Congress, Brussels, May 2002; María Lúcia Amaral, "Problemas da *Judicial Review* em Portugal," *Themis*, *Revista da Faculdade de Direito da UNL*, Year VI, 10, 2005, 67–90, 70.

2 Wording from Maria Lúcia Amaral, "Problemas da *Judicial Review* em Portugal," *op. cit.*, 88.

relation to the President of the Republic,[3] national and local referenda,[4] political parties,[5] political officeholders, and elections.

All procedures concerning the constitutionality review begin with the submission of a request addressed to the Constitutional Court. Abstract control procedures must be laid down by a selected list of officials and entities mentioned previously. Concrete control procedures have to be brought by litigants in a pending judicial proceeding in which such a norm was applied or refused to be applied on grounds of unconstitutionality (it should be noted that the procedure followed in the concrete control is different in most European countries, where the judge halts the judicial proceedings *a quo* and raises the question of the law's possible unconstitutionality before the constitutional court).

The Court can declare the unconstitutionality of rules only in relation to which a review has been requested, but it can do so on the grounds of constitutional rules or principles other than those whose breach was alleged (articles 51(5) and 79-C of the Law Governing the Constitutional Court).

Besides decisions of a procedural nature (chiefly as to whether to admit a request), the Constitutional Court issues two types of ruling: it either pronounces the (total or partial) unconstitutionality of the rules submitted to it or does not pronounce such unconstitutionality. There are, however, some (infrequent) decisions that do not fit in with this dualism, namely, when the concrete norm under review is upheld by the Constitutional Court as compatible with the Constitution but only on the basis of a certain interpretation, excluding other variants interpreting the norm as unconstitutional, as explained hereafter.

The effects of a decision pronouncing the unconstitutionality of a rule vary depending on the type of procedure.[6]

In prior control of legislative drafts, the Court's decision declaring the unconstitutionality of a rule can be overcome by a special vote of the competent legislative organ, as pointed out earlier. However, until now, there has been but one case in which the Court's decision was prevailed over.[7]

3 In proceedings involving the death, permanent physical incapacity, temporary impediment, removal from office, or dismissal of the President of the Republic.

4 The Court verifies the constitutionality and legality of draft referenda and hears appeals concerning alleged irregularities during the voting.

5 Such as registration of new parties or coalitions and application of fines to political parties.

6 On this subject, see *Replies to the questionnaire on the execution of constitutional review decisions (Portugal)*, at http://www.venice.coe.int.

7 In Ruling nº 190/1987, the Court upheld the unconstitutionality of all norms of a draft regional legislative decree, which was subsequently vetoed by the Representative of the Republic.

And as far as the Assembly of the Republic is concerned, it has always deleted or changed the wording of those draft norms declared unconstitutional to meet the terms of the Court's decision. Still, this is law in action not imposed by written law.

In successive abstract review of legislation, if the norm is declared contrary to the Constitution, it is considered null and void and ceases automatically to produce any effect, and the other courts and public or private entities should act in conformity, meaning that such norm is no longer applicable. In this regard, the Court's decisions are self-executing.

Such declaration of unconstitutionality with generally binding force shall take effects as of the moment at which the rule declared unconstitutional came into force (*ex tunc* effects), with the exception of the cases protected by the *res judicata* principle (article 282 of the Constitution).

When required for the purposes of legal certainty, reasons of fairness, or an exceptionally important public interest, the grounds for which shall be given, the Constitutional Court may rule safeguarding the effects that were produced by the norm until the decision of the Court (*ex nunc* effects) (article 282(4) of the Constitution). The Constitutional Court often limits the temporal effects of the declaration of unconstitutionality with general binding force, namely establishing that it will produce effects only from that date on, that is, from the date of the publishing of its decision in the official journal (*Diário da República*). The Court has never postponed the effects of its ruling by safeguarding effects produced after the declaration of unconstitutionality (and according to the prevailing opinion on this subject the effects of annulment could not be postponed).

The declaration of unconstitutionality with general binding force has negative force of law, because it annuls directly the unconstitutional rule. Furthermore, the legal provisions that had been amended or repealed by the norm declared unconstitutional are revived from the date on which the decision of the Constitutional Court becomes effective, unless the Constitutional Court determines otherwise (article 282 (1 and 4) of the Constitution).

The Portuguese review of constitutionality can be said to be one step ahead of the negative legislator model, as it grants the Constitutional Court

However, the Legislative Assembly of the Azores confirmed it and maintained the exact same norms, voted by the majority, as established in article 279(2) of the Constitution. After its entering in force, at the request of the Attorney-General, the Court held unconstitutional such regional legislative decree with general binding force (Ruling nº 151/1993).

the power to limit *ex tunc* effects of unconstitutionality decisions and consequently to bound the revalidation of prior legal provisions.

Decisions taken in the concrete review of constitutionality have effects only on the case for which the constitutionality issue was raised (*inter partes* effects). The decision on the appeal determines *res judicata* regarding the question of unconstitutionality. As a result, the court whose decision was submitted to Constitutional Court must comply with the latest ruling (it must review the case taken in consideration the decision on the constitutional issue) but only in that specific case. In other similar cases, no court is submitted to such ruling. The Constitutional Court itself may decide differently when reviewing the same norm in a different procedure of concrete review of constitutionality (this type of appeal is heard in sections of five Justices, except when the President decides that the case should be heard in plenary session because this is necessary to avoid conflicting jurisprudence, or when the nature of the issue at stake justifies it – Article 79-A of the Law Governing the Constitutional Court).

Still, when the same norm has been deemed unconstitutional in three different concrete cases, the Public Prosecutor's Office may initiate an abstract review procedure that allows the Constitutional Court to declare the unconstitutionality of such norm with *erga omnes* effects.

3. *Interpretation of Statute in Harmony with the Constitution*

Article 80(3) of the Law Governing the Constitutional Court provides that the judgment of unconstitutionality in concrete review procedures can be founded on a particular interpretation of the rule alleged to be unconstitutional. In other words, the Constitutional Court can determine a conform-interpretation of the rule to avoid any unconstitutionality, and the court *a quo* will be bound by it, having to apply such interpretation of the norm in the case in question.

The Constitutional Court has set conform-interpretation in rare cases. For instance, in Ruling No. 35/2008, the Court put together a unique interpretation of several norms concerning the expenses of judicial proceedings and declares it to be the only one to comply with the Constitution. Also in Ruling No. 651/2005, the Court avoided a judgment of unconstitutionality by determining a certain interpretation of a rule concerning secondary liability for payment of administrative penalties prescribed in the Highway Code (*Código da Estrada*).

In both those cases, the conform-interpretation set in the Court's decision would be the only one applicable by the court *a quo*. However, the courts may be inclined to voluntarily carry out such conform-interpretation in similar cases.

Some legal doctrine argues that the Constitutional Court should not have the supremacy to issue interpretations that are binding to other courts and that the latter should maintain the power to interpret ordinary law by themselves.[8]

4. *Manipulative and Additive Decisions*

As mentioned before, the Court has important powers in what concerns the temporal effects of the declaration of the unconstitutional character of norms and the revalidation of prior legal provisions. It is in the Court's power to modified the effects of such declarations by establishing *ex nunc* effects instead of *ex tunc* effects.

Furthermore, in some exceptional cases, the Court's decisions are thought to have normative effects.

A special situation may arise under the Constitution's equal protection clause (principle of equality). If a norm granting favors to certain groups of persons while excluding (or omitting) others in violation of an equal protection clause, this exclusion (omission) is unconstitutional. The Court may then, as the case may be, declare the norm unconstitutional and declare that noninclusion of the relevant group is unconstitutional.

The Court does not have the power to admonish the legislator to bring about an equal solution for the excluded group. However, in some rare cases, the Court's ruling by itself made possible the inclusion of certain groups under the scope of rules that omitted or excluded them. For instance, in Ruling No. 449/87, the Court held unconstitutional a norm that established different allowances for the widower and widow in case of death caused by work accident. Furthermore, it stated that the only solution that would comply with the Constitution would be one that granted equal treatment to both, meaning that the favor granted to the widow should be extended to the widower.

In Ruling No. 359/91, the Court considered and ruled on a request from the Ombudsman for not only a successive abstract review of the rules laid down by the Civil Code concerning the transmission of the position of the tenant in the event of divorce when interpreted as not applicable to *de facto*

[8] Gomes Canotilho, *Direito Constitucional e Teoria da Constituição*, 7th ed., Coimbra, 2003, 1313; Rui Medeiros, *A decisão de inconstitucionalidade*, Lisbon, 1999, 381.

unions, even if the couple in question has underage children, but also a review of the "unconstitutionality by omission of a legislative measure which expressly states that those rules are applicable, with the necessary adaptations, to *de facto* unions of couples with underage children." In this decision, the Court issued a declaration with generally binding force of the unconstitutionality of that interpretation for breaching the principle of nondiscrimination against children born outside wedlock, but it decided against the existence of unconstitutionality by omission. As a result of the Court's decision, the said rules of the Civil Code were thereafter understood as including such *de facto* unions.

The related decisions can be considered additive decisions[9] as their implementation changes the scope of legislative rules regardless of any amendment to the wording of such rules. It should be underlined, though, that the Court's ruling does not put up a norm *ex nihilo*. Those decisions only put forward a solution imposed by the Constitution provisions and principles by extending a rule already chosen by the legislator.[10]

5. *The Impact of Constitutional Case Law*

In its twenty-five years of existence, the Court's ruling has proved to have consequences other than those standard effects pointed out.

Even though the Constitutional Court does not play a part in the lawmaking process, many amendments made to existing legislation are the result of its ruling, either to incorporate or to set aside the Court's ruling on the subject.

An example of the former, among many others, is Ruling No. 23/2006,[11] which held unconstitutional, with general binding force, a norm of the Portuguese Civil Code concerning the deadline for filing court cases on the investigation or paternity and maternity. Later, the norm was modified to provide an extended time limit (Law 14/2009).

Sometimes the legislator acknowledges this influence by alluding to Constitutional Court's ruling while summarizing the intention of the legislature in passing the measure. An illustration is the preamble to Decree Law 64-A/89 (regarding termination of labor contract) in which Ruling No.

9 On the possibility of additive decisions under certain circumstances, see Carlos Blanco De Morais, "Sobre o conteúdo possível das sentenças aditivas constitucionalmente obrigatórias," at http://www.icjp.pt/estudos.

10 See Rui Medeiros, *A decisão*, *op. cit.*, 504.

11 All Court decisions can be found at its Web site (http://www.tribunalconstitutional.pt).

107/88 (taken in a prior review case) is referred to as giving bounding guidelines.

And even some amendments to the Constitution were a result of constitutional case law. That is the case of the wording of article 33(4) of the Constitution, concerning the extradition for crimes that are punishable under the applicant state's law by a sentence or security measure that deprives or restricts freedom in perpetuity or for an undefined duration. The introduction of this provision (in the constitutional revision of 1997) reflects the ruling of the Constitutional Court on this subject. In Ruling No. 474/95, the Court upheld that, although the wording of article 33 of the Constitution only prohibited, at that time, extradition for crimes for which the death penalty is legally possible, the Constitution principles also prohibited the extradition for a crime publishable by life imprisonment. Furthermore, the Court's ruling provides the keystone for the interpretation of the conditions that must be fulfilled to allow the extradition of persons charged with crimes for which a sentence of death sentence or life imprisonment is nominally prescribed.[12]

Also the wording of constitutional provisions concerning the autonomous regions' legislative autonomy was changed in part because of the Constitutional Court's ruling on the subject, but this turn the changes intended to reverse such ruling, which was supposed to be a limiting view of the regional autonomies.

Some of the most impressive examples of a silent dialogue between Constitutional Court and legislator regard the control of breaches of the Constitution by means of omission of legislative measures.

The Court's decision in such procedure is known to have merely declarative effects, as it only verifies or recognizes the situation of lack of provision needed to make constitutional rules executable (article 283 of the Constitution). In this case, the legislative authorities are bound to legislate, but the Court cannot substitute itself for those authorities by creating the missing rules, nor can it urge them to act by indicating the timing or content of such action.

As underlined by Portuguese legal doctrine, the decisions regarding unconstitutionality by omission have no biding effect, purely providing a sort of formalized critical publicity on breaches of the Constitution.

[12] See Ruling nº 384/05, summary of which can be found in *Bulletin on Constitutional Case-Law*, Venice Commission, Edition 2005, Volume 2, 269-271

Despite all that, the pending of such a procedure in the Constitutional Court has been encouragement enough for legislative authorities to overcome the omission of legislative measures in question.

So far, the Constitutional Court has handed down only seven decisions involving a review of unconstitutionality by omission, all of them at the request of the Ombudsman.[13]

In the only two situations in which the Constitutional Court determined that unconstitutionality by omission existed, the legislative authorities comply with its judgment. In Ruling No. 182/89, the Court held that article 35(4) of the Constitution (concerning the use of computers and prohibition of third-party access to files containing personal data) was not being complied with because of a lack of legislative measure defining the concept of personal data. This ruling was followed by immediate parliamentary initiatives, and a law on the subject was passed (Law 10/91). In Ruling No. 474/2002, the Court held that article 59(1-e) of the Constitution was not being complied with because of omission of legislative measures needed to provide for a social benefit for Public Administration workers who involuntarily found themselves unemployed. This ruling was published in December 2002, and some years later, after several unsuccessful initiatives to overcome the legislative gap and public justification for the delay, the Assembly of the Republic passed a law on the subject (Law 11/2008).

In another four cases presented to the Constitutional Court, the expectation of the Court's decision was effective by itself, given that the needed legislative measures were approved while the procedure was pending and before the Court's decision. The Court decided to hear the requests and ruled that no unconstitutionality by omission existed because, at that time, a legislative act had already overcome the omission in question – Ruling Nos. 276/89 (omission of legislative act specifying the special crimes for which political officeholders may be held liable), 36/90 (local referenda), 638/95 (constitutional right of *actio popularis*), and 424/01 (nominations for election to local authority bodies submitted by groups of registered electors).

Regarding the relations between the Constitutional Court and other courts, it should be emphasized once more that in Portugal (unlike many European countries), the courts cannot refer a preliminary question to the Constitutional Court, given that all Portuguese courts are empowered to decide whether the rules they have to apply comply with the Constitution. It

13 For further development of this subject, see "Problems of Legislative Omission in Constitutional Jurisprudence," Portuguese Report, *XIVth Congress of the Conference of European Constitutional Court*, Reports II, 704–743.

is up to the concerned parties to file an appeal in the Constitutional Court challenging the other court's decision on the constitutionality issue. In such a concrete review procedure, the Constitutional Court's ruling applies only in that specific case in which it is handed down.

However, the impact of the Constitutional Court's decisions is not confined to its legal force (*inter partes* effect), namely because all other courts tend to follow closely the constitutional case law in concrete review (which represents about 90 percent of the Court's decisions) and frequently carry on its *rationes decidendi* of past cases.

In Portugal, as in most European countries, the influence of constitutional jurisdiction is considerable and extends to all legal disciplines, which are experiencing an ever-growing constitutionalization effect.

SERBIA

A CONSTITUTIONAL COURT IN TRANSITION: MAKING SENSE OF CONSTITUTIONAL ADJUDICATION IN POSTAUTHORITARIAN SERBIA

Boško Tripković
Lecturer and Researcher, European University Institute (Florence)
tripkovicb@yahoo.com

INTRODUCTION

The breakdown of communist regimes in Eastern Europe has resulted in the emergence of constitutional courts throughout the region. The introduction of constitutional courts rested on a belief that judiciary is the least dangerous branch of government and on profound distrust in politicians. Such ideas emanated from previous experiences of authoritarian governance and a lack of democratic heritage. The constitution was viewed as a legal act designed to keep politics within boundaries of law, whereas the ideal guardian of constitution was found in an independent judicial authority. In most cases, establishing Kelsenian judicial review created activist courts, which derived legitimacy from their role in democratic transition and from the new democratic constitutional structure. Although this type of strong and centralized judicial review of legislation existed in transitional Serbia as well, there were obvious specificities of both democratic transition and constitutional adjudication that make Serbia a case worthy of detailed exploration.

In contrast to the omnipresent Eastern European narrative, democratic transition in Serbia did not commence immediately after the fall of communism. The transition was not pervasive, but incremental, all while burdened by a multitude of problems. The first postcommunist constitution introduced a multiparty system in 1990; nevertheless, it did not lead to establishment of democracy. Instead, it took a decade of wars and authoritarian rule before democratic revolution ensued in 2000. This did not conclude the problems created by the heritage of dictatorship, as Serbia was only beginning to face new challenges: assassination of the prime minister, a state of emergency, dissolution of federation with Montenegro and secession of Kosovo. In a formal sense, transition to democracy started in 2006 with the adoption of the new constitution, which was a result of a compromise with political forces of the past and a clear expression of formal continuity with the previous constitution.

Apart from general factors that conditioned democratic transition, constitutional adjudication was distinguished by further specificities. The Serbian constitutional court was not introduced as a symbol or tool of democratic transition after the political changes, but was established in 1963, amid communist rule. Two obvious differences with regard to other constitutional courts in Eastern Europe emanate from this: first, the Serbian constitutional court lacked straightforward legitimacy that would be based on morality of new political and legal order, or at least on public expectations from a novel institution; second, having operated within an authoritarian environment for almost forty years, it developed a specific deferential legal culture.

Having these specificities in mind, the purpose of this report is to assess the performance of the court and to account for factors that determined its decision making. I develop the argument as follows. In the first section, I devise a theoretical framework comprising different normative goals that are said to be consequences or aims of judicial review. In the second section, I evaluate the performance of the court against those goals, basing my analysis on the relevant case law. I particularly investigate whether the court was activist while pursuing specific normative goals or whether there other factors that can explain its decision making. I conclude by analyzing the determinants of judicial performance and assert that, even though the constitutional court fostered some of the normative goals, this was a consequence of various factors and neither was exclusively determined by these normative goals as such nor was a corollary of institutionally strong and centralized judicial review.

I. NORMATIVE GOALS OF JUDICIAL REVIEW

Judicial review of legislation is one of the most contested issues in constitutional law. Scholars disagree even on its desirability or legitimacy, and arguments range from the most abstract to empirically verifiable. It would do injustice to complex philosophical arguments to address them here, but strong judicial review is certainly a disputed instrument, mostly because courts are considered unsuitable for resolving moral disagreements about the substance of rights.[1] I do not claim that such perceptions are true or false, as my argument is different – it entails a view that there is a need to adjust these conceptions to specific empirical setting. This argument has two limbs. First, the transitional environment may change some of the propositions on which general theories of judicial review rely. Political branches in developing democracies sometimes leave the judiciary with morally simpler choices when compared to established democracies. For instance, legislatures in transitional countries can impair basic and minimal principles of human rights and minority protection or – even more obvious – can violate fundamental democratic rules that guarantee equal participation. Second, if judicial review cannot be rejected on the basis of philosophical argumentation, its performance must be evaluated on the basis of empirical evidence. Such evidence can be only assessed against a normative framework of values that may be attained through judicial review of legislation. Therefore, the question is not one of *a priori* justification for judicial review but one of determining under what conditions judicial review generates desired results. This kind of inquiry inevitably entails defining normative goals that judicial review should produce.

In literature, there are several arguments in favor of judicial review, which are based on factual conditions that ought to be fulfilled. They can be roughly classified in two groups. First, there are democratic reasons for judicial review. Within that group, there are arguments of representation, deliberation, and responsiveness. According to one cluster of literature, judicial review is justified if it remedies fallibilities of democratic process and contributes to better representation.[2] For the other group of authors, judicial review may, under certain conditions, provide for an independent forum in which legislative decisions can be contested on the basis of reason and thus improve the deliberative democratic element of a polity.[3]

1 This academic discussion has its most sophisticated expression in the work of Ronald Dworkin and Jeremy Waldron. See, e.g., J. Waldron, "The Core of the Case against Judicial Review" (2006) 115 *Yale LJ* 1346; J. Waldron, *Law and Disagreement* (OUP, Oxford 1999) 211–312; J. Waldron, "Moral Truth and Judicial Review" (1998) 43 *Am J Juris* 75; R. Dworkin, *Law's Empire* (Fontana, London 1986) 355–99; R. Dworkin, *Taking Rights Seriously* (Duckworth, London 1997) 81–130; R. Dworkin, *Freedom's Law: The Moral Reading of the American Constitution* (OUP, Oxford 1996) 1–38.

2 J. H. Ely, *Democracy and Distrust: A Theory of Judicial Review* (Harvard University Press, Cambridge, MA 1980).

3 A. Kavanagh, "Participation and Judicial Review: A Reply to Jeremy Waldron" (2003) 22 *Law and Philosophy* 451; M. Kumm, "Democracy Is Not Enough: Rights, Proportionality and the Point of Judicial Review" (2009) NYU School of Law Public Law Research Paper n°

Furthermore, some scholars argue that judicial review may contribute to responsiveness of government, by bringing in line the will of the electorate and governmental action between elections.[4]

Second, there is a liberal argument that opposes the majoritarian democratic paradigm. Judicial review is justified if it reduces the possibility of human rights infringements and enhances political legitimacy of the regime, conceived not only as a procedural matter but also as a substantive one – it exists when citizens have reasons to obey government even when they disagree with a particular decision.[5] The term *liberal* is used in the broadest possible sense, and this group of normative objectives can include a range of values, from protection of constitutional rights and distinct conceptions of good life to the safeguarding of institutional preconditions for human rights protection.

In contrast, there are arguments against judicial review that are based on negative effects that it may produce. Judicial review can remove from the public debate the issue of rights and lead to legislative irresponsibility in that area. Furthermore, it can serve as a legitimating factor for regimes that do not respect the rule of law or that seek to justify unpopular policies as constitutionally inevitable.[6] As a consequence, democratic institutions may not fully develop and judicial review can be detrimental to democratic transition.

This short overview of main perceptions of judicial review is modest in several ways. Notably, it does not give due concern to partial artificiality of the distinction between protection of democratic and liberal values. It may imply that there is a tension between two sets of protected values, although this need not be the case – there is significant overlap between them, in the sense that sometimes courts can foster democracy and protect liberal rights. Also, this framework does not provide a categorical answer to the question of which ends should prevail in case they come into collision or offer a solution to the background question of incommensurability of values. It merely states what ends judicial review might serve.

09-10, http://ssrn.com/abstract=1356793 (accessed 15 December 2009); J. Habermas, *Between Facts and Norms: Contributions to a Discourse Theory of Law and Democracy* (Polity Press, Cambridge 1996) 194–286.

4 K. L. Scheppele, "Democracy by Judiciary. Or Why Courts Can Be More Democratic Than Parliaments" in A. Czarnota, M. Krygier, and W. Sadurski (eds.), *Rethinking the Rule of Law after Communism* (Central European University Press, Budapest 2005).

5 R. H. Fallon, "The Core of an Uneasy Case for Judicial Review" (2008) 121 *Harv LR* 1693.

6 M. Tushnet, "Policy Distortion and Democratic Debilitation: Comparative Illumination of the Countermajoritarian Difficulty" (1995) 94 *Mich L Rev* 245.

However, such a framework can be useful when exploring transitional judicial review. On the one hand, this is because democratic procedures are fragile during the first years of transition, so the courts play an important part in democratic consolidation. On the other hand, there are competing interests of human rights protection and improving responsiveness by taking into account public preferences. Even though this dilemma is not novel or exclusive to transitional constitutional adjudication, it can become more acute in such circumstances. It is no surprise that authors disagree on whether judicial review has beneficial effects on one or both of these levels. For example, Wojciech Sadurski is skeptical about the performance of transitional constitutional courts in the protection of liberal values and is also concerned with negative effects that strong judicial review may have on development of democratic institutions.[7] Conversely, Cindy Skach asserts that there are reasons for robust judicial review during democratic transition, as it can be beneficial for democratic consolidation.[8]

Potential tension between these values also influences the view of how the courts should decide hard cases. Namely, should they protect rights at all costs, or should they act strategically to strengthen judicial review and protection of rights in the long run, as suggested by Tom Ginsburg?[9] Courts can act so as to stabilize their position or the position of other institutions in the fragile political system, which, to a certain extent, suggests a consequentialist reasoning. As a result, their possible role as a substitute for nonoperational civil society and institutionalized party system can be a justification for not pursuing their primary responsibility of human rights protection. Conversely, through deontological reasoning and decision making, the courts may jeopardize their position and hence the protection of liberal rights.

The prescriptive question about deciding hard cases has an analogous empirical counterpart – what motives and factors guide the courts in practice, and are there any general trends that can be established? According to Alec

7 W. Sadurski, *Rights before Courts: A Study of Constitutional Courts in Postcommunist States of Central and Eastern Europe* (Springer, Dordrecht 2008) 289–99. See also S. Holmes and C. R. Sunstein, "The Politics of Constitutional Revision in Eastern Europe" in S. Levinson (ed.), *Responding to Imperfection: The Theory and Practice of Constitutional Amendment* (Princeton University Press, Princeton 1995) 299–301.

8 S. Skach, "Rethinking Judicial Review: Shaping the Toleration of Difference?" in Czarnota, Krygier, and Sadurski (n 4) 66–71.

9 T. Ginsburg, *Judicial Review in New Democracies: Constitutional Courts in Asian Cases* (CUP, Cambridge 2003) 72–5.

Stone Sweet, courts tend to act to reinforce their position for the future.[10] Both Stone Sweet and Sunstein claim that one of the strategies that courts use to this end is a formalistic interpretation and covering of intrinsically moral decisions in allegedly neutral legal reasoning.[11] Tom Ginsburg's empirical study of transitional judicial review shows that courts change this strategy, tend to engage in activism, and depart from strictly formalistic interpretation or deference to legislature in situations of diffused politics when outcomes of upcoming elections are uncertain. He argues that concentration of political power constrains constitutional courts, whereas situations of divided government, electoral unpredictability, and equalized strength of political forces expand judicial power.[12] Not only does the judiciary have additional incentives to be activist because diffused politics create more conflicts that must be adjudicated on; it also sometimes follows the preferences of incoming political majority and hence opposes the government of the day.

Departing from this theoretical framework, I examine the performance of the constitutional court by focusing on the democratic and liberal sphere. In the democratic context, I concentrate on representation and deliberation aspects. I do not deal with responsiveness argument separately, because the issue of responsiveness or answerability becomes less of a virtue and more of a crosscutting facilitating or detrimental factor in pursuance of other values.[13] Therefore, I examine responsiveness in the context of determinants of judicial behavior, as transitional courts tend to follow public opinion in diffused political situations. On a liberal axis, I focus on both protection of institutional preconditions for securing human rights and the human rights protection itself.

10 A. Stone Sweet, *Governing with Judges: Constitutional Politics in Europe* (OUP, Oxford 2000) 200.

11 *Id.*; C. R. Sunstein, *Legal Reasoning and Political Conflict* (OUP, Oxford 1996) 24–6.

12 Ginsburg (n. 9) 89 and 261. For similar arguments about the expansion of judicial power, see C. N. Tate, "Why the Expansion of Judicial Power?" in C. N. Tate and T. Vallinder (eds.), *The Global Expansion of Judicial Power* (New York University Press, New York 1995); R. Hirschl, *Towards Juristocracy: The Origins and Consequences of the New Constitutionalism* (Harvard University Press, Cambridge 2004).

13 Text to n. 4.

II. PERFORMANCE OF THE SERBIAN CONSTITUTIONAL COURT

1. *General Features of the System of Judicial Review*

In determining how the constitutional court acted, what goals it pursued, and what the driving forces were behind its decision making, it is necessary to make some preliminary remarks. There are two dominant characteristics of judicial review in Serbia. On the one hand, institutional arrangements set the stage for judicial activism and robust judicial review. On the other hand, judicial review has generally been deferential. Thus, there is a sharp contrast between institutional variables that would suggest an activist role of the court and jurisprudence of the court, which has been dominated by the philosophy of restraint.

There are a number of features at the institutional level that could make the court a significant constitutional and political factor. These are connected to the competences of the court, access to the court, effects of decisions, lack of precedents, and judicial appointments. First, the court acts as a sole defender of the principles of constitutionality and legality, as far as general legal acts are considered. Not only does the court decide on the constitutionality of legislation; it also has jurisdiction over the constitutionality and legality of all general legal acts brought by any body with public authority.[14] The system of judicial review is completely centralized, and the extensive jurisdiction of the constitutional court leaves no space for ordinary judges to declare unconstitutional acts null and void with *inter partes* effect.

Second, access to the court is virtually unlimited. *A posteriori* review of general acts can be put in motion by two instruments – initiative and proposal. Initiative is a type of *actio popularis*, as it belongs to all domestic natural and legal persons. Although they do not formally start the procedure, as a further ruling of the court on the acceptance of the initiative is needed, initiatives were in practice as effective as direct actions, because the court gave full reasoning every time an initiative was rejected.[15] Proposal, as a direct action for control of the constitutionality and legality, must be

14 Constitution of the Republic of Serbia 1990 OJRS 1/1990 art. 125 (Constitution of 1990); Constitution of the Republic of Serbia 2006 OJRS 83/06 art. 167(1) (Constitution of 2006). Constitutions of 1990 and 2006, as well as respective legislative frameworks, share a number of similarities and I thus examine them together, except when differences are of significance.

15 Constitution of 1990 (n. 14) art. 128(1); Constitution of 2006 (n. 14) art. 168(2). See, e.g., IU-290/2002 of 8 May 2003; IU-271/2002 of 17 April 2003; IU-268/2002 of 17 July 2003; IU-57/2002 of 26 June 2003.

submitted by the authorized proposer, which includes all state authorities and organs. The range of authorized proposers is additionally expanded by the right of the constitutional court to start the procedure itself.[16] Moreover, the constitutional court is not constrained by the request of the authorized proposer or initiator. Once the procedure starts, the court can consider other provisions of the act in question, which need not be challenged by the initial proposal, and decide *ultra petita*. The court is allowed to continue with the proceeding even when the claimant has withdrawn the request.[17] Finally, abstract control of constitutionality of legal acts can occur as an auxiliary consequence of other proceedings – especially through individual constitutional complaint procedure established in 2006 and by incidental review through the *ex officio* referral of an ordinary judge *a quo*.[18]

Third, decisions on constitutionality have *erga omnes* effects. They are "final, enforceable and generally binding,"[19] and when a general act is found to be unconstitutional or unlawful, it ceases to be effective from the day of publication of the court's decision.[20] Dialogical decisions, such as mere declaration of unconstitutionality, do not exist. Hence, the only possibility for the legislature to engage in the dialogue with the constitutional court is to initiate revision of the entrenched constitution.

Fourth, there is neither a legal obligation nor a culture of precedent. Although integrity in judicial decision making would entail a certain amount of respect for previous decisions, the court is not constrained by them. Only decisions brought in *ex ante* judicial review procedure have *res judicata* effects.[21] Lack of precedents could also facilitate a stronger position of the court, as the only way to overturn the court's decision is through its own activity or through an unlikely change of the constitution. Furthermore, a court that is not constrained by precedents could engage in activism, knowing that its doctrines and reasoning can be transformed through subsequent decision making.

Finally, there is nothing in the appointment and tenure of judges that would suggest significant political influence over the court. Under the old

16 Constitution of 1990 (n. 14) art. 128(2); Constitution of 2006 (n. 14) art. 168(1).

17 Law on the Procedure before the Constitutional Court and Legal Effects of Its Decisions 1991 OJRS 32/91, 67/93, 101/2005 art. 24 (Constitutional Court Act 1991); Law on Constitutional Court 2007 OJRS 109/2007 art. 54 (Constitutional Court Act 2007).

18 Constitution of 2006 (n. 14) art. 170; Constitutional Court Act 2007 (n. 17) ch. 8 and art. 63.

19 Constitution of 2006 (n. 14) art. 166(2).

20 Constitution of 1990 (n 14) art. 130; Constitutional Court Act 1991 (n. 17) art. 51; Constitution of 2006 (n. 14) art. 168(3); Constitutional Court Act 2007 (n. 17) art. 58.

21 Constitution of 2006 (n. 14) art. 169.

constitution of 1990, the judges were elected by the parliament, based on the proposal of the president, for life tenure. Thus, the appointment procedure was divided between the legislature and part of the executive (which is independently elected), and judges were more or less irremovable.[22] Under the constitution of 2006, the appointment procedure is divided evenly among three powers – executive, legislative, and judicial. Five judges are elected by the parliament, among ten candidates proposed by the president. Another five are appointed by the president, who chooses between ten contenders nominated by the parliament. The last five judges are selected by the highest ordinary court in the country among ten candidates nominated by independent judicial bodies, whose main function is related to judicial appointments.[23] Their term is shortened to nine years, but it is still longer than the parliamentary (four years) and presidential (five years) mandate.[24]

However, despite these institutional features, the court's role was not as prominent as could be expected. Two reasons for this can be identified, which I refer to as the culture of restraint and ideology of legalism. Although there is no formal obligation for the court to follow judicial practices developed under previous constitutional settings, there is a strong heritage of deference that characterized case law in the authoritarian period. For example, in the time span between the constitutions of 1963 and 1974, the court did not declare a single statute unconstitutional, and from 1974 to 1990, there were only eight such decisions.[25] Even under the first pluralist constitution of 1990, the level of restraint decreased slightly, with only a few decisions on unconstitutionality per year. This was largely a consequence of an increase in claims of unconstitutionality before the court.[26] However, this court also preserved continuity with the previous constitutional regime. First, it continued to assess constitutionality of laws brought before constitutional change against the old, communist constitution. Second, there was a personal continuity with the old court, as eight (out of a total of nine) judges from the communist period survived the constitutional change and stayed on the bench after 1990.[27] As a general rule, politically important acts were kept

22 Constitution of 1990 (n. 14) arts. 73(1)(10), 83(1)(2), 126, and 127.

23 Constitution of 2006 (n. 14) art. 172.

24 Constitution of 2006 (n. 14) arts. 102(1), 116(1), and 172(1).

25 For facts and figures, see S Vučetić, "Četiri decenije Ustavnog Suda Srbije, sa posebnim osvrtom na njegovu ulogu i značaj u savremenom ustavnom sistemu Republike Srbije" in Ustavni sud Republike Srbije, Ustavni sud Srbije: četrdeset godina postojanja (Ustavni sud Republike Srbije, Belgrade 2003) 15–19.

26 *Id.* 28.

27 *Id.* 41–2.

intact and were declared unconstitutional only after they ceased to be positive law through political action. There was no effort on the part of the court to foster democratic transition, and Milosevic's political influence on the court remained strong until the revolution of 2000. After the changes, the newly established democratic regime obtained a majority in the court, given the retirement of several judges in February 2001. Nevertheless, the institutional setting was not altered. Modes of operation were well entrenched, and the culture of restraint, which had developed during forty years of authoritarian rule, was strong enough to survive, as changes in the political realm were not institutionally effectuated through constitutional revision.

It is not surprising that the court, in general, did not make use of institutional mechanisms for robust judicial review. The culture of restraint was almost a convention that required every possible way of keeping the statute valid to be used. The court would rarely commence the procedure on its own. In practice, the *ne bis in idem* principle was strictly respected, and the court never found that there were enough new reasons and proofs to decide on an already-adjudicated issue.[28] The court never developed techniques through which other constitutional courts extend their role beyond the original, negative legislator character – it did not deliver interpretative, manipulative, additive, or substitutive decisions.[29]

The culture of restraint led to a development of the ideology of legalism, which highly influenced interpretative techniques of the court. The difference between the culture of restraint and the ideology of legalism is that the former describes the factual operation of the court and only creates a convention that has no additional normative value, whereas the latter aspires to become a sound political philosophy behind decision making and a value in itself. However, legalism as a political ideology of the court has not come about only as a corollary of restraint, although it suits deferential decision making. One of the main reasons for the occurrence of legalism is the lack of tradition in the rule of law, which was, in turn, wrongly conceived after democratic changes. The ideology of legalism has at least two consequences on the operation of the constitutional court – first, it implies strict constructionism in interpretation, which determines boundaries in the reading of the constitution set out by a dictionary-style understanding of

[28] See, e.g., IU-222/2001 of 3 October 2002; IU-71/2002 of 17 July 2003; IU-295/2005 of 9 March 2006; IU-163/2004 of 15 May 2008.

[29] For types of decisions, see A. R. - , *Judicial Review in Comparative Law* (CUP, Cambridge 1989); R. B. Llorente, "Constitutional Jurisdiction as Law Making" in A. Pizzorusso (ed.), *Law in the Making: A Comparative Survey* (Springer-Verlag, Berlin 1988).

constitutional text; second, constitutionality is conceived of in a predominantly formal sense, as adherence to constitutional procedures, without exploring the substance of potentially unconstitutional decisions. The ideology in question is based not on a belief that rule-of-law principles have inner morality regardless of the substance of the law, but on the conviction that formal understanding of legal propositions is morally good.

Legalism in constitutional interpretation can be recognized in many of the firmly established doctrines of the court. For example, the notion of equality in the case law is conceived as general application of laws. The court regularly held that equality means equal application of the law on subjects who are "in the same legal situation."[30] This doctrine, however, does not involve Aristotelian propositions (treat alike cases alike; treat different cases differently); on the contrary, the court refuses to engage in the issue of what cases are alike and leaves it to the legislator to decide what the "same legal situation" standard means. The court does not engage in a strict scrutiny or rationality analysis of policies that differentiate categories of people on the basis of sex, religion, ethnic origin, and so on, but allows the legislator to decide when such differences are justified.[31] The standard of equality protection remains low, because the doctrine allows for all differentiations except those between people in identical legal positions, which would possibly occur only in some sort of a bill of attainder.

Formalism characterizes understanding of the rule-of-law desiderata as well. For instance, retroactive effects of laws have been forbidden by both constitutions and *vacatio legis* cannot be shorter than eight days, except if, respectively, "general interest" or "reasons particularly justified" are determined when legal acts are brought.[32] The court restricted its scrutiny only to the formal elements of these provisions. Thus, it was enough for a rule-making body to demonstrate that some interest or reason is mentioned in the decision-making process to justify retroactive effects or absence of *vacatio legis*. The court did not engage in exploration of whether such interest is actually general or whether such reasons are in fact particularly

[30] For example, IU-37/2001 of 19 December 2002; IU-424/2003 of 4 March 2004; IU-439/2003 of 17 March 2005; IU-363/2004 of 16 March 2006; IU-433/2005 of 25 September 2008.

[31] IU-420/2003 of 1 July 2004; IU-247/2003 of 10 November 2005; IU-88/2005 of 15 June 2006.

[32] Constitution of 1990 (n 14) arts. 120 and 121(2); Constitution of 2006 (n 14) arts. 196(4) and 197(2).

justified.[33] The notion of constitutionality is strictly formal in such cases – it is enough that the procedure is followed regardless of the constitutional proposition that demands substantive inquiry into the issue.

The constitutional court's understanding of its procedure and competences was also formalistic. The procedure always remained abstract, regardless of the way in which the case was brought before the court – by direct facial challenge or through the incidental method, in which a controversy arose in a case pending before an ordinary court. On a number of occasions, the court also refused to address the issue of application of laws.[34] The only concern for the court was abstract, logical, and textual compatibility of statutes with the constitution, even though in practice laws had unconstitutional effects. Similarly, the court ignored problems that occurred as a consequence of ambiguity or incoherence within a statute, as the principle of constitutionality operated only on a vertical scale, as determined by the Kelsenian hierarchy of legal acts.[35] Still, even though such hierarchy would in theory include legal acts that are above the constitution (e.g., the federal constitution when Serbia was a part of federal state with Montenegro) or would require respect for international law whatever its position in that hierarchy, the court adhered to purely formal understanding of legal sources that it should take into account. For instance, ratified international treaties, which had legal force and the form of ordinary laws under the constitution of 1990, had been largely disregarded as a source of law until the constitution of 2006 explicitly assigned a place for ratified international treaties above ordinary statutes.[36] Likewise, the court in most cases took no notice of the federal constitution, because it was not explicitly mentioned among the competences of the court, even in periods when the federal constitutional judiciary did not function.[37]

An interconnection between the culture of restraint and ideology of legalism brought about the policy-issues doctrine. This is an underdeveloped, incompletely reasoned doctrine, according to which the court characterizes an issue as a question of legislative concern without

33 IU-120/2002 of 19 June 2003; IU-73/2007 of 13 November 2008; IU-125/2006 of 17 July 2008.

34 IU-319/2004 of 6 October 2005; IU-148/2006 of 26 June 2008; IU-70/2007 of 3 July 2008; IU-102/2007 of 17 July 2008; IU-63/2008 of 3 July 2008; IU-47/2008 of 12 June 2008.

35 For example, IU-187/2003 of 3 February 2005.

36 IU-354/2003 of 15 April 2004; IU-371/2005 of 26 January 2006; IU-168/2004 of 9 February 2006.

37 IU-138/2001 of 14 November 2002; IU-196/2003 of 29 April 2004; IU-134/97 of 16 October 2003; IU-301/2003 of 11 March 2004; IU-251/2003 of 21 April 2005; IU-111/2005 of 16 February 2006.

specifically justifying its decision. The margin of appreciation left for the legislator is broad, and legalistic rationalization was generally found in article 72 of the constitution of 1990, which defines competences of the republic. This provision was first included in the constitution because Serbia was a part of the dissolving Yugoslav Federation at that time, to protect competences from possible intrusion coming from the federal level. However, a similar provision is incorporated again in the constitution of 2006 without obvious reason (article 97), as Serbia became independent and remained a unitary state. The court used that article as the most usual way of justifying its deference to the legislature, pointing out how the republic has competence to regulate certain matters listed in the constitution.[38] In this way, the court on many occasions reduced the issue of constitutionality to the issue of having a competence to act, even though particular controversy was not connected to the conflict of competence between different levels of government, but one of constitutionality of a statute.

The culture of restraint and ideology of legalism were overarching and predominant determinants of the court's behavior. In the following passages, I examine how and why the court changed these practices in light of the normative framework of judicial review. A role in protection of democratic and liberal values included activism both toward political branches of government and prevailing legal culture and toward ideology of the court.

2. *Constitutional Adjudication and Democratic Process*

A. Representation

The thesis that strong systems of judicial review are by definition undemocratic is contested famously in the work of John H. Ely, who claims that judicial review may be countermajoritarian but still not undemocratic. Ely recognizes that most constitutional provisions are principally procedural guarantees and not rights of substantive nature that would entrench a distinct view of moral values.[39] Departing from that premise, he criticizes judicial activism that imposes judicial values on the legislator. However, Ely strongly supports judicial protection of democratic process. There are at least two ways in which courts can reinforce representative democracy: first, by clearing the channels of political change, that is, by preventing a particular

[38] IU-391/2004 of 16 June 2005; IU-70/2007 (n. 34); IU-48/2008 of 17 July 2008; IU-83/2005 of 17 July 2008.

[39] Ely (n. 2) 92.

majority from preserving its position in power through misuse or abuse of procedure; second, by protection of political participation and representation of minorities that are discriminated against or do not enjoy the same amount of protection with regard to their participatory rights. Therefore, he is opposed to judicial substitution of legislative policy making but considers the judiciary to be in a better position to police procedural aspects of policy process. He does not claim that the judiciary should replace accountability mechanisms completely or at all, which is therefore different from the responsiveness argument. Government should be able to implement even unpopular policies, and the judiciary should interfere only if the decision-making process is untrustworthy. Furthermore, his theory is not descriptive but prescriptive: he claims not that courts act so as to protect the representative democratic process but that they ought to do so.[40]

Countries in democratic transition may be insufficiently protective of democratic procedures, and a lack of democratic heritage may encourage political elites to jeopardize participatory rights of minorities. Accordingly, courts functioning in a transitional milieu may confront controversies arising from infringements of democratic procedures more often. The Serbian constitutional court was faced with such challenges in the sphere of both of Ely's propositions. First, there is a group of cases in which some political groups tried to exclude the representation of others, and second, there are cases in which judicial protection of minorities in the political realm was required.

Most of the first type of controversies arose as a consequence of a split in political coalition that overthrew Milosevic following the elections of September 2000. Although broad coalitions tend to break up in the first years after democratic changes,[41] this effect was further strengthened by the dualism of levels across which the political power was distributed. On the federal level, the Democratic Party of Serbia (DSS) held a presidential post, and its leader – Vojislav Kostunica, who won the elections against Milosevic – enjoyed massive popular support. However, the real political power remained at the level of the Serbian government, as the Yugoslav Federation was largely dysfunctional and without significant competences. At the Serbian level, Prime Minister Zoran Djindjic and his Democratic Party (DS), with other parties of the former oppositional block, gained principal influence after the elections of December 2000. Political differences and

[40] *Id.* 101–4.

[41] H. Kitschelt, "The Formation of Party Systems in East Central Europe" (1992) 20 *Politics & Society* 7.

frustration with the discrepancy between popular support and the amount of political influence culminated when DSS stepped out of the Serbian government in August 2001 and when their parliamentary seats were taken by other coalition partners by mid-2002.[42]

The constitutional court dealt with this political controversy through a facial challenge to the electoral law.[43] Under the electoral law, the term of a member of Parliament (MP) would end when membership in a political party or coalition that nominated him or her came to an end.[44] The court annulled this provision, which was supposed to strengthen the position of political parties and reinforce party discipline. There are numerous reasons this case was groundbreaking, both in terms of the change in reasoning of the court and in terms of its willingness to engage itself in a politically controversial issue. First, the court unusually commenced the procedure *ex officio*.[45] Second, the parliament submitted its reply, a rare example of it using this procedural opportunity, which resulted in substantial political pressure on the court. Third, the decision was brought in spite of several doctrines that the court had applied beforehand.

The constitution explicitly left it to the legislator to decide on the conditions under which the term of a MP could end. This would undoubtedly have removed the issue from the constitutional court's scrutiny according to the previous case law.[46] The court usually found it sufficient that the legislator had a general competence to legislate in some area, let alone such a clear constitutional authorization. The court reached its decision through interpretation of general constitutional principles – a move never invoked before – because the principles, according to the ideology of legalism, were regarded as political declarations rather than clear legal rules. The principles include popular sovereignty, direct parliamentary elections, and political representation.[47] Furthermore, the court found that several human rights guarantees were violated – equality, freedom of association, and electoral rights.[48] The understanding of equality changed, as the court did not apply

[42] Z. Stojiljković, "Izborne koalicije i proces formiranja vlasti u Srbiji" in S. Mihajlović (ed.), *Oko izbora 17: Parlamentarni izbori u Republici Srbiji*, 11 May 2008 godine (CeSID), Belgrade 2008).

[43] IU-197/2002 of 27 May 2003.

[44] Law on Election of Deputies 2000 OJRS 35/2000 art. 88(1)(1).

[45] IU-197/2002 of 24 October 2002.

[46] Constitution of 1990 (n. 14) art. 74(3).

[47] Constitution of 1990 (n. 14) arts. 2, 74(2), and 76.

[48] Constitution of 1990 (n. 14) arts. 13, 42, and 44.

previous case law that allowed for virtually unlimited margin of appreciation for the legislator. Thus, differentiation between MPs who are members of a political party from those who are not was considered unconstitutional. The same decisions were later reached in cases concerning laws on local self-government and local elections, where the court accentuated constitutional principles of equality and political representation.[49]

Similarly, a politically induced case concerning presidential elections pushed the court outside the legalistic constitutional interpretation.[50] According to the election law, presidential elections were valid only if 50 percent turnout is reached in both rounds.[51] This allowed for a relatively easy boycotting of elections that would prevent election of the president. After two unsuccessful elections in the autumn of 2002, in which DSS leader Kostunica did not manage to overcome the lack of support among his former allies gathered around DS, the country operated with an acting president until mid-2004. This was possible because the DS political majority in the parliament, together with the president of the parliament (acting president), construed the constitutional provision as to allow for discretion of acting president to call the elections. The constitutional court decided that the 50 percent turnout threshold was not unconstitutional *per se*, given explicit constitutional authorization for the legislator to regulate presidential elections.[52] However, the discretionary power of the president of the parliament to call elections was found unconstitutional. The constitution stipulated that the president of parliament "must call elections" and electoral law prescribed that he "decide[] on calling the elections."[53] Strict legalistic interpretation would imply that the condition is fulfilled if the acting president calls elections at least once, which he in fact did. The court held that his right was not constitutive but declaratory, and therefore could not be discretionary. It annulled the provision of election law on the basis of principle of separation of powers and systemic interpretation of the "entirety of constitutional provisions." However, the court rendered the decision after the issue became politically insignificant and therefore did not directly interfere with the electoral process.

[49] IU-66/2002, IU-201/2003, and IU-249/2003 of 25 September 2003.

[50] IU-23/2003 of 18 September 2003.

[51] Law on Elections of the President of the Republic 1990 OJRS 1/90, 79/92 and 73/02 (Presidential Elections Act 1990) arts. 5z(1) and 5z(3).

[52] Constitution of 1990 (n. 14) art. 87(7).

[53] Constitution of 1990 (n. 14) art. 87(4); Presidential Elections Act 1990 (n. 51) art. 5i(3).

The court also actively protected democratic procedure in two decisions concerning governmental attempts to foster democratic reforms at the expense of inclusiveness of the decision-making process. In the first case, the court found that the law on amending constitutional revision procedure was unconstitutional.[54] Because Milosevic's constitution of 1990 provided for procedure that made constitutional revision practically impossible, government enacted a law providing for a less strict procedure that was still inclusive and democratic enough because it prescribed an obligatory referendum.[55] The court found this new procedure unconstitutional, but only after the law lost its political significance following the change in government in early 2004. In the second case, the court declared changes in parliamentary rules of procedure unconstitutional.[56] The government initiated these changes to prevent obstruction from the opposition. The new rules restricted rights of MPs to participate in the debate on amendments they did not submit. The rules also provided for sanction of removal of MPs up to ninety days in case of serious violations of public order.[57] The court again used general constitutional values to justify its decision, so the act was rendered unconstitutional on the basis of principles of popular sovereignty and democratic representation. However, the decision was also rendered after a change in government and when challenged rules were no longer politically valid.

The second type of cases is connected with Ely's other proposition, that is, protection of minority's participatory rights. Decisions in these cases were not directed against the will of parliamentary majority, but, conversely, the court upheld the challenged acts. However, by doing so, it acted against some of its established doctrines. The first case concerned affirmative action measures aimed at achieving substantive equality in the political realm.[58] The contested provisions of the electoral law prescribed a quota system for women and abolished the general threshold of 5 percent for political parties of ethnic minorities.[59] It was consistent with the equality jurisprudence of the court to defer to the legislator's judgment on legitimate differentiation on the

54 IU-168/2003 of 25 March 2004.

55 Constitution of 1990 (n. 15) arts. 132–4; Law on Method and Procedure of Constitutional Revision 2003 OJRS 39/2003.

56 IU-61/2001 of 12 February 2004.

57 Decision on Amending the Rules of Procedure of the National Assembly of the Republic of Serbia 2001 OJRS 59/01 arts. 14 and 33; Decision on Amending the Rules of Procedure of the National Assembly of the Republic of Serbia 2002 OJRS 30/02 art. 14.

58 IU-110/2004 of 15 July 2004.

59 Law That Amends the Law on Election of Deputies 2004 OJRS 18/2004 arts. 8 and 13.

basis of sex or ethnic origin. However, the court departed from its usual restraint in equality cases and determined how the federal constitution allows for affirmative action, even though it explicitly refused to draw on the federal constitution before. The court also established that international law stipulates an obligation for states to adopt affirmative action measures. Moreover, it found that the constitutional equality clause, even though it does not mention affirmative action specifically, not only inherently allows for affirmative action but also creates an obligation for introduction of affirmative action. This doctrine was subsequently confirmed in the case relating to affirmative action for ethnic minorities on a regional level.[60] After the constitution of 2006 explicitly allowed for affirmative action, the court upheld the law on local elections that specified this constitutional provision in the case of ethnic minorities.[61]

However, in a recent decision the court issued an injunction to suspend enforcement of the electoral commission instruction according to which political parties of ethnic minorities did not need to obtain a minimal level of signatures to nominate their candidates lists in elections.[62] This instruction presented an attempt by the ruling coalition to accept criticism coming from ethnic minorities' parties with regard to the discriminatory effect electoral law had on their chances to participate in elections. As the parliament was dissolved at that time, the only way of doing so was through the electoral commission, but this was clearly against the electoral law. The court reached a rather unusual decision – first, it issued an injunction, a tool it had almost never used before, and second, it did so one month before the elections and quickly after the proposal had been submitted by the largest opposition party. The court acted extraordinarily in this case, both in terms of its efficacy and in contrast to pro–affirmative action jurisprudence. In the face of upcoming elections with uncertain outcomes, the court had a strong incentive to uphold the initiative of the single largest party in the parliament. At the same time, ethnic minorities' parties did not have comparable political weight. Furthermore, the legalistic philosophy of the court perfectly fit the decision as hierarchy of legal acts was clearly breached, so the court had enough formal reasons to issue an injunction.

Almost all of the cases concerning democratic procedure were highly influenced by politics. The only decision that was brought against the current

[60] IU-334/2004 of 2 December 2004.

[61] IU-97/2008 of 18 December 2008.

[62] IU-42/2008 of 8 April 2008; Instruction on the Implementation of the Law on Election of Deputies 2008 OJRS 28/08 art. 28(8).

legislative majority was the one related to the parliamentary seats.[63] Other decisions were brought after the changes in government that either rendered respective legislation unimportant (cases concerning presidential elections and rules of procedure)[64] or in which legislation became contrary to the political preferences of the new majority (law on constitutional revision case).[65] This thesis is confirmed by case law on the protection of participation of minorities.[66] The court followed legislative policy on these issues, except when benefits of such deference were overcome by potential costs arising from possible change in government. There are several reasons the court exercised activism in the parliamentary seats case: there was a significant discrepancy between popular will and actions of the parliamentary majority, the breach of democratic procedure was major, restitution could be provided only by the constitutional court, and the split in the coalition led to a split among judges appointed after the changes. In any case, the court acted against the parliamentary majority only to follow closely the will of the electorate and the views of incoming government. This shows that political diffusion leads to judicial activism; however, activism was limited by the court's perception of public opinion and probable future government. Although the court preserved responsiveness, it merely followed the will of the incoming majority. In other cases, when outcomes of the political process were more uncertain, it tended to postpone decision making until the political situation had been clarified.

B. Deliberation

Constitutional adjudication is often praised for its alleged tendency to foster democratic deliberation and bring rights-based arguments of principle in public focus. There are two main claims on which this thesis is based. First, judicial review could present an instrument of public participation in decision making. As Aileen Kavanagh notes, participatory rights should be redefined as to include effective participation. Equal dignity implies not only formal procedures but also substantive impact of every individual, which may require a departure from mere formal equality of participatory rights. Having in mind deficiencies of democratic procedures where real influence of an individual on policy may be limited, constitutional courts could be fora

63 IU-197/2002 (n 43).

64 IU-23/2003 (n 50); IU-61/2001 (n 56).

65 IU-168/2003 (n 54).

66 IU-110/2004 (n 58); IU-334/2004 (n 60); IU-97/2008 (n 61); IU-42/2008 (n 62).

in which individuals can directly challenge these policies and enter the public domain without resources that are otherwise distributed unequally.[67] Second, availability of the procedure to individuals is not itself sufficient. There is a strong argument that proportionality analysis by its very structure fosters deliberation on reasons for legislative decisions. Mattias Kumm describes this procedure as "Socratic contestation," whereby an individual critically challenges authorities, and judicial decision making moves from deductive application of rules or distinct legalistic reasoning to arguments of principle.[68] In other words, there is a "turn from interpretation to justification" in judicial reasoning.[69] Even those who oppose this trend agree that it significantly changes the way the judiciary operates. Aleinikoff argues that "balancing is undermining our usual understanding of constitutional law as an interpretive enterprise," and "in so doing, it is transforming constitutional discourse into a general discussion of the reasonableness of governmental conduct."[70]

The balancing of rights mechanisms could potentially be of special importance for transitional democracies. As Stone Sweet and Mathews demonstrate, a move to rights-based constitutionalism and proportionality analysis was often linked to democratization.[71] They suggest that proportionality analysis provides "judges with a flexible means of managing sensitive legal questions in potentially explosive political environments."[72] Even though their study shows that proportionality analysis serves as a doctrinal foundation for global expansion of judicial power, there are considerable differences in contexts in which courts operate, which influence the use of these mechanisms.[73] The case of the Serbian constitutional court supports this point, as it shows that pure institutional change will not lead to the use of proportionality method when contextual factors do not foster the change.

Whereas the judicial review process in Serbia remained open for individuals throughout the transitional period, the proportionality analysis

[67] Kavanagh (n. 3) 479–86.

[68] Kumm (n. 3) 15–27.

[69] *Id.* 6.

[70] T. A. Aleinikoff, "Constitutional Law in the Age of Balancing" (1987) 96 *Yale LJ* 943, 987.

[71] A. Stone Sweet and J. Mathews, "Proportionality Balancing and Global Constitutionalism" (2008) 47 *Colum JTL* 72, 160.

[72] *Id.* 161.

[73] *Id.* 160–3.

clause was first included in the constitution of 2006.[74] Moreover, the process itself became more inclusive, with the introduction of the constitutional complaint procedure by which one can bring about rights-based challenges of individual legal acts. Even though this instrument does not present a direct challenge to a general act that contains legislative policies, there are institutional reasons that suggest that it could actually lead to greater scrutiny of general legal acts. First, openness of the procedure and motives of individuals to use it to protect their rights resulted in a rise in individual claims before the court. Initiative as a facial challenge could not have led to such an increase, as individuals recognize that their rights are more often breached by individual acts of public authorities than by general policies, of which they are commonly unaware. Second, a facial challenge of an act can be included in the complaint, and the court can put the procedure in motion *ex officio*. There is a strong incentive for the claimant to challenge the general act as well, because it could increase the chances of success of the complaint. However, as the court's case law demonstrates, the introduction of constitutional complaint did not lead to such additional scrutiny of constitutionality.[75]

Moreover, the court did not use the proportionality clause in a way that would foster deliberation on public policies. The main test of constitutionality of laws with regard to human rights before the adoption of the new constitution was a formalistic analysis of the parliament's competence to legislate in this area. The test encompassed the distinction between the manner of exercising rights, where the legislator had freedom to legislate, and conditions for their attainment, that was a part of *materiae constitutionis*.[76] The same provision is included in the constitution of 2006, together with the introduction of classical proportionality clause.[77] In contrast to suggestions that proportionality analysis would lead to deliberation on public policies or increase in judicial activism, the court largely ignored the new instrument.[78]

74 Constitution of 2006 (n. 14) art. 20.

75 The court only once decided on constitutionality of a law following such challenge (UŽ-1429/2008 of 16 July 2009) and refused to consider constitutional complaints wrongly addressed against general acts as *de facto* initiatives for the assessment of constitutionality (UŽ-1388/2008 of 25 December 2008; UŽ-785/2008 of 30 October 2008).

76 Constitution of 1990 (n.14) arts. 12(1) and 12(2).

77 Constitution of 2006 (n. 14) arts. 18(2) and 20.

78 Proportionality clause is usually mentioned as a point of law but never actually used (see, e.g., IU-70/2007 (n. 34); IU-54/2008 of 24 April 2008). The court balanced two rights between themselves only once (UŽ-904/2008 of 25 December 2008).

There are several reasons for this. First, the court understood constitutional complaint as a part of regular criminal or civil procedure. Instead of becoming an instrument for the challenge of constitutionality, in practice, the court limited its scrutiny to the question of whether the ordinary court applied the law correctly and not whether such application or the very legislation that is applied is constitutional.[79] In that way, judges of the constitutional court, who are most commonly recruited from the ordinary judiciary, did what they knew best – they applied the law to concrete circumstances.[80] Therefore, the violation of rights was found in incorrect interpretation or application of legislation, not in the unconstitutionality of laws.

Second, the old test that includes the distinction between manner of exercising rights and conditions for obtaining them suited the deferential character of judicial scrutiny better. The court actually never provided a complete explanation of the doctrine and applied it rather randomly. As it is hard to differentiate between the manner and conditions, because both can prevent someone from exercising a certain right, the court applied a sort of proportionality analysis, without having to justify its decision. For example, in a case concerning local elections, the court found that a residency requirement for exercising voting rights is not a new condition but only a manner in which the rights are used.[81] In another case, residency was found to be a condition for obtaining the right to work as a taxi driver.[82] With all the questionable consequences it has, proper proportionality analysis includes justification not only of legislative policies but also of judicial decisions. It works both ways – the court is compelled to uncover the reasons for the decision and to provide sound justification for it.

Third, there were no political reasons that would foster the use of the proportionality clause. Public attention to these issues is not as high as in the case of violations of democratic procedure. Apart from the lack of transparency in the work and decisions of the court, the main reason for that is the very nature of human rights claims. They are mostly put forward by individuals, without big political controversies in the background.

[79] UŽ-112/2007 of 18 December 2008.

[80] Half of the current ten judges have background in the ordinary courts or prosecutor's office.

[81] IU-214/99 of 15 May 2003. See also IU-23/2003 (n. 50).

[82] IU-169/2002 of 25 December 2003.

3. *Constitutional Court and Liberal Values*

When judicial review is contested, the critique is mostly based on the belief that moral disagreement about what rights people have should not be decided by the judiciary, the only principled solution being procedural equality, which gives everyone formally equal impact in the public domain.[83] Constitution makers are in original position when they draft constitutional rights, so rights are often vague (there is disagreement on their meaning in a particular case) and minimal (so the agreement on their constitutionalization can be reached among many conflicting interests). Yet human rights protection is the single most important justification for judicial review.

In contrast to proponents of procedural democratic values, those who claim that judicial review is beneficial for the protection of liberal values are concerned with outcomes of democratic process. Ronald Dworkin argues that political process in constitutional as opposed to majoritarian democracy should produce outcomes that citizens would support if they were absolutely rational and informed.[84] Such policies ought to treat people with equal concern and respect, thereby protecting both equality and liberty.[85] Similarly, Richard H. Fallon argues that, if judicial review reduces the possibility of human rights violations, the whole regime becomes more legitimate.[86] The main objection to these views is that the answer to the question of which results are morally better must be informed by necessarily partisan beliefs on what the right answer to constitutional controversy should be. However, as Fallon notices, legitimacy is a matter of degree, and judicial review is legitimate if it leads to morally better decisions and outcomes on the whole, regardless of controversial cases that involve vague rights.[87] The focus on hard cases conceals the reality of ordinary human rights adjudication that may not involve vague rights. Hence, empirical claims about the court's efficacy in protection of human rights need not include moral bias in each and every case.

In a transitional society, dangers of the imposition of popular morality can be even greater, and challenges that constitutional courts face are less

[83] Waldron, "The Core of the Case against Judicial Review" (n. 1).

[84] Dworkin, *Freedom's Law: The Moral Reading of the American Constitution* (n. 1) 17.

[85] *Id.*

[86] Fallon (n. 5) 1699.

[87] *Id.* 1727.

controversial in terms of the "right answer."[88] Additionally, judicial review is usually established with a view to protect human rights. It is not surprising that courts in transitional societies show more willingness toward activism when resolving human rights issues than when adjudicating on triadic disputes on competences for which they may be better equipped.[89] However, even though a rights-based review is less costly for the court's position in the political system than for highly politicized issues, it often includes collision of interests between individual-minority and government, which can lead to a reduced level of protection.[90]

The Serbian constitutional court is specific in this respect. Human rights protection was not conceived of as its raison d'être, because it existed during communism and Milosevic's dictatorship as well. Its human rights performance was therefore highly influenced by various exogenous factors, such as public opinion or international pressure. In the case law of the Serbian constitutional court, there were generally two types of challenges to human rights. The first could be termed *direct*, which includes human rights violations through both general and individual acts of the state. The second group consists of indirect (or institutional) challenges, and it comprises alleged encroachments on the independence of the judiciary or prosecution, which can, in the long run, worsen human rights protection.

A. Direct Protection of Liberal Values

In general, the constitutional court has not been very active in human rights protection when direct infringements of rights are concerned. However, there are several typical cases in which it protected human rights, and almost all include some sort of political or other pressure that generated such protection. Without additional impetus, the court exercised the usual restraint.

First of these cases includes the assessment of constitutionality of measures that were deployed during the state of emergency declared after the Prime Minister Djindjic was assassinated in March 2003.[91] The court faced a complex legal and political situation. On the one hand, the state of

[88] Dworkin argues that in divided societies judges should disregard public views and take into account only their own political morality. R. Dworkin, "Response to Overseas Commentators" (2003) 1 *ICON* 651, 655.

[89] Sadurski (n. 7) 36.

[90] Ginsburg (n. 9) 86-9.

[91] IU-93/2003 of 8 July 2004.

emergency enjoyed almost-undivided popular support[92] and presented the final attempt of the new democratic government to dismantle forces of the past, especially by fighting organized crime that had become deeply entrenched in governmental structures, thus effectively ending the revolution started in 2000. Besides, Serbia gained further international approval for these efforts, by being admitted to the Council of Europe during the state of emergency. On the other hand, numerous rights were violated – some twelve thousand people were arrested and kept in custody without judicial approval, freedom of the press was restricted only to publishing governmental briefings, and so on.[93] The court declared unconstitutional the violations of freedom of expression, personal liberty, due process, right to strike, and privacy of communication, drawing extensively on international law and federal human rights documents. The strategy the court adopted was to wait until the change in government occurred, and it rendered the decision sixteen months after the state of emergency had been declared. In that way, it practically endorsed the view of the new government, according to which the state of emergency was not justified.

In other cases that are connected to transitional circumstances, the court's strategy included deference when important policy decisions were in question. The court lacked transitional legitimacy and refrained from remedying past human rights violations. For example, the court repeatedly refused to address the constitutionality of communist nationalization of property, with the reasoning that these were "historical laws," although such laws never existed in the legal system or in theory.[94] The real issue was the lack of political will and financial resources to deal with restitution. Similarly, the court did not interfere when the government tried to alleviate consequences of autocratic rule, except when political pressure was high after the change in government. For instance, the court upheld partial lustration in universities that provided for retroactive reconsideration of academic appointments after 1998, when Milosevic instated complete control over universities,[95] but it annulled the governmental decree on public access to secret service files.[96] In the latter case, the court used the well-known strategy – it rendered the decision three years after the decree had

[92] Stojiljković (n. 42) 135.

[93] *Id.*

[94] IU-178/2004 of 3 March 2005; IU-177/2004 of 25 November 2004; IU-70/2005 of 23 February 2006.

[95] IU-120/2002 (n. 33); Law on University 2002 OJRS 21/2002 arts. 141 and 142.

[96] IU-149/2001 of 19 June 2003; Ordinance on the Access to Certain Files Kept on Citizens of Serbia by the State Security Agency 2001 OJRS 30/2001, 31/2001.

been brought and after the political parties that were opposed to opening of files had won the elections.

Without external pressures, the court upheld almost every governmental policy that affected human rights. For example, the court did not find that the law establishing facultative religious education in state schools only for seven "traditional" religious communities violated equality or freedom of religion.[97] In cases concerning the right to effective remedy, the court held that this right did not extend to situations where "only facts are determined"[98] and did not consider obligatory lawyer's assistance for filing an extraordinary remedy in civil cases an unjustified limitation of this right.[99]

The court annulled only those laws that were brought by the previous regime and that were not also politically significant for contemporary government. Under these conditions, the court remedied violations of human rights conducted before democratic changes. In one case, Milosevic's law that prohibited military deserters from inheriting property was declared unconstitutional,[100] and in another, a limitation of the right to political association for public servants was annulled.[101] In both cases, the court rather unusually based its decisions on novel reading of the equality provision, according to which differentiations must be "reasonable," and alike cases must be treated alike.

Apart from facial challenges of legislation, human rights adjudication also emerged through constitutional complaints against individual legal acts. Since the adoption of the constitution of 2006, the court acted as the last domestic instance of human rights protection before the application could be filed to the European Court of Human Rights (ECtHR). The new role of the court brought significant momentum for human rights protection. However, out of all cases in which the court found violation of a human right, 92.5 percent pertained to liberty and security in relation to detention, fair trial, and the right to an effective remedy.[102] The most probable explanation for this is that 68.65 percent of cases in which the ECtHR held that Serbia violated the European Convention (ECHR) include articles 5, 6, and 13.[103] This statistic

[97] IU-214/2002 of 4 November 2003.

[98] IU-2/2004 of 7 July 2005.

[99] IU-181/2005 of 28 September 2006.

[100] IU-358/95 of 25 September 2003.

[101] IU-353/1995 of 14 April 2005.

[102] Calculated on the basis of decisions available at http://www.ustavni.sud.rs (accessed on 21 April 2010).

[103] Convention for the Protection of Human Rights and Fundamental Freedoms 213 UNTS 222 (ECHR). Percentage is calculated on the basis of ECtHR, "Violation by Article and by

may not provide conclusive evidence that the ECtHR's influence was significant; it may be that these rights were those most often violated, that individuals frequently complained about infringements of these rights, or that the data may merely point out the fact that the majority of all successful applications before the ECtHR concern articles 5, 6, and 13.[104] Still, such a significant percentage and higher ratio of these rights violations in the constitutional court's case law demonstrates that the influence of the ECtHR decisively determined the substance of domestic human rights protection. This tendency is also evident when decisions are examined more closely – readiness to include the ECtHR case law in reasoning is obvious when these rights are in question. This is a consequence of both the court's judicial philosophy and international influence. Because these rights do not entail the kind of proportionality analysis that the court constantly refused to apply, the court in such cases openly used the ECtHR's cases and doctrines, at the same time preventing the potential liability of the state before the international court.[105]

The court exercised more activism in cases concerning political representation, although the political costs tend to be lower in human rights adjudication. This is certainly because the court's legitimacy was not based on human rights protection from the beginning of its operation. But it also shows that the court's deferential default position generated by the culture of restraint changed only when some additional, external factors for activism were present. In cases concerning human rights, these incentives were often absent. Moreover, the court's authority building was mainly defensive and followed the actions of political forces. Activism was a corollary of self-protecting strategies, by which the court strived not to oppose the dominant political actors rather than establish itself as an important institution in the political system through independent decision making. Such a strategy changed only when the court considered its position threatened, as exemplified by cases concerning indirect protection of liberal values.

Country: 2003-2009" (December 2009) 2, at http://www.echr.coe.int/NR/rdonlyres/E26094FC-46E7-41F4-91D2-32B1EC143721/0/Tableau_de_violations_19592009_ENG.pdf (accessed on 21 April 2010).

104 *Id.*

105 See, e.g., UŽ-261/2007 of 25 December 2008; UŽ-372/2008 of 16 October 2008; UŽ-536/2008 of 11 December 2008; UŽ-687/2008 of 25 December 2008.

B. Indirect Protection of Liberal Values

In contrast to the direct protection of human rights, the Serbian constitutional court has been very active in preserving the conditions in which human rights can be effectively exercised. These cases include protection of the judiciary from possible influence of the executive. In such instances, the court was ready not only to oppose the legislator but also to depart from its well-established doctrines. On a number of occasions, the court decided on the manner in which ordinary judges should be appointed. The constitution of 1990 prescribed that judges are to be elected by the parliament, but it remained silent on the question of who should nominate the candidates, so the legislator was free to decide on possible nominators.[106]

The first of the cases included a facial challenge to a new law on the judiciary, which established the High Judicial Council as a new independent body responsible for proposing candidates for judicial positions.[107] However, the law stipulated that if the proposal of this body turned out to be unsuccessful, the competence would be transferred to the parliamentary committee.[108] This solution could have resulted in the legislature establishing complete control over judicial appointments, but at the same time, it would not have been *stricto sensu* unconstitutional. The court annulled this provision, basing its decision on the principle of separation of powers. According to the court, the process of proposing candidates for judges must remain a competence of the judiciary, which includes the High Judicial Council. However, this body was not substantially a judicial organ because it did not resolve legal disputes and did not perform judicial functions. The separation-of-powers principle was strictly construed, notwithstanding the constitutional provision that explicitly empowered the parliament to appoint judges. Article 8(4) of the constitution stipulated that "judicial power belongs to the courts," and it in fact defined separation of powers in functional, not organizational, terms. It merely stated that adjudication should be performed by the judiciary, not that the judiciary should independently nominate candidates for judicial appointments. Apart from basing its decision in a general separation-of-powers principle, the court also uncommonly drew on international soft-law documents, including those

106 Constitution of 1990 (n. 14) art. 73(1)(10).

107 IU-122/2002 of 11 February 2003.

108 Law Amending the Law on Judges 2002 OJRS 42/02 art. 10.

adopted within the Council of Europe, even though Serbia was not a member at that time.[109]

The court confirmed such understanding of separation of powers in other cases concerning judicial appointments. For example, it held that establishment of the Council for Judicial Administration that was supposed to appoint presidents of courts was unconstitutional, because the parliament elected members of the Council.[110] This was another case of the court basing its decision on international soft-law. Even after the new constitution was brought, the court continued with the same understanding of separation of powers. In a recent case, it concluded that the provision that allows the minister of justice to initiate the procedure for termination of judicial office was unconstitutional.[111] In a similar manner, the court applied the separation-of-powers doctrine to prohibit the government's influence over appointments and removals of public prosecutors from office.[112]

However, the protection of judiciary was not consistent. Even though the constitutional court included prosecutors in the notion of judiciary, and thus extended the protection of the separation-of-powers principle, this was not the case with magistrates. On two occasions, governmental appointments of magistrates were declared constitutional, even though magistrates' courts perform judicial function and can even impose sanctions.[113] There is no sound legal justification for such reasoning, and the experience with Milosevic's use of magistrates to suppress freedom of expression would have suggested caution with governmental appointments to these organs. Inconsistency and preferential treatment of ordinary courts and prosecutors is even more obvious in a case concerning the constitutional complaint of a judge who had been mistakenly retired three months ahead of time. In that case, the court expanded its understanding of human rights to include "a right to permanency of judicial position" and decided in favor of the claimant.[114] Conversely, in another case, the court explicitly established that constitutional complaint procedure was restricted only to those rights

[109] These documents include the European Charter on the Statute for Judges DAJ/DOC 98 (23); Basic Principles on the Independence of the Judiciary, General Assembly of the United Nations resolutions 40/32 of 29 November 1985 and 40/146 of 13 December 1985.

[110] IU-232/2003 of 18 March 2004; Law Amending the Law on Judges 2003 OJRS 27/03 art. 70.

[111] IU-28/2006 of 19 February 2009.

[112] IU-167/2003 of 22 April 2004.

[113] IU-264/98 of 3 April 2003; IU-392/2005 of 16 March 2006.

[114] UŽ-134/2007 of 10 July 2008.

guaranteed among human rights provisions.[115] The so-called right to permanency of judicial position is not explicitly guaranteed in the constitution, neither among human rights provisions nor among other parts of the constitution; the court derived such a right from a general principle of permanency of judicial office.[116]

There are two possible reasons the constitutional court protected the independence of judiciary more vigorously than any other constitutional value. First, half of current and a third of previous judges have been recruited from the judiciary and prosecutor's office. Therefore, there is a strong sentiment on the bench that the judiciary needs additional protection from possible encroachments of other powers. Second, by protecting the judiciary, the constitutional court has been trying to guard its own position in the political system. Although the nature of the constitutional court cannot be understood only as judicial,[117] if the court were to increase its power and compliance among purely political branches of government, one of the ways to do so would be to enhance respect for other nonpolitical branches, such as the judiciary. Nonetheless, when interests of power building collided with the most important policies of the government, the court refrained from activism. In a recent case, the court faced a dilemma of this kind. After the new constitution was established, the government seized the opportunity to deal with corrupt and inefficient judiciary and provided for reappointment of all ordinary judges. The court upheld the constitutionality of such reappointment.[118] This was such an important political issue that the court refused to be activist and at the same time altered some of the doctrines from previous cases: first, it undermined the importance and refused to take into account the same international soft-law documents on which it based decisions in previous cases;[119] second, it abandoned strict application of separation of powers principle and understood it as balance and mutual control of powers.

CONCLUSION

Democratic transition in Serbia brought about many challenges for the constitutional court. Perhaps one of the most substantial was intrinsic to the

[115] UŽ-785/2008 of 30 October 2008.

[116] Constitution of 2006 (n. 14) art. 146(1).

[117] Stone Sweet (n. 10) 61–91.

[118] IUz-43/2009 of 9 July 2009.

[119] See n. 109.

court itself. It had to change its role from a court that served as a façade for authoritarian rule to a protector of liberal and democratic values. Thus, the burden was twofold – on the one hand, the culture of restraint and ideology of legalism prevented the court from active engagement in the political process, and on the other hand, transitional circumstances put the court in the position to remedy fallibilities of political decision making.

The performance of the court hence depended on many different variables. Its institutional position, which would suggest an important role in the legal and political system, was not enough to secure protection of democratic and liberal values. On the democratic level, the court protected procedural principles of representative democracy but only when politics was diffused and electoral outcomes uncertain. More precisely, the most important determinant of judicial activism was the perception of possible electoral outcomes. When guarding democratic procedure coincided with preferences of present or future government, the court was ready to depart from its usual deferential role or interpretative techniques. Without additional impetus, the court failed to serve as a facilitator of democratic consolidation, which is exemplified by its insignificant role in fostering democratic deliberation. With regard to the protection of liberal values, adjudication was determined by similar factors. The court lacked direct transitional authority and did not derive its legitimacy from preeminence of human rights. Thus, on most occasions, it failed to protect human rights and engaged directly in their protection mainly when it was politically opportune or when international pressure was high. However, while protecting the independence of the judiciary and prosecution, the court openly opposed the legislature and was ready to engage in activist decision making. This was largely because the court, by so doing, tried to stabilize its own position. Even in these cases, if political pressure was considerable, the court deferred to the legislature. This shows that the main cause of judicial activism or restraint was authority building in a politically and legally unstable transitional environment.

The question remains as to how the performance of the court should be evaluated. On the one hand, it is certain that its role was not as prominent as it could have been and that it did not vigorously protect liberal-democratic values. On the other hand, even though it often reacted after political changes that would have remedied previous infringements of these values, the court had an important standard-setting role. After the court renders its decision, even if it comes late and when the issue loses political importance, a certain standard of protection is established. Although the court failed many times on the integrity and consistency agenda, overturning its decisions would at least demand a sound justification, especially in cases with high public attention. In that sense, the existence of the court has had beneficial effects on democratic consolidation. However, the influence has not been as important as general theories of judicial review or experiences of other transitional countries would suggest. Future achievements of the court will depend on the elimination of conditions that have been detrimental so far. In that sense, stabilization of the court as a guardian of the constitution will occur when democratic consolidation is achieved, when the court has good reason to believe that compliance is secured, and when the influence of international institutions is intensified.

SLOVAK REPUBLIC

CONSTITUTIONAL COURT OF THE SLOVAK REPUBLIC AS POSITIVE LEGISLATOR VIA APPLICATION AND INTERPRETATION OF THE CONSTITUTION

Ján Svák,
Professor, Bratislava School of Law
rektor@uninova.sk

Lucia Berdisová,
Research Fellow, Slovak Academy of Sciences, Institute of State and Law
lucia.berdisova@yahoo.com

The position of the Constitutional Court of the Slovak Republic (hereafter "Constitutional Court") as a positive legislator has been widely influenced by two factors. The first is the fact that Slovakia had only fractional practical experience with constitutional judiciary, and furthermore only within the common state with the Czechs.

The first experience dates back to the period of the establishment of the first Czechoslovak Republic between the two world wars, when the Constitutional Court was created on the basis of the Constitution of Czechoslovakia of 1920, which was strongly influenced by Hans Kelsen's theory. It has been one of the first practical experiments that came from this doctrine, and it is also an exemplary illustration of the fact that practical realization of a theoretical construction can be scholastic in practice. The factual activity of this court had only marginal effect on the state's constitutional life. The second attempt was the establishment of the Constitutional Court of the Czechoslovak Socialist Republic. This court was incorporated into the Constitution of a totalitarian state within the time of political warming, the so-called Prague Spring, in 1968–69. The failure of the experiment of socialism with a human face was also the gravedigger of the actual founding of this constitutional court. At last, in the third attempt, the Constitutional Court of the Czech and Slovak Federal Republic was created in 1992 after the fall of the totalitarian regime. This federal state existed for only a short time; for this reason, the Constitutional Court could not considerably influence the tradition of constitutional judiciary. Despite this fact, some of its decisions concerning the so-called material rule of law in connection with review of the legal order before 1989 became the theoretical basis for the Constitutional Court's jurisdiction created after the establishment of the independent Slovak Republic.

The second factor that influenced the position of the Constitutional Court as a positive legislator was the dynamic establishment of a new state – the Slovak Republic. The Constitution of the Slovak Republic[1] was made in an unbelievably short period of time (only a few weeks). This Constitution found its historical inspiration in the Constitution of Czechoslovakia of 1920. This fact was manifest in two determinants. The first was the natural tension between institutions that were embedded in the Constitution at the beginning of the twentieth century and the same institutions at the end of the century. This was especially reflected by the mechanical adoption of the classical doctrine of Ch. L. De Montesquieu on the separation of powers – the Governing power, the Legislative power, and the Judicative power, which was the core of the Constitution of Czechoslovakia of 1920. However, the constitutional life at the end of the twentieth century in Slovakia was affected by the issues such as the growth of importance of direct democracy forms, transfer of the real power in the state onto political parties, growth of importance of the judiciary, and other law-protecting institutions (e.g., public prosecution, ombudsman).

The second determinant was the resignation concerning detailed codification of some constitutional institutions, often caused by different visions of their future. A fine example is the public prosecution, which, even though it is incorporated in the Constitution of the Slovak Republic, was not only excluded from the branches of power (executive power, judicial power) but the Constitution also completely abstained from any kind of its constitutional definition.

The result of such a legal and political background connected with the formation of a new state and the creation of its Constitution was also the fact

1 The Constitution of the Slovak Republic promulgated under n° 460/1992 Coll, as amended.

that the immense power of active (direct or indirect) formation of constitutional text was given to the Constitutional Court.

The direct way is the constitutional authorization of the Constitutional Court to interpret the Slovak Constitution. The indirect one is the abstract control of constitutionality, whereby the Constitutional Court, just like other constitutional courts and tribunals in continental countries, decides on the conformity of the law with the Constitution, as well as concrete control of constitutionality, whereby the Constitutional Court decides on infringement of fundamental rights or freedoms in individual cases.

I. INTERPRETATION OF THE CONSTITUTION

According to article 128 of the Constitution of the Slovak Republic, "the Constitutional Court shall give an interpretation of the Constitution or constitutional law if the matter is disputable," and this interpretation is generally binding from the date of its promulgation in the Collection of Law, as the Constitution states explicitly. As a result, the decisions of the Constitutional Court directly complement the normative text of the Slovak Constitution, and its wording has the identical legal power and binding effect as the text of the Constitution itself.[2]

As the case law of the Constitutional Court developed, it was determined that the Constitutional Court was entitled to interpret constitutional statutes (including the Constitution) if two conditions are fulfilled.

First, the matter must be disputable, what means that there has to be an actual and specific dispute. Second, the dispute has to involve two different constitutional bodies, i.e., the National Council of the Slovak Republic (at

2 The Constitutional Court stated with regard to this competence (decision nº II. ÚS 69/99): "By the exercise of the competence according to art. 128 para. 1 of the Constitution of SR the Constitutional Court of the Slovak Republic carries out the activity that is an abstract control of constitutionality. The aim of proceeding on interpretation of constitutional statutes (according to art. 128 para. 1) is to eliminate the possibility of repeated disputes on legally binding interpretation of the constitutional provision in the future after the actual emergence of the dispute. The Constitutional Court does not decide whether the state bodies did violate the Constitution by the wrong interpretation. The legal effect of interpretation as to art. 128 para. 1 is not explicitly stated. It is so because in the proceeding on interpretation of constitutional statutes according to art. 128 par.1 of the Constitution, the Constitutional Court of the Slovak Republic neither assesses nor decides on constitutionality (i.e., the conformity with the Constitution of SR) of the action, omission or decision of state body, which brought about the dispute. The court only provides the interpretation of disputed part of constitutional statute. It follows that the decisions on interpretation of the Constitutional Court of Slovak Republic do not have and cannot have any legal effects on actions, omissions or decisions of state bodies that brought about the dispute.

least one-fifth of the members of the Parliament), the President of the Slovak Republic, the Government of the Slovak Republic, a court, the Attorney General, and the Public Defender of Rights.[3]

Thus, private subjects (natural and legal persons) do not initiate a proceeding on the interpretation of the Constitution.

The interpretation of the Constitution of the Slovak Republic made directly by the Constitutional Court was used especially often[4] after the establishment of the Slovak Republic (in the first office of justice from 1993 to 1999), and it considerably influenced the constitutional order of the Slovak Republic. One can find good examples in the decisions of the Constitutional Court concerning the position and authority of the President of Slovak Republic.

The original text of the Constitution of the Slovak Republic comes from the project of classical parliamentary form of the government, where the head of the state has the position of *porvoir neuter* and a relatively weak position, as far as its competence is concerned. However, the Constitutional Court directly strengthened the Slovak President's position by interpreting the Constitution of the Slovak Republic. The court stated in the decision No. I. ÚS 39/93 that, "even if the Government of the Slovak Republic ("government") is the highest executive body (art. 108), the constitutional position of the President of Slovak Republic is in fact dominant towards constitutional position of the government." The object of the decision was the interpretation of the notion "he shall appoint and recall" the Prime Minister and other members of Government of the Slovak Republic. The grammatical form of those verbs in Slovak does not provide a univocal answer to the question whether the president has the right or the constitutional obligation to appoint members of the government based on the motion of the Prime Minister. The Constitutional Court added that, "in order

3 See decision of the Constitutional Court nº I. ÚS 30/97, which states "the word 'disputable' stands for proceedings on matters where the dispute occurs and where there are two opponents, i.e. there are two state bodies with different opinion on interpretation of the constitutional provision. . . . The proceeding, as to art. 128 para. 1 of the Constitution requires the actual existence of a dispute. The legal effects according to art. 128 para. 1 of the Constitution can't be connected with any kind of dispute on interpretation of the Constitution, but only with constitutionally relevant one. The relevant dispute … cannot arise between any subject entitled to submit a motion in accordance with art. 130 para. 3 letter a) of the Constitution. Constitutionally relevant dispute on interpretation of the Constitution is a dispute on rights or duties between bodies of the state which do have such rights and duties prescribed in the Constitution."

4 See, e.g., decisions of the Constitutional Court nº I. ÚS 39/93, nº II. ÚS 81/ 93, nº I. ÚS 5/94, nº I. ÚS 20/94, nº I. ÚS 58/94, nº I. ÚS 7/96, nº I. ÚS 61/ 96, nº II. ÚS 31/97, nº I. ÚS 40/ 99.

to create inner balance within the executive power, the Constitution of the Slovak Republic assigns the President of the Slovak Republic only the obligation to deal with the motion of the Prime Minister, it is not his obligation to comply with it."

The previously described decision of the Constitutional Court implied serious consequences for the constitutional system of the Slovak Republic. First, the legitimacy of the government *de facto* is decided not by the parliament (as in a classical parliamentary government) but by the president. So the position of the President of the Slovak Republic was extraordinarily strengthened, and the Constitutional Court became the direct creator of the constitutional system of the Slovak Republic.

II. ABSTRACT CONTROL OF CONSTITUTIONALITY

The Constitutional Court executes traditional continental competence of the constitutional judiciary based on art. 125 of the Constitution of the Slovak Republic, as it decides on the conformity of the statutes and other legal sources with legal power that is below statutes (e.g. decrees issued by the Government, legal regulation issued by the ministries) with the Constitution. If the Constitutional Court holds that there is inconformity with the law or part of the law with the Constitution, the respective regulation or its part shall lose effect and the parliament will be obliged to harmonize the law and/or statute with the Constitution (i.e., with the opinion of the Constitutional Court). Only the *obiter dictum* part of the decision is generally binding – this part states that there is inconformity of the statute, or part of it, with the particular clauses of the Constitution. The *ratio decidendi* part of the decision provides the instructions of the court as to the manner of eliminating the unconstitutionality of the statute and results from the interpretation of the Constitution. The *ratio decidendi* part is of great importance in practice. Just recently, the Constitutional Court decided that there is inconformity of two important statutes with the Constitution – act No. 335/2005 Coll. on proving the origin of a property[5] and Act No. 458/2003 Coll. on the establishment of the Special Court and of the Office of Special Prosecution.[6] In the case of the latter, Parliament did follow *ratio decidendi* of the decision to eliminate unconstitutional features of the

5 Decision of the Constitutional Court nº PL. ÚS 29/05.

6 Decision of the Constitutional Court nº PL ÚS 17/08.

original statute, and it adopted the new Act No. 291/2009 Coll. on Specialized Criminal Court.

Apart from the methodical sphere of activity of the Constitutional Court as to creation of the laws that are in conformity with the Constitution, the Court also plays the role of positive legislator via interpretation of the Constitution as provided within the abstract control of constitutionality. We can demonstrate it again on the decision of the Constitutional Court regarding the position of the President. Even here the Court kept its trend and strengthened the President's competence. The good example is the court's supervision of the conformity of Act No. 3/1993 Coll., on the establishment of the Army of the Slovak Republic with the Constitution. The core of the case was the matter of the competence to appoint the Chief of the General Staff of the army, which was given to the Government by original law. However, according to Art. 102 of the Constitution of the Slovak Republic, the competence to appoint and recall "higher state officials" belongs to the President. So the interpretation of the constitutional notion of higher state official was at stake. As to the opinion of the Constitutional Court manifested in the decision No. PL. ÚS 32/95, there is no "obstacle that could keep the President from the execution of his competence towards Chief of the General Staff of the army as a higher state official." This decision in connection with the direct interpretation of the Constitution by the Constitutional Court has *de facto* transformed the classical parliamentary form of government into some kind of semipresidential form, and yet without changing the normative text of Constitution. This fact also brought the Parliament (as the constituent/constitutional body) to adjust the "new" powers of the President to his legitimacy . The constitutional law No. 9/1999 Coll., on the direct election of the President by citizens of the Slovak Republic, was introduced. However, the following development remains a historical rarity, because the Parliament weakened the authority of the President by the next major amendment of the Constitution (constitutional law No. 90/2001 Coll.), and so it relativized the significance of the previous decisions of the Constitutional Court regarding to this matter.[7]

[7] Another interesting case within the abstract control of constitutionality where the Constitutional Court interpreted the paragraph of the Constitution *prima facie* in conflict with the normative text of the Constitution is decision nº PL. ÚS 38/03. The task of the court was to decide on the conformity of the statute that implemented charge for "services connected with health care" with art. 40 of the Constitution. This article states that "the citizens shall have the right to free health care and medical equipment for disabilities on the basis of medical insurance under the terms to be laid down by a law." A majority of the Constitutional Court decided that the word "free" does not imply that health care is *gratis* (cost free), because there is an obligatory medical insurance.

1. *Effect of the Ruling of the Constitutional Court Regarding the Unconformity Between Legal Regulations*

The act on the organization of the Constitutional Court of the Slovak Republic, the Proceedings before the Constitutional Court, and the status of its Judges[8] ("act on the Constitutional Court") also includes the issue of the *inter partes* effect of the finding of the Constitutional Court on unconformity of legal regulation with the Constitution, that is, the influence of such a decision on a judgment issued in a civil, administrative, and criminal proceeding on the basis of legal regulation that was later found to be in inconformity with the Constitution.

Paragraph 41b of the mentioned act states that if a judgment issued in a criminal proceeding based on the regulation in inconformity with the Constitution has not been executed, then the ruling of the Constitutional Court on inconformity is a reason for a retrial. The valid decisions issued in civil and administrative proceedings remains unaffected, but obligations imposed by such a decision cannot be subject to enforcement.

Thanks to the fact that legal provisions do not specify the effects of a ruling on inconformity of statutes with the Constitution on cases before the courts that are not yet validly decided., a dispute concerning such a effects arose. Namely, it was dispute about effects of the ruling No. PL. ÚS 38/03 on inconformity of § 38 (4) of the medical insurance act with the Constitution.[9] Different general courts applied the above mentioned ruling in different ways according to (i) the substantive effect of the ruling No. PL. ÚS 38/03 as to the cases that *have not been* validly decided and § 38 (4) of the act on medical insurance should be applied to them, and (ii) the

The majority also said that the distinction between health care and services connected with care is reasonable. But a minority of the court criticized the majority in its dissenting opinion: "As to our opinion, wording of the art. 40, second sentence, of the Constitution does not allow the legislator to impose any charge (no matter how it is called) on health care based on medical insurance (for natural persons, policy holders).That is to say the term 'for free' used in the art. 40 of the Constitution does not allow (by its substance) any extent or scale of exemption from charges. . . . We proceed from the assumption that the Constitutional Court shall follow evident and strict meaning of the words which they undoubtedly have (without the need to interpret or amend them) have one."

8 Act nº 38/1993 Coll.

9 Act nº 273/1994 Coll.

restitution of validity and legal effect of the previous wording of § 38 (4) of the act on medical insurance.[10]

Even single Senates of the Constitutional Court did not have the same opinion on substantive effects of the ruling No. PL. ÚS 38/03 as they decided on complaints according to art. 127 of the Constitution when complainants were pleading infringement of their fundamental rights by application of § 38 (4) by a court. That is why the Constitutional Court used its competence to decide on the unification of different legal opinions of the Senates (§ 6 of the Act on Constitutional Court) within the Plenary Session in PLz. ÚS 1/06, and it acted as positive legislator.

In fact, the Constitutional Court had to decide whether it would protect the legal certainty and thus not allow the retroactive effect of the ruling (decision on *ex nunc* effect) or protect the principle of constitutionality and not allow any application of the regulation known to be unconstitutional (decision on *ex tunc* effect). Not only the principle of legal certainty but also the principle of constitutionality are fundamental principles of rule of law, and thus the Constitutional Court faced an uneasy task. One of the constitutional justices later said that he felt as if he were between Scylla and Charybdis. Finally, the Constitutional Court decided to protect the principle of constitutionality also because it is inadmissible to apply the principle of legal certainty absolutely, and it decided that the mentioned ruling has *ex tunc* substantive effect. It means that judge of the ordinary court must not apply regulation that is in inconformity with the Constitution. The Constitutional Court, by doing so *de facto*, set up a doctrine on the substantial effects of the rulings on inconformity between legal regulation, which is not yet deeply developed.[11]

10 The latter question was answered by the Constitutional Court in a simple way, because the court held that as to the Act on Constitutional Court: "the loss of effect or validity of legal provission on the basis of ruling of the Constitutional Court, does not entail renewal of the validity of legal regulations annulled by it; if on the other hand a legal provision is merely amended, then the previous legal provision shall be considered valid in the wording prior to this amendments" (§ 41a (3) of the Act on the Constitutional Court).

11 A little bit more "sophisticated" doctrine advocates, for example, the Constitutional Court of the Czech Republic. To put it simply, the court prefers *ex tunc* substantive effects of the rulings on inconformity of legal provisions with Constitution on the proceedings that are not validly decided only if the *ex nunc* effect would infringe the fundamental rights and freedoms of aggrieved persons. It means that a judge of an ordinary court can apply unconstitutional provision if the fundamental rights and freedoms will not be infringed. See, e.g., the decision of the Constitutional Court of the Czech Republic nº IV.ÚS 1777/07 and other decisions mentioned there.

We can summarize the situation by quoting III. ÚS 164/07:[12] "The act on the Constitutional Court distinguishes effects of the rulings of the Constitutional Court on inconformity of the legal regulations on proceedings before the courts and other bodies of public power in the individual issues on those that has become validly decided before the promulgation of the ruling (§ 41b of the Act on the Constitutional Court) and those that has not been validly decided before the promulgation of the ruling." In the first case, the ruling has *ex nunc* effect, and in the second case, it has *ex tunc* effect. Despite this, we can find some decisions of the Constitutional Court that curtly claim general *ex nunc* effects of the rulings of Constitutional Court according to art. 125 of the Constitution (e.g., PL.ÚS 15/08).

Regarding the issue of the effects of the ruling of the Constitutional Court on inconformity of legal provisions with the Constitution, it is important to point out certain *ultra vires* excesses of the Constitutional Court in the forementioned ruling on inconformity of the act No. 458/2003 Coll. on establishing the Special Court and the Office of the Special Prosecution, with the Constitution (decision No. PL. ÚS 17/08). In the verdict the court claimed that this ruling on inconformity of the statute with the Constitution does not become a reason for a retrial as to the judgments of the Special Court in criminal proceedings that have not been executed. But it is in direct conflict with the mentioned wording of § 41b of the Act on the Constitutional Court.

III. CONCRETE CONTROL OF CONSTITUTIONALITY

The constitutional basis of concrete control of constitutionality is formed by art. 127 of the Constitution, which in para. 1 states that "the Constitutional Court shall decide on complaints of natural persons and legal persons if they are pleading the infringement of their fundamental rights and freedoms, or human rights and fundamental freedoms resulting from the international treaty which has been ratified by the Slovak Republic and promulgated in the manner laid down by law, save another court shall decide on protection of these rights and freedoms."

The law that is in force now was introduced by amendment of the Constitution by constitutional law No. 90/2001 Coll. In connection with the theme of this report, a very interesting situation occurred in connection with the entry into force of mentioned amendment, and the Constitutional Court

12 This decision fully respects doctrine of the decision PLz. ÚS 1/06.

stepped into the position of positive legislator to save the existence of concrete control of constitutionality (defined as protection of constitutional rights and freedoms of natural persons and legal persons).

Constitutional law N° 90/2001 Coll. entered into force on January 1, 2002, in the part that amended art. 127 and thus introduced the complaint as an effective means of protecting fundamental rights and freedoms. Meanwhile, the previous means of protection – the petition under art. 130, para. 3,[13] of the Constitution, was repealed by this law, with effect from July 1, 2001.

Thus, from July 1, 2001, until December 31, 2001, there did not exist a national means by which natural or legal persons could plead the infringement of their fundamental rights and freedoms before the Constitutional Court. The Constitutional Court filled this vacuum of protection by extensive interpretation of art. 124 of the Constitution, which states that "the Constitutional Court shall be an independent judicial authority vested with the mandate to protect constitutionality." The court deduced from this article that it has the competence to deal with individual motions by natural persons and legal persons that are pleading infringement of their constitutional rights (no matter how they were called – petition or complaint) even from July 1, 2001, until December 31, 2001. The Constitutional Court argued: "The Constitutional Court is according to the art. 124 of the Constitution the judicial authority for protection of constitutionality. This article constitutes the competence of the Constitutional Court to protect mainly fundamental rights and freedoms guaranteed by the Constitution. The Constitutional Court is led by this imperative even after the nullification of the paragraphs about petition (from July 1, 2001) until the entry into force of art. 127 of the Constitution (January 1, 2002) and so it is entitled and obliged to provide individual protection of fundamental rights and freedoms while the court also relies on art. 1 of the Constitution, which states that Slovak Republic is the state governed by the rule of law. That is why fundamental rights and freedoms cannot be even temporarily deprived of judicial protection as to the art. 124 of the Constitution in connection with other articles that guarantee fundamental rights and freedoms."[14]

13 This means of protection were hold ineffective by the European Court of Human Rights (ECtHR), which is why there was no need to exhaust themt. And so a plaintiff from the Slovak Republic could "skip" the Constitutional Court of Slovak Republic. See, e.g., *Bánošová v. Slovak Republic*, n° 38798/98, April 27, 2000.

14 Decision of the Constitutional Court n° III. ÚS 117/01. The court similarly justifies its decision in III. ÚS 124/01: "In the period from July 1, 2001 to December 31, 2001 the competence of the

The Constitutional Court thus acted as if the institution of petition had been repealed not from July 1, 2001, but from January 1, 2002!

Also, some other decisions of the Constitutional Court within the abstract control of constitutionality can prove that the Constitutional Court interprets the Constitution in such a manner that it *de facto* forms and complements constitutional institutions. We provide at least a few examples. From the sphere of the right to personal freedom and physical integrity, for example, decisions I. ÚS 6/02, I. ÚS 100/04, II. ÚS 111/08, and II. ÚS 8/96 are relevant.

In the first of those cases, the Constitutional Court decided on the violation of the complainants rights according to art. 17 of the Constitution[15] and art. 5 of the Convention on Protection of Human Rights and Fundamental Freedoms ("Convention").[16] The matter of the case was whether the complainant was in detention without a required decision of the court. The Code of Criminal Procedures that was valid in the decisive period did not require a separate decision of the court on the extension of the duration of the pretrial detention if a claim was filed (thus, the detention could be extended by a sole decision on prosecution). The Constitutional Court played the role of the positive legislator when interpreting the wording of the Constitution "detention can be imposed only on the grounds and for the period provided by a law and determined by the court." It held that the quoted provision means that a required decision of the court ("determined by the court") cannot be the decision that charges person with a crime but only the separate decision on the extension of the duration of the detention. That is why, regardless of the wording of the Code of Criminal Procedures, the Constitutional Court did not allow "automatic" extension of duration of the detention on the basis of decision on prosecution.[17]

Constitutional Court is founded on the art. 124 in connection with art. 1 of the Constitution. It is so in order to provide protection of constitutionality including protection of guaranteed fundamental rights and freedoms of natural persons and legal persons." See also II. ÚS 80/01, III. ÚS 100/01, III. ÚS 116/01.

15 As to art. 17 of the Constitution, personal liberty of every individual shall be guaranteed (para. 1), no one shall be deprived of liberty safe for reasons and by means laid down by a law (part of para. 2) and detention can be imposed only on the grounds and for the period provided by a law and determined by the court (para. 5).

16 The Convention is in Slovak Republic promulgated by Act n° 209/1992 Coll.

17 The Constitutional Court held that it "took the dissimilarity of the statutory provisions into account. But it also took into account that the ordinary courts are obliged to interpret and apply respective statutes on the concrete cases in conformity with the Constitution and international treaties on human rights and they have to do it in such a way that they will pay attention to

In 2004, the Constitutional Court decided on the complaint pleading the violation of art. 17 of the Constitution and art. 5 of the Convention. The dispute concerned the fact that courts have not examined his application to be released on warranty which he submitted together with the application for release from arrest (I. ÚS 100/04). The Code of Criminal Procedures that was in force at the time did not permit release from arrest based on warranty in the case of remand for collusion, which was applicable to the plaintiff. The courts applied the valid Code of Criminal Procedures. But the Constitutional Court stressed that the international treaties that provide a greater scope of constitutional rights and freedoms shall have precedence over national laws (art. 154c of the Constitution) and it held that the courts should consider art. 5 of the Convention and the relevant case law of ECtHR. The case law of ECtHR became consistent as allowed exemption of some crimes from the possibility of release from arrest on warranty. The ECtHR maintains that national law cannot exempt some crimes or some reasons for detention from the possibility of release for warranty. It means that courts in Slovak Republic have to apply the Convention preferentially (in spite of the wording of the Code of Criminal Procedures), and so they *de facto* have to follow also judicial precedents – i.e., case law of ECtHR.. This was the explicit recognition of the fact that the judicial power may be a positive legislator because it can eliminate the application of valid national law with legal force below the Constitution. It may do so through certain and specific interpretation of constitutional provisions (and the Convention) exhibited in its judicial precedent within a concrete control of constitutionality.

The next case we focus on is *Labsi* (II. ÚS 111/08). Mr. Labsi filled the complaint pleading the infringement of the right not to be subject to torture or cruel, inhuman, or degrading treatment or punishment, guaranteed by art. 3 of the Convention and art. 16 para. 2 of the Constitution. The mentioned right was, in his opinion, violated by a decision of the Supreme Court of the Slovak Republic (Supreme Court), which authorized his extradition to Algeria for prosecution. Based on the court's decision, Mr. Labsi was to be extradited to Algeria, but as to the Code of Criminal Procedures the Minister of Justice could subsequently decide that he will not permit an extradition in the case of existence of a reasonable concern that the criminal proceedings in a country which requested extradition does not follow the principles stated in

effective satisfaction of fundamental rights guaranteed by the Constitution" (I. ÚS 6/02). The Constitutional Court widely relied on the case law of ECtHR as it decided this case.

art. 3 and art. 6 of the Convention.[18] The valid Code of Criminal Procedures did not (and does not) give the court that decides on the authorization of extradition (the regional courts and the Supreme Court) the competence to consider a danger of torture or inhuman treatment of the person, even if those facts can be considered by the Minister of Justice in deciding whether to permit extradition.[19] The Constitutional Court, in spite of the provisions of the Code of Criminal Procedures, stated that "ordinary courts are bound by norms on human rights when they decide on authorisation of extradition. In other words, the conditions of authorisation of extradition (the substantive extraditional law) which are considered by ordinary courts (as their obligation) are extended by the condition of conformity with human rights. The core of conformity with human right is created by the text of the Convention and respect case law of the European Court of Human Rights."

This means that, even if conditions of authorization of extradition are enumerated in the Code of Criminal Procedures, the ordinary courts are obliged to consider the danger of violation of human rights because, according to the Constitutional Court, "the literal interpretation and the classical conception of enumeration cannot always stand the conception of direct applicability of the Constitution and international treaties on human rights." That is why the Constitutional Court held that the Supreme Court violated the human rights of Mr. Labsi and found the doctrine of the court in the field of extradition, which was later followed.

The issue of the case No. II. ÚS 8/96 was the petition on the infringement of the right to enter and leave the territory of the Slovak Republic freely, which was guaranteed in art. 23, para. 4, of the Constitution. The Constitutional Court interpreted this right in such a way that it deduced an obligation of state bodies to actively participate in its protection. According to the Constitutional Court, it does not only mean that state bodies are not allowed to create obstacles to free return of a citizen to the territory of Slovak Republic but also that those bodies are obliged to actively help a citizen to return to the territory. And so the bodies of the Slovak Republic (e.g., the Ministry of Foreign Affairs of the Slovak Republic) had an obligation to help the citizen return to the Slovak Republic because he was

[18] See § 509 and § 510 of the Code of Criminal Procedures (Act n° 301/2005 Coll.)

[19] *Id.*

kept abroad against his will, even if this obligation was not enumerated in the law and they did not have the explicit authority to do so.[20]

We analyze one more example of the case (II. ÚS 5/03) in which the Constitutional Court of the Slovak Republic formed law – Act No. 185/2002 Coll. on the Judiciary Council of the Slovak Republic ("Act on Judiciary Council") became a positive legislator. The Constitutional Court was to decide on the complaint of the candidate for the Chief Justice who lost. The candidate was pleading infringement of the right to access the elected and public offices under equal conditions guaranteed in art. 30, para. 4, of the Constitution by the resolution of the Judicial Council of the Slovak Republic ("the Judicial Council"), which certified the results of the election of the Chief Justice. This resolution was also a relevant proposal addressed to the President to appoint the successful candidate for the Chief Justice. Unlike the candidate who won, the candidate who lost was not a member of the Judiciary Council and so was at a disadvantage before and during the election. The winner of this election could (and did) vote for himself. The given action of the Judiciary Council was not explicitly in conflict with the Act on the Judiciary Council, since also the Constitutional Court said that "the Constitution, Act on the Judiciary Council and other law concerning courts and judges do not embrace detailed provisions about procedure of proposal and appointment of the Chief of Justice. This can be considered to be lacuna (loophole) in the laws or the delegation of this matter on the Judiciary Council (as a demonstration of its independence and autonomy." In contrast, the loopholes in the law do not liberate the Judiciary Council from the obligation to respect fundamental rights and freedoms and so the Judiciary Council "was not liberated from an obligation to choose and follow the procedure of a proposal of candidate for the Chief Justice that is undoubtedly in conformity with the Constitution, on the contrary, this obligation was even strengthened." It means that, even if the Act on the Judiciary Council allows a member of Judiciary Council to vote for himself for the elections for Chief Justice, the Constitutional Court formed and indirectly amended the wording of this act (and *de facto* the wording of the Constitution) in a way that such a procedure is not permitted.

[20] This case was of the kidnapped son of the former President of the Slovak Republic, Michal Kováč Jr. Michal Kováč Jr. wanted to return to the territory of the Republic, but state bodies did not help him to do so. The offenders stayed unknown because this act was amnestied by Prime Minister Vladimír Mečiar, who exercised some power of the President when the office of President had been vacant.

Concerning the methods of interpretation the Constitutional Court employs, the widest occasion to become a positive legislator is provided by teleological interpretation and argumentation. In 2005, the Constitutional Court used teleological interpretation 127 times and argumentation with principles 292 times.[21] The court often justified its decision by principle of subsidiarity[22] (153 times); principle of legal certainty (30 times); and principles of rightful procedure, equality before the law and *denegatio justitiae* (each 10 times). Even though the case law of the Constitutional Court digresses some from the text of the Constitution and other laws, we can sum up (on the basis of the examples we provided here) that the court does so mostly to fill the loopholes in the laws and to protect principles of the rule of law.

21 See PRUSÁK, J. et al.: *Sociologicko-právny výskum prameňov práva a justifikácia súdnych rozhodnutí* in Acta Universitatis Tyrnaviensis, Iuridica: ročenka Právnickej fakulty Trnavskej univerzity v. Trnave 2007. 4. – 1. ed. – Bratislava: Iura Edition, 2008, p. 122 ff. (PRUSÁK, J. et al., *Sociological and Juridical Research of Sources of Law and Judicial Justification*).

22 That is, the Constitutional Court is not a court of appeal, and so it acts only if ordinary courts are violating fundamental human rights.

SWITZERLAND

CONSTITUTIONAL COURTS AS POSITIVE LEGISLATORS

Tobias Jaag [*]
Professor, University of Zürich
tobias.jaag@rwi.uzh.ch

I. INTRODUCTION

1. *Courts as Legislators in General*

This report examines the legal situation in Switzerland in view of an international comparative law study on constitutional courts as positive legislators.

One speaks of a judge or court as a legislator whenever no legislative rule exists for a question arising within the scope of court proceedings. In such cases, the court must close the gap in the law. Pursuant to Article 1, paragraph 2, of the Swiss Civil Code, in such cases "the judge shall decide according to customary law and, in the absence of such customary law, according to the rule he would establish as a legislator."[1]

* Prof. Dr. iur., LL.M., University of Zurich, Switzerland. I acknowledge the excellent help and support provided by Dr. iur. Julia Hänni in the preparation of this text and by Rebecca Brunner-Peters, J.D., in the translation of the text from German to English. – This article was first published in 2010 in Lukas Heckendorn Urscheler/Annelot Peters (eds.), *Swiss Reports Presented at the XVIIIth International Congress of Comparative Law*, Publications of the Swiss Institute of Comparative Law 66, Geneva/Zürich/Basel (Schulthess), p. 221 et seq. (www.schulthess.com). It is republished with the permission of Schulthess éditions romandes

1 Swiss Civil Code of December 10, 1907 ("ZGB"; SR 210). Cf. Arthur Meier-Hayoz, Art. 1, in Berner Kommentar zum schweizerischen Privatrecht, Band I, 1. Abteilung, Einleitung, Art. 1-10 ZGB, Berne 1966, 78 et seq.; Hutter, 45 et seq. In terms of case law, e.g., Decisions of the Federal Supreme Court (BGE) 131/2005 I 321, 329; 127/2001 II 69, 78.

The power, or even the obligation, to close the gap – which is available to all courts – results from the prohibition against the denial of justice. Although the provision of law is set out in the Civil Code, it applies to all areas of law; Article 1, paragraph 2, of the Civil Code reflects a general principle of law.[2]

A gap may result because a problem was not recognized in connection with the adoption of the provision and, for that reason, was not regulated (original gap), or because the need for the regulation did not arise until after the provision was adopted (subsequent gap).[3] No gap in the law exists in the case of qualified silence in the statute, that is, when a rule has been intentionally omitted.[4]

As to the extent to which it is permissible to close a gap in the law where a legislative rule exists but would lead to an offensive result in the specific case of application (pseudo gap), there are differing opinions. Based on the view gaining support in Switzerland, the closure of a gap is permissible in each case in which a statute, contrary to plan, is incomplete.[5] However, the precept to apply federal statutes takes precedence.[6]

The closure of a gap may occur not only at the legislative but also at the constitutional level. In the latter case, one speaks of constitutional development. This is primarily carried out by the Federal Supreme Court; it is of paramount importance in Switzerland.[7]

2. *The Federal Supreme Court as a Constitutional Court*

A. Judicial Review in General

In contrast to numerous other States, Switzerland does not have any special constitutional court. Instead, the Federal Supreme Court is the highest court for civil, criminal, administrative, and constitutional matters.[8]

2 As to the closure of gaps in public law, cf. in particular Rhinow, 37 ff; Häfelin/Haller/Keller, N. 137 et seq.; Hutter, 91 et seq.

3 Hans Michael Riemer, Die Einleitungsartikel des Schweizerischen Zivilgesetzbuches, 2nd ed., Berne 2003, § 4 N. 76 et seq. In terms of case law, cf., e.g., BGE 101/1975 II 11, 12.

4 Cf. BGE 130/2004 II 137, 144 et seq.; Rhinow, 40.

5 Häfelin/Haller/Keller, N. 141 et seq.; BGE 128/2002 I 34, 40 et seq.; Administrative Court Aargau, in ZBl 88/1987, 552, 556 et seq.

6 Art. 190 of the Swiss Constitution of April 18, 1999 (Const.; SR 101). Cf. *infra*, I.B.2.

7 Cf. Biaggini, Richterrecht; Chiariello, 11 et seq.

8 Art. 188 para. 1 Const.

Since 2007, the Supreme Court has been handling constitutional issues in connection with the public law appeal, the public law action, and the subsidiary constitutional appeal.[9] Until 2006, it dealt with the constitutional law appeal, the administrative court appeal, and constitutional and administrative actions.[10]

In addition to the Supreme Court, other courts may also act as constitutional courts, such as the Federal Administrative Court and cantonal courts.[11] The Federal Assembly (the Federal Parliament, that is, the National Council and the Council of States) is also responsible to a limited extent for constitutional review, for example, in connection with the guarantee of the cantonal constitutions.[12] The Federal Parliament and the cantonal parliaments also review popular initiatives in terms of their constitutionality.[13] Even administrative authorities sporadically perform duties of constitutional review, particularly within the scope of the review of regulations of the cantons and municipalities (abstract judicial review) and of the control of norms in connection with the application of law (concrete judicial review).[14] Therefore, judicial review is not just limited to the Federal Supreme Court; a diffuse system of judicial review applies in Switzerland.

Switzerland is also subject to the jurisdiction of the European Court of Human Rights (ECtHR), which – on request by individuals – reviews the compatibility of decisions of the Swiss Federal Supreme Court with the European Human Rights Convention (EHRC). The case law of the ECtHR has a decisive influence on Swiss legislation and case law.[15]

B. Limitations on Judicial Review

The Federal Supreme Court is not a comprehensive constitutional court. Its authority to enforce the constitution is limited in different respects.

9 Arts. 82 et seq., 113 et seq., and 120 of the Law on the Swiss Federal Supreme Court (BGG) of June 17, 2005 (SR 173.110). Cf. the legal commentaries on the BGG of Niggli/Uebersax/Wiprächtiger as well as of Seiler/von Werdt/Güngerich.

10 Arts. 83, 84 et seq., 97 et seq., and 116 et seq. of the Federal Law on the Organization of the Federal Judiciary of December 16, 1943 (no longer in effect). As to the constitutional appeal, cf. in particular Kälin, Beschwerde.

11 For examples, cf. Hänni, 595 et seq.

12 Art. 51 para. 1 Const.

13 For the federal level, Art. 139 para. 3 Const.

14 Cf. Biaggini, Normenkontrolle 174 et seq.

15 Cf. Haller, Constitution N. 2, 461.

Resolutions of the Federal Assembly cannot be contested by means of any legal action whatsoever. Neither the political parties nor defeated members of Parliament or private individuals may submit decisions of the Federal Parliament to the Supreme Court for a ruling. In contrast to other States, political disputes in Switzerland may be carried on before the Federal Supreme Court only to a limited extent.[16]

In general, federal statutes (and public international law) are precluded not only by an abstract control of norms but also by indirect (concrete) judicial review. Under Article 190 of the Federal Constitution, the provisions of law adopted by the Federal Assembly that were subject to an optional referendum must be applied by courts and authorities, even if they are in contravention of the Federal Constitution.[17] Therefore, enforcement of the supremacy of the Federal Constitution is not ensured.[18] Thus, the principle of direct democracy prevails over the rule of law.

According to case law, the Federal Court is also in part precluded from reviewing cantonal constitutions. Because the Federal Assembly is responsible for the review and guarantee of the provisions of cantonal constitutions, the Supreme Court rejects any abstract control of norms of the cantonal constitutions, and a concrete review takes place only with respect to federal law that has been adopted after the decision on the guarantee of the Federal Assembly.[19]

3. *The Federal Supreme Court as Legislator*

A. Negative Legislation

Whenever the role of the constitutional court as legislator is discussed, the primary question relates to the extent to which supplements and amendments to legislation may be carried out within the scope of judicial review.

[16] Cf. Biaggini, Normenkontrolle 177; Haller, Verfassungsfortbildung 5; Haller, Bundesgericht 179 et seq. In general, as regards legislation on the federal level, there is no abstract control of norms; this also applies with respect to ordinances of the Federal Council and of the administration (cf. *infra*, C.1).

[17] Cf. Haller, Art. 113 N. 142 et seq.; Haller, Constitution nº 561 et seq. The *Etoilauto* case represents a vivid example from the case law of the Federal Supreme Court; cf. Kaufmann, 139 et seq.

[18] As to the exception in connection with the European Human Rights Convention (EHRC), cf. *infra*, III.D.

[19] BGE 111/1985 Ia 239 et seq.; 116/1990 Ia 359, 366 et seq.; 118/1992 Ia 124, 126 et seq. Haller, Constitution N. 119.

The constitutional court may engage in legislative functions in a negative or a positive way. One speaks of negative legislation if the constitutional court is able to annul legislative provisions.[20] This is always possible if the court has authority to undertake abstract control of norms, that is, to review legislation in terms of its conformity with superior law, regardless of a specific case of application, based on direct actions to control the constitutionality of statutes. If an appeal is upheld within the scope of an abstract control of norms, the court annuls the contested legislative provision. According to the currently prevailing view, the annulment applies only prospectively (*ex nunc*), not retroactively (*ex tunc*).[21] An abstract control of norms exists in Switzerland only with respect to cantonal legislation (with the exception of the cantonal constitution),[22] not with respect to statutes and ordinances at the federal level.

The same effect as in connection with the annulment of provisions of law within the scope of the abstract control of norms can be achieved in connection with the indirect (concrete or specific) control of norms, when a legislative rule is reviewed by means of a preliminary question in connection with its application in an individual case and is determined to be unlawful. In these cases, although the unlawful norm is not formally annulled by the court, application of the norm will be rejected; the norm is declared unconstitutional, but not annulled.[23] Through the rejection of application in the individual case, the norm will be *de facto* deprived of effect in all future cases as well. The legislator will thereby be required to repeal or amend the provision.

The annulment or refusal to apply legal norms, however, often results not merely in negative legislation. Through the annulment of individual provisions, the rules that have been upheld may take on a different meaning. If, for example, exemption clauses are annulled, the scope of application will usually be expanded as a result, and the law will thereby be transfigured. This is tantamount, at least in terms of result, to positive legislation.[24]

[20] Cf. Rütsche, 275 et seq., 281 et seq. Critical as to the concept of negative legislation, Biaggini, Normenkontrolle 171. As to the annulment of norms by the Federal Supreme Court in general, cf. Gerber, 105 et seq.; Camprubi, 143 et seq.

[21] Strehle, 95 et seq.; Haller, Art. 113 N. 129; Kälin, Beschwerde 398 et seq.; Haefliger, 360 et seq.

[22] For an example, cf. BGE 123/1997 I 112 relating to a Geneva law on the removal and transplantation of organs and tissues.

[23] As mentioned in I.B.2., under Art. 190 Const., this is not permitted with respect to federal statutes.

[24] Rütsche, 282 et seq.

The annulment of unconstitutional rules is not suitable to restore the lawful status if the annulment results in a worsening, rather than an improvement, of the legal situation.[25]

B. Positive Legislation

One speaks of positive legislation on the part of the constitutional court when a legal norm is capable not only of being annulled but also of being modified by the court, and/or when the court has the authority to close gaps in the law.[26] This is the main issue of the present contribution.

4. *Federal and Cantonal Law*

The Swiss Federal Supreme Court deals with legal disputes arising both under federal law and under the law of the cantons (constituent states). The power of review, however, is not the same.

As mentioned already, under Article 190 of the Swiss Constitution, there is a duty to apply federal statutes even if they contravene the Federal Constitution or public international law;[27] in Switzerland, federal legislation is not subject to judicial review. The duty to apply, however, does not preclude the Federal Supreme Court from criticizing a legislative rule and thereby signaling to the legislator that an amendment of the law would be required.[28] This constitutional clause also does not preclude the closing of a gap in the law.

In contrast, the Federal Supreme Court is permitted to undertake both an abstract review and a specific review of cantonal statutes in terms of their conformity with superior law.[29] This is the case even if the cantonal rule corresponds to a rule under federal law.[30] Judicial review in Switzerland is, thus, to a large extent limited to cantonal legislation and decisions.

[25] Rütsche, 284 et seq. Cf. *infra*, II.B.

[26] Rütsche, 288 et seq.

[27] *Supra*, I.B.2. Cf. the exception with respect to violations of the EHRC *infra* III.D.

[28] Cf., e.g., BGE 103/1977 Ia 53, 55; Haller, Art. 113 N. 206; Häfelin/Haller/Keller, nº 2089.

[29] Art. 82(b) of the BGG.

[30] BGE 130/2004 I 26, 33; different result: BGE 106/1980 Ib 102 et seq.

II. REFUSAL OF THE FEDERAL SUPREME COURT TO ACT AS POSITIVE LEGISLATOR

1. *Principle*

The Swiss Federal Supreme Court repeatedly emphasizes that it cannot issue rules in place of the legislator. The Supreme Court – like all other courts – is not a legislative body: "Lié par le principe de l'effet cassatoire du recours de droit public, le Tribunal fédéral ne peut modifier lui-même le texte de la loi cantonale."[31] This applies not only in connection with the specific review of rules but also within the scope of the abstract control of norms with respect to cantonal legislation.

Under the former constitutional appeal to the Federal Supreme Court,[32] the competence of the Court was limited to the power to annul the contested provision in the event that the appeal against cantonal legislation was upheld. It is true that, based on current law, the Supreme Court may also issue a decision replacing the one against which the appeal was directed.[33] Nonetheless, at least in complex cases, the Supreme Court will, if it upholds an appeal, continue to remand such cases to the prior or the first instance. On the one hand, the Federal Court would not be in a position to regulate complex issues.[34] On the other hand, if more than one regulatory option is available, the Court rule would also encroach on the discretionary power, and thus the autonomy, of the relevant Canton.[35]

2. *Examples*

Probably the most famous example for the refusal of the Federal Court to assume the role of legislator is the *Hegetschweiler* case.[36] On the basis of the appeal of a married couple, the Supreme Court concluded that a cantonal regulation relating to income and property taxes for married couples was unconstitutional because married couples owed higher taxes than unmarried couples living together in the same household having similar financial

31 BGE 110/1984 Ia 99, 105. Cf. also BGE 125/1999 I 104, 107.

32 Cf., e.g., BGE 118/1992 Ia 64, 69; Auer, Effets 560 et seq.; Haefliger, 361 et seq.; Camprubi, 143 et seq.

33 Art. 107 para. 2 BGG.

34 BGE 117/1991 V 318, 324 et seq. Cf. Rütsche, 279 et seq.

35 Kälin, Beschwerde 397; von Werdt, in Handkommentar BGG, Art. 107 nº 11; Rütsche, 281.

36 BGE 110/1984 Ia 7. Cf. e.g., Hänni, 593 et seq.; Auer, Caprices; Auer, Effet 562 et seq.; Weber-Dürler, 340 et seq.; Teygeler, 49 et seq.

means; this constituted a breach of the equal treatment precept.[37] The subject matter of the appeal for an abstract control of norms was a new rule that actually represented, in substance, an improvement over the previous legal situation. If the Supreme Court had annulled the contested rule, the former rule would have again entered into effect, unless the Court were to decide on a substitute rule. It refused to do so, referring to the nature of the former constitutional appeal that was limited to the annulment of rules and decisions. The Supreme Court rejected the appeal and limited itself to stating that the contested rule was not in full conformity with the Constitution; in this manner, the cantonal legislator was asked to remedy the unconstitutional situation. For the couple that appealed, such an outcome of the proceedings was most dissatisfactory.[38]

In another case, the Supreme Court found that a cantonal regulation imposing a lower retirement age for women than for men was in breach of the constitutional right to equal treatment of women and men. The Supreme Court, however, left it at that, reasoning that the cantonal legislator needed time to establish the constitutional status. The equal treatment precept was included in the Federal Constitution in 1981, and the decision was issued in 1986.[39]

The Supreme Court likewise protected the complaint of a federal official that a rule permitting only women, but not men, to take early retirement after thirty-five years of service violated the right to equal treatment of women and men. The Court did not view itself as having competence, however, to issue a correct rule; the petition of the federal official for permission to take early retirement was therefore rejected.[40] In a similar case relating to the equal treatment of boys and girls during school lessons, the Court explicitly held: "it would, however, be out of the question for the Supreme Court, on its own initiative, to create a rule in lieu of the cantonal legislator."[41]

During the past years, several cantonal voting systems have been held to be unconstitutional because the equal treatment of the voters (equal weight of each individual vote) was not guaranteed.[42] In these cases, the Supreme

37 Now Art. 8 para. 1 Const.

38 Biaggini, 171 et seq.

39 Sup.Ct. in ZBl 87/1986, 482 et seq.

40 BGE 109/1983 Ib 86, 88 et seq.; cf. Haefliger, 95.

41 Sup.Ct. in ZBl 86/1985, 492, 495 (translation from the German original). Cf. Weber-Dürler, 339 et seq.; Hänni, 591 et seq.

42 BGE 131/2005 I 74 et seq.; 129/2003 I 185 et seq. Cf. Bernhard Rütsche, Grenzen der Verfassungsgerichtsbarkeit. Besprechung von BGE 129 I 185, ius.full 2003, 160 et seq.

Court contented itself with declaring that the voting systems were unconstitutional and asking the cantonal legislators to amend the rule that was objected to.[43]

Such judgments are decisions with an appeal to the legislator.[44]

III. THE FEDERAL SUPREME COURT AS POSITIVE LEGISLATOR

1. *In General*

Even though the Federal Supreme Court, under established case law, refuses to function as a legislator, the Court has nonetheless in numerous areas taken on the function of a constitution maker and legislator, not always in a formal fashion, but on a *de facto* basis. This can be illustrated by various examples.[45]

At the forefront is the recognition of fundamental rights that were not listed in the former Federal Constitution of 1874.[46] The rules on political rights at the cantonal level are decisively shaped by the case law of the Federal Supreme Court. Through a generous interpretation of Article 4 of the former Federal Constitution, the Supreme Court developed numerous procedural rights before these were expressly enshrined in the Constitution or in a law. In the area of the delimitation of competence and avoidance of conflicts in the federal State, the Supreme Court is likewise allotted the role of a legislator. Finally, in specific subject areas, the Court has developed rules because corresponding legislative regulations were lacking and in part continue to be lacking today, as, for example, in the area of expropriation.

2. *Fundamental Rights*

A. New Fundamental Rights

The Federal Constitution of 1874 only included a few fundamental rights. Therefore, the question arose as to whether the constitutional catalog of fundamental rights was exhaustive. Constitutional law doctrine took the view

43 BGE 131/2005 I 74, 84 et seq.; 129/2003 I 185, 205 et seq. Also cf. *infra*, III.C.

44 BGE 131/2005 I 74, 85. Cf. Rütsche, 298 et seq.

45 Cf. also Rütsche, 289 et seq.; Chiariello, 11 et seq.

46 Federal Constitution of May 24, 1874 (Const. 1874; replaced by the Federal Constitution of 1999 as per January 1, 2000).

quite early on that the Federal Constitution only included, by way of illustration, the fundamental rights that were of practical significance at the time of the formation of the Constitution. It was assumed that other, unwritten fundamental rights existed to the extent that there was a practical need for the same.

The Federal Supreme Court followed this doctrine.[47] In 1960, it recognized the guarantee of property as an unwritten fundamental right under the Federal Constitution.[48] This guarantee was then embodied in the Federal Constitution in 1969, together with the federal competence for purposes of land use planning.[49]

The Federal Constitution of 1874 expressly guaranteed the freedom of the press. In 1961, the Federal Supreme Court generally recognized *freedom of expression* as an unwritten constitutional right.[50] In 1970, recognition of freedom to assemble followed, which, together with the freedom of expression, also encompasses the right to hold public demonstrations.[51] However, the Supreme Court rejected the freedom to demonstrate as an independent unwritten constitutional right.[52] Later, the freedom of science and the freedom of artistic expression,[53] as well as the protection of editorial secrecy,[54] were recognized as independent, unwritten rights under the Constitution.

In 1963, the Federal Supreme Court recognized for the first time, as an unwritten constitutional right, the right to personal freedom within the meaning of a right to physical and mental integrity.[55] The recognition of the right to personal freedom by the Supreme Court served, for example, to increase the minimum time contemplated in a prison ordinance for walks by prisoners.[56] Within the scope of proceedings concerning the detention of foreigners, the Supreme Court concluded that the Swiss legal system did not sufficiently protect the right of asylum seekers to protection of their freedom.

47 Jörg Paul Müller, in Kommentar aBV, Einführung zu den Grundrechten, N. 10 et seq.; Rossinelli, 67 et seq.; Kley, 301 et seq.; Tschannen, 226 et seq.; Chiariello, 17 et seq., 91 et seq.

48 Sup.Ct. in ZBl 62/1961, 69, 72; cf. already BGE 35/1909 I 571 et seq.

49 Article 22 Const. 1874. Now Art. 26 Const.

50 BGE 87/1961 I 114, 117. Now Art. 16 Const.

51 BGE 96/1970 I 219, 223 et seq. Now Art. 22 Const.

52 BGE 100/1974 Ia 392, 400 et seq.

53 BGE 101/1975 Ia 252, 255. Now Arts. 20 and 21 Const. Cf. also Haller, Verfassungsfortbildung.

54 BGE 123/1997 IV 236, 247. Now Art. 17 para. 3 Const.

55 BGE 89/1963 I 92, 97 et seq. Now Art. 10 Const.

56 BGE 102/1976 Ia 279, 292; Rütsche, 285.

After mentioning that the legislator must act immediately, the Court continued that it was "not prevented from establishing principles, for a transitional period until the effective date of a new rule of law, such that at least . . . the right to freedom pursuant to Article 5 clause 1 of the EHRC will be guaranteed to a sufficient extent."[57]

In 1965, recognition of the freedom of language as an unwritten constitutional right followed.[58] This includes the right to use one's native language in the private sphere; in contacts with public authorities, however, the right is restricted by the obligation to use the official language of the respective Canton or community (i.e., German, French, Italian, or Romansh, according to the location).[59]

Finally, in 1995, the Federal Supreme Court recognized an unwritten right to existence and care, which encompasses minimum financial assistance by the government in case of need.[60]

B. Interpretation and Substantiation of Fundamental Rights

The recognition and substantiation of fundamental rights leads to the establishment of rules that can be assigned a function similar to legislation. Thus, for example, the Federal Supreme Court derived from the freedom of religion and the State's duty to religious neutrality the prohibition of crucifixes on the premises of public schools and the prohibition of headscarves for female teachers. Similarly, the right to dispensation from school lessons on religious holidays[61] and a right to dispensation for religious reasons from mixed-sex swimming instruction in school was approved; the latter was rejected later.[62]

3. *Political Rights*

In long-established case law, the Federal Supreme Court has developed rules for guaranteeing proper elections and votes in the cantons and has recognized the freedom to elect and vote as a constitutional right.[63] This

[57] BGE 123/1997 II 193, 201 et seq. (translation from the German original).

[58] BGE 91/1965 I 480, 485 et seq. Now Art. 18 Const.

[59] Art. 70 Const. Cf. Haller, Constitution N. 94 and 421.

[60] BGE 121/1995 I 367, 370 et seq. Now Art. 12 Const.

[61] BGE 116/1990 Ia 252 et seq.; 123/1997 I 296 et seq.; 134/2008 I 114 et seq.

[62] BGE 119/1993 Ia 178 et seq.; 135/2009 I 79 et seq.

[63] Cf. BGE 121/1995 I 138, 141 et seq. Now Art. 34 Const.

includes, among other aspects, rules on governmental propaganda in connection with elections and votes, as well as the principle of the unity of subject matter in connection with popular initiatives; this means that an initiative must not comprise several proposals that have no interrelationship.[64]

The most important example of positive legislation by the Federal Supreme Court in the area of political rights relates to the right of women to participate in the Landsgemeinde (assembly of the citizens as the highest legislative body) of the Canton Appenzell-Innerrhoden.[65] The Constitution of Appenzell-Innerrhoden provided that only men could participate in the Landsgemeinde. The government and parliament petitioned to the Landsgemeinde in 1990 for introduction of the right to vote for women. The Landsgemeinde, however, rejected the petition. Numerous citizens, both female and male, lodged an appeal against this decision with the Federal Supreme Court and objected to the infringement of the constitutional right to equal treatment of women and men.[66] The Supreme Court declared the provision of the Constitution of Appenzell-Innerrhoden, as it had been interpreted to date, to be in contravention of the Federal Constitution and declared women to be immediately entitled to vote. Since then, women in Canton Appenzell-Innerrhoden participate in the Landsgemcinde and are entitled to vote and elect, as in all other cantons.[67]

In connection with the structuring of proportional representation, the principle of the equal right to vote must be observed. Thus, based on the case law of the Federal Supreme Court, electoral districts must be of similar size so that the citizens' votes carry a similar weight (equality in magnitude of success), and for this reason as well, exclusion clauses are permissible only to a limited extent. The Supreme Court has developed these principles, but has not itself placed them into effect, in connection with its review of cantonal voting systems. Instead, it has requested the affected cantons, through decisions with an appeal to the legislators, to modify their voting systems accordingly.[68]

64 Haller, Constitution N. 237.

65 BGE 116/1990 Ia 359 et seq.

66 Now Art. 8 para. 3 Const.

67 Cf. Auer, Effet 564 et seq.; Biaggini, Einführung 65 et seq.; Biaggini, Verfassungsfortbildung 134 et seq.; Weber-Dürler, 346 et seq.; already before the referenced decision, Auer, Frauenstimmrecht 141 et seq. In a similar case, in 1957, the Federal Supreme Court had refused to introduce the right to vote for women in Canton Vaud through a new interpretation of Article 4 of the Federal Constitution of 1874; BGE 83/1957 I 173 et seq. Cf. Hänni 602 et seq.

68 Cf., e.g., BGE 131/2005 I 74 et seq. and 85 et seq.; 129/2003 I 185 et seq.

In a recent decision, a popular initiative was at stake demanding that decisions on naturalization in the City of Zurich by the City Parliament be made subject to a poll. The popular initiative was declared invalid by the municipal and cantonal authorities because decisions on naturalization are individual, specific orders that require substantiation, and the rejection of an application for naturalization in a popular vote cannot be substantiated. The Federal Supreme Court confirmed the cantonal decisions and declared polls on applications for naturalization unconstitutional.[69] Although this decision related to one specific case, it *de facto* annulled all cantonal and municipal regulations that provided for a poll on decisions on naturalization. In a later judgment, the Supreme Court declared decisions of the municipal voters' assembly on applications for naturalization to be permissible because it is possible there to substantiate the decision.[70]

4. *Procedural Guarantees*

Article 4 of the Federal Constitution of 1874 guaranteed equality before the law.[71] Numerous other constitutional rights were derived from this guarantee over the course of time.[72] Thus, from the outset, the Federal Supreme Court based the prohibition against arbitrary conduct on equality before the law.[73] The principle of good faith as well as the protection of legitimate expectations were likewise derived from the guarantee of equality before the law;[74] this guarantee also includes the prohibition against excessive formalism.[75] The prohibition against legal measures having retroactive effect as well as the presumption of innocence under criminal law

69 BGE 129/2003 I 232, 236 et seq. Cf., e.g., Andreas Auer/Nicolas von Arx, Direkte Demokratie ohne Grenzen? Ein Diskussionsbeitrag zur Frage der Verfassungsmässigkeit von Einbürgerungsbeschlüssen durch das Volk, AJP 9/2000, 923 et seq.; Daniel Thürer/Michael Frei, Einbürgerung im Spannungsfeld zwischen direkter Demokratie and Rechtsstaatlichkeit, ZSR 123/2004 I, 205 et seq.; Doris Bianchi, Paradigmenwechsel im Einbürgerungsrecht. Vom politischen Einbürgerungsentscheid zum Verwaltungsakt, ZBl 105/2004, 401 et seq.; Tobias Jaag, Aktuelle Entwicklungen im Einbürgerungsrecht, ZBl 106/2005, 113, 125 et seq.; Chiariello, 75 et seq.

70 BGE 130/2004 I 140 et seq. Cf. today Art. 15a of the Law on Citizenship of September 29, 1952 (SR 141.0).

71 Now Art. 8 para. 1 Const.

72 Cf. Chiariello, 33 et seq., 103 et seq.

73 Now Art. 9 Const. Cf. Felix Uhlmann, Das Willkürverbot (Art. 9 BV), Habil., Bern 2005, nº 24 et seq.

74 BGE 115/1989 Ia 12, 18; 118/1992 Ib 367, 379. Now Art. 5 para. 3 and Art. 9 Const.

75 BGE 114/1988 V 203, 207.

were also based on the guarantee of equal treatment.[76] Furthermore, even before being enshrined in the Federal Constitution of 1999, the right to access records, the right to be heard, the obligation for decisions to be substantiated, as well as the right to be exempted from costs of proceedings and to free legal counsel in case of indigence were all derived from the guarantee of equal treatment under the previous Federal Constitution.[77]

On the basis of the European Human Rights Convention (EHRC), the Supreme Court has flouted the limitation on judicial review set out under Article 190 of the current Federal Constitution. It refused to apply a provision of a federal law excluding an appeal to the Federal Supreme Court in matters of foreign and national security and proceeded to deal with such an appeal to accommodate the right to a judicial decision pursuant to Article 6, paragraph 1, of the EHRC.[78] In so doing, it introduced an exception from the precept to apply federal statutes violating superior law and therefore introduced limited judicial review for federal statutes.

5. *Federal Conflicts*

Already the Federal Constitution of 1874 instructed the federal legislator to adopt rules against intercantonal *double taxation.*[79] Following the failure of various efforts to enact provisions of law against double taxation, the Federal Supreme Court developed corresponding principles in its case law over the years.[80] This was possible because the obligation of the legislator to adopt provisions against double taxation is treated as an individual right. Therefore, taxpayers may contest double taxation by means of an appeal to the Supreme Court.

Because the competence to regulate child and family allowances for employees rests with the cantons, there is a risk that overlaps or gaps in coverage may arise in connection with professional activities in more than one canton. There is considerable interest, therefore, in rules to ensure the avoidance of duplication or gaps in the intercantonal context. The Federal Supreme Court has posed the question of whether, in the absence of a

[76] BGE 122/1996 II 113, 124; 123/1997 I 221, 228. Today, the presumption of innocence is enshrined in Art. 32 para. 1 Const.

[77] Now Art. 29 para. 2 and 3 Const.; BGE 99/1973 Ia 325, 330.

[78] BGE 125/1999 I 417, 425. Cf. Chiariello, 64 et seq., 116 et seq.

[79] Art. 46 para. 2 Const. 1874. Now Art. 127 para. 3 Const.

[80] Cf. Ernst Höhn, in Kommentar aBV, Art. 46 para. 2, N. 19 et seq.; Teygeler, 4 et seq.; Chiariello, 44 et seq., 108 et seq.

legislative rule, it could develop corresponding principles; it has, however, left this question open.[81]

The Federal Constitution of 1874 obligated the cantons to recognize credentials issued in other cantons on the qualification to practice academic professions.[82] The federal legislation contemplated for this, however, failed to be adopted for many years. The determinative principles in this area were developed by the Federal Supreme Court as well.[83]

With respect to the resolution of conflicts between the cantons, there is no legislative rule. The Supreme Court has closed the gap by declaring that the rules under public international law are applicable by way of analogy.[84]

6. *Compensation for Infringement of Property Rights*

The guarantee of property does not preclude the State from carrying out expropriations to perform public duties. Expropriation, however, is only permissible against full compensation. This applies not only with respect to formal expropriations but also with respect to limitations on property that are tantamount to expropriation (quasi expropriation).[85]

The Federal Law on Expropriations sets out the necessary rules for formal expropriations.[86] The legislative rule is tailored to the classic case of the compulsory deprivation of property. However, it has gaps with respect to the expropriation of rights of defense under the law governing the respective interests of neighbors; furthermore, the compensation for limitations on property that are tantamount to an expropriation (quasi expropriation) is not regulated at all in the Law on Expropriations.[87] The conditions and modalities of these forms of expropriation have been developed by the

81 BGE 129/2003 I 265, 274 et seq.

82 Art. 33 in conjunction with Art. 5 of the Transitory Provisions (UeB) Const. 1874. Cf. Philippe Bois, in Kommentar aBV, Art. 33 N. 24 et seq. and Art. 5 UeB N. 1 et seq.

83 Cf., e.g., BGE 111/1985 Ia 108, 111 et seq.

84 BGE 106/1980 Ib 154, 159 et seq.

85 Now Art. 26 para. 2 Const.

86 Federal Law on Expropriations of June 20, 1930 (SR 711).

87 Art. 5 para. 2 of the Land Use Planning Law of June 22, 1979 (SR 700) merely repeats the constitutional provision.

Federal Supreme Court.[88] Even today, the Supreme Court case law in these areas continues to play the role of legislative rules.[89]

7. *Further Examples*

In deviating from the Planning and Construction Law of the Canton of Zurich, the Federal Supreme Court approved a zone for public buildings outside of the construction zone to enable sports facilities to be erected; the Court held the legislative rule to be manifestly incomplete to the extent that, contrary to its meaning, it fails to make distinctions that "according to all reason . . . were to be drawn."[90] For the introduction of the *numerus clausus* at universities, the Supreme Court, in the absence of a legislative rule, formulated strict requirements.[91] For telephone monitoring within the scope of criminal investigations, the Supreme Court likewise developed rules by requiring that affected persons be notified afterward and by providing for exceptions from this requirement.[92]

CONCLUSIONS

Although the Federal Supreme Court repeatedly emphasizes that it cannot adopt rules that rest within the competence of the legislator, it nonetheless consistently acts as a positive legislator. This applies to a large extent in terms of the development of the Constitution, as shown, in particular, by the examples of the recognition of unwritten fundamental rights as well as the derivation of numerous procedural guarantees based on Article 4 of the Federal Constitution of 1874. The Supreme Court has also engaged in the implementation of constitutional norms at the legislative level in various areas, such as the substantiation of the double taxation prohibition and the regulation of the conditions for compensation based on infringements of property rights (quasi expropriation) and based on the expropriation of rights of defense under the law governing the respective interests of neighbors.

88 BGE 91/1965 I 329 et seq. (quasi expropriation); BGE 94/1968 I 286 et seq. (appropriation of rights of neighbors).

89 Cf., e.g., the numerous decisions of the Federal Supreme Court of 2008 as to compensation based on aircraft noise: BGE 134/2008 II 49 et seq. and 145 et seq.

90 BGE 108/1982 Ia 295, 297 (translation from the German original).

91 BGE 121/1995 I 22 et seq.

92 BGE 109/1983 Ia 273, 298 et seq.

The performance of legislative tasks by the Federal Supreme Court suggests itself whenever the Constitution lays down rights for individuals enabling them to action against the State and the legislative rules necessary in this regard have not been enacted.[93] If one does not wish to simply violate such rights, the Court must have the ability to act in lieu of the legislator.

Judicial lawmaking is always problematic, or even precluded, whenever considerable financial resources or infrastructures must be made available for implementation of the rule decided on by the court, as well as whenever a court rule would prejudice later decisions on the part of the legislators.[94] In these cases, the court must content itself with ascertaining the unconstitutionality, combined with an appeal to the competent political instances to restore the lawful status.[95]

Because the Federal Supreme Court not only annuls unconstitutional rules but also issues rules on its own, it participates in a decisive fashion in the realization of the Constitution.[96] It is true that, from the viewpoint of democracy, it is problematic that the ordinary legislative process is circumvented in this manner. However, judicial lawmaking is merely a temporary solution because it only becomes effective if the legislator failed to decide on a required rule and the legislation therefore suffers from a lack of completeness, contrary to plan. The legislator has the ability at all times to replace the court-made rules with its own rules – within the constitutional framework – and thereby rectify the democratic deficiency.[97]

Judicial lawmaking is therefore not to be viewed as an impurity in the constitutional state; it is an important component of the same. No objection is to be raised against it as long as the institutional parameters are correct, to the extent that the judge selection process meets high standards, to the extent that the independence of the judges is guaranteed, and to the extent that the Court acts only if it is clearly necessary (judicial self-restraint).[98]

93 Rütsche, 284.

94 Rütsche, 291.

95 Rütsche, 297 et seq.

96 Chiariello, 353 et seq.

97 Rütsche, 290 et seq.

98 Art. 191c Const.; Haller, Verfassungsfortbildung 19 et seq.; Chiariello, 382 et seq.

BIBLIOGRAPHY

AUBERT, JEAN-FRANÇOIS/EICHENBERGER KURT/MÜLLER JÖRG PAUL/RHINOW RENÉ/SCHINDLER DIETRICH (eds.), Kommentar zur Bundesverfassung vom 24. Mai 1874, Zurich/Basel/Berne 1986 et seq. (*Kommentar aBV*).

AUER, ANDREAS, Die Bundesverfassung und das *Frauenstimmrecht* in Appenzell, ZSR 108/1989 I, 141 et seq.

AUER, ANDREAS, Les caprices de la nature cassatoire du recours de droit public. Réflexions sur l'arrêt *Hegetschweiler*, in: Festschrift für Ulrich Häfelin, Zürich 1989, 33 et seq.

AUER, ANDREAS, L'effet des décisions d'inconstitutionnalité du Tribunal fédéral, AJP 1/1992, 559 et seq.

BIAGGINI, GIOVANNI, Verfassung und *Richterrecht*. Verfassungsrechtliche Grenzen der Rechtsfortbildung im Wege der bundesgerichtlichen Rechtsprechung, Diss., Basel/Frankfurt a.M. 1991.

BIAGGINI, GIOVANNI, Die *Einführung* des Frauenstimmrechts im Kanton Appenzell I. Rh. kraft bundesgerichtlicher Verfassungsinterpretation, recht 1992, 65 et seq.

BIAGGINI, GIOVANNI, Abstrakte und konkrete *Normenkontrolle*. Überprüfung von Erlassen auf ihre Rechtmässigkeit im Rahmen der abstrakten und konkreten Normenkontrolle, ius.full 2006, 164 et seq.

BIAGGINI, GIOVANNI, Verfahren und Methoden der *Verfassungsfortbildung*, in: Giovanni Biaggini/Georg Müller/Jörg Paul Müller/Felix Uhlmann (eds.), Demokratie, Regierungsreform, Verfassungsfortbildung. Symposium für René Rhinow zum 65. Geburtstag, Basel 2009, 125 et seq.

CAMPRUBI, MADELEINE, Kassation und positive Anordnungen bei der staatsrechtlichen Beschwerde. Wirkungen und Grenzen des Grundrechtsschutzes in Praxis und Theorie, Diss., Zurich 1999.

CHIARIELLO, ELISABETH, Der Richter als Verfassungsgeber? Zur Fortbildung von Grundlagen des Rechtsstaats und der Demokratie durch höchste Gerichte, Habil., Zurich/St. Gallen 2009.

GERBER, PHILIPPE, La nature cassatoire du recours de droit public, Mythe et réalité, Diss., Geneva/Basel/Frankfurt a.M. 1997.

HÄFELIN, ULRICH/HALLER WALTER/KELLER HELEN, Schweizerisches Bundesstaatsrecht, 7th ed., Zurich/Basel/Geneva 2008.

HAEFLIGER, ARTHUR, Die Rechtsfolgen der Gutheissung einer staatsrechtlichen Beschwerde, in: Festschrift für O.K. Kaufmann, Berne/Stuttgart 1989, 357 et seq.

HALLER, WALTER, in: Kommentar aBV, Art. 113.

HALLER, WALTER, *Verfassungsfortbildung* durch Richterrecht, ZSR 124/2005 I, 5 et seq.

HALLER, WALTER, Das schweizerische *Bundesgericht* als Verfassungsgericht, in: Christian Starck/Albrecht Weber (eds.), Verfassungsgerichtsbarkeit in Westeuropa, Teilband I, Baden-Baden 2007, 179 et seq.

HALLER, WALTER, The Swiss *Constitution* in a Comparative Context, Zurich/St. Gallen 2009.

Handkommentar BGG, see SEILER/VON WERDT/GÜNGERICH.

HÄNNI, PETER, Grenzen richterlicher Möglichkeiten bei der Durchsetzung von Gleichheitsansprüchen gemäss Art. 4 BV, ZSR 107/1988 I, 591 et seq.

HUTTER, SILVAN, Die Gesetzeslücke im Verwaltungsrecht, Diss., Fribourg 1989.

KÄLIN, WALTER, *Verfassungsgerichtsbarkeit* in der Demokratie. Funktionen der staatsrechtlichen Beschwerde, Berne 1987.

KÄLIN, WALTER, Das Verfahren der staatsrechtlichen *Beschwerde*, 2nd ed., Berne 1994.

KAUFMANN, OTTO K., Etoilauto S.A. c. Confédération, in: Mélanges Henri Zwahlen, Lausanne 1977, 139 et seq.

KLEY, ANDREAS, Der Grundrechtskatalog der nachgeführten Bundesverfassung – ausgewählte Neuerungen, ZBJV 135/1999, 301 et seq.

Kommentar aBV, see AUBERT/EICHENBERGER/MÜLLER/RHINOW/SCHINDLER.

Kommentar BGG, see NIGGLI/UEBERSAX/WIPRÄCHTIGER.

NIGGLI, MARCEL ALEXANDER/UEBERSAX PETER/WIPRÄCHTIGER HANS (eds.), Bundesgerichtsgesetz, Basler Kommentar, Basel 2008.

RHINOW, RENÉ, Rechtsetzung und Methodik. Rechtstheoretische Untersuchungen zum gegenseitigen Verhältnis von Rechtsetzung und Rechtsanwendung, Habil., Basel 1979.

ROSSINELLI, MICHEL, Les libertés non écrites. Contribution à l'étude du pouvoir créateur du juge constitutionnel, Diss., Lausanne 1987.

RÜTSCHE, BERNHARD, Rechtsfolgen von Normenkontrollen. Entwicklungen in Praxis und Lehre seit dem Fall Hegetschweiler vor zwei Jahrzehnten, ZBl 106/2005, 273 et seq.

SEILER, HANSJÖRG/VON WERDT NICOLAS/GÜNGERICH ANDREAS, Bundesgerichtsgesetz (BGG), Stämpflis Handkommentar, Berne 2007 (*Handkommentar BGG*).

STREHLE, BARBARA, Rechtswirkungen verfassungsgerichtlicher Normenkontrollentscheidungen. Eine vergleichende Darstellung der Entscheidungswirkungen des schweizerischen Bundesgerichts, des deutschen

Bundesverfassungsgerichts und des österreichischen Verfassungsgerichtshofs, Diss., Zurich 1980.

TEYGELER, JACOBA, Rechtswirkungen verfassungsgerichtlicher Normenkontrollentscheidungen (im Lichte der Durchsetzung der verfassungsmässigen Rechte durch das Bundesgericht und durch die kantonalen Gerichte), Diss., Basel 1993.

TSCHANNEN, PIERRE, Die Auslegung der neuen Bundesverfassung, in: Ulrich Zimmerli (ed.), Die neue Bundesverfassung. Konsequenzen für Praxis und Wissenschaft, Berne 2000, 223 et seq.

WEBER-DÜRLER, BEATRICE, Grenzen des Rechtsschutzes bei der Gleichberechtigung, in: Festschrift für Margrith Bigler-Eggenberger, Basel/Frankfurt a.M. 1993, 337 et seq.

ABBREVIATIONS

AJP	Aktuelle Juristische Praxis
BGE	Decisions of the Federal Supreme Court
BGG	Federal Law on the Federal Supreme Court (Federal Supreme Court Law) of June 17, 2005 (SR 173.110)
Const.	Constitution of the Swiss Federation of April 19, 1999 (SR 101)
Const. 1874	Constitution of the Swiss Federation of May 24, 1874 (out of force since 2000)
ECtHR	European Court on Human Rights
EHRC	European Human Rights Convention
Habil.	Habilitation thesis
N	Paragraph
SR	Systematic Collection of Federal Laws
Sup.Ct.	Federal Supreme Court
VVDStRL	Veröffentlichungen der Vereinigung der Deutschen Staatsrechtslehrer
ZBJV	Zeitschrift des Bernischen Juristenvereins
ZBl	Schweizerisches Zentralblatt für Staats- und Verwaltungsrecht
ZSR	Zeitschrift für Schweizerisches Recht

UNITED KINGDOM

CONSTITUTIONAL COURTS AS POSITIVE LEGISLATORS

John Bell
Professor, University of Cambridge
jsb48@cam.ac.uk

INTRODUCTION AND TERMINOLOGY

Particularly English lawyers have problems with the terminology of *constitution* and *constitutional judge*. It is perhaps symptomatic that in a major reflective work on the British Constitution in the twentieth century,[1] the editor's introduction does not discuss the courts at all and the writer of the report on the courts focuses on the "Government and the Judiciary" and begins by saying, "For much of the twentieth century the judiciary has been thought of more as a dignified than an effective element in the constitution."[2]

Constitution: There is a British Constitution, even though it does not consist of a single consistent and overarching document. Trevor Allan[3] talks of a "common law constitution" as a set of legal principles and rules which have been laid down from time to time, typically by judges. In addition and of increasing importance are statutes. There is no procedural or formal distinction between a "constitutional" statute and an ordinary statute. For example, the Constitutional Reform Act 2005 was passed by exactly the same procedure as any other public and general statute, despite its

1 V. Bogdanor (ed.), *The British Constitution in the Twentieth Century* (London: British Academy 2003).

2 Robert Stevens, *Ibid.*, p. 333. See also David Robertson, *Judicial Discretion in the House of Lords* (Oxford: Oxford UP 1998).

3 T. Allan, *Law, Liberty and Justice: The Legal Foundations of British Constitutionalism* (Oxford: Oxford UP 1993).

acknowledged constitutional importance. In these respects, the British Constitution is now unusual, but it has very similar features to the French Third Republic (1870–1940), which was the longest lasting of the fifteen French constitutions to date.

The result of these features is that the very label "constitutional" attached to a legal rule or principle can be controversial. There are no agreed-on criteria by which such rules and principles can be identified, other than by agreement of the legal and political communities.

A further complication is the fact that British jurists attach the label "constitutional" to nonlegal rules, especially conventions of the Constitution. These conventions are rules of political morality and not merely practices or habits.[4] Such conventions are not merely supplementary to the law but may contradict it. For example, in law, the Queen has a discretion to refuse to sign an Act of Parliament, but well-established convention denies her any discretion in the matter.[5] Again, this is not a peculiarity of the British Constitution.[6] But the application of the label "constitutional rule" to both legal and nonlegal values can make legal debate confusing for outsiders. For example, the prime ministers of the British Empire (as it then was) agreed in 1931 that the U.K. Parliament would not legislate for Dominions without the consent of their Parliaments. When this was implemented in relation to the repatriation of the Canadian Constitution in 1981, the question arose as to the legal implications of the 1931 agreement, passed as the Statute of Westminster.

It is typical that one of the most important constitutional reforms in recent years, the introduction of sets of ethics for the conduct of public affairs, should have been achieved without legislation or any legal constitutional text. The "Nolan principles" governing standards in public life[7] introduced in 1995 a set of values governing the holders of a range of public offices. These principles have led to major changes in the procedures for appointing all kinds of public official (including judges). Some of the specific changes were introduced by law, but most have not needed more than convention as guidance. The key feature of the process for this report is that the person who chaired the Commission was a judge (Lord Nolan, a member of the

4 G. Marshall, *Constitutional Conventions* (Oxford: Oxford UP 1984), pp. 8–9.

5 *Ibid.*, pp. 21–23.

6 See P. Avril, *Les Conventions de la constitution* (Paris: Leviathan 1998).

7 *Standards in Public Life* (Cm 2850-I, 1995); see generally J. Jowell and D. Oliver, *The Changing Constitution* (6th ed., Oxford: Oxford UP 2007), ch. 17, and the Committee on Standards in Public Life, http://www.public-standards.gov.uk.

House of Lords). He was chosen because a judge gave the required status of independence to the process. But at the end of the day, the actual rules produced were not legal.[8]

Constitutional Judge: There is no special court to deal with constitutional matters as such. As will be seen, there is no formal process of "constitutional review," and so it is not surprising that there is no special judge for such matters. Even the creation of the Supreme Court from 1 October 2009 does not significantly change this position.[9]

The term "judicial review" in Britain is normally restricted to the review of administrative action by government or other public bodies. For that reason, the term "constitutional review" is preferred in this report.

The General Reporter writes that "the main purpose of the Report is also to analyze in a comparative way, the most important cases of judicial activism and decisions issued by constitutional judges or constitutional courts or tribunals that have contributed to shape these new functions of the constitutional judges when interpreting the Constitution, well beyond their original 'Negative Legislator' character."

In one sense, Britain has neither "specific constitutional or statutory provisions that empower constitutional judges, by means of interpreting the Constitution, to adopt obligatory decisions on constitutional matters" nor specific decisions on constitutional matters. But this would be too simplistic an approach. The nature of a common law constitution is that the basic "rules of recognition"[10] are not contained in statute but are in the common law. The principles are rather like the "fundamental principles recognized by the laws of the Republic" in French law, which are not laid down by statute but which are judicially identified, even if formally not created by judges.[11] There do arise a number of issues on which ordinary judges have to take decisions which are binding and which could be characterized as constitutional.

[8] For further comment, see R. Stevens, *The English Judges* (Oxford: Hart, 2002), pp. 55, 70–1, and 84.

[9] See http://www.supremecourt.gov.uk.

[10] H. L. A. Hart, *The Concept of Law* (2nd ed., Oxford UP 1994), pp. 153–4, 256.

[11] See J. Bell, *French Constitutional Law* (Oxford: Oxford UP 1992), pp. 68–73.

I. CONSTITUTIONAL (JUDICIAL) REVIEW, CONCENTRATED OR DISTRIBUTED

Constitutional review is essentially distributed. The absence of formally distinct constitutional rules makes this more or less inevitable. All legal disputes go to ordinary judges. For example, the compatibility of a British statute concerning the limits for fishing with European Union law was raised and decided by the lowest tier of criminal law courts, the magistrates' court.[12] Matters may be appealed up to the highest courts within the national (English and Welsh, Scottish and Northern Irish) jurisdictions and, in many cases, on to the British Supreme Court, but there is no preliminary reference procedure.

There are three exceptions. First, in relation to devolution matters, the question of the validity of the legislation of the three devolved assemblies (Wales, Scotland, and Northern Ireland) can be referred to the Supreme Court either by the British Secretary of State, the British Attorney-General, or the national Attorneys-General (or equivalent) or by the national courts before which the issue is raised.

Second, courts in any part of Britain can refer to the Supreme Court questions concerning the interpretation of the Human Rights Act 1998. This statute is a major constitutional statute on fundamental rights. The Act implements the European Convention on Human Rights, and it can lead to either the narrowing of the scope of legislation by means of an interpretation which makes the statute compatible with the Convention or a declaration of incompatibility, which empowers a minister to amend or repeal an incompatible statutory provision.[13]

Third, as in any Member State of the European Union, a court seized of a question concerning the compatibility of British law with EU law can refer the issue to the European Court of Human Rights, or if the matter does not give rise to a serious difficulty (it is an *acte clair*) in interpretation, it can apply European law directly itself. Either as a result of a ruling from the ECJ or on application of the *acte clair* doctrine, the British court may refuse to apply a British statute.[14] This was not explicitly decided by Parliament in the European Communities Act 1972, s. 2(4). It remained discussed by the

12 E.g., Case 63/83, *R v. Kirk* [1984] ECR 2689; [1984] 3 CMLR 522.

13 See N. Bamforth, "Parliamentary Sovereignty and the Human Rights Act 1998" [1998] *Public Law* 572.

14 Case 283/81, *Srl CILFIT v. Minister of Health* [1982] ECR 3415, E. Mancini and D. Keeling, "From *CILFIT* to *ERT*: The Constitutional Challenge Facing the European Court of Justice" (1991) 11 *Yearbook of European Law* 1.

British judges but was not definitively adopted until the European Court of Justice had specifically stated that the British courts ought to disapply a British Act of Parliament incompatible with European legislation.[15] In that case, the issue was raised by way of an action for judicial review against the decision of a minister. In subsequent cases, the courts have accepted that a declaration can be granted where British legislation is incompatible with European Union law.[16] Craig notes that in this case, the House of Lords made its ruling about the incompatibility of national legislation with EU law without the need for a reference to the ECJ.

In these three ways in particular, the British courts are creating rules, mainly through interpretation of key constitutional statutes, which are obligatory.

II. SPECIFIC ISSUES

1. *Constitutional Review Procedures*

Apart from devolution issues, where certain ministers can raise issues by way of abstract review without needing to have a specific interest, all other questions have to be raised by way of ordinary litigation for which the person will require an interest.

There have been some cases of public interest litigation concerning the validity of legislation. Most recently, in *Jackson v. Attorney-General*,[17] the applicant alleged that an Act of Parliament had been passed by a wrong use of the procedures laid down in the Parliament Acts 1911 and 1949. The House of Lords was prepared to examine the argument, only to reject it by deciding on limited grounds that there was no valid challenge to the validity of the Hunting Act 2004. The House was unwilling to discuss the broader questions of how far an Act of Parliament could redefine parliamentary procedures for the future. It certainly did not provide future guidance about how Parliament should vote on bills in the future. In general, there needs to

[15] Compare *R v. Secretary of State for Transport, ex parte Factortame Ltd* [1990] 2 AC 85 with *R v. Secretary of State for Transport, ex parte Factortame Ltd (No.2)* [1991] 1 AC 603. See further P. P. Craig, "Sovereignty of the United Kingdom Parliament after *Factortame*" (1991) 11 *Yearbook of European Law* 221.

[16] *R v. Secretary of State for Employment, ex p. Equal Opportunities Commission* [1995] 1 AC 1; see generally Jowell and Oliver, *op. cit.*, ch. 4.

[17] [2006] 1 AC 262. See A. L. Young, "Hunting and Sovereignty: *Jackson v. Her Majesty's Attorney-General* [2006] Public Law 187; R. Cooke, "A Constitutional Retreat" (2006) 122 *Law Quarterly Review* 224.

be a specific interest (e.g., as a person who is involved in hunting). But occasionally, the issue is so important that any voter has the right to bring a challenge to the law's validity.[18] But generally, a personal interest is required.

A number of key issues are not considered to be justiciable and are resolved only by the internal processes of Parliament. The key issues are first the process within Parliament for the passing of legislation,[19] and second the designation of specific legislation as a "money bill" (finance law), which allows certain more rapid procedures to be used within Parliament under the Parliament Act 1911.[20] In many other countries, both issues would give rise to constitutional litigation, and the courts could serve as positive legislators in prescribing principles for the use of procedures. In Britain, decisions on such issues with regard to the Westminster Parliament are strictly for the Speaker. In relation to devolved Parliaments, the only matters that can be challenged in the courts are matters concerning the competence of the legislature, not the failure to follow rules of parliamentary procedure.

2. *Judicial Decisions*[21]

Courts in the United Kingdom have limited competence to undertake any of the declaration of the unconstitutional character of statutes, annulment (total or partial) of unconstitutional statutes, constitutional mutations, and constitutional manipulations.

The U.K. judges have no power to strike down legislation of the Westminster Parliament, except in the limited area of the compatibility with EU law. There have been few decisions in this respect. Nearly all the decisions have involved a decision from the European Court of Justice. No legislation of the Scottish Parliament or of the Northern Ireland Assembly has been annulled on this ground.

No legislation of any of the devolved assemblies has been annulled, and there have been only a few decisions, mainly on human rights issues that

18 *R v. Secretary of State for Foreign Affairs, ex p. Rees-Mogg* [1994] QB 552.

19 *Pickin v. British Railways Board* [1974] AC 765. This applies only to the passing of U.K. legislation of the Westminster Parliament. The legislation of subordinate parliaments, such as the Scottish Parliament, is subject to constitutional review: *Anderson et al v. Scottish Ministers* [2001] UKPC D5; [2003] 2 AC 602.

20 This is decided by the Speaker. See W. McKay (ed.), *Erskine May's Treatise on The Law, Privileges, Proceedings and Usage of Parliament* (23rd ed., London: LexisNexis 2004), pp. 928–9.

21 See generally J. Bell, *Judiciaries within Europe* (Cambridge: Cambridge UP 2006).

have discussed the possible constitutional invalidity of the legislation of devolved assemblies.[22] So the only area in which the judge has had scope to be a positive legislator is in the area of human rights.

A. Human Rights and Judicial Activism

The Human Rights Act 1998 was, according to Stevens, predominantly psychological in its impact.[23] For many years, judges had already been using the European Convention as a benchmark for the interpretation of English law. The interpretative obligation in s. 3 of the Act did not add anything formally new. But the formal power to give a declaration of incompatibility provided an additional way of altering the government's agenda. When a declaration is given, then the Government has to decide whether to propose an amendment of the law to bring it in line with the Convention or to take other action to maintain the incompatibility, such as by registering a formal derogation from the Convention. This is the nearest that English judges come to a constitutional review.[24] An example was *A (FC) and others. v. Secretary of State for the Home Department,*[25] in which a number of individuals challenged their detention without trial. They were held because they were suspected of being a danger to national security, but they could not be expelled to another country. The House of Lords held that s. 23 of the Anti-Terrorism, Crime and Security Act 2001 was incompatible with articles 5 and 14 of the European Convention insofar as it is disproportionate and permits detention of suspected international terrorists in a way that discriminates on the ground of nationality or immigration status, and it quashed the Government's derogation from the Convention. Lord Bingham[26] stated:

> [T]he function of independent judges charged to interpret and apply the law is universally recognised as a cardinal feature of the modern democratic state, a cornerstone of the rule of law itself. The Attorney General is fully

22 See B. K. Winetrobe, in Jowell and Oliver, ch. 9 at pp. 223–4; C. McCrudden, *Ibid.*, ch. 10. The most significant effect of the human rights provisions of the devolution legislation was to lead the courts to quash predevolution legislation which permitted the appointment of temporary judges ("sheriffs") and was held to be contrary to the independence of the judiciary: *Starrs v. Ruxton* 2000 JC 208.

23 R. Stevens, *The English Judges*, 115.

24 See C. Gearty and A. Tomkins in D. Hayton (ed.), *Law's Futures* (Oxford: Oxford UP 2000), ch. 4.

25 [2004] HL 56.

26 [2004] HL 56, para. 42.

> entitled to insist on the proper limits of judicial authority, but he is wrong to stigmatise judicial decision-making as in some way undemocratic. It is particularly inappropriate in a case such as the present in which Parliament has expressly legislated in section 6 of the [Human Rights Act] 1998 … to render unlawful any act of a public authority, including a court, incompatible with a Convention right, has required courts (in section 2) to take account of relevant Strasbourg jurisprudence, has (in section 3) required courts, so far as possible, to give effect to Convention rights and has conferred a right of appeal on derogation issues. The effect is not, of course, to override the sovereign legislative authority of the Queen in Parliament, since if primary legislation is declared to be incompatible the validity of the legislation is unaffected (section 4(6)) and the remedy lies with the appropriate minister (section 10), who is answerable to Parliament. The 1998 Act gives the courts a very specific, wholly democratic, mandate.

The significance of human rights cases in the recent case load of the House of Lords suggests that the new Supreme Court will have a significant constitutional function.[27] The criticism of the legislature in this case covered both the substance of the legislation (detention without trial) and the derogation from the European Convention. In effect, the judges prevented the legislature carrying out a policy in relation to terrorist suspects, which they considered to be disproportionate to the demonstrated threat the individuals posed.

Stevens[28] demonstrates the importance of the judiciary in relation to the protection of prisoners against harsh treatment. Particular areas of concern have been indefinite sentences, where the executive had traditionally made the final decision on release. In relation to prisoners on indefinite sentences (usually minors) and life sentence prisoners, the exercise of judicial review of administrative action by the courts even before the Human Rights Act (but influenced by the European Convention) ensured that the executive set out criteria for the detention of individuals. One particular area of conflict was in relation to the management of life sentences. When the young killers of a child had been sentenced to detention at Her Majesty's pleasure, the Home Secretary sought to impose a minimum period of detention without examining the interests of the child killers in question. The minister was under immense political pressure in this case, but the House of Lords held that he needed to act like a judge and was wrong to be inflexible in the

[27] See Jowell, in V. Bogdanor, *The British Constitution in the Twentieth Century* at pp. 390–5, and D. Feldman, *Ibid.*, ch. 11.

[28] Stevens, *English Judges*, pp. 71–2 and 129–36.

exercise of his discretion.[29] In this respect, the judiciary forced an approach on government that was more focused on the merits of individual prisoners and their need for future punishment, as opposed to the generality of prisoners of a particular category.

More typical is the decision in *R (James) v. Secretary of State for Justice*,[30] in which a claim was made by prisoners on indeterminate sentences that they were being denied reasonable access to courses of treatment which would enable them to show at the end that they were ready for release. The claimants succeeded at first instance. The Secretary of State conceded before the House of Lords that he had failed in his duty to make reasonable provision for such courses. But the prisoners failed in their claim that the continuation of their detention as a result of this failure made their detention unlawful.

B. Judicial Substitution

The basic principle is that the court does not substitute itself for the legislature.

Increasingly, human rights litigation gives the judge the power to make decisions which supplement the jurisdiction of the legislator or the administration. There are three areas in which judicial decisions have become important: the rights of asylum seekers, the release of prisoners, and moral matters concerning the beginning and end of life.

Moral matters of social controversy which is not party political are typically raised by way of a claim for a declaration. Parliament is often unwilling to engage in these matters, which are socially divisive and where no broad political consensus can be reached. Thus, the decision of a minister to approve the distribution of contraceptives by doctors to children younger than sixteen without the consent of their parents was examined by the courts and upheld.[31] Equally, the application of the abortion law to new techniques which permitted the medical process to be supervised by a nurse and not a doctor, was examined.[32] In both cases, the legality of governmental circulars was tested and supported by the courts. In other cases, there is no established policy issuing from government, and so the courts are invited by the parties

29 *R v. Secretary of State for the Home Department, ex p. Venables* [1998] AC 407.

30 [2009] UKHL 22.

31 *Gillick v. West Norfolk and Wisbech Health Authority* [1986] AC 112.

32 *Royal College of Nursing v. DHSS* [1981] AC 800; J. Bell, *Policy Arguments in Judicial Decisions* (Oxford: Oxford UP 1983), pp. 88–90.

to lay down guidelines. For example, in relation to the sterilization of intellectually handicapped adults,[33] the House of Lords laid down principles that would govern the approval of such cases. In a more individual case, the Court of Appeal approved the separation of conjoined twins, even though one of them would die as a result.[34] A very good example of this area is *Airedale NHS Trust v. Bland.*[35] In this case, a man was in a permanent vegetative state, but his body was still functioning, provided that he was fed through a tube. The House of Lords decided the circumstances in which the doctors could lawfully accede to the wishes of his parents that the feeding stop and that he be allowed to die. Clearly, the judges were having to establish policies on medical treatment and the point at which actions of the doctor would amount to murder, which were extremely controversial. These are clear cases of the judges making the law in areas where there was inadequate previous precedent or statute.[36] The policy laid down was then to be applied to other situations in the future where doctors would be called upon to decide to terminate treatment. Unlike in the parole cases, there is no conflict between the executive and the courts.

In relation to assistance for suicide, there have been several attempts to use human rights legislation, especially the protection of private life (art. 8 of the Convention) to require prosecutors to declare their policy in dealing with future assistance for suicide. The first of the leading cases, *R (Pretty) v. Director of Public Prosecutions (Secretary of State for the Home Department Intervening)*,[37] concerned the question of whether the Director of Public Prosecutions could be required to rule in advance whether a husband would be prosecuted for assisting his wife to commit suicide when she was physically unable to take all the steps herself. Aiding and abetting suicide is an offence contrary to s. 2(1) of the Suicide Act 1961. The European Court of Human Rights decided that the decision did not breach Mrs. Pretty's right to a private life (and thus to self-determination). More recently, in *R (Purdy) v. Director of Public Prosecutions*,[38] the House of Lords was invited to rule that the Director of Public Prosecutions should set out his policy in relation to a husband who might accompany his wife to

33 *Re F (Mental Patient: Sterilisation)* [1990] 2 AC 173.

34 *Re A (Conjoined Twins: Surgical Separation)* [2000] 4 All ER 961.

35 [1993] 1 All ER 821.

36 For a political analysis, see D. Robertson, *Judicial Discretion in the House of Lords* (Oxford 1998), 381–90.

37 [2001] UKHL 61, [2002] 1 AC 800.

38 [2009] UKHL 45.

Switzerland, where she could lawfully commit suicide. Here the majority of the members of the House of Lords held that it was unreasonable of the Director to refuse to set out the principles on which he would exercise his discretion to prosecute in such cases, when there was legal uncertainty. The decision is all the more important because, on 7 July 2009, the House of Lords in its legislative capacity had refused to vote for an amendment to a bill that would have made it lawful for a person to assist another to leave the country to commit suicide elsewhere. The House of Lords in its judicial capacity decided *Purdy* on 30 July 2009 and was very clear that it was not making such assistance lawful. It was merely requiring the DPP to make his prosecution policy explicit. Human rights considerations, as well as broader principles of legal certainty, led the House of Lords to put the matter back on the agenda of the executive. But the House refused to give guidance to the DPP on how to frame his discretion. Lord Hope remarked, "We do not venture into that arena [of whether to legalize giving assistance to travel abroad to commit suicide], nor would it be right for us to do so. Our function as judges is to say what the law is and, if it is uncertain, to do what we can to clarify it."[39]

So in relation to the moral issues, the courts have generally not written the policy but rather have endorsed the policy of the relevant ministers. But in relation to comatose individuals, they have produced rules in *Bland* or with sterilization which have provided rules for future application in the absence of any authoritative pronouncement by government (e.g., in the form of a ministerial circular). There is a particular niche within the British political process for the courts to be a forum in which certain moral issues are determined.[40]

3. *Effect of Decisions*

Apart from specific powers under EU law where the ECJ can declare decisions applicable *ex nunc*, all decisions are applicable *ex tunc*. The retrospective effect of human rights decisions can obviously pose problems. In practice, the principal forms of action giving rise to review of the decisions of the legislature will be in the form of declarations. This allows the administration time to come up with a solution. The ECJ can make

39 [2009] UKHL 45, para. 26.

40 In some areas, such as bioethics, a similar function is performed by the Human Fertilization and Embryology Authority.

rulings that are *ex tunc* or that are suspended in their application.[41] So the combination of these features limits the retrospective application of wide-ranging decisions.

[41] See *Case 262/88, Barber v. Guardian Royal Exchange* [1990] ECR 1889 on redundancy pay and occupational pensions was effective *ex tunc* only as an interpretation of Community law.

UNITED STATES OF AMERICA

CONSTITUTIONAL COURTS AS POSITIVE LEGISLATORS IN THE UNITED STATES*

***Laurence Claus,*•**
Professor of Law, University of San Diego
lclaus@sandiego.edu

Richard S. Kay,
Wallace Stevens Professor of Law, University of Connecticut
richer.kay@law.uconn.edu

This Report asks whether American courts that decide constitutional cases, and ultimately the Justices of the U.S. Supreme Court, may be characterized as legislators, and in particular, as "positive" legislators. After defining the terms, the report reviews the Supreme Court's practice of constitutional lawmaking and considers academic and political reactions to that practice. The Report concludes with an account of challenges that the Court has encountered in crafting remedies fit to fulfill the promise of its constitutional rulings.

I. LEGISLATORS AND POSITIVE LEGISLATORS

The topic of this Report engages two analytically distinct ideas – legislation and "positive legislation." By legislation, we mean any action that adds a rule to a given system of law.[1] Historically, American jurisprudence

* DOI 105131/ajcl.2009.0018.

• We are grateful for excellent research assistance from Annie Hu of the University of San Diego School of Law.

1 We need not, for the purposes of this Report, state more precisely what it takes to be a "rule" in a given legal system. Any attempt to do so depends in part on certain disputed assumptions about the operation of the particular legal system. See H. L. A. Hart, "Definition and Theory in

has displayed an ambivalent attitude to the idea that judges legislate in this sense. Judicial lawmaking is, of course, an entirely familiar feature of common law adjudication, but until the latter part of the nineteenth century, this proposition was widely considered heretical. The orthodox view was that what might look like judicially created rules were, in fact, deductions from a preexisting body of common law principles.[2] By the middle of the twentieth century, however, this idea had been fully debunked, and there was common agreement that "judges do and must legislate," although they can "do so only interstitially; they are confined from molar to molecular motions."[3] Critically, moreover, such judge-made law was universally acknowledged to be subject to correction and revision by elected legislatures.

A narrow view of the judicial role was even more widely held with respect to adjudication pursuant to a formally enacted text. According to the conventional wisdom, the job of the judge in that situation was in no way legislative. The act of legislation had been completed by the time the courts came into the picture. Their job was to apply the existing rule to a particular set of facts. In this respect, the judges, notwithstanding their constitutional independence, could be perceived as performing an executive function.[4] Thomas Jefferson expressed this view when he declared that the judge should be a "mere machine."[5] As it involved the judicial application of a written text, the same understanding extended to constitutional adjudication. In the foundational case of *Marbury v. Madison*,[6] Chief Justice Marshall depicted the invalidation of an unconstitutional statute not as a discretionary exercise of power, but as an inescapable duty.[7] When asked about certain

Jurisprudence," in *Essays in Jurisprudence and Philosophy* 21 (1983). The entitlement of the examples given here to be called rules is relatively uncontroversial.

2 This is not to say that more skeptical views were ever entirely absent. See Brian Z. Tamanaha, *Beyond the Formalist-Realist Divide: The Role of Politics in Judging* (Princeton Univ. Press, 2009).

3 *S. Pac. Co. v. Jensen*, 244 U.S. 205, 221 (1917) (Holmes, J., dissenting). The classic American treatment is Benjamin N. Cardozo, *The Nature of the Judicial Process* (1921).

4 See Laurence Claus, "Montesquieu's Mistakes and the True Meaning of Separation," 25 *Oxford J. Legal Stud.* 419, 421–23 (2005).

5 1 Thomas Jefferson, "Thomas Jefferson to Edmund Pendleton, August 26, 1776," in *The Papers of Thomas Jefferson* 503, 505 (Julian P. Boyd et al. eds., 1950).

6 Marbury v. Madison, 5 U.S. (1 Cranch) 137 (1803).

7 *Id.* at 180 ("Why does a judge swear to discharge his duties agreeably to the constitution of the United States, if that constitution forms no rule for his government?"). Philip Hamburger has recently stressed the historical primacy of judges' duty to apply the law in his thorough history of the development of judicial constitutional review. See generally Philip Hamburger, *Law and Judicial Duty* (2008).

constitutional judgments of the Supreme Court, Justice Hugo Black replied: "Well, the court didn't do it. . . . The Constitution did it."[8]

This is a view of the function of courts in constitutional litigation that has few defenders today. The Constitution, it is reasoned, must be interpreted and interpretation is not and cannot be a mechanical process. The preoccupation of American constitutional scholars with judicial interpretation is well known. It is enough here to note that most commentators, even most of those attached to a method of interpretation tethered to the original meaning of the constitutional language, see constitutional judges as faced with inevitable choices in adjudicating claims under the Constitution.[9] Without regard to the correctness of this assumption as a matter of theory, no candid observer can deny that, in fact, the history of American constitutional law is, in critical measure, one of judicial choice.

In this sense, judges may be lawmakers, and often are. But are they in any sense *positive* lawmakers? We will treat judges as engaged in positive lawmaking when they *originate* a scheme of law as opposed to merely considering, revising, or rejecting schemes conceived by other legislative actors. As we hope our examination of American constitutional law will show, this is a question of degree, not of absolute characterization. We need to ask, that is, not "was this positive legislation?" but "to what extent was this positive legislation?"

This sense of positive legislation resonates with the famous dictum of Hans Kelsen that a constitutional court which can declare enacted laws ineffective functions as a "negative legislator."[10] Kelsen's characterization followed from his liberal definition of legislation as any "creation of general norms."[11] A judgment that effectively invalidates a statute changes the content of the set of legal norms. For Kelsen, this was enough to amount to legislation.[12] Kelsen was clear that such a judgment had "a constitutive, not a declaratory character."[13] This way of looking at things was in direct

8 *Justice Black and the Bill of Rights* (CBS Television Broadcast, Dec. 3, 1968).

9 See, e.g., Michael J. Perry, *The Constitution in the Courts: Law or Politics?*, 55–57, 95–102 (1994). We discuss the current state of the debate on "originalist" constitutional interpretation *infra* text accompanying notes 53–61.

10 Hans Kelsen, *General Theory of Law and State* 268 (Anders Wedberg trans., 1949).

11 *Id.* at 270.

12 Other scholars, focusing on other distinctive aspects of such adjudication, have denied that it involves legislation. See, e.g., Allan R. Brewer-Carías, *Études de droit public comparé* 685 (2001) (noting that constitutional courts use "legal methods and criteria, in a process initiated by a party with the required standing").

13 Hans Kelsen, "Judicial Review of Legislation: A Comparative Study of the Austrian and the American Constitution," 4 *J. Pol.* 183, 190 (1942).

contradiction to the classic American view of constitutional adjudication, according to which a judicial holding of unconstitutionality amounted to an authoritative statement that the statute was void *ab initio*.[14] A judgment could not repeal or "abolish" statutes. The Austrian Constitution of 1920, in language drafted by Kelsen, on the other hand, refers to the power of the Constitutional Court to cancel or undo (*aufheben*) a law – not merely to declare it to be without effect.[15] While Kelsen himself sometimes used the somewhat more ambiguous English word "annul," he was in no doubt that when a constitutional court held a law invalid, it was legislating.[16] In the same vein, the Austrian Constitution called for a judgment of the Constitutional Court invalidating an enactment to be published in the official journal of new legislation, a practice followed in numerous national constitutions adopting the Austrian model of constitutional review.[17]

Kelsen, in fact, gave little attention to the ways that legislation might be negative or positive. If anything, his insistence that annulment of legislative enactments amounted to lawmaking depended on an assumption that there was no essential difference between creating and removing an official norm. Rescinding a law was legislation whether it was done by a constitutional court or by an elected assembly; indeed, there is nothing intrinsically more important about the creation of a rule than its elimination. What does distinguish these two forms of lawmaking is the universe of possibilities open to the legislator in each case. The potential agenda of the ordinary lawmaker includes any form of regulation that he or she can constitutionally conceive. The constitutional judge as a negative lawmaker, on the other hand, appears strictly limited to subjects already considered and addressed by nonjudicial legislators. For a constitutional court to be a positive lawmaker under this terminology would involve the court in considering, propounding, and creating a scheme of regulation of its own conception.

The formal characteristics of adjudication, of course, limit the lawmaking potential of constitutional courts. The agenda of such courts is largely set by

14 See *Norton v. Shelby County*, 118 U.S. 425, 442 (1886). As discussed below, this pristine view has been considerably modified.

15 The official English translation of the Austrian Constitution, in this respect unchanged since 1920, uses the even more suggestive "rescinded"; available at http://www.ris.bka.gv.at/Dokumente/Erv/ERV_1930_1/ERV_1930_1.html (last visited Sept. 3, 2009).

16 See Kelsen, *supra* note 13, at 187–90. Later Kelsen sometimes used the English word "abolish." *See* Hans Kelsen, *General Theory of Law and State* 268 (Anders Wedberg trans., 1949).

17 See Venice Commission, *Decisions of Constitutional Courts and Equivalent Bodies and their Execution*, May 17, 2001, available at http://www.venice.coe.int/docs/2001/CDL-INF(2001)009-e.asp.

the choices of other people, although in some systems, liberal rules on standing to litigate or the sheer number of potential litigants mean that there are few important questions of public policy that may not, at some point, present themselves for decision.[18] In any event, once a court has taken jurisdiction, a substantial range of possible lawmaking may arise within the scope of the subject matter before it.

It is worth noting briefly a second sense of "positive lawmaking" that may be relevant in our discussion. A constitutional court may be said to engage in positive constitutional lawmaking when the rule it formulates creates "affirmative" public duties. Students of comparative constitutional law are familiar with the distinction between "first generation," or negative, constitutional rights debarring state interference with private activity and "second generation," or positive, constitutional rights obliging the state to provide certain benefits.[19] When American courts have engaged in positive constitutional lawmaking in the first sense, they have mainly produced "negative" constitutional law in the second sense. That is, they have pronounced limits on what the state may do. But there is a relationship. Positive judicial lawmaking in the first sense may raise some of the problems that have been particularly associated with the enforcement of affirmative social and economic rights. In particular, commentators have worried about the ability of courts to provide adequate remedies in light of the limited capacity of courts to administer the necessary programs or to compel others to do so.[20] Kelsen, noting the presence in some constitutions of provisions "prescribing a certain content for future laws," assumed that they could have no legal (that is, justiciable) effect since "it is hardly possible to attach legal consequences to such an omission [to legislate]."[21]

[18] See generally Richard S. Kay, *Standing to Raise Constitutional Issues: Comparative Perspectives* (2005). Allan R. Brewer-Carías has questioned the usefulness of referring to constitutional courts as "legislators" in light of the formal limits on the way courts do business. See Allan R. Brewer-Carías, *supra* note 12, at 684. It is also worth pointing out that *sua sponte* legal declarations by constitutional courts are not unknown. See *In re* 42 Pa. C. S. § 1703, 394 A.2d 444 (Pa. 1978); Wojciech Sadurski, *Twenty Years after the Transition: Constitutional Review in Central and Eastern Europe* (Sydney Law School Research Paper nº 09/69, 2009, available at http://ssrn.com/abstract=1437843 (discussing self-initiated constitutional review in Hungary and Russia).

[19] There are now references to third-generation rights, the beneficiaries of which are groups and communities. See David S. Law, "Globalization and the Future of Constitutional Rights," 102 *NW. U. L. Rev.* 1277, 1282 n.15 (2008).

[20] See generally Ross Sandler and David Schoenbrod, *Democracy by Decree: What Happens When Courts Run Government* (2003).

[21] Kelsen, *supra* note 10, at 262.

When a court engages in true "negative" legislation in the classic Kelsenian sense, the remedy of invalidation is simple enough. The legal system goes on without the law in question. When a court creates a new legal regulation, however, its effectiveness often depends on more than passive acquiescence. It requires the active cooperation of other agents. So, as we will see in Part III, when American courts formulated certain procedural rules for the apprehension and detention of persons accused of crimes, the effectiveness of those rules depended on changing police practices. And when they enunciated constitutional standards for the treatment of incarcerated persons, it proved necessary for courts to oversee the operation of prison facilities. These challenges are similar whether the rules formulated impose negative or affirmative duties.

II. HOW AMERICAN COURTS LEGISLATE THROUGH CONSTITUTIONAL ADJUDICATION

In this part, we review the development of lawmaking by American courts in the process of constitutional adjudication and briefly consider some of the significant subjects of policy and value in which those courts have taken a leading role. We will look briefly as well at the academic and political responses to such judicial legislation. It should go without saying that we can do no more here than adumbrate a complex and multifaceted phenomenon.

We have referred to the long-standing tradition of elaborating law in common law adjudication, elaboration which, when practiced apart from a controlling enacted text, has come to be universally recognized as a kind of lawmaking. That elaboration was effected in opinions issued by judges explaining their decisions. Neither English nor American courts abandoned that format for decision-making when resolving legal disputes in which the law invoked was a formally enacted text. American courts have from the beginning issued written reasons in their constitutional judgments. That written reasoning, in the context of constitutional dispute resolution, expounds what the Constitution requires. Exposition is elaboration. Elaboration is lawmaking. Judicial resolution of constitutional disputes has added to the words that count as American constitutional law – the words to which later courts, and others wishing to know what American constitutional law is, have turned to find answers to their legal questions.

The American founders posited distinct executive, legislative, and judicial departments of government, relying in substantial measure on Montesquieu's tripartite schema. But when Montesquieu used "the Constitution of

England"[22] as his heuristic for distinguishing legislative, executive, and judicial powers, he displayed no awareness of the opinion-writing practices of the English judges.[23] His own judicial experience in France had left him aware that dispute resolvers sometimes needed to investigate the "spirit" of the laws they applied,[24] but he contemplated less need for that in England. The English, after all, regularly convened a representative body to legislate and so could readily rectify their written law's deficiencies. If laws needed elaboration, Parliament could achieve that through later laws. Montesquieu did not see that English courts were, in fact, contributing to the process of elaborating law by issuing reasoned opinions for their decisions.[25] They were not, *pace* Jefferson, "mere machines."

Of what, then, did Montesquieu's judicial power consist? Montesquieu made that clear by identifying those whom he thought were exercising it. They were . . . juries.[26] Montesquieu's "power of judging"[27] was a power to resolve questions of *fact*. That English judges were resolving questions of law, were writing opinions explaining the reasons for their decisions on those questions of law, and were receiving deference from later courts resolving later disputes, Montesquieu seemed not to notice. Had he realized that English judges were issuing writings that elaborated upon the effect of existing laws and that, under the doctrine of precedent, later dispute resolvers were treating those elaborative words as *part of the law*, there is little doubt how Montesquieu would have classified the issuance of those writings. They were exercises of *legislative* power, analogous to the Roman rescripts that Montesquieu called "a bad method of legislation," but legislation nonetheless.[28]

During debates over the ratification of the U.S. Constitution, the more insightful among the Constitution's opponents worried that Article III's "one supreme Court," vested with the power to resolve all disputes "arising under this Constitution," might "make" the law of the Constitution.[29] Alexander Hamilton aptly summarized their critique:

[22] Charles de Secondat, Baron de Montesquieu, *The Spirit of the Laws* (Thomas Nugent trans.), Bk. XI, Ch. VI. (ed. rev. 1873, first published 1748).

[23] See Claus, *supra* note 4, at 422–23, 431–33.

[24] Montesquieu, *supra* note 22, at Bk. VI, Ch. III, 85–86.

[25] *Id.*; *Id.* at Bk. XI, Ch. VI, 182.

[26] *Id.* at 175–76.

[27] *Id.* at 173–74.

[28] *Id.* at Bk. XXIX, Ch. XVII, 290–91.

[29] See Brutus, Nos. 12 and 15, *in* Herbert J. Storing, *The Complete Antifederalist* 423–26, 437–42 (1981).

> The authority of the proposed Supreme Court of the United States, which is to be a separate and independent body, will be superior to that of the legislature. The power of construing the laws according to the spirit of the Constitution, will enable that court to mould them into whatever shape it may think proper; especially as its decisions will not be in any manner subject to the revision or correction of the legislative body. This is as unprecedented as it is dangerous. In Britain, the judicial power, in the last resort, resides in the House of Lords, which is a branch of the legislature; and this part of the British government has been imitated in the State constitutions in general. The Parliament of Great Britain, and the legislatures of the several States, can at any time rectify, by law, the exceptionable decisions of their respective courts. But the errors and usurpations of the Supreme Court of the United States will be uncontrollable and remediless.[30]

Hamilton disputed this analysis, famously countering that the judiciary would "have neither *force* nor *will*, but merely judgment; and must ultimately depend upon the aid of the executive arm even for the efficacy of its judgments."[31] As he must have known, the idea that courts exercised only case-confined judgment was false, and his ensuing citation of Montesquieu was a mischievous exploitation of the French theorist's inadequate understanding of common law adjudication and of the doctrine of precedent. *Juries* might have only judgment, for their fact-finding has no significance beyond the outcome for the parties before them, and the legal rules applied to their fact-finding are exogenously established. Subject to their understandings of morality in constitutional interpretation, on the other hand, *judges* are presented with ample opportunities to exercise will. Through their written reasons for decision, they can will law into being, as surely as congressmen and senators do when voting for bills. And in a system that apportions legislative and executive powers within a national government and federally between that government and state governments, the other constitutional actors might well find that according force to judicial exercises of will is the only way to preserve the Constitution's scheme for authentically apportioned power.

The text of the U.S. Constitution, consisting at critical points of "majestic generalities,"[32] might be read as offering its expositors a linguistic basis for

30 Alexander Hamilton, John Jay, and James Madison, *The Federalist: A Commentary on the Constitution of the United States Being a Collection of Essays Written in Support of the Constitution Agreed upon September 17, 1787, by the Federal Convention* 502 (1888) (nº 81) (Alexander Hamilton).

31 *The Federalist*, nº 78, *supra* note 30.

32 *W. Va. State Bd. of Educ. v. Barnette*, 319 U.S. 624, 639 (1943).

elaborating the great moral ideas of liberty and equality. The U.S. Supreme Court's elaboration of those ideas provides perhaps the most salient example of positive lawmaking in the course of American constitutional adjudication. On its face, the equal protection clause of the Fourteenth Amendment[33] provides a plausible textual basis for licensing courts to expound the nature of equality. The Court's choice to treat the more obscure constitutional guarantee of "due process"[34] as a linguistic invitation to expound "liberty," on the other hand, has been more controversial.[35] Some commentators have treated the Ninth Amendment[36] as supplying linguistic support for a general constitutional guarantee of liberty,[37] although this is arguably not the reading best supported by the amendment's history,[38] and not one that the Court has ever clearly endorsed.[39]

The Constitution's guarantee of equal protection has been interpreted to guarantee equal treatment by the law, not just equal application of the law.[40] Expounding that guarantee has involved American courts in the highly controvertible enterprise of deciding which distinctions drawn in laws are morally acceptable and which are unacceptable.[41] The Constitution's insistence that no person be deprived of liberty "without due process of law" has, with less linguistic basis,[42] been held by the Supreme Court to guarantee

33 "No state shall . . . deny to any person within its jurisdiction the equal protection of the laws." U.S. Const. amend. XIV § 1.

34 There are two due process clauses in the U.S. Constitution. Amendment V of the U.S. Constitution ("No person shall be . . . deprived of life, liberty, or property, without due process of law") applies to the United States, and amendment XIV ("[N]or shall any State deprive any person of life, liberty, or property, without due process of law") to the state governments. With few exceptions they have been applied consistently with each other.

35 See most prominently *Roe v. Wade*, 410 U.S. 113 (1973).

36 "The enumeration in the Constitution, of certain rights, shall not be construed to deny or disparage others retained by the people." U.S. Const. amend. IX.

37 See Daniel A. Farber, *Retained by the People: The "Silent" Ninth Amendment and the Constitutional Rights Americans Don't Know They Have* (2007); Randy E. Barnett, "The Ninth Amendment: It Means What It Says," 85 *Tex. L. Rev.* 1 (2006).

38 See Laurence Claus, "Protecting Rights from Rights: Enumeration, Disparagement, and the Ninth Amendment," 79 *Notre Dame L. Rev.* 585 (2004); Kurt T. Lash, "A Textual-Historical Theory of the Ninth Amendment," 60 *Stan. L. Rev.* 895 (2008); Kurt T. Lash, "The Lost Original Meaning of the Ninth Amendment," 83 *Tex. L. Rev.* 331 (2004).

39 Kurt T. Lash, *The Lost Jurisprudence of the Ninth Amendment*, 83 *Tex. L. Rev.* 597 (2005). Cf. *Griswold v. Conn.*, 381 U.S. 479, 486–99 (1965) (Goldberg, J., joined by Warren, C.J. and Brennan, J., concurring).

40 *Yick Wo v. Hopkins*, 118 U.S 356, 369 (1886) ("[T]he equal protection of the laws is a pledge of the protection of equal laws.").

41 See, e.g., *Brown v. Bd. of Educ.*, 347 U.S. 483 (1954); *Romer v. Evans*, 517 U.S. 620 (1996).

42 The clause has its roots in chapter 39 of Magna Carta, which recited an array of adverse government actions not to be done to any "free man . . . except by the lawful judgment of his

liberty outright,[43] thus allowing courts to decide which freedoms are so important that government is limited or precluded from removing those freedoms. The case law expounding the clause moved meaning through three stages.

The first stage of due process exposition saw judicial expositors conclude, after some initial uncertainty,[44] that the due process clause constrained legislatures in their choice of content for enacted law. Those early cases pointed to a limitation redolent of the Constitution's prohibitions of bills of attainder[45] and of cruel and unusual punishments.[46] It was a limitation that implemented more comprehensively the separation-of-powers principle, later reflected in the equal protection clause, that legislation should be general in character, not targeted by legislators to kill, lock up, or take property from particular disfavored individuals.[47] Broader judicial power to protect liberty and property from legislative encroachment was, in this period, sometimes directly attributed to extra-textual natural rights.[48]

Expounding the due process clause moved into a second stage when American courts began holding that the clause precluded legislatures from impairing existing property rights even by general legislation,[49] a principle congruent with the protection for liberty provided more specifically in the

peers or by the law of the land." The more general guarantee of due process was in Magna Carta explicitly in the alternative to one particular procedure for removing someone's life, liberty, or property, namely, "lawful judgment of his peers." The first American state constitution adopted that phraseology: "[T]hat no man be deprived of his liberty, except by the law of the land or the judgment of his peers." VA. CONST., art. I, § 8 (1776). That clause could be satisfied by a jury verdict, and *liberty* in the clause clearly just meant not being locked up. The alternative, more general promise of due process would thus also appear to have been simply about legally required procedures for deciding whether someone should be imprisoned. *Liberty* was something that a jury could plausibly vote to remove – the term was used in the narrow sense of freedom from jail, not in the quite distinct and sweeping sense of freedom from legal restrictions on action.

43 See *Roe v. Wade*, 410 U.S. 113 (1973); *Griswold v. Connecticut*, 381 U.S. 479 (1965); *Lochner v. New York*, 198 U.S. 45 (1905).

44 See, e.g., *Mayo v. Wilson*, 1 N.H. 53, 57 (1817) (treating duly enacted legislation as necessarily due process of law).

45 U.S. Const. art. I, § 9, cl. 3; U.S. Const. art. I, § 10, cl. 1.

46 U.S. Const. amend. VIII.

47 See, e.g., *Dartmouth College v. Woodward*, 4 Wheat. 518, 581 (1819) (submissions of Daniel Webster); *Hoke v. Henderson*, 15 N.C. 1, 14–15 (1833) (Ruffin, C.J.).

48 See *Calder v. Bull*, 3 U.S. (3 Dall.) 386, 387–89 (1798) (Chase, J.). Cf. *id.* at 398–99 (Iredell, J., concurring). See also *Wilkinson v. Leland*, 27 U.S. (2 Pet.) 627, 657 (1829) (Story, J.); *Terrett v. Taylor*, 13 U.S. (9 Cranch) 43, 52 (1815) (Story, J.); *Fletcher v. Peck*, 10 U.S. (6 Cranch) 87, 135–36 (1810) (Marshall, C.J.).

49 See *Wynehamer v. People*, 13 N.Y. 378 (1856).

Constitution's prohibition of *ex post facto* laws.[50] Laws could prevent property rights from arising in the future and could provide for loss of liberty or property based on future conduct,[51] but could not simply confiscate or imprison. But then came stage three, in which courts began treating "liberty" in the clause not just as a modest reference to being out of jail but as an expansive expression of freedom to live one's life free from unjustified government regulation.[52] So read, the clause condemns any government restriction that the courts – and ultimately, five Justices of the Supreme Court – consider morally unjustified. And so the law of liberty and equality in America is now, in large measure, ultimately created and shaped by the Supreme Court.

Those who consider such open-ended moral decision-making an inapt allocation of power to courts have expressed their concern, in part, as following from theories of interpretive morality. Prominent in this context are principles of so-called originalist interpretation that require judges to take the meaning of a constitutional rule as fixed at the moment of its promulgation. But originalism does not necessarily obviate broad moral decision-making that in turn makes law for the nation. The most prominent and widely-endorsed contemporary theory of originalism, "original public meaning originalism," calls for interpretation to be based on the meaning that the language of the Constitution had for a (variously defined) typical American reader or speaker of English at the time of enactment.[53] This approach draws support from the fact that we make law as a community to serve an essentially predictive function and that law cannot fulfill that function if it lacks meaning-fixedness across its audience community and over time. But the original public meaning of "equal protection", for

50 U.S. Const. art. I, § 9, cl. 3; U.S. CONST. art. I, § 10, cl. 1. At an early date, the Supreme Court held this provision to apply only to retroactive imposition or enhancement of criminal penalties. *Calder*, 3 U.S. (3 Dall.) at 386.

51 Cf. *Dred Scott v. Sandford,* 60 U.S. (19 How.) 393, 450 (1856) (Taney, C.J.), which signaled that even future conduct (in that case, bringing a slave into a free state) might not always be sufficient ground for removing property rights.

52 See, e.g., *Allgeyer, v. Louisiana*, 165 U.S. 578 (1897) (affirming, unanimously, the "liberty to contract").

53 See, e.g., Randy E. Barnett, *Restoring the Lost Constitution: The Presumption of Liberty* (2004); Antonin Scalia, *A Matter of Interpretation: Federal Courts and the Law* (1997); Keith E. Whittington, *Constitutional Construction: Divided Powers and Constitutional Meaning* (1999); Keith E. Whittington, *Constitutional Interpretation: Textual Meaning, Original Intent, and Judicial Review* (1999); Lawrence B. Solum, *Semantic Originalism* 120 (Illinois Public Law Research Paper nº 07-24, 2008), available at http://ssrn.com/abstract=1120244. Various specifications for the typical reader have been posited in the literature. See Richard S. Kay, "Original Intention and Public Meaning in Constitutional Interpretation," 103 *Nw. U. L. Rev.* 703, 721–23 (2009).

example, provides enormous opportunities for judicial legislation insofar as it hands to expositors the job of deciding, without much restriction, which distinctions morally matter. Likewise, the original public meaning of the Second Amendment's "right to bear arms"[54] hands to the courts the chance for elaborative decision making about which weapons count as "arms."[55] In identifying original public meaning, one can no more justify limiting "equal protection" to prohibiting race discrimination than one can justify limiting "arms" to muskets.

The apparent judicial discretion to legislate national morality entailed by original public meaning interpretation is less obvious in a different strain of originalism, which we might call intentionalism and which identifies the original meaning with the meaning the text had for the actual enactors of a constitutional provision (as opposed to the hypothetical community member of public meaning originalism).[56] Intentionalism might appear a more appealing interpretive principle for those who wish to limit the Constitution's reach to something resembling the "original expected application"[57] of constitutional guarantees. In order to ascertain the intended meaning, this approach calls for consulting, among other sources, legislative history to a degree that English common law courts declined to do until 1992.[58] But confining meaning to original expected application need not be the consequence of intentionalism, depending on what was intended by those whose views intentionalists think we should care about. Choice to express oneself at a level of abstraction above one's concrete concerns suggests an intention to address future counterparts to those concerns, counterparts perhaps not yet adequately appreciated at the time of enactment. The Second Amendment's adopters could have explicitly confined themselves to the weapons that they personally valued. The Fourteenth Amendment's adopters could have explicitly confined themselves to the particular immoral discrimination that was bothering them. They chose, instead, to express

54 "A well regulated Militia, being necessary to the security of a free State, the right of the people to keep and bear Arms, shall not be infringed." U.S. Const. amend. II.

55 See *District of Columbia v. Heller*, 128 S.Ct. 2783 (2008).

56 See, e.g., Richard S. Kay, "Adherence to the Original Intentions in Constitutional Adjudication: Three Objections and Responses," 82 *Nw. U. L. Rev.*. 226 (1988).

57 See Jack M. Balkin, "Abortion and Original Meaning," 24 *Const. Comment.* 291, 293 (2007); Jack M. Balkin, "Original Meaning and Constitutional Redemption," 24 *Const. Comment.* 427 (2007).

58 See *Pepper v. Hart* [1992] A.C. 593 (H.L.) (U.K.). Public meaning originalists also consult drafting and ratification history, but they do so to gather evidence of usage in the period of enactment. See Vasan Kesavan and Michael Stokes Paulsen, "The Interpretive Force of the Constitution's Secret Drafting History," 91 *Geo. L.J.* 1113, 1118 (2003).

themselves at a higher level of abstraction. Whether or not that choice of language reflected a decision to delegate broad elaborative discretion to later expositors is itself a historical fact, one that intentionalist interpreters need to investigate.

The debate between proponents of intentionalism and proponents of original public meaning may ultimately turn on differing perceptions of the nature and function of law. Particularly relevant is the question whether lawmakers have "authority," in the sense of moral right, to be obeyed. One of us finds moral support for intentionalism in widely-endorsed notions about what creates a moral duty to obey the U.S. Constitution,[59] while the other of us favors original public meaning on the basis that law is, in Holmes' terms, just a body of "systematized prediction."[60] On that view, notions of lawgivers' moral right to be obeyed are superfluous to law's true nature.[61]

In any event, theories of morality in interpretation have not had much effect in constraining the courts, which have, as the examples given illustrate, appropriated a wide range of fundamental social and political decision-making. What else might constrain? For much of its history, the U.S. Congress has been dubiously treated as having power to create "Exceptions" to the Supreme Court's jurisdiction to decide constitutional questions.[62] But this alleged ability to deprive the Court of constitutional

59 See Kay, *supra* note 53, *passim*.

60 Oliver Wendell Holmes, Jr., "The Path of the Law," 10 *Harv. L. Rev.* 457, 458 (1897) ("lay[ing] down some first principles for the study of this body of dogma or systematized prediction which we call the law.").

61 Laurence Claus, "The Empty Idea of Authority," 2009 *U. Ill. L. Rev.* 1301.

62 *See* U.S. Const. art. III, § 2, cl. 2. For a range of views on the scope of the power, see Martin H. Redish, *Federal Jurisdiction: Tensions in the Allocation of Judicial Power*, 24–45 (2d ed. 1990); Akhil Reed Amar, "Article III and the Judiciary Act of 1789: The Two-Tiered Structure of the Judiciary Act of 1789," 138 *U. Pa. L. Rev.* 1499 (1990); Akhil Reed Amar, "A Neo-Federalist View of Article III: Separating the Two Tiers of Federal Jurisdiction," 65 *B.U. L. Rev.* 205 (1985); Charles L. Black, *Decision According to Law*, 37–39 (1981); Steven G. Calabresi and Gary Lawson, "The Unitary Executive, Jurisdiction Stripping, and the Hamdan Opinions: A Textualist Response to Justice Scalia," 107 *Colum. L. Rev.* 1002 (2007); Laurence Claus, "The One Court that Congress Cannot Take Away: Singularity, Supremacy, and Article III," 96 *Geo. L.J.* 59 (2007); Laurence Claus, "Constitutional Guarantees of the Judiciary: Jurisdiction, Tenure, and Beyond," 54 *Am. J. Comp. L.* 459, 460–76 (2006); Barry Friedman, "A Different Dialogue: The Supreme Court, Congress and Federal Jurisdiction," 85 *Nw. U. L. Rev.* 1 (1990); Gerald Gunther, "Congressional Power to Curtail Federal Court Jurisdiction: An Opinionated Guide to the Ongoing Debate," 36 *Stan. L. Rev.* 895 (1984); John Harrison, "The Power of Congress to Limit the Jurisdiction of Federal Courts and the Text of Article III," 64 *U. Chi. L. Rev.* 203, 243–44 (1997); Henry M. Hart, Jr., "The Power of Congress to Limit the Jurisdiction of Federal Courts: An Exercise in Dialectic," 66 *Harv. L. Rev.* 1362, 1365 (1953); Daniel J. Meltzer, "The History and Structure of Article III," 138 *U. Pa. L. Rev.* 1569 (1990); James E. Pfander, "Marbury, Original Jurisdiction, and the Supreme Court's Supervisory Powers," 101

lawmaking power has lain largely in desuetude, thanks to Congress's need for judicial policing of the Constitution's apportionment of powers. That apportionment between Congress, the President, and the state governments, must be the subject of elaborative judicial lawmaking regardless of the Constitution's linguistic vagueness. Umpiring the apportionment of power among American government institutions has rendered the Supreme Court's expositions of the Constitution an indispensable feature of American public life. When the issue is *which* of multiple competing elected government actors is allowed to act, the Justices lack the option of being pervasively pro-democratic "minimalists" who routinely resolve vagueness and ambiguity in favor of the validity of action by elected institutions.[63] However unclear the Constitution, the Court must decide who gets to act, and its decisions must succeed in affecting what the competing actors do. The American system of separated branches and levels of government cannot otherwise survive.

Secure in its almost universally recognized indispensability, the Supreme Court has elaborated with similar latitude upon the constitutional vaguenesses and ambiguities that concern relations between government and the individual. For the most part, Congress has not been tempted to truncate the Court's jurisdiction to do this. The exceptional circumstances in which Congress has seriously threatened use of its "Exceptions" power have been occasions on which the Court had protected, or looked likely to protect, "discrete and insular minorities"[64] from government action. Until recently, Congress's most notorious use of the power was to strip the Court of jurisdiction to hear challenges to federal measures of doubtful constitutionality adopted in the wake of the American Civil War.[65] In this century and decade, the "Exceptions" power has been invoked in Congress

Colum. L. Rev. 1515 (2001); James E. Pfander, "Jurisdiction-Stripping and the Supreme Court's Power to Supervise Inferior Tribunals," 78 *Tex. L. Rev.* 1433, 1455 n.8 (2000); Lawrence Gene Sager, "The Supreme Court 1980 Term, Foreword: Constitutional Limitations on Congress' Authority to Regulate the Jurisdiction of the Federal Courts," 95 *Harv. L. Rev.* 17 (1981); Herbert Wechsler, "The Courts and the Constitution," 65 *Colum. L. Rev.* 1001, 1005–06 (1965).

63 James Bradley Thayer argued that the Supreme Court should resolve constitutional underdeterminacy in favor of the validity of Congressional action but that the Court should accord no comparable favor to state government action. See James B. Thayer, "The Origin and Scope of the American Doctrine of Constitutional Law," 7 *Harv. L. Rev.* 129, 150, 154–55 (1893). Thayerian minimalism rests, then, not on deference to democratic choice, but on whether institutions enjoy coordinate status with the Court. On that premise, how should the Court resolve demarcation disputes *between* the Court's two elected coordinates?

64 *United States v. Carolene Prods. Co.*, 304 U.S. 144, 152 n.4 (1938) (Stone, J., opinion of the Court).

65 *Ex parte McCardle*, 74 U.S. (7 Wall.) 506 (1869).

in connection with proposals to stop the Court hearing claims from aliens,[66] atheists,[67] and gay people.[68] Notwithstanding substantial support for some of these measures, the breadth of the Supreme Court's jurisdiction has escaped largely untouched. Measured by durability and depth of influence in shaping constitutional values, the Justices may well be the most powerful sitting lawmakers in the nation.

III. ENFORCING JUDICIAL LEGISLATION

The impressive enterprise of positive lawmaking by American courts in the course of constitutional adjudication has, necessarily, raised questions about how to enforce the resulting law. Kelsen expected enforcement of "negative" law that emerged from constitutional courts to be fairly straightforward. The condemned measure would be erased from the statute book, just as if it had been repealed by the legislature.

The American constitutional experience, however, has shown that complexities arise when enforcing even decisions that simply hold legislative acts invalid. There has been controversy, for example, concerning the effect that such decisions have on the legal status of actions taken pursuant to law before that law's invalidation.[69] Under the classic understanding of constitutional judicial review derived from *Marbury v. Madison*, a judgment

66 Detainee Treatment Act of 2005 §§ 1005(e), 1005(h); Military Commissions Act of 2006 § 7. The Court's decisions holding aspects of the Acts invalid did not directly address the reach of the "Exceptions" power. See *Hamdan v. Rumsfeld*, 548 U.S. 557 (2006); *Boumediene v. Bush*, 128 S.Ct. 2229 (2008).

67 *Pledge Protection Act* of 2004 § 2 (passed by the House of Representatives as H.R. 2028 on Sept. 23, 2004) and Pledge Protection Act of 2005 § 2 (introduced to the House of Representatives and Senate respectively as H.R. 2389 and S. 1046 on May 17, 2005) (purporting to eliminate the Supreme Court's jurisdiction to determine the constitutionality of the Pledge of Allegiance as defined in 4 U.S.C. § 4 or of that pledge's recitation). See also *Constitution Restoration Act* of 2005 § 101 (introduced to the House of Representatives and Senate respectively as H.R. 1070 and S. 520 on Mar. 3, 2005) (purporting to eliminate the Supreme Court's jurisdiction to determine the constitutionality of government actors' "acknowledgment of God as the sovereign source of law, liberty, or government").

68 Marriage Protection Act of 2004 § 2 (passed by the House of Representatives as H.R. 3313 on July 22, 2004) and Marriage Protection Act of 2005 § 2 (introduced to the House of Representatives as H.R. 1100 on Mar. 3, 2005) (purporting to eliminate the Supreme Court's jurisdiction to determine the constitutionality of the Defense of Marriage Act, 28 U.S.C. § 1738C).

69 A related question attaches to the case of a statute held invalid in a judgment subsequently overruled. Does the law in question spring back into life, or is a new enactment necessary? The Supreme Court, to the extent it has considered the question, seems to have assumed such a statute is once more automatically effective. See Legal Tender Cases, 79 U.S. (12 Wall.) 457 (1870). The issue is discussed in William Michael Treanor and Gene B. Sperling, "Prospective Overruling and the Revival of 'Unconstitutional' Statutes," 93 *Colum. L. Rev.* 1902 (1993).

of unconstitutionality holds that the unconstitutional enactment was, *contra* Kelsen, never law at all. This orthodox view was expressed in a nineteenth-century decision of the U.S. Supreme Court: "An unconstitutional act is not a law; it confers no rights; it imposes no duties; it affords no protection; it creates no office; it is, in legal contemplation, as inoperative as though it had never been passed."[70] The unsettling results of such a policy with respect to actions undertaken in reliance on an apparently valid law have persuaded the Supreme Court to abandon this absolute rule. It will now, sometimes, declare its holdings to operate only prospectively, based on an evaluation of the particular interests of individuals, society, and the legal system.[71] This kind of holding, of course, makes the legislative character of the judicial action dramatically clear.[72]

The remedial complexities of negative judicial lawmaking are minor, however, when compared with those that attend the judicial creation of legal rules. When a legislature creates a body of law, it is in a position to provide the means by which that law is to be made effective. The new scheme may use existing agencies of law administration and enforcement, or create new ones. It may also provide the necessary resources by appropriating public funds and raising new revenues. Sometimes, as when conduct is regulated by criminal sanction, the existing law enforcement and criminal justice system may be adequate. But in other situations, as has been the case, for example, with respect to new rules protecting the environment, a large new bureaucratic apparatus may be required.[73] In contrast, the instrumentalities of administration and enforcement available to *judicial* legislators are radically limited. It is for this reason that Kelsen dismissed the potential for judicial enforcement of positive constitutional rights.[74] The way in which judicially

70 *Norton v. Shelby County*, 118 U.S. 425, 442 (1886).

71 See, e.g., *Lemon v. Kurtzman*, 411 U.S. 192, 197–201 (1973).

72 "That concept is quite foreign to the American legal and constitutional tradition. It would have struck John Marshall as an extraordinary assertion of raw power. . . . Fully retroactive decision making was considered a principal distinction between the judicial and the legislative power: '[I]t is said that that which distinguishes a judicial from a legislative act is, that the one is a determination of what the existing law is in relation to some existing thing already done or happened, while the other is a predetermination of what the law shall be for the regulation of all future cases.' T. Cooley, *Constitutional Limitations* *91." *Harper v. Va. Dep't of Taxation*, 509 U.S. 86, 106–07 (1993) (Scalia, J., dissenting in part).

73 Alexandra B. Klass, "Modern Public Trust Principles: Recognizing Rights and Integrating Standards," 82 *Notre Dame L. Rev.* 699, 719–20 (2006) (discussing the creation of agencies to implement environmental laws). See generally Peter L. Strauss, Todd D. Rakoff, Cynthia R. Farina, and Walter Gellhorn, *Gellhorn and Byse's Administrative Law: Cases and Comments* 13–23 (Robert C. Clark ed., 10th ed. 2003).

74 See Kelsen, *supra* note 10, at 262.

created rules have been implemented in the United States has been deeply affected by the courts' institutional limitations.[75]

Much depends, of course, on the kind of law the courts have made. Some judge-made law regulates government actors who cannot achieve their goals without judicial confirmation. In such cases, those other officials must comply with the judicial legislation or risk failing in their objectives. The U.S. Supreme Court, invoking the Fourth, Fifth, and Sixth Amendments to the Constitution, has created a fairly detailed set of rules regulating the conditions for lawful search and arrest in connection with investigating and prosecuting crime. These decisions have resulted in a substantial and relatively complex body of law controlling police behavior.[76] The means for assuring the effectiveness of this law are direct and obvious. Courts may simply reverse the convictions of defendants who have been treated other than in accordance with the judicially produced rules.[77] Law enforcement agencies interested in securing convictions, therefore, have an interest in compliance. To a significant extent, police departments have adopted procedures and trained their personnel to follow these rules – a result familiar to any viewer of American television police dramas.[78]

Judicial lawmaking is not so easy to implement when it relates to behavior that does not contemplate some subsequent judicial process. It may happen that, on a statement of the law by a court, the relevant actors, and especially the holders of government power, will conform their behavior to the rules announced. Sometimes, moreover, elected legislators will reenact the court's law in statutory form. The Supreme Court's various and changing pronouncements on the death penalty (whose implementation does require

75 The most famous summary of the limited abilities of the courts is Alexander Hamilton's in *The Federalist* nº 78, noting that the judiciary has "no influence over either the sword or the purse; no direction either of the strength or of the wealth of the society; and can take no active resolution whatever. It may truly be said to have neither Force nor Will, but merely judgment; and must ultimately depend upon the aid of the executive arm even for the efficacy of its judgments." See *The Federalist*, nº 78, *supra* note 30.

76 See Joshua Dressler and Alan C. Michaels, *Understanding Criminal Procedure*, 149–89 (2006).

77 This is a substantial simplification of the actual practice. Not every deviation from the prescribed procedures results in a reversal of the subsequent conviction. One important qualification is the "harmless error" rule whereby a conviction may be affirmed if the reviewing court concludes that it would have resulted even if the police had acted properly. See *id.* at 44. On the uncertain status of these rules in the American legal hierarchy, see Henry P. Monaghan, "The Supreme Court 1974 Term, Foreword: Constitutional Common Law," 89 *Harv. L. Rev.* 1 (1975).

78 See Myron W. Orfield, Jr., "The Exclusionary Rule and Deterrence: An Empirical Study of Chicago Narcotics Officers," 54 U. *Chi. L. Rev.* 1016 (1987) (discussing changes in police training and record-keeping in response to judicial constitutional rulings); Corey Fleming Hirokawa, Comment, "Making the 'Law of the Land' the Law on the Street: How Police Academies Teach Evolving Fourth Amendment Law," 49 *Emory L.J.* 295 (2000) (same).

some judicial confirmation) have generally been followed by conforming legislation.[79] Indeed, in the United States, respect for, and deference to, the constitutional mandates of the courts is much more the norm than the exception.[80] Judges have come to learn, however, that adequate cooperation is not always forthcoming. In such situations, the question arises as to how the judges, lacking the powers of "the sword or the purse," may give substance to the law declared.

This issue has to be seen against the background of Anglo-American law concerning remedies available to successful litigants. That law is, in part, a product of the historic division between courts of common law and courts of equity. Generally speaking, in noncriminal proceedings at common law, courts were limited to remedies reaching the property of the defendant, whereas courts of equity could act "on the person," ordering even a nongovernmental defendant to act or to refrain from acting. From the uneasy coexistence of these systems there eventually emerged a practice whereby resort to equity – and the *in personam* relief it offered – was available only when remedies at law were deemed inadequate to redress the violation of the plaintiff's rights.[81] When, in the last century, both law and equity were lodged in unitary court systems, the priority of remedies was, at least formally, retained. Equitable remedies, including injunctions decreeing a course of conduct by the defendant, were treated as exceptional, to be granted only where law damages were inadequate and, even then, only in the discretion of the court.[82]

The preference for damages remedies raised obvious difficulties in the enforcement of constitutional law in which the wrongs involved so often resist pecuniary measurement. Moreover, until about fifty years ago, an action for money damages premised on a violation of constitutional rights was generally unavailable in federal courts.[83] The quintessential relief

[79] Christine Holdeman, Sandi Mather, and Judith A. Young, Case Note, "Roper v. Simmons: The Death Penalty Was Banned for Juvenile Offenders," 35 *Lincoln L. Rev.* 43, 43 (2007) (noting that thirty-five states amended their death penalty statutes after the Supreme Court's first major decision in 1972).

[80] For a survey of the history of Congressional resistance and acquiescence see Charles G. Geyh, "Judicial Independence, Judicial Accountability, and the Role of Constitutional Norms in Congressional Regulation of the Courts," 78 *Ind. L.J.* 153 (2003).

[81] See Henry L. McClintock, *Handbook of Equity*, 25–26 (1936).

[82] See *Beacon Theatres, Inc. v. Westover*, 359 U.S. 500, 506–11 (1959). Among the factors weighing against the exercise of such discretion is the need for continuous supervision by the court of any decrees that might be issued. See McClintock, *supra* note 81, at 94.

[83] Such an action was not recognized as authorized by federal statute law until 1961. *Monroe v. Pape*, 365 U.S. 167 (1961).

accorded in constitutional cases, exemplified in *Marbury v. Madison*, was, as we have seen, the negative one of finding an unconstitutional act to be without legal effect. Still, the judicial power created in Article III of the Constitution extended to "all cases, in law and equity, arising under this Constitution [and] laws of the United States," suggesting the availability of equitable relief in proper cases. In the early part of the twentieth century, federal courts began issuing injunctions against state officials to bar the enforcement of unconstitutional state laws.[84] Such orders were, however, clearly inadequate to redress constitutional violations that required affirmative changes in the way a state operated. The extent to which U.S. courts have exploited their equitable powers to move beyond prohibitory to mandatory relief is one of the most striking developments in modern constitutional law.

We begin our account of this phenomenon with the Supreme Court's momentous judgments in *Brown v. Board of Education*. In 1954, the Court held that racial segregation in public education was a denial of the "equal protection of the laws," which, under the Fourteenth Amendment, no state was to deny to any person within the state's jurisdiction.[85] At the time of the decision, racially segregated schools operated in thousands of districts, affecting tens of thousands of children in twenty states and the District of Columbia.[86] Under the best circumstances, the necessary reassignment of students and personnel would have been complicated. But, as the Court knew well, circumstances were far from the best. The decision in *Brown* would be bitterly resented and resisted by much of the white population of the American South. The Justices understood that it would take more than a declaration of law to end the dual system of education.[87]

The case was argued before the Supreme Court in December 1952, but in June 1953, the Court issued an order setting the case for reargument the following term and asking the parties to address five questions set by the Court. Questions four and five dealt with the content of any decree the Court might issue should it find segregation unconstitutional. Should that decree order that African-American children "forthwith be admitted to schools of

84 *Ex parte Young*, 209 U.S. 123 (1908).

85 *Brown v. Bd. of Educ.*, 347 U.S. 483 (1954).

86 See Charles T. Clotfelter, *After Brown: The Rise and Retreat of School Desegregation*, 14–22 (2004).

87 The unwillingness of other government actors to implement fully a mere judicial declaration of law was a critical factor leading courts to undertake the kind of extensive managerial functions discussed in this section. For a sensitive discussion, see Paul Gewirtz, "Remedies and Resistance," 92 *Yale L.J.* 585 (1983).

their choice" or should the court "in the exercise of its equity powers, permit an effective gradual adjustment" to unitary systems? And if the latter course were chosen, should the Court "formulate detailed decrees"?[88] Notwithstanding these inquiries and the parties' responses to them, when the Supreme Court, in May 1954, declared racial segregation incompatible with the Fourteenth Amendment, it *again* postponed formulating a remedial order and set down the question for further argument.[89] The Court did not issue its decree in the case until May 1955, two and one-half years after the initial argument.[90]

The Court's opinion in this second *Brown* opinion displays an obvious uncertainty as to what exactly should happen next. It plainly declined to treat the case as ordinary. Rather than particularized relief, the Court foresaw a "transition to a system of public education freed from racial discrimination." This was going to be a process, not an event. Although the "primary responsibility" belonged to local school authorities, their actions would be subject to "judicial appraisal" by lower courts applying "equitable principles":

> Traditionally, equity has been characterized by a practical flexibility in shaping its remedies and by a facility for adjusting and reconciling public and private needs . . . . At stake is the personal interest of the plaintiffs in admission to public schools as soon as practicable on a nondiscriminatory basis. To effectuate this interest may call for elimination of a number of obstacles. . . . Courts of equity may properly take into account the public interest in the elimination of such obstacles in a systematic and effective manner. . . . To that end, the courts may consider problems related to administration, arising from the physical condition of the school plant, the school transportation system, personnel, revision of school districts and attendance areas into compact units to achieve a system of determining admission to the public schools on a nonracial basis. . . . During this period of transition, the courts will retain jurisdiction of these cases.[91]

The *Brown* cases were remanded to the trial courts with instructions to issue orders to the states to admit the plaintiffs to public schools on a nondiscriminatory basis not "forthwith," but "with all deliberate speed."[92] This obscure prescription implicitly recognized that the Court's judgment

88 *Brown v. Bd. of Educ.*, 345 U.S. 972, 972 (1953).

89 *Brown v. Bd. of Educ.*, 347 U.S. 483, 495–96 (1954).

90 *Brown v. Bd. of Educ.*, 349 U.S. 294 (1955).

91 *Id.* at 300–01.

92 *Id.*

amounted to the promulgation of a new national policy to apply across a wide variety of circumstances and into an extended future. Implementing that policy required the machinery of law administration and enforcement. In a memorandum to his colleagues while the case was under consideration, Justice Felix Frankfurter noted that the decree "would be radically different from decrees enforcing merely individual rights," for the Court would be, "broadly speaking, promoting a process of social betterment. . . . [S]preading the adjustment over time will more effectively accomplish the desired end."[93]

The subsequent history of the desegregation of schools in the United States bore out the expectation implicit in the Supreme Court's decision. Desegregation was a painfully slow process. By one count, in 1963, almost a decade after the Court's initial pronouncement, only 1.06 percent of African American children in the South attended school with whites.[94] By that time, the federal courts, and the Supreme Court in particular, began to understand that the complex process of readjustment could not be left to the local school authorities, the defendants in the desegregation cases. An important turning point was reached in 1968 in *Green v. County School Board*.[95] The local school district had responded to a desegregation action by adopting a freedom-of-choice attendance policy honoring any student's request to change schools. But after three years, the previously all-black school was still all-black, although some African-American students had enrolled in the previously white school. The Supreme Court declared that the order in *Brown* obliged any school board that had operated a "dual system . . . to take whatever steps might be necessary to convert to a unitary system in which racial discrimination would be eliminated *root and branch*."[96] It was not enough, that is, to discontinue the policies that had led to unconstitutional segregation. The school district had to "undo" the segregation that those policies had created.[97] The district was obliged to take further measures, such

[93] Quoted in Richard Kluger, *Simple Justice: The History of* Brown v. Board of Education *and Black America's Struggle for Equality* 866–67 (1975). See also Michael J. Klarman, *From Jim Crow to Civil Rights: The Supreme Court and the Struggle for Racial Equality* 313 (2004) ("The justices chose vagueness and gradualism."). In argument before the Court, Thurgood Marshall, one of the counsel for the plaintiffs in *Brown*, and later a Justice of the Supreme Court, argued for an order setting a fixed date for full desegregation no later than one year after the judgment: "I submit that a longer period would get the lower court into the legislative field." Doug Rendleman, "Brown II's 'All Deliberate Speed' at Fifty: A Golden Anniversary or a Mid-Life Crisis for the Constitutional Injunction as a School Desegregation Remedy?" 41 *San Diego L. Rev.* 1575, 1585 (2004).

[94] Some of the statistics are collected in Klarman, *supra* note 93, at 344–63.

[95] *Green v. County Sch. Bd.*, 391 U.S. 430 (1968).

[96] *Id.* at 437–38 (emphasis added).

[97] *Id.* at 440 (quoting the dissenting opinion in the Court of Appeals).

as creating compulsory attendance zones, that would eliminate the racial character of the system.[98] Supervising courts had to evaluate the measures taken "in light of the facts at hand and in light of any alternatives which may be shown as feasible and more promising in their effectiveness." District courts "should retain jurisdiction until it is clear that state-imposed segregation has been completely removed."[99]

What this would mean for the ongoing involvement of courts in administering desegregation plans became clear three years later in *Swann v. Charlotte-Mecklenburg Board of Education.*[100] The Supreme Court approved a detailed decree issued by a district court, based on the recommendation of an expert in educational administration. The Supreme Court endorsed decrees calling for such measures as designing oddly shaped attendance zones, pairing or clustering of black and white schools to produce better racial balance, compulsorily transporting students to schools outside their neighborhoods, reassigning teachers and other personnel to reduce the racial specificity of individual schools, and requiring that new schools be constructed in locations that would not contribute to the persistence of segregation.[101] All of these tools, however, were to be employed with discretion and sensitivity to the particular conditions present in a particular time and place, taking into account both "individual and collective interests."[102]

Over the following twenty years, federal courts repeatedly had to reconcile the constitutional imperative with the practical realities of operating a school system, a task often made more difficult by the passive or active resistance of the local authorities. The practical and political questions associated with managing a desegregation regime returned regularly to the Supreme Court, whose subsequent judgments were largely concerned with defining limits on the broad judicial mandate sketched out in *Brown*, *Green*, and *Swann*. The kinds of issues involved were illustrated by the Supreme Court's judgment in *Missouri v. Jenkins*[103] in 1995, one of the Court's last significant statements on the remedial authority of federal courts in desegregation cases. The

98 *Id.* at 441–42.

99 *Id.* at 439.

100 *Swann v. Charlotte-Mecklenburg Bd. of Educ.*, 402 U.S. 1 (1971).

101 *Id.* at 19–25.

102 *Id.* at 16. The court quoted *Hecht Co. v. Bowles*, 321 U.S. 321, 329–30 (1944) for the proposition that equity was an "instrument for nice adjustment and reconciliation between the public interest and private needs as well as competing private claims."

103 *Missouri v. Jenkins*, 515 U.S. 70 (1995).

district court in that case had found that unconstitutional segregation had affected the quality of the education offered in the schools in issue. Over a ten-year period, the district court judge had, consequently, ordered that class sizes be reduced, that a full-time kindergarten be instituted, that summer programs be expanded, that before- and after-school tutoring be provided, and that an early childhood development program be established. The district court also ordered a major capital improvement program and salary increases for teachers and other school employees.[104] The Supreme Court held that, since many of these actions sought to remedy a racial disparity among school districts, they were not part of a proper remedy for the constitutional violation that had been found within a particular district.[105]

The issues emerging from the remedial approaches developed in desegregation litigation suggest more general themes applicable when constitutional courts make public law. What the substantive constitutional prohibition of racial segregation required may have seemed clear enough when *Brown* was decided in 1954. But the idea, enunciated in *Green*, that an adequate remedy required eliminating every "vestige" of discrimination meant that the supervising courts had to determine what counted as vestiges, how vestiges could be identified, and what measures were appropriate to eliminate them.

The desegregation cases have provided the remedial model for a number of important categories of modern constitutional litigation. The Eighth Amendment's prohibition of "cruel and unusual punishments" has been the predicate for widespread constitutional challenges to the operation of prisons. The same features we have already noted – the need for extended time to reform facilities, the technical complexities of institutional change, the uncertain outcomes of alternative measures and the sometimes reluctant compliance of the responsible officials – have resulted in long-term supervision of numerous institutions. In litigation challenging the constitutionality of aspects of Arkansas state correctional institutions, federal judges ordered, among other things, that institutions be closed, maximum numbers of inmates for particular facilities and for individual cells, detailed procedures for determining disciplinary violations, and limits on the punishments administered. The courts also required employment of full-time psychiatrists or psychologists, affirmative action to recruit more minority personnel, and mandatory training of employees to improve race relations in the prisons. The practice of using armed inmates as "trusty" guards was

[104] *Id.* at 74–80.

[105] *Id.* at 90–100.

prohibited. Inmates were to be provided with educational opportunities and a fair procedure for filing grievances. The courts retained jurisdiction for more than ten years.[106] Mental hospitals have been the subject of similar decrees[107] and, in somewhat more contained proceedings, so has the process of apportioning legislative representation.[108]

Remedial measures of this scope and complexity, especially when combined with such procedural innovations as class actions, flexible rules on joinder of parties, and liberal standing requirements for associations, constitute a new category of judicial action. In an influential article published in 1976, Abram Chayes contrasted the attributes of "public law litigation" with those of traditional adjudication. The object in the new actions was not the well-defined settlement of a discrete dispute between identified parties. It was "not a terminal, compensatory transfer, but an effort to devise a program to contain future consequences in a way that accommodates the range of interests involved."[109] Chayes made clear how these decrees blurred the difference between adjudication and legislation:

> The whole process begins to looks like the traditional description of legislation: Attention is drawn to a "mischief," existing or threatened, and the activity of the parties and court is directed to the development of on-going measures designed to cure that mischief. Indeed, if, as is often the case, the decree sets up an affirmative regime governing the activities in controversy for the indefinite future and having binding force for persons within its ambit, then it is not very much of a stretch to see it as, pro tanto, a legislative act.[110]

106 See *Hutto v. Finney*, 437 U.S. 678 (1978) (dealing with limited aspects of the case). Details and citations are set forth in Malcolm M. Feeley and Edward L. Rubin, *Judicial Policy Making and the Modern State: How the Courts Reformed America's Prisons* 59–74 (1998).

107 *Wyatt v. Stickney*, 344 F. Supp. 373 (1972). See Jules B. Gerard, "A Restrained Perspective on Activism," 64 *Chi.-Kent L. Rev.* 605, 613 (1988) ("The full flavor of the order he did enter is impossible to capture in a summary. It covers eight printed pages and is divided into five major sections. Beside definitions, it contains thirty-five paragraphs, some with as many as sixteen subparagraphs, and some subparagraphs with as many as five sub-subparagraphs. It lists thirty-five different kinds of employees, ranging from psychiatrists and psychologists to messengers and vehicle drivers, and how many of each, every Alabama institution was ordered to have on its staff. It contains detailed instructions with respect to physical facilities – how hot the water must be (110F at the fixture), for example. And so on – and on." (citing *Wyatt*, at 379–86)).

108 See *Branch v. Smith*, 538 U.S. 254 (2003) (upholding a district court injunction ordering adoption of a Congressional district reapportionment plan of the district court's own devising).

109 Abram Chayes, "The Role of the Judge in Public Law Litigation," 89 *Harv. L. Rev.* 1281, 1294 (1976).

110 *Id.* at 1297.

An essential aspect of this development was the elimination or even reversal of the historic priority of legal over equitable remedies. In this category of litigation, at least, the primary remedy is the injunction. Courts often choose, moreover, not a simple command to do or refrain from doing a particular act. Rather, as exemplified by the desegregation cases, they issue continuing injunctions directed at a vaguely expressed goal. They allow for repeated recourse to further judicial review for modification as circumstances change, or as one or another solution proves inadequate to the long-term elimination of the objectionable conditions.[111] The result, at least sometimes, is what Donald Horowitz has called a "chameleon case, ever-new, ever-changing, never-ending."[112]

The actual management of such remedial regimes necessarily occurs in the trial courts, although, as we have seen, their orders are subject to periodic correction by appellate tribunals. The administrative and bureaucratic functions of the trial courts are, in that way, manifestations of the lawmaking activities of the appellate courts. Even more than occurs in modern legislatures, much of the lawmaking by American courts in constitutional litigation involves promulgating broad standards of constitutional conduct.[113] The lower courts thus play a role analogous to that of administrative agencies in giving specific shape to the "soft rights" they have been directed to enforce.[114] Again, the lower courts' experiences working out the practicalities of the Supreme Court's general mandate to eliminate racially segregated schools are exemplary.

The new remedial regimes have been sharply criticized for their radical departure from the ordinary judicial role. Some of the critics may have been motivated merely by disagreement with the substantive changes that the courts have engineered. This was surely the case with many of the shrillest complaints about the courts' involvement in the desegregation of the

111 See *id.* at 1292. See generally Owen M. Fiss, *The Civil Rights Injunction* (1978). Fiss posited the utility of the "structural injunction, which seeks to effectuate the reorganization of an ongoing social institution." *Id.* at 7.

112 Donald L. Horowitz, "Decreeing Organizational Change: Judicial Supervision of Public Institutions," 1983 *Duke L.J.* 1265, 1297 (1983).

113 Michael Dorf draws a connection between broad, indeterminate legal norms and "experimentalist" trial courts that creatively solve problems rather than merely applying controlling rules, although he does not refer explicitly to the judicial administration of structural injunctions. See Michael C. Dorf, "Legal Indeterminacy and Institutional Design," 78 *N.Y.U. L. Rev.* 875, 885–87, 940–43 (2003).

114 See Sandler and Schoenbrod, *supra* note 20, at 99–103. While the subject of this Report is limited to the law emerging from constitutional adjudication, the greater part of public law litigation involves the attempted judicial enforcement of personal rights arising from ordinary legislation. See generally *id.*

schools. But some academic critique focused distinctly on the redefinition of judicial authority that such litigation has produced. According to those critics, such developments transgressed the constitutionally defined limits of the judicial power and involved an unwarranted assumption of both legislative and executive responsibility.[115] Some of the defenses of the expanded judicial role helped to generate this concern. "Civil litigation," according to an early and prominent proponent of structural reform litigation, "is an institutional arrangement for using state power to bring a recalcitrant reality closer to our chosen ideals."[116] Critics questioned whether the unambiguous evil of segregation and its legacy was sufficient moral justification for catapulting the courts into an essentially different institutional role. Given the breadth and complexity of the issues involved, critics contended, courts were necessarily making decisions without full benefit of argument on behalf of all relevant interests, potentially compromising the appearance of disinterestedness that supports judicial authority.[117] Critics charged, moreover, that even strictly in terms of achieving judicially identified social progress, the courts were proving to be crude and clumsy managers of institutional reform.[118]

Worries about judicial overreaching have sometimes manifested themselves in legislative efforts to limit remedial decrees. The Civil Rights Act of 1964 significantly increased the opportunities for judicial intervention in school administration by authorizing the federal government to initiate legal action against segregated systems.[119] Subsequently, however, Congress prescribed a set of priorities for federal courts issuing desegregation orders, including limits on the circumstances in which those courts may order the transportation of students.[120] Unhappiness with intervention in the operation of prisons led to enactment of the Prison Litigation Reform Act in 1996. That legislation limited federal court decrees in prisoner rights cases to "narrowly drawn" relief employing "the least intrusive means necessary to

[115] John Choon Yoo, "Who Measures the Chancellor's Foot? The Inherent Remedial Authority of the Federal Courts," 84 *Cal. L. Rev.* 1121, 1144–71 (1996).

[116] Owen M. Fiss, Comment, "Against Settlement," 93 *Yale L.J.* 1073, 1089 (1984).

[117] See Sandler and Schoenbrod, *supra* note 20, at 123–38.

[118] *See* Horowitz, *supra* note 112. This article remains one of the most perceptive critical reviews of institutional public litigation. See also Gerald N. Rosenberg, *The Hollow Hope: Can Courts Bring About Social Change?* 30–36 (1991) (surveying limitations to courts' ability to effect social reform); Sandler and Schoenbrod, *supra* note 20, at 113–162. See generally Peter H. Schuck, "Judging Remedies: Judicial Approaches to Housing Segregation," 37 *Harv. C.R.-C.L. L. Rev.* 289 (2002).

[119] 42 U.S.C. § 2000c-6(a).

[120] Equal Educational Opportunities Act of 1974, 20 U.S.C. §§ 1721, et seq.

correct violation of the Federal right." The Act also set in place various procedural devices to ensure that the supervising court paid attention to the Act's limitations.[121] But insofar as we are dealing with the implementation of legal rules promulgated by the courts in the name of the Constitution, any attempt at legislative correction that was found to thwart the effectiveness of those rules would itself be unconstitutional.[122]

In recent years, the Supreme Court has itself stressed the limits rather than the reach of judicial remedial authority.[123] Commentators perceive a significant reduction in the number of cases where courts have retained supervisory authority over public institutions.[124] It would be wrong, however, to conclude that public law litigation and "structural injunctions" are now of mere historical significance. Courts continue to be confronted with requests for specific relief ordering the reform of public institutions alleged to be operating unconstitutionally. In July 2009, the U.S. Department of Justice had a list of 208 "open cases" concerning the discriminatory administration of public schools.[125]

Some commentators have noted a change in the techniques of judicial control of public administration, whereby detailed management has been replaced by more flexible processes that allow the various "stakeholders" to participate in formulating methods of reform.[126] But this is a far cry from the elimination of judicial authority, final judicial authority, in determining the way government operates in important sectors of public activity. The Supreme Court has moderated, but it has never renounced, the kind of ongoing structural relief that we have described, despite the doubts of some

[121] 42 U.S.C. §§ 3626(a)–3626(b). A constitutional challenge to one of these devices was rejected by the Supreme Court in *Miller v. French*, 530 U.S. 327 (2000).

[122] On whether Congress can preclude judicial findings of unconstitutionality, see the range of views expressed at note 62, *supra*.

[123] See *Lewis v. Casey*, 518 U.S. 347 (1996); *Missouri v. Jenkins*, 515 U.S. 70 (1995).

[124] See Myriam Gilles, "An Autopsy of the Structural Reform Injunction: Oops . . It's Still Moving!," 58 *U. Miami L. Rev.* 143, 144 (2003); Wendy Parker, "The Decline of Judicial Decision-Making: School Desegregation and District Court Judges," 81 *N.C. L. Rev.* 1623, 1626–44 (2003); Russell L. Weaver, "The Rise and Decline of Structural Remedies," 41 *San Diego L. Rev.* 1617, 1623–28 (2004).

[125] List on file with authors. We are grateful to John Brittain for providing this information.

[126] See Charles F. Sabel and William H. Simon, "Destabilization Rights: How Public Law Litigation Succeeds," 117 *Harv. L. Rev.* 1016, 1067–73 (2004). "The judge's role changes from that of directly determining the merits to facilitating a process of deliberation and negotiations among the stakeholders." *Id.* at 1055.

of its members.[127] It may, in fact, be fair to say that the role of the constitutional judge as policy maker and potential administrator of public institutions has now become a permanent feature of American constitutional law.

[127] See *Missouri v. Jenkins*, 515 U.S. 70, 124–25 (Thomas, J. concurring). See also *id.* at 112 (O'Connor, J. concurring) (expressing doubts about judicial capacity to manage institutional reform).

VENEZUELA

CONSTITUTIONAL COURTS AS POSITIVE LEGISLATORS: THE VENEZUELAN EXPERIENCE

Daniela Urosa Maggi *

Professor, Central University of Venezuela,
Catholic University Andrés Bello and Monteávila Universitys
Caracas
urosadaniela7@gmail.com

Title VIII, Chapter I, of the Venezuelan Constitution of 1999 is named "Guarantee of this Constitution." As stated in the Preliminary Recitals of said Fundamental Text, said Chapter sets forth the main dispositions of constitutional justice as a jurisdictional mechanism for guaranteeing the supremacy and normative force principles of the Constitution, which are also stated in article 7 of the Constitution of 1999.

Constitutional justice is exercised in Venezuela through different mechanisms that complement one another. On the one hand, the Constitution assigns to every judge, in the scope of his or her corresponding competencies, the obligation to "assure the integrity of the Constitution" (article 334 of the Constitution). This obligation must be complied with by all judges of the Republic in different ways: (i) in the course of the actions and processes that they must hear according to their competency; (ii) by the hearing of amparo actions for the protection of fundamental rights and guarantees; and (iii) through the diffuse control of the constitutionality, under which "in case of incompatibility between this Constitution and a statute or any other legal norm, the constitutional dispositions will be

* Doctor in Law of the Universidad Complutense de Madrid

applicable,"[1] leaving without effect, for this specific case, the application of the norm contrary to the Constitution, even if the same is made *ex officio*.

On the other hand, Venezuelan constitutional justice, which has been qualified as a mixed or integral system, also includes the concentrated control of the constitutionality of the acts and omissions of the Public Power with rank of law. Given its nature, this control is exercised exclusively by a jurisdictional organ that, in the case of Venezuela, is the Constitutional Chamber of the Supreme Tribunal of Justice (hear on Constitutional Chamber). This way, the 1999 Constitution is the first Venezuelan Constitution that sets a Constitutional Chamber as a specialized jurisdictional entity to which corresponds, exclusively, the concentrated power of the constitutionality of the acts of the Public Power having rank of law. Said Chamber is established in the Venezuelan constitutional jurisdiction. Article 334 of the 1999 Constitution clearly states: "it corresponds exclusively to the Constitutional Chamber of the Supreme Tribunal of Justice, as constitutional jurisdiction, to declare the nullity of the statutes and other acts of the organs that exercise the Public Power issued in direct and immediate execution of this Constitution or that have rank of law, when they collide with it." This is the exclusive exercise of the concentrated control of the constitutionality of the acts with rank of law that as added by the Preliminary Recitals, "do not hinder the Constitution or the statutes, to grant them other competencies in constitutional matters."

In 1999, the Constitutional Chamber was born in the Venezuelan legal system as a jurisdictional entity having exclusive exercise of the constitutional jurisdiction, that is, concentrated control of the constitutionality of the rank of law of the Public Power acts, which is the jurisdictional entity within the structure of the Supreme Tribunal of Justice, at the top of the Venezuelan Judicial Power. The creation of this Chamber does not imply that no concentrated control of the constitutionality existed before. On the contrary, the Venezuelan constitution of 1858 granted to the Supreme Court of Justice the competency to "annul provincial statutes contrary to the Constitution." This competency was exercised beginning with the Constitution of 1925, through a specific procedural mean, such as the unconstitutionality action against the general effects acts – afterward specified as acts with rank of law – which was an exclusive competency of all the Chambers of the former Supreme Court of Justice ruling together until the 1999 Constitution, that as indicated before, created the Constitutional Chamber. Therefore, the novelty of the 1999 Constitution, regarding the

1 Article 334 of the 1999 Constitution.

concentrated control of the constitution, was to create a special jurisdictional entity which main function is the exercise of said control over the constitutionality of the acts and commissions having rank of law, that is, creating the constitutional jurisdiction.

Among the powers that the 1999 Constitution granted to the Constitutional Chamber, that are set in its article 336, stands out the competency to "declare the total or partial nullity" of the local, state, and municipal statutes and of the acts having rank of law or in direct and immediate execution of the Constitution of the National Executive and of "any other state entity in the exercise of the Public Power," when such acts collide with the Constitution.[2] The purpose of said nullity claim, is, as the Constitution indicates, the partial or total nullity of the act, when the act collides with the Constitution. The Organic Law of the Supreme Tribunal of 2004 sets forth in the same terms the competency of the Constitutional Chamber to declare the nullity of the acts of rank of law and adds only that, in cases estimating nullity, the Chamber will determine the effects of the decision along the time and will order its publication in the official Gazette.

Even if these are the terms that the legislator and the constituent have used to set the nullifying power of the Constitutional Chamber, which we could say coincide with the original characteristics that Hans Kelsen granted to the concentrated control of the acts of the Public Power generally used by a negative legislator,, that leaves without effect and erases from the legal world the legal acts that are contrary to the Constitution; the fact is that the jurisprudence of the Constitutional Chamber has demonstrated, from the beginning, a systematic and growing broadening of its nullifying powers. This can be evidenced in many situations in which the Chamber, does not limit itself to declaring the nullity of the norm or act contrary to the Constitution, but also carries out its substitution, modification or addition.

This judicial activism that is translated, in many cases, in expressions of the Constitutional Chamber as a positive legislator is based in the exercise of the "normative jurisdiction" that the Chamber has assumed within its powers. The precedents issued in this sense may be organized in two great scopes: (i) those where the Chamber has acted as positive legislator in the granting and determination of its own competencies and (ii) those where the Constitutional Chamber has acted as positive legislator in substantive matters it has heard of, integrating and modifying the legal system.

2 Article 336, sections 1 to 4, of the 1999 Constitution.

Therefore, in the following pages we must analyze, on a preliminary basis, the so-called normative jurisdiction as a basis or justification of the Venezuelan Constitutional Chamber to act as positive legislator, its origin, contents, and scope. Second, we indicate the precedents in which said normative jurisdiction has been applied on the issuing of interpretative, additive, and amending decisions of legal norms currently in force instead of other norms. Third, we note those cases where the Constitutional Chamber has refrained from practicing its normative jurisdiction and the reasons for said refrains. Finally, we analyze to what extent the exercise of said normative jurisdiction and the acts as positive legislator are contrary or not to the 1999 Venezuelan Constitution.

I. THE NORMATIVE JURISDICTION ACCORDING TO THE JURISPRUDENCE OF THE CONSTITUTIONAL CHAMBER

From the first decision issued by the Constitutional Chamber of the Venezuelan Supreme Tribunal of Justice since its creation by the 1999 Venezuelan Constitution, it has acted as positive legislator. This has been, as already mentioned, a constant characteristic in its decisions. Said way to act has been based in the exercise of a "normative jurisdiction" that the Chamber has attributed to itself and that consists in the fact that, while the statutes that develop certain constitutional precepts are not enacted, the Chamber on its own will regulate normative and temporarily the matter, which gives way to immediate application and force to the constitutional norm.

The decision of the Constitutional Chamber where it was affirmed and explained the scope of said "normative jurisdiction" was decision no. 1571, dated August 22, 2001 (*Asodeviprilara* case),[3] which has been reiterated many times. Because article 335 of the 1999 Constitution has been the basis given by the Chamber to the existence of said normative jurisdiction, it is worth noting the contents of said constitutional norm: "The Supreme Tribunal of Justice will guarantee the supremacy and effectiveness of the constitutional norms and principles; it will be the highest and final interpreter of this Constitution and shall watch over its uniform interpretation and application. The interpretations set forth by the Constitutional Chamber over the contents or scope of the constitutional norms and principles are binding for the other Chambers of the Supreme Tribunal of Justice and other courts of Republic."

3 See text at http://www.tsj.gov.ve/decisiones/scon/Agosto/1571-220801-01-1274%20.htm.

Thus, based on said article 335 of the Constitution and departing from the argument where constitutional norms have a direct application and their effectiveness cannot be subject to the eventual development set by the legislator, the Constitutional Chamber set in said decision no. 1571/01 that, "in the specific cases where a constitutional infraction arises, the Chamber has exercised the jurisdiction in a normative manner, giving immediate force to the constitutional norm and indicating its scopes or forms of exercise, even if there are no statutes that can develop it directly."

Therefore, the Constitutional Chamber justifies the exercise of the normative jurisdiction in the nonprogrammatic nature of the constitutional norms, especially those that regulate fundamental rights. Therefore, given the absence of a statute, it deems that the Chamber is obliged to exercise the normative jurisdiction to give direct operability to the fundamental right, or in general, to the constitutional norm. For the Constitutional Chamber, the 1999 Constitution in its article 335, "allows the normative jurisdiction, specifically regarding the existing programmatic norms within the Constitution that would remain in undefined suspense until the legislator decides to develop them, remaining in suspense its effectiveness in time," thus hindering what the Chamber defines as constitutional immobilization.

In this sense, the Constitutional Chamber considers that the general principles of procedural law are not applicable, specifically the dispositive principle, but that because the "direct application of the constitutional rights" is at play, the constitutional jurisdiction acts in a more inquisitive manner.

Given the normative jurisdiction that the Constitutional Chamber has kept, the precedents where the Chamber has acted as positive legislator have been frequent. That nature has been specially expressed in three scopes: (i) positive legislator in the granting and determination of its own competencies; (ii) as positive legislator in the determination and phases of several judicial processes; and (iii) as positive legislator in substantive matters it has known, integrating or modifying the constitutional legal system. We analyze each one of them.

II. CASES WHERE THE CONSTITUTIONAL CHAMBER HAS EXTENDED ITS OWN COMPETENCIES THROUGH THE PRACTICING OF THE NORMATIVE JURISDICTION

As stated earlier, article 336 of the Constitution established the competencies of the Constitutional Chamber and among them the power to anull statutes and the acts issued by any the Public Power entities in direct and immediate execution of the Constitution; the prior control of the constitutionality of the international treaties before its ratification; the prior control of the constitutionality of the legislative omissions; the resolutions of collisions among legal norms; the resolution of constitutional controversies between the entities of the Public Power; the review of the final decisions of constitutional amparo and of control over the constitutionality of statutes or legal norms enacted by courts of the Republic and "the other ones set in this Constitution and the Law," which affirms the nature of legal reserve of the granting of its competencies acting as Public Power entity.

Said competencies have been added to other ones that the jurisprudence of the Constitutional Chamber has set, that is, competencies that the Constitutional Chamber has kept and that we analyze in the following sections.[4]

1. *Competencies in Constitutional Amparo Matters*

One of the procedural means that exist in the Venezuelan legal system to exercise constitutional justice, even under the scope of Constitution of 1961, is the so-called constitutional amparo action. The object of said claim is the brief, summary, and efficient protection of fundamental rights, and it is exercised by all courts of the Republic according to the relation with the affected parties. The constitutional amparo has been traditionally understood in Venezuela not only from its procedural point of view but also as a fundamental right as the right of all the inhabitants to demand before the courts, the protection and reestablishment of the enjoyment and exercise of their fundamental rights through a brief and summary procedure.

The development of the procedural aspects of said fundamental right was made in the Venezuelan legal system through the Organic Law of Amparo over Constitutional Rights and Guarantees in 1988. Article 27 of the Constitution of 1999 establishes the fundamental right to the constitutional amparo of the constitutional rights and guarantees, even of those inherent to the persons who do not appear in an express manner in the Constitution or in the international instruments regarding human rights, that must be guaranteed through brief, gratuitous and antiformalist judicial means. In this way, the 1999 Constitution kept, in essence, the traditional conception of the traditional constitutional amparo.

4 See on this matter, in the jurisprudence, Allan R. Brewer-Carías, "Quis Custodiet ipsos Custodes: De la interpretación constitucional a la inconstitucionalidad de la interpretación," *Revista de Derecho Público* nº 104, Caracas, 2006, pp. 7 ff. See also Allan R. Brewer-Carías, "La ilegítima mutación de la constitución por el juez constitucional: La inconstitucional ampliación y modificación de su propia competencia en materia de control de constitucionalidad," in *Libro homenaje a Josefina Calcaño de Temeltas*, Fundación de Estudios de Derecho Administrativo (FUNEDA), Caracas 2009, pp. 319–362.

However, in the first decisions issued by the Constitutional Chamber after its creation, said Chamber considered that the Law of Amparo over Constitutional Rights and Guarantees had to be adapted to the new conception of the amparo of the 1999 Constitution; therefore, it modified the Organic Law of Amparo over Constitutional Rights and Guarantees, regarding the competencies and the procedure set in said law.

A. Modification of the Competencies to Hear the Amparo Claims

We make specific reference to decisions no. 1 and 2, both dated January 20, 2000 (*Emery Mata Millán* and *Domingo Ramírez Monja* cases),[5] through which the Constitutional Chamber modified, *ex officio*, articles 7 and 8 of the Organic Law of Amparo over Constitutional Rights and Guarantees and redistributed the competency of the first and second instance courts and of the Chamber in constitutional amparo matters. At the end, after the decisions, the competency of the courts in the first and second instance of the different modes of constitutional amparo (amparo against judicial decisions, amparo against administrative acts, amparo against normative acts), as well as in consultation and review of all the amparo decisions issued by said Chamber, is the one set forth in said decisions and no longer the ones set forth in the Organic Law of Amparo, even when, ten years after the new Constitution was enacted, it is still in force, because it has not been formally abrogated or annulled.

B. Modification of the Procedure of the Constitutional Amparo Claim

In decision no. 7, dated February 1, 2000 (*José Amando Mejía* case),[6] the Constitutional Chamber considered, again *ex officio*, that the "immediate

[5] The text of the decision nº 1/2000 is available at http://www.tsj.gov.ve/decisiones/scon/Enero/01-200100-00-002.htm, and decision nº 2/2000 at http://www.tsj.gov.ve/decisiones/scon/Enero/02-200100-00-001.htm. See the initial comments to the decisions in Allan R. Brewer-Carías, *El sistema de justicia constitucional en la Constitución de 1999 (Comentarios sobre su desarrollo jurisprudencial y su explicación, a veces errada, en la Exposición de Motivos)*, Editorial Jurídica Venezolana, Caracas 2000, pp. 28–35.

[6] The text of this decision can be found at http://www.tsj.gov.ve/decisiones/scon/Febrero/07-010200-00-0010.htm. See the initial comments on this decision in Allan R. Brewer-Carías, *El sistema de justicia constitucional en la Constitución de 1999 (Comentarios sobre su desarrollo jurisprudencial y su explicación, a veces errada, en la Exposición de Motivos)*, Editorial Jurídica Venezolana, Caracas 2000, pp. 49–58. From the same author, "El juez constitucional como legislador positivo y la inconstitucional reforma de la Ley Orgánica de Amparo mediante sentencias interpretativas," in A.A.V.V., Eduardo Ferrer Mac-Gregor and Arturo Zaldívar Lelo de Larrea (coords.), *La ciencia del derecho procedural constitucional. Estudios en homenaje a Héctor Fix-Zamudio en sus cincuenta años como investigador del derecho*, Instituto de

application of article 27 of the Constitution currently in force, leads the Chamber to adapt the amparo procedure set forth in the Organic Law of Amparo over Constitutional Rights and Guarantees of the dispositions of article 27" and to the dispositions of article 49 *ejusdem*. For this purpose, the Chamber used its conditions of "highest interpreter of the Constitution."

Said reform of the amparo procedure was more substantial than formal, as it modified the procedural phases, it set the holding of two oral hearings, it modified the procedural terms of the discovery phase and the opportunity to issue the decisions – also differentiating the case when the amparo is against judicial decisions of the rest of amparo types – all this having a binding nature for the rest of the courts of the Republic.

Finally, the procedural aspects of the constitutional amparo claim, especially those related to the competency and the procedure to be followed, are at the present time those that have been established by the Constitutional Chamber in the decisions it has issued, although this praetorian regulation collides with the Organic Law of Amparo over Constitutional Rights and Guarantees that is currently in force, and there is no previous declaration of the nullity of that Law. The Constitutional Chamber, *ex officio* and with a binding nature, acted as positive legislator and modified substantially the adjective regime of the constitutional amparo set forth in the Organic Law of Amparo over Constitutional Rights and Guarantees.

2. *Competencies in the Special Recourse to Review Decisions*

Before the 1999 Constitution entered into force, the diffuse control of the constitutionality was exercised by all the judges of the Republic. However, their decisions in these matters were reviewed only by the corresponding judge of second instance through the appeal recourse and, if applicable, through the special recourse of cassation. Also in this way, the decisions issued by the judges of the Republic in matters of constitutional amparo were subject to impugnation through a decision of second instance, whether through appeal or through consultation.

The Constitution of 1999 modified this situation. This way, with the creation of the Constitutional Chamber, it was granted, among other

Investigaciones Jurídicas, Universidad Nacional Autónoma de México, Mexico City 2008, Vol. V, pp. 63–80; also from the same author, *Crónica sobre la "in"justicia constitucional: La Sala Constitucional y el autoritarismo en Venezuela*, Editorial Jurídica Venezolana, Caracas, 2007, p. 550. Also in this sense, see Jesús María Casal, "La protección de la Constitución frente a las omisiones legislativas," *Constitución y justicia constitucional*, Universidad Católica Andrés Bello, Caracas, 2004, p. 223.

competencies, the competency to "review the final decisions of constitutional amparo and of the control over the constitutionality of the statutes of legal norms enacted by the courts of the Republic, in the terms set by the corresponding organic law" (Article 336.10). The basis of this competency is article 335 of the same Constitution, according to which the Constitutional Chamber must watch over a uniform interpretation and application of the Constitution. That is why for the constituent, the decisions that exercise diffuse control of the constitutionality and the final constitutional amparo decisions are susceptible to review by the Chamber "in the terms set forth by the corresponding organic law."

However, before said Organic Law was enacted, the Constitutional Chamber, through decision no. 93 dated February 6, 2001, (*CORPOTURISMO* case),[7] exercising what it calls "interpretative jurisprudence" and based "in its nature of highest interpreter of the Constitution," determined "which is the scope of the special review of final decisions power granted by the Constitution."

In that sense, the decision established that the Constitutional Chamber has the power to review not only the decisions issued by the "courts of the Republic" – that is the disposition of article 336.10 – but also the decisions issued by the other Chambers of the Supreme Tribunal of Justice. Therefore, the Constitutional Chamber broadened the subjective scope of its competencies of review of other courts, to decisions of other Chambers of the Supreme Tribunal of Justice.

It also broadened the objective scope of this competency, when in the same decision no. 93 of 2001 it established that it may review not only the final decisions of constitutional amparo and of diffuse control but also any "final decisions contrary to the interpretative criteria of the constitutional norm that this Chamber has previously established," regardless of the nature of the case where they have been issued. This "interpretation" of its competencies, translated into a self-attribution of competencies that are not expressly established in article 336.10, of the Constitution, where based again in article 335 *ejusdem* establishing the Constitutional Chamber as the "highest and final binding interpreter of the Constitution."

[7] See text at http://www.tsj.gov.ve/decisiones/scon/Febrero/93-060201-00-1529%20.htm. See initial comments of these decisions in Allan R. Brewer-Carías, *La Constitución de 1999: Derecho constitucional venezolano*, Vol. II, Editorial Jurídica Venezolana, Caracas 2004, pp. 983–988. From the same author, *Crónica sobre la "in"justicia constitucional: La Sala Constitucional and el autoritarismo en Venezuela, op. cit.*, p. 56.

It must be indicated that after said decision no. 93/01 of the Constitutional Chamber, the Organic Law of the Supreme Tribunal of Justice was enacted in 2004. This Law established as competencies of the Constitutional Chamber the review of final decisions of the other Chambers of the Supreme Tribunal of Justice and other courts of the Republic in constitutional amparo matters, where a diffuse control was exercised or "decisions issued *by one of the Chambers,* when it is claimed grounded on the violation of the fundamental legal principles contained in the Constitution . . . Treaties, Agreements or International Agreements . . . or that has been issued as a consequence of an inexcusable error, fraud, corruption or breach of public duty" (article 5, sections 4, 16, and 22, of the Organic Law of the Supreme Tribunal of Justice).

Please note that the Organic Law of the Supreme Tribunal of Justice reduced the competencies of the Constitutional Chamber in review of decisions matters, as this Law did not include the competency to review the decisions of any court of the Republic that contradict the interpretations of said Chamber.

Regardless of said reduction of competencies by the statute, the Constitutional Chamber established, through decision no. 1992 dated September 8, 2004 (*Peter Hofle* case),[8] that its competency in review of decisions matters is still the one that before the sanctioning of the statute, was determined in its decision 93/2001, under the criteria that it developed article 336.10 of the Constitution, regardless, as we previously stated, that the grounds of said decision of 2001 went beyond the content of said article 336.10 of the Constitution.

3. *Competencies to Hear the Interpretation of the Constitution Recourse*

Article 336 of the 1999 Constitution, which is the norm that lists the competencies of the Constitutional Chamber, does not include any power that allows said jurisdictional entity to make an *in abstracto* interpretation of the Constitution through a petition or constitutional interpretation claim.

However, the Constitutional Chamber exercised its normative jurisdiction and understood that it has competency to hear petitions or constitutional norms interpretation recourse. Specifically, through decision no. 1077, dated September 22, 2000 (*Servio Tulio León* case),[9] the Chamber declared the

8 See text at http://www.tsj.gov.ve/decisiones/scon/Septiembre/1992-080904-03-2332%20.htm.

9 See text at http://www.tsj.gov.ve/decisiones/scon/Septiembre/1077-220900-00-1289.htm. See the comments to this decision and to the interpretation recourse in Allan R. Brewer-Carías, "Le

existence of a procedural mean that is not expressly foreseen in our legal system, or in the Constitution, or in the Law, which was named as "constitutional interpretation recourse," attributing to itself the competency to hear it, again, based on its condition of being the "highest and final interpreter of the Constitution" according to article 335 of the Constitution.

In that same decision no. 1077/00 that created the constitutional interpretation recourse, apart from determining that the competency to hear is exclusive of the Constitutional Chamber, it also established its scope, the legitimacy, and procedure to follow. Thus, the substantive and adjective aspects of this new procedural mean were regulated.[10] Said aspects were then complemented in decision no. 1415 dated November 22, 2000 (*Freddy Rangel Rojas* case).[11]

It must be pointed out that the Organic Law of the Supreme Tribunal enacted in 2004, as mentioned, did not state among the competencies of the Constitutional Chamber the hearing of constitutional interpretation recourses. This way, its article 5.52 following the guidelines of article 266.6 of the 1999 Constitution, regulated the interpretation recourse of legal texts and distributed the competency according to "the applicable Chamber related to the matters to be discussed." In this way, the constitutional interpretation

recours d'interprétation abstrait de la Constitution au Vénézuéla," in *Le renouveau du droit constitutionnel, Mélanges en l'honneur de Louis Favoreu*, Dalloz, Paris, 2007, pp. 61–70; from the same author, "El recurso abstracto de interpretación constitucional en Venezuela," in *Estudios sobre el Estado Constitucional (2005-2006)*, Editorial Jurídica Venezolana, Caracas, 2007, pp. 699–706.

10 Decision nº 1077/2000 had a concurrent vote, which stated that the new procedural "constitutional interpretation recourse," apart from not being set in the Constitution or in the Law, was inapplicable because the interpretation of of the constitutional norms by the Constitutional Chamber must not be, ever, in abstract or for academic purposes. Its decisions must be adopted within the frame of the competencies of constitutionality control of the acts having rank of law that do correspond to it in the exercise of the constitutional jurisdiction. The Venezuelan doctrine has also echoed the excess the jurisprudence incurred in "creating" the constitutional interpretation and has indicated: "we are facing a broadening of own competencies that the Chamber has arrogated through an unconstitutional interpretation of the Constitution that does not establish the possibility of this autonomous recourse for the abstract interpretation of the constitutional norms. Additionally, nothing similar exists in the known constitutional justice systems." Cf. Allan R. Brewer-Carías, *Crónica sobre la 'in'justicia constitucional: La Sala Constitucional and el autoritarismo en Venezuela*, *op. cit.*, p. 56. Likewise see Luis Alfonso, Herrera Orellana, "El 'recurso de interpretación' de la Constitución: Reflexiones críticas desde la argumentación jurídica y la teoría del discurso," *Revista de Derecho Público* nº 113, Caracas, pp. 7 ff.; and Marianella Villegas Salazar, "Comentarios sobre el recurso de interpretación constitucional en la jurisprudencia de la Sala Constitucional," *Revista de Derecho Público* nº 84, Caracas, 2000, pp. 417 ff.

11 This decision is available at http://www.tsj.gov.ve/decisiones/scon/Noviembre/1415-221100-00-1725.htm.

recourse still is a consequence of the exercise of the normative jurisdiction of the Constitutional Chamber and lacks constitutional and legal base.

Last, we must mention a recent decision of the Constitutional Chamber, no. 1939, dated December 18, 2008 (case of nonexecution of the decision of the Interamerican Court of Human Rights),[12] through which – as we previously stated – the scope of this praetorian-granted competency of constitutional interpretation was broadened more. In this new occasion, the majority of the Chamber – counting with a dissenting vote – attributed, based on this same constitutional interpretation competency, the possibility to determine "the scope and intelligence of the execution of a decision issued by an international entity based on a treaty of constitutional hierarchy, facing the alleged antinomy between this International Convention and the National Constitution."

In this specific case, it deals with the "interpretation of the constitutional conformity of the decision of the Interamerican Court of Human Rights, dated August 05, 2008 where it was ordered the reincorporation of ex-judges of the First Court in Contentious Administrative Matters to their offices," so it included, as object of said interpretation of constitutional norms recourse, not a norm but a decision issued also by an international entity.

Said questionable inclusion arises, as it deals not with the hypothesis – also questionable – of interpretation of a supranational precept but with a decision, that is, a jurisdictional act of an international entity, such as the Interamerican Court of Human Rights. It is a principle that jurisdictional acts are not susceptible to being interpreted; they are executive acts and are of mandatory compliance by the parties, who, in case of doubt, can request the

[12] See http://www.tsj.gov.ve/decisiones/scon/Diciembre/1939-181208-2008-08-1572.html. Also see the critics the Venezuelan doctrine has made to this decision: Carlos Ayala Corao, *La "inejecución" de las sentencias internacionales en la jurisprudencia constitucional de Venezuela (1999-2009)*, Fundación Manuel García-Pelayo, Caracas, 2009, pp. 69 ff.; Allan Brewer-Carías, "El juez constitucional vs. La justicia internacional en materia de derechos humanos," *Revista de Derecho Público* nº 116, Caracas, 2008, pp. 248 ff.; from the same author "La interrelación entre los Tribunales Constitucionales de América Latina y la Corte Interamericana de Derechos Humanos, y la cuestión de la inejecutabilidad de sus decisiones en Venezuela," in *Gaceta Constitucional*, Análisis multidisciplinario de la jurisprudencia del Tribunal Constitucional, Gaceta Jurídica, Vol. 16, 2009, Lima 2009, pp. 17–48; "La interrelación entre los Tribunales Constitucionales de América Latina y la Corte Interamericana de Derechos Humanos, y la cuestión de la inejecutabilidad de sus decisiones en Venezuela," in Armin von Bogdandy, Flavia Piovesan, and Mariela Morales Antonorzi (coords.), *Direitos humanos, democracia e integracao jurídica na América do Sul*, Umen Juris Editora, Rio de Janeiro 2010, pp. 661–701; "La interrelación entre los Tribunales Constitucionales de América Latina y la Corte Interamericana de Derechos Humanos, y la cuestión de la inejecutabilidad de sus decisiones en Venezuela," *Anuario Iberoamericano de Justicia Constitucional*, Centro de Estudios Políticos and Constitucionales, nº 13, Madrid 2009, pp. 99–136.

clarification before the court that issues the decision. The nonapplicability of said interpretation was so evident that the dispositive part of decision no. 1939/08 of the Constitutional Chamber did not interpret anything and just declared "unenforceable" the decision of the Interamerican Court.

So this decision constitutes an example of the legal insecurity that implies that a competency –the interpretation competency– does not have a constitutional or legal base, but only a jurisprudential one, and therefore, that same jurisprudence may go on "modeling" and broadening the interpretation competency to new cases according to the circumstances of the specific cases and not in general and *a priori*, as the granting of competencies should be.

4. *Competencies in Matters of Concentrated Control of the Constitutionality of Statutes and Other Acts Having Rank of Law*

A. Jurisprudential Inclusion of the Competency of Incidental Control over Statutes

The incidental control is the kind of concentrated control of the statutes and other acts of legal rank that is exercised, normally *ex officio*, during the course of a judicial procedure, the initial object of which is not the action of nullity of said statute.[13]

The 1999 Constitution did not establish among the competencies of the Constitutional Chamber the possibility to exercise incidental control, and it limited the concentrated control of constitutionality through the action or nullity for unconstitutionality recourse, which is posterior control of constitutionality, exercised by the interested party, where the main object of the claim is the nullity of the statute.

However, at least two times, the Constitutional Chamber considered applicable the exercise of incidental control of the constitutionality of the statutes. This way, in decision no. 2588, dated December 11, 2001 (case *Yrene Martínez*),[14] the Constitutional Chamber declared, through incidental means and *ex officio*, the invalidity of a legal norm. In this way, the

13 In this regard, see Margarita Escudero León, *El control judicial de constitucionalidad sobre las ramas legislativa y ejecutiva del Poder Público*, Universidad Central de Venezuela, Caracas, 2005, pp. 162 ff.; Allan R. Brewer-Carías, *La Constitución de 1999: Derecho constitucional venezolano*, Vol. II, Editorial Jurídica Venezolana, Caracas 2004, pp. 959 ff.; *Ley Orgánica del Tribunal Supremo de Justicia*, Editorial Jurídica Venezolana, Caracas 2004, pp. 90 ff.

14 The text of the decision is available at http://www.tsj.gov.ve/decisiones/scon/Diciembre/2588-111201-01-1096.htm.

Constitutional Chamber recognized that, although the Constitution does not establish expressly its competence to exercise the incidental control of the constitutionality, said attribution is "congruent" with the nature of its functions and therefore "declares" its own power.[15]

In a later opportunity, the Constitutional Chamber exercised again said incidental control, specifically in decision no. 806, dated April 24, 2002, (*Sintracemento* case),[16] which declared incidentally the nullity of article 43 of the Organic Law of the Supreme Tribunal of Justice.

In any case, take it must be mentioned that said power to exercise the incidental control of the constitutionality was later on prohibited in the Organic Law of the Supreme Tribunal Justice 2004, which in the second paragraph of article 5 sets forth that "the concentrated control of constitutionality will only correspond to the Constitutional Chamber in the terms set forth in this Law, which will not be able to hear it incidentally in other actions, but only when an unconstitutionality popular recourse is exercised."

That legal prohibition of the exercise of incidental control of constitutionality is, in our opinion, correct, as said mode of control has been justified in comparative law and in legal systems where no diffuse control of the constitutionality (e.g., Spain); therefore, it is a recourse for the unconstitutionality of the norms that is used during the course of a judicial process being followed by instance judges, who in consequence place the incident of unconstitutionality or matter of unconstitutionality to the constitutional court. However, in the case of Venezuela, where all the courts of the Republic, including the Constitutional Chamber, are empowered not to apply to the specific case the unconstitutional norm through diffuse control, there is no reason to foresee the incidental control of constitutionality.

15 Regarding the criteria established in this decision, it can be affirmed that "this doctrine of the Chamber, of course, is not applicable in Venezuela, where the concentrated control of the constitutionality of the laws demands, the process to be initiated by a party (popular action) and a contradictory constitutional process (*litis*) where the service of process of the entity producing the norm must be guaranteed and the participation as parties of all those who have procedural interest in the matter." Cf. Allan R. Brewer-Carías, *Crónica sobre la "in"justicia constitucional: La Sala Constitucional el autoritarismo en Venezuela*, *op. cit.*, p. 71.

16 See the contents of this decision at http://www.tsj.gov.ve/decisiones/scon/Abril/806-240402-00-3049.htm.

B. Modification of the Procedure of the Nullity Cases

The Organic Law of the Supreme Tribunal of Justice of 2004 established the procedure to be followed to file a recourse for nullity for unconstitutionality of statutes and other acts of rank of law, specifically its article 21.9 that is a provision that was applied not only in the nullity cases ruled by the constitutional jurisdiction but also by the contentious – administrative jurisdiction regarding administrative acts.

However, a few months after said Statute came into force, the Constitutional Chamber issued decision no. 1645, dated August 19, 2004, (*Gregorio Pérez Vargas* case),[17] through which it substantially modified the procedure set forth for the following of the nullity of statutes and other acts of direct execution of the Constitution cases and established the "new" procedure to be followed in these cases.

Please note that this jurisprudential regulation of a new procedure for the nullity of statutes and other acts having legal rank cases, was made without there existing any declaration of nullity for unconstitutionality of the Organic Law of the Supreme Tribunal of Justice, or nonapplication through diffuse controls of its norms; only a simple "modification" through an "interpretative decision" exercising the "normative jurisdiction," and its publication was ordered in the Official Gazette.[18]

Complementing that decision, the Constitutional Chamber issued a second decision, decision no. 1795, dated July 19, 2005 (case *Promotora San Gabriel*),[19] where other procedural aspects were detailed that were not included in the previous decision, such as the case of the filing of the nullity procedures when actions or precautionary measures are accumulated;

17 The text of this decision is available at http://www.tsj.gov.ve/decisiones/scon/ Agosto/1645-190804-04-0824.htm; see also the comments to it by Allan R. Brewer-Carías, *Ley Orgánica del Tribunal Supremo de Justicia*, *op. cit.*, pp. 257 ff.

18 That decision of the Constitutional Chamber had a dissenting vote, stating various reasons the modification of the procedure legally established through a judicial decision exceeded by far, the attributions of the Constitutional Chamber. Thus, the vote indicated that the decision that modifies a legal text without there existing an unconstitutionality case against it, and without there existing any vacuum, ambiguity, or obscurity that requires an interpretation or integration by the judge, violates the principle of separation of powers and implies an usurpation of functions. This becomes worse when the matter modified has a strict legal reserve nature, such as the case of the regime of the cases and judicial procedures following article 156, numeral 32, of the 1999 Constitution. Therefore, the vote concludes indicating "instead of a benefit for those searching justice, an unwished element of legal insecurity has been introduced shortly after the entering into force of the Organic Law of the Supreme Tribunal of Justice."

19 This is available at http://www.tsj.gov.ve/decisiones/scon/Julio/1795-190705-05-0159.htm.

likewise, it indicated the terms for the publication of the summons notice of the interested parties that want to become a party of the case.

In this way, it is evidenced how the Constitutional Chamber has also modeled its competencies in matters of remedies for nullity and constitutional control of the statutes and other acts of legal rank. In this case, what happened with the so-called constitutional interpretation recourse or the review recourse did not happen; that is, in this case, it was an auto attribution of competencies, it did not regulate the substantive aspect of the competency, but it did regulate its adjective aspect: the procedure to be followed, although the existing statute regulated sufficiently and in detail a procedure for those cases. The deficiencies of the procedure established by the legislator – which we cannot deny – were not enough reason for the Constitutional Chamber to modify and substitute said procedure for the one the Chamber created in a praetorian manner.

5. *Competencies in Matters of Control over Unconstitutionality for Omission*

Article 336.7, of the Constitution, sets the competition of the Constitutional Chamber to declare the unconstitutionality of the omissions of the legislative power. It is a certainly innovative attribution that incorporated for the first time the Constitution of 1999. However, the Organic Law of the Supreme Tribunal of Justice reiterated, within the competencies of the Constitutional Chamber, the control of the legislative omissions and even broadened substantially the scope of said control when including the behaviors of omission of "any of the entities that exercise the Public Power of national scope, regarding obligations or duties directly established by the Constitution."

Now, neither the Constitution nor the Organic Law of the Supreme Tribunal of Justice regulated any of the procedural aspects of said constitutionality for omission control, but, as it was said, it was limited to enunciate the competence of the Constitutional Chamber. Given said absence of legislation, the Chamber determined, through decision no. 1556 dated July 9, 2002 (case *Alfonso Albornoz and Gloria de Vicentini*)[20] the procedural regulation of said claim, applicable until it is regulated by the Statute. To establish that regulation, the Constitutional Chamber invoked the exercise of its normative jurisdiction, to which we made reference before.

[20] This is available at http://www.tsj.gov.ve/decisiones/scon/Julio/1556-090702-01-2337%20.htm.

Even if the Constitutional Chamber expressed that the determination of all those cases corresponded to it in exercise of the normative jurisdiction, it is true that, in our opinion, it was not necessary the exercise of said supposed power, given that the competencies were sufficiently determined in the 1999 Constitution and afterward complemented in the Organic Law of the Supreme Tribunal of Justice of 2004, the determination of the procedure could be made following article 19 of said Organic Law, according to which "when the legal system does not contemplate a special procedure, the one that is deem more convenient for the realization of justice may be applicable, provided it has its legal juridical basis." Because in the case of the exercise of the power of constitutional control for omission there did not exist a special procedure legally established, the Constitutional Chamber could, according to said norm –and not exercising any other legal norm– determine the application of another procedure by analogy, as happened in this case, with the procedure of the nullity of the statute's recourse.

6. *Competency in Matters of Claims for Protection of Diffuse and Collective Interests*

A. Creation of a Claim for Protection of Diffuse and Collective Interests

From the 1999 Constitution, the right to effective judicial protection is extended, as expressly indicated in its article 26, to the individual and collective interests. Jurisprudence of the Constitutional Chamber has interpreted this disposition, specifically, since decision no. 656, dated June 30, 2000 (case *Dilia Parra Guillén*),[21] admitting that the diffuse or collective rights may legitimate certain persons – with specific links regarding said rights – to file any kind of action, including a constitutional amparo.

In that decision, the Constitutional Chamber established that said fundamental right must have immediate operability and not be subject to the prior legislative development. Therefore, it established that until the corresponding legislation that regulates the exercise and procedural regime of the supraindividual rights and obligations, its judicial protection would be made through a protection of diffuse and collective interests claim and that it must be heard exclusively by said Chamber, through the procedure it determines for such purpose.

[21] See http://www.tsj.gov.ve/decisiones/scon/Junio/656-300600-00-1728%20.htm.

In this case, once again, the Constitutional Chamber uses its normative jurisdiction, under the justification of the immediate operability of the fundamental rights, and with that it created a procedural mean: the claim for protection of diffuse and collective interests It determined that this claim will be of exclusive competency of said Chamber, and it set the procedural requirements and the scope of the decision in these cases.[22]

B. Procedure to Be Followed and Legitimacy in Claims for Protection of Diffuse and Collective Interests

In decision no. 1571, dated August 22, 2001 (case *Asodeviprilara*), mentioned earlier, the Constitutional Chamber determined the procedure to be followed in these claims for protection of diffuse and collective interests, and for such purpose, it applied the oral hearing of the Civil Procedure Code.

Likewise, through decision no. 1395, dated November 21, 2000 (case *William Dávila*),[23] the Constitutional Chamber established who can legitimately file this claim and which persons, whether individuals or legal entities, public or private entities, or even entities having no legal capacity, may be holders of collective or diffuse rights.

7. *Competencies in Matters of* Habeas Data

Article 28 of the Venezuelan Constitution of 1999 recognized the right to have access to information and data of the individuals or goods that are evidenced in official or private records, as well as the right to judicially request the updating, rectification, or destruction of erroneous data or data that illegitimately affect their rights. Likewise, it sets the right of communities and groups of persons to have access to documents that contain information that may be of their interest.

Given that it is a right of recent incorporation in the Venezuelan Constitutional frame, it did not have a legal regime that developed a special mean to exercise its jurisdictional guarantee, leaving intact of course, the applicability of the constitutional amparo, which is always possible because it is a fundamental right.

22 On the regulation of the procedural aspects of this claim, keep in mind decision nº 3648, dated December 19, 2003 (case *Fernando Asenjo*), available at http://www.tsj.gov.ve/decisiones/scon/Diciembre/3648-191203-03-0831.htm.

23 See http://www.tsj.gov.ve/decisiones/scon/Noviembre/1395-211100-00-1901%20.htm.

Through decision No. 332, dated March 14, 2001 (case *INSACA*),[24] the Constitutional Chamber established that the exercise of said right could be protected not only through the constitutional amparo but also though an autonomous claim of *habeas data*. In this case, the Chamber would establish the procedure to be followed and would always assume the competency to hear the claim "allowing this way that situations founded in article 28 of the Constitution, but that do not fall within the cases of constitutional amparo , may be solved."

The creation of said *habeas data* claim and the self-attribution of the competency to hear the cause was based by the Constitutional Chamber on the same criteria it has maintained in other cases where it has exercised the normative jurisdiction: the direct application of the constitutional norms "and that when the statutes have developed their exercise and require to attend to the courts of justice due to the direct application of said norms, it is the constitutional jurisdiction, represented by this Constitutional Chamber, the one that will know the controversies that arise due to the constitutional norms that have not been developed legislatively."

In this way, decision No. 332/01 set, also with a binding nature, all the procedural aspects of said *habeas data* claim created by it. However, those procedural aspects, specifically the procedure to be followed in these cases, have been modified in several opportunities since. First, through decision no. 2551, dated September 24, 2003 (case *Jaime Ojeda*),[25] and second through decision No. 1511, dated November 9, 2009 (case *Mercedes Josefina Ramírez*),[26] to establish "a more brief procedure that allows a prompt judicial decision" in order to expedite the protection of the constitutional rights indicated in article 28 of the Constitution.

In our opinion, it was not necessary to jurisprudentially create a new procedural mean, or for the Constitutional Chamber to have exclusive competency over it. As it was previously stated, given that it is a fundamental right –the right to have access to data and individual information and to the rectification thereof– its guarantee is totally covered by the constitutional amparo. A different matter is that the legislator, not the jurisprudence, established and regulated a *habeas data* claim where a

24 See http://www.tsj.gov.ve/decisiones/scon/Marzo/332-140301-00-1797%20.htm.

25 Cf. http://www.tsj.gov.ve/decisiones/scon/Septiembre/2551-240903-03-0980.htm.

26 Cf. http://www.tsj.gov.ve/decisiones/scon/Noviembre/1511-91109-2009-09-0369.html.

protection different to the amparo was given, for example, that it would allow indemnification actions.[27]

III. CASES OF JUDICIAL ACTIVISM ON MATTERS OF CONSTITUTIONAL INTERPRETATION: THE CONSTITUTIONAL CHAMBER AS POSITIVE CONSTITUENT

One of the cases that the Venezuelan doctrine considers characteristic of the Venezuelan constitutional judge's judicial activism is the case of the exercise of the constitutional interpretation authority, which competency,[28] as already mentioned, has been claimed for itself by the Constitutional Chamber. Therefore, in some decisions issued as a result of recourses or petitions for constitutional interpretation, relevant modifications to the content of specific constitutional principles may observed that give rise to actual constitutional mutations.[29]

Many of the decisions mentioned here, such as decision No. 1077/00 (case *Servio Tulio León*), decision No. 93/01 (case *CORPOTURISMO*), and decision no. 1939/08 (case *Non Execution of the Interamerican Court of Human Rights*), as well as decision no. 1942/03 (case *Rafael Chavero*),[30] are examples of decisions in which the Constitutional Chamber made modifications to the textual content –and with no ambiguities– of constitutional rules. We make reference to others of the most relevant cases

27 In this sense, see also in the Venezuelan doctrine, Cosimina Pellegrino Pacera, "El derecho a la intimidad en la nueva era informática, el derecho a la autodeterminación informativa y el habeas data a la luz de la Constitución venezolana de 1999," *Revista de Derecho Público* nº 85–86/87–88, Caracas, 2001, pp. 5 ff.

28 On this matter, see Margarita Escudero León, *El control judicial de constitucionalidad sobre las ramas legislativa y ejecutiva del Poder Público, op. cit.*, pp. 282 ff.

29 On the jurisprudence of the Constitutional Chamber of the Supreme Tribunal of Justice, see Allan R. Brewer-Carías, "El juez constitucional al servicio del autoritarismo y la ilegítima mutación de la Constitución: El caso de la Sala Constitucional del Tribunal Supremo de Justicia de Venezuela (1999-2009)," *Revista de Administración Pública*, nº 180, Madrid 2009, pp. 383–418; "La ilegítima mutación de la Constitución por el juez constitucional y la demolición del estado de derecho en Venezuela," *Revista de Derecho Político*, nos. 75–76, *Homenaje a Manuel García Pelayo*, Universidad Nacional de Educación a Distancia, Madrid, 2009, pp. 289–325; "El juez constitucional al servicio del autoritarismo y la ilegítima mutación de la Constitución: El caso de la Sala Constitucional del Tribunal Supremo de Justicia de Venezuela (1999-2009)," in *IUSTEL, Revista General de Derecho Administrativo*, nº 21, June 2009, Madrid; "La fraudulenta mutación de la Constitución en Venezuela, o de cómo el juez constitucional usurpa el poder constituyente originario," *Anuario de Derecho Público*, Centro de Estudios de Derecho Público de la Universidad Monteávila, Year 2, Caracas 2009, pp. 23–65.

30 This text is available at http://www.tsj.gov.ve/decisiones/scon/Julio/1942-150703-01-0415.htm.

in which such Chamber has acted as positive constituent for modifying or adding circumstances or legal consequences of rules having constitutional rank.

1. *Decisions No. 6 of January 27, 2000 (case* Milagros Gómez et al.*) and No. 180 of March 28, 2000 (case* Allan Brewer-Carías et al.*):*[31] *Legitimization of the Constitutional Transition Regime Approved by the National Constituent Assembly on December 1999 and Legitimization of the Acts Performed by Such Assembly in the Execution of Such Transition Regimen*

On December 15, 1999, the Venezuelan electors approved a new Constitutional Text drafted and approved by the National Constituent Assembly, which authority derived from a performance statute approved through a consultative referendum held on April 1999. The duties of such National Constituent Assembly were therefore the drafting and approval of a new Constitution that would be submitted to the final approval of electors.

However, after the popular approval of December 15, 1999, the National Constituent Assembly issued, on the twenty-ninth day of such same month and year, a Decree of the Regime of Transition of the Public Power to facilitate the "immediate applicability of the Constitution" (Art. 1). In virtue of this regime, several rules for "developing" and "complementing" the Transitory Provisions of the new Constitution (Art. 2 of the Decree) were issued, eliminating the former national legislative organ (Congress of the Republic) and appointing, in lieu thereof, a National Legislative Commission – not provided for by the Constitution – until the legislative elections took place; the Legislative Assemblies of States were abolished; the regional executive and legislative organs were abolished and modified; the former Supreme Court of Justice was abolished; the judicial statutory regime was intervened and modified; the assembly established the number of Judges to be appointed to the Chambers of the Supreme Tribunal of Justice and who were subsequently appointed; being none of such duties provided by the 1999 Constitution as competencies of the National Constituent Assembly, but, instead, of the National Assembly, a higher legislative organ, once the latter was constituted after the parliamentary elections.

31 The text of decision nº 6/2000 is available at http://www.tsj.gov.ve/decisiones/scon/Enero/ 06-270100-000011.htm and for decision nº 180/2000 at http://www.tsj.gov.ve/decisiones/scon/Marzo/180-280300-00-0737%20.htm On these decisions, see Allan R. Brewer-Carías, *La Constitución de 1999: Derecho constitucional venezolano*, Vol. II, *op. cit.*, pp. 1035 ff.

Such Decree of the National Constituent Assembly was challenged before the Constitutional Chamber through an nullity action seeking its annulment for the violation of the 1999 Constitution, as a result thereof, the Chamber established, through decision no. 6 of January 27, 2000, that the acts of the National Constituent Assembly had supraconstitutional nature and therefore were not subject to the 1961 Constitution or to the 1999 Constitution, as the challenged Decree was published in the *Official Gazette* before the publication of the new Constitutional Text and therefore the latter was not applicable thereto. In a few words, these are acts by the Public Power which are not subject to any constitutional rule whatsoever and are therefore not subject to any limitation whatsoever; nevertheless, the challenged Decree was issued for purposes of facilitating the immediate applicability of the Constitution and making new changes to the organization and distribution of the Public Power established by the new Constitution.

Finally, in this case, we may speak of a constitutional mutation from the moment in which the Constitutional Chamber admitted that the National Constituent Assembly had issued rules of constitutional –or supraconstitutional– rank based on competencies not provided for by the Constitution and not approved through popular elections.[32]

2. *Decision No. 34 of January 26, 2004 (case* Vestalia Araujo*):*[33] *Interpretation of Article 203 of the Constitution*

A recourse of interpretation for Article 203 of the 1999 Constitution was filed in order that the Constitutional Chamber clarified "if, pursuant to such rule, it is required the favorable vote of two thirds of the Representatives of the National Assembly for beginning the discussion of the organic law project of the Supreme Tribunal of Justice which would repeal the Organic Law of the Supreme Court of Justice, independently of whether the organic nature comes from a constitutional denomination."

The petitioners' doubt arose as a result of a specific case, the reform of the Organic Law of the Supreme Court of Justice and its replacement by the Organic Law of the Supreme Tribunal of Justice. Thus, the petitioners alleged that, although the project of the Organic Law of the Supreme

32 Such decisions have been questioned by the doctrine. For all of them, see Allan R. Brewer-Carías, *Crónica sobre la "in"justicia constitucional. La Sala Constitucional y el autoritarismo en Venezuela, op. cit.*, pp. 23ff.

33 See http://www.tsj.gov.ve/decisiones/scon/Enero/34-260104-03-2109%20.htm and comments in Allan R. Brewer-Carías, *La Constitución de 1999: Derecho constitucional venezolano*, Vol. I, *op. cit.*, pp. 451 ff.

Tribunal of Justice represented an Organic Law by constitutional denomination and, consequently, according to Article 203, would not require the favorable vote of two-thirds of Parliament to begin its discussion, such a law would modify an organic law and therefore would be subject to the final condition provided by such Article of the Constitution in the sense that the qualified majority voting of the Representatives "would also apply to the modification of organic laws."

Nevertheless, the decision reached another interpretation of the rule and concluded that, "pursuant to Article 203 of the Constitution in force, it is not necessary the favorable vote of two thirds (2/3) of the members of the National Assembly for beginning the discussion of projects related to organic laws, denominated as such by constitutional classification those which seek modifying organic laws in force."

Consequently, and based on the considerations expressed in the dissenting vote issued in this decision, such precedent intervened the textual interpretation of the rule, which expressly sets forth, in its final part, that the modification of any organic law requires the qualified majority of votes, and the rule in question made no reference for understanding that, even though the case involved the modification of an organic law, the qualified quorum would not be required if the new Law had organic nature as per the constitutional denomination.

3. *Decision No. 565 of April 15, 2008 (case* Attorney General of the Republic*):*[34] *Interpretation of Article 164.10, of the 1999 Constitution*

The Attorney General of the Republic, judicial and extrajudicial representative of the patrimonial interests of the Republic of Venezuela, filed a recourse for interpretation before the Constitutional Chamber of Article 164.10 of the 1999 Constitution, related to the "legal uncertainty regarding the scope and limitations of its competency . . . regarding the coordination with the states of the administration, conservation and exploitation of national roads and highways, as well as commercial ports and airports." Consequently, the Attorney General requested that the Chamber establish the terms of the coordination relationship between the Republic and the states (regional entities) regarding the competency over the conservation, administration, and exploitation of roads and highways, as well as commercial ports and airports.

[34] The text of this decision is available at http://www.tsj.gov.ve/decisiones/scon/Abril/565-150408-07-1108.htm.

Despite the fact that the 1999 Constitution provided, in its Article 164, number 10, the exclusive competency of states over the conservation, administration, and exploitation of national roads and highways, as well as commercial ports and airports, decision no. 565/08 ruled that "the National Government, through the President of the Republic in Council of Ministers, could decree the intervention for purposes of taking over the rendering of the services and assets of the national roads and highways, as well as commercial ports and airports" in those cases in which the services provided "by the States are deficient or nonexistent."

Such interpretation implies a substantial modification of the Constitutional Text because it involved the conversion of the exclusive nature of the already mentioned competency of the states into a concurrent competency among these and the Government, a competency that in the event of decentralization may be subject to intervention, reversion, and retaking over by the National Government.

Finally, decision no. 565/08 involved a relevant modification of the Constitutional Text, in such a manner that the decision itself recognizes that "this binding interpretation gives rise to a necessary revision and modification of great scope and extent of the legal system in force" and, consequently, exhorted the National Legislative Power to "proceed to the revision and corresponding modification of the legal regulation related to the binding interpretation established in this decision, in order to establish a congruent legal regulation with the constitutional rights and based on the interpretation made by this Chamber while exercising its competencies. Likewise, the Chamber exhorts the overall revision of the Organic Law of Decentralization, Delimitation and Assignment of Competencies of the Public Power, General Law of Ports and Law of Civil Aviation, without prejudice to the necessary consideration of other legal texts for adapting their content to the valid interpretation."[35]

In other words, because the changes made by the Constitutional Chamber to the Constitutional Text itself are really substantial, changes that exceed by

[35] See the comments on this decision by Allan R. Brewer-Carías, "La ilegítima mutación de la Constitución y la legitimidad de la jurisdicción constitucional: la "reforma" de la forma federal del Estado en Venezuela mediante interpretación constitucional" in *Memoria del X Congreso Iberoamericano de Derecho Constitucional*, Instituto Iberoamericano de Derecho Constitucional, Asociación Peruana de Derecho Constitucional, Instituto de Investigaciones Jurídicas-UNAM and Maestría en Derecho Constitucional-PUCP, IDEMSA, Lima 2009, vol. 1, pp. 29-51; from the same author, "La Sala Constitucional como poder constituyente: La modificación de la forma federal del estado y del sistema constitucional de división territorial del poder público," *Revista de Derecho Público*, nº 114 (April–June 2008), Editorial Jurídica Venezolana, Caracas 2008, pp. 247–262.

far a mere interpretation of the regulation and imply an unlawful replacement in the constituent itself, it was necessary to reform the legal system so that it be adapted to such decision that, by virtue of its relevance, required also its publication in the *Official Gazette*.

IV. PRECEDENTS OF THE CONSTITUTIONAL CHAMBER IN WHICH IT ACTED AS POSITIVE LEGISLATOR FOR ADDING TO THE LEGAL SYSTEM REGULATORY PRINCIPLES THAT DID NOT EXIST BEFORE

Many decisions issued by the Constitutional Chamber have as a characteristic the creation of formally mandatory considerations to which they grant binding nature. Such precedents may be understood as additive rulings, as they do not modify or substitute previously established rules, but instead add new legal provisions to the legal system. Most of the decisions previously mentioned fall in this category, although these were analyzed separately, taking into consideration the common denominator they had regarding the attribution of competencies they all involve. But there are also other precedents in which legal provisions are added to the matters of each specific case, such as those detailed here.

1. *Decision No. 1013 of June 12, 2001 (case* Elias Santana*): Interpretation and Limitation of Rights Related to Freedom of Expression and Right to Rebuttal*

In this case, a constitutional amparo proceeding was filed for the protection of the right to rebuttal and the rectification of untrue or offending information in order that the plaintiff be granted "a period of ten minutes in the radio show 'Aló Presidente' so the plaintiff could exercise the right to rebuttal to the information concerning him and the civil association Queremos Elegir."

Even though the decision declared the amparo proceeding inadmissible, it established several considerations, to which it granted binding nature, regarding the content and scope of Articles 57 and 58 of the 1999 Constitution, rules that set forth the right to free expression of thought; the right to timely, true, impartial and uncensored information; and the right to rebuttal and rectification.

In this decision, the Constitutional Chamber, *ex officio*, not only interpreted the scope of these two constitutional dispositions but also imposed limitations or exceptions thereon that were not established by the

Constitution, and ruled the exercise of such right even though all such aspects are evidently matters of legal reserve.

Thus, the doctrine has pointed out that, in this precedence, the Constitutional Chamber "abused of its competency when establishing binding interpretations regarding the content and scope of the constitutional rules and principles";[36] violated the principle of separation of powers when establishing rules that regulate and condition fundamental rights, which regulation is a matter of legal reserve; and, moreover, the content of the limitations assumed by the Chamber implied an inappropriate reduction of the scope of fundamental rights in the terms in which these are recognized by international treaties and the 1999 Constitution.

2. *Decision No. 978 of April 30, 2003 (case* Bolívar Banco*):*[37] *Resolution of the Method and Opportunity for Exercising the State Tax Authority on Tax Stamp Matters Pending the Issuing of the Relevant National Legislation*

An action was filed before the Constitutional Chamber for conflict of laws among Article 28 of the Decree with Force of Law on Tax Stamps, Article 19 of the Ordinance on Tax Stamps of the Metropolitan District of Caracas, and the Law on Tax Stamps of the Miranda State in virtue of the overlapping of taxable bases and tax burdens established by the three laws; that is, the three laws imposed, in a substantially identical manner, the same tax obligation for specific civil and mercantile proceedings.

The decision declared the action admissible and resolved the case on the basis of which of the rules would prevail according to the different circumstances brought up and the different territorial entities. It also resolved the case on the basis of a legal gap due to the omission of the National Assembly in the issue of a legislation that governed the State Internal Revenue and the Law on Tax Coordination. Consequently, the decision established that "pending issue of the national legal regime provided by Article 164.4 of the Constitution, which includes both the Law on State Internal Revenue and the Law on Tax Coordination," it would proceed by means of case law to determine fundamental aspects of this legal regime.

36 See Allan R. Brewer-Carías, *Crónica sobre la "in"justicia constitucional. La Sala Constitucional y el autoritarismo en Venezuela*, *op. cit.*, pp. 424 ff.

37 This text is available at http://www.tsj.gov.ve/decisiones/scon/Abril/978-300403-01-1535%20.htm.

As a result, the decision filled in several legal gaps that it listed as follows: "1. When can States jointly exercise their power of creating taxes and their power of collecting taxes on fiscal stamp matters based on Article 164, Numeral 7, of the Constitution of the Bolivarian Republic of Venezuela, without being obliged by Article 164, Numeral 4, to wait for the issuing of the federal legal framework which permits the coordinated exercise by States and the Metropolitan District of Caracas of such tax competency?" and "When can States exercise only their power to collect taxes on tax stamp matters based on Article 164, Numeral 7, of the Constitution of the Bolivarian Republic of Venezuela and the substantive rules established by the National Power in the Decree with Force of Law on Tax Stamps pending issue of the Organic Law on State Internal Revenue?"

As an answer to those questions, decision no. 978/03 itself established a series of declaratory legal considerations and, moreover, established a series of rules "which shall be strictly complied with pending issue of the abovementioned tax laws."[38]

Take into consideration that, in this specific case, even though the Constitutional Chamber issued a series of parameters to which it granted the value of general rules of mandatory compliance, that is, it acted as a positive legislator and integrated the legal system, doing so acted on a provisional basis, that is, until the legislator issues the corresponding laws. The provisional measures were issued by the Chamber considering it possible within its authority of controlling legislative omissions.

3. *Decision No. 511 of April 5, 2004 (case* Maira Rincón Lugo*):*[39] *Decision on the Taking over Proceeding of Cases from Lower Courts (Avocamiento), Having Binding Nature for All Other Courts of the Supreme Tribunal of Justice*

In this precedent, a petition was filed before the Constitutional Chamber for the revision of a decision issued by the Civil Cassation Chamber of the same Supreme Tribunal. The Constitutional Chamber declared inadmissible the petition of revision because it did not meet the requirements for its admission. Notwithstanding this decision – which was the only applicable one pursuant to the congruency principle of the decision regarding the petitions filed – the Constitutional Chamber in this precedent established, *ex*

[38] Textual reference of the decision.

[39] This decision is available at http://www.tsj.gov.ve/decisiones/scon/Abril/511-050404-04-0418..%20.htm.

officio, and with no relation to the specific case, the proceeding to be followed when any of the Chambers of the Supreme Tribunal of Justice exercises the power of taking over the cases from lower courts (*avocamiento*). Moreover, it granted binding nature to this interpretation for its mandatory compliance by the other courts.

The decision was issued with two dissenting votes, which expressed solid arguments for having rejected such unlawful legislation issued by the Constitutional Chamber. First of all, these pointed out that, pursuant to Article 335 of the Constitution, the binding nature of the decisions issued by the Constitutional Chamber is limited to those cases that make an interpretation regarding the scope or content of constitutional rules and principles, a matter that evidently does not apply in this case, as no constitutional rule is interpreted and the taking over of cases from lower courts (*avocamiento*) is not even provided for by the Constitution. Second, the votes condemned the usurpation of powers and the invasion of legislative competencies by the court.

We agree with the dissenting votes that, in fact, the case involved a decision ruling over matters not related to the specific case (*ultrapetita*) in which the Constitutional Chamber usurped powers from the legislative power and established the proceeding for taking over cases from lower courts (*avocamiento*) with the intention of making it a proceeding of regulatory force, binding and mandatory for the other courts. The Chamber in this cases of proceedings for taking over the case of a lower court (*avocamiento*) in which the Law provided no proceeding whatsoever for its resolution, should have only limited to apply by analogy to the specific case any other means provided by another law – as indeed it was allowed in Article 19 of the Organic Law of the Supreme Tribunal of Justice –,, instead of creating a proceeding and granting it a "mandatory and binding" nature for other courts, such as if it were a law.

4. *Decision No. 1682 of July 15, 2005 (case* Carmela Manpieri*): Interpretation of Article 77 of the Constitution – Comparison between Men and Women De Facto and Men and Women Marriage – and the Praetorian Development of Its Legal Regime*

Article 77 of the 1999 Constitution sets forth that those stable relations between men and women that meet the requirements provided by the law "shall have the same effects of marriage." Resolving on a recourse of interpretation filed regarding this rule, the Constitutional Chamber established its scope, and moreover, although the decision made no reference to the exercise of normative jurisdiction, it developed, in jurisprudential terms, the entire legal regime of *de facto* stable relations between men and women, establishing which of the civil effects of marriage are applicable to such relations and which are not.

Consequently, the decision ruled on the legal regime of many rights, such as the right to pensions, retirement benefits, use of the partner's name, economic regime, community property, and succession rights within the framework *de facto* stable relations between men and women. In the end, it developed the legal effects of Article 77 of the Constitution regarding concubinary relations, granted it a binding nature and ordered its publication in *Official Gazette*.

Such regulation represents a clear performance as positive legislator and a substitution by the Constitutional Chamber of the legislator's functions, as such regulation of rights and duties included *ex officio* in the decision is a matter of legal reserve pursuant to Article 156, number 32, for being the legal regime applicable to civil rights.

5. *Decision No. 1456 of July 27, 2006 (case* Yamilex Núñez de Godoy*)*[40] *and the Praetorian Development of the Legal Regime of Assisted Reproduction*

In this specific case, a constitutional amparo was filed against a fertility clinic because of the refusal of the medical center to "complete the cycle of in vitro fertilization in [a] person with the sperm sample of her late spouse"; the Clinic's refusal was based on the lack of an express wish by the donor regarding this fertilization alternative.

The Constitutional Chamber declared admissible the amparo proceeding and even recognized "the legitimate relationship of a child born from this assisted reproduction and ordered its registration in the Civil Registry Office with such condition." For reaching such a conclusion, the Chamber expressly based its decision on its normative jurisdiction and made several legal considerations – of binding nature – regarding assisted reproduction and its methods, specifically regarding in vitro fertilization. In the case, the Chamber ruled on matters related to the decision of a legitimate relationship in assisted reproduction, to nonconsented fecundation, to retributive donation, to cases of surrogate mothers and to the feasibility of successions in these cases.[41]

[40] See http://www.tsj.gov.ve/decisiones/scon/Julio/1456-270706-05-1471.htm.

[41] In contrast with the majority's criteria, the dissenting vote of this decision expressed that, for the resolution of a case, "there is no need of applying what is known as 'normative jurisdiction'

Finally, and as expressed in the dissenting vote, in this precedent, the Constitutional Chamber legislated on a matter that required an exhaustive legal treatment through a formal law issued by means of a constitutional proceeding for the creation of laws, a matter in which it is specially relevant the analysis of many ethical, moral, and scientific principles that are impossible to cover within a decision. In addition thereto, it is reprehensible the inappropriate use of the normative jurisdiction for issuing binding legal precepts to be applied in the same specific case to be resolved on in this occasion. This implies the usurpation of the Legislator's power, the violation to the principle of non-retroactivity of the law and the violation to the principle of legal reserve since, as mentioned above, the regulation of civil rights is a matter of national legal reserve pursuant to Article 156.32, of the 1999 Constitution.

V. PRECEDENTS OF THE CONSTITUTIONAL CHAMBER THAT ACTS AS POSITIVE LEGISLATOR TO MODIFY PREEXISTING LAWS

1. *Decisions That Modify Legal Rules through Substitutive Decisions on No Prior Declaration of Annulment of the Rule*

In multiple precedents, the Constitutional Chamber has changed the content of legal rules in force through decisions that may be referred to as substitutive because they modify the content of a legal provision with no prior declaration of annulment for unconstitutionality; that is, they change the principle through the partial substitution of the initially established circumstance or legal consequence for a new one, granting binding nature to the new text as well. Some of them were previously mentioned, such as the case of the decisions that modify the Organic Law on Amparo regarding Constitutional Rights and Guarantees (decisions no. 1 and 2/00, cases *Emery Mata Millán* and *Domingo Ramírez Monja*, no. 7/00, case *José Amado Mejía*, no. 1555/00 case *Yoslena Chanchamire*)[42] as well as decision no. 1645/04, case *Gregorio Pérez*, which modified the proceeding of actions for

since, although there is no special regulation, such as in other countries, there is no lack of regulation on the matter, as recognized, in its several analysis, the verdict itself" and that "what is known, under different denominations, as 'normative jurisdiction' in Comparative Law, is the interpretative activity of the constitutional judge of the existing legal system – and which has democratic legitimacy due to its legislative origin – in order to develop new rules or different rules from it through several universal interpretation techniques, but not for such same judge's free creation of rules."

42 Available at http://www.tsj.gov.ve/decisiones/scon/Diciembre/1555-081200-00-0779%20.htm.

the annulment of laws and other acts with force of law. To those, which were also classified as decisions that attribute or modify the competencies of the Constitutional Chamber, we may add the following decisions in which the change was made regarding substantive laws applicable to each specific case.

A. Decision No. 2855 of November 20, 2002 (case *FEDENAGA*):[43] Constitutionality of Articles 40 and 43 of the Decree with Force of Law on Rural Lands and Agrarian Development

This was a case of a recourse for annulment filed before the Constitutional Chamber for unconstitutionality against several articles of the Decree with Force of Law on Lands and Agrarian Development. Among other allegations of unconstitutionality, it was alleged that Articles 40 and 43 of the Law established the publication of a service of process in the Agrarian Official Gazette as a means to notify the interested parties about the administrative proceedings filed against them, as well as a means for notifying the administrative proceedings of specific effects that declare lands inactive and, consequently, affect their legal sphere, instead of the personal notification of the interested party that, in its judgment, was a violation to the right to defense and due process.

The Constitutional Chamber opted to not annul the challenged rules but to grant them a constitutional and binding interpretation; that is, it annulled Articles 40 and 43 of the Decree Law on Rural Lands and kept the publication of the service of process in the Agrarian Official Gazette as a means to publish the initiation of an administrative file or final proceeding, but it added that it is indispensable to perform the personal notification of interested parties as well if known.

It is our opinion that this decision, in principle, does not legislate – that is, it does not add a new legal provision – but instead it makes a constitutional interpretation to the challenged articles, stating that they do not violate the right to defense, declaring that the requirement to be applied as well was the personal notification governed by the Organic Law on Administrative Proceedings. This Law establishes the general framework on matters of administrative proceedings and performance of the Public Administration in Venezuela, providing in Article 73 as general principle, the personal notification of interested parties of all administrative proceedings affecting their legal sphere. Therefore, it may be considered that the decision, in

[43] See http://www.tsj.gov.ve/decisiones/scon/Noviembre/2855-201102-02-0311.htm.

addition to legislating, interpreted the Decree Law on Rural Lands and Agrarian Development on the basis of the Constitution, establishing the application of the Organic Law on Administrative Proceedings as a supplement or complement thereof.

However, the decision itself pointed out that the obligation to perform the personal notification was a direct consequence of the decision and from the supplemental application of the Organic Law on Administrative Proceedings, a supplemental application which, to its judgment, was not applicable in this case.

B. Decision No. 2560 of August 5, 2005 (case *Rómulo Pacheco*):[44] Modification of Article 172 of the Organic Code of Criminal Procedure

A constitutional amparo proceeding was filed before the Constitutional Chamber against a decision issued by the Court of Appeals of the Criminal Judicial Circuit of Anzoategui State, under the allegation that the decision violated the right to an effective judicial protection because it declared that the recourse of appeal was extemporaneous.

Decision No. 2560/05 declared admissible the constitutional review and annulled the decision issued by the Court of Appeals because it violated, in the Chamber's judgment, the right to an effective judicial protection, deciding to hear the appeal initially dismissed. To reach such a conclusion, the decision had to reinterpret Article 172 of the Organic Code of Criminal Procedure for being the rule that established how to calculate the terms within the preparation phase of criminal proceedings. The text of this rule reads as follows: "For the hearing of criminal matters during the preparation phase all days shall be considered court days. During the intermediate phases and oral trial, Saturdays, Sundays and holidays established by the law, as well as those in which the court resolves upon not working, shall not be counted."

The Constitutional Chamber, with no prior declaration of annulment of the rule – which, in any case, did not apply within the scope of a constitutional amparo proceeding – established, with binding nature, that, even though the rule sets forth in general that for the hearing of criminal matters during the preparation phase, all days are considered court days, for the recourse of

[44] This text is available at http://www.tsj.gov.ve/decisiones/scon/Agosto/2560-050805-03-1309.htm.

appeal, the term is calculated according to the court days even though it is a procedural act of such preparation phase of a trial.

The praetorian modification of the rule is made on the basis of a partial declaration of unconstitutionality thereof, even though there was no declaration of annulment. It is therefore a "reducing" decision; that is, it removes a circumstance from the original scope of application of the principle – in this case, the term for filing recourse of appeal – and grants it a different legal treatment established by the decision itself. In addition, the Chamber granted a binding nature to the modification of the text's content and ordered its publication in the *Official Gazette*, all of which implies legislative performance by the constitutional judge.[45]

C. Decision No. 301 of February 27, 2007 (case *Adriana Vigilanza*):[46] Modification of the Sense and Scope of Article 31 of the Income Tax Law

A petition for annulment for unconstitutionality was filed before the Constitutional Chamber against Articles 67, 68, 69, 72, 74, and 79 of the 1999 Decree Law on Income Tax. On issuing the final decision, the Chamber verified that the challenged rules were repealed and had no effect –at least not on the record– and, consequently, it declared the subsequent inadmissibility of the action.

45 Decision nº 2560/05 had a dissenting vote that expressed the valid reasons for rejecting the normative proceeding, pointing out that it is reprehensible that the Constitutional Chamber modified the legal consequence provided by the law to a specific circumstance, with the aggravating factor that, in this case, there was no declaration of annulment of the legal rule.

46 See http://www.tsj.gov.ve/decisiones/scon/Febrero/301-270207-01-2862.htm. On this decision, see Allan R. Brewer-Carías, "El juez constitucional en Venezuela como legislador positivo de oficio en materia tributaria," *Revista de Derecho Público*, nº 109 (January–March 2007), Editorial Jurídica Venezolana, Caracas 2007, pp. 193-212; "Régimen y alcance de la actuación judicial de oficio en materia de justicia constitucional en Venezuela," *Revista IURIDICA*, nº 4, Centro de Investigaciones Jurídicas Dr. Aníbal Rueda, Universidad Arturo Michelena, Valencia, July–December 2006, pp. 13–40; "El juez constitucional como legislador positivo de oficio en materia tributaria: La legitimación activa en la acción popular y la impugnación de leyes derogadas" in *Crónica sobre la "In"justicia constitucional: La Sala Constitucional y el autoritarismo en Venezuela, op. cit.*, pp. 565–592; "El juez constitucional en Venezuela como legislador positivo de oficio en materia tributaria," in *Homenaje a Tomás Enrique Carrillo Batalla*, (Coordinator Azdrúbal Grillet Correa), Vol. I, Universidad Central de Venezuela, Caracas 2009, pp. 163–189; "De cómo la Jurisdicción constitucional en Venezuela, no sólo legisla de oficio, sino subrepticiamente modifica las reformas legales que 'sanciona,' a espaldas de las partes en el proceso: El caso de la aclaratoria de la sentencia de Reforma de la Ley de Impuesto sobre la Renta de 2007," *Revista de Derecho Público*, nº 114, Editorial Jurídica Venezolana, Caracas 2008, pp. 267–276.

However, and even though such a decision would resolve the petition, the Constitutional Chamber proceeded, *ex officio*, to analyze the constitutionality of a rule that was not object of the recourse of annulment – Article 31 of the 2001 Income Tax Law – invoking Article 5, paragraph 2, of the Organic Law of the Supreme Tribunal of Justice, and the decision pointed out that "in matters related to the concentrated control of constitutionality the dispositive principle does not prevail for its nature of public order."

Certainly, the rule invoked by the Constitutional Chamber allows it "to substitute *ex officio* the deficiencies of the petitioner regarding the dispositions challenged"; that is, it allows it to take into consideration arguments or allegations of unconstitutionality not challenged by the parties but related to the rules object of the petition for annulment, which was not this specific case for which the court analyzed *ex officio* the unconstitutionality of an unchallenged rule provided by a law other than the law initially challenged.

On the basis of such statements, the Constitutional Chamber analyzed the content of Article 31 of the Income Tax Law, the original content of which was as follows:

> Article 31. Net enrichments are deemed as the wages, salaries, payments, allowances, bonuses and other similar remunerations, other than travel expenses, gained for the rendering of personal services under a dependence relationship. Net enrichments are also considered those interests derived from loans and other credits granted by financial institutions located abroad or not domiciled in the country, as well as shares subject to proportional taxes pursuant to the terms of this Law.

Thus, the decision considered that such a legal disposition collides with constitutional rights of salaried workers; consequently, given the "conflict" between the disposition of Article 31 of the Income Tax Law and the Constitution, the decision modified the content of the principle and established a new wording:

> Article 31. *Net enrichments are deemed as the salaries gained on a regular and permanent basis for the rendering of personal services under a dependence relationship*. Net enrichments are also considered those interests derived from loans and other credits granted by financial institutions located abroad or not domiciled in the country, as well as shares subject to proportional taxes pursuant to the terms of this Law.

> For purposes of this Article, *provisional earnings, earnings derived from seniority benefits and those which the Law considers non-salary payments are considered excluded from the salary.*[47]

It is our opinion that this precedent usurped the powers of the legislative power, because the constitutional judge, with no declaration of annulment, modified the content of a legal rule, thus suppressing a part of the principle, including circumstances that were not previously established. The difference between the original content of Article 31 of the Income Tax Law and the content provided by the decision evidences that they are two completely different principles.

Take into consideration that this precedent caused the National Assembly, Venezuela's national legislative organ, to issue the Agreement of March 22, 2007, for "categorically rejecting" decision no. 301/2007 for, among other reasons, the implicit usurpation of powers of the decision.[48]

2. *Decisions of the Constitutional Chamber That Annulled and Established the New Wording of Legal Provisions*

A. Decision no. 80 of February 1, 2001 (Case of Procedural Terms):[49] Modification of Article 197 of the Civil Procedure Code Regarding the Calculation of Procedural Terms

In this case, a petition for annulment was filed on the unconstitutionality of Article 197 of the Civil Procedure Code, which governs the calculation of procedural terms and periods.

[47] The "new"text is in Italic. This decision nº 301/07 was subject to a subsequent clarification through decision nº 390 of March 9, 2007, in which the Constitutional Chamber partially modified the new interpretation and content given to Article 31 of the Income Tax Law (http://www.tsj.gov.ve/decisiones/scon/Marzo/390-090307-01-2862.htm).

[48] On this decision, see Allan R. Brewer-Carías, *Crónica sobre la "in"justicia constitucional: La Sala Constitucional y el autoritarismo en Venezuela, op. cit.*, pp. 565 ff.; from the same author, "El juez constitucional en Venezuela como legislador positivo de oficio en materia tributaria," *Revista de Derecho Público*, nº 109, Caracas, 2007, pp. 194 ff.; José Antonio Muci Borjas, "La base imponible del impuesto sobre la renta de las personas naturales y la sentencia nº 301/2007 de la Sala Constitucional del Tribunal Supremo de Justicia," *Revista de Derecho Público*, nº 116, Caracas, 2008, pp. 267 ff.

[49] This text is available at http://www.tsj.gov.ve/decisiones/scon/Febrero/80-010201-00-1435%20.htm. On this sentence and the modification of the procedural terms, see Allan R. Brewer-Carías, "Los primeros pasos de la Jurisdicción Constitucional como 'legislador positivo,' y el régimen legal de cómputo de los lapsos procesales," in *Crónica sobre la "in"justicia constitucional: La Sala Constitucional y el autoritarismo en Venezuela, op. cit.*, pp. 511–543.

The petitioner alleged that the rule, for purposes of calculating the procedural terms, differentiated between the terms for the submission of evidences, which are calculated taking into account consecutive calendar days, even though – in the opinion of the petitioners – the rest of the procedural terms, especially those related to the exercise of recourses against decisions, should also be calculated according to court days. The contrary was considered to violated the right to defense of the parties involved in a proceeding.

The Constitutional Chamber declared admissible the allegation, considering that the legal rule violated the right to defense. Consequently, it declared the partial annulment of Article 197 of the Civil Procedure Code regarding the phrase "the terms for submitting evidences, in which the calculation shall not include," and in the disposition of the decision, the Chamber required that "Article 197 of the Civil Procedure Code be reworded."

This is a decision in which the partial annulment of the rule completely changes its original sense. In principle, the Constitutional Chamber should not have reworded the content of the legal provision, which is an inherent and exclusive competency of the legislator; instead, it should have limited itself to declaring its annulment and exhorting or ordering the legislator to establish a new principle according to constitutional guidelines.

B. Decision No. 1264 of June 11, 2002 (case *Jesús Rendón*):[50] Partial Annulment of Article 201 of the Civil Procedure Code That Governs Judicial Holidays

In this precedent, a petition for annulment was filed on the unconstitutionality of Article 201 of the Civil Procedure Code due to the alleged violation of the right to access justice, right to equality, and right to work by this legal provision, which established the annual periods in which courts were in recess, known as court holidays. The rule that was object of the petition established two holiday periods: from August 15 to September 15 and from December 24 to January 6 each year.

In this context, the Constitutional Chamber considered the violation of the right to access justice and the right to defense by Article 201 of the Civil Procedure Code to the extent that justice cannot be paralyzed and must be administered without delays. Consequently, it declared the partial annulment

[50] The text of this decision is available at http://www.tsj.gov.ve/decisiones/scon/Junio/1264-110602-00-1281.htm.

of the rule, specifically regarding part of the phrase that made reference to the period from August 15 to September 15 and established, in the decision, the new wording of the disposition pursuant to which the sole period of judicial holidays shall be from December 24 to January 6 of each year.

This decision is a a decision declaring the nullity of the provision, in which the original scope of application of the rule has been reduced but in which the legislator's discretion was not respected, because after the declaration of annulment of the judicial holiday period, the National Assembly could have opted for multiple legislative options – establishing, for example, several shorter periods. However, the decision substituted for the legislator and immediately established the new wording and content of the partially annulled disposition. This inappropriate substitution for the legislator by the decision was expressed in the dissenting vote issued with the decision.

C. Decision No. 2241 of September 24, 2002 (case *Andrés Velázquez*):[51] Partial Annulment of Article 80 of the Organic Law on the Financial Administration of the Public Sector

In this case, a petition for annulment was filed on the unconstitutionality of Article 80 of the Organic Law on the Financial Administration of the Public Sector under the allegation that such rule infringed the first paragraph of Articles 150 and number 9 of Article 187 of the 1999 Constitution by establishing a control mechanism – periodical information – from the National Executive to the National Assembly of the public credit transactions performed by the former, in a way different to those provided in such constitutional provisions – prior authorization – in those cases in which the public credit transaction involves the subscription of agreements of national public interest with States, foreign official entities, or companies not domiciled in Venezuela.

The Constitutional Chamber took into consideration the arguments of the petitioners and established the partial unconstitutionality of the rule for not including, in the last paragraph of Article 80 of the Organic Law of the Financial Administration of the Public Sector, an exception or reference to the mandatory control or authorization of the National Assembly regarding the public credit transactions performed by the National Executive and those involving agreements of national public interest. Instead, it established "a general authorization through the approval of the Law of Annual Indebtedness and a regime of periodical information to the National

[51] See http://www.tsj.gov.ve/decisiones/scon/Septiembre/2241-240902-00-2874%20.htm.

Assembly, infringing therefore the sense, purpose and basis of the constitutional dispositions provided by the abovementioned articles."

Consequently, the Chamber declared the partial annulment of Article 80 of the Organic Law on the Financial Administration of the Public Sector and established the new wording of the rule.

Considering that even though it is a decision declaring the nullity of the challenged provision, and even though it declares the partial annulment of the disposition, it actually makes no annulment whatsoever but represents a typical additive decision, to the extent that it adds to the legal disposition circumstances and/or legal consequences not previously established by the legislator for purposes of its adaptation to the constitutional rule; this is a typical case in which the judge acts as positive legislator.[52]

D. Decision No. 3241 of December 12, 2002 (case *COVEIN*):[53] Partial Annulment of Article 1 of the Ordinance on the Industry and Commerce License Tax of the Bolivar Municipality of the Anzoátegui State

A petition was filed for the partial annulment of a municipal rule, Article 1 of the Ordinance on the Industry and Commerce License Tax of the Bolivar Municipality of the Anzoátegui State, specifically because the rule established, among the economic activities subject to the local tax, the rendering of professional services, which, in the opinion of the petitioner, violated the Constitution, because the imposition of taxes over such economic activity was beyond the Municipality's tax competency.

The Constitutional Chamber admitted the petition, partially annulled the rule, and established its new wording, in which it deleted the reference to "professional activities" among the activities originally subject to the municipal tax to make the disposition coherent according to the dispositions of the decision.

The Constitutional Chamber did not legislate in this case because it did not establish new content for the law beyond its partial annulment. In other words, the decision declared the partial annulment of the rule and transcribed how its wording would remain after deleting the annulled phrase, making no additional modification to its sense or content. Such practice of the Constitutional Chamber of partially annulling a rule and establishing, in the

[52] Francisco Javier Díaz Revorio, *Las sentencias interpretativas del Tribunal Constitucional*, *op. cit.*, pp. 133 ff.

[53] See http://www.tsj.gov.ve/decisiones/scon/Diciembre/3241-121202-00-0824.htm.

decision, the wording by deleting only the phrase annulled, has been common, as evidenced, among other decisions, by decision no. 15 of February 15, 2005 (case *Tomás Arenciba*); however, this does not involve the creation of any legislation by the jurisdictional organ but only the transcription of the wording of a rule resulting from the declaration of its partial annulment.

E. Decision No. 865 of April 22, 2003 (case *Ernesto José Rodríguez Casares*):[54] Annulment of Article 48 of the Ordinance on Urban and Rural Common and Personal Lands for the Bolivar District of the Zulia State

The petitioner requested the annulment of Article 48 of the Ordinance on Urban and Rural Common and Personal Lands for the Bolívar District of the Zulia State, alleging the violation of the constitutional right to property for establishing a preferential right for the Municipality to reacquire lands considered common properties and paying the same price for which they were sold within up to a period of twenty years after the sale was made, which, according to the petitioner, caused significant financial damage because of inflationary effects. Likewise, it was alleged that the rule also violated the right to property "for requiring the persons subject to the rule the obligation to provide fifty percent (50%) of the price obtained in the sale if the value of the common land has increased regarding its price when the initial sale took place."

The Constitutional Chamber found that there was a violation to the right to property because the requirements represented a violation of the *ius abutendi*, or right to disposal, granted to every owner for the disposal of his or property and for limiting the owner's wish to carry out the disposal of his or her own assets.

Consequently, the rule was partially annulled, specifically the reference regarding which the Municipality could reacquire the common land "at the same price [at] which it was sold" and the entire second paragraph, which set forth the obligation of providing the Municipality 50 percent of the price obtained in the sale if the value of the common land had increased in price when the initial sale took place. In its decision, the Chamber, in addition to partially annulling the rule, established new wording, which simply reproduced the text and deleted those phrases and paragraphs that were subject to annulment. Therefore, this is an annulling decision, which reduced

[54] This text is available at http://www.tsj.gov.ve/decisiones/scon/Abril/865-220403-00-0718.htm.

the circumstances of the rule by partially annulling its unconstitutional portion and did not involve the creation of legislation but the restatement of a disposition, which does not modify its sense and content beyond the phrase annulled.

F. Decision No. 1104 of May 23, 2006 (case *Carlos Brender*):[55] Partial Annulment of Article 90 of the Organic Law of the Attorney General of the Republic

In this case, a petition was filed for annulment of Article 90 of the Organic Law on the Attorney General of the Republic. The allegation of unconstitutionality referred to the fact that the legal rule established the possibility of the Republic's counterparty in trial to deposit a bail for the precautionary measures issued against it to be lifted; however, the rule also established that "such bail must be approved by the attorney general of the Republic." Such approval, in the opinion of the petitioner, was unconstitutional because it violates the right to procedural equality, the right to effective judicial protection, and the right to due process, and because it implies a reduction of the powers of the judge, who should be responsible for approving bail.

The Chamber admitted the allegation of the violation to the right to defense and due process and, consequently, partially annulled the rule, specifically in reference to "this bail must be approved by the attorney general of the Republic." Likewise, it established new wording for the Article in the following terms: "This bail must be approved by the corresponding judge."

In our opinion, it is certainly questionable that the decision established new wording and changed the terms of the legal rule being annulled. In this case, because of the legal gap that resulted from this annulled disposition, the correct proceeding was to apply by analogy the general principles of civil procedure provided for in the Civil Procedure Code, specifically Article 590 of the Code. Therefore, it was not necessary to legislate, that is, to modify the terms of the rule's original wording, only to apply by analogy – or even in a supplementary manner – the general procedural rules provided for in the Civil Procedure Code.

55 This text is available at http://www.tsj.gov.ve/decisiones/scon/Mayo/1104-230506-02-1688.htm.

G. Decision No. 163 of February 28, 2008 (case *Ciro Ramón Araujo*):[56] Partial Annulment of the Organic Law of Public Defense

This precedent evidences several types of legislative performance by the Constitutional Chamber, which we will analyze separately:

a. *Partial Annulment and Modification of the Text of Article 3 of the Organic Law of Public Defense*

A petition for annulment for unconstitutionality was filed against Article 3 of the Organic Law of Public Defense. The alleged reason for unconstitutionality was that the rule ascribed, through an organic law, the Public Defense Service to the Public Defender's Office, even though the Public Defense Service was one of the organs part of the judicial system as provided by the 1999 Constitution. The petitioner thus alleged that such organ should be attached to the Supreme Tribunal of Justice.

Decision no. 163/08 partially annulled Article 3 of the Organic Law of Public Defense, specifically the part that established its attachment to the Public Defender's Office, and it established the new wording of such rule according to which the Public Defense Service will be attached to the Supreme Tribunal of Justice.

b *Partial Annulment and Modification of Articles 11, 12, and 13 of the Organic Law of Public Defense*

As a direct consequence of the declaration of annulment of Article 3, the decision, *ex officio*, analyzed the constitutionality of other articles from the same law and partially annulled Articles 11–13, which established the competency and proceeding for the appointment and removal of the head of the Public Defense Service, and it established a new wording.

The dissent vote of the decision expressed the excess of annulling, *ex officio*, rules that established the competency and proceeding for the appointment of the maximum authority of the Public Defense Service and establishing a completely different competency and proceeding.

[56] This available at http://www.tsj.gov.ve/decisiones/scon/Febrero/163-280208-07-0124.htm.

c. *Partial Annulment and Modification of Article 15 of the Organic Law of Public Defense*

Finally, decision no. 163/08 *ex officio* annulled Article 15, sections 5 and 7, of the same law, which obligated the Executive Director of the Public Defense Service to submit a budget plan for the Public Defense Service and to submit an annual report of his or her performance as the head of the Public Defender's Office. It also established new wording for such dispositions by replacing the reference to the Public Defender's Office with a reference to the Supreme Tribunal of Justice with all Chambers acting jointly:

> 5. Submit the budget plan to all the Chambers acting jointly of the Supreme Tribunal of Justice. . . .
>
> 7. Submit an annual report of his/her performance to the Supreme Tribunal of Justice with all the Chambers acting jointly.

In our opinion, the Constitutional Chamber certainly had reasons for declaring unconstitutional Article 3 of the Organic Law of Public Defense: according to the 1999 Constitution, that organ of the Public Power is part of the judicial system and must be attached to the Supreme Tribunal of Justice and not to the Public Defender's Office, an organ that is part of the Citizen Power. However, the appropriate proceeding was for the decision to be limited to declaring unconstitutionality and, consequently, establishing a period of time for the National Assembly, the national legislative organ, to adapt the Law to the Constitutional text according to the disposition of the decision. Likewise, to avoid a legal gap while the Law in question was being reformed, the decision could have been limited to declaring the Law unconstitutional and not annulling Article 3, so that the Public Defense Service would remain ascribed to the Public Defender's Office until the rule's reform was complete.

This is a solution commonly used in comparative law, as in Germany, where declarations of unconstitutionality without annulment or of mere incompatibility (*Unvereinbarket*) exhort the legislator to modify them within a specific period. This avoids the undesirable consequence of a legislative gap and avoids the constitutional courts's usurping of the legislative function.[57]

[57] On this matter, see the considerations of Francisco Javier Díaz Revorio, *Las sentencias interpretativas del Tribunal Constitucional, op. cit.*, pp. 260 ff.

VI. BRIEF CONCLUSIONS REGARDING THE UNCONSTITUTIONALLITY OF THE EXCERCISE OF THE NORMATIVE POWERS BY THE CONSTITUTIONAL CHAMBER OF THE SUPREME TRIBUNAL OF JUSTICE

The study of the jurisprudence of the Constitutional Chamber shows that, since its creation, it has been constant in the exercise of the normative jurisdiction, through which it has issued many decisions of a normative nature, such as modifying preexisting norms without prior declaration of nullity, integrating the legal system in areas where no legislation existed, and substituting precepts that were declared null with other precepts that, in the Chambert's criteria, better fit the Constitution. Thus, it stands out how many of the competencies that the Constitutional Chamber currently has are a result of said normative jurisdiction; that is, they have been self-attributed by the Constitutional Chamber. However, there is not a systematic application of said normative jurisdiction, as there exist several precedents in which the Chamber has abstained from substituting itself in the legislative function.[58]

The exercise of the normative jurisprudence does not have in Venezuela a constitutional base; that is, there is no norm in the Constitution that expressly grants the Constitutional Chamber competencies to enact or modify legal norms, only competencies to annul acts having rank of law contrary to the Constitution. The Chamber certainly is the highest and final interpreter of the Constitution; however, that power is what allows it to interpret, that is, to determine the scope that has to be given to the constitutional norms, not to fill in the "constitutional vacuums" or enact precepts having intended rank of law.[59]

Therefore, the exercise of normative jurisdiction in Venezuela is against (i) the principle of separation of powers, as it implies an usurpation of functions of the legislative power by the judicial power; (ii) the principle of legal reserve, as the legal norms that are a result of the normative jurisdiction must

58 See references to decisions nº 3118, dated November 6, 2003 (case *Ley Orgánica del Poder Público Municipal*); nº 1168, dated June 15, 2004 (case *FENIATRIDE*); nº 91, dated March 2, 2005 (case *PROVEA*); nº 1043, dated May 31, 2004 (case *Ley Orgánica del Poder Municipal II*); nº 74, dated January 25, 2006 (case *Las morochas*); nº 1682, dated July 15, 2005 (case *Carmela Manpieri*); decision nº 190, dated February 28, 2008 (case *Unión Afirmativa de Venezuela*).

59 See the comments by Jesús María Casal, "La protección de la Constitución frente a las omisiones legislativas," *op. cit.*, pp. 226–227; and Mario Pesci-Feltri, "La jurisdicción normativa y los artículos 335 y 336 de la Constitución," in A.A.V.V. *El derecho público a comienzos del siglo XXI, Estudios en homenaje al Profesor Allan R. Brewer-Carías*, Vol. I, Civitas, Madrid, 2003, p. 1035.

have been enacted through precepts having rank of law through the procedure to create statutes set forth in the Constitution; (iii) the principle of judicial security, as there is not always enough certainty or publicity regarding the modification of the legal norms;[60] and (iv) following the application of the fundamental principles of the Procedural Law to the constitutional Procedural Law, the normative jurisdiction is also against the right to due process, as it implies a wrongful declarative substitution for the decision regarding the political option of the legislator and an unacceptable suppression of the voluntary execution phase of every judicial decision. In this voluntary execution the legislator could enact a new legal norm that fits the Constitution in substitution of the one that is declared unconstitutional by the judge.

The existence in the Venezuelan legal system of a complete system of control of the constitutionality of State acts having rank of law also makes unnecessary the application of normative jurisdiction, particularly because the different means that conform such control – concentrated control, diffuse control, constitutional amparo – are sufficient in order to guarantee the principles of constitutional supremacy and efficacy, within the limits of the exercise of the jurisdictional function. Likewise, in many of the exposed precedents, the exercise of the normative jurisdiction has been possible to be avoided through the application of the traditional methods to fulfill legal vacuums, such as the case of the replacement and the analogy (decisions no. 1556/02, 1456/06, 2855/02 and 1104/06, among others), or by means of the issuing of precautionary measures in order to guarantee the effectiveness of the Constitution until the legislative entity enacts the due norms, which the Constitutional Chamber has done in some opportunities, such as the case of decision no. 3418, dated November 8, 2005 (case *Ordenanza de Contraloría Municipal del Municipio Rafael Rangel del Estado Trujillo*)[61] or decision no.

60 In this sense, Jesús María Casal states that "without denying the admission of declarations that contain binding constitutional interpretation that are closely linked to the decided case, but that are not composed by the precedent in its own sense, is important to warn about the risks that can lead regarding the values such as the legal security and the constitutional distribution of the public functions, specifically what refers to the limits between the constitutional jurisdiction and the legislative power, the so called normative jurisdiction." In "Cosa Juzgada y efecto vinculante en la justicia constitucional," in *Constitución y justicia Constitucional*, Universidad Católica Andrés Bello, Caracas, 2004, p. 271.

61 This text is available at http://www.tsj.gov.ve/decisiones/scon/Noviembre/3418-081105-03-1504.htm.

PART THREE

SYNTHESIS REPORT: CONSTITUTIONAL COURTS AS POSITIVE LEGISLATORS IN COMPARATIVE LAW[*]

PRELIMINARY REMARKS

1. *The Subordination of Constitutional Courts to the Constitution*

In all democratic countries, constitutional courts[1] have the same role of interpreting and applying the Constitution to preserve its supremacy by testing the constitutionality or conventionality of statutes,[2] and to ensure the prevalence of the democratic principle and of fundamental rights, they even have the role of adapting the Constitution when societal changes and time impose such a task.

This is true in all systems of constitutional judicial review, where a progressive convergence of principles and solutions has consolidated over

[*] Synthesis of the General Report, Subject IV.B.2, Constitutional Courts as "Positive Legislators," *XVIII International Congress of Comparative Law,* International Academy of Comparative Law, Washington, July 27, 2010.

[1] For the purpose of the General Report, because of the variety of solutions, I have used the phrase "constitutional court" in a general sense to refer to any court acting as constitutional judge.

[2] For the purpose of the General Report, I have used the phrase "control of constitutionality" to include not only judicial review of statutes regarding their conformity with the Constitution but also control of conventionality, in the sense of their conformity with international conventions – particularly on matters of human rights, as in the Netherlands, the United Kingdom, France, and many Latin American countries – and their conformity with Constitutional Conventions (what John Bell calls constitutional review in the *United Kingdom National Report*). See generally Ernesto Rey Cantor, *El control de convencionalidad de las leyes y derechos humanos*, Ed. Porrúa, Mexico City 2008; Juan Carlos Hitters, "Control de constitucionalidad y control de convencionalidad: Comparación (Criterios fijados por la Corte Interamericana de Derechos Humanos)," in *Estudios Constitucionales*, Year 7, nº 2, Santiago de Chile 2009, pp. 109–128.

the past decades.[3] Today it is difficult even to draw clearly the classic distinction between the concentrated and the diffuse systems of judicial review,[4] which were so commonly used during many decades.[5]

In all the systems, the basic principle that can be identified is that constitutional courts, in accomplishing their roles, must always be subordinated to the Constitution, not allowed to invade the field of the Legislator or of the constituent power. The contrary would be, as asserted by Sandra Morelli in the Colombia National Report, to develop an "irresponsible judicial totalitarianism,"[6] which of course is part of the pathology of judicial review.

[3] See Lucio Pegoraro, "Clasificaciones y modelos de justicia constitucional en la dinámica de los ordenamientos," *Revista Iberoamericana de Derecho Procesal Constitucional*, nº 2, Instituto Iberoamericano de Derecho Procesal Constitucional, Editorial Porrúa, Mexico City 2004, pp. 131 ff.; Alfonse Celotto, "La justicia constitucional en el mundo: Formas y modalidades," *Revista Iberoamericana de Derecho Procesal Constitucional*, nº 1, Instituto Iberoamericano de Derecho Procesal Constitucional, Editorial Porrúa, Mexico City 2004, pp. 3 ff.

[4] See, e.g., Francisco Fernández Segado, *La justicia constitucional ante el siglo XXI: La progresiva convergencia de los sistemas americano y europeo-kelseniano*, Librería Bonomo Editrice, Bologna 2003, pp. 40 ff.; Francisco Fernández Segado, "La obsolecencia de la bipolaridad 'modelo Americano-modelo europeo-kelseniano' como criterio analítico del control de constitucionalidad y la búsqueda de una nueva tipología explicativa," in *La justicia constitucional: Una visión de derecho comparado*, Vol. I, Ed. Dykinson, Madrid 2009, pp. 129–220; Guillaume Tusseau, *Contre les "modèles" de justice constitutionnelle: Essai de critique métodologique*, Bononia University Press, bilingual edition (French-Italian), Universitá di Bologna, Bologna, 2009; Guillaume Tusseau, "Regard critique sur les outils méthodologique du comparatisme. L'example des modèles de justice constitutionnelle," *IUSTEL, Revista General de Derecho Público Comparado*, nº 4, Madrid, January 2009, pp. 1–34.

[5] See Mauro Cappelletti, *Judicial Review in Contemporary World*, Bobbs-Merrill, Indianapolis 1971, p. 45; Mauro Cappelletti and J. C. Adams, "Judicial Review of Legislation: European Antecedents and Adaptations," in *Harvard Law Review*, 79, 6, April 1966, p. 1207; Mauro Cappelletti, "El control judicial de la constitucionalidad de las leyes en el derecho comparado," *Revista de la Facultad de Derecho de México*, 61, 1966, p. 28; Allan R. Brewer-Carías, *Judicial Review in Comparative Law*, Cambridge University Press, Cambridge 1989; Allan R. Brewer-Carías, *Étutes de droit pubic comparé*, Bruylant, Brussels 2000, pp. 653 ff. On the distinction, it can be said that the only aspect of it that remains is the one referred to as the organ of control, in the sense that, in the diffuse system of judicial review, all courts are constitutional judges without the need for their powers to be expressly established in the Constitution. In the concentrated system, the Constitution must expressly establish constitutional jurisdiction, assigning to a single Constitutional Court, Tribunal, or Council, or to the existing Supreme or High Court or Tribunal of Justice, the power to control the constitutionality of statutes and to annul them.

[6] See Sandra Morelli, *La Corte Constitucional: Un papel por definir*, Academia Colombiana de Jurisprudencia, Bogota, 2002; and "The Colombian Constitutional Court: from Institutional Leadership, to Conceptual Audacity," *Colombian National Report*, XVIII International Congress of Comparative Law, Washington, DC, July 2010, p. 3. See also Allan R. Brewer-Carías, "*Quis Custodiet Ipsos Custodes*: De la interpretación constitucional a la inconstitucionalidad de la interpretación," in *VIII Congreso Nacional de Derecho Constitucional, Perú*, Fondo Editorial 2005, Colegio de Abogados de Arequipa, Arequipa, September 2005, pp. 463–489, and *Revista de Derecho Público*, nº 105, Editorial Jurídica Venezolana, Caracas 2006, pp. 7–27; *Crónica*

That is, constitutional courts can assist the legislators in accomplishing their functions, but they cannot substitute for the Legislators and enact legislation – nor do they have any discretionary political basis for creating legal norms or provisions that cannot be deducted from the Constitution itself.

It is in this sense that it is possible to affirm as a general principle that constitutional courts still are considered – as Hans Kelsen used to say – negative legislators;[7] they are not positive legislators in the sense that, as affirmed by Richard Kay and Laurence Claus, in the United States National Report, they are not able to consider, propound, or create *ex novo* pieces of legislation "of their own conception" or to introduce "reforms" for statutes conceived of by other legislative actors.[8]

2. *New Role of Constitutional Courts and the Question of Acting as Positive Legislators*

Although the general principle in comparative law continues to be to consider constitutional courts as not able to create *ex novo* pieces of legislation, the fact is that during the past decades, the role of constitutional courts has dramatically changed, because their role is not limited to declare the unconstitutionality of statutes or to annul or not annul a statute on the grounds of its unconstitutionality.

In all systems, new approaches have been developed, such as those based on the principle of conservation of statutes, given their presumption of constitutionality, which empowers constitutional courts not to annul or declare them unconstitutional (even though they are contrary to the Constitution) but to interpret them according to the Constitution or in harmony with the Constitution. This has allowed the Courts to avoid creating any legislative vacuum and, in some cases, to fill permanently or temporarily the vacuums that annulment could cause.

sobre la "in"justicia constitucional: La Sala Constitucional y el autoritarismo en Venezuela, Editorial Jurídica Venezolana, Caracas 2007; and *Reforma constitucional y fraude a la Constitución*, Academia de Ciencias Políticas y Sociales, Caracas 2009.

7 See Hans. Kelsen, "La garantie juridictionnelle de la constitution (La Justice constitutionnelle)," in *Revue du droit public et de la science politique en France et a l'ètranger*, Librairie Général de Droit et the Jurisprudence, Paris 1928, pp. 197–257; Hans Kelsen, *La garantía jurisdiccional de la Constitución (La justicia constitucional)*, Universidad Nacional Autónoma de México, Mexico City 2001.

8 See Laurence Claus and Richard S. Kay, "Constitutional Courts as 'Positive Legislators' in the United States," *U.S. National Report*, XVIII International Congress of Comparative Law, Washington, DC, July 2010, pp. 3, 5.

In addition, it is now more frequent to see constitutional courts, instead of dealing with existing statutes, dealing with the absence of statutes or with absolute or relative omissions or abstention incurred by the Legislator. By controlling these omissions, constitutional courts in many cases assume the role of legislative assistant or auxiliaries, thus creating norms they normally deduct from the Constitution; in some cases, they substitute for the Legislator by assuming an open role of positive legislators, issuing temporary or provisional rules to be applied on specific matters pending the enactment of legislation.

Among the main tools for triggering this new role of constitutional courts has been the principles of progressiveness and the prevalence of human rights,[9] as has occurred in many cases with the rediscovery of the right to equality and nondiscrimination. In these cases, in the interest of the protection of citizens' rights and guarantees, there have been no doubts in accepting the legitimacy of constitutional courts' activism interfering with the Legislative functions and applying constitutional principles and values.

In these matters, the main discussion today is directed not toward rejecting the legislative activities by the courts but toward determining the extent and limits of constitutional courts' decisions and the degree of interference allowed regarding Legislative functions, as expressed by Francisco Fernandez Segado, in the Spain National Report, to avoid "transforming the guardian of the Constitution into sovereign."[10]

My analysis of the subject of constitutional courts as positive legislators in comparative law[11] has allowed me to identify four main trends regarding the relations of the constitutional courts not only with the Legislator but also with the Constitutional Legislator, which can be considered as expressions of their activities acting as positive legislators.

9 See Pedro Nikken, *La protección internacional de los derechos humanos: Su desarrollo progresivo*, Instituto Interamericano de Derechos Humanos, Ed. Civitas, Madrid 1987; Mónica Pinto, "El principio *pro homine*: Criterio hermenéutico y pautas para la regulación de los derechos humanos," in *La aplicación de los tratados sobre derechos humanos por los tribunales locales*, Centro de Estudios Legales y Sociales, Buenos Aires, 1997, p. 163.

10 See Francisco Fernández Segado, "Algunas reflexiones generales en torno a los efectos de las sentencias de inconstitucionalidad y a la relatividad de ciertas fórmulas esterotipadas vinculadas a ellas," *Anuario Iberoamericano de Justicia Constitucional*, Centro de Estudios Políticos y Constitucionales, nº 12, Madrid 2008, p. 161.

11 For the preparation of the General Report, I received thirty-six National Reports from thirty-one countries: nineteen from Europe (including six from Eastern Europe), ten from the Americas (three from North America, five from South America, and two from Central America), one from Asia, and one from Australia.

First is the role of constitutional courts interfering with the Constituent Power by enacting constitutional rules and even mutating the Constitution. Second is the role of constitutional courts interfering with existing legislation, assuming the task of being assistants to the Legislator, complementing statutes, adding to them new provisions, and determining the temporal effects of legislation. Third is the role of constitutional courts interfering with the absence of Legislation due to absolute and relative legislative omissions, acting in some cases as provisional Legislators. Fourth is the role of constitutional courts as Legislators on matters of judicial review.

FIRST TREND: CONSTITUTIONAL COURTS INTERFERING WITH THE CONSTITUENT POWER

The first trend that comparative law shows us is the role of constitutional courts interfering with the constitutional Legislator, that is, with the Constituent Power, in some cases enacting constitutional rules, as when resolving constitutional disputes between State organs; when exercising constitutional control over constitutional provisions or over constitutional amendments; and when legitimately "mutating" the Constitution by means of adapting provisions to current times and thus giving them concrete meaning.

1. *Constitutional Courts Resolving Constitutional Federal Disputes and Enacting Constitutional Rules*

The first case refers to constitutional courts interfering with the Constituent Power when they resolve constitutional conflicts or disputes between State organs, which is a common role in Federal States, as highlighted by Konrad Lachmayer, in the Austrian National Report, referring to the Austrian Constitutional Court as having acted as a positive legislator, "enacting constitutional law" when exercising positive powers regarding the division of competences between the Federation and the *Länder*, having the final say on the matter.[12] It has also been the case in the United States, where on the basis of the commerce clause, the Supreme Court has been progressively determining the powers of the federal government regarding the states; it is difficult nowadays to imagine anything that Congress could not regulate.[13]

[12] See Konrad Lachmayer, "Constitutional Courts as 'Positive Legislators,'" *Austrian National Report*, XVIII International Congress of Comparative Law, Washington, DC, July 2010, pp. 1–2.

[13] See Erwin Chemerinsky, *Constitutional Law: Principles and Policies*, Aspen Publishers, New York 2006, pp. 259–260.

By means of the case law on matters related to the federal State, the Supreme Court's decisions, without doubt, eventually have enacted constitutional rules; although in some cases, they have distorted the constitutional frame of power distribution, as has been the case in Venezuela.[14]

2. *Constitutional Courts Exercising Judicial Review on Constitutional Provisions*

The second way constitutional courts can participate in the enactment of constitutional rules is when they are empowered to review the Constitution itself, as is the case in Austria, where the Constitutional Court is empowered to confront the Constitution with its own basic principles, like the principle of democracy, the federal state, the *Rechtsstaat*, separation of powers, and the general system of human rights.[15]

3. *Constitutional Courts Exercising Judicial Review on Constitutional Reforms and Amendments*

The third way constitutional courts interfere with the Constituent Power is when they are empowered to review constitutional amendments, as is the case in Colombia, Ecuador, and Bolivia, although the power there is limited to its procedural aspects.[16]

In other countries, discussions have developed regarding the powers of constitutional courts to exercise judicial review powers on the merits of constitutional reforms or amendments, for instance, regarding the unchangeable constitutional clauses (*cláusulas pétreas*) expressly defined in the Constitution. The basic principle is that, in such cases, the courts' powers

14 Decision of the Constitutional Chamber nº 565 of April 15, 2008, Case: Procurador General de la República, *Interpretación del artículo 164.10 de la Constitución de 1999*, available at http://www.tsj.gov.ve/decisio-nes/scon/Abril/565-150408-07-1108.htm. See comments in Allan R. Brewer-Carías, "La ilegítima mutación de la Constitución y la legitimidad de la jurisdicción constitucional: La 'reforma' de la forma federal del Estado en Venezuela mediante interpretación constitucional," in *Memoria del X Congreso Iberoamericano de Derecho Constitucional*, Instituto Iberoamericano de Derecho Constitucional, Asociación Peruana de Derecho Constitucional, Instituto de Investigaciones Jurídicas-UNAM and Maestría en Derecho Constitucional-PUCP, IDEMSA, Lima 2009, Vol. 1, pp. 29–51.

15 Decision of the Constitutional Court, VfSlg 16.327/2001. See Konrad Lachmayer, "Constitutional Courts as Positive Legislators," *Austrian National Report*, XVIII International Congress of Comparative Law, Washington, DC, July 2010, p. 6 (footnote 20).

16 See the references in Allan R. Brewer-Carías, *Reforma constitucional y fraude a la Constitución: Venezuela 1999-2009*, Academia de Ciencias Políticas y Sociales, Caracas 2009, pp. 78 ff.

derive from the supremacy of those constitutional clauses. In such cases, to not confront the will of the people and not substitute the constituent power, the control must be exercised before the reform has been enacted through popular vote, when required.[17]

Nonetheless, even in the absence of constitutional authorization, there are cases of constitutional courts exercising judicial review regarding constitutional amendments. This was the case in Colombia, where the Constitutional Court (February 26, 2010) annulled a Law convening a referendum for the purpose of approving a reform of an article of the Constitution directed to allow the reelection for a third period of the President of the Republic, by considering that such reform contained "substantial violations of the democratic principle," introducing reforms implying the "substitution or subrogation of the Constitution."[18]

In other cases, as in India, the Supreme Court has imposed "implied" limits on the power of Parliament to amend the Constitution, excluding basic features or basic structure of the Constitution,[19] such as the scope of judicial review powers;[20] as a result, the Supreme Court has become, according to Surya Deva, author of the Indian National Report, "probably the most powerful court in any democracy."[21]

[17] See Allan R. Brewer-Carías, *Reforma constitucional y fraude a la Constitución: Venezuela 1999-2009*, Academia de Ciencias Políticas y Sociales, Caracas 2009, pp. 78 ff.; and "La reforma constitucional en América Latina y el control de constitucionalidad," in *Reforma de la Constitución y control de constitucionalidad: Congreso Internacional, Pontificia Universidad Javeriana, Bogotá Colombia, junio 14 al 17 de 2005*, Bogotá, 2005, pp. 108–159.

[18] The decision, in September 2010, has not been published. See the communiqué of the text of the decision (nº 9) published by the Constitutional Court on February 26, 2010, available at http://www.corteconstitucional.com. See the comments in Sandra Morelli, "The Colombian Constitutional Court: From Institutional Leadership, to Conceptual Audacity," *Colombian National Report*, XVIII International Congress of Comparative Law, Washington, DC, July 2010, pp. 13–16.

[19] Case *Kesvananda Bharti v. State of Kerala*, Supreme Court of India, in Surya Deva, "Constitutional Courts as 'Positive Legislators: The Indian Experience," *Indian National Report*, XVIII International Congress of Comparative Law, Washington, DC, July 2010, pp. 5–6.

[20] Cases *Waman Rao v. Union of India* AIR 1981 SC 271; *S P Sampath Kumar v. Union of India* AIR 1987 SC 386; and *L Chandra Kumar v. Union of India* AIR 1997 SC 1125, in *id.*, p. 6 (footnote 41).

[21] *Id.*, p. 6.

4. *The Role of Constitutional Courts Adapting the Constitution on Matters of Fundamental Rights*

In the fourth case, constitutional courts interfere with the Constituent Power when they assume the role of adapting constitutional provisions by means of their interpretation, particularly on matters of fundamental rights. In these cases, according to Laurence Claus and Richard S. Kay, in the United States National Report, Constitutional, Courts "engage in positive constitutional lawmaking," particularly when the rule they "formulate, creates 'affirmative' public duties."[22]

This role of constitutional courts has been the result of a discovering process of fundamental rights not expressly enlisted in the Constitutions, thus enlarging the scope of provisions to maintain a "living" Constitution.[23] Referring to the U.S. Supreme Court's role in elaborating constitutional principles and values, Claus and Kay state that it "provides perhaps the most salient example of positive lawmaking in the course of American constitutional adjudication."[24] This was the case, for instance, beginning with *Brown v. Board of Education of Topeka*, 347 U.S. 483 (1954), when the Supreme Court interpreted the equal protection clause of the Fourteenth Amendment to expound the nature of equality; or when having argued about the constitutional guarantee of due process (Amendments 5 and 14), or the open clause of Amendment 9, to construct the sense of liberty. This process has converted the Court, it has been said, into "the most powerful sitting [constitutional] lawmaker in the nation."[25]

The same has happened in France, where the Constitution does not have a declaration of fundamental rights; the role of the Constitutional Council during the past decades has been precisely to mutate the Constitution, enlarging the *bloc de constitutionnalité* by giving constitutional rank, through the Preamble of the 1958 Constitution, the Preamble of the 1946

22 See Laurence Claus and Richard S. Kay, "Constitutional Courts as 'Positive Legislators' in the United States," *U.S. National Report*, XVIII International Congress of Comparative Law, Washington, DC, July 2010, p. 6.

23 See Mauro Cappelletti, "El formidable problema del control judicial y la contribución del análisis comparado," *Revista de Estudios Políticos*, 13, Madrid 1980, p. 78; "'The Mighty Problem' of Judicial Review and the Contribution of Comparative Analysis," *Southern California Law Review*, 1980, p. 409.

24 See Laurence Claus and Richard S. Kay, "Constitutional Courts as 'Positive Legislators' in the United States," *U.S. National Report*, XVIII International Congress of Comparative Law, Washington, DC, July 2010, pp. 12–13.

25 *Id.*, p. 20.

Constitution, and eventually the 1789 Declaration of Rights of Man and Citizen.[26]

This role of constitutional courts adapting the Constitution to guarantee fundamental rights is a significant trend in comparative law, which can be identified in many countries with different systems of judicial review, as is the case in Switzerland, Germany, Portugal, Austria, Poland, Croatia, Greece, and India, where constitutional courts have introduced important changes in the Constitution and have expanded the scope of fundamental rights.[27]

5. *The Mutation of the Constitution on Institutional Matters*

On matters other than fundamental rights, it is possible to find legitimate constitutional mutations made by constitutional courts referring to other key constitutional matters related to the organization and functioning of the State. The German Federal Constitutional Tribunal, for instance, in the case *AWACS-Urteil* of July 12, 1994,[28] ruled on the deployment in time of peace of missions of German Armed Forces to foreign countries, detailing a substitute legislation (provisional measures) ordering the Legislator and the Executive to proceed according to it, thus imposing the formal participation of the Legislator.

[26] See Louis Favoreu, "Le principe de Constitutionalité: Essai de definition d'apres la jurisprudence du Conseil Constitutionnel," *Recueil d'étude en hommage a Charles Eisenman*, Paris 1977, p. 34. On comparative law, see also Francisco Zúñiga Urbina, *Control de constitucionalidad y sentencia*, Cuadernos del Tribunal Constitucional, nº 34, Santiago de Chile 2006, pp. 46–68.

[27] See Tobias Jaag, "Constitutional Courts as 'Positive Legislators:' Switzerland," *Swiss National Report*, XVIII International Congress of Comparative Law, Washington, DC, July 2010, p. 11; I. Härtel, "Constitutional Courts as Positive Legislators," *German National Report*, XVIII International Congress of Comparative Law, Washington, DC, July 2010, p. 12; Marek Safjan, "The Constitutional Courts as a Positive Legislator," *Polish National Report*, XVIII International Congress of Comparative Law, Washington, DC, July 2010, p. 9; Sanja Barić and Petar Bačić, "Constitutional Courts as Positive Legislators – National Report: Croatia," *Croatian National Report*, XVIII International Congress of Comparative Law, Washington, DC, July 2010, pp. 23 ff.; Julia Iliopoulos-Strangas and Stylianos-Ioannis G. Koutnatzis, "Constitutional Courts as Positive Legislators. *Greek National Report*," XVIII International Congress of Comparative Law, Washington, DC, July 2010, p. 14; Joaquim de Sousa Ribeiro and Esperança Mealha, "The Constitutional Courts as a Positive Legislator," *Portuguese National Report*, XVIII International Congress of Comparative Law, Washington, DC, July 2010, pp. 9–10; Surya Deva, "Constitutional Courts as 'Positive Legislators: The Indian Experience," *Indian National Report*, XVIII International Congress of Comparative Law, Washington, DC, July 2010, p. 4.

[28] Cases: BVferG, July 12, 1994, BVeffGE 90, 585–603, in Christian Behrendt, *Le judge constitutionnel, un législateur-cadre positif: Un analyse comparative en droit francais, belge et allemande*, Bruylant, Brussels 2006, pp. 352–356.

The Constitutional Court of Austria has even created a new constitutional framework to be followed by Parliament in areas not expressly provided in the Constitution, like the privatization process, imposing rules to all State authorities.[29]

The Council of State of Greece has also imposed limits on matters of privatization excluding for instance police powers.[30] The Constitutional Court of the Slovak Republic has reshaped the constitutional provisions regarding the position and authority of the President of the Republic within the general organization of the State; the Court is considered by Ján Svák and Lucia Bertisová, in the Slovak Republic National Report, as "the direct creator of the constitutional system of the Slovak Republic."[31]

Finally, the Supreme Court of Canada, through the important instrument of reference judgments, has created and declared constitutional rules, for instance, governing important constitutional processes as the patriation of Canada's Constitution from the United Kingdom (*Patriation Reference,* 1981);[32] and the possible secession of Quebec from Canada (*Quebec Secession Reference*, 1998),[33] laying down as mentioned by Kent Roach, in the Canadian National Report, some basic rules to guide constitutional change and to avoid potential constitutional crises.

In these matters, unfortunately, there are also examples of constitutional courts mutating the Constitution with the purpose of destroying the democratic principle, as happened in Venezuela when the Constitutional

[29] Cases: "Austro Control" VfSlg 14.473/1996; "Bundeswertpapieraufsicht" (Federal Bond Authority) VfSlg 16.400/2001; "E-Control" VfSlg 16.995/2003; "Zivildienst-GmbH" (Compulsory Community Service Ltd), VfSlg 17.341/2004, in Konrad Lachmayer, "Constitutional Courts as 'Positive Legislators" *Austrian National Report*, XVIII International Congress of Comparative Law, Washington, DC, July 2010, p. 11 (footnote 31).

[30] Decision of the Council of State nº 1934/1998, *ToS* 1998, 598 (602–603), in Julia Iliopoulos-Strangas and Stylianos-Ioannis G. Koutnatzis, "Constitutional Courts as Positive Legislators," *Greek National Report*, XVIII International Congress of Comparative Law, Washington, DC, July 2010, p. 16 (footnote 125).

[31] Decision nº I. ÚS 39/93, in Ján Svák and Lucia Berdisová, "Constitutional Court of the Slovak Republic as Positive Legislator via Application and Interpretation of the Constitution," *Slovak National Report*, XVIII International Congress of Comparative Law, Washington, DC, July 2010, p. 4.

[32] Decision [1981] 1 S.C.R. 753, in Kent Roach, "Constitutional Courts as Positive Legislators," *Canadian National Report*," XVIII International Congress of Comparative Law, Washington, DC, July 2010, p. 9.

[33] Decision [1998] 2 S.C.R. 217, in Kent Roach, "Constitutional Courts as Positive Legislators," *Canadian National Report*," XVIII International Congress of Comparative Law, Washington, DC, July 2010, p. 9.

Chamber implemented a rejected 2007 constitutional reform by means of constitutional interpretation.[34]

SECOND TREND: CONSTITUTIONAL COURTS INTERFERING WITH EXISTING LEGISLATION

The most important and common role of constitutional courts is regarding existing legislation, not only declaring their unconstitutionality but also interpreting statutes in conformity to or in harmony with the Constitution and giving directives or guidelines to the Legislator.

1. *Constitutional Courts Complementing Legislative Functions by Interpreting Statutes in Harmony with the Constitution*

Constitutional courts have moved beyond the classical binomial of unconstitutionality-invalidity (or unconstitutionality-nullity) that confirmed the initial activity of constitutional courts as negative legislators.[35] On the contrary, constitutional courts progressively have assumed a more active role interpreting the Constitution and statutes, not only to annul or not apply them when unconstitutional but also to preserve the Legislator's actions and the statutes it enacts by interpreting them in harmony with the Constitution.[36]

[34] See the comments on some cases in Allan R. Brewer-Carías, "El juez constitucional al servicio del autoritarismo y la ilegítima mutación de la Constitución: El caso de la Sala Constitucional del Tribunal Supremo de Justicia de Venezuela (1999-2009)," *Revista de Administración Pública*, nº 180, Centro de Estudios Constitucionales, Madrid 2009, pp. 383–418; "El juez constitucional vs. la alternabilidad republicana (La reelección continua e indefinida)," *Revista de Derecho Público*, nº 117, Editorial Jurídica Venezolana, Caracas 2009, pp. 205–211; "La ilegítima mutación de la constitución por el juez constitucional: La inconstitucional ampliación y modificación de su propia competencia en materia de control de constitucionalidad," in *Libro Homenaje a Josefina Calcaño de Temeltas*, Fundación de Estudios de Derecho Administrativo (FUNEDA), Caracas 2009, pp. 319–362; "La ilegitima mutación de la Constitución y la legitimidad de la jurisdicción constitucional: La 'reforma' de la forma federal del Estado en Venezuela mediante interpretación constitucional," in *Memoria del X Congreso Iberoamericano de Derecho Constitucional*, Instituto Iberoamericano de Derecho Constitucional, Asociación Peruana de Derecho Constitucional, Instituto de Investigaciones Jurídicas-UNAM and Maestría en Derecho Constitucional-PUCP, IDEMSA, Lima 2009, Vol. 1, pp. 29–51.

[35] See F. Fernández Segado, "El Tribunal Constitucional como legislador positivo," *Spanish National Report*, XVIII International Congress of Comparative Law, Washington, DC, July 2010, pp. 8 ff.

[36] *Ashwander v. TVA,* 297 U.S. 288, 346–48 (1936) (Justice Brandeis). The principle was formulated for the first time in the case *Crowell v. Benson,* 285 U.S. 22, 62 (1932). See "Notes: Supreme Court Interpretation of Statutes to Avoid Constitutional Decision," in *Columbia Law Review*, Vol. 53, nº 5, New York, May 1953, pp. 633–651.

Thus, constitutional courts have become important constitutional institutions that assist and cooperate with the Legislator in its legislative functions.

These sorts of interpretative decisions have been widely used by the constitutional courts in Italy, Spain, France, and Hungary,[37] where in many cases courts have not annulled the challenged law and instead have ruled to modify its meaning by establishing new content, thus making the law constitutional as a result of the constitutional interpretation.[38]

In all these cases, the interference of constitutional courts with existing legislation has followed two main courses of action: first, they complement legislative functions as provisional Legislators or add rules to existing legislation through interpretative decisions; second, they interfere with the temporal effects of existing legislation.

2. *Constitutional Courts Complementing the Legislator by Adding New Rules (and a New Meaning) to the Existing Legislative Provision*

When interpreting statutes in harmony with the Constitution and testing their unconstitutionality, constitutional courts, to avoid invalidating statutes, frequently create new legislative rules. On some occasions, they alter the meaning of the particular provision and add to its wording what it considers lacking.

These are so-called additive decisions, which have been extensively issued by the Italian Constitutional Court – as explained by Gianpaolo Parodi in the Italian National Report – through decisions that leave unaltered the text of the provision declared unconstitutional but transform "its normative meaning, at times reducing, at others extending the sphere of application, not without introducing a new norm into the legal system," or creating new

37 See Gianpaolo Parodi, "The Italian Constitutional Court as 'Positive Legislator,'" Italian *National Report*, XVIII International Congress of Comparative Law, Washington, DC, July 2010, p. 3; Francisco Fernández Segado, "El Tribunal Constitucional como legislador positivo," *Spanish National Report*, XVIII International Congress of Comparative Law, Washington, DC, July 2010, p. 34; Bertrand Mathieu, "Le Conseil constitutionnel 'législateur positif. Ou la question des interventions du juge constitutionnel français dans l'exercise de la function legislative," *French National Report*, XVIII International Congress of Comparative Law, Washington, DC, July 2010, p. 13; Lóránt Csink, Józef Petrétei, and Péter Tilk, "Constitutional Court as Positive Legislator," *Hungarian National Report*, XVIII International Congress of Comparative Law, Washington, DC, July 2010, p. 4.

38 See Francisco Javier Díaz Revorio, *Las sentencias interpretativas del Tribunal Constitucional*, Lex Nova, Valladolid 2001, pp. 59 ff.; and José Julio Fernández Rodríguez, *La justicia constitucional europea ante el siglo XXI*, Tecnos, Madrid 2007, pp. 129 ff.

norms.[39] Additive decisions have also been applied in Germany by the Federal Constitutional Court and in Peru by the Constitutional Tribunal.

Additive decision have been regularly applied in cases related to protecting the right to equality and nondiscrimination, as courts seek to eliminate the differences established in the law. This is the case in Spain, where the Constitutional Tribunal extended to "sons and brothers" the benefit of Social Security pensions granted to "daughters and sisters";[40] it also extended rights of married people to those living in a *de facto* marriage.[41] These are cases in which Francisco Fernandez Segado, in the Spanish National Report, has said that is possible to consider the Spanish Constitutional Tribunal a "real positive legislator."[42]

A similar situation is found in Portugal, where the Constitutional Tribunal has extended to widowers the allowances assigned to widows;[43] to *de facto* unions, rights of married persons; and legal protection given to children of *de facto* unions, the allowances to children born to married parents.[44]

Similarly, in South Africa, the Constitutional Court extended some rights of married couples to same-sex partners in long-term relationships.[45]

In Canada, to allow same-sex marriages, the Ontario Court of Appeal struck down a definition of marriage as a union of a man and a woman and substituted for that the definition of marriage as a gender-neutral concept of a union between persons. These decisions, as affirmed in the Canadian

[39] See Gianpaolo Parodi, "The Italian Constitutional Court as 'Positive Legislator,'" *Italian National Report*, XVIII International Congress of Comparative Law, Washington, DC, July 2010, p. 6.

[40] Decision STC 3/1993, January 14, 1993, in Francisco Javier Díaz Revorio, *Las sentencias interpretativas del Tribunal Constitucional*, Lex Nova, Valladolid 2001, pp. 177, 274; F. Fernández Segado, "El Tribunal Constitucional como legislador positivo," *Spanish National Report*, XVIII International Congress of Comparative Law, Washington, DC, July 2010, p. 42.

[41] Decision STC 222/1992, December 11, 1992, in Francisco Javier Díaz Revorio, *Las sentencias interpretativas del Tribunal Constitucional*, Lex Nova, Valladolid 2001, pp. 181, 182, 275; F. Fernández Segado, "El Tribunal Constitucional como legislador positivo," *Spanish National Report*, XVIII International Congress of Comparative Law, Washington, DC, July 2010, p. 41.

[42] See F. Fernández Segado, "El Tribunal Constitucional como legislador positivo," *Spanish National Report*, XVIII International Congress of Comparative Law, Washington, DC, July 2010, p. 48.

[43] Decision nº 449/87 del Tribunal Constitucional, in Joaquim de Sousa Ribeiro and Esperança Mealha, "Constitutional Courts as Positive Legislators," *Portuguese National Report*, International Congress of Comparative Law, Washington, DC, July 2010, p. 8.

[44] *Id.*, p. 9.

[45] See Iván Escobar Fornos, "Las sentencias constitucionales y sus efectos en Nicaragua," *Anuario Iberoamericano de Justicia Constitucional*, Centro de Estudios Políticos y Constitucionales, nº 12, 2008, Madrid 2008, pp. 111–112.

National Report by Kent Roach, "amount to judicial amendments or additions to legislation."[46]

A similar solution of additive decisions to enforce the right to equality and nondiscrimination is found in many similar cases in the Netherlands, Peru, Costa Rica, Argentina, Poland, the Czech Republic, and France,[47] where, in a particular case regarding the right to respond on matters of television communications, as mentioned by Bertrand Mathieu, in the French National Report, the Constitutional Council substituted for the will of the Legislator.[48]

3. *Constitutional Courts Complementing Legislative Functions by Interfering with the Temporal Effects of Legislation*

The second role of constitutional courts interfering with existing legislation pertains to the power of said Courts to determine the temporal effects of legislation. Decades ago, the matter of the temporal effects of decisions issued by constitutional courts was one of the main aspects of the distinction between the diffuse and the concentrated systems of judicial review. Nowadays, this distinctive element has completely disappeared, and all the systems are converging, so the role of constitutional courts on matters of interfering with the temporal effects of legislation is common.

This can be seen, in comparative law, in three different situations: in postponing the effects of the Courts' decisions, in extending retroactively or

46 See Kent Roach, "Constitutional Courts as Positive Legislator," *Canadian National Report*, XVIII International Congress of Comparative Law, Washington, DC, July 2010, p. 7.

47 See, e.g., Marek Safjan, "The Constitutional Courts as a Positive Legislator," *Polish National Report*, XVIII International Congress of Comparative Law, Washington, DC, July 2010, pp. 13–14; Lóránt Csink, Józef Petrétei, and Péter Tilk, "Constitutional Court as Positive Legislator," *Hungarian National Report*, XVIII International Congress of Comparative Law, Washington, DC, July 2010, p. 5; Zdenek Kühn, "Czech Constitutional Court as Positive Legislator," *Czech National Report*, XVIII International Congress of Comparative Law, Washington, DC, July 2010, p. 9; J. Uzman T. Barkhuysen and M. L. van Emmerik, "The Dutch Supreme Court: A Reluctant Positive Legislator?" *Dutch National Report*, XVIII International Congress of Comparative Law, Washington, DC, July 2010, p. 14; Fernán Altuve Febres, "El juez constitucional como legislador positivo en el Perú," *Peruvian National Report*, XVIII International Congress of Comparative Law, Washington, July 2010, pp. 14–15; Rubén Hernández Valle, "Las Cortes Constitucionales como legisladores positivos," *Costa Rican National Report*, XVIII International Congress of Comparative Law, Washington, DC, July 2010, p. 38; Alejandra Rodríguez Galán and Alfredo Mauricio Vítolo, "Constitutional Courts as Positive Legislators," *Argentinean National Report*, XVIII International Congress of Comparative Law, Washington, DC, July 2010, p. 17.

48 See Bertrand Mathieu, "Le Conseil constitutionnel 'législateur positif. Ou la question des interventions du juge constitutionnel français dans l'exercise de la function legislative," *French National Report*, XVIII International Congress of Comparative Law, Washington, DC, July 2010, p. 16.

prospectively the effects of the Courts' decisions, and in reviving repealed legislation as a consequence of the constitutional control.

A. The Power of the Constitutional Courts to Determine When Annulled Legislation Will Cease to Have Effect: Postponing the Effect of the Courts' Ruling

The first of the cases in which constitutional courts interfere with the legislative function in modulating the temporal effects of a decision declaring unconstitutional or null a statute is when constitutional court establishes *vacatio sentenciae*, determining when annulled legislation will cease to have effects by postponing the effects of its own decision and extending the application of the invalidated statute. This is the situation in Austria, Greece, Belgium, the Czech Republic, France, Croatia, Brazil, Poland, and Peru.[49] In Mexico, if in principle the Supreme Court's decisions have general effects starting on the date of a decision's publication, the Court can establish another date to avoid legislative vacuums, thus giving time to the Legislator to enact new legislation to substitute for the annulled one.[50]

[49] See Konrad Lachmayer, "Constitutional Courts as Positive Legislators," *Austrian National Report*, XVIII International Congress of Comparative Law, Washington, DC, July 2010, p. 7; Julia Iliopoulos-Strangas and Stylianos-Ioannis G. Koutnatzis, "Constitutional Courts as Positive Legislators," *Greek National Report*, XVIII International Congress of Comparative Law, Washington, DC, July 2010, p. 20; Christian Behrendt, *Le judge constitutionnel, un législateur-cadre positif. Un analyse comparative en droit francais, belge et allemande*, Bruylant, Brussels 2006, p. 87, 230, 235, 286, 309; P. Popelier, "L'activité du judge constitutional belge comme législateur," *Belgium National Report*, XVIII International Congress of Comparative Law, Washington, DC, July 2010, pp. 4–7; Zdenek Kühn, "Czech Constitutional Court as Positive Legislator," *Czech National Report*, XVIII International Congress of Comparative Law, Washington, DC, July 2010, p. 12; Sanja Barić and Petar Bačić, "Constitutional Courts as positive legislators," *National Report: Croatia*, XVIII International Congress of Comparative Law, Washington, DC, July 2010, p. 17; Jairo Gilberto Schäfer and Vânia Hack de Almeida, "O controle de constitutionalidade no dereitto brasileiro e a possibilidade de modular os efeitos da decisão de inconstitutionalidade," *Anuario Iberoamericano de Justicia Constitucional*, nº 12, 2008, Centro de Estudios Políticos y Constitucionales, Madrid 2008, p. 384; Domingo García Belaúnde and Gerardo Eto Cruz, "Efectos de las sentencias constitucionales en el Perú," *Anuario Iberoamericano de Justicia Constitucional*, nº 12, 2008, Centro de Estudios Políticos y Constitucionales, Madrid 2008, pp. 283–284.

[50] See "Tesis jurisprudencial" P./J 11/2001, in SJFG, Vol. XIV, September 2001, p. 1008, in Héctor Fix Zamudio and Eduardo Ferrer Mac Gregor, *Las sentencias de los Tribunales Constitucionales*, Ed. Porrúa, Mexico City, pp. 69; and "Las sentencias de los tribunales constitucionales en el ordenamiento mexicano," *Anuario Iberoamericano de Justicia Constitucional*, nº 12, 2008, Centro de Estudios Políticos y Constitucionales, Madrid 2008, pp. 247–248.

The same solution is found in Germany; however, without a clear provision and only based in the article of the Federal Constitutional Tribunal Law that gives the Tribunal the power to establish the way in which the execution of its decisions will take place.[51]

Also, in Italy, although the Constitution clearly establishes that, when the Constitutional Court declares unconstitutional a statutory provision, its effects cease the day after its publication (Article 136),[52] there are important decisions of the Constitutional Court that have deferred the effects of such a declaration.[53] The same has happened in Spain and Canada; in the absence of any legal rule on the matter, constitutional courts have assumed the power to postpone the beginning of the effects of annulment decisions.[54] In Argentina this has also happened, despite the diffuse system of judicial review.[55]

B. The Power of the Constitutional Courts to Determine When Annulled Legislation Will Cease to Have Effects: The Retroactive or Nonretroactive Effects of Their Own Decisions

Another aspect of the temporal effects of Constitutional Courts' decisions are their retroactive or nonretroactive effects. Again, all systems of judicial review are converging, and it is not possible to find rigid solutions.

[51] Case BVferG, May 22, 1963 (*Electoral Circuits*), in Christian Behrendt, *Le judge constitutionnel, un législateur-cadre positif. Un analyse comparative en droit francais, belge et allemande*, Bruylant, Brussels 2006, pp. 299–300. Case BVferG, November 7, 2006 (State Tax), in I. Härtel, "Constitutional Courts as Positive Legislators," *German National Report*, International Congress of Comparative Law, Washington, DC, July 2010, p. 7.

[52] The unapproved constitutional reform draft seeks to authorize the Constitutional Tribunal to postpone for up to one year the effects of its annulment decisions. See Francisco Javier Díaz Revorio, *Las sentencias interpretativas del Tribunal Constitucional*, Lex Nova, Valladolid 2001, p. 125 (footnote 166).

[53] Decision nos. 370/2003; 13 and 423/2004 (on matter of education), in Gianpaolo Parodi, "The Italian Constitutional Court as Positive Legislator," *Italian National Report*, XVIII International Congress of Comparative Law, Washington, DC, July 2010, p. 13.

[54] Case *Manitoba Language Reference* [1985] 1 S.C.R. 721, in Kent Roach, "Constitutional Courts as Positive Legislator," *Canadian National Report*, XVIII International Congress of Comparative Law, Washington, DC, July 2010, p. 7 (footnote 8).

[55] Case *Rosza, Jurisprudencia Argentina*, 2007-III-414, in Néstor P. Sagües, "Los efectos de las sentencias constitucionales en el derecho argentino," *Anuario Iberoamericano de Justicia Constitucional*, Centro de Estudios Políticos y Constitucionales, nº 12, 2008, Madrid 2008, p. 352.

a. *The Possibility of Limiting the Retroactive* Ex Tunc *Effects of Declarative Decisions*

The classic approach to these matters was that, as a matter of principle, in a diffuse system of judicial review, the judicial review decisions were considered declarative ones, with *ex tunc*, *ab initio*, and retroactive effects. This was the traditional principle, for instance, in the United States, where the U.S. Supreme Court's decisions had retroactive effects, particularly in criminal matters.[56] Nonetheless, the principle has been progressively relaxed as a result of its possible negative or unjust effects given the effects already produced by the unconstitutional statute. Thus, the former absolute rule has been abandoned, in recognition of its authority to give or to deny retroactive effects to its ruling on constitutional issues. The same solution has been followed in Argentina,[57] and in the Netherlands, regarding the control of conventionality of statutes.[58]

The principle has also been relaxes in countries with a concentrated system of judicial review where the same possibility of retroactive principle was adopted for decisions annulling statutes. This is the case in Germany, where although the rule is for the declarative effects of the Federal Constitutional Tribunal, in practice it is uncommon to find decisions annulling statutes with purely *ex tunc* effects.[59] In Poland and Brazil, the constitutional courts are authorized to restrict the retroactive effects of their decisions and to give *ex nunc, pro futuro* effects to their decisions.[60]

[56] Case *Norton v. Selby County*, 118 U.S. 425 (1886), p. 442. See the critique of this decision in J. A. C. Grant, "The Legal Effect of a Ruling That a Statute Is Unconstitutional," *Detroit College of Law Review*, 1978, 2, p. 207.

[57] Case Itzcovich, *Jurisprudencia Argentina* 2005-II-723, in Néstor P. Sagües, "Los efectos de las sentencias constitucionales en el derecho argentino," *Anuario Iberoamericano de Justicia Constitucional*, Centro de Estudios Políticos y Constitucionales, nº 12, 2008, Madrid 2008, p. 351.

[58] Case *Boon v. Van Loon*, November 27, 1981, *NJ* 1982/503, in J. Uzman T. Barkhuysen and M. L. van Emmerik, "The Dutch Supreme Court: A Reluctant Positive Legislator?" Dutch *National Report*, XVIII International Congress of Comparative Law, Washington, DC, July 2010, p. 42 (footnote 138).

[59] See Francisco Fernández Segado, "El Tribunal Constitucional como legislador positivo," *Spanish National Report*, XVIII International Congress of Comparative Law, Washington, DC, July 2010, pp. 8, 14.

[60] See, e.g., Marek Safjan, "The Constitutional Courts as a Positive Legislator," *Polish National Report*, XVIII International Congress of Comparative Law, Washington, DC, July 2010, p. 5; María Fernanda Palma, "O Legislador negativo e o interprete da Constitucão," *Anuario Iberoamericano de Justicia Constitucional*, Centro de Estudios Políticos y Constitucionales, nº 12, 2008, Madrid 2008, pp. 174, 329; Francisco Fernández Segado, "Algunas reflexiones generales en torno a los efectos de las sentencias de inconstitucionalidad y a la relatividad de ciertas fórmulas esterotipadas vinculadas a ellas," *Anuario Iberoamericano de Justicia*

b. *The Possibility of Retroactive Effects for* Ex Nunc *Constitutive Decisions*

In countries with concentrated systems of judicial review, although the initial principle, following Kelsen, in the 1920 Austrian Constitution was that decisions of the Constitutional Court to annul a statute would have in principle *ex nunc, pro futuro,* or prospective effects,[61] such principle has also been mitigated, particularly in criminal cases, to accept the retroactive effects of annulment. This general trend is commonly applied in Spain, Peru, France, Croatia, Serbia, the Slovak Republic, Mexico, and Bolivia.[62] In other countries, like Venezuela, Brazil, Colombia, and Costa Rica, the constitutional courts are authorized to determine the temporal effects of its judicial review decisions, which can have or not have retroactive effects.[63]

Constitucional, Centro de Estudios Políticos y Constitucionales, nº 12, 2008, Madrid 2008, p. 174; Iván Escovar Fornos, *Estudios Jurídicos*, Vol. I, Ed. Hispamer, Managua 2007, p. 493; Joaquim de Sousa Ribeiro and Esperança Mealha, "Constitutional Courts as Positive Legislators," *Portuguese National Report*, XVIII International Congress of Comparative Law, Washington, DC, July 2010, p. 6; Thomas Bustamante and Evanlida de Godoi Bustamante, "Constitutional Courts as 'Negative Legislators': The Brazilian Case," *Brazilian National Report*, XVIII International Congress of Comparative Law, Washington, DC, July 2010, p. 26.

61 See Konrad Lachmayer, "Constitutional Courts as Positive Legislators," *Austrian National Report*, XVIII International Congress of Comparative Law, Washington, DC, July 2010, pp. 7–8.

62 See, e.g., Francisco Javier Díaz Revorio, *Las sentencias interpretativas del Tribunal Constitucional*, Ed. Lex Nova, Valladolid, 2001, pp. 104–105, 126–127; Francisco Fernández Segado, "Algunas reflexiones generales en torno a los efectos de las sentencias de inconstitucionalidad y a la relatividad de ciertas fórmulas esterotipadas vinculadas a ellas," *Anuario Iberoamericano de Justicia Constitucional*, Centro de Estudios Políticos y Constitucionales, nº 12, 2008, Madrid 2008, pp. 192–194; Domingo García Belaúnde and Gerardo Eto Cruz, "Efectos de las sentencias constitucionales en el Perú," *Anuario Iberoamericano de Justicia Constitucional*, Centro de Estudios Políticos y Constitucionales, nº 12, 2008, Madrid 2008, pp. 281–282.

63 See, e.g., Allan R. Brewer-Carías, "Algunas consideraciones sobre el control jurisdiccional de la constitucionalidad de los actos estatales en el derecho venezolano," *Revista de Administración Pública*, nº 76, Madrid 1975, pp. 419–446, and *Justicia constitucional: Procesos y procedimientos constitucionales*, Universidad Nacional Autónoma de México, Mexico City 2007, pp. 343 ff.; Jairo Gilberto Schäfer and Vânia Hack de Almeida, "O controle de constitucionalidade no dereito brasileiro e a possibilitade de modular os effeitos de decisão de inconstitucionalidade," *Anuario Iberoamericano de Justicia Constitucional*, Centro de Estudios Políticos y Constitucionales, nº 12, 2008, Madrid 2008, pp. 383–384; Héctor Fix Zamudio and Eduardo Ferrer Mac Gregor, *Las sentencias de los Tribunales Constitucionales*, Ed. Porrúa, Mexico City, p. 69; "Las sentencias de los Tribunales Constitucionales en el ordenamiento mexicano," *Anuario Iberoamericano de Justicia Constitucional*, Centro de Estudios Políticos y Constitucionales, nº 12, 2008, Madrid 2008, p. 248.

4. *The Power of Constitutional Courts to Revive Repealed Legislation*

Finally, as a matter of principle – and according to Hans Kelsen's 1928 writings[64] – judicial review decisions declaring null a statutory provision adopted by constitutional courts do not imply the revival of the former legislation, but the contrary has been adopted in Austria and applied in Portugal and Belgium.[65] In Poland, Mexico, and Costa Rica, it is for the constitutional courts to decide on the matter.[66]

THIRD TREND: CONSTITUTIONAL COURTS INTERFERING WITH THE ABSENCE OF LEGISLATION OR WITH LEGISLATIVE OMISSIONS

In the contemporary world, one of the most important roles of constitutional courts is controlling not the constitutionality of existing legislation but the absence of such legislation or the omissions of statutes, which results when the Legislator does not comply with its constitutional obligation to legislate on specific matters or issues incomplete or discriminatory legislation.

Two sorts of legislative omissions are generally distinguished: absolute and relative. Both are subject to judicial review.[67]

1. *Constitutional Courts Filling In Absolute Legislative Omissions*

Regarding judicial review over absolute legislative omissions, constitutional courts have carried out constitutional control through two

64 See Hans Kelsen, *La garantía jurisdiccional de la Constitución (La justicia constitucional)*, Universidad Nacional Autónoma de México, Mexico City 2001, p. 84.

65 See, e.g., Christian Behrendt, *Le judge constitutionnel, un législateur-cadre positif. Un analyse comparative en droit francais, belge et allemande*, Bruylant, Brussels 2006, pp. 280, 281, 436–437.

66 See, e.g., Héctor Fix Zamudio and Eduardo Ferrer Mac Gregor, *Las sentencias de los Tribunales Constitucionales*, Ed. Porrúa, Mexico City, pp. 63–64, 74; "Las sentencias de los Tribunales Constitucionales en el ordenamiento mexicano," *Anuario Iberoamericano de Justicia Constitucional*, Centro de Estudios Políticos y Constitucionales, nº 12, 2008, Madrid 2008, p. 252.

66 See Iván Escovar Fornos, *Estudios Jurídicos*, Vol. I, Ed. Hispamer, Managua 2007, p. 513; and "Las sentencias constitucionales y sus efectos en Nicaragua," *Anuario Iberoamericano de Justicia Constitucional*, Centro de Estudios Políticos y Constitucionales, nº 12, 2008, Madrid 2008, p. 114.

67 See José Julio Fernández Rodríguez, *La inconstitucionalidad por omisión: Teoría general, Derecho comparado, El caso español*, Civitas, Madrid 1998, pp. 33, 114 ff.

judicial means: in deciding a direct action filed against the unconstitutional absolute omission of the Legislator and in deciding a particular action or complaint for the protection of fundamental rights filed against an omission of the Legislator that, in a particular case, prevents the possibility of enjoying such right.

A. Direct Action against Absolute Legislative Omissions

The direct action to seek judicial review of unconstitutional absolute legislative omissions was first established in the 1974 Constitution of the former Yugoslavia. Two years later, it was incorporated in the 1976 Constitution of Portugal, with standing to sue to some high public officials.[68] The decisions of the Constitutional Tribunal could only inform the competent legislative organ of its findings conduct.[69]

A few years later, direct action for judicial review of absolute unconstitutional legislative omissions was adopted in a few Latin American countries, particularly Brazil (1988),[70] Costa Rica, Ecuador, and Venezuela, where it has been used extensively. Nonetheless, the main difference among these countries is the case of Venezuela, where the action is conceived of as a popular action,[71] and the Constitutional Chamber of the Supreme Tribunal of Justice has been granted express powers to establish not only the unconstitutionality of the omission but also the terms and, if necessary, the guidelines for correcting the omission. Nonetheless, the Constitutional Chamber has enlarged its powers controlling the legislative omission regarding nonlegislative acts, and in 2004, after the National Assembly failed to appoint the members of the National Electoral Council, the Chamber not only declared the omission unconstitutional but also proceeded to appoint directly the high officials. In doing so, it usurped the Assembly's exclusive powers and ensured the complete control of the Electoral branch of

68 See Jorge Campinos, "Brevísimas notas sobre a fiscalizacão da constitucionalidade des leis em Portugal," in Giorgo Lombardi (coord.), *Constituzione e giustizia constitutionale nel diritto comparato*, Maggioli, Rímini, 1985, and *La Constitution portugaise de 1976 et sa garantie*, UNAM, Congreso sobre La Constitución y su Defensa, (mimeo) Mexico City, August 1982, p. 42.

69 See José Julio Fernández Rodríguez, *La inconstitucionalidad por omisión: Teoría general – Derecho comparado, El caso español*, Civitas, Madrid 1998, pp. 265–266.

70 See, e.g., Marcia Rodrigues Machado, "Inconstitutionalidade por omissão," *Revista da Procuradoria Geral de São Paulo*, nº 30, 1988, pp. 41 ff.

71 See Allan R. Brewer-Carías and Víctor Hernández Mendible, *Ley Orgánica del Tribunal Supremo de Justicia*, Caracas 2010.

government by the National Executive.[72] This case, also, goes to the pathology of judicial review.

Also in Hungary, the Constitution grants the Constitutional Court the power to decide *ex officio* or at anyone's petition on the unconstitutionality of legislative omissions; thus, it is able to instruct the Legislator to fulfill its task within a specific deadline and even to define the contents of the rules to be sanctioned.[73] This power has also been attributed in Croatia to the Constitutional Court, which can also proceed *ex officio*.[74]

B. The Protection of Fundamental Rights from Absolute Legislative Omissions by Means of Actions or Complaints for Their Protection

Constitutional courts commonly exercise judicial review regarding unconstitutional legislative omissions through the specific actions of amparo,[75] or complaints for the protection of fundamental rights filed against the harms or threats that such omissions can cause to such rights.

This is the case in Germany, where the complaint for the constitutional protection of fundamental rights (*Verfassungsbeschwerde*)[76] has been used by the Federal Constitutional Tribunal as a means for judicial review of absolute legislative omissions. It has been applied, for instance, in cases regarding rights of illegitimate children, where the Tribunal has imposed the application of the same conditions that extend to children born in wedlock

[72] See the comments on Decisions nº 2073 of August 4, 2003 (Case: *Hermánn Escarrá Malaver y otros*) and nº 2341 of August 25, 2003 (Case: *Hermánn Escarrá M. y otros*), in Allan R. Brewer-Carías, "El secuestro del Poder Electoral y la confiscación del derecho a la participación política mediante el referendo revocatorio presidencial: Venezuela 2000-2004," *Boletín Mexicano de Derecho Comparado*, nº 112, January–April 2005, Instituto de Investigaciones Jurídicas, Universidad Nacional Autónoma de México, Mexico City, pp. 11–73.

[73] See Lóránt Csink, Józef Petrétei, and Péter Tilk, "Constitutional Court as Positive Legislator," *Hungarian National Report*, XVIII International Congress of Comparative Law, Washington, DC, July 2010, pp. 5–6.

[74] See Sanja Barić and Petar Bačić, "Constitutional Courts as Positive Legislators," *Croatian National Report*, XVIII International Congress of Comparative Law, Washington, DC, July 2010, pp. 12–13.

[75] On comparative law, see generally Allan R. Brewer-Carías, *Constitutional Protection of Human Rights in Latin America: A Comparative Study of Amparo Proceeding*, Cambridge University Press, New York 2009, pp. 324 ff.

[76] See generally Francisco Fernández Segado, "El control de las omisiones legislativas por el Bundesverfassungsgericht," *Revista de Derecho*, nº 4, Universidad Católica del Uruguay, Konrad Adenauer Stiftung, Montevideo 2009, pp. 137–186.

and has exhorted the Legislator to reform the Civil Code giving the parliament a specific term to approve the reform.[77]

In India, the Supreme Court has controlled the legislative omissions by ruling in cases of complaints for the protection of fundamental rights, as in the important case regarding ragging (i.e., bullying) at universities. Here, the Court not only urged the Legislator to enact the omitted legislation but also prescribed detailed steps to curb the practice and outlined diverse modes of punishment that educational authorities may take. The Indian Supreme Court even directly appointed, in 2006, a Committee to suggest remedial measures; in 2007, it ordered the implementation of its recommendations.[78]

Similarly, and through equitable remedies like injunctions, the U.S. Supreme Court has progressively developed the protection of fundamental rights by filling in gaps of legislative omissions, particularly with coercive and preventive remedies, as well as structural injunctions.[79] This was very important after the Supreme Court's decision in *Brown v. Board of Education*, 347 U.S. 483 (1954); 349 U.S. 294 (1955), which declared the dual school system discriminatory and allowed courts to undertake supervision of institutional State policies and practices to prevent discrimination.[80] This activism by injunction was later applied in other important cases of civil rights litigation involving electoral reappointments, mental hospitals, prisons, trade practices, and the environment. Also, in deciding on equitable remedies for the protection of fundamental rights, the U.S. Supreme Court has created complementary judicial legislation, as in the conditions for lawful search and arrest in connection with investigation of and prosecution for a crime.

[77] Decision of the Federal Constitutional Tribunal nº 26/1969 of January 29, 1969, in I. Härtel, "Constitutional Courts as Positive Legislators," *German National Report*, XVIII International Congress of Comparative Law, Washington, DC, July 2010, p. 19.

[78] Cases *Vishwa Jagriti Mission v. Central Government* AIR 2001 SC 2793, and *University of Kerala v. Council of Principals of Colleges of Kerala*, in Surya Deva, "Constitutional Courts as Positive Legislators: The Indian Experience," *Indian National Report*, XVIII International Congress of Comparative Law, Washington, DC, July 2010, p. 9 (footnote 58).

[79] See William Tabb and Elaine W. Shoben, *Remedies*, Thomson West, 2005, p. 13; Owen M. Fiss, *The Civil Rights Injunctions*, Indiana University Press, 1978, pp. 4–5; Owen M. Fiss and Doug Rendelman, *Injunctions*, Foundation Press, 1984, pp. 33–34; Allan R. Brewer-Carías, *Constitutional Protection of Human Rights in Latin America*, Cambridge University Press, New York 2009, pp. 69 ff.

[80] Missouri v. Jenkins, 515 U.S. 70 (1995), in Laurence Claus and Richard S. Kay, "Constitutional Courts as Positive Legislators in the United States," *U.S. National Report*, XVIII, International Congress of Comparative Law, Washington, DC, July 2010, p. 31 (footnote 104).

In Latin America, these complaints for the protection of legislative omissions have also been used.[81] This is the case of the Brazilian *mandado de injunção*, a writ of injunction granted whenever the lack of regulatory provision makes the exercise of constitutional rights and freedoms unfeasible. The courts not only can give Congress a term within which it must repair its omission but also can establish the rules, sometimes by analogy, to be applied if the omission persists. This has occurred in matters of the country's social security regime and strike rights of public-sector employees.[82]

The same general approach of the constitutional courts in complementing the Legislator on matters of protecting fundamental rights is also found in amparo actions in Argentina.[83] Also, in Colombia, deciding actions of *tutela*, in the case of massive violations of human rights regarding displaced persons, the Constitutional Court created *ex officio* a factual state of unconstitutionality (*estado de cosas inconstitucionales*), which it uses to substitute itself for ordinary judges, the Legislator, and the Administration in defining and coordinating public policies.[84]

In Canada, similar to the Latin American amparo proceeding, according to the Charter, the Courts have the power to issue a wide variety of remedies, including declarations and injunctions that require the government to take positive action to comply with the Constitution and to remedy the effects of past constitutional violations. These judicial powers have been widely used to enforce protection of minority language, to ensure bilingualism in the Provinces; on matters of criminal justice, given the absence of legislative response to enact statutory standards for speedy trials and disclosure of evidence to the accused by the prosecutor; and in matters of extradition of a person who could face death penalty in the requesting state.[85]

[81] See Allan R. Brewer-Carías, *Constitutional Protection of Human Rights in Latin America*, Cambridge University Press, New York 2009.

[82] See Thomas Bustamante and Evanlida de Godoi Bustamante, "Constitutional Courts as Negative Legislators: The Brazilian Case," *Brazilian National Report*, XVIII, International Congress of Comparative Law, Washington, DC, July 2010, p. 19.

[83] See Alejandra Rodríguez Galán and Alfredo Mauricio Vítolo, "Constitutional Courts as Positive Legislators," *Argentinean National Report*, XVIII, International Congress of Comparative Law, Washington, DC, July 2010, p. 17.

[84] See Sandra Morelli, "The Colombian Constitutional Court: From Institutional Leadership, to Conceptual Audacity," *Colombian National Report*, XVIII, International Congress of Comparative Law, Washington, DC, July 2010, p. 5.

[85] Cases: *Reference re Manitoba Language Rights* [1985] 1 S.C.R. 721; [1985] 2 S.C.R. 347; [1990] 3 S.C.R. 1417n; [1992] 1 S.C.R. 212; *R. v. Stinchcombe* [1991] 3 S.C.R. 326, in Kent Roach, "Constitutional Courts as Positive Legislators," *Canadian National Report*, XVIII, International Congress of Comparative Law, Washington, DC, July 2010, pp. 11–12.

In the United Kingdom, although in general the Courts do not substitute themselves for the legislature, it is possible to identify important activity the Courts have developed on matters of constitutional review regarding the protection of human rights. They have issued decisions with guidelines that supplement the jurisdiction of the Legislator or the Administration, as in matters related to sterilization of intellectually handicapped adults and persons in a permanent vegetative state, thus providing rules for future application.[86]

In the Czech Republic, the Constitutional Court has filled the gap derived from legislative omission on specific matters like the one related to rent increases in apartment houses, where the Court considered that "its role of protector of constitutionality cannot limit its function to the mere position of a 'negative' legislator."[87]

2. *Constitutional Courts Filling In the Gap of Relative Legislative Omissions*

In the case of judicial review regarding relative legislative omissions, when dealing with poor, deficient, or inadequate legislative regulations affecting the enjoyment of fundamental rights, during the past decades, particularly in the concentrated system of judicial review, constitutional courts have developed the technique of declaring unconstitutional insufficient provisions but not annulling them. Instead, they send them to the Legislator, with directives, guidelines, recommendations, and even orders to correct unconstitutional legislative omissions. In all these cases, the constitutional courts have developed a role of assisting and collaborating with the Legislator, particularly to protect the right to equality and nondiscrimination. The instructions or directives sent by constitutional courts to the Legislator are in some cases nonbinding recommendations; in other cases, they are obligatory; in others still, they are provisional pieces of legislation.

[86] Cases *Re F (Mental Patient: Sterilisation)* [1990] 2 *AC 173; and Airedale NHS Trust v Bland,* in John Bell, "Constitutional Courts as Positive Legislators: United Kingdom," *British National Report,* XVIII, International Congress of Comparative Law, Washington, DC, July 2010, p. 7.

[87] Decision Pl. ÚS 8/02, *Rent Control II*, nº 528/2002 Sb. Of November 20, 2002; and Pl. ÚS 2/03, *Rent Control III*, nº 84/2003 Sb, of March 19, 2003, in Zdenek Kühn, "Czech Constitutional Court as Positive Legislator," *Czech National Report*, XVIII, International Congress of Comparative Law, Washington, DC, July 2010, p. 14 (footnote 58).

A. Constitutional Courts' Issuing of Nonbinding Directives to the Legislator

In general terms, regarding noncompulsory judicial recommendations – known as exhortative decisions, delegate decisions, or *sentenze indiritzzo* in Italy[88] – the Constitutional Court declares unconstitutional a provision but does not introduce the norm to be applied through interpretation, thus leaving this task to the Legislator. In other cases, the instruction directed to the Legislator can be conditional regarding the judicial review power of the Constitutional Court. For example, in Italy, through the so-called *doppia pronuncia* formula,[89] if the Legislator fails to execute the recommendations of the Court, in a second decision, the Court can declare unconstitutional the impugned statute.

This sort of exhortative judicial review is also accepted in Germany, known as appellate decisions, where the Federal Constitutional Tribunal can issue "admonitions to the Legislator," containing legislative directives that give a term within which the Legislator must enact the omitted provision.[90]

This same technique has been applied in France and Belgium, where the Constitutional Council and Court have issued directives addressed to the Legislator, which even without normative direct effects, can establish a framework for future legislative action.[91] A similar technique has been applied in Poland, known as signalizations, through which the Constitutional Tribunal directs the Legislator's attention to problems of general nature;[92] and it has been applied in Serbia, the Czech Republic, and Mexico.[93]

88 See L. Pegoraro, *La Corte e il Parlamento. Sentenze-indirizzo e attivitá legislativa*, Cedam, Padova 1987, pp. 3 ff.; Francisco Javier Díaz Revorio, *Las sentencias interpretativas del Tribunal Constitucional*, Ed. Lex Nova, Valladolid, 2001, p. 268.

89 See Iván Escovar Fornos, *Estudios Jurídicos*, Vol. I, Ed. Hispamer, Managua 2007, p. 504.

90 See Francisco Javier Díaz Revorio, *Las sentencias interpretativas del Tribunal Constitucional*, Ed. Lex Nova, Valladolid, 2001, p. 264; Iván Escovar Fornos, *Estudios Jurídicos*, Vol. I, Ed. Hispamer, Managua 2007, p. 505.

91 Decision BVerfG, July 19, 1966, BVerfGE 20, 56 (114–115), in Christian Behrendt, *Le judge constitutionnel, un législateur-cadre positif. Un analyse comparative en droit francais, belge et allemande*, Bruylant, Brussels 2006, pp. 176–179, 185 ff.

92 See, e.g., the signalization on tenants' protection of June 29, 2005, OTK ZU 2005/6A/77, in Marek Safjan, "The Constitutional Courts as a Positive Legislator," *Polish National Report*, International Congress of Comparative Law, Washington, DC, July 2010, p. 16 (footnote 45).

93 See, e.g., Héctor Fix Zamudio and Eduardo Ferrer Mac Gregor, "Las sentencias de los tribunales constitucionales en el ordenamiento mexicano," *Anuario Iberoamericano de Justicia Constitucional*, nº 12, 2008, Centro de Estudios Políticos y Constitucionales, Madrid 2008, p. 252.

In countries with diffuse systems of judicial review, like Argentina, exhortative rulings have also been issued by the Supreme Courts in cases related to collective *habeas corpus* petition. The Courts exhort the involved authorities to sanction new legal provisions to take care, for instance, overcrowding in prisons.[94] These powers have also been used in cases of judicial review of conventionality regarding the American Convention of Human Rights. A similar position has been adopted by the Supreme Court of the Netherlands in giving its "expert advice" to the Legislator.[95]

B. Constitutional Courts' Issuing of Binding Orders and Directives to the Legislator

In many other cases of judicial review that pertain to relative legislative omissions, generally based on the violation of the right to nondiscrimination and to equality, constitutional courts, in declaring unconstitutional a provision without annulling it, have progressively assumed a more positive role, issuing the Legislator not only directives but also orders or instructions, for it to reform or correct pieces of legislation. This has transformed constitutional courts into an auxiliary of the Legislator, imposing on them certain tasks and establishing a precise term for their performance.

This judicial review technique has been used in Germany, where the Federal Constitutional Tribunal, through injunctive decisions, has issued orders to the Legislator on matters related to alimony, professional incompatibilities, reimbursement of electoral expenses in electoral campaigns, professors' tenure, abortion, and alternative civilian service, even indicating what the Legislator should not do to aggravate the unconstitutional inequalities.[96] Similar decisions are found in Belgium, Austria, Croatia, and Colombia.[97]

[94] Case *Verbitsky*, CSIJ, Fallos 328:1146, in Néstor P. Sagües, "Los efectos de las sentencias constitucionales en el derecho argentino," *Anuario Iberoamericano de Justicia Constitucional*, Centro de Estudios Políticos y Constitucionales, nº 12, 2008, Madrid 2008, p. 340.

[95] Case *Harmonisation Act* de 1989, in J. Uzman T. Barkhuysen and M.L. van Emmerik, "The Dutch Supreme Court: A Reluctant Positive Legislator?" *Dutch National Report*, XVIII International Congress of Comparative Law, Washington, DC, July 2010, p. 6.

[96] Decisions BVerfG, of July 14, 1981, BVerfGE 57, 381; BVerfG, of February 15, 1967, BVerfGE 21, 183; BVerfG, of March 9, 1976, BVerfGE 41, 414, in I. Härtel, "Constitutional Courts as Positive Legislators," *German National Report*, XVIII, International Congress of Comparative Law, Washington, DC, July 2010, p. 9.; Christian Behrendt, *Le judge constitutionnel, un législateur-cadre positif. Un analyse comparative en droit francais, belge et allemande*, Bruylant, Brussels 2006, pp. 259–288.

[97] See, e.g., Mónica Liliana Ibagón, "Control jurisdiccional de las omisiones legislativas en Colombia," in Juan Vega Gómez and Edgar Corzo Sosa, *Instrumentos de tutela y justicia*

In France, given the traditional *a priori* judicial review of legislation exercised by the Constitutional Council, one of the most important means to ensure the enforcement of the Council's decisions are the directives called *réserves d'interprétation* or *réserves d'application*, which are directed to the administrative authorities that must issue the regulations of the law and to the judges who must apply the law.[98]

3. *Constitutional Courts as Provisional Legislators*

Finally, in many other cases on relative legislative omissions, constitutional courts have not limited themselves to issue orders to the Legislator to enact legislative provisions but have assumed the direct role of being provisional Legislators by including in their decisions that declare a statute unconstitutional provisional measures or regulations to be applied in the specific matter considered unconstitutional, until the Legislator sanctions the statute it is obliged to produce.[99] In these cases, the courts immediately stops the application of the unconstitutional provision, but to avoid the vacuum that annulment can originate, it temporarily establishes certain rules until the enactment of new legislation occurs. Constitutional courts, in these cases, act as substitute Legislators; they do not usurp the Legislator's functions but preserve the legislative freedom of parliament.[100]

This technique has been applied also in Germany by the Federal Constitutional Tribunal in assuming "an auxiliary legislative power" and acting as a "parliamentary reparation enterprise,"[101] on a matter like the one resolved in 1975 on the partial decriminalization of abortion. In that case, after declaring unconstitutional the provisions of the Criminal Code, the Tribunal considered that, "in the interest of the clarity of law," it was suitable

constitucional: Memoria del VII Congreso Iberoamericano de Derecho Constitucional, Universidad Nacional Autónoma de México, Mexico City 2002, pp. 322–323.

98 See Bertrand Mathieu, "Le Conseil constitutionnel 'législateur positif. Ou la question des interventions du juge constitutionnel français dans l'exercise de la function legislative," *French National Report*, XVIII International Congress of Comparative Law, Washington, DC, July 2010, p. 10.

99 See Christian Behrendt, *Le judge constitutionnel, un législateur-cadre positif. Un analyse comparative en droit francais, belge et allemande*, Bruylant, Brussels 2006, pp. 333 ff.

100 See Otto Bachof, "Nuevas reflexiones sobre la jurisdicción constitucional entre derecho y política," *Boletín Mexicano de Derecho Comparado*, Vol. 19, nº 57, Mexico City 1986, pp. 848–849.

101 See Christian Behrendt, *Le judge constitutionnel, un législateur-cadre positif. Un analyse comparative en droit francais, belge et allemande*, Bruylant, Brussels 2006, p. 341 (footnotes 309 and 310).

for it to establish "provisory regulation" to apply until the new provisions were enacted by the Legislator."[102] It proceeded to enact detailed provisional legislation on the matter, which applied for nearly fifteen years, until 1992. In 1993, after the corresponding reform, the Federal Constitutional Tribunal issued a new decision considering the new provisions to be contrary to the Constitution[103] and establishing once more in an extremely detailed regulation, as "real legislator," all the rules applicable to abortion in the country.

In Switzerland, the Supreme Court has also provided rules to fill the gaps of legislative omissions concerning enforcement of constitutional rights, as has happened, for instance, regarding the proceedings concerning the detention of foreigners, the right of asylum, and rules on expropriation.[104]

In India, the Supreme Court has assumed the role of provisional legislator on matters of protecting fundamental rights related to police arrest and detention. It has issued notices to all state governments and established detail requirements to be followed in all cases of arrest or detention till legal provisions are made. In this case, even though the requirements were seemingly intended to be temporary, they have continued to be the main rules applicable on the matter.[105] The Supreme Court has also exercised the same powers to protect the rights of working women from sexual harassment at workplace, issuing "for the protection of these rights *to fill the legislative vacuum*."[106]

Among these judicial review decisions that include provisional regulations by interpreting the Constitution are the cases of *súmula vinculante* issued by

[102] Decision BVerfG, of February 25, 1975, BVerfGE 39, 1, (68), in Christian Behrendt, *Le judge constitutionnel, un législateur-cadre positif. Un analyse comparative en droit francais, belge et allemande*, Bruylant, Brussels 2006, pp. 342 ff.; I. Härtel, "Constitutional Courts as Positive Legislators," *German National Report*, XVIII International Congress of Comparative Law, Washington, DC, July 2010, p. 14.

[103] Decisions BVerfG, of March 25, 1993 (*Schwangerrschaftsabbruch II*), and BVerfGE 88, 203, de of February 25, 1975, in Christian Behrendt, *Le judge constitutionnel, un législateur-cadre positif. Un analyse comparative en droit francais, belge et allemande*, Bruylant, Brussels 2006, pp. 346–351.

[104] Decisions BGE 91 I 329 ff. (Substantive Expropriation); BGE 94 I 286 ff. (Taking Neighbors' Rights). See Tobias Jaag, "Constitutional Courts as Positive Legislators: Switzerland, " *Swiss National Report*, XVIII International Congress of Comparative Law, Washington, DC, July 2010, p. 16 (footnote 89).

[105] Case *D K Basu v. State of West Bengal*, (1997) 1 SCC 416, in Surya Deva, "Constitutional Courts as Positive Legislators: The Indian Experience," *Indian National Report*, XVIII International Congress of Comparative Law, Washington, DC, July 2010, pp. 6–7.

[106] Case *Vishaka v. State of Rajasthan*, 1997 SC 3011, in Surya Deva, "Constitutional Courts as Positive Legislators: The Indian Experience," *Indian National Report*, XVIII International Congress of Comparative Law, Washington, July 2010, p. 8 (footnote 49).

the Federal Supreme Tribunal of Brazil on, for instance, the prohibition of nepotism in the Judiciary and the demarcation of indigenous people's land.[107]

In Venezuela, there are cases in which the Constitutional Chamber of the Supreme Tribunal, in the absence of the corresponding statutes, has issued decisions containing legislation in the exercise of what the Chamber has called its normative jurisdiction. In so doing, it established complete regulations on, for instance, the *de facto* marital relations between men and women and on matters of in vitro fertilization.[108]

FOURTH TREND: CONSTITUTIONAL COURTS AS LEGISLATORS ON MATTERS OF JUDICIAL REVIEW

The fourth and final trend that can be identified in comparative law regarding the role of constitutional courts as positive legislators is related to matters of legislation on judicial review, not only regarding the powers of the courts when exercising judicial review and the actions that can be filed before them but also regarding the rules of procedure applicable to the judicial review. This situation varies according to the system of judicial review adopted.

1. *Constitutional Courts' Creating of Their Own Judicial Review Powers*

A. The Judge-Made Law on the Diffuse System of Judicial Review

In the diffuse or decentralized system of judicial review, being the power attributed to all courts to disregard the application of statutes they deem unconstitutional giving preference to the Constitution, a power that derives from the principle of the supremacy of the Constitution and the duty of the

[107] *Súmula vinculante* nº 13, STF, *DJ* 1º.set.2006, ADC 12 MC/DF, Rel. Min. Carlos Britto; STF, *DJ* 25.set.2009, Pet 3388/RR, Rel. Min. Carlos Britto, in Luis Roberto Barroso et al., "Notas sobre a questão do Legislador Positivo" (*Brazil*), XVIII International Congress of Comparative Law, Washington, DC, July 2010, pp. 33–37, 43–46.

[108] Decision nº 1682 of July 15, 2005, Case *Carmela Manpieri, Interpretación del artículo 77 de la Constitución*, available at http://www.tsj.gov.ve/decisiones/scon/Julio/1682-150705-04-3301.htm; and Decision nº 1456 of July 27, 2006, Case *Yamilex Núñez de Godoy*, available at http://www.tsj.gov.ve/decisiones/scon/Julio/1456-270706-05-1471.htm. See Daniela Urosa Maggi, "Cortes Constitucionales como legisladores positivos: La experiencia venezolana," *Venezuelan National Report*, XVIII International Congress of Comparative Law, Washington, DC, July 2010, pp. 19–20.

courts not to apply statutes contrary to the Constitution, such power does not need to be expressly established in the Constitution. This was the main doctrine established by Chief Justice Marshall in *Marbury* v. *Madison*, 1 Cranch 137 (1803). Consequently, in the United States, because of this essential link between the supremacy of the Constitution and judicial review, judicial review was a creation of the courts, as was also the case a few decades later in Norway, Greece, and Argentina,[109] where judicial review was also a creation of the respective Supreme of High Courts.

B. The Extension of Judicial Review Powers to Ensure the Protection of Fundamental Rights

In the same sense, and particularly regarding the protection of fundamental rights and liberties, constitutional courts in many Latin American countries, in their character of supreme interpreter of the Constitution, have created the amparo action in the absence of legislation as a special means for protecting fundamental rights. This was also the case in Argentina in 1957; the Dominican Republic in 1999;[110] and the Slovak Republic, where the constitutional courts "created" a specific means of protection.[111]

In Venezuela, the Constitutional Chamber of the Supreme Tribunal has admitted the direct amparo action for the protection of diffused and collective rights and interests established in the Constitution,[112] and in India, the Supreme Court has expanded the action for the protection of fundamental rights to the protection of collective or diffused rights, called public interest litigation (PIL).[113]

[109] See Allan R. Brewer-Carías, *Judicial Review in Comparative Law*, Cambridge University Press, Cambridge 1989.

[110] See Allan R. Brewer-Carías, *Constitutional Protection of Human Rights in Latin America*, Cambridge University Press, New York, 2010.

[111] Decision of the Constitutional Court nº III. ÚS 117/01, in Ján Svák and Lucia Berdisová, "Constitutional Court of the Slovak Republic as Positive Legislator via Application and Interpretation of the Constitution," *Slovak National Report*, XVIII International Congress of Comparative Law, Washington, DC, July 2010, p. 9.

[112] Decisions nº 656 of June 30, 2000, Case *Dilia Parra Guillen (Peoples' Defender)*, in http://www.tsj.gov.ve/decisiones/scon/Junio/656-300600-00-1728%20.htm; nº 1395 of November 21, 2000, Case *William Dávila, Revista de Derecho Público*, nº 84, Editorial Jurídica Venezolana, Caracas, 2000, pp. 330; nº 1571 of August 22, 2001, Case *Asodeviprilara*, available at http://www.tsj.gov.ve/decisiones/scon/Agosto/1571-220801-01-1274%20.htm. See Daniela Urosa Maggi, "Cortes Constitucionales como legisladores positivos: La experiencia venezolana," *Venezuelan National Report*, XVIII International Congress of Comparative Law, Washington, DC, July 2010, pp. 11–12.

[113] Cases *S P Gupta v. Union of India* AIR 1982 SC 149; *PUDR v. Union of India* AIR 1982 SC 1473; *Bandhua Mukti Morcha v. Union of India* (1984) 3 SCC 161, in Surya Deva,

2. *The Need for the Express Provision in the Constitution of Judicial Review Powers of the Constitutional Jurisdiction and Its Deviation*

Nonetheless, and specifically with respect to the concentrated system of judicial review, the power to judge the control of constitutionality of legislative acts when reserved to a supreme court of justice or to a constitutional court must be accomplished as expressly provided for in the Constitution; it cannot be developed by deduction through court decisions.[114]

Nonetheless, regarding judicial review powers, in some cases, constitutional courts have extended or adapted them, as in, for example, declaring unconstitutional a statute but not annulling it; extending the application of an unconstitutional statute for a term; and issuing directives to the Legislator to legislate in harmony with the Constitution. This was a technique developed in Germany, as mentioned by Ines Härtel, in the Germany National Report, "without statutory authorization, in fact *contra legem*".[115] In Spain, the Constitutional Tribunal has applied the technique despite the contrary provision in the Organic Law of the Constitutional. Tribunal.[116]

In other cases, constitutional courts have created their own judicial review powers not established in the Constitution, as in Venezuela, where the Constitutional Chamber of the Supreme Tribunal created as a new means of judicial review not envisaged in the Constitution, the so-called abstract recourse for constitutional interpretation,[117] through which, at the Attorney

"Constitutional Courts as Positive Legislators: The Indian Experience," *Indian National Report*, XVIII International Congress of Comparative Law, Washington, DC, July 2010, pp. 2, 4–5.

[114] See Allan R. Brewer-Carías, *Judicial Review in Comparative Law*, Cambridge University Press, Cambridge 1989, pp. 185 ff.; Jorge Carpizo, *El Tribunal Constitucional y sus límites*, Grijley Ed., Lima 2009, p. 41.

[115] See I. Härtel, "Constitutional Courts as Positive Legislators," *German National Report*, XVIII International Congress of Comparative Law, Washington, DC, July 2010, p. 8; Francisco Fernández Segado, "Algunas reflexiones generales en torno a los efectos de las sentencias de inconstitucionalidad y a la relatividad de ciertas fórmulas esterotipadas vinculadas a ellas," *Anuario Iberoamericano de Justicia Constitucional*, Centro de Estudios Políticos y Constitucionales, nº 12, 2008, Madrid 2008, p. 162.

[116] See F. Fernández Segado, "El Tribunal Constitucional como Legislador Positivo," *Spanish National Report*, XVIII International Congress of Comparative Law, Washington, DC, July 2010, p. 6, 11.

[117] Decision nº 1077 of September 22, 2000, Case *Servio Tulio León*, *Revista de Derecho Público*, nº 83, Editorial Jurídica Venezolana, Caracas 2000, pp. 247 ff. See Allan R. Brewer-Carías, "Le recours d'interprétation abstrait de la Constitution au Vénézuéla," in *Renouvau du droit constitutionnel: Mélanges en l'honneur de Louis Favoreu*, Paris 2007, pp. 61–70; "La ilegítima mutación de la constitución por el juez constitucional: La inconstitucional ampliación y modificación de su propia competencia en materia de control de constitucionalidad," in *Libro*

General's request, the Constitutional Chamber has distorted important constitutional provisions. This was the case, for instance, in the decisions adopted regarding the consultative and repeal referenda between 2002 and 2004, where the Chamber transformed the repeal referendum into a ratification referendum not established in the Constitution.[118] These are cases that go to the pathology of judicial review.

3. *Constitutional Courts' Creation of Procedural Rules on Judicial Review*

Finally, regarding constitutional courts' interference in legislative functions, the creation of procedural rules for the exercise of their constitutional attributions, when not established in the legislation regulating their functions, must also be mentioned.

Constitutional courts, as is the case of the Constitutional Tribunal of Peru, have claimed to have "procedural autonomy" in the exercise of their extended powers to develop and complement the procedural rules applicable in judicial review process not expressly regulated in the statutes.[119]

In Germany, the same principle of procedural autonomy (*Verfahrensautonomie*) has been used to explain the powers developed by the Federal Constitutional Tribunal to complement procedural rules on

Homenaje a Josefina Calcaño de Temeltas, Fundación de Estudios de Derecho Administrativo (FUNEDA), Caracas 2009, pp. 319–362.

[118] The constitutional mutation occurred precisely for the purpose of preventing the repeal of the mandate of President Chávez in 2004. He was elected in August 2000 with 3,757,744 votes, enough to repeal his mandate according to the Constitution, and the votes for revocation were more than that figure. The number of votes in favor of the repeal cast on August 15, 2004, was 3,989,008, so the mandate was constitutionally repealed. Nonetheless, the national Electoral Council on August 27, 2004 – with 5,800,629 votes for the revocation – decided to ratify the President in his post until the end of his term in January 2007. See *El Nacional*, Caracas, August 28, 2004, pp. A-1 and A-2. See comments on this case in Allan R. Brewer-Carías, "La Sala Constitucional vs. El derecho ciudadano a la revocatoria de mandatos populares o de cómo un referendo revocatorio fue inconstitucionalmente convertido en un 'referendo ratificatorio,'" in *Crónica sobre la "in"justicia constitucional. La Sala Constitucional y el autoritarismo en Venezuela*, Colección Instituto de Derecho Público, Universidad Central de Venezuela, nº 2, Editorial Jurídica Venezolana, Caracas 2007, pp. 350 ff.

[119] Decision of the Constitutional Tribunal, nº 0020-2005-AI/TC, FJ 2, in Francisco Eguiguren and Liliana Salomé, "Función contra-mayoritaria de la jurisdicción constitucional, su legitimidad democrática y los conflictos entre el Tribunal Constitucional y el legislador," *Peruvian National Report*, XVIII International Congress of Comparative Law, Washington, DC, July 2010, p. 14; Fernán Altuve-Febres, "El Juez Constitucional como legislador positivo en el Perú," *Peruvian National Report II*, XVIII International Congress of Comparative Law, Washington, DC, July 2010, pp. 22–23.

judicial review process based on the interpretation of article 35 of the Law of the Federal Constitutional Tribunal related to the execution of its decisions.

In other cases, judicial interference in legislative matters related to rules of procedures on matters of judicial review has been more intense, as in Colombia, where the Constitutional Court has assumed the exclusive competency to establish the effects of its own decisions.[120] In Venezuela, the Constitutional Chamber of the Supreme Tribunal of Justice has also invoked normative jurisdiction to establish procedural rules for judicial review when not regulated in statutes, particularly regarding the control of absolute legislative omission[121] and on matters of *habeas data*, establishing detail procedural regulations "in order to fill the existing vacuum."[122]

FINAL REMARKS

The main conclusion that we can deduct from this comparative law study of constitutional courts as positive legislators is that, in the contemporary world, constitutional courts have progressively assumed roles that decades ago corresponded only to the Constituent power or to the Legislator. In some cases, they discovered and deducted constitutional rules, particularly on matters of human rights not expressively enshrined in the Constitution and that could not even be considered to have been the intention of an ancient and original Constituent when sanctioning a Constitution conceived for other time in history.

[120] See Decision C-113/93, in Germán Alfonso López Daza, "Le juge constitutionnel colombien, législateur-cadre positif: un gouvernement des juges," *Colombian National Report I*, XVIII International Congress of Comparative Law, Washington, DC, July 2010, p. 9.

[121] Decision nº 1556 of July 9, 2002, Case *Alfonzo Albornoz y Gloria de Vicentini*, available at http://www.tsj.gov.ve/decisiones/scon/Julio/1556-090702-01-2337%20.htm. See Daniela Urosa Maggi, "Cortes Constitucionales como legisladores positivos: La experiencia venezolana," *Venezuelan National Report*, XVIII International Congress of Comparative Law, Washington, DC, July 2010, pp. 10–11.

[122] Decision nº 1511 of November 9, 2009, Case *Mercedes Josefina Ramírez, Acción de Habeas Data*, available at http://www.tsj.gov.ve/decisiones/scon/Noviembre/1511-91109-2009-09-0369.html. See Allan R. Brewer-Carías, "El proceso constitucional de las acciones de habeas data en Venezuela: Las sentencias de la Sala Constitucional como fuente del Derecho Procesal Constitucional," in Eduardo Andrés Velandia Canosa (coord.), *Homenaje al Maestro Héctor Fix Zamudio: Derecho Procesal Constitucional – Memorias del Primer Congreso Colombiano de Derecho Procesal Constitucional*, May 26–28, 2010, Bogotá, pp. 289–295; Daniela Urosa Maggi, "Cortes Constitucionales como legisladores positivos: La experiencia venezolana," *Venezuelan National Report*, XVIII International Congress of Comparative Law, Washington, DC, July 2010, p. 13.

In other cases, constitutional courts have progressively performed legislative functions, complementing the Legislator in its role of lawmaker, filling in the gaps from legislative omissions, sending guidelines and orders to the Legislator, and even issuing provisional legislation resulting from the exercise of their functions.

These common trends, found in different countries and in all legal systems, are of course more numerous and important than the possible differences that could exist. That is why, in these matters of judicial review, constitutional courts in many countries – to develop their own competencies and exercise their powers to control the constitutionality of statutes, to protect fundamental rights, and to ensure the supremacy of the Constitution – have progressively begun to study and analyze the similar work developed in other Courts and in other countries, thus enriching their rulings.

Consequently, it is possible to say that, perhaps with the exception of the U.S. Supreme Court, it is common to find, in constitutional courts' decisions, constant references to decisions issued on similar matters or cases by other constitutional courts. Thus, in general, there is no aversion to using foreign law to interpret, when applicable, the Constitution.

On the contrary, in the United States, for example, Justice Sonia Sotomayor, in her Senate confirmation hearings, affirmed that "American Law does not permit the use of foreign law or international law to interpret the Constitution," and that this was a "given" question regarding which "there is no debate."[123] U.S. Justice Ruth Bader Ginsburg has said that she "frankly [doesn't] understand all the brouhaha lately from Congress and even from some of my colleagues about referring to foreign law," explaining that the controversy was based in the misunderstanding that citing a foreign precedent means for the court to considers itself bound by foreign law as opposed to merely being influenced by such power as its reasoning holds. That is why she formulated the following question: "Why shouldn't we look to the wisdom of a judge from abroad with at least as much ease as we would read a law review article written by a professor?"[124]

And this is precisely what is now common in all Constitutional Jurisdiction all over the world where constitutional courts commonly consider foreign law when they have to decide on the same matter and on the basis of the same principles. In such cases, in the same sense of studying the matter

[123] See the comments of Justice Sonia Sotomayor in the Senate confirmation hearings on July 15, 2009, in "Sotomayor on the Issues," *New York Times*, July 16, 2009, p. A18.

[124] See Adam Liptak, "Ginsburg Shares Views on Influence of Foreign Law on Her Court, and Vice Versa," in *New York Times*, April 12, 2009, p. 14.

according to authors' opinion and analysis in books and articles, they can also rely on courts' decisions from other countries, which can be useful because those courts dealt not only with a theoretical proposition but also with a specific solution already applied by a court to resolve a particular case. And it is here, precisely, where comparative law is a very important and useful tool.

APPENDIX

LIST OF NATIONAL REPORTS AND PAPERS

The following were the National Reports and Papers received by the author for *XVIII International Congress of Comparative Law,* Washington, DC, July 2010:

ARGENTINA: Alejandra Rodríguez Galán and Alfredo Mauricio Vítolo, "*Constitutional Courts as Positive Legislators (Argentina)*" (18 pp.).

-Néstor Pedro Sagües, "*La Corte Suprema Argentina como legislador positivo*" (24 pp.).

AUSTRALIA: Cherryl Saunders, "*Interpretation and Review*" (54 pp.).

AUSTRIA: Konrad Lachmayer, "*Constitutional Courts as Positive Legislators*" (13 pp.).

BELGIUM: Patricia Popelier, "*L'activité du judge constitutional belge comme législateur*" (16 pp.).

BRAZIL: Thomas Bustamante and Evanilda de Godoi Bustamante, "*Constitutional Courts as Negative Legislators: The Brazilian Case*" (29 pp.).

-Marcelo Figuereido, "*Judicial Remedies Aimed to Fill the Legislative Gaps resulting from State Omissions under Brazilian Law*" (12 pp.).

-Luis Roberto Barroso, Thiago Magalhães, and Felipe Drummond, "*Notas sobre a questão do Legislador Positivo*" (47 pp.).

CANADA: Kent Roach, "Constitutional Courts as Positive Legislators: Canada Country Report" (25 pp.).

COLOMBIA: Germán Alfonso López Daza, "*Le juge constitutionnel colombien, législateur-cadre positif: un gouvernement des juges*" (16 pp.).

-Sandra Morelli, "*The Colombian Constitutional Court: from Institutional Leadership, to Conceptual Audacity*" (20 pp.).

COSTA RICA: Rubén Hernández Valle, "Las Cortes Constitucitnales como Legisladores positivos" (43 pp.).

CROATIA: Sanja Barić and Petar Bačić, "Constitutional Courts as Positive Legislators. National Report: Croatia" (29 pp).

CZECH REPUBLIC: Zdenek Kühn, "Czech Constitutional Court as Positive Legislator? " (17 pp.).

FRANCE: Bertrand Mathieu, "Le Conseil constitutionnel 'législateur positif. Ou la question des interventions du juge constitutionnel français dans l'exercise de la function legislative" (18 pp.).

GERMANY: Ines Härtel, "Constitutional Courts as Positive Legislators" (22 pp.).

GREECE: Julia Iliopoulos-Strangas and Stylianos-Ioannis G. Koutnatzis, "Constitutional Courts as Positive Legislators. Greek National Report" (24 pp.).

HUNGARY: Lóránt Csink, Józef Petrétei and Péter Tilk, "Constitutional Court as Positive Legislator. Hungarian National Report" (7 pp).

INDIA: Surya Deva, "Constitutional Courts as Positive Legislators: The Indian Experience," (11 pp.).

ITALY: Giampaolo Parodi, "The Italian Constitutional Court as Positive Legislator" (13 pp.).

MEXICO: Eduardo Ferrer Mac-Gregor, "La Corte Suprema de Justicia como Tribunal Constitucional" (27 pp.).

NETHERLAND: Jerfi Uzman, Tom Barkhuysen and Michiel L. van Emmerik, "The Dutch Supreme Court: A Reluctant Positive Legislator?" (54 pp).

NICARAGUA: Sergio J. Cuarezma Terán and Francisco Enríquez Cabistán, "La estructura normativa de la Constitución Política de Nicaragua y sus mecanismos de tutela" (55 pp.).

NORWAY, Eivind Smith, "Constitutional Courts as 'Positive Legislators:" Norway" (7 pp.).

PERU: Fernán Altuve Febres, "El Juez Constitucional como legislador positivo en el Perú" (30 pp.).

-Francisco Eguiguren and Liliana Salomé, "Función contra-mayoritaria de la Juridicción Constitucional, su legitimidad democrática y los conflictos entre el Tribunal Constitucional y el Legislador" (18 pp.).

POLAND, Marek Safjan, "The Constitutional Courts as a Positive Legislator" (18 pp.).

PORTUGAL: Joaquim de Sousa Ribeiro and Esperança Mealha, "Constitutional Courts as Positive Legislators" (11 pp.).

SERBIA: Boško Tripković, "*A National Report for Serbia on the topic Constitutional Courts as "Positive Legislators*" (19 pp.).

SLOVAK REPUBLIC: Ján Svák and Lucia Berdisová, "*Constitutional Court of the Slovak Republic as Positive Legislator via Application and Interpretation of the Constitution*" (14 pp.).

SPAIN: Francisco Fernández Segado, "*El Tribunal Constitucional como Legislador Positivo (Spain)*" (48 pp.).

SWEDEN: Joakim Nergelius, "*Human Rights and Judicial Review*" (29 pp.).

SWITZERLAND, Tobias Jaag, "*Constitutional Courts as Positive Legislators: Switzerland*" (23 pp.).

UNITED KINGDOM: John Bell, "*Constitutional Courts as 'Positive Legislators': United Kingdom*" (8 pp.).

UNITED STATES: Laurence Claus and Richard S Kay, "*Constitutional Courts as Positive Legislators' in the United States*" (38 pp.).

VENEZUELA: Daniela Urosa, "*Cortes Constitucionales como Legisladores Positivos: La experiencia venezolana*" (30 pp.).

INDEX

-H-

-I-

-J-